MyEconLab® Provides the Power of Practice

Optimize your study time with **MyEconLab**, the online assessment and tutorial system. When you take a sample test online, **MyEconLab** gives you targeted feedback and a personalized Study Plan to identify the topics you need to review.

Study Plan

The Study Plan shows you the sections you should study next, gives easy access to practice problems, and provides you with an automatically generated quiz to prove mastery of the course material.

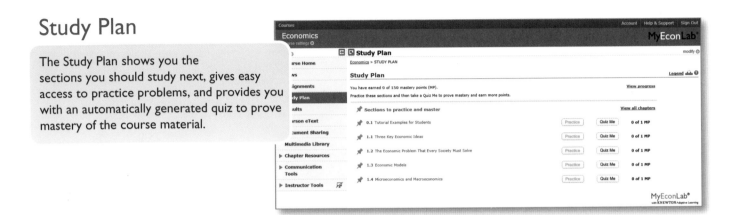

Unlimited Practice

As you work each exercise, instant feedback helps you understand and apply the concepts. Many Study Plan exercises contain algorithmically generated values to ensure that you get as much practice as you need.

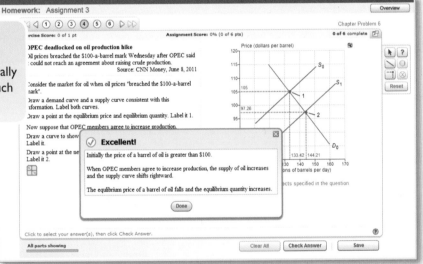

Learning Resources

Study Plan problems link to learning resources that further reinforce concepts you need to master.

- **Help Me Solve This** learning aids help you break down a problem much the same way as an instructor would do during office hours. Help Me Solve This is available for select problems.

- **eText links** are specific to the problem at hand so that related concepts are easy to review just when they are needed.

- A **graphing tool** enables you to build and manipulate graphs to better understand how concepts, numbers, and graphs connect.

Find out more at www.myeconlab.com

Real-Time Data Analysis Exercises

Up-to-date macro data is a great way to engage in and understand the usefulness of macro variables and their impact on the economy. Real-Time Data Analysis exercises communicate directly with the Federal Reserve Bank of St. Louis's FRED® site, so every time FRED posts new data, students see new data.

End-of-chapter exercises accompanied by the Real-Time Data Analysis icon ⓜ include Real-Time Data versions in **MyEconLab**.

Select in-text figures labeled **MyEconLab** Real-Time Data update in the electronic version of the text using FRED data.

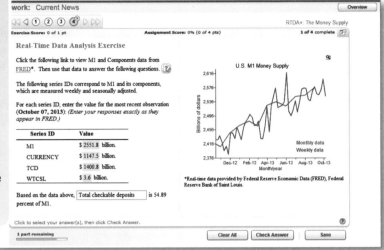

Current News Exercises

Posted weekly, we find the latest microeconomic and macroeconomic news stories, post them, and write auto-graded multi-part exercises that illustrate the economic way of thinking about the news.

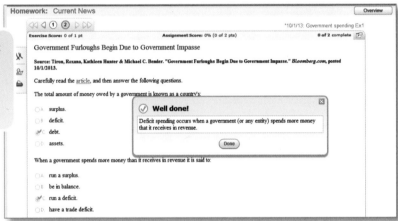

Interactive Homework Exercises

Participate in a fun and engaging activity that helps promote active learning and mastery of important economic concepts.

Pearson's experiments program is flexible and easy for instructors and students to use. For a complete list of available experiments, visit *www.myeconlab.com*.

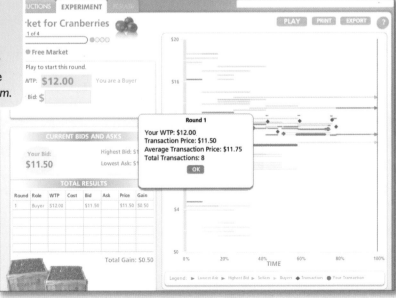

 **PEARSON Choices**   Providing Options and Value in Economics

Microeconomics

The Pearson Series in Economics

Abel/Bernanke/Croushore
*Macroeconomics**

Bade/Parkin
*Foundations of Economics**

Berck/Helfand
The Economics of the Environment

Bierman/Fernandez
Game Theory with Economic Applications

Blanchard
*Macroeconomics**

Blau/Ferber/Winkler
The Economics of Women, Men, and Work

Boardman/Greenberg/Vining/Weimer
Cost-Benefit Analysis

Boyer
Principles of Transportation Economics

Branson
Macroeconomic Theory and Policy

Bruce
Public Finance and the American Economy

Carlton/Perloff
Modern Industrial Organization

Case/Fair/Oster
*Principles of Economics**

Chapman
Environmental Economics: Theory, Application, and Policy

Cooter/Ulen
Law & Economics

Daniels/VanHoose
International Monetary & Financial Economics

Downs
An Economic Theory of Democracy

Ehrenberg/Smith
Modern Labor Economics

Farnham
Economics for Managers

Folland/Goodman/Stano
The Economics of Health and Health Care

Fort
Sports Economics

Froyen
Macroeconomics

Fusfeld
The Age of the Economist

Gerber
*International Economics**

González-Rivera
Forecasting for Economics and Business

Gordon
*Macroeconomics**

Greene
Econometric Analysis

Gregory
Essentials of Economics

Gregory/Stuart
Russian and Soviet Economic Performance and Structure

Hartwick/Olewiler
The Economics of Natural Resource Use

Heilbroner/Milberg
The Making of the Economic Society

Heyne/Boettke/Prychitko
The Economic Way of Thinking

Holt
Markets, Games, and Strategic Behavior

Hubbard/O'Brien
*Economics**

*Money, Banking, and the Financial System**

Hubbard/O'Brien/Rafferty
*Macroeconomics**

Hughes/Cain
American Economic History

Husted/Melvin
International Economics

Jehle/Reny
Advanced Microeconomic Theory

Johnson-Lans
A Health Economics Primer

Keat/Young/Erfle
Managerial Economics

Klein
Mathematical Methods for Economics

Krugman/Obstfeld/Melitz
*International Economics: Theory & Policy**

Laidler
The Demand for Money

Leeds/von Allmen
The Economics of Sports

Leeds/von Allmen/Schiming
*Economics**

Lynn
Economic Development: Theory and Practice for a Divided World

Miller
*Economics Today**

Understanding Modern Economics

Miller/Benjamin
The Economics of Macro Issues

Miller/Benjamin/North
The Economics of Public Issues

Mills/Hamilton
Urban Economics

Mishkin
*The Economics of Money, Banking, and Financial Markets**

*The Economics of Money, Banking, and Financial Markets, Business School Edition**

*Macroeconomics: Policy and Practice**

Murray
Econometrics: A Modern Introduction

O'Sullivan/Sheffrin/Perez
*Economics: Principles, Applications and Tools**

Parkin
*Economics**

Perloff
*Microeconomics**

*Microeconomics: Theory and Applications with Calculus**

Perloff/Brander
*Managerial Economics and Strategy**

Phelps
Health Economics

Pindyck/Rubinfeld
*Microeconomics**

Riddell/Shackelford/Stamos/Schneider
Economics: A Tool for Critically Understanding Society

Roberts
The Choice: A Fable of Free Trade and Protection

Rohlf
Introduction to Economic Reasoning

Roland
Development Economics

Scherer
Industry Structure, Strategy, and Public Policy

Schiller
The Economics of Poverty and Discrimination

Sherman
Market Regulation

Stock/Watson
Introduction to Econometrics

Studenmund
Using Econometrics: A Practical Guide

Tietenberg/Lewis
Environmental and Natural Resource Economics

Environmental Economics and Policy

Todaro/Smith
Economic Development

Waldman/Jensen
Industrial Organization: Theory and Practice

Walters/Walters/Appel/Callahan/Centanni/Maex/O'Neill
Econversations: Today's Students Discuss Today's Issues

Weil
Economic Growth

Williamson
Macroeconomics

*denotes MyEconLab titles   Visit www.myeconlab.com to learn more.

Microeconomics

Fifth Edition

R. Glenn Hubbard
Columbia University

Anthony Patrick O'Brien
Lehigh University

PEARSON

Boston   Columbus   Indianapolis   New York   San Francisco   Upper Saddle River
Amsterdam   Cape Town   Dubai   London   Madrid   Milan   Munich   Paris   Montréal   Toronto
Delhi   Mexico City   São Paulo   Sydney   Hong Kong   Seoul   Singapore   Taipei   Tokyo

Editor in Chief: Donna Battista
AVP/Executive Editor: David Alexander
Executive Development Editor: Lena Buonanno
Senior Editorial Project Manager: Lindsey Sloan
Editorial Assistant: Patrick Henning
AVP/Executive Marketing Manager: Lori DeShazo
Managing Editor: Jeff Holcomb
Production Project Manager: Carla Thompson
Supplements Project Manager: Andra Skaalrud
Procurement Specialist: Carol Melville
Senior Art Director: Jonathan Boylan
Cover Design: Jonathan Boylan
Image Manager: Rachel Youdelman

Photo Research: Aptara, Inc.
Text Permissions Associate Project Manager: Samantha Graham
Text Permissions Research: Khalid Shakhshir, Electronic Publishing
  Services, Inc.
Director of Media: Susan Schoenberg
Content Leads, MyEconLab: Courtney Kamauf and Noel Lotz
Senior Media Producer: Melissa Honig
Audio and Video Editing: Hodja Media, Inc.
Full-Service Project Management/Composition:
  PreMediaGlobal
Printer/Binder: Courier, Kendallville
Cover Printer: Courier, Kendallville
Text Font: Minion

Credits and acknowledgments borrowed from other sources and reproduced, with permission, in this textbook appear on appropriate page within text or on page 621.

FRED® is a registered trademark and the FRED® Logo and ST. LOUIS FED are trademarks of the Federal Reserve Bank of St. Louis. http://research.stlouisfed.org/fred2/

Microsoft and/or its respective suppliers make no representations about the suitability of the information contained in the documents and related graphics published as part of the services for any purpose. All such documents and related graphics are provided "as is" without warranty of any kind. Microsoft and/or its respective suppliers hereby disclaim all warranties and conditions with regard to this information, including all warranties and conditions of merchantability, whether express, implied or statutory, fitness for a particular purpose, title and non-infringement. In no event shall Microsoft and/or its respective suppliers be liable for any special, indirect or consequential damages or any damages whatsoever resulting from loss of use, data or profits, whether in an action of contract, negligence or other tortious action, arising out of or in connection with the use or performance of information available from the services.

 The documents and related graphics contained herein could include technical inaccuracies or typographical errors. Changes are periodically added to the information herein. Microsoft and/or its respective suppliers may make improvements and/or changes in the product(s) and/or the program(s) described herein at any time. Partial screen shots may be viewed in full within the software version specified.

Microsoft®, Excel®, PowerPoint®, Windows®, and Word® are registered trademarks of the Microsoft Corporation in the U.S.A. and other countries. This book is not sponsored or endorsed by or affiliated with the Microsoft Corporation.

Many of the designations by manufacturers and sellers to distinguish their products are claimed as trademarks. Where those designations appear in this book, and the publisher was aware of a trademark claim, the designations have been printed in initial caps or all caps.

Cataloging-in-Publication Data is on file at the Library of Congress

10 9 8 7 6 5 4 3 2 1

ISBN 10: 0-13-345554-8
ISBN 13: 978-0-13-345554-0

For Constance, Raph, and Will
—*R. Glenn Hubbard*

For Cindy, Matthew, Andrew, and Daniel
—*Anthony Patrick O'Brien*

Glenn Hubbard, policymaker, professor, and researcher. R. Glenn Hubbard is the dean and Russell
L. Carson Professor of Finance and Economics in the Graduate School of Business at Columbia University and professor of economics in Columbia's Faculty of Arts and Sciences. He is also a research associate of the National Bureau of Economic Research and a director of Automatic Data Processing, Black Rock Closed-End Funds, KKR Financial Corporation, and MetLife. He received his Ph.D. in economics from Harvard University in 1983. From 2001 to 2003, he served as chairman of the White House Council of Economic Advisers and chairman of the OECD Economic Policy Committee, and from 1991 to 1993, he was deputy assistant secretary of the U.S. Treasury Department. He currently serves as co-chair of the nonpartisan Committee on Capital Markets Regulation. Hubbard's fields of specialization are public economics, financial markets and institutions, corporate finance, macroeconomics, industrial organization, and public policy. He is the author of more than 100 articles in leading journals, including American Economic Review, Brookings Papers on Economic Activity, Journal of Finance, Journal of Financial Economics, Journal of Money, Credit, and Banking, Journal of Political Economy, Journal of Public Economics, Quarterly Journal of Economics, RAND Journal of Economics, and Review of Economics and Statistics. His research has been supported by grants from the National Science Foundation, the National Bureau of Economic Research, and numerous private foundations.

Tony O'Brien, award-winning professor and researcher. Anthony Patrick O'Brien is a professor of
economics at Lehigh University. He received his Ph.D. from the University of California, Berkeley, in 1987. He has taught principles of economics for more than 15 years, in both large sections and small honors classes. He received the Lehigh University Award for Distinguished Teaching. He was formerly the director of the Diamond Center for Economic Education and was named a Dana Foundation Faculty Fellow and Lehigh Class of 1961 Professor of Economics. He has been a visiting professor at the University of California, Santa Barbara, and the Graduate School of Industrial Administration at Carnegie Mellon University. O'Brien's research has dealt with issues such as the evolution of the U.S. automobile industry, the sources of U.S. economic competitiveness, the development of U.S. trade policy, the causes of the Great Depression, and the causes of black–white income differences. His research has been published in leading journals, including American Economic Review, Quarterly Journal of Economics, Journal of Money, Credit, and Banking, Industrial Relations, Journal of Economic History, and Explorations in Economic History. His research has been supported by grants from government agencies and private foundations.

BRIEF CONTENTS

*These end-of-chapter resource materials repeat in all chapters. Chapter 8 includes two Real-Time Data Exercises.

PART 2: Markets in Action: Policy and Applications

PART 3: Firms in the Domestic and International Economies

FLEXIBILITY CHART

The following chart helps you organize your syllabus based on your teaching preferences and objectives:

Core	Optional	Policy
Chapter 1: Economics: Foundations and Models	**Chapter 1 Appendix:** Using Graphs and Formulas	
Chapter 2: Trade-offs, Comparative Advantage, and the Market System		
Chapter 3: Where Prices Come From: The Interaction of Demand and Supply		
	Chapter 4 Appendix: Quantitative Demand and Supply Analysis	**Chapter 4:** Economic Efficiency, Government Price Setting, and Taxes
		Chapter 5: Externalities, Environmental Policy, and Public Goods
Chapter 6: Elasticity: The Responsiveness of Demand and Supply		
		Chapter 7: The Economics of Health Care
	Chapter 8: Firms, the Stock Market, and Corporate Governance	
	Chapter 8 Appendix: Tools to Analyze Firms' Financial Information	
Chapter 9: Comparative Advantage and the Gains from International Trade		
	Chapter 10: Consumer Choice and Behavioral Economics	
	Chapter 10 Appendix: Using Indifference Curves and Budget Lines to Understand Consumer Behavior	

Core	Optional	Policy
Chapter 11: Technology, Production, and Costs	**Chapter 11 Appendix:** Using Isoquants and Isocost Lines to Understand Production and Cost	
Chapter 12: Firms in Perfectly Competitive Markets		
Chapter 13: Monopolistic Competition: The Competitive Model in a More Realistic Setting		
Chapter 14: Oligopoly: Firms in Less Competitive Markets		
Chapter 15: Monopoly and Antitrust Policy		
	Chapter 16: Pricing Strategy	
Chapter 17: The Markets for Labor and Other Factors of Production		
		Chapter 18: Public Choice, Taxes, and the Distribution of Income

PREFACE

Our approach in this new edition remains what it was in the first edition, published more than 10 years ago: To provide students and instructors with an economics text that delivers complete economics coverage with many real-world business examples. Our goal has been to teach economics in a "widget-free" way by using real-world business and policy examples. We are gratified by the enthusiastic response from students and instructors who used the first four editions of this book, which has made it one of the best-selling economic textbooks in the world. Much has happened, though, in the U.S. and world economies since we prepared the previous edition. We have incorporated many of these developments in the new real-world examples used in this edition.

New to the Fifth Edition

While our basic approach of placing applications in the forefront of the discussion remains the same, this new edition has been thoroughly revised. One exciting new addition is the significant expansion of the digital resources available to students and instructors with either the e-text version of the book or the MyEconLab supplement to the printed text.

New digital features located in MyEconLab

MyEconLab is a unique online course management, testing, and tutorial resource. It is included with the e-text version of the book or as a supplement to the print book. Students and instructors will find the following new online resources to accompany the fifth edition:

- **Videos:** There are approximately 60 *Making the Connection* features in the book that provide real-world reinforcement of key concepts. Each feature is now accompanied by a short video of the author explaining the key point of that *Making the Connection*. Each video is less than two minutes long and includes visuals, such as new photos or graphs, that are not in the main book. The goal of these videos is to summarize key content and bring the applications to life. Related assessment is included with each video. Our experience is that many students benefit from this type of online learning.

- **Concept Checks:** Each section of each learning objective concludes with an online Concept Check that contains one or two multiple choice, true/false, or fill-in questions. These checks act as "speed bumps" that encourage students to stop and check their understanding of fundamental terms and concepts before moving on to the next section. The goal of this digital resource is to help students assess their progress on a section-by-section basis, so they can be better prepared for homework, quizzes, and exams.

- **Animations:** Graphs are the backbone of introductory economics, but many students struggle to understand and work with them. Each numbered figure in the text has a supporting animated version online. The goal of this digital resource is to help students understand shifts in curves, movements along curves, and changes in equilibrium values. Having an animated version of a graph helps students who have difficulty interpreting the static version found in the printed text. Graded practice exercises are included with the animations. Our experience is that many students benefit from this type of online learning.

- **Interactive Solved Problems:** Many students have difficulty applying economic concepts to solving problems. The goal of this digital resource is to help students overcome this hurdle by giving them a model of how to solve an economic problem by breaking it down step by step. Each *Solved Problem* in the printed text is accompanied by a similar problem online, so students can have more practice and build their problem-solving skills. These interactive tutorials help students learn to think like economists and apply basic problem-solving skills to homework, quizzes, and exams. The goal is for students to build skills they can use to analyze real-world economic issues they hear and read about in the news. Each Solved Problem in MyEconLab and the digital eText also includes at least one additional graded practice exercise for students.

- **Graphs Updated with Real-Time Data from FRED:** Figure 7.5, "Spending on Health Care around the World," Figure 8.2, "Movements in Stock Market Indexes," and Figures 9.1 and 9.3, both on international trade, are continuously updated online with the latest available data from FRED (Federal Reserve Economic Data), which is a comprehensive, up-to-date data set maintained by the Federal Reserve Bank of St. Louis. Students can display a pop-up graph that shows new data plotted in the graph. The goal of this digital feature is to help students understand how to work with data and understand how including new data affects graphs.

- **Interactive Problems and Exercises Updated with Real-Time Data from FRED:** Chapter 8, "Firms, the Stock Market, and Corporate Governance," includes two real-time data exercises that use the latest data from FRED. The goal of this digital feature is to help students become familiar with this key data source, learn how to locate data, and develop skills in interpreting data.

Summary of Changes to Chapters

- Chapter 5, "Externalities, Environmental Policy, and Public Goods," includes new coverage of the end of the sulfur dioxide cap-and-trade program. This discussion helps reinforce the interaction between economic analysis and politics in the formation of government policies.

- Chapter 7, "The Economics of Health Care," was introduced in the fourth edition and proved popular with instructors and students. In revising the chapter for this edition, we added several new demand and supply graphs. Our purpose was to make the content more analytical and to make the chapter more effective as an example of applied demand and supply analysis. We also extensively updated the discussion of the debate over President Obama's Patient Protection and Affordable Care Act. Figure 7.5, "Spending on Health Care around the World," is now continuously updated online with the latest available data from FRED.

- Chapter 8, "Firms, the Stock Market, and Corporate Governance," includes Figure 8.2, "Movements in Stock Market Indexes." This figure is now continuously updated online with the latest available data from FRED. The chapter also includes 2 new end-of-chapter *Real-Time-Data Exercises* that help students become familiar with a key data source, learn how to locate data, and develop skills in interpreting data. The exercise marked with a ⊕ allows students and instructors to use the very latest data from FRED.

- Chapter 9, "Comparative Advantage and the Gains from International Trade," includes two figures that are continuously updated online with the latest available data from FRED: Figure 9.1, "International Trade Is of Increasing Importance to the United States," and Figure 9.3, "International Trade As a Percentage of GDP."

- Chapter 10, "Consumer Choice and Behavioral Economics," has already provided extensive coverage of behavioral economics. We have found that many students find this material among the most interesting in the microeconomic chapters. We took advantage of the problems Ron Johnson encountered as CEO of J.C. Penney to include a new section on "The Behavioral Economics of Shopping." This section includes discussion of several behavioral studies of consumer choice.

- Chapter 18, "Public Choice, Taxes, and the Distribution of Income," includes a new *Making the Connection*, "What Explains the 1 Percent?" that summarizes the recent debate over increasing income inequality in the United States.

Other Changes to Chapters

- All companies in the chapter openers have been either replaced with new companies or updated with current information.

- Chapters 1–4 include new An Inside Look newspaper articles and analyses to help students apply economic thinking to current events and policy debates. Additional newspaper articles and analysis are updated weekly on MyEconLab.

- There are 13 new Making the Connection features to help students tie economic concepts to current events and policy issues.

- There are 6 new *Solved Problems*. This feature helps students break down and answer an economic problem down step by step.

- To make room for the new content described earlier, we have cut approximately 14 *Making the Connections* and 4 *Solved Problems* from the previous edition and transferred them to the book's Instructor's Manual where they are available for instructors who wish to continue using them.

- Figures and tables have been updated, using the latest data available.

- Many of the end-of-chapter problems have been either replaced or updated. To most chapters, we have added one or two new problems that include a graph for students to analyze. Chapter 8, "Firms, the Stock Market, and Corporate Governance," includes a new category entitled *Real-Time-Data Exercises*.

- Finally, we have gone over the text literally line by line, tightening the discussion, rewriting unclear points, and making many other small changes. We are grateful to the many instructors and students who made suggestions for improvements in the previous edition. We have done our best to incorporate as many of those suggestions as possible.

New Chapter Openers, *Making the Connections, Solved Problems,* and *Inside Looks*

Here are the new or heavily revised chapter-opening business cases and accompanying *Inside Look* newspaper articles. The business or issue introduced in the chapter opener is revisited within the chapter in either a *Making the Connection* feature or a *Solved Problem* feature. The following are the features new to this edition. Please see the detailed table of contents for the list of features for all chapters.

Chapter 1, "Economics: Foundations and Models," opens with a new discussion of why some doctors are leaving private practice and closes with *An Inside Look* newspaper article and analysis of how technology, such as the smartphone, may change the way doctors and patients will interact.

Chapter 2, "Trade-offs, Comparative Advantage, and the Market System," opens with a new discussion of the manufacturing decisions facing managers at Tesla Motors and closes with *An Inside Look* that discusses how managers at Mercedes-Benz face those same decisions. New *Solved Problem 2.1* asks students to use a production possibilities frontier to analyze some of the choices managers at Tesla Motors face. This chapter also has a new *Making the Connection* on comparative advantage and housework.

Chapter 3, "Where Prices Come From: The Interaction of Demand and Supply," opens with a new discussion of the market for smartphones and closes with *An Inside Look* about challenges Google and Apple face in this market. This chapter has three new *Making the Connections*: "Forecasting the Demand for iPhones," "Are Tablet Computers Substitutes for E-Readers?" and "Coke and Pepsi Are Hit by U.S. Demographics."

Chapter 4, "Economic Efficiency, Government Price Setting, and Taxes," opens with a new discussion of how the sharing economy for rooms affects rent control policy and closes with *An Inside Look* about how the sharing economy affects efficiency.

Chapter 5, "Externalities, Environmental Policy, and Public Goods," opens with an updated discussion of how people respond to changes in the price of gasoline. New *Solved Problem 5.3* is on the externalities of car driving.

Chapter 6, "Elasticity: The Responsiveness of Demand and Supply," opens with a revised and updated discussion of the price elasticity of gasoline. The chapter includes an entirely rewritten *Making the Connection* on "Price Elasticity, Cross-Price Elasticity, and Income Elasticity in the Market for Alcoholic Beverages."

Chapter 7, "The Economics of Health Care," opens with a new discussion of how much businesses and employees pay for health insurance and the role of the Patient Protection and Affordable Care Act of 2010. New *Solved Problem 7.3* explores whether young, healthy people should buy health insurance. The chapter includes new Figure 7.4 on the externalities of vaccinations and new Figure 7.8 on the third-party payer system. It also includes a *Making the Connection* on how paying for health insurance affects the competitiveness of U.S. firms.

Chapter 8, "Firms, the Stock Market, and Corporate Governance," opens with a new discussion of the benefits and costs of becoming a publicly owned firm. New *Solved Problem 8.2* explores whether a CEO should also be a chairman of the board of the same firm. There's also a new *Making the Connection* that explores the performance of Facebook's stock.

Chapter 9, "Comparative Advantage and the Gains from International Trade," opens with a new discussion of the U.S. tariff on Chinese tires. The chapter includes a new *Making the Connection* on how the tire tariff affected Goodyear and a new *Making the Connection* on how the tariff affected the wider economy.

Chapter 10, "Consumer Choice and Behavioral Economics," opens with a new discussion of the failed pricing strategy at J.C. Penney. A new section discusses the behavioral economics of shopping. A new *Making the Connection* uses behavioral economics to explore consumer reaction to the J.C. Penney pricing strategy.

Chapter 11, "Technology, Production, and Costs," opens with a new discussion of fracking, marginal costs, and energy prices.

Chapter 12, "Firms in Perfectly Competitive Markets," opens with an updated discussion of organic foods at farmers' markets. The chapter includes a new *Making the Connection* on the solar panel industry and a new *Solved Problem 12.4* on when a movie studio should stop production of a movie.

Chapter 13, "Monopolistic Competition: The Competitive Model in a More Realistic Setting," opens with an updated discussion of the challenges Starbucks faces from other coffeehouses and includes a new *Making the Connection* on e-cigarettes.

Chapter 14, "Oligopoly: Firms in Less Competitive Markets," opens with a discussion of the video game console market and the competition between Sony's PlayStation and Microsoft's Xbox. A new *Solved Problem 14.2* explores competition between Wal-Mart and Amazon over same-day delivery.

Chapter 15, "Monopoly and Antitrust Policy," opens with a discussion of a lobster restaurant in Maine and includes a new *Making the Connection* on trademark disputes involving Hasbro's Monopoly game.

Chapter 16, "Pricing Strategy," opens with an updated coverage of pricing strategy at Walt Disney and includes a new *Making the Connection* on price discrimination and online shoppers.

Chapter 17, "The Markets for Labor and Other Factors of Production," opens with a discussion of pitcher Zach Greinke of the Los Angeles Dodgers. The chapter includes a new *Making the Connection* that uses demand and supply to analyze the falling incomes of veterinarians.

Chapter 18, "Public Choice, Taxes, and the Distribution of Income," opens with an updated coverage of the debate about tax policy and includes a new *Making the Connection* about the "1 percenters."

The Foundation:
Contextual Learning and Modern Organization

We believe a course is a success if students can apply what they have learned to both their personal lives and their careers, and if they have developed the analytical skills to understand what they read in the media. That's why we explain economic concepts by using many real-world business examples and applications in the chapter openers, graphs, Making the Connection features, An Inside Look features, and end-of-chapter problems. This approach helps both business majors and liberal arts majors become educated consumers, voters, and citizens. In addition to our widget-free approach, we have a modern organization and place interesting policy topics early in the book to pique student interest.

We are convinced that students learn to apply economic principles best if they are taught in a familiar context. Whether they open an art studio, do social work, trade on Wall Street, work for the government, or tend bar, students benefit from understanding the economic forces behind their work. Though business students will have many opportunities to see economic principles in action in various courses, liberal arts students may not. We therefore use many diverse real-world business and policy examples to illustrate economic concepts and develop educated consumers, voters, and citizens:

- **A strong set of introductory chapters.** The introductory chapters provide students with a solid foundation in the basics. We emphasize the key ideas of marginal analysis and economic efficiency. In Chapter 4, "Economic Efficiency, Government Price Setting, and Taxes," we use the concepts of consumer and producer surplus to measure the economic effects of price ceilings and price floors as they relate to the familiar examples of rental properties and the minimum wage. (We revisit consumer and producer surplus in Chapter 9, "Comparative Advantage and the Gains from International Trade," where we discuss outsourcing and analyze government policies that affect trade; in Chapter 15, "Monopoly and Antitrust Policy," where we examine the effect of market power on economic efficiency; and in Chapter 16, "Pricing Strategy," where we examine the effect of firm pricing policy on economic efficiency.) In Chapter 8, "Firms, the Stock Market, and Corporate Governance," we provide students with a basic understanding of how firms are organized, raise funds, and provide information to investors. We also illustrate how in a market system entrepreneurs meet consumer wants and efficiently organize production.

- **Early coverage of policy issues.** To expose students to policy issues early in the course, we discuss health care policy in Chapter 1, "Economics: Foundations and Models"; rent control and the minimum wage in Chapter 4, "Economic Efficiency, Government Price Setting, and Taxes"; air pollution, global warming, and public goods in Chapter 5, "Externalities, Environmental Policy, and Public Goods"; government policy toward illegal drugs in Chapter 6, "Elasticity: The Responsiveness of Demand and Supply"; and health care policy in Chapter 7, "The Economics of Health Care."

- **Complete coverage of monopolistic competition.** We devote a full chapter, Chapter 13, "Monopolistic Competition: The Competitive Model in a More Realistic Setting," to monopolistic competition prior to covering oligopoly and monopoly in Chapter 14, "Oligopoly: Firms in Less Competitive Markets," and Chapter 15, "Monopoly and Antitrust Policy." Although many instructors cover monopolistic competition very briefly or dispense with it entirely, we think it is an overlooked tool for reinforcing the basic message of how markets work in a context that is much more familiar to students than are the agricultural examples that dominate other discussions of perfect competition. We use the monopolistic competition model to introduce the downward-sloping demand curve material usually introduced in a monopoly chapter. This approach helps students grasp the important point that nearly all firms—not just monopolies—face downward-sloping demand curves. Covering monopolistic competition directly after perfect competition also allows for the early discussion of topics such as brand management and sources of competitive success. Nevertheless, we wrote the chapter so that instructors who prefer to cover monopoly (Chapter 15, "Monopoly and Antitrust Policy") directly after perfect competition (Chapter 12, "Firms in Perfectly Competitive Markets") can do so without loss of continuity.

- **Extensive, realistic game theory coverage.** In Chapter 14, "Oligopoly: Firms in Less Competitive Markets," we use game theory to analyze competition among oligopolists.

Game theory helps students understand how companies with market power make strategic decisions in many competitive situations. We use familiar companies such as Apple, Hewlett-Packard, Coca-Cola, PepsiCo, and Dell in our game theory applications.

- **Unique coverage of pricing strategy.** In Chapter 16, "Pricing Strategy," we explore how firms use pricing strategies to increase profits. Students encounter pricing strategies everywhere—when they buy a movie ticket, book a flight for spring break, or research book prices online. We use these relevant, familiar examples to illustrate how companies use strategies such as price discrimination, cost-plus pricing, and two-part tariffs.

Special Features:
A Real-World, Hands-on Approach to Learning Economics

Business Cases and *An Inside Look* News Articles

Each chapter-opening case provides a real-world context for learning, sparks students' interest in economics, and helps unify the chapter. The case describes an actual company facing a real situation. The company is integrated in the narrative, graphs, and pedagogical features of the chapter. Many of the chapter openers focus on the role of entrepreneurs in developing new products and bringing them to the market. For example, Chapter 2 discusses Elon Musk of Tesla Motors and Chapter 8 discusses Mark Zuckerberg of Facebook. Here are a few examples of companies we explore in the chapter openers:

- Tesla Motors (Chapter 2, "Trade-offs, Comparative Advantage, and the Market System")
- Apple (Chapter 3, "Where Prices Come From: The Interaction of Demand and Supply")
- Facebook (Chapter 8, "Firms, the Stock Market, and Corporate Governance")

An *Inside Look* is a two-page feature that shows students how to apply the concepts from the chapter to the analysis of a news article. The feature appears at the end of Chapters 1–4. An *Inside Look* feature presents an excerpt from an article, analysis of the article, a graph(s), and critical thinking questions. Additional articles are located on MyEconLab, where they are continuously updated.

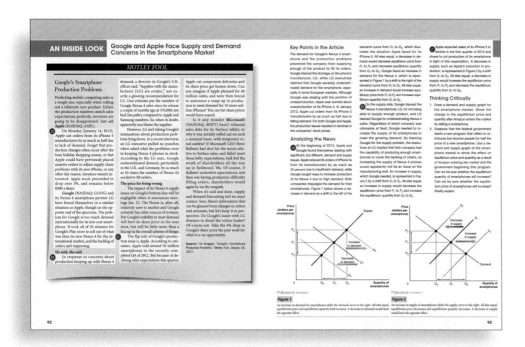

Economics in Your Life

After the chapter-opening real-world business case, we include a personal dimension to the chapter opener with a feature titled *Economics in Your Life*, which asks students to consider how economics affects their lives. The feature piques the interest of students and emphasizes the connection between the material they are learning and their experiences.

Economics in Your Life

Will You Buy an Apple iPhone or a Samsung Galaxy?

Suppose you want to buy a smartphone and are choosing between an Apple iPhone and a Samsung Galaxy S. If you buy an iPhone, you will have access to more applications—or "apps"—that can increase the enjoyment and performance of your smartphone. In addition, the iPhone is thin, lightweight, and sleek looking. One strategy Samsung can use to overcome these advantages is to compete based on price and value. Would you choose to buy a Galaxy S if it had a lower price than a comparable iPhone? If your income increased, would it affect your decision about which smartphone to buy? As you read this chapter, try to answer these questions. You can check your answers against those we provide on **page 91** at the end of this chapter.

At the end of the chapter, we use the chapter concepts to answer the questions asked at the beginning of the chapter.

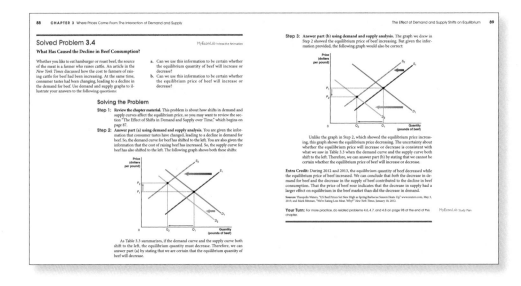

Continued from page 69

Economics in Your Life

Will You Buy an Apple iPhone or a Samsung Galaxy?

At the beginning of this chapter, we asked you to consider two questions: Would you choose to buy a Samsung Galaxy S if it had a lower price than a comparable Apple iPhone? and Would your decision be affected if your income increased? To determine the answer to the first question, you have to recognize that the iPhone and the Galaxy S are substitutes. If you consider the two smartphones to be close substitutes, then you are likely to buy the one with the lower price. In the market, if consumers generally believe that the iPhone and the Galaxy S are close substitutes, a fall in the price of the iPhone will increase the quantity of iPhones demanded and decrease the demand for Galaxy Ss. Suppose that you are currently leaning toward buying the Galaxy S because its price is lower than the price of the iPhone. If an increase in your income would cause you to change your decision and buy the iPhone, then the Galaxy S is an inferior good for you.

The following are examples of the topics we cover in the *Economics in Your Life* feature:

- Will you buy an Apple iPhone or a Samsung Galaxy? (Chapter 3, "Where Prices Come From: The Interaction of Demand and Supply")
- Is your take-home pay affected by what your employer spends on your health insurance? (Chapter 7, "The Economics of Health Care")
- Why can't you find a cheap PlayStation 4? (Chapter 14, "Oligopoly: Firms in Less Competitive Markets")

Solved Problems

Many students have great difficulty handling applied economics problems. We help students overcome this hurdle by including in each chapter two or three worked-out problems tied to select chapter-opening learning objectives. Our goals are to keep students focused on the main ideas of each chapter and give them a model of how to solve an economic problem by breaking it down step by step. Additional exercises in the end-of-chapter *Problems and Applications* section are tied to every *Solved Problem*. Additional *Solved Problems* appear in the *Instructor's Manual* and the print *Study Guide*. In addition, the Test Item File includes problems tied to the *Solved Problems* in the main book.

Don't Let This Happen to You

We know from many years of teaching which concepts students find most difficult. Each chapter contains a box feature called *Don't Let This Happen to You* that alerts students to the most common pitfalls in that chapter's material. We follow up with a related question in the end-of-chapter *Problems and Applications* section.

Making the Connection

Each chapter includes two to four *Making the Connection* features that provide real-world reinforcement of key concepts and help students learn how to interpret what they read on the Web and in newspapers. Most *Making the Connection* features use relevant, stimulating, and provocative news stories focused on businesses and policy issues. One-third of them are new to this edition, and most others have been updated. Several discuss health care, which remains a pressing policy issue. Each *Making the Connection* has at least one supporting end-of-chapter problem to allow students to test their understanding of the topic discussed.

Don't Let This Happen to You

Remember: A Change in a Good's Price Does *Not* Cause the Demand or Supply Curve to Shift

Suppose a student is asked to draw a demand and supply graph to illustrate how an increase in the price of oranges would affect the market for apples, with other variables being constant. He draws the graph on the left and explains it as follows: "Because apples and oranges are substitutes, an increase in the price of oranges will cause an initial shift to the right in the demand curve for apples, from D_1 to D_2. However, because this initial shift in the demand curve for apples results in a higher price for apples, P_2, consumers will find apples less desirable, and the demand curve will shift to the left, from D_2 to D_3, resulting in a final equilibrium price of P_3." Do you agree or disagree with the student's analysis?

You should disagree. The student has correctly understood that an increase in the price of oranges will cause the demand curve for apples to shift to the right. But, the second demand curve shift the student describes, from D_2

to D_3, will not take place. Changes in the price of a product do not result in shifts in the product's demand curve. Changes in the price of a product result only in movements along a demand curve.

The graph on the right shows the correct analysis. The increase in the price of oranges causes the demand curve for apples to increase from D_1 to D_2. At the original price, P_1, the increase in demand initially results in a shortage of apples equal to $Q_3 - Q_1$. But, as we have seen, a shortage causes the price to increase until the shortage is eliminated. In this case, the price will rise to P_2, where both the quantity demanded and the quantity supplied are equal to Q_2. Notice that the increase in price causes a decrease in the *quantity demanded*, from Q_3 to Q_2, but does *not* cause a decrease in demand.

MyEconLab Study Plan

Your Turn: Test your understanding by doing related problems 4.13 and 4.14 on pages 98–99 at the end of this chapter.

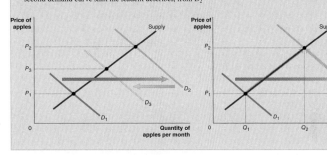

Graphs and Summary Tables

Graphs are an indispensable part of a principles of economics course but are a major stumbling block for many students. Every chapter except Chapter 1 includes end-of-chapter problems that require students to draw, read, and interpret graphs. Interactive graphing exercises appear on the book's supporting Web site. We use four devices to help students read and interpret graphs:

1. Detailed captions
2. Boxed notes
3. Color-coded curves
4. Summary tables (see pages 76, 81, 195, and 371 for examples)

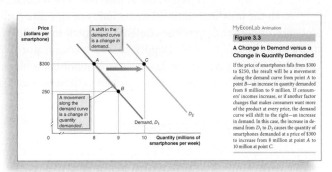

MyEconLab Animation

Figure 3.3

A Change in Demand versus a Change in Quantity Demanded

If the price of smartphones falls from $300 to $250, the result will be a movement along the demand curve from point A to point B—an increase in quantity demanded from 8 million to 9 million. If consumers' incomes increase, or if another factor changes that makes consumers want more of the product at every price, the demand curve will shift to the right—an increase in demand. In this case, the increase in demand from D_1 to D_2 causes the quantity of smartphones demanded at a price of $300 to increase from 8 million at point A to 10 million at point C.

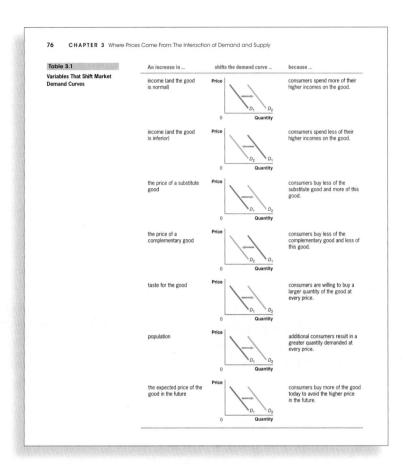

Review Questions and Problems and Applications— Grouped by Learning Objective to Improve Assessment

All the end-of-chapter material—Summary, Review Questions, and Problems and Applications—is grouped under learning objectives. The goals of this organization are to make it easier for instructors to assign problems based on learning objectives, both in the book and in MyEconLab, and to help students efficiently review material that they find difficult. If students have difficulty with a particular learning objective, an instructor can easily identify which end-of-chapter questions and problems support that objective and assign them as homework or discuss them in class. Every exercise in a chapter's Problems and Applications section is available in MyEconLab. Using MyEconLab, students can complete these and many other exercises online, get tutorial help, and receive instant feedback and assistance on exercises they answer incorrectly. Also, student learning will be enhanced by having the summary material and problems grouped together by learning objective, which will allow them to focus on the parts of the chapter they find most challenging. Each major section of the chapter, paired with a learning objective, has at least two review questions and three problems.

As in the previous editions, we include one or more end-of-chapter problems that test students' understanding of the content presented in the Solved Problem, Making the Connection, and Don't Let This Happen to You special features in the chapter. Instructors can cover a feature in class and assign the corresponding problem for homework. The Test Item Files also include test questions that pertain to these special features.

Real-Time-Data Exercises

Chapter 8, "Firms, the Stock Market, and Corporate Governance," includes two *Real-Time-Data Exercises* that help students become familiar with a key data source, learn how to locate data, and develop skills in interpreting data. The exercise marked with 🌐 allows students and instructors to use the very latest data from FRED.

Integrated Supplements

The authors and Pearson Education/Prentice Hall have worked together to integrate the text, print, and media resources to make teaching and learning easier.

MyEconLab is a unique online course management, testing, and tutorial resource.

MyEconLab

For the Instructor

Instructors can choose how much or how little time to spend setting up and using MyEcon-Lab. Here is a snapshot of what instructors are saying about MyEconLab:

> MyEconLab offers [students] a way to practice every week. They receive immediate feedback and a feeling of personal attention. As a result, my teaching has become more targeted and efficient.—Kelly Blanchard, Purdue University

> Students tell me that offering them MyEconLab is almost like offering them individual tutors.—Jefferson Edwards, Cypress Fairbanks College

> MyEconLab's eText is great—particularly in that it helps offset the skyrocketing cost of textbooks. Naturally, students love that.—Doug Gehrke, Moraine Valley Community College

Each chapter contains two preloaded homework exercise sets that can be used to build an individualized study plan for each student. These study plan exercises contain tutorial resources, including instant feedback, links to the appropriate learning objective in the eText, pop-up definitions from the text, and step-by-step guided solutions, where appropriate. After the initial setup of the course by the instructor, student use of these materials requires no further instructor setup. The online grade book records each student's performance and time spent on the tests and study plan and generates reports by student or chapter.

Alternatively, instructors can fully customize MyEconLab to match their course exactly, including reading assignments, homework assignments, video assignments, current news assignments, and quizzes and tests. Assignable resources include:

- Preloaded exercise assignments sets for each chapter that include the student tutorial resources mentioned earlier
- Preloaded quizzes for each chapter that are unique to the text and not repeated in the study plan or homework exercise sets
- Study plan problems that are similar to the end-of-chapter problems and numbered exactly like the book to make assigning homework easier
- *Real-Time-Data Analysis Exercises*, marked with ⬤, in Chapter 8 allow students and instructors to use the very latest data from FRED. By completing the exercises, students become familiar with a key data source, learn how to locate data, and develop skills in interpreting data.
- In the eText available in MyEconLab, select figures labeled MyEconLab Real-time data allow students to display a pop-up graph updated with real-time data from FRED.
- *Current News Exercises* provide a turnkey way to assign gradable news-based exercises in MyEconLab. Each week, Pearson scours the news, finds a current microeconomics article, creates an exercise around this news article, and then automatically adds it to MyEconLab. Assigning and grading current news-based exercises that deal with the latest micro events and policy issues has never been more convenient.

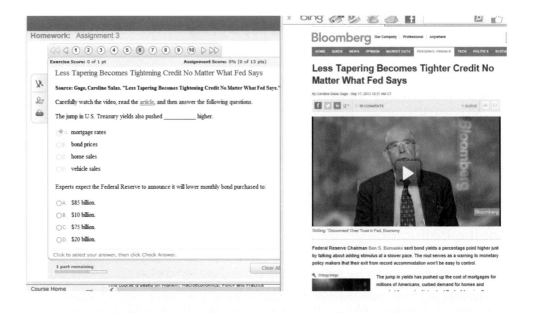

- *Experiments in MyEconLab* are a fun and engaging way to promote active learning and mastery of important economic concepts. Pearson's Experiments program is flexible and easy for instructors and students to use.
  - Single-player experiments allow your students to play against virtual players from anywhere at any time so long as they have an Internet connection.
  - Multiplayer experiments allow you to assign and manage a real-time experiment with your class.
  - Pre- and post-questions for each experiment are available for assignment in MyEconLab.

For a complete list of available experiments, visit www.myeconlab.com.

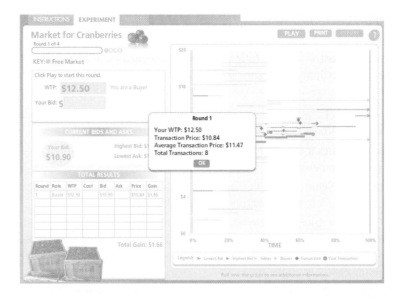

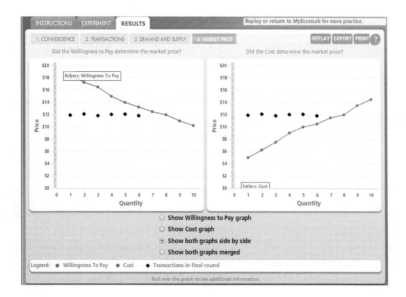

- Test Item File questions that allow you to assign quizzes or homework that will look just like your exams
- Econ Exercise Builder, which allows you to build customized exercises

Exercises include multiple-choice, graph drawing, and free-response items, many of which are generated algorithmically so that each time a student works them, a different variation is presented.

MyEconLab grades every problem type except essays, even problems with graphs. When working homework exercises, students receive immediate feedback, with links to additional learning tools.

Customization and Communication

MyEconLab in MyLab/Mastering provides additional optional customization and communication tools. Instructors who teach distance-learning courses or very large lecture sections find the MyLab/Mastering format useful because they can upload course documents and assignments, customize the order of chapters, and use communication features such as Document Sharing, Chat, ClassLive, and Discussion Board.

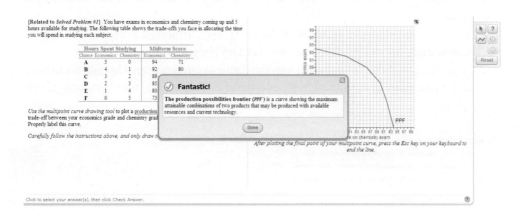

For the Student

MyEconLab puts students in control of their learning through a collection of testing, practice, and study tools tied to the online, interactive version of the textbook and other media resources. Here is a snapshot of what students are saying about MyEconLab:

- It was very useful because it had EVERYTHING, from practice exams to exercises to reading. Very helpful.—student, Northern Illinois University
- I would recommend taking the quizzes on MyEconLab because it gives you a true account of whether or not you understand the material.—student, Montana Tech
- It made me look through the book to find answers, so I did more reading.—student, Northern Illinois University

Students can study on their own or can complete assignments created by their instructor. In MyEconLab's structured environment, students practice what they learn, test their understanding, and pursue a personalized study plan generated from their performance on sample tests and from quizzes created by their instructors. In Homework or Study Plan mode, students have access to a wealth of tutorial features, including:

- Instant feedback on exercises that helps students understand and apply the concepts
- Links to the eText to promote reading of the text just when the student needs to revisit a concept or an explanation
- Step-by-step guided solutions that force students to break down a problem in much the same way an instructor would do during office hours

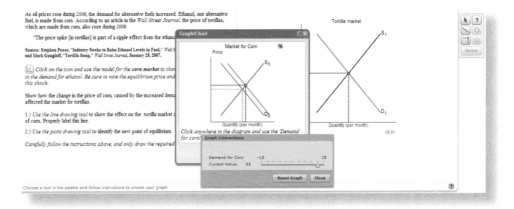

- Pop-up key term definitions from the eText to help students master the vocabulary of economics
- Links to the important features of the eText, such as Solved Problem, Making the Connection, An Inside Look, and Don't Let This Happen to You
- A graphing tool that is integrated into the various exercises to enable students to build and manipulate graphs to better understand how concepts, numbers, and graphs connect

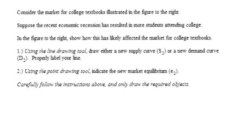
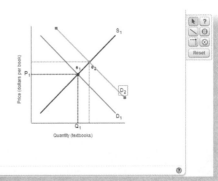

Additional MyEconLab Tools

MyEconLab includes the following additional features:

- **eText**—In addition to the portions of eText available as pop-ups or links, a fully searchable eText is available for students who wish to read and study in a fully electronic environment.

- **Print upgrade**—For students who wish to complete assignments in MyEconLab but read in print, Pearson offers registered MyEconLab users a loose-leaf version of the print text at a significant discount.

- **Glossary flashcards**—Every key term is available as a flashcard, allowing students to quiz themselves on vocabulary from one or more chapters at a time.

- **MySearchLab**—**MySearchLab** provides extensive help on the research process and four exclusive databases of credible and reliable source material, including the New York Times, the Financial Times, and peer-reviewed journals.

MyEconLab content has been created through the efforts of Chris Annala, State University of New York–Geneseo; Charles Baum, Middle Tennessee State University; Peggy Dalton, Frostburg State University; Carol Dole, Jacksonville University; David Foti, Lone Star College; Sarah Ghosh, University of Scranton; Satyajit Ghosh, Universtity of Scranton; Melissa Honig, Pearson Education; Woo Jung, University of Colorado; Courtney Kamauf, Pearson Education; Chris Kauffman, University of Tennessee–Knoxville; Russell Kellogg, University of Colorado–Denver; Noel Lotz, Pearson Education; Katherine McCann, University of Delaware; Daniel Mizak, Frostburg State University; Christine Polek, University of Massachusetts–Boston; Mark Scanlan, Stephen F. Austin State University; Leonie L. Stone, State University of New York–Geneseo; and Bert G. Wheeler, Cedarville University.

Other Resources for the Instructor

Instructor's Manual

Edward Scahill of the University of Scranton prepared the *Instructor's Manual*, which includes chapter-by-chapter summaries, learning objectives, extended examples and class exercises, teaching outlines incorporating key terms and definitions, teaching tips, topics for class discussion, new *Solved Problems*, new *Making the Connection* features, and solutions to all review questions and problems. The *Instructor's Manual* is available in print and for download from the Instructor's Resource Center (www.pearsonhighered.com/hubbard). The authors, Harry Ellis of the University of North Texas, and Robert Gillette of the University of Kentucky prepared the solutions to the end-of-chapter review questions and problems.

Test Item File

Randy Methenitis of Richland College prepared the Test Item File, which includes 4,000 multiple-choice, true/false, short-answer, and graphing questions. There are questions to support each key feature in the book. The Test Item File is available in print and for download from the Instructor's Resource Center (www.pearsonhighered.com/hubbard). Test questions are annotated with the following information:

- **Difficulty:** 1 for straight recall, 2 for some analysis, 3 for complex analysis
- **Type:** multiple-choice, true/false, short-answer, essay
- **Topic:** the term or concept the question supports
- **Learning outcome**
- **AACSB** (see description that follows)
- **Page number** in the text
- **Special feature in the main book:** chapter-opening business example, *Economics in Your Life, Solved Problem, Making the Connection*, and *Don't Let This Happen to You*

The Association to Advance Collegiate Schools of Business (AACSB)

The Test Item File author has connected select questions to the general knowledge and skill guidelines found in the AACSB Assurance of Learning Standards.

What Is the AACSB?

AACSB is a not-for-profit corporation of educational institutions, corporations, and other organizations devoted to the promotion and improvement of higher education in business administration and accounting. A collegiate institution offering degrees in business administration or accounting may volunteer for AACSB accreditation review. The AACSB makes initial accreditation decisions and conducts periodic reviews to promote continuous quality improvement in management education. Pearson Education is a proud member of the AACSB and is pleased to provide advice to help you apply AACSB Assurance of Learning Standards.

What Are AACSB Assurance of Learning Standards?

One of the criteria for AACSB accreditation is the quality of curricula. Although no specific courses are required, the AACSB expects a curriculum to include learning experiences in the following categories of Assurance of Learning Standards:

- Communication
- Ethical Reasoning
- Analytic Skills
- Use of Information Technology
- Multicultural and Diversity
- Reflective Thinking

Questions that test skills relevant to these standards are tagged with the appropriate standard. For example, a question testing the moral questions associated with externalities would receive the Ethical Reasoning tag.

How Can Instructors Use the AACSB Tags?

Tagged questions help you measure whether students are grasping the course content that aligns with the AACSB guidelines noted earlier. This in turn may suggest enrichment activities or other educational experiences to help students achieve these skills.

TestGen

The computerized TestGen package allows instructors to customize, save, and generate classroom tests. The test program permits instructors to edit, add, or delete questions from the Test Item File; analyze test results; and organize a database of tests and student results. This software allows for extensive flexibility and ease of use. It provides many options for organizing and displaying tests, along with search and sort features. The software and the Test Item File can be downloaded from the Instructor's Resource Center (www.pearson-highered.com/hubbard).

PowerPoint Lecture Presentation

Three sets of PowerPoint slides, prepared by Paul Holmes of State University of New York–Fredonia, are available:

1. A comprehensive set of PowerPoint slides can be used by instructors for class presentations or by students for lecture preview or review. These slides include all the graphs, tables, and equations in the textbook. Two versions are available—step-by-step mode, in which you can build graphs as you would on a blackboard, and automated mode, in which you use a single click per slide.
2. A comprehensive set of PowerPoint slides have Classroom Response Systems (CRS) questions built in so that instructors can incorporate CRS "clickers" into their classroom lectures. For more information on Pearson Education's partnership with CRS, see the section "Classroom Response Systems." Instructors can download these

PowerPoint presentations from the Instructor's Resource Center (www.pearsonhigh-ered.com/hubbard).

3. A student version of the PowerPoint slides is available as .pdf files. This version allows students to print the slides and bring them to class for note taking. Instructors can download these PowerPoint presentations from the Instructor's Resource Center (www.pearsonhighered.com/hubbard).

Classroom Response Systems

Classroom Response Systems (CRS) is an exciting new wireless polling technology that increases the interactivity of large and small classrooms by enabling instructors to pose questions to their students, record results, and display the results instantly. Students can answer questions easily, using compact remote-control transmitters. Pearson Education has partnerships with leading CRS providers and can show you everything you need to know about setting up and using CRS. Pearson Education will provide the classroom hardware, text-specific PowerPoint slides, software, and support, and will also show you how your students can benefit! Please contact your local Pearson Education sales representative for more information.

Other Resources for the Student

In addition to MyEconLab, Pearson provides the following resources.

Study Guide

Fatma Abdel-Raouf from Goldey-Beacom College prepared the Study Guide, which reinforces the textbook and provides students with the following:

- Chapter summaries
- Discussion of each learning objective
- Section-by-section reviews of the concepts presented
- Helpful study hints
- Additional Solved Problems to supplement those in the text
- Key terms with definitions
- Self-tests for each chapter, which include 40 multiple-choice questions plus a number of short-answer and true/false questions, with accompanying answers and explanations

PowerPoint Slides

For student use as a study aid or note-taking guide, PowerPoint slides, prepared by Paul Holmes of State University of New York–Fredonia, can be downloaded from MyEconLab or the Instructor's Resource Center and made available to students. The slides include:

- All graphs, tables, and equations in the text
- Figures in step-by-step mode and automated modes, using a single click per graph curve
- End-of-chapter key terms with hyperlinks to relevant slides

Instructors

CourseSmart goes beyond traditional expectations, providing instant online access to the textbooks and course materials you need, at a lower cost to students. And, even as students save money, you can save time and hassle with a digital textbook that allows you to search the most relevant content at the very moment you need it. Whether it's evaluating textbooks or creating lecture notes to help students with difficult concepts, CourseSmart can make life a little easier. See how when you visit www.coursesmart.com.

Students

CourseSmart goes beyond traditional expectations, providing instant, online access to the textbooks and course materials students need, at lower cost. They can also search, highlight, and take notes anywhere, any time. See all the benefits to students at www.coursesmart.com.

Accuracy Review Board and Reviewers

The guidance and recommendations of the following instructors helped us develop the revision plans for the fifth edition and the supplements package. While we could not incorporate every suggestion from every consultant board member, reviewer, or accuracy checker, we do thank each and every one of you and acknowledge that your feedback was indispensable in developing this text. We greatly appreciate your assistance in making this the best text it could be; you have helped teach a whole new generation of students about the exciting world of economics.

Accuracy Review Board

Our accuracy checkers did a particularly painstaking and thorough job of helping us proof the graphs, equations, and features of the text and supplements. We are grateful for their time and commitment:

Fatma Abdel-Raouf, Goldey-Beacom College
Lee A. Craig, North Carolina State University
Harold Elder, University of Alabama
Robert Gillette, University of Kentucky
Anthony Gyapong, Pennsylvania State University
Kristen Keith, University of Toledo
Randy Methenitis, Richland College
Edward Scahill, University of Scranton
Julianne Treme, University of North Carolina–Wilmington
David N. van der Goes, University of New Mexico

Reviewers

The guidance and thoughtful recommendations of many instructors helped us develop and implement a revision plan that improved the book's content, enhanced the figures, and strengthened the assessment features. We extend special thanks to Edward Scahill of the University of Scranton for helping us revise the chapter openers, to Randy Methenitis of Richland College for helping us revise the An Inside Look feature in Chapters 1–4, and to Robert Gillette of the University of Kentucky and Harry Ellis of University of North Texas for helping us revise the end-of-chapter questions. We are grateful for the comments and many helpful suggestions received from the following reviewers:

Frank Albritton, Seminole State College
William P. Aldridge, University of Alabama

Genevieve Briand, Washington State University
Shirley Cassing, University of Pittsburgh
David Davenport, McLennan Community College
John Dogbey, University of Nebraska at Omaha
Kirk Doran, University of Notre Dame
Harold W. Elder, University of Alabama
Rudy Fichtenbaum, Wright State University
Alejandro Gelves, Midwestern State University
Robert Gillette, University of Kentucky
Allen C. Goodman, Wayne State University
Jamal G. Husein, Angelo State University
Mark Jablonowski, University of Hartford
Kristen Keith, University of Toledo
Carrie B. Kerekes, Florida Gulf Coast University
Michael H. Lampert, Truckee Meadows Community College
Keith D. Malone, University of North Alabama
Abraham Mathew, Indiana University–Purdue University Indianapolis
Barbara A. Moore, University of Central Florida
Shofiqur Rahman, University of Texas at El Paso
Edward Scahill, University of Scranton
Dosse Toulaboe, Fort Hays State University
Julianne Treme, University of North Carolina–Wilmington
Tara Westerhold, Western Illinois University
Zhen Zhu, University of Central Oklahoma

Previous Edition Class Testers, Accuracy Reviewers, and Consultants

Class Testers

We are grateful to both the instructors who class-tested manuscript of the first edition and their students for providing useful recommendations on how to make chapters more interesting, relevant, and comprehensive:

Charles A. Bennett, Gannon University

Anne E. Bresnock, University of California–Los Angeles, and California State Polytechnic University–Pomona

Linda Childs-Leatherbury, Lincoln University, Pennsylvania

John Eastwood, Northern Arizona University

David Eaton, Murray State University

Paul Elgatian, St. Ambrose University

Patricia A. Freeman, Jackson State University

Robert Godby, University of Wyoming

Frank Gunter, Lehigh University

Ahmed Ispahani, University of LaVerne

Brendan Kennelly, Lehigh University and National University of Ireland–Galway

Ernest Massie, Franklin University

Carol McDonough, University of Massachusetts–Lowell

Shah Mehrabi, Montgomery College

Sharon Ryan, University of Missouri–Columbia

Bruce G. Webb, Gordon College

Madelyn Young, Converse College

Susan Zumas, Lehigh University

Accuracy Review Boards

We are grateful to the following accuracy checkers of the previous editions for their hard work on the book and supplements:

Fatma Abdel-Raouf, Goldey-Beacom College

Anne Alexander, University of Wyoming

Mohammad Bajwa, Northampton Community College

Cynthia Bansak, St. Lawrence University

Hamid Bastin, Shippensburg University

Kelly Hunt Blanchard, Purdue University

Don Bumpass, Sam Houston State University

Charles Callahan III, State University of New York–Brockport

Mark S. Chester, Reading Area Community College

Kenny Christianson, Binghamton University

Ishita Edwards, Oxnard College

Harold Elder, University of Alabama

Harry Ellis, University of North Texas

Can Erbil, Brandeis University

Marc Fusaro, Arkansas Tech University

Sarah Ghosh, University of Scranton

Robert Gillette, University of Kentucky

Maria Giuili, Diablo Valley College

Mark Gius, Quinnipiac University

Robert Godby, University of Wyoming

William L. Goffe, Pennsylvania State University

Anthony Gyapong, Pennsylvania State University—Abington

Travis Hayes, University of Tennessee–Chattanooga

Carol Hogan, University of Michigan–Dearborn

Anisul M. Islam, University of Houston–Downtown

Aaron Jackson, Bentley College

Nancy Jianakoplos, Colorado State University

Thomas C. Kinnaman, Bucknell University

Mary K. Knudson, University of Iowa

Faik A. Koray, Louisiana State University

Stephan Kroll, California State University–Sacramento

Tony Lima, California State University–East Bay

Randy Methenitis, Richland College

Normal C. Miller, Miami University

David Mitch, University of Maryland–Baltimore County

James A. Moreno, Blinn College

Michael Potepan, San Francisco State University

Mary L. Pranzo, California State University–Fresno

Fernando Quijano, Dickinson State University

Matthew Rafferty, Quinnipiac University

Ratha Ramoo, Diablo Valley College

Jeff Reynolds, Northern Illinois University

Brian Rosario, University of California–Davis

Joseph M. Santos, South Dakota State University

Edward Scahill, University of Scranton

Mark V. Siegler, California State University–Sacramento

Rachel Small, University of Colorado–Boulder

Stephen Smith, Bakersfield College

Rajeev Sooreea, Pennsylvania State University–Altoona

Rebecca Stein, University of Pennsylvania

Ed Steinberg, New York University

Michael Stone, Quinnipiac University

Arlena Sullivan, Jones County Junior College

Wendine Thompson–Dawson, University of Utah

Julianne Treme, University of North Carolina–Wilmington

Robert Whaples, Wake Forest University

Consultant Boards

We received guidance from a dedicated consultant board during the development of the previous editions at several critical junctures. We relied on the board for input on content, figure treatment, and design:

Kate Antonovics, University of California–San Diego
Robert Beekman, University of Tampa
Valerie Bencivenga, University of Texas–Austin
Kelly Blanchard, Purdue University
Susan Dadres, Southern Methodist University
Harry Ellis, Jr., University of North Texas
Sherman T. Folland, Oakland University
Robert Gillette, University of Kentucky
Robert Godby, University of Wyoming
William L. Goffe, Pennsylvania State University
Jane S. Himarios, University of Texas–Arlington
Donn M. Johnson, Quinnipiac University
Mark Karscig, Central Missouri State University
Jenny Minier, University of Kentucky
David Mitch, University of Maryland–Baltimore County
Nicholas Noble, Miami University
Michael Potepan, San Francisco State University
Matthew Rafferty, Quinnipiac University
Helen Roberts, University of Illinois–Chicago
Robert Rosenman, Washington State University
Joseph M. Santos, South Dakota State University
Stephen Snyder, University of Pittsburgh
Martin C. Spechler, Indiana University–Purdue University Indianapolis
Robert Whaples, Wake Forest University
Jonathan B. Wight, University of Richmond

Reviewers

The guidance and recommendations of the following instructors helped us shape the previous editions.

ALABAMA
Doris Bennett, Jacksonville State University
Harold W. Elder, University of Alabama–Tuscaloosa
Wanda Hudson, Alabama Southern Community College
Edward Merkel, Troy University
James L. Swofford, University of Southern Alabama

ARIZONA
Doug Conway, Mesa Community College
John Eastwood, Northern Arizona University
Price Fishback, University of Arizona
Anne Williams, Gateway Community College

ARKANSAS
Jerry Crawford, Arkansas State University
Marc Fusaro, Arkansas Tech University
Randall Kesselring, Arkansas State University
Dan Marburger, Arkansas State University

CALIFORNIA
Shawn Abbott, College of the Siskiyous
Renatte Adler, San Diego State University
Ercument Aksoy, Los Angeles Valley College
Maneeza Aminy, Golden Gate University
Kate Antonovics, University of California–San Diego
Becca Arnold, Mesa College
Asatar Bair, City College of San Francisco
Diana Bajrami, College of Alameda
Robert Bise, Orange Coast Community College
Victor Brajer, California State University–Fullerton
Anne E. Bresnock, University of California–Los Angeles, and California State Polytechnic University–Pomona
David Brownstone, University of California–Irvine
Maureen Burton, California State Polytechnic University–Pomona
Annette Chamberlin, National College
Anoshua Chaudhuri, San Francisco State University
James G. Devine, Loyola Marymount University
Jose Esteban, Palomar College
Roger Frantz, San Diego State University
Craig Gallet, California State University–Sacramento
Andrew Gill, California State University–Fullerton
Maria Giuili, Diablo Valley College
Julie Gonzalez, University of California–Santa Cruz
Lisa Grobar, California State University–Long Beach
Steve Hamilton, California State University–Fullerton
Dewey Heinsma, Mt. San Jacinto Community College
Jessica Howell, California State University–Sacramento
Greg Hunter, California State University–Pomona
John Ifcher, Santa Clara University
Ahmed Ispahani, University of LaVerne
George A. Jouganatos, California State University–Sacramento
Jonathan Kaplan, California State University–Sacramento
Leland Kempe, California State University–Fresno
Philip King, San Francisco State University
Lori Kletzer, University of California, Santa Cruz
Stephan Kroll, California State University–Sacramento
David Lang, California State University–Sacramento
Carsten Lange, California State Polytechnic University–Pomona
Don Leet, California State University–Fresno
Rose LeMont, Modesto Junior College
Tony Lima, California State University–East Bay
Solina Lindahl, California Polytechnic State University–San Luis Obispo
Roger Mack, DeAnza College
Michael Marlow, California Polytechnic State University
Kristen Monaco, California State University–Long Beach
W. Douglas Morgan, University of California, Santa Barbara
Nivedita Mukherji, Oakland University

Solomon Namala, Cerritos College

Andrew Narwold, University of San Diego

Hanna Paulson, West Los Angeles College

Joseph M. Pogodzinksi, San Jose State University

Michael J. Potepan, San Francisco State University

Mary L. Pranzo, California State University–Fresno

Sasha Radisich, Glendale Community College

Ratha Ramoo, Diablo Valley College

Scott J. Sambucci, California State University–East Bay

Ariane Schauer, Marymount College

Frederica Shockley, California State University–Chico

Mark Siegler, California State University–Sacramento

Jonathan Silberman, Oakland University

Lisa Simon, California Polytechnic State University–
San Louis Obispo

Stephen Smith, Bakersfield College

Rodney B. Swanson, University of California–Los Angeles

Martha Stuffler, Irvine Valley College

Lea Templer, College of the Canyons

Kristin A. Van Gaasbeck, California State University–
Sacramento

Va Nee Van Vleck, California State University–Fresno

Michael Visser, Sonoma State University

Steven Yamarik, California State University–Long Beach

Guy Yamashiro, California State University–Long Beach

Kevin Young, Diablo Valley College

Anthony Zambelli, Cuyamaca College

COLORADO

Mohammed Akacem, Metropolitan State College of Denver

Rhonda Corman, University of Northern Colorado

Dale DeBoer, University of Colorado–Colorado Springs

Debbie Evercloud, University of Colorado–Denver

Karen Gebhardt, Colorado State University

Scott Houser, Colorado School of Mines

Murat Iyigun, University of Colorado at Boulder

Nancy Jianakoplos, Colorado State University

Jay Kaplan, University of Colorado–Boulder

William G. Mertens, University of Colorado–Boulder

Rachael Small, University of Colorado–Boulder

Stephen Weiler, Colorado State University

CONNECTICUT

Christopher P. Ball, Quinnipiac University

Mark Gius, Quinnipiac University

Donn M. Johnson, Quinnipiac University

Robert Martel, University of Connecticut

Judith Mills, Southern Connecticut State University

Matthew Rafferty, Quinnipiac University

Christian Zimmermann, University of Connecticut

DISTRICT OF COLUMBIA

Colleen Callahan, American University

Robert Feinberg, American University

Walter Park, American University

DELAWARE

Fatma Abdel-Raouf, Goldey-Beacom College

Ali Ataiifar, Delaware County Community College

Andrew T. Hill, University of Delaware

FLORIDA

Herman Baine, Broward Community College

Robert L. Beekman, University of Tampa

Eric P. Chiang, Florida Atlantic University

Martine Duchatelet, Barry University

Hadley Hartman, Santa Fe Community College

Richard Hawkins, University of West Florida

Brad Kamp, University of South Florida

Brian Kench, University of Tampa

Thomas McCaleb, Florida State University

Barbara A. Moore, University of Central Florida

Augustine Nelson, University of Miami

Jamie Ortiz, Florida Atlantic University

Deborah Paige, Santa Fe Community College

Robert Pennington, University of Central Florida

Bob Potter, University of Central Florida

Jerry Schwartz, Broward Community College–North

William Stronge, Florida Atlantic University

Nora Underwood, University of Central Florida

Zhiguang Wang, Florida International University

Joan Wiggenhorn, Barry University

GEORGIA

Greg Brock, Georgia Southern University

Donna Fisher, Georgia Southern University

Shelby Frost, Georgia State University

John King, Georgia Southern University

Constantin Ogloblin, Georgia Southern University

Dr. Greg Okoro, Georgia Perimeter College–Clarkston

Michael Reksulak, Georgia Southern University

Bill Yang, Georgia Southern University

IDAHO

Cynthia Hill, Idaho State University

Don Holley, Boise State University

Tesa Stegner, Idaho State University

ILLINOIS

Teshome Abebe, Eastern Illinois University

Ali Akarca, University of Illinois–Chicago

Zsolt Becsi, Southern Illinois University–Carbondale

James Bruehler, Eastern Illinois University

Louis Cain, Loyola University Chicago and Northwestern
University

Rosa Lea Danielson, College of DuPage

Kevin Dunagan, Oakton Community College

Scott Gilbert, Southern Illinois University

Rajeev K. Goel, Illinois State University

David Gordon, Illinois Valley Community College

Alan Grant, Eastern Illinois University

Rik Hafer, Southern Illinois University–Edwardsville

Alice Melkumian, Western Illinois University
Christopher Mushrush, Illinois State University
Jeff Reynolds, Northern Illinois University
Helen Roberts, University of Illinois–Chicago
Thomas R. Sadler, Western Illinois University
Eric Schulz, Northwestern University
Dennis Shannon, Southwestern Illinois College
Charles Sicotte, Rock Valley Community College
Neil T. Skaggs, Illinois State University
Kevin Sylwester, Southern Illinois University–Carbondale
Wendine Thompson-Dawson, Monmouth College
Tara Westerhold, Western Illinois University
Mark Witte, Northwestern University
Laurie Wolff, Southern Illinois University–Carbondale
Paula Worthington, Northwestern University

INDIANA
Kelly Blanchard, Purdue University
Cecil Bohanon, Ball State University
Kirk Doran, University of Notre Dame
Thomas Gresik, University of Notre Dame
Robert B. Harris, Indiana University–Purdue University, Indianapolis
Fred Herschede, Indiana University–South Bend
John Pomery, Purdue University
Curtis Price, University of Southern Indiana
Rob Rude, Ivy Tech Community College
James K. Self, Indiana University–Bloomington
Esther-Mirjam Sent, University of Notre Dame
Virginia Shingleton, Valparaiso University
Martin C. Spechler, Indiana University–Purdue University Indianapolis
Arun K. Srinivasan, Indiana University–Southeast Campus
Geetha Suresh, Purdue University–West Lafayette

IOWA
Terry Alexander, Iowa State University
Paul Elgatian, St. Ambrose University
Jennifer Fuhrman, University of Iowa
Ken McCormick, University of Northern Iowa
Andy Schuchart, Iowa Central Community College
John Solow, University of Iowa
Jonathan Warner, Dordt College

KANSAS
Guatam Bhattacharya, University of Kansas
Amanda Freeman, Kansas State University
Dipak Ghosh, Emporia State University
Alan Grant, Baker University
Wayne Oberle, St. Ambrose University
Jodi Messer Pelkowski, Wichita State University
Martin Perline, Wichita State University
Joel Potter, Kansas State University
Joshua Rosenbloom, University of Kansas
Shane Sanders, Kansas State University
Bhavneet Walia, Kansas State University

KENTUCKY
Tom Cate, Northern Kentucky University
Nan-Ting Chou, University of Louisville
David Eaton, Murray State University
Ann Eike, University of Kentucky
Robert Gillette, University of Kentucky
Barry Haworth, University of Louisville
Gail Hoyt, University of Kentucky
Donna Ingram, Eastern Kentucky University
Waithaka Iraki, Kentucky State University
Hak Youn Kim, Western Kentucky University
Martin Milkman, Murray State University
Jenny Minier, University of Kentucky
David Shideler, Murray State University
John Vahaly, University of Louisville

LOUISIANA
Lara Gardner, Southeastern Louisiana University
Jay Johnson, Southeastern Louisiana University
Faik Koray, Louisiana State University
Paul Nelson, University of Louisiana–Monroe
Sung Chul No, Southern University and A&M College
Tammy Parker, University of Louisiana–Monroe
Wesley A. Payne, Delgado Community College
Nancy Rumore, University of Louisiana at Lafayette

MARYLAND
Carey Borkoski, Anne Arundel Community College
Kathleen A. Carroll, University of Maryland–Baltimore County
Jill Caviglia-Harris, Salisbury University
Dustin Chambers, Salisbury University
Karl Einolf, Mount Saint Mary's University
Marsha Goldfarb, University of Maryland–Baltimore City
Bruce Madariaga, Montgomery College
Shah Mehrabi, Montgomery College
Gretchen Mester, Anne Arundel Community College
David Mitch, University of Maryland–Baltimore County
John Neri, University of Maryland
Henry Terrell, University of Maryland

MASSACHUSETTS
William L. Casey, Jr., Babson College
Arthur Schiller Casimir, Western New England College
Michael Enz, Western New England College
Can Erbil, Brandeis University
Lou Foglia, Suffolk University
Gerald Friedman, University of Massachusetts
Todd Idson, Boston University
Aaron Jackson, Bentley College
Russell A. Janis, University of Massachusetts–Amherst
Anthony Laramie, Merrimack College
Carol McDonough, University of Massachusetts–Lowell
William O'Brien, Worcester State College
Ahmad Saranjam, Bridgewater State College

Howard Shore, Bentley College
Janet Thomas, Bentley College
Gregory H. Wassall, Northeastern University
Bruce G. Webb, Gordon College
Gilbert Wolpe, Newbury College
Jay Zagorsky, Boston University

MICHIGAN

Eric Beckman, Delta College
Jared Boyd, Henry Ford Community College
Victor Claar, Hope College
Dr. Sonia Dalmia, Grand Valley State University
Daniel Giedeman, Grand Valley State University
Steven Hayworth, Eastern Michigan University
Gregg Heidebrink, Washtenaw Community College
Carol Hogan, University of Michigan–Dearborn
Marek Kolar, Delta College
Susan J. Linz, Michigan State University
James Luke, Lansing Community College
Ilir Miteza, University of Michigan–Dearborn
John Nader, Grand Valley State University
Norman P. Obst, Michigan State University
Laudo M. Ogura, Grand Valley State University
Robert J. Rossana, Wayne State University
Michael J. Ryan, Western Michigan University
Charles A. Stull, Kalamazoo College
Michael J. Twomey, University of Michigan–Dearborn
Mark Wheeler, Western Michigan University
Wendy Wysocki, Monroe County Community College

MINNESOTA

Mary Edwards, Saint Cloud State University
Phillip J. Grossman, Saint Cloud State University
Monica Hartman, University of St. Thomas
Matthew Hyle, Winona State University
David J. O'Hara, Metropolitan State University–Minneapolis
Kwang Woo (Ken) Park, Minnesota State University–Mankato
Artatrana Ratha, Saint Cloud State University
Ken Rebeck, Saint Cloud State University
Katherine Schmeiser, University of Minnesota

MISSISSIPPI

Becky Campbell, Mississippi State University
Randall Campbell, Mississippi State University
Patricia A. Freeman, Jackson State University
Arlena Sullivan, Jones County Junior College

MISSOURI

Chris Azevedo, University of Central Missouri
Ariel Belasen, Saint Louis University
Catherine Chambers, University of Central Missouri
Paul Chambers, University of Central Missouri
Kermit Clay, Ozarks Technical Community College
Ben Collier, Northwest Missouri State University
John R. Crooker, University of Central Missouri

Jo Durr, Southwest Missouri State University
Julie H. Gallaway, Southwest Missouri State University
Terrel Gallaway, Southwest Missouri State University
Mark Karscig, Central Missouri State University
Nicholas D. Peppes, Saint Louis Community College–Forest Park
Steven T. Petty, College of the Ozarks
Sharon Ryan, University of Missouri–Columbia
Ben Young, University of Missouri–Kansas City

MONTANA

Agnieszka Bielinska-Kwapisz, Montana State University–Bozeman
Jeff Bookwalter, University of Montana–Missoula

NEBRASKA

Allan Jenkins, University of Nebraska–Kearney
James Knudsen, Creighton University
Craig MacPhee, University of Nebraska–Lincoln
Kim Sosin, University of Nebraska–Omaha
Mark E. Wohar, University of Nebraska–Omaha

NEVADA

Bernard Malamud, University of Nevada–Las Vegas
Bill Robinson, University of Nevada–Las Vegas

NEW HAMPSHIRE

Evelyn Gick, Dartmouth College
Neil Niman, University of New Hampshire

NEW JERSEY

Len Anyanwu, Union County College
Maharuk Bhiladwalla, Rutgers University–New Brunswick
Giuliana Campanelli-Andreopoulos, William Paterson University
Gary Gigliotti, Rutgers University–New Brunswick
John Graham, Rutgers University–Newark
Berch Haroian, William Paterson University
Paul Harris, Camden County College
Jeff Rubin, Rutgers University
Henry Ryder, Gloucester County College
Donna Thompson, Brookdale Community College

NEW MEXICO

Donald Coes, University of New Mexico
Kate Krause, University of New Mexico
Curt Shepherd, University of New Mexico

NEW YORK

Seemi Ahmad, Dutchess Community College
Chris Annala, State University of New York–Geneseo
Erol Balkan, Hamilton College
John Bockino, Suffolk County Community College–Ammerman
Charles Callahan III, State University of New York–Brockport
Michael Carew, Baruch College
Sean Corcoran, New York University
Ranjit S. Dighe, City University of New York–Bronx Community College

Debra Dwyer, Stony Brook University
Glenn Gerstner, Saint John's University–Queens
Susan Glanz, Saint John's University–Queens
Wayne A. Grove, LeMoyne College
Nancy Howe, Hudson Valley Community College
Christopher Inya, Monroe Community College
Ghassan Karam, Pace University
Clifford Kern, State University of New York–Binghamton
Mary Lesser, Iona College
Anna Musatti, Columbia University
Theodore Muzio, St. John's University, New York
Emre Ozsoz, Fashion Institute of Technology
Howard Ross, Baruch College
Ed Steinberg, New York University
Leonie Stone, State University of New York–Geneseo
Ganti Subrahmanyam, University of Buffalo
Jogindar S. Uppal, State University of New York–Albany
Susan Wolcott, Binghamton University

NORTH CAROLINA

Rita Balaban, University of North Carolina
Otilia Boldea, North Carolina State University
Robert Burrus, University of North Carolina–Wilmington
Lee A. Craig, North Carolina State University
Alexander Deshkovski, North Carolina Central University
Kathleen Dorsainvil, Winston–Salem State University
Lydia Gan, School of Business, University of North Carolina–Pembroke
Michael Goode, Central Piedmont Community College
Salih Hakeem, North Carolina Central University
Melissa Hendrickson, North Carolina State University
Haiyong Liu, East Carolina University
Kosmas Marinakis, North Carolina State University
Todd McFall, Wake Forest University
Shahriar Mostashari, Campbell University
Jonathan Phillips, North Carolina State University
Bobby Puryear, North Carolina State University
Jeff Sarbaum, University of North Carolina–Greensboro
Peter Schuhmann, University of North Carolina–Wilmington
Robert Shoffner, Central Piedmont Community College
Catherine Skura, Sandhills Community College
Carol Stivender, University of North Carolina–Charlotte
Vera Tabakova, East Carolina University
Eric Taylor, Central Piedmont Community College
Hui-Kuan Tseng, University of North Carolina at Charlotte
Robert Whaples, Wake Forest University
John Whitehead, Appalachian State University
Gary W. Zinn, East Carolina University
Rick Zuber, University of North Carolina at Charlotte

OHIO

John P. Blair, Wright State University
Bolong Cao, Ohio University–Athens
Kyongwook Choi, Ohio University

James D'Angelo, University of Cincinnati
Darlene DeVera, Miami University
Tim Fuerst, Bowling Green University
Harley Gill, Ohio State University
Leroy Gill, Ohio State University
Steven Heubeck, Ohio State University
Daniel Horton, Cleveland State University
Jean Kujawa, Lourdes College
Ernest Massie, Franklin University
Ida A. Mirzaie, Ohio State University
Jay Mutter, University of Akron
Mike Nelson, University of Akron
Nicholas Noble, Miami University
Dennis C. O'Neill, University of Cincinnati
Joseph Palardy, Youngstown State University
Charles Reichheld, Cuyahoga Community College
Teresa Riley, Youngstown State University
Rochelle Ruffer, Youngstown State University
Kate Sheppard, University of Akron
Richard Stratton, University of Akron
Albert Sumell, Youngstown State University
Steve Szheghi, Wilmington College
Melissa Thomasson, Miami University
Yaqin Wang, Youngstown State University
Bert Wheeler, Cedarville University
Kathryn Wilson, Kent State University
Sourushe Zandvakili, University of Cincinnati

OKLAHOMA

David Hudgins, University of Oklahoma
Bill McLean, Oklahoma State University
Denny Myers, Oklahoma City Community College
Ed Price, Oklahoma State University
Abdulhamid Sukar, Cameron University

OREGON

Bill Burrows, Lane Community College
Tom Carroll, Central Oregon Community College
Tim Duy, University of Oregon
B. Starr McMullen, Oregon State University
Ted Scheinman, Mount Hood Community College
Larry Singell, University of Oregon
Ayca Tekin-Koru, Oregon State University

PENNSYLVANIA

Bradley Andrew, Juniata College
Mohammad Bajwa, Northampton Community College
Gustavo Barboza, Mercyhurst College
Charles A. Bennett, Gannon University
Cynthia Benzing, West Chester University
Howard Bodenhorn, Lafayette College
Milica Bookman, St. Joseph's University
Robert Brooker, Gannon University
Eric Brucker, Widener University
Linda Childs-Leatherbury, Lincoln University

Scott J. Dressler, Villanova University

Satyajit Ghosh, University of Scranton

William L. Goffe, Pennsylvania State University

Anthony Gyapong, Pennsylvania State University–Abington

Mehdi Haririan, Bloomsburg University

Andrew Hill, Federal Reserve Bank of Philadelphia

Steven Husted, University of Pittsburgh

James Jozefowicz, Indiana University of Pennsylvania

Stephanie Jozefowicz, Indiana University of Pennsylvania

Nicholas Karatjas, Indiana University of Pennsylvania

Mary Kelly, Villanova University

Brendan Kennelly, Lehigh University

Thomas C. Kinnaman, Bucknell University

Christopher Magee, Bucknell University

Katherine McCann, Penn State

Judy McDonald, Lehigh University

Ranganath Murthy, Bucknell University

Hong V. Nguyen, University of Scranton

Cristian Pardo, Saint Joseph's University

Iordanis Petsas, University of Scranton

Denis Raihall, West Chester University

Adam Renhoff, Drexel University

Nicole Sadowski, York College of Pennsylvania

Edward Scahill, University of Scranton

Ken Slaysman, York College of Pennsylvania

Rajeev Sooreea, Pennsylvania State University–Altoona

Rebecca Stein, University of Pennsylvania

Sandra Trejos, Clarion University

Peter Zaleski, Villanova University

Ann Zech, Saint Joseph's University

Lei Zhu, West Chester University of Pennsylvania

Susan Zumas, Lehigh University

RHODE ISLAND

Jongsung Kim, Bryant University

Leonard Lardaro, University of Rhode Island

Nazma Latif-Zaman, Providence College

SOUTH CAROLINA

Calvin Blackwell, College of Charleston

Ward Hooker, Orangeburg–Calhoun Technical College

Woodrow W. Hughes, Jr., Converse College

John McArthur, Wofford College

Chad Turner, Clemson University

Madelyn Young, Converse College

SOUTH DAKOTA

Joseph M. Santos, South Dakota State University

Jason Zimmerman, South Dakota State University

TENNESSEE

Sindy Abadie, Southwest Tennessee Community College

Charles Baum, Middle Tennessee State University

John Brassel, Southwest Tennessee Community College

Bichaka Fayissa, Middle Tennessee State University

Michael J. Gootzeit, University of Memphis

Travis Hayes, University of Tennessee–Chattanooga

Christopher C. Klein, Middle Tennessee State University

Leila Pratt, University of Tennessee at Chattanooga

Millicent Sites, Carson-Newman College

TEXAS

Carlos Aguilar, El Paso Community College

Rashid Al-Hmoud, Texas Tech University

William Beaty, Tarleton State University

Klaus Becker, Texas Tech University

Alex Brown, Texas A&M University

Jack A. Bucco, Austin Community College–Northridge and Saint Edward's University

Don Bumpass, Sam Houston State University

Marilyn M. Butler, Sam Houston State University

Mike Cohick, Collin County Community College

Cesar Corredor, Texas A&M University

Steven Craig, University of Houston

Patrick Crowley, Texas A&M University–Corpus Christi

Richard Croxdale, Austin Community College

Susan Dadres, Southern Methodist University

Harry Ellis, Jr., University of North Texas

Paul Emberton, Texas State University

Diego Escobari, Texas A&M University

Nicholas Feltovich, University of Houston–Main

Charles Harold Fifield, Baylor University

Mark Frank, Sam Houston State University

Edgar Ghossoub, University of Texas at San Antonio

Richard Gosselin, Houston Community College–Central

Sheila Amin Gutierrez de Pineres, University of Texas–Dallas

Tina J. Harvell, Blinn College–Bryan Campus

James W. Henderson, Baylor University

Jane S. Himarios, University of Texas–Arlington

James Holcomb, University of Texas–El Paso

Jamal Husein, Angelo State University

Ansul Islam, University of Houston–Downtown

Karen Johnson, Baylor University

Kathy Kelly, University of Texas–Arlington

Thomas Kemp, Tarrant County College–Northwest

Jim Lee, Texas A&M University–Corpus Christi

Ronnie W. Liggett, University of Texas–Arlington

Akbar Marvasti, University of Houston–Downtown

James Mbata, Houston Community College

Kimberly Mencken, Baylor University

Randy Methenitis, Richland College

Carl Montano, Lamar University

James Moreno, Blinn College

Camille Nelson, Texas A&M University

Michael Nelson, Texas A&M University

Charles Newton, Houston Community College–Southwest College

John Pisciotta, Baylor University

Sara Saderion, Houston Community College–Southwest College

George E. Samuels, Sam Houston State University

David Schutte, Mountain View College

Ivan Tasic, Texas A&M University

David Torres, University of Texas–El Paso

Ross vanWassenhove, University of Houston

Roger Wehr, University of Texas–Arlington

Jim Wollscheid, Texas A&M University–Kingsville

J. Christopher Wreh, North Central Texas College

David W. Yoskowitz, Texas A&M University–Corpus Christi

Inske Zandvliet, Brookhaven College

UTAH

Chris Fawson, Utah State University

Lowell Glenn, Utah Valley State College

Aric Krause, Westminster College

Arden Pope, Brigham Young University

VERMONT

Nancy Brooks, University of Vermont

VIRGINIA

Lee Badgett, Virginia Military Institute

Lee A. Coppock, University of Virginia

Janelle Davenport, Hampton University

Philip Heap, James Madison University

George E. Hoffer, Virginia Commonwealth University

Oleg Korenok, Virginia Commonwealth University

Larry Landrum, Virginia Western Community College

Frances Lea, Germanna Community College

Carrie Meyer, George Mason University

John Min, Northern Virginia Community College

Eugene Bempong Nyantakyi, West Virginia University

James Roberts, Tidewater Community College–Virginia Beach

Robert Rycroft, University of Mary Washington

Araine A. Schauer, Mary Mount College

Sarah Stafford, The College of William & Mary

Bob Subrick, James Madison University

Susanne Toney, Hampton University

Michelle Vachris, Christopher Newport University

James Wetzel, Virginia Commonwealth University

George Zestos, Christopher Newport University

WASHINGTON

Andrew Ewing, University of Washington

Stacey Jones, Seattle University

Dean Peterson, Seattle University

Robert Rosenman, Washington State University

WEST VIRGINIA

Jacqueline Agesa, Marshall University

Richard Agesa, Marshall University

WISCONSIN

Peng Huang, Ripon College

Marina Karabelas, Milwaukee Area Technical College

Elizabeth Sawyer Kelly, University of Wisconsin–Madison

Pascal Ngoboka, University of Wisconsin–River Falls

Kevin Quinn, St. Norbert College

John R. Stoll, University of Wisconsin–Green Bay

WYOMING

Robert Godby, University of Wyoming

DISTRICT OF COLUMBIA

Leon Battista, American Enterprise Institute

Michael Bradley, George Washington University

Colleen M. Callahan, American University

INTERNATIONAL

Minh Quang Dao, Carleton University–Ottawa, Canada

A Word of Thanks

Once again, we benefited greatly from the dedication and professionalism of the Pearson Economics team. Executive Editor David Alexander's energy and support were indispensable. David helped mold the presentation and provided words of encouragement whenever our energy flagged. Executive Development Editor Lena Buonanno worked tirelessly to ensure that this text was as good as it could be and to coordinate the many moving parts involved in a project of this magnitude. This new edition posed particular challenges, and we remain astonished at the amount of time, energy, and unfailing good humor she brings to this project. As we worked on the first edition, Director of Key Markets David Theisen provided invaluable insight into how best to structure a principles text. His advice helped shape nearly every chapter. We have worked with Executive Marketing Manager Lori DeShazo on three different books: principles of economics, money and banking, and intermediate macroeconomics, and we continue to be amazed at her energy and creativity in promoting the field of economics. Lindsey Sloan helped create the videos that accompany the *Making the Connections*, and she and Andra Skaalrud managed the extensive supplement package that accompanies the book. Carla Thompson and Jonathan Boylan turned our manuscript pages into a beautiful published book. We received excellent research assistance from Ed Timmons, Matthew Saboe, David N. van der Goes, and Jason Hockenberry. We thank Pam Smith, Elena Zeller, Jennifer Brailsford, and Cindy O'Brien for their careful proofreading of first- and second-round page proofs.

As instructors, we recognize how important it is for students to view graphs that are clear and accessible. We are fortunate to have Fernando Quijano of Dickinson State University render all the figures in our books and also our supplements. Market feedback on the figures continues to be positive. We extend our thanks to Fernando not only for collaborating with us and creating the best figures possible but also for his patience with our demanding schedule.

This fifth edition has several new media components, which required skilled and patient creators and developers. We extend special thanks to Andy Taylor of Hodja Media for preparing the video clips and to Paul Graf of the University of Indiana–Bloomington for preparing the graph animations. In addition to preparing the graphs for the book, Fernando Quijano also prepared the many layered, step-by-step graphs that appear in these animations. These videos and animations are an important part of our revision.

A good part of the burden of a project of this magnitude is borne by our families. We appreciate the patience, support, and encouragement of our wives and children.

Economics:
Foundations and Models

Chapter Outline
and Learning Objectives

Is the Private Doctor's Office Going to Disappear?

Traditionally, most doctors in the United States have worked in private practices that they owned themselves or in partnership with other doctors. Like other businesspeople, a doctor hires workers—nurses, physician's assistants, and receptionists—and buys or rents machinery and equipment. A doctor's income represents the profits from his or her practice, or the difference between the revenue received from patients and their health insurance plans and the costs to the doctor of wages, rent, loans, and insurance.

Increasingly, rather than owning a private practice, many doctors have chosen to work as salaried employees of hospitals. Although in 2000 nearly 60 percent of doctors were in private practice, by 2013 fewer than 40 percent were. What explains the increasing number of doctors who are giving up their private practices to become salaried employees of hospitals? Some doctors choose private practice because they like being their own boss. Other doctors prefer the more regular hours of working for a hospital, where they are less likely to be woken up at 2 A.M. to treat a patient with a medical emergency. Economists believe, though, that the best explanation for doctors abandoning private practice is that the doctors are acting in response to changing *economic incentives*. In fact, one of the key ideas that we will explore in this book is that we can often predict behavior by assuming that people respond to economic incentives.

The economic incentives doctors face have changed in a number of ways. For example, soaring health care costs have led many private insurance companies, as well as the federal and state governments, to reduce the payments they make to doctors in return for treating patients. As a result, doctors in private practice have found their incomes fluctuating, which makes the steady income from a hospital salary more attractive. Congress passed President Barack Obama's package of health care changes in 2010. One rule requires most doctors and hospitals to convert to electronic medical record keeping. Although this change may improve the quality of health care, the computer systems required are expensive. Doctors can avoid this cost by leaving private practice for hospital employment. Other new rules have increased the amount of paperwork doctors must complete to be paid for treating patients.

AN INSIDE LOOK on page 18 discusses how technological change is affecting medical care.

Sources: Robert Kocher and Nikhil R. Sahni, "Hospitals' Race to Employ Physicians," *New England Journal of Medicine*, Vol. 364, No. 19, May 12, 2011, pp. 1790–1793; Julie Creswell and Reed Abelson, "A Hospital War Reflects a Bind for Doctors in the U.S.," *New York Times*, November 30, 2012; and Scott Gottlieb, "The Doctor Won't See You Now: He's Clocked Out," *Wall Street Journal*, March 14, 2013.

Economics in Your Life

Will There Be Plenty of Jobs Available in the Health Care Industry?

The U.S. Health Resources and Services Administration (HRSA) forecasts that there will be 866,400 doctors in the United States in 2020. The HRSA also forecasts that 922,000 doctors will be needed in 2020. In other words, this federal government agency forecasts that there will be a shortage of about 56,000 doctors in 2020. The U.S. Bureau of Labor Statistics forecasts that 9 of the 20 fastest growing occupations over the next 10 years will be in the medical field. But the availability of these jobs depends on the reliability of the forecasts. What is the basis for the forecasts on the availability of jobs in health care, and how reliable are the forecasts? As you read this chapter, try to answer this question. You can check your answer against the one we provide on **page 17** at the end of this chapter.

I n this book, we use economics to answer questions such as the following:

- How are the prices of goods and services determined?
- Why have health care costs risen so rapidly?
- Why do firms engage in international trade, and how do government policies affect international trade?
- Why does the government control the prices of some goods and services, and what are the effects of those controls?

Economists do not always agree on the answers to every question. In fact, as we will see, economists engage in lively debate on some issues. In addition, new problems and issues are constantly arising. So, economists are always at work developing new methods to analyze economic questions.

All the topics we discuss in this book illustrate a basic fact of life: To attain our goals, we must make choices. We must make choices because we live in a world of **scarcity**, which means that although our wants are *unlimited*, the resources available to fulfill those wants are *limited*. You might like to own a BMW and spend each summer vacationing at five-star European hotels, but unless Bill Gates is a close and generous relative, you probably lack the funds to fulfill these dreams. Every day, you make choices as you spend your limited income on the many goods and services available. The finite amount of time you have also limits your ability to attain your goals. If you spend an hour studying for your economics midterm, you have one hour less to study for your history midterm. Firms and the government are in the same situation as you: They must also attain their goals with limited resources. **Economics** is the study of the choices consumers, business managers, and government officials make to attain their goals, given their scarce resources.

We begin this chapter by discussing three important economic ideas that we will return to many times in the following chapters: *People are rational, people respond to economic incentives*, and *optimal decisions are made at the margin*. Then, we consider the three fundamental questions that any economy must answer: *What* goods and services will be produced? *How* will the goods and services be produced? and *Who* will receive the goods and services produced? Next, we consider the role of *economic models* in analyzing economic issues. **Economic models** are simplified versions of reality used to analyze real-world economic situations. We will explore why economists use models and how they construct them. Finally, we will discuss the difference between microeconomics and macroeconomics, and we will preview some important economic terms.

Scarcity A situation in which unlimited wants exceed the limited resources available to fulfill those wants.

Economics The study of the choices people make to attain their goals, given their scarce resources.

Economic model A simplified version of reality used to analyze real-world economic situations.

1.1 LEARNING OBJECTIVE

Explain these three key economic ideas: People are rational; people respond to economic incentives; and optimal decisions are made at the margin.

Market A group of buyers and sellers of a good or service and the institution or arrangement by which they come together to trade.

Three Key Economic Ideas

As you try to achieve your goals, whether they involve buying a new computer or finding a part-time job, you will interact with other people in *markets*. A **market** is a group of buyers and sellers of a good or service and the institution or arrangement by which they come together to trade. Examples of markets are the markets for smartphones, houses, haircuts, stocks and bonds, and labor. Most of economics involves analyzing what happens in markets. Throughout this book, as we study how people make choices and interact in markets, we will return to three important ideas:

1. People are rational.
2. People respond to economic incentives.
3. Optimal decisions are made at the margin.

People Are Rational

Economists generally assume that people are rational. This assumption does *not* mean that economists believe everyone knows everything or always makes the "best" decision. It means that economists assume that consumers and firms use all available information as they act to achieve their goals. Rational individuals weigh the benefits and costs of each action, and they choose an action only if the benefits outweigh the costs. For example, if Apple charges a price of $299 for its latest iPhone, economists assume that the managers at Apple have estimated that this price will earn Apple the most profit. The managers may be wrong; perhaps a price of $325 would be more profitable, but economists assume that the managers at Apple have acted rationally, on the basis of the information available to them, in choosing the price. Of course, not everyone behaves rationally all the time. Still, the assumption of rational behavior is very useful in explaining most of the choices that people make.   MyEconLab Concept Check

People Respond to Economic Incentives

Human beings act from a variety of motives, including envy, compassion, and religious belief. While not ignoring other motives, economists emphasize that consumers and firms consistently respond to *economic incentives*. This point may seem obvious, but it is often overlooked. For example, according to an article in the *Wall Street Journal*, the FBI couldn't understand why banks were not taking steps to improve security in the face of an increase in robberies: "FBI officials suggest that banks place uniformed, armed guards outside their doors and install bullet-resistant plastic, known as a 'bandit barrier,' in front of teller windows." FBI officials were surprised that few banks took their advice. But the article also reported that installing bullet-resistant plastic costs $10,000 to $20,000, and a well-trained security guard receives $50,000 per year in salary and benefits. The average loss in a bank robbery is only about $1,200. The economic incentive to banks is clear: It is less costly to put up with bank robberies than to take additional security measures. FBI agents may be surprised by how banks respond to the threat of robberies—but economists are not.

In each chapter, the *Making the Connection* feature discusses a news story or another application related to the chapter material. Read this *Making the Connection* for a discussion of whether people respond to economic incentives even when deciding how much to eat and how much to exercise.   MyEconLab Concept Check

Making the Connection	Does Health Insurance Give People an Incentive to Become Obese?

Making the Connection
MyEconLab Video

Does Health Insurance Give People an Incentive to Become Obese?

Obesity is an increasing problem in the United States. The U.S. Centers for Disease Control and Prevention (CDC) defines obesity for an adult as having a body mass index (BMI) of 30 or greater. The BMI measures a person's weight relative to the person's height. (The exact formula is: BMI = (Weight in pounds/Height in inches$^2 \times 703$.) A BMI of 30 is equivalent to a person 5'4" being 30 pounds overweight. Obesity is related to a variety of diseases, including heart disease, stroke, diabetes, and hypertension.

These two maps show the dramatic increase in obesity between 1994 and 2011. In 1994, in a majority of states between 10 percent and 14 percent of the adult population was obese, and in no state was more than 20 percent of the adult population obese. By 2011, in every state at least 20 percent of the adult population was obese, and in about three-quarters of the states, at least 25 percent of the adult population was obese.

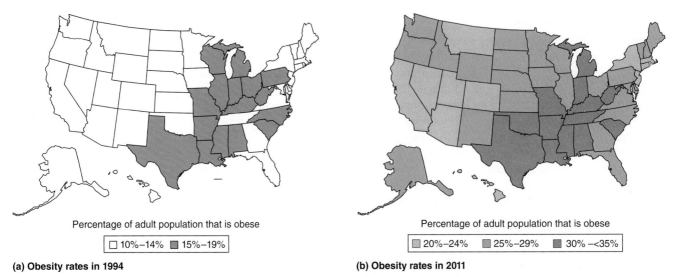

Percentage of adult population that is obese

☐ 10%–14% ■ 15%–19%

(a) Obesity rates in 1994

Percentage of adult population that is obese

☐ 20%–24% ■ 25%–29% ■ 30% –<35%

(b) Obesity rates in 2011

Source: Centers for Disease Control and Prevention, "Prevalence of Self-Reported Obesity among U.S. Adults."

Many people who suffer from obesity have underlying medical conditions. For these people, obesity is an unfortunate medical problem that they cannot control. The fact that obesity is increasing, though, indicates that for some people obesity is the result of diet and lifestyle choices. Potential explanations for the increase in obesity include greater intake of high-calorie fast foods, insufficient exercise, and a decline in the physical activity associated with many jobs. The CDC recommends that teenagers get a minimum of 60 minutes of aerobic exercise per day, a standard that only 15 percent of high school students were meeting in 2013. In 1960, 50 percent of jobs in the United States required at least moderate physical activity. By 2013, only 20 percent of jobs did. As a result, a typical worker was burning off about 130 fewer calories per workday.

In addition to eating too much and not exercising enough, could health insurance be a cause of obesity? Obese people tend to suffer more medical problems and so incur higher medical costs. Obese people with health insurance that will reimburse them for only part of their medical bills or who have no health insurance must pay some or all of these higher medical bills themselves. People with health insurance that covers most of their medical bills will not suffer as large a monetary cost from being obese. In other words, by reducing some of the costs of obesity, health insurance may give people an economic incentive to gain weight.

At first glance, this argument may seem implausible. Some people suffer from medical conditions that can make physical activity difficult or that can cause weight gain even with moderate eating, so they may become obese whether they have health insurance or not. Some people are obese because of poor eating habits or lack of exercise, and they probably don't consider health insurance when deciding whether to have another slice of chocolate cake or to watch television instead of going to the gym. But if economists are correct about the importance of economic incentives, then we would expect that if we hold all other personal characteristics—such as age, gender, and income—constant, people with health insurance will be more likely to be overweight than people without health insurance.

Jay Bhattacharya and Kate Bundorf of Stanford University, Noemi Pace of the University of Venice, and Neeraj Sood of the University of Southern California, have analyzed the effects of health insurance on weight. Using a sample that followed nearly 80,000 people from 1989 to 2004, they found that after controlling for income, education, race, gender, age, and other factors, people with health insurance were significantly more likely to be overweight than people without health insurance. Having private health insurance increased BMI by 1.3 points, and having public health insurance, such as Medicaid, which is a program under which the government provides health care to low-income people, increased BMI by 2.3 points. These findings suggest that people respond to economic incentives even when making decisions about what they eat and how much they exercise.

Sources: Centers for Disease Control and Prevention, "Prevalence of Self-Reported Obesity among U.S. Adults," www.cdc .gov; Katherine M. Flegal, Margaret D. Caroll, Cynthia L. Ogden, and Lester R. Curtin, "Prevalence and Trends in Obesity among U.S. Adults, 1999–2008," *Journal of the American Medical Association*, Vol. 303, No. 3, January 20, 2010, pp. 235–241; Jay Bhattacharya, Kate Bundorf, Noemi Pace, and Neeraj Sood, "Does Health Insurance Make You Fat?" in Michael Grossman and Naci H. Mocan, eds., *Economic Aspects of Obesity*, Chicago: University of Chicago Press, 2011; and Tara Parker-Pope, "Less Active at Work, Americans Have Packed on Pounds," *New York Times*, May 25, 2011.

Your Turn: Test your understanding by doing related problems 1.6 and 1.7 on page 20 at the end of this chapter.

MyEconLab Study Plan

Optimal Decisions Are Made at the Margin

Some decisions are "all or nothing." For instance, when an entrepreneur decides whether to open a new restaurant, she starts the new restaurant or she doesn't. When you decide whether to enter graduate school or to take a job, you enter graduate school or you don't. But rather than being all or nothing, most decisions in life involve doing a little more or a little less. If you are trying to decrease your spending and increase your saving, the decision is not really between saving all the money you earn or spending it all. Rather, many small choices are involved, such as whether to buy a caffè mocha at Starbucks every day or just three times per week.

Economists use the word *marginal* to mean "extra" or "additional." Should you watch another hour of television or spend that hour studying? The *marginal benefit (MB)* of watching more television is the additional enjoyment you receive. The *marginal cost (MC)* is the lower grade you receive from having studied a little less. Should Apple produce an additional 300,000 iPhones? Firms receive *revenue* from selling goods. Apple's marginal benefit is the additional revenue it receives from selling 300,000 more iPhones. Apple's marginal cost is the additional cost—for wages, parts, and so forth—of producing 300,000 more iPhones. *Economists reason that the optimal decision is to continue any activity up to the point where the marginal benefit equals the marginal cost—* MB = MC. Often we apply this rule without consciously thinking about it. Usually you will know whether the additional enjoyment from watching a television program is worth the additional cost involved in not spending that hour studying, without giving the decision a lot of thought. In business situations, however, firms often have to make careful calculations to determine, for example, whether the additional revenue received from increasing production is greater or less than the additional cost of the production. Economists refer to analysis that involves comparing marginal benefits and marginal costs as **marginal analysis**.

In each chapter, you will see the feature *Solved Problem*. This feature will increase your understanding of the material by leading you through the steps of solving an applied economic problem. After reading the problem, test your understanding by doing the related problems that appear at the end of the chapter and in the study guide that accompanies this book. You can also complete Solved Problems on **www.myeconlab.com** and receive tutorial help.

MyEconLab Concept Check

Marginal analysis Analysis that involves comparing marginal benefits and marginal costs.

Solved Problem 1.1

MyEconLab Interactive Animation

A Doctor Makes a Decision at the Margin

A doctor receives complaints from patients that her office isn't open enough hours. So the doctor asks her office manager to analyze the effect of keeping her office open 9 hours per day rather than 8 hours. The doctor's office manager tells her: "Keeping the office open an extra hour is a good idea because the revenue from your practice will increase by $300,000 per year when the office is open 9 hours per day." Do you agree with the office manager's reasoning? What, if any, additional information do you need to decide whether the doctor should keep her office open an additional hour per day?

Solving the Problem

Step 1: **Review the chapter material.** This problem is about making decisions, so you may want to review the section "Optimal Decisions Are Made at the Margin," which begins on page 7.

Step 2: **Explain whether you agree with the office manager's reasoning.** We have seen that any activity should be continued to the point where the marginal benefit is equal to the marginal cost. In this case, the doctor should keep her office open up to the point where the additional revenue she receives from seeing more patients is equal to the marginal cost of keeping her office open an additional hour. The office manager has provided information on marginal revenue but not on marginal cost. So the office manager has not provided enough information to make a decision, and you should not agree with the office manager's reasoning.

Step 3: **Explain what additional information you need.** To make a correct decision, you would need information on the marginal cost of remaining open an extra hour per day. The marginal cost would include the additional salary to be paid to the office staff, any additional medical supplies that would be used, as well as any additional electricity or other utilities. The doctor would also need to take into account the nonmonetary cost of spending another hour working rather than spending time with her family and friends or in other leisure activities. The marginal revenue would depend on how many more patients the doctor can see in the extra hour. The doctor should keep her office open an additional hour if the marginal revenue of doing so is greater than the marginal cost. If the marginal cost is greater than the marginal revenue, then the doctor should continue to keep her office open for 8 hours.

MyEconLab Study Plan

Your Turn: For more practice, do related problems 1.8, 1.9, and 1.10 on page 21 at the end of this chapter.

1.2 LEARNING OBJECTIVE

Discuss how an economy answers these questions: What goods and services will be produced? How will the goods and services be produced? Who will receive the goods and services produced?

Trade-off The idea that, because of scarcity, producing more of one good or service means producing less of another good or service.

Opportunity cost The highest-valued alternative that must be given up to engage in an activity.

The Economic Problem That Every Society Must Solve

Because we live in a world of scarcity, any society faces the *economic problem* that it has only a limited amount of economic resources—such as workers, machines, and raw materials—and so can produce only a limited amount of goods and services. Therefore, every society faces **trade-offs**: Producing more of one good or service means producing less of another good or service. In fact, the best measure of the cost of producing a good or service is the value of what has to be given up to produce it. The **opportunity cost** of any activity—such as producing a good or service—is the highest-valued alternative that must be given up to engage in that activity. The concept of opportunity cost is very important in economics and applies to individuals as much as it does to firms or society as a whole. Consider the example of a doctor who could receive a salary of $100,000 per year working as an employee of a hospital but decides to open his own private practice instead. In that case, the opportunity cost of the physician services he supplies to his own firm is the $100,000 he gives up by not working for the hospital, *even if he does not explicitly pay himself a salary.* As in this example, opportunity costs often do not involve actual payments of money.

Trade-offs force society to make choices when answering the following three fundamental questions:

1. *What* goods and services will be produced?
2. *How* will the goods and services be produced?
3. *Who* will receive the goods and services produced?

Throughout this book, we will return to these questions many times. For now, we briefly introduce each question.

What Goods and Services Will Be Produced?

How will society decide whether to produce more economics textbooks or more Blu-ray players? More daycare facilities or more football stadiums? Of course, "society" does not make decisions; only individuals make decisions. The answer to the question of what will be produced is determined by the choices that consumers, firms, and the government make. Every day, you help decide which goods and services firms will produce when you choose to buy an iPhone instead of a Samsung Galaxy or a caffè mocha rather than a chai tea. Similarly, Apple must choose whether to devote its scarce resources to making more iPhones or more iPads. The federal government must choose whether to spend more of its limited budget on breast cancer research or on repairing highways. In each case, consumers, firms, and the government face the problem of scarcity by trading off one good or service for another. And each choice made comes with an opportunity cost, measured by the value of the best alternative given up.   MyEconLab Concept Check

How Will the Goods and Services Be Produced?

Firms choose how to produce the goods and services they sell. In many cases, firms face a trade-off between using more workers or using more machines. For example, a local service station has to choose whether to provide car repair services using more diagnostic computers and fewer auto mechanics or fewer diagnostic computers and more auto mechanics. Similarly, movie studios have to choose whether to produce animated films using highly skilled animators to draw them by hand or fewer animators and more computers. In deciding whether to move production offshore to China, firms may need to choose between a production method in the United States that uses fewer workers and more machines and a production method in China that uses more workers and fewer machines.   MyEconLab Concept Check

Who Will Receive the Goods and Services Produced?

In the United States, who receives the goods and services produced depends largely on how income is distributed. The higher a person's income, the more goods and services he or she can buy. Often, people are willing to give up some of their income—and, therefore, some of their ability to purchase goods and services—by donating to charities to increase the incomes of poorer people. Each year, Americans donate about $300 billion to charity, or an average donation of $2,650 for each household in the country. An important policy question, however, is whether the government should intervene to make the distribution of income more equal. Such intervention already occurs in the United States, because people with higher incomes pay a larger fraction of their incomes in taxes and because the government makes payments to people with low incomes. There is disagreement over whether the current attempts to redistribute income are sufficient or whether there should be more or less redistribution.   MyEconLab Concept Check

Centrally Planned Economies versus Market Economies

To answer the three questions—what, how, and who—societies organize their economies in two main ways. A society can have a **centrally planned economy** in which the government decides how economic resources will be allocated. Or a society can have a **market economy** in which the decisions of households and firms interacting in markets allocate economic resources.

From 1917 to 1991, the most important centrally planned economy in the world was that of the Soviet Union, which was established when Vladimir Lenin and the Communist Party staged a revolution and took control of the Russian Empire. In the Soviet Union, the government decided what goods to produce, how the goods would be produced, and who would receive the goods. Government employees managed factories and stores. The objective of these managers was to follow the government's orders rather than to satisfy the wants of consumers. Centrally planned economies like that of the Soviet Union have not been successful in producing low-cost, high-quality goods and services. As a result, the standard of living of the average person in a centrally planned economy tends to be low. All centrally planned economies have also been political

Centrally planned economy An economy in which the government decides how economic resources will be allocated.

Market economy An economy in which the decisions of households and firms interacting in markets allocate economic resources.

dictatorships. Dissatisfaction with low living standards and political repression finally led to the collapse of the Soviet Union in 1991. Today, only North Korea still has a completely centrally planned economy.

All high-income democracies, including the United States, Canada, Japan, and the countries of Western Europe, have market economies. Market economies rely primarily on privately owned firms to produce goods and services and to decide how to produce them. Markets, rather than the government, determine who receives the goods and services produced. In a market economy, firms must produce goods and services that meet the wants of consumers, or the firms will go out of business. In that sense, it is ultimately consumers who decide what goods and services will be produced. Because firms in a market economy compete to offer the highest-quality products at the lowest price, they are under pressure to use the lowest-cost methods of production. For example, in the past 10 years, some U.S. firms have been under pressure to reduce their costs to meet competition from Chinese firms.

In a market economy, the income of an individual is determined by the payments he receives for what he has to sell. If he is a civil engineer, and firms are willing to pay a salary of $85,000 per year for engineers with his training and skills, he will have this amount of income to purchase goods and services. If the engineer also owns a house that he rents out, his income will be even higher. One of the attractive features of markets is that they reward hard work. Generally, the more extensive the training a person has received and the longer the hours the person works, the higher the person's income will be. Of course, luck—both good and bad—also plays a role here, as elsewhere in life. Someone might have a high income because she won the state lottery, while someone else might have a low income because he has severe medical problems. We can conclude that market economies respond to the question: "Who receives the goods and services produced?" with the answer: "Those who are most willing and able to buy them."   MyEconLab Concept Check

The Modern "Mixed" Economy

In the nineteenth and early twentieth centuries, the U.S. government engaged in relatively little regulation of markets for goods and services. Beginning in the middle of the twentieth century, government intervention in the economy dramatically increased in the United States and other market economies. This increase was primarily caused by the high rates of unemployment and business bankruptcies during the Great Depression of the 1930s. Some government intervention was also intended to raise the incomes of the elderly, the sick, and people with limited skills. For example, in the 1930s, the United States established the Social Security system, which provides government payments to retired and disabled workers, and minimum wage legislation, which sets a floor on the wages employers can pay workers in many occupations. In more recent years, government intervention in the economy has also expanded to meet goals such as the protection of the environment, the promotion of civil rights, and the provision of medical care to low-income people and the elderly.

Mixed economy An economy in which most economic decisions result from the interaction of buyers and sellers in markets but in which the government plays a significant role in the allocation of resources.

Some economists argue that the extent of government intervention makes it no longer accurate to refer to the U.S., Canadian, Japanese, and Western European economies as pure market economies. Instead, they should be referred to as *mixed economies*. A **mixed economy** is still primarily a market economy because most economic decisions result from the interaction of buyers and sellers in markets. However, the government plays a significant role in the allocation of resources. As we will see in later chapters, economists continue to debate the role government should play in a market economy.

One of the most important developments in the international economy in recent years has been the movement of China from being a centrally planned economy to being a more mixed economy. The Chinese economy suffered decades of economic stagnation following the takeover of the government in 1949 by Mao Zedong and the Communist Party. Although China remains a political dictatorship, the production of most goods and services is now determined in the market rather than by the government. The result has been rapid economic growth that in the future may lead to total production of goods and services in China surpassing total production in the United States.   MyEconLab Concept Check

Efficiency and Equity

Market economies tend to be more efficient than centrally planned economies. There are two types of efficiency. **Productive efficiency** occurs when a good or service is produced at the lowest possible cost. **Allocative efficiency** occurs when production is in accordance with consumer preferences. Markets tend to be efficient because they promote competition and facilitate voluntary exchange. With **voluntary exchange**, both the buyer and the seller of a product are made better off by the transaction. We know that they are both made better off because, otherwise, the buyer would not have agreed to buy the product or the seller would not have agreed to sell it. Productive efficiency is achieved when competition among firms forces them to produce goods and services at the lowest cost. Allocative efficiency is achieved when the combination of competition among firms and voluntary exchange between firms and consumers results in firms producing the mix of goods and services that consumers prefer the most. Competition will force firms to continue producing and selling goods and services as long as the additional benefit to consumers is greater than the additional cost of production. In this way, the mix of goods and services produced will match consumer preferences.

Although markets promote efficiency, they don't guarantee it. Inefficiency can arise from various sources. To begin with, it may take some time to achieve an efficient outcome. When Blu-ray players were introduced, for example, firms did not instantly achieve productive efficiency. It took several years for firms to discover the lowest-cost method of producing this good. As we will discuss in later chapters, governments sometimes reduce efficiency by interfering with voluntary exchange in markets. For example, many governments limit the imports of some goods from foreign countries. This limitation reduces efficiency by keeping goods from being produced at the lowest cost. The production of some goods damages the environment. In this case, government intervention can increase efficiency because without such intervention, firms may ignore the costs of environmental damage and thereby fail to produce the goods at the lowest possible cost.

An economically efficient outcome is not necessarily desirable. Many people prefer economic outcomes that they consider fair or equitable, even if those outcomes are less efficient. **Equity** is harder to define than efficiency because there isn't an agreed upon definition of fairness. For some people, equity involves a more equal distribution of economic benefits than would result from an emphasis on efficiency alone. For example, some people support raising taxes on people with higher incomes to provide the funds for programs that aid the poor. Although governments may increase equity by reducing the incomes of high-income people and increasing the incomes of the poor, efficiency may be reduced. People have less incentive to open new businesses, supply labor, and save if the government takes a significant amount of the income they earn from working or saving. The result is that fewer goods and services are produced, and less saving takes place. As this example illustrates, *there is often a trade-off between efficiency and equity.* Government policymakers often confront this trade-off. MyEconLab Concept Check

Productive efficiency A situation in which a good or service is produced at the lowest possible cost.

Allocative efficiency A state of the economy in which production is in accordance with consumer preferences; in particular, every good or service is produced up to the point where the last unit provides a marginal benefit to society equal to the marginal cost of producing it.

Voluntary exchange A situation that occurs in markets when both the buyer and the seller of a product are made better off by the transaction.

Equity The fair distribution of economic benefits.

MyEconLab Study Plan

Economic Models

1.3 LEARNING OBJECTIVE

Understand the role of models in economic analysis.

Economists rely on economic theories, or models (the words *theory* and *model* are used interchangeably), to analyze real-world issues, such as those involved with health care. As mentioned earlier, economic models are simplified versions of reality. Economists are certainly not alone in relying on models: An engineer may use a computer model of a bridge to help test whether it will withstand high winds, or a biologist may make a physical model of a nucleic acid to better understand its properties. One purpose of economic models is to make economic ideas sufficiently explicit and concrete so that individuals, firms, or the government can use them to make decisions. For example, we will see in Chapter 3 that the model of demand and supply is a simplified version of how the prices of products are determined by the interactions among buyers and sellers in markets.

Economists use economic models to answer questions. For example, will the United States have a sufficient number of doctors in 2020? For such a complicated question, economists often use several models to examine different aspects of the issue. For example, economists at the U.S. Bureau of Labor Statistics (BLS) build models that allow them to forecast future employment in different occupations. These models allow the BLS to forecast how many doctors there are likely to be at a future date. Economists also use models to forecast the demand for medical services. By separately forecasting the number of doctors and the demand for medical services, these models provide a forecast of whether there will be a sufficient number of doctors in 2020. As mentioned on page 3, economists at the U.S. Health Resources and Services Administration (HRSA) have used models to forecast that there will be a shortage of about 56,000 doctors in 2020.

Sometimes economists use an existing model to analyze an issue, but in other cases, they have to develop a new model. To develop a model, economists generally follow these steps:

1. Decide on the assumptions to use in developing the model.
2. Formulate a testable hypothesis.
3. Use economic data to test the hypothesis.
4. Revise the model if it fails to explain the economic data well.
5. Retain the revised model to help answer similar economic questions in the future.

The Role of Assumptions in Economic Models

Any model is based on making assumptions because models have to be simplified to be useful. We cannot analyze an economic issue unless we reduce its complexity. For example, economic models make *behavioral assumptions* about the motives of consumers and firms. Economists assume that consumers will buy the goods and services that will maximize their well-being or their satisfaction. Similarly, economists assume that firms act to maximize their profits. These assumptions are simplifications because they do not describe the motives of every consumer and every firm. How can we know if the assumptions in a model are too simplified or too limiting? We can determine the usefulness of assumptions by forming hypotheses based on the assumptions and then testing the hypotheses using real-world information.   MyEconLab Concept Check

Forming and Testing Hypotheses in Economic Models

Economic variable Something measurable that can have different values, such as the incomes of doctors.

An **economic variable** is something measurable that can have different values, such as the incomes of doctors. In an economic model, a hypothesis is a statement that may be either correct or incorrect about an economic variable. An example of a hypothesis in an economic model is the statement that the falling incomes earned by primary care physicians—often referred to as *family doctors*—will result in a decline in the number of physicians choosing to enter primary care in the United States in 2020. An economic hypothesis is usually about a causal relationship; in this case, the hypothesis states that lower incomes cause, or lead to, fewer doctors entering primary care.

Before we can accept a hypothesis, we have to test it. To test a hypothesis, we analyze statistics on the relevant economic variables. In our example, we would gather statistics on the incomes of family doctors, the number of family doctors, and perhaps other variables as well. Testing a hypothesis can be tricky. For example, showing that the number of family doctors declined at a time when the average income of these doctors declined would not be enough to demonstrate that the decline in income *caused* the decline in the number of family doctors. Just because two things are correlated—that is, they happen at the same time—does not mean that one caused the other. For example, before entering practice, a doctor spends time in a teaching hospital as a resident in his or her field. Teaching hospitals determine how many residencies they will offer in a particular field. Suppose that teaching hospitals decreased the number of residencies in primary care at the same time that the incomes of family doctors were declining. In that case, the declining number of residencies, rather than the declining incomes, might have caused the decline in the number of family doctors. Over a period of time, many economic variables change, which complicates the testing of hypotheses. In fact, when economists disagree about a hypothesis, such as the effect of falling incomes on the number of family doctors, it is often because of disagreements over interpreting the statistical analysis used to test the hypothesis.

Note that hypotheses must be statements that could, in principle, turn out to be incorrect. Statements such as "Increasing the number of family doctors is good" or "Increasing the number of family doctors is bad" are value judgments rather than hypotheses because it is not possible to disprove them.

Economists accept and use an economic model if it leads to hypotheses that are confirmed by statistical analysis. In many cases, the acceptance is tentative, however, pending the gathering of new data or further statistical analysis. In fact, economists often refer to a hypothesis having been "not rejected," rather than having been "accepted," by statistical analysis. But what if statistical analysis clearly rejects a hypothesis? For example, what if a model leads to a hypothesis that declining incomes of family doctors will cause a decline in the number of these doctors, but the data reject this hypothesis? In this case, the model must be reconsidered. It may be that an assumption used in the model was too simplified or too limiting. For example, perhaps the model ignored the fact that family doctors were moving from owning their own practices to becoming salaried employees of hospitals, where they would be freed from the responsibilities involved in running their own businesses. This change in how primary care physicians are employed might explain why the data rejected the hypothesis.

The BLS has analyzed the accuracy of the projections it had made in 1996 of employment levels in 2006. Some projections were quite accurate, while others were less so. For instance, the BLS had projected that 677,917 physicians and surgeons would be employed in 2006, but actual employment was only 633,292, or about 7 percent less than projected. The error with respect to physician's assistants was much larger, with the projection being that 93,485 physician's assistants would be employed in 2006, but actual employment was only 65,628, or about 30 percent less than expected. Analyzing the errors in these projections helps the BLS to improve the models it uses to make projections of occupational employment.

The process of developing models, testing hypotheses, and revising models occurs not just in economics but also in disciplines such as physics, chemistry, and biology. This process is often referred to as the *scientific method*. Economics is a *social science* because it applies the scientific method to the study of the interactions among individuals. MyEconLab Concept Check

Positive and Normative Analysis

Throughout this book, as we build economic models and use them to answer questions, bear in mind the following important distinction: **Positive analysis** is concerned with *what is*, and **normative analysis** is concerned with *what ought to be*. Economics is about positive analysis, which measures the costs and benefits of different courses of action.

We can use the federal government's minimum wage law to compare positive and normative analysis. In 2013, under this law, it was illegal for an employer to hire a worker at a wage less than $7.25 per hour. Without the minimum wage law, some firms and workers would voluntarily agree to a lower wage. Because of the minimum wage law, some workers have difficulty finding jobs, and some firms end up paying more for labor than they otherwise would have. A positive analysis of the federal minimum wage law uses an economic model to estimate how many workers have lost their jobs because of the law, its effect on the costs and profits of businesses, and the gains to workers receiving the minimum wage. After economists complete this positive analysis, the decision as to whether the minimum wage law is a good or a bad idea is a normative one and depends on how people evaluate the trade-off involved. Supporters of the law believe that the losses to employers and workers who are unemployed as a result of the law are more than offset by the gains to workers who receive higher wages than they would without the law. Opponents of the law believe the losses are greater than the gains. The assessment by any individual depends, in part, on that person's values and political views. The positive analysis an economist provides would play a role in the decision but can't by itself decide the issue one way or the other.

In each chapter, you will see a *Don't Let This Happen to You* box like the one on page 14. These boxes alert you to common pitfalls in thinking about economic ideas. After reading this box, test your understanding by working the related problem that appears at the end of the chapter. MyEconLab Concept Check

Positive analysis Analysis concerned with what is.

Normative analysis Analysis concerned with what ought to be.

Don't Let This Happen to You

Don't Confuse Positive Analysis with Normative Analysis

"Economic analysis has shown that the minimum wage law is a bad idea because it causes unemployment." Is this statement accurate? As of 2013, the federal minimum wage law prevents employers from hiring workers at a wage of less than $7.25 per hour. This wage is higher than some employers are willing to pay some workers. If there were no minimum wage law, some workers who currently cannot find any firm willing to hire them at $7.25 per hour would be able to find employment at a lower wage. Therefore, positive economic analysis indicates that the minimum wage law causes unemployment (although economists disagree about how much unemployment the minimum wage law causes). But, some workers who have jobs benefit from the minimum wage law because they are paid a higher wage than they otherwise would be. In other words, the minimum wage law creates both losers (the workers who become unemployed and the firms that have to pay higher wages) and winners (the workers who receive higher wages).

Should we value the gains to the winners more than we value the losses to the losers? The answer involves normative analysis. Positive economic analysis can show the consequences of a particular policy, but it cannot tell us whether the policy is "good" or "bad." So, the statement at the beginning of this box is inaccurate.

MyEconLab Study Plan

Your Turn: Test your understanding by doing related problem 3.9 on page 23 at the end of this chapter.

Economics as a Social Science

Because economics studies the actions of individuals, it is a social science. Economics is therefore similar to other social science disciplines, such as psychology, political science, and sociology. As a social science, economics considers human behavior—particularly decision-making behavior—in every context, not just in the context of business. Economists have studied issues such as how families decide on the number of children to have, why people have difficulty losing weight or attaining other desirable goals, and why people often ignore relevant information when making decisions. Economics also has much to contribute to questions of government policy. As we will see throughout this book, economists have played an important role in formulating government policies in areas such as the environment, health care, and poverty. MyEconLab Concept Check

Making the Connection
MyEconLab Video

Should Medical School Be Free?

The U.S. population continues to increase, which by itself would increase the demand for medical services. In addition, the average age of the population is rising, and older people need more medical care than do younger people. So, over time, the number of doctors needs to increase. As mentioned at the beginning of this chapter, the U.S. Health Resources and Services Administration (HRSA) estimates that the number of doctors needed to provide patient care will rise from about 805,000 in 2010 to 922,000 in 2020.

Can we be sure that these additional doctors will be available in 2020? The HRSA forecasts that, in fact, there will be a shortage of 56,000 doctors in 2020. The bulk of that shortage is likely to be in primary care physicians, or family doctors. As we will discuss in later chapters, ordinarily we expect that when consumers want more of a product, higher wages and salaries and more job openings will attract workers to that industry. For example, during the U.S. housing boom of the mid-2000s, the number of workers in the building trades—carpenters, plumbers, roofers, and others—increased rapidly. But producing more doctors is a long process. After completing his or her undergraduate education, a doctor spends four years in medical school and then three to five years at

Should these medical students have to pay tuition?

a teaching hospital, pursuing a residency in a particular field of medicine. Apparently convinced that hospitals will not train enough doctors unless they get help, Congress contributes $10 billion per year to teaching hospitals, based on the number of residents they train.

Peter Bach of the Sloan-Kettering Cancer Center and Robert Kocher of the Brookings Institution have proposed that medical schools should charge no tuition. They argue that nearly all students graduate from medical school owing money on student loans, with the average student owing more than $160,000. We might expect that these debts, although large, would not deter students from applying to medical school, because in 2013, the average income of physicians was more than $250,000 per year. Bach and Kocher argue, though, that the high cost of medical school has two bad outcomes: Some good students do not apply because they either do not want to be saddled with such large debts or are unable to borrow sufficient money, and many students avoid going into primary care—where average incomes are $190,000—in favor of specialties such as plastic surgery or anesthesiology—where average incomes are $325,000. Teaching hospitals pay doctors a salary of about $50,000 per year during their residencies. Bach and Kocher propose that hospitals continue to pay residents who pursue primary care but not pay residents who specialize. The money that hospitals would otherwise pay to these residents would be paid to medical schools instead to finance the free tuition. The plan would give residents an incentive to pursue primary care rather than to specialize. Critics of the Bach and Kocher proposal have questioned whether many students capable of being admitted to medical school actually are deterred by medical school tuition. They also question whether many residents who intend to specialize would choose primary care instead, even if specializing means they have to borrow to meet living expenses rather than paying for them with a hospital salary.

Like many other policy debates, the debate over whether changes should be made in how medical school is paid for has positive and normative elements. By gathering data and using economic models, we can assess some of the quantitative claims made by each side in the debate: What role does tuition play in a student's decision about whether to attend medical school? Have tuition increases had a large or a small effect on the number of applications to medical school? How do changes in expected future incomes affect the decisions of medical students about which specialty to choose? These are all positive questions, so it is possible to formulate quantitative answers. Ultimately, though, this debate also has a normative element. For instance, some doctors, economists, and policymakers argue that it is important that people living in low-income or rural areas have improved access to health care, so they are willing to support policies that would redirect medical students away from specialized fields and toward primary care. Other doctors, economists, and policymakers believe that medical students who enter specialized fields make a larger contribution to society than do students who enter primary care. A disagreement of this type is unlikely to be resolved by building models and analyzing data because the issue involved is essentially normative.

In 2010, President Obama and Congress enacted the Patient Protection and Affordable Care Act, which made major changes to the U.S. health care system. Most of the changes were in effect by 2014. Additional changes are likely as policymakers grapple with the rapidly escalating costs of health care. Whether Congress and the president will enact policies intended to increase the number of family doctors remains to be seen.

Sources: Uwe E. Reinhardt, "Producing More Primary-Care Doctors," *New York Times,* June 10, 2011; Uwe E. Reinhardt, "The Debt of Medical Students," *New York Times,* September 14, 2012; and Peter B. Bach and Robert Kocher, "Why Medical School Should Be Free," *New York Times,* May 28, 2011.

Your Turn: Test your understanding by doing related problem 3.6 on page 23 at the end of this chapter.

MyEconLab Study Plan

Microeconomics and Macroeconomics

1.4 LEARNING OBJECTIVE

Distinguish between microeconomics and macroeconomics.

Economic models can be used to analyze decision making in many areas. We group some of these areas together as *microeconomics* and others as *macroeconomics*. **Microeconomics** is the study of how households and firms make choices, how they interact in markets, and how the government attempts to influence their choices. Microeconomic issues include explaining how consumers react to changes in product prices and how firms decide what prices to charge for the products they sell. Microeconomics

Microeconomics The study of how households and firms make choices, how they interact in markets, and how the government attempts to influence their choices.

Macroeconomics The study of the economy as a whole, including topics such as inflation, unemployment, and economic growth.

MyEconLab Study Plan

Define important economic terms.

also involves policy issues, such as analyzing the most efficient way to reduce teenage smoking, analyzing the costs and benefits of approving the sale of a new prescription drug, and analyzing the most efficient way to reduce air pollution.

Macroeconomics is the study of the economy as a whole, including topics such as inflation, unemployment, and economic growth. Macroeconomic issues include explaining why economies experience periods of recession and increasing unemployment and why, over the long run, some economies have grown much faster than others. Macroeconomics also involves policy issues, such as whether government intervention can reduce the severity of recessions.

The division between microeconomics and macroeconomics is not hard and fast. Many economic situations have *both* a microeconomic and a macroeconomic aspect. For example, the level of total investment by firms in new machinery and equipment helps to determine how rapidly the economy grows—which is a macroeconomic issue. But to understand how much new machinery and equipment firms decide to purchase, we have to analyze the incentives individual firms face—which is a microeconomic issue.   MyEconLab Concept Check

A Preview of Important Economic Terms

In the following chapters, you will encounter certain important terms again and again. Becoming familiar with these terms is a necessary step in learning economics. Here we provide a brief introduction to some of these terms. We will discuss them all in greater depth in later chapters.

- *Firm, company, or business.* A *firm* is an organization that produces a good or service. Most firms produce goods or services to earn profits, but there are also nonprofit firms, such as universities and some hospitals. Economists use the terms *firm*, *company*, and *business* interchangeably.

- *Entrepreneur.* An *entrepreneur* is someone who operates a business. In a market system, entrepreneurs decide what goods and services to produce and how to produce them. An entrepreneur starting a new business puts his or her own funds at risk. If an entrepreneur is wrong about what consumers want or about the best way to produce goods and services, his or her funds can be lost. Losing money in a failed business is not unusual: In the United States, about half of new businesses close within four years. Without entrepreneurs willing to assume the risk of starting and operating businesses, economic progress would be impossible in a market system.

- *Innovation.* There is a distinction between an *invention* and an *innovation*. An *invention* is a new good or a new process for making a good. An *innovation* is the practical application of an invention. (*Innovation* may also be used more broadly to refer to any significant improvement in a good or in the means of producing a good.) Much time often passes between the appearance of a new idea and its development for widespread use. For example, the Wright brothers first achieved self-propelled flight at Kitty Hawk, North Carolina, in 1903, but the Wright brothers' plane was very crude, and it wasn't until the introduction of the DC-3 by Douglas Aircraft in 1936 that regularly scheduled intercity airline flights became common in the United States. Similarly, the first digital electronic computer—the ENIAC—was developed in 1945, but the first IBM personal computer was not introduced until 1981, and widespread use of computers did not have a significant effect on the productivity of U.S. business until the 1990s.

- *Technology.* A firm's *technology* is the processes it uses to produce goods and services. In the economic sense, a firm's technology depends on many factors, such as the skill of its managers, the training of its workers, and the speed and efficiency of its machinery and equipment.

- *Goods.* *Goods* are tangible merchandise, such as books, computers, or Blu-ray players.

- *Services.* *Services* are activities done for others, such as providing haircuts or investment advice.

- *Revenue.* A firm's *revenue* is the total amount received for selling a good or service. We calculate it by multiplying the price per unit by the number of units sold.

- *Profit.* A firm's *profit* is the difference between its revenue and its costs. Economists distinguish between *accounting profit* and *economic profit.* In calculating accounting profit, we exclude the cost of some economic resources that the firm does not pay for explicitly. In calculating economic profit, we include the opportunity cost of all resources used by the firm. When we refer to *profit* in this book, we mean economic profit. It is important not to confuse *profit* with *revenue.*

- *Household.* A *household* consists of all persons occupying a home. Households are suppliers of factors of production—particularly labor—used by firms to make goods and services. Households also demand goods and services produced by firms and governments.

- *Factors of production, economic resources, or inputs.* Firms use *factors of production* to produce goods and services. The main factors of production are labor, capital, natural resources—including land—and entrepreneurial ability. Households earn income by supplying the factors of production to firms. Economists use the terms *factors of production, economic resources,* and *inputs* interchageably.

- *Capital.* In everyday speech, the word *capital* can refer to *financial capital* or to *physical capital.* Financial capital includes stocks and bonds issued by firms, bank accounts, and holdings of money. In economics, though, *capital* refers to physical capital, which includes manufactured goods that are used to produce other goods and services. Examples of physical capital are computers, factory buildings, machine tools, warehouses, and trucks. The total amount of physical capital available in a country is referred to as the country's *capital stock.*

- *Human capital. Human capital* refers to the accumulated training and skills that workers possess. For example, college-educated workers generally have more skills and are more productive than workers who have only high school degrees; therefore, college-educated workers have more human capital.   MyEconLab Concept Check   MyEconLab Study Plan

Continued from page 3

Economics in Your Life

Will There Be Plenty of Jobs Available in the Health Care Industry?

At the beginning of this chapter, we posed the question: "What is the basis for the forecasts on the availability of jobs in health care, and how reliable are the forecasts?" As the U.S. population increases and as the average age of the population rises, it seems likely that there will be an increase in the number of doctors, nurses, physician's assistants, and other health care workers. The U.S. Bureau of Labor Statistics (BLS) publishes the most widely used occupational forecasts. Economists at the BLS base these forecasts on economic models. The forecasts can be inaccurate, however. For example, in 1996, the BLS forecast that 93,485 physician's assistants would be employed in 2006, when in fact only 65,628 were. The BLS analyzes errors like these in attempting to improve its forecasts. So, it is likely that the BLS's forecasts will become more accurate over time, but it would be a mistake to expect the forecasts to be exact.

Conclusion

Economics is a group of useful ideas about how individuals make choices. Economists have put these ideas into practice by developing economic models. Consumers, business managers, and government policymakers use these models every day to help make choices. In this book, we explore many key economic models and give examples of how to apply them in the real world.

Reading newspapers and other periodicals is an important part of understanding the current business climate and learning how to apply economic concepts to a variety of real-world events. At the end of the first four chapters, you will see a two-page feature titled *An Inside Look.* This feature consists of an excerpt from an article that relates to the company or economic issue introduced at the start of the chapter and also to the concepts discussed in the chapter. A summary and an analysis with supporting graphs highlight the key economic points of the article. Read *An Inside Look* for a discussion of how technological changes, such as smartphones, affect how doctors provide health care. Test your understanding by answering the *Thinking Critically* questions.

FORBES

The Year 2020: The Doctor Will (NOT) See You Now!

It's the year 2020. 20/20, just like perfect vision.

And interestingly, it's also *your* vision. In today's world of health and wellness, computer-guided laser vision correction is so commonplace that eye glasses are hardly necessary and almost pure fashion. Except for the occasional "Google Glasses" that early innovators still wear as a badge of adoption.

The Exam Room of the Future

Today is the first time you've been to a doctor's office in two years. Yet, surprisingly, you're as compliant and up to date as can be. Over the past two years, you've had several interactions with your doctor including an ECG, simplified physical exam and evaluation of a sore throat. However, these evaluations were done from your home with one of the most essential components of care for both you and your physician–the smartphone. As you arrive, one of the first things you notice is that the waiting room is almost empty. Advances in digital appointments and off site care have changed the practice dynamics significantly. In fact, your family physician sees more patients virtually than in the real world. The digital receptionist acknowledges you by first name as you approach this holographic image. Face recognition has instantly identified you and a thermal scan has checked your body temperature to screen for the potential of any infectious conditions that would immediately shuttle you off to an isolation area.

You pick up an electronic tablet and have a seat in the specific color-coded, pod-like chair that the receptionist has indicated. There are some quick questions to answer on the tablet as electronic sensors built into the chair begin to analyze your weight, blood oxygen, and other key elements of your physiology. You're asked to do some basic tasks including standing, looking into a small scanner and to grasp two sensor handles. The analysis is compared directly with your electronic medical records and prompt questions about unusual changes or variations. Once the basic analysis has been completed, supplemental questions–culled from an extensive clinical database–are asked to preemptively identify health issues and problems that can be addressed much earlier.

You might be surprised to know that most of your "history and-physical" is now complete. An entire "healthprint" is on your physician's desktop. It contains a comprehensive physical exam that has been cross indexed against your past history and a large database of patients. Any outlying concerns can be addressed the good old-fashioned way. But leaving that up to the unpredictable and error-prone abilities of a nurse or doctor can be problematic!

"Looks like you're doing great!" Those are the first words you hear from an actual human–your doctor. And you're done…. But as you leave you can't stop and wonder if this "carwash" type doctor visit is sub-optimal. What happened to the face time and human component of good old-fashioned medicine?

Examining the Exam

Let's take a closer look at what just happened in the future:

- It took 17 minutes–from start to finish. It's effective *and* efficient.
- The analytical and diagnostic acumen of the technology is, in many respects, superior to the physical skill set of your doctor.
- The data used for diagnosis and therapeutic recommendations are always current and reflect the best and brightest thinking in medicine.
- The depth and breadth of the database used for predictive information is massive. No individual physician can ever have the experience, intuition or processing power to come close.
- The human touch is still there–it's just reserved for more specific and valuable use.

Healthcare is in a great state of transition now. Financial concerns, reimbursement and coverage, and an aging population will be powerful drivers of change. Technology will be a beacon of innovation that will help address many of these concerns without the compromise of care. The innovation, and the rate of change, is simply amazing and the future is looking very healthy indeed.

Source: John Nosta, "The Year 2020: The Doctor Will (NOT) See You Now!" *Forbes*, August 15, 2012.

Key Points in the Article

Advances in technology may change the way patients interact with their doctors in 2020. Today, many people visit a doctor's office for routine physical exams or treatment of conditions such as the flu. This article predicts that by the end of this decade, many medical evaluations will be performed via smartphone from the convenience of the patient's home. There will still be occasions when an actual visit to the doctor's office is necessary, so the doctor's office will not disappear, but it will be drastically transformed as a result of technology. These changes, including electronic evaluations and diagnoses based on extensive, current databases, not only will reduce the amount of time required for a typical doctor's appointment but may also dramatically improve the quality of analysis and level of care that patients receive.

Analyzing the News

a Advances in technology continue to change many facets of the economy, and the doctor's office is no exception. Economic incentives are changing for both doctors and patients. Granted, the author of the article is speculating as to how basic medical care will be handled by the end of this decade, but based on ongoing improvements in technology, his ideas read more like fact than fiction. Smartphone technology has improved greatly over the past few years, so it is not hard to imagine these devices playing an ever-increasing role in our everyday lives. Being able to

have routine medical tests and diagnoses performed electronically via smartphone will save time and money for doctors, laboratories, and patients, thereby increasing efficiency and potentially reducing costs.

b Imagine a routine trip to the doctor's office taking 17 minutes—from start to finish—and happening only once every two years. No more taking off an entire day from work or school every time a minor ailment arises. (You may not be interested in this improvement now, but your professors and your future employer will appreciate it.) Lost time from work or school can have a negative effect on productivity, decreasing economic efficiency. One key to the scenario presented in the article is that efficiency will be improved without sacrificing quality. The author also argues that the quality of medical care will be enhanced as well. Should this outcome occur, the additional benefits received from this way of delivering medical care would seem to outweigh the additional costs, including having less personal interaction with the doctor.

c The health care industry is changing and, with the passage of the Affordable Care Act in 2010, will continue to change. The chapter opener discusses the increasing number of doctors leaving private practice to become salaried employees of hospitals because of changes in health care laws and financial concerns. Other factors that will significantly affect health care in the coming years and that may also be a reason for doctors choosing hospital employment are the aging population and the increasing number

of people covered by health insurance. The figure below shows recent data on the number of people aged 65 and older, the number of uninsured people, and projections for 2020. These numbers indicate a significant increase in demand for health care services in the coming years. Technological innovations such as those discussed in the article could prove invaluable in efficiently providing quality medical care to this growing number of patients.

Thinking Critically

1. One key economic idea is that people respond to economic incentives. Explain how the improvements in technology discussed in the article, along with the expected increase in the demand for health care, may affect the incentives for doctors leaving private practice for employment in hospitals.

2. The article speculates that improvements in technology will increase efficiency in the health care industry without compromising the quality of customer care. Suppose you want to develop an economic model to analyze the relationship between the increased efficiency resulting from the changes in technology used in a doctor's office and the corresponding level of care patients receive. Use information from the article to explain the steps you would take to develop this model.

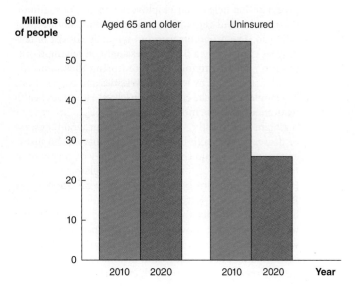

Technological innovations could help increase availability of health care to an aging population and the uninsured.

Data for people aged 65 and older and the uninsured are for 2010 and projected for 2020.

Source: U.S. Census Bureau and Congressional Budget Office.

Chapter Summary and Problems

Key Terms

Allocative efficiency, p. 11

Centrally planned economy, p. 9

Economic model, p. 4

Economic variable, p. 12

Economics, p. 4

Equity, p. 11

Macroeconomics, p. 16

Marginal analysis, p. 7

Market, p. 4

Market economy, p. 9

Microeconomics, p. 16

Mixed economy, p. 10

Normative analysis, p. 13

Opportunity cost, p. 8

Positive analysis, p. 13

Productive efficiency, p. 11

Scarcity, p. 4

Trade-off, p. 8

Voluntary exchange, p. 11

 1.1

Three Key Economic Ideas, pages 4–8

LEARNING OBJECTIVE: Explain these three key economic ideas: People are rational; people respond to economic incentives; and optimal decisions are made at the margin.

Summary

Economics is the study of the choices consumers, business managers, and government officials make to attain their goals, given their scarce resources. We must make choices because of **scarcity**, which means that although our wants are unlimited, the resources available to fulfill those wants are limited. Economists assume that people are rational in the sense that consumers and firms use all available information as they take actions intended to achieve their goals. Rational individuals weigh the benefits and costs of each action and choose an action only if the benefits outweigh the costs. Although people act from a variety of motives, ample evidence indicates that they respond to economic incentives. Economists use the word **marginal** to mean extra or additional. The optimal decision is to continue any activity up to the point where the marginal benefit equals the marginal cost.

MyEconLab   Visit **www.myeconlab.com** to complete these exercises online and get instant feedback.

Review Questions

1.1 Briefly discuss each of the following economic ideas: People are rational, people respond to economic incentives, and optimal decisions are made at the margin.

1.2 What is scarcity? Why is scarcity central to the study of economics?

Problems and Applications

1.3 Do you agree with the following statement: "The problem with economics is that it assumes that consumers and firms always make the correct decisions. But we know that everyone makes mistakes."

1.4 According to the FBI Bank Crime Statistics, there were more than 5,000 bank robberies in the United States in 2012. The FBI claims that banks have allowed themselves to become easy targets by refusing to install clear acrylic partitions, called *bandit barriers*, that separate bank tellers from the public. According to a special agent with the FBI, "Bandit barriers are a great deterrent. We've talked to guys who rob banks, and as soon as they see a bandit barrier, they go find another bank." Despite this finding, many banks have been reluctant to install these barriers. Wouldn't banks have a strong incentive to install bandit barriers to deter robberies? Why, then, do so many banks not do so?

Sources: "FBI Bank Crime Statistics 2012," www.fbi.gov; and Richard Cowen, "FBI: Banks Are to Blame for Rise in Robberies," NorthJersey.com, March 10, 2009.

1.5 The grading system plays an important role in student learning. In their book *Effective Grading: A Tool for Learning and Assessment in College*, Barbara Walvoord and Virginia Anderson state that "grading infuses everything that happens in the classroom." They also argue that grading "needs to be acknowledged and managed from the first moment that an instructor begins planning a class."
  a. How could the grading system a teacher uses affect the incentives of students to learn the course material?
  b. If teachers put too little weight in the grading scale on a certain part of the course, such as readings outside the textbook, how might students respond?
  c. Teachers often wish that students came to class prepared, having read the upcoming material. How could a teacher design the grading system to motivate students to come to class prepared?

Source: Barbara E. Walvoord and Virginia Johnson Anderson, *Effective Grading: A Tool for Learning and Assessment in College*, 2nd edition, San Francisco: Jossey-Bass, 2010, p. 1.

1.6 **[Related to the** Making the Connection **on page 5]** Many universities and corporations offer a health wellness program that helps their employees improve or maintain their health and get paid (a relatively small amount) for doing so. The programs vary but typically consist of employees completing a health assessment, receiving a program for healthy living, and monitoring their monthly health activities. Why would universities and corporations pay employees to take care of themselves? How does health insurance affect the incentive of employees to improve or maintain their health? Would a wellness program increase or decrease the health insurance premiums that an insurance company would charge the university or corporation to provide insurance coverage? Briefly explain.

1.7 **[Related to the** Making the Connection **on page 5]** Jay Bhattacharya and Kate Bundorf of Stanford University have found evidence that people who are obese and who work for firms that provide health insurance receive lower wages than workers at those firms who are not obese. At firms that do not provide health insurance, obese workers do not receive lower wages than workers who are not obese.

a. Why might firms that provide workers with health insurance pay a lower wage to obese workers than to workers who are not obese?

b. Is Bhattacharya and Bundorf's finding relevant to the question of whether health insurance provides people with an incentive to become obese? Briefly explain.

Source: Jay Bhattacharya and M. Kate Bundorf, "The Incidence of the Health Care Costs of Obesity," *Journal of Health Economics*, Vol. 28, No. 3, May 2009, pp. 649–658.

1.8 **[Related to** Solved Problem 1.1 **on page 7]** In 2013, the president and chief executive officer of McDonald's, Don Thompson, said that McDonald's was considering serving breakfast all day, instead of stopping at 10:30 A.M. on weekdays and 11:00 A.M. on weekends. Several owners of McDonald's restaurants, however, point out that offering breakfast 24 hours a day presents two logistical problems: (1) Burgers and other meats need to be cooked at a higher temperature than eggs, so it would be difficult for employees to set the grill at the right temperature for both foods, and (2) scrambled eggs require employees to continually stir, while hamburgers don't require this attention. In addition, some customers might buy the cheaper breakfast rather than the more expensive lunch or dinner meals. If you were the president and chief executive officer of McDonald's, discuss how you would go about deciding whether to serve breakfast all day. Would your decision have to be all or nothing—either serve breakfast up to 10:30 A.M. or serve breakfast all day? Would you have to serve the entire breakfast menu all day?

Source: Susan Berfield and Leslie Patton, "What's So Hard About a 24/7 McMuffin?" *Bloomberg BusinessWeek*, May 6–12, 2013.

1.9 **[Related to** Solved Problem 1.1 **on page 7]** Two students are discussing Solved Problem 1.1:

Joe: I think the key additional information you need to know in deciding whether the doctor should keep the medical practice open 9 hours per day rather than 8 hours is the amount of profit she is currently making while being open 8 hours. Then, she can compare the profit earned from being open 9 hours with the profit earned from being open 8 hours. This information is more important than the additional revenue and additional cost of being open 1 more hour.

Jill: Actually, Joe, knowing how much profits change when the medical practice stays open 1 more hour is exactly the same as knowing the additional revenue and the additional cost.

Briefly evaluate their discussion.

1.10 **[Related to** Solved Problem 1.1 **on page 7]** Late in the semester, a friend tells you, "I was going to drop my psychology course so I could concentrate on my other courses, but I had already put so much time into the course that I decided not to drop it." What do you think of your friend's reasoning? Would it make a difference to your answer if your friend has to pass the psychology course at some point to graduate? Briefly explain.

1.11 In a paper written by Bentley College economists Patricia M. Flynn and Michael A. Quinn, the authors state:

> We find evidence that Economics is a good choice of major for those aspiring to become a CEO [chief executive officer]. When adjusting for size of the pool of graduates, those with undergraduate degrees in Economics are shown to have had a greater likelihood of becoming an S&P 500 CEO than any other major.

A list of famous economics majors published by Marietta College includes business leaders Warren Buffett, Donald Trump, Ted Turner, Diane von Furstenberg, Steve Ballmer, and Sam Walton, as well as former presidents George H.W. Bush, Gerald Ford, and Ronald Reagan. Why might studying economics be particularly good preparation for being the top manager of a corporation or a leader in government?

Sources: Patricia M. Flynn and Michael A. Quinn, "Economics: A Good Choice of Major for Future CEOs," *Social Science Research Network*, November 28, 2006; and *Famous Economics Majors*, Marietta College, Marietta, Ohio, May 15, 2012.

1.2 The Economic Problem That Every Society Must Solve, pages 8–11

LEARNING OBJECTIVE: Discuss how an economy answers these questions: What goods and services will be produced? How will the goods and services be produced? Who will receive the goods and services produced?

Summary

Society faces **trade-offs**: Producing more of one good or service means producing less of another good or service. The **opportunity cost** of any activity—such as producing a good or service—is the highest-valued alternative that must be given up to engage in that activity. The choices of consumers, firms, and governments determine what goods and services will be produced. Firms choose how to produce the goods and services they sell. In the United States, who receives the goods and services produced depends largely on how income is distributed in the marketplace. In a **centrally planned economy**, most economic decisions are made by the government. In a **market economy**, most economic decisions are made by consumers and firms. Most economies, including that of the United States, are **mixed economies** in which most economic decisions are made by consumers and firms but in which the government also plays a significant role. There are two types of efficiency: productive efficiency and allocative efficiency. **Productive efficiency** occurs when a good or service is produced at the lowest possible cost. **Allocative efficiency** occurs when production corresponds with consumer preferences. **Voluntary exchange** is a situation that occurs in markets when both the buyer and the seller of a product are made better off by the transaction. **Equity** is more difficult to define than efficiency, but it usually involves a fair distribution of economic benefits. Government policymakers often face a trade-off between equity and efficiency.

 MyEconLab   Visit **www.myeconlab.com** to complete these exercises online and get instant feedback.

Review Questions

2.1 Why does scarcity imply that every society and every individual face trade-offs?

2.2 What are the three economic questions that every society must answer? Briefly discuss the differences in how centrally planned, market, and mixed economies answer these questions?

2.3 What is the difference between productive efficiency and allocative efficiency?

2.4 What is the difference between efficiency and equity? Why do government policymakers often face a trade-off between efficiency and equity?

Problems and Applications

2.5 When the price of Microsoft stock increased more than 27 percent in the first part of 2013, Bill Gates, who owns 436 million shares of Microsoft stock, once again became the world's richest person. Does Bill Gates face scarcity? Does everyone? Are there any exceptions?

Source: "Bill Gates Surpasses Carlos Slim to Become Richest Man in the World," Huffingtonpost.com, May 16, 2013.

2.6 Consider an organization that exists to help the poor. The members of the organization are discussing alternative methods of aiding the poor, when a proponent of one particular method asserts that: "If even one poor person is helped with this method, then all our time and money would have been worth it." If you were a member of the organization, how would you reply to this assertion?

2.7 In a market economy, why does a firm have a strong incentive to be productively efficient and allocatively efficient? What does the firm earn if it is productively and allocatively efficient, and what happens if it is not?

2.8 Would you expect new and better machinery and equipment to be adopted more rapidly in a market economy or in a centrally planned economy? Briefly explain.

2.9 Centrally planned economies have been less efficient than market economies.
   a. Has this difference in efficiency happened by chance, or is there some underlying reason?
   b. If market economies are more economically efficient than centrally planned economies, would there ever be

a reason to prefer having a centrally planned economy rather than a market economy?

2.10 Would you expect a centrally planned economy to be better at productive efficiency or allocative efficiency? Briefly explain.

2.11 Leonard Fleck, a philosophy professor at Michigan State University, has written:

> When it comes to health care in America, we have limited resources for unlimited health care needs. We want everything contemporary medical technology can offer that will improve the length or quality of our lives as we age. But as presently healthy taxpayers, we want costs controlled.

Why is it necessary for all economic systems to limit services such as health care? How does a market system prevent people from getting as many goods and services as they want?

Source: Leonard Fleck, *Just Caring: Health Care Rationing and Democratic Deliberation*, New York: Oxford University Press, 2009.

2.12 Suppose that your local police department recovers 100 tickets to a big NASCAR race in a drug raid. Police decide to distribute the tickets to residents and announce that tickets will be given away at 10 A.M. Monday at City Hall.
   a. What groups of people will be most likely to try to get the tickets? Think of specific examples and then generalize.
   b. What is the opportunity cost of distributing the tickets this way?
   c. Productive efficiency occurs when a good or service (such as the distribution of tickets) is produced at the lowest possible cost. Is this an efficient way to distribute the tickets? If possible, think of a more efficient method of distributing the tickets.
   d. Is this an equitable way to distribute the tickets? Explain.

1.3	**Economic Models, pages 11–15**

LEARNING OBJECTIVE: Understand the role of models in economic analysis.

Summary

An **economic variable** is something measurable that can have different values, such as the wages of software programmers. Economists rely on economic models when they apply economic ideas to real-world problems. **Economic models** are simplified versions of reality used to analyze real-world economic situations. Economists accept and use an economic model if it leads to hypotheses that are confirmed by statistical analysis. In many cases, the acceptance is tentative, however, pending the gathering of new data or further statistical analysis. Economics is a *social science* because it applies the scientific method to the study of the interactions among individuals. Economics is concerned with positive analysis rather than normative analysis. **Positive analysis** is concerned with what is. **Normative analysis** is concerned with what ought to be. As a social science, economics considers human behavior in every context of decision making, not just in business.

Review Questions

3.1 Why do economists use models? How are economic data used to test models?

3.2 Describe the five steps by which economists arrive at a useful economic model.

3.3 What is the difference between normative analysis and positive analysis? Is economics concerned mainly with normative analysis or positive analysis? Briefly explain.

Problems and Applications

3.4 Suppose an economist develops an economic model and finds that "it works great in theory, but it fails in practice." What should the economist do next?

3.5 Dr. Strangelove's theory is that the price of mushrooms is determined by the activity of subatomic particles that exist in another universe parallel to ours. When the subatomic particles are emitted in profusion, the price of mushrooms is high. When subatomic particle emissions are low, the price of mushrooms is also low. How would you go about testing Dr. Strangelove's theory? Discuss whether this theory is useful.

3.6 **[Related to the** Making the Connection **on page 14]** This feature explains that there are both positive and normative elements to the debate over whether medical schools should charge tuition and whether hospitals should continue to pay residents who pursue primary care but not residents who specialize. What economic statistics would be most useful in evaluating the positive elements in this debate? Assuming that these statistics are available or could be gathered, are they likely to resolve the normative issues in this debate?

3.7 **[Related to the** Chapter Opener **on page 3]** In recent years, many doctors have decided to give up running their private practices as small businesses and have become salaried employees of hospitals.

   a. What important differences exist between doctors' private practices and other small businesses, such as restaurants and hardware stores?

   b. How have the economic incentives a doctor faces when considering whether to operate a private practice or become a salaried employee of a hospital changed over the years?

3.8 **[Related to the** Chapter Opener **on page 3]** According to an article in the *New York Times*, hospitals sometimes complain that doctors do not work as hard when they become hospital employees as they do when they operate a private practice. How do the economic incentives a doctor faces to work hard change when the doctor closes a private practice and becomes a salaried employee of a hospital?

Source: Julie Crewell and Reed Abelson, "A Hospital War Reflects a Bind for Doctors in the U.S.," *New York Times*, November 30, 2012.

3.9 **[Related to the** Don't Let This Happen to You **on page 14]** Explain which of the following statements represent positive analysis and which represent normative analysis.

   a. A 50-cent-per-pack tax on cigarettes will lead to a 12 percent reduction in smoking by teenagers.

   b. The federal government should spend more on AIDS research.

   c. Rising wheat prices will increase bread prices.

   d. The price of coffee at Starbucks is too high.

3.10 In the United States, to receive a medical license, a doctor must complete a residency program at a hospital. Hospitals are not free to expand their residency programs in a particular medical specialty without approval from a Residency Review Committee (RRC), which is made up of physicians in that specialty. A hospital that does not abide by the rulings of the RRC runs the risk of losing its accreditation from the Accreditation Council for Graduate Medical Education (ACGME). The ACGME and the RRCs argue that this system makes it possible to ensure that residency programs do not expand to the point where they are not providing residents with high-quality training.

   a. How does this system help protect consumers?

   b. How might this system protect the financial interests of doctors more than the well-being of consumers?

   c. Briefly discuss whether you consider this system to be a good one. Is your conclusion an example of normative economics or of positive economics? Briefly explain.

Sources: Brian Palmer, "We Need More Doctors, Stat!" *Slate*, June 27, 2011; and Sean Nicholson, "Barriers to Entering Medical Specialties," Wharton School, September 2003.

1.4 | **Microeconomics and Macroeconomics, pages 15–16**
LEARNING OBJECTIVE: Distinguish between microeconomics and macroeconomics.

Summary

Microeconomics is the study of how households and firms make choices, how they interact in markets, and how the government attempts to influence their choices. **Macroeconomics** is the study of the economy as a whole, including topics such as inflation, unemployment, and economic growth.

 MyEconLab   Visit **www.myeconlab.com** to complete these exercises online and get instant feedback.

Review Question

4.1 Briefly discuss the difference between microeconomics and macroeconomics.

4.2 Is every economic issue either strictly microeconomic or strictly macroeconomic? Briefly explain.

Problems and Applications

4.3 Briefly explain whether each of the following is primarily a microeconomic issue or a macroeconomic issue.

   a. The effect of higher cigarette taxes on the quantity of cigarettes sold.

   b. The effect of higher income taxes on the total amount of consumer spending.

   c. The reasons the economies of East Asian countries grow faster than the economies of sub-Saharan African countries.

   d. The reasons for low rates of profit in the airline industry.

4.4 Briefly explain whether you agree with the following assertion: "Microeconomics is concerned with things that happen in one particular place, such as the unemployment rate in one city. In contrast, macroeconomics is concerned with things that affect the country as a whole, such as how the rate of teenage smoking in the United States would be affected by an increase in the tax on cigarettes."

1.5 | **A Preview of Important Economic Terms, pages 16–17**
LEARNING OBJECTIVE: Define important economic terms.

Summary

Becoming familiar with important terms is a necessary step in learning economics. These important economic terms include *capital, entrepreneur, factors of production, firm, goods, household, human capital, innovation, profit, revenue, services,* and *technology.*

Appendix

Using Graphs and Formulas

Graphs are used to illustrate key economic ideas. Graphs appear not just in economics textbooks but also on Web sites and in newspaper and magazine articles that discuss events in business and economics. Why the heavy use of graphs? Because they serve two useful purposes: (1) They simplify economic ideas, and (2) they make the ideas more concrete so they can be applied to real-world problems. Economic and business issues can be complicated, but a graph can help cut through complications and highlight the key relationships needed to understand the issue. In that sense, a graph can be like a street map.

Suppose you take a bus to New York City to see the Empire State Building. After arriving at the Port Authority Bus Terminal, you will probably use a map similar to the one shown here to find your way to the Empire State Building.

Maps are very familiar to just about everyone, so we don't usually think of them as being simplified versions of reality, but they are. This map does not show much more than the streets in this part of New York City and some of the most important buildings. The names, addresses, and telephone numbers of the people who live and work in the area aren't given. Almost none of the stores and buildings those people work and live in are shown either. The map doesn't indicate which streets allow curbside parking and which don't. In fact, the map shows almost nothing about the messy reality of life in this section of New York City, except how the streets are laid out, which is the essential information you need to get from the Port Authority Bus Terminal to the Empire State Building.

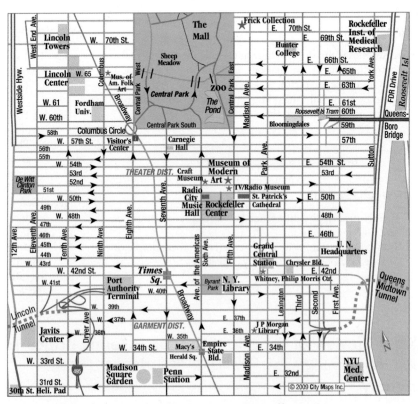

Street map of New York City. Copyright © 2011 City Maps Inc. Reprinted by permission.

Think about someone who says, "I know how to get around in the city, but I just can't figure out how to read a map." It certainly is possible to find your destination in a city without a map, but it's a lot easier with one. The same is true of using graphs in economics. It is possible to arrive at a solution to a real-world problem in economics and business without using graphs, but it is usually a lot easier if you use them.

Often, the difficulty students have with graphs and formulas is a lack of familiarity. With practice, all the graphs and formulas in this text will become familiar to you. Once you are familiar with them, you will be able to use them to analyze problems that would otherwise seem very difficult. What follows is a brief review of how graphs and formulas are used.

Graphs of One Variable

Figure 1A.1 displays values for *market shares* in the U.S. automobile market, using two common types of graphs. Market shares show the percentage of industry sales accounted for by different firms. In this case, the information is for groups of firms: the "Big Three"—Ford, General Motors, and Chrysler—as well as Japanese, European, and Korean firms. Panel (a) displays the information on market shares as a *bar graph*, where the market share of each group of firms is represented by the height of its bar. Panel (b) displays the same information as a *pie chart*, where the market share of each group of firms is represented by the size of its slice of the pie.

Information on economic variables is also often displayed in *time-series graphs*. Time-series graphs are displayed on a coordinate grid. In a coordinate grid, we can measure the value of one variable along the vertical axis (or *y*-axis) and the value of another variable along the horizontal axis (or *x*-axis). The point where the vertical axis intersects the horizontal axis is called the *origin*. At the origin, the value of both variables is zero. The points on a coordinate grid represent values of the two variables. In Figure 1A.2, we measure the number of automobiles and trucks sold worldwide by Ford Motor Company on the vertical axis, and we measure time on the horizontal axis. In time-series graphs, the height of the line at each date shows the value of the variable measured on the vertical axis. Both panels of Figure 1A.2 show Ford's worldwide sales during each year from 2001 to 2012. The difference between panel (a) and panel (b) illustrates the importance of the scale used in a time-series graph. In panel (a), the vertical axis starts at 0 and the distance between each value shown is the same. In this panel, the decline in

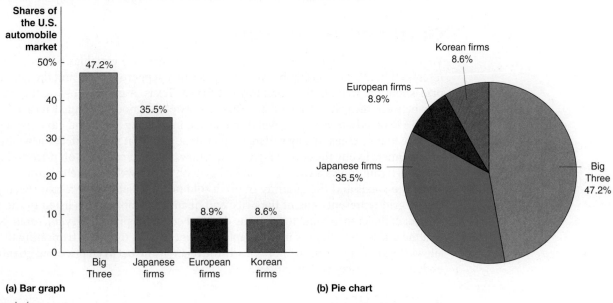

(a) Bar graph

(b) Pie chart

MyEconLab Animation

Figure 1A.1 Bar Graphs and Pie Charts

Values for an economic variable are often displayed as a bar graph or a pie chart. In this case, panel (a) shows market share data for the U.S. automobile industry as a bar graph, where the market share of each group of firms is represented by the height of its bar. Panel (b) displays the same information as a pie chart, where the market share of each group of firms is represented by the size of its slice of the pie. **Source:** "Auto Sales," *Wall Street Journal*, May 1, 2013.

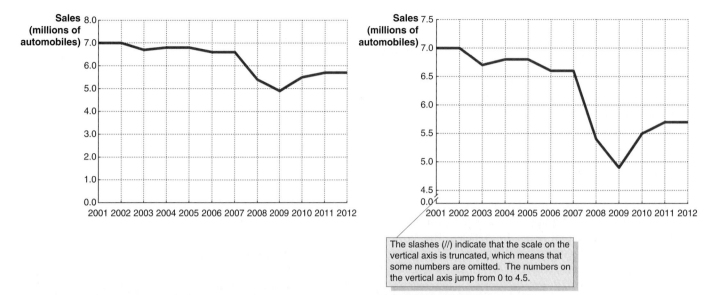

(a) Time-series graph where the scale is not truncated

(b) Time-series graph with truncated scale

The slashes (//) indicate that the scale on the vertical axis is truncated, which means that some numbers are omitted. The numbers on the vertical axis jump from 0 to 4.5.

MyEconLab Animation

Figure 1A.2 **Time-Series Graphs**

Both panels present time-series graphs of Ford Motor Company's worldwide sales during each year from 2001 to 2012. In panel (a), the vertical axis starts at 0 and the distance between each pair of values shown is the same. In panel (b), the scale on the vertical axis is truncated, which means that although it starts at zero, it then jumps to 4.5 million. As a result, the fluctuations in Ford's sales appear smaller in panel (a) than in panel (b).

Source: Ford Motor Company, *Annual Report*, various years.

Ford's sales during 2008 and 2009 appears relatively small. In panel (b), the scale on the vertical axis is truncated, which means that although it starts at zero, it jumps to 4.5 million. As a result, the distance on the vertical axis from 0 to 4.5 million is much smaller than the distance from 4.5 million to 5.0 million. The slashes (//) near the bottom of the axis indicate that the scale is truncated. In panel (b), the decline in Ford's sales during 2008 and 2009 appears much larger than in panel (a). (Technically, the horizontal axis in both panels is also truncated because we start with 2001, not 0.) MyEconLab Concept Check

Graphs of Two Variables

We often use graphs to show the relationship between two variables. Suppose you are interested in the relationship between the price of a pepperoni pizza and the quantity of pizzas sold per week in the small town of Bryan, Texas. A graph showing the relationship between the price of a good and the quantity of the good demanded at each price is called a *demand curve*. (As we will discuss later, in drawing a demand curve for a good, we have to hold constant any variables other than price that might affect the willingness of consumers to buy the good.) Figure 1A.3 shows the data collected on price and quantity. The figure shows a two-dimensional grid on which we measure the price of pizza along the *y*-axis and the quantity of pizza sold per week along the *x*-axis. Each point on the grid represents one of the price and quantity combinations listed in the table. We can connect the points to form the demand curve for pizza in Bryan, Texas. Notice that the scales on both axes in the graph are truncated. In this case, truncating the axes allows the graph to illustrate more clearly the relationship between price and quantity by excluding low prices and quantities.

Slopes of Lines

Once you have plotted the data in Figure 1A.3, you may be interested in how much the quantity of pizza sold increases as the price decreases. The *slope* of a line tells us how much the variable we are measuring on the *y*-axis changes as the variable we are measuring on the *x*-axis changes. We can use the Greek letter delta (Δ) to stand for the

Price (dollars per pizza)	Quantity (pizzas per week)	Points
$15	50	A
14	55	B
13	60	C
12	65	D
11	70	E

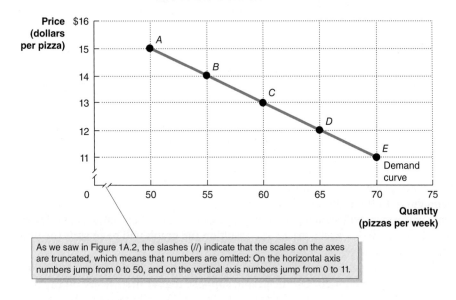

As we saw in Figure 1A.2, the slashes (//) indicate that the scales on the axes are truncated, which means that numbers are omitted: On the horizontal axis numbers jump from 0 to 50, and on the vertical axis numbers jump from 0 to 11.

MyEconLab Animation

Figure 1A.3

Plotting Price and Quantity Points in a Graph

The figure shows a two-dimensional grid on which we measure the price of pizza along the vertical axis (or *y*-axis) and the quantity of pizza sold per week along the horizontal axis (or *x*-axis). Each point on the grid represents one of the price and quantity combinations listed in the table. By connecting the points with a line, we can better illustrate the relationship between the two variables.

change in a variable. The slope is sometimes referred to as the rise over the run. So, we have several ways of expressing slope:

$$\text{Slope} = \frac{\text{Change in value on the vertical axis}}{\text{Change in value on the horizontal axis}} = \frac{\Delta y}{\Delta x} = \frac{\text{Rise}}{\text{Run}}.$$

Figure 1A.4 reproduces the graph from Figure 1A.3. Because the slope of a straight line is the same at any point, we can use any two points in the figure to calculate the slope of the line. For example, when the price of pizza decreases from $14 to $12, the quantity of pizza sold increases from 55 per week to 65 per week. Therefore, the slope is:

$$\text{Slope} = \frac{\Delta \text{Price of pizza}}{\Delta \text{Quantity of pizza}} = \frac{(\$12 - \$14)}{(65 - 55)} = \frac{-2}{10} = -0.2.$$

The slope of this line shows us how responsive consumers in Bryan, Texas, are to changes in the price of pizza. The larger the value of the slope (ignoring the negative sign), the steeper the line will be, which indicates that not many additional pizzas are sold when the price falls. The smaller the value of the slope, the flatter the line will be, which indicates a greater increase in pizzas sold when the price falls.   MyEconLab Concept Check

Taking into Account More Than Two Variables on a Graph

The demand curve graph in Figure 1A.4 shows the relationship between the price of pizza and the quantity of pizza demanded, but we know that the quantity of any good demanded depends on more than just the price of the good. For example, the quantity of pizza demanded in a given week in Bryan, Texas, can be affected by other variables—the price of hamburgers, whether an advertising campaign by local pizza parlors has begun that week, and so on. Allowing the values of any other variables to change will cause the position of the demand curve in the graph to change.

Figure 1A.4

Calculating the Slope of a Line

We can calculate the slope of a line as the change in the value of the variable on the *y*-axis divided by the change in the value of the variable on the *x*-axis. Because the slope of a straight line is constant, we can use any two points in the figure to calculate the slope of the line. For example, when the price of pizza decreases from $14 to $12, the quantity of pizza demanded increases from 55 per week to 65 per week. So, the slope of this line equals −2 divided by 10, or −0.2.

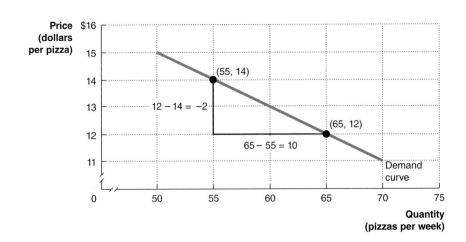

Suppose that the demand curve in Figure 1A.4 were drawn holding the price of hamburgers constant, at $1.50. If the price of hamburgers rises to $2.00, some consumers will switch from buying hamburgers to buying pizza, and more pizzas will be demanded at every price. The result on the graph will be to shift the line representing the demand curve to the right. Similarly, if the price of hamburgers falls from $1.50 to $1.00, some consumers will switch from buying pizza to buying hamburgers, and fewer pizzas will be demanded at every price. The result on the graph will be to shift the line representing the demand curve to the left.

The table in Figure 1A.5 shows the effect of a change in the price of hamburgers on the quantity of pizza demanded. On the graph, suppose that at first we are on the line labeled Demand curve₁. If the price of pizza is $14 (point *A*), an increase in the price of

Figure 1A.5

Showing Three Variables on a Graph

The demand curve for pizza shows the relationship between the price of pizzas and the quantity of pizzas demanded, *holding constant other factors that might affect the willingness of consumers to buy pizza.* If the price of pizza is $14 (point *A*), an increase in the price of hamburgers from $1.50 to $2.00 increases the quantity of pizzas demanded from 55 to 60 per week (point *B*) and shifts us to Demand curve₂. Or, if we start on Demand curve₁ and the price of pizza is $12 (point *C*), a decrease in the price of hamburgers from $1.50 to $1.00 decreases the quantity of pizza demanded from 65 to 60 per week (point *D*) and shifts us to Demand curve₃.

Price (dollars per pizza)	Quantity (pizzas per week)		
	When the Price of Hamburgers = $1.00	When the Price of Hamburgers = $1.50	When the Price of Hamburgers = $2.00
$15	45	50	55
14	50	55	60
13	55	60	65
12	60	65	70
11	65	70	75

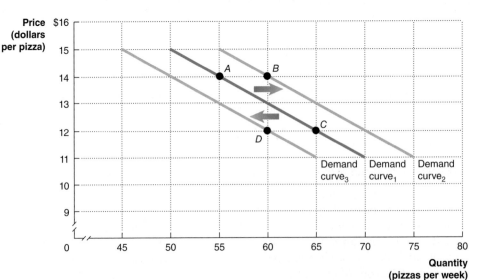

hamburgers from $1.50 to $2.00 increases the quantity of pizzas demanded from 55 to 60 per week (point *B*) and shifts us to Demand curve$_2$. Or, if we start on Demand curve$_1$ and the price of pizza is $12 (point *C*), a decrease in the price of hamburgers from $1.50 to $1.00 decreases the quantity of pizzas demanded from 65 to 60 per week (point *D*) and shifts us to Demand curve$_3$. By shifting the demand curve, we have taken into account the effect of changes in the value of a third variable—the price of hamburgers. We will use this technique of shifting curves to allow for the effects of additional variables many times in this book.   MyEconLab Concept Check

Positive and Negative Relationships

We can use graphs to show the relationships between any two variables. Sometimes the relationship between the variables is *negative*, meaning that as one variable increases in value, the other variable decreases in value. This was the case with the price of pizza and the quantity of pizzas demanded. The relationship between two variables can also be *positive*, meaning that the values of both variables increase or decrease together. For example, when the level of total income—or *disposable personal income*—received by households in the United States increases, the level of total *consumption spending*, which is spending by households on goods and services, also increases. The table in Figure 1A.6 shows the values (in billions of dollars) for income and consumption spending for 2009–2012. The graph plots the data from the table, with disposable personal income measured along the horizontal axis and consumption spending measured along the vertical axis. Notice that the points for 2010 and 2011 do not all fall exactly on the line. To examine the relationship between two variables, economists often use the straight line that best fits the data.   MyEconLab Concept Check

Determining Cause and Effect

When we graph the relationship between two variables, we usually want to draw conclusions about whether changes in one variable are causing changes in the other variable. Doing so can, however, lead to mistakes. Suppose you graph over the course of a year the number of homes in a neighborhood that have a fire burning in the fireplace and the number of leaves on trees in the neighborhood. You would get a relationship like

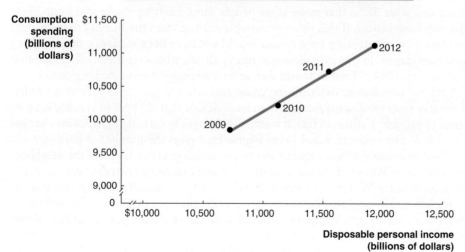

Year	Disposable Personal Income (billions of dollars)	Consumption Spending (billions of dollars)
2009	$10,722	$9,846
2010	11,127	10,216
2011	11,549	10,729
2012	11,931	11,120

MyEconLab Animation

Figure 1A.6

Graphing the Positive Relationship between Income and Consumption

In a positive relationship between two economic variables, as one variable increases, the other variable also increases. This figure shows the positive relationship between disposable personal income and consumption spending. As disposable personal income in the United States has increased, so has consumption spending.

Source: U.S. Department of Commerce, Bureau of Economic Analysis.

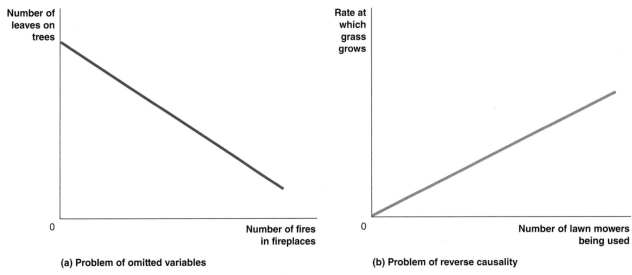

(a) Problem of omitted variables

(b) Problem of reverse causality

MyEconLab Animation

Figure 1A.7   Determining Cause and Effect

Using graphs to draw conclusions about cause and effect can be hazardous. In panel (a), we see that there are fewer leaves on the trees in a neighborhood when many homes have fires burning in their fireplaces. We cannot draw the conclusion that using fireplaces causes the leaves to fall because we have an *omitted*

variable—the season of the year. In panel (b), we see that more lawn mowers are used in a neighborhood during times when the grass grows rapidly and fewer lawn mowers are used when the grass grows slowly. Concluding that using lawn mowers *causes* the grass to grow faster would be making the error of *reverse causality*.

that shown in panel (a) of Figure 1A.7: The more fireplaces in use in the neighborhood, the fewer leaves the trees have. Can we draw the conclusion from this graph that using a fireplace causes trees to lose their leaves? We know, of course, that such a conclusion would be incorrect. In spring and summer, there are relatively few fireplaces being used, and the trees are full of leaves. In the fall, as trees begin to lose their leaves, fireplaces are used more frequently. And in winter, many fireplaces are being used and many trees have lost all their leaves. The reason that the graph in Figure 1A.7 is misleading about cause and effect is that there is obviously an *omitted variable* in the analysis—the season of the year. An omitted variable is one that affects other variables, and its omission can lead to false conclusions about cause and effect.

Although in our example the omitted variable is obvious, there are many debates about cause and effect where the existence of an omitted variable has not been clear. For instance, it has been known for many years that people who smoke cigarettes suffer from higher rates of lung cancer than do nonsmokers. For some time, tobacco companies and some scientists argued that there was an omitted variable—perhaps a failure to exercise or a poor diet—that made some people more likely to smoke and more likely to develop lung cancer. If this omitted variable existed, then the finding that smokers were more likely to develop lung cancer would not have been evidence that smoking *caused* lung cancer. In this case, however, nearly all scientists eventually concluded that the omitted variable did not exist and that, in fact, smoking does cause lung cancer.

A related problem in determining cause and effect is known as *reverse causality*. The error of reverse causality occurs when we conclude that changes in variable *X* cause changes in variable *Y* when, in fact, it is actually changes in variable *Y* that cause changes in variable *X*. For example, panel (b) of Figure 1A.7 plots the number of lawn mowers being used in a neighborhood against the rate at which grass on lawns in the neighborhood is growing. We could conclude from this graph that using lawn mowers *causes* the grass to grow faster. We know, however, that in reality, the causality is in the other direction. Rapidly growing grass during the spring and summer causes the increased use of lawn mowers. Slowly growing grass in the fall or winter or during periods of low rainfall causes the decreased use of lawn mowers.

Once again, in our example, the potential error of reverse causality is obvious. In many economic debates, however, cause and effect can be more difficult to determine.

For example, changes in the money supply, or the total amount of money in the economy, tend to occur at the same time as changes in the total amount of income people in the economy earn. A famous debate in economics was about whether the changes in the money supply caused the changes in total income or whether the changes in total income caused the changes in the money supply. Each side in the debate accused the other side of committing the error of reverse causality. MyEconLab Concept Check

Are Graphs of Economic Relationships Always Straight Lines?

The graphs of relationships between two economic variables that we have drawn so far have been straight lines. The relationship between two variables is *linear* when it can be represented by a straight line. Few economic relationships are actually linear. For example, if we carefully plot data on the price of a product and the quantity demanded at each price, holding constant other variables that affect the quantity demanded, we will usually find a curved—or *nonlinear*—relationship rather than a linear relationship. In practice, however, it is often useful to approximate a nonlinear relationship with a linear relationship. If the relationship is reasonably close to being linear, the analysis is not significantly affected. In addition, it is easier to calculate the slope of a straight line, and it is also easier to calculate the area under a straight line. So, in this textbook, we often assume that the relationship between two economic variables is linear, even when we know that this assumption is not precisely correct. MyEconLab Concept Check

Slopes of Nonlinear Curves

In some situations, we need to take into account the nonlinear nature of an economic relationship. For example, panel (a) of Figure 1A.8 shows the hypothetical relationship between Apple's total cost of producing iPhones and the quantity of iPhones produced. The relationship is curved rather than linear. In this case, the cost of production is increasing at an increasing rate, which often happens in manufacturing. In other words, as we move up the curve, its slope becomes larger. (Remember that with a straight line, the slope is always constant.) To see why, first remember that we calculate the slope of a curve by dividing the change in the variable on the y-axis by the change in the variable on the x-axis. As we move from point A to point B, the quantity produced increases by 1 million iPhones, while the total cost of production increases by $50 million. Farther up the curve, as we move from point C to point D, the change in quantity is the same—1 million iPhones—but the change in the total cost of production is now much larger—$250 million. Because the change in the y variable has increased, while the change in the x variable has remained the same, we know that the slope has increased.

To measure the slope of a nonlinear curve at a particular point, we measure the slope of the line that is tangent to that curve at that point. This tangent line will touch the curve only at that point. We can measure the slope of the tangent line just as we would measure the slope of any other straight line. In panel (b), the tangent line at point B has a slope equal to:

$$\frac{\Delta \text{Cost}}{\Delta \text{Quantity}} = \frac{75}{1} = 75.$$

The tangent line at point C has a slope equal to:

$$\frac{\Delta \text{Cost}}{\Delta \text{Quantity}} = \frac{150}{1} = 150.$$

Once again, we see that the slope of the curve is larger at point C than at point B. MyEconLab Concept Check

Formulas

We have just seen that graphs are an important economic tool. In this section, we will review several useful formulas and show how to use them to summarize data and to calculate important relationships.

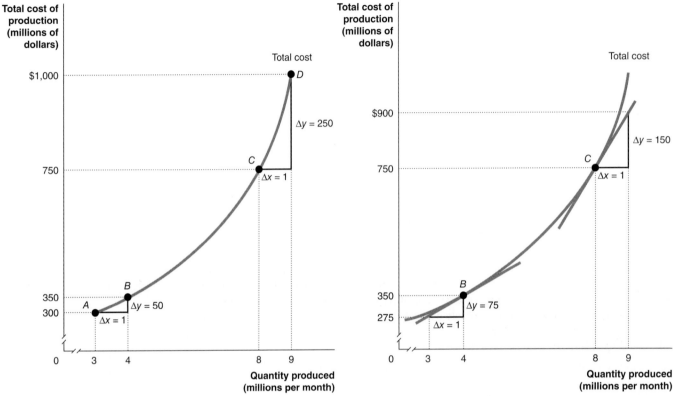

(a) The slope of a nonlinear curve is not constant

(b) The slope of a nonlinear curve is measured by the slope of the tangent line

MyEconLab Animation

Figure 1A.8   **The Slope of a Nonlinear Curve**

The relationship between the quantity of iPhones produced and the total cost of production is curved rather than linear. In panel (a), when we move from point *A* to point *B*, the quantity produced increases by 1 million iPhones, while the total cost of production increases by $50 million. Farther up the curve, as we move from point *C* to point *D*, the change in quantity is the same—1 million iPhones—but the change in the total cost of production is now much larger—$250 million.

Because the change in the *y* variable has increased, while the change in the *x* variable has remained the same, we know that the slope has increased. In panel (b), we measure the slope of the curve at a particular point by calculating the slope of the tangent line at that point. The slope of the tangent line at point *B* is 75, and the slope of the tangent line at point *C* is 150.

Formula for a Percentage Change

One important formula is the percentage change. The *percentage change* is the change in some economic variable, usually from one period to the next, expressed as a percentage. A key macroeconomic measure is the real gross domestic product (GDP). GDP is the value of all the final goods and services produced in a country during a year. "Real" GDP is corrected for the effects of inflation. When economists say that the U.S. economy grew 2.8 percent during 2012, they mean that real GDP was 2.8 percent higher in 2012 than it was in 2011. The formula for making this calculation is:

$$\left(\frac{\text{GDP}_{2012} - \text{GDP}_{2011}}{\text{GDP}_{2011}} \right) \times 100,$$

or, more generally, for any two periods:

$$\text{Percentage change} = \left(\frac{\text{Value in the second period} - \text{Value in the first period}}{\text{Value in the first period}} \right) \times 100.$$

In this case, real GDP was $15,052 billion in 2011 and $15,471 billion in 2012. So, the growth rate of the U.S. economy during 2012 was:

$$\left(\frac{\$15,471 - \$15,052}{\$15,052} \right) \times 100 = 2.8\%.$$

Notice that it doesn't matter that in using the formula, we ignored the fact that GDP is measured in billions of dollars. In fact, when calculating percentage changes, *the units don't matter*. The percentage increase from $15,052 billion to $15,471 billion is exactly the same as the percentage increase from $15,052 to $15,471.   MyEconLab Concept Check

Formulas for the Areas of a Rectangle and a Triangle

Areas that form rectangles and triangles on graphs can have important economic meaning. For example, Figure 1A.9 shows the demand curve for Pepsi. Suppose that the price is currently $2.00 and that 125,000 bottles of Pepsi are sold at that price. A firm's *total revenue* is equal to the amount it receives from selling its product, or the quantity sold multiplied by the price. In this case, total revenue will equal 125,000 bottles times $2.00 per bottle, or $250,000.

The formula for the area of a rectangle is:

$$\text{Area of a rectangle} = \text{Base} \times \text{Height}.$$

In Figure 1A.9, the shaded rectangle also represents the firm's total revenue because its area is given by the base of 125,000 bottles multiplied by the price of $2.00 per bottle.

We will see in later chapters that areas that are triangles can also have economic significance. The formula for the area of a triangle is:

$$\text{Area of a triangle} = \frac{1}{2} \times \text{Base} \times \text{Height}.$$

The shaded area in Figure 1A.10 is a triangle. The base equals 150,000 − 125,000, or 25,000. Its height equals $2.00 − $1.50, or $0.50. Therefore, its area equals 1/2 × 25,000 × $0.50, or $6,250. Notice that the shaded area is a triangle only if the demand curve is a straight line, or linear. Not all demand curves are linear. However, the formula for the area of a triangle will usually still give a good approximation, even if the demand curve is not linear.   MyEconLab Concept Check

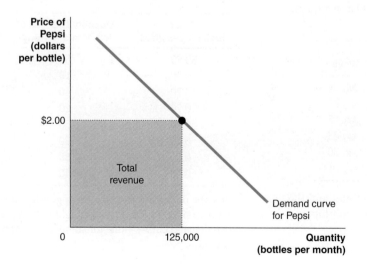

MyEconLab Animation

Figure 1A.9

Showing a Firm's Total Revenue on a Graph

The area of a rectangle is equal to its base multiplied by its height. Total revenue is equal to quantity multiplied by price. Here, total revenue is equal to the quantity of 125,000 bottles times the price of $2.00 per bottle, or $250,000. The area of the shaded rectangle shows the firm's total revenue.

Figure 1A.10

The Area of a Triangle

The area of a triangle is equal to 1/2 multiplied by its base multiplied by its height. The area of the shaded triangle has a base equal to 150,000 − 125,000, or 25,000, and a height equal to $2.00 − $1.50, or $0.50. Therefore, its area is equal to 1/2 × 25,000 × $0.50, or $6,250.

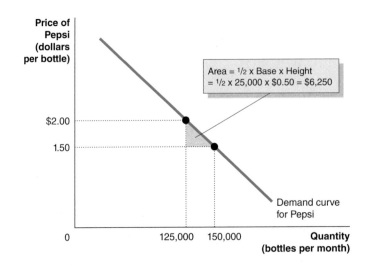

Summary of Using Formulas

You will encounter several other formulas in this book. Whenever you use a formula, you should follow these steps:

1. Make sure you understand the economic concept the formula represents.
2. Make sure you are using the correct formula for the problem you are solving.
3. Make sure the number you calculate using the formula is economically reasonable. For example, if you are using a formula to calculate a firm's revenue and your answer is a negative number, you know you made a mistake somewhere. MyEconLab Concept Check

MyEconLab Study Plan

| 1A | **Using Graphs and Formulas, pages 24–34** |

LEARNING OBJECTIVE: Review the use of graphs and formulas.

MyEconLab   Visit www.myeconlab.com to complete these exercises online and get instant feedback.

Problems and Applications

1A.1 The following table shows the relationship between the price of custard pies and the number of pies Jacob buys per week:

Price (dollars per pie)	Quantity of pies	Week
$3.00	6	July 2
2.00	7	July 9
5.00	4	July 16
6.00	3	July 23
1.00	8	July 30
4.00	5	August 6

a. Is the relationship between the price of pies and the number of pies Jacob buys a positive relationship or a negative relationship?

b. Plot the data from the table on a graph similar to Figure 1A.3 on page 27. Draw a straight line that best fits the points.

c. Calculate the slope of the line.

1A.2 The following table gives information on the quantity of glasses of lemonade demanded on sunny and overcast days:

Price (dollars per glass)	Quantity (glasses of lemonade per day)	Weather
$0.80	30	Sunny
0.80	10	Overcast
0.70	40	Sunny
0.70	20	Overcast
0.60	50	Sunny
0.60	30	Overcast
0.50	60	Sunny
0.50	40	Overcast

Plot the data from the table on a graph similar to Figure 1A.5 on page 28. Draw two straight lines representing the two demand curves—one for sunny days and one for overcast days.

1A.3 Using the information in Figure 1A.2 on page 26, calculate the percentage change in Ford's auto sales from one year to the next. During which year did sales fall at the highest rate?

1A.4 Real GDP in 2008 was $14,834 billion. Real GDP in 2009 was $14,418 billion. What was the percentage change in real GDP from 2008 to 2009. What do economists call the percentage change in real GDP from one year to the next?

1A.5 Assume that the demand curve for Pepsi passes through the following two points:

Price per bottle of Pepsi (in dollars)	Number of bottles demanded
$2.50	100,000
1.25	200,000

a. Draw a graph with a linear demand curve that passes through these two points.
b. Show on the graph the areas representing total revenue at each price. Give the value for total revenue at each price.

1A.6 What is the area of the triangle shown in the following figure?

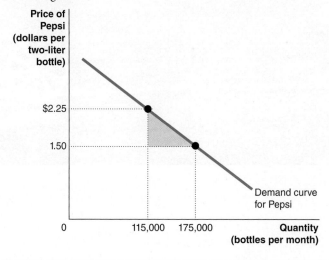

1A.7 Calculate the slope of the total cost curve at point *A* and at point *B* in the following figure.

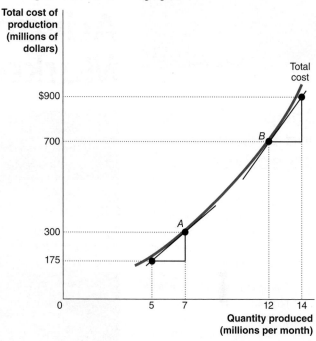

Trade-offs, Comparative Advantage, and the Market System

Chapter Outline and Learning Objectives

Managers at Tesla Motors Face Trade-Offs

Are all-electric cars the wave of the future? If you're like most drivers, you probably like the idea of skipping the gas station in favor of powering up your car by plugging it into an electric outlet. Yet, all-electric cars, such as the Chevrolet Volt and Nissan Leaf, have struggled to succeed in the marketplace for two key reasons: (1) The lithium batteries that power electric cars are costly, forcing up the prices of the cars, and (2) available batteries need to be recharged every 300 miles or so, making all-electric cars difficult to use on long trips.

Many people were therefore surprised when Tesla Motors announced in early 2013 that sales of its all-electric cars had been higher than expected and that it had made a profit for the first time. Tesla was founded in 2003 by billionaire Elon Musk, who also started the online payment system PayPal and the private space firm SpaceX. As many investors began to believe that Tesla was likely to become the first successful electric car company, the value of the firm soared to more than $200 billion.

Tesla manufactures its cars in Fremont, California. To compete in the automobile market, Tesla's managers must make many strategic decisions, such as whether to introduce new car models. In 2013, Tesla's only model, the Model S sedan, received the highest car rating ever from *Consumer Reports* and won the 2013 award for World Green Car of the Year. In 2014, Tesla introduced a second model, the Model X, a cross between a sport utility vehicle (SUV) and a minivan. The Model X was designed for families who would otherwise buy traditional gasoline-powered SUVs or minivans.

Tesla's managers must also decide how to sell and service its cars. Most cars are sold through dealerships, which also provide service for those cars. In 2013, however, Tesla had no dealerships. Instead, the company sold all of its cars online and relied on company-owned service centers to provide maintenance and repair services. Some economists have questioned whether Tesla will be able to meet its future sales goals without selling cars through dealerships.

Managers also make smaller-scale decisions. For instance, in scheduling production at its Fremont plant, Tesla's managers must decide each month the quantity of Model S sedans and Model X SUVs to manufacture. Like other decisions managers make, this one involves a trade-off: Producing more of one of these two models means producing fewer of the other.

AN INSIDE LOOK on **page 60** discusses how managers at Mercedes-Benz decide which models to manufacture and why the company chose to partner with Tesla Motors to develop electric-vehicle components.

Sources: Steven Russolillo, "Four Reasons Morgan Stanley Loves Tesla," *Wall Street Journal*, May 14, 2013; and Christopher F. Schuetze, "Will 2013 Be the Year of the Electric Car?" *New York Times*, January 7, 2013.

Economics in Your Life

The Trade-offs When You Buy a Car

When you buy a traditional gasoline-powered car, you probably consider factors such as safety and fuel efficiency. To increase fuel efficiency, automobile manufacturers make cars that are small and light. Large cars absorb more of the impact of an accident than do small cars. As a result, people are usually safer driving large cars than small cars. What can we conclude from these facts about the relationship between safety and fuel efficiency? Under what circumstances would it be possible for automobile manufacturers to make cars that are both safer and more fuel efficient? As you read the chapter, try to answer these questions. You can check your answers against those provided on **page 58** at the end of this chapter.

Scarcity A situation in which unlimited wants exceed the limited resources available to fulfill those wants.

I n a market system, managers at most firms must make decisions like those made by Tesla's managers. These decisions reflect a key fact of economic life: *Scarcity requires trade-offs*. **Scarcity** exists because we have unlimited wants but only limited resources available to fulfill those wants. Goods and services are scarce. So, too, are the economic resources, or *factors of production*—workers, capital, natural resources, and entrepreneurial ability—used to make goods and services. Your time is scarce, which means you face trade-offs: If you spend an hour studying for an economics exam, you have one less hour to spend studying for a psychology exam or going to the movies. If your university decides to use some of its scarce budget to buy new computers for the computer labs, those funds will not be available to buy new books for the library or to resurface the student parking lot. If Tesla decides to devote some of the scarce workers and machinery in its Fremont assembly plant to producing more Model X SUVs, those resources will not be available to produce more Model S sedans.

Households and firms make many of their decisions in markets. Trade is a key activity that takes place in markets. Trade results from the decisions of millions of households and firms spread around the world. By engaging in trade, people can raise their incomes. In this chapter, we provide an overview of how the market system coordinates the independent decisions of these millions of households and firms. We begin our analysis of the economic consequences of scarcity and the working of the market system by introducing an important economic model: the *production possibilities frontier*.

2.1 LEARNING OBJECTIVE

Use a production possibilities frontier to analyze opportunity costs and trade-offs.

Production possibilities frontier (*PPF*) A curve showing the maximum attainable combinations of two products that may be produced with available resources and current technology.

Production Possibilities Frontiers and Opportunity Costs

As we saw in the chapter opener, Tesla operates an automobile factory in Fremont, California, where it assembles two car models. Because the firm's resources—workers, machinery, materials, and entrepreneurial skills—are limited, Tesla faces a trade-off: Resources devoted to producing one model are not available for producing the other model. Chapter 1 explained that economic models can be useful in analyzing many questions. We can use a simple model called the *production possibilities frontier* to analyze the trade-offs Tesla faces in its Fremont plant. A **production possibilities frontier (*PPF*)** is a curve showing the maximum attainable combinations of two products that may be produced with available resources and current technology. In Tesla's case, the company produces only Model S sedans and Model X SUVs at the Fremont plant, using workers, materials, robots, and other machinery.

Graphing the Production Possibilities Frontier

Figure 2.1 uses a production possibilities frontier to illustrate the trade-offs that Tesla faces. The numbers from the table are plotted in the graph. The line in the graph represents Tesla's production possibilities frontier. If Tesla uses all its resources to produce Model S sedans, it can produce 80 per day—point *A* at one end of the production possibilities frontier. If Tesla uses all its resources to produce Model X SUVs, it can produce 80 per day—point *E* at the other end of the production possibilities frontier. If Tesla devotes resources to producing both vehicles, it could be at a point like *B*, where it produces 60 sedans and 20 SUVs.

All the combinations either on the frontier—like points *A*, *B*, *C*, *D*, and *E*—or inside the frontier—like point *F*—are *attainable* with the resources available. Combinations on the frontier are *efficient* because all available resources are being fully utilized,

Tesla's Production Choices at Its Fremont Plant		
Choice	Quantity of Sedans Produced	Quantity of SUVs Produced
A	80	0
B	60	20
C	40	40
D	20	60
E	0	80

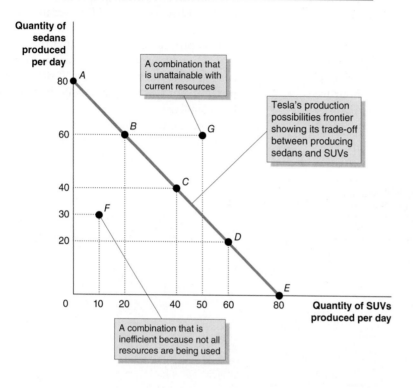

MyEconLab Animation

Figure 2.1

Tesla's Production Possibilities Frontier

Tesla faces a trade-off: To build one more sedan, it must build one fewer SUV. The production possibilities frontier illustrates the trade-off Tesla faces. Combinations on the production possibilities frontier—like points *A*, *B*, *C*, *D*, and *E*—are *technically efficient* because the maximum output is being obtained from the available resources. Combinations inside the frontier—like point *F*—are *inefficient* because some resources are not being used. Combinations outside the frontier—like point *G*—are *unattainable* with current resources.

and the fewest possible resources are being used to produce a given amount of output. Combinations inside the frontier—like point *F*—are *inefficient* because maximum output is not being obtained from the available resources—perhaps because the assembly line is not operating at its capacity. Tesla might like to be beyond the frontier—at a point like *G*, where it would be producing 60 sedans and 50 SUVs per day—but points beyond the production possibilities frontier are *unattainable*, given the firm's current resources. To produce the combination at *G*, Tesla would need more machines and more workers.

Notice that if Tesla is producing efficiently and is on the production possibilities frontier, the only way to produce more of one vehicle is to produce fewer of the other vehicle. Recall from Chapter 1 that the **opportunity cost** of any activity is the highest-valued alternative that must be given up to engage in that activity. For Tesla, the opportunity cost of producing one more SUV is the number of sedans the company will not be able to produce because it has shifted those resources to producing the SUV. For example, in moving from point *B* to point *C*, the opportunity cost of producing 20 more SUVs per day is the 20 fewer sedans that Tesla can produce.

What point on the production possibilities frontier is best? We can't tell without further information. If consumer demand for SUVs is greater than the demand for sedans, the company is likely to choose a point closer to *E*. If demand for sedans is greater than the demand for SUVs, the company is likely to choose a point closer to *A*.   MyEconLab Concept Check

Opportunity cost The highest-valued alternative that must be given up to engage in an activity.

Solved Problem 2.1

Drawing a Production Possibilities Frontier for Tesla Motors

Suppose, for simplicity, that during any given week, the machinery and number of workers at Tesla Motors' Fremont plant cannot be increased. So the number of sedans or SUVs the company can produce during the week depends on how many hours are devoted to assembling each of the different models. Assume that SUVs are more difficult to assemble, so if Tesla devotes an hour to assembling sedans, it will produce 15 vehicles, but if Tesla devotes an hour to producing SUVs, it will produce only 10 vehicles. Assume that the plant can run for 8 hours per day.

a. Use the information given to complete the following table:

Choice	Hours Spent Making Sedans	Hours Spent Making SUVs	Quantity Produced per Day Sedans	Quantity Produced per Day SUVs
A	8	0	_____	_____
B	7	1	_____	_____
C	6	2	_____	_____
D	5	3	_____	_____
E	4	4	_____	_____
F	3	5	_____	_____
G	2	6	_____	_____
H	1	7	_____	_____
I	0	8	_____	_____

b. Use the data in the table to draw a production possibilities frontier graph illustrating Tesla's trade-off between assembling sedans and assembling SUVs. Label the vertical axis "Quantity of sedans produced per day." Label the horizontal axis "Quantity of SUVs produced per day." Make sure to label the values where Tesla's production possibilities frontier intersects the vertical and horizontal axes.

c. Label the points representing choice D and choice E. If Tesla is at choice D, what is its opportunity cost of making 10 more SUVs?

Solving the Problem

Step 1: Review the chapter material. This problem is about using production possibilities frontiers to analyze trade-offs, so you may want to review the section "Graphing the Production Possibilities Frontier," which begins on page 38.

Step 2: Answer part (a) by filling in the table. If Tesla can assemble 15 sedans in 1 hour, then with choice A, it can assemble 120 sedans and 0 SUVs. Because Tesla can assemble 10 SUVs in 1 hour, with choice B, it will produce 105 sedans and 10 SUVs. Using similar reasoning, you can fill in the remaining cells in the table as follows:

Choice	Hours Spent Making Sedans	Hours Spent Making SUVs	Quantity Produced per Day Sedans	Quantity Produced per Day SUVs
A	8	0	120	0
B	7	1	105	10
C	6	2	90	20
D	5	3	75	30
E	4	4	60	40
F	3	5	45	50
G	2	6	30	60
H	1	7	15	70
I	0	8	0	80

Step 3: Answer part (b) by drawing the production possibilities frontier graph.
Using the data in the table in Step 2, you should draw a graph that looks like this:

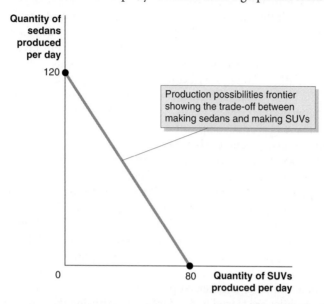

If Tesla devotes all 8 hours to assembling sedans, it will produce 120 sedans.
Therefore, Tesla's production possibilities frontier will intersect the vertical
axis at 120 sedans produced. If Tesla devotes all 8 hours to assembling SUVs,
it will produce 80 SUVs. Therefore, Tesla's production possibilities frontier
will intersect the horizontal axis at 80 SUVs produced.

Step 4: Answer part (c) by labeling choices *D* and *E* on your graph. The points for
choices *D* and *E* can be plotted using the information from the table:

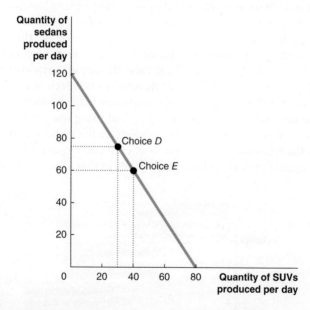

Moving from choice *D* to choice *E* increases Tesla's production of SUVs by 10
but lowers its production of sedans by 15. Therefore, Tesla's opportunity cost
of producing 10 more SUVs is making 15 fewer sedans.

Your Turn: For more practice, do related problem 1.10 on page 63 at the end of this chapter.   MyEconLab Study Plan

Increasing Marginal Opportunity Costs

We can use the production possibilities frontier to explore issues concerning the economy as a whole. Suppose we divide all the goods and services produced in the economy into just two types: military goods and civilian goods. In Figure 2.2, we let tanks represent military goods and automobiles represent civilian goods. If all the country's resources are devoted to producing military goods, 400 tanks can be produced in one year. If all resources are devoted to producing civilian goods, 500 automobiles can be produced in one year. Devoting resources to producing both goods results in the economy being at other points along the production possibilities frontier.

Notice that this production possibilities frontier is bowed outward rather than being a straight line. Because the curve is bowed out, the opportunity cost of automobiles in terms of tanks depends on where the economy currently is on the production possibilities frontier. For example, to increase automobile production from 0 to 200—moving from point *A* to point *B*—the economy has to give up only 50 tanks. But to increase automobile production by another 200 vehicles—moving from point *B* to point *C*—the economy has to give up 150 tanks.

As the economy moves down the production possibilities frontier, it experiences *increasing marginal opportunity costs* because increasing automobile production by a given quantity requires larger and larger decreases in tank production. Increasing marginal opportunity costs occur because some workers, machines, and other resources are better suited to one use than to another. At point *A*, some resources that are well suited to producing automobiles are forced to produce tanks. Shifting these resources into producing automobiles by moving from point *A* to point *B* allows a substantial increase in automobile production, without much loss of tank production. But as the economy moves down the production possibilities frontier, more and more resources that are better suited to tank production are switched to automobile production. As a result, the increases in automobile production become increasingly smaller, while the decreases in tank production become increasingly larger. We would expect in most situations that production possibilities frontiers will be bowed outward rather than linear as in the Tesla example discussed earlier.

The idea of increasing marginal opportunity costs illustrates an important economic concept: *The more resources already devoted to an activity, the smaller the payoff to devoting additional resources to that activity.* For example, the more hours you have already spent studying economics, the smaller the increase in your test grade from each additional hour you spend—and the greater the opportunity cost of using the hour in that way. The more funds a firm has devoted to research and development during a given year, the smaller the amount of useful knowledge it receives from each additional dollar—and the greater the opportunity cost of using the funds in that way. The more funds the federal government spends cleaning up the environment during a given year, the smaller the reduction in pollution from each additional dollar—and, once again, the greater the opportunity cost of using the funds in that way. MyEconLab Concept Check

MyEconLab Animation

Figure 2.2

Increasing Marginal Opportunity Costs

As the economy moves down the production possibilities frontier, it experiences *increasing marginal opportunity costs* because increasing automobile production by a given quantity requires larger and larger decreases in tank production. For example, to increase automobile production from 0 to 200—moving from point *A* to point *B*—the economy has to give up only 50 tanks. But to increase automobile production by another 200 vehicles—moving from point *B* to point *C*—the economy has to give up 150 tanks.

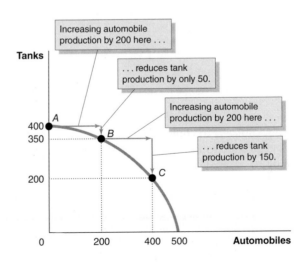

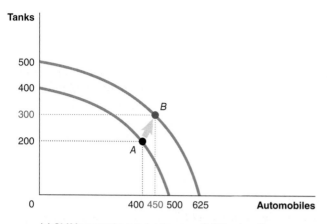

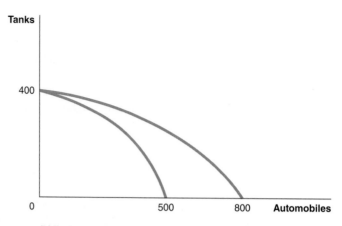

(a) Shifting out the production possibilities frontier   **(b) Technological change in the automobile industry**

MyEconLab Animation

| Figure 2.3 | Economic Growth |

Panel (a) shows that as more economic resources become available and technological change occurs, the economy can move from point A to point B, producing more tanks and more automobiles. Panel (b) shows the results of technological change in the automobile industry that increases the quantity of vehicles workers can produce per year while leaving unchanged the maximum quantity of tanks they can produce. Outward shifts in the production possibilities frontier represent *economic growth*.

Economic Growth

At any given time, the total resources available to any economy are fixed. Therefore, if, for example, the United States produces more automobiles, it must produce less of something else—tanks in our example. Over time, though, the resources available to an economy may increase. For example, both the labor force and the capital stock—the amount of machinery and other physical capital available in the country—may increase. The increase in the available labor force and the capital stock shifts the production possibilities frontier outward for the U.S. economy and makes it possible to produce both more automobiles and more tanks. Panel (a) of Figure 2.3 shows that the economy can move from point A to point B, producing more tanks and more automobiles.

Similarly, technological change makes it possible to produce more goods with the same number of workers and the same amount of machinery, which also shifts the production possibilities frontier outward. Technological change need not affect all sectors equally. Panel (b) of Figure 2.3 shows the results of technological change in the automobile industry that increases the quantity of automobiles workers can produce per year while leaving unchanged the quantity of tanks they can produce.

Outward shifts in the production possibilities frontier represent **economic growth** because they allow the economy to increase the production of goods and services, which ultimately raises the standard of living. In the United States and other high-income countries, the market system has aided the process of economic growth, which over the past 200 years has greatly increased the well-being of the average person.   MyEconLab Concept Check

Economic growth The ability of the economy to increase the production of goods and services.

MyEconLab Study Plan

Comparative Advantage and Trade

We can use the concepts of the production possibilities frontier and opportunity costs to understand the basic economic activity of *trade*. Markets are fundamentally about **trade**, which is the act of buying and selling. Sometimes we trade directly, as when children trade one baseball card for another baseball card. But often we trade indirectly: We sell our labor services as, say, an accountant, a salesperson, or a nurse for money, and then we use the money to buy goods and services. Although in these cases trade takes place indirectly, ultimately the accountant, salesperson, or nurse is trading his or her services for food, clothing, and other goods and services. One of the great benefits of trade is that it makes it possible for people to become better off by increasing both their production and their consumption.

2.2 LEARNING OBJECTIVE

Describe comparative advantage and explain how it serves as the basis for trade.

Trade The act of buying and selling.

Specialization and Gains from Trade

Consider the following situation: You and your neighbor both have fruit trees on your properties. Initially, suppose you have only apple trees and your neighbor has only cherry trees. In this situation, if you both like apples and cherries, there is an obvious opportunity for both of you to gain from trade: You trade some of your apples for some of your neighbor's cherries, making you both better off. But what if there are apple and cherry trees growing on both of your properties? In that case, there can still be gains from trade. For example, your neighbor might be very good at picking apples, and you might be very good at picking cherries. It would make sense for your neighbor to concentrate on picking apples and for you to concentrate on picking cherries. You can then trade some of the cherries you pick for some of the apples your neighbor picks. But what if your neighbor is actually better at picking both apples and cherries than you are?

We can use production possibilities frontiers (*PPF*s) to show how your neighbor can benefit from trading with you *even though she is better than you are at picking both apples and cherries*. (For simplicity, and because it will not have any effect on the conclusions we draw, we will assume that the *PPF*s in this example are straight lines.) The table in Figure 2.4 shows how many apples and how many cherries you and your neighbor can pick in one week. The graph in the figure uses the data from the table to construct *PPF*s. Panel (a) shows your *PPF*. If you devote all your time to picking apples, you can pick 20 pounds of apples per week. If you devote all your time to picking cherries, you can pick 20 pounds per week. Panel (b) shows that if your neighbor devotes all her time to picking apples, she can pick 30 pounds. If she devotes all her time to picking cherries, she can pick 60 pounds.

The *PPF*s in Figure 2.4 show how many apples and cherries you and your neighbor can consume, *without trade*. Suppose that when you don't trade with your neighbor, you pick and consume 8 pounds of apples and 12 pounds of cherries per week. This

	You		Your Neighbor	
	Apples	Cherries	Apples	Cherries
Devote all time to picking apples	20 pounds	0 pounds	30 pounds	0 pounds
Devote all time to picking cherries	0 pounds	20 pounds	0 pounds	60 pounds

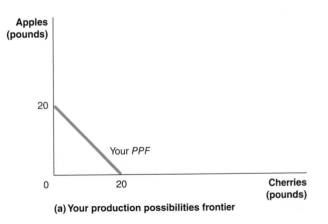

(a) Your production possibilities frontier

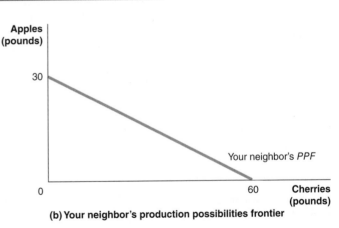

(b) Your neighbor's production possibilities frontier

MyEconLab Animation

Figure 2.4 **Production Possibilities for You and Your Neighbor, without Trade**

The table shows how many pounds of apples and how many pounds of cherries you and your neighbor can each pick in one week. The graphs use the data from the table to construct *PPF*s for you and your neighbor. Panel (a) shows your *PPF*. If you devote all your time to picking apples and none to picking cherries, you can pick 20 pounds. If you devote all your time to picking cherries, you can pick 20 pounds. Panel (b) shows that if your neighbor devotes all her time to picking apples, she can pick 30 pounds. If she devotes all her time to picking cherries, she can pick 60 pounds.

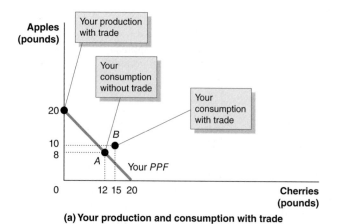

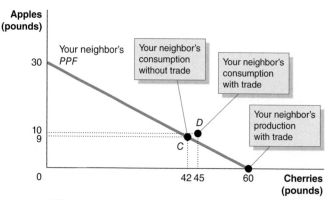

Figure 2.5   Gains from Trade

When you don't trade with your neighbor, you pick and consume 8 pounds of apples and 12 pounds of cherries per week—point A in panel (a). When your neighbor doesn't trade with you, she picks and consumes 9 pounds of apples and 42 pounds of cherries per week—point C in panel (b). If you specialize in picking apples, you can pick 20 pounds. If your neighbor specializes in picking cherries, she can pick 60 pounds. If you trade 10 pounds of your apples for 15 pounds of your neighbor's cherries, you will be able to consume 10 pounds of apples and 15 pounds of cherries—point B in panel (a). Your neighbor can now consume 10 pounds of apples and 45 pounds of cherries—point D in panel (b). You and your neighbor are both better off as a result of the trade.

combination of apples and cherries is represented by point A in panel (a) of Figure 2.5. When your neighbor doesn't trade with you, she picks and consumes 9 pounds of apples and 42 pounds of cherries per week. This combination of apples and cherries is represented by point C in panel (b).

After years of picking and consuming your own apples and cherries, suppose your neighbor comes to you one day with the following proposal: She offers to trade you 15 pounds of her cherries for 10 pounds of your apples the next week. Should you accept this offer? As we can show, you should accept because you will end up with more apples and more cherries to consume. To take advantage of her proposal, you should specialize in picking only apples rather than splitting your time between picking apples and picking cherries. We know specializing will allow you to pick 20 pounds of apples. You can trade 10 pounds of apples to your neighbor for 15 pounds of her cherries. The result is that you will be able to consume 10 pounds of apples and 15 pounds of cherries (point B in panel (a) of Figure 2.5). You are clearly better off as a result of trading with your neighbor: You can now consume 2 more pounds of apples and 3 more pounds of cherries than you were consuming without trading. You have moved beyond your *PPF*!

Your neighbor has also benefited from the trade. By specializing in picking only cherries, she can pick 60 pounds. She trades 15 pounds of cherries to you for 10 pounds of apples. She can then consume 10 pounds of apples and 45 pounds of cherries (point D in panel (b) of Figure 2.5). This combination is 1 more pound of apples and 3 more pounds of cherries than she was consuming before trading with you. She also has moved beyond her *PPF*. Table 2.1 summarizes the changes in production and consumption that result from your trade with your neighbor. (In this example, we chose one specific rate of trading cherries for apples—15 pounds of cherries for 10 pounds of apples. There are, however, many other rates of trading cherries for apples that would also make you and your neighbor better off.)

Absolute Advantage versus Comparative Advantage

Perhaps the most remarkable aspect of the preceding example is that your neighbor benefits from trading with you even though she is better than you at picking both apples and cherries. **Absolute advantage** is the ability of an individual, a firm, or a country to produce more of a good or service than competitors, using the same amount of resources. Your neighbor has an absolute advantage over you in picking both apples and

Absolute advantage The ability of an individual, a firm, or a country to produce more of a good or service than competitors, using the same amount of resources.

Table 2.1

A Summary of the Gains from Trade

	You		Your Neighbor	
	Apples (in pounds)	Cherries (in pounds)	Apples (in pounds)	Cherries (in pounds)
Production *and* consumption *without* trade	8	12	9	42
Production *with* trade	20	0	0	60
Consumption *with* trade	10	15	10	45
Gains from trade (increased consumption)	2	3	1	3

cherries because she can pick more of each fruit than you can in the same amount of time. Although it seems that your neighbor should pick her own apples *and* her own cherries, we have just seen that she is better off specializing in picking cherries and leaving picking apples to you.

We can consider further why both you and your neighbor benefit from specializing in picking only one fruit. First, think about the opportunity cost to each of you of picking the two fruits. We saw from the *PPF* in Figure 2.4 that if you devoted all your time to picking apples, you would be able to pick 20 pounds of apples per week. As you move down your *PPF* and shift time away from picking apples to picking cherries, you have to give up 1 pound of apples for each pound of cherries you pick (the slope of your *PPF* is −1. For a review of calculating slopes, see the appendix to Chapter 1.) Therefore, your opportunity cost of picking 1 pound of cherries is 1 pound of apples. By the same reasoning, your opportunity cost of picking 1 pound of apples is 1 pound of cherries. Your neighbor's *PPF* has a different slope, so she faces a different trade-off: As she shifts time from picking apples to picking cherries, she has to give up 0.5 pound of apples for every 1 pound of cherries she picks (the slope of your neighbor's *PPF* is −0.5). As she shifts time from picking cherries to picking apples, she gives up 2 pounds of cherries for every 1 pound of apples she picks. Therefore, her opportunity cost of picking 1 pound of apples is 2 pounds of cherries, and her opportunity cost of picking 1 pound of cherries is 0.5 pound of apples.

Table 2.2 summarizes the opportunity costs for you and your neighbor of picking apples and cherries. Note that even though your neighbor can pick more apples in a week than you can, the *opportunity cost* of picking apples is higher for her than for you because when she picks apples, she gives up more cherries than you do. So, even though she has an absolute advantage over you in picking apples, it is more costly for her to pick apples than it is for you. The table also shows that her opportunity cost of picking cherries is lower than yours. **Comparative advantage** is the ability of an individual, a firm, or a country to produce a good or service at a lower opportunity cost than competitors. In picking apples, your neighbor has an *absolute advantage* over you, while you have a *comparative advantage* over her. Your neighbor has both an absolute advantage and a comparative advantage over you in picking cherries. As we have seen, you are better off specializing in picking apples, and your neighbor is better off specializing in picking cherries. MyEconLab Concept Check

Comparative advantage The ability of an individual, a firm, or a country to produce a good or service at a lower opportunity cost than competitors.

Comparative Advantage and the Gains from Trade

We have just arrived at an important economic principle: *The basis for trade is comparative advantage, not absolute advantage.* The fastest apple pickers do not necessarily do

Table 2.2

Opportunity Costs of Picking Apples and Cherries

	Opportunity Cost of Picking 1 Pound of Apples	Opportunity Cost of Picking 1 Pound of Cherries
You	1 pound of cherries	1 pound of apples
Your Neighbor	2 pounds of cherries	0.5 pound of apples

Don't Let This Happen to You

Don't Confuse Absolute Advantage and Comparative Advantage

First, make sure you know the definitions:

- **Absolute advantage.** The ability of an individual, a firm, or a country to produce more of a good or service than competitors, using the same amount of resources. In our example, your neighbor has an absolute advantage over you in both picking apples and picking cherries.
- **Comparative advantage.** The ability of an individual, a firm, or a country to produce a good or service at a lower opportunity cost than competitors. In our example, your neighbor has a comparative advantage in picking cherries, but you have a comparative advantage in picking apples.

Keep these two key points in mind:

1. It is possible to have an absolute advantage in producing a good or service without having a comparative advantage. This is the case with your neighbor picking apples.
2. It is possible to have a comparative advantage in producing a good or service without having an absolute advantage. This is the case with your picking apples.

MyEconLab Study Plan

Your Turn: Test your understanding by doing related problem 2.5 on page 64 at the end of this chapter.

---

much apple picking. If the fastest apple pickers have a comparative advantage in some other activity—picking cherries, playing Major League Baseball, or being industrial engineers—they are better off specializing in that activity. Individuals, firms, and countries are better off if they specialize in producing goods and services for which they have a comparative advantage and obtain the other goods and services they need by trading. We will return to the important concept of comparative advantage in Chapter 9, which is devoted to the subject of international trade.

MyEconLab Concept Check

Solved Problem 2.2

MyEconLab Interactive Animation

Comparative Advantage and the Gains from Trade

Suppose that Canada and the United States both produce maple syrup and honey, which are sold for the same price in both countries. These are the combinations of the two goods that each country can produce in one day using the same amounts of capital and labor:

Canada		United States	
Honey (in tons)	Maple Syrup (in tons)	Honey (in tons)	Maple Syrup (in tons)
0	60	0	50
10	45	10	40
20	30	20	30
30	15	30	20
40	0	40	10
		50	0

a. Which country has a comparative advantage in producing maple syrup? Which country has a comparative advantage in producing honey?
b. Suppose that Canada is currently producing 30 tons of honey and 15 tons of maple syrup, and the United States is currently producing 10 tons of honey and 40 tons of maple syrup. Demonstrate that Canada and the United States can both be better off if they specialize in producing only one good and trade for the other.
c. Illustrate your answer to question (b) by drawing a *PPF* for the United States and a *PPF* for Canada. Show on your *PPF*s the combinations of honey and maple syrup produced and consumed in each country before and after trade.

Solving the Problem

Step 1: **Review the chapter material.** This problem is about comparative advantage, so you may want to review the section "Absolute Advantage versus Comparative Advantage," which begins on page 45.

Step 2: **Answer part (a) by calculating which country has a comparative advantage in each activity.** Remember that a country has a comparative advantage in producing a good if it can produce the good at the lowest opportunity cost. When Canada produces 1 more ton of honey, it produces 1.5 tons less of maple syrup. When the United States produces 1 more ton of honey, it produces 1 ton less of maple syrup. Therefore, the United States' opportunity cost of producing honey—1 ton of maple syrup—is lower than Canada's—1.5 tons of maple syrup. When Canada produces 1 more ton of maple syrup, it produces 0.67 ton less of honey. When the United States produces 1 more ton of maple syrup, it produces 1 ton less of honey. Therefore, Canada's opportunity cost of producing maple syrup—0.67 ton of honey—is lower than that of the United States—1 ton of honey. We can conclude that the United States has a comparative advantage in the production of honey and Canada has a comparative advantage in the production of maple syrup.

Step 3: **Answer part (b) by showing that specialization makes Canada and the United States better off.** We know that Canada and the United States should each specialize where it has a comparative advantage. If both countries specialize, Canada will produce 60 tons of maple syrup and 0 tons of honey, and the United States will produce 0 tons of maple syrup and 50 tons of honey. After both countries specialize, the United States could then trade 30 tons of honey to Canada for 40 tons of maple syrup. (Other mutually beneficial trades are possible as well.) We can summarize the results in a table:

	Before Trade		After Trade	
	Honey (in tons)	Maple Syrup (in tons)	Honey (in tons)	Maple Syrup (in tons)
Canada	30	15	30	20
United States	10	40	20	40

The United States is better off after trade because it can consume the same amount of maple syrup and 10 more tons of honey. Canada is better off after trade because it can consume the same amount of honey and 5 more tons of maple syrup.

Step 4: **Answer part (c) by drawing the PPFs.**

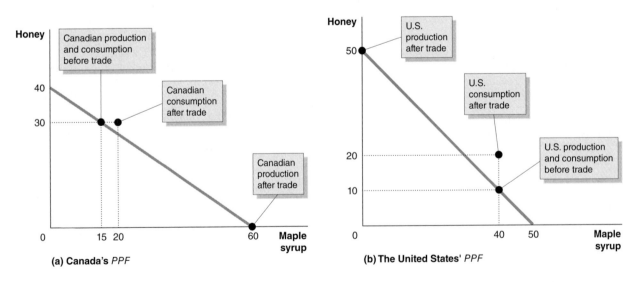

(a) Canada's *PPF*

(b) The United States' *PPF*

MyEconLab Study Plan   **Your Turn:** For more practice, do related problems 2.6 and 2.7 on pages 64–65 at the end of this chapter.

Making the Connection
MyEconLab Video

Comparative Advantage, Opportunity Cost, and Housework

Among roommates, married couples, and other people living together, dividing up the household chores can be a source of stress. Traditionally among married couples, women did most of the housework, such as preparing meals, cleaning, and doing the laundry. In 1965, married women with children averaged about 32 hours of housework per week, while married men averaged only 4 hours. Today, women average about 18 hours of housework, while men average about 10 hours.

Housework doesn't seem to be part of buying, selling, and the usual topics of business and economics. In fact, we can use basic economic concepts to analyze housework. Consider first the most efficient way to divide up household chores. Suppose Jack and Jill need to decide how they will get the cooking and laundry done. Assume Jack has an absolute advantage over Jill in both chores, but he has a big advantage over Jill in cooking—he takes much less time to prepare very tasty meals—but is only a little faster than Jill in doing the laundry. In other words, assuming they have the same amount of time available to do housework, Jack has a comparative advantage in cooking, while Jill has a comparative advantage in doing the laundry. So rather than Jack and Jill both doing some of the cooking and some of the laundry, they would be better off if Jack follows his comparative advantage and does all the cooking, while Jill follows her comparative advantage and does all the laundry.

Economics can also provide some insight into the decline in the number of hours spent on housework since the 1960s. Combined, men and women now spend more than 20 percent fewer hours on housework. This decline has been partly driven by technology, particularly improvements in household appliances, such as dishwashers and microwave ovens. The decline in the number of hours women devote to housework also reflects the greater job opportunities available to women today compared with the 1960s. The opportunity cost to a woman of spending time on housework and childcare is the wage she gives up by not spending that time in paid work. If a woman could work for an hour at a wage of $20 but spends that hour doing household chores, the opportunity cost of the time spent on chores is $20. As job opportunities for women and the wages those jobs pay have increased, so has the opportunity cost of doing housework. So in addition to taking advantage of improved appliances, many families have found that the cost of hiring specialists in household chores, such as cleaning services and lawn care services, is lower than the cost of the wife (or husband) performing those chores.

As women's wages have risen relative to men's wages, the opportunity cost to women of doing housework has increased more than has the opportunity cost to men. So we would expect that in addition to women devoting fewer hours to housework, the gap between the hours women and men devote would narrow. In fact, between 1965 and 2011, the average number of hours women devote to housework declined from 32 hours per week to 18 hours. The average number of hours women devote to paid work increased from 8 hours per week to 21 hours.

Of course, changes in social attitudes also help explain changes in how men and women allocate their time. But we have seen that the basic economic concepts of comparative advantage and opportunity cost provide important insights into the not-so-wonderful world of household chores.

Sources: Kim Parker and Wendy Wang, "Modern Parenthood: Roles of Moms and Dads Converge as They Balance Work and Family," pewsocialtrends.org, March 13, 2013; Emily Oster, "You're Dividing the Chores Wrong," *Slate*, November 21, 2012; and Ellen Byron, "A Truce in the Chore Wars," *New York Times*, December 4, 2012.

What's the most efficient way to divide up household chores?

Your Turn: Test your understanding by doing related problems 2.14 and 2.15 on page 65 at the end of this chapter.

MyEconLab Study Plan

The Market System

We have seen that households, firms, and the government face trade-offs and incur opportunity costs because resources are scarce. We have also seen that trade allows people to specialize according to their comparative advantage. By engaging in trade, people can raise their incomes and their standard of living. Of course, trade in the modern world is much more complex than the examples we have considered so far. Trade today involves the decisions of millions of people around the world. How are the decisions of these millions of people coordinated? In the United States and most other countries, trade is carried out in markets. Markets also determine the answers to the three fundamental questions discussed in Chapter 1: What goods and services will be produced? How will the goods and services be produced? and Who will receive the goods and services produced?

Recall that a **market** is a group of buyers and sellers of a good or service and the institution or arrangement by which they come together to trade. Markets take many forms: They can be physical places, such as a local pizza parlor or the New York Stock Exchange, or virtual places, such as eBay or iTunes. In a market, the buyers are demanders of goods or services, and the sellers are suppliers of goods or services. Households and firms interact in two types of markets: *product markets* and *factor markets*. **Product markets** are markets for goods—such as computers—and services—such as medical treatment. In product markets, households are demanders and firms are suppliers. **Factor markets** are markets for the *factors of production*. **Factors of production** are the inputs used to make goods and services. Factors of production are divided into four broad categories:

Market A group of buyers and sellers of a good or service and the institution or arrangement by which they come together to trade.

Product market A market for goods—such as computers—or services—such as medical treatment.

Factor market A market for the factors of production, such as labor, capital, natural resources, and entrepreneurial ability.

Factors of production The inputs used to make goods and services.

- *Labor* includes all types of work, from the part-time labor of teenagers working at McDonald's to the work of senior managers in large corporations.
- *Capital* refers to physical capital, such as computers and machine tools, that is used to produce other goods.
- *Natural resources* include land, water, oil, iron ore, and other raw materials (or "gifts of nature") that are used in producing goods.
- An *entrepreneur* is someone who operates a business. *Entrepreneurial ability* is the ability to bring together the other factors of production to successfully produce and sell goods and services.

The Circular Flow of Income

Two key groups participate in markets:

- A *household* consists of all the individuals in a home. Households are suppliers of factors of production—particularly labor—employed by firms to make goods and services. Households use the income they receive from selling the factors of production to purchase the goods and services supplied by firms. We are familiar with households as suppliers of labor because most people earn most of their income by going to work, meaning they are selling their labor services to firms in the labor market. But households own the other factors of production as well, either directly or indirectly, by owning the firms that own these resources. All firms are owned by households. Small firms, like a neighborhood restaurant, might be owned by one person. Large firms, like Apple, are owned by millions of households that own shares of stock in them. When firms pay profits to the people who own them, the firms are paying for using the capital and natural resources that are supplied to them by those owners. So, we can generalize by saying that in factor markets, households are suppliers and firms are demanders.
- *Firms* are suppliers of goods and services. Firms use the funds they receive from selling goods and services to buy or hire the factors of production needed to make the goods and services.

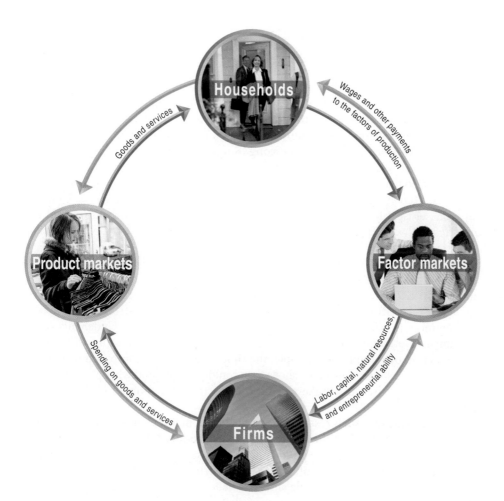

MyEconLab Animation

Figure 2.6

The Circular-Flow Diagram

Households and firms are linked together in a circular flow of production, income, and spending. The blue arrows show the flow of the factors of production. In factor markets, households supply labor, entrepreneurial ability, and other factors of production to firms. Firms use these factors of production to make goods and services that they supply to households in product markets. The red arrows show the flow of goods and services from firms to households. The green arrows show the flow of funds. In factor markets, households receive wages and other payments from firms in exchange for supplying the factors of production. Households use these wages and other payments to purchase goods and services from firms in product markets. Firms sell goods and services to households in product markets, and they use the funds to purchase the factors of production from households in factor markets.

We can use a simple economic model called the **circular-flow diagram** to see how participants in markets are linked. Figure 2.6 shows that in factor markets, households supply labor and other factors of production in exchange for wages and other payments from firms. In product markets, households use the payments they earn in factor markets to purchase the goods and services supplied by firms. Firms produce these goods and services using the factors of production supplied by households. In the figure, the blue arrows show the flow of factors of production from households through factor markets to firms. The red arrows show the flow of goods and services from firms through product markets to households. The green arrows show the flow of funds from firms through factor markets to households and the flow of spending from households through product markets to firms.

Like all economic models, the circular-flow diagram is a simplified version of reality. For example, Figure 2.6 leaves out the important role of government in buying goods from firms and in making payments, such as Social Security or unemployment insurance payments, to households. The figure also leaves out the roles played by banks, the stock and bond markets, and other parts of the *financial system* in aiding the flow of funds from lenders to borrowers. Finally, the figure does not show that some goods and services purchased by domestic households are produced in foreign countries and some goods and services produced by domestic firms are sold to foreign households. (We explore the government, the financial system, and the international sector further in later chapters.) Despite these simplifications, the circular-flow diagram in Figure 2.6 is useful for seeing how product markets, factor markets, and their participants are linked together. One of the great wonders of the market system is that it manages to successfully coordinate the independent activities of so many households and firms.   MyEconLab Concept Check

Circular-flow diagram A model that illustrates how participants in markets are linked.

Free market A market with few government restrictions on how a good or service can be produced or sold or on how a factor of production can be employed.

The Gains from Free Markets

A **free market** exists when the government places few restrictions on how goods and services can be produced or sold or on how factors of production can be employed. Governments in all modern economies intervene more than is consistent with a fully free market. In that sense, we can think of the free market as being a benchmark against which we can judge actual economies. There are relatively few government restrictions on economic activities in the United States, Canada, the countries of Western Europe, Hong Kong, Singapore, and Estonia. So these countries come close to the free market benchmark. In countries such as Cuba and North Korea, the free market system has been rejected in favor of centrally planned economies with extensive government control over product and factor markets. Countries that come closest to the free market benchmark have been more successful than countries with centrally planned economies in providing their people with rising living standards.

The Scottish philosopher Adam Smith is considered the father of modern economics because his book *An Inquiry into the Nature and Causes of the Wealth of Nations*, published in 1776, was an early and very influential argument for the free market system. Smith was writing at a time when extensive government restrictions on markets were common. In many parts of Europe, the *guild system* prevailed. Under this system, governments would give guilds, or organizations of producers, the authority to control the production of a good. For example, the shoemakers' guild controlled who was allowed to produce shoes, how many shoes they could produce, and what price they could charge. In France, the cloth makers' guild even dictated the number of threads in the weave of the cloth.

Smith argued that such restrictions reduced the income, or wealth, of a country and its people by restricting the quantity of goods produced. Some people at the time supported the restrictions of the guild system because it was in their financial interest to do so. If you were a member of a guild, the restrictions served to reduce the competition you faced. But other people sincerely believed that the alternative to the guild system was economic chaos. Smith argued that these people were wrong and that a country could enjoy a smoothly functioning economic system if firms were freed from guild restrictions. MyEconLab Concept Check

The Market Mechanism

In Smith's day, defenders of the guild system worried that if, for instance, the shoemakers' guild did not control shoe production, either too many or too few shoes would be produced. Smith argued that prices would do a better job of coordinating the activities of buyers and sellers than the guilds could. A key to understanding Smith's argument is the assumption that *individuals usually act in a rational, self-interested way*. In particular, individuals take those actions that are most likely to make themselves better off financially. This assumption of rational, self-interested behavior underlies nearly all economic analysis. In fact, economics can be distinguished from other disciplines that study human behavior—such as sociology and psychology—by its emphasis on the assumption of self-interested behavior. Adam Smith understood—as economists today understand—that people's motives can be complex. But when we analyze people in the act of buying and selling, the motivation of financial reward usually provides the best explanation for the actions people take.

For example, suppose that a significant number of consumers switch from buying regular gasoline-powered cars to buying gasoline/electric-powered hybrid cars, such as the Toyota Prius, or all-electric cars, such as the Tesla Model S. Firms will find that they can charge relatively higher prices for hybrid cars and electric cars than they can for regular cars. The self-interest of these firms will lead them to respond to consumers' wishes by producing more hybrid and electric cars and fewer regular cars. Or suppose that consumers decide that they want to eat less bread, pasta, and other foods that are high in carbohydrates. Then the prices firms can charge for bread and pasta will fall.

The self-interest of firms will lead them to produce less bread and pasta, which, in fact, is what has happened over the past 10 years.

Note that for the market mechanism to work in response to changes in consumers' wants, *prices must be flexible*. Changes in *relative prices*—the price of one good or service relative to the prices of other goods or services—provide information, or a signal, to both consumers and firms. For example, during 2010, consumers worldwide increased their demand for cattle and poultry. Because corn is fed to cattle and poultry, prices for corn soared relative to prices for other crops. Many farmers in the United States received this price signal and responded by increasing the amount of corn they planted and decreasing the amount of soybeans and wheat. One Kansas farmer was quoted as saying, "It seemed to me there was $100 to $150 per acre more money in the corn than there was in the beans. That's the kind of math that a lot of guys were using." By 2013, the United States was experiencing record corn crops. Similarly, falling prices for DVDs or music CDs in the 2000s were a signal to movie studios and record companies to devote fewer resources to these products and more resources to making movies and music available online.

In the United States today, governments at the federal, state, and local levels set or regulate the prices of only about 10 to 20 percent of goods and services. The prices of other goods and services are free to change as consumer wants change and as costs of production change.

In the case where consumers want more of a product, and in the case where they want less of a product, the market system responds without a guild or the government giving orders about how much to produce or what price to charge. In a famous phrase, Smith said that firms would be led by the "invisible hand" of the market to provide consumers with what they want. Firms respond *individually* to changes in prices by making decisions that *collectively* end up satisfying the wants of consumers.　　　　　　　　　　　　　　　　　　　　MyEconLab Concept Check

Making the Connection
MyEconLab Video

A Story of the Market System in Action: How Do You Make an iPad?

Apple produces the iPad. Because Apple's headquarters are in Cupertino, California, it seems reasonable to assume that iPads are also manufactured in that state. A poll by the *New York Times* showed that, in fact, a majority of people interviewed believed that iPads were manufactured in the United States, if not specifically in California. Although engineers at Apple designed the iPad, the company produces none of the components of the iPad, nor does it assemble the components into a finished product. Far from being produced entirely by one company in one country, the iPad requires the coordinated activities of thousands of workers and dozens of firms spread around the world.

Foxconn, which is based in Taiwan, assembles the iPad in factories in Shenzhen and Chengdu, China, and Jundiai, São Paulo, Brazil, and ships them to Apple for sale in the United States. Although Foxconn does final assembly, it doesn't make any of the components and, in fact, charges Apple less than $15 for assembling each iPad.

The following table lists some of the many suppliers of iPad components.

Each of these suppliers in turn relies on its own suppliers. For example, Broadcom designs the touchscreen controller for the iPad and supplies it to Apple, but it does not manufacture the components of the controller or assemble them. To manufacture the components, Broadcom relies on SilTerra, based in Malaysia; SMIC, based in mainland China; and Taiwan Semiconductor Manufacturing Corporation (TSMC) and UMC, based in Taiwan. TSMC's factories are for the most part not in Taiwan but in mainland China and Eastern Europe. To assemble the components, Broadcom uses several companies, including Amkor Technology, based in Chandler, Arizona, and STATS ChipPAC, based in Singapore.

The market coordinates the activities of the many people spread around the world who contribute to making an iPad.

Firm	Location of the Firm	iPad Component the Firm Supplies
AKM	Japan	Motion sensor
AU Optronics	Taiwan	Display
Broadcom	United States (California)	Touchscreen controller and wireless chip
Cirrus Logic	United States (Texas)	Audio chip
Corning	United States (New York)	Glass screen cover
Elpida	Japan	System memory
SK Hynix	South Korea	Flash memory
Infineon Technologies	Germany	Semiconductors
LG Electronics	South Korea	Display
Quicomm	United Kingdom	Wireless section
Samsung	South Korea	Display, flash memory, and applications processor
Sharp	Japan	Display
STMicroelectronics	France/Italy	Motion sensors
Texas Instruments	United States (Texas)	Touchscreen controller
Toshiba	Japan	Flash memory

All told, an iPad contains hundreds of parts that are designed, manufactured, and assembled by firms around the world. Many of these firms are not even aware of which other firms are also producing components for the iPad. Few of the managers of these firms have met managers of the other firms or shared knowledge of how their particular components are produced. In fact, no one person from Tim Cook, the chief executive officer of Apple, on down possesses the knowledge of how to produce all the components that are assembled into an iPad. Instead, the invisible hand of the market has led these firms to contribute their knowledge and resources to the process that ultimately results in an iPad available for sale in a store in the United States. Apple has so efficiently organized the process of producing the iPad that you can order a custom iPad with a personal engraving and have it delivered from an assembly plant in China or Brazil to your doorstep in the United States in as little as three days.

Sources: Marjorie Connelly, "Poll Finds Consumer Confusion on Where Apple Devices Are Made," *New York Times*, January 25, 2012; Andrew Rassweiler, "New iPad 32GB + 4G Carries $364.35 Bill of Materials," iSuppli.com, March 16, 2012; and Arik Hesseldahl, "Teardown Shows Apple iPad Mini Costs at Least $188 to Build," allthingsd.com, November 3, 2012.

MyEconLab Study Plan

Your Turn: Test your understanding by doing related problems 3.8 and 3.9 on page 66 at the end of this chapter.

The Role of the Entrepreneur

Entrepreneurs are central to the working of the market system. An **entrepreneur** is someone who operates a business. Entrepreneurs first determine what goods and services they believe consumers want and then decide how to produce those goods and services most profitably, using the available factors of production—labor, capital, and natural resources. Successful entrepreneurs are able to search out opportunities to provide new goods and services. Frequently these opportunities are created by new technology. Consumers and existing businesses often do not at first realize that the new technology makes new products feasible. For example, even after the development of the internal combustion engine had made automobiles practicable, Henry Ford remarked, "If I had asked my customers what they wanted, they would have said a faster horse." Because consumers often cannot evaluate a new product before it exists, some of the most successful entrepreneurs, such as the late Steve Jobs

Entrepreneur Someone who operates a business, bringing together the factors of production—labor, capital, and natural resources—to produce goods and services.

of Apple, rarely use *focus groups*, or meetings with consumers in which the consumers are asked what new products they would like to see. Instead, entrepreneurs think of products that consumers may not even realize they need, such as, in Jobs's case, an MP3 player—iPod—or a tablet computer—iPad. Entrepreneurs are important to the economy because they are often responsible for making new products widely available to consumers, as Henry Ford did with the automobile and Steve Jobs did with the iPod.

The firms entrepreneurs found are typically small at first, as Apple and Ford were. Table 2.3 lists some of the important products entrepreneurs at small firms introduced during the twentieth century.

Entrepreneurs put their own funds at risk when they start businesses. If they are wrong about what consumers want or about the best way to produce goods and services, they can lose those funds. In fact, it is not unusual for entrepreneurs who eventually achieve great success to fail at first. For instance, early in their careers, both Henry Ford and Sakichi Toyoda, who eventually founded the Toyota Motor Corporation, started companies that quickly failed. Research by Richard Freeman of Harvard University has shown that a typical entrepreneur earns less than an employee at a large firm who has the same education and other characteristics. Few entrepreneurs make the fortunes earned by Mark Zuckerberg, Steve Jobs, or Bill Gates.

Product	Inventor
Air conditioning	William Haviland Carrier
Airplane	Orville and Wilbur Wright
Automobile, mass produced	Henry Ford
Biomagnetic imaging	Raymond Damadian
Biosynthetic insulin	Herbert Boyer
DNA fingerprinting	Alec Jeffries
FM radio	Edwin Howard Armstrong
Helicopter	Igor Sikorsky
High-resolution CAT scanner	Robert Ledley
Hydraulic brake	Malcolm Lockheed
Integrated circuit	Jack Kilby
Microprocessor	Ted Hoff
Optical scanner	Everett Franklin Lindquist
Oral contraceptives	Carl Djerassi
Overnight delivery service	Fred Smith
Personal computer	Steve Jobs and Steve Wozniak
Quick-frozen foods	Clarence Birdseye
Safety razor	King Gillette
Soft contact lens	Kevin Tuohy
Solid fuel rocket engine	Robert Goddard
Supercomputer	Seymour Cray
Vacuum tube	Philo Farnsworth
Zipper	Gideon Sundback

Table 2.3

Important Products Introduced by Entrepreneurs at Small Firms

Source: William J. Baumol, *The Microtheory of Innovative Entrepreneurship*, Princeton, NJ: Princeton University Press, 2010, and various sources. Note that the person who first commercially developed a particular product is sometimes disputed by historians.

Entrepreneurs make a vital contribution to economic growth through their roles in responding to consumer demand and introducing new products. Government policies that encourage entrepreneurship are also likely to increase economic growth and raise the standard of living. In the next section, we consider the legal framework required for a successful market in which entrepreneurs can succeed.   MyEconLab Concept Check

The Legal Basis of a Successful Market System

In a free market, government does not restrict how firms produce and sell goods and services or how they employ factors of production. But the absence of government intervention is not enough for the market system to work well. Government has to take active steps to provide a *legal environment* that will allow markets to operate efficiently.

Protection of Private Property   For the market system to work well, individuals must be willing to take risks. Someone with $250,000 can be cautious and keep it safely in a bank—or even in cash, if the person doesn't trust banks. But the market system won't work unless a significant number of people are willing to risk their funds by investing them in businesses. Investing in businesses is risky in any country. Many businesses fail every year in the United States and other high-income countries. But in high-income countries, someone who starts a new business or invests in an existing business doesn't have to worry that the government, the military, or criminal gangs might decide to seize the business or demand payments for not destroying the business. Unfortunately, in many poor countries, owners of businesses are not well protected from having their businesses seized by the government or from having their profits taken by criminals. Where these problems exist, opening a business can be extremely risky. Cash can be concealed easily, but a business is difficult to conceal or move.

Property rights The rights individuals or firms have to the exclusive use of their property, including the right to buy or sell it.

Property rights are the rights individuals or firms have to the exclusive use of their property, including the right to buy or sell it. Property can be tangible, physical property, such as a store or factory. Property can also be intangible, such as the right to an idea. Two amendments to the U.S. Constitution guarantee property rights: The Fifth Amendment states that the federal government shall not deprive any person "of life, liberty, or property, without due process of law." The Fourteenth Amendment extends this guarantee to the actions of state governments: "No state … shall deprive any person of life, liberty, or property, without due process of law." Similar guarantees exist in every high-income country. Unfortunately, in many developing countries, such guarantees do not exist or are poorly enforced.

In any modern economy, *intellectual property rights* are very important. Intellectual property includes books, films, software, and ideas for new products or new ways of producing products. To protect intellectual property, the federal government grants a *patent* that gives an inventor—often a firm—the exclusive right to produce and sell a new product for a period of 20 years from the date the patent was filed. For instance, because Microsoft has a patent on the Windows operating system, other firms cannot sell their own versions of Windows. The government grants patents to encourage firms to spend money on the research and development necessary to create new products. If other companies could freely copy Windows, Microsoft would not have spent the funds necessary to develop it. Just as a new product or a new method of making a product receives patent protection, new books, films, and software receive *copyright* protection. Under U.S. law, the creator of a book, film, or piece of music has the exclusive right to use the creation during the creator's lifetime. The creator's heirs retain this exclusive right for 50 years after the death of the creator.

In providing copyright protection for only a limited time, Congress provides economic incentives to creators while eventually—after the period of copyright has ended—allowing the creators' works to be freely available. The longer the period of copyright, the more likely it is that some consumers will not gain access to the copyrighted work and the longer the wait before others can use the copyrighted work in their own work, for instance, by writing a sequel to a copyrighted book.

| **Making the Connection** MyEconLab Video | ### Who Owns *The Wizard of Oz*? The U.S. Congress provides copyright protection to authors to give them an economic incentive to invest the time and effort required to write a book. While a book is under copyright, only the author—or whoever the author sells the copyright to—can |

legally publish a paper or digital copy of the book. Once the copyright expires, however, the book enters the *public domain* and anyone is free to publish the book. Copies of classic books, such as *Huckleberry Finn* or *Oliver Twist*, are usually available from many publishers.

L. Frank Baum wrote *The Wonderful Wizard of Oz* in 1900. The copyright on the book expired years ago and many publishers now sell their own versions of the book. While these publishers can't claim copyright of Baum's words, because those words are in the public domain, they can claim copyright on a new design of the book or on any new illustrations they create.

The Wonderful Wizard of Oz is a classic book from 1900 that became a classic film in 1939. A remake of the film in 2013 raised copyright issues.

A similar situation exists with the famous 1939 MGM film *The Wizard of Oz*. Warner Brothers, which now owns the copyright to the film, does not have a legal right to any of the words or incidents in the film that were taken directly from Baum's book. However, Warner Brothers does have a copyright on any dialogue or incidents that were written specifically for the film as well as the design of the film sets and the actors' costumes. Warner Brothers was aggressive in defending its copyright when Walt Disney announced that it was making a film called *Oz The Great and Powerful*. As a copyright lawyer put it: "The MGM film presented the story in a certain way, and it's those things—the embellishments, the creative decisions—that Disney cannot use."

Disney had to be careful even in minor details to avoid violating Warner Brothers' copyright. For example, it made the green makeup of the Wicked Witch of the West a different shade from that in the earlier film. Disney also changed the location of the Yellow Brick Road and the name of Munchkin Country to avoid infringing on Warner Brothers' copyright. Shortly before the film was released in early 2013, Disney's lawyers decided that the hairstyles of some of the Munchkins in the completed film had to be digitally altered because they appeared too close to the hairstyles in the earlier film.

Most economists believe that copyrights provide needed protection for authors and creators of movies or other artistic works. However, the roadblocks Warner Brothers placed in the way of Disney making a new *Oz* film show that copyrights may deter others from producing new work that might infringe on a copyrighted work.

Sources: Brooks Barnes, "We Aren't in the Old Kansas, Toto," *New York Times*, February 28, 2013; and Eriq Gardner, "Disney, Warner Bros. Fighting Over 'Wizard of Oz' Trademarks," *Hollywood Reporter*, February 12, 2012.

Your Turn: Test your understanding by doing related problem 3.17 on page 67 at the end of this chapter.

MyEconLab Study Plan

Enforcement of Contracts and Property Rights Business activity often involves someone agreeing to carry out some action in the future. For example, you may borrow $20,000 to buy a car and promise the bank—by signing a loan contract—that you will pay back the money over the next five years. Or Facebook may sign a licensing agreement with a small technology company, agreeing to use that company's technology for a period of several years in return for a fee. Usually these agreements take the form of legal contracts. For the market system to work, businesses and individuals have to rely on these contracts being carried out. If one party to a legal contract does not fulfill its obligations—perhaps the small company had promised Facebook exclusive use of its technology but then began licensing it to other companies—the other party can go to court to have the agreement enforced. Similarly, if property owners in the United States believe that the federal or state government has violated their rights under the Fifth or Fourteenth Amendments, they can go to court to have their rights enforced.

But going to court to enforce a contract or private property rights will be successful only if the court system is independent and judges are able to make impartial decisions on the basis of the law. In the United States and other high-income countries, the court systems have enough independence from other parts of the government and enough protection from intimidation by outside forces—such as criminal gangs—that they are able to make their decisions based on the law. In many developing countries, the court systems lack this independence and will not provide a remedy if the government violates private property rights or if a person with powerful political connections decides to violate a business contract.

If property rights are not well enforced, fewer goods and services will be produced. This reduces economic efficiency, leaving the economy inside its production possibilities frontier.

MyEconLab Study Plan

MyEconLab Concept Check

Continued from page 37

Economics in Your Life

The Trade-offs When You Buy a Car

At the beginning of the chapter, we asked you to think about two questions: With respect to traditional gasoline-powered cars, what is the relationship between safety and fuel efficiency? and Under what circumstances would it be possible for automobile manufacturers to make cars safer and more fuel efficient? To answer the first question, you have to recognize that there is a trade-off between safety and fuel efficiency. With the technology available at any particular time, an automobile manufacturer can increase fuel efficiency by making a car smaller and lighter. But driving a lighter car increases your chances of being injured if you have an accident. The trade-off between safety and fuel efficiency would look much like the relationship in Figure 2.1 on page 39. To get more of both safety and gas mileage, automobile makers would have to discover new technologies that allow them to make cars lighter and safer at the same time. Such new technologies would make points like G in Figure 2.1 attainable.

Conclusion

We have seen that by trading in markets, people are able to specialize and pursue their comparative advantage. Trading on the basis of comparative advantage makes all participants in trade better off. The key role of markets is to facilitate trade. In fact, the market system is a very effective means of coordinating the decisions of millions of consumers, workers, and firms. At the center of the market system is the consumer. To be successful, firms must respond to the desires of consumers. These desires are communicated to firms through prices. To explore how markets work, we must study the behavior of consumers and firms. We continue this exploration of markets in Chapter 3, when we develop the model of demand and supply.

Before moving on to Chapter 3, read *An Inside Look* on the next page to explore the trade-offs managers face at luxury carmaker Mercedes-Benz and why the company chose to partner with Tesla Motors to develop electric-vehicle components.

CAR AND DRIVER

Mercedes-Benz Execs Talk 13 New Models, Electric Cars, and Hybrid AMGs

Mercedes-Benz has never had a stronger first quarter in the United States than it has had in 2013, but the German automaker isn't about to slow down. The company is taking strides to secure its position over the long term and to bolster its global sales with 13 all-new new models by 2020. These vehicles aren't just refreshes and redesigns; the Stuttgart-based marque will introduce 13 new nameplates—vehicles without a predecessor. We know there will be the front-drive-based GLA-class crossover and the S-class will add coupe and convertible variants, but the bulk of the plan remains a mystery. Hoping to fill in some of the unknowns, we sat down with four of the most influential executives at Mercedes-Benz: Thomas Weber, head of R&D; Dieter Zetsche, Daimler chairman and head of Mercedes-Benz cars; Jörg Prigl, vice president of small-car development; and Ola Källenius, chairman of Mercedes-Benz AMG. Here's what they had to say about the future of Mercedes:

Car and Driver [C/D]: We're struggling to find 13 obvious holes in the Mercedes-Benz lineup. What kinds of vehicles are coming? Should we expect Mercedes versions of BMW's Gran Turismos?

Thomas Weber: To build such a vehicle is easy. To be successful is the name of the game. You also must be careful not to say a current trend is a trend forever. We will certainly add long-wheelbase models targeting the Asian markets. As we look at these new models, we need to beat our competitors in three areas: design, powertrains, and environmental and safety technologies.

(a) *C/D: Is there any concern that the $30,825 CLA250 might dilute the brand image in the U.S. or cannibalize C-class sales?*

Dieter Zetsche: Our more-mature, more-affluent customers are very good to us. At the same time, the A-class has an average age drop of 10 years [in Europe]. It's all about striking the right balance. The new S-class will move into Rolls-Royce Ghost territory. Just as we introduce small cars, we keep the light shining on the brand.

Jörg Prigl: If we saw that as a risk, we shouldn't have done the CLA. We are not fighting for the loyal customers we have.

(b) *C/D: Electric vehicles have failed to take off in the U.S. Why bring the electric B-class to market?*

Prigl: Technology leadership in a potential future drivetrain is a must for us. The partnership with Tesla will help us speed up and beat the competition. If you believe you can do this alone as an automaker, you will fail. The battery cell should not be done by the OEM [Auto Parts]. There should be huge competition among suppliers to get the cell right. The specific know-how for the automaker is in the packaging and the battery management. Tesla provides the complete powertrain for the B-class Electric Drive, but the calibration is split between Tesla and Mercedes-Benz.

C/D: The Geneva auto show was dominated by a pair of hybrid supercars, the McLaren P1 and the Ferrari LaFerrari. At what point will tightening environmental regulations force AMG to adopt hybrid powertrains?

Ola Källenius: The SLS AMG Electric Drive is a glimpse of the future, but we took two steps forward to take one step back. Hybrids are the next logical step, likely in five to seven years. For now, with conventional gas measures we can reduce emissions another 20 percent. The immediate future is relatively clear. Downsize and direct injection is where combustion is headed, but it is inevitable that we will have to electrify these cars.

(c) *C/D: Why isn't Mercedes making a big investment in carbon fiber like BMW and the Volkswagen Group have?*

Källenius: Carbon fiber is for a hypercar. Taking out weight is a decathlon. You need to work with all the materials. Right now, the industry is at a peak; every new car going forward will shave off weight ….

Source: Eric Tingwall, "Mercedes-Benz Execs Talk 13 New Models, Electric Cars, and Hybrid AMGs," *Car and Driver*, April 10, 2013.

Key Points in the Article

Mercedes is planning 13 new models by 2020, including a new crossover vehicle; new variations of its S-class automobile; redeveloped entry-level vehicles; and the introduction of an electric car. With these new models, the managers at Mercedes are making choices about how to use new designs, upgraded powertrains, and advances in technology to deal with environmental and safety concerns. In addition, these managers have also chosen to partner with Tesla Motors to develop electric-vehicle components. Making the optimal choices will be important for Mercedes to remain one of the most competitive and successful high-end automobile manufacturers in the world.

Analyzing the News

a Automobile manufacturers must decide what type of cars to bring to market. Mercedes has two challenges in introducing a new entry-level car in the United States. First, for a high-end manufacturer like Mercedes, image is very important, and even the perception that the company is catering to a lower-income consumer can be damaging. Second, Mercedes does not want to sacrifice sales of its more profitable C-class models for these new lower-price A-class models. Suppose Mercedes produced only A-class and C-class vehicles and in 2013 had the capability of producing a total of 30,000 vehicles. This capacity is represented by PPF_{2013} in the figure below. This curve shows that Mercedes would have to sacrifice production (and therefore sales) of one type of vehicle to produce more of the other. The executives at Mercedes expect their market to continue to grow, and they do not believe that introducing the new A-class model will take sales away from the C-class. Mercedes will therefore have to produce a larger number of automobiles, which is represented by PPF_{2020} in the figure.

b Despite disappointing sales figures for electric vehicles, Mercedes has decided to introduce its electric B-class model in the U.S. market. Mercedes believes that the market for electric vehicles will grow, and it needs to be at the forefront of development in order to beat the competition. Mercedes faced a trade-off when deciding on the development of its electric vehicle. Rather than build this vehicle completely in-house, Mercedes chose to partner with Tesla, believing that Tesla's experience in producing electric vehicles would be advantageous for both companies and make the B-class a success. In choosing to take advantage of Tesla's expertise and technology, Mercedes gave up some level of control, but it chose this path believing it would increase the potential for building a vehicle that would have strong sales.

c As emissions standards continue to tighten and gas-mileage requirements continue to grow, lighter-weight cars will become a bigger part of our future. One decision Mercedes has made is to *not* invest heavily in lightweight carbon fiber for use in production, but rather to reduce the weight of all materials over the next several years. Here again, Mercedes faced a trade-off between investing in one specific technology and waiting to see what the future holds in terms of other lighter-weight production options that it can use in its manufacturing.

Thinking Critically

1. Suppose that from 2013 to 2020, the resources Mercedes-Benz uses to produce its automobiles remain constant, while improvements in technology in 2020 allow Mercedes to produce the additional quantity of A-class models shown in the figure below, but no additional C-class models. Draw a graph that illustrates this technology change. Be sure to show both the 2013 and new 2020 *PPF*s. What is the opportunity cost to Mercedes-Benz of producing one C-class model in 2013? In 2020?

2. Assume that the figure below accurately represents Mercedes-Benz's *PPF*s for 2013 and 2020, and that in 2020 it has customer orders for 35,000 A-class models and 20,000 C-class models. Explain whether Mercedes can fill all of these orders.

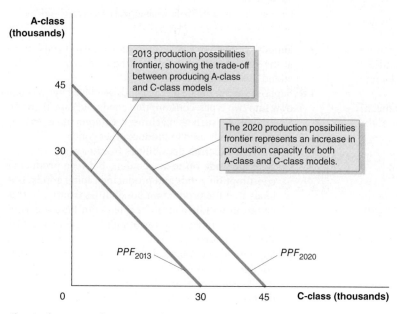

Choosing between producing a Mercedes A-class model and producing a C-class model.

Chapter Summary and Problems

Key Terms

Absolute advantage, p. 45

Circular-flow diagram, p. 51

Comparative advantage, p. 46

Economic growth, p. 43

Entrepreneur, p. 54

Factor market, p. 50

Factors of production, p. 50

Free market, p. 52

Market, p. 50

Opportunity cost, p. 39

Product market, p. 50

Production possibilities frontier (*PPF*), p. 38

Property rights, p. 56

Scarcity, p. 38

Trade, p. 43

2.1 **Production Possibilities Frontiers and Opportunity Costs, pages 38–43**

LEARNING OBJECTIVE: Use a production possibilities frontier to analyze opportunity costs and trade-offs.

Summary

The **production possibilities frontier** (*PPF*) is a curve that shows the maximum attainable combinations of two products that may be produced with available resources. The *PPF* is used to illustrate the trade-offs that arise from **scarcity**. Points on the frontier are technically efficient. Points inside the frontier are inefficient, and points outside the frontier are unattainable. The **opportunity cost** of any activity is the highest-valued alternative that must be given up to engage in that activity. Because of increasing marginal opportunity costs, production possibilities frontiers are usually bowed out rather than straight lines. This illustrates the important economic concept that the more resources that are already devoted to any activity, the smaller the payoff from devoting additional resources to that activity is likely to be. **Economic growth** is illustrated by shifting a production possibilities frontier outward.

MyEconLab   Visit www.myeconlab.com to complete these exercises online and get instant feedback.

Review Questions

1.1 What do economists mean by *scarcity*? Can you think of anything that is not scarce according to the economic definition?

1.2 What is a production possibilities frontier? How can we show efficiency on a production possibilities frontier? How can we show inefficiency? What causes a production possibilities frontier to shift outward?

1.3 What does increasing marginal opportunity costs mean? What are the implications of this idea for the shape of the production possibilities frontier?

Problems and Applications

1.4 Draw a production possibilities frontier that shows the trade-off between the production of cotton and the production of soybeans.
  a. Show the effect that a prolonged drought would have on the initial production possibilities frontier.
  b. Suppose genetic modification makes soybeans resistant to insects, allowing yields to double. Show the effect of this technological change on the initial production possibilities frontier.

1.5 **[Related to the** Chapter Opener **on page 37]** One of the trade-offs Tesla faces is between safety and the maximum range someone can drive an all-electric car before having to recharge it. For example, adding steel to a car makes it safer but also heavier, which results in fewer miles between recharges. Draw a hypothetical production possibilities frontier that Tesla engineers face that shows this trade-off.

1.6 **[Related to** Chapter Opener **on page 37]** According to an article on *CNNMoney*, in May 2013 CEO Elon Musk of Tesla Motors announced plans for a large expansion of Tesla's network of supercharger stations by the end of the year. The network of supercharger stations will stretch from Los Angeles to New York and cover most metropolitan areas in the United States and Supercharger stations allow the all-electric cars to be recharged in about an hour. Musk stated that: "It is very important to address this issue of long-distance travel."
  a. Why is it important for Tesla Motors to address the issue of long-distance travel?
  b. Tesla Motors, like other firms, faces many strategic decisions and trade-offs. What would be the opportunity cost to Tesla Motors to expanding the supercharger networks?

Source: Chris Isidore, "Tesla Tripling Supercharger Network for LA to NY Trip," *CNNMoney*, May 31, 2013.

1.7 Suppose you win free tickets to a movie plus all you can eat at the snack bar for free. Would there be a cost to you to attend this movie? Explain.

1.8 Suppose we can divide all the goods produced by an economy into two types: consumption goods and capital goods. Capital goods, such as machinery, equipment, and computers, are goods used to produce other goods.
  a. Use a production possibilities frontier graph to illustrate the trade-off to an economy between producing consumption goods and producing capital goods. Is it likely that the production possibilities frontier in this situation will be a straight line (as in Figure 2.1 on page 39) or bowed out (as in Figure 2.2 on page 42)? Briefly explain.
  b. Suppose a technological change occurs that has a favorable effect on the production of capital goods but not consumption goods. Show the effect on the production possibilities frontier.

c. Suppose that Lichtenstein and Luxembourg currently have identical production possibilities frontiers but that Lichtenstein devotes only 5 percent of its resources to producing capital goods over each of the next 10 years, while Luxembourg devotes 30 percent. Which country is likely to experience more rapid economic growth in the future? Illustrate using a production possibilities frontier graph. Your graph should include production possibilities frontiers for Lichtenstein and Luxembourg today and in 10 years.

1.9 Use the following production possibilities frontier for a country to answer the questions.

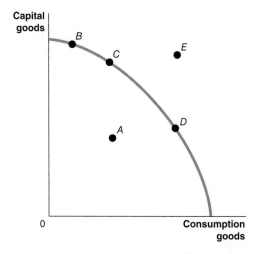

a. Which point or points are unattainable? Briefly explain why.

b. Which point or points are efficient? Briefly explain why.

c. Which point or points are inefficient? Briefly explain why.

d. At which point is the country's future growth rate likely to be the highest? Briefly explain why.

1.10 **[Related to** Solved Problem 2.1 **on page 40]** You have exams in economics and chemistry coming up, and you have 5 hours available for studying. The following table shows the trade-offs you face in allocating the time you will spend in studying each subject:

Hours Spent Studying			Midterm Score	
Choice	Economics	Chemistry	Economics	Chemistry
A	5	0	95	70
B	4	1	93	78
C	3	2	90	84
D	2	3	86	88
E	1	4	81	90
F	0	5	75	91

a. Use the data in the table to draw a production possibilities frontier graph. Label the vertical axis "Score on economics exam," and label the horizontal axis "Score on chemistry exam." Make sure to label the values where your production possibilities frontier intersects the vertical and horizontal axes.

b. Label the points representing choice C and choice D. If you are at choice C, what is your opportunity cost of increasing your chemistry score by 4 points?

c. Under what circumstances would choice A be a sensible choice?

1.11 Suppose the U.S. president is attempting to decide whether the federal government should spend more on research to find a cure for heart disease. He asks you, one of his economic advisors, to prepare a report discussing the relevant factors he should consider. Use the concepts of opportunity cost and trade-offs to discuss some of the main issues you would deal with in your report.

1.12 Suppose that the federal government is deciding which of two cancer treatment therapies it will allow Medicare to pay for (assuming that only one treatment therapy will be funded): Therapy A, which will prolong the average life span of patients receiving the treatment by 24 months and will cost $750,000 per patient treated, or therapy B, which will prolong the average life span of patients receiving the treatment by 20 months and will cost $25,000 per patient treated. What factors should the federal government take into consideration in making its decision?

1.13 Lawrence Summers served as secretary of the Treasury in the Clinton administration from 1999 to 2001 and as director of the National Economic Council in the Obama administration from 2009 to 2010. He has been quoted as giving the following defense of the economic approach:

> There is nothing morally unattractive about saying: We need to analyze which way of spending money on health care will produce more benefit and which less, and using our money as efficiently as we can. I don't think there is anything immoral about seeking to achieve environmental benefits at the lowest possible costs.

Would it be more ethical to reduce pollution without worrying about the cost, or by taking the cost into account? Briefly explain.

Source: David Wessel, "Precepts from Professor Summers," *Wall Street Journal*, October 17, 2002.

1.14 In *The Wonderful Wizard of Oz* and his other books about the Land of Oz, L. Frank Baum observed that if people's wants were limited enough, most goods would not be scarce. According to Baum, this was the case in Oz:

> There were no poor people in the Land of Oz, because there was no such thing as money.... Each person was given freely by his neighbors whatever he required for his use, which is as much as anyone may reasonably desire. Some tilled the lands and raised great crops of grain, which was divided equally among the whole population, so that all had enough. There were many tailors and dressmakers and shoemakers and the like, who made things that any who desired them might wear. Likewise there were jewelers who made ornaments for the person, which pleased and beautified the people, and these ornaments also were free to those who asked for them. Each man and woman, no

matter what he or she produced for the good of the community, was supplied by the neighbors with food and clothing and a house and furniture and ornaments and games. If by chance the supply ever ran short, more was taken from the great storehouses of the Ruler, which were afterward filled up again when there was more of any article than people needed... .

You will know, by what I have told you here, that the Land of Oz was a remarkable country. I do not suppose such an arrangement would be practical with us.

Do you agree with Baum that the economic system in Oz wouldn't work in the contemporary United States? Briefly explain why or why not.

Source: L. Frank Baum, *The Emerald City of Oz*, 1910, pp. 30–31.

2.2 Comparative Advantage and Trade, pages 43–49

LEARNING OBJECTIVE: Describe comparative advantage and explain how it serves as the basis for trade.

Summary

Fundamentally, markets are about **trade**, which is the act of buying or selling. People trade on the basis of comparative advantage. An individual, a firm, or a country has a **comparative advantage** in producing a good or service if it can produce the good or service at the lowest opportunity cost. People are usually better off specializing in the activity for which they have a comparative advantage and trading for the other goods and services they need. It is important not to confuse comparative advantage with absolute advantage. An individual, a firm, or a country has an **absolute advantage** in producing a good or service if it can produce more of that good or service using the same amount of resources. It is possible to have an absolute advantage in producing a good or service without having a comparative advantage.

MyEconLab   Visit **www.myeconlab.com** to complete these exercises online and get instant feedback.

Review Questions

2.1 What is absolute advantage? What is comparative advantage? Is it possible for a country to have a comparative advantage in producing a good without also having an absolute advantage? Briefly explain.

2.2 What is the basis for trade: absolute advantage or comparative advantage? How can an individual or a country gain from specialization and trade?

Problems and Applications

2.3 Look again at the information in Figure 2.4 on page 44. Choose a rate of trading cherries for apples different from the rate used in the text (15 pounds of cherries for 10 pounds of apples) that will allow you and your neighbor to benefit from trading. Prepare a table like Table 2.1 on page 46 to illustrate your answer.

2.4 Using the same amount of resources, the United States and Canada can both produce lumberjack shirts and lumberjack boots, as shown in the following production possibilities frontiers:

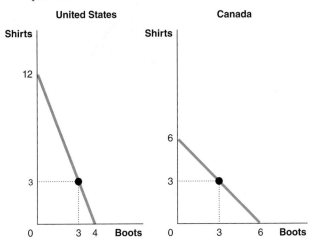

a. Who has a comparative advantage in producing lumberjack boots? Who has a comparative advantage in producing lumberjack shirts? Explain your reasoning.

b. Does either country have an absolute advantage in producing both goods? Explain.

c. Suppose that both countries are currently producing three pairs of boots and three shirts. Show that both can be better off if they each specialize in producing one good and then trade for the other.

2.5 **[Related to** Don't Let This Happen to You **on page 47]** In the 1950s, the economist Bela Balassa compared 28 manufacturing industries in the United States and Britain. In every one of the 28 industries, Balassa found that the United States had an absolute advantage. In these circumstances, would there have been any gain to the United States from importing any of these products from Britain? Explain.

2.6 **[Related to** Solved Problem 2.2 **on page 47]** Suppose Iran and Iraq both produce oil and olive oil, which are sold for the same prices in both countries. The following table shows the combinations of both goods that each country can produce in a day, measured in thousands of barrels, using the same amounts of capital and labor:

Iraq		Iran	
Oil	Olive Oil	Oil	Olive Oil
0	8	0	4
2	6	1	3
4	4	2	2
6	2	3	1
8	0	4	0

a. Who has the comparative advantage in producing oil? Explain.

b. Can these two countries gain from trading oil and olive oil? Explain.

2.7 [Related to Solved Problem 2.2 **on page 47**] Suppose that France and Germany both produce schnitzel and wine. The following table shows combinations of the goods that each country can produce in a day:

France		Germany	
Wine (bottles)	Schnitzel (pounds)	Wine (bottles)	Schnitzel (pounds)
0	8	0	15
1	6	1	12
2	4	2	9
3	2	3	6
4	0	4	3
		5	0

a. Who has a comparative advantage in producing wine? Who has a comparative advantage in producing schnitzel?

b. Suppose that France is currently producing 1 bottle of wine and 6 pounds of schnitzel, and Germany is currently producing 3 bottles of wine and 6 pounds of schnitzel. Demonstrate that France and Germany can both be better off if they specialize in producing only one good and then trade for the other.

2.8 Can an individual or a country produce beyond its production possibilities frontier? Can an individual or a country consume beyond its production possibilities frontier? Explain.

2.9 If Nicaragua can produce with the same amount of resources twice as much coffee as Columbia, explain how Columbia could have a comparative advantage in producing coffee.

2.10 Imagine that the next time the Indianapolis Colts play the New England Patriots at Lucas Oil Stadium in Indianapolis, Colts star quarterback Andrew Luck has a temporary lack of judgment and plans to sell Colts memorabilia during the game because he realizes that he can sell five times more Colts products than any other player. Likewise, imagine that you are a creative and effective manager at work and that you tell your employees that during the next six months, you plan to clean the offices because you can clean five times better than the cleaning staff. What error in judgment are both Andrew and you making? Why shouldn't Andrew and you do what you are better than anyone else at doing?

2.11 Is specialization and trade between individuals and countries more about having a job or about obtaining a higher standard of living? Individually, if you go from a situation of not trading with others (you produce everything yourself) to a situation of trading with others, do you still have a job? Does your standard of living increase? Likewise, if a country goes from not trading with other countries to trading with other countries, does it still have jobs? Does its standard of living increase?

2.12 In colonial America, the population was spread thinly over a large area, and transportation costs were very high because it was difficult to ship products by road for more than short distances. As a result, most of the free population lived on small farms, where they not only grew their own food but also usually made their own clothes and very rarely bought or sold anything for money. Explain why the incomes of these farmers were likely to rise as transportation costs fell. Use the concept of comparative advantage in your answer.

2.13 During the 1928 presidential election campaign, Herbert Hoover, the Republican candidate, argued that the United States should import only products that could not be produced here. Do you believe that this would be a good policy? Explain.

2.14 [Related to the Making the Connection **on page 49**] In discussing dividing up household chores, Emily Oster, an economist at the University of Chicago, advises that: "No, you shouldn't always unload the dishwasher because you're better at it." If you are better at unloading the dishwasher, why shouldn't you be the one to unload it?

Source: Emily Oster, "Your're Dividing the Chores Wrong," *Slate*, November 21, 2012.

2.15 [Related to the Making the Connection **on page 49**] According to the U.S. Bureau of Labor Statistics, the amount of time men devote to housework has been increasing, while the amount of time women devote to housework has been decreasing. Briefly explain whether there is an economic explanation for these trends.

Source: U.S. Bureau of Labor Statistics, *American Time Use Survey.*

2.3 The Market System, pages 50–58
LEARNING OBJECTIVE: Explain the basic idea of how a market system works.

Summary

A **market** is a group of buyers and sellers of a good or service and the institution or arrangement by which they come together to trade. **Product markets** are markets for goods and services, such as computers and medical treatment. **Factor markets** are markets for the **factors of production**, such as labor, capital, natural resources, and entrepreneurial ability. A **circular-flow diagram** shows how participants in product markets and factor markets are linked. Adam Smith argued in his 1776 book *The Wealth of Nations* that in a **free market**, where the government does not control the production of goods and services, changes in prices lead firms to produce the goods and services most desired by consumers. If consumers demand more of a good, its price will rise. Firms respond to rising prices by increasing production. If consumers demand less of a good, its price will fall. Firms respond to falling prices by producing less of a good. An **entrepreneur** is someone who operates a business. In the market system, entrepreneurs are responsible for organizing the production of goods and services. The market system will work well only if there is protection for **property rights**, which are the rights of individuals and firms to use their property.

MyEconLab   Visit **www.myeconlab.com** to complete these exercises online and get instant feedback.

Review Questions

3.1 What is a circular-flow diagram, and what does it demonstrate?

3.2 What are the two main categories of participants in markets? Which participants are of greatest importance in determining what goods and services are produced?

3.3 What is a free market? In what ways does a free market economy differ from a centrally planned economy?

3.4 What is an entrepreneur? Why do entrepreneurs play a key role in a market system?

3.5 Under what circumstances are firms likely to produce more of a good or service? Under what circumstances are firms likely to produce less of a good or service?

3.6 What are private property rights? What role do they play in the working of a market system? Why are independent courts important for a well-functioning economy?

Problems and Applications

3.7 Identify whether each of the following transactions will take place in the factor market or in the product market and whether households or firms are supplying the good or service or demanding the good or service:
a. George buys a Tesla Model S.
b. Tesla increases employment at its Fremont plant.
c. George works 20 hours per week at McDonald's.
d. George sells the land he owns to McDonald's so that it can build a new restaurant.

3.8 [Related to the Making the Connection **on page 53**] In *The Wealth of Nations*, Adam Smith wrote the following (Book I, Chapter II): "It is not from the benevolence of the butcher, the brewer, or the baker, that we expect our dinner, but from their regard to their own interest." Briefly discuss what he meant by this.

3.9 [Related to the Making the Connection **on page 53**] According to an article in the *Wall Street Journal*, the parts contained in the BlackBerry Torch smartphone include a power management chip made by Texas Instruments (United States); a memory chip made by Samsung (South Korea); a GPS receiver made by CSR (United Kingdom); a radio frequency (RF) transceiver made by Dialog Semiconductor (Germany); an RF transceiver made by Renesas (Japan); an application and communications processor made by Marvell (United States); a video image processor made by STMicroelectronics (Switzerland); and plastic and stamped metal parts made by several firms in China. A firm in Mexico carries out final assembly of the Torch before it is shipped to BlackBerry for sale in the United States and other countries. Is it necessary for the managers in all these firms to know how the components of the Torch are manufactured and how the components are assembled into a smartphone? Is it necessary for the chief executive officer (CEO) of BlackBerry to know this information? Briefly explain.
Source: Jennifer Valentino-DeVries and Phred Dvorak, "Piece by Piece: The Suppliers Behind the New BlackBerry Torch Smartphone," *Wall Street Journal*, August 16, 2010.

3.10 In many parts of Europe during the mid-1770s, governments gave guilds, or organizations of producers, the authority to control who was allowed to produce a good, the amount of the good produced, and the price charged for the good. Would you expect more competition among producers in a *guild system* or in a market system? Was the consumer or the producer at the center of the guild system, and which is at the center of the market system? How would the two systems compare over time in terms of innovation of new products and technologies?

3.11 In a speech at the New York University Law School, Federal Reserve Chairman Ben Bernanke stated:
> Writing in the eighteenth century, Adam Smith conceived of the free-market system as an "invisible hand" that harnesses the pursuit of private interest to promote the public good. Smith's conception remains relevant today, notwithstanding the enormous increase in economic complexity since the Industrial Revolution.

Briefly explain the idea of the invisible hand. What is so important about the idea of the invisible hand?
Source: Ben S. Bernanke, "Financial Regulation and the Invisible Hand," speech made at the New York University Law School, New York, New York, April 11, 2007.

3.12 Evaluate the following argument: "Adam Smith's analysis is based on a fundamental flaw: He assumes that people are motivated by self-interest. But this isn't true. I'm not selfish, and most people I know aren't selfish."

3.13 Writing in the *New York Times*, Michael Lewis argued that "a market economy is premised on a system of incentives designed to encourage an ignoble human trait: self-interest." Do you agree that self-interest is an "ignoble human trait"? What incentives does a market system provide to encourage self-interest?

Source: Michael Lewis, "In Defense of the Boom," *New York Times*, October 27, 2002.

3.14 Some economists have been puzzled that although entrepreneurs take on the risk of losing money by starting new businesses, on average their incomes are lower than those of people with similar characteristics who go to work at large firms. Economist William Baumol believes part of the explanation for this puzzle may be that entrepreneurs are like people who buy lottery tickets. On average, people who don't buy lottery tickets are left with more money than people who buy tickets because lotteries take in more money than they give out. Baumol argues that "the masses of purchasers who grab up the [lottery] tickets are not irrational if they receive an adequate payment in another currency: psychic rewards."

    a. What are "psychic rewards"?

    b. What psychic rewards might an entrepreneur receive?

    c. Do you agree with Baumol that an entrepreneur is like someone buying a lottery ticket? Briefly explain.

Source: William J. Baumol, *The Microtheory of Innovative Entrepreneurship*, Princeton, NJ: Princeton University Press, 2010.

3.15 The 2009 International Property Rights Index study states:

> [T]hose developing countries that respect property rights grow on average faster than those that fail to provide sound legal and political environments and protection for physical property rights.

Why would the protection of property rights be likely to increase economic growth in a developing, or low-income, country?

Source: Gaurav Tiwari, "Report: Property Rights Linked to Economic Security," *International Property Rights Index 2012 Report*.

3.16 According to an article on Phillyburbs.com, some farmers in rural Pennsylvania are causing a "stink" by using pig manure for fertilizer. The farmers purchase the pig manure, which is an organic fertilizer, from a nearby pork processing plant and spread it across the fields where they grow corn and soybeans. The article asserts that the farmers switched to pig manure because of the skyrocketing price of chemical fertilizers. Some of the residents of Milford, however, have complained about the smell, but the "farmers are likely protected under Pennsylvania's Right to Farm Act, which allows farmers to engage in practices that are common to agriculture."

    a. What price signal did the farmers respond to in their switch to the organic pig manure fertilizer?

    b. According to the Pennsylvania Right to Farm Act, do the farmers or the townspeople have the property right to the smell of the air around the farms? (Some of the residents did ask the township to urge the farmers to plow under the manure to reduce its stench.)

Source: Amanda Cregan, "Milford Farmers Switch to Pig Manure Causing a Stink for Neighbors," Phillyburbs.com, March 6, 2013.

3.17 **[Related to the** Making the Connection **on page 57]** The British historian Thomas Macaulay once remarked that copyrights are "a tax on readers." In what sense are copyrights a tax on readers? If copyrights are a tax on readers, why do governments enact them?

Where Prices Come From: The Interaction of Demand and Supply

Chapter Outline and **Learning Objectives**

Smartphones: The Indispensible Product?

If you're like most students, professors, and businesspeople, you carry your cellphone or smartphone everywhere you go. With a cellphone, you can make and receive phone calls and text messages. With a smartphone, you can do much more: send and receive e-mails, check Facebook and other social media sites, share photos, and stream videos. By 2013, more than two million smartphones were being sold *per day* worldwide.

Ten years ago, the BlackBerry, sold by the Canadian-based firm Research in Motion, was the only widely used smartphone. The BlackBerry was expensive, though, and most buyers were businesspeople who wanted to send and answer e-mails while away from the office. When Apple introduced the iPhone in 2007, smartphones started to become popular with a wider market of consumers, including students. With the release of the iPhone 3G in 2008, Apple announced that a section of its immensely popular iTunes music and video store would be devoted to applications (or "apps") for the iPhone. Major software companies, as well as individuals writing their first software programs, have posted games, calendars, dictionaries, and many other types of apps to the iTunes store. Apple sold more than 3 million iPhones within a month of launching the iPhone 3G.

Although initially Apple had a commanding share of the smartphone market, competitors soon appeared. Companies such as Samsung, Nokia, HTC, LG, Huawei, Microsoft, Sony, ZTE, and Panasonic introduced smartphones. Most of these manufacturers followed Apple in developing apps or providing users access to online app stores.

The intense competition among firms selling smartphones is a striking example of how the market responds to changes in consumer tastes. As many consumers indicated that they would pay more for a smartphone than a regular cellphone, firms scrambled to meet the demand for smartphones. Although intense competition is not always good news for firms trying to sell products, it is great news for consumers because it increases the available choice of products and lowers the prices consumers pay for those products.

AN INSIDE LOOK on page 92 discusses how Google faced the problem of not having enough of its Nexus 4 smartphones to meet customer demand, while Apple worried about overproduction of its iPhone 5.

Sources: Brian X. Chen, "Smartphones Finally Surpass the Feature Phone," *New York Times*, April 26, 2013; Eric Pfanner, "Competition Designed to Spread Basic Technologies," *New York Times*, April 18, 2013; and Brad Reed, "A Brief History of Smartphones," pcworld.com, June 18, 2010.

Economics in Your Life

Will You Buy an Apple iPhone or a Samsung Galaxy?

Suppose you want to buy a smartphone and are choosing between an Apple iPhone and a Samsung Galaxy S. If you buy an iPhone, you will have access to more applications—or "apps"—that can increase the enjoyment and performance of your smartphone. In addition, the iPhone is thin, lightweight, and sleek looking. One strategy Samsung can use to overcome these advantages is to compete based on price and value. Would you choose to buy a Galaxy S if it had a lower price than a comparable iPhone? If your income increased, would it affect your decision about which smartphone to buy? As you read this chapter, try to answer these questions. You can check your answers against those we provide on **page 91** at the end of this chapter.

I n Chapter 1, we explored how economists use models to predict human behavior. In Chapter 2, we used the model of production possibilities frontiers to analyze scarcity and trade-offs. In this chapter and the next, we explore the model of demand and supply, which is the most powerful tool in economics, and use the model to explain how prices are determined.

Recall from Chapter 1 that because economic models rely on assumptions, the models are simplifications of reality. In some cases, the assumptions of a model may not seem to describe exactly the economic situation being analyzed. For example, the model of demand and supply assumes that we are analyzing a **perfectly competitive market**, which is a market where there are many buyers and sellers, all the products sold are identical, and there are no barriers to new firms entering the market. These assumptions are very restrictive and apply exactly to only a few markets, such as the markets for wheat and other agricultural products. Experience has shown, however, that the model of demand and supply can be very useful in analyzing markets where competition among sellers is intense, even if there are relatively few sellers and the products being sold are not identical. In fact, in recent studies, the model of demand and supply has been successful in analyzing markets with as few as four buyers and four sellers. In the end, the usefulness of a model depends on how well it can predict outcomes in a market. As we will see in this chapter, this model is often successful in predicting changes in quantities and prices in many markets.

We begin studying the model of demand and supply by discussing consumers and the demand side of the market, before turning to firms and the supply side. Throughout this book, we will apply this model to understand business, the economy, and economic policy.

Perfectly competitive market A market that meets the conditions of (1) many buyers and sellers, (2) all firms selling identical products, and (3) no barriers to new firms entering the market.

3.1 LEARNING OBJECTIVE

Discuss the variables that influence demand.

The Demand Side of the Market

Chapter 2 explained that in a market system consumers ultimately determine which goods and services will be produced. The most successful businesses are the ones that respond best to consumer demand. But what determines consumer demand for a product? Certainly, many factors influence the willingness of consumers to buy a particular product. For example, consumers who are considering buying a smartphone, such as an Apple iPhone or a Samsung Galaxy S, will make their decisions based on, among other factors, the income they have available to spend and the effectiveness of the advertising campaigns of the companies that sell smartphones. The main factor in most consumer decisions, though, is the price of the product. So, it makes sense to begin with price when analyzing how consumers decide to buy a product. It is important to note that when we discuss demand, we are considering not what a consumer *wants* to buy but what the consumer is both willing and *able* to buy.

Demand Schedules and Demand Curves

Demand schedule A table that shows the relationship between the price of a product and the quantity of the product demanded.

Quantity demanded The amount of a good or service that a consumer is willing and able to purchase at a given price.

Demand curve A curve that shows the relationship between the price of a product and the quantity of the product demanded.

Market demand The demand by all the consumers of a given good or service.

Tables that show the relationship between the price of a product and the quantity of the product demanded are called **demand schedules**. The table in Figure 3.1 shows the number of smartphones consumers would be willing to buy over the course of a week at five different prices. The amount of a good or service that a consumer is willing and able to purchase at a given price is called the **quantity demanded**. The graph in Figure 3.1 plots the numbers from the table as a **demand curve**, which shows the relationship between the price of a product and the quantity of the product demanded. (Note that, for convenience, we made the demand curve in Figure 3.1 a straight line, or linear. There is no reason that all demand curves need to be straight lines.) The demand curve in Figure 3.1 shows the **market demand**, which is the demand by all the consumers of a given good or service. The market for a product, such as restaurant meals, that is sold locally would include all the consumers in a city or a relatively small area. The market for a product, such as smartphones, that is sold internationally would include all the consumers in the world.

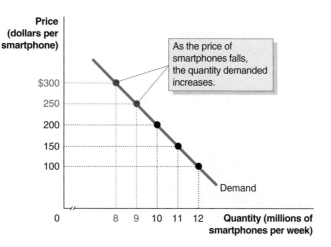

MyEconLab Animation

Figure 3.1

A Demand Schedule and Demand Curve

As the price changes, consumers change the quantity of smartphones they are willing to buy. We can show this as a *demand schedule* in a table or as a *demand curve* on a graph. The table and graph both show that as the price of smartphones falls, the quantity demanded increases. When the price of smartphones is $300, consumers buy 8 million smartphones per week. When the price falls to $250, consumers buy 9 million. Therefore, the demand curve for smartphones is downward sloping.

The demand curve in Figure 3.1 slopes downward because consumers will buy more smartphones as the price falls. When the price of smartphones is $300, consumers buy 8 million smartphones per week. When the price falls to $250, consumers buy 9 million. Buyers demand a larger quantity of a product as the price falls because the product becomes less expensive relative to other products and because they can afford to buy more at a lower price. MyEconLab Concept Check

The Law of Demand

The inverse relationship between the price of a product and the quantity of the product demanded is called the **law of demand**: Holding everything else constant, when the price of a product falls, the quantity demanded of the product will increase, and when the price of a product rises, the quantity demanded of the product will decrease. The law of demand holds for any market demand curve. Economists have found only a very few exceptions to this law. MyEconLab Concept Check

Law of demand The rule that, holding everything else constant, when the price of a product falls, the quantity demanded of the product will increase, and when the price of a product rises, the quantity demanded of the product will decrease.

What Explains the Law of Demand?

It makes sense that consumers will buy more of a good when its price falls and less of a good when its price rises, but let's look more closely at why this result holds. When the price of a product falls, consumers buy a larger quantity because of the *substitution effect* and the *income effect*.

Substitution Effect The **substitution effect** refers to the change in the quantity demanded of a good that results from a change in price making the good more or less expensive *relative* to other goods that are *substitutes*. When the price of smartphones falls, people will substitute buying smartphones for other goods, such as regular cellphones or even tablet computers, such as the iPad.

Substitution effect The change in the quantity demanded of a good that results from a change in price making the good more or less expensive relative to other goods that are substitutes.

Income Effect The **income effect** of a price change refers to the change in the quantity demanded of a good that results from the effect of a change in the good's price on consumers' *purchasing power*. Purchasing power is the quantity of goods a consumer can buy with a fixed amount of income. When the price of a good falls, the increased purchasing power of consumers' incomes will usually lead them to purchase a larger quantity of the good. When the price of a good rises, the decreased purchasing power of consumers' incomes will usually lead them to purchase a smaller quantity of the good.

Income effect The change in the quantity demanded of a good that results from the effect of a change in the good's price on consumers' purchasing power.

Note that although we can analyze them separately, the substitution effect and the income effect occur simultaneously whenever a price changes. So, a fall in the price of smartphones leads consumers to buy more smartphones both because the smartphones are now less expensive relative to substitute products and because the purchasing power of consumers' incomes has increased. MyEconLab Concept Check

Holding Everything Else Constant: The *Ceteris paribus* Condition

Notice that the definition of the law of demand contains the phrase *holding everything else constant*. In constructing the market demand curve for smartphones, we focused only on the effect that changes in the price of smartphones would have on the quantity consumers would be willing and able to buy. We were holding constant other variables that might affect the willingness of consumers to buy smartphones. Economists refer to the necessity of holding all variables other than price constant in constructing a demand curve as the ***ceteris paribus* condition**. *Ceteris paribus* means "all else equal" in Latin.

What would happen if we allowed a change in a variable—other than price—that might affect the willingness of consumers to buy smartphones? Consumers would then change the quantity they demanded at each price. We can illustrate this effect by shifting the market demand curve. A shift of a demand curve is *an increase or a decrease in demand*. A movement along a demand curve is *an increase or a decrease in the quantity demanded*. As Figure 3.2 shows, we shift the demand curve to the right if consumers decide to buy more smartphones at each price, and we shift the demand curve to the left if consumers decide to buy less at each price.   MyEconLab Concept Check

Variables That Shift Market Demand

Many variables other than price can influence market demand. These five are the most important:

- Income
- Prices of related goods
- Tastes
- Population and demographics
- Expected future prices

We next discuss how changes in each of these variables affect the market demand curve.

Income   The income that consumers have available to spend affects their willingness and ability to buy a good. Suppose that the market demand curve in Figure 3.1 on page 71 represents the willingness of consumers to buy smartphones when average household income is $50,000. If average household income rises to $52,000, the demand for smartphones will increase, which we show by shifting the demand curve to the right. A good is a **normal good** when the demand for the good increases following a rise in

Ceteris paribus **("all else equal")** **condition**   The requirement that when analyzing the relationship between two variables—such as price and quantity demanded—other variables must be held constant.

Normal good   A good for which the demand increases as income rises and decreases as income falls.

MyEconLab Animation

Figure 3.2

Shifting the Demand Curve

When consumers increase the quantity of a product they want to buy at a given price, the demand curve shifts to the right, from D_1 to D_2. When consumers decrease the quantity of a product they want to buy at a given price, the demand curve shifts to the left, from D_1 to D_3.

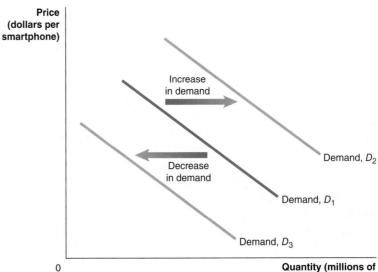

income and decreases following a fall in income. Most goods are normal goods, but the demand for some goods falls when income rises and rises when income falls. For instance, as your income rises, you might buy less canned tuna or fewer instant noodles and buy more shrimp or whole grain pasta. A good is an **inferior good** when the demand for the good decreases following a rise in income and increases following a fall in income. So, for you, canned tuna and instant noodles would be examples of inferior goods—not because they are of low quality but because you buy less of them as your income increases.

Inferior good A good for which the demand increases as income falls and decreases as income rises.

Prices of Related Goods The prices of other goods can also affect consumers' demand for a product. Consumers who would use a smartphone primarily for making phone calls could use a regular cellphone instead. Consumers who would use a smartphone to answer e-mails or surf the Web could use a tablet computer instead. Goods and services that can be used for the same purpose are called **substitutes**. When two goods are substitutes, the more you buy of one, the less you will buy of the other. A decrease in the price of a substitute causes the demand curve for a good to shift to the left. An increase in the price of a substitute causes the demand curve for a good to shift to the right.

Substitutes Goods and services that can be used for the same purpose.

Suppose that the market demand curve in Figure 3.1 on page 71 represents the willingness and ability of consumers to buy smartphones during a week when the average price of tablet computers is $700. If the average price of tablets falls to $600, how will the market demand for smartphones change? Consumers will demand fewer smartphones at every price. We show this change by shifting the demand curve for smartphones to the left.

Making the Connection
MyEconLab Video

Are Tablet Computers Substitutes for E-Readers?

Two products are rarely perfect substitutes for each other in the sense that consumers use them for exactly the same purpose. For example, if you want to read e-books, you would buy an e-reader, such as Barnes & Noble's Nook, Amazon's Kindle, or Kobo's Aura HD. If you want to send and receive e-mails, check your Facebook page, or watch a video, you would probably buy a tablet computer, such as Apple's iPad or Samsung's Galaxy Tab. Although you could use tablet computers to read e-books, tablets have higher prices and are often heavier than e-readers, which makes them less comfortable to hold for an extended period of reading. In addition, tablets typically don't display text as sharply as e-readers.

So e-readers and tablets are substitutes—but they aren't perfect substitutes. To correctly forecast sales and produce the correct quantity of e-readers, firms that produce them need to evaluate how close a substitute consumers consider e-readers and tablets to be. If people who read a lot of e-books strongly prefer e-readers to tablets, then e-reader sales are likely to be higher than if those people consider e-readers and tablets close substitutes.

By 2013, it had become clear that consumers considered the two products close substitutes. E-reader sales were falling much faster than many industry analysts had been expecting. Although 23 million e-readers were sold worldwide in 2011, only 16 million were sold in 2012, and as few as 5.8 million were expected to be sold in 2013. In July 2013, Barnes & Noble's CEO William Lynch resigned after losses from selling the Nook e-reader more than offset the company's profits from its retail stores. As one analyst explained: "It's looking like e-readers were a device for a particular moment in time that, more rapidly than we or anyone else thought, has been replaced by a new technology." Unfortunately for firms selling e-readers, consumers decided that tablets were a close substitute.

By 2013, many consumers saw the tablet computer as a close substitute for the e-reader.

Sources: Jeffrey A. Trachtenberg, "Barnes & Noble Pulls Back After Losses In Tablet Wars," *Wall Street Journal*, June 25, 2013; Brian X. Chen, "E-Reader Market Shrinks Faster Than Many Predicted," *New York Times*, December 20, 2012; Tom Gara, "The Future of the Nook," *Wall Street Journal*, May 9, 2013; Erik Sofge, "The Best E-Reader: Kobo's Aura HD," *Wall Street Journal*, May 3, 2013; and Tom Gara, "One More Casualty Of Barnes & Noble's Nook Problems: Its CEO," *Wall Street Journal*, July 8, 2013.

Your Turn: Test your understanding by doing related problem 1.12 on page 95 at the end of this chapter.

MyEconLab Study Plan

Complements Goods and services that are used together.

Goods and services that are used together—such as hot dogs and hot dog buns—are called **complements**. When two goods are complements, the more consumers buy of one, the more they will buy of the other. A decrease in the price of a complement causes the demand curve for a good to shift to the right. An increase in the price of a complement causes the demand curve for a good to shift to the left.

Many people use applications, or "apps," on their smartphones. So, smartphones and apps are complements. Suppose the market demand curve in Figure 3.1 represents the willingness of consumers to buy smartphones at a time when the average price of an app is $2.99. If the average price of apps falls to $0.99, consumers will buy more apps *and* more smartphones, and the demand curve for smartphones will shift to the right.

Tastes Consumers can be influenced by an advertising campaign for a product. If Apple, Samsung, LG, and other firms making smartphones begin to advertise heavily, consumers are more likely to buy smartphones at every price, and the demand curve will shift to the right. An economist would say that the advertising campaign has affected consumers' *taste* for smartphones. Taste is a catchall category that refers to the many subjective elements that can enter into a consumer's decision to buy a product. A consumer's taste for a product can change for many reasons. Sometimes trends play a substantial role. For example, the popularity of low-carbohydrate diets caused a decline in demand for some goods, such as bread and donuts, and an increase in demand for beef. In general, when consumers' taste for a product increases, the demand curve will shift to the right, and when consumers' taste decreases, the demand curve will shift to the left.

Population and Demographics As the population of a country increases, the number of consumers and the demand for most products will increase. The **demographics** of a population refers to its characteristics, with respect to age, race, and gender. As the demographics of a country or region change, the demand for particular goods will increase or decrease because different categories of people tend to have different preferences for those goods. For instance, Hispanics are expected to increase from 17 percent of the U.S. population in 2012 to 29 percent in 2050. This increase will expand demand for Spanish-language books and cable television channels, among other goods and services.

Demographics The characteristics of a population with respect to age, race, and gender.

Younger consumers are buying more water and juice and less Coke and Pepsi than previous generations.

Making the Connection
MyEconLab Video

Coke and Pepsi Are Hit by U.S. Demographics

Traditionally, consumption of soft drinks, such as Coca-Cola and Pepsi-Cola, has been much higher among people aged 30 and below than among older consumers. For many years, the demographics of soft drink consumption did not pose a problem for U.S. soft drink companies. As one generation aged and moved on to drinking coffee, tea, and other beverages, another generation of soft drink buyers took its place. In recent years, though, soft drink companies have begun to experience gradually decreasing sales in the United States.

One reason for declining soft drink sales is that the average age of the U.S. population is increasing. Following the end of World War II in 1945, the United States experienced a "baby boom," as birthrates rose and remained high through the early 1960s. Falling birthrates after 1965 mean that the baby boom generation is larger than the generations before and after it. As the baby boomers have aged and reduced their soft drink consumption, the generations that have followed have been smaller.

Even worse news for the soft drink companies is that younger consumers are not buying as much Coke, Pepsi, and other soft drinks as their parents and grandparents did. Younger consumers are more likely to buy energy drinks, water, juice, coffee, or tea than past generations. Part of the move away from soda is due to increased publicity about the potential health problems resulting from drinking soda. Some public health advocates argue that the amount of added sugars in many soft drinks make them unsafe and have called on the federal government to regulate the ingredients in soft drinks. Many schools have reduced the availability of sodas in cafeterias and vending machines. As a result, consumption per person of carbonated soft drinks declined by more than 15 percent in the United States between 2005 and 2013. In early 2013, Pepsi announced that in just the past year, its soda sales in North America had declined by about 5 percent. The double problem of an aging population and a younger population not as inclined to drink soda led an article in the *Wall Street Journal* to ask: "Is This the End of the Soft-Drink Era?"

There were, however, some rays of sunshine for U.S. soft drink companies. Although demographics were hurting the demand for soft drinks in the United States, a growing population of young people worldwide meant that the global demand for soft drinks, particularly in developing countries, was increasing. U.S. soft drink companies responded to this opportunity. Coca-Cola announced a multiyear plan to increase sales in foreign markets, including investments of $5 billion in new bottling plants in India and $4 billion in China. As Indra K. Nooyi, PepsiCo's chairman and chief executive officer, put it in the company's *Annual Report*: "Looking back to 2006, emerging and developing markets accounted for 24 percent of our net revenue; in 2012, they represented 35 percent of our net revenue. And over the long term, we are looking to grow our business in these markets at high single digits to low double digits."

Clearly, soft drink companies needed to be aware of the effects of changing demographics on the demand for their products.

Sources: Mike Esterl, "Is This the End of the Soft-Drink Era?" *Wall Street Journal*, January 18, 2013; "PepsiCo Beats Expectations Despite Soda Struggles," Associated Press, April 13, 2013; PepsiCo, *2012 Annual Report*, www.pepsico.com /annual12/; and Stephanie Strom, "Health Officials Urge F.D.A. to Limit Sweeteners in Sodas," *New York Times*, February 13, 2013.

Your Turn: Test your understanding by doing related problem 1.13 on page 95 at the end of this chapter.   MyEconLab Study Plan

---

Expected Future Prices Consumers choose not only which products to buy but also when to buy them. For instance, if enough consumers become convinced that houses will be selling for lower prices in three months, the demand for houses will decrease now, as some consumers postpone their purchases to wait for the expected price decrease. Alternatively, if enough consumers become convinced that the price of houses will be higher in three months, the demand for houses will increase now, as some consumers try to beat the expected price increase.

Table 3.1 on page 76 summarizes the most important variables that cause market demand curves to shift. Note that the table shows the shift in the demand curve that results from an *increase* in each of the variables. A *decrease* in these variables would cause the demand curve to shift in the opposite direction.   MyEconLab Concept Check

A Change in Demand versus a Change in Quantity Demanded

It is important to understand the difference between a *change in demand* and a *change in quantity demanded*. A change in demand refers to a shift of the demand curve. A shift occurs if there is a change in one of the variables—*other than the price of the product*—that affects the willingness of consumers to buy the product. A change in quantity demanded refers to a movement along the demand curve as a result of a change in the product's price. Figure 3.3 on page 77 illustrates this important distinction. If the price of smartphones falls from $300 to $250, the result will be a movement along the demand curve from point *A* to point *B*—an increase in quantity demanded from 8 million to 9 million. If consumers' incomes increase, or if another factor changes that makes consumers want more of the product at every price, the demand curve will shift to the right—an increase in demand. In this case, the increase in demand from D_1 to D_2 causes the quantity of smartphones demanded at a price of $300 to increase from 8 million at point *A* to 10 million at point *C*.   MyEconLab Concept Check

Table 3.1

Variables That Shift Market Demand Curves

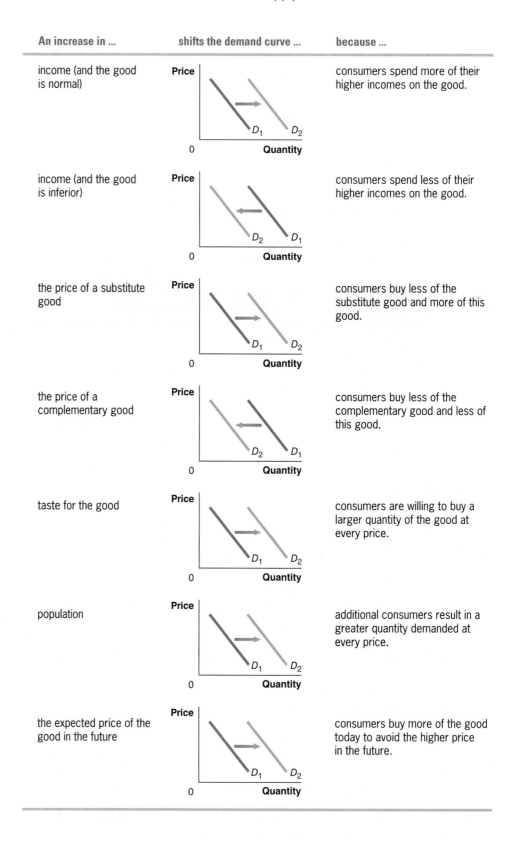

An increase in ...	shifts the demand curve ...	because ...
income (and the good is normal)		consumers spend more of their higher incomes on the good.
income (and the good is inferior)		consumers spend less of their higher incomes on the good.
the price of a substitute good		consumers buy less of the substitute good and more of this good.
the price of a complementary good		consumers buy less of the complementary good and less of this good.
taste for the good		consumers are willing to buy a larger quantity of the good at every price.
population		additional consumers result in a greater quantity demanded at every price.
the expected price of the good in the future		consumers buy more of the good today to avoid the higher price in the future.

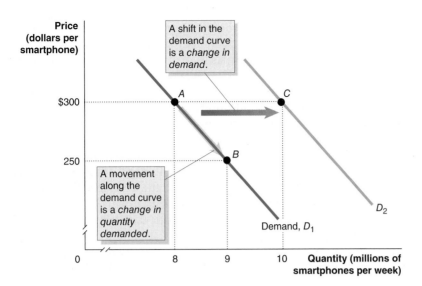

MyEconLab Animation

Figure 3.3

A Change in Demand versus a Change in Quantity Demanded

If the price of smartphones falls from $300 to $250, the result will be a movement along the demand curve from point A to point B—an increase in quantity demanded from 8 million to 9 million. If consumers' incomes increase, or if another factor changes that makes consumers want more of the product at every price, the demand curve will shift to the right—an increase in demand. In this case, the increase in demand from D_1 to D_2 causes the quantity of smartphones demanded at a price of $300 to increase from 8 million at point A to 10 million at point C.

Making the Connection

MyEconLab Video

Forecasting the Demand for iPhones

One of the most important decisions that managers of any large firm face is which new products to develop. A firm must devote people, time, and money to design a new product, negotiate with suppliers, formulate a marketing campaign, and perform many other tasks. But any firm has only limited resources and so faces a trade-off: Resources used to develop one product will not be available to develop another product. Ultimately, the products a firm chooses to develop will be those that it believes will be the most profitable. So, to decide which products to develop, firms need to forecast the demand for those products.

David Sobotta, who worked at Apple for 20 years and eventually became its national sales manager, has described discussions at Apple during 2002 about whether to develop a tablet computer. According to Sobotta, representatives of the U.S. National Institutes of

Will demand for iPhones continue to grow despite increasing competition?

Health urged Apple to develop a tablet computer, arguing that it would be particularly useful to doctors, nurses, and hospitals. In 2001, Bill Gates, chairman of Microsoft, had predicted that "within five years … [tablet PCs] will be the most popular form of PC sold in America." Apple's managers decided not to develop a tablet computer, however, because they believed the technology available at that time was too complex for an average computer user, and they also believed that the demand from doctors and nurses would be small. Apple's forecast was correct. Despite Bill Gates's prediction, in 2006 tablet computers made up only 1 percent of the computer market. According to Sobotta, "Apple executives had a theory that the route to success will not be through selling thousands of relatively expensive things, but millions of very inexpensive things like iPods."

Apple continued to work on smartphones, developing the technology to eliminate keyboards in favor of touchscreen displays. Rather than proceeding immediately to build a tablet computer, Steve Jobs, then Apple's CEO, realized he could use this technology in a different way: "I thought 'My God we can build a phone out of this.'" From its introduction in 2007, the iPhone was an immediate success. By mid-2013, Apple had sold more than 350 million iPhones worldwide.

As Apple attempts to forecast demand for its iPhone, it needs to consider two factors: competition from other firms producing smartphones and competition from substitute goods. By 2013, industry analysts were divided as to whether Apple would be able to maintain its share of the smartphone market in the face of increasing competition from other firms. The outlook for substitute goods was also mixed. Smartphones were an increasing share of the overall worldwide cellphone market. Many consumers were shifting from regular cellphones and music players, such as iPods, to smartphones. The increasing availability of apps, including new mobile payment apps that can be used in place of credit cards, was increasing the usefulness of smartphones. Some consumers, though, preferred the use of tablets, such as Apple's iPad or Samsung's Galaxy Tab, with their larger screens, for checking e-mails or surfing the Web. Installing the Skype app even made it possible to use a tablet to make phone calls.

Taking these factors together, Apple was optimistic that its iPhone sales would double by 2016 in comparison with 2012. As any firm does in forecasting demand, Apple faced a trade-off: If it was too cautious in expanding capacity or buying components for smartphones, other firms might seize a large share of the market. But, if Apple was too optimistic, it ran the risk of spending on capacity to produce more units than it could actually sell—an outcome that might turn potential profits into losses. Apple spent several billion dollars to buy large quantities of motion sensors, screens, and other components from suppliers. That will be money well spent … if the forecast of demand turns out to be accurate. Time will tell whether the future demand for smartphones will be as large as Apple and other firms were forecasting.

Source: "Apple Reports Second Quarter Results: 37.4 Million iPhones Sold; 19.5 Million iPads Sold," www.apple.com, April 23, 2013; Jérémie Bouchaud, "Apple and Samsung Are Top Buyers of MEMS Motion Sensors in Handsets and Tablets," www.isuppli.com, April 1, 2013; Jay Yarow, "CITI: Apple Is Pretty Much Doomed," www.businessinsider.com, March 6, 2013; David Sobotta, "What Jobs Told Me on the iPhone," *Guardian* (London), January 3, 2007; "Jobs Says iPad Idea Came Before iPhone," Associated Press, January 2, 2010; and "More Smartphones Were Shipped in Q1 2013 Than Feature Phones, an Industry First According to IDC," www.idc.com, April 25, 2013.

MyEconLab Study Plan

Your Turn: Test your understanding by doing related problem 1.17 on page 95 at the end of this chapter.

related problem 1.17 on page 95

3.2 LEARNING OBJECTIVE

Discuss the variables that influence supply.

Quantity supplied The amount of a good or service that a firm is willing and able to supply at a given price.

Supply schedule A table that shows the relationship between the price of a product and the quantity of the product supplied.

Supply curve A curve that shows the relationship between the price of a product and the quantity of the product supplied.

The Supply Side of the Market

Just as many variables influence the willingness and ability of consumers to buy a particular good or service, many variables influence the willingness and ability of firms to sell a good or service. The most important of these variables is price. The amount of a good or service that a firm is willing and able to supply at a given price is the **quantity supplied**. Holding other variables constant, when the price of a good rises, producing the good is more profitable, and the quantity supplied will increase. When the price of a good falls, selling the good is less profitable, and the quantity supplied will decrease. In addition, as we saw in Chapter 2, devoting more and more resources to the production of a good results in increasing marginal costs. If, for example, Apple, Samsung, LG, and other firms increase production of smartphones during a given time period, they are likely to find that the cost of producing additional smartphones increases as their suppliers run existing factories for longer hours and pay higher prices for components and higher wages for workers. With higher marginal costs, firms will supply a larger quantity only if the price is higher.

Supply Schedules and Supply Curves

A **supply schedule** is a table that shows the relationship between the price of a product and the quantity of the product supplied. The table in Figure 3.4 is a supply schedule showing the quantity of smartphones that firms would be willing to supply per month at different prices. The graph in Figure 3.4 plots the numbers from the table as a **supply curve**, which shows the relationship between the price of a product and the quantity of

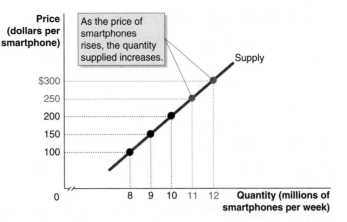

Supply Schedule	
Price (dollars per smartphone)	Quantity (millions of smartphones per week)
$300	12
250	11
200	10
150	9
100	8

Figure 3.4

A Supply Schedule and Supply Curve

As the price changes, Apple, Samsung, LG, and other firms producing smartphones change the quantity they are willing to supply. We can show this as a *supply schedule* in a table or as a *supply curve* on a graph. The supply schedule and supply curve both show that as the price of smartphones rises, firms will increase the quantity they supply. At a price of $250 per smartphone, firms will supply 11 million smartphones per week. At a price of $300, firms will supply 12 million.

the product supplied. The supply schedule and supply curve both show that as the price of smartphones rises, firms will increase the quantity they supply. At a price of $250 per smartphone, firms will supply 11 million smartphones per week. At a higher price of $300, firms will supply 12 million. (Once again, we are assuming for convenience that the supply curve is a straight line, even though not all supply curves are actually straight lines.)   MyEconLab Concept Check

The Law of Supply

The *market supply curve* in Figure 3.4 is upward sloping. We expect most supply curves to be upward sloping, according to the **law of supply**, which states that, holding everything else constant, increases in price cause increases in the quantity supplied, and decreases in price cause decreases in the quantity supplied. Notice that the definition of the law of supply—like the definition of the law of demand—contains the phrase *holding everything else constant*. If only the price of the product changes, there is a movement along the supply curve, which is *an increase or a decrease in the quantity supplied.* As Figure 3.5 shows, if any other variable that affects the willingness of firms to supply a good changes, the supply curve will shift, which is *an increase or a decrease in supply.* When firms increase the quantity of a product they want to sell at a given price, the supply curve shifts to the right. The shift from S_1 to S_3 represents *an increase in supply.* When firms decrease the quantity of a product they want to sell at a given price, the supply curve shifts to the left. The shift from S_1 to S_2 represents *a decrease in supply.*   MyEconLab Concept Check

Law of supply The rule that, holding everything else constant, increases in price cause increases in the quantity supplied, and decreases in price cause decreases in the quantity supplied.

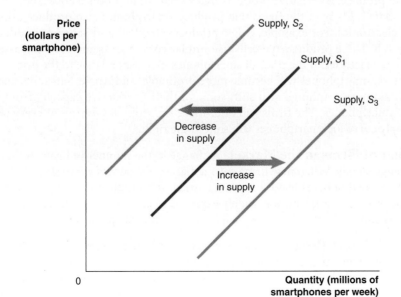

Figure 3.5

Shifting the Supply Curve

When firms increase the quantity of a product they want to sell at a given price, the supply curve shifts to the right. The shift from S_1 to S_3 represents an *increase in supply*. When firms decrease the quantity of a product they want to sell at a given price, the supply curve shifts to the left. The shift from S_1 to S_2 represents a *decrease in supply*.

Variables That Shift Market Supply

The following are the most important variables that shift market supply:

- Prices of inputs
- Technological change
- Prices of substitutes in production
- Number of firms in the market
- Expected future prices

We next discuss how changes in each of these variables affect the market supply curve.

Prices of Inputs The factor most likely to cause the supply curve for a product to shift is a change in the price of an *input*. An input is anything used in the production of a good or service. For instance, if the price of a component of smartphones, such as memory chips, rises, the cost of producing smartphones will increase, and smartphones will be less profitable at every price. The supply of smartphones will decline, and the market supply curve for smartphones will shift to the left. Similarly, if the price of an input declines, the supply of smartphones will increase, and the market supply curve will shift to the right.

Technological change A positive or negative change in the ability of a firm to produce a given level of output with a given quantity of inputs.

Technological Change A second factor that causes a change in supply is **technological change**, which is a positive or negative change in the ability of a firm to produce a given level of output with a given quantity of inputs. Positive technological change occurs whenever a firm is able to produce more output using the same amount of inputs. In other words, the *productivity* of the firm's workers or machines has increased. If a firm can produce more output with the same amount of inputs, its costs will be lower, and the good will be more profitable to produce at any given price. As a result, when positive technological change occurs, the firm will increase the quantity supplied at every price, and its supply curve will shift to the right.

Negative technological change is relatively rare, although it could result from an earthquake or another natural disaster or from a war that reduces the ability of firms to supply as much output with a given amount of inputs. Negative technological change will raise firms' costs, and firms will earn lower profits from producing the good. Therefore, negative technological change will cause the market supply curve to shift to the left.

Prices of Substitutes in Production Firms often choose which good or service they will produce. Alternative products that a firm could produce are called *substitutes in production*. Many of the firms that produce smartphones also produce other consumer electronics. For example, Apple produces the iPad and Samsung produces the Galaxy Tab. These products typically use similar components and are often assembled in the same factories. If the price of smartphones increases relative to the price of tablet computers, smartphones will become more profitable, and Apple, Samsung, and other firms making smartphones will shift some of their productive capacity from tablets toward smartphones. The firms will offer more smartphones for sale at every price, so the supply curve for smartphones will shift to the right.

Number of Firms in the Market A change in the number of firms in the market will change supply. When new firms *enter* a market, the supply curve shifts to the right, and when existing firms leave, or *exit*, a market, the supply curve shifts to the left. In 2013, for instance, Amazon was widely expected to enter the market for smartphones. Amazon's entry will shift the market supply curve for smartphones to the right.

Expected Future Prices If a firm expects that the price of its product will be higher in the future, it has an incentive to decrease supply now and increase it in the future. For instance, if Apple believes that prices for smartphones are temporarily low—perhaps because of a recession—it may store some of its production today to sell later on, when it expects prices to be higher.

Table 3.2

Variables That Shift Market Supply Curves

An increase in ...	shifts the supply curve ...	because ...
the price of an input	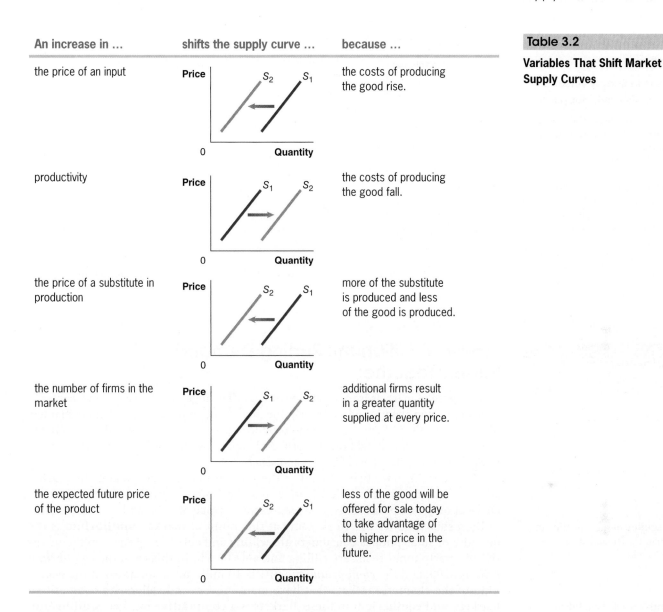	the costs of producing the good rise.
productivity		the costs of producing the good fall.
the price of a substitute in production		more of the substitute is produced and less of the good is produced.
the number of firms in the market		additional firms result in a greater quantity supplied at every price.
the expected future price of the product		less of the good will be offered for sale today to take advantage of the higher price in the future.

Table 3.2 summarizes the most important variables that cause market supply curves to shift. Note that the table shows the shift in the supply curve that results from an *increase* in each of the variables. A *decrease* in these variables would cause the supply curve to shift in the opposite direction.   MyEconLab Concept Check

A Change in Supply versus a Change in Quantity Supplied

We noted earlier the important difference between a change in demand and a change in quantity demanded. There is a similar difference between a *change in supply* and a *change in quantity supplied*. A change in supply refers to a shift of the supply curve. The supply curve will shift when there is a change in one of the variables—*other than the price of the product*—that affects the willingness of suppliers to sell the product. A change in quantity supplied refers to a movement along the supply curve as a result of a change in the product's price. Figure 3.6 illustrates this important distinction. If the price of smartphones rises from $200 to $250, the result will be a movement up the supply curve from point *A* to point *B*—an increase in quantity supplied from 10 million to 11 million. If the price of an input decreases, or if another factor changes that causes sellers to supply more of a product at every price, the supply curve will shift to the right—an increase in supply. In this case, the increase in supply from S_1 to S_2 causes the quantity of smartphones supplied at a price of $250 to increase from 11 million at point *B* to 13 million at point *C*.   MyEconLab Concept Check

MyEconLab Animation

Figure 3.6

A Change in Supply versus a Change in Quantity Supplied

If the price of smartphones rises from $200 to $250, the result will be a movement up the supply curve from point A to point B—an increase in quantity supplied by Apple, Samsung, Nokia, and other firms from 10 million to 11 million. If the price of an input decreases, or if another factor changes that causes sellers to supply more of the product at every price, the supply curve will shift to the right—an increase in supply. In this case, the increase in supply from S_1 to S_2 causes the quantity of smartphones supplied at a price of $250 to increase from 11 million at point B to 13 million at point C.

MyEconLab Study Plan

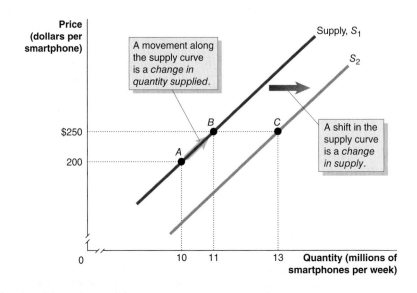

3.3 LEARNING OBJECTIVE

Use a graph to illustrate market equilibrium.

Market equilibrium A situation in which quantity demanded equals quantity supplied.

Competitive market equilibrium A market equilibrium with many buyers and sellers.

Market Equilibrium: Putting Demand and Supply Together

The purpose of markets is to bring buyers and sellers together. As we saw in Chapter 2, instead of being chaotic and disorderly, the interaction of buyers and sellers in markets ultimately results in firms being led to produce the goods and services that consumers want most. To understand how this process happens, we first need to see how markets work to reconcile the plans of buyers and sellers.

In Figure 3.7, we bring together the market demand curve and the market supply curve for smartphones. Notice that the demand curve crosses the supply curve at only one point. This point represents a price of $200 and a quantity of 10 million smartphones per week. Only at this point of **market equilibrium** is the quantity of smartphones consumers are willing and able to buy equal to the quantity of smartphones firms are willing and able to sell. In this case, the *equilibrium price* is $200, and the *equilibrium quantity* is 10 million. As we noted at the beginning of the chapter, markets that have many buyers and sellers are competitive markets, and equilibrium in these markets is a **competitive market equilibrium**. In the market for smartphones, there are many buyers but only about 20 firms. Whether 20 firms are enough for our model of demand and supply to apply to this

MyEconLab Animation

Figure 3.7

Market Equilibrium

Where the demand curve crosses the supply curve determines market equilibrium. In this case, the demand curve for smartphones crosses the supply curve at a price of $200 and a quantity of 10 million smartphones. Only at this point is the quantity of smartphones consumers are willing to buy equal to the quantity that Apple, Samsung, LG, and other firms are willing to sell: The quantity demanded is equal to the quantity supplied.

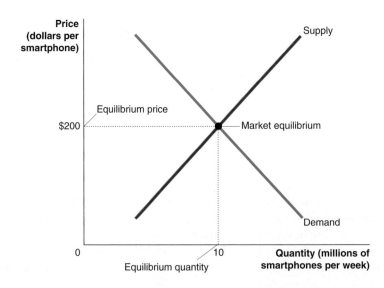

market is a matter of judgment. In this chapter, we are assuming that the market for smartphones has enough sellers to be competitive.

How Markets Eliminate Surpluses and Shortages

A market that is not in equilibrium moves toward equilibrium. Once a market is in equilibrium, it remains in equilibrium. To see why, consider what happens if a market is not in equilibrium. Suppose that the price in the market for smartphones was $250 rather than the equilibrium price of $200. As Figure 3.8 shows, at a price of $250, the quantity of smartphones supplied would be 11 million, and the quantity of smartphones demanded would be 9 million. When the quantity supplied is greater than the quantity demanded, there is a **surplus** in the market. In this case, the surplus is equal to 2 million smartphones (11 million − 9 million = 2 million). When there is a surplus, firms will have unsold goods piling up, which gives them an incentive to increase their sales by cutting the price. Cutting the price will simultaneously increase the quantity demanded and decrease the quantity supplied. This adjustment will reduce the surplus, but as long as the price is above $200, there will be a surplus, and downward pressure on the price will continue. Only when the price falls to $200 will the market be in equilibrium.

If, however, the price were $100, the quantity demanded would be 12 million, and the quantity supplied would be 8 million, as shown in Figure 3.8. When the quantity demanded is greater than the quantity supplied, there is a **shortage** in the market. In this case, the shortage is equal to 4 million smartphones (12 million − 8 million = 4 million). When a shortage occurs, some consumers will be unable to buy smartphones at the current price. In this situation, firms will realize that they can raise the price without losing sales. A higher price will simultaneously increase the quantity supplied and decrease the quantity demanded. This adjustment will reduce the shortage, but as long as the price is below $200, there will be a shortage, and upward pressure on the price will continue. Only when the price rises to $200 will the market be in equilibrium.

At a competitive market equilibrium, all consumers willing to pay the market price will be able to buy as much of the product as they want, and all firms willing to accept the market price will be able to sell as much of the product as they want. As a result, there will be no reason for the price to change unless either the demand curve or the supply curve shifts.

MyEconLab Concept Check

Surplus A situation in which the quantity supplied is greater than the quantity demanded.

Shortage A situation in which the quantity demanded is greater than the quantity supplied.

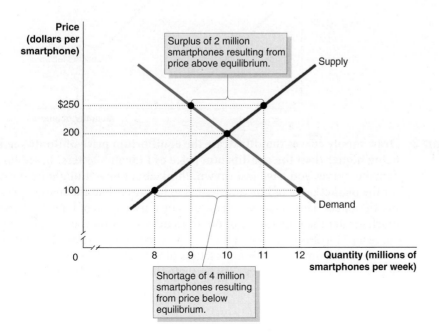

MyEconLab Animation

Figure 3.8

The Effect of Surpluses and Shortages on the Market Price

When the market price is above equilibrium, there will be a *surplus*. A price of $250 for smartphones results in 11 million smartphones being supplied but only 9 million being demanded, or a surplus of 2 million. As Apple, Nokia, LG, and other firms cut the price to dispose of the surplus, the price will fall to the equilibrium of $200. When the market price is below equilibrium, there will be a *shortage*. A price of $100 results in 12 million smartphones being demanded but only 8 million being supplied, or a shortage of 4 million. As firms find that consumers who are unable to find smartphones available for sale are willing to pay higher prices to get them, the price will rise to the equilibrium of $200.

Demand and Supply Both Count

Keep in mind that the interaction of demand and supply determines the equilibrium price. Neither consumers nor firms can dictate what the equilibrium price will be. No firm can sell anything at any price unless it can find a willing buyer, and no consumer can buy anything at any price without finding a willing seller. MyEconLab Concept Check

Solved Problem 3.3

MyEconLab Interactive Animation

Demand and Supply Both Count: A Tale of Two Letters

Which letter is likely to be worth more: one written by Abraham Lincoln or one written by his assassin, John Wilkes Booth? Lincoln is one of the greatest presidents, and many people collect anything he wrote. The demand for letters written by Lincoln surely would seem to be much greater than the demand for letters written by Booth. Yet, when R.M. Smythe and Co. auctioned off on the same day a letter written by Lincoln and a letter written by Booth, the Booth letter sold for $31,050, and the Lincoln letter sold for only $21,850. Use a demand and supply graph to explain how the Booth letter has a higher market price than the Lincoln letter, even though the demand for letters written by Lincoln is greater than the demand for letters written by Booth.

Solving the Problem

Step 1: **Review the chapter material.** This problem is about prices being determined at market equilibrium, so you may want to review the section "Market Equilibrium: Putting Demand and Supply Together," which begins on page 82.

Step 2: **Draw demand curves that illustrate the greater demand for Lincoln's letters.** Begin by drawing two demand curves. Label one "Demand for Lincoln's letters" and the other "Demand for Booth's letters." Make sure that the Lincoln demand curve is much farther to the right than the Booth demand curve.

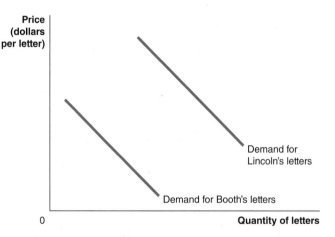

Step 3: **Draw supply curves that illustrate the equilibrium price of Booth's letters being higher than the equilibrium price of Lincoln's letters.** Based on the demand curves you have just drawn, think about how it might be possible for the market price of Lincoln's letters to be lower than the market price of Booth's letters. This outcome can occur only if the supply of Lincoln's letters is much greater than the supply of Booth's letters. Draw on your graph a supply curve for Lincoln's letters and a supply curve for Booth's letters that will result in an equilibrium price of Booth's letters of $31,050 and an equilibrium price of Lincoln's letters of $21,850. You have now solved the problem.

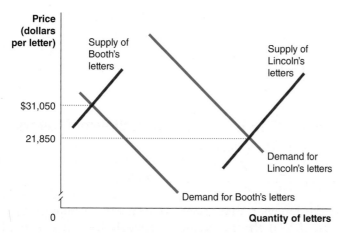

Extra Credit: The explanation for this puzzle is that both demand and supply count when determining market price. The demand for Lincoln's letters is much greater than the demand for Booth's letters, but the supply of Booth's letters is very small. Historians believe that only eight letters written by Booth exist today. (Note that the supply curves for letters written by Booth and by Lincoln are upward sloping, even though only a fixed number of each of these letters is available and, obviously, no more can be produced. The upward slope of the supply curves occurs because the higher the price, the larger the quantity of letters that will be offered for sale by people who currently own them.)

Your Turn: For more practice, do related problems 3.5, 3.6, and 3.7 on pages 96–97 at the end of this chapter.

MyEconLab Study Plan

The Effect of Demand and Supply Shifts on Equilibrium

3.4 LEARNING OBJECTIVE

Use demand and supply graphs to predict changes in prices and quantities.

We have seen that the interaction of demand and supply in markets determines the quantity of a good that is produced and the price at which it is sold. We have also seen that several variables cause demand curves to shift and other variables cause supply curves to shift. As a result, demand and supply curves in most markets are constantly shifting, and the prices and quantities that represent equilibrium are constantly changing. In this section, we look at how shifts in demand and supply curves affect equilibrium price and quantity.

The Effect of Shifts in Supply on Equilibrium

If Amazon enters the market for smartphones, the market supply curve for smartphones will shift to the right. Figure 3.9 shows the supply curve shifting from S_1 to S_2.

MyEconLab Animation

Figure 3.9

The Effect of an Increase in Supply on Equilibrium

If a firm enters a market, as Amazon is expected to enter the market for smartphones, the equilibrium price will fall, and the equilibrium quantity will rise:

1. As Amazon enters the market for smartphones, a larger quantity of smartphones will be supplied at every price, so the market supply curve shifts to the right, from S_1 to S_2, which causes a surplus of smartphones at the original price, P_1.

2. The equilibrium price falls from P_1 to P_2.

3. The equilibrium quantity rises from Q_1 to Q_2.

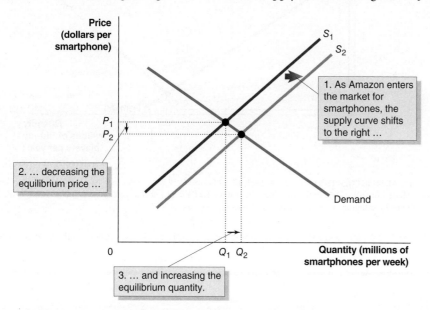

When the supply curve shifts to the right, there will be a surplus at the original equilibrium price, P_1. The surplus is eliminated as the equilibrium price falls to P_2, and the equilibrium quantity rises from Q_1 to Q_2. If an existing firm exits the market, the supply curve will shift to the left, causing the equilibrium price to rise and the equilibrium quantity to fall.

MyEconLab Concept Check

Making the Connection

MyEconLab Video

The Falling Price of Blu-ray Players

The technology for playing prerecorded movies has progressed rapidly during the past 30 years. Video cassette recorders (VCRs) were introduced in Japan in 1976 and in the United States in 1977. As the first way of recording TV programs or playing prerecorded movies, VHS players were immensely popular. In 1997, though, digital video disc (DVD) players became available in the United States. DVDs could store more information than could the VHS tapes played on VCRs and could produce a crisper picture. Within a few years, sales of DVD players were greater than sales of VCRs, and by 2006 the movie studios had stopped releasing films on VHS tapes. In 2006, Blu-ray players were introduced. Because Blu-ray discs can store up to 50 gigabytes of data, compared with fewer than 5 gigabytes on a typical DVD, Blu-ray players can reproduce high-definition images that DVD players cannot.

When firms began selling VCRs, DVD players, and Blu-ray players, they initially charged high prices that declined rapidly within a few years. As this figure shows, the average price of a Blu-ray player was about $800 in May 2006, but it had declined to about $95 in 2013. Sales of Blu-ray players rose from about 425,000 in 2006 to 13.3 million in 2013. The figure shows that the decline in price and increase in quantity resulted from a large shift to the right of the supply curve. The supply curve in 2013 was much farther to the right than the supply curve in 2006 for two reasons: First, after Samsung introduced the first Blu-ray player—at a price of $999—other firms entered the industry, increasing the quantity supplied at every price. Second, the prices of the parts used in manufacturing Blu-ray players, particularly the laser components, declined sharply. As the cost of manufacturing the players declined, the quantity supplied at every price increased.

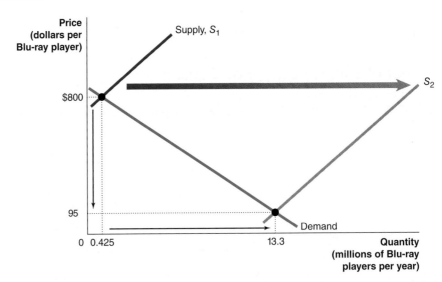

Source: Sarah McBride, "New DVD Players Resolve Battle of Formats," *Wall Street Journal*, January 4, 2007; Yukari Iwatani Kane and Miguel Bustillo, "Dreaming of a Blu Christmas," *Wall Street Journal*, December 23, 2009; and "DEG 2012 Year-End Home Entertainment Report," www.degonline.org.

MyEconLab Study Plan

Your Turn: Test your understanding by doing related problem 4.5 on page 97 at the end of this chapter.

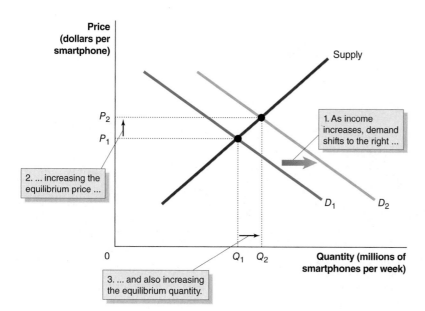

MyEconLab Animation

Figure 3.10

The Effect of an Increase in Demand on Equilibrium

Increases in income will cause the equilibrium price and quantity to rise:

1. Because smartphones are a normal good, as income increases, the quantity demanded increases at every price, and the market demand curve shifts to the right, from D_1 to D_2, which causes a shortage of smartphones at the original price, P_1.
2. The equilibrium price rises from P_1 to P_2.
3. The equilibrium quantity rises from Q_1 to Q_2.

The Effect of Shifts in Demand on Equilibrium

Because smartphones are a normal good, when incomes increase, the market demand curve shifts to the right. Figure 3.10 shows the effect of a demand curve shifting to the right, from D_1 to D_2. This shift causes a shortage at the original equilibrium price, P_1. To eliminate the shortage, the equilibrium price rises to P_2, and the equilibrium quantity rises from Q_1 to Q_2. In contrast, if the price of a substitute good, such as tablet computers, were to fall, the demand for smartphones would decrease, shifting the demand curve to the left. When the demand curve shifts to the left, both the equilibrium price and quantity will decrease.   MyEconLab Concept Check

The Effect of Shifts in Demand and Supply over Time

Whenever only demand or only supply shifts, we can easily predict the effect on equilibrium price and quantity. But, what happens if *both* curves shift? For instance, in many markets, the demand curve shifts to the right over time as population and income increase. The supply curve also often shifts to the right as new firms enter the market and positive technological change occurs. Whether the equilibrium price in a market rises or falls over time depends on whether demand shifts to the right more than does supply. Panel (a) of Figure 3.11 shows that when demand shifts to the right more than supply, the equilibrium price rises, while panel (b) shows that when supply shifts to the right more than demand, the equilibrium price falls.

Table 3.3 summarizes all possible combinations of shifts in demand and supply over time and the effects of the shifts on equilibrium price (*P*) and quantity (*Q*). For example, the entry in red in the table shows that if the demand curve shifts to the right and the supply curve also shifts to the right, the equilibrium quantity will increase, while the equilibrium price may increase, decrease, or remain unchanged. To make sure you understand each entry in the table, draw demand and supply graphs to check whether you can reproduce the predicted changes in equilibrium price and quantity. If the entry in the table says the predicted change in equilibrium price or quantity can be either an increase or a decrease, draw two graphs similar to panels (a) and (b) of Figure 3.11, one showing the equilibrium price or quantity increasing and the other showing it decreasing. Note also that in the ambiguous cases where either price or quantity might increase or decrease, it is also possible that price or quantity might remain unchanged. Be sure you understand why this is true.   MyEconLab Concept Check

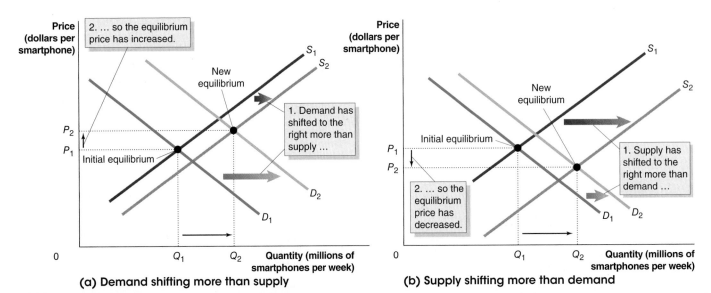

MyEconLab Animation

Figure 3.11   Shifts in Demand and Supply over Time

Whether the price of a product rises or falls over time depends on whether demand shifts to the right more than supply.

In panel (a), demand shifts to the right more than supply, and the equilibrium price rises:
1. Demand shifts to the right more than supply.
2. The equilibrium price rises from P_1 to P_2.

In panel (b), supply shifts to the right more than demand, and the equilibrium price falls:
1. Supply shifts to the right more than demand.
2. The equilibrium price falls from P_1 to P_2.

Table 3.3 **How Shifts in Demand and Supply Affect Equilibrium Price (P) and Quantity (Q)**		**Supply Curve Unchanged**	**Supply Curve Shifts to the Right**	**Supply Curve Shifts to the Left**
	Demand Curve Unchanged	Q unchanged P unchanged	Q increases P decreases	Q decreases P increases
	Demand Curve Shifts to the Right	Q increases P increases	Q increases P increases or decreases	Q increases or decreases P increases
	Demand Curve Shifts to the Left	Q decreases P decreases	Q increases or decreases P decreases	Q decreases P increases or decreases

Solved Problem 3.4

MyEconLab Interactive Animation

What Has Caused the Decline in Beef Consumption?

Whether you like to eat hamburger or roast beef, the source of the meat is a farmer who raises cattle. An article in the *New York Times* discussed how the cost to farmers of raising cattle for beef had been increasing. At the same time, consumer tastes had been changing, leading to a decline in the demand for beef. Use demand and supply graphs to illustrate your answers to the following questions:

a. Can we use this information to be certain whether the equilibrium quantity of beef will increase or decrease?

b. Can we use this information to be certain whether the equilibrium price of beef will increase or decrease?

Solving the Problem

Step 1:   Review the chapter material. This problem is about how shifts in demand and supply curves affect the equilibrium price, so you may want to review the section "The Effect of Shifts in Demand and Supply over Time," which begins on page 87.

Step 2: **Answer part (a) using demand and supply analysis.** You are given the information that consumer tastes have changed, leading to a decline in demand for beef. So, the demand curve for beef has shifted to the left. You are also given the information that the cost of raising beef has increased. So, the supply curve for beef has also shifted to the left. The following graph shows both these shifts:

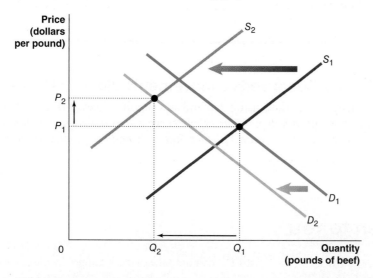

As Table 3.3 summarizes, if the demand curve and the supply curve both shift to the left, the equilibrium quantity must decrease. Therefore, we can answer part (a) by stating that we are certain that the equilibrium quantity of beef will decrease.

Step 3: **Answer part (b) using demand and supply analysis.** The graph we drew in Step 2 showed the equilibrium price of beef increasing. But given the information provided, the following graph would also be correct:

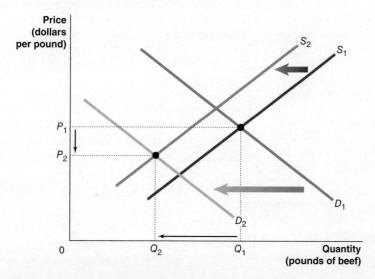

Unlike the graph in Step 2, which showed the equilibrium price increasing, this graph shows the equilibrium price decreasing. The uncertainty about whether the equilibrium price will increase or decrease is consistent with what we saw in Table 3.3 when the demand curve and the supply curve both shift to the left. Therefore, we can answer part (b) by stating that we cannot be certain whether the equilibrium price of beef will increase or decrease.

Extra Credit: During 2012 and 2013, the equilibrium quantity of beef decreased while the equilibrium price of beef increased. We can conclude that *both* the decrease in demand for beef and the decrease in the supply of beef contributed to the decline in beef consumption. That the price of beef rose indicates that the decrease in supply had a larger effect on equilibrium in the beef market than did the decrease in demand.

Sources: Theopolis Waters, "US Beef Prices Set New High as Spring Barbecue Season Heats Up," www.reuters.com, May 3, 2013; and Mark Bittman, "We're Eating Less Meat. Why?" *New York Times*, January 10, 2012.

MyEconLab Study Plan

Your Turn: For more practice, do related problems 4.6, 4.7, and 4.8 on page 98 at the end of this chapter.

Shifts in a Curve versus Movements along a Curve

When analyzing markets using demand and supply curves, it is important to remember that *when a shift in a demand or supply curve causes a change in equilibrium price, the change in price does not cause a further shift in demand or supply.* Suppose an increase in

Don't Let This Happen to You

Remember: A Change in a Good's Price Does *Not* Cause the Demand or Supply Curve to Shift

Suppose a student is asked to draw a demand and supply graph to illustrate how an increase in the price of oranges would affect the market for apples, with other variables being constant. He draws the graph on the left and explains it as follows: "Because apples and oranges are substitutes, an increase in the price of oranges will cause an initial shift to the right in the demand curve for apples, from D_1 to D_2. However, because this initial shift in the demand curve for apples results in a higher price for apples, P_2, consumers will find apples less desirable, and the demand curve will shift to the left, from D_2 to D_3, resulting in a final equilibrium price of P_3." Do you agree or disagree with the student's analysis?

You should disagree. The student has correctly understood that an increase in the price of oranges will cause the demand curve for apples to shift to the right. But, the second demand curve shift the student describes, from D_2

to D_3, will not take place. Changes in the price of a product do not result in shifts in the product's demand curve. Changes in the price of a product result only in movements along a demand curve.

The graph on the right shows the correct analysis. The increase in the price of oranges causes the demand curve for apples to increase from D_1 to D_2. At the original price, P_1, the increase in demand initially results in a shortage of apples equal to $Q_3 - Q_1$. But, as we have seen, a shortage causes the price to increase until the shortage is eliminated. In this case, the price will rise to P_2, where both the quantity demanded and the quantity supplied are equal to Q_2. Notice that the increase in price causes a decrease in the *quantity demanded*, from Q_3 to Q_2, but does *not* cause a decrease in demand.

MyEconLab Study Plan

Your Turn: Test your understanding by doing related problems 4.13 and 4.14 on pages 98–99 at the end of this chapter.

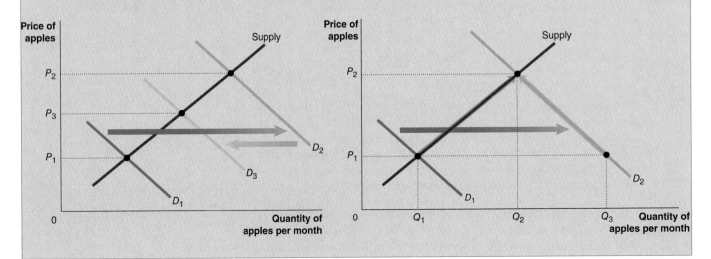

supply causes the price of a good to fall, while everything else that affects the willingness of consumers to buy the good is constant. The result will be an increase in the quantity demanded but not an increase in demand. For demand to increase, the whole curve must shift. The point is the same for supply: If the price of the good falls but everything else that affects the willingness of sellers to supply the good is constant, the quantity supplied decreases, but the supply does not. For supply to decrease, the whole curve must shift.

MyEconLab Concept Check   MyEconLab Study Plan

Continued from page 69

Economics in Your Life

Will You Buy an Apple iPhone or a Samsung Galaxy?

At the beginning of this chapter, we asked you to consider two questions: Would you choose to buy a Samsung Galaxy S if it had a lower price than a comparable Apple iPhone? and Would your decision be affected if your income increased? To determine the answer to the first question, you have to recognize that the iPhone and the Galaxy S are substitutes. If you consider the two smartphones to be close substitutes, then you are likely to buy the one with the lower price. In the market, if consumers generally believe that the iPhone and the Galaxy S are close substitutes, a fall in the price of the iPhone will increase the quantity of iPhones demanded and decrease the demand for Galaxy Ss. Suppose that you are currently leaning toward buying the Galaxy S because its price is lower than the price of the iPhone. If an increase in your income would cause you to change your decision and buy the iPhone, then the Galaxy S is an inferior good for you.

Conclusion

The interaction of demand and supply determines market equilibrium. The model of demand and supply is a powerful tool for predicting how changes in the actions of consumers and firms will cause changes in equilibrium prices and quantities. As we have seen in this chapter, we can use the model to analyze markets that do not meet all the requirements for being perfectly competitive. As long as there is intense competition among sellers, the model of demand and supply can often successfully predict changes in prices and quantities. We will use this model in the next chapter to analyze economic efficiency and the results of government-imposed price floors and price ceilings.

Before moving on to Chapter 4, read *An Inside Look* on the next page for a discussion of how Google dealt with the problem of not having enough of its Nexus 4 smartphones to meet customer demand, and how Apple dealt with overproduction of its iPhone 5.

Google and Apple Face Supply and Demand Concerns in the Smartphone Market

MOTLEY FOOL

Google's Smartphone Production Problems

Predicting mobile computing sales is a tough one, especially when rolling out a relatively new product. Unless the production numbers match sales expectations perfectly, investors are going to be disappointed. Just ask **Apple** (NASDAQ: AAPL).

(a) On Monday [January 14, 2013], Apple cut orders from its iPhone 5 manufacturers by as much as half due to lack of demand. Forget that production changes often occur after the busy holiday shopping season, or that Apple could have previously placed massive orders to adjust supply chain problems with its new iPhone, or any other fair reason. Investors weren't interested. Apple stock proceeded to drop over 3%, and remains below $500 a share.

Google (NASDAQ: GOOG) and its Nexus 4 smartphone partner LG have found themselves in a similar situation as Apple, though on the opposite end of the spectrum. The problem for Google is too much demand internationally for its low-cost smartphone. It took all of 20 minutes for Google's Play store to sell out of what was then its new Nexus 4 for the international market, and the backlog of orders isn't improving.

He said, she said

(b) In response to concerns about production keeping up with Nexus 4 demand, a director in Google's U.K. offices said, "Supplies with the manufacturer [LG] are erratic," not exactly a glowing recommendation for LG. One estimate put the number of Google Nexus 4 sales since its release a couple of months ago at 370,000; not bad, but paltry compared to Apple and Samsung numbers. So, when in doubt, apparently you blame the supplier.

However, LG isn't taking Google's insinuations about production problems lying down. In a recent interview, an LG executive pulled no punches when asked what the problems were in keeping Nexus 4 phones in stock. According to the LG exec, Google underestimated demand, particularly in the U.K. and Germany, by as much as 10 times the number of Nexus 4's needed to fill orders.

The price for being wrong

The impact of its Nexus 4 supply issues on Google's bottom line will be negligible when it announces earnings Jan. 22. The Nexus is, after all, relatively new to market and Google certainly has other sources of revenue. But Google's inability to meet demand will hurt its share price in the near term, but will be little more than a hiccup in the overall scheme of things.

(c) The flip side of Google's production issue is Apple. According to estimates, Apple sold around 50 million smartphones in the recently completed Q4 of 2012. But because of declining sales expectations this quarter, Apple cut component deliveries and its share price got beaten down. Can you imagine if Apple planned for 40 million units, and were then forced to announce a ramp-up in production to meet demand for 10 more million iPhones? You can bet share prices would have soared.

Is it any wonder **Microsoft** (NASDAQ: MSFT) hasn't released sales data for its Surface tablet, or why it was initially rolled out on such a minimal basis, with temporary retail outlets? If Microsoft CEO Steve Ballmer had shot for the moon relative to Surface sales, and didn't meet those lofty expectations, he'd feel the wrath of shareholders all the way up in Redmond, Wa. Of course, if Ballmer undershot expectations, and then was having production difficulty filling orders, shareholders would again be on the warpath.

When it's said and done, supply and demand forecasting isn't an exact science. Sure, there's information that can be gleaned from changes in orders and amounts, but let's keep it in perspective. Do Google's issues with LG threaten to derail the online leader? Of course not. Take the 4% drop in Google's share price the past week for what it is: an opportunity.

Source: Tim Brugger, "Google's Smartphone Production Problems," *Motley Fool*, January 18, 2013.

Key Points in the Article

The demand for Google's Nexus 4 smartphone and the production problems prevented the company from supplying enough of the product to fill its orders. Google blamed the shortage on the phone's manufacturer, LG, while LG executives claimed that Google severely underestimated demand for the smartphone, especially in some European markets. Although Google was dealing with the problem of underproduction, Apple was worried about overproduction of its iPhone 5. In January 2013, Apple cut orders from its iPhone 5 manufacturers by as much as half due to falling demand. For both Google and Apple, the production issues resulted in declines in the companies' stock prices.

Analyzing the News

ⓐ At the beginning of 2013, Apple and Google found themselves dealing with significant, but different, demand and supply issues. Apple reduced its orders of iPhone 5s from its manufacturers by as much as 50 percent due to insufficient demand, while Google sought ways to increase production of its Nexus 4 due to high demand. Both companies misjudged the demand for their smartphones. Figure 1 below shows a decrease in demand as a shift to the left of the demand curve from D_1 to D_3, which illustrates the situation Apple faced for its iPhone 5. All else equal, a decrease in demand would decrease equilibrium price from P_1 to P_3 and decrease equilibrium quantity from Q_1 to Q_3. Google faced an increase in demand for the Nexus 4, which is represented in Figure 1 by a shift to the right of the demand curve from D_1 to D_2. All else equal, an increase in demand would increase equilibrium price from P_1 to P_2 and increase equilibrium quantity from Q_1 to Q_2.

ⓑ On the supply side, Google blamed the Nexus 4 manufacturer, LG, for not being able to supply enough product, and LG blamed Google for underestimating Nexus 4 sales. Regardless of which company was ultimately at fault, Google needed to increase the supply of its smartphones to meet the growing demand. By blaming Google for the supply problem, the executives at LG implied that their company had the capability of producing enough smartphones to cover the backlog of orders, so increasing the supply of Nexus 4 phones would apparently not be an issue on the manufacturing end. An increase in supply, which Google needed, is represented in Figure 2 by a shift from S_1 to S_2. All else equal, an increase in supply would decrease the equilibrium price from P_1 to P_3 and increase the equilibrium quantity from Q_1 to Q_2.

ⓒ Apple expected sales of its iPhone 5 to decline in the first quarter of 2013 and chose to cut production of its smartphone in light of this expectation. A decrease in supply, such as Apple's reduction in production, is represented in Figure 2 by a shift from S_1 to S_3. All else equal, a decrease in supply would increase the equilibrium price from P_1 to P_2 and decrease the equilibrium quantity from Q_1 to Q_3.

Thinking Critically

1. Draw a demand and supply graph for the smartphone market. Show the change in the equilibrium price and quantity after Amazon enters the market by selling a smartphone.

2. Suppose that the federal government starts a new program that offers to reimburse low-income people for half the price of a new smartphone. Use a demand and supply graph of the smartphone market to show the effect on equilibrium price and quantity as a result of Amazon entering the market and the government beginning this program. Can we be sure whether the equilibrium quantity of smartphones will increase? Can we be sure whether the equilibrium price of smartphones will increase? Briefly explain.

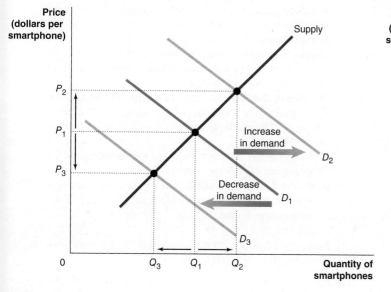

MyEconLab Animation

Figure 1

An increase in demand for smartphones shifts the demand curve to the right. All else equal, equilibrium price and equilibrium quantity both increase. A decrease in demand would have the opposite effect.

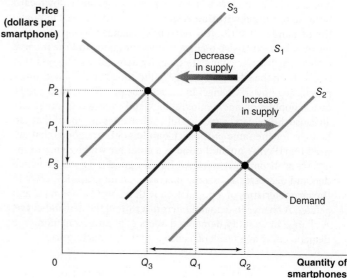

MyEconLab Animation

Figure 2

An increase in supply of smartphones shifts the supply curve to the right. All else equal, equilibrium price decreases and equilibrium quantity increases. A decrease in supply would have the opposite effect.

Chapter Summary and Problems

Key Terms

Ceteris paribus ("all else equal") condition, p. 72

Competitive market equilibrium, p. 82

Complements, p. 74

Demand curve, p. 70

Demand schedule, p. 70

Demographics, p. 74

Income effect, p. 71

Inferior good, p. 73

Law of demand, p. 71

Law of supply, p. 79

Market demand, p. 70

Market equilibrium, p. 82

Normal good, p. 72

Perfectly competitive market, p. 70

Quantity demanded, p. 70

Quantity supplied, p. 78

Shortage, p. 83

Substitutes, p. 73

Substitution effect, p. 71

Supply curve, p. 78

Supply schedule, p. 78

Surplus, p. 83

Technological change, p. 80

3.1 **The Demand Side of the Market, pages 70–78**
LEARNING OBJECTIVE: Discuss the variables that influence demand.

Summary

The model of demand and supply is the most powerful tool in economics. The model applies exactly only to **perfectly competitive markets**, where there are many buyers and sellers, all the products sold are identical, and there are no barriers to new sellers entering the market. But, the model can also be useful in analyzing markets that don't meet all these requirements. The **quantity demanded** is the amount of a good or service that a consumer is willing and able to purchase at a given price. A **demand schedule** is a table that shows the relationship between the price of a product and the quantity of the product demanded. A **demand curve** is a graph that shows the relationship between the price of a product and the quantity of the product demanded. **Market demand** is the demand by all consumers of a given good or service. The **law of demand** states that *ceteris paribus*—holding everything else constant—the quantity of a product demanded increases when the price falls and decreases when the price rises. Demand curves slope downward because of the **substitution effect**, which is the change in quantity demanded that results from a price change making one good more or less expensive relative to another good, and the income effect, which is the change in quantity demanded of a good that results from the effect of a change in the good's price on consumer purchasing power. Changes in income, the prices of related goods, tastes, population and demographics, and expected future prices all cause the demand curve to shift. **Substitutes** are goods that can be used for the same purpose. **Complements** are goods that are used together. A **normal good** is a good for which demand increases as income increases. An **inferior good** is a good for which demand decreases as income increases. **Demographics** refers to the characteristics of a population with respect to age, race, and gender. A change in demand refers to a shift of the demand curve. A change in quantity demanded refers to a movement along the demand curve as a result of a change in the product's price.

MyEconLab   Visit **www.myeconlab.com** to complete these exercises online and get instant feedback.

Review Questions

1.1 What is a demand schedule? What is a demand curve?

1.2 What do economists mean when they use the Latin expression *ceteris paribus*?

1.3 What is the difference between a change in demand and a change in quantity demanded?

1.4 What is the law of demand? Use the substitution effect and the income effect to explain why an increase in the price of a product causes a decrease in the quantity demanded.

1.5 What are the main variables that will cause the demand curve to shift? Give an example of each.

Problems and Applications

1.6 For each of the following pairs of products, state which are complements, which are substitutes, and which are unrelated.
  a. New cars and used cars
  b. Houses and washing machines
  c. UGG boots and Kindle e-readers
  d. iPads and Kindle e-readers

1.7 **[Related to the** Chapter Opener **on page 69]** When smartphones based on the Android operating system were first introduced, there were relatively few applications, or "apps," available for them. Now, there are many more apps available for Android-based smartphones. Are these apps substitutes or complements for smartphones? How has the increase in the availability of apps for these smartphones affected the demand for Apple iPhones? Briefly explain.

1.8 **[Related to the** Chapter Opener **on page 69]** Smart TVs, unlike traditional TVs, can connect directly to the Internet. Smart TVs made up 27 percent of all televisions sold worldwide in 2012.
  a. Should smart TVs be considered a substitute good for smartphones? Briefly explain.
  b. If smart TVs are a substitute for smartphones, how would a decline in the price of smart TVs affect the demand curve for smartphones? Include a graph in your answer.

  Source: Greg Tarr, "Smart TVs Rise to 27% of TV Shipments," www.twice.com, February 21, 2013.

1.9 State whether each of the following events will result in a movement along the demand curve for McDonald's Big Mac hamburgers or whether it will cause the curve to shift. If the demand curve shifts, indicate whether it will shift to the left or to the right and draw a graph to illustrate the shift.
  a. The price of Burger King's Whopper hamburger declines.
  b. McDonald's distributes coupons for $1.00 off the purchase of a Big Mac.

c. Because of a shortage of potatoes, the price of French fries increases.

d. Fast-food restaurants post nutrition warning labels.

e. The U.S. economy enters a period of rapid growth in incomes.

1.10 Suppose that the following table shows the quantity demanded of UGG boots at five different prices in 2014 and 2015:

| Price | Quantity Demanded (thousands of pairs of boots) | |
	2014	2015
$160	5,000	4,000
170	4,500	3,500
180	4,000	3,000
190	3,500	2,500
200	3,000	2,000

Name two different variables that could cause the quantity demanded of UGG boots to change from 2014 to 2015 as indicated in the table.

1.11 Suppose that the curves in the following graph represent two demand curves for traditional wings (basket of six) at Buffalo Wild Wings. What would cause a movement from point *A* to point *B* on D_1? Name two variables that would cause a movement from point *A* to point *C*.

1.12 [Related to the Making the Connection **on page 73**] Are smartphones a closer substitute for tablet computers, such as the iPad, or for e-readers, such as the Kindle? Briefly explain.

1.13 [Related to the Making the Connection **on page 74**] Since 1979, China has had a policy that allows couples to have only one child. This policy has caused a change in the demographics of China. Between 1980 and 2011, the share of the population under age 14 decreased from 36 percent to 19 percent. And, as parents attempt to ensure that the lone child is a son, the number of newborn males relative to females has increased. Choose three goods and explain how the demand for them has been affected by China's one-child policy.

Sources: World Bank, *World Development Indicators*, May 2013; and "China's Family Planning: Illegal Children Will Be Confiscated" and "China's Population: Only and Lonely," *Economist*, July 21, 2011.

1.14 Suppose the following table shows the price of a base model Toyota Prius hybrid and the quantity of Priuses sold for three years. Do these data indicate that the demand curve for Priuses is upward sloping? Explain.

Year	Price	Quantity
2012	$31,880	35,265
2013	30,550	33,250
2014	33,250	36,466

1.15 The following statement appeared in an article in the *New York Times* on the effects of changes in college tuition: "Some private colleges said that applications actually increased when they bolstered prices, apparently because families equated higher prices with quality." If applications increased when these colleges raised the tuition price they charged, did these colleges face upward sloping demand curves? Briefly explain.

Source: Andrew Martin, "Colleges Expect Lower Enrollment," *New York Times*, January 10, 2013.

1.16 Richard Posner is a federal court judge who also writes on economic topics. A newspaper reporter summarized Posner's views on the effect of online bookstores and e-books on the demand for books:

> Posner's [argument] is that the disappearance of bookstores is to be celebrated and not mourned, partly because e-books and online stores will reduce the cost of books and thus drive up demand for them.

Do you agree with Posner's statement, as given by the reporter? Briefly explain.

Source: Christopher Shea, "Judge Posner Hails the Demise of Bookstores," *Wall Street Journal*, January 13, 2011.

1.17 [Related to the Making the Connection **on page 77**] An article in the *Wall Street Journal* in 2013 was titled "In India, iPhone Lags Far Behind." According to the article, the difficulty Apple was having selling iPhones in India was "no small matter as Apple's growth slows in the U.S. and other mature markets."

a. What does the article mean by "mature markets"?

b. Why would sales of iPhones be likely to be slower in mature markets than in countries such as India?

c. Would forecasting sales in mature markets be easier or harder than forecasting sales in countries such as India? Briefly explain.

Source: Dhanya Ann Thoppil, Amol Sharma, and Jessica E. Lessin, "In India, iPhone Lags Far Behind," *Wall Street Journal*, February 26, 2013.

3.2 | # The Supply Side of the Market, pages 78–82

LEARNING OBJECTIVE: Discuss the variables that influence supply.

Summary

The **quantity supplied** is the amount of a good that a firm is willing and able to supply at a given price. A **supply schedule** is a table that shows the relationship between the price of a product and the quantity of the product supplied. A **supply curve** is a curve that shows the relationship between the price of a product and the quantity of the product supplied. When the price of a product rises, producing the product is more profitable, and a greater amount will be supplied. The **law of supply** states that, holding everything else constant, the quantity of a product supplied increases when the price rises and decreases when the price falls. Changes in the prices of inputs, technology, the prices of substitutes in production, expected future prices, and the number of firms in a market all cause the supply curve to shift. **Technological change** is a positive or negative change in the ability of a firm to produce a given level of output with a given quantity of inputs. A change in supply refers to a shift of the supply curve. A change in quantity supplied refers to a movement along the supply curve as a result of a change in the product's price.

MyEconLab   Visit www.myeconlab.com to complete these exercises online and get instant feedback.

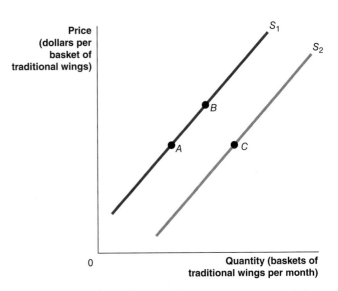

Review Questions

2.1 What is a supply schedule? What is a supply curve?

2.2 What is the difference between a change in supply and a change in the quantity supplied?

2.3 What is the law of supply? What are the main variables that will cause a supply curve to shift? Give an example of each.

Problems and Applications

2.4 Briefly explain whether each of the following statements describes a change in supply or a change in the quantity supplied:

   a. To take advantage of high prices for snow shovels during a snowy winter, Alexander Shovels, Inc., decides to increase output.

   b. The success of the Apple iPhone leads more firms to begin producing smartphones.

   c. In the six months following the Japanese earthquake and tsunami in 2011, production of automobiles in Japan declined by 20 percent.

2.5 Suppose that the curves in the following graph represent two supply curves for traditional wings (basket of six) at Buffalo Wild Wings. What would cause a movement from point A to point B on S_1? Name two variables that would cause a movement from point A to point C.

2.6 Suppose that the following table shows the quantity supplied of UGG boots at five different prices in 2014 and 2015:

Price	Quantity Supplied (thousands of pairs of boots)	
	2014	2015
$160	3,000	2,000
170	3,500	2,500
180	4,000	3,000
190	4,500	3,500
200	5,000	4,000

Name two different variables that would cause the quantity supplied of UGG boots to change from 2014 to 2015 as indicated in the table.

2.7 Will each firm in the smartphone industry always supply the same quantity as every other firm at each price? What factors might cause the quantity of smartphones supplied by different firms to be different at a particular price?

2.8 If the price of a good increases, is the increase in the quantity of the good supplied likely to be smaller or larger, the longer the time period being considered? Briefly explain.

3.3 ## Market Equilibrium: Putting Demand and Supply Together, pages 82–85

LEARNING OBJECTIVE: Use a graph to illustrate market equilibrium.

Summary

Market equilibrium occurs where the demand curve intersects the supply curve. A **competitive market equilibrium** has a market equilibrium with many buyers and sellers. Only at this point is the quantity demanded equal to the quantity supplied. Prices above equilibrium result in **surpluses**, with the quantity supplied being greater than the quantity demanded. Surpluses cause the market price to fall. Prices below equilibrium result in **shortages**, with the quantity demanded being greater than the quantity supplied. Shortages cause the market price to rise.

MyEconLab   Visit www.myeconlab.com to complete these exercises online and get instant feedback.

Review Questions

3.1 What do economists mean by *market equilibrium*?

3.2 What do economists mean by a *shortage*? By a *surplus*?

3.3 What happens in a market if the current price is above the equilibrium price? What happens if the current price is below the equilibrium price?

Problems and Applications

3.4 Briefly explain whether you agree with the following statement: "When there is a shortage of a good, consumers eventually give up trying to buy it, so the demand for the good declines, and the price falls until the market is finally in equilibrium."

3.5 **[Related to** Solved Problem 3.3 **on page 84]** In *The Wealth of Nations*, Adam Smith discussed what has come to be known as the "diamond and water paradox":

   Nothing is more useful than water: but it will purchase scarce anything; scarce anything can be had in exchange for it. A diamond, on the contrary, has scarce any value in use; but a very great quantity of other goods may frequently be had in exchange for it.

Graph the market for diamonds and the market for water. Show how it is possible for the price of water to be much lower than the price of diamonds, even though the demand for water is much greater than the demand for diamonds.

Source: Adam Smith, *An Inquiry into the Nature and Causes of the Wealth of Nations*, Vol. I, Oxford, UK: Oxford University Press, 1976; original edition, 1776.

3.6 **[Related to** Solved Problem 3.3 **on page 84]** An article discusses the market for autographs by Mickey Mantle, the superstar centerfielder for the New York Yankees during the 1950s and 1960s: "At card shows, golf outings, charity dinners, Mr. Mantle signed his name over and over." One expert on sport autographs is quoted as saying, "He was a real good signer.… He is not rare." Yet the article quotes another expert as saying, "Mr. Mantle's autograph ranks No. 3 of most-popular autographs, behind Babe Ruth and Muhammad Ali." A baseball signed by Mantle is likely to sell for the relatively high price of $250 to $400. By contrast, baseballs signed by Whitey Ford, a teammate of Mantle's on the Yankees, typically sell for less than $150. Use one graph to show both the demand and supply for autographs by Whitey Ford and the demand and supply for autographs by Mickey Mantle. Show how it is possible for the price of Mantle's autographs to be higher than the price of Ford's autographs, even though the supply of Mantle autographs is larger than the supply of Ford autographs.

Source: Beth DeCarbo, "Mantle Autographs Not Rare, but Collectors Don't Care," *Wall Street Journal*, August 4, 2008.

3.7 **[Related to** Solved Problem 3.3 **on page 84]** Comic book fans eagerly compete to buy copies of *Amazing Fantasy* No. 15, which contains the first appearance of the superhero Spider-Man. At the same time the publisher printed copies of the comic for the U.S. market, with the price printed on the cover in cents, it printed copies for the U.K. market, with the price printed on the cover in British pence. About 10 times as many U.S. copies of *Amazing Fantasy* No. 15 have survived as U.K. copies. Yet in auctions that occurred at about the same time in 2013, a U.S. copy sold for $29,000, while a U.K. copy in the same condition sold for only $10,755. Use a demand and supply graph to explain how the U.S. version of the comic has a higher price than the U.K. version, even though the supply of the U.S. version is so much greater than the supply of the U.K. version.

Source: Auction price data from: *GPA Analysis for CGC Comics*, www.comics.gpanalysis.com.

3.8 If a market is in equilibrium, is it necessarily true that all buyers and sellers are satisfied with the market price? Briefly explain.

3.9 During 2013, an article in the *Wall Street Journal* stated: "Steel prices have slumped this month, setting off a scramble among steelmakers to maintain prices … despite a nationwide glut."
   a. What does the article mean by a "glut"? What does a glut imply about the quantity demanded of steel relative to the quantity supplied?
   b. Why would steel prices slump if there is a glut in the steel market?
   c. Is it likely that steel companies would succeed in maintaining steel prices in the face of a glut in the market? Briefly explain.

Source: John W. Miller, "Steelmakers Pinched by Price Plunge," *Wall Street Journal*, April 26, 2013.

3.4 | The Effect of Demand and Supply Shifts on Equilibrium, pages 85–91

LEARNING OBJECTIVE: Use demand and supply graphs to predict changes in prices and quantities.

Summary

In most markets, demand and supply curves shift frequently, causing changes in equilibrium prices and quantities. Over time, if demand increases more than supply, equilibrium price will rise. If supply increases more than demand, equilibrium price will fall.

 MyEconLab   Visit www.myeconlab.com to complete these exercises online and get instant feedback.

Review Questions

4.1 Draw a demand and supply graph to show the effect on the equilibrium price in a market in the following situations:
   a. The demand curve shifts to the right.
   b. The supply curve shifts to the left.

4.2 If, over time, the demand curve for a product shifts to the right more than the supply curve does, what will happen to the equilibrium price? What will happen to the equilibrium price if the supply curve shifts to the right more than the demand curve? For each case, draw a demand and supply graph to illustrate your answer.

Problems and Applications

4.3 According to an article in the *Wall Street Journal*, one of the effects of an increase in the demand for corn was a decline in the number of U.S. farmers growing rice: "The number of acres dedicated to rice likely will decline 3% this spring compared with last year, to 2.61 million acres." Use a demand and supply graph to analyze the effect on the equilibrium price of rice resulting from the increase in the demand for corn.

Source: Owen Fletcher, "Farmers Lose Their Taste for Rice," *Wall Street Journal*, April 1, 2013.

4.4 According to an article on the wine market in the *Wall Street Journal*, "many farmers in recent years stopped planting new [grape] vines, and some even switched to nuts, vegetables and other fruit." But at the same time, "Americans kept drinking more wine." Use demand and supply graphs to illustrate your answers to the following questions:
   a. Can we use this information to be certain whether the equilibrium quantity of wine will increase or decrease?
   b. Can we use this information to be certain whether the equilibrium price of wine will increase or decrease?

Source: Mike Esterl, "Fewer Grapes, More Drinkers," *Wall Street Journal*, June 8, 2012.

4.5 **[Related to the** Making the Connection **on page 86]** More than half of homes in the United States are heated by burning natural gas. According to an article in the *Wall Street Journal*, demand for natural gas decreased during the winter of 2012 because of unusually warm weather. At the same time, "robust production [of natural gas] from U.S. shale fields has created record supplies." Use demand and supply graphs to illustrate your answers to the following questions:

a. Can we use this information to be certain whether the equilibrium quantity of natural gas increased or decreased?

b. Can we use this information to be certain whether the equilibrium price of natural gas increased or decreased?

Source: Christian Berthelsen, "Natural-Gas Futures Slide," *Wall Street Journal*, January 11, 2012.

4.6 **[Related to** Solved Problem 3.4 **on page 88]** The demand for watermelons is highest during summer and lowest during winter. Yet, watermelon prices are normally lower in summer than in winter. Use a demand and supply graph to demonstrate how this is possible. Be sure to carefully label the curves in your graph and to clearly indicate the equilibrium summer price and the equilibrium winter price.

4.7 **[Related to** Solved Problem 3.4 **on page 88]** According to one observer of the lobster market: "After Labor Day, when the vacationers have gone home, the lobstermen usually have a month or more of good fishing conditions, except for the occasional hurricane." Use a demand and supply graph to explain whether lobster prices are likely to be higher or lower during the fall than during the summer.

Source: Jay Harlow, "Lobster: An Affordable Luxury," www.Sallybernstein.com.

4.8 **[Related to** Solved Problem 3.4 **on page 88]** An article in the *Wall Street Journal* discussed the market for gasoline in the United States during the summer of 2013. Compared with the previous summer, the article stated that there will be "lower demand, as cars become more efficient" and "growth in oil production from hydraulic fracturing of shale deposits in the U.S."

a. Draw a demand and supply graph of the market for gasoline to analyze the situation described in this article. Be sure to indicate the equilibrium price and quantity of gasoline in the summer of 2012, the equilibrium price and quantity of gasoline in the summer of 2013, and any shifts in the demand curve and supply curve for gasoline.

b. Can you be certain from your analysis whether the equilibrium price of gasoline would increase or decrease? Can you be certain whether the equilibrium quantity of gasoline would increase or decrease? Briefly explain.

Source: Ángel González, "Drivers Can Expect a Break On Summer Gas Prices," *Wall Street Journal*, April 14, 2013.

4.9 Years ago, an apple producer argued that the United States should enact a tariff, or a tax, on imports of bananas. His reasoning was that "the enormous imports of cheap bananas into the United States tend to curtail the domestic consumption of fresh fruits produced in the United States."

a. Was the apple producer assuming that apples and bananas are substitutes or complements? Briefly explain.

b. If a tariff on bananas acts as an increase in the cost of supplying bananas in the United States, use two demand and supply graphs to show the effects of the apple producer's proposal. One graph should show the effect on the banana market in the United States, and the other graph should show the effect on the apple market in the United States. Be sure to label the change in equilibrium price and quantity in each market and any shifts in the demand and supply curves.

Source: Douglas A. Irwin, *Peddling Protectionism: Smoot-Hawley and the Great Depression*, Princeton, NJ: Princeton University Press, 2011, p. 22.

4.10 An article in the *Wall Street Journal* noted that the demand for video Internet advertising was increasing at the same time that the number of Internet sites accepting advertising was also increasing. After reading the article, a student argues: "From this information, we know that the price of Internet ads should rise, but we don't know whether the total quantity of Internet ads will increase or decrease." Is the student's analysis correct? Illustrate your answer with a demand and supply graph.

Source: Suzanne Vranica, "Web Video: Bigger and Less Profitable," *Wall Street Journal*, March 14, 2013.

4.11 Historically, the production of many perishable foods, such as dairy products, was highly seasonal. As the supply of those products fluctuated, prices tended to fluctuate tremendously—typically by 25 to 50 percent or more—over the course of the year. One effect of mechanical refrigeration, which was commercialized on a large scale in the last decade of the nineteenth century, was that suppliers could store perishables from one season to the next. Economists have estimated that as a result of refrigerated storage, wholesale prices rose by roughly 10 percent during peak supply periods, while they fell by almost the same amount during the off season. Use a demand and supply graph for each season to illustrate how refrigeration affected the market for perishable food.

Source: Lee A. Craig, Barry Goodwin, and Thomas Grennes, "The Effect of Mechanical Refrigeration on Nutrition in the U.S.," *Social Science History*, Vol. 28, No. 2, Summer 2004, pp. 327–328.

4.12 If the equilibrium price and quantity of a product were $100 and 1,000 units per month in 2013 and are $150 and 800 units per month in 2014, did this product experience a larger shift in its demand curve or supply curve from 2013 to 2014? Briefly explain.

4.13 **[Related to the** Don't Let This Happen to You **on page 90]** A student writes the following: "Increased production leads to a lower price, which in turn increases demand." Do you agree with his reasoning? Briefly explain.

4.14 **[Related to the** Don't Let This Happen to You **on page 90]** A student was asked to draw a demand and supply graph to illustrate the effect on the market for smartphones of a fall in the price of displays used in smartphones, holding everything else constant. She drew the following graph and explained it as follows:

> Displays are an input to smartphones, so a fall in the price of displays will cause the supply curve for smartphones to shift to the right (from S_1 to S_2). Because this shift in the supply curve results in a lower price (P_2), consumers will want to buy more smartphones, and the demand curve will shift to the right (from D_1 to D_2). We know that

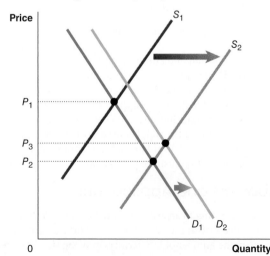

more smartphones will be sold, but we can't be sure whether the price of smartphones will rise or fall. That depends on whether the supply curve or the demand curve has shifted farther to the right. I assume that the effect on supply is greater than the effect on demand, so I show the final equilibrium price (P_3) as being lower than the initial equilibrium price (P_1).

Explain whether you agree or disagree with the student's analysis. Be careful to explain exactly what—if anything—you find wrong with her analysis.

4.15 Following are four graphs and four market scenarios, each of which would cause either a movement along the supply curve for Pepsi or a shift of the supply curve. Match each scenario with the appropriate graph.

  a. A decrease in the supply of Coke

  b. A drop in the average household income in the United States from $52,000 to $50,000

  c. An improvement in soft drink bottling technology

  d. An increase in the prices of sugar and high-fructose corn syrup

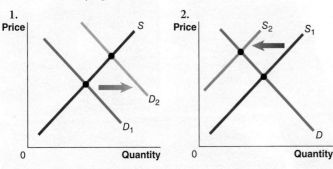

4.16 Proposals have been made to increase government regulation of firms providing childcare services by, for instance, setting education requirements for childcare workers. Suppose that these regulations increase the quality of childcare and cause the demand for childcare services to increase. At the same time, assume that complying with the new government regulations increases the costs of firms providing childcare services. Draw a demand and supply graph to illustrate the effects of these changes in the market for childcare services. Briefly explain whether the total quantity of childcare services purchased will increase or decrease as a result of regulation.

4.17 Which of the following graphs best represents what happens in the market for hotel rooms at a ski resort during the winter? Briefly explain. From the graph that you picked, what would be the result during the winter if hotel rates stayed at their summer level?

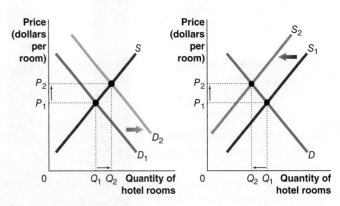

4.18 The following graphs show the supply and demand curves for two markets. One of the markets is for Tesla automobiles, and the other is for a cancer-fighting drug, without which lung cancer patients will die. Briefly explain which graph most likely represents which market.

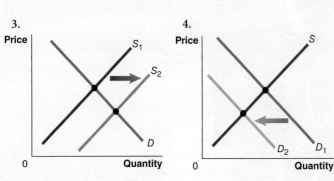

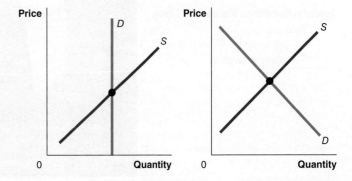

Economic Efficiency, Government Price Setting, and Taxes

Chapter Outline and Learning Objectives

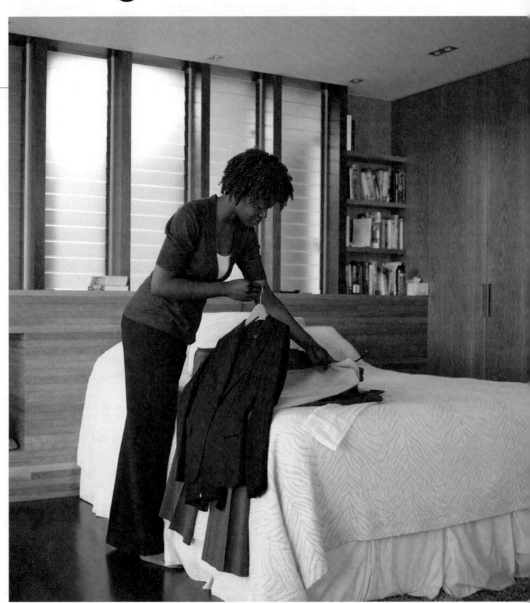

The Sharing Economy, Phone Apps, and Rent Control

The role of markets is to bring together buyers and sellers. Recently, Internet start-up companies have created rental markets for short-term use of apartments, cars, boats, bicycles, and other goods. For example, people who download the Airbnb app can search for short-term room rentals in 30,000 cities in 192 countries. The suppliers in this market typically want to earn extra money by renting their house, apartment, or sometimes just a single room, for a few days. Airbnb, Roomorama, Getaround, RelayRides, and SnapGoods, among other sites, facilitate peer-to-peer rentals. The *Economist* magazine has referred to the rapid increase in the number of people using these sites as the rise of the "sharing economy."

Airbnb was founded in 2008 and is based in San Francisco. More than 2.5 million people rented rooms using the site in 2012. Despite this success, Airbnb has run into problems, particularly in cities that have rent control regulations. In New York, San Francisco, Los Angeles, and nearly 200 smaller cities in the United States, apartments are subject to rent control by the local government. Rent control puts a legal limit on the rent that landlords can charge for an apartment. Supporters of rent control argue it is necessary to preserve affordable apartments in cities where equilibrium market rents would be above what middle- and lower-income people are willing and able to pay. But, as we will see in this chapter, rent controls cause a shortage of apartments and give people an incentive to list their apartments on Airbnb or other sites at rents far above the controlled rents. In San Francisco, a number of landlords complain that some high-income renters have moved out of the city but have kept their rent-controlled apartments in order to rent them using the apartment-sharing sites.

Some observers argue that the difficulty governments face regulating peer-to-peer rental sites will make it impossible to enforce rent control rules. Rent control supporters argue that city governments should do a better job of enforcing regulations that they believe some users of Airbnb and other sites are violating. As the head of the San Francisco Tenants Union noted: "All you have to do is sit in front of the computer for a few hours, and you can identify a lot of the lawbreakers. But there's no enforcement by the city."

AN INSIDE LOOK AT POLICY on page 122 explains how the sharing economy is benefiting consumers by giving them access to previously unavailable products and services, including rooms to rent from homeowners.

Sources: "The Rise of the Sharing Economy" and "All Eyes on the Sharing Economy," *Economist*, March 9, 2013; "NYC Judge: Renting Apartments Using Airbnb Illegal," Associated Press, May 22, 2013; Steven T. Jones, "Airbnb's Tax and Tenant Law Violations Headed for Hearings," sfbg.com, March 28, 2013; and C.W. Nevius, "Rent Control Sometimes Benefitting the Rich," *San Francisco Chronicle*, June 16, 2012.

Economics in Your Life

Does Rent Control Make It Easier for You to Find an Affordable Apartment?

Suppose you have job offers in two cities. One factor in deciding which job to accept is whether you can find an affordable apartment. If one city has rent control, are you more likely to find an affordable apartment in that city, or would you be better off looking for an apartment in a city without rent control? As you read the chapter, try to answer this question. You can check your answer against the one we provide on **page 121** at the end of this chapter.

Price ceiling A legally determined maximum price that sellers may charge.

Price floor A legally determined minimum price that sellers may receive.

W e have seen that in a competitive market the price adjusts to ensure that the quantity demanded equals the quantity supplied. Stated another way, in equilibrium, every consumer willing to pay the market price is able to buy as much of the product as the consumer wants, and every firm willing to accept the market price can sell as much as it wants. Even so, consumers would naturally prefer to pay a lower price, and sellers would prefer to receive a higher price. Normally, consumers and firms have no choice but to accept the equilibrium price if they wish to participate in the market. Occasionally, however, consumers succeed in having the government impose a **price ceiling**, which is a legally determined maximum price that sellers may charge. Rent control is an example of a price ceiling. Firms also sometimes succeed in having the government impose a **price floor**, which is a legally determined minimum price that sellers may receive. In markets for farm products such as milk, the government has been setting price floors that are above the equilibrium market price since the 1930s.

Another way the government intervenes in markets is by imposing taxes. The government relies on the revenue raised from taxes to finance its operations. Unfortunately, whenever the government imposes a price ceiling, a price floor, or a tax, there are predictable negative economic consequences. It is important for government policymakers and voters to understand the negative consequences when evaluating these policies. Economists have developed the concepts of *consumer surplus*, *producer surplus*, and *deadweight loss* to analyze the economic effects of price ceilings, price floors, and taxes.

4.1 LEARNING OBJECTIVE

Distinguish between the concepts of consumer surplus and producer surplus.

Consumer Surplus and Producer Surplus

Consumer surplus measures the dollar benefit consumers receive from buying goods or services in a particular market. Producer surplus measures the dollar benefit firms receive from selling goods or services in a particular market. Economic surplus in a market is the sum of consumer surplus and producer surplus. As we will see, *when the government imposes a price ceiling or a price floor, the amount of economic surplus in a market is reduced*; in other words, price ceilings and price floors reduce the total benefit to consumers and firms from buying and selling in a market. To understand why this is true, we need to understand how consumer surplus and producer surplus are determined.

Consumer Surplus

Consumer surplus The difference between the highest price a consumer is willing to pay for a good or service and the actual price the consumer pays.

Consumer surplus is the difference between the highest price a consumer is willing to pay for a good or service and the actual price the consumer pays. Suppose you are in Wal-Mart, and you see a DVD of *World War Z* on the shelf. The DVD doesn't have a price sticker, so you take it to the register to check the price. As you walk to the register, you think to yourself that $18 is the highest price you would be willing to pay. At the register, you find out that the price is actually $12, so you buy the DVD. Your consumer surplus in this example is $6: the difference between the $18 you were willing to pay and the $12 you actually paid.

We can use the demand curve to measure the total consumer surplus in a market. Demand curves show the willingness of consumers to purchase a product at different prices. Consumers are willing to purchase a product up to the point where the marginal benefit of consuming a product is equal to its price. The **marginal benefit** is the additional benefit to a consumer from consuming one more unit of a good or service. As a simple example, suppose there are only four consumers in the market for chai tea: Theresa, Tom, Terri, and Tim. Because these four consumers have different tastes for tea and different incomes, the marginal benefit each of them receives from consuming a cup of tea will be different. Therefore, the highest price each is willing to pay for a cup of tea is also different. In Figure 4.1, the information from the table is used to construct a demand curve for chai tea. For prices above $6 per cup, no tea is sold because $6 is the highest price any of the consumers is willing to pay. At a price of $5, both Theresa and

Marginal benefit The additional benefit to a consumer from consuming one more unit of a good or service.

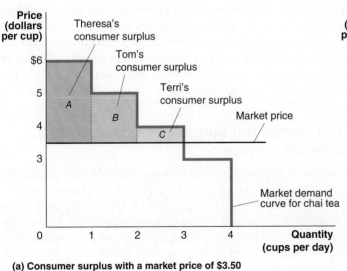

Consumer	Highest Price Willing to Pay
Theresa	$6
Tom	5
Terri	4
Tim	3

MyEconLab Animation

Figure 4.1

Deriving the Demand Curve for Chai Tea

With four consumers in the market for chai tea, the demand curve is determined by the highest price each consumer is willing to pay. For prices above $6, no tea is sold because $6 is the highest price any consumer is willing to pay. For prices of $3 and below, each of the four consumers is willing to buy a cup of tea.

Tom are willing to buy tea, so two cups are sold. At prices of $3 and below, all four consumers are willing to buy tea, and four cups are sold.

Suppose the market price of tea is $3.50 per cup. As Figure 4.2 shows, the demand curve allows us to calculate the total consumer surplus in this market. Panel (a) shows that the highest price Theresa is willing to pay is $6, but because she pays only $3.50, her consumer surplus is $2.50 (shown by the area of rectangle *A*). Similarly, Tom's consumer surplus is $1.50 (rectangle *B*), and Terri's consumer surplus is $0.50 (rectangle *C*). Tim is

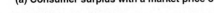

(a) Consumer surplus with a market price of $3.50

(b) Consumer surplus with a market price of $3.00

MyEconLab Animation

Figure 4.2   Measuring Consumer Surplus

Panel (a) shows the consumer surplus for Theresa, Tom, and Terri when the price of tea is $3.50 per cup. Theresa's consumer surplus is equal to the area of rectangle *A* and is the difference between the highest price she would pay—which is $6—and the market price of $3.50. Tom's consumer surplus is equal to the area of rectangle *B*, and

Terri's consumer surplus is equal to the area of rectangle *C*. Total consumer surplus in this market is equal to the sum of the areas of rectangles *A*, *B*, and *C*, or the total area below the demand curve and above the market price. In panel (b), consumer surplus increases by the dark blue area as the market price declines from $3.50 to $3.00.

Figure 4.3

Total Consumer Surplus in the Market for Chai Tea

The demand curve shows that most buyers of chai tea would have been willing to pay more than the market price of $2.00. For each buyer, consumer surplus is equal to the difference between the highest price he or she is willing to pay and the market price actually paid. Therefore, the total amount of consumer surplus in the market for chai tea is equal to the area below the demand curve and above the market price. Consumer surplus represents the benefit to consumers in excess of the price they paid to purchase a product.

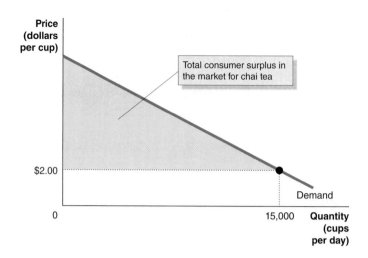

unwilling to buy a cup of tea at a price of $3.50, so he doesn't participate in this market and receives no consumer surplus. In this simple example, the total consumer surplus is equal to $2.50 + $1.50 + $0.50 = $4.50 (or the sum of the areas of rectangles *A*, *B*, and *C*). Panel (b) shows that a lower price will increase consumer surplus. If the price of tea falls from $3.50 per cup to $3.00, Theresa, Tom, and Terri each receive $0.50 more in consumer surplus (shown by the dark blue areas), so the total consumer surplus in the market rises to $6.00. Tim now buys a cup of tea but doesn't receive any consumer surplus because the price is equal to the highest price he is willing to pay. In fact, Tim is indifferent between buying the cup or not—his well-being is the same either way.

The market demand curves shown in Figures 4.1 and 4.2 do not look like the typical smooth demand curve because in this case we have only a small number of consumers, each consuming a single cup of tea. With many consumers, the market demand curve for chai tea will have the normal smooth shape shown in Figure 4.3. In this figure, the quantity demanded at a price of $2.00 is 15,000 cups per day. We can calculate total consumer surplus in Figure 4.3 the same way we did in Figures 4.1 and 4.2—by adding up the consumer surplus received on each unit purchased. Once again, we can draw an important conclusion: *The total amount of consumer surplus in a market is equal to the area below the demand curve and above the market price.* Consumer surplus is shown as the shaded area in Figure 4.3 and represents the benefit to consumers in excess of the price they paid to purchase a product—in this case, chai tea.   MyEconLab Concept Check

Making the Connection

MyEconLab Video

The Consumer Surplus from Broadband Internet Service

Consumer surplus allows us to measure the benefit consumers receive in excess of the price they paid to purchase a product. Shane Greenstein of Northwestern University and Ryan McDevitt of the University of Rochester estimated the consumer surplus that households receive from subscribing to broadband Internet service. To carry out the analysis, they estimated the demand curve for broadband Internet service and then computed the shaded area shown in the following graph.

In the year they analyzed, 47 million consumers paid an average price of $36 per month to subscribe to a broadband Internet service. The demand curve shows the marginal benefit consumers receive from subscribing to a broadband Internet service rather than using dialup or doing without access to the Internet. The area below the demand curve and above the $36 price line represents the difference between the price consumers would have paid rather than do without broadband service and the $36 they did pay. The shaded area on the graph represents the total consumer surplus in the market for broadband Internet service. Greenstein and McDevitt estimate that the value of this

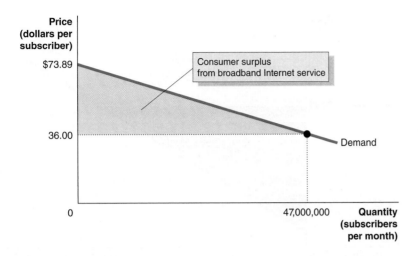

area is $890.4 million. This value is one month's benefit to the consumers who subscribe to a broadband Internet service.

Source: Shane Greenstein and Ryan C. McDevitt, "The Broadband Bonus: Estimating Broadband Internet's Economic Value," *Telecommunications Policy*, Vol. 35, No. 7, August 2011, pp. 617–632.

Your Turn: For more practice do related problem 1.11 on page 125 at the end of this chapter.

MyEconLab Study Plan

Producer Surplus

Just as demand curves show the willingness of consumers to buy a product at different prices, supply curves show the willingness of firms to supply a product at different prices. The willingness to supply a product depends on the cost of producing it. Firms will supply an additional unit of a product only if they receive a price equal to the additional cost of producing that unit. **Marginal cost** is the additional cost to a firm of producing one more unit of a good or service. Consider the marginal cost to the firm Heavenly Tea of producing one more cup of tea: In this case, the marginal cost includes the ingredients to make the tea and the wages paid to the worker preparing the tea. Often, the marginal cost of producing a good increases as more of the good is produced during a given period of time. Increasing marginal cost is the key reason that supply curves are upward sloping.

> **Marginal cost** The additional cost to a firm of producing one more unit of a good or service.

Panel (a) of Figure 4.4 shows Heavenly Tea's producer surplus. For simplicity, we show Heavenly producing only a small quantity of tea. The figure shows that Heavenly's marginal cost of producing the first cup of tea is $1.25, its marginal cost of producing the second cup is $1.50, and so on. The marginal cost of each cup of tea is the lowest price Heavenly is willing to accept to supply that cup. The supply curve, then, is also a marginal cost curve. Suppose the market price of tea is $2.00 per cup. On the first cup of tea, the price is $0.75 higher than the lowest price that Heavenly is willing to accept. **Producer surplus** is the difference between the lowest price a firm would be willing to accept for a good or service and the price it actually receives. Therefore, Heavenly's producer surplus on the first cup is $0.75 (shown by the area of rectangle *A*), its producer surplus on the second cup is $0.50 (rectangle *B*), and its producer surplus on the third cup is $0.25 (rectangle *C*). Heavenly will not be willing to supply the fourth cup because the marginal cost of producing it is greater than the market price. Heavenly Tea's total producer surplus is equal to $0.75 + $0.50 + $0.25 = $1.50 (or the sum of the areas of rectangles *A*, *B*, and *C*). A higher price will increase producer surplus. For example, if the market price of chai tea rises from $2.00 to $2.25, Heavenly Tea's producer surplus will increase from $1.50 to $2.25. (Make sure you understand how the new level of producer surplus was calculated.)

> **Producer surplus** The difference between the lowest price a firm would be willing to accept for a good or service and the price it actually receives.

The supply curve shown in panel (a) of Figure 4.4 does not look like the typical smooth curve because we are looking at a single firm producing only a small quantity of tea. With

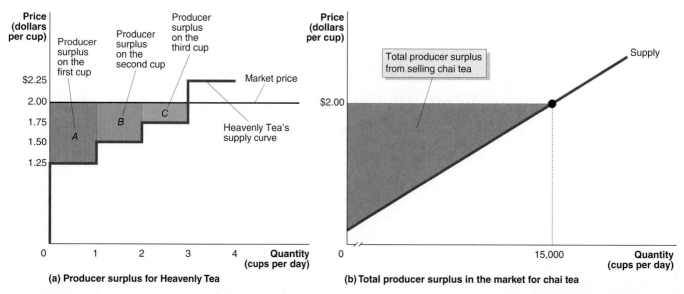

MyEconLab Animation

Figure 4.4 **Measuring Producer Surplus**

Panel (a) shows Heavenly Tea's producer surplus. The lowest price Heavenly Tea is willing to accept to supply a cup of tea is equal to its marginal cost of producing that cup. When the market price of tea is $2.00, Heavenly receives producer surplus of $0.75 on the first cup (the area of rectangle *A*), $0.50 on the second cup (rectangle *B*), and $0.25 on the third cup (rectangle *C*).

In panel (b), the total amount of producer surplus tea sellers receive from selling chai tea can be calculated by adding up for the entire market the producer surplus received on each cup sold. In the figure, total producer surplus is equal to the shaded area above the supply curve and below the market price.

many firms, the market supply curve for chai tea will have the normal smooth shape shown in panel (b) of Figure 4.4. In panel (b), the quantity supplied at a price of $2.00 is 15,000 cups per day. We can calculate total producer surplus in panel (b) the same way we did in panel (a): by adding up the producer surplus received on each cup sold. Therefore, *the total amount of producer surplus in a market is equal to the area above the market supply curve and below the market price.* The total producer surplus tea sellers receive from selling chai tea is shown as the shaded area in panel (b) of Figure 4.4. **MyEconLab** Concept Check

What Consumer Surplus and Producer Surplus Measure

We have seen that consumer surplus measures the benefit to consumers from participating in a market, and producer surplus measures the benefit to producers from participating in a market. It is important to be clear about what these concepts are measuring. In a sense, consumer surplus measures the *net* benefit to consumers from participating in a market rather than the *total* benefit. That is, if the price of a product were zero, the consumer surplus in a market would be all of the area under the demand curve. When the price is not zero, consumer surplus is the area below the demand curve and above the market price. So, consumer surplus in a market is equal to the total benefit consumers receive minus the total amount they must pay to buy the good or service.

Similarly, producer surplus measures the *net* benefit received by producers from participating in a market. If producers could supply a good or service at zero cost, the producer surplus in a market would be all of the area below the market price. When cost is not zero, producer surplus is the area below the market price and above the supply curve. So, producer surplus in a market is equal to the total amount firms receive from consumers minus the cost of producing the good or service. **MyEconLab** Concept Check

MyEconLab Study Plan

4.2 LEARNING OBJECTIVE

Understand the concept of economic efficiency.

The Efficiency of Competitive Markets

Recall that a *competitive market* is a market with many buyers and many sellers. An important advantage of the market system is that it results in efficient economic outcomes. But what does *economic efficiency* mean? The concepts we have developed so far in this chapter give us two ways to think about the economic efficiency of competitive markets. We can think in terms of marginal benefit and marginal cost. We can also think in terms of consumer surplus and producer surplus. As we will see, these two approaches lead to the same outcome, but using both can increase our understanding of economic efficiency.

Marginal Benefit Equals Marginal Cost in Competitive Equilibrium

Figure 4.5 again shows the market for chai tea. Recall from our discussion that the demand curve shows the marginal benefit received by consumers, and the supply curve shows the marginal cost of production. For this market to achieve economic efficiency, the marginal benefit from the last unit sold should equal the marginal cost of production. The figure shows that this equality occurs at competitive equilibrium where 15,000 cups per day are produced and marginal benefit and marginal cost are both equal to $2.00. Why is this outcome economically efficient? Because every cup of chai tea has been produced where the marginal benefit to buyers is greater than or equal to the marginal cost to producers.

Another way to see why the level of output at competitive equilibrium is efficient is to consider what the situation would be if output were at a different level. Suppose that output of chai tea was 14,000 cups per day. Figure 4.5 shows that at this level of output, the marginal benefit from the last cup sold is $2.20, while the marginal cost is only $1.80. This level of output is not efficient because 1,000 more cups could be produced for which the additional benefit to consumers would be greater than the additional cost of production. Consumers would willingly purchase those cups, and tea sellers would willingly supply them, making both consumers and sellers better off. Similarly, if the output of chai tea were 16,000 cups per day, the marginal cost of the 16,000th cup is $2.20, while the marginal benefit is only $1.80. Tea sellers would only be willing to supply this cup at a price of $2.20, which is $0.40 higher than consumers would be willing to pay. In fact, consumers would not be willing to pay the price tea sellers would need to receive for any cup beyond the 15,000th.

To summarize, we can say this: *Equilibrium in a competitive market results in the economically efficient level of output, at which marginal benefit equals marginal cost.*

MyEconLab Concept Check

Economic Surplus

Economic surplus in a market is the sum of consumer surplus and producer surplus. In a competitive market, with many buyers and sellers and no government restrictions, economic surplus is at a maximum when the market is in equilibrium. To see this point, let's look one

Economic surplus The sum of consumer surplus and producer surplus.

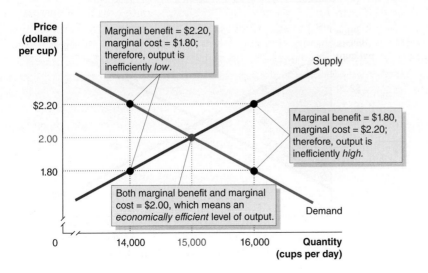

MyEconLab Animation

Figure 4.5

Marginal Benefit Equals Marginal Cost Only at Competitive Equilibrium

In a competitive market, equilibrium occurs at a quantity of 15,000 cups and a price of $2.00 per cup, where marginal benefit equals marginal cost. This level of output is economically efficient because every cup has been produced for which the marginal benefit to buyers is greater than or equal to the marginal cost to producers.

Figure 4.6

Economic Surplus Equals the Sum of Consumer Surplus and Producer Surplus

The economic surplus in a market is the sum of the blue area, representing consumer surplus, and the red area, representing producer surplus.

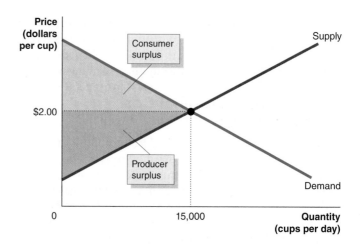

more time at the market for chai tea shown in Figure 4.6. The consumer surplus in this market is the blue area below the demand curve and above the line indicating the equilibrium price of $2.00. The producer surplus is the red area above the supply curve and below the price line.   MyEconLab Concept Check

Deadweight Loss

To show that economic surplus is maximized at equilibrium, consider a situation in which the price of chai tea is *above* the equilibrium price, as shown in Figure 4.7. At a price of $2.20 per cup, the number of cups consumers are willing to buy per day falls from 15,000 to 14,000. At competitive equilibrium, consumer surplus is equal to the sum of areas A, B, and C. At a price of $2.20, fewer cups are sold at a higher price, so consumer surplus declines to just the area of A. At competitive equilibrium, producer surplus is equal to the sum of areas D and E. At the higher price of $2.20, producer surplus changes to be equal to the sum of areas B and D. The sum of consumer and producer surplus—economic surplus—has been reduced to the sum of areas A, B, and D.

Figure 4.7

When a Market Is Not in Equilibrium, There Is a Deadweight Loss

Economic surplus is maximized when a market is in competitive equilibrium. When a market is not in equilibrium, there is a deadweight loss. For example, when the price of chai tea is $2.20 instead of $2.00, consumer surplus declines from an amount equal to the sum of areas A, B, and C to just area A. Producer surplus increases from the sum of areas D and E to the sum of areas B and D. At competitive equilibrium, there is no deadweight loss. At a price of $2.20, there is a deadweight loss equal to the sum of triangles C and E.

	At Competitive Equilibrium	At a Price of $2.20
Consumer Surplus	A + B + C	A
Producer Surplus	D + E	B + D
Deadweight Loss	None	C + E

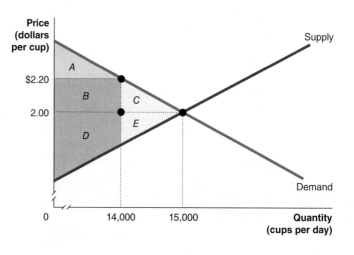

Notice that this sum is less than the original economic surplus by an amount equal to the sum of triangles *C* and *E*. Economic surplus has declined because at a price of $2.20, all the cups between the 14,000th and the 15,000th, which would have been produced in competitive equilibrium, are not being produced. These "missing" cups are not providing any consumer or producer surplus, so economic surplus has declined. The reduction in economic surplus resulting from a market not being in competitive equilibrium is called the **deadweight loss**. In the figure, deadweight loss is equal to the sum of the triangles *C* and *E*.   MyEconLab Concept Check

> **Deadweight loss** The reduction in economic surplus resulting from a market not being in competitive equilibrium.

Economic Surplus and Economic Efficiency

Consumer surplus measures the benefit to consumers from buying a particular product, such as chai tea. Producer surplus measures the benefit to firms from selling a particular product. Therefore, economic surplus—which is the sum of the benefit to firms plus the benefit to consumers—is the best measure we have of the benefit to society from the production of a particular good or service. This gives us a second way of characterizing the economic efficiency of a competitive market: *Equilibrium in a competitive market results in the greatest amount of economic surplus, or total net benefit to society, from the production of a good or service.* Anything that causes the market for a good or service not to be in competitive equilibrium reduces the total benefit to society from the production of that good or service.

Now we can give a more general definition of *economic efficiency* in terms of our two approaches: **Economic efficiency** is a market outcome in which the marginal benefit to consumers of the last unit produced is equal to its marginal cost of production and in which the sum of consumer surplus and producer surplus is at a maximum.   MyEconLab Concept Check

> **Economic efficiency** A market outcome in which the marginal benefit to consumers of the last unit produced is equal to its marginal cost of production and in which the sum of consumer surplus and producer surplus is at a maximum.
>
> MyEconLab Study Plan

> **4.3 LEARNING OBJECTIVE**
>
> Explain the economic effect of government-imposed price floors and price ceilings.

Government Intervention in the Market: Price Floors and Price Ceilings

Notice that we have *not* concluded that every *individual* is better off if a market is at competitive equilibrium. We have concluded only that economic surplus, or the *total* net benefit to society, is greatest at competitive equilibrium. Any individual producer would rather receive a higher price, and any individual consumer would rather pay a lower price, but usually producers can sell and consumers can buy only at the competitive equilibrium price.

Producers or consumers who are dissatisfied with the competitive equilibrium price can lobby the government to legally require that a different price be charged. In the United States, the government only occasionally overrides the market outcome by setting prices. When the government does intervene, it can attempt to aid either sellers by requiring that a price be above equilibrium—a price floor—or buyers by requiring that a price be below equilibrium—a price ceiling. To affect the market outcome, the government must set a price floor that is above the equilibrium price or set a price ceiling that is below the equilibrium price. Otherwise, the price ceiling or price floor will not be *binding* on buyers and sellers. The preceding section demonstrates that moving away from competitive equilibrium will reduce economic efficiency. We can use the concepts of consumer surplus, producer surplus, and deadweight loss to understand more clearly the economic inefficiency of price floors and price ceilings.

Price Floors: Government Policy in Agricultural Markets

The Great Depression of the 1930s was the worst economic disaster in U.S. history, affecting every sector of the economy. Many farmers could sell their products only at very low prices. Farmers were able to convince the federal government to set price floors for many agricultural products. Government intervention in agriculture—often referred to as the *farm program*—has continued ever since. To understand how a price floor in

Figure 4.8

The Economic Effect of a Price Floor in the Wheat Market

If wheat farmers convince the government to impose a price floor of $8.00 per bushel, the amount of wheat sold will fall from 2.0 billion bushels per year to 1.8 billion. If we assume that farmers produce 1.8 billion bushels, producer surplus then increases by rectangle *A*—which is transferred from consumer surplus—and falls by triangle *C*. Consumer surplus declines by rectangle *A* plus triangle *B*. There is a deadweight loss equal to triangles *B* and *C*, representing the decline in economic efficiency due to the price floor. In reality, a price floor of $8.00 per bushel will cause farmers to expand their production from 2.0 billion to 2.2 billion bushels, resulting in a surplus of wheat.

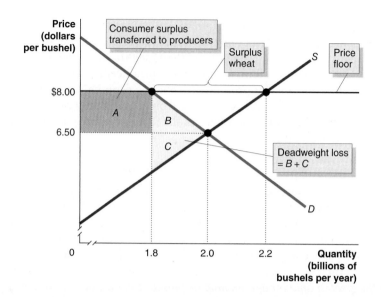

an agricultural market works, suppose that the equilibrium price in the wheat market is $6.50 per bushel, but the government decides to set a price floor of $8.00 per bushel. As Figure 4.8 shows, the price of wheat rises from $6.50 to $8.00, and the quantity of wheat sold falls from 2.0 billion bushels per year to 1.8 billion. Initially, suppose that production of wheat also falls to 1.8 billion bushels.

The producer surplus received by wheat farmers increases by an amount equal to the area of rectangle *A* and decreases by an amount equal to the area of triangle *C*. (This is the same result we saw in the market for chai tea in Figure 4.7) The area of rectangle *A* represents a transfer from consumer surplus to producer surplus. The total fall in consumer surplus is equal to the sum of the areas of rectangle *A* and triangle *B*. Wheat farmers benefit from this program, but consumers lose. There is also a deadweight loss equal to the areas of triangles *B* and *C* because economic efficiency declines as the price floor reduces the amount of economic surplus in the market for wheat. In other words, the price floor has caused the marginal benefit of the last bushel of wheat to be greater than the marginal cost of producing it. We can conclude that a price floor reduces economic efficiency.

We assumed initially that farmers reduce their production of wheat to the amount consumers are willing to buy. In fact, as Figure 4.8 shows, a price floor will cause the quantity of wheat that farmers want to supply to increase from 2.0 billion to 2.2 billion bushels. Because the higher price also reduces the amount of wheat consumers want to buy, the result is a surplus of 0.4 billion bushels of wheat (the 2.2 billion bushels supplied minus the 1.8 billion demanded).

The federal government's farm programs have often resulted in large surpluses of wheat and other agricultural products. In response, the government has usually either bought the surplus food or paid farmers to restrict supply by taking some land out of cultivation. Because both of these options are expensive, Congress passed the Freedom to Farm Act of 1996. The intent of the act was to phase out price floors and government purchases of surpluses and return to a free market in agriculture. To allow farmers time to adjust, the federal government began paying farmers *subsidies*, or cash payments based on the number of acres planted. Although the subsidies were originally scheduled to be phased out, Congress has passed additional farm bills that have resulted in the continuation of subsidies involving substantial federal government spending. In 2013, the Congressional Budget Office estimated that the farm bill then under consideration by Congress would result in federal spending of more than $960 billion over the following 10 years.

**Making
the
Connection**
MyEconLab Video

Price Floors in Labor Markets: The Debate over Minimum Wage Policy

The minimum wage may be the most controversial "price floor." Supporters see the minimum wage as a way of raising the incomes of low-skilled workers. Opponents argue that it results in fewer jobs and imposes large costs on small businesses.

Since 2009, the national minimum wage as set by Congress has been $7.25 per hour for most occupations. It is illegal for an employer to pay less than this wage in these occupations. For most workers, the minimum wage is irrelevant because it is well below the wage employers are voluntarily willing to pay them. In 2013, only about 3 percent of workers in the United States earned the minimum wage or less. But for some low-skilled workers—such as workers in fast-food restaurants—the minimum wage is above the wage they would otherwise receive. The following figure shows the effect of the minimum wage on employment in the market for low-skilled labor.

Without a minimum wage, the equilibrium wage would be W_1 and the number of workers hired would be L_1. With a minimum wage set above the equilibrium wage, the number of workers employers demand declines from L_1 to L_2, and the quantity of labor supplied increases to L_3, leading to a surplus of workers unable to find jobs equal to $L_3 - L_2$. The quantity of labor supplied increases because the higher wage attracts more people to work. For instance, some teenagers may decide that working after school is worthwhile at the minimum wage of $7.25 per hour but would not be worthwhile at a lower wage.

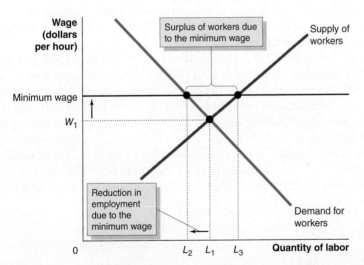

This analysis is very similar to our analysis of the wheat market in Figure 4.8. Just as a price floor in the wheat market leads to less wheat being consumed, a price floor in the labor market should lead to fewer workers being hired. Views differ sharply among economists, however, concerning how large a reduction in employment the minimum wage causes. For instance, David Card of the University of California, Berkeley, and Alan Krueger of Princeton University, conducted a study of fast-food restaurants in New Jersey and Pennsylvania. Their study indicated that the effect of minimum wage increases on employment is very small. This study has been controversial, however. Other economists have examined similar data and have come to the different conclusion that the minimum wage leads to a significant decrease in employment.

Whatever the extent of employment losses from the minimum wage, because it is a price floor, it will cause a deadweight loss, just as a price floor in the wheat market does. Therefore, many economists favor alternative policies for attaining the goal of raising the incomes of low-skilled workers. One policy many economists support is the *earned income tax credit*. The earned income tax credit reduces the amount of tax that low-income wage earners would otherwise pay to the federal government. Workers with very low incomes who do not owe any tax receive a payment from the government. Compared with the minimum wage, the earned income tax credit can increase the incomes of low-skilled workers without reducing employment. The earned income tax credit also places a lesser burden on the small businesses that employ many low-skilled workers and may cause a smaller loss of economic efficiency.

Sources: David Card and Alan B. Krueger, *Myth and Measurement: The New Economics of the Minimum Wage*, Princeton, J: Princeton University Press, 1995; David Neumark and William Wascher, "Minimum Wages and Employment: A Case Study of the Fast-Food Industry in New Jersey and Pennsylvania: Comment," *American Economic Review*, Vol. 90, No. 5, December 2000, pp. 1362–1396; and David Card and Alan B. Krueger, "Minimum Wages and Employment: A Case Study of the Fast-Food Industry in New Jersey and Pennsylvania: Reply," *American Economic Review*, Vol. 90, No. 5, December 2000, pp. 1397–1420.

MyEconLab Study Plan   **Your Turn:** Test your understanding by doing related problem 3.10 on page 127 at the end of this chapter.

Price Ceilings: Government Rent Control Policy in Housing Markets

Support for governments setting price floors typically comes from sellers, and support for governments setting price ceilings typically comes from consumers. For example, when there is a sharp increase in gasoline prices, proposals are often made for the government to impose a price ceiling on the market for gasoline. As we saw in the chapter opener, a number of cities impose rent control, which puts a ceiling on the maximum rent that landlords can charge for an apartment. Figure 4.9 shows the market for apartments in a city that has rent control.

Without rent control, the equilibrium rent would be $2,500 per month, and 2,000,000 apartments would be rented. With a maximum legal rent of $1,500 per month, landlords reduce the quantity of apartments supplied to 1,900,000. The fall in the quantity of apartments supplied can be the result of landlords converting some apartments into offices, selling some off as condominiums, or converting some small apartment buildings into single-family homes. Over time, landlords may even abandon some apartment buildings. At one time in New York City, rent control resulted in landlords abandoning whole city blocks because they were unable to cover their costs with the rents the government allowed them to charge. In London, when rent controls were

MyEconLab Animation

Figure 4.9

The Economic Effect of a Rent Ceiling

Without rent control, the equilibrium rent is $2,500 per month. At that price, 2,000,000 apartments would be rented. If the government imposes a rent ceiling of $1,500 per month, the quantity of apartments supplied decreases to 1,900,000, and the quantity of apartments demanded increases to 2,100,000, resulting in a shortage of 200,000 apartments. Producer surplus equal to the area of rectangle *A* is transferred from landlords to renters, and there is a deadweight loss equal to the areas of triangles *B* and *C*.

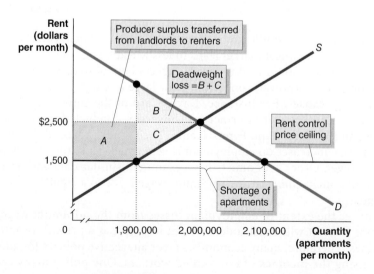

Don't Let This Happen to You

Don't Confuse "Scarcity" with "Shortage"

At first glance, the following statement seems correct: "There is a shortage of every good that is scarce." In everyday conversation, we describe a good as "scarce" if we have trouble finding it. For instance, if you are looking for a gift for a child, you might call the latest hot toy "scarce" if you are willing to buy it at its listed price but can't find it online or in any store. But recall that economists have a broader definition of *scarce*. In the economic sense, almost everything—except undesirable things like garbage—is scarce.

A shortage of a good occurs only if the quantity demanded is greater than the quantity supplied at the current price. Therefore, the preceding statement—"There is a shortage of every good that is scarce"—is incorrect. In fact, there is no shortage of most scarce goods.

MyEconLab Study Plan
Your Turn: Test your understanding by doing related problem 3.14 on page 128 at the end of this chapter.

applied to rooms and apartments located in a landlord's own home, the quantity of these apartments supplied decreased by 75 percent.

In Figure 4.9, with the rent ceiling of $1,500 per month, the quantity of apartments demanded rises to 2,100,000, resulting in a shortage of 200,000 apartments. Consumer surplus increases by rectangle *A* and falls by triangle *B*. Rectangle *A* would have been part of producer surplus if rent control were not in place. With rent control, it is part of consumer surplus. Rent control causes the producer surplus landlords receive to fall by rectangle *A* plus triangle *C*. Triangles *B* and *C* represent the deadweight loss, which results from rent control reducing the amount of economic surplus in the market for apartments. Rent control has caused the marginal benefit of the last apartment rented to be greater than the marginal cost of supplying it. We can conclude that a price ceiling, such as rent control, reduces economic efficiency. The appendix to this chapter shows how we can make quantitative estimates of the deadweight loss and provides an example of the changes in consumer surplus and producer surplus that can result from rent control.

Renters as a group benefit from rent controls—total consumer surplus is larger—but landlords lose. Because of the deadweight loss, the total loss to landlords is greater than the gain to renters. Notice also that although renters as a group benefit, the number of renters is reduced, so some renters are made worse off by rent controls because they are unable to find an apartment at the legal rent.   MyEconLab Concept Check

Black Markets and Peer-to-Peer Sites

To this point, our analysis of rent controls is incomplete. In practice, renters may be worse off and landlords may be better off than Figure 4.9 makes it seem. We have assumed that renters and landlords actually abide by the price ceiling, but sometimes they don't. Because rent control leads to a shortage of apartments, renters who would otherwise not be able to find apartments have an incentive to offer landlords rents above the legal maximum. When governments try to control prices by setting price ceilings or price floors, buyers and sellers often find a way around the controls. The result is a **black market** in which buying and selling take place at prices that violate government price regulations.

Airbnb and other peer-to-peer rental sites have provided landlords and tenants another way to avoid rent controls. Landlords can use these sites to convert a regular yearly rental into a series of short-term rentals for which they can charge above the legal maximum rent. Tenants can also use the sites to make a profit from rent controls. As we saw in the chapter opener, in San Francisco some tenants moved out of the city while keeping their rent-controlled apartments. They then rented out their apartments using

Black market A market in which buying and selling take place at prices that violate government price regulations.

peer-to-peer rental sites. Both San Francisco and New York have taken actions against peer-to-peer rental sites because some government officials believe the sites undermine rent control. Both cities have laws that prohibit landlords for renting apartments for less than 30 days. San Francisco also announced that anyone renting rooms through Airbnb and similar sites must pay the city's 14 percent hotel tax.

Some government officials in both cities, however, were reluctant to take actions that might limit the growth of the sharing economy of peer-to-peer rental sites. The sharing economy has the potential to improve economic efficiency and make available to consumers goods, such as cars, bikes, boats, and apartments, at lower prices. When cities have rent control laws, though, peer-to-peer sites perform a somewhat different function by making apartments available at rents higher than the legal price ceiling— apartments that renters might otherwise have difficulty finding because of the shortage caused by rent control. It remains to be seen whether local policymakers can resolve the conflict between putting legal ceilings on rents and encouraging peer-to-peer sites to operate in their cities.

MyEconLab Concept Check

Solved Problem 4.3

MyEconLab Interactive Animation

What's the Economic Effect of a Black Market in Renting Apartments?

In many cities that have rent controls, such as New York and San Francisco, the actual rents paid can be much higher than the legal maximum. Because rent controls cause a shortage of apartments, desperate tenants are often willing to pay landlords rents that are higher than the law allows, perhaps by writing a check for the legally allowed rent and paying an additional amount in cash. Look again at Figure 4.9

on page 112. Suppose that competition among tenants results in the black market rent rising to $3,500 per month. At this rent, tenants demand 1,900,000 apartments. Draw a graph showing the market for apartments and compare this situation with the one shown in Figure 4.9. Be sure to note any differences in consumer surplus, producer surplus, and deadweight loss.

Solving the Problem

Step 1: **Review the chapter material.** This problem is about price controls in the market for apartments, so you may want to review the section "Price Ceilings: Government Rent Control Policy in Housing Markets," which begins on page 112.

Step 2: **Draw a graph similar to Figure 4.9,** with the addition of the black market price.

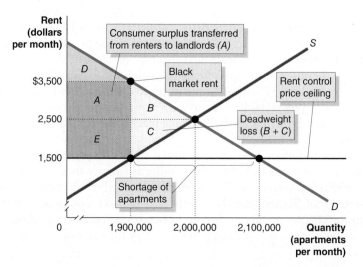

Step 3: **Analyze the changes from Figure 4.9.** The black market rent is now $3,500 per month—even higher than the original competitive equilibrium rent shown in Figure 4.9. So, consumer surplus declines by an amount equal to the sum of the areas of rectangle *A* and rectangle *E*. The remaining consumer surplus is triangle *D*. Note that rectangle *A*, which would have been part of consumer surplus without rent control, represents a transfer from renters to landlords. Compared with the situation shown in Figure 4.9, producer surplus has increased by an amount equal to the sum of the areas of rectangles *A* and *E*, and consumer surplus has declined by the same amount. Deadweight loss is equal to the sum of the areas of triangles *B* and *C*, the same as in Figure 4.9.

Extra Credit: This analysis leads to a surprising result: With an active black market in apartments, rent control may leave renters as a group worse off—with less consumer surplus—than if there were no rent control. There is one more possibility to consider, however. If enough landlords become convinced that they can get away with charging rents above the legal ceiling, the quantity of apartments supplied will increase. Eventually, the market could even end up at the competitive equilibrium, with an equilibrium rent of $2,500 and equilibrium quantity of 2,000,000 apartments. In that case, the rent control price ceiling becomes nonbinding, not because it was set below the equilibrium price but because it was not legally enforced.

Your Turn: For more practice, do related problem 3.15 on page 128 at the end of this chapter.   MyEconLab Study Plan

---

Rent controls can also lead to an increase in racial and other types of discrimination. With rent controls, more renters are looking for apartments than there are apartments to rent. Landlords can afford to indulge their prejudices by refusing to rent to people they don't like. In cities without rent controls, landlords face more competition, which makes it more difficult to turn down tenants on the basis of irrelevant characteristics, such as race.

The Results of Government Price Controls: Winners, Losers, and Inefficiency

When the government imposes price floors or price ceilings, three important results occur:

- Some people win.
- Some people lose.
- There is a loss of economic efficiency.

The winners with rent control are the people who are paying less for rent because they live in rent-controlled apartments. Landlords may also gain if they break the law by charging rents above the legal maximum for their rent-controlled apartments, provided that those illegal rents are higher than the competitive equilibrium rents would be. The losers from rent control are the landlords of rent-controlled apartments who abide by the law and renters who are unable to find apartments to rent at the controlled price. Rent control reduces economic efficiency because fewer apartments are rented than would be rented in a competitive market (refer again to Figure 4.9, on page 112). The resulting deadweight loss measures the decrease in economic efficiency.   MyEconLab Concept Check

Positive and Normative Analysis of Price Ceilings and Price Floors

Are rent controls, government farm programs, and other price ceilings and price floors bad? As we saw in Chapter 1, questions of this type have no right or wrong answers. Economists are generally skeptical of government attempts to interfere with competitive market equilibrium. Economists know the role competitive markets have played in raising the average person's standard of living. They also know that too much government intervention has the potential to reduce the ability of the market system to produce similar increases in living standards in the future.

But recall the difference between positive and normative analysis. Positive analysis is concerned with *what is*, and normative analysis is concerned with *what should be*. Our analysis of rent control and the federal farm programs in this chapter is positive analysis. We discussed the economic results of these programs. Whether these programs are desirable or undesirable is a normative question. Whether the gains to the winners more than make up for the losses to the losers and for the decline in economic efficiency is a matter of judgment and not strictly an economic question. Price ceilings and price floors continue to exist partly because people who understand their downside still believe they are good policies and therefore support them. The policies also persist because many people who support them do not understand the economic analysis in this chapter and so do not understand the drawbacks to these policies.

MyEconLab Study Plan | MyEconLab Concept Check

4.4 LEARNING OBJECTIVE

Analyze the economic impact of taxes.

The Economic Impact of Taxes

Supreme Court Justice Oliver Wendell Holmes once remarked: "Taxes are what we pay for a civilized society." When the government taxes a good or service, however, it affects the market equilibrium for that good or service. Just as with a price ceiling or price floor, one result of a tax is a decline in economic efficiency. Analyzing taxes is an important part of the field of economics known as *public finance*. In this section, we will use the model of demand and supply and the concepts of consumer surplus, producer surplus, and deadweight loss to analyze the economic impact of taxes.

The Effect of Taxes on Economic Efficiency

Whenever a government taxes a good or service, less of that good or service will be produced and consumed. For example, a tax on cigarettes will raise the cost of smoking and reduce the amount of smoking that takes place. We can use a demand and supply graph to illustrate this point. Figure 4.10 shows the market for cigarettes.

Without the tax, the equilibrium price of cigarettes would be $5.00 per pack, and 4 billion packs of cigarettes would be sold per year (point *A*). If the federal government requires sellers of cigarettes to pay a $1.00-per-pack tax, then their cost of selling cigarettes will increase by $1.00 per pack. This increase in costs causes the supply curve for cigarettes to shift up by $1.00 because sellers will now require a price that is $1.00 greater to supply the same quantity of cigarettes. In Figure 4.10, the supply curve shifts up by $1.00 to show the effect of the tax, and there is a new equilibrium price of $5.90 and a new equilibrium quantity of 3.7 billion packs (point *B*).

The federal government will collect tax revenue equal to the tax per pack multiplied by the number of packs sold, or $3.7 billion. The area shaded in green in Figure 4.10 represents the government's tax revenue. Consumers will pay a higher price of $5.90 per pack. Although sellers appear to be receiving a higher price per pack, once they have paid the tax, the price they receive falls from $5.00 per pack to $4.90 per pack. There is a loss of consumer surplus because consumers are paying a higher price. The price producers receive falls, so there is also a loss of producer surplus. Therefore, the tax on cigarettes has reduced *both* consumer surplus and producer surplus. Some of the reduction in consumer and producer surplus becomes tax revenue for the government. The rest of the reduction in consumer and producer surplus is equal to the deadweight loss from the tax, shown by the yellow-shaded triangle in the figure.

We can conclude that the true burden of a tax is not just the amount consumers and producers pay the government but also includes the deadweight loss. The deadweight loss from a tax is referred to as the *excess burden* of the tax. *A tax is efficient if it imposes a small excess burden relative to the tax revenue it raises.* One contribution economists make to government tax policy is to advise policymakers on which taxes are most efficient.

MyEconLab Concept Check

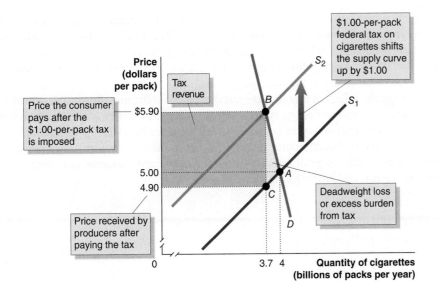

MyEconLab Animation

Figure 4.10

The Effect of a Tax on the Market for Cigarettes

Without the tax, market equilibrium occurs at point *A*. The equilibrium price of cigarettes is $5.00 per pack, and 4 billion packs of cigarettes are sold per year. A $1.00-per-pack tax on cigarettes will cause the supply curve for cigarettes to shift up by $1.00, from S_1 to S_2. The new equilibrium occurs at point *B*. The price of cigarettes will increase by $0.90, to $5.90 per pack, and the quantity sold will fall to 3.7 billion packs. The tax on cigarettes has increased the price paid by consumers from $5.00 to $5.90 per pack. Producers receive a price of $5.90 per pack (point *B*), but after paying the $1.00 tax, they are left with $4.90 (point *C*). The government will receive tax revenue equal to the green-shaded box. Some consumer surplus and some producer surplus will become tax revenue for the government, and some will become deadweight loss, shown by the yellow-shaded area.

Tax Incidence: Who Actually Pays a Tax?

The answer to the question "Who pays a tax?" seems obvious: Whoever is legally required to send a tax payment to the government pays the tax. But there can be an important difference between who is legally required to pay the tax and who actually *bears the burden* of the tax. The actual division of the burden of a tax between buyers and sellers is referred to as **tax incidence**. For example, the federal government currently levies an excise tax of 18.4 cents per gallon of gasoline sold. Gas station owners collect this tax and forward it to the federal government, but who actually bears the burden of the tax?

Tax incidence The actual division of the burden of a tax between buyers and sellers in a market.

Determining Tax Incidence on a Demand and Supply Graph
Suppose that currently the federal government does not impose a tax on gasoline. In Figure 4.11, equilibrium in the retail market for gasoline occurs at the intersection of the demand curve and supply curve, S_1. The equilibrium price is $3.50 per gallon, and the equilibrium quantity is 144 billion gallons per year. Now suppose that the federal government imposes a 10-cents-per-gallon tax. As a result of the tax, the supply curve for gasoline will shift up by 10 cents per gallon. At the new equilibrium, where the demand curve intersects the supply curve, S_2, the price has risen by 8 cents per gallon, from $3.50 to

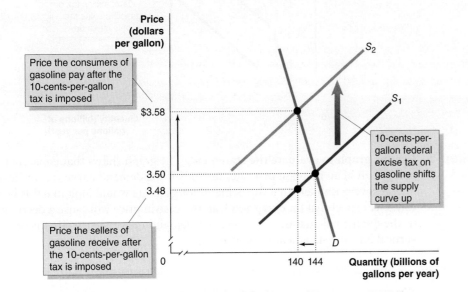

MyEconLab Animation

Figure 4.11

The Incidence of a Tax on Gasoline

With no tax on gasoline, the price would be $3.50 per gallon, and 144 billion gallons of gasoline would be sold each year. A 10-cents-per-gallon excise tax shifts up the supply curve from S_1 to S_2, raises the price consumers pay from $3.50 to $3.58, and lowers the price sellers receive from $3.50 to $3.48. Therefore, consumers pay 8 cents of the 10-cents-per-gallon tax on gasoline, and sellers pay 2 cents.

$3.58. Notice that only in the extremely unlikely case that demand is a vertical line will the market price rise by the full amount of the tax. Consumers are paying 8 cents more per gallon. Sellers of gasoline receive a new higher price of $3.58 per gallon, but after paying the 10-cents-per-gallon tax, they are left with $3.48 per gallon, or 2 cents less than they were receiving in the old equilibrium.

Although the sellers of gasoline are responsible for collecting the tax and sending the tax receipts to the government, they do not bear most of the burden of the tax. In this case, consumers pay 8 cents of the tax because the market price has risen by 8 cents, and sellers pay 2 cents of the tax because after sending the tax to the government, they are receiving 2 cents less per gallon of gasoline sold. Expressed in percentage terms, consumers pay 80 percent of the tax, and sellers pay 20 percent of the tax.

Solved Problem 4.4

MyEconLab Interactive Animation

When Do Consumers Pay All of a Sales Tax Increase?

A student makes the following statement: "If the federal government raises the sales tax on gasoline by $0.25, then the price of gasoline will rise by $0.25. Consumers can't get by without gasoline, so they have to pay the whole amount of any increase in the sales tax." Under what circumstances will the student's statement be true? Illustrate your answer with a graph of the market for gasoline.

Solving the Problem

Step 1: **Review the chapter material.** This problem is about tax incidence, so you may want to review the section "Tax Incidence: Who Actually Pays a Tax?" that begins on page 117.

Step 2: **Draw a graph like Figure 4.11 to illustrate the circumstances when consumers will pay all of an increase in a sales tax.**

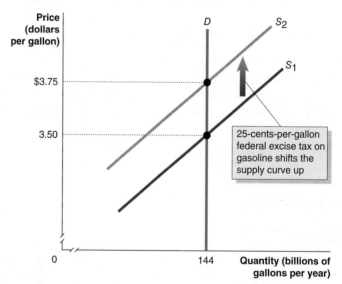

Step 3: **Use the graph to evaluate the statement.** The graph shows that consumers will pay all of an increase in a sales tax only if the demand curve is a vertical line. It is very unlikely that the demand for gasoline would look like this because we expect that for every good, an increase in price will cause a decrease in the quantity demanded. Because the demand curve for gasoline is not a vertical line, the statement is incorrect.

MyEconLab Study Plan   **Your Turn:** For more practice, do related problem 4.7 on page 130 at the end of the chapter.

MyEconLab Animation

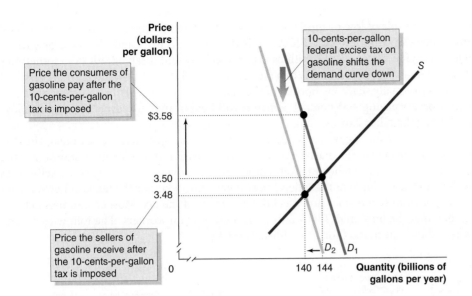

Figure 4.12

The Incidence of a Tax on Gasoline Paid by Buyers

With no tax on gasoline, the demand curve is D_1. If a 10-cents-per-gallon tax is imposed that consumers are responsible for paying, the demand curve shifts down by the amount of the tax, from D_1 to D_2. In the new equilibrium, consumers pay a price of \$3.58 per gallon, including the tax. Producers receive \$3.48 per gallon. The result is the same as when producers were responsible for paying the tax.

Does It Make a Difference Whether the Government Collects a Tax from Buyers or Sellers?

We have already seen the important distinction between who is legally required to pay a tax and who actually *bears the burden* of a tax. We can reinforce this point by noting explicitly that the incidence of a tax does *not* depend on whether the government collects a tax from the buyers of a good or from the sellers. Figure 4.12 illustrates this point by showing the effect on equilibrium in the market for gasoline if a 10-cents-per-gallon tax is imposed on buyers rather than on sellers. That is, we are now assuming that instead of sellers having to collect the 10-cents-per-gallon tax at the pump, buyers are responsible for keeping track of how many gallons of gasoline they purchase and sending the tax to the government. (Of course, it would be very difficult for buyers to keep track of their purchases or for the government to check whether they were paying all of the taxes they owe. That is why the government collects the tax on gasoline from sellers.)

Figure 4.12 is similar to Figure 4.11 except that it shows the gasoline tax being imposed on buyers rather than on sellers. In Figure 4.12, the supply curve does not shift because nothing has happened to change the quantity of gasoline sellers are willing to supply at any given price. The demand curve has shifted, however, because consumers now have to pay a 10-cent tax on every gallon of gasoline they buy. Therefore, at every quantity, they are willing to pay a price 10 cents less than they would have without the tax. In the figure, we indicate the effect of the tax by shifting the demand curve down by 10 cents, from D_1 to D_2. Once the tax has been imposed and the demand curve has shifted down, the new equilibrium quantity of gasoline is 140 billion gallons, which is exactly the same as in Figure 4.11.

The new equilibrium price after the tax is imposed appears to be different in Figure 4.12 than in Figure 4.11, but if we include the tax, buyers will pay the same price and sellers will receive the same price in both figures. To see this point, notice that in Figure 4.11, buyers pay sellers a price of \$3.58 per gallon. In Figure 4.12, they pay sellers only \$3.48, but they must also pay the government a tax of 10 cents per gallon. So, the total price buyers pay remains \$3.58 per gallon. In Figure 4.11, sellers receive \$3.58 per gallon from buyers, but after they pay the tax of 10 cents per gallon, they are left with \$3.48, which is the same amount they receive in Figure 4.12.   MyEconLab Concept Check

Making the Connection
MyEconLab Video

Is the Burden of the Social Security Tax Really Shared Equally between Workers and Firms?

Most people who receive paychecks have several different taxes withheld by their employers, who forward these taxes directly to the government. In fact, after getting their first job, many people are shocked when they discover the gap between their gross pay and their net pay after taxes have been deducted. The largest tax many people of low or moderate income pay is FICA, which stands for the Federal Insurance Contributions Act. FICA funds the Social Security and Medicare programs, which provide income and health care to the elderly and disabled. FICA is sometimes referred to as the *payroll tax*. When Congress passed the act, it wanted employers and workers to equally share the burden of the tax. Currently, FICA is 15.3 percent of wages, with workers paying 7.65 percent, which is withheld from their paychecks, and employers paying the other 7.65 percent.

But does requiring workers and employers to each pay half the tax mean that the burden of the tax is also shared equally? Our discussion in this chapter shows that the answer is "no." In the labor market, employers are buyers, and workers are sellers. As we saw in the example of the federal tax on gasoline, whether the tax is collected from buyers or from sellers does not affect the incidence of the tax. Most economists believe, in fact, that the burden of FICA falls almost entirely on workers. The following figure, which shows the market for labor, illustrates why.

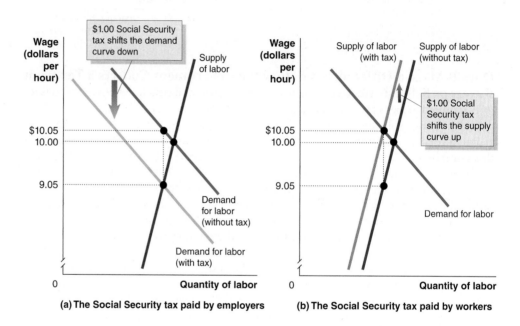

(a) The Social Security tax paid by employers   (b) The Social Security tax paid by workers

In the market for labor, the demand curve represents the quantity of labor demanded by employers at various wages, and the supply curve represents the quantity of labor supplied by workers at various wages. The intersection of the demand curve and the supply curve determines the equilibrium wage. In both panels, the equilibrium wage without a Social Security payroll tax is $10 per hour. For simplicity, let's assume that the payroll tax equals $1 per hour of work. In panel (a), we assume that employers must pay the tax. The tax causes the demand for labor curve to shift down by $1 at every quantity of labor because firms must now pay a $1 tax for every hour of labor they hire. We have drawn the supply curve for labor as being very steep because most economists believe the quantity of labor supplied by workers does not change much as the wage rate changes. In panel (a), after the tax is imposed, the equilibrium wage declines from $10 per hour to $9.05 per hour. Firms are now paying a total of $10.05 for every hour of work they hire: $9.05 in wages to workers and $1 in tax to the government. In other words, workers have paid $0.95 of the $1 tax, and firms have paid only $0.05.

Panel (b) shows that this result is exactly the same when the tax is imposed on workers rather than on firms. In this case, the tax causes the supply curve for labor to shift up by $1 at every quantity of labor because workers must now pay a tax of $1 for every hour they work. After the tax is imposed, the equilibrium wage increases to $10.05 per hour. But workers receive only $9.05 after they have paid the $1.00 tax. Once again, workers have paid $0.95 of the $1 tax, and firms have paid only $0.05.

Although the figure presents a simplified analysis, it reflects the conclusion of most economists who have studied the incidence of FICA: Even though Congress requires employers to pay half the tax and workers to pay the other half, in fact, the burden of the tax falls almost entirely on workers. This conclusion would not be changed even if Congress revised the law to require either employers or workers to pay all of the tax. The forces of demand and supply working in the labor market, and not Congress, determine the incidence of the tax.

Your Turn: Test your understanding by doing related problems 4.8 and 4.9 on page 130 at the end of this chapter.

MyEconLab Study Plan

Continued from page 101

Economics in Your Life

Does Rent Control Make It Easier for You to Find an Affordable Apartment?

At the beginning of the chapter, we posed the following question: If you have job offers in two different cities, one with rent control and one without, will you be more likely to find an affordable apartment in the city with rent control? In answering the question, this chapter has shown that although rent control can keep rents lower than they might otherwise be, it can also lead to a permanent shortage of apartments. You may have to search for a long time to find a suitable apartment, and landlords may even ask you to give them payments "under the table," which would make your actual rent higher than the controlled rent. Finding an apartment in a city without rent control should be much easier, although the rent may be higher.

Conclusion

Our discussion of the model of demand and supply shows that markets free from government intervention eliminate surpluses and shortages and do a good job of responding to the wants of consumers. As we have seen in this chapter, both consumers and firms sometimes try to use the government to change market outcomes in their favor. The concepts of consumer surplus, producer surplus, and deadweight loss allow us to measure the benefits consumers and producers receive from competitive market equilibrium. These concepts also allow us to measure the effects of government price floors and price ceilings and the economic impact of taxes.

Read *An Inside Look at Policy* on the next page for an example of regulatory and legal challenges facing companies like Airbnb and Uber that promote the sharing economy.

WASHINGTON POST

The Sharing Economy: How Do You Stop Something You Can't Keep Up With?

At one time, the sharing economy looked unstoppable.

In the aftermath of the 2008 recession, everybody was looking for ways to save and generally be smarter about using the diminishing amount of what they had. By some accounts the total value of everything people are sharing today—from apartments to cars to used clothing to unused parking spaces—is close to $26 billion. Yet, even the icons of the sharing economy—companies such as Airbnb and Uber—continue to face a host of regulatory and legal challenges that could impede, if not completely foil, their plans for future growth faster than they can disrupt the markets of the incumbents.

(a) The more recent signs that the sharing economy may not be unstoppable are the new legal troubles swirling around Airbnb, the international couchsurfing community that already has a Tumblr- and Instagram-like valuation of $1 billion. In New York City, where apartment vacancy rates remain around 2 percent—regulators and lawmakers are concerned that Airbnb might be violating New York City's "illegal hotel" laws that prohibit apartment owners from renting out rooms for less than 29 days at a time. The laws, which were originally intended to dissuade greedy landlords from drying up the housing supply even more by transforming residential buildings into pricey boutique hotels—now seem to apply equally as well to the cash-strapped condo owner with an extra room to let out for a few days.

With regard to its regulatory headaches, Airbnb is not alone. Think of mobile car-hailing business Uber, which has been involved in legal battles with regulators since Day 1. Even after Uber cleared initial regulatory hurdles in Washington, it still didn't make it any easier for a ride-sharing company like Sidecar to enter the market in its wake. If a company with access to a fleet of cars scared regulators, imagine what they felt when they learned that anyone could start picking up total strangers in their personal cars ....

(b) You can see where this is going—whether it's apartments, condos, cars or bikes—market incumbents are making no secret of the fact that they don't like the sharing economy. Fundamentally, "sharing" means that they will sell less of whatever they offer to consumers. Therefore, incumbents have an incentive to convince regulators and lawmakers that sharing economy start-ups are somehow "illegal." In the name of protecting the interests of the consumer, they trot out all the regulations, codes and laws that are potentially being violated. In the case of Airbnb, it's easy to see how lawmakers and regulators might be convinced to shut down certain economic activity if there's the implied specter of transients coming and going from seedy apartments all over the city at all hours of the day and night.

(c) But all of that assumes these sharing economy companies are something fundamentally new, a radical change to how the economy operates. That's not quite true. What's actually happening is that these sharing economy companies are going places where Adam Smith's "invisible hand" cannot. They are re-calibrating supply and demand, giving consumers access to otherwise unused capacity or idle assets. Instead of representing an entirely new underground economy, the companies of the sharing economy represent more of a supplement, adding capacity while driving down prices in ways that help consumers.

So, no, don't worry, the sharing economy is not illegal. Until the pace of regulatory change catches up to the pace of technological change, though, we can expect more of these legal and regulatory challenges to the likes of Airbnb and Uber. Until regulators understand how a route calculated via GPS might differ from the mileage calculated by a car's odometer or a taxi's taximeter, how could it be otherwise? The good news is that, as long as the entrenched market incumbents continue to argue that they're only acting to protect the interests of consumers, you can rest assured that the sharing economy is not going away anytime soon.

Source: Dominic Basulto, "The Sharing Economy: How Do You Stop Something You Can't Keep Up with?" *Washington Post*, May 24, 2013.

Key Points in the Article

Recent regulatory and legal challenges threaten the existence of Airbnb and Uber, two relatively new companies that are a part of the sharing economy. New York City lawmakers are exploring the possibility that Airbnb, a company that facilitates short-term room rentals in private residences, may be violating the city's hotel laws, which prohibit homeowners from renting rooms for less than 29 consecutive days. Uber, an on-demand car service company, is also involved in legal battles in several cities for potentially violating taxicab regulations. Established businesses in these industries argue that these new companies are not being subjected to the same level of regulatory laws, thereby gaining an unfair advantage.

Analyzing the News

ⓐ Airbnb's primary business is matching homeowners who want to rent out rooms for a short period with travelers looking for short-term rentals. In New York City, hotel laws prohibit the renting of private rooms for less than 29 consecutive days, so some hotel and government regulators have accused Airbnb and the homeowners of violating these laws. In New York City, hotel rooms are subject to a 15 percent tax. Customers renting rooms through Airbnb are not subject to these taxes, and this loss of tax revenue may be a concern for lawmakers. The figure below shows a hypothetical example of a tax on the market for these private rooms. Without the tax, the equilibrium price is $100 per night, with a quantity of 5,000 rooms being rented each week. With a 15 percent tax ($15), the supply curve shifts up by $15, increasing the price the consumer pays to $107.50, decreasing the price the homeowner receives to $92.50, and decreasing the quantity of rooms rented to 4,200. The tax revenue is equal to $63,000 ($15 per room × 4,200 rooms).

ⓑ Airbnb is competing with the established hotel industry, which is concerned that this new sharing economy will hurt their business. Customers using companies like Airbnb to rent rooms will cause a decrease in the demand for hotel rooms, which, all else equal, will decrease the equilibrium price and equilibrium quantity of hotel rooms. This loss of business and drop in revenue are certainly factors in the decision of the hotel industry to push lawmakers to apply regulations to companies conducting business in the sharing economy.

ⓒ Businesses in the sharing economy are benefiting consumers by giving them access to previously unavailable products and services. With Airbnb, consumers are able to choose from a wider variety of options when it comes to renting a room, which could lower the equilibrium price of rooms. This access has the potential to increase efficiency in the market by increasing consumer surplus.

Thinking Critically About Policy

1. The figure below shows the market for private rooms before and after the imposition of a 15 percent tax. What can you tell about the burden of the tax from the figure? What effect does the tax have on economic efficiency? Use the figure to show any change in efficiency resulting from the imposition of the tax.

2. Suppose that you are a legislator in New York considering whether to exempt people using Airbnb from the rule that rooms in private homes have to be rented for at least 29 consecutive days. What considerations would you take into account in making a decision? Briefly explain whether your analysis of this issue is entirely positive, entirely normative, or a mixture of the two.

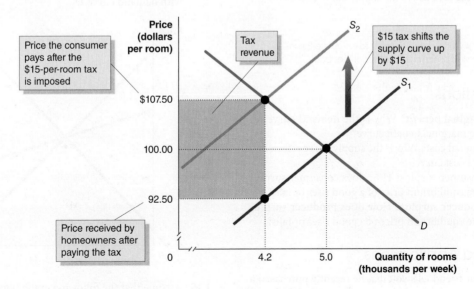

The market for private rooms before and after the imposition of a 15 percent hotel tax.

Chapter Summary and Problems

Key Terms

 4.1 Consumer Surplus and Producer Surplus, pages 102–106

LEARNING OBJECTIVE: Distinguish between the concepts of consumer surplus and producer surplus.

Summary

Although most prices are determined by demand and supply in markets, the government sometimes imposes *price ceilings* and *price floors*. A **price ceiling** is a legally determined maximum price that sellers may charge. A **price floor** is a legally determined minimum price that sellers may receive. Economists analyze the effects of price ceilings and price floors using *consumer surplus, producer surplus,* and *deadweight loss*. **Marginal benefit** is the additional benefit to a consumer from consuming one more unit of a good or service. The demand curve is also a marginal benefit curve. **Consumer surplus** is the difference between the highest price a consumer is willing to pay for a good or service and the actual price the consumer pays. The total amount of consumer surplus in a market is equal to the area below the demand curve and above the market price. **Marginal cost** is the additional cost to a firm of producing one more unit of a good or service. The supply curve is also a marginal cost curve. **Producer surplus** is the difference between the lowest price a firm is willing to accept for a good or service and the price it actually receives. The total amount of producer surplus in a market is equal to the area above the supply curve and below the market price.

MyEconLab   Visit **www.myeconlab.com** to complete these exercises online and get instant feedback.

Review Questions

1.1 What is marginal benefit? Why is the demand curve referred to as a marginal benefit curve?

1.2 What is marginal cost? Why is the supply curve referred to as a marginal cost curve?

1.3 What is consumer surplus? How does consumer surplus change as the equilibrium price of a good rises or falls?

1.4 What is producer surplus? How does producer surplus change as the equilibrium price of a good rises or falls?

Problems and Applications

1.5 Suppose your friend tells you that he recently purchased a particular product for $1,000 but that the product was "priceless." Although your friend is probably exaggerating, what would the consumer surplus equal for his "priceless" product?

1.6 Suppose that a frost in Florida reduces the size of the orange crop, which causes the supply curve for oranges to shift to the left. Briefly explain whether consumer surplus will increase or decrease and whether producer surplus will increase or decrease. Use a demand and supply graph to illustrate your answers.

1.7 A student makes the following argument: "When a market is in equilibrium, there is no consumer surplus. We know this because in equilibrium, the market price is equal to the price consumers are willing to pay for the good." Briefly explain whether you agree with the student's argument.

1.8 How does consumer surplus differ from the total benefit consumers receive from purchasing products? Similarly, how does producer surplus differ from the total revenue that firms receive from selling products? Under what special case will consumer surplus equal the total benefit consumers receive from consuming a product? Under what special case will producer surplus equal the total revenue firms receive from selling a product?

1.9 In the graph below, is the consumer surplus larger with demand curve D_1 or demand curve D_2? Briefly explain. Compare the producer surplus with demand curve D_1 and with demand curve D_2.

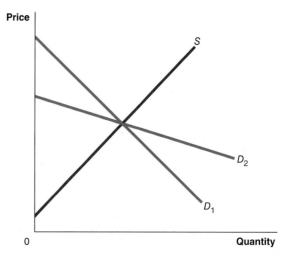

1.10 Assume that the following graph illustrates the market for a breast cancer–fighting drug, without which breast cancer patients cannot survive. What is the consumer surplus in this market? How does it differ from the consumer surplus in the markets you have studied up to this point?

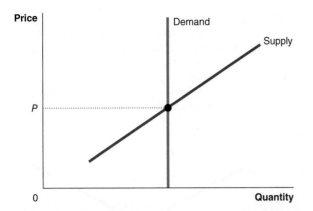

1.11 **[Related to the** Making the Connection **on page 104]** The *Making the Connection* states that the value of the area representing consumer surplus from broadband Internet service is $890.4 million. Use the information from the graph in the *Making the Connection* to show how this value was calculated. (For a review of how to calculate the area of a triangle, see the appendix to Chapter 1.)

1.12 The following graph shows the market for tickets to a concert that will be held in a local arena that seats 15,000 people. What is the producer surplus in this market? How does it differ from the producer surplus in the markets you have studied up to this point?

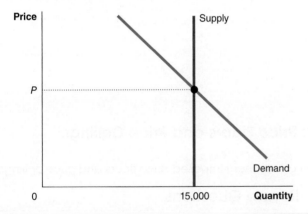

1.13 A study estimates that the total consumer surplus gained by people participating in auctions on eBay in a recent year was $7 billion. Is it likely that the total consumer surplus for the items bought in these auctions was higher or lower than it would have been if consumers had purchased these items for fixed prices in retail stores?

Source: Ravi Bapna, Wolfgang Jank, and Galit Shmueli, "Consumer Surplus in Online Auctions," *Information Systems Research*, Vol. 19, No. 4, December 2008, pp. 400–416.

1.14 Movies, songs, and books are covered by copyrights, which allow the creators of these works to keep other people from reproducing them without permission. Many people, though, violate copyright laws by using file-sharing services that allow them to download copies of songs and movies at a zero price.

   a. Does file sharing increase the consumer surplus from consuming existing songs and movies? Draw a demand curve to illustrate your answer. The demand curve should indicate the price when file sharing is not possible, the zero price with file sharing, and the amount of consumer surplus with and without file sharing.

   b. What are the likely effects of file sharing in the long run? Is file sharing likely to increase the total consumer surplus from consuming songs and movies in the long run? Briefly explain.

Source: Joel Waldfogel, "Bye, Bye, Miss American Pie? The Supply of New Recorded Music Since Napster," National Bureau of Economic Research Working Paper 16882, March 2011.

<table>
<tr><td>**4.2**</td><td>**The Efficiency of Competitive Markets, pages 106–109**
LEARNING OBJECTIVE: Understand the concept of economic efficiency.</td></tr>
</table>

Summary

Equilibrium in a competitive market is **economically efficient**. **Economic surplus** is the sum of consumer surplus and producer surplus. Economic efficiency is a market outcome in which the marginal benefit to consumers from the last unit produced is equal to the marginal cost of production and in which the sum of consumer surplus and producer surplus is at a maximum. When the market price is above or below the equilibrium price, there is a reduction in economic surplus. The reduction in economic surplus resulting from a market not being in competitive equilibrium is called the **deadweight loss**.

 MyEconLab   Visit **www.myeconlab.com** to complete these exercises online and get instant feedback.

Review Questions

2.1 Define *economic surplus* and *deadweight loss*.

2.2 What is economic efficiency? Why do economists define *efficiency* in this way?

Problems and Applications

2.3 Briefly explain whether you agree with the following statement: "A lower price in a market always increases economic efficiency in that market."

2.4 Briefly explain whether you agree with the following statement: "If at the current quantity, marginal benefit is greater than marginal cost, there will be a deadweight loss in the market. However, there is no deadweight loss when marginal cost is greater than marginal benefit."

2.5 Using a demand and supply graph, illustrate and briefly explain the effect on consumer surplus and producer surplus of the price in a market being below the equilibrium price. Show any deadweight loss on your graph.

2.6 Briefly explain whether you agree with the following statement: "If consumer surplus in a market increases, producer surplus must decrease."

2.7 Does an increase in economic surplus in a market always mean that economic efficiency in the market has increased? Briefly explain.

2.8 Using the following graph, show the effects on consumer surplus and producer surplus of an increase in supply from S_1 to S_2. By how much does economic surplus increase?

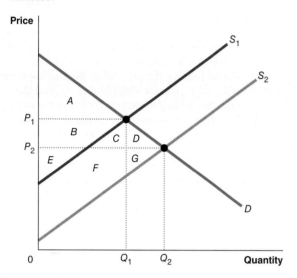

2.9 A student argues: "Economic surplus is greatest at the level of output where the difference between marginal benefit and marginal cost is largest." Do you agree? Briefly explain.

2.10 Using the following graph, explain why economic surplus would be smaller if Q_1 or Q_3 were the quantity produced than if Q_2 is the quantity produced.

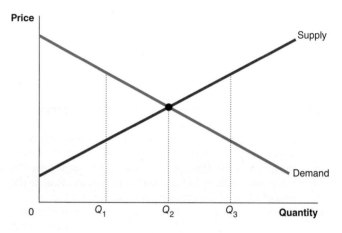

4.3 | Government Intervention in the Market: Price Floors and Price Ceilings, pages 109–116

LEARNING OBJECTIVE: Explain the economic effect of government-imposed price floors and price ceilings.

Summary

Producers or consumers who are dissatisfied with the equilibrium in a market can attempt to convince the government to impose a price floor or a price ceiling. Price floors usually increase producer surplus, decrease consumer surplus, and cause a deadweight loss. Price ceilings usually increase consumer surplus, reduce producer surplus, and cause a deadweight loss. The results of the government imposing price ceilings and price floors are that some people win, some people lose, and a loss of economic efficiency occurs. Price ceilings and price floors can lead to a **black market**, in which buying and selling take place at prices that violate government price regulations. Positive analysis is concerned with *what is*, and normative analysis is concerned with *what should be*. Positive analysis shows that price ceilings and price floors cause deadweight losses. Whether these policies are desirable or undesirable, though, is a normative question.

Review Questions

3.1 Why do some consumers tend to favor price controls while others tend to oppose them?

3.2 Do producers tend to favor price floors or price ceilings? Briefly explain.

3.3 What is a black market? Under what circumstances do black markets arise?

3.4 Can economic analysis provide a final answer to the question of whether the government should intervene in markets by imposing price ceilings and price floors? Briefly explain.

Problems and Applications

3.5 The following graph shows the market for apples. Assume that the government has imposed a price floor of $10 per crate.

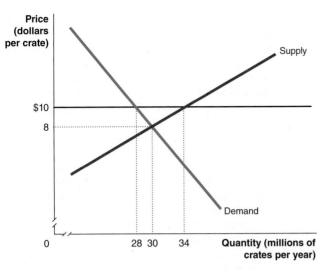

a. How many crates of apples will be sold to consumers after the price floor has been imposed?

b. Will there be a shortage or a surplus? If there is a shortage or a surplus, how large will it be?

c. Will apple producers benefit from the price floor? If so, explain how they will benefit.

3.6 Use the information on the kumquat market in the table to answer the following questions:

Price (per Crate)	Quantity Demanded (Millions of Crates per Year)	Quantity Supplied (Millions of Crates per Year)
$10	120	20
15	110	60
20	100	100
25	90	140
30	80	180
35	70	220

a. What are the equilibrium price and quantity? How much revenue do kumquat producers receive when the market is in equilibrium? Draw a graph showing the market equilibrium and the area representing the revenue kumquat producers receive.

b. Suppose the federal government decides to impose a price floor of $30 per crate. Now how many crates of kumquats will consumers purchase? How much revenue will kumquat producers receive? Assume that the government does not purchase any surplus kumquats. On your graph from question (a), show the price floor, the change in the quantity of kumquats purchased, and the revenue kumquat producers receive after the price floor is imposed.

c. Suppose the government imposes a price floor of $30 per crate and purchases any surplus kumquats from producers. Now how much revenue will kumquat producers receive? How much will the government spend on purchasing surplus kumquats? On your graph from question (a), show the area representing the amount the government spends to purchase the surplus kumquats.

3.7 Suppose that the government sets a price floor for milk that is above the competitive equilibrium price and that the government does not purchase any surplus milk.

a. Draw a graph showing this situation. Be sure your graph shows the competitive equilibrium price, the price floor, the quantity that would be sold in competitive equilibrium, and the quantity that would be sold with the price floor.

b. Compare the economic surplus in this market when there is a price floor and when there is not.

3.8 A newspaper headline reads: "State Officials Take on Pricing Regulations to Try to Provide Better, Dependable Income to Dairy Farmers." Is providing dependable income to dairy farmers a good policy goal for government officials? How are government officials likely to try to achieve this goal using pricing regulations? Should government officials use regulations to try to provide dependable incomes to every business in the country?

Source: Tim Darragh, "Thirsty for More Milk," *Morning Call*, (Allentown, PA) July 12, 2010.

3.9 According to an article in the *New York Times*, the Venezuelan government "imposes strict price controls that are intended to make a range of foods and other goods more affordable for the poor. They are often the very products that are the hardest to find."

a. Why would imposing price controls on goods make them hard to find?

b. One of the goods subject to price controls was toothpaste. Draw a graph to illustrate this situation. On your graph, be sure to indicate the areas representing consumer surplus, producer surplus, and deadweight loss.

Source: William Neuman, "With Venezuelan Cupboards Bare, Some Blame Price Controls," *New York Times*, April 20, 2012.

3.10 [Related to the Making the Connection **on page 111]** Some economists studying the effects of the minimum wage law have found that it tends to reduce the employment of black teenagers relative to white teenagers. Does the graph in the *Making the Connection* help you understand why black teenagers may have been disproportionately affected by the minimum wage law? Briefly explain.

3.11 [Related to the Chapter Opener **on page 101]** The cities of Peabody and Woburn are five miles apart. Woburn enacts a rent control law that puts a ceiling on rents well below their competitive market value. Predict the effect of this law on the competitive equilibrium rent in Peabody, which does not have a rent control law. Illustrate your answer with a demand and supply graph.

3.12 [Related to the Chapter Opener **on page 101]** If San Francisco were to repeal its rent control law, would the prices for short-term rentals in the city listed on Airbnb and other peer-to-peer sites be likely to rise or fall? Briefly explain.

3.13 [Related to the Chapter Opener **on page 101]** The competitive equilibrium rent in the city of Lowell is currently $1,000 per month. The government decides to enact rent control and establish a price ceiling of $750 per month for apartments. Briefly explain whether rent control is likely to make each of the following people better or worse off:

a. Someone currently renting an apartment in Lowell

b. Someone who will be moving to Lowell next year and who intends to rent an apartment

c. A landlord who intends to abide by the rent control law

d. A landlord who intends to ignore the law and illegally charge the highest rent possible for his apartments

3.14 **[Related to the** Don't Let This Happen to You **on page 113]** Briefly explain whether you agree with the following statement: "If there is a shortage of a good, it must be scarce, but there is not a shortage of every scarce good."

3.15 **[Related to** Solved Problem 4.3 **on page 114]** Use the information on the market for apartments in Bay City in the table to answer the following questions:

Rent	Quantity Demanded	Quantity Supplied
$500	375,000	225,000
600	350,000	250,000
700	325,000	275,000
800	300,000	300,000
900	275,000	325,000
1,000	250,000	350,000

a. In the absence of rent control, what is the equilibrium rent and what is the equilibrium quantity of apartments rented? Draw a demand and supply graph of the market for apartments to illustrate your answer. In equilibrium, will there be any renters who are unable to find an apartment to rent or any landlords who are unable to find a renter for an apartment?

b. Suppose the government sets a ceiling of $600 per month on rents. What is the quantity of apartments demanded, and what is the quantity of apartments supplied?

c. Assume that all landlords abide by the law. Use a demand and supply graph to illustrate the effect of this price ceiling on the market for apartments. Be sure to indicate on your graph each of the following: (i) the area representing consumer surplus after the price ceiling has been imposed, (ii) the area representing producer surplus after the price ceiling has been imposed, and (iii) the area representing the deadweight loss after the price ceiling has been imposed.

d. Assume that the quantity of apartments supplied is the same as you determined in (b). But now assume that landlords ignore the law and rent this quantity of apartments for the highest rent they can get. Briefly explain what this rent will be.

3.16 A student makes the following argument:

A price floor reduces the amount of a product that consumers buy because it keeps the price above the competitive market equilibrium. A price ceiling, though, increases the amount of a product that consumers buy because it keeps the price below the competitive market equilibrium.

Do you agree with the student's reasoning? Use a demand and supply graph to illustrate your answer.

3.17 University towns with major football programs experience an increase in demand for hotel rooms during home football weekends. Hotels respond to the increase in demand by increasing the prices they charge for rooms. Periodically, there is an outcry against the higher prices and accusations of "price gouging."

a. Draw a demand and supply graph of the market for hotel rooms in Boostertown for weekends with home football games and another graph for weekends without home football games. If the Boostertown city council passes a law stating that prices for rooms are not allowed to rise, what would happen to the market for hotel rooms during home football game weekends? Show your answer on your graph.

b. If the prices of hotel rooms are not allowed to increase, what will be the effect on out-of-town football fans?

c. How might the city council's law affect the supply of hotel rooms over time? Briefly explain.

d. University towns are not the only places that face peak and nonpeak "seasons." Can you think of other locations that face a large increase in demand for hotel rooms during particular times of the year? Why do we typically not see laws limiting the prices hotels can charge during peak seasons?

3.18 Suppose that initially the gasoline market is in equilibrium, at a price of $3.50 per gallon and a quantity of 45 million gallons per month. Then a war in the Middle East disrupts imports of oil into the United States, shifting the supply curve for gasoline from S_1 to S_2. The price of gasoline begins to rise, and consumers protest. The federal government responds by setting a price ceiling of $3.50 per gallon. Use the graph to answer the following questions:

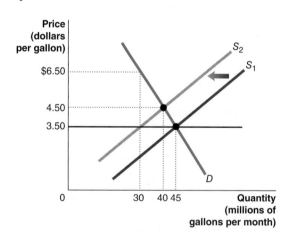

a. If there were no price ceiling, what would be the equilibrium price of gasoline, the quantity of gasoline demanded, and the quantity of gasoline supplied? Now assume that the price ceiling is imposed and that there is no black market in gasoline. What are the price of gasoline, the quantity of gasoline demanded, and the quantity of gasoline supplied? How large is the shortage of gasoline?

b. Assume that the price ceiling is imposed, and there is no black market in gasoline. Show on the graph the areas representing consumer surplus, producer surplus, and deadweight loss.

c. Now assume that there is a black market, and the price of gasoline rises to the maximum that consumers are willing to pay for the amount supplied by producers, at $3.50 per gallon. Show on the graph the areas representing producer surplus, consumer surplus, and deadweight loss.

d. Are consumers made better off with the price ceiling than without it? Briefly explain.

3.19 An editorial in the *Economist* magazine discusses the fact that in most countries—including the United States—it is illegal for individuals to buy or sell body parts, such as kidneys.

a. Draw a demand and supply graph for the market for kidneys. Show on your graph the legal maximum price of zero and indicate the quantity of kidneys

supplied at this price. (*Hint:* Because we know that some kidneys are donated, the quantity supplied will not be zero.)

b. The editorial argues that buying and selling kidneys should be legalized:

> With proper regulation, a kidney market would be a big improvement over the current sorry state of affairs. Sellers could be checked for disease and drug use, and cared for after operations…. Buyers would get better kidneys, faster. Both sellers and buyers would do better than in the illegal market, where much of the money goes to middlemen.

Do you agree with this argument? Should the government treat kidneys like other goods and allow the market to determine the price?

Source: "Psst, Wanna Buy a Kidney?" *Economist*, November 18, 2006, p. 15.

4.4 **The Economic Impact of Taxes, pages 116–121**
LEARNING OBJECTIVE: Analyze the economic impact of taxes.

Summary

Most taxes result in a loss of consumer surplus, a loss of producer surplus, and a deadweight loss. The true burden of a tax is not just the amount consumers and producers pay to the government but also includes the deadweight loss. The deadweight loss from a tax is called the excess burden of the tax. **Tax incidence** is the actual division of the burden of a tax. In most cases, consumers and firms share the burden of a tax levied on a good or service.

MyEconLab   Visit **www.myeconlab.com** to complete these exercises online and get instant feedback.

Review Questions

4.1 What is meant by *tax incidence*?

4.2 What do economists mean by an *efficient tax*?

4.3 Does who is legally responsible for paying a tax—buyers or sellers—make a difference in the amount of tax each pays? Briefly explain.

Problems and Applications

4.4 As explained in the chapter, economic efficiency is a market outcome in which the marginal benefit to consumers of the last unit produced is equal to its marginal cost of production. Using this explanation of economic efficiency, explain why a tax creates a deadweight loss.

4.5 Suppose the current equilibrium price of a quarter-pound hamburger is $5, and 10 million quarter-pound hamburgers are sold per month. After the federal government imposes a tax of $0.50 per hamburger, the equilibrium

price of hamburgers rises to $5.20, and the equilibrium quantity falls to 9 million. Illustrate this situation with a demand and supply graph. Be sure your graph shows the equilibrium price before and after the tax; the equilibrium quantity before and after the tax; and the areas representing consumer surplus after the tax, producer surplus after the tax, tax revenue collected by the government, and deadweight loss.

4.6 Use the following graph of the market for cigarettes to answer the questions:

a. According to the graph, how much is the government tax on cigarettes?

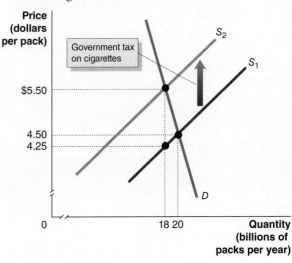

b. What price do producers receive after paying the tax?

c. How much tax revenue does the government collect?

d. How would the graph be different if the tax were collected from the buyers of cigarettes?

e. If the tax were collected from buyers, what would be the new equilibrium price that buyers pay producers of cigarettes?

f. Including the tax, what would be the total amount that cigarette buyers pay per pack?

4.7 **[Related to** Solved Problem 4.4 **on page 118]** Suppose the federal government decides to levy a sales tax of $1.00 per pie on pizza. Briefly explain whether you agree with the following statement, made by a representative of the pizza industry:

> The pizza industry is very competitive. As a result, pizza sellers will have to pay the whole tax because they are unable to pass any of it on to consumers in the form of higher prices. Therefore, a sales tax of $1.00 per pie will result in pizza sellers receiving $1.00 less on each pie sold, after paying the tax.

Illustrate your answer with a graph.

4.8 **[Related to the** Making the Connection **on page 119]** If the price consumers pay and the price sellers receive are not affected by whether consumers or sellers collect a tax on a good or service, why does the government usually collect a tax from sellers rather than from consumers?

4.9 **[Related to the** Making the Connection **on page 119]** Suppose the government imposes a payroll tax of $1 per hour of work and collects the tax from employers. Use a graph for the market for labor to show the effect of the payroll tax, assuming the special case of a vertical supply

curve of labor. By how much does the new equilibrium wage that employers pay workers fall?

4.10 The following graph shows the effect of a tax imposed on soft drinks. Use this graph to answer the questions:

a. Which areas in the graph represent the excess burden (deadweight loss) of the tax?

b. Which areas represent the revenues collected by the government from the tax?

c. Would this tax on soft drinks be considered efficient? Briefly explain.

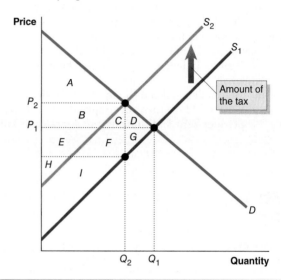

Appendix

Quantitative Demand and Supply Analysis

LEARNING OBJECTIVE

Use quantitative demand and supply analysis.

Graphs help us understand economic change *qualitatively*. For instance, a demand and supply graph can tell us that if household incomes rise, the demand curve for a normal good will shift to the right, and the price of the good will rise. Often, though, economists, business managers, and policymakers want to know more than the qualitative direction of change; they want a *quantitative estimate* of the size of the change.

In this chapter, we carried out a qualitative analysis of rent controls. We saw that imposing rent controls involves a trade-off: Renters as a group gain, but landlords lose, and the market for apartments becomes less efficient, as shown by the deadweight loss. To better evaluate rent controls, we need to know more than just that these gains and losses exist; we need to know how large they are. A quantitative analysis of rent controls will tell us how large the gains and losses are.

Demand and Supply Equations

The first step in a quantitative analysis is to supplement our use of demand and supply curves with demand and supply *equations*. Economists use data on prices, quantities, and other economic variables to statistically estimate equations for demand and supply curves. For example, suppose that economists have estimated that the demand for apartments in New York City is:

$$Q^D = 4,750,000 - 1,000P,$$

and the supply of apartments is:

$$Q^S = -1,000,000 + 1,300P.$$

We have used Q^D for the quantity of apartments demanded per month, Q^S for the quantity of apartments supplied per month, and P for the apartment rent, in dollars per month. In reality, both the quantity of apartments demanded and the quantity of apartments supplied will depend on more than just the rental price of apartments in New York City. The demand for apartments in New York City will also depend, for instance, on the average incomes of families in the New York area and on the rents of apartments in the surrounding cities. For simplicity, we will ignore these other factors.

With no government intervention, we know that at competitive market equilibrium, the quantity demanded must equal the quantity supplied, or:

$$Q^D = Q^S.$$

We can use this equation, which is called an *equilibrium condition*, to solve for the equilibrium monthly apartment rent by setting the quantity demanded from the demand equation equal to the quantity supplied from the supply equation:

$$4,750,000 - 1,000P = -1,000,000 + 1,300P$$

$$5,750,000 = 2,300P$$

$$P = \frac{5,750,000}{2,300} = \$2,500.$$

Figure 4A.1

Graphing Supply and Demand Equations

After statistically estimating supply and demand equations, we can use the equations to draw supply and demand curves. In this case, the equilibrium rent for apartments is $2,500 per month, and the equilibrium quantity of apartments rented is 2,250,000. The supply equation tells us that at a rent of $769, the quantity of apartments supplied will be zero. The demand equation tells us that at a rent of $4,750, the quantity of apartments demanded will be zero. The areas representing consumer surplus and producer surplus are also indicated on the graph.

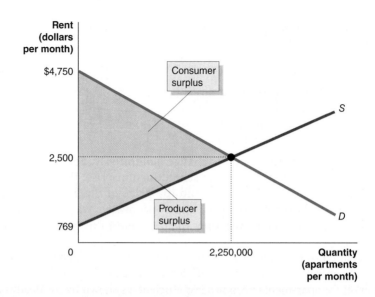

We can then substitute this price back into either the supply equation or the demand equation to find the equilibrium quantity of apartments rented:

$$Q^D = 4,750,000 - 1,000P = 4,750,000 - 1,000\,(2,500) = 2,250,000,$$

or

$$Q^S = -1,000,000 + 1,300P = -1,000,000 + 1,300\,(2,500) = 2,250,000.$$

Figure 4A.1 illustrates the information from these equations in a graph. The figure shows the values for rent when both the quantity supplied and the quantity demanded are zero. These values can be calculated from the demand and supply equations by setting Q^D and Q^S equal to zero and solving for price:

$$Q^D = 0 = 4,750,000 - 1,000P$$

$$P = \frac{4,750,000}{1,000} = \$4,750$$

and:

$$Q^S = 0 = -1,000,000 + 1,300P$$

$$P = \frac{-1,000,000}{-1,300} = \$769.23.$$

Calculating Consumer Surplus and Producer Surplus

Figure 4A.1 shows consumer surplus and producer surplus in this market. Recall that the sum of consumer surplus and producer surplus equals the net benefit that renters and landlords receive from participating in the market for apartments. We can use the values from the demand and supply equations to calculate the value of consumer surplus and producer surplus. Remember that consumer surplus is the area below the demand curve and above the line representing market price. Notice that this area forms a right triangle because the demand curve is a straight line—it is *linear*. As we noted in the appendix to Chapter 1, the area of a triangle is equal to ½ × Base × Height. In this case, the area is:

$$\frac{1}{2} \times (2,250,000) \times (4,750 - 2,500) = \$2,531,250,000.$$

So, this calculation tells us that the consumer surplus in the market for rental apartments in New York City is about $2.5 billion per month.

We can calculate producer surplus in a similar way. Remember that producer surplus is the area above the supply curve and below the line representing market price.

Because the supply curve is also a straight line, producer surplus in the figure is equal to the area of the right triangle:

$$\tfrac{1}{2} \times 2,250,000 \times (2,500 - 769) = \$1,947,375,000.$$

This calculation tells us that the producer surplus in the market for rental apartments in New York City is about $1.9 billion per month.

We can use the same type of analysis to measure the effect of rent control on consumer surplus, producer surplus, and economic efficiency. For instance, suppose the city imposes a rent ceiling of $1,500 per month. Figure 4A.2 can help guide us as we measure the effect.

First, we can calculate the quantity of apartments that will actually be rented by substituting the rent ceiling of $1,500 into the supply equation:

$$Q^S = -1,000,000 + (1,300 \times 1,500) = 950,000.$$

We also need to know the price on the demand curve when the quantity of apartments is 950,000. We can do this by substituting 950,000 for quantity in the demand equation and solving for price:

$$950,000 = 4,750,000 - 1,000P$$

$$P = \frac{-3,800,000}{-1,000} = \$3,800.$$

Compared with its value in competitive equilibrium, consumer surplus has been reduced by a value equal to the area of triangle B but increased by a value equal to the area of rectangle A. The area of triangle B is:

$$\tfrac{1}{2} \times (2,250,000 - 950,000) \times (3,800 - 2,500) = \$845,000,000,$$

and the area of rectangle A is Base × Height, or:

$$(\$2,500 - \$1,500) \times (950,000) = \$950,000,000.$$

The value of consumer surplus in competitive equilibrium was $2,531,250,000. As a result of the rent ceiling, it will be increased to:

$$(\$2,531,250,000 + 950,000,000) - \$845,000,000 = \$2,636,250,000.$$

Compared with its value in competitive equilibrium, producer surplus has been reduced by a value equal to the sum of the areas of triangle C and rectangle A. The area of triangle C is:

$$\tfrac{1}{2} \times (2,250,000 - 950,000) \times (2,500 - 1,500) = \$650,000,000.$$

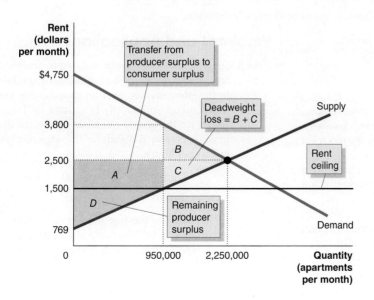

Figure 4A.2

Calculating the Economic Effect of Rent Controls

Once we have estimated equations for the demand and supply of rental housing, a diagram can guide our numerical estimates of the economic effects of rent control. Consumer surplus falls by an amount equal to the area of triangle B and increases by an amount equal to the area of rectangle A. Producer surplus falls by an amount equal to the sum of the areas of rectangle A and triangle C. The remaining producer surplus is equal to the area of triangle D. Deadweight loss is equal to the sum of the areas of triangles B and C.

We have already calculated the area of rectangle *A* as $950,000,000. The value of producer surplus in competitive equilibrium was $1,947,375,000. As a result of the rent ceiling, it will be reduced to:

$$\$1,947,375,000 - \$650,000,000 - \$950,000,000 = \$347,375,000.$$

The loss of economic efficiency, as measured by the deadweight loss, is equal to the value represented by the areas of triangles *B* and *C*, or:

$$\$845,000,000 + \$650,000,000 = \$1,495,000,000$$

The following table summarizes the results of the analysis (the values are in millions of dollars):

Consumer Surplus		Producer Surplus		Deadweight Loss	
Competitive Equilibrium	Rent Control	Competitive Equilibrium	Rent Control	Competitive Equilibrium	Rent Control
$2,531	$2,636	$1,947	$347	$0	$1,495

Qualitatively, we know that imposing rent control will make consumers better off, make landlords worse off, and decrease economic efficiency. The advantage of the analysis we have just gone through is that it puts dollar values on the qualitative results. We can now see how much consumers have gained, how much landlords have lost, and how great the decline in economic efficiency has been. Sometimes the quantitative results can be surprising. Notice, for instance, that after the imposition of rent control, the deadweight loss is actually much greater than the remaining producer surplus. Of course, these results are dependent on the numbers we chose for the demand and supply curve equations. Choosing different numbers would have changed the results.

Economists often study issues where the qualitative results of actions are apparent, even to non-economists. You don't have to be an economist to understand who wins and who loses from rent control or that if a company cuts the price of its product, its sales will increase. Business managers, policymakers, and the general public do, however, need economists to measure quantitatively the effects of different actions—including policies such as rent control—so that they can better assess the results of these actions.

MyEconLab Study Plan

MyEconLab Concept Check

Quantitative Demand and Supply Analysis, pages 131–134

LEARNING OBJECTIVE: Use quantitative demand and supply analysis.

MyEconLab   Visit **www.myeconlab.com** to complete these exercises online and get instant feedback.

Review Questions

4A.1 In a linear demand equation, what economic information is conveyed by the intercept on the price axis? Similarly, what economic information is conveyed by the intercept on the price axis in a linear supply equation?

4A.2 Suppose you were assigned the task of choosing a price that maximizes economic surplus in a market. What price would you choose? Why?

4A.3 Consumer surplus is used as a measure of a consumer's net benefit from purchasing a good or service. Explain why consumer surplus is a measure of net benefit.

4A.4 Why would economists use the term *deadweight loss* to describe the impact on consumer surplus and producer surplus from a price control?

Problems and Applications

4A.5 Suppose that you have been hired to analyze the impact on employment from the imposition of a minimum wage in the labor market. Further suppose that you estimate the demand and supply functions for labor, where *L* stands for the quantity of labor (measured in thousands of workers) and *W* stands for the wage rate (measured in dollars per hour):

$$\text{Demand:} \quad L^D = 100 - 4W$$
$$\text{Supply:} \quad L^S = 6W$$

First, calculate the free market equilibrium wage and quantity of labor. Now suppose the proposed minimum wage is $12. How large will the surplus of labor in this market be?

4A.6 The following graphs illustrate the markets for two different types of labor. Suppose an identical minimum wage is imposed in both markets. In which market will the minimum wage have the largest impact on employment? Why?

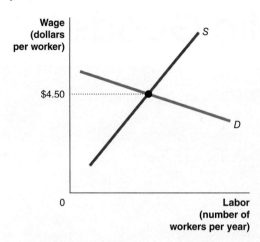

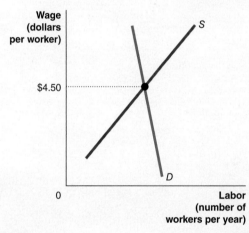

4A.7 Suppose that you are the vice president of operations of a manufacturing firm that sells an industrial lubricant in a competitive market. Further suppose that your economist gives you the following demand and supply functions:

Demand: $Q^D = 45 - 2P$

Supply: $Q^S = -15 + P$

What is the consumer surplus in this market? What is the producer surplus?

4A.8 The following graph shows a market in which a price floor of $3.00 per unit has been imposed. Calculate the values of each of the following:

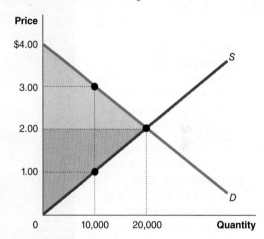

  a. The deadweight loss
  b. The transfer of producer surplus to consumers or the transfer of consumer surplus to producers
  c. Producer surplus after the price floor is imposed
  d. Consumer surplus after the price floor is imposed

4A.9 Construct a table like the one in this appendix on page 134, but assume that the rent ceiling is $2,000 rather than $1,500.

Externalities, Environmental Policy, and Public Goods

Chapter Outline and **Learning Objectives**

Can Economic Policy Help Protect the Environment?

Most scientists believe that burning fossil fuels generates carbon dioxide and other greenhouse gases that can increase global warming and cause potentially costly changes in climate. Should the government act to reduce greenhouse gases? If so, what policy would be best? In 2013, Duke University conducted a public opinion poll that found that about two-thirds of those surveyed believed that the government should regulate greenhouse gases. A large majority believed that the government should attempt to directly control the emission of greenhouse gases by, for instance, requiring that new cars have better gas mileage.

According to a poll conducted by the business school at the University of Chicago, most economists agreed that government policy should attempt to reduce greenhouse gases but they disagreed with the public about which government policies would be best. When the federal government orders firms to use particular methods to reduce pollution—for example, by requiring that automobile companies produce cars with better gas mileage—the government is using *command-and-control policies*. Many economists argue that a more efficient way to reduce pollution is through *market-based policies* that rely on economic incentives rather than on administrative rules.

A carbon tax is an example of a market-based policy. If the government taxes oil, coal, and other carbon-based fuels that generate carbon dioxide when burned, households and firms would have an economic incentive to reduce their use of those fuels. Government policies to reduce pollution, including the carbon tax, have been controversial, however. Some businesses oppose the carbon tax because they believe it will raise their costs of production. For example, the National Corn Growers Association stated that if a carbon tax were enacted, "every corn grower in the country will experience increased costs of production." Similarly, a spokesman for the American Fuel & Petrochemical Manufacturers argued against a carbon tax because "energy consumption can't simply be quit nor can it be reduced without considerable costs to consumers and especially to the nation's most vulnerable populations." Other businesses view the carbon tax favorably, particularly in comparison with command-and-control policies that they see as more costly and less effective. The Pacific Gas and Electric Company, a utility based in California, has praised "the flexibility and power of market incentives to promote a cleaner environment and more sustainable economy."

As we will see in this chapter, economic analysis has an important role to play in the debate over environmental policies.

Sources: "Americans Want Climate Rules but Not Taxes," UPI, February 7, 2013; Jonathan Marshall, "California's Cap-and-Trade Program: In Good Company," *Currents: News and Perspectives from Pacific Gas and Electric Company*, November 20, 2012; "NCDA Says Cap and Trade Will Hurt Corn Growers," www.agwired.com, January 20, 2010; Paoloa Sapienza and Luigi Zingales, "Economic Experts vs. Average Americans," University of Chicago, Booth School of Business, Working Paper 13-11; and Charles Drevna, "Energy Experts Blog," www.energy.nationaljournal.com, November 19, 2012.

Economics in Your Life

What's the "Best" Level of Pollution?

Policymakers debate alternative approaches for achieving the goal of reducing carbon dioxide emissions. But how do we know the "best" level of carbon emissions? If carbon dioxide emissions hurt the environment, should the government take action to eliminate them completely? As you read this chapter, try to answer these questions. You can check your answers against those we provide on **page 161** at the end of this chapter.

Pollution is a part of economic life. Consumers create air pollution by burning gasoline to power their cars and natural gas to heat their homes. Firms create air pollution when they produce electricity, pesticides, or plastics, among other products. Utilities produce sulfur dioxide when they burn coal to generate electricity. Sulfur dioxide contributes to acid rain, which can damage trees, crops, and buildings. The burning of fossil fuels generates carbon dioxide and other greenhouse gases that can increase global warming.

Pollution is just one example of an *externality*. An **externality** is a benefit or cost that affects someone who is not directly involved in the production or consumption of a good or service. In the case of air pollution, there is a *negative externality* because, for example, people with asthma may bear a cost even though they were not involved in the buying or selling of the electricity that caused the pollution. *Positive externalities* are also possible. For instance, medical research can provide a positive externality because people who are not directly involved in producing it or paying for it can benefit. A competitive market usually does a good job of producing the economically efficient amount of a good or service. This result may not hold, though, if there is an externality in the market. When there is a negative externality, the market may produce a quantity of the good that is greater than the efficient amount. When there is a positive externality, the market may produce a quantity that is less than the efficient amount. Government interventions in the economy—such as price floors on agricultural products or price ceilings on rents—can reduce economic efficiency (see Chapter 4). But, when there are externalities, government intervention may actually increase economic efficiency and enhance the well-being of society. The way in which government intervenes is important, however. Economists can help policymakers ensure that government programs are as efficient as possible.

In this chapter, we explore how best to deal with the problem of pollution and other externalities. We also look at *public goods*, which may not be produced at all unless the government produces them.

Externality A benefit or cost that affects someone who is not directly involved in the production or consumption of a good or service.

5.1 LEARNING OBJECTIVE

Identify examples of positive and negative externalities and use graphs to show how externalities affect economic efficiency.

Externalities and Economic Efficiency

When you consume a Big Mac, only you benefit, but when you consume a college education, other people also benefit. College-educated people are less likely to commit crimes, and by being better-informed voters, they are more likely to contribute to better government policies. So, although you capture most of the benefits of your college education, you do not capture all of them.

When you buy a Big Mac, the price you pay covers all of McDonald's costs of producing the Big Mac. When you buy electricity from a utility that burns coal and generates acid rain, the price you pay does not cover the cost of the damage caused by the acid rain.

So, there is a *positive externality* in the production of college educations because people who do not pay for them will nonetheless benefit from them. There is a *negative externality* in the generation of electricity because, for example, people with homes on a lake from which fish and wildlife have disappeared because of acid rain have incurred a cost, even though they might not have bought their electricity from the polluting utility.

The Effect of Externalities

Externalities interfere with the *economic efficiency* of a market equilibrium. A competitive market achieves economic efficiency by maximizing the sum of consumer surplus and producer surplus (see Chapter 4). *But that result holds only if there are no externalities in production or consumption.* An externality causes a difference between the *private cost* of production and the *social cost*, or the *private benefit* from consumption and the *social benefit*. The **private cost** is the cost borne by the producer of a good or service. The

Private cost The cost borne by the producer of a good or service.

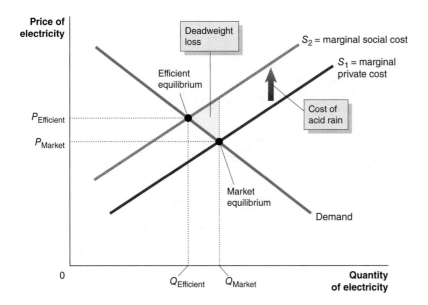

MyEconLab Animation

Figure 5.1

The Effect of Pollution on Economic Efficiency

Because utilities do not bear the cost of acid rain, they produce electricity beyond the economically efficient level. Supply curve S_1 represents just the marginal private cost that the utility has to pay. Supply curve S_2 represents the marginal social cost, which includes the costs to those affected by acid rain. If the supply curve were S_2 rather than S_1, market equilibrium would occur at price $P_{Efficient}$ and quantity $Q_{Efficient}$, the economically efficient level of output. But, when the supply curve is S_1, the market equilibrium occurs at price P_{Market} and quantity Q_{Market} where there is a deadweight loss equal to the area of the yellow triangle. Because of the deadweight loss, this equilibrium is not efficient.

social cost is the total cost of producing a good or service, and it is equal to the private cost plus any external cost, such as the cost of pollution. Unless there is an externality, the private cost and the social cost are equal. The **private benefit** is the benefit received by the consumer of a good or service. The **social benefit** is the total benefit from consuming a good or service, and it is equal to the private benefit plus any external benefit, such as the benefit to others resulting from your college education. Unless there is an externality, the private benefit and the social benefit are equal.

How a Negative Externality in Production Reduces Economic Efficiency

Consider how a negative externality in production reduces economic efficiency. Typically, economists assume that the producer of a good or service must bear all the costs of production. We now know that this observation is not always true. In the production of electricity, private costs are borne by the utility, but some external costs of pollution are borne by people who are not customers of the utility. The social cost of producing electricity is the sum of the private cost plus the external cost. Figure 5.1 shows the effect on the market for electricity of a negative externality in production.

S_1 is the market supply curve and represents only the private costs that utilities have to bear in generating electricity. Firms will supply an additional unit of a good or service only if they receive a price equal to the additional cost of producing that unit, so a supply curve represents the *marginal cost* of producing a good or service (see Chapter 4). If utilities also had to bear the cost of pollution, the supply curve would be S_2, which represents the true marginal social cost of generating electricity. The equilibrium with price $P_{Efficient}$ and quantity $Q_{Efficient}$ is efficient. The equilibrium with price P_{Market} and quantity Q_{Market} is not efficient.

To see why, remember that an equilibrium is economically efficient if economic surplus—which is the sum of consumer surplus plus producer surplus—is at a maximum (see Chapter 4). When economic surplus is at a maximum, the net benefit to society from the production of the good or service is at a maximum. With an equilibrium quantity of $Q_{Efficient}$, economic surplus is at a maximum, and the equilibrium is efficient. But, with an equilibrium quantity of Q_{Market}, economic surplus is reduced by the deadweight loss, shown in Figure 5.1 by the yellow triangle, and the equilibrium is not efficient. The deadweight loss occurs because the supply curve is above the demand curve for the production of the units of electricity between $Q_{Efficient}$ and Q_{Market}. That is, the additional cost—including the external cost—of producing these units is greater than the marginal benefit to consumers, as represented by the demand curve. In other words, because of the cost of the pollution, economic efficiency would be improved if less electricity were produced.

Social cost The total cost of producing a good or service, including both the private cost and any external cost.

Private benefit The benefit received by the consumer of a good or service.

Social benefit The total benefit from consuming a good or service, including both the private benefit and any external benefit.

MyEconLab Animation

Figure 5.2

The Effect of a Positive Externality on Economic Efficiency

People who do not consume college educations can still benefit from them. As a result, the marginal social benefit from a college education is greater than the marginal private benefit to college students. Because only the marginal private benefit is represented in the market demand curve D_1, the quantity of college educations produced, Q_{Market}, is too low. If the market demand curve were D_2 instead of D_1, the level of college educations produced would be $Q_{Efficient}$, which is the efficient level. At the market equilibrium of Q_{Market}, there is a deadweight loss equal to the area of the yellow triangle.

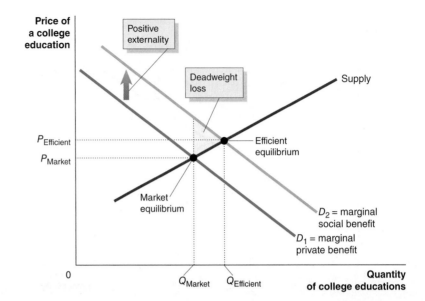

We can conclude the following: *When there is a negative externality in producing a good or service, too much of the good or service will be produced at market equilibrium.*

How a Positive Externality in Consumption Reduces Economic Efficiency

We have seen that a negative externality interferes with achieving economic efficiency. The same holds true for a positive externality. In earlier chapters, we assumed that the demand curve represents all the benefits that come from consuming a good. But a college education generates benefits that are not captured by the student receiving the education and so are not included in the market demand curve for college educations. Figure 5.2 shows the effect of a positive externality in consumption on the market for college educations.

If students receiving a college education could capture all its benefits, the demand curve would be D_2, which represents the marginal social benefits. The actual demand curve is D_1, however, which represents only the marginal private benefits received by students. The efficient equilibrium would come at price $P_{Efficient}$ and quantity $Q_{Efficient}$. At this equilibrium, economic surplus is maximized. The market equilibrium, at price P_{Market} and quantity Q_{Market}, will not be efficient because the demand curve is above the supply curve for production of the units between Q_{Market} and $Q_{Efficient}$. That is, the marginal benefit—including the external benefit—for producing these units is greater than the marginal cost. As a result, there is a deadweight loss equal to the area of the yellow triangle. Because of the positive externality, economic efficiency would be improved if more college educations were produced.

We can conclude the following: *When there is a positive externality in consuming a good or service, too little of the good or service will be produced at market equilibrium.*
MyEconLab Concept Check

Externalities and Market Failure

We have seen that because of externalities, the efficient level of output may not occur in either the market for electricity or the market for college educations. These are examples of **market failure**: situations in which the market fails to produce the efficient level of output. Later, we will discuss possible solutions to problems of externalities. But, first, we need to consider why externalities occur.
MyEconLab Concept Check

Market failure A situation in which the market fails to produce the efficient level of output.

What Causes Externalities?

Governments need to guarantee *property rights* in order for a market system to function well (see Chapter 2). **Property rights** refer to the rights individuals or businesses have to the exclusive use of their property, including the right to buy or sell it. Property can be tangible or physical, such as a store or factory. Property can also be intangible, such as the right to an idea. Most of the time, the governments of the United States and other

Property rights The rights individuals or businesses have to the exclusive use of their property, including the right to buy or sell it.

high-income countries do a good job of enforcing property rights, but in certain situations, property rights do not exist or cannot be legally enforced.

Consider the following situation: Lee owns land that includes a lake. A paper company wants to lease some of Lee's land to build a paper mill. The paper mill will discharge pollutants into Lee's lake. Because Lee owns the lake, he can charge the paper company the cost of cleaning up the pollutants. The result is that the cost of the pollution is a private cost to the paper company and is included in the price of the paper it sells. There is no externality, the efficient level of paper is produced, and there is no market failure.

Now suppose that the paper company again builds its paper mill on privately owned land but discharges its pollutants into a lake that is owned by the state government rather than by an individual. In the absence of any government regulations, the company can discharge pollutants into the lake without having to pay a fee. The cost of the pollution will be external to the company because it doesn't have to pay the cost of cleaning it up. The paper mill will produce a quantity of paper that is greater than the economically efficient level, and a market failure will occur. Or, suppose that Lee owns the lake, but the pollution is caused by acid rain generated by an electric utility hundreds of miles away. The law does not allow Lee to charge the electric utility for the damage caused by the acid rain. Even though someone is damaging Lee's property, he cannot enforce his property rights in this situation. Once again, there is an externality, and the market failure will result in too much electricity being produced.

If you buy a house, the government will protect your right to exclusive use of that house. No one else can use the house without your permission. Because of your property rights in the house, your private benefit from the house and the social benefit are the same. When you buy a college education, however, other people are able to benefit from it. You have no property right that will enable you to prevent them from benefiting or to charge them for the benefits they receive. As a result, there is a positive externality, and the market failure will result in too few college educations being supplied.

We can conclude the following: *Externalities and market failures result from incomplete property rights or from the difficulty of enforcing property rights in certain situations.*

MyEconLab Concept Check

MyEconLab Study Plan

Private Solutions to Externalities: The Coase Theorem

5.2 LEARNING OBJECTIVE

Discuss the Coase theorem and explain how private bargaining can lead to economic efficiency in a market with an externality.

As noted at the beginning of this chapter, government intervention may actually increase economic efficiency and enhance the well-being of society when externalities are present. It is also possible, however, for people to find private solutions to the problem of externalities.

Can the market cure market failure? In an influential article written in 1960, Ronald Coase of the University of Chicago, winner of the 1991 Nobel Prize in Economics, argued that under some circumstances, private solutions to the problem of externalities will occur. To understand Coase's argument, it is important to recognize that completely eliminating an externality usually is not economically efficient. Consider pollution, for example. There is, in fact, an *economically efficient level of pollution reduction*. At first, this seems paradoxical. Pollution is bad, and you might think the efficient amount of a bad thing is zero. But it isn't zero.

The Economically Efficient Level of Pollution Reduction

Chapter 1 introduced the important idea that the optimal decision is to continue any activity up to the point where the marginal benefit equals the marginal cost. This idea applies to reducing pollution just as much as it does to other activities. Sulfur dioxide emissions contribute to smog and acid rain. As sulfur dioxide emissions—or any other type of pollution—decline, society benefits: Fewer trees die, fewer buildings are damaged, and fewer people suffer breathing problems. But, a key point is that the additional benefit—that is, the *marginal benefit*—received from eliminating another ton of sulfur dioxide declines as sulfur dioxide emissions are reduced. To see why, consider what happens if utilities generate electricity without attempting to reduce sulfur dioxide emissions. In this situation, many smoggy days will occur in the cities of the Midwest and Northeast. Even healthy people may experience breathing problems. As sulfur dioxide emissions are reduced, the number of smoggy days will fall, and healthy people will no longer experience breathing problems. Eventually, if sulfur dioxide emissions fall to low levels, people with asthma will no longer be affected. Further reductions in sulfur dioxide emissions will have little additional benefit. The same will be true of the other benefits from reducing sulfur dioxide emissions: As the reductions increase, the additional benefits from fewer buildings and trees being damaged and lakes polluted will decline.

Making the Connection
MyEconLab Video

The Clean Air Act: How a Government Policy Reduced Infant Mortality

The following bar graphs show that the United States has made tremendous progress in reducing air pollution since Congress passed the Clean Air Act in 1970: Total emissions of the six main air pollutants have fallen dramatically. Over the same period, real U.S. gross domestic product (GDP)—which measures the value, corrected for inflation, of all the final goods and services produced in the country—more than tripled, energy consumption increased by half, and the number of miles traveled by all vehicles doubled.

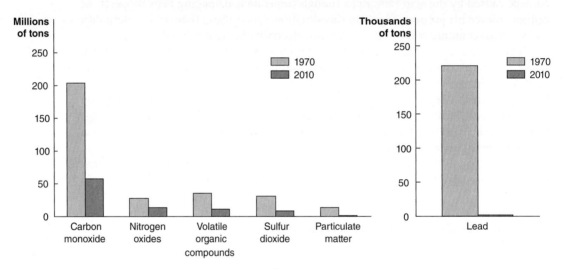

Source: U.S. Environmental Protection Agency, "Air Quality Trends," www.epa.gov/airtrends/aqtrends.html.

As we have seen, when levels of pollution are high, the marginal benefit of reducing pollution is also high. We would expect, then, that the benefit of reducing air pollution in 1970 was much higher than the benefit from a proportional reduction in air pollution would be today, when the level of pollution is much lower. Kenneth Y. Chay of Brown University and Michael Greenstone of MIT have shown that the benefits from the reductions in air pollution that occurred in the period immediately after passage of the Clean Air Act were indeed high. They argue that the exposure of pregnant women to high levels of air pollution can be damaging to their unborn children, possibly by reducing lung functioning. This damage would increase the chance that the infant would die in the first weeks after being born. In the two years following passage of the Clean Air Act, there was a sharp reduction in air pollution and also in infant mortality. The decline in infant mortality was mainly due to a reduction in deaths within one month of birth. Of course, other factors may also have been responsible for the decline in infant mortality, but Chay and Greenstone use statistical analysis to isolate the effect of the decline in air pollution. They conclude that: "1,300 fewer infants died in 1972 than would have in the absence of the Clean Air Act."

Source: Kenneth Y. Chay and Michael Greenstone, "Air Quality, Infant Mortality, and the Clean Air Act of 1970," National Bureau of Economic Research Working Paper 10053, October 2003.

MyEconLab Study Plan   **Your Turn:** Test your understanding by doing related problem 2.8 on pages 164–165 at the end of this chapter.

What about the marginal cost to electric utilities of reducing pollution? To reduce sulfur dioxide emissions, utilities have to switch from burning high-sulfur coal to burning more costly fuel, or they have to install pollution control devices, such as scrubbers. As the level of pollution falls, further reductions become increasingly costly. Reducing emissions or other types of pollution to very low levels can require complex and expensive new technologies. For example, Arthur Fraas, formerly of the federal Office of Management and Budget, and Vincent Munley, of Lehigh University, have shown that the marginal cost of removing 97 percent of pollutants from municipal wastewater is more than twice as high as the marginal cost of removing 95 percent.

The *net benefit* to society from reducing pollution is equal to the difference between the benefit of reducing pollution and the cost. To maximize the net benefit to society, sulfur dioxide emissions—or any other type of pollution—should be reduced up to the point where the marginal benefit from another ton of reduction is equal to the marginal cost. Figure 5.3 illustrates this point.

In Figure 5.3, we measure *reductions* in sulfur dioxide emissions on the horizontal axis. We measure the marginal benefit and marginal cost in dollars from eliminating another ton of sulfur dioxide emissions on the vertical axis. As reductions in pollution increase, the marginal benefit declines and the marginal cost increases. The economically efficient amount of pollution reduction occurs where the marginal benefit equals the marginal cost. The figure shows that, in this case, the economically efficient reduction of sulfur dioxide emissions is 8.5 million tons per year. In a program begun in 1990, this is the amount of reduction Congress decided should occur by 2010. At that level of emission reduction, the marginal benefit and the marginal cost of the last ton of sulfur dioxide emissions eliminated are both $200 per ton. Suppose instead that the emissions target was only 7.0 million tons. The figure shows that, at that level of reduction, the last ton of reduction has added $250 to the benefits received by society, but it has added only $175 to the costs of utilities. There has been a net benefit to society from this ton of pollution reduction of $75. In fact, the figure shows a net benefit to society from pollution reduction for every ton from 7.0 million to 8.5 million. Only when sulfur dioxide

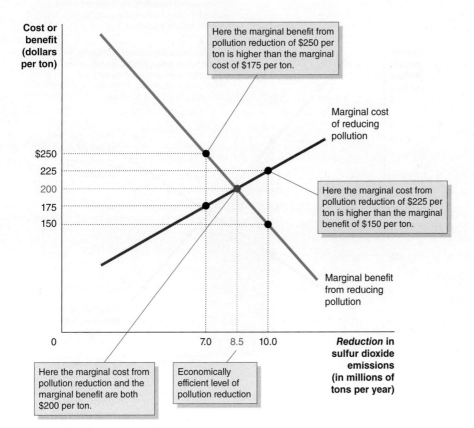

MyEconLab Animation

Figure 5.3

The Marginal Benefit from Pollution Reduction Should Equal the Marginal Cost

If the reduction of sulfur dioxide emissions is at 7.0 million tons per year, the marginal benefit of $250 per ton is greater than the marginal cost of $175 per ton. Further reductions in emissions will increase the net benefit to society. If the reduction of sulfur dioxide emissions is at 10.0 million tons, the marginal cost of $225 per ton is greater than the marginal benefit of $150 per ton. An increase in sulfur dioxide emissions will increase the net benefit to society. Only when the reduction is at 8.5 million tons is the marginal benefit equal to the marginal cost. This level is the economically efficient level of pollution reduction.

emissions are reduced by 8.5 million tons per year will marginal benefit fall enough and marginal cost rise enough that the two are equal.

Now suppose Congress had set the target for sulfur dioxide emissions reduction at 10 million tons per year. Figure 5.3 shows that the marginal benefit at that level of reduction has fallen to only $150 per ton and the marginal cost has risen to $225 per ton. The last ton of reduction has actually *reduced* the net benefit to society by $75 per ton. In fact, every ton of reduction beyond 8.5 million reduces the net benefit to society.

To summarize: If the marginal benefit of reducing sulfur dioxide emissions is greater than the marginal cost, further reductions will make society better off. But if the marginal cost of reducing sulfur dioxide emissions is greater than the marginal benefit, further reductions will actually make society worse off.   MyEconLab Concept Check

The Basis for Private Solutions to Externalities

In arguing that private solutions to the problem of externalities were possible, Ronald Coase emphasized that when more than the optimal level of pollution is occurring, the benefits from reducing the pollution to the optimal level are greater than the costs. Figure 5.4 illustrates this point.

The marginal benefit curve shows the additional benefit from each reduction in a ton of sulfur dioxide emissions. The area under the marginal benefit curve between the two emission levels is the *total* benefit received from reducing emissions from one level to another. For instance, in Figure 5.4, the total benefit from increasing the reduction in sulfur dioxide emissions from 7.0 million tons to 8.5 million tons is the sum of the areas of *A* and *B*. The marginal cost curve shows the additional cost from each reduction in a ton of emissions. The *total* cost of reducing emissions from one level to another is the

MyEconLab Animation

Figure 5.4

The Benefits of Reducing Pollution to the Optimal Level Are Greater than the Costs

Increasing the reduction in sulfur dioxide emissions from 7.0 million tons to 8.5 million tons results in total benefits equal to the sum of the areas of *A* and *B* under the marginal benefit curve. The total cost of this decrease in pollution is equal to the area of *B* under the marginal cost curve. The total benefits are greater than the total costs by an amount equal to the area of *A*. Because the total benefits from reducing pollution are greater than the total costs, it is possible for those receiving the benefits to arrive at a private agreement with polluters to pay them to reduce pollution.

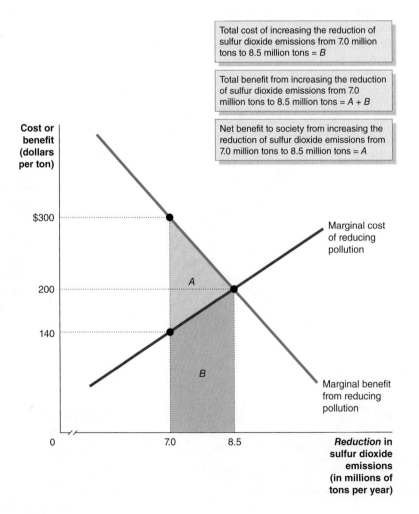

Total cost of increasing the reduction of sulfur dioxide emissions from 7.0 million tons to 8.5 million tons = B

Total benefit from increasing the reduction of sulfur dioxide emissions from 7.0 million tons to 8.5 million tons = A + B

Net benefit to society from increasing the reduction of sulfur dioxide emissions from 7.0 million tons to 8.5 million tons = A

Don't Let This Happen to You

Remember That It's the *Net* Benefit That Counts

Why would we not want to *completely* eliminate anything unpleasant? As long as any person suffers any unpleasant consequences from air pollution, the marginal benefit of reducing air pollution will be positive. Therefore, removing every particle of air pollution will result in the largest *total* benefit to society. But removing every particle of air pollution is not optimal for the same reason that it is not optimal to remove every particle of dirt or dust from a room when cleaning it. The cost of cleaning your room is not just the price of the cleaning products but also the opportunity cost of your time. The more time you devote to cleaning your room, the less time you have for other activities. As

you devote more and more additional hours to cleaning your room, the alternative activities you have to give up are likely to increase in value, raising the opportunity cost of cleaning: Cleaning instead of watching television may not be too costly, but cleaning instead of eating any meals or getting any sleep is very costly. Optimally, you should eliminate dirt in your room up to the point where the marginal benefit of the last dirt removed equals the marginal cost of removing it. Society should take the same approach to air pollution. The result is the largest *net* benefit to society.

MyEconLab Study Plan

Your Turn: Test your understanding by doing related problem 2.9 on page 165 at the end of this chapter.

---

area under the marginal cost curve between the two emission levels. The total cost from increasing the reduction in emissions from 7.0 million tons to 8.5 million tons is the area of *B*. The net benefit from reducing emissions is the difference between the total cost and the total benefit, which is equal to the area of *A*.

In Figure 5.4, the benefits from further reductions in sulfur dioxide emissions are much greater than the costs. In the appendix to Chapter 1, we reviewed the formula for calculating the area of a triangle, which is ½ × Base × Height, and the formula for the area of a rectangle, which is Base × Height. Using these formulas, we can calculate the value of the total benefits from the reduction in emissions and the value of the total costs. The value of the benefits $(A + B)$ is $375 million. The value of the costs (B) is $255 million. If the people who would benefit from a reduction in pollution could get together, they could offer to pay the electric utilities $255 million to reduce the pollution to the optimal level. After making the payment, they would still be left with a net benefit of $120 million. In other words, a private agreement to reduce pollution to the optimal level is possible, without any government intervention.   MyEconLab Concept Check

Making the Connection
MyEconLab Video

The Fable of the Bees

Apple trees must be pollinated by bees to bear fruit. Bees need the nectar from apple trees (or other plants) to produce honey. In an important article published in the early 1950s, the British economist James Meade, winner of the 1977 Nobel Prize in Economics, argued that there were positive externalities in both apple growing and beekeeping. The more apple trees growers planted, the more honey would be produced in the hives of local beekeepers. And the more hives beekeepers kept, the larger the apple crops in neighboring apple orchards. Meade assumed that apple growers were not compensating beekeepers for the pollination services they were providing for apple crops and that beekeepers were not compensating apple growers for the use of their nectar in honey making. Therefore, he concluded that unless the government intervened, the market would not supply enough apple trees and beehives.

Steven Cheung of the University of Washington showed, however, that government intervention was not necessary because beekeepers and apple growers had long since arrived at private agreements. In fact, in Washington State, farmers with fruit orchards had been renting beehives to pollinate their trees since at least as early as 1917. According to Cheung, "Pollination contracts usually include stipulations regarding the number

Some apple growers and beekeepers make private arrangements to arrive at an economically efficient outcome.

and strength of the [bee] colonies, the rental fee per hive, the time of delivery and removal of hives, the protection of bees from pesticide sprays, and the strategic placing of hives."

Today, honeybees pollinate more than $14 billion worth of crops annually, from blueberries in Maine to almonds in California. Increasing demand for almonds has expanded the crop in California until it now stretches for 300 miles, across 800,000 acres, producing 80 percent of the country's almonds. Currently, about 1.6 million beehives are required to pollinate the California almond crop. Beehives are shipped into the state in February and March to pollinate the almond trees, and then they are shipped to Oregon and Washington to pollinate the cherry, pear, and apple orchards during April and May.

A mysterious disease that began wiping out beehives beginning in 2005 was still reducing the bee population in 2013. But private agreements between beekeepers and farmers continued to play an important role in U.S. agriculture.

Sources: James E. Meade, "External Economies and Diseconomies in a Competitive Situation," *Economic Journal*, Vol. 62, March 1952, pp. 54–67; Steven N. S. Cheung, "The Fable of the Bees: An Economic Investigation," *Journal of Law and Economics*, Vol. 16, No. 1, April 1973, pp. 11–33; and Michael Wines, "Mystery Malady Kills More Bees, Heightening Worry on Farms," *New York Times*, March 18, 2013.

MyEconLab Study Plan

Your Turn: Test your understanding by doing related problem 2.11 on page 165 at the end of this chapter.

Do Property Rights Matter?

In discussing the bargaining between the electric utilities and the people suffering the effects of the utilities' pollution, we assumed that the electric utilities were not legally liable for the damage they were causing. In other words, the victims of pollution could not legally enforce the right of their property not to be damaged, so they would have to pay the utilities to reduce the pollution. But would it make any difference if the utilities were legally liable for the damages? Surprisingly, as Coase was the first to point out, it does not matter for the amount of pollution reduction. The only difference would be that now the electric utilities would have to pay the victims of pollution for the right to pollute rather than the victims having to pay the utilities to reduce pollution. Because the marginal benefits and marginal costs of pollution reduction would not change, the bargaining should still result in the efficient level of pollution reduction—in this case, 8.5 million tons.

In the absence of the utilities being legally liable, the victims of pollution have an incentive to pay the utilities to reduce pollution up to the point where the marginal benefit of the last ton of reduction is equal to the marginal cost. If the utilities are legally liable, they have an incentive to pay the victims of pollution to allow them to pollute up to the same point. MyEconLab Concept Check

The Problem of Transactions Costs

Unfortunately, there are frequently practical difficulties that interfere with a private solution to the problem of externalities. In cases of pollution, for example, there are often both many polluters and many people suffering from the negative effects of pollution. Negotiating an agreement between the people suffering from pollution and the firms causing the pollution often fails because of the *transactions costs* involved. **Transactions costs** are the costs in time and other resources that parties incur in the process of agreeing to and carrying out an exchange of goods or services. In this case, the transactions costs would include the time and other costs of negotiating an agreement, drawing up a binding contract, and monitoring the agreement. Unfortunately, when many people are involved, the transactions costs are often higher than the net benefits from reducing the externality. In that case, the cost of transacting ends up exceeding the gain from the transaction, and a private solution to an externality problem is not feasible. MyEconLab Concept Check

Transactions costs The costs in time and other resources that parties incur in the process of agreeing to and carrying out an exchange of goods or services.

The Coase Theorem

Coase's argument that private solutions to the problem of externalities are possible is summed up in the **Coase theorem**: *If transactions costs are low, private bargaining will result in an efficient solution to the problem of externalities.* We have seen the basis for the Coase theorem in the preceding example of pollution by electric utilities: Because the benefits from reducing an externality are often greater than the costs, private bargaining can lead to an efficient outcome. But we have also seen that this outcome will occur only if transactions costs are low, and in the case of pollution, they usually are not. In general, private bargaining is most likely to reach an efficient outcome if the number of parties bargaining is small.

In practice, we must add a couple of other qualifications to the Coase theorem. In addition to low transactions costs, private solutions to the problem of externalities will occur only if all parties to the agreement have full information about the costs and benefits associated with the externality, and all parties must be willing to accept a reasonable agreement. For example, if those suffering from the effects of pollution do not have information on the costs of reducing pollution, it is unlikely that the parties can reach an agreement. Unreasonable demands can also hinder an agreement. For instance, in the example of pollution by electric utilities, we saw that the total benefit of reducing sulfur dioxide emissions was $375 million. Even if transactions costs are very low, if the utilities insist on being paid more than $375 million to reduce emissions, no agreement will be reached because the amount paid exceeds the value of the reduction to those suffering from the emissions.   MyEconLab Concept Check

Coase theorem The argument of economist Ronald Coase that if transactions costs are low, private bargaining will result in an efficient solution to the problem of externalities.

MyEconLab Study Plan

Government Policies to Deal with Externalities

When private solutions to externalities are not feasible, how should the government intervene? British economist A. C. Pigou of Cambridge University was the first to analyze market failure systematically. Pigou argued that to deal with a negative externality in production, the government should impose a tax equal to the cost of the externality. The effect of such a tax is shown in Figure 5.5, which reproduces the negative externality from acid rain shown in Figure 5.1 on page 139.

By imposing a tax on the production of electricity equal to the cost of acid rain, the government will cause electric utilities to *internalize* the externality. As a consequence, the cost of the acid rain will become a private cost borne by the utilities, and the supply

5.3 LEARNING OBJECTIVE

Analyze government policies to achieve economic efficiency in a market with an externality.

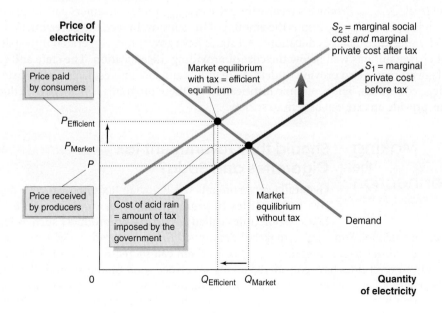

MyEconLab Animation

Figure 5.5

When There Is a Negative Externality, a Tax Can Lead to the Efficient Level of Output

Because utilities do not bear the cost of acid rain, they produce electricity beyond the economically efficient level. If the government imposes a tax equal to the cost of acid rain, the utilities will internalize the externality. As a consequence, the supply curve will shift up, from S_1 to S_2. The market equilibrium quantity changes from Q_{Market}, where an inefficiently high level of electricity is produced, to $Q_{\text{Efficient}}$, the economically efficient equilibrium quantity. The price of electricity will rise from P_{Market}—which does not include the cost of acid rain—to $P_{\text{Efficient}}$—which does include the cost. Consumers pay the price $P_{\text{Efficient}}$, while producers receive the price P, which is equal to $P_{\text{Efficient}}$ minus the amount of the tax.

Figure 5.6

When There Is a Positive Externality, a Subsidy Can Bring about the Efficient Level of Output

People who do not consume college educations can benefit from them. As a result, the social benefit from a college education is greater than the private benefit to college students. If the government pays a subsidy equal to the external benefit, students will internalize the externality. The subsidy will cause the demand curve to shift up, from D_1 to D_2. As a result, the market equilibrium quantity will shift from Q_{Market}, where an inefficiently low level of college educations is supplied, to $Q_{Efficient}$, the economically efficient equilibrium quantity. Producers receive the price $P_{Efficient}$, while consumers pay the price P, which is equal to $P_{Efficient}$ minus the amount of the subsidy.

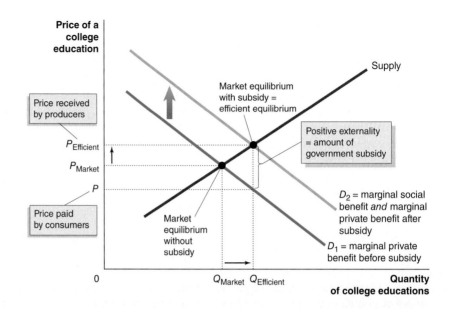

curve for electricity will shift from S_1 to S_2. The result will be a decrease in the equilibrium output of electricity from Q_{Market} to the efficient level, $Q_{Efficient}$. The price consumers pay for electricity will rise from P_{Market} —which does not include the cost of acid rain—to $P_{Efficient}$—which does include the cost. Producers will receive a price P, which is equal to $P_{Efficient}$ minus the amount of the tax.

Pigou also reasoned that the government can deal with a positive externality in consumption by giving consumers a subsidy, or payment, equal to the value of the externality. The effect of the subsidy is shown in Figure 5.6, which reproduces the positive externality from college education shown in Figure 5.2 on page 140.

By paying college students a subsidy equal to the external benefit from a college education, the government will cause students to *internalize* the externality. That is, the external benefit from a college education will become a private benefit received by college students, and the demand curve for college educations will shift from D_1 to D_2. The equilibrium number of college educations supplied will increase from Q_{Market} to the efficient level, $Q_{Efficient}$. Producers receive the price $P_{Efficient}$, while consumers pay the price P, which is equal to $P_{Efficient}$ minus the amount of the subsidy. In fact, the government does heavily subsidize college educations. All states have government-operated universities that charge tuitions well below the cost of providing the education. The state and federal governments also provide students with grants and low-interest loans that subsidize college educations. The economic justification for these programs is that college educations provide an external benefit to society.

| Making the Connection | **Should the Government Tax Cigarettes and Soda?** |

MyEconLab Video

Generally, governments use Pigovian taxes to deal with negative externalities in *production*. Governments also impose taxes—sometimes called *sin taxes*—on products such as cigarettes and alcohol. Some policymakers have argued that these products generate negative externalities in *consumption*, so a tax on them can increase economic efficiency. Recently, several cities have considered taxing sweetened soda, on the grounds that these sodas cause a negative externality by raising medical costs. Just as governments can deal with a positive externality in consumption by giving consumers a subsidy, they can deal with a negative externality by imposing a tax.

The effect of a tax on soda is shown in the following figure. By imposing a tax on soda, the government will cause consumers to internalize the externality. That is, the external cost to drinking soda will become a private cost paid by consumers. Because consumers now have to pay a tax on soda, at every quantity they are willing to pay less than they would have without the tax, so the demand curve for soda will shift down by the amount of the tax, from D_1 to D_2. The equilibrium quantity of sodas consumed will decrease from Q_{Market} to the efficient level, $Q_{Efficient}$. (Note that as we saw in Chapter 4, pages 119–121, we get the same result whether the government imposes a tax on the buyers of a good or on the sellers.)

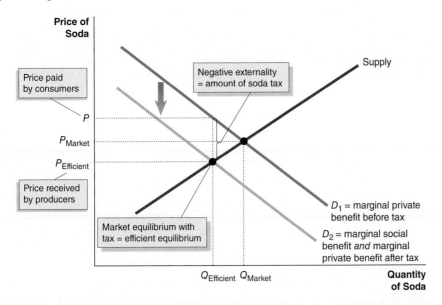

But do people actually cause a negative externality by smoking and drinking sweetened sodas? It might seem that they don't because consumers of cigarettes and sodas bear the costs of any health problems they experience. In fact, though, the higher medical expenses from treating the complications of cigarette smoking or obesity are not paid entirely by the smokers or soda drinkers. A smoker who receives health insurance through his employer may increase the costs of that insurance, which all the workers at the firm will pay. Similarly, taxpayers partly pay for the health care of someone who is over age 65 and is enrolled in the federal government's Medicare program. The costs of medical care that smokers or soda drinkers do not pay themselves represent a negative externality.

There is a complication to this conclusion, however: Smokers and people who are obese tend to die early. This tragic outcome means that smokers and the obese may have been paying taxes to help pay for Social Security and Medicare benefits that they will never receive. They may also have made payments into company and public employee pension plans and purchased long-term care insurance, but they may not have lived long enough to receive many pension payments or to have spent time in a nursing home. So, there are offsetting effects: While alive, smokers and obese people may impose costs on others who bear the expense of their higher medical costs, but because they are likely to die early, they provide a financial gain to recipients of Social Security, Medicare, company and public employee pension plans, and purchasers of long-term care insurance.

W. Kip Viscusi of Vanderbilt University has studied the case of tobacco smoking and concluded that the external costs and benefits roughly offset each other, meaning that there doesn't appear to be a significant negative externality from smoking. Studies of obesity have arrived at somewhat conflicting results: A study of obesity in the Netherlands found that the cost savings from premature death offset the additional lifetime medical costs of obese people. But another study on U.S. data found that obesity did lead to a net increase in lifetime medical costs, even taking into account the shorter average life spans of obese people.

There may also be costs to smoking and obesity beyond additional medical costs. Smokers may inflict costs on others because of secondhand smoke or because smoking during pregnancy can lead to low birth weights and other health problems for babies. Airlines have noted that they spend more on fuel costs because of the increasing weight of passengers.

In the end, economists and policymakers continue to debate whether the government should use taxes to deal with negative externalities in consumption.

Sources: David Leonhardt, "Obama Likes Some Sin Taxes More Than Others," *New York Times*, April 10, 2013; W. Kip Viscusi, "Cigarette Taxation and the Social Consequences of Smoking," in James Poterba, ed., *Tax Policy and the Economy*, Vol. 9, Cambridge: MIT Press, 1995; Pieter H. M. van Baal, et al., "Lifetime Medical Costs of Obesity: Prevention No Cure for Increasing Health Expenditure," *PLoS Medicine*, Vol. 5, No. 2, February 2008, pp. 242–249; Pierre-Carl Michaud, "Understanding the Economic Consequences of Shifting Trends in Population Health," National Bureau of Economic Research Working Paper 15231, August 2009; and "Feds Say Obesity Epidemic Hurts Airlines by Increasing Fuel Costs," Associated Press, November 5, 2004.

MyEconLab Study Plan

Your Turn: Test your understanding by doing related problem 3.12 on page 166 at the end of this chapter.

Solved Problem 5.3

MyEconLab Interactive Animation

Dealing with the Externalities of Car Driving

When you drive a car, you generate several negative externalities: You cause some additional air pollution, you increase the chances that other drivers will have an accident, and you cause some additional congestion on roads, causing other drivers to waste time in traffic. Ian Parry of the International Monetary Fund and Kenneth Small of the University of California, Irvine, have estimated that these external costs amount to about $1.00 per gallon of gasoline. Taxes on gasoline are currently about $0.50 per gallon.

a. Draw a graph showing the gasoline market. Indicate the efficient equilibrium quantity and the market equilibrium quantity.

b. Given this information, if the federal government wanted to bring about the efficient level of gasoline production, how large a tax should the government impose on gasoline? Will the price consumers pay for gasoline rise by the full amount of the tax? Briefly explain using your graph from part (a).

Solving the Problem

Step 1: Review the chapter material. This problem is about the government using a tax to deal with a negative externality, so you may want to review the section "Government Policies to Deal with Externalities," which begins on page 147.

Step 2: Answer part (a) by drawing a graph of the gasoline market. In this case, the tax is levied on the consumption of gasoline rather than on its production, so your graph can show the demand curve representing marginal social benefit being below the demand curve showing marginal private benefit. (Of course, the government actually collects the tax from sellers rather than from consumers, but we get the same result whether the government imposes a tax on the buyers of a good or on the sellers.) Your graph should also show the market equilibrium quantity of gasoline, Q_{Market}, being greater than the efficient equilibrium quantity, $Q_{\text{Efficient}}$.

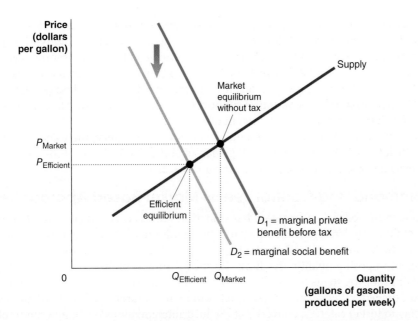

Step 3: **Answer part (b) by explaining the size of the necessary tax, indicating the tax on your graph from part (a), and explaining the effect of the tax on the equilibrium price.** If Parry and Small are correct that the external cost from consuming gasoline is $1.00 per gallon, then the tax per gallon should be raised from $0.50 to $1.00 per gallon. You should show the effect of the increase in the tax on your graph.

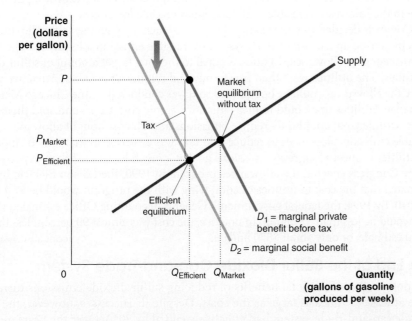

The graph shows that although the tax shifts down the demand curve for gasoline by $0.50 per gallon, the price consumers pay increases by less than $0.50. To see this, note that the price consumers pay rises from P_{Market} to P, which is smaller than the $0.50 per gallon tax, which equals the vertical distance between $P_{Efficient}$ and P.

Source: Ian W. H. Parry and Kenneth A. Small, "Does Britain or the United States Have the Right Gasoline Tax?" *American Economic Review*, Vol. 95, No. 4, September 2005, pp. 1276–1289.

Your Turn: For more practice, do related problems 3.9, 3.10, and 3.11 on page 166 at the end of this chapter.   MyEconLab Study Plan

Pigovian taxes and subsidies
Government taxes and subsidies intended to bring about an efficient level of output in the presence of externalities.

Because Pigou was the first economist to propose using government taxes and subsidies to deal with externalities, they are sometimes referred to as **Pigovian taxes and subsidies**. Note that a Pigovian tax eliminates deadweight loss and improves economic efficiency, unlike most taxes, which are intended simply to raise revenue and can reduce consumer surplus and producer surplus and create a deadweight loss (see Chapter 4). In fact, one reason that economists support Pigovian taxes as a way to deal with negative externalities is that the government can use the revenues raised by Pigovian taxes to lower other taxes that reduce economic efficiency. For instance, the Canadian province of British Columbia has enacted a Pigovian tax on carbon dioxide emissions and uses the revenue raised to reduce personal income taxes.

Command-and-Control versus Market-Based Approaches

Command-and-control approach
A policy that involves the government imposing quantitative limits on the amount of pollution firms are allowed to emit or requiring firms to install specific pollution control devices.

Although the federal government has sometimes used taxes and subsidies to deal with externalities, in dealing with pollution, it has traditionally used a *command-and-control approach*. A **command-and-control approach** to reducing pollution involves the government imposing quantitative limits on the amount of pollution firms are allowed to emit or requiring firms to install specific pollution control devices. For example, in the 1980s, the federal government required auto manufacturers such as Ford and General Motors to install catalytic converters to reduce auto emissions on all new automobiles.

Congress could have used direct pollution controls to deal with the problem of acid rain. To achieve its objective of a reduction of 8.5 million tons per year in sulfur dioxide emissions by 2010, Congress could have required every utility to reduce sulfur dioxide emissions by the same specified amount. However, this approach would not have been an economically efficient solution to the problem because utilities can have very different costs of reducing sulfur dioxide emissions. Some utilities that already used low-sulfur coal could reduce emissions further only at a high cost. Other utilities, particularly those in the Midwest, were able to reduce emissions at a lower cost.

Congress decided to use a market-based approach to reducing sulfur dioxide emissions by setting up a *cap-and-trade system* of tradable emission allowances. The federal government gave allowances to utilities equal to the total target amount of sulfur dioxide emissions. The utilities were then free to buy and sell the allowances. An active market where the allowances could be bought and sold was conducted on the Chicago Mercantile Exchange. Utilities that could reduce emissions at low cost did so and sold their allowances. Utilities that could only reduce emissions at high cost bought allowances. Using tradable emission allowances to reduce acid rain was a success in that it made it possible for utilities to meet Congress's emissions goal at a much lower cost than expected. Just before Congress enacted the allowances program in 1990, the Edison Electric Institute estimated that the cost to utilities of complying with the program would be $7.4 billion by 2010. By 1994, the federal government's General Accounting Office estimated that the cost would be less than $2 billion. In practice, the cost was almost 90 percent less than the initial estimate, or only about $870 *million*.   MyEconLab Concept Check

The End of the Sulfur Dioxide Cap-and-Trade System

The dollar value of the total benefits of reducing sulfur dioxide emissions turned out to be at least 25 times as large as the costs. Despite its successes, however, the sulfur dioxide cap-and-trade system had effectively ended by 2013. Over the years, research showed that the amount of illnesses caused by sulfur dioxide emissions was greater than had been thought. In response to these findings, President George W. Bush proposed legislation lowering the cap on sulfur dioxide emissions, but Congress did not pass the legislation. Court rulings kept the Environmental Protection Agency (EPA) from using regulations to set up a new trading system for sulfur dioxide allowances with a lower cap. As a result, the EPA reverted to the previous system of setting limits on sulfur dioxide emissions at the state or the individual power plant level.

Because nationwide trading of emission allowances was no longer possible, the allowances lost their value. Many economists continue to believe that market-based policies, such as the sulfur dioxide cap-and-trade system, are an efficient way to deal with the externalities of pollution. But in the end, any policy requires substantial political support to be enacted and maintained.   MyEconLab Concept Check

Are Tradable Emission Allowances Licenses to Pollute?

Tradable emission allowances also face a political problem because some environmentalists have criticized them for being "licenses to pollute." These environmentalists argue that just as the government does not issue licenses to rob banks or drive drunk, it should not issue licenses to pollute. But, this criticism ignores one of the central lessons of economics: Resources are scarce, and trade-offs exist. Resources that are spent on reducing one type of pollution are not available to reduce other types of pollution or for any other use. Because reducing acid rain using tradable emission allowances has cost utilities $870 million per year, rather than $7.4 billion, as originally estimated, society has saved more than $6.5 billion per year.   MyEconLab Concept Check

Making the Connection
MyEconLab Video

Can a Carbon Tax Reduce Global Warming?

In the past 35 years, the global temperature has increased about 0.75 degree Fahrenheit (or 0.40 degree Centigrade) compared with the average for the period between 1951 and 1980. The following graph shows changes in temperature over the years since 1880.

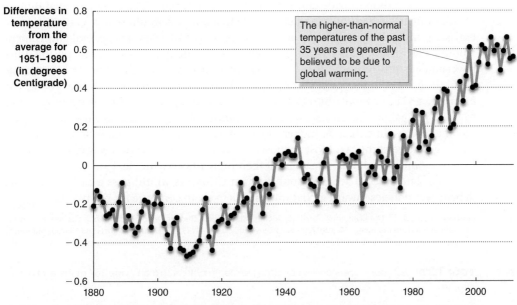

Source: NASA, Goddard Institute for Space Studies, data.giss.nasa.gov/gistemp/tabledata_v3/GLB.Ts.txt.

Over the centuries, global temperatures have gone through many long periods of warming and cooling. Nevertheless, many scientists are convinced that the recent warming trend is not part of the natural fluctuations in temperature but is primarily caused by the burning of fossil fuels, such as coal, natural gas, and petroleum. Burning these fuels releases carbon dioxide, which accumulates in the atmosphere as a "greenhouse gas." Greenhouse gases cause some of the heat released from the earth to be reflected back, increasing temperatures. Annual carbon dioxide emissions have increased from about 50 million metric tons of carbon in 1850 to 1,600 million metric tons in 1950 and to nearly 9,500 million metric tons in 2011.

If greenhouse gases continue to accumulate in the atmosphere, according to some estimates global temperatures could increase by 3 degrees Fahrenheit or more during the next 100 years. Such an increase in temperature could lead to significant changes in climate, which might result in more hurricanes and other violent weather conditions, disrupt farming in many parts of the world, and lead to increases in sea levels, which could lead to flooding in coastal areas.

Although most economists and policymakers agree that emitting carbon dioxide results in a significant negative externality, there has been an extensive debate over which policies should be adopted. Part of the debate arises from disagreements over how rapidly global warming is likely to occur and what the economic cost will be. In addition, carbon dioxide emissions are a global problem; sharp reductions in carbon dioxide emissions only in the United States and Europe, for instance, would not be enough to stop global warming. But coordinating policy across countries has proven difficult. Finally, policymakers and economists debate the relative effectiveness of different policies.

Governments have used several approaches to reducing carbon dioxide emissions. In 2005, 24 countries in the European Union established a cap-and-trade system, similar to the one used successfully in the United States to reduce sulfur dioxide emissions. Under this program, each country issues emission allowances that can be freely traded among firms in different countries. In 2013, the system suffered a setback when the European Parliament voted against a plan to reduce the number of allowances available. Without a reduction in allowances, it was unclear how the system could be used to further reduce carbon dioxide emissions. In 2009, President Barack Obama proposed a cap-and-trade system for the United States to reduce carbon dioxide emissions to their 1990 level by 2020. However, Congress failed to approve the plan. California has introduced its own carbon dioxide cap-and-trade system, as have Australia, South Korea, and several provinces in China.

In 2013, members of Congress introduced a bill to reduce carbon dioxide emissions. Economists working at federal government agencies have estimated that the marginal social cost of carbon dioxide emissions is about $21 per ton. The Congressional Budget Office estimates that a Pigovian tax equal to that amount would reduce carbon dioxide emissions in the United States by about 8 percent over 10 years. The federal government would collect about $1.2 trillion in revenues from the tax over the same period. One government study indicates that 87 percent of a carbon tax would be borne by consumers in the form of higher prices for gasoline, electricity, natural gas, and other goods. For example, a $21 per ton carbon tax would increase the price of gasoline by about $0.18 to $0.20 per gallon. Because lower-income households spend a larger fraction of their incomes on gasoline than do higher income households, they would bear a proportionally larger share of the tax. Most proposals for a carbon tax include a way of refunding to lower-income households some part of their higher tax payments.

As of late 2013, it seemed doubtful that Congress would pass a carbon tax. The debate over policies toward global warming is likely to continue for many years.

Sources: "ETS, RIP?" *The Economist*, April 20, 2013; Congressional Budget Office, "Effects of a Carbon Tax on the Economy and the Environment," May 2013, www.cbo.gov/publication/44223; and Daniel F. Morris and Clayton Munnings, "Progressing to a Fair Carbon Tax," Resources for the Future, April 2013, www.rff.org/RFF/Documents/RFF-IB-13-03.pdf.

MyEconLab Study Plan

Your Turn: Test your understanding by doing related problem 3.16 on page 167 at the end of this chapter.

5.4 LEARNING OBJECTIVE

Explain how goods can be categorized on the basis of whether they are rival or excludable and use graphs to illustrate the efficient quantities of public goods and common resources.

Rivalry The situation that occurs when one person consuming a unit of a good means no one else can consume it.

Excludability The situation in which anyone who does not pay for a good cannot consume it.

Private good A good that is both rival and excludable.

Four Categories of Goods

We can explore further the question of when the market is likely to succeed in supplying the efficient quantity of a good by understanding that goods differ on the basis of whether their consumption is *rival* and *excludable*. **Rivalry** occurs when one person consuming a unit of a good means no one else can consume it. If you consume a Big Mac, for example, no one else can consume it. **Excludability** means that anyone who does not pay for a good cannot consume it. If you don't pay for a Big Mac, McDonald's can exclude you from consuming it. The consumption of a Big Mac is therefore rival and excludable. The consumption of some goods, however, can be either *nonrival* or *nonexcludable*. Nonrival means that one person's consumption does not interfere with another person's consumption. Nonexcludable means that it is impossible to exclude others from consuming the good, whether they have paid for it or not. Figure 5.7 shows four possible categories into which goods can fall.

We next consider each of the four categories:

1. A **private good** is both rival and excludable. Food, clothing, haircuts, and many other goods and services fall into this category. One person consuming a unit of these goods precludes other people from consuming that unit, and no one can consume these goods

	Excludable	Nonexcludable
Rival	**Private Goods** *Examples:* *Big Macs* *Running shoes*	**Common Resources** *Examples:* *Tuna in the ocean* *Public pasture land*
Nonrival	**Quasi-Public Goods** *Examples:* *Cable TV* *Toll road*	**Public Goods** *Examples:* *National defense* *Court system*

MyEconLab Animation

Figure 5.7

Four Categories of Goods

Goods and services can be divided into four categories on the basis of whether people can be excluded from consuming them and whether they are rival in consumption. A good or service is rival in consumption if one person consuming a unit of a good means that another person cannot consume that unit.

without buying them. Although we didn't state it explicitly, when we analyzed the demand and supply for goods and services in earlier chapters, we assumed that the goods and services were all private goods.

2. A **public good** is both nonrival and nonexcludable. Public goods are often, although not always, supplied by a government rather than private firms. The classic example of a public good is national defense. Your consuming national defense does not interfere with your neighbor consuming it, so consumption is nonrival. You also cannot be excluded from consuming it, whether you pay for it or not. No private firm would be willing to supply national defense because everyone can consume national defense whether they pay for it or not. The behavior of consumers in this situation is called **free riding** because individuals benefit from a good—in this case, the provision of national defense—without paying for it.

3. A *quasi-public good* is excludable but not rival. An example is cable television. People who do not pay for cable television do not receive it, but one person watching it doesn't affect other people watching it. The same is true of a toll road. Anyone who doesn't pay the toll doesn't get on the road, but one person using the road doesn't interfere with someone else using the road (unless so many people are using the road that it becomes congested). Goods that fall into this category are called *quasi-public goods*.

4. A **common resource** is rival but not excludable. Forest land in many poor countries is a common resource. If one person cuts down a tree, no one else can use the tree. But if no one has a property right to the forest, no one can be excluded from using it. As we will discuss in more detail later, people often overuse common resources.

Public good A good that is both nonrival and nonexcludable.

Free riding Benefiting from a good without paying for it.

Common resource A good that is rival but not excludable.

We discussed the demand and supply for private goods in earlier chapters. For the remainder of this chapter, we focus on the categories of public goods and common resources. To determine the optimal quantity of a public good, we have to modify our usual demand and supply analysis to take into account that a public good is both nonrival and nonexcludable.

The Demand for a Public Good

We can determine the market demand curve for a good or service by adding up the quantity of the good demanded by each consumer at each price. To keep things simple, let's consider the case of a market with only two consumers. Figure 5.8 shows that the market demand curve for hamburgers depends on the individual demand curves of Jill and Joe.

At a price of $4.00, Jill demands 2 hamburgers per week and Joe demands 4. Adding horizontally, the combination of a price of $4.00 per hamburger and a quantity demanded of 6 hamburgers will be a point on the market demand curve for hamburgers. Similarly, adding horizontally at a price of $1.50, we have a price of $1.50 and a quantity demanded of 11 as another point on the market demand curve. A consumer's demand curve for a good represents the marginal benefit the consumer receives from the good, so when we add together the consumers' demand curves, we have not only the market demand curve but also the marginal social benefit curve for this good, assuming that there is no externality in consumption.

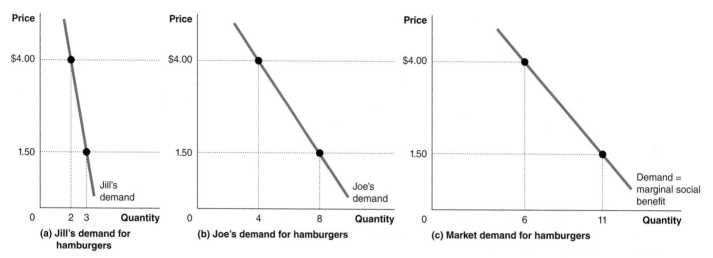

MyEconLab Animation

Figure 5.8 **Constructing the Market Demand Curve for a Private Good**

The market demand curve for private goods is determined by adding horizontally the quantity of the good demanded at each price by each consumer. For instance, in panel (a), Jill demands 2 hamburgers when the price is $4.00, and in panel (b),

Joe demands 4 hamburgers when the price is $4.00. So, a quantity of 6 hamburgers and a price of $4.00 is a point on the market demand curve in panel (c).

How can we find the demand curve or marginal social benefit curve for a public good? Once again, for simplicity, assume that Jill and Joe are the only consumers. Unlike with a private good, where Jill and Joe can end up consuming different quantities, with a public good, they will consume *the same quantity*. Suppose that Jill owns a service station on an isolated rural road, and Joe owns a car dealership next door. These are the only two businesses around for miles. Both Jill and Joe are afraid that unless they hire a security guard at night, their businesses may be burgled. Like national defense, the services of a security guard are in this case a public good: Once hired, the guard will be able to protect both businesses, so the good is nonrival. It also will not be possible to exclude either business from being protected, so the good is nonexcludable.

To arrive at a demand curve for a public good, we don't add quantities at each price, as with a private good. Instead, we add the price each consumer is willing to pay for each quantity of the public good. This value represents the total dollar amount consumers as a group would be willing to pay for that quantity of the public good. In other words, to find the demand curve, or marginal social benefit curve, for a private good, we add the demand curves of individual consumers horizontally; for public goods, we add individual demand curves vertically. Figure 5.9 shows how the marginal social benefit curve for security guard services depends on the individual demand curves of Jill and Joe.

The figure shows that Jill is willing to pay $8 per hour for the guard to provide 10 hours of protection per night. Joe would suffer a greater loss from a burglary, so he is willing to pay $10 per hour for the same amount of protection. Adding the dollar amount that each is willing to pay gives us a price of $18 per hour and a quantity of 10 hours as a point on the marginal social benefit curve for security guard services. The figure also shows that because Jill is willing to spend $4 per hour for 15 hours of guard services and Joe is willing to pay $5, a price of $9 per hour and a quantity of 15 hours is another point on the marginal social benefit curve for security guard services. MyEconLab Concept Check

The Optimal Quantity of a Public Good

We know that to achieve economic efficiency, a good or service should be produced up to the point where the sum of consumer surplus and producer surplus is maximized, or, alternatively, where the marginal social cost equals the marginal social benefit. Therefore, the optimal quantity of security guard services—or any other public good—will

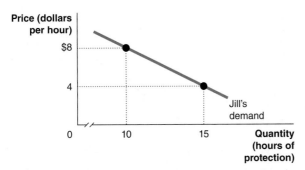

(a) Jill's demand for security guard services

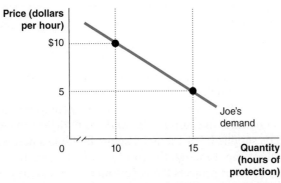

(b) Joe's demand for security guard services

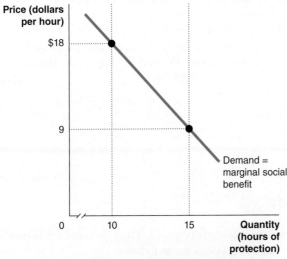

(c) Total demand for security guard services

MyEconLab Animation

Figure 5.9

Constructing the Demand Curve for a Public Good

To find the demand curve for a public good, we add up the price at which each consumer is willing to purchase each quantity of the good. In panel (a), Jill is willing to pay $8 per hour for a security guard to provide 10 hours of protection. In panel (b), Joe is willing to pay $10 for that level of protection. Therefore, in panel (c), the price of $18 per hour and the quantity of 10 hours will be a point on the demand curve for security guard services.

occur where the marginal social benefit curve intersects the supply curve. As with private goods, in the absence of an externality in production, the supply curve represents the marginal social cost of supplying the good. Figure 5.10 shows that the optimal quantity of security guard services supplied is 15 hours, at a price of $9 per hour.

Will the market provide the economically efficient quantity of security guard services? One difficulty is that the individual preferences of consumers, as shown by their demand curves, are not revealed in this market. This difficulty does not arise with private goods because consumers must reveal their preferences in order to purchase private goods. If the market price of Big Macs is $4.00, Joe either reveals that he is willing to pay that much by buying it or he does without it. In our example, neither Jill nor Joe can be excluded from consuming the services provided by a security guard once either hires one, and, therefore, neither has an incentive to reveal her or his preferences. In this

MyEconLab Animation

Figure 5.10

The Optimal Quantity of a Public Good

The optimal quantity of a public good is produced where the sum of consumer surplus and producer surplus is maximized, which occurs where the demand curve intersects the supply curve. In this case, the optimal quantity of security guard services is 15 hours, at a price of $9 per hour.

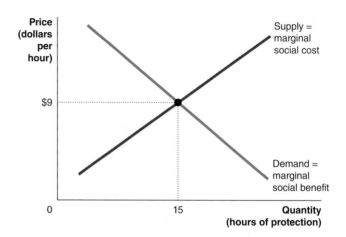

case, though, with only two consumers, it is likely that private bargaining will result in an efficient quantity of the public good. This outcome is not likely for a public good—such as national defense—that is supplied by the government to millions of consumers.

Governments sometimes use *cost–benefit analysis* to determine what quantity of a public good should be supplied. For example, before building a dam on a river, the federal government will attempt to weigh the costs against the benefits. The costs include the opportunity cost of other projects the government cannot carry out if it builds the dam. The benefits include improved flood control or new recreational opportunities on the lake formed by the dam. However, for many public goods, including national defense, the government does not use a formal cost–benefit analysis. Instead, the quantity of national defense supplied is determined by a political process involving Congress and the president. Even here, of course, Congress and the president realize that trade-offs are involved: The more resources used for national defense, the fewer resources available for other public or private goods.   MyEconLab Concept Check

Solved Problem 5.4   MyEconLab Interactive Animation

Determining the Optimal Level of Public Goods

Suppose, once again, that Jill and Joe run businesses that are next door to each other on an isolated road and both need a security guard. Their demand schedules for security guard services are as follows:

Joe		Jill	
Price (dollars per hour)	Quantity (hours of protection)	Price (dollars per hour)	Quantity (hours of protection)
$20	0	$20	1
18	1	18	2
16	2	16	3
14	3	14	4
12	4	12	5
10	5	10	6
8	6	8	7
6	7	6	8
4	8	4	9
2	9	2	10

The supply schedule for security guard services is as follows:

Price (dollars per hour)	Quantity (hours of protection)
$8	1
10	2
12	3
14	4
16	5
18	6
20	7
22	8
24	9

a. Draw a graph that shows the optimal level of security guard services. Be sure to label the curves on the graph.

b. Briefly explain why 8 hours of security guard protection is not an optimal quantity.

Solving the Problem

Step 1: Review the chapter material. This problem is about determining the optimal level of public goods, so you may want to review the section "The Optimal Quantity of a Public Good," which begins on page 156.

Step 2: Begin by deriving the demand curve or marginal social benefit curve for security guard services. To calculate the marginal social benefit of guard services, we need to add the prices that Jill and Joe are willing to pay at each quantity:

Demand or Marginal Social Benefit

Price (dollars per hour)	Quantity (hours of protection)
$38	1
34	2
30	3
26	4
22	5
18	6
14	7
10	8
6	9

Step 3: Answer part (a) by plotting the demand (marginal social benefit) and supply (marginal social cost) curves. The graph shows that the optimal level of security guard services is 6 hours.

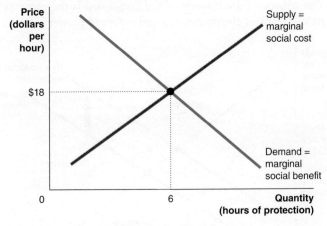

Step 4: Answer part (b) by explaining why 8 hours of security guard protection is not an optimal quantity. For each hour beyond 6, the supply curve is above the demand curve. Therefore, the marginal social benefit received will be less than the marginal social cost of supplying these hours. This results in a deadweight loss and a reduction in economic surplus.

Your Turn: For more practice, do related problem 4.4 on page 168 at the end of this chapter.   MyEconLab Study Plan

Common Resources

In England during the Middle Ages, each village had an area of pasture, known as the *commons*, on which any family in the village was allowed to graze its cows or sheep without charge. Of course, the grass one family's cow ate was not available for another family's cow, so consumption was rival. But every family in the village had the right to use the commons, so it was nonexcludable. Without some type of restraint on usage, the commons would be overgrazed. To see why, consider the economic incentives facing a family that was thinking of buying another cow and grazing it on the commons. The family would gain the benefits from increased milk production, but adding another cow to the commons would create a negative externality by reducing the amount of grass available for the cows of other families. Because this family—and the other families in the village—did not take this negative externality into account when deciding whether to add another cow to the commons, too many cows would be added. The grass on the commons would eventually be depleted, and no family's cow would get enough to eat.

Tragedy of the commons The tendency for a common resource to be overused.

The Tragedy of the Commons The tendency for a common resource to be overused is called the **tragedy of the commons**. The forests in many poor countries are a modern example. When a family chops down a tree in a public forest, it takes into account the benefits of gaining firewood or wood for building, but it does not take into account the costs of deforestation. Haiti, for example, was once heavily forested. Today, 80 percent of the country's forests have been cut down, primarily to be burned to create charcoal for heating and cooking. Because the mountains no longer have tree roots to hold the soil, heavy rains lead to devastating floods.

Figure 5.11 shows that with a common resource such as wood from a forest, the efficient level of use, $Q_{Efficient}$, is determined by the intersection of the demand curve, which represents the marginal social benefit received by consumers, and S_2, which represents the marginal social cost of cutting the wood. As in our discussion of negative externalities, the social cost is equal to the private cost of cutting the wood plus the external cost. In this case, the external cost represents the fact that the more wood each person cuts, the less wood there is available for others and the greater the deforestation, which increases the chances of floods. Because each individual tree cutter ignores the external cost, the equilibrium quantity of wood cut is Q_{Actual}, which is greater than the efficient quantity. At the actual equilibrium level of output, there is a deadweight loss, as shown in Figure 5.11 by the yellow triangle.

Is There a Way out of the Tragedy of the Commons? Notice that our discussion of the tragedy of the commons is very similar to our earlier discussion of negative externalities. The source of the tragedy of the commons is the same as the source of negative externalities: lack of clearly defined and enforced property rights. For instance,

MyEconLab Animation

Figure 5.11

Overuse of a Common Resource

For a common resource such as wood from a forest, the efficient level of use, $Q_{Efficient}$, is determined by the intersection of the demand curve, which represents the marginal benefit received by consumers, and S_2, which represents the marginal social cost of cutting the wood. Because each individual tree cutter ignores the external cost, the equilibrium quantity of wood cut is Q_{Actual}, which is greater than the efficient quantity. At the actual equilibrium level of output, there is a deadweight loss, as shown by the yellow triangle.

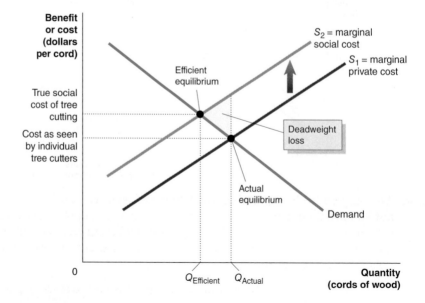

suppose that instead of being held as a collective resource, a piece of pastureland is owned by one person. That person will take into account the effect of adding another cow on the grass available to cows already using the pasture. As a result, the optimal number of cows will be placed on the pasture. Over the years, most of the commons lands in England were converted to private property. Most of the forestland in Haiti and other developing countries is actually the property of the government. The failure of the government to protect the forests against trespassers or convert them to private property is the key to their overuse.

In some situations, though, enforcing property rights is not feasible. An example is the oceans. Because no country owns the oceans beyond its own coastal waters, the fish and other resources of the ocean will remain a common resource. In situations in which enforcing property rights is not feasible, two types of solutions to the tragedy of the commons are possible. If the geographic area involved is limited and the number of people involved is small, access to the commons can be restricted through community norms and laws. If the geographic area or the number of people involved is large, legal restrictions on access to the commons are required. As an example of the first type of solution, the tragedy of the commons was avoided in the Middle Ages by traditional limits on the number of animals each family was allowed to put on the common pasture. Although these traditions were not formal laws, they were usually enforced adequately by social pressure.

With the second type of solution, the government imposes restrictions on access to the common resources. These restrictions can take several different forms, of which taxes, quotas, and tradable permits are the most common. By setting a tax equal to the external cost, governments can ensure that the efficient quantity of a resource is used. Quotas, or legal limits, on the quantity of the resource that can be taken during a given time period have been used in the United States to limit access to pools of oil that are beneath property owned by many different persons.   MyEconLab Concept Check   MyEconLab Study Plan

Continued from page 137

Economics in Your Life

What's the "Best" Level of Pollution?

At the beginning of this chapter, we asked you to think about what is the "best" level of carbon emissions. Conceptually, this is a straightforward question to answer: The efficient level of carbon emissions is the level for which the marginal benefit of reducing carbon emissions exactly equals the marginal cost of reducing carbon emissions. In practice, however, this question is very difficult to answer. For example, scientists disagree about how much carbon emissions are contributing to climate change and what the damage from climate change will be. In addition, the cost of reducing carbon emissions depends on the method of reduction used. As a result, neither the marginal cost curve nor the marginal benefit curve for reducing carbon emissions is known with certainty. This uncertainty makes it difficult for policymakers to determine the economically efficient level of carbon emissions and is the source of much of the current debate. In any case, economists agree that the total cost of *completely* eliminating carbon emissions is much greater than the total benefit.

Conclusion

Government interventions in the economy, such as imposing price ceilings and price floors, can reduce economic efficiency. But in this chapter, we have seen that the government plays an indispensable role in the economy when the absence of well-defined and enforceable property rights keeps the market from operating efficiently. For instance, because no one has a property right for clean air, in the absence of government intervention, firms will produce too great a quantity of products that generate air pollution. We have also seen that public goods are nonrival and nonexcludable and are, therefore, often supplied directly by the government.

Visit MyEconLab for a news article and analysis related to the concepts in this chapter.

Chapter Summary and Problems

Key Terms

Coase theorem, p. 147

Command-and-control approach, p. 152

Common resource, p. 155

Excludability, p. 154

Externality, p. 138

Free riding, p. 155

Market failure, p. 140

Pigovian taxes and subsidies, p. 152

Private benefit, p. 139

Private cost, p. 138

Private good, p. 154

Property rights, p. 140

Public good, p. 155

Rivalry, p. 154

Social benefit, p. 139

Social cost, p. 139

Tragedy of the commons, p. 160

Transactions costs, p. 146

 5.1

Externalities and Economic Efficiency, pages 138–141

LEARNING OBJECTIVE: Identify examples of positive and negative externalities and use graphs to show how externalities affect economic efficiency.

Summary

An **externality** is a benefit or cost to parties who are not involved in a transaction. Pollution and other externalities in production cause a difference between the **private cost** borne by the producer of a good or service and the **social cost**, which includes any external cost, such as the cost of pollution. An externality in consumption causes a difference between the **private benefit** received by the consumer and the **social benefit**, which includes any external benefit. If externalities exist in production or consumption, the market will not produce the optimal level of a good or service. This outcome is referred to as **market failure**. Externalities arise when property rights do not exist or cannot be legally enforced. **Property rights** are the rights individuals or businesses have to the exclusive use of their property, including the right to buy or sell it.

MyEconLab   Visit www.myeconlab.com to complete these exercises online and get instant feedback.

Review Questions

1.1 What is an externality? Give an example of a positive externality, and give an example of a negative externality.

1.2 When will the private cost of producing a good differ from the social cost? Give an example. When will the private benefit from consuming a good differ from the social benefit? Give an example.

1.3 What is economic efficiency? How do externalities affect the economic efficiency of a market equilibrium?

1.4 What is market failure? When is market failure likely to arise?

1.5 Briefly explain the relationship between property rights and the existence of externalities.

Problems and Applications

1.6 The chapter states that your consuming a Big Mac does not create an externality. But suppose you arrive at your favorite McDonald's at lunchtime and get in a long line to be served. By the time you reach the counter, there are 10 people in line behind you. Because you decided to have a Big Mac for lunch—instead of, say, a pizza—each of those 10 people must wait in line an additional 2 minutes. Is it still correct to say that your consuming a Big Mac creates no externalities? Might there be a justification here for the government to intervene in the market for Big Macs? Briefly explain.

1.7 A neighbor's barking dog can be both a positive externality and a negative externality. Under what circumstances would the barking dog serve as a positive externality? Under what circumstances would the barking dog be a negative externality?

1.8 Yellowstone National Park is in bear country. The National Park Service, at its Yellowstone Web site, states the following about camping and hiking in bear country:

> Do not leave packs containing food unattended, even for a few minutes. Allowing a bear to obtain human food even once often results in the bear becoming aggressive about obtaining such food in the future. Aggressive bears present a threat to human safety and eventually must be destroyed or removed from the park. Please obey the law and do not allow bears or other wildlife to obtain human food.

What negative externality does obtaining human food pose for bears? What negative externality do bears obtaining human food pose for future campers and hikers?

Source: National Park Service, Yellowstone National Park, "Backcountry Camping and Hiking," June 7, 2013, www.nps.gov/yell/planyourvisit/backcountryhiking.htm.

1.9 Every year at the beginning of flu season, many people, including the elderly, get a flu shot to reduce their chances of contracting the flu. One result is that people who do *not* get a flu shot are less likely to contract the flu.

a. What type of externality (negative or positive) arises from getting a flu shot?

b. On the graph that follows, show the effects of this externality by drawing in and labelling any additional curves that are needed and by labeling the efficient quantity and the efficient price of flu shots. Label the area representing deadweight loss in this market.

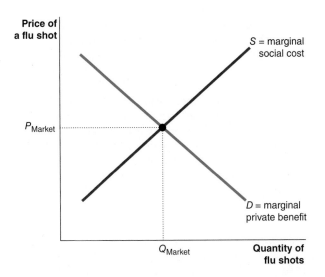

1.10 John Cassidy, a writer for the *New Yorker* magazine, wrote a blog post arguing against New York City's having installed bike lanes. Cassidy complained that the bike lanes had eliminated traffic lanes on some streets as well as some on-street parking. A writer for the *Economist* magazine disputed Cassidy's argument with the following comment: "I hate to belabour the point, but driving, as it turns out, is associated with a number of negative externalities." What externalities are associated with driving? How do these externalities affect the debate over whether big cities should install more bike lanes?

Sources: John Cassidy, "Battle of the Bike Lanes," *New Yorker*, March 8, 2011; and "The World Is His Parking Spot," *Economist*, March 9, 2011.

1.11 In a study at a large state university, students were randomly assigned roommates. Researchers found that, on average, males assigned to roommates who reported drinking alcohol in the year before entering college had GPAs one-quarter point lower than those assigned to nondrinking roommates. For males who drank frequently before college, being assigned to a roommate who also drank frequently before college reduced their GPAs by two-thirds of a point. Draw a graph showing the price of alcohol and the quantity of alcohol consumption on college campuses. Include in the graph the demand for drinking and the private and social costs of drinking. Label any deadweight loss that arises in this market.

Source: Michael Kremer and Dan M. Levy, "Peer Effects and Alcohol Use among College Students," *Journal of Economic Perspectives*, Vol. 22, No. 3, Summer 2008, pp. 189–206.

1.12 Tom and Jacob are college students. Each of them will probably get married later and have two or three children. Each knows that if he studies more in college, he'll get a better job and earn more money. Earning more will enable them to spend more on their future families for things such as orthodontia, nice clothes, admission to expensive colleges, and travel. Tom thinks about the potential benefits to his potential children when he decides how much studying to do. Jacob doesn't.
  a. What type of externality arises from studying?
  b. Draw a graph showing this externality, contrasting the responses of Tom and Jacob. Who studies more? Who acts more efficiently? Briefly explain.

1.13 Fracking, or hydraulic fracturing, has been used more frequently in recent years to drill for oil and natural gas that previously was too expensive to obtain. According to an article in the *New York Times*, "horizontal drilling has enabled engineers to inject millions of gallons of high-pressure water directly into layers of shale to create the fractures that release the gas. Chemicals added to the water dissolve minerals, kill bacteria that might plug up the well, and insert sand to prop open the fractures." Experts are divided about whether fracking results in significant pollution, but some people worry that chemicals used in fracking might lead to pollution of underground supplies of water used by households and farms.
  a. First, assume that fracking causes no significant pollution. Use a demand and supply graph to show the effect of fracking on the market for natural gas.
  b. Now assume that fracking does result in pollution. On your graph from part (a), show the effect of fracking. Be sure to carefully label all curves and all equilibrium points.
  c. In your graph in part (b), what has happened to the efficient level of output and the efficient price in the market for natural gas compared with the situation before fracking? Can you be certain that the efficient level of output and the efficient price have risen or fallen as a result of fracking? Briefly explain.

Source: Susan L. Brantley and Anna Meyendorff, "The Facts on Fracking," *New York Times*, March 13, 2013.

1.14 The following information regarding cable television is from the Federal Communications Commission Web site:

> In general, a cable television operator has the right to select the channels and services that are available on its cable system. With the exception of certain channels like local broadcast television channels which are required to be carried by federal law, the cable operator has broad discretion in choosing which channels will be available and how those channels will be packaged and marketed to subscribers.... With the exception of broadcast channels that elect "must carry" status and PEG channels, all other programming on the cable system is based on terms negotiated between the cable operator and the entity that owns the channel or programming service. Terms may include whether the channel or service will be offered in a package with other programming or whether the channel or service will be offered on a per-channel or pay-per-view basis....

Suppose you are a fan of *The Daily Show* with Jon Stewart and *The Colbert Report*, both on the Comedy

Central cable channel, but the only way you can get Comedy Central from your local cable provider is to subscribe to a package that includes 30 other channels. Is there an externality involved here? If so, is it an externality in production or consumption, and is it positive or negative? If there is an externality, discuss possible solutions.

Source: Consumer and Government Affairs Bureau, "Choosing Cable Channels," June 7, 2013, www.fcc.gov/cgb/consumerfacts /cablechannels.html.

1.15 In an article in the agriculture magazine *Choices*, Oregon State University economist JunJie Wu made the following observation about the conversion of farmland to urban development:

> Land use provides many economic and social benefits, but often comes at a substantial cost to the environment. Although most economic costs are figured into land use decisions, most environmental externalities

are not. These environmental "externalities" cause a divergence between private and social costs for some land uses, leading to an inefficient land allocation. For example, developers may not bear all the environmental and infrastructural costs generated by their projects. Such "market failures" provide a justification for private conservation efforts and public land use planning and regulation.

What does the author mean by *market failures* and *inefficient land allocation*? Explain why the author describes inefficient land allocation as a market failure. Illustrate your argument with a graph showing the market for land to be used for urban development.

Source: JunJie Wu, "Land Use Changes: Economic, Social, and Environmental Impacts," *Choices*, Vol. 23, No. 4, Fourth Quarter 2008, pp. 6–10.

5.2 | **Private Solutions to Externalities: The Coase Theorem, pages 141–147**

LEARNING OBJECTIVE: Discuss the Coase theorem and explain how private bargaining can lead to economic efficiency in a market with an externality.

Summary

Externalities and market failures result from incomplete property rights or from the difficulty of enforcing property rights in certain situations. When an externality exists, and the efficient quantity of a good is not being produced, the total cost of reducing the externality is usually less than the total benefit. According to the **Coase theorem**, if **transactions costs** are low, private bargaining will result in an efficient solution to the problem of externalities.

MyEconLab   Visit www.myeconlab.com to complete these exercises online and get instant feedback.

Review Questions

2.1 What do economists mean by "an economically efficient level of pollution"?

2.2 What is the Coase theorem? Why do the parties involved in an externality have an incentive to reach an efficient solution?

2.3 What are transactions costs? When are we likely to see private solutions to the problem of externalities?

Problems and Applications

2.4 Is it ever possible for an *increase* in pollution to make society better off? Briefly explain, using a graph like Figure 5.3 on page 143.

2.5 If the marginal cost of reducing a certain type of pollution is zero, should all that type of pollution be eliminated? Briefly explain.

2.6 Discuss the factors that determine the marginal cost of reducing crime. Discuss the factors that determine the marginal benefit of reducing crime. Would it be economically efficient to reduce the amount of crime to zero? Briefly explain.

2.7 In discussing the reduction of air pollution in the developing world, Richard Fuller of the Blacksmith Institute, an environmental organization, observed, "It's the 90/10 rule. To do 90 percent of the work only costs 10 percent of the money. It's the last 10 percent of the cleanup that costs 90 percent of the money." Why should it be any more costly to clean up the last 10 percent of polluted air than to clean up the first 90 percent? What trade-offs would be involved in cleaning up the final 10 percent?

Source: Tiffany M. Luck, "The World's Dirtiest Cities," *Forbes*, February 28, 2008.

2.8 **[Related to the** Making the Connection **on page 142]** In the first years following the passage of the Clean Air Act in 1970, air pollution declined sharply, and there were important health benefits, including a decline in infant mortality. According to an article in the *Economist* magazine, however, recently some policymakers "worry that the EPA is constantly tightening restrictions on pollution, at ever higher cost to business but with diminishing returns in terms of public health."

a. Why might additional reductions in air pollution come at "ever higher cost"? What does the article mean that these reductions will result in "ever diminishing returns in terms of public health"?

b. How should the federal government decide whether further reductions in air pollution are needed?

Source: "Soaring Emissions," *Economist*, June 2, 2011.

2.9 [Related to the Don't Let This Happen to You **on page 145]** Briefly explain whether you agree or disagree with the following statement: "Sulfur dioxide emissions cause acid rain and breathing difficulties for people with respiratory problems. The total benefit to society is greatest if we completely eliminate sulfur dioxide emissions. Therefore, the economically efficient level of emissions is zero."

2.10 According to the Coase theorem, why would a steel plant that creates air pollution agree to curtail production (and, therefore, pollution) if it were not legally liable for the damage the pollution was causing? Must the property right to clean air be assigned to the victims of air pollution for the steel plant to agree to reduce pollution?

2.11 [Related to the Making the Connection **on page 145]** We know that owners of apple orchards and beehives are able to negotiate private agreements. Is it likely that as a result of these private agreements, the market supplies the efficient quantities of apple trees and beehives? Are there any real-world difficulties that might stand in the way of achieving this efficient outcome?

5.3 | ## Government Policies to Deal with Externalities, pages 147–154
LEARNING OBJECTIVE: Analyze government policies to achieve economic efficiency in a market with an externality.

Summary

When private solutions to externalities are unworkable, the government sometimes intervenes. One way to deal with a negative externality in production is to impose a tax equal to the cost of the externality. The tax causes the producer of the good to internalize the externality. The government can deal with a positive externality in consumption by giving consumers a subsidy, or payment, equal to the value of the externality. Government taxes and subsidies intended to bring about an efficient level of output in the presence of externalities are called **Pigovian taxes and subsidies**. Although the federal government has sometimes used subsidies and taxes to deal with externalities, in dealing with pollution it has more often used a command-and-control approach. A **command-and-control approach** involves the government imposing quantitative limits on the amount of pollution allowed or requiring firms to install specific pollution control devices. Direct pollution controls of this type are not economically efficient, however. As a result, economists generally prefer reducing pollution by using market-based policies.

 MyEconLab   Visit **www.myeconlab.com** to complete these exercises online and get instant feedback.

Review Questions

3.1 What is a Pigovian tax? At what level must a Pigovian tax be set to achieve efficiency?

3.2 What does it mean for a producer or consumer to internalize an externality? What would cause a producer or consumer to internalize an externality?

3.3 Why do most economists prefer tradable emission allowances to the command-and-control approach to pollution?

Problems and Applications

3.4 The author of a newspaper article remarks that many economists "support Pigovian taxes because, in some sense, we are already paying them." In what sense might consumers in a market be "paying" a Pigovian tax even if the government hasn't imposed an explicit tax?

Source: Adam Davidson, "Should We Tax People for Being Annoying?" *New York Times*, January 8, 2013.

3.5 The federal government's nutrition guidelines urge adults to eat at least five cups of fruits and vegetables each day. Does consuming fruits and vegetables have a positive externality? Should the government subsidize the consumption of fruits and vegetables? Briefly explain.

3.6 Many antibiotics that once were effective in eliminating infections no longer are because bacteria have evolved to become resistant to them. Some bacteria are now resistant to all but one or two existing antibiotics. Some policymakers have argued that pharmaceutical companies should receive subsidies for developing new antibiotics. A newspaper article states:

> While the notion of directly subsidizing drug companies may be politically unpopular in many quarters, proponents say it is necessary to bridge the gap between the high value that new antibiotics have for society and the low returns they provide to drug companies.

Is there a positive externality in the production of antibiotics? Should firms producing every good where there is a gap between the value of the good to society and the profit to the firms making the good receive subsidies? Briefly explain.

Source: Andrew Pollack, "Antibiotics Research Subsidies Weighed by U.S.," *New York Times*, November 5, 2010.

3.7 A newspaper article has the headline: "Should We Tax People for Being Annoying?"

   a. Do annoying people cause a negative externality? Should they be taxed? Do crying babies on a bus or plane cause a negative externality? Should the babies (or their parents) be taxed?

   b. Do people who plant flowers and otherwise have beautiful gardens visible from the street cause a positive externality? Should these people receive a government subsidy?

   c. Should every negative externality be taxed? Should every positive externality be subsidized? How might the government decide whether using Pigovian taxes and subsidies is appropriate?

   Source: Adam Davison, "Should We Tax People for Being Annoying?" *New York Times*, January 8, 2013.

3.8 Writing in the *New York Times*, Michael Lewis argued, "Good new technologies are a bit like good new roads: Their social benefits far exceed what any one person or company can get paid for creating them." Does this observation justify the government subsidizing the production of new technologies? If so, how might the government do this?

   Source: Michael Lewis, "In Defense of the Boom," *New York Times*, October 27, 2002.

3.9 **[Related to** Solved Problem 5.3 **on page 150]** Solved Problem 5.3 contains the statement: "Of course, the government actually collects the tax from sellers rather than from consumers, but we get the same result whether the government imposes a tax on the buyers of a good or on the sellers." Demonstrate that this statement is correct by solving the problem assuming that the increase in the tax on gasoline shifts the supply curve rather than the demand curve.

3.10 **[Related to** Solved Problem 5.3 **on page 150]** The fumes from dry cleaners can contribute to air pollution. Suppose the following graph illustrates the situation in the dry cleaning market.

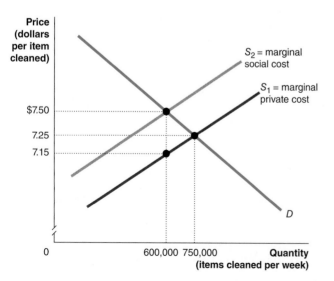

   a. Explain how a government can use a tax on dry cleaning to bring about the efficient level of production. What should the value of the tax be?

   b. How large is the deadweight loss (in dollars) from excessive dry cleaning, according to the figure?

3.11 **[Related to** Solved Problem 5.3 **on page 150]** Companies that produce toilet paper bleach the paper to make it white. Some paper plants discharge the bleach into rivers and lakes, causing substantial environmental damage. Suppose the following graph illustrates the situation in the toilet paper market.

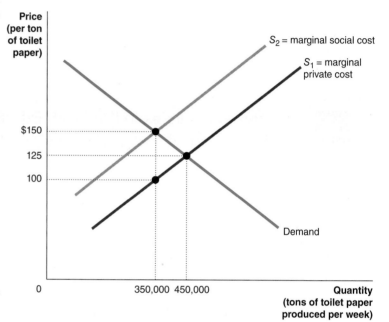

   Explain how the federal government can use a tax on toilet paper to bring about the efficient level of production. What should be the value of the tax?

3.12 **[Related to the** Making the Connection **on page 148]** Eric Finklestein, an economist at Duke University, has argued that the external costs from being obese are larger than the external costs from smoking because "the mortality effect for obesity is much smaller than it is for smoking and the costs start much earlier in life."

   a. What does Finklestein mean by the "mortality effect"? Why would the mortality effect of obesity being smaller than the mortality effect of smoking result in obesity having a larger external cost?

   b. Tobacco taxes have been more politically popular than taxes on soda. Why might the general public be more willing to support cigarette taxes than soda taxes?

   Source: David Leonhardt, "Obama Likes Some Sin Taxes More Than Others," *New York Times*, April 10, 2013.

3.13 A few years ago, Governor Deval Patrick of Massachusetts proposed that criminals would have to pay a "safety fee" to the government. The size of the fee would be based on the seriousness of the crime (that is, the fee would be larger for more serious crimes).

a. Is there an economically efficient amount of crime? Briefly explain.

b. Briefly explain whether the "safety fee" is a Pigovian tax of the type discussed in this chapter.

Source: Michael Levenson, "Patrick Proposes New Fee on Criminals," *Boston Globe*, January 14, 2007.

3.14 The following graph illustrates the situation in the dry cleaning market assuming that the marginal social cost of the pollution *increases* as the quantity of items cleaned per week increases. The graph includes two demand curves: one for a smaller city, D_S, and the other for a larger city, D_L.

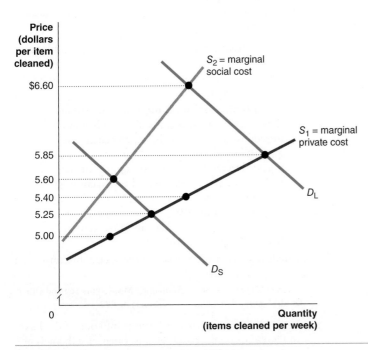

a. Explain why the marginal social cost curve has a different slope than the marginal private cost curve.

b. What tax per item cleaned will achieve economic efficiency in the smaller city? In the larger city? Explain why the efficient tax is different in the two cities.

3.15 **[Related to the** Chapter Opener **on page 137]** According to an article in the *New York Times*: "Top economists agree a tax on fuels and the carbon they spew into the atmosphere would be the cheapest way to combat climate change." Why would a carbon tax be a cheaper way to reduce carbon dioxide emissions than the command-and-control approach of ordering utilities to emit less carbon dioxide and automobile companies to produce more fuel-efficient cars?

Source: Eduardo Porter, "In Energy Taxes, Tools to Help Tackle Climate Change," *New York Times*, January 29, 2013.

3.16 **[Related to the** Making the Connection **on page 153]** According to a Congressional Budget Office report, the burden of a carbon tax would fall disproportionately on low-income households.

a. What does the report mean by the "burden" of the tax?

b. Why would the burden of a carbon tax fall disproportionately on low-income households? What actions might the government take to reduce the burden on these households?

Source: Congressional Budget Office, "Effects of a Carbon Tax on the Economy and the Environment," May 2013, p. 8.

5.4 ## Four Categories of Goods, pages 154–161

LEARNING OBJECTIVE: Explain how goods can be categorized on the basis of whether they are rival or excludable and use graphs to illustrate the efficient quantities of public goods and common resources.

Summary

There are four categories of goods: private goods, public goods, quasi-public goods, and common resources. **Private goods** are both rival and excludable. **Rivalry** means that when one person consumes a unit of a good, no one else can consume that unit. **Excludability** means that anyone who does not pay for a good cannot consume it. **Public goods** are both nonrival and nonexcludable. Private firms are usually not willing to supply public goods because of free riding. **Free riding** involves benefiting from a good without paying for it. *Quasi-public goods* are excludable but not rival. **Common resources** are rival but not excludable. The **tragedy of the commons** refers to the tendency for a common resource to be overused. The tragedy of the commons results from a lack of clearly defined and enforced property rights. We find the market demand curve for a private good by adding the quantity of the good demanded by each consumer at each price. We find the demand curve for a public good by adding vertically the price each consumer would be willing to pay for each quantity of the good. The optimal quantity of a public good occurs where the demand curve intersects the curve representing the marginal cost of supplying the good.

MyEconLab   Visit www.myeconlab.com to complete these exercises online and get instant feedback.

Review Questions

4.1 Define *rivalry* and *excludability* and use these terms to discuss the four categories of goods.

4.2 What is free riding? How is free riding related to the tendency of a public good to create market failure?

4.3 What is the tragedy of the commons? How can it be avoided?

Problems and Applications

4.4 **[Related to** Solved Problem 5.4 **on page 158]** Suppose that Jill and Joe are the only two people in the small town of Andover. Andover has land available to build a park of no more than 9 acres. Jill and Joe's demand schedules for the park are as follows:

Joe

Price per Acre	Number of Acres
$10	0
9	1
8	2
7	3
6	4
5	5
4	6
3	7
2	8
1	9

Jill

Price per Acre	Number of Acres
$15	0
14	1
13	2
12	3
11	4
10	5
9	6
8	7
7	8
6	9

The supply curve is as follows:

Price per Acre	Number of Acres
$11	1
13	2
15	3
17	4
19	5
21	6
23	7
25	8
27	9

a. Draw a graph showing the optimal size of the park. Be sure to label the curves on the graph.

b. Briefly explain why a park of 2 acres is not optimal.

4.5 Commercial whaling has been described as a modern example of the tragedy of the commons. Briefly explain whether you agree.

4.6 Nancy Folbre, an economist at the University of Massachusetts, Amherst, argued, "We must take responsibility for governing the commons—not just the quaint old-fashioned village green, but things that cannot easily be privatized—[such as] clean air." Do you agree that clean air is like a common pasture in England in the Middle Ages? Briefly explain.

Source: Nancy Folbre, "Taking Responsibility for the Commons," *New York Times*, February 26, 2009.

4.7 The more frequently bacteria are exposed to antibiotics, the more quickly the bacteria will develop resistance to the antibiotics. An article from MayoClinic.com includes the following about antibiotic use:

> If antibiotics are used too often for things they can't treat—like colds, flu or other viral infections—not only are they of no benefit, they become less effective against the bacteria they're intended to treat…. Nearly all significant bacterial infections in the world are becoming resistant to commonly used antibiotics. When you misuse antibiotics, you help create resistant microorganisms that can cause new and hard-to-treat infections.

Briefly discuss in what sense antibiotics can be considered a common resource.

Source: Mayo Clinic Staff, "Antibiotics: Misuse Puts You and Others at Risk," www.MayoClinic.com, February 4, 2012.

4.8 Put each of these goods or services into one of the boxes in Figure 5.7 on page 155. That is, categorize them as private goods, public goods, quasi-public goods, or common resources.

a. A television broadcast of baseball's World Series
b. Home mail delivery
c. Education in a public school
d. Education in a private school
e. Hiking in a park surrounded by a fence
f. Hiking in a park not surrounded by a fence
g. An apple

4.9 Explain whether you agree with the following statement:

> Health care is obviously a public good. If one person becomes ill and doesn't receive treatment, that person may infect many other people. If many people become ill, then the output of the economy will be negatively affected. Therefore, health care is a public good that the government should supply.

4.10 Deer-hunting clubs in southeast Virginia impose a fine on anyone harvesting a buck with antlers below a certain size on land where those clubs have exclusive rights to hunt. The hunt clubs, however, do not impose a fine for harvesting a buck with small antlers on land where several clubs have the right to hunt. Why would the hunt clubs treat the harvesting of bucks on the two lands differently?

4.11 In the early 1800s, more than 60 million American bison (commonly known as the buffalo) roamed the Great Plains. By the late 1800s, the buffalo was nearly extinct. Considering the four categories of goods discussed in this chapter, why might it be that hunters nearly killed buffalo to extinction but not cattle?

4.12 William Easterly in *The White Man's Burden* shares the following account by New York University Professor Leonard Wantchekon of how Professor Wantchekon's village in Benin, Africa, managed the local fishing pond when he was growing up:

> To open the fishing season, elders performed ritual tests at Amlé, a lake fifteen kilometers from the village. If the fish were large enough, fishing was allowed for two or three days. If they were too small, all fishing was forbidden, and anyone who secretly fished the lake at this time was outcast, excluded from the formal and informal groups that formed the village's social structure. Those who committed this breach of trust were often shunned by the whole community; no one would speak to the offender, or even acknowledge his existence for a year or more.

What economic problem were the village elders trying to prevent? Do you think their solution was effective?

Source: William Easterly, *The White Man's Burden: Why the West's Efforts to Aid the Rest Have Done So Much Ill and So Little Good*, New York: Penguin Books, 2006, p. 94.

CHAPTER 6

Elasticity: The Responsiveness of Demand and Supply

Chapter Outline and Learning Objectives

Do People Respond to Changes in the Price of Gasoline?

"Get ready for a roller coaster." This advice came from Steve Mosby, a partner with Admo Energy, a supplier of gasoline to retailers. Mr. Mosby was referring to swings in gasoline prices that were predicted for the summer of 2013. The fluctuations in gasoline prices over the previous few years had been much larger than normal.

But do fluctuations in gas prices have much effect on sales of gasoline? Some people would say that they don't. These people argue that consumers don't vary the quantity of gas they buy as the price fluctuates because the number of miles they need to drive to get to work or school or to run errands is roughly constant. Actual consumer behavior contradicts this argument. For example, in September 2012, when the average price of gasoline was $3.91 per gallon, U.S. consumers bought about 5 percent less gasoline than they had during September 2011, when the average price of gasoline was $3.66 per gallon.

When gasoline prices have reached $4 per gallon on several occasions in recent years, consumers found many ways to cut back on the quantity they purchased. As Dennis Jacobe, chief economist of Gallup,

a public opinion poll firm, put it: "At $4 a gallon, you get people who might have money to spend, but with the amount gasoline costs, they start to cut back in response to the price. At $4 a gallon … they make fewer trips." In California, rising gas prices have resulted in a decline in the number of cars crossing the Golden Gate Bridge, as commuters switch to using buses and ferries. Car dealers report that sales of smaller, more fuel-efficient cars are increasing compared with sales of SUVs and other less fuel-efficient vehicles.

All businesses have a strong interest in knowing how much their sales will decrease as prices rise. Governments are also interested in knowing how consumers will react if the price of a product such as gasoline rises following a tax increase. In this chapter, we will explore what determines the responsiveness of the quantity demanded and the quantity supplied to changes in the market price.

Sources: Steve Everly, "'Get Ready for a Roller Coaster' as Gas Prices Swing Wildly," *Kansas City Star*, April 21, 2013; Meg Handley, "Memorial Day 2013: Higher Gas Prices, Fewer Travelers," *U.S. News & World Report*, May 23, 2013; and data on gasoline prices and consumption from the U.S. Energy Information Administration.

Economics in Your Life

How Much Do Gas Prices Matter to You?

What factors would make you more or less responsive to price when purchasing gasoline? Have you responded differently to price changes during different periods of your life? Why do consumers seem to respond more to changes in gas prices at a particular service station but seem less sensitive when gas prices rise or fall at all service stations? As you read this chapter, try to answer these questions. You can check your answers against those we provide on **page 194** at the end of this chapter.

W hether you are managing a service station, a pizza parlor, or a coffee shop, you need to know how an increase or a decrease in the price of your products will affect the quantity consumers are willing to buy. We know that cutting the price of a good increases the quantity demanded and that raising the price reduces the quantity demanded. But the critical question is: *How much* will the quantity demanded change as a result of a price increase or decrease? Economists use the concept of **elasticity** to measure how one economic variable—such as the quantity demanded—responds to changes in another economic variable—such as the price. For example, the responsiveness of the quantity demanded of a good to changes in its price is called the *price elasticity of demand*. Knowing the price elasticity of demand allows you to compute the effect of a price change on the quantity demanded.

We also know that the quantity of a good that consumers demand depends not just on the price of the good but also on consumer income and on the prices of related goods. As a manager, you would also be interested in measuring the responsiveness of demand to these other factors. As we will see, we can use the concept of elasticity here as well. We are also interested in the responsiveness of the quantity supplied of a good to changes in its price, which is called the *price elasticity of supply*.

Elasticity is an important concept not just for business managers but for policymakers as well. If the government wants to discourage teenage smoking, it can raise the price of cigarettes by increasing the tax on them. If we know the price elasticity of demand for cigarettes, we can calculate how many fewer packs of cigarettes will be demanded at a higher price. In this chapter, we will also see how policymakers use the concept of elasticity.

Elasticity A measure of how much one economic variable responds to changes in another economic variable.

Define price elasticity of demand and understand how to measure it.

Price elasticity of demand The responsiveness of the quantity demanded to a change in price, measured by dividing the percentage change in the quantity demanded of a product by the percentage change in the product's price.

The Price Elasticity of Demand and Its Measurement

We know from the law of demand that when the price of a product falls, the quantity demanded of the product increases. But the law of demand tells firms only that the demand curves for their products slope downward. More useful is a measure of the responsiveness of the quantity demanded to a change in price. This measure is called the **price elasticity of demand**.

Measuring the Price Elasticity of Demand

We might measure the price elasticity of demand by using the slope of the demand curve because the slope of the demand curve tells us how much quantity changes as price changes. Using the slope of the demand curve to measure price elasticity has a drawback, however: The measurement of slope is sensitive to the units chosen for quantity and price. For example, suppose a $1 per gallon decrease in the price of gasoline leads to an increase in the quantity demanded from 10.1 million gallons to 10.2 million gallons per day. The change in quantity is 0.1 million gallons, and the change in price is −$1, so the slope is $0.1/-1 = -0.1$. But if we measure price in cents, rather than in dollars, the slope is $0.1/-100 = -0.001$. If we measure price in dollars and gallons in thousands, instead of millions, the slope is $100/-1 = -100$. Clearly, the value we compute for the slope can change dramatically, depending on the units we use for quantity and price.

To avoid this confusion over units, economists use *percentage changes* when measuring the price elasticity of demand. Percentage changes are not dependent on units of measurement. (For a review of calculating percentage changes, see the appendix to Chapter 1.) No matter what units we use to measure the quantity of gasoline, 10 percent more gasoline is 10 percent more gasoline. Therefore, the price elasticity of demand is measured by dividing the percentage change in the quantity demanded by the percentage change in the product's price. Or:

$$\text{Price elasticity of demand} = \frac{\text{Percentage change in quantity demanded}}{\text{Percentage change in price}}.$$

It's important to remember that *the price elasticity of demand is not the same as the slope of the demand curve.*

If we calculate the price elasticity of demand for a price cut, the percentage change in price will be negative, and the percentage change in quantity demanded will be positive. Similarly, if we calculate the price elasticity of demand for a price increase, the percentage change in price will be positive, and the percentage change in quantity demanded will be negative. Therefore, the price elasticity of demand is always negative. In comparing elasticities, though, we are usually interested in their relative size. So, we often drop the minus sign and compare their *absolute values*. For example, although −3 is actually a smaller number than −2, we say that a price elasticity of −3 is larger than a price elasticity of −2. MyEconLab Concept Check

Elastic Demand and Inelastic Demand

If the quantity demanded is very responsive to changes in price, the percentage change in quantity demanded will be *greater* than the percentage change in price, and the price elasticity of demand will be greater than 1 in absolute value. In this case, demand is **elastic**. For example, if a 10 percent decrease in the price of bagels results in a 20 percent increase in the quantity of bagels demanded, then:

$$\text{Price elasticity of demand} = \frac{20\%}{-10\%} = -2,$$

and we can conclude that the demand for bagels is elastic.

When the quantity demanded is not very responsive to price, however, the percentage change in quantity demanded will be *less* than the percentage change in price, and the price elasticity of demand will be less than 1 in absolute value. In this case, demand is **inelastic**. For example, if a 10 percent decrease in the price of wheat results in a 5 percent increase in the quantity of wheat demanded, then:

$$\text{Price elasticity of demand} = \frac{5\%}{-10\%} = -0.5,$$

and we can conclude that the demand for wheat is inelastic.

In the special case where the percentage change in quantity demanded is equal to the percentage change in price, the price elasticity of demand equals −1 (or 1 in absolute value). In this case, demand is **unit elastic**. MyEconLab Concept Check

An Example of Computing Price Elasticities

Suppose you own a service station, and you are trying to decide whether to cut the price you are charging for a gallon of gas. You are currently at point *A* in Figure 6.1, selling 1,000 gallons per day at a price of $4.00 per gallon. How many more gallons you will sell by cutting the price to $3.70 depends on the price elasticity of demand for gasoline at your service station. Let's consider two possibilities: If D_1 is the demand curve for gasoline at your station, your sales will increase to 1,200 gallons per day, point *B*. But if D_2 is your demand curve, your sales will increase only to 1,050 gallons per day, point *C*. We might expect—correctly, as we will see—that between these points, demand curve D_1 is *elastic*, and demand curve D_2 is *inelastic*.

To confirm that D_1 is elastic between these points and that D_2 is inelastic, we need to calculate the price elasticity of demand for each curve. In calculating price elasticity between two points on a demand curve, though, we face a problem because we get a different value for price increases than for price decreases. Suppose we calculate the price elasticity for D_1 as the price is cut from $4.00 to $3.70. This 7.5 percent price cut increases the quantity demanded from 1,000 gallons to 1,200 gallons, or by 20 percent. Therefore, the price elasticity of demand between points *A* and *B* is 20/−7.5 = −2.7. Now let's calculate the price elasticity for D_1 as the price is *increased* from $3.70 to $4.00. This 8.1 percent price increase causes a decrease in the quantity demanded from 1,200 gallons to 1,000 gallons, or by 16.7 percent. So, now our measure of the price elasticity of demand between points *A* and *B* is −16.7/8.1 = −2.1. It can be confusing to have different

Elastic demand Demand is elastic when the percentage change in the quantity demanded is *greater* than the percentage change in price, so the price elasticity is *greater* than 1 in absolute value.

Inelastic demand Demand is inelastic when the percentage change in quantity demanded is *less* than the percentage change in price, so the price elasticity is *less* than 1 in absolute value.

Unit-elastic demand Demand is unit elastic when the percentage change in quantity demanded is *equal to* the percentage change in price, so the price elasticity is equal to 1 in absolute value.

MyEconLab Animation

Figure 6.1

Elastic and Inelastic Demand

Along D_1, cutting the price from $4.00 to $3.70 increases the number of gallons demanded from 1,000 to 1,200 per day. Because the percentage change in quantity demanded is greater than the percentage change in price (in absolute value), demand is elastic between point A and point B. Along D_2, cutting the price from $4.00 to $3.70 increases the number of gallons demanded only from 1,000 to 1,050 per day. Because the percentage change in quantity demanded is smaller than the percentage change in price (in absolute value), demand is inelastic between point A and point C.

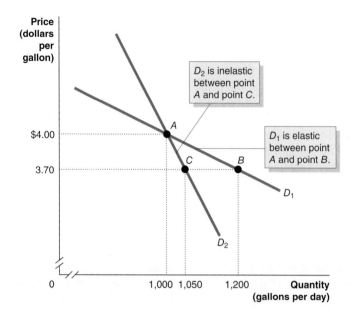

values for the price elasticity of demand between the same two points on the same demand curve. As we will see in the next section, economists use a formula that allows them to avoid this confusion when calculating elasticities.   MyEconLab Concept Check

The Midpoint Formula

We can use the *midpoint formula* to ensure that we have only one value of the price elasticity of demand between the same two points on a demand curve. The midpoint formula uses the *average* of the initial and final quantities and the initial and final prices. If Q_1 and P_1 are the initial quantity and price, and Q_2 and P_2 are the final quantity and price, the midpoint formula is:

$$\text{Price elasticity of demand} = \frac{(Q_2 - Q_1)}{\left(\dfrac{Q_1 + Q_2}{2}\right)} \div \frac{(P_2 - P_1)}{\left(\dfrac{P_1 + P_2}{2}\right)}.$$

The midpoint formula may seem challenging at first, but the numerator is just the change in quantity divided by the average of the initial and final quantities, and the denominator is just the change in price divided by the average of the initial and final prices.

Let's apply the formula to calculating the price elasticity of D_1 in Figure 6.1. Between point A and point B on D_1, the change in quantity is 200, and the average of the two quantities is 1,100. Therefore, there is an 18.2 percent change in quantity demanded. The change in price is −$0.30, and the average of the two prices is $3.85. Therefore, there is a −7.8 percent change in price. So, the price elasticity of demand is 18.2/−7.8 = −2.3. Notice these three results from calculating the price elasticity of demand using the midpoint formula:

1. As we suspected from examining Figure 6.1, demand curve D_1 is elastic between points A and B.
2. The value for the price elasticity calculated using the midpoint formula is between the two values we calculated earlier.
3. The midpoint formula will give us the same value whether we are moving from the higher price to the lower price or from the lower price to the higher price.

We can also use the midpoint formula to calculate the elasticity of demand between point A and point C on D_2. In this case, there is a 4.9 percent change in quantity and a −7.8 percent change in price. So, the elasticity of demand is 4.9/−7.8 = −0.6. Once again, as we suspected, demand curve D_2 is price inelastic between points A and C.   MyEconLab Concept Check

Solved Problem 6.1

Calculating the Price Elasticity of Demand

Suppose you own a service station, and you are currently selling gasoline for $3.50 per gallon. At this price, you can sell 2,000 gallons per day. You are considering cutting the price to $3.30 to attract drivers who have been buying their gas at competing stations. The following graph shows two possible increases in the quantity of gasoline sold as a result of your price cut. Use the information in the graph to calculate the price elasticity between these two prices on each of the demand curves. Use the midpoint formula in your calculations. State whether each demand curve is elastic or inelastic between these two prices.

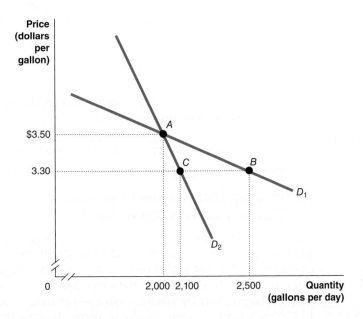

Solving the Problem

Step 1: **Review the chapter material.** This problem requires calculating the price elasticity of demand, so you may want to review the material in the section "The Midpoint Formula," which begins on page 174.

Step 2: **To begin using the midpoint formula, calculate the average quantity and the average price for demand curve D_1.**

$$\text{Average quantity} = \frac{2,000 + 2,500}{2} = 2,250$$

$$\text{Average price} = \frac{\$3.50 + \$3.30}{2} = \$3.40$$

Step 3: **Now calculate the percentage change in the quantity demanded and the percentage change in price for demand curve D_1.**

$$\text{Percentage change in quantity demanded} = \frac{2,500 - 2,000}{2,250} \times 100 = 22.2\%$$

$$\text{Percentage change in price} = \frac{\$3.30 - \$3.50}{\$3.40} \times 100 = -5.9\%$$

Step 4: **Divide the percentage change in the quantity demanded by the percentage change in price to arrive at the price elasticity for demand curve D_1.**

$$\text{Price elasticity of demand} = \frac{22.2\%}{-5.9\%} = -3.8$$

Because the elasticity is greater than 1 in absolute value, D_1 is price *elastic* between these two prices.

Step 5: **Calculate the price elasticity of demand curve D_2 between these two prices.**

$$\text{Percentage change in quantity demanded} = \frac{2,100 - 2,000}{2,050} \times 100 = 4.9\%$$

$$\text{Percentage change in price} = \frac{\$3.30 - \$3.50}{\$3.40} \times 100 = -5.9\%$$

$$\text{Price elasticity of demand} = \frac{4.9\%}{-5.9\%} = -0.8$$

Because the elasticity is less than 1 in absolute value, D_2 is price *inelastic* between these two prices.

MyEconLab Study Plan

Your Turn: For more practice, do related problem 1.7 on page 196 at the end of this chapter.

When Demand Curves Intersect, the Flatter Curve Is More Elastic

Remember that elasticity is not the same thing as slope. While slope is calculated using changes in quantity and price, elasticity is calculated using percentage changes. But it *is* true that if two demand curves intersect, the one with the smaller slope (in absolute value)—the flatter demand curve—is more elastic, and the one with the larger slope (in absolute value)—the steeper demand curve—is less elastic. In Figure 6.1, for a given change in price, demand curve D_1 is more elastic than demand curve D_2.   MyEconLab Concept Check

Polar Cases of Perfectly Elastic and Perfectly Inelastic Demand

Perfectly inelastic demand The case where the quantity demanded is completely unresponsive to price and the price elasticity of demand equals zero.

Although they do not occur frequently, you should be aware of the extreme, or polar, cases of price elasticity. If a demand curve is a vertical line, it is **perfectly inelastic**. In this case, the quantity demanded is completely unresponsive to price, and the price elasticity of demand equals zero. No matter how much price may increase or decrease, the quantity remains the same. For only a very few products will the quantity demanded be completely unresponsive to the price, making the demand curve a vertical line. The drug insulin is an example. Some diabetics must take a certain amount of insulin each day. If the price of insulin declines, it will not affect the required dose and therefore will not increase the quantity demanded. Similarly, a price increase will not affect the required dose or decrease the quantity demanded. (Of course, some diabetics may not be able to afford insulin at a higher price. If so, even in this case the demand curve may not be completely vertical and, therefore, not perfectly inelastic.)

Perfectly elastic demand The case where the quantity demanded is infinitely responsive to price and the price elasticity of demand equals infinity.

If a demand curve is a horizontal line, it is **perfectly elastic**. In this case, the quantity demanded is infinitely responsive to price, and the price elasticity of demand equals infinity. If a demand curve is perfectly elastic, an increase in price causes the quantity demanded to fall to zero. Once again, perfectly elastic demand curves are rare, and it is important not to confuse *elastic* with *perfectly elastic*. Table 6.1 summarizes the different price elasticities of demand.   MyEconLab Concept Check

Table 6.1

Summary of the Price Elasticity of Demand

if demand is …	then the absolute value of price elasticity is …
elastic	greater than 1
inelastic	less than 1
unit elastic	equal to 1
perfectly elastic	equal to infinity
perfectly inelastic	equal to 0

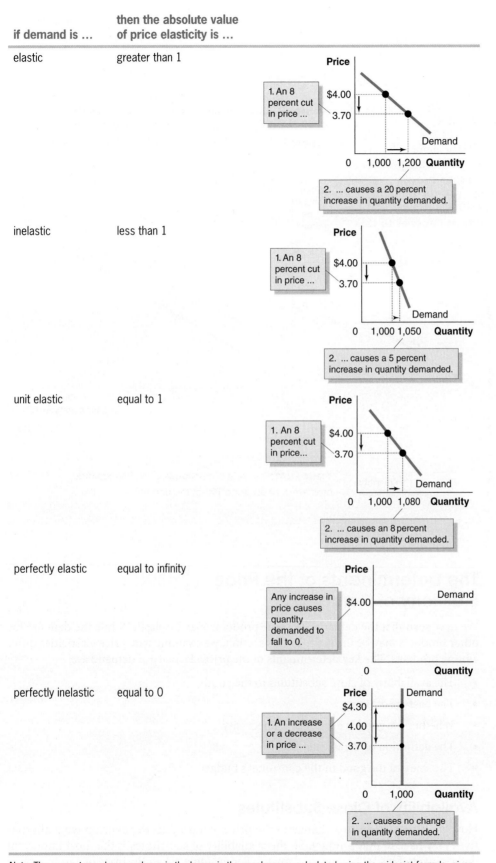

MyEconLab Study Plan

Note: The percentage changes shown in the boxes in the graphs were calculated using the midpoint formula, given on page 174, and are rounded to the nearest whole number.

Don't Let This Happen to You

Don't Confuse Inelastic with Perfectly Inelastic

You may be tempted to simplify the concept of elasticity by assuming that any demand curve described as being inelastic is *perfectly* inelastic. You should never make this assumption because perfectly inelastic demand curves are rare. For example, consider the following problem: "Use a demand and supply graph to show how a decrease in supply affects the equilibrium quantity of gasoline. Assume that the demand for gasoline is inelastic." The following graph would be an *incorrect* answer to this problem.

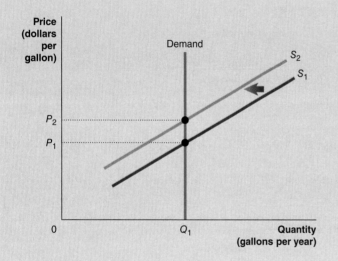

The demand for gasoline is inelastic, but it is not *perfectly* inelastic. When the price of gasoline rises, the quantity demanded falls. So, the correct answer to this problem would use a graph showing a typical downward-sloping demand curve rather than a vertical demand curve.

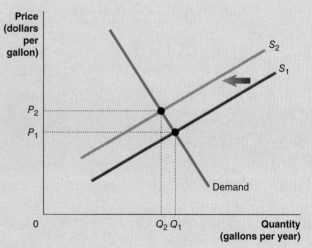

MyEconLab Study Plan

Your Turn: Test your understanding by doing related problem 1.10 on page 197 at the end of this chapter.

6.2 LEARNING OBJECTIVE

Understand the determinants of the price elasticity of demand.

The Determinants of the Price Elasticity of Demand

We have seen that the demand for some products may be elastic, while the demand for other products may be inelastic. In this section, we examine why price elasticities differ among products. The key determinants of the price elasticity of demand are:

- The availability of close substitutes to the good
- The passage of time
- Whether the good is a luxury or a necessity
- The definition of the market
- The share of the good in the consumer's budget

Availability of Close Substitutes

How consumers react to a change in the price of a product depends on what alternatives they have to that product. So the availability of substitutes is the most important determinant of price elasticity of demand. For example, when the price of gasoline rises, consumers have few alternatives, so the quantity demanded falls only a little. But if the price of pizza rises, consumers have many alternative foods they can eat, so the quantity demanded is likely to fall substantially. In fact, a key constraint on a firm's pricing policies is how many close substitutes exist for its product. In general, *if a product has more substitutes available, it will have more elastic demand. If a product has fewer substitutes available, it will have less elastic demand.*   MyEconLab Concept Check

Passage of Time

It usually takes consumers some time to adjust their buying habits when prices change. If the price of chicken falls, for example, it takes a while before consumers decide to change from eating chicken for dinner once a week to eating it twice a week. If the price of gasoline increases, it also takes a while for consumers to decide to begin taking public transportation, to buy more fuel-efficient cars, or to find new jobs closer to where they live. *The more time that passes, the more elastic the demand for a product becomes.*   MyEconLab Concept Check

Luxuries versus Necessities

Goods that are luxuries usually have more elastic demand curves than goods that are necessities. For example, the demand for bread is inelastic because bread is a necessity, and the quantity that people buy is not very dependent on its price. Tickets to a concert are a luxury, so the demand for concert tickets is much more elastic than the demand for bread. *The demand curve for a luxury is more elastic than the demand curve for a necessity.*   MyEconLab Concept Check

Definition of the Market

In a narrowly defined market, consumers have more substitutes available. For example, if you own a service station and raise the price you charge for gasoline, many of your customers will switch to buying from a competitor. So, the demand for gasoline at one particular station is likely to be elastic. The demand for gasoline as a product, on the other hand, is inelastic because consumers have few alternatives (in the short run) to buying it. *The more narrowly we define a market, the more elastic demand will be.*   MyEconLab Concept Check

Share of a Good in a Consumer's Budget

Goods that take only a small fraction of a consumer's budget tend to have less elastic demand than goods that take a large fraction. For example, most people buy table salt infrequently and in relatively small quantities. The share of an average consumer's budget that is spent on salt is very low. As a result, even a doubling of the price of salt is likely to result in only a small decline in the quantity of salt demanded. "Big-ticket items," such as houses, cars, and furniture, take up a larger share in the average consumer's budget. Increases in the prices of these goods are likely to result in significant declines in the quantity demanded. In general, *the demand for a good will be more elastic the larger the share of the good in the average consumer's budget.*   MyEconLab Concept Check

Some Estimated Price Elasticities of Demand

Table 6.2 shows some estimated short-run price elasticities of demand. It's important to remember that estimates of the price elasticities of different goods can vary, depending on the data used and the time period over which the estimates were made. The results given in the table are consistent with our discussion of the determinants of price elasticity. Goods for which there are few substitutes, such as cigarettes, gasoline, and health insurance, are price inelastic, as are broadly defined goods, such as bread or beer. Particular brands of products such as Coca-Cola, Tide, or Post Raisin Bran

Table 6.2

Estimated Real-World Price Elasticities of Demand

Product	Estimated Elasticity	Product	Estimated Elasticity
Books (Barnes & Noble)	−4.00	Bread	−0.40
Books (Amazon)	−0.60	Water (residential use)	−0.38
DVDs (Amazon)	−3.10	Chicken	−0.37
Post Raisin Bran	−2.50	Cocaine	−0.28
Automobiles	−1.95	Cigarettes	−0.25
Tide (liquid detergent)	−3.92	Beer	−0.29
Coca-Cola	−1.22	Catholic school attendance	−0.19
Grapes	−1.18	Residential natural gas	−0.09
Restaurant meals	−0.67	Gasoline	−0.06
Health insurance (low-income households)	−0.65	Milk	−0.04
		Sugar	−0.04

See Text Credits at the back of the book for complete source list.

are price elastic. (This point is discussed further in the *Making the Connection* on the price elasticity of breakfast cereal.)

The table shows that the demand for books or DVDs bought from a particular retailer is typically price elastic. Note, though, that the demand for books from Amazon is inelastic, which indicates that consumers do not consider ordering from other online sites to be good substitutes for ordering from Amazon.

An increase in the price of grapes will lead some consumers to substitute other fruits, so demand for grapes is price elastic. Similarly, an increase in the price of new automobiles will lead some consumers to buy used automobiles or to continue driving their current cars, so demand for automobiles is also price elastic. The demand for necessities, such as natural gas and water, is price inelastic.   MyEconLab Concept Check

Making the Connection

MyEconLab Video

The Price Elasticity of Demand for Breakfast Cereal

MIT economist Jerry Hausman has estimated the price elasticity of demand for breakfast cereal. He divided breakfast cereals into three categories: children's cereals, such as Trix and Froot Loops; adult cereals, such as Special K and Grape-Nuts; and family cereals, such as Corn Flakes and Raisin Bran. Some of the results of his estimates are given in the following table:

Cereal	Price Elasticity of Demand
Post Raisin Bran	−2.5
All family breakfast cereals	−1.8
All types of breakfast cereals	−0.9

Just as we would expect, the price elasticity for a particular brand of raisin bran was larger in absolute value than the elasticity for all family cereals, and the elasticity for all family cereals was larger than the elasticity for all types of breakfast cereals. If Post increases the price of its raisin bran by 10 percent, sales will decline by 25 percent, as many consumers switch to another brand of raisin bran. If the prices of all family breakfast cereals rise by 10 percent, sales will decline by 18 percent, as consumers switch to child or adult cereals. In both of these cases, demand is elastic.

But if the prices of all types of breakfast cereals rise by 10 percent, sales will decline by only 9 percent. Demand for all breakfast cereals is inelastic.

Source: Jerry A. Hausman, "Valuation of New Goods under Perfect and Imperfect Competition," in Timothy F. Bresnahan and Robert J. Gordon, eds., *The Economics of New Goods*, Chicago: University of Chicago Press, 1997.

Your Turn: Test your understanding by doing related problem 2.4 on page 197 at the end of this chapter.

MyEconLab Study Plan

The Relationship between Price Elasticity of Demand and Total Revenue

6.3 LEARNING OBJECTIVE

Understand the relationship between the price elasticity of demand and total revenue.

Knowing the price elasticity of demand allows a firm to calculate how changes in price will affect its **total revenue**, which is the total amount of funds it receives from selling a good or service. Total revenue is calculated by multiplying price per unit by the number of units sold. When demand is inelastic, price and total revenue move in the same direction: An increase in price raises total revenue, and a decrease in price reduces total revenue. When demand is elastic, price and total revenue move inversely: An increase in price reduces total revenue, and a decrease in price raises total revenue.

To understand the relationship between price elasticity and total revenue, consider Figure 6.2. Panel (a) shows a demand curve for gasoline that is inelastic between point A and point B. (It was demand curve D_2 in Figure 6.1 on page 174.) The total revenue received by the service station owner at point A equals the price of $4.00 multiplied by the 1,000 gallons sold, or $4,000. This amount equals the areas of rectangles C and D in the figure because together the rectangles have a height of $4.00 and a base of 1,000 gallons. Because this demand curve is inelastic between point A and point B, cutting

Total revenue The total amount of funds a seller receives from selling a good or service, calculated by multiplying price per unit by the number of units sold.

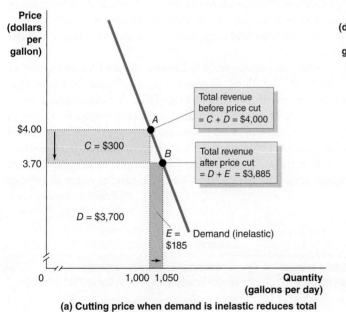

(a) Cutting price when demand is inelastic reduces total revenue.

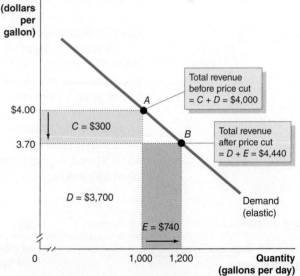

(b) Cutting price when demand is elastic increases total revenue.

MyEconLab Animation

Figure 6.2   **The Relationship between Price Elasticity and Total Revenue**

When demand is inelastic, a cut in price will decrease total revenue. In panel (a), at point A, the price is $4.00, 1,000 gallons are sold, and total revenue received by the service station equals $4.00 × 1,000 gallons, or $4,000. At point B, cutting the price to $3.70 increases the quantity demanded to 1,050 gallons, but the fall in price more than offsets the increase in quantity. As a result, revenue falls to

$3.70 × 1,050 gallons, or $3,885. When demand is elastic, a cut in the price will increase total revenue. In panel (b), at point A, the areas of rectangles C and D are still equal to $4,000. But at point B, the areas of rectangles D and E are equal to $3.70 × 1,200 gallons, or $4,440. In this case, the increase in the quantity demanded is large enough to offset the fall in price, so total revenue increases.

the price to $3.70 (point *B*) reduces total revenue. The new total revenue is shown by the areas of rectangles *D* and *E* and is equal to $3.70 multiplied by 1,050 gallons, or $3,885. Total revenue falls because the increase in the quantity demanded is not large enough to make up for the decrease in price. As a result, the $185 increase in revenue gained as a result of the price cut—rectangle *E*—is less than the $300 in revenue lost—rectangle *C*.

Panel (b) of Figure 6.2 shows a demand curve that is elastic between point *A* and point *B*. (It was demand curve D_1 in Figure 6.1.) With this demand curve, cutting the price increases total revenue. At point *A*, the areas of rectangles *C* and *D* are still equal to $4,000, but at point *B*, the areas of rectangles *D* and *E* are equal to $3.70 multiplied by 1,200 gallons, or $4,440. Here, total revenue rises because the increase in the quantity demanded is large enough to offset the lower price. As a result, the $740 increase in revenue gained as a result of the price cut—rectangle *E*—is greater than the $300 in revenue lost—rectangle *C*.

The third, less common possibility is that demand is unit elastic. In that case, a small change in price is exactly offset by a proportional change in the quantity demanded, leaving revenue unaffected. Therefore, when demand is unit elastic, neither a decrease nor an increase in price affects revenue. Table 6.3 summarizes the relationship between price elasticity and revenue.

Elasticity and Revenue with a Linear Demand Curve

Along most demand curves, elasticity is not constant at every point. For example, a straight-line, or linear, demand curve for gasoline is shown in panel (a) of Figure 6.3. (For simplicity, small quantities are used.) The numbers from the table are plotted in the graphs. The demand curve shows that when the price drops by $1 per gallon, consumers always respond by buying 2 more gallons per day. When the price is high and the quantity demanded is low, demand is elastic. Demand is elastic because a $1 drop in price is a smaller percentage change when the price is high, and an increase of 2 gallons is a larger percentage change when the quantity of gasoline purchased is low. By similar reasoning, we can see why demand is inelastic when the price is low and the quantity demanded is high.

Panel (a) in Figure 6.3 shows that when price is between $8 and $4 and quantity demanded is between 0 gallons and 8 gallons, demand is elastic. Panel (b) shows that over this same range, total revenue will increase as price falls. For example, in panel (a), as price falls from $7 to $6, the quantity demanded increases from 2 to 4, and in panel (b), total revenue increases from $14 to $24. Similarly, when price is between $4 and $0 and the quantity demanded is between 8 and 16, demand is inelastic. Over this same range, total revenue will decrease as price falls. For example, as price falls from $3 to $2 and the quantity demanded increases from 10 to 12, total revenue decreases from $30 to $24.   MyEconLab Concept Check

Table 6.3	If demand is ...	then ...	because ...
The Relationship between Price Elasticity and Revenue	elastic	an increase in price reduces revenue	the decrease in quantity demanded is proportionally *greater* than the increase in price.
	elastic	a decrease in price increases revenue	the increase in quantity demanded is proportionally *greater* than the decrease in price.
	inelastic	an increase in price increases revenue	the decrease in quantity demanded is proportionally *smaller* than the increase in price.
	inelastic	a decrease in price reduces revenue	the increase in quantity demanded is proportionally *smaller* than the decrease in price.
	unit elastic	an increase in price does not affect revenue	the decrease in quantity demanded is proportionally *the same as* the increase in price.
	unit elastic	a decrease in price does not affect revenue	the increase in quantity demanded is proportionally *the same as* the decrease in price.

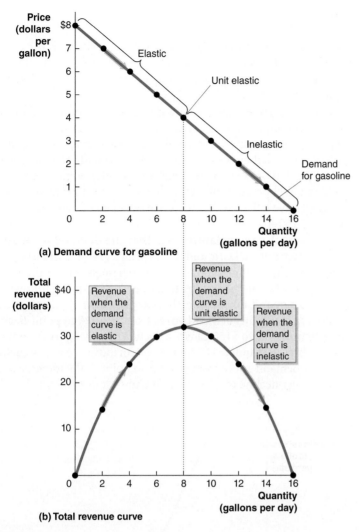

Price	Quantity Demanded	Total Revenue
$8	0	$0
7	2	14
6	4	24
5	6	30
4	8	32
3	10	30
2	12	24
1	14	14
0	16	0

MyEconLab Animation

Figure 6.3   Elasticity Is Not Constant along a Linear Demand Curve

The data from the table are plotted in the graphs. Panel (a) shows that as we move down the demand curve for gasoline, the price elasticity of demand declines. In other words, at higher prices, demand is elastic, and at lower prices, demand is inelastic. Panel (b) shows that as the quantity of gasoline purchased increases from 0, revenue will increase until it reaches a maximum of $32 when 8 gallons are purchased. As purchases increase beyond 8 gallons, revenue falls because demand is inelastic on this portion of the demand curve.

Solved Problem 6.3

MyEconLab Interactive Animation

Price and Revenue Don't Always Move in the Same Direction

New York City officials believed they needed more revenue to maintain 35 city-owned recreation centers. To raise the additional revenue, the city's parks department increased the annual membership fee to use the centers from $75 to $150. According to an article in the *New York Times*, "the department had hoped to realize $4 million in new revenue, but in fact, it lost about $200,000." The article also explains that the parks department had expected a 5 percent decline in memberships due to the price increase.

a. What did the parks department believe about the price elasticity of demand for memberships in its recreation centers?

b. Is demand for memberships actually elastic or inelastic? Briefly explain. Illustrate your answer with a graph showing the demand curve for memberships as the parks department believed it to be and as it actually is.

Solving the Problem

Step 1: Review the chapter material. This problem deals with the effect of a price change on a firm's revenue, so you may want to review the section "The Relationship between Price Elasticity of Demand and Total Revenue," which begins on page 181.

Step 2: Answer part (a) by explaining how the parks department viewed the demand for memberships. Looking at Table 6.3, we can conclude that managers at the parks department must have thought the demand for memberships was inelastic because they believed that revenue would increase if they raised the price. The managers estimated that the quantity of memberships demanded would fall by 5 percent following the 100 percent price increase. Therefore, they must have believed that the price elasticity of demand for memberships was $-5\% / 100\% = -0.05$.

Step 3: Answer part (b) by explaining whether the demand for memberships is actually elastic or inelastic and by drawing a graph to illustrate your answer. Because revenue fell when the parks department raised the price, we know that demand for memberships must be elastic. In the following graph, D_1 shows the demand for memberships as the parks department believed it to be. Moving along this demand curve from point A to point B, an increase in the price from \$75 to \$150 causes a decline of only Q_1 to Q_2 in the quantity of memberships demanded. D_2 shows the demand curve as it actually is. Moving along this demand curve from point A to point C, the increase in price causes a much larger decline of Q_1 to Q_3 in memberships demanded.

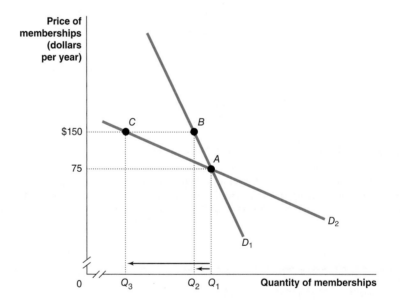

MyEconLab Study Plan **Your Turn:** For more practice, do related problems 3.8 and 3.9 on page 199 at the end of this chapter.

Estimating Price Elasticity of Demand

To estimate the price elasticity of demand, a firm needs to know the demand curve for its product. For a well-established product, economists can use historical data to statistically estimate the demand curve. To calculate the price elasticity of demand for a new product, firms often rely on market experiments, trying different prices and observing the change in quantity demanded that results.

For example, Apple introduced the first-generation iPhone in June 2007, at a price of $599. But demand for the iPhone was more elastic than Apple had expected, and when sales failed to reach Apple's projections, the company cut the price to $399 just two months later. Similarly, when 3D televisions were introduced into the U.S. market in early 2010, Sony and other manufacturers believed that sales would be strong despite prices being several hundred dollars higher than those for other high-end ultra-thin televisions. Once again, though, demand turned out to be more elastic than expected, and by December firms were cutting prices 40 percent or more in an effort to increase revenue. MyEconLab Concept Check

MyEconLab Study Plan

Other Demand Elasticities

Elasticity is an important concept in economics because it allows us to quantify the responsiveness of one economic variable to changes in another economic variable. In addition to price elasticity, two other demand elasticities are important: *cross-price elasticity of demand* and *income elasticity of demand*.

Cross-Price Elasticity of Demand

Suppose you work at Apple, and you need to predict the effect of an increase in the price of Samsung's Galaxy Tab on the quantity of iPads demanded, holding other factors constant. You can do this by calculating the **cross-price elasticity of demand**, which is the percentage change in the quantity of iPads demanded divided by the percentage change in the price of Galaxy Tabs—or, in general:

$$\text{Cross-price elasticity of demand} = \frac{\text{Percentage change in quantity demanded of one good}}{\text{Percentage change in price of another good}}.$$

The cross-price elasticity of demand is positive or negative, depending on whether the two products are substitutes or complements. Recall that substitutes are products that can be used for the same purpose, such as two brands of tablet computers. Complements are products that are used together, such as tablet computers and applications that can be downloaded from online stores. An increase in the price of a substitute will lead to an increase in the quantity demanded, so the cross-price elasticity of demand will be positive. An increase in the price of a complement will lead to a decrease in the quantity demanded, so the cross-price elasticity of demand will be negative. Of course, if the two products are unrelated—such as tablet computers and peanut butter—the cross-price elasticity of demand will be zero. Table 6.4 summarizes the key points concerning the cross-price elasticity of demand.

Cross-price elasticity of demand is important to firm managers because it allows them to measure whether products sold by other firms are close substitutes for their products. For example, Pepsi-Cola and Coca-Cola spend heavily on advertising with the hope of convincing consumers that each cola tastes better than its rival. How can these firms tell whether their advertising campaigns have been effective? One way is by seeing whether the cross-price elasticity of demand has changed. If, for instance, Coca-Cola has a successful advertising campaign, when it increases the price of Coke, the percentage increase in sales of Pepsi should be smaller. In other words, the value of the cross-price elasticity of demand should have declined. MyEconLab Concept Check

Cross-price elasticity of demand
The percentage change in the quantity demanded of one good divided by the percentage change in the price of another good.

Table 6.4

Summary of Cross-Price Elasticity of Demand

If the products are …	then the cross-price elasticity of demand will be …	Example
substitutes	positive.	Two brands of tablet computers
complements	negative.	Tablet computers and applications downloaded from online stores
unrelated	zero.	Tablet computers and peanut butter

Table 6.5	If the income elasticity of demand is …	then the good is …	Example
Summary of Income Elasticity of Demand	positive but less than 1	normal and a necessity.	Bread
	positive and greater than 1	normal and a luxury.	Caviar
	negative	inferior.	High-fat meat

Income elasticity of demand A measure of the responsiveness of the quantity demanded to changes in income, measured by the percentage change in the quantity demanded divided by the percentage change in income.

Income Elasticity of Demand

The **income elasticity of demand** measures the responsiveness of the quantity demanded to changes in income. It is calculated as follows:

$$\text{Income elasticity of demand} = \frac{\text{Percentage change in quantity demanded}}{\text{Percentage change in income}}.$$

We know that if the quantity demanded of a good increases as income increases, then the good is a *normal good* (see Chapter 3). Normal goods are often further subdivided into *luxuries* and *necessities*. A good is a luxury if the quantity demanded is very responsive to changes in income, so that a 10 percent increase in income results in more than a 10 percent increase in the quantity demanded. Expensive jewelry and vacation homes are examples of luxuries. A good is a necessity if the quantity demanded is not very responsive to changes in income, so that a 10 percent increase in income results in less than a 10 percent increase in the quantity demanded. Food and clothing are examples of necessities. A good is *inferior* if the quantity demanded falls when income increases. Ground beef with a high fat content is an example of an inferior good. We should note that *normal good*, *inferior good*, *necessity*, and *luxury* are just labels economists use for goods with different income elasticities; the labels are not intended to be value judgments about the worth of these goods.

Because most goods are normal goods, during periods of economic expansion when consumer income is rising, most firms can expect—holding other factors constant—that the quantity demanded of their products will increase. Sellers of luxuries can expect particularly large increases. During recessions, falling consumer income can cause firms to experience increases in demand for inferior goods. For example, the demand for bus trips increases as consumers cut back on air travel, and supermarkets find that the demand for canned tuna increases relative to the demand for fresh salmon. Table 6.5 summarizes the key points about the income elasticity of demand.   MyEconLab Concept Check

Making the Connection
MyEconLab Video

Price Elasticity, Cross-Price Elasticity, and Income Elasticity in the Market for Alcoholic Beverages

Many public policy issues are related to the consumption of alcoholic beverages. These issues include underage drinking, drunk driving, and the possible beneficial effects of red wine in lowering the risk of heart disease. Knowing how responsive the demand for alcohol is to changes in price provides insight into these policy issues. Christopher Ruhm of the University of Virginia and colleagues have estimated statistically the following elasticities. (*Spirits* refers to all beverages that contain alcohol, other than beer and wine.)

Price elasticity of demand for beer	−0.30
Cross-price elasticity of demand between beer and wine	−0.83
Cross-price elasticity of demand between beer and spirits	−0.50
Income elasticity of demand for beer	0.09

These results indicate that the demand for beer is inelastic. A 10 percent increase in the price of beer will result in a 3 percent decline in the quantity of beer demanded.

Somewhat surprisingly, both wine and spirits are complements for beer rather than substitutes. A 10 percent increase in the price of wine will result in an 8.3 percent *decrease* in the quantity of beer demanded. Previous studies of the price elasticity of beer had found that beer was a substitute for other alcoholic drinks. Ruhm and his colleagues argue that their results are more reliable because they use Uniform Product Code (UPC) scanner data on prices and quantities sold in grocery stores. They argue that these price data are more accurate than the data used in many previous studies that included the prices of only one brand each of beer, wine, and whiskey.

The results in the table also show that a 10 percent increase in income will result in a 0.9 percent *increase* in the quantity of beer demanded. So, beer is a normal good. According to the definitions given earlier, beer would be classified as a necessity because it has an income elasticity that is positive but less than 1.

Source: Christopher J. Ruhm, et al., "What U.S. Data Should Be Used to Measure the Price Elasticity of Demand for Alcohol," *Journal of Health Economics*, Vol. 31, No. 16, December 2012.

Your Turn: Test your understanding by doing related problem 4.8 on page 200 at the end of this chapter.

MyEconLab Study Plan

Using Elasticity to Analyze the Disappearing Family Farm

6.5 LEARNING OBJECTIVE

Use price elasticity and income elasticity to analyze economic issues.

The concepts of price elasticity and income elasticity can help us understand many economic issues. For example, some people are concerned that the family farm is becoming an endangered species in the United States. Although food production continues to grow rapidly, the number of farms and farmers continue to dwindle. In 1950, the United States was home to more than 5 million farms, and more than 23 million people lived on farms. By 2013, only about 2 million farms remained, and fewer than 3 million people lived on them. The federal government has several programs that are intended to aid farmers (see Chapter 4). Many of these programs have been aimed at helping small, family-operated farms, but rapid growth in farm production, combined with low price and income elasticities for most food products, have made family farming difficult in the United States.

Productivity measures the ability of firms to produce goods and services with a given amount of economic inputs, such as workers, machines, and land. Productivity has grown very rapidly in U.S. agriculture. In 1950, the average U.S. wheat farmer harvested about 17 bushels from each acre of wheat planted. By 2013, because of the development of superior strains of wheat and improvements in farming techniques, the average American wheat farmer harvested 46 bushels per acre. So, even though the total number of acres devoted to growing wheat declined from about 62 million to about 56 million, total wheat production rose from about 1.0 billion bushels to about 2.3 billion.

Unfortunately for U.S. farmers, this increase in wheat production resulted in a substantial decline in wheat prices. Two key factors explain this decline: (1) The demand for wheat is inelastic, and (2) the income elasticity of demand for wheat is low. Even though the U.S. population has increased greatly since 1950 and the income of the average American is much higher than it was in 1950, the demand for wheat has increased only moderately. For all of the additional wheat to be sold, the price has had to decline. Because the demand for wheat is inelastic, the price decline has been substantial. Figure 6.4 illustrates these points.

A large shift in supply, a small shift in demand, and an inelastic demand curve combined to drive down the price of wheat from $19.29 per bushel in 1950 to $7.80 in 2013. (We measure the price in 1950 in terms of prices in 2013, to adjust for the general increase in prices since 1950.) With low prices, only the most efficiently run farms have been able to remain profitable. Small family–run farms have found it difficult to survive, and many of these farms have disappeared. The markets for most other food products are similar to the market for wheat. They are characterized by rapid output growth and low income and price elasticities. The result is the paradox of American farming: ever more abundant and cheaper food, supplied by fewer and fewer farms. American consumers have benefited, but most family farmers have not.   MyEconLab Concept Check

MyEconLab Animation

Figure 6.4

Elasticity and the Disappearing Family Farm

In 1950, U.S. farmers produced 1.0 billion bushels of wheat at a price of $19.29 per bushel. Over the next 60 years, rapid increases in farm productivity caused a large shift to the right in the supply curve for wheat. The income elasticity of demand for wheat is low, so the demand for wheat increased relatively little over this period. Because the demand for wheat is also inelastic, the large shift in the supply curve and the small shift in the demand curve resulted in a sharp decline in the price of wheat, from $19.29 per bushel in 1950 to $7.80 in 2013.
Source: U.S. Department of Agriculture, *Wheat Yearbook Tables*, May 21, 2013.

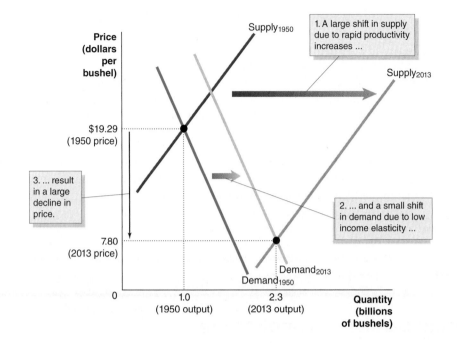

Solved Problem 6.5

MyEconLab Interactive Animation

Using Price Elasticity to Analyze a Policy of Taxing Gasoline

If the consumption of a product results in a negative externality, taxing the product may improve economic efficiency (see Chapter 5). Some economists and policymakers argue that driving cars and trucks involves a negative externality because burning gasoline increases emissions of greenhouse gases and contributes to the congestion that clogs many highways in and around big cities and to the accidents that take more than 30,000 lives per year. Some economists have suggested substantially increasing the federal excise tax on gasoline, which in 2013 was 18.4 cents per gallon. How much the tax would cause consumption to fall and how much revenue the tax would raise depend on the price elasticity of demand. Suppose that the price of gasoline is currently $4.00 per gallon, the quantity of gasoline demanded

is 140 billion gallons per year, the price elasticity of demand for gasoline is −0.06, and the federal government decides to increase the excise tax on gasoline by $1.00 per gallon. The price of a product will not rise by the full amount of a tax increase unless the demand for the product is perfectly inelastic (see Chapter 4). In this case, suppose that the price of gasoline increases by $0.80 per gallon after the $1.00 excise tax is imposed.

a. What is the new quantity of gasoline demanded after the tax is imposed? How effective would a gas tax be in reducing consumption of gasoline in the short run?

b. How much revenue does the federal government receive from the tax?

Solving the Problem

Step 1: **Review the chapter material.** This problem deals with applications of the price elasticity of demand formula, so you may want to review the section "Measuring the Price Elasticity of Demand," which begins on page 172.

Step 2: **Answer the first question in part (a) using the formula for the price elasticity of demand to calculate the new quantity demanded.**

$$\text{Price elasticity of demand} = \frac{\text{Percentage change in quantity demanded}}{\text{Percentage change in price}}.$$

We can plug into the midpoint formula the values given for the price elasticity, the original price of $4.00, and the new price of $4.80 (= $4.00 + $0.80).

$$-0.06 = \frac{\text{Percentage change in quantity demanded}}{\left(\dfrac{(\$4.80 - \$4.00)}{\left(\dfrac{\$4.00 + \$4.80}{2}\right)}\right)}.$$

Or, rearranging and writing out the expression for the percentage change in the quantity demanded:

$$-0.011 = \frac{(Q_2 - 140 \text{ billion})}{\left(\dfrac{140 \text{ billion} + Q_2}{2}\right)}.$$

Solving for Q_2, the new quantity demanded is:

$$Q_2 = 138.5 \text{ billion gallons.}$$

Step 3: **Answer the second question in part (a).** Because the price elasticity of demand for gasoline is so low, −0.06, even a substantial increase in the gasoline tax of $1.00 per gallon would reduce gasoline consumption by only a small amount: from 140 billion gallons of gasoline per year to 138.5 billion gallons. Note, though, that price elasticities typically increase over time. Economists estimate that the long-run price elasticity of gasoline is in the range of −0.40 to −0.60, so in the long run, the decline in the consumption of gasoline would be larger.

Step 4: **Calculate the revenue earned by the federal government to answer part (b).** The federal government would collect an amount equal to the tax per gallon multiplied by the number of gallons sold: $1 per gallon × 138.5 billion gallons = $138.5 billion.

Extra Credit: The tax of $138.5 billion calculated in Step 4 is substantial: about 12 percent of all the revenue the federal government raised from the personal income tax in 2012. It is also much larger than the roughly $25 billion the federal government receives each year from the existing 18.4-cents-per-gallon gasoline tax. We can conclude that raising the federal excise tax on gasoline would be a good way to raise revenue for the federal government, but, at least in the short run, increasing the tax would not greatly reduce the quantity of gasoline consumed. Notice that if the demand for gasoline were elastic, this result would be reversed: The quantity of gasoline consumed would decline much more, but so would the revenue that the federal government would receive from the tax increase.

Your Turn: For more practice, do related problems 5.2 and 5.3 on pages 200–201 at the end of this chapter.

MyEconLab Study Plan

The Price Elasticity of Supply and Its Measurement

6.6 LEARNING OBJECTIVE

Define price elasticity of supply and understand its main determinants and how it is measured.

We can use the concept of elasticity to measure the responsiveness of firms to a change in price, just as we used it to measure the responsiveness of consumers. We know from the law of supply that when the price of a product increases, the quantity supplied increases. To measure how much the quantity supplied increases when price increases, we use the *price elasticity of supply.*

Measuring the Price Elasticity of Supply

Just as with the price elasticity of demand, we calculate the **price elasticity of supply** by using percentage changes:

$$\text{Price elasticity of supply} = \frac{\text{Percentage change in quantity supplied}}{\text{Percentage change in price}}.$$

Price elasticity of supply The responsiveness of the quantity supplied to a change in price, measured by dividing the percentage change in the quantity supplied of a product by the percentage change in the product's price.

Notice that because supply curves are upward sloping, the price elasticity of supply will be a positive number. We categorize the price elasticity of supply the same way we categorized the price elasticity of demand: If the price elasticity of supply is less than 1, then supply is *inelastic.* For example, the price elasticity of supply of gasoline from U.S. oil refineries is about 0.20, and so it is inelastic; a 10 percent increase in the price of gasoline will result in only a 2 percent increase in the quantity supplied. If the price elasticity of supply is greater than 1, then supply is *elastic.* If the price elasticity of supply is equal to 1, the supply is *unit elastic.* As with other elasticity calculations, when we calculate the price elasticity of supply, we hold constant the values of other factors.   MyEconLab Concept Check

Determinants of the Price Elasticity of Supply

Whether supply is elastic or inelastic depends on the ability and willingness of firms to alter the quantity they produce as price increases. Often, firms have difficulty increasing the quantity of the product they supply during any short period of time. For example, a pizza parlor cannot produce more pizzas on any one night than is possible using the ingredients on hand. Within a day or two, it can buy more ingredients, and within a few months, it can hire more cooks and install additional ovens. As a result, the supply curve for pizza and most other products will be inelastic if we measure it over a short period of time, but the supply curve will be increasingly elastic the longer the period of time over which we measure it. Products that require resources that are themselves in fixed supply are an exception to this rule. For example, a French winery may rely on a particular variety of grape. If all the land on which that grape can be grown is already planted in vineyards, then the supply of that wine will be inelastic even over a long period. MyEconLab Concept Check

Making the Connection MyEconLab Video

Why Are Oil Prices So Unstable?

Bringing oil to market is a long process. Oil companies hire geologists to locate fields for exploratory oil well drilling. If significant amounts of oil are present, the company begins full-scale development of the field. The process from exploration to pumping significant amounts of oil can take years. This long process is the reason for the very low short-run price elasticity of supply for oil.

During the period from 2003 to mid-2008, the worldwide demand for oil increased rapidly as India, China, and some other developing countries increased both their manufacturing production and their use of automobiles. As the following graph shows, when supply is inelastic, an increase in demand can cause a large increase in price. The shift in the demand curve from D_1 to D_2 causes the equilibrium quantity of oil to increase only by 5 percent, from 80 million barrels per day to 84 million, but the equilibrium price rises by 75 percent, from $80 to $140 per barrel.

The world oil market is heavily influenced by the Organization of the Petroleum Exporting Countries (OPEC). OPEC has 11 members, including Saudi Arabia, Kuwait, Iran, Venezuela, and Nigeria. Together OPEC members own 75 percent of the world's proven oil reserves. Periodically, OPEC has attempted to force up the price of oil by reducing the quantity of oil its members supply. Since the 1970s, OPEC's attempts to reduce the quantity of oil in world markets have been successful only sporadically. As a result, the supply curve for oil shifts fairly frequently. Combined with the low price elasticities of oil supply and demand, these shifts in supply have caused the price of oil to fluctuate significantly over the past 40 years, from as low as $10 per barrel to more than $140.

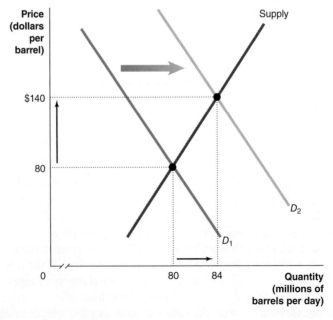

By mid-2008, the financial crisis that began in the United States had spread to other countries, resulting in a severe recession. As production and incomes fell during the recession, the worldwide demand for oil declined sharply. Over the space of a few months, the equilibrium price of oil fell from $140 per barrel to $40. As the following graph shows, once again, the extent of the price change reflected not only the size of the decline in demand but also the low short-run price elasticity of supply for oil.

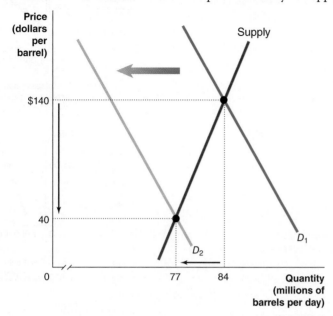

Over the long run, the elasticity of supply for oil is much higher than in the short run. High oil prices give oil companies an incentive to devise ways to extract oil from shale formations. Increases in the quantity of shale oil being pumped have led to forecasts that the United States could become the world's largest oil producer by 2020.

Your Turn: Test your understanding by doing related problem 6.3 on page 201 at the end of this chapter.

MyEconLab Study Plan

Polar Cases of Perfectly Elastic and Perfectly Inelastic Supply

Although it occurs infrequently, it is possible for supply to fall into one of the polar cases of price elasticity. If a supply curve is a vertical line, it is *perfectly inelastic*. In this case, the quantity supplied is completely unresponsive to price, and the price elasticity of supply equals zero. Regardless of how much price may increase or decrease, the quantity remains the same. Over a brief period of time, the supply of some goods and services may be perfectly inelastic. For example, a parking lot may have only a fixed number of parking spaces. If demand increases, the price to park in the lot may rise, but no more spaces will become available. Of course, if demand increases permanently, over a longer period of time, the owner of the lot may buy more land and add additional spaces.

If a supply curve is a horizontal line, it is *perfectly elastic*. In this case, the quantity supplied is infinitely responsive to price, and the price elasticity of supply equals infinity. If a supply curve is perfectly elastic, a very small increase in price causes a very large increase in the quantity supplied. Just as with demand curves, it is important not to confuse a supply curve being elastic with its being perfectly elastic and not to confuse a supply curve being inelastic with its being perfectly inelastic. Table 6.6 summarizes the different price elasticities of supply.

MyEconLab Concept Check

Table 6.6

Summary of the Price Elasticity of Supply

If supply is...	then the value of price elasticity is ...	
elastic	greater than 1	

1. An 8 percent increase in price ...

$4.00
3.70

Supply

0   1,000   1,200   **Quantity**

2. ... causes a 20 percent increase in quantity supplied.

inelastic	less than 1	

1. An 8 percent increase in price ...

$4.00
3.70

Supply

0   1,000 1,050   **Quantity**

2. ... causes a 5 percent increase in quantity supplied.

unit elastic	equal to 1	

1. An 8 percent increase in price ...

$4.00
3.70

Supply

0   1,000 1,080   **Quantity**

2. ... causes an 8 percent increase in quantity supplied.

perfectly elastic	equal to infinity	

Any increase in price causes the percentage change in quantity supplied to become infinite.

$4.00

Supply

0   **Quantity**

perfectly inelastic	equal to 0	

1. An increase or a decrease in price ...

$4.30
4.00
3.70

Supply

0   1,000   **Quantity**

2. ... causes no change in quantity supplied.

Note: The percentage increases shown in the boxes in the graphs were calculated using the midpoint formula, given on page 174.

Using Price Elasticity of Supply to Predict Changes in Price

Figure 6.5 illustrates the important point that, when demand increases, the amount by which price increases depends on the price elasticity of supply. The figure shows the demand and supply for parking spaces at a beach resort. In panel (a), on a typical summer weekend, equilibrium occurs at point *A*, where Demand$_{Typical}$ intersects a supply curve that is inelastic. The increase in demand for parking spaces on July 4th shifts the demand curve to the right, moving the equilibrium to point *B*. Because the supply curve is inelastic, the increase in demand results in a large increase in price—from $2.00 per hour to $4.00—but only a small increase in the quantity of spaces supplied—from 1,200 to 1,400.

In panel (b), supply is elastic, perhaps because the resort has vacant land that can be used for parking during periods of high demand. As a result, the change in equilibrium from point *A* to point *B* results in a smaller increase in price and a larger increase in the quantity supplied. An increase in price from $2.00 per hour to $2.50 is sufficient to increase the quantity of parking spaces supplied from 1,200 to 2,100. Knowing the price elasticity of supply makes it possible to predict more accurately how much price will change following an increase or a decrease in demand.

MyEconLab Concept Check   MyEconLab Study Plan

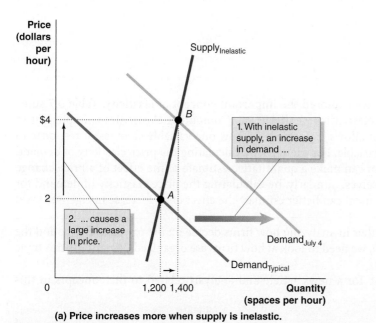

(a) Price increases more when supply is inelastic.

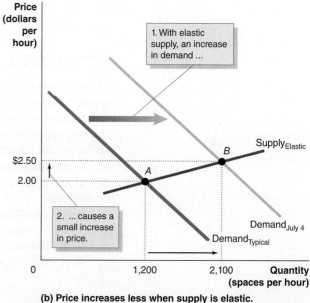

(b) Price increases less when supply is elastic.

Figure 6.5   **Changes in Price Depend on the Price Elasticity of Supply**   MyEconLab Animation

In panel (a), Demand$_{Typical}$ represents the typical demand for parking spaces on a summer weekend at a beach resort. Demand$_{July\ 4}$ represents demand on July 4th. Because supply is inelastic, the shift in equilibrium from point *A* to point *B* results in a large increase in price—from $2.00 per hour to $4.00—but only a small increase in the quantity of spaces supplied—from 1,200 to 1,400.

In panel (b), supply is elastic. As a result, the change in equilibrium from point *A* to point *B* results in a smaller increase in price and a larger increase in the quantity supplied. An increase in price from $2.00 per hour to $2.50 is sufficient to increase the quantity of parking supplied from 1,200 to 2,100.

Continued from page 171

Economics in Your Life

How Much Do Gas Prices Matter to You?

At the beginning of the chapter, we asked you to think about three questions: What factors would make you more or less sensitive to price when purchasing gasoline? Have you responded differently to price changes during different periods of your life? and Why do consumers seem to respond more to changes in gas prices at a particular service station but seem less sensitive when gas prices rise or fall at all service stations? A number of factors are likely to affect your sensitivity to changes in gas prices, including how high your income is (and, therefore, how large a share of your budget is taken up by gasoline purchases), whether you live in an area with good public transportation (which can be a substitute for having to use your own car), and whether you live within walking distance of your school or job. Each of these factors may change over the course of your life, making you more or less sensitive to changes in gas prices. Finally, consumers respond to changes in the price of gas at a particular service station because gas at other service stations is a good substitute. But there are presently few good substitutes for gasoline as a product, so consumers respond much less to changes in prices at all service stations.

Conclusion

In this chapter, we have explored the important concept of elasticity. Table 6.7 summarizes the various elasticities we discussed. Computing elasticities is important in economics because it allows us to measure how one variable changes in response to changes in another variable. For example, by calculating the price elasticity of demand for its product, a firm can make a quantitative estimate of the effect of a price change on the revenue it receives. Similarly, by calculating the price elasticity of demand for cigarettes, the government can better estimate the effect of an increase in cigarette taxes on smoking.

Before going further in analyzing how firms decide on the prices to charge and the quantities to produce, we need to look at how firms are organized. We discuss this topic in the next chapter.

Visit MyEconLab for a news article and analysis related to the concepts in this chapter.

Price Elasticity of Demand

Table 6.7

Summary of Elasticities

Formula: $\dfrac{\text{Percentage change in quantity demanded}}{\text{Percentage change in price}}$

Midpoint formula: $\dfrac{(Q_2 - Q_1)}{\left(\dfrac{Q_1 + Q_2}{2}\right)} \div \dfrac{(P_2 - P_1)}{\left(\dfrac{P_1 + P_2}{2}\right)}$

	Absolute Value of Price Elasticity	Effect on Total Revenue of an Increase in Price
Elastic	Greater than 1	Total revenue falls
Inelastic	Less than 1	Total revenue rises
Unit elastic	Equal to 1	Total revenue unchanged

Cross-Price Elasticity of Demand

Formula: $\dfrac{\text{Percentage change in quantity demanded of one good}}{\text{Percentage change in price of another good}}$

Types of Products	Value of Cross-Price Elasticity
Substitutes	Positive
Complements	Negative
Unrelated	Zero

Income Elasticity of Demand

Formula: $\dfrac{\text{Percentage change in quantity demanded}}{\text{Percentage change in income}}$

Types of Products	Value of Income Elasticity
Normal and a necessity	Positive but less than 1
Normal and a luxury	Positive and greater than 1
Inferior	Negative

Price Elasticity of Supply

Formula: $\dfrac{\text{Percentage change in quantity supplied}}{\text{Percentage change in price}}$

	Value of Price Elasticity
Elastic	Greater than 1
Inelastic	Less than 1
Unit elastic	Equal to 1

Chapter Summary and Problems

Key Terms

Cross-price elasticity of demand, p. 185

Elastic demand, p. 173

Elasticity, p. 172

Income elasticity of demand, p. 186

Inelastic demand, p. 173

Perfectly elastic demand, p. 176

Perfectly inelastic demand, p. 176

Price elasticity of demand, p. 172

Price elasticity of supply, p. 189

Total revenue, p. 181

Unit-elastic demand, p. 173

6.1 ## The Price Elasticity of Demand and Its Measurement, pages 172–178
LEARNING OBJECTIVE: Define *price elasticity of demand* and understand how to measure it.

Summary

Elasticity measures how much one economic variable responds to changes in another economic variable. The **price elasticity of demand** measures how responsive the quantity demanded is to changes in price. The price elasticity of demand is equal to the percentage change in the quantity demanded divided by the percentage change in price. If the quantity demanded changes more than proportionally when price changes, the price elasticity of demand is greater than 1 in absolute value, and demand is **elastic**. If the quantity demanded changes less than proportionally when price changes, the price elasticity of demand is less than 1 in absolute value, and demand is **inelastic**. If the quantity demanded changes proportionally when price changes, the price elasticity of demand is equal to 1 in absolute value, and demand is **unit elastic**. **Perfectly inelastic demand** curves are vertical lines, and **perfectly elastic demand** curves are horizontal lines. Relatively few products have perfectly elastic or perfectly inelastic demand curves.

 MyEconLab   Visit www.myeconlab.com to complete these exercises online and get instant feedback.

Review Questions

1.1 Write the formula for the price elasticity of demand. Why isn't elasticity just measured by the slope of the demand curve?

1.2 If a 10 percent increase in the price of Cheerios causes a 25 percent reduction in the number of boxes of Cheerios demanded, what is the price elasticity of demand for Cheerios? Is the demand for Cheerios elastic or inelastic?

1.3 What is the midpoint formula for calculating price elasticity of demand? How else can you calculate the price elasticity of demand? What is the advantage of using the midpoint formula?

1.4 Draw a graph of a perfectly inelastic demand curve. Think of a product that would have a perfectly inelastic demand curve. Explain why demand for this product would be perfectly inelastic.

Problems and Applications

1.5 In the 2010 holiday season, Steve Richardson decided to cut the prices of his handcrafted wooden puzzles to increase sales. According to a newspaper account, "the number of orders at Stave Puzzles Inc., his Norwich, Vermont, business, hasn't been enough to offset the price cuts." Is the demand for these puzzles elastic or inelastic? Briefly explain.
Source: Emily Maltby, "In Season of Big Discounts, Small Shops Suffer," *Wall Street Journal*, November 24, 2010.

1.6 Suppose that the following table gives data on the price of rye and the number of bushels of rye sold in 2013 and 2014:

Year	Price (dollars per bushel)	Quantity (bushels)
2013	$3.00	8 million
2014	2.00	12 million

  a. Calculate the change in the quantity of rye demanded divided by the change in the price of rye. Measure the quantity of rye in bushels.

  b. Calculate the change in the quantity of rye demanded divided by the change in the price of rye, but this time measure the quantity of rye in millions of bushels. Compare your answer to the one you computed in (a).

  c. Assuming that the demand curve for rye did not shift between 2013 and 2014, use the information in the table to calculate the price elasticity of demand for rye. Use the midpoint formula in your calculation. Compare the value for the price elasticity of demand to the values you calculated in (a) and (b).

1.7 [Related to Solved Problem 6.1 **on page 175**] You own a hot dog stand that you set up outside the student union every day at lunchtime. Currently, you are selling hot dogs for a price of $3 each, and you sell 30 hot dogs a day. You are considering cutting the price to $2. The following graph shows two possible increases in the quantity sold as a result of your price cut. Use the information in the graph to calculate the price elasticity between these two prices on each of the demand curves. Use the midpoint formula to calculate the price elasticities.

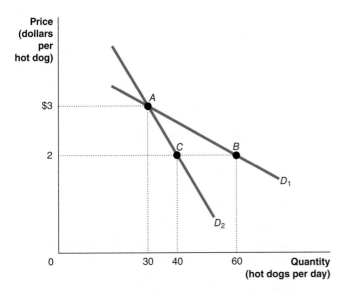

in Pace's freshman class elastic or inelastic? Did the total amount of tuition Pace received from its freshman class rise or fall in 2006 compared with 2005?

Source: Karen W. Arenson, "At Universities, Plum Post at Top Is Now Shaky," *New York Times*, January 9, 2007.

1.9 In 1916, the Ford Motor Company sold 500,000 Model T Fords at a price of $440 each. Henry Ford believed that he could increase sales of the Model T by 1,000 cars for every dollar he cut the price. Use this information to calculate the price elasticity of demand for Model T Fords. Use the midpoint formula in your calculation.

1.10 **[Related to the** Don't Let This Happen to You **on page 178]** The publisher of a magazine gives his staff the following information:

Current price	$2.00 per issue
Current sales	150,000 copies per month
Current total costs	$450,000 per month

He tells the staff, "Our costs are currently $150,000 more than our revenues each month. I propose to eliminate this problem by raising the price of the magazine to $3.00 per issue. This will result in our revenue being exactly equal to our cost." Do you agree with the publisher's analysis? Explain. (*Hint:* Remember that a firm's revenue is calculated by multiplying the price of the product by the quantity sold.)

1.8 In the fall of 2006, Pace University in New York raised its annual tuition from $24,751 to $29,454. Freshman enrollment declined from 1,469 in the fall of 2005 to 1,131 in the fall of 2006. Assuming that the demand curve for places in the freshman class at Pace did not shift between 2005 and 2006, calculate the price elasticity of demand. Use the midpoint formula in your calculation. Is the demand for places

---

<table>
<tr><td>**6.2**</td><td>**Determinants of the Price Elasticity of Demand, pages 178–181**
LEARNING OBJECTIVE: Understand the determinants of the price elasticity of demand.</td></tr>
</table>

Summary

The main determinants of the price elasticity of demand for a good are the availability of close substitutes, the passage of time, whether the good is a necessity or a luxury, how narrowly the market for the good is defined, and the share of the good in the consumer's budget.

 MyEconLab   Visit www.myeconlab.com to complete these exercises online and get instant feedback.

Review Questions

2.1 Is the demand for most agricultural products elastic or inelastic? Briefly explain.

2.2 What are the key determinants of the price elasticity of demand for a product? Which determinant is the most important?

Problems and Applications

2.3 Briefly explain whether the demand for each of the following products is likely to be elastic or inelastic:
   a. Milk
   b. Frozen cheese pizza
   c. Cola
   d. Prescription medicine

2.4 **[Related to the** Making the Connection **on page 180]** One study found that the price elasticity of demand for soda is −0.78, while the price elasticity of demand for

Coca-Cola is −1.22. Coca-Cola is a type of soda, so why isn't its price elasticity the same as the price elasticity for soda as a product?

Source: Kelly D. Brownell and Thomas R. Frieden, "Ounces of Prevention—The Public Policy Case for Taxes on Sugared Beverages," *New England Journal of Medicine*, April 30, 2009, pp. 1805–1808.

2.5 The price elasticity of demand for crude oil in the United States has been estimated to be −0.06 in the short run and −0.45 in the long run. Why would the demand for crude oil be more price elastic in the long run than in the short run?

Source: John C. B. Cooper, "Price Elasticity of Demand for Crude Oil: Estimate for 23 Countries," *OPEC Review*, March 2003, pp. 1–8.

2.6 **[Related to the** Chapter Opener **on page 171]** An article in the *Dallas Morning News* discussed the market for green cars—hybrid gasoline and electric cars, electric cars, and diesel cars. One factor the article mentioned as affecting the market for green cars was the increasing gas mileage of conventional gasoline-powered cars. How would this factor be likely to affect the price elasticity of demand for green cars?

Source: Terry Box and Troy Oxford, "Green Cars Still a Small Part of New-Car Sales," *Dallas Morning News*, May 26, 2013.

2.7 The entrance fee into Yellowstone National Park in northwestern Wyoming is "$25 for a private, noncommercial vehicle; $20 for each snowmobile or motorcycle; or $12 for each visitor 16 and older entering by foot, bike, ski, etc." The fee provides the visitor with a seven-day entrance permit into Yellowstone and nearby Grand Teton National Park.

a. Would you expect the demand for entry into Yellowstone National Park for visitors in private, noncommercial vehicles to be elastic or inelastic? Briefly explain.

b. There are three general ways to enter the park: in a private, noncommercial vehicle; on a snowmobile or motorcycle; and by foot, bike, or ski. Which way would you expect to have the largest price elasticity of demand, and which would you expect to have the smallest price elasticity of demand? Briefly explain.

Source: National Park Service, Yellowstone National Park, "Fees, Reservations, and Permits," http://www.nps.gov/yell/planyourvisit/feesandreservations.htm, June 12, 2013.

6.3 The Relationship between Price Elasticity of Demand and Total Revenue, pages 181–185

LEARNING OBJECTIVE: Understand the relationship between the price elasticity of demand and total revenue.

Summary

Total revenue is the total amount of funds received by a seller of a good or service. When demand is inelastic, a decrease in price reduces total revenue, and an increase in price raises total revenue. When demand is elastic, a decrease in price increases total revenue, and an increase in price decreases total revenue. When demand is unit elastic, an increase or a decrease in price leaves total revenue unchanged.

MyEconLab   Visit **www.myeconlab.com** to complete these exercises online and get instant feedback.

Review Questions

3.1 If the demand for orange juice is inelastic, will an increase in the price of orange juice increase or decrease the revenue orange juice sellers receive?

3.2 The price of organic apples falls, and apple growers find that their revenue increases. Is the demand for organic apples elastic or inelastic?

Problems and Applications

3.3 **[Related to the** Chapter Opener **on page 171]** The Energy Information Administration estimated that in 2012 American consumers spent 4 percent of their incomes on gasoline. Would the elasticity of demand likely be greater or less if consumers had spent 8 percent of their incomes on gasoline? Briefly explain.

Source: Steve Everly, "'Get Ready for a Roller Coaster' as Gas Prices Swing Wildly," *Kansas City Star*, April 21, 2013.

3.4 Economists' estimates of price elasticities can differ somewhat, depending on the time period and on the markets in which the price and quantity data used in the estimates were gathered. An article in the *New York Times* contained the following statement from the Centers for Disease Control and Prevention: "A 10 percent increase in the price of cigarettes reduces consumption by 3 percent to 5 percent." Given this information, compute the range of the price elasticity of demand for cigarettes. Explain whether the demand for cigarettes is elastic, inelastic, or unit elastic. If cigarette manufacturers raise prices, will their revenue increase or decrease? Briefly explain.

Source: Shaila Dewan, "States Look at Tobacco to Balance the Budget," *New York Times*, March 20, 2009.

3.5 According to an article in the *New York Times*, in 2011 the Port Authority of New York and New Jersey was planning to increase the tolls on the bridges and tunnels crossing the Hudson River by as much as 50 percent. According to the article, "Revenue from the ... higher tolls would raise an additional $720 million for the agency ...." Is the Port Authority assuming that the demand for using bridges and tunnels crossing the Hudson is elastic or inelastic? Why might the Port Authority be reasonably confident in this assumption?

Source: Michael M. Grynbaum, "Port Authority Seeks Big Toll Increase," *New York Times*, August 5, 2011.

3.6 Use the following graph for Yolanda's Frozen Yogurt Stand to answer the questions.

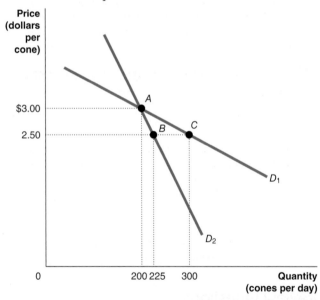

a. Use the midpoint formula to calculate the price elasticity of demand for D_1 between point A and point C and the price elasticity of demand for D_2 between point A and point B. Which demand curve is more elastic, D_1 or D_2? Briefly explain.

b. Suppose Yolanda is initially selling 200 cones per day at a price of $3.00 per cone. If she cuts her price to $2.50 per cone and her demand curve is D_1, what will be the change in her revenue? What will be the change in her revenue if her demand curve is D_2?

3.7 A sportswriter writing about the Cleveland Indians baseball team made the following observation: "If the Indians suddenly slashed all tickets to $10, would their attendance actually increase? Not all that much and revenue would drop dramatically." What is the sportswriter assuming about the price elasticity of demand for Indians' tickets?

Source: David Schoenfiel, "Chat with David Schoenfield," espn.com, November 27, 2012.

3.8 [**Related to** Solved Problem 6.3 **on page 183**] Briefly explain whether you agree with Manager 2's reasoning:

Manager 1: "The only way we can increase the revenue we receive from selling our frozen pizzas is by cutting the price."

Manager 2: "Cutting the price of a product never increases the amount of revenue you receive. If we want to increase revenue, we have to increase price."

3.9 [**Related to** Solved Problem 6.3 **on page 183**] If a firm increases the price of its product and its total revenue increases, will further increases in its price necessarily lead to further increases in its total revenue? Briefly explain.

3.10 According to an article in the *Wall Street Journal*, some small publishers have argued that Amazon has been increasing the prices it sells their books for on its Web site. Amazon was increasing the prices by reducing the discount it offered consumers on the retail prices of the books. One small nonfiction publisher said that Amazon had reduced the discount on its books from about 30 percent to about 16 percent. According to the author of the article: "For this publisher, that means less revenue and less profit as some buyers reject the more expensive books."

  a. Does the fact that some buyers will no longer buy the publisher's books at a higher price necessarily mean the publisher will earn less revenue? Briefly explain.

  b. What must be true about the price elasticity of demand for the publisher's books for the author's statement to be correct?

  Source: David Streitfield, "As Competition Wanes, Amazon Cuts Back Its Discounts," *Wall Street Journal*, July 4, 2013.

3.11 After parking rates were increased substantially from $10 to $16 per day at the "Big Blue Deck" at Detroit's Metro Airport, parking revenue increased from the previous December. Use the information in the following table to calculate the price elasticity of demand for parking spaces at the Big Blue Deck, using the midpoint formula. Assume that nothing happened between December 2007 and December 2008 to shift the demand curve for parking spaces. Be sure to state whether demand is elastic or inelastic.

Month	Rate	Revenue
December 2007	$10	$1,387,000
December 2008	16	1,448,000

Sources: Mary Francis Masson, "Metro Airport Parking Rate Hikes Worry Employees," *Detroit Free Press*, February 14, 2009; and Tanveer Ali, "Parking Dips; Revenue Soars," *Detroit News*, February 13, 2009.

3.12 The Delaware River Joint Toll Bridge Commission increased the toll from $0.50 to $1.00 on the bridges on Route 22 and Interstate 78 from New Jersey to Pennsylvania. Use the information in the following table to answer the questions. (Assume that besides the toll change, nothing occurred during the months that would affect consumer demand.)

		Number of Vehicles Crossing the Bridge	
Month	Toll	Route 22 Bridge	Interstate 78 Bridge
November	$0.50	519,337	728,022
December	1.00	433,691	656,257

  a. Calculate the price elasticity of demand for each bridge, using the midpoint formula.

  b. How much total revenue did the commission collect from these bridges in November? How much did it collect in December? Relate your answer to your answer in (a).

  Source: Garrett Therolf, "Frugal Drivers Flood Free Bridge," *The Morning Call*, January 20, 2003.

6.4 **Other Demand Elasticities, pages 185–187**

LEARNING OBJECTIVE: Define *cross-price elasticity of demand* and *income elasticity of demand* and understand their determinants and how they are measured.

Summary

In addition to the elasticities already discussed, other important demand elasticities are the **cross-price elasticity of demand**, which is equal to the percentage change in the quantity demanded of one good divided by the percentage change in the price of another good, and the **income elasticity of demand**, which is equal to the percentage change in the quantity demanded divided by the percentage change in income.

 Visit **www.myeconlab.com** to complete these exercises online and get instant feedback.

Review Questions

4.1 Define the *cross-price elasticity of demand*. What does it mean if the cross-price elasticity of demand is negative? What does it mean if the cross-price elasticity of demand is positive?

4.2 Define the *income elasticity of demand*. Use income elasticity to distinguish a normal good from an inferior good.

Is it possible to tell from the income elasticity of demand whether a product is a luxury good or a necessity good?

Problems and Applications

4.3 When lettuce prices doubled, from about $1.50 per head to about $3.00, the reaction of one consumer was quoted in a newspaper article: "I will not buy [lettuce] when it's $3 a head," she said, adding that other green vegetables can fill in for lettuce. "If bread were $5 a loaf we'd still have to buy it. But lettuce is not that important in our family."

  a. For this consumer's household, which product has the higher price elasticity of demand: bread or lettuce? Briefly explain.

  b. Is the cross-price elasticity of demand between lettuce and other green vegetables positive or negative for this consumer? Briefly explain.

  Source: Justin Bachman, "Sorry, Romaine Only," *Associated Press*, March 29, 2002.

4.4 In the following graph, the demand for hot dog buns has shifted to the right because the price of hot dogs has fallen from $2.20 to $1.80 per package. Calculate the cross-price elasticity of demand between hot dogs and hot dog buns.

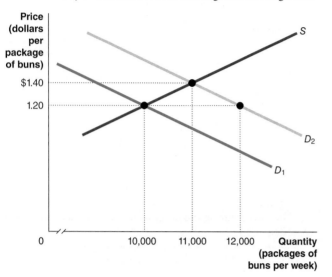

4.5 Are the cross-price elasticities of demand between the following pairs of products likely to be positive or negative? Briefly explain.
   a. Iced coffee and iced tea
   b. French fries and ketchup
   c. Steak and chicken
   d. Blu-ray players and Blu-ray discs

4.6 **[Related to the** Chapter Opener **on page 171]** During the spring of 2008, gasoline prices increased sharply in the United States. According to a newspaper article, rising gas prices had the following effect on the car market:

> Sales of Toyota's subcompact Yaris increased 46 percent, and Honda's tiny Fit had a record month. Ford's compact Focus model jumped 32 percent in April from a year earlier. All those models are rated at more than 30 miles per gallon for highway driving....

Sales of traditional SUVs are down more than 25 percent this year. In April, for example, sales of GM's Chevrolet Tahoe fell 35 percent. Full-size pickup sales have fallen more than 15 percent this year, with Ford's industry-leading F-Series pickup dropping 27 percent in April alone.

   a. Is the cross-price elasticity of demand between gasoline and high-mileage subcompact cars positive or negative? Is the cross-price elasticity of demand between gasoline and low-mileage SUVs and full-size pickups positive or negative? Briefly explain.
   b. How can we best think of the relationships among gasoline, subcompact cars, and SUVs? Briefly discuss which can be thought of as substitutes and which can be thought of as complements.

Source: Bill Vlasic, "As Gas Costs Soar, Buyers Flock to Small Cars," *New York Times*, May 2, 2008.

4.7 Rank the following four goods from lowest income elasticity of demand to highest income elasticity of demand. Briefly explain your ranking.
   a. Bread
   b. Pepsi
   c. Mercedes-Benz automobiles
   d. Laptop computers

4.8 **[Related to the** Making the Connection **on page 186]** The elasticities reported in this *Making the Connection* were calculated using price data for many brands of beer. Why might price elasticity estimates for a product be less reliable if they use data for only one brand of that product?

4.9 Consider firms selling three goods—one firm sells a good with an income elasticity of demand less than zero, one firm sells a good with an income elasticity of demand greater than zero but less than one, and one firm sells a good with an income elasticity of demand greater than one. In a recession, which firm is likely to see its sales decline the most? Which firm is likely to see its sales increase the most? Briefly explain.

6.5 **Using Elasticity to Analyze the Disappearing Family Farm, pages 187–189**
LEARNING OBJECTIVE: Use price elasticity and income elasticity to analyze economic issues.

Summary

Price elasticity and income elasticity can be used to analyze many economic issues. One example is the disappearance of the family farm in the United States. Because the income elasticity of demand for food is low, the demand for food has not increased proportionally as incomes in the United States have grown. As farmers have become more productive, they have increased the supply of most foods. Because the price elasticity of demand for food is low, increasing supply has resulted in continually falling food prices.

 MyEconLab Visit **www.myeconlab.com** to complete these exercises online and get instant feedback.

Review Questions

5.1 The demand for agricultural products is inelastic, and the income elasticity of demand for agricultural products is low. How do these facts help explain the decline of the family farm in the United States?

Problems and Applications

5.2 **[Related to** Solved Problem 6.5 **on page 188]** According to a study by the U.S. Centers for Disease Control and Prevention, the price elasticity of demand for cigarettes is −0.25. Americans purchase about 360 billion cigarettes each year.
   a. If the federal tax on cigarettes were increased enough to cause a 50 percent increase in the price of cigarettes, what would be the effect on the quantity of cigarettes demanded?

b. Is raising the tax on cigarettes a more effective way to reduce smoking if the demand for cigarettes is elastic or if it is inelastic? Briefly explain.

Source: "Response to Increases in Cigarette Prices by Race/Ethnicity, Income, and Age Groups—United States, 1976–1993," *Morbidity and Mortality Weekly Report*, July 31, 1998.

5.3 **[Related to** Solved Problem 6.5 **on page 188]** Suppose that the long-run price elasticity of demand for gasoline is −0.55. Assume that the price of gasoline is currently $4.00 per gallon, the quantity of gasoline is 140 billion gallons per year, and the federal government decides to increase the excise tax on gasoline by $1.00 per gallon. Suppose that in the long run the price of gasoline increases by $0.70 per gallon after the $1.00 excise tax is imposed.

  a. What is the new quantity of gasoline demanded after the tax is imposed? How effective would a gas tax be in reducing consumption of gasoline in the long run?

  b. How much does the federal government receive from the tax?

  c. Compare your answers to those in *Solved Problem 6.5* on page 188.

5.4 Corruption has been a significant problem in Iraq. Opening and running a business in Iraq usually requires paying multiple bribes to government officials. We can think of there being a demand and supply for bribes, with the curves having the usual shapes: The demand for bribes will be downward sloping because the smaller the bribe, the more business owners will be willing to pay it. The supply of bribes will be upward sloping because the larger the bribe, the more government officials will be willing to run the risk of breaking the law by accepting the bribe.

Suppose that the Iraqi government introduces a new policy to reduce corruption that raises the cost to officials of accepting bribes—perhaps by increasing the jail term for accepting a bribe. As a result, the supply curve for bribes will shift to the left. If we measure the burden on the economy from corruption by the total value of the bribes paid, what must be true of the demand for bribes if the government policy is to be effective? Illustrate your answer with a demand and supply graph. Be sure to show on your graph the areas representing the burden of corruption before and after the government policy is enacted.

Source: Frank R. Gunter, *The Political Economy of Iraq: Restoring Balance in a Post-Conflict Society*, Cheltenham, UK: Edward Elgar, 2013, Chapter 4.

5.5 The head of the United Kumquat Growers Association makes the following statement:

> The federal government is considering implementing a price floor in the market for kumquats. The government will not be able to buy any surplus kumquats produced at the price floor or to pay us any other subsidy. Because the demand for kumquats is elastic, I believe this program will make us worse off, and I say we should oppose it.

Explain whether you agree or disagree with this reasoning.

5.6 Review the concept of economic efficiency from Chapter 4 before answering the following question: Will there be a greater loss of economic efficiency from a price ceiling when demand is elastic or inelastic? Illustrate your answer with a demand and supply graph.

6.6	**The Price Elasticity of Supply and Its Measurement, pages 189–195**

LEARNING OBJECTIVE: Define *price elasticity of supply* and understand its main determinants and how it is measured.

Summary

The **price elasticity of supply** is equal to the percentage change in quantity supplied divided by the percentage change in price. The supply curves for most goods are inelastic over a short period of time, but they become increasingly elastic over longer periods of time. Perfectly inelastic supply curves are vertical lines, and perfectly elastic supply curves are horizontal lines. Relatively few products have perfectly elastic or perfectly inelastic supply curves.

 MyEconLab   Visit **www.myeconlab.com** to complete these exercises online and get instant feedback.

Review Questions

6.1 Write the formula for the price elasticity of supply. If an increase of 10 percent in the price of frozen pizzas results in a 9 percent increase in the quantity of frozen pizzas supplied, what is the price elasticity of supply for frozen pizzas? Is the supply of pizzas elastic or inelastic?

6.2 What is the main determinant of the price elasticity of supply?

Problems and Applications

6.3 **[Related to the** Making the Connection **on page 190]** Refer again to the first graph in the *Making the Connection* on page 190. Suppose that demand had stayed at the level indicated in the graph, with the equilibrium price of oil remaining at $140 per barrel. Over long periods of time, high oil prices lead to greater increases in the quantity of oil supplied. In other words, the price elasticity of supply for oil increases. This happens because higher prices provide an economic incentive to recover oil from more costly sources, such as under the oceans, from tar sands, or from shale formations. If the supply of oil becomes more elastic, explain how the increase in demand shown in the figure will result in a lower equilibrium price than $140 per barrel and a higher equilibrium quantity than 84 million barrels per day. Illustrate your answer with a demand and supply graph.

6.4 Use the midpoint formula for calculating elasticity to calculate the price elasticity of supply between point *A* and point *B* for each panel of Figure 6.5 on page 193.

6.5 Briefly explain whether you agree with the following statement: "The longer the period of time following an increase in the demand for apples, the greater the increase in the equilibrium quantity of apples and the smaller the increase in the equilibrium price."

6.6 Consider an increase in the demand for petroleum engineers in the United States. How would the supply of these engineers respond in the short run and in the long run? Conversely, consider a decrease in demand for lawyers. How would the supply of lawyers respond in the short run and in the long run?

6.7 On most days, the price of a rose is $1, and 8,000 roses are purchased. On Valentine's Day, the price of a rose jumps to $2, and 30,000 roses are purchased.
  a. Draw a demand and supply graph that shows why the price jumps.
  b. Based on this information, what do we know about the price elasticity of demand for roses? What do we know about the price elasticity of supply for roses? Calculate values for the price elasticity of demand and the price elasticity of supply or explain why you can't calculate these values.

6.8 Use the following graph of the market for basketball tickets at State University to answer these questions:
  a. What is the price elasticity of supply?
  b. Suppose the basketball team at State University goes undefeated in the first half of the season, and the demand for basketball tickets increases. Show the effects of this increase in demand on the graph. What happens to the equilibrium price and quantity of tickets? Briefly explain.

  c. If the State University basketball team continues to do very well in future years, what is likely to happen to the price elasticity of supply of tickets to its games? Briefly explain.

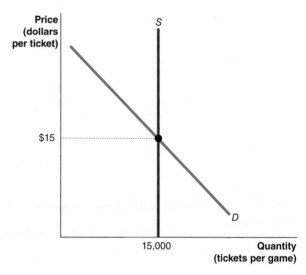

The Economics of Health Care

Chapter Outline and **Learning Objectives**

How Much Will You Pay for Health Insurance?

When you take a full-time job, how much will you pay for health insurance? In 2013, David Goldhill, president and chief executive officer of the Game Show Network (GSN), wrote a newspaper column about how much a 23-year-old new hire at his company pays for health care. Many firms buy health insurance for their workers from private insurance companies such as Blue Cross or Aetna. In the case of Goldhill's employee, out of her $35,000 annual salary, she paid $2,600 for health insurance, while GSN paid $6,190 on her behalf. Goldhill pointed out that the amount the company paid for the worker's health insurance might otherwise have been paid to her in salary. In addition, GSN withholds $1,500 from its employees' paycheck in federal and state taxes to support two federal programs: Medicare, which provides health insurance to people aged 65 and older, and Medicaid, which provides health insurance to low-income people. Employees are frequently unaware of the big bite that health care costs take out of their paychecks.

For many small firms, providing health insurance for their workers represents their most rapidly increasing cost. Health care spending increased from 5.2 percent of gross domestic product (GDP) in 1960 to 17.9 percent in 2013, an upward trend that is expected to continue. The U.S. Congressional Budget Office projects that Medicare and Medicaid spending will increase from 6 percent of GDP in 2013 to nearly 12 percent in 2050.

In 2010, President Barack Obama and Congress enacted the Patient Protection and Affordable Care Act (ACA), which made major changes to the U.S. health care system. Most of the changes were in place by 2014. Included in the act was a provision that businesses with 50 or more full-time employees (those working 30 or more hours per week) must provide health insurance to all full-time employees or face fines. Under the act, states were also to set up health insurance exchanges to make health insurance less expensive for small businesses and individuals by allowing them to enter an insurance pool where both healthy and sick people will be in the same insurance plan and pay the same insurance premium. As ACA went into effect, it remained to be seen whether the health insurance exchanges would lower health care premiums.

Sources: David Goldhill, "The Health Benefits That Cut Your Pay," *New York Times*, February 16, 2013; Karen Blumenthal, "Tackling the New Health-Care Rules," *Wall Street Journal*, May 31, 2013; U.S. Centers for Medicare & Medicaid Studies, "National Health Expenditure Data," www.cms.gov; and U.S. Congressional Budget Office, "Updated Budget Projections," May 14, 2013.

Economics in Your Life

Is Your Take-Home Pay Affected by What Your Employer Spends on Your Health Insurance?

If you work for a firm that provides you health insurance, the firm will withhold some amount from each of your paychecks to pay for the insurance. Typically, firms pay the majority of the cost of health insurance for their employees. In 2012, employees paid only 18 percent of the cost of coverage for themselves or 28 percent of the cost of coverage for their family. Your paycheck doesn't show the amount your employer pays on your behalf for health insurance, but does that amount affect your take-home pay? As you read this chapter, try to answer this question. You can check your answer against the one we provide on **page 229** at the end of this chapter.

Source: The Kaiser Family Foundation and Health Research and Educational Trust, *Employer Health Benefits, 2012 Annual Survey*, September 11, 2012.

Health care Goods and services, such as prescription drugs, consultations with a doctor, and surgeries, that are intended to maintain or improve a person's health.

Health care refers to goods and services, such as prescription drugs, consultations with a doctor, and surgeries, that are intended to maintain or improve a person's health. In 2013, health care made up more than one-sixth of the U.S. economy—about the size of the entire economy of France. Improvements in health care are an important part of the tremendous increase in living standards people in the United States and other high-income countries have experienced over the past 100 years. Health care has seen rapid technological change with new products, such as MRI units and other diagnostic equipment; prescription drugs to treat cancer, high blood pressure, and AIDS; vaccinations for meningitis; and new surgical techniques, such as cardiac catheterizations for treatment of heart disease.

Health care is provided through markets, just as are most other goods and services such as hamburgers and haircuts. So, we can apply to health care the tools of economic analysis we used in previous chapters. But the market for health care is different from other markets. In the United States, doctors and hospitals that supply most health care are primarily private firms, but the government also provides some health care services directly through the Veterans Health Administration, which is part of the U.S. Department of Veterans Affairs, and indirectly through the *Medicare* and *Medicaid* programs. In addition to having a large government role, the market for health care differs from most markets in other ways. Most importantly, a typical consumer of health care doesn't pay its full price. Most people either have private health insurance—most often provided through their employers—or are enrolled in the Medicare or Medicaid programs. Consumers who have insurance make different decisions about the quantity of health care they wish to consume than they would if they were paying the full cost of the services. So, to analyze the market for health care, we will need to use economic tools beyond those introduced in previous chapters. We begin our analysis of health care with an overview of health care around the world.

7.1 LEARNING OBJECTIVE

Discuss trends in U.S. health over time.

The Improving Health of People in the United States

Two hundred years ago, the whole world was very poor by modern standards. Today, an average person in a high-income country has a standard of living well beyond what even the richest people in the past could have imagined. One aspect of this higher standard of living is the improved health the average person enjoys. For example, in the late 1700s, England had the highest level of income per person of any large country. But the average person in England had a short life span and suffered from diseases—such as cholera, yellow fever, dysentery, and smallpox—that have disappeared from high-income countries today. The average life expectancy at birth was only 38 years, and 30 percent of the population died before reaching the age of 30. Even people who survived to age 20 could expect to live only an average of 34 more years. In 2014, the average life expectancy at birth in the United Kingdom and other high-income countries was around 80 years. People in eighteenth-century England were also short by modern standards. The average height of an adult male was 5 feet, 5 inches compared with 5 feet, 9 inches today.

In this section, we discuss the health of people in the United States. In Section 7.2, we discuss the health of people in other countries.

Changes over Time in U.S. Health

When economists measure changes over time in the standard of living in a country, they usually look first at increases in income per person. However, changes in health are also

Variable	1850	2013
Life expectancy at birth	38.3 years	78.7 years
Average height (adult males)	5'7"	5'9"
Infant mortality (death of a child aged 1 year or less)	228.9 per 1,000 live births	5.9 per 1,000 live births

Table 7.1

Health in the United States, 1850 and 2013

Note: The data on heights for 1850 include only native-born white and black citizens. The data on height for 2013 were gathered in 2007–2010 and represent the median height of adult males 20 years and older.

Sources: Susan B. Carter et al., eds., *Historical Statistics of the United States: Millennium Edition*; U.S. National Center for Health Statistics, *Anthropometric Reference Data for Children and Adults: United States, 2007–2010*, October 2012; and U.S. Central Intelligence Agency, *World Factbook*.

important because a person's health is an essential part of the person's well-being and, therefore, of his or her standard of living. The health of the average person in the United States improved significantly during the nineteenth and twentieth centuries, and by and large, it continues to improve today.

Table 7.1 compares some indicators of health in the United States in 1850 and 2013. Individuals in the United States today are taller, live much longer, and are much less likely to die in the first months of life than was true 160 years ago. Economists often look at heights as a measure of long-run changes in the average well-being of a population. A person's height relies partly on genetics—that is, tall parents tend to have tall children—but also on a person's *net nutritional status*. Net nutritional status depends on a person's food intake relative to the work the person has to perform, whether the person is able to remain warm in cold weather, and the diseases to which the person is exposed. Over time, people in the United States and other high-income countries have, on average, become taller, which is an indication that their nutritional status has improved.

MyEconLab Concept Check

Reasons for Long-Run Improvements in U.S. Health

For most of the country's history, the health of people in the United States has steadily improved, with life expectancies increasing and death rates decreasing. Panel (a) of Figure 7.1 shows for the years 1900–2011 the increase in life expectancy and the decline in the mortality rate, or death rate, measured as deaths per 100,000 people. Note that the mortality rate is "age adjusted," which means that it is not affected by changes in the age structure of the population. Life expectancy at birth in the United States increased from 47.3 years in 1900 to 78.7 years in 2013. Panel (b) shows for recent years the change in the overall mortality rate of the U.S. population, measured as deaths per 100,000 people, and the age-adjusted mortality rates for several diseases. The overall mortality rate decreased by more than 25 percent between 1981 and 2011. Over this same period, deaths from cancer, cardiovascular disease, such as heart attacks and strokes, and diseases of the liver all declined significantly. For example, cancer deaths were 20 percent lower in 2011 than they had been in 1981, while deaths from cardiovascular disease declined by more than half. Deaths from diabetes and kidney disease both increased slightly during this period, largely due to the effects of increasing obesity. The overall decline in death rates in the United States since 1981 was due to changes in lifestyle, particularly a decline in smoking, and advances in new diagnostic equipment, prescription drugs, and surgical techniques.

What explains the long-run increases in life expectancy and declines in death rates? Improvements in sanitation and in the distribution of food during the late nineteenth and early twentieth centuries led to better health during that period. More generally, the late Nobel Laureate Robert Fogel of the University of Chicago and Roderick Floud of

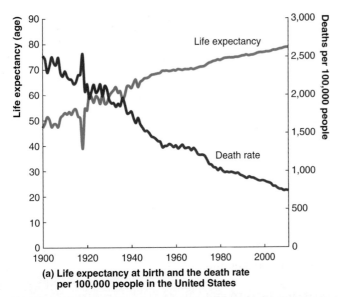

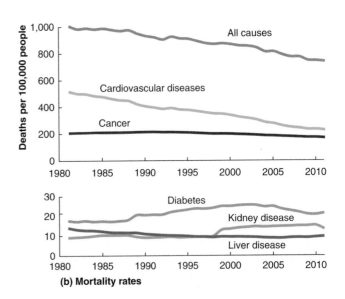

(a) Life expectancy at birth and the death rate per 100,000 people in the United States

(b) Mortality rates

MyEconLab Animation

Figure 7.1 **The Improving Health of the U.S. Population**

Since 1900, life expectancy has increased and mortality rates have decreased in the United States. Since 1981, there have been significant decreases in rates of death due to cancer, cardiovascular diseases, and diseases of the liver. Rates of death due to kidney disease and diabetes increased slightly because of an increase in obesity. Note that, in panel (a), the increase in mortality and decrease in life expectancy in 1918 are due to the severe influenza epidemic of that year.

Sources: For panel (a): Susan B. Carter et al., eds., *Historical Statistics of the United States: Millennium Edition*, Series Ab644; and Centers for Disease Control and Prevention, National Vital Statistics Reports, various issues; for panel (b): "Age-Adjusted Mortality per 100,000 by Underlying and Multiple Cause, Ages 181: US, 1981–2009"; Centers for Disease Control and Prevention, National Center for Health Statistics, "VitalStats: Mortality," www.cdc.gov/nchs/vitalstats.htm.

Gresham College, along with coauthors, have described a process by which better health makes it possible for people to work harder as they become taller, stronger, and more resistant to disease. Working harder raises a country's total income, making it possible for the country to afford better sanitation, more food, and a better system for distributing the food. In effect, improving health shifts out a country's production possibilities frontier. Higher incomes also allow the country to devote more resources to research and development, including medical research. The United States has been a pioneer in the development of medical technology, new surgical techniques, and new pharmaceuticals, which have played important roles in lengthening life spans and reducing the death toll from diseases.

MyEconLab Study Plan

MyEconLab Concept Check

7.2 LEARNING OBJECTIVE

Compare the health care systems and health care outcomes in the United States and other countries.

Health Care around the World

In the United States, private firms provide most health care, through either doctors' practices or hospitals. The main exception is the care the government provides through the network of hospitals operated by the federal government's Veterans Administration, although some cities also own and operate hospitals. Governments in most countries outside of the United States have a more substantial direct role in paying for or providing health care. Policymakers and economists debate the effects of greater government involvement in the health care system on health outcomes such as life expectancy, infant mortality, and successful treatment of diseases.

The U.S. Health Care System

Health insurance A contract under which a buyer agrees to make payments, or *premiums*, in exchange for the provider agreeing to pay some or all of the buyer's medical bills.

One important difference among health care systems in different countries is how people pay for their health care. Most people in the United States have *health insurance* that helps them to pay their medical bills. **Health insurance** is a contract under which a buyer agrees to make payments, or *premiums*, in exchange for the provider

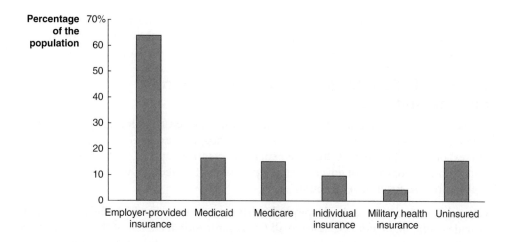

MyEconLab Animation

Figure 7.2

Sources of Health Insurance in the United States, March 2012

In 2012, about 64 percent of people received health insurance through their employer and about 10 percent directly purchased an individual or family health insurance policy from an insurance company. About 36 percent of people received health insurance through a government program including Medicaid, Medicare, and the program run by the Department of Veteran Affairs. About 16 percent of people were uninsured. *Note:* Because some people have more than one type of health insurance, the sum of the values for each category shown is greater than 100 percent.

Sources: Carmen DeNavas-Walt, Bernadette D. Proctor, and Jessica C. Smith, U.S. Census Bureau, Current Population Reports, P60-243, *Income, Poverty, and Health Insurance Coverage in the United States: 2011*, Washington, DC: U.S. Government Printing Office, September 2012, Table 8.

agreeing to pay some or all of the buyer's medical bills. Figure 7.2 shows the sources of health insurance in the United States in 2012. Some people have insurance of more than one type by, for example, participating in a government insurance program such as Medicare as well as having a private insurance policy. About 64 percent of people receive health insurance through their employer, and about 10 percent directly purchase an individual or family health insurance policy from an insurance company. About 36 percent of people receive health insurance through a government program including Medicaid, Medicare, and the program run by the Department of Veterans Affairs.

Most people who have private health insurance receive it through their employer. In 2012, about 98 percent of firms employing more than 200 workers and about 61 percent of firms employing between 3 and 199 workers offered health insurance as a fringe benefit (that is, a type of non-wage compensation) to their employees. Private health insurance companies can be either not-for-profit firms, such as some of the Blue Cross and Blue Shield organizations, or for-profit firms, such as Aetna and John Hancock, which typically also sell other types of insurance. Private health insurance firms sell *group plans* to employers to cover all of their employees or individual plans directly to the public. Some health insurance plans reimburse doctors and hospitals on a **fee-for-service** basis, which means that doctors and hospitals receive a payment for each service they provide. Other health insurance plans are organized as *health maintenance organizations* (HMOs), which typically reimburse doctors mainly by paying a flat fee per patient, rather than paying a fee for each individual office visit or other service provided.

About 16 percent of people were not covered by health insurance in 2012. Many people lack health insurance because their incomes are low, and they believe they cannot afford to buy private health insurance. Some low-income people either do not qualify for Medicaid or choose not to participate in that program. About two-thirds of the uninsured live in families in which at least one member has a job. These individuals either were not offered health insurance through their employers or chose not to purchase it. Some young people opt out of employer-provided health insurance because they are healthy and do not believe that the cost of the premium their employer charges for the insurance is worth the benefit of having the insurance. In 2011, 54 percent of the uninsured were younger than age 34. Although 98 percent of firms with 200 or more employees offer health insurance to their employees, only about 62 percent of employees accept the coverage. The remaining employees are covered by a spouse's policy, are not eligible for coverage, or have decided to go uninsured because they do not want to pay the premium for the insurance. The uninsured must pay for their own medical bills *out of pocket*, with money from their own income, just as they pay their other bills, or

Fee-for-service A system under which doctors and hospitals receive a payment for each service they provide.

receive care from doctors or hospitals either free or below the normal price. As we will see, addressing the problems of the uninsured was one of the motivations for the federal government's health care legislation enacted in 2010. MyEconLab Concept Check

The Health Care Systems of Canada, Japan, and the United Kingdom

In many countries, such as Canada, Japan, and the United Kingdom, the government either supplies health care directly by operating hospitals and employing doctors and nurses, or pays for most health care expenses, even if hospitals are not government owned and doctors are not government employees. In this section, we look briefly at the health care systems in several countries.

Single-payer health care system A system, such as the one in Canada, in which the government provides health insurance to all of the country's residents.

Canada Canada has a **single-payer health care system** in which the government provides *national health insurance* to all Canadian residents. Each of the 10 Canadian provinces has its own system, although each system must meet the federal government's requirement of covering 100 percent of the cost of all medically necessary procedures. Individuals pay nothing for doctor's visits or hospital stays; instead, they pay for medical care indirectly through the taxes they pay to the provincial and federal governments. As in the United States, most doctors and hospitals are private businesses, but unlike in the United States, doctors and hospitals are required to accept the fees that are set by the government. Also as in the United States, doctors and hospitals are typically reimbursed on a fee-for-service basis.

Japan Japan has a system of *universal health insurance* under which every resident of the country is required to enroll either in one of the many nonprofit health insurance societies that are organized by industry or profession or in the health insurance program provided by the national government. The system is funded by a combination of premiums paid by employees and firms and a payroll tax similar to the tax that funds the Medicare program in the United States. Unlike the Canadian system, the Japanese system requires substantial *co-payments* under which patients pay as much as 30 percent of their medical bills, while health insurance pays for the rest. Japanese health insurance does not pay for most preventive care, such as annual physical exams, or for medical expenses connected with pregnancies, unless complications result. Health insurance in the United States and Canada typically does cover these expenses. As in the United States, most doctors in Japan do not work for the government, and there are many privately owned hospitals. The number of government-run hospitals, though, is greater than in the United States.

Socialized medicine A health care system under which the government owns most of the hospitals and employs most of the doctors.

The United Kingdom In the United Kingdom, the government, through the National Health Service (NHS), owns nearly all hospitals and directly employs nearly all doctors. This system contrasts with those in the United States, Canada, and Japan, where the government employs relatively few doctors and owns relatively few hospitals. Because there are few private insurance plans and private hospitals in the United Kingdom, its health care system is often called **socialized medicine**. With 1.7 million employees, the NHS is the largest government-run health care system in the world. Apart from a small co-payment for prescriptions, the NHS supplies health care services without charge to patients, receiving its funding from income taxes. The NHS concentrates on preventive care and care for acute conditions. Nonemergency care, also called elective care—such as hip replacements, knee surgery following a sports injury, or reconstructive surgery following a mastectomy—is a low priority. The NHS's goals result in waiting lists for elective procedures that can be very long, with patients sometimes waiting a year or more for a procedure that would be available in a few weeks or less in the United States. To avoid the waiting lists, more than 10 percent of the population also has private health insurance, frequently provided by employers, which the insured use to pay for elective procedures. The NHS essentially trades off broader coverage for longer waiting times and performing fewer procedures, particularly nonemergency surgeries. MyEconLab Concept Check

Comparing Health Care Outcomes around the World

We have seen that the way health care systems are organized varies significantly across countries. Health care outcomes and the amounts countries spend on health care are also quite different. As Figure 7.3 shows, typically, the higher the level of income per person in a country, the higher the level of spending per person on health care. This result is not surprising because health care is a *normal good*. We know that as income increases, so does spending on normal goods (see Chapter 3). The line in the figure shows the average relationship between income per person and health care spending per person. The dots for most countries are fairly close to the line, but note that the dot representing the United States is significantly above the line. Being well above the line indicates that health care spending per person in the United States is higher than in other countries, even taking into account the relatively high income levels in the United States. Later in this chapter, we will discuss explanations for the high levels of health care spending in the United States.

Have the high levels of spending on health care in the United States resulted in better health outcomes? Are people in the United States healthier, and do they have their medical problems addressed more rapidly than do people in other countries? Table 7.2 compares several health care outcomes for the countries that are members of the Organization for Economic Cooperation and Development (OECD), a group of 34 high-income countries. The table shows that the United States does relatively poorly with respect to infant mortality, while it does about average with respect to life expectancy. People in the United States are more likely to be obese than are people in other countries, which can lead to developing diabetes and other health problems.

The United States rates well in the availability of medical equipment that can be used in diagnosing and treating illness. Table 7.2 shows that the United States has more than twice as many MRI units and over 50 percent more CT scanners than the average of European countries, although the United States has relatively fewer of these machines than does Japan. The United States also appears to do well in cancer treatment. People in the United States have a lower rate of cancer deaths and a lower probability of dying from cancer before age 75 than in most OECD countries, although higher than in Japan. The United States also has a relatively low mortality ratio from cancer. The mortality ratio measures the rate at which people die from cancer relative to the rate at which they are diagnosed with cancer. A low cancer mortality ratio indicates that the U.S. health care system does a relatively good job of reducing the death rate among people diagnosed with cancer.

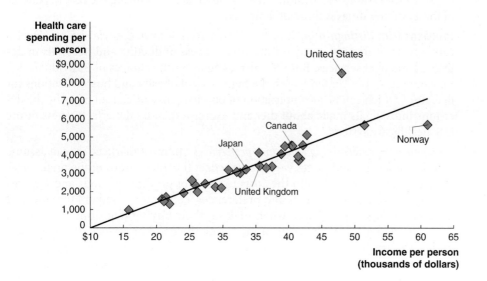

MyEconLab Animation

Figure 7.3

Levels of Income per Person and Spending per Person on Health Care

The United States is well above the line showing the average relationship between income per person and health care spending per person, which indicates that the United States spends more on health care per person than do other countries, even taking into account the relatively high levels of income in the United States.

Note: Income per person is measured as real GDP per person.

Source: Organization for Economic Co-operation and Development, *OECD Health Data 2013*, June 2013.

Table 7.2   **Health Outcomes in High-Income Countries**

Health Care Outcome	United States	Canada	Japan	United Kingdom	OECD Average
Life Expectancy					
Life expectancy at birth	78.7 years	80.8 years	83.0 years	80.6 years	77.6 years
Male life expectancy at age 65	17.7 years	18.3 years	18.9 years	18.3 years	17.2 years
Female life expectancy at age 65	20.3 years	21.5 years	23.9 years	20.9 years	20.5 years
Infant mortality (deaths per 1,000 live births)	6.1	5.1	2.3	4.2	3.6
Health Problems					
Obesity (percentage of the population with BMI > 30)	35.7%	25.6%	2.9%	26.2%	13.1%
Diagnostic Equipment					
MRI units per 1,000,000 population	25.9	8.0	43.1	5.6	10.3
CT scanners per 1,000,000 population	34.3	13.9	97.3	7.4	20.4
Cancer					
Deaths from cancer per 100,000 population	104.1	113.3	94.8	115.8	114.7
Risk of dying of cancer before age 75	11.2%	11.8%	9.7%	11.9%	12.0%
Mortality ratio for cancer	39.5%	40.4%	52.3%	47.6%	48.1%

How useful are cross-country comparisons of health care outcomes in measuring the effectiveness of different health care systems? Health economists and other researchers disagree strongly about the answer to this question. We can consider some of the difficulties in making cross-country comparisons in health care outcomes:

- *Data problems.* Countries do not always collect data on diseases and other health problems in the same way. So, there are not enough consistent data available to compare health care outcomes for more than a few diseases.

- *Problems with measuring health care delivery.* The easiest outcomes to measure are deaths because a specific event has occurred. So, measures of life expectancy, infant mortality, and mortality rates from some diseases, such as cancer, are available across countries. But much of health care involves treatment for injuries, simple surgical procedures, writing pharmaceutical prescriptions, and other activities where outcomes are difficult to measure. For example, although the United Kingdom does well in many of the measures shown in Table 7.2, patients have long waiting times for elective surgical procedures that can be arranged much more quickly in some other countries, including the United States. Measuring the cost to patients of these waiting times is difficult, however.

- *Problems with distinguishing health care effectiveness from lifestyle choices.* Health care outcomes depend partly on the effectiveness of doctors and hospitals in delivering medical services. But they also depend on the choices of individuals. So, for example, in the United States, the high rates of obesity and hospitalizations for diabetes—which can be a complication of obesity—may be caused more by the decisions individuals make about diet and exercise than by the effectiveness of the U.S. health care system.

- *Problems with determining consumer preferences.* In most markets, we can assume that the quantities and prices we observe reflect the interactions of the preferences of consumers (demand) with the costs to firms of producing goods and services (supply). Given their incomes and preferences, consumers compare the prices of different goods and services when making their buying decisions. The prices firms charge represent the costs of providing the good or service. In the market for health care, however, the government plays the dominant role in supplying the service in most countries other than the United States, so the cost of the service is not fully represented in its price, which in some countries is zero. Even in countries where consumers must pay for medical services, the prices they pay usually do not represent the cost of providing the service. In the United States, for instance, consumers with private health insurance typically pay only 10 to 20 percent of the price as a co-payment. For these reasons, it is difficult to determine whether some countries do a better job than others in providing health care services whose cost and effectiveness are consistent with consumer preferences.   MyEconLab Concept Check   MyEconLab Study Plan

Information Problems and Externalities in the Market for Health Care

7.3 LEARNING OBJECTIVE

Discuss how information problems and externalities affect the market for health care.

The market for health care is significantly affected by the problem of **asymmetric information**, which occurs when one party to an economic transaction has less information than the other party. Understanding the concept of asymmetric information can help us analyze the actions of buyers and sellers of health care and health care insurance and the actions of the government in the health care market. The consequences of asymmetric information may be easier to understand if we first consider its effect on the market for used automobiles, which was the market in which economists first began to carefully study the problem of asymmetric information.

Asymmetric information A situation in which one party to an economic transaction has less information than the other party.

Adverse Selection and the Market for "Lemons"

Nobel Laureate George Akerlof of the University of California, Berkeley, pointed out that the seller of a used car will always have more information on the true condition of the car than will potential buyers. A car that has been poorly maintained—by, for instance, not having its oil changed regularly—may have damage that even a trained mechanic would have difficulty detecting.

If potential buyers of used cars know that they will have difficulty separating the good used cars from the bad used cars, or "lemons," they will take this into account in the prices they are willing to pay. Consider the following simple example: Suppose that half of the 2011 Volkswagen Jettas offered for sale have been well maintained and are good, reliable used cars. The other half have been poorly maintained and are lemons that will be unreliable. Suppose that potential buyers of 2011 Jettas would be willing to pay $10,000 for a reliable one but only $5,000 for an unreliable one. The sellers know how well they have maintained their cars and whether they are reliable, but the buyers do not have this information and so have no way of distinguishing the reliable used cars from the unreliable ones.

In this situation, buyers will generally offer a price somewhere between the price they would be willing to pay for a good car and the price they would be willing to pay for a lemon. With a 50–50 chance of buying a good car or a lemon, buyers might offer $7,500, which is halfway between the price they would pay if they knew for certain the car was a good one and the price they would pay if they knew it was a lemon.

Unfortunately for used car buyers, a major glitch arises at this point. From the buyers' perspective, given that they don't know whether any particular car offered for sale is a good car or a lemon, an offer of $7,500 seems reasonable. But the sellers do know whether the cars they are offering are good cars or lemons. To a seller of a good car, an offer of $7,500 is $2,500 below the true value of the car, and the seller will be reluctant to sell. But to a seller of a lemon, an offer of $7,500 is $2,500 above the true value of the car, and the seller will be quite happy to sell. As sellers of lemons take advantage of knowing more about the cars they are selling than buyers do, the used car market will fall victim to **adverse selection**: Most used cars offered for sale will be lemons. In other words, because of asymmetric information, the market has selected adversely the cars that will be offered for sale. Notice as well that the problem of adverse selection reduces the total quantity of used cars bought and sold in the market because few good cars are offered for sale.   MyEconLab Concept Check

Adverse selection The situation in which one party to a transaction takes advantage of knowing more than the other party to the transaction.

Asymmetric Information in the Market for Health Insurance

Asymmetric information problems are particularly severe in the markets for all types of insurance, including health insurance. To understand this point, first consider how insurance works. Insurance companies provide the service of *risk pooling* when they sell policies to households. For example, if you own a $150,000 house but do not have a fire insurance policy, a fire that destroys your house can be a financial catastrophe. But an insurance company can pool the risk of your house burning down by selling fire insurance policies to you and thousands of other homeowners. Homeowners are willing to accept the certain cost represented by the premium they pay for insurance in return for eliminating the uncertain—but potentially very large—cost should their house burn down. Notice that for the insurance company to cover all of its costs, the total amount it receives in premiums must be greater than the amount it pays out in claims to policyholders. To survive, insurance companies have to predict accurately the amount they are likely to pay out to policyholders. For instance, if an insurance company predicts that the houses of only 2 percent of policyholders will burn down during a year when 5 percent of houses actually burn down, the company will suffer losses. On the other hand, if the company predicts that 8 percent of houses will burn down when only 5 percent actually do, the company will have charged premiums that are too high. A company that charges premiums that are too high will lose customers to other companies and may eventually be driven out of business.

Adverse Selection in the Market for Health Insurance One obstacle to health insurance companies accurately predicting the number of claims policyholders will make is that buyers of health insurance policies always know more about the state of their health—and, therefore, how likely they are to submit medical bills for payment—than will the insurance companies. In other words, insurance companies face an adverse selection problem because sick people are more likely to want health insurance than are healthy people. If insurance companies have trouble determining who is healthy and who is sick, they are likely to sell policies to more sick people than they had expected, with the result that their premiums will be too low to cover their costs. An insurance company faces a financial problem if the premiums it is charging are too low to cover the costs of the claims being submitted. The company might try to increase the premiums it charges, but this may make the adverse selection problem worse. If premiums rise, then younger, healthier people who rarely visit the doctor may respond to the increase in premiums by dropping their insurance. The insurance company will then find its adverse selection problem has been made worse because its policyholders will be less healthy on average than they were before the premium increase. The situation is similar to that facing a used car buyer who knows that adverse selection is a problem in the used car market and decides to compensate for it by lowering the price he is willing to pay for a car. The lower price will reduce the number of sellers of good cars willing to sell to him, making his adverse selection problem worse.

One way to deal with the problem of adverse selection is for the government to require every person to buy insurance. Most states require all drivers to buy automobile insurance, so that both high-risk and low-risk drivers will carry insurance. The Patient Protection and Affordable Care Act (ACA) passed in 2010 requires that beginning in 2014 residents of the United States must carry insurance or pay a fine. This provision of the law is known as the *individual mandate* and has been controversial. We discuss it further later in the chapter.

Moral Hazard in the Market for Health Insurance The insurance market is subject to a second consequence of asymmetric information. **Moral hazard** refers to actions people take after they have entered into a transaction that make the other party to the transaction worse off. Moral hazard in the insurance market occurs when people change their behavior after becoming insured. For example, once a firm has taken out a fire insurance policy on a warehouse, its managers might be reluctant to install an expensive sprinkler system. Similarly, someone with health insurance may visit the doctor for treatment of a cold or other minor illness, when he would not do so without the insurance. Or someone with health insurance might engage in risky activities, such as riding a motorcycle, that she would avoid if she lacked insurance.

One way to think about the basic moral hazard problem with insurance is to note that normally there are two parties to an economic transaction: the buyer and the seller.

Moral hazard The actions people take after they have entered into a transaction that make the other party to the transaction worse off.

Don't Let This Happen to You

Don't Confuse Adverse Selection with Moral Hazard

The two key consequences of asymmetric information are adverse selection and moral hazard. It is easy to mix up these concepts. One way to keep the concepts straight is to remember that adverse selection refers to what happens at the time of entering into a transaction. An example would be an insurance company that sells a life insurance policy to a terminally ill person because the company lacks full information on the person's health. Moral hazard refers to what happens after entering into a transaction. For example, a nonsmoker buys a life insurance policy and then starts smoking four packs of cigarettes a day. (It may help to remember that *a* comes before *m* alphabetically just as *a*dverse selection comes before *m*oral hazard.)

MyEconLab Study Plan

Your Turn: Test your understanding by doing related problems 3.9 and 3.10 on pages 231–232 at the end of this chapter.

The insurance company becomes a third party to the purchase of medical services because the insurance company, rather than the patient, pays for some or all of the service. For this reason, economists refer to traditional health insurance as a *third-party payer* system. Because of this system, consumers of health care do not pay a price that reflects the full cost of providing the service. This lower price leads consumers to use more health care than they otherwise would.

Third-party payer health insurance can also lead to another consequence of moral hazard known as the *principal–agent problem* because doctors may be led to take actions that are not necessarily in the best interests of their patients, such as increasing their incomes by prescribing unnecessary tests or other treatments for which the doctors receive payment. The **principal–agent problem** results from agents—in this case, doctors—pursuing their own interests rather than the interests of the principals—in this case, patients—who hired them. If patients had to pay the full price of lab tests, MRI scans, and other procedures, they would be more likely to question whether the procedures were really necessary. Because health insurance pays most of the bill for these procedures, patients are more likely to accept them. Note that the fee-for-service aspect of most health insurance in the United States can make the principal–agent problem worse because doctors and hospitals are paid for each service performed, whether or not the service was effective.

Principal–agent problem A problem caused by agents pursuing their own interests rather than the interests of the principals who hired them.

The number of medical procedures performed in the United States has been continually increasing. Many doctors argue that the increasing number of medical procedures is not the result of third-party payer health insurance. Instead, the increase reflects the improved effectiveness of the procedures in diagnosing illness and the tendency of some doctors to practice "defensive medicine" because they fear that if they fail to correctly diagnose an illness, a patient may file a malpractice lawsuit against them.

How Insurance Companies Deal with Adverse Selection and Moral Hazard Insurance companies can take steps to reduce adverse selection and moral hazard problems. For example, insurance companies can use deductibles and coinsurance to reduce moral hazard. A deductible requires the policyholder to pay a certain dollar amount of a claim. With coinsurance, the insurance company pays only a percentage of any claim. Suppose you have a health insurance policy with a $200 deductible and 20 percent coinsurance, and you receive a medical bill for $1,000. You must pay the first $200 of the bill and 20 percent of the remaining $800. Deductibles and coinsurance make the policies less attractive to people who intend to file many claims, thereby reducing the adverse selection problem. Deductibles and coinsurance also provide policyholders with an incentive to avoid filing claims, thereby reducing the moral hazard problem. Notice, though, that deductibles and coinsurance reduce, but do not eliminate, adverse selection and moral hazard. People who anticipate having large medical bills will still have a greater incentive than healthy people to buy insurance, and people with health insurance are still more likely to visit the doctor even for a minor illness than are people without health insurance.

To reduce the problem of adverse selection, someone applying for an individual health insurance policy is usually required to submit his or her medical records to the insurance company. Insurance companies often also carry out their own medical examinations. Prior to the passage of the ACA in 2010, companies typically limited coverage of *pre-existing conditions*, which are medical problems, such as heart disease or cancer, that the buyer already has before purchasing the insurance. Health insurance companies typically would not cover pre-existing conditions for a year or two after a consumer purchased insurance, although sometimes they would permanently decline to cover these conditions. Limits on coverage of pre-existing conditions have been very common in health insurance policies for individuals, but were also sometimes included in *group policies*, such as the policies companies sell to businesses providing coverage to their employees. Exclusions and limits on coverage of pre-existing conditions have been controversial. Critics argue that by excluding coverage of pre-existing conditions, insurance companies were forcing people with serious illnesses to pay the entire amount of what might be very large medical bills or to go without medical care. Some people with chronic or terminal illnesses found it impossible to buy an individual health insurance policy. The insurance companies argued that if they did not exclude coverage of pre-existing conditions, they might have been unable to offer any health insurance policies or might have been forced to charge premiums that were so high as to cause relatively healthy people to not renew their policies, which would have made adverse selection problems worse. To some extent, the debate over coverage of pre-existing conditions is a normative one. Ordinarily, in a market system, people who cannot afford a good or service must do without it. Many people are reluctant to see people not have access to health insurance because they cannot afford it. As we will discuss in the next section, Congress included significant restrictions on the ability of insurance companies to limit coverage of pre-existing conditions when it passed the ACA. MyEconLab Concept Check

---

Solved Problem 7.3

MyEconLab Interactive Animation

If You Are Young and Healthy, Should You Buy Health Insurance?

New York Times columnist David Brooks wrote about the implementation of the Patient Protection and Affordable Care Act (ACA) and described a possible adverse selection *cascade*: "the young may decide en masse that it is completely irrational for them to get health insurance that subsidizes others."

a. Why might it be irrational for young and healthy people to buy health insurance?

b. In what sense do young and healthy people who buy health insurance provide a subsidy to people who are older or who are ill?

c. What do you think Brooks meant by an adverse selection *cascade*? How might the actions of young and healthy people contribute to adverse selection problems in the health insurance system?

Solving the Problem

Step 1: **Review the chapter material.** This problem is about adverse selection, so you may want to review the section "Adverse Selection in the Market for Health Insurance," which is on page 214, and "How Insurance Companies Deal with Adverse Selection and Moral Hazard," which begins on page 215.

Step 2: **Answer part (a) by explaining why a young and healthy person might decide not to buy health insurance.** When you buy health insurance, you (or your employer on your behalf) make premium payments to an insurance company. If you are healthy and rarely visit the doctor or buy prescription medicines, you are likely to pay more in premiums—possibly much more—than you receive back in benefits. Therefore, a young and healthy person might rationally decide that he or she would be better off not buying health insurance. People who don't buy health insurance, though, are taking on the risk of having to pay big medical bills if they are in an accident or encounter an unexpected medical problem. Under the ACA, people who don't buy health insurance are also subject to a fine, although the value of the fine—which starts at $95 per year in 2014 and rises to $695 per year in 2016—is typically less than the amount paid for insurance.

Step 3: **Answer part (b) by explaining why young people who buy health insurance may be providing a subsidy for people who are older or who are ill.** The basis of insurance is risk pooling, with insurance companies pooling the risks of a catastrophic event, such as injuries from a car accident or expensive treatment for disease, across many people. The people who benefit most from insurance are those who have the greatest likelihood of making an insurance claim for payment of large medical bills. These people are likely to receive more in benefits than they paid in insurance premiums. Young and healthy people are in the opposite situation of being likely to pay more in premiums than they receive in benefits. The only way an insurance plan can make payments to people who are ill and make many claims is to have healthy people enrolled in the insurance plan who do not make many claims. In that sense, young and healthy people provide a subsidy to other people in the plan.

Step 4: **Answer part (c) by explaining how the actions of young people might lead to an adverse selection _cascade_ in the health insurance system.** Brooks is referring to a process also sometimes called an adverse selection _death spiral_. If young and healthy people who pay premiums but make few claims drop out of an insurance system, then companies have to raise premiums on the people remaining in the plan. But higher premiums make the insurance an even worse deal for healthy people, causing even more of them to drop out of the plan. Over time, the proportion of ill people to healthy people in the insurance plan continues to increase, undermining the risk pooling services the plan can provide.

Extra Credit: The authors of the ACA law were well aware of the potential for adverse selection problems in the health insurance system, particularly because the law sharply limits the ability of insurance companies to deny coverage to people with pre-existing conditions. The law attempted to reduce adverse selection problems by requiring that everyone have health insurance. Those who refuse are subject to a fine. There is some question, however, whether the fines will provide enough incentive for young and healthy people to buy health insurance.

Source: David Brooks, "Health Chaos Ahead," _New York Times_, April 25, 2013.

Your Turn: For more practice, do related problems 3.12, 3.13, and 3.14 on page 232 at the end of this chapter.

MyEconLab Study Plan

Externalities in the Market for Health Care

For most goods and services, we assume that the consumer receives all the benefits from consuming the good and that the firm producing the good bears all of the costs of production. Some goods or services, though, involve an _externality_, which is a benefit or cost that affects someone who is not directly involved in the production or consumption of a good or service. For example, if a utility burns coal to produce electricity, the result will be air pollution, which causes a _negative externality_ because people with asthma or other breathing problems may bear a cost even though they were not involved in buying or selling the electricity that caused the pollution. College education may result in a _positive externality_ because college-educated people are less likely to commit crimes and, by being better-informed voters, more likely to contribute to better government policies. So, although you receive most of the benefits of your college education, other people also receive some of the benefits.

Externalities interfere with the economic efficiency of a market equilibrium. A competitive market achieves economic efficiency by maximizing the sum of consumer surplus and producer surplus (see Chapter 4). But when there is a negative externality in production, as with air pollution, the market will produce more than the efficient quantity. When there is a positive externality in consumption, as with college educations, the market will produce less than the efficient quantity. (A more complete discussion of externalities appears in Chapter 5, "Externalities, Environmental Policy, and Public Goods.")

Are there externalities involved with medicine and health care? Many economists believe several aspects of health care involve externalities. For example, anyone vaccinated against a communicable disease not only protects himself or herself but also reduces the chances that people who have not been vaccinated will contract the disease. The positive externality from vaccinations causes a difference between the *private benefit* from being vaccinated and the *social benefit*. The *private benefit* is the benefit received by the consumer of a good or service. The *social benefit* is the total benefit from consuming a good or service, and it is equal to the private benefit plus any external benefit, such as the benefit to others from a reduced chance of getting a disease for which you have been vaccinated. Because of the positive externality, the social benefit of vaccinations is greater than the private benefit.

Figure 7.4 shows the market for vaccinations. If people receiving vaccinations could capture all the benefits, the demand curve would be D_2, which represents the marginal social benefit. The actual demand curve is D_1, however, which represents only the marginal private benefit received by people receiving vaccinations. The efficient equilibrium would occur at price $P_{\text{Efficient}}$ and quantity $Q_{\text{Efficient}}$. At this equilibrium, economic surplus is maximized (see Chapter 4). The market equilibrium, at price P_{Market} and quantity Q_{Market}, will not be efficient because the demand curve is above the supply curve for production of the vaccinations between Q_{Market} and $Q_{\text{Efficient}}$. That is, the marginal benefit—including the external benefit—for producing these vaccinations is greater than the marginal cost. As a result, there is a deadweight loss equal to the area of the yellow triangle. Because of the positive externality, economic efficiency would be improved if more people were vaccinated.

Figure 7.4 assumes that the market for vaccinations is like the market for goods such as hamburgers, with consumers paying the full price of the vaccinations. In practice, people with health insurance pay a reduced price for vaccinations and the government

MyEconLab Animation

Figure 7.4

The Effect of a Positive Externality on the Market for Vaccinations

People who do not get vaccinated still benefit from other people being vaccinated. As a result, the marginal social benefit from vaccinations is greater than the marginal private benefit to people being vaccinated. Because only the marginal private benefit is represented in the market demand curve D_1, the quantity of vaccinations produced, Q_{Market}, is too low. If the market demand curve were D_2 instead of D_1, the level of vaccinations would be $Q_{\text{Efficient}}$, which is the efficient level. At the market equilibrium of Q_{Market}, there is a deadweight loss equal to the area of the yellow triangle.

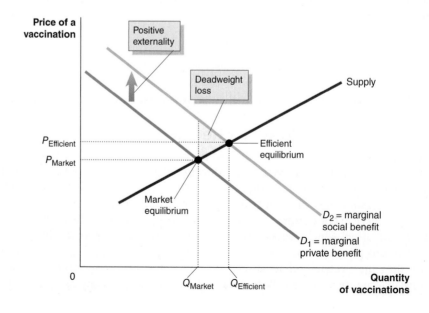

often provides further subsidies to the firms that produce vaccines. One reason for the government subsidies is to overcome the effects of the positive externality.

Externalities are important in health care markets, though economists and policy-makers continue to debate the extent to which they require significant government involvement in health care.   MyEconLab Concept Check

Making the Connection
MyEconLab Video

Should the Government Run the Health Care System?

During the debate over President Barack Obama's health care plan, some members of Congress pro-posed expanding the federal government's role in health care by adopting a system similar to the single-payer sys-tem used in Canada under which the government would provide health care to all residents of the United States. What role the federal government should play in health care remains a controversial public policy issue.

Economists categorize goods on the basis of whether they are *rival* and *excludable*. Rivalry occurs when one person consuming a unit of a good means no one else can consume it. If you consume a taco, for ex-ample, no one else can consume it. Excludability means that anyone who does not pay for a good cannot con-sume it. If you don't pay for a taco, for example, Taco Bell can exclude you from consuming it. A *public good* is both nonrival and nonex-cludable. Public goods are often, although not always, supplied by a government rather than by private firms. The classic example of a public good is national defense. Your consuming national defense does not interfere with your neighbor consuming it, so consumption is nonrivalrous. You also cannot be excluded from consuming it, whether you pay for it or not. No private firm would be willing to supply national defense be-cause everyone can consume national defense without paying for it.

Congress passed, and President Obama signed, the Patient Protection and Affordable Care Act in 2010.

Is health care a public good that government should supply—or, at least, pay for? Is it a private good, like furniture, clothing, or computers, that private firms should supply and consumers should pay for without government aid? Should private firms supply most health care, subject to some government regulation? Economists differ in their answers to these questions because the delivery of health care involves a num-ber of complex issues, but we can consider briefly some of the most important points. Because public goods must be both nonrivalrous and nonexcludable, health care does not qualify as a public good under the usual definition. More than one person cannot simultaneously consume the same surgical operation, for example. And someone who will not pay for an operation can be excluded from consuming it. (Most states require hospitals to treat patients who are too poor to pay for treatment, and many doctors will treat poor people at a reduced price. But because there is nothing in the nature of health care that keeps people who do not pay for it from being excluded from consuming it, health care does not fit the definition of a public good.)

There are aspects of the delivery of health care that have convinced some econ-omists that government intervention is justified, however. For example, consuming certain types of health care generates positive externalities. Being vaccinated against a communicable disease, such as influenza or meningitis, reduces not only the chance that the person vaccinated will catch the disease but also the probability that an epi-demic of the disease will occur. Therefore, the market may supply an inefficiently small quantity of vaccinations unless vaccinations receive a government subsidy.

Information problems can also be important in the market for private health insur-ance. Consumers as buyers of health insurance often know much more about the state of their health than do the companies selling health insurance. This information problem may raise costs to insurance companies when the pool of people being insured is small, making insurance companies less willing to offer health insurance to consumers the companies suspect may file too many claims. Economists debate how important information problems are in health care markets and whether government intervention is required to reduce them.

Many economists believe that market-based solutions are the best approach to improving the health care system. As we saw in Table 7.2 on page 212, the United States has a mixed record with respect to health care outcomes. The United States is, however, a world leader in innovation in medical technology and prescription drugs. The market-oriented approach to reforming health care starts with the goal of improving health care outcomes while preserving incentives for U.S. firms to continue with innovations in medical screening equipment, surgical procedures, and prescription drugs. Presently, markets are delivering inaccurate signals to consumers because when buying health care, unlike when buying most other goods and services, consumers pay a price well below the true cost of providing the service. Under current tax laws, people do not pay taxes on health insurance benefits they receive from their employers, and this benefit encourages them to want very generous coverage that reduces incentives to control costs. As we will discuss later in the chapter, market-based approaches to health care reform attempt to address these issues.

It remains an open question whether the U.S. health care system will continue to move toward greater government intervention, which is the approach adopted in most other countries, or whether market-based reforms will be implemented. Because health care is so important to consumers and because health care spending looms so large in the U.S. economy, the role of the government in the health care system is likely to be the subject of intense debate for some time to come.

MyEconLab Study Plan

Your Turn: Test your understanding by doing related problem 3.15 on page 232 at the end of this chapter.

7.4 LEARNING OBJECTIVE

Explain the major issues involved in the debate over health care policy in the United States.

The Debate over Health Care Policy in the United States

Shortly after taking office in January 2009, President Barack Obama proposed far-reaching changes in the U.S. health care system. The result was the Patient Protection and Affordable Care Act (ACA), which Congress passed in March 2010. The act was controversial, with every Republican member of Congress and 34 Democratic members voting against it. Economists vigorously debated its likely effects on health care and the economy. In the next section, we explore the issue of rising health care costs, which played an important role in the health care debate, before discussing the details of the ACA and the debate over the legislation's effect.

The Rising Cost of Health Care

Figure 7.5 illustrates a key fact underlying the debate over health care policy in the United States: Health care's share of gross domestic product (GDP), which is the total value of output in the economy, is increasing. Panel (a) shows that spending on health care was less than 6 percent of GDP in 1965, but had risen to about 17.3 percent in 2013, and is projected to rise to about 19.6 percent in 2019. In other words, an increasing percentage of total production in the United States is being devoted to health care. Panel (b) shows increases in health care spending per person in the United States and 10 other high-income countries. Spending on health care has grown faster in the United States than in other countries.

Does it matter that spending on health care is an increasing share of total spending and output in the U.S. economy? The shares of different products in total spending change frequently. For instance, in the United States, the shares of spending on cellphones or LCD televisions were much greater in 2014 than in 2000. Spending on food as a share of total spending has been declining for decades. Economists interpret these changes as reflecting in part consumers' preferences—consumers choose to spend relatively more of their incomes on cellphones and relatively less on food. As we have seen, though, most people pay for health care by relying on third-party payers, such as employer-provided health insurance or government-provided Medicare or Medicaid.

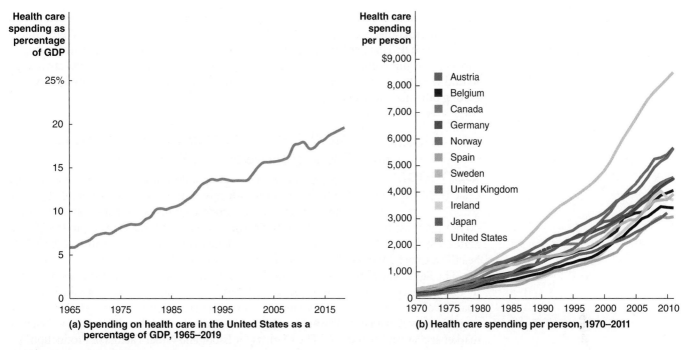

(a) Spending on health care in the United States as a percentage of GDP, 1965–2019

(b) Health care spending per person, 1970–2011

MyEconLab Real-time data

Figure 7.5 Spending on Health Care around the World

Panel (a) shows that health care spending has been a rising percentage of GDP in the United States. Health care spending rose from less than 6 percent of GDP in 1965 to about 17.3 percent in 2013, and it is projected to rise to about 19.6 percent in 2019.

Panel (b) shows that health care spending per person has been growing faster in the United States than in other high-income countries.
Sources: For panel (a): U.S. Department of Health and Human Services, Centers for Medicare & Medicaid Services; for panel (b): Organization for Economic Cooperation and Development, *OECD Health Data 2013*, June 2013.

Out-of-pocket spending, spending on health care that consumers pay out of their own incomes rather than through health insurance, has been declining.

Figure 7.6 shows that out-of-pocket spending on health care as a percentage of all spending on health care has steadily declined since 1960. In 1960, 48 percent of all health care spending was out of pocket, while in 2011, only 11 percent was. As a result, in recent years, consumers of health care have been directly paying for only a small fraction of the true cost of providing health care, with third-party payers picking up the remainder. As average incomes rise, consumers might be expected to spend a rising share of the increase on health care. But because consumers do not pay the full cost of increases in health care spending, they may not be willing to buy as much health care as they currently receive if they had to pay the full price.

Because the federal and state governments in the United States pay for just over half of health care spending through Medicare, Medicaid, and other programs, increases in

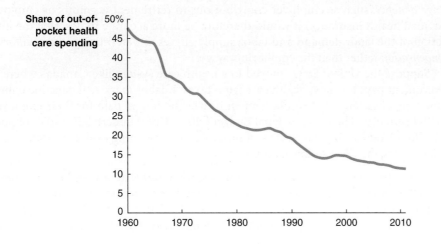

MyEconLab Animation

Figure 7.6

The Declining Share of Out-of-Pocket Health Care Spending

Out-of-pocket spending on health care has declined sharply as a fraction of all health care spending, while the fraction of spending accounted for by third-party payers, such as firms or the government, has increased.
Source: U.S. Department of Health and Human Services, Centers for Medicare & Medicaid Services.

health care spending can cause problems for government budgets. The Medicare and Medicaid programs began in 1965. By 2013, spending on these programs had grown to 6 percent of GDP. That percentage is expected to double over the next 40 years unless health care costs begin to grow at a slower rate. In 2013, the federal government was struggling to find ways to pay for the projected increases in Medicare and Medicaid without severely cutting other federal spending or sharply raising taxes.   MyEconLab Concept Check

| Making the Connection | Are U.S. Firms Handicapped by Paying for Their Employees' Health Insurance? |

MyEconLab Video

Some members of Congress and some business leaders argue that the high cost of health care in the United States handicaps U.S. firms in competition with foreign firms. In many countries, firms do not purchase health insurance for their workers, as most large firms do in the United States. Do foreign firms in fact have an advantage over U.S. firms because of high U.S. health care costs? We can analyze this assertion using the demand and supply for labor.

The figure illustrates the market for labor in a particular industry (for example, automobiles). The demand curve is downward sloping because the lower the wage, the larger the quantity of workers firms will demand. The supply curve is upward sloping because as the wage rises, more workers will want to work in this industry. (A fuller discussion of the labor market appears in Chapter 17, "The Markets for Labor and Other Factors of Production.")

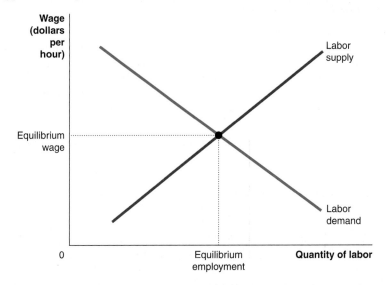

Equilibrium in this labor market occurs where the quantity of labor demanded equals the quantity of labor supplied. On the vertical axis, we measure the wage, so the graph shows the determination of the equilibrium wage. When choosing among jobs, however, workers don't just consider the wage firms offer, they also take into account *fringe benefits*, such as employer contributions to retirement accounts or employer-provided health insurance. It would therefore be more accurate to describe the intersection of the labor demand and labor supply curves as determining *the equilibrium compensation* rather than the equilibrium wage.

Suppose the United States moved to a health care system like Canada's where the government pays for most health care from taxes. If labor markets determine equilibrium compensation, what would happen if firms no longer paid for their employees' health insurance? The Congressional Budget Office (CBO) undertakes studies of policy issues for Congress. In an overview of proposals for reforming health insurance in the United States, the CBO addressed this question:

> Some observers have asserted that domestic producers that provide health insurance to their workers face higher costs for compensation than competitors based in countries where insurance is not employment based and that fundamental changes to the health insurance system could reduce or eliminate that disadvantage. However, such

a cost reduction is unlikely to occur. . . . The equilibrium level of overall compensation in the economy is determined by the supply of and the demand for labor. Fringe benefits (such as health insurance) are just part of that compensation. Consequently, the costs of fringe benefits are borne by workers largely in the form of lower cash wages than they would receive if no such benefits were provided by their employer. Replacing employment-based health care with a government-run system could reduce employers' payments for their workers' insurance, but the amount that they would have to pay in overall compensation would remain essentially unchanged.

To give an example, suppose a firm was paying its workers $50,000 in wages and paying $10,000 per worker for health insurance, thereby providing total compensation of $60,000. If the government began paying all health care expenses, it might appear that the firm's labor costs would drop by $10,000 per worker. But if the firm offered its employees only $50,000 in wages as their total compensation, many would leave to work for other firms. The firm would have to pay its employees an additional $10,000 in wages so that the total compensation it offered would be at the equilibrium level of $60,000 for the industry. In other words, basic demand and supply analysis indicates that having firms rather than the government provide health insurance to workers changes the *composition* of the compensation the firms pay, but does not change its level.

Source: Congress of the United States, Congressional Budget Office, *Key Issues in Analyzing Major Health Insurance Proposals*, December 2008, p. 167.

Your Turn: Test your understanding by doing related problem 4.10 on page 233 at the end of this chapter.

MyEconLab Study Plan

Explaining Rapid Increases in Health Care Spending

In this section, we briefly discuss some reasons economists believe that health care spending has been increasing rapidly in the United States. We start by reviewing explanations that are sometimes offered by policymakers and journalists, but that are unlikely to account for most of the increases in health care costs.

Factors That Do *Not* Explain Sustained Increases in Health Care Spending
The two panels of Figure 7.5 show that spending on health care has been growing faster than the economy as a whole for at least the past several decades. Explaining the rapid growth of health care spending requires identifying factors that have more than a one-time effect. For example, because the U.S. health care system relies on many independent hospitals, medical practices, and insurance companies, some observers argue that it generates more paperwork, duplication, and waste than systems in other countries. Even if this observation is correct, it cannot account for health care's rising share of GDP unless paperwork and waste are *increasing* year after year, which seems unlikely.

Unlike in most countries, it is relatively easy in the United States for patients who have been injured by medical errors to sue doctors and hospitals for damages. The Congressional Budget Office (CBO) estimates, though, that the payments to settle malpractice lawsuits plus the premiums doctors pay for malpractice insurance amount to less than 1 percent of health care costs. Other economists believe the CBO estimate is too low and that the costs of malpractice lawsuits, including the costs of unnecessary tests and procedures doctors order to avoid being sued, are as much as 7 percent of total health care costs. Still, these costs have not been significantly increasing over time.

Somewhere between 1 and 4 percent of health care costs are due to uninsured patients receiving treatments at hospital emergency rooms that could have been provided less expensively in doctors' offices. But once again, this cost has not been increasing rapidly enough to account for much of the increase in health care as a percentage of GDP.

"Cost Disease" in the Health Care Sector Some economists argue that health care suffers from a problem often encountered in service industries. In some sectors of the economy, particularly manufacturing and the production of goods, *productivity*, or the amount of output each worker can produce in a given period, increases steadily. These increases in productivity occur because over time firms provide workers with more machinery and equipment, including computers, with which to work, and because technological progress results in improvements in machinery and equipment and in other parts of the production process. As workers produce more goods, firms are able to pay them higher wages. In service-producing industries, increasing output per worker is more difficult. In medicine, MRI units, CT scanners, and other medical technology have improved diagnosis and treatment, but most medicine still requires a face-to-face meeting between a doctor and a patient. As wages rise in industries in which productivity is increasing rapidly, service industries in which productivity is increasing less rapidly must match these wage increases or lose workers. Because increases in wages are not offset by increases in productivity in service industries, the cost to firms of supplying services increases.

William Baumol of New York University has labeled the tendency for low productivity in service industries to lead to higher costs in those industries as "the cost disease of the service sector." There is good reason to think that health care suffers from this cost disease because growth in labor productivity in health care has been less than half as fast as labor productivity growth in the economy as a whole. This slow growth in productivity can help explain why the cost of health care has been rising so rapidly, thereby increasing health care's share of total spending and output.

The Aging of the Population and Advances in Medical Technology As people age, they increase their spending on health care. Firms continue to develop new prescription drugs and medical equipment that typically have higher costs than the drugs and equipment they replace. The aging of the U.S. population and the introduction of higher cost drugs and medical equipment interact to drive up spending on the federal government's Medicare program and on health care generally. Many newly introduced drugs and diagnostic tools are used disproportionately by people over age 65. Partly as a result, health care spending on people over age 65 is six times greater than spending on people aged 18 to 24 and four times greater than on people aged 25 to 44. In 2013, more than 50 million people were enrolled in Medicare, and that number is expected to grow to 80 million by 2030. As we have seen, even in the absence of the development of new drugs and other medical technology, low rates of productivity in the health care sector could be expected to drive up costs. In fact, as Figure 7.7 illustrates, the CBO estimates that most of the increase in federal spending on Medicare and Medicaid benefits will be due to increases in the cost of providing health care, rather than to the aging of the population. In the figure, "effect of excess cost growth" refers to the extent to which health care costs per person grow faster than GDP per person. So, the combination of an aging population and increases in the cost of providing health care are an important reason why health care spending is an increasing percentage of GDP.

Distorted Economic Incentives As we noted earlier, some part of the increase in health care spending over the years represents consumers choosing to allocate more of their incomes to health care as their incomes rise. But as we have also seen, consumers usually pay less than the true cost of medical treatment because a third party—typically, an insurance

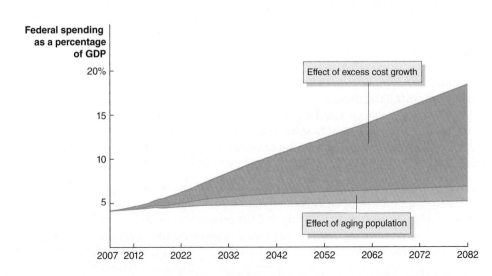

MyEconLab Animation

Figure 7.7

Reasons for Rising Federal Spending on Medicare and Medicaid

Although the aging of the U.S. population will increase federal government spending on the Medicare and Medicaid programs, increases in the cost of providing health care will have a larger effect on government spending on these programs.
Source: U.S. Congressional Budget Office.

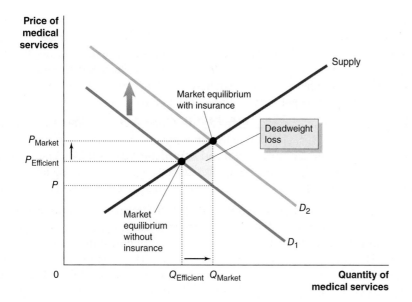

MyEconLab Animation

Figure 7.8

The Effect of the Third-Party Payer System on the Demand for Medical Services

If consumers paid the full price of medical services, their demand would be D_1 and the equilibrium quantity would be at the efficient level $Q_{Efficient}$. Because consumers pay only a fraction of the true cost of medical services, their demand is D_2, and the equilibrium quantity of medical services produced increases to Q_{Market}, which is beyond the efficient level. There is a deadweight loss equal to the yellow triangle. Doctors and other suppliers of medical services receive a price, P_{Market}, that is well above the price, P, paid by consumers.

company or the government—often pays most of the bill. For example, consumers who have health insurance provided by their employers usually pay only a small amount—perhaps $20—for a visit to a doctor's office, when the true cost of the visit might be $80 or $90. The result is that consumers demand a larger quantity of health care services than they would if they paid a price that better represented the cost of providing the services.

Figure 7.8 illustrates this situation. If consumers paid the full price of medical services, their demand would be D_1. The marginal benefit to consumers from medical services would equal the marginal cost of producing the services, and the equilibrium quantity would be at the efficient level $Q_{Efficient}$. However, because consumers pay only a fraction of the true cost of medical services, their demand increases to D_2. In this equilibrium, the quantity of medical services produced increases to Q_{Market}, which is beyond the efficient level. The marginal cost of producing these additional units is greater than the marginal benefit consumers receive from them. As a result, there is a deadweight loss equal to the yellow triangle. Doctors and other suppliers of medical services receive a price, P_{Market}, that is well above the price, P, paid by consumers. Note that the effect of a third-party payer is common to nearly all health care systems, whether the government provides health care directly, as is done in the United Kingdom, or whether most people have private health insurance, as in the United States.

In important ways, health insurance is different from other types of insurance. As we discussed earlier, the basic idea of insurance is that the risk of an unpredictable, high-cost event—a house fire or a serious car accident—is pooled among the many consumers who buy insurance. Health insurance, though, also typically covers many planned expenses, such as routine health checkups, annual physicals, vaccinations, and other low-cost events, such as treatment for minor illnesses. By disguising the true cost of these routine expenses, health insurance encourages overuse of health care services.

We discuss further the role of economic incentives in health care in the next section.   MyEconLab Concept Check

The Continuing Debate over Health Care Policy

As we have seen, the United States has been unusual among high-income countries in relying on private health insurance—mostly offered by employers—to provide health care coverage to the majority of the population. Most other high-income countries either provide health care directly, as the United Kingdom does, through government-owned hospitals and government-employed doctors, or they provide health insurance to all residents, as Canada does, without directly employing doctors or owning hospitals. There have been several attempts to reorganize the U.S. health care system to make it more like the systems in other countries. In 1945, President Harry Truman proposed a plan for *national health insurance* under which anyone could purchase health insurance from the federal government. The health insurance would cover treatment received from doctors and hospitals that agreed to enroll in the system. Congress declined to enact the plan. In 1993, President Bill Clinton proposed a health care plan intended to provide universal coverage. While somewhat complex, the plan was based on requiring most businesses to provide health insurance to their employees and new government-sponsored health alliances that would ensure coverage for anyone who otherwise would not have health insurance. After a prolonged political debate, Congress chose not to enact President Clinton's plan.

The Patient Protection and Affordable Care Act In 2009, President Barack Obama proposed health care legislation that after much debate and significant changes was signed into law as the **Patient Protection and Affordable Care Act (ACA)** in March 2010. The act was long and complex, taking up over 20,000 pages and touching nearly every aspect of health care in the United States. Here is a summary of only the act's main provisions:

> **Patient Protection and Affordable Care Act (ACA)** Health care reform legislation passed by Congress and signed by President Barack Obama in 2010.

- *Individual mandate.* The act required that, with limited exceptions, every resident of the United States have health insurance that meets certain basic requirements. Beginning in 2014, individuals who do not acquire health insurance are subject to a fine. The fine will rise from $95 per adult in 2014 to $695 or 2.5 percent of income, whichever is greater, in 2016. For example, in 2016 an adult with an income of $40,000 per year will pay a fine of $1,000 if he or she refuses to buy health insurance.

- *State health exchanges.* Beginning in October 2013, each state had to establish an Affordable Insurance Exchange. Separate exchanges were to be established for individuals and small businesses with fewer than 50 employees. The exchanges offer health insurance policies that meet certain specified requirements. Although the exchanges were intended to be run by a state government agency or a nonprofit firm, a number of states decided to allow the federal government to run the exchange in their state. Private insurance companies compete by offering policies on the exchanges to individuals and small businesses. Low-income individuals and small businesses with 25 or fewer employees are eligible for tax credits to offset the costs of buying health insurance. The purpose of the exchanges is to allow greater risk pooling and lower administrative costs than had existed in the market for health insurance policies sold to individuals or small businesses. If successful, greater risk pooling and lower administrative costs will make it possible for individuals and small businesses to buy polices with lower premiums than had been available.

- *Employer mandate.* Every firm with more than 200 full-time employees must offer health insurance to its employees and must automatically enroll them in the plan. Firms with 50 or more full-time employees must offer health insurance or pay a fee of $3,000 to the federal government for every employee who receives a tax credit from the federal government for obtaining health insurance through a health exchange. A worker is a full-time employee if he or she works at least 30 hours per week. Although the requirement for firms with 50 or more employees was originally scheduled to go into effect on January 1, 2014, in July 2013 the Obama Administration announced a one-year delay to January 1, 2015.

- *Regulation of health insurance.* Insurance companies are required to participate in a high-risk pool that will insure individuals with pre-existing medical conditions who have been unable to buy health insurance for at least six months. All individual and group policies must provide coverage for dependent children up to age 26. Lifetime dollar maximums on coverage are prohibited. Limits are also placed on the size of deductibles and on the waiting period before coverage becomes effective.

- *Medicare and Medicaid.* Eligibility for Medicaid was originally expanded to persons with incomes up to 138 percent of the federal poverty line, although a 2012 Supreme Court decision resulted in the states being allowed to opt out of this requirement. In an attempt to control increases in health care costs, an Independent Payment Advisory Board (IPAB) was established with the power to reduce Medicare payments for prescription drugs and the use of diagnostic equipment and other technology if Medicare spending exceeds certain levels. Some Medicare reimbursements to hospitals and doctors were reduced.

- *Taxes.* Several new taxes will help fund the program. Workers earning more than $200,000 will have their Medicare payroll tax increase from 1.45 percent to

2.35 percent, and investors who earn more than $200,000 will pay a new 3.8 percent tax on their investment income. Beginning in 2018, a tax will be imposed on employer-provided health insurance plans that have a value above $10,200 for an individual or $27,500 for a family. Pharmaceutical firms, health insurance firms, and firms producing medical devices will also pay new taxes.

The ACA is scheduled to be fully implemented by 2019, at which point more than 30 million additional individuals are expected to have health care coverage. The Congressional Budget Office (CBO) has estimated that the law will increase federal government spending by about $938 billion over 10 years. The CBO estimates that the additional taxes and fees enacted under the law will raise more than $1 trillion, which would be enough to pay for the plan and reduce the federal government's budget deficit by more than $100 billion over 10 years. Many economists have disputed this estimate, arguing that the law's new spending will increase the deficit.

The Debate over the ACA   Any law as far-reaching and complex as the ACA is bound to draw criticism. The congressional debate over the law was highly partisan with every Republican ultimately voting against it and most Democrats voting in favor of it. Critics of the act can be divided into two broad groups: Those who argue that health care reform should involve a greater movement toward a system similar to the British, Canadian, and Japanese systems, and those who argue that health care reform should include more market-based changes.

As we discussed in the *Making the Connection* on page 219, some economists and policymakers believe that information problems and externalities in the market for health care are sufficiently large that the government should either provide health care directly through government-owned hospitals and government-employed doctors or pay for health care through national health insurance, sometimes called a *single-payer system*. Although the ACA significantly increased the federal government's involvement in the health care system, it stopped short of the degree of government involvement that exists in Canada, Japan, or the United Kingdom. Those in favor of moving toward greater government involvement typically argue that doing so would reduce the paperwork and waste caused by the current system. They argue that the current Medicare system—which is essentially a single-payer system for people over age 65—has proved to have lower administrative costs than have private health insurance companies. Supporters of greater government involvement in the health care system have also argued that the Canadian and British systems have had lower levels of health care spending per person and lower rates of increase in total health care spending, while providing good health care outcomes.

Market-based reforms of health care involve changing the market for health care so that it becomes more like the markets for other goods and services. As in other markets, the prices consumers pay and suppliers receive would do a better job of conveying information on consumer demand and supplier costs. The expectation is that increased competition among doctors, hospitals, pharmaceutical companies, and other providers of health care would reduce costs and increase economic efficiency. Economists who support market-based reforms as the best approach to improving the health care system were disappointed that the ACA did not adopt this approach. Currently, markets are delivering inaccurate signals to consumers because when buying health care, unlike when buying most other goods and services, consumers pay a price well below the true cost of providing the service.

MyEconLab Concept Check

Market-based reforms Changes in the market for health care that would make it more like the markets for other goods and services.

Making the Connection
MyEconLab Video

How Much Is That MRI Scan?

Magnetic resonance imaging (MRI) units play an important role in modern medicine. First introduced in the early 1980s, they allow doctors to see inside the body's soft tissues to identify tumors, torn muscles, and other medical problems. As we noted earlier, MRI units are more widely available in the United States than in most other countries. We would normally expect that when a product is widely available, competition among firms results in the price of the product being about the same everywhere. Customers would not buy a best-selling book from Amazon.com if the price was 50 percent higher than on BarnesandNoble.com.

Does competition equalize the prices of medical services? The data in the table below indicate that the prices of abdominal MRI scans vary widely. In most cities in the United States, the most expensive MRI scan has a price that is more than double the least expensive scan. For example, in 2013, the highest price for an MRI in New York City was $10,000, while the lowest price was only $1,650. Two reporters looking at prices for shoulder MRI scans in Pensacola, Florida, found that Sacred Heart Hospital was charging $800 for a shoulder MRI scan, while Pensacola Open MRI & Imaging, a private firm located less than one mile away, was charging $450 for the same scan. Pensacola Open MRI & Imaging was actually using newer MRI units that give higher resolution images, so they were charging less for a better service.

City	Highest Price	Lowest Price	Difference
New York, New York	$10,000	$1,650	$8,350
San Francisco, California	7,800	2,000	5,800
Orlando, Florida	7,300	2,325	4,975
Houston, Texas	7,000	1,450	5,550
Chicago, Illinois	6,500	1,450	5,050
Omaha, Nebraska	6,200	2,100	4,100
Baton Rouge, Louisiana	6,000	2,175	3,825
Atlanta, Georgia	5,900	2,175	3,725
Lexington, Kentucky	5,400	925	4,475
Charlotte, North Carolina	4,800	2,000	2,800

How can some providers of medical services charge hundreds or thousands of dollars more than competitors and remain in business? The answer is that most patients are not concerned about prices because they either do not pay them or they pay only a small fraction of them. Patients typically rely on doctors to refer them to a facility for an MRI scan or other procedure and make little or no effort to determine the price the facility charges. A goal of market-based reforms of the health care system is to give patients an incentive to pay more attention to the prices of medical services.

Sources: Caitlin Kenney, "Shopping for an MRI," www.npr.org, November 6, 2009; MRI prices from newchoicehealth.com, June 3, 2013.

MyEconLab Study Plan   **Your Turn:** Test your understanding by doing related problem 4.11 on page 233 at the end of this chapter.

Supporters of market-based reforms note that employees have to pay federal income and payroll taxes on the wages their employers pay them, but in most circumstances they do not pay taxes on the value of the health insurance their employers provide them. This feature of the tax laws encourages employees to want very generous health care coverage; in fact, if offered the choice between a $1,000 salary increase or increased health care coverage that was worth $1,000, many people would choose the increased health care coverage because it would be tax free (although someone who was young and healthy and did not expect to have medical bills would probably choose the increase in salary). The size of this tax break is quite substantial—more than $250 billion in 2013. But individuals typically get no tax break when buying an individual health insurance policy or when they spend money on health care out of pocket.[1]

Some economists have proposed making the tax treatment of employer-provided health insurance the same as the tax treatment of individually purchased health insurance and out-of-pocket health care spending. They argue that this change could, potentially, significantly reduce spending on health care without reducing the effectiveness of the health care received. Such tax law changes would make it more likely that employer-provided health insurance would focus on large medical bills—such as those resulting

[1]Individuals receive a deduction on their federal income tax only if their medical expenses are greater than 7.5 percent of their income. Only a relatively small number of individuals have expenses high enough to make use of that deduction. The threshold is being raised under the ACA to 10 percent.

from hospitalizations—while consumers would pay prices closer to the costs of providing routine medical care. John Cogan of the Hoover Institution, Glenn Hubbard of Columbia University, and Daniel Kessler of Stanford University estimate that repealing the tax preference for employer-provided health insurance would reduce spending by people enrolled in these programs by 33 percent.

Currently, the U.S. health care system is a world leader in innovation in medical technology and prescription drugs. About two-thirds of pharmaceutical patents are issued to U.S. firms and about two-thirds of research on new medicines is carried out in the United States. One goal of market-based reforms would be to ensure that U.S. firms continue with innovations in medical screening equipment, surgical procedures, and prescription drugs. Executives of U.S. pharmaceutical firms have voiced concern over whether aspects of the ACA will affect their ability to profitably bring new prescription drugs to market. In particular, managers at these firms worry that the new Independent Payment Advisory Board (IPAB) might reduce the payments Medicare would make for new prescription drugs.

Both critics of the ACA who favor greater government involvement in health care and those who favor market reforms raise questions about the act's individual mandate. The individual mandate requires every U.S. resident to have health insurance. The mandate was considered necessary because otherwise healthy people might avoid buying insurance until they become ill. Because insurance companies would not be allowed to deny coverage for pre-existing conditions, they would end up paying large medical bills for people who had not been paying premiums to support the system while they were healthy. There were questions about whether the requirement to buy health insurance would be enforceable. Although people who do not buy insurance are subject to fines under the act, there was no mechanism set up to collect the fines if people refused to pay them voluntarily.

MyEconLab Study Plan

Continued from page 205

Economics in Your Life

Is Your Take-Home Pay Affected by What Your Employer Spends on Your Health Insurance?

At the beginning of this chapter, we asked: "Your paycheck doesn't show the amount your employer pays on your behalf for health insurance, but does that amount affect your take-home pay?" The *Making the Connection* on page 219 shows that the equilibrium compensation that workers receive in labor markets is made up partly of wages and partly of fringe benefits such as health insurance. So, while the amount that a firm pays on your behalf for health insurance may not affect your total compensation, it will affect the amount of your take-home pay. For a given level of compensation, the more a firm pays for your health insurance, the less it will pay you in wages. A related question is why a firm would buy health insurance for you rather than increasing your wages by the same amount and letting you buy your own insurance? We have seen that there are two important reasons why so many people receive health insurance from their employers: (1) The wage an employer pays you is taxable income to you, but the money an employer spends to buy health insurance for you is not taxable; and (2) insurance companies are typically willing to charge lower premiums for group insurance, particularly to large employers, because risk pooling is improved and adverse selection and moral hazard problems are lower when compared with individual policies.

Conclusion

In this chapter, we have seen that economic analysis can provide important insights into the market for health care. As with many other policy issues, though, economic analysis can help inform the debate, but cannot resolve it. Because health care is so important to consumers and health care spending looms so large in the U.S. economy, the role of the government in the health care system is likely to be the subject of intense debate for years to come.

Visit MyEconLab for a news article and analysis related to the concepts in this chapter.

Chapter Summary and Problems

Key Terms

Adverse selection, p. 213

Asymmetric information, p. 213

Fee-for-service, p. 209

Health care, p. 206

Health insurance, p. 208

Market-based reforms, p. 227

Moral hazard, p. 214

Patient Protection and Affordable Care Act (ACA), p. 226

Principal–agent problem, p. 215

Single-payer health care system, p. 210

Socialized medicine, p. 210

7.1 **The Improving Health of People in the United States, pages 206–208**
LEARNING OBJECTIVE: Discuss trends in U.S. health over time.

Summary

Health care refers to goods and services, such as prescription drugs and consultations with a doctor, that are intended to maintain or improve health. Over time, the health of people in most countries has improved. In the United States, as a result of improving health, life expectancy has increased, death rates have decreased, infant mortality has decreased, and the average person has become taller.

 Visit **www.myeconlab.com** to complete these exercises online and get instant feedback.

Review Questions

1.1 Briefly discuss the most important differences between the market for health care and the markets for other goods and services.

1.2 Briefly describe changes over time in the health of the average person in the United States.

1.3 How can improvements in health increase a country's total income? How can increases in a country's total income improve health?

Problems and Applications

1.4 In what sense have improvements in the health of the average American caused the U.S. production possibilities frontier to shift out? Panel (a) in Figure 7.1 on page 208 indicates that life expectancy in the United States declined in 1918. What effect did this decline in life expectancy likely have on the U.S. production possibilities frontier? Briefly explain.

1.5 The widespread acceptance in the late nineteenth century that bacteria causes diseases helped lead to a public health movement in the late nineteenth and early twentieth centuries. This movement eventually brought sewers, clean drinking water, and garbage removal to all U.S. cities. What effect did the public health movement in the United States in the late nineteenth and early twentieth centuries have on the country's production possibilities frontier?

1.6 Between 1830 and 1890, the height of the average adult male in the United States declined by about two inches at the same time that average incomes more than tripled. Did the standard of living in the United States increase during this period? What insight into the health and well-being of the U.S. population might the decline in height provide? Briefly explain.

7.2 **Health Care around the World, pages 208–213**
LEARNING OBJECTIVE: Compare the health care systems and health care outcomes in the United States and other countries.

Summary

Health insurance is a contract under which a buyer agrees to make payments, or premiums, in exchange for the provider agreeing to pay some or all of the buyer's medical bills. A majority of people in the United States live in households that have private health insurance, which they typically obtain through an employer. Other people have health insurance through the Veteran's Administration or the Medicare and Medicaid programs. In 2012, about 16 percent of people in the United States lacked health insurance. Many health insurance plans operate on a **fee-for-service** basis under which doctors and hospitals receive a payment for each service they provide. Most countries outside of the United States have greater government involvement in their health care systems. Canada has a **single-payer health care system**, in which the government provides national health insurance to all Canadian residents. In the United Kingdom, the government owns most hospitals and employs most doctors, and the health care system is referred to as **socialized medicine**. The United States spends more

per person on health care than do other high-income countries. The United States has lower life expectancy, higher infant mortality, and a greater incidence of obesity than do other high-income countries. The United States has more medical technology per person and has lower mortality rates for people diagnosed with cancer than do other high-income countries. Data and other problems make it difficult to compare health care outcomes across countries.

 Visit **www.myeconlab.com** to complete these exercises online and get instant feedback.

Review Questions

2.1 Define the following terms:
  a. Health insurance
  b. Fee-for-service
  c. Single-payer health care system
  d. Socialized medicine

2.2 What are the main sources of health insurance in the United States?

2.3 Briefly compare the health care systems in Canada, Japan, and the United Kingdom with the health care system in the United States.

2.4 What is meant by the phrase "health care outcome"? How do health care outcomes in the United States compare with those of other high-income countries? What problems arise in attempting to compare health care outcomes across countries?

Problems and Applications

2.5 According to an article in the *Economist* about the health care system in the United Kingdom: "A defining principle of the National Health Service is that it is 'free at the point of delivery.'" What does "free at the point of delivery" mean? Is health care actually free to residents of the United Kingdom? Briefly explain.

Source: "Free-for-All," *Economist*, June 1, 2013.

2.6 Why do comparisons of health care outcomes across countries often concentrate on measures such as life expectancy and infant mortality? Are there other measures of the quality of health care systems? Briefly explain.

2.7 Two health care analysts argue that in the United States, "we have arrived at a moment where we are making little headway in defeating various kinds of diseases. Instead, our main achievements today consist of devising ways to marginally extend the lives of the very sick."

a. Should "marginally extend[ing] the lives of the very sick" be an important goal of a health care system? What other goals should have a higher priority? (Note: This question is basically a normative one without a definitive correct or incorrect answer. You are being asked to consider what the goals of a health care system *should be*.)

b. Would it be possible to measure how successful the health care systems of different countries are in extending the lives of the very sick? If so, how might it be done?

Source: David Brooks, "Death and Budgets," *New York Times*, July 14, 2011.

7.3 **Information Problems and Externalities in the Market for Health Care, pages 213–220**
LEARNING OBJECTIVE: Discuss how information problems and externalities affect the market for health care.

Summary

The market for health care is affected by the problem of **asymmetric information**, which occurs when one party to an economic transaction has less information than the other party. **Adverse selection**, the situation in which one party to a transaction takes advantage of knowing more than the other party to the transaction, is a problem for firms selling health insurance policies because it results in people who are less healthy being more likely to buy insurance than people who are healthier. **Moral hazard**, actions people take after they have entered into a transaction that make the other party to the transaction worse off, is also a problem for insurance companies because once people have health insurance they are likely to make more visits to their doctors and in other ways increase their use of medical services. Moral hazard can also involve a **principal–agent problem** in which doctors may order more lab tests, MRI scans, and other procedures than they would if their patients lacked health insurance. Insurance companies use deductibles, co-payments, and restrictions on coverage of patients with pre-existing conditions to reduce the problems of adverse selection and moral hazard. There may be externalities involved with medicine and health care because, for example, people who are vaccinated against influenza or other diseases may not receive all of the benefits from having been vaccinated and people who become obese may not bear all of the costs from their obesity.

MyEconLab   Visit www.myeconlab.com to complete these exercises online and get instant feedback.

Review Questions

3.1 Define the following terms:
a. Asymmetric information
b. Adverse selection
c. Moral hazard
d. Principal–agent problem

3.2 What are the asymmetric information problems in the market for health insurance?

3.3 How do health insurance companies deal with asymmetric information problems?

3.4 What is an externality? Are there externalities in the market for health care? Briefly explain.

Problems and Applications

3.5 Suppose you see a 2010 Volkswagen Jetta GLS Turbo Sedan advertised in the campus newspaper for $10,000. If you knew the car was reliable, you would be willing to pay $12,000 for it. If you knew the car was unreliable, you would be willing to pay $8,000 for it. Under what circumstances should you buy the car?

3.6 What is the *lemons problem*? Is there a lemons problem with health insurance? Briefly explain.

3.7 Michael Kinsley, a political columnist, observes: "The idea of insurance is to share the risks of bad outcomes." In what sense does insurance involve sharing risks? How does the problem of adverse selection affect the ability of insurance to provide the benefit of sharing risk?

Source: Michael Kinsley, "Congress on Drugs," *Slate*, August 1, 2002.

3.8 Under the Social Security retirement system, the federal government collects a tax on most people's wage income and makes payments to retired workers above a certain age who are covered by the system. (The age to receive full Social Security retirement benefits varies based on the year the worker was born.) The Social Security retirement system is sometimes referred to as a program of social insurance. Is Social Security an insurance program in the same sense as a health insurance policy that a company provides to its workers? Briefly explain.

3.9 **[Related to the** Don't Let This Happen to You **on page 215]** Briefly explain whether you agree with the following statement: "The reluctance of healthy young adults to buy health insurance creates a moral hazard problem for insurance companies."

3.10 **[Related to the** Don't Let This Happen to You **on page 215]**
While teaching the concepts of asymmetric information, a professor asked his students for examples of adverse selection or moral hazard in marriage. One of the students, who happened to be married, replied: "Your spouse doesn't bring you flowers any more!" Would the student's reply be an example of adverse selection or moral hazard? Briefly explain.

3.11 An opinion column in the *Wall Street Journal* observes about "defensive medicine" that: "Many physicians maintain that fear of lawsuits significantly affects the practice of medicine, and that reform of the malpractice system is crucial for containing costs."

Is there another economic explanation—apart from fear of lawsuits—for why doctors may end up ordering unnecessary tests and other medical procedures? Briefly explain.

Source: Amitabh Chandra, Anupam B. Jena, and Seth A. Seabury, "Defensive Medicine May Be Costlier Than It Seems," *Wall Street Journal*, February 7, 2013.

3.12 **[Related to** Solved Problem 7.3 **on page 216]** An article in the *Economist* magazine argues that the real problem with health insurance is:

> The healthy people who decide not to buy insurance out of rational self-interest, and who turn out to be right. By not buying insurance, those (largely young) healthy people will be failing to subsidize the people insurance is meant for: the ones who end up getting sick.

  a. Why is it rational for healthy people not to buy health insurance?

  b. Do you agree that health insurance is meant for people who end up getting sick?

  c. Why is the situation described here a problem for a system of health insurance? If it is a problem, suggest possible solutions.

Source: "Romney on Health Care: To Boldly Go Where He Had Already Been Before," *Economist*, May 13, 2011.

3.13 **[Related to** Solved Problem 7.3 **on page 216]** An article in the *Economist* magazine contains the following description of the "classic adverse selection spiral": "because [health insurance] premiums go higher, healthy people become even less likely to buy insurance, which drives premiums higher yet, and so on until the whole thing winks out. . . ." Why does an adverse selection spiral develop? What steps can insurance companies take to avoid it?

Source: "Romney on Health Care: To Boldly Go Where He Had Already Been Before," *Economist*, May 13, 2011.

3.14 **[Related to** Solved Problem 7.3 **on page 216]** An article in the *Los Angeles Times* describes a healthy 23-year-old woman who has decided not to buy health insurance as "exactly the type of person insurance plans, states and the federal government are counting on to make health reform work." Why are healthy 23-year-olds needed to make health reform work?

Source: Anna Gorman, "Affordable Care Act's Challenge: Getting Young Adults Enrolled," *Los Angeles Times*, June 2, 2013.

3.15 **[Related to the** Making the Connection **on page 219]**
Explain whether you agree with the following statement:

> Providing health care is obviously a public good. If one person becomes ill and doesn't receive treatment, that person may infect many other people. If many people become ill, then the output of the economy will be negatively affected. Therefore, providing health care is a public good that should be supplied by the government.

The Debate over Health Care Policy in the United States, pages 220–229

LEARNING OBJECTIVE: Explain the major issues involved in the debate over health care policy in the United States.

Summary

In March 2010, Congress passed the Patient Protection and Affordable Care Act (ACA), which significantly reorganized the U.S. health care system. Spending on health care in the United States has been growing rapidly as a percentage of GDP, and spending per person on health care has been growing more rapidly than in other high-income countries. Third-party payers, such as employer-provided health insurance and the Medicare and Medicaid programs, have financed an increasing fraction of health care spending, while out-of-pocket payments have sharply declined as a fraction of total health care spending. Several explanations have been offered for the rapid increase in health care spending in the United States: Slow rates of growth of labor productivity in health care may be driving up costs, the U.S. population is becoming older, medical technology and new prescription drugs have higher costs, and the tax system and the reliance on third-party payers have distorted the economic incentives of consumers and suppliers of health care. The ACA has several important provisions: (1) an individual mandate that requires every resident of the United States to obtain health insurance or be fined; (2) the establishment of health exchanges that will be run by the state or federal governments and provide a means for individuals and small businesses to purchase health insurance; (3) an employer mandate that requires every firm with more than 200 employees to offer health insurance to them; (4) increased regulation of health insurance companies; (5) expansion of eligibility for Medicaid and the establishment of the Independent Payment Advisory Board (IPAB), which has the power to reduce Medicare payments for prescription drugs and for the use of diagnostic equipment and other technology if Medicare spending exceeds certain levels; and (6) increased taxes on people with incomes above $200,000. Some critics of the ACA argue that it does not go far enough in increasing government involvement in the health care system, while other critics argue that health care reform should rely more heavily on **market-based reforms**, which involve changing the market for health care so that it becomes more like the markets for other goods and services.

MyEconLab   Visit www.myeconlab.com to complete these exercises online and get instant feedback.

Review Questions

4.1 What is the Patient Protection and Affordable Care Act (ACA)? Briefly list its major provisions.

4.2 In the United States, what has been the trend in health care spending as a percentage of GDP? Compare the increases in health care spending per person in the United States with the increases in health care spending per person in other high-income countries. What implications do current trends in health care spending have for the growth of federal government spending in the United States?

4.3 Briefly discuss how economists explain the rapid increases in health care spending.

4.4 What arguments do economists and policymakers who believe that the federal government should have a larger role in the health care system make in criticizing the ACA?

4.5 What arguments do economists and policymakers who believe that market-based reforms are the key to improving the health care system make in criticizing the ACA?

Problems and Applications

4.6 Figure 7.7 on page 224 shows that the Congressional Budget Office forecasts that only about 10 percent of future increases in spending on Medicare as a percentage of GDP will be due to the aging of the population. What factors explain the other 90 percent of the increase?

4.7 Some economists and policymakers have argued that one way to control federal government spending on Medicare is to have a board of experts decide whether new medical technologies are worth their higher costs. If the board decides that they are *not* worth the costs, Medicare would not pay for them. Other economists and policymakers argue that the costs to beneficiaries should more closely represent the costs of providing medical services. This result might be attained by raising premiums, deductibles, and co-payments or by "means testing," which would limit the Medicare benefits high-income individuals receive. Political columnist David Brooks has summarized these two ways to restrain the growth of spending on Medicare: "From the top, a body of experts can be empowered to make rationing decisions. . . . Alternatively, at the bottom, costs can be shifted to beneficiaries with premium supports to help them handle the burden."

    a. What are "rationing decisions"? How would these decisions restrain the growth of Medicare spending?

    b. How would shifting the costs of Medicare to beneficiaries restrain the growth of Medicare spending? What does Brooks mean by "premium supports"?

    c. Should Congress and the president be concerned about the growth of Medicare spending? If so, which of these approaches should they adopt, or is there a third approach that might be better? (Note: This last question is normative and has no definitive answer. It is

intended to lead you to consider possible approaches to the Medicare program.)

Source: David Brooks, "The Missing Fifth," *New York Times*, May 9, 2011.

4.8 Ross Douthat, a political columnist, offers the following observations about the Medicare program:

> Certainly telling seniors to buy *all* their own health care is a complete political (and ethical) non-starter. But telling seniors to pay for *more* of their own health care—well, it's hard to see how else we can hope to reduce Medicare's fiscal burden.

    a. What does Douthat mean by Medicare's "fiscal burden"?

    b. How could the government change the Medicare program so that seniors would pay for more of their own health care? How would this change restrain growth in the spending on Medicare? How would this change affect very low-income seniors?

Source: Ross Douthat, "We're All Rationers," *New York Times*, May 19, 2011.

4.9 Nobel Laureate Robert Fogel of the University of Chicago argued that: "Expenditures on health care are driven by demand, which is spurred by income and by advances in biotechnology that make health interventions increasingly effective."

    a. If Fogel was correct, should policymakers be concerned by projected increases in health care spending as a percentage of GDP?

    b. What objections do some economists raise to Fogel's analysis of what is driving increases in spending on health care?

Source: Robert Fogel, "Forecasting the Cost of U.S. Healthcare," *The American*, September 3, 2009.

4.10 [Related to the Making the Connection **on page 222**] Employees in most circumstances do not pay taxes on the value of the health insurance provided by their employers. If employees were taxed on the value of the employer-provided health insurance, what would you expect to happen to the overall compensation employers pay employees? To the value of health insurance provided by employers? To the wages paid to employees? Briefly explain.

4.11 [Related to the Making the Connection **on page 227**] A column in the *Wall Street Journal* observes that: "Independent websites like Edmunds.com, AutoTrader.com and Kelley Blue Book publish detailed pricing information [on automobiles] for consumers and do so for free. Consumers want such information and businesses see opportunity in providing it, even for free, in order to attract eyeballs for advertising. … Such information doesn't exist in health care…" Why aren't there Web sites that offer pricing data on health care and make a profit from selling advertisements?

Source: Holman W. Jenkins, Jr., "The Young Won't Buy ObamaCare," *Wall Street Journal*, June 18, 2013.

4.12 [Related to the Chapter Opener **on page 205**] Working conditions in developing countries are often considerably worse than working conditions in developed countries. If working conditions are analogous to fringe benefits, would requiring companies in developing countries to substantially improve working conditions necessarily increase the well-being of their workers? How might the improved working conditions affect wages? Might workers in low-income countries have a different trade-off between wages and working conditions than workers in affluent countries?

4.13 Suppose consumers pay less than the true cost of medical services because a third party, such as an insurance company or the government, pays most of the bill. In the graph, D_1 represents the demand for medical services if consumers paid the full price of medical services; D_2 represents the demand for medical services when consumers pay only a fraction of the true cost of medical services; and S represents the supply of medical services. Use the graph to answer the following questions. Briefly explain your answers.

a. What is the equilibrium market price received by doctors and other suppliers of medical services?

b. What is the efficient quantity of medical services?

c. What is the price paid by consumers of medical services?

d. Which area represents the deadweight loss resulting from consumers not paying the full price of medical services?

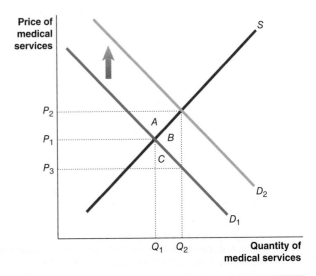

Firms, the Stock Market, and Corporate Governance

Chapter Outline and Learning Objectives

Facebook Learns the Benefits and Costs of Becoming a Publicly Owned Firm

When Mark Zuckerberg started Facebook in 2004, he was a sophomore in college. Just nine years later, Facebook had 1.1 billion active users worldwide. Zuckerberg started Facebook because he believed that people were less interested in meeting new friends online—the assumption built into other social networking sites—than they were in staying in touch with the friends they already had. On Facebook, pages are typically visible only to people the user has linked to, or "friended," which reduces the problem of fake identities that plagued other sites.

By the fall of 2011, Zuckerberg faced a decision: Any business experiencing the runaway success of Facebook needs to raise funds quickly to finance its expansion. Some businesses raise funds by borrowing from banks. Large firms, as Facebook has become, have the ability to sell stocks and bonds to investors in financial markets. Firms that sell stock that is traded in financial markets such as the New York Stock Exchange are called public firms, while firms that do not sell stock are called private firms. For Zuckerberg, turning Facebook into a public firm and selling stock would raise revenue, but buyers of the stock would have partial ownership of the firm and a claim on its profits and might question Zuckerberg's leadership. Zuckerberg would retain control but feared that he might no longer have a completely free hand to continue Facebook's expansion.

Finally, in May 2012, Facebook sold shares of stock to the general public. Many individual investors were eager to buy shares at the initial price of $38 per share. During the following year, though, as more people began using Facebook on smartphones and tablets than on computers, Facebook had difficulty selling advertisements, and its revenue grew more slowly than expected. As a result, Facebook's stock price fluctuated. In 2013, Facebook's stock finally rose above its initial price of $38 per share, providing investors who had bought at that price with significant gains.

As we will see in this chapter, financial markets are an important source of funds to many firms and an important source of investment opportunities to households. More generally, a well-functioning financial system is crucial to the health of the economy.

Sources: Based on Jessi Hempel, "How Facebook Is Taking over Our Lives," *Fortune*, March 11, 2009; Khadeeja Safdar, "Facebook, One Year Later: What Really Happened in the Biggest IPO Flop Ever," *Atlantic*, May 20, 2013; and Evelyn Rusli, "After IPO, Facebook Gets Serious about Making Money," *Wall Street Journal*, May 16, 2013.

Economics in Your Life

Do Corporate Managers Act in the Best Interests of Shareholders?

Although stockholders legally own corporations, managers often have a great deal of freedom in deciding how corporations are run. As a result, managers can make decisions, such as spending money on large corporate headquarters or decorating their offices with expensive paintings, that are in their interests but not in the interests of the shareholders. If managers make decisions that waste money and lower the profits of a firm, the price of the firm's stock will fall, which hurts the investors who own the stock. Suppose you are considering buying stock in a corporation. Why will it be difficult to get the managers to act in your interests rather than in their own? Given this problem, should you ever take on the risk of buying stock? As you read this chapter, try to answer these questions. You can check your answers against those we provide on **page 255** at the end of this chapter.

I n this chapter, we look at firms: how they are organized, how they raise funds, and the information they provide to investors. As we have discussed in earlier chapters, firms in a market system are responsible for organizing the factors of production to produce goods and services. Firms are the vehicles entrepreneurs use to earn profits. To succeed, entrepreneurs must meet consumers' wants by producing new or better goods and services or by finding ways to produce existing goods and services at a lower cost so that they can be sold at a lower price. Entrepreneurs also need access to sufficient funds, and they must be able to efficiently organize production. As the typical firm in many industries has become larger over the past 100 years, the task of efficiently organizing production has become more difficult. In the final section of this chapter, we look at problems of *corporate governance* that have occurred in recent years. We also look at the steps firms and the government have taken to avoid similar problems in the future.

8.1 LEARNING OBJECTIVE

Categorize the major types of firms in the United States.

Sole proprietorship A firm owned by a single individual and not organized as a corporation.

Partnership A firm owned jointly by two or more persons and not organized as a corporation.

Corporation A legal form of business that provides owners with protection from losing more than their investment should the business fail.

Asset Anything of value owned by a person or a firm.

Limited liability The legal provision that shields owners of a corporation from losing more than they have invested in the firm.

Types of Firms

In studying a market economy, it is important to understand the basics of how firms operate. In the United States, there are three main categories of firms: *sole proprietorships*, *partnerships*, and *corporations*. A **sole proprietorship** is a firm owned by a single individual. Although most sole proprietorships are small, some employ many workers and earn large profits. **Partnerships** are firms owned jointly by two or more—sometimes many—persons. Most law and accounting firms are partnerships. Some of them can be quite large. For instance, in 2013, the Baker & McKenzie law firm based in Chicago had 1,400 partners. Most large firms, though, are organized as *corporations*. A **corporation** is a legal form of business that provides owners with protection from losing more than their investment in the firm should the business fail.

Who Is Liable? Limited and Unlimited Liability

A key distinction among the three types of firms is that the owners of sole proprietorships and partnerships have unlimited liability, which means that there is no legal distinction between the personal assets of the owners of the firm and the assets of the firm. An **asset** is anything of value owned by a person or a firm. If a sole proprietorship or a partnership owes a lot of money to the firm's suppliers or employees, the suppliers and employees have a legal right to sue the firm for payment, even if in order to pay their debts the firm's owners have to sell some of their personal assets, such as stocks or bonds. In other words, with sole proprietorships and partnerships, the owners are not legally distinct from the firms they own.

It may only seem fair that the owners of a firm be responsible for the firm's debts. But early in the nineteenth century, it became clear to many state legislatures in the United States that unlimited liability was a significant problem for any firm that was attempting to raise funds from large numbers of investors. An investor might be interested in making a relatively small investment in a firm but be unwilling to become a partner in the firm, for fear of placing at risk all of his or her personal assets if the firm were to fail. To get around this problem, state legislatures began to pass *general incorporation laws*, which allowed firms to be organized as corporations. Under the corporate form of business, the owners of a firm have **limited liability**, which means that if the firm fails, the owners can never lose more than the amount they have invested in the firm. The personal assets of the owners of the firm are not affected by the failure of the firm. In fact, in the eyes of the law, a corporation is a legal "person," separate from its owners. Limited liability has made it possible for corporations to raise funds by issuing shares of stock to large numbers of investors. For example, if you buy a share of Facebook stock, you are a part owner of the firm, but even if Facebook were to go bankrupt, you would

	Sole Proprietorship	Partnership	Corporation
Advantages	• Control by owner • No layers of management	• Ability to share work • Ability to share risks	• Limited personal liability • Greater ability to raise funds
Disadvantages	• Unlimited personal liability • Limited ability to raise funds	• Unlimited personal liability • Limited ability to raise funds	• Costly to organize • Possible double taxation of income

Table 8.1

Differences among Business Organizations

not be personally responsible for any of Facebook's debts. Therefore, you could not lose more than the amount you paid for the stock.

Organizing a firm as a corporation also has some disadvantages. In the United States, corporate profits are taxed twice—once at the corporate level and again when investors in the firm receive a share of the firm's profits. Corporations generally are larger than sole proprietorships and partnerships and are therefore more difficult to organize and run. Table 8.1 reviews the advantages and disadvantages of different forms of business organization. MyEconLab Concept Check

Corporations Earn the Majority of Revenue and Profits

Figure 8.1 gives basic statistics on the three types of business organizations. Panel (a) shows that almost three-quarters of all firms are sole proprietorships. Panels (b) and (c) show that although only 18 percent of all firms are corporations, they account for a majority of the revenue and profits earned by all firms. *Profit* is the difference between revenue and the total cost to a firm of producing the goods and services it offers for sale.

There are more than 5.8 million corporations in the United States, but only 35,000 have annual revenues of more than $50 million. We can think of these 35,000 firms—including Apple, McDonald's, and Facebook—as representing "big business." These large firms earn more than 80 percent of the total profits of all corporations in the United States. MyEconLab Concept Check

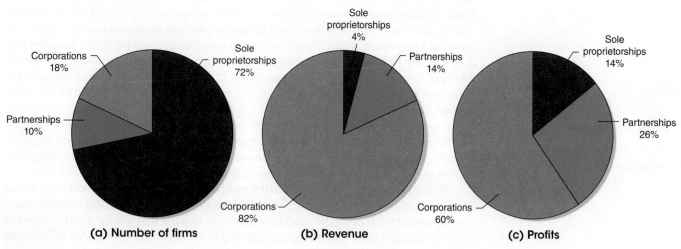

MyEconLab Animation

Figure 8.1   **Business Organizations: Sole Proprietorships, Partnerships, and Corporations**

The three types of firms in the United States are sole proprietorships, partnerships, and corporations. Panel (a) shows that only 18 percent of all firms are corporations. Yet, as panels (b) and (c) show, corporations account for a majority of the revenue and profits earned by all firms.

Source: Internal Revenue Service, *Statistics on Income.*

**Making
the
Connection**
MyEconLab Video

How Important Are Small Businesses to the U.S. Economy?

We have seen that although a large majority of all firms are sole proprietorships, they account for only a small fraction of total revenues and profits earned by all firms. In addition, as the following figure shows, more than 70 percent of people work at firms that have 50 or more employees. Does this mean that small businesses are not important to the U.S. economy?

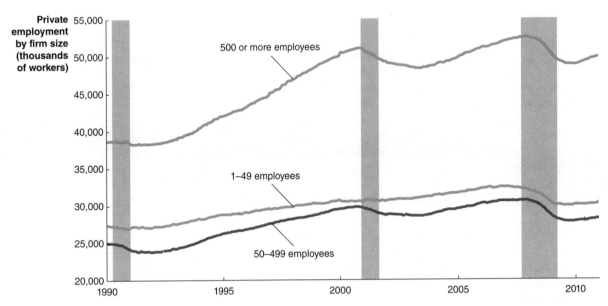

Note: The shaded areas represent periods of recession.
Source: U.S. Bureau of Labor Statistics, "Experimental Size Class Employment, Hours, and Earnings Series from the Current Employment Statistics Survey," July 26, 2012.

On the contrary, most economists would argue that small firms are vital to the health of the economy. Starting a small firm provides an entrepreneur with a vehicle for bringing a new product or process to market. Finding funds to start a small firm is often difficult, though, because a new firm lacks a record of operating profitably, so banks and other lenders worry that the firm won't be able to pay back borrowed money. As a result, more than 80 percent of small firms are started using funds provided by the founders and their families, by borrowing on credit cards, or by taking out loans against the value of the founders' homes. While anyone starting a new firm hopes to become successful, perhaps even wealthy, founding a company can also provide employment opportunities for workers and new goods and services for consumers. In most years, more than 600,000 new firms open in the United States, and, of these, more than 95 percent employ fewer than 20 workers. In a typical year, new small firms create 3.3 million jobs. Forty percent of all new jobs are created by small firms, and in some years more than half are. Strikingly, more than 85 percent of all jobs created by new firms of all sizes are created by small firms.

Although, on average, jobs at small firms pay lower wages than jobs at large firms and are less likely to provide fringe benefits, such as health insurance and retirement accounts, workers at small firms tend to be younger, and the first job for many workers is often with a small firm. Small firms are also less likely than large firms to lay off workers during a recession.

Entrepreneurs founding small firms have been the source of many important new goods and services, even though large firms spend much more on research and development than do small firms. Some economists have argued that although spending on research and development by large firms frequently leads to important improvements in existing products, innovative new products are often introduced by small firms. For instance, during the late nineteenth and early twentieth centuries, Thomas Edison, Henry Ford, and the Wright Brothers were all responsible for introducing important products shortly after starting what were initially very small firms. In more recent years, Bill Gates, Steve Jobs, Michael Dell, and Mark Zuckerberg decided that the best way to develop their ideas was by founding Microsoft, Apple, Dell Computer, and Facebook, rather than by choosing to work for large corporations. Each of these firms began with a handful of employees, and the key products and processes they pioneered were developed long before they evolved into the large firms they are today.

Sources: David Neumark, Brandon Wall, and Junfu Zhang, "Do Small Businesses Create More Jobs? New Evidence for the United States from the National Establishment Time Series," *Review of Economics and Statistics*, Vol. 93, No. 1, February 2011, pp. 16–29; Ben Casselman, "Small Business Tops in Job Creation, but Also Job Cuts," *Wall Street Journal*, January 29, 2013; Amar Bhidé, *The Origins and Evolution of New Businesses*, New York: Oxford University Press, 2003; Giuseppe Moscarini and Fabien Postel-Vinay, "The Contribution of Large and Small Employers to Job Creation at Times of High and Low Unemployment," *American Economic Review*, Vol. 102, No. 6, October 2012, pp. 2509–2539; data are from *The Statistical Abstract of the United States*; the U.S. Small Business Administration; and the U.S. Bureau of Labor Statistics.

Your Turn: Test your understanding by doing related problems 1.8 and 1.9 on page 256 at the end of this chapter.

MyEconLab Study Plan

The Structure of Corporations and the Principal–Agent Problem

8.2 LEARNING OBJECTIVE

Describe the typical management structure of corporations and understand the concepts of separation of ownership from control and the principal–agent problem.

Because large corporations account for a majority of sales and profits in the economy, it is important to know how they are managed. Most large corporations have a similar management structure. The way in which a corporation is structured and the effect that structure has on the corporation's behavior is referred to as **corporate governance**.

Corporate Structure and Corporate Governance

Corporations are legally owned by their *shareholders*, the owners of the corporation's stock. Unlike with a sole proprietorship, a corporation's shareholders, although they are the firm's owners, do not manage the firm directly. Instead, they elect a *board of directors* to represent their interests. The board of directors appoints a *chief executive officer* (CEO) to run the day-to-day operations of the corporation. Sometimes the board of directors also appoints other members of *top management*, such as the *chief financial officer* (CFO). At other times, the CEO appoints other members of top management. Members of top management, including the CEO and CFO, often serve on the board of directors. They are called *inside directors*. Members of the board of directors who do not have a direct management role in the firm are called *outside directors*. The outside directors are intended to act as a check on the decisions of top managers, but the distinction between an outside director and an inside director is not always clear. For example, the CEO of a firm that sells a good or service to a large corporation may sit on the corporation's board of directors. Although technically an outside director, this person may be reluctant to oppose the top managers because they have the power to stop purchasing from his or her firm. In some instances, top managers have effectively controlled their firms' boards of directors.

Unlike the owners of family businesses, the top management of a large corporation does not generally own a large share of the firm's stock, so large corporations have a **separation of ownership from control**. Although the shareholders actually own the firm, the top management controls the firm's day-to-day operations. Because top managers own only a small percentage of the firm's stock, they may decrease the firm's profits by spending money to purchase private jets or schedule management meetings at luxurious resorts. Economists refer to the conflict between the interests of shareholders and the interests of the top management as a **principal–agent problem**.[1] This problem occurs when agents—in this case, a firm's top management—pursue their own interests rather than the interests of the principal who hired them—in this case, the shareholders

Corporate governance The way in which a corporation is structured and the effect that structure has on the corporation's behavior.

Separation of ownership from control A situation in a corporation in which the top management, rather than the shareholders, controls day-to-day operations.

Principal–agent problem A problem caused by an agent pursuing his own interests rather than the interests of the principal who hired him.

[1]In Chapter 7, we saw that the principal–agent problem arises from moral hazard that can occur because of asymmetric information. In this case, the asymmetric information involves top managers knowing more about how the firm is actually run than do the firm's shareholders.

of the corporation. To reduce the effect of the principal–agent problem, many boards of directors in the 1990s began to tie the salaries of top managers to the profits of the firm or to the price of the firm's stock. They hoped this step would give top managers an incentive to make the firm as profitable as possible, thereby benefiting its shareholders. Sometimes, though, top managers act in ways that increase the profits of the firm in the short run—and the salaries and bonuses of the top managers—but that actually reduce the profits of the firm in the long run.   MyEconLab Concept Check

Solved Problem 8.2

MyEconLab Interactive Animation

Should a Firm's CEO Also Be the Chairman of the Board?

James Dimon has served as both CEO of JP Morgan Chase bank and the chairman of the firm's board of directors. A resolution at the 2013 shareholders' meeting proposed separating the two positions so that one person could not serve in both roles. Jeffrey Sonnenfeld, a professor at the Yale School of Management, argued against the resolution, contending that it is easier for a CEO to provide strong leadership to a firm if he or she is also the chairman of the board: "In the town square of villages in almost every nation, there is a statue celebrating not a board committee but a courageous individual leader." Briefly discuss whether you believe the shareholders of JP Morgan Chase should have approved the resolution.

Solving the Problem

Step 1: **Review the chapter material.** This problem is about the principal–agent problem, so you may want to review the section "Corporate Structure and Corporate Governance" on page 241.

Step 2: **Answer the question by discussing the pros and cons of having the positions of CEO and chairman of the board held by different people.** Corporations face a principal–agent problem because their top managers run the firm but rarely own more than a small amount of the firm's stock. This separation of ownership from control may result in CEOs taking actions that are in their interests but not in the interest of the shareholders.

The argument in favor of having two people fill these positions is that the role of the board of directors is to monitor the CEO and other top managers. If the CEO runs the board of directors as its chair, it may be more difficult for the board to effectively monitor that person. Jeffrey Sonnenfeld and others argue, though, that unless the CEO is also the chairman, the CEO will lack the undivided authority to make decisions and successfully lead the firm.

Economists disagree about how to structure a corporation: Some economists argue that the CEO should not also serve as chairman, while other economists recommend that one person should fill both roles.

Extra Credit: JP Morgan Chase's shareholders rejected the proposal to require different people to serve in the two positions. Fewer than 25 percent of the 500 largest U.S. firms have an independent director serving as chairman of the board.

Source: Jeffrey A. Sonnenfeld, "The Jamie Dimon Witch Hunt," *New York Times*, May 8, 2013.

MyEconLab Study Plan

Your Turn: For more practice, do related problems 2.7 and 2.8 on page 257 at the end of this chapter.

8.3 LEARNING OBJECTIVE

Explain how firms raise the funds they need to operate and expand.

How Firms Raise Funds

Owners and managers of firms try to earn a profit. To earn a profit, a firm must raise funds to pay for its operations, including paying its employees and buying or renting computers and other machinery and equipment. Indeed, a central challenge for anyone running a firm, whether that person is a sole proprietor or a top manager of a large corporation, is raising the funds needed to operate and expand the business. Suppose you decide to open an online social networking site using $100,000 you have saved in a bank. You use the $100,000 to rent an office for your firm, buy computers, and pay other startup expenses. Your firm is a great success, and you decide to expand it by moving to a larger office and buying more computers. As the owner of a small business, you can raise the funds for this expansion in three ways:

1. If you are making a profit, you could reinvest the profits back into your firm. Profits that are reinvested in a firm rather than taken out of the firm and paid to the firm's owners are referred to as *retained earnings*.
2. You could raise funds by recruiting additional owners to invest in the firm. This arrangement would increase the firm's *financial capital*.
3. Finally, you could borrow the funds from relatives, friends, or a bank.

The managers of a large public firm have some additional ways to raise funds, as we will see in the next section.

Sources of External Funds

Unless firms rely on retained earnings, they have to raise the *external funds* they need from those who have funds available to invest. It is the role of an economy's *financial system* to transfer funds from savers to borrowers.

Most firms raise external funds in two ways. The first way, called **indirect finance**, relies on financial intermediaries such as banks. If you put $1,000 in a checking account or in a certificate of deposit (CD), the bank will loan most of those funds to borrowers. The bank will combine your funds with those of other depositors and, for example, make a $100,000 loan to a local business. Small businesses rely heavily on bank loans as their primary source of external funds.

> **Indirect finance** A flow of funds from savers to borrowers through financial intermediaries such as banks. Intermediaries raise funds from savers to lend to firms (and other borrowers).

A second way for firms to acquire external funds is through *financial markets*. Raising funds in these markets, such as the New York Stock Exchange on Wall Street in New York City, is called **direct finance**. Direct finance usually takes the form of the borrower selling the lender a *financial security*. A financial security is a document—sometimes in electronic form—that states the terms under which the funds are passed from the buyer of the security (who is lending funds) to the borrower. *Bonds* and *stocks* are the two main types of financial securities. Typically, only large corporations are able to sell bonds and stocks on financial markets. Investors are generally unwilling to buy securities issued by small and medium-sized firms because the investors lack sufficient information on the financial health of smaller firms.

> **Direct finance** A flow of funds from savers to firms through financial markets, such as the New York Stock Exchange.

Bonds Bonds are financial securities that represent promises to repay a fixed amount of funds. When Apple sells a bond to raise funds, it promises to pay the purchaser of the bond an interest payment each year for the term of the bond, as well as a payment of the loan amount, or the *principal*, at the end of the term. Apple may need to raise many millions of dollars to build new offices, but each individual bond has a principal, or *face value*, of $1,000, which is the amount each bond purchaser is lending Apple. So, Apple must sell many bonds to raise all the funds it needs. Suppose Apple promises it will pay interest of $40 per year to anyone who buys one of its bonds. The interest payments on a bond are called **coupon payments**. The **interest rate** is the cost of borrowing funds, usually expressed as a percentage of the amount borrowed. We can calculate the interest rate on the bond, called the *coupon rate*, by dividing the coupon by the face value of the bond. In this case, the coupon rate is:

> **Bond** A financial security that represents a promise to repay a fixed amount of funds.

$$\frac{\$40}{\$1,000} = 0.04, \text{ or } 4\%.$$

> **Coupon payment** An interest payment on a bond.
>
> **Interest rate** The cost of borrowing funds, usually expressed as a percentage of the amount borrowed.

Many bonds that corporations issue have terms, or *maturities*, of 30 years. In this example, if you bought a bond from Apple, Apple would pay you $40 per year for 30 years, and at the end of the thirtieth year, Apple would repay the $1,000 principal to you.

The interest rate that a borrower selling a bond has to pay depends on how likely bond buyers—investors—think that the bond seller is to default, or not make the promised coupon or principal payments. The higher the *default risk* on a bond, the higher the interest rate will be. For example, investors see the federal government as being very unlikely to default on its bonds, so federal government bonds pay a lower interest rate than do bonds of a firm such as Apple. In turn, Apple pays a lower interest rate on its bonds than does a corporation that investors believe is not as likely to make its bond payments.

Making the Connection
MyEconLab Video

The Rating Game: Is the U.S. Treasury Likely to Default on Its Bonds?

Federal regulations require that before they can sell bonds to investors, firms and governments must first have bonds rated by one of the credit-rating agencies. The three largest rating agencies are Moody's Investors Service, Standard & Poor's Corporation, and Fitch Ratings. These private firms rate bonds by giving them letter grades—AAA or Aaa being the highest—that reflect the likelihood that the firm or government will be able to make the payments on the bond. The following table shows the ratings:

	Moody's Investors Service	Standard & Poor's (S&P)	Fitch Ratings	Meaning of the Ratings
Investment-grade bonds	Aaa	AAA	AAA	Highest credit quality
	Aa	AA	AA	Very high credit quality
	A	A	A	High credit quality
	Baa	BBB	BBB	Good credit quality
Non-investment-grade bonds	Ba	BB	BB	Speculative
	B	B	B	Highly speculative
	Caa	CCC	CCC	Substantial default risk
	Ca	CC	CC	Very high levels of default risk
	C	C	C	Exceptionally high levels of default risk
	—	D	D	Default

Note: The entries in the "Meaning of the Ratings" column are slightly modified from those that Fitch uses. The other two rating agencies have similar descriptions. For each rating from Aa to Caa, Moody's adds a numerical modifier of 1, 2, or 3. The rating Aa1 is higher than the rating Aa2, and the rating Aa2 is higher than the rating Aa3. Similarly, Standard & Poor's and Fitch Ratings add a plus (+) or minus (−) sign. The rating AA+ is higher than the rating AA, and the rating AA is higher than the rating AA−.

Source: *Money, Banking, and the Financial System*, 2nd edition by R. Glenn Hubbard and Anthony P. O'Brien. Copyright © 2014 by Pearson Education, Inc. Reprinted and electronically reproduced by permission of Pearson Education, Inc., Upper Saddle River, New Jersey.

Investors can use the ratings in deciding how much risk they are willing to accept when buying a bond. Generally, the lower the rating, the higher the interest rate an investor will receive, but also the higher the risk that the issuer of the bond will default.

The rating agencies charge firms and governments—rather than investors—for their services. This arrangement raises the question of whether rating agencies face a conflict of interest. Because firms issuing bonds can choose which of the agencies to hire to rate their bonds, the agencies may have an incentive to give higher ratings than might be justified in order to keep the firms' business. During the housing boom of the mid-2000s, some financial firms issued *mortgage-backed bonds*. These bonds were similar to regular corporate bonds except that the interest payments came from mortgage loans people had taken out to buy houses. The money from those mortgage payments was passed along to investors who had bought the mortgage-backed bonds. The rating agencies gave many of these bonds AAA ratings, even though when housing prices began to decline in 2006, many homeowners stopped making their mortgage payments and the value of the bonds declined sharply. Some economists and policymakers believe the rating agencies provided the high ratings primarily to ensure that the firms that issued the bonds would continue to hire them.

Standard & Poor's (S&P) became involved in another controversy in August 2011, when it downgraded U.S. Treasury bonds from AAA to AA+. Never before had a rating agency given Treasury bonds less than a AAA rating. S&P downgraded the Treasury's rating because of the size of the federal government's budget deficit. Whenever the federal government runs a budget deficit, the Treasury must borrow an amount equal to the deficit by issuing bonds. In 2011, the federal government was spending much more than it was collecting in taxes, which resulted in a large budget deficit. The budget deficit reflected the lower tax receipts and increased government spending resulting from the 2007–2009 economic recession. But forecasts from the U.S. Congressional Budget Office indicated that even after the effects of the recession had disappeared, large budget deficits would remain because spending on Social Security, Medicare, Medicaid, and other government programs were expected to increase faster than tax revenues. When prolonged negotiations between President Barack Obama and Congress failed to make much of a dent in the problem, S&P announced the rating downgrade. In the months following the announcement, interest rates on Treasury bonds actually fell rather than rose, as might have been expected if investors had believed that a default was possible.

So, is it likely that the U.S. Treasury will default on its bonds? S&P argued that while a default is still unlikely, the continuing large deficits increased the chance that someday the Treasury might not make the interest payments on its bonds. As the federal deficit shrank during 2013, most economists believed that the chance of a Treasury default was low. Like the Ghost of Christmas Yet to Come in Charles Dickens's *A Christmas Carol*, S&P was giving a warning of something that might happen rather than something that necessarily must happen.

Sources: Mary Williams Walsh, "Credit Ratings Services Give Mixed Reviews to Tax Deal," *New York Times*, January 3, 2013; and Andrew Ross Sorkin, "S.E.C. Urges Changes to Ratings-Agency Rules," *New York Times*, August 29, 2010.

Your Turn: Test your understanding by doing related problem 3.8 on page 258 at the end of this chapter.

MyEconLab Study Plan

Stocks When you buy a newly issued bond from a firm, you are lending funds to that firm. When you buy **stock** issued by a firm, you are actually buying part ownership of the firm. When a corporation sells stock, it is doing the same thing the owner of a small business does when he or she takes on a partner: The firm is increasing its financial capital by bringing additional owners into the firm. Any one shareholder usually owns only a small fraction of the total shares of stock issued by a corporation.

Stock A financial security that represents partial ownership of a firm.

Many small investors buy shares of *mutual funds* rather than directly buying stocks of companies. Mutual funds, such as Fidelity Investment's Magellan Fund, sell shares to investors and use the funds to invest in a portfolio of financial assets, such as stocks and bonds. By buying shares in a mutual fund, small investors reduce the costs they would pay to buy many individual stocks and bonds. Small savers who have only enough money to buy a few individual stocks and bonds can also lower their investment risk by buying shares in a mutual fund because most mutual funds hold a large number of stocks and bonds. If a firm issuing a stock or bond declares bankruptcy, causing the stock or bond to lose all of its value, the effect on a mutual fund's portfolio is likely to be small. The effect might be devastating, though, to a small investor who had invested most of his or her savings in the stock or bond. Because mutual funds are willing to buy back their shares at any time, they also provide savers with easy access to their money.

A shareholder is entitled to a portion of the corporation's profits, if there are any. Corporations generally keep some of their profits as retained earnings to finance future expansion. The remaining profits are paid to shareholders as **dividends**. If a firm uses its retained earnings to grow and earn economic profits, its share price rises, which provides a *capital gain* for investors. If a corporation is unable to make a profit, it usually does not pay a dividend. Under the law, corporations must make payments on any debt they have before making payments to their owners. That is, a corporation must make promised payments to bondholders before it can make any dividend payments to shareholders. Unlike bonds, stocks do not have a maturity date, so the firm is not obliged to return the investor's funds at any particular date.

Dividends Payments by a corporation to its shareholders.

MyEconLab Concept Check

Stock and Bond Markets Provide Capital—and Information

The original purchasers of stocks and bonds may resell them to other investors. In fact, most of the buying and selling of stocks and bonds that takes place each day involves investors reselling existing stocks and bonds to each other rather than corporations selling new stocks and bonds to investors. The buyers and sellers of stocks and bonds together make up the *stock and bond markets*. There is no single place where stocks and bonds are bought and sold. Some trading of stocks and bonds takes place in buildings known as *exchanges*, such as the New York Stock Exchange or the Tokyo Stock Exchange. In the United States, the stocks and bonds of the largest corporations are traded on the New York Stock Exchange. The development of computer technology has spread the trading of stocks and bonds outside exchanges to *securities dealers* linked by computers. These dealers comprise the *over-the-counter market*. The stocks of many computer and other high-technology firms—including Apple, Google, and Facebook—are traded in the most important of the over-the-counter markets, the *National Association of Securities Dealers Automated Quotations* system, which is referred to by its acronym, NASDAQ.

Shares of stock represent claims on the profits of the firms that issue them. Therefore, as the fortunes of the firms change and they earn more or less profit, the prices of the stock the firms have issued should also change. Similarly, bonds represent claims to receive coupon payments and one final payment of the principal. Therefore, a particular bond that was issued in the past may have its price go up or down, depending on whether the coupon payments being offered on newly issued bonds are higher or lower than those on existing bonds. If you hold a bond with a coupon of $30 per year, and newly issued bonds have coupons of $40 per year, the price of your bond will fall because it is less attractive to investors. The price of a bond will also be affected by changes in *default risk*, which reflects investors' perceptions of the issuing firm's ability to make the coupon payments. For example, if investors begin to believe that a firm may soon go out of business and stop making coupon payments to its bondholders, the price of the firm's bonds will fall to very low levels.

Changes in the value of a firm's stocks and bonds offer important information for a firm's managers, as well as for investors. An increase in the stock price means that investors are

Don't Let This Happen to You

When Facebook Shares Are Sold, Facebook Doesn't Get the Money

Facebook is a popular investment, with investors buying and selling shares often as their views about the value of the firm shift. That's great for Facebook, right? Think of Facebook collecting all that money as shares change hands and the stock price goes up. *Wrong.* Facebook raises funds in a primary market, but its shares trade in a secondary market. Those trades don't put money into Facebook's hands, but they do give important information to the firm's managers. Let's see why.

Primary markets are those in which firms sell newly issued stocks and bonds to initial buyers. Businesses can raise funds in a primary financial market in two ways— by borrowing (selling bonds) or selling shares of stock— which result in different types of claims on the borrowing firm's future income. Although you may hear about the stock market fluctuations every day in news updates, bonds actually account for more of the funds raised by borrowers. The total value of bonds in the United States is typically about twice the value of stocks.

In *secondary markets*, stocks and bonds that have already been issued are sold by one investor to another. If Facebook sells shares to the public, it is turning to a primary market for new funds. Once Facebook shares are issued, investors trade the shares in the secondary market. Facebook does not receive any new funds when its shares are traded on secondary markets. The initial seller of a stock or bond raises funds from an investor only in the primary market. Secondary markets convey information to firms' managers and investors by determining the price of stocks and bonds. For example, a major increase in Facebook's stock price conveys the market's good feelings about the firm, and the firm may decide to raise funds to expand. So, secondary markets are valuable sources of information for corporations that are considering raising funds.

Primary and secondary markets are both important, but they play different roles. As an investor, you principally trade stocks and bonds in a secondary market. As a corporate manager, you may help decide how to raise new funds to expand the firm where you work.

MyEconLab Study Plan

Your Turn: Test your understanding by doing related problem 3.11 on page 258 at the end of this chapter.

more optimistic about the firm's profit prospects, and the firm's managers might want to expand the firm's operations as a result. By contrast, a decrease in the firm's stock price indicates that investors are less optimistic about the firm's profit prospects, so management may want to shrink the firm's operations. Similarly, changes in the value of the firm's bonds imply changes in the cost of external funds to finance the firm's investment in research and development or in new factories. A higher bond price indicates a lower cost of new external funds, while a lower bond price indicates a higher cost of new external funds.   MyEconLab Concept Check

Why Do Stock Prices Fluctuate So Much?

The performance of the U.S. stock market is often measured using *stock market indexes.* Stock market indexes are averages of stock prices, with the value of the index set equal to 100 in a particular year, called the *base year.* Because the stock indexes are intended to show movements in prices from one year to the next, rather than the actual dollar values of the underlying stocks, the year chosen for the base year is unimportant. Figure 8.2 shows movements from January 1996 to June 2013 in the three most widely followed stock indexes:

- The Dow Jones Industrial Average, which is an index of the stock prices of 30 large U.S. corporations.

- The S&P 500, which is an index prepared by Standard & Poor's Corporation and includes the stock prices of 500 large U.S. firms.

- The NASDAQ Composite Index, which includes the stock prices of more than 4,000 firms whose shares are traded in the NASDAQ stock market. NASDAQ is an over-the-counter market, meaning that buying and selling on NASDAQ is carried out between dealers who are linked together by computer. The listings on NASDAQ are dominated by high-tech firms such as Apple, Facebook, and Google.

As we have seen, ownership of a firm's stock represents a claim on the firm's profits. So, the larger the firm's profits are, the higher its stock price will be. When the overall economy is expanding, incomes, employment, and spending will all increase, as will corporate profits. When the economy is in a recession, incomes, employment, and spending will fall, as will corporate profits. Therefore, we would expect that stock prices will rise when the economy is expanding and fall when the economy is in recession. We see this pattern reflected in the three stock market indexes shown in Figure 8.2. All three indexes follow a roughly similar pattern: increases in stock prices during the

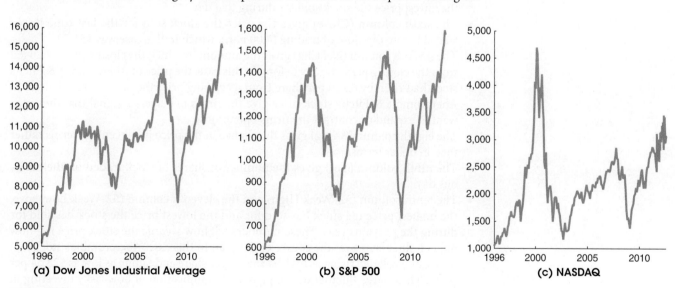

MyEconLab Real-time data

Figure 8.2   Movements in Stock Market Indexes, January 1996 to June 2013

The performance of the U.S. stock market is often measured by market indexes, which are averages of stock prices. The three most important indexes are the Dow Jones Industrial Average, the S&P 500, and the NASDAQ. During the period from 1996 to 2013, the three indexes followed similar patterns, rising when the U.S. economy was expanding and falling when the economy was in recession. Note that in all three panels the vertical axis does not start at zero.

economic expansion of the late 1990s, declines after the "dot-com crash" of 2000 and the recession of 2001, increases from late 2001 to late 2007, declines as the U.S. economy entered a recession at the end of 2007, and then increases beginning in early 2009.

The stock prices of many early Internet companies soared in the late 1990s, as some analysts made what turned out to be overly optimistic predictions about how rapidly online retailing would grow. In 2000, when investors came to believe that many dot-coms would never be profitable, their stock prices crashed. Because the NASDAQ is dominated by high-tech stocks, it experienced greater swings during the dot-com boom and bust of the late 1990s and early 2000s than did the other two indexes. The sharp declines in all three indexes beginning in late 2007 reflected the severity of the recession that began in December of that year. The severity of the recession was due in part to problems with financial firms, which we will discuss later in this chapter. During 2013, as recovery from the recession continued, the Dow Jones Industrial Average and the S&P 500 both reached their highest values ever.   MyEconLab Concept Check

---

Making the Connection
MyEconLab Video

Following Abercrombie & Fitch's Stock Price in the Financial Pages

If you read the online stock listings on the *Wall Street Journal's* Web site or on another site, you will notice that the listings pack into a small space a lot of information about what happened to stocks during the previous day's trading. The following figure reproduces a small portion of the listings from the *Wall Street Journal* on June 8, 2013, for stocks listed on the New York Stock Exchange. The listings provide information on the buying and selling of stocks of five firms during the previous day. Let's focus on the highlighted listing for Abercrombie & Fitch, the clothing store, and examine the information in each column:

- The first column gives the name of the company.
- The second column gives the firm's "ticker" symbol (ANF), which you may have seen scrolling along the bottom of the screen on cable financial news channels.
- The third column (Open) gives the price (in dollars) of the stock at the time when trading began, which is 9:30 A.M., on the New York Stock Exchange. Abercrombie & Fitch opened for trading at a price of $51.11.
- The fourth column (High) and the fifth column (Low) give the highest price and the lowest price the stock sold for during that day.
- The sixth column (Close) gives the price the stock sold for the last time it was traded before the close of trading (4:00 P.M.), which in this case was $51.70.
- The seventh column (Net Chg) gives the amount by which the closing price changed from the closing price the day before. In this case, the price of Abercrombie & Fitch's stock had risen by $2.10 per share from its closing price the day before. Changes in Abercrombie & Fitch's stock price give the firm's managers a signal that they may want to expand or contract the firm's operations.
- The eighth column (%Chg) gives the change in the price in percentage terms rather than in dollar terms.
- The ninth column (Vol) gives the number of shares of stock traded on the previous day.
- The tenth column (52-Week High) and the eleventh column (52-Week Low) give, the highest price the stock has sold for and the lowest price the stock has sold for during the previous year. These numbers tell how *volatile* the stock price is—how much it fluctuates over the course of the year. In this case, Abercrombie's stock had been quite volatile, rising as high as $55.23 per share and falling as low as $28.64 per share. These large fluctuations in price are an indication of how risky investing in the stock market can be.
- The twelfth column (Div) gives the dividend, expressed in dollars. In this case, 0.80 means that Abercrombie paid a dividend of $0.80 per share.

- The thirteenth column (Yield) gives the *dividend yield*, which is calculated by dividing the dividend by the *closing price* of the stock—the price at which Abercrombie's stock last sold before the close of trading on the previous day.
- The fourteenth column (PE) gives the *P–E ratio* (or *price–earnings ratio*), which is calculated by dividing the price of the firm's stock by its earnings per share. (Remember that because firms retain some earnings, earnings per share is not necessarily the same as dividends per share.) Abercrombie's P–E ratio was 27, meaning that its price per share was 27 times its earnings per share. So, you would have to pay $27 to buy $1 of Abercrombie & Fitch's earnings.
- The final column (Year-to-Date %Chg) gives the percentage change in the price of the stock from the beginning of the year to the previous day. In this case, the price of Abercrombie's stock had increased by 7.8 percent since the beginning of 2013.

	Symbol	Open	High	Low	Close	Net Chg	%Chg	Vol	52-Week High	52-Week Low	Div	Yield	PE	Year-to-Date % Chg
Abbott Laboratories	ABT	36.95	37.55	36.90	37.51	0.87	2.37	5,971,945	38.77	29.22	0.56	1.49	11.25	19.69
AbbVie	ABBV	43.72	44.27	43.50	44.00	0.50	1.15	5,421,935	48.00	32.51	1.60	3.64	...	28.81
Abercrombie & Fitch	ANF	51.11	52.25	51.07	51.70	2.10	4.23	2,060,682	55.23	28.64	0.80	1.55	27.27	7.78
ABM Industries	ABM	24.85	24.90	24.51	24.66	0.02	0.08	196,680	26.38	17.85	0.60	2.43	18.54	23.61
Acadia Realty Trust	AKR	26.44	26.64	25.96	26.40	0.05	0.19	415,048	29.32	22.27	0.84	3.18	...	5.26

Source: "Closing Quote Tables" from *Wall Street Journal*. Copyright © 2013 by Dow Jones & Company, Inc. Reproduced with permission of Dow Jones & Company, Inc.

Your Turn: Test your understanding by doing related problems 3.12 and 3.13 on page 258 at the end of this chapter.

MyEconLab Study Plan

Using Financial Statements to Evaluate a Corporation

8.4 LEARNING OBJECTIVE

Understand the information provided in corporations' financial statements.

To raise funds, a firm's managers must persuade potential lenders or investors that it will be profitable. Before a firm can sell new issues of stocks or bonds, it must first provide investors and financial regulators with information about its finances. To borrow from a bank, the firm must also provide the bank with financial information.

In most high-income countries, government agencies require firms to disclose specific financial information to the public before they are allowed to sell securities such as stocks or bonds in financial markets. In the United States, the Securities and Exchange Commission (SEC) requires publicly owned firms to report their performance in financial statements prepared using standard accounting methods, often referred to as *generally accepted accounting principles*. Such disclosure reduces the cost to investors of gathering information about firms, but it doesn't eliminate these costs—for two reasons. First, some firms may be too young to have much information for potential investors to evaluate. Second, managers may try to present the required information in the most favorable way so that investors will overvalue their securities.

Private firms also collect information on business borrowers and sell the information to lenders and investors. If the information-gathering firms do a good job, lenders and investors purchasing the information will be better able to judge the quality of borrowing firms. Some firms—including Moody's Investors Service, Standard & Poor's Corporation, Value Line, and Dun & Bradstreet—collect information from businesses and sell it to subscribers. Buyers include individual investors, libraries, and financial intermediaries. You can find some of these publications in your college library or through online information services.

What kind of information do investors and firm managers need? A firm must answer three basic questions: What to produce? How to produce it? What price to charge? To answer these questions, a firm's managers need two pieces of information: The first is the firm's revenues and costs, and the second is the value of the property and other assets the firm owns and the firm's debts, or other **liabilities**, that it owes to households and other firms. Potential investors in the firm also need this information to decide whether to buy the firm's stocks or bonds. The information can be found in the firm's *financial statements*, principally its income statement and balance sheet, which we discuss next.

Liability Anything owed by a person or a firm.

MyEconLab Concept Check

The Income Statement

A firm's **income statement** shows its revenues, costs, and profit over a period of time. Corporations issue annual income statements, although the 12-month *fiscal year* covered may be different from the calendar year to better represent the seasonal pattern of the business. We explore income statements in greater detail in the appendix to this chapter.

Income statement A financial statement that shows a firm's revenues, costs, and profit over a period of time.

Accounting Profit An income statement shows a firm's revenue, costs, and profit for the firm's fiscal year. To determine profitability, the income statement starts with the firm's revenue and subtracts its operating expenses and taxes paid. The remainder, *net income*, is the **accounting profit** of the firm.

Accounting profit A firm's net income, measured as revenue minus operating expenses and taxes paid.

Economic Profit Accounting profit provides information on a firm's current net income, measured according to accepted accounting standards. Accounting profit is not, however, the ideal measure of a firm's profits because it neglects some of the firm's costs. *Economic profit* provides a better indication than accounting profit of how successful a firm is because economic profit is calculated using all of a firm's costs. Firms making an economic profit will remain in business and may even expand. Firms making an *economic loss* are unlikely to remain in business in the long run. To understand how economic profit is calculated, remember that economists always measure cost as *opportunity cost*. The **opportunity cost** of any activity is the highest-valued alternative that must be given up to engage in that activity. Costs are either *explicit* or *implicit*. When a firm spends money, an **explicit cost** results. If a firm incurs an opportunity cost but does not spend money, an **implicit cost** results. For example, firms incur an explicit labor cost when they pay wages to employees. Firms have many other explicit costs as well, such as the cost of the electricity used to light their buildings or the costs of advertising or insurance.

Opportunity cost The highest-valued alternative that must be given up to engage in an activity.

Explicit cost A cost that involves spending money.

Implicit cost A nonmonetary opportunity cost.

Some costs are implicit, however. The most important of these is the opportunity cost to investors of the funds they have invested in the firm. Economists use the term *normal rate of return* to refer to the minimum amount that investors must earn on the funds they invest in a firm, expressed as a percentage of the amount invested. If a firm fails to provide investors with at least a normal rate of return, it will not be able to remain in business over the long run because investors will not continue to invest their funds in the firm. For example, Borders was once the second-largest bookstore chain in the United States and a very profitable firm, with stock that sold for more than $40 per share. By 2010, investors became convinced that the firm's difficulty competing with Amazon and other online booksellers and its loss of sales to e-books meant that the firm would never be able to provide investors with a normal rate of return. Many investors expected that the firm would eventually have to declare bankruptcy, and as a result, the price of Border's stock plummeted to less than $1 per share. Within a year, the firm declared bankruptcy, and its remaining assets were sold off. The return (in dollars) that investors require to continue investing in a firm is a true cost to the firm and should be subtracted from the firm's revenues to calculate its profits.

The rate of return that investors require to continue investing in a firm varies from firm to firm. If the investment is risky—as would be the case with a biotechnology startup—investors may require a high rate of return to compensate them for the risk. Investors in firms in more established industries, such as electric utilities, may require lower rates of return. The exact rate of return investors require to invest in any particular firm is difficult to calculate, which also makes it difficult for an accountant to include the return as a cost on an income statement. Firms have other implicit costs, besides the return investors require, that can also be difficult to calculate. As a result, the rules of accounting generally require that only explicit costs be included in the firm's financial records. *Economic costs* include both explicit costs *and* implicit costs. **Economic profit** is equal to a firm's revenues minus its economic costs. Because accounting profit excludes some implicit costs, it is larger than economic profit.   MyEconLab Concept Check

Economic profit A firm's revenues minus all of its implicit and explicit costs.

The Balance Sheet

A firm's **balance sheet** sums up its financial position on a particular day, usually the end of a quarter or year. Recall that an asset is anything of value that a firm owns and a liability is a debt or an obligation owed by a firm. Subtracting the value of a firm's liabilities from the value of its assets leaves its *net worth*. We can think of the net worth as what the firm's owners would be left with if the firm were closed, its assets were sold, and its liabilities were paid off. Investors can determine a firm's net worth by inspecting its balance sheet. We analyze a balance sheet in more detail in the appendix to this chapter.   MyEconLab Concept Check

Balance sheet A financial statement that sums up a firm's financial position on a particular day, usually the end of a quarter or year.

MyEconLab Study Plan

Corporate Governance Policy and the Financial Crisis of 2007–2009

8.5 LEARNING OBJECTIVE

Discuss the role that corporate governance problems may have played in the financial crisis of 2007–2009.

A firm's financial statements provide important information on the firm's ability to create value for investors and the economy. Accurate and easy-to-understand financial statements are inputs to decisions by the firm's managers and by investors. In fact, the information in financial statements helps guide resource allocation in the economy.

Firms disclose financial statements in periodic filings to the federal government and in *annual reports* to shareholders. An investor is more likely to buy a firm's stock if the firm's income statement shows a large after-tax profit and if its balance sheet shows a large net worth. The top management of a firm has at least two reasons to attract investors and keep the firm's stock price high. First, a higher stock price increases the funds the firm can raise when it sells a given amount of stock. Second, to reduce the principal–agent problem, boards of directors often tie the salaries of top managers to the firm's stock price or to the profitability of the firm.

Top managers clearly have an incentive to maximize the profits reported on the income statement and the net worth reported on the balance sheet. If top managers make good decisions, the firm's profits will be high, and the firm's assets will be large relative to its liabilities. Problems that surfaced during the early 2000s, however, revealed that some top managers have inflated profits and hidden liabilities that should have been listed on their balance sheets. At other firms, managers took on more risk than they disclosed to investors. We will explore recent problems with corporate governance and the government's reaction to these problems by discussing the accounting scandals of the early 2000s and problems that many financial firms encountered during 2007–2009.

The Accounting Scandals of the Early 2000s

In the early 2000s, the top managers of several well-known firms, including Enron, an energy trading firm, and WorldCom, a telecommunications firm, falsified their firms' financial statements in order to mislead investors about how profitable the firms actually were. Several top managers were sentenced to long jail terms, and some of the firms, including Enron, went out of business.

How was it possible for corporations such as Enron and WorldCom to falsify their financial statements? The federal government regulates how financial statements are prepared, but this regulation cannot by itself guarantee the accuracy of the statements. All firms that issue stock to the public have certified public accountants working for outside firms *audit* their financial statements. Unfortunately, as the Enron and WorldCom scandals revealed, top managers who are determined to deceive investors about the true financial condition of their firms can also deceive outside auditors.

To guard against future scandals, new federal legislation was enacted in 2002. The landmark *Sarbanes-Oxley Act* of 2002 requires that CEOs personally certify the accuracy of financial statements. The Sarbanes-Oxley Act also requires that financial analysts and auditors disclose whether any conflicts of interest might exist that would limit their independence in evaluating a firm's financial condition. On balance, most observers acknowledge that the Sarbanes-Oxley Act increased confidence in the U.S. corporate governance system. However, as we will discuss in the next section, problems during 2007–2009 at financial firms again raised questions of whether corporations were adequately disclosing information to investors. MyEconLab Concept Check

The Financial Crisis of 2007–2009

Beginning in 2007 and lasting into 2009, the U.S. economy suffered the worst financial crisis since the Great Depression of the 1930s. At the heart of the crisis was a problem in the market for home mortgages. When people buy houses, they typically borrow the money by taking out a mortgage loan from a bank or another financial institution. The house they are buying is pledged as collateral for the loan, meaning that the bank can take possession of the house and sell it if the borrower defaults by failing to make the payments on the loan.

For many years, a bank or other financial institution granting a mortgage would keep the loan until the borrower had paid it off. Beginning in the 1970s, financial institutions began *securitizing* some mortgage loans, which means that groups of mortgages were bundled together and sold to investors. These *mortgage-backed securities* are very similar to bonds in that the investor who buys one receives regular interest payments, which in this case come from the payments being made on the original mortgage loans. At first, the securitization process was carried out by the Federal National Mortgage Association ("Fannie Mae") and the Federal Home Loan Mortgage Corporation ("Freddie Mac"), which Congress had established to help increase the volume of lending in the home mortgage market. Fannie Mae and Freddie Mac would buy mortgages granted to creditworthy borrowers and bundle them into securities that were then sold to investors.

Beginning in the 1990s, private financial firms, primarily investment banks, started to securitize mortgages. By the early 2000s, many mortgages were being granted by banks and other financial institutions to "subprime" borrowers, whose credit histories include failures to make payments on bills, and "Alt-A" borrowers, who failed to document that their incomes were high enough to afford their mortgage payments. Both subprime and Alt-A borrowers were more likely to default on loans than were conventional borrowers. Fueled by the ease of obtaining a mortgage, housing prices in the United States soared before beginning a sharp downturn in mid-2006. By 2007, many borrowers—particularly subprime and Alt-A borrowers—began to default on their mortgages. These defaults were bad news for anyone owning mortgage-backed securities because the value of these securities depended on steady payments being made on the underlying mortgages. As prices of these securities plunged, many financial institutions suffered heavy losses, and some of the largest of them remained in business only because they received aid from the federal government.

During the financial crisis, many investors complained that they weren't aware of the riskiness of some of the assets—particularly mortgage-backed securities—on the balance sheets of financial firms. Some observers believed that the managers of many financial firms had intentionally misled investors about the riskiness of these assets. Others argued that the managers themselves had not understood how risky the assets were. In the fall of 2008, Fannie Mae and Freddie Mac were brought under direct control of the government. As the crisis passed, in July 2010, Congress overhauled the regulation of the financial system with the passage of the **Wall Street Reform and Consumer Protection Act**, referred to as the **Dodd-Frank Act**. Among its provisions, the act created the Consumer Financial Protection Bureau, housed in the Federal Reserve—the central bank of the United States—to write rules intended to protect consumers in their borrowing and investing activities. The act also established the Financial Stability Oversight Council, which includes representatives from all the major federal financial regulatory bodies, including the SEC and the Federal Reserve. The council is intended to identify and act on risks to the financial system. Economists are divided in their opinions about whether the Dodd-Frank Act will significantly reduce the risk of future financial crises.   MyEconLab Concept Check

Wall Street Reform and Consumer Protection Act (Dodd-Frank Act) Legislation passed during 2010 that was intended to reform regulation of the financial system.

Did Principal–Agent Problems Help Cause the 2007–2009 Financial Crisis?

As we have seen, the process of securitizing mortgages played an important role in the financial crisis of 2007–2009. Beginning in the 1990s, private investment banks began to securitize mortgages. Unlike commercial banks, whose main activities are accepting deposits and making loans, investment banks had traditionally concentrated on providing advice to corporations on selling new stocks and bonds and on *underwriting* the issuance of stocks and bonds by guaranteeing a price to the firm selling them. Investment banking is considered riskier than commercial banking because investment banks can suffer substantial losses on underwriting. To address this greater risk, Congress passed the *Glass-Steagall Act* in 1933. The act prevented financial firms from being both commercial banks and investment banks.

Some economists and policymakers argued that Glass-Steagall reduced competition for investment banking services by prohibiting commercial banks from offering these services. Congress repealed the Glass-Steagall Act in 1999, after which some commercial banks began engaging in investment banking. Many of the largest, best-known investment banks, such as Lehman Brothers, Bear Stearns, Goldman Sachs, Merrill Lynch, and Morgan Stanley, remained exclusively investment banks. The mortgage-backed securities originated by the investment banks were mostly sold to investors, but some were retained as investments by these firms. As a result, when the prices of these securities declined beginning in 2007, the investment banks suffered heavy losses. Lehman Brothers was forced to declare bankruptcy; Merrill Lynch and Bear Stearns were sold to commercial banks in deals arranged by the U.S. government; and Goldman Sachs and Morgan Stanley became bank holding companies, which allowed them to engage in commercial banking activity.

Why did investment banks take on so much risk by originating securities backed by mortgages granted to borrowers who had a high likelihood of defaulting on the loans? Michael Lewis, a financial journalist and former Wall Street bond salesman, has argued that a key reason was a change in how the investment banks were organized. Traditionally, large Wall Street investment banks had been organized as partnerships, but by 2000 they had all converted to being publicly traded corporations. As we have seen, in a partnership the funds of the relatively small group of owners are put directly at risk, and the principal–agent problem is reduced because there is little separation of ownership from control. With a publicly traded corporation, on the other hand, the principal–agent problem can be severe. Lewis argues:

> No investment bank owned by its employees would have . . . bought and held
> $50 billion in [exotic mortgage-backed securities]. . . . or even allow [these securities]
> to be sold to its customers. The hoped-for short-term gain would not have justified
> the long-term hit.

Issues of corporate governance will clearly continue to be a concern for economists, policymakers, and investors.   MyEconLab Concept Check

The Ups and Downs of Investing in Facebook

The first time a company sells stock, the sale is called an *initial public offering* (IPO). In 2012, Mark Zuckerberg announced his plan to take Facebook public with an IPO. There was widespread anticipation among both ordinary investors and institutional investors, such as managers of mutual funds. Many small investors hoped they would be getting in on the ground floor of a high-tech company whose profits—and stock price—would soar, as had happened with firms like Microsoft and Apple. Unfortunately, as the following graph shows, during the year following the IPO these investors were disappointed.

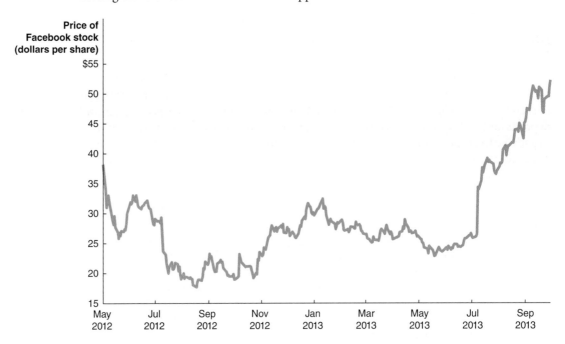

Investors who bought at the IPO price of $38 per share found that the price of the stock had fallen by 10 percent by the second day of trading. More than a year later, in mid-June 2013, Facebook stock was selling for about $23 per share, a decline of nearly 40 percent from the IPO price. But then the stock price began to rise and by October 2013 reached $54 per share, well above the IPO price. What explains the swings in Facebook's stock?

First, stock prices are very difficult to predict. As we have seen, the price of a firm's stock reflects the firm's profitability. But it is not just the firm's current profitability—which is known—that counts; the firm's future profitability—which is not known with certainty—matters even more. Investors are willing to pay much higher prices for stock issued by firms that they expect to be highly profitable in the future than they are for stock issued by firms that they expect will be less profitable. Many investors were willing to pay the IPO price of $38 per share because they expected that Facebook's rapid growth of the previous few years and increasing profits would continue into the future. In fact, though, Facebook was beginning to encounter difficulties because more people were accessing the site on their phones or tablets and Facebook was having trouble selling advertising on the mobile version of its site. When it appeared that Facebook's profits would not be increasing as rapidly as many investors had expected, the firm's stock price dropped well below the IPO level and stayed there. But then, unexpectedly, in July 2013 Facebook reported that its revenue from ads on the mobile version of its site had soared. As a result, Facebook's stock price rose more than 30 percent in one day.

There was still controversy, though, about Facebook's IPO. Some investors argued that Facebook was aware that its future profits were likely to be lower than expected and had made this information available before the IPO to the Morgan Stanley investment bank, which was underwriting the IPO, and to some investment analysts at other financial firms. Although Facebook and Morgan Stanley argued that Facebook had made all relevant information publicly available before the IPO, some investors filed lawsuits because they believed the company had taken advantage of them. The SEC launched an investigation. Morgan Stanley, without admitting or denying guilt, agreed to pay the state of Massachusetts a $5 million fine to settle a lawsuit brought by the secretary of the commonwealth of Massachusetts.

In late 2013, the outcome of the SEC's investigation of the Facebook IPO remained uncertain. Because Facebook's stock price eventually rose above its IPO price, investors had become less critical of the firm. Some investors, though, continued to doubt whether firms launching IPOs were fully disclosing information. The question remained important as Twitter and other firms prepared for IPOs.

Sources: Vindu Goel, "Facebook's Stock Soars Amid Rosy Growth Expectations," *New York Times*, July 25, 2013; Paul Vigna, "Facebook IPO Anniversary: No Sugarcoating It," *Wall Street Journal*, May 17, 2013; Jessica E. Lessin, Pui-Wing Tam, and Telis Demos, "Pace Picks Up on Tech IPOs," *Wall Street Journal*, May 16, 2013; and Susanne Craig and Ben Protess, "Massachusetts Fines Morgan Stanley over Facebook IPO," *New York Times*, December 17, 2012.

Your Turn: Test your understanding by doing related problem 5.6 on page 260 at the end of this chapter.

MyEconLab Study Plan

Continued from page 237

Economics in Your Life

Do Corporate Managers Act in the Best Interests of Shareholders?

At the beginning of the chapter, we asked you to consider two questions: Why is it difficult to get the managers of a firm to act in your interests rather than in their own? and Given this problem, should you ever take on the risk of buying stock? The reason managers may not act in shareholders' interest is that in large corporations there is separation of ownership from control: The shareholders own the firm, but the top managers actually control it. This results in the principal–agent problem discussed in the chapter. The principal–agent problem clearly adds to the risk you would face by buying stock rather than doing something safe with your money, such as putting it in the bank. But the rewards to owning stock can also be substantial, potentially earning you far more over the long run than if you keep your money in a bank account.

Buying the stock of well-known firms, such as Google, that are closely followed by Wall Street investment analysts helps to reduce the principal–agent problem. It is less likely that the managers of these firms will take actions that are clearly not in the best interests of shareholders because the managers' actions are difficult to conceal. Buying the stock of large, well-known firms certainly does not completely eliminate the risk from the principal–agent problem, however. Enron, WorldCom, and some of the other firms that were involved in the scandals discussed in this chapter were all well known and closely followed by Wall Street analysts, as were the large financial firms that ran into difficulties during the financial crisis of 2007–2009, but their stock turned out to be very poor investments.

Conclusion

In a market system, firms make independent decisions about which goods and services to produce, how to produce them, and what prices to charge. In modern high-income countries, such as the United States, large corporations account for a majority of the sales and profits earned by firms. Generally, the managers of these corporations do a good job of representing the interests of stockholders while providing the goods and services demanded by consumers. As the business scandals of the early 2000s and the problems with financial firms in 2007–2009 showed, however, the principal–agent problem can sometimes become severe. Economists debate the costs and benefits of regulations proposed to address these problems.

Visit MyEconLab for a news article and analysis related to the concepts in this chapter.

Chapter Summary and Problems

Key Terms

Accounting profit, p. 250	Direct finance, p. 243	Interest rate, p. 243	Separation of ownership from control, p. 241
Asset, p. 238	Dividends, p. 245	Liability, p. 250	Sole proprietorship, p. 238
Balance sheet, p. 251	Economic profit, p. 251	Limited liability, p. 238	Stock, p. 245
Bond, p. 243	Explicit cost, p. 250	Opportunity cost, p. 250	Wall Street Reform and Consumer Protection Act (Dodd-Frank Act), p. 253
Corporate governance, p. 241	Implicit cost, p. 250	Partnership, p. 238	
Corporation, p. 238	Income statement, p. 250	Principal–agent problem, p. 241	
Coupon payment, p. 243	Indirect finance, p. 243		

8.1 Types of Firms, pages 238–241

LEARNING OBJECTIVE: Categorize the major types of firms in the United States.

Summary

There are three types of firms: A **sole proprietorship** is a firm owned by a single individual and not organized as a corporation. A **partnership** is a firm owned jointly by two or more persons and not organized as a corporation. A **corporation** is a legal form of business that provides the owners with limited liability. An **asset** is anything of value owned by a person or a firm. The owners of sole proprietorships and partnerships have unlimited liability, which means there is no legal distinction between the personal assets of the owners of the business and the assets of the business. The owners of corporations have **limited liability**, which means they can never lose more than their investment in the firm. Although only 18 percent of firms are corporations, they account for the majority of revenue and profits earned by all firms.

MyEconLab   Visit **www.myeconlab.com** to complete these exercises online and get instant feedback.

Review Questions

1.1 What are the three major types of firms in the United States? Briefly discuss the most important characteristics of each type.

1.2 What is limited liability? Why does the government grant limited liability to the owners of corporations?

1.3 Why is limited liability more important for firms trying to raise funds from a large number of investors than for firms trying to raise funds from a small number of investors?

Problems and Applications

1.4 Suppose that shortly after graduating from college, you decide to start your own business. Will you be likely to organize the business as a sole proprietorship, a partnership, or a corporation? Explain your reasoning.

1.5 How would the establishment of limited liability for the owners of corporations affect the production possibilities frontier of a country over time?

1.6 Evaluate the following argument:

> I would like to invest in the stock market, but I think that buying shares of stock in a corporation is too risky. Suppose I buy $10,000 of Facebook stock, and the company ends up going bankrupt. Because as a stockholder I'm part owner of the company, I might be responsible for paying hundreds of thousands of dollars of the company's debts.

1.7 According to an article in the *Economist* magazine, historian David Faure has argued that the Chinese economy failed to grow rapidly during the nineteenth century because "family-run companies . . . could not raise sufficient capital to exploit the large-scale opportunities tied to the rise of the steam engine, notably railways and (with limited exceptions) global shipping and automated manufacturing." How did the United States solve the problem of firms raising enough funds to operate railroads and other large-scale businesses?
Source: "The PCCW Buy-Out in Court," *Economist*, April 21, 2009.

1.8 **[Related to the** Making the Connection **on page 240]** Why might large existing firms be more likely to focus on improving existing goods and services than on introducing new ones? Why might small new firms take the opposite approach?

1.9 **[Related to the** Making the Connection **on page 240]** Muhammad Yunus is a Ph.D. economist and winner of the Nobel Peace Prize in 2006. He founded the Grameen Bank and was an innovator in using microcredit, or small loans—often of $100 or less—to spur growth in developing countries. "Yunus realized that very small loans to very poor people could make a big difference" in the ability of entrepreneurs in developing countries to start new businesses. Why would the funding to start small firms be more difficult in developing countries than in the United States? How do most entrepreneurs in the United States obtain funds to start new firms?
Source: William Easterly, *The White Man's Burden: Why the West's Efforts to Aid the Rest Have Done So Much Ill and So Little Good*, New York: Penguin Books, 2006, pp. 58–59.

8.2 **The Structure of Corporations and the Principal-Agent Problem, pages 241–242**

LEARNING OBJECTIVE: Describe the typical management structure of corporations and understand the concepts of separation of ownership from control and the principal–agent problem.

Summary

Corporate governance refers to the way in which a corporation is structured and the effect a corporation's structure has on the firm's behavior. Most corporations have a similar management structure: The shareholders elect a board of directors that appoints the corporation's top managers, such as the chief executive officer (CEO). Because top managers often do not own a large fraction of the stock in the corporation, large corporations have a **separation of ownership from control**. When top managers have less incentive to increase the corporation's profits than to increase their own salaries and their own enjoyment, corporations can suffer from the **principal–agent problem**. The principal–agent problem exists when the principals—in this case, the shareholders of the corporation—have difficulty getting the agent—the corporation's top management—to carry out their wishes.

MyEconLab   Visit **www.myeconlab.com** to complete these exercises online and get instant feedback.

Review Questions

2.1 What does it mean to say that there is a separation of ownership from control in large corporations?

2.2 How is the separation of ownership from control related to the principal–agent problem?

2.3 Why is it important for a board of directors to have outside directors, as opposed to only inside directors?

Problems and Applications

2.4 The principal–agent problem arises almost everywhere in the business world, and it also crops up even closer to home. Discuss the principal–agent problem that exists in the college classroom. Who is the principal? Who is the agent? What potential conflicts in objectives exist between this principal and this agent?

2.5 In a public corporation, the principal–agent problem between ownership and top management results from asymmetric information. What information, if known, would prevent this principal–agent problem?

2.6 Sales personnel, whether selling life insurance, automobiles, or pharmaceuticals, typically get paid on commission instead of a straight hourly wage. How does paying a commission help solve the principal–agent problem between the owners of a business and the sales force?

2.7 **[Related to** Solved Problem 8.2 **on page 242]** Briefly explain whether you agree with the following argument: "The separation of ownership from control in large corporations and the principal–agent problem mean that top managers can work short days, take long vacations, and otherwise slack off."

2.8 **[Related to** Solved Problem 8.2 **on page 242]** The members of many corporate boards of directors have to be reelected by the firm's stockholders every year. Some corporations, though, have staggered elections for their boards of directors, with only one-half or one-third of the members being up for election each year. According to an article in the *Economist* magazine, studies have found that firms that have staggered elections for their boards of directors are less profitable than similar firms where all members of the boards of directors are elected each year. Provide a possible explanation for this finding.
Source: "A Different Class," *Economist*, February 18, 2011.

2.9 Private equity firms, such as Blackstone and Kohlberg Kravis Roberts & Co., search for firms where the managers appear not to be maximizing profits. A private equity firm can buy stock in these firms and have its employees elected to the firms' boards of directors and may even acquire control of the targeted firm and replace the top management. Does the existence of private equity firms reduce any problems in corporate governance? Briefly explain.

 8.3 **How Firms Raise Funds, pages 242–249**

LEARNING OBJECTIVE: Explain how firms raise the funds they need to operate and expand.

Summary

Firms rely on retained earnings—which are profits retained by the firm and not paid out to the firm's owners—or on using the savings of households for the funds they need to operate and expand. With **direct finance**, the savings of households flow directly to businesses when investors buy **stocks** and **bonds** in financial markets. With **indirect finance**, savings flow indirectly to businesses when households deposit money in saving and checking accounts in banks and the banks lend these funds to businesses. Federal, state, and local governments also sell bonds in financial markets, and households also borrow funds from banks. When a firm sells a bond, it is borrowing money from the buyer of the bond. Firms make **coupon payments** to buyers of bonds. The **interest rate** is

the cost of borrowing funds, usually expressed as a percentage of the amount borrowed. When a firm sells stock, it is selling part ownership of the firm to the buyer of the stock. **Dividends** are payments by a corporation to its shareholders. The original purchasers of stocks and bonds may resell them in stock and bond markets, such as the New York Stock Exchange. The performance of the U.S. stock market is often measured using stock market indexes. The three most widely followed stock indexes are the Dow Jones Industrial Average, the S&P 500, and the NASDAQ Composite Index.

MyEconLab   Visit **www.myeconlab.com** to complete these exercises online and get instant feedback.

Review Questions

3.1 What is the difference between direct finance and indirect finance? If you borrow money from a bank to buy a new car, are you using direct finance or indirect finance?

3.2 Why is a bond considered to be a loan but a share of stock is not? Why do corporations issue both bonds and shares of stock?

3.3 How do the stock and bond markets provide information to businesses? Why do stock and bond prices change over time?

Problems and Applications

3.4 Suppose that a firm in which you have invested is losing money. Would you rather own the firm's stock or the firm's bonds? Briefly explain.

3.5 Suppose you originally invested in a firm when it was small and unprofitable. Now the firm has grown to be large and profitable. Would you be better off if you had bought the firm's stock or the firm's bonds? Briefly explain.

3.6 If you deposit $20,000 in a savings account at a bank, you might earn 1 percent interest per year. Someone who borrows $20,000 from a bank to buy a new car might have to pay an interest rate of 6 percent per year on the loan. Knowing this, why don't you just lend your money directly to the car buyer, cutting out the bank?

3.7 **[Related to the** Chapter Opener **on page 237]** Were the shares of stock issued as a result of Facebook's initial public offering (IPO) sold in a primary market or a secondary market? Was the IPO an example of direct finance or indirect finance?

3.8 **[Related to the** Making the Connection **on page 244]** In 2013, the government of Thailand was suffering large losses on a rice subsidy program introduced to raise the incomes of rice farmers. An article in the *Wall Street Journal* reported that: "Moody's Investors Service on Monday warned that losses from the subsidy could threaten Thailand's stable Baa1 rating."

    a. What is Moody's top bond rating? Why might Thailand not have received this rating even before the Thai government began to suffer large losses on the rice subsidy program?

    b. If Moody's decides to downgrade Thailand's debt rating, what will be the likely result for the interest rate the Thai government will have to pay when it sells bonds? Briefly explain.

    Source: James Hookway and Sameer Mohindru, "Thailand's Credibility Risks Beating over Rice Dispute," *Wall Street Journal*, June 7, 2013.

3.9 What effect would the following events be likely to have on the price of Google's stock?

    a. A competitor launches a search engine that is better than Google's.

    b. The corporate income tax is abolished.

    c. Google's board of directors becomes dominated by close friends and relatives of its top management.

    d. The price of wireless Internet connections in developing countries unexpectedly drops, so more and more people world wide use the Internet.

    e. Google announces a profit of $10 billion, but investors anticipated that Google would earn a profit of $11 billion.

3.10 The following appeared in an article in the *Wall Street Journal* about the bond market in high-income (or developed) countries (that is, the United States and countries in Europe) and the emerging-market countries (that is, Latin American and Asian countries):

> "In the developed markets, it's been about analyzing the business cycle, and in emerging markets, it's been about solvency," says David Rolley, the co-manager of the Loomis Sayles Global Bond fund. "Now it's not. You have to do both for both." . . . It could ultimately mean that developed economies, the U.S. included, could face extra penalties for the perceived, even if ever-so-slight, risk that they may not repay their debts.

    a. What does it mean to say that the emerging markets have been about "solvency"?

    b. What are the "extra penalties" the developed economies could face from the increase in perceived risk?

    Source: Matthieu Wirz and Matt Phillips, "Sea Change in Map of Global Risk," *Wall Street Journal*, August 1, 2011.

3.11 **[Related to the** Don't Let This Happen to You **on page 246]** Briefly explain whether you agree with the following statement: "The total value of the shares of Microsoft stock traded on the NASDAQ last week was $250 million, so the firm actually received more revenue from stock sales than from selling software."

3.12 **[Related to the** Making the Connection **on page 248]** Loans from banks are the most important external source of funds to businesses because most businesses are too small to borrow in financial markets by issuing stocks or bonds. Most investors are reluctant to buy the stocks or bonds of small businesses because of the difficulty of gathering accurate information on the financial strength and profitability of these businesses. Nevertheless, news about the stock market is included in nearly every network news program and is often the lead story in the business section of most newspapers. Is there a contradiction here? Why is the average viewer of TV news or the average reader of a newspaper interested in the fluctuations in prices in the stock market?

3.13 **[Related to the** Making the Connection **on page 248]** The following table shows information on June 7, 2013 on the stock price of Starbucks Corporation:

    a. How much did the price of Starbucks' stock change from the day before?

    b. Did the Starbucks' stock price vary much during this day's trading?

    c. Did the price of Starbucks' stock vary much over the preceding 52 weeks?

    d. How many shares of Starbucks' stock were traded on this day?

Symbol	Open	High	Low	Close	Net Chg	Volume	52-Week High	52-Week Low	Div
SBUX	63.41	65.09	63.41	65.04	0.01	6,794,623	65.09	43.04	0.84

8.4 Using Financial Statements to Evaluate a Corporation, pages 249-251

LEARNING OBJECTIVE: Understand the information provided in corporations' financial statements.

Summary

A firm's **income statement** sums up its revenues, costs, and profit over a period of time. A firm's **balance sheet** sums up its financial position on a particular day, usually the end of a quarter or year. A balance sheet records a firm's assets and liabilities. A **liability** is anything owed by a person or a firm. Firms report their **accounting profit** on their income statements. Accounting profit does not always include all of a firm's **opportunity cost**. **Explicit cost** is a cost that involves spending money. **Implicit cost** is a nonmonetary opportunity cost. Because accounting profit excludes some implicit costs, it is larger than **economic profit**.

MyEconLab   Visit www.myeconlab.com to complete these exercises online and get instant feedback.

Review Questions

4.1 What is the difference between a firm's assets and its liabilities? Give an example of an asset and an example of a liability.

4.2 What is the difference between a firm's balance sheet and its income statement?

4.3 Distinguish between a firm's explicit costs and its implicit costs and between a firm's accounting profit and its economic profit.

4.4 Would a business be expected to survive in the long run if it earned a positive accounting profit but a negative economic profit? Briefly explain.

Problems and Applications

4.5 Paolo currently has $100,000 invested in bonds that earn him 10 percent interest per year. He wants to open a pizza restaurant and is considering either selling the bonds and using the $100,000 to start his restaurant or borrowing $100,000 from a bank, which would charge him an annual interest rate of 7 percent. He finally decides to sell the bonds and not take out the bank loan. He reasons, "Because I already have the $100,000 invested in the bonds, I don't have to pay anything to use the money. If I take out the bank loan, I have to pay interest, so my costs of producing pizza will be higher if I take out the loan than if I sell the bonds." What do you think of Paolo's reasoning?

4.6 Paolo and Alfredo are twins who both want to open pizza restaurants. Their parents have always liked Alfredo best, and they buy two pizza ovens and give both to him. Unfortunately, Paolo must buy his own pizza ovens. Does Alfredo have a lower cost of producing pizza than Paolo does because Alfredo received his pizza ovens as a gift, while Paolo had to pay for his? Briefly explain.

4.7 Dane decides to give up a job earning $200,000 per year as a corporate lawyer and converts the duplex that he owns into a UFO museum. (He had been renting out the duplex for $20,000 a year.) His direct expenses include $75,000 per year paid to his assistants and $10,000 per year for utilities. Fans flock to the museum to see his collection of extraterrestrial paraphernalia, which he could easily sell on eBay for $1,000,000. Over the course of the year, the museum brings in revenues of $200,000.

a. How much is Dane's accounting profit for the year?

b. Is Dane earning an economic profit? Explain.

4.8 The Securities and Exchange Commission requires that every firm that wishes to issue stocks and bonds to the public make available its balance sheet and income statement. Briefly explain how information useful to investors can be found in these financial statements.

8.5 Corporate Governance Policy and the Financial Crisis of 2007-2009, pages 251-255

LEARNING OBJECTIVE: Discuss the role that corporate governance problems may have played in the financial crisis of 2007-2009.

Summary

Because their compensation often rises with the profitability of the corporation, top managers have an incentive to overstate the profits reported on their firm's income statements. During the early 2000s, it became clear that the top managers of several large corporations had done this, even though intentionally falsifying financial statements is illegal. The *Sarbanes-Oxley Act* of 2002 took several steps intended to increase the accuracy of financial statements and increase the penalties for falsifying them. The financial crisis of 2007-2009 revealed that many financial firms held assets that were far riskier than investors had realized. Congress passed the **Wall Street Reform and Consumer Protection Act (Dodd-Frank Act)** in July 2010 to address some of the issues raised by the financial crisis of 2007-2009.

MyEconLab   Visit www.myeconlab.com to complete these exercises online and get instant feedback.

Review Questions

5.1 What is the Sarbanes-Oxley Act? Why was it passed?

5.2 What was the source of the problems encountered by many financial firms during the crisis of 2007-2009?

Problems and Applications

5.3 The following is from an article in *USA Today*:

In what some call a worldwide corporate-governance movement, shareholders are pushing for stronger corporate-governance laws, teaming with investors from different countries and negotiating behind the scenes with businesses.

What is corporate governance? Why would shareholders push for stronger corporate governance laws?

Source: Edward Iwata, "Corporate Governance Gets More Transparent Worldwide," *USA Today*, February 17, 2008.

5.4 According to an article in the *Wall Street Journal*: "Companies in Standard & Poor's 500 stock index elected the smallest number of new directors last year [2012] in 10 years . . . ." Is having members of boards of directors serve for longer periods likely to be good news or bad news for corporate governance? Briefly explain.

Source: Joann S. Lublin, "The 40-Year Club: America's Longest-Serving Directors," *Wall Street Journal*, July 16, 2013.

5.5 An article in the *Wall Street Journal* observes: "Being on the board of directors of a publicly traded company isn't as much fun as it used to be. You're tied up in accounting red tape as a result of reforms under the Sarbanes-Oxley Act of 2002 . . . ." Is it possible to put a dollar value on the benefits to the economy of corporations complying with Sarbanes-Oxley? Which groups are likely to receive the most benefits from Sarbanes-Oxley: investors, corporations, or some other group?

Source: Jason Zweig, "Would You Want to Be a Director of This Company?" *Wall Street Journal*, July 24, 2013.

5.6 **[Related to the** Making the Connection **on page 254]** Jay Ritter, a professor at the University of Florida, was quoted in the *Wall Street Journal* as saying about Facebook: "It's entirely possible for a company to have solid growth prospects while its stock is overvalued."
a. What does it mean to say that a stock is "overvalued"?
b. Why might a firm's stock be overvalued despite the firm having "solid growth prospects"?

Source: Mark Hulbert, "A Year after Its Debut, Facebook Still Looks Overpriced," *Wall Street Journal*, May 17, 2013.

5.7 An article about corporate fraud on forbes.com stated that "misleading accounting and disclosure practices weaken the integrity of capital markets." The article noted that using incentive contracts for top managers can create a "'perverse' incentive to manipulate stock prices because their (executive) total package is based on stock price appreciation."
a. Why do financial markets depend on accurate accounting and disclosure practices? Why can misleading accounting and disclosure practices weaken the integrity of financial markets?
b. Why do corporate boards of directors sometimes link top managers' compensation to the corporations' stock prices? Briefly explain how tying compensation too closely to stock prices might create an incentive for corporate fraud.

Source: John Wasik, "How Corporate Fraud Costs You Money: Four Red Flags," forbes.com, June 17, 2013.

Real-Time-Data Exercises

D8.1 **[The stock market and recessions]** Go to the Web site of the Federal Reserve Bank of St. Louis (FRED) (research.stlouisfed.org/fred2/) and download and graph the data series for the S&P 500 stock index (SP500) from January 1957 until the most recent day available. Go to the Web site of the National Bureau of Economic Research (nber.org) and find the dates for business cycle peaks and troughs (the period between a business cycle peak and trough is a recession). Describe how stock prices move just before, during, and just after a recession. Is the pattern the same across recessions?

D8.2 **[Exploring dividends]** Go to wsj.com and find the dividend per share for each of the following firms:
a. Microsoft
b. Apple
c. Coca-Cola
d. Facebook
To find the dividend per share, enter the company's name in the search box on the home page. Which pays the highest dividend? Which has the highest dividend yield? Which does not pay a dividend? Why might a firm not pay a dividend? Why would investors buy the stock of a firm that does not pay a dividend?

Appendix

Tools to Analyze Firms' Financial Information

8A LEARNING OBJECTIVE

Understand the concept of present value and the information contained on a firm's income statement and balance sheet.

As we saw in the chapter, modern business firms are not just "black boxes" transforming inputs into output. The majority of business revenues and profits are earned by large corporations. Unlike founder-dominated firms, the typical large corporation is run by managers who generally do not own a controlling interest in the firm. Large firms raise funds from outside investors, and outside investors seek information on firms and the assurance that the managers of firms will act in the interests of the investors.

This chapter shows how corporations raise funds by issuing stocks and bonds. This appendix provides more detail to support that discussion. We begin by analyzing *present value* as a key concept in determining the prices of financial securities. We then provide greater information on *financial statements* issued by corporations, using Facebook as an example.

Using Present Value to Make Investment Decisions

Firms raise funds by selling equity (stock) and debt (bonds and loans) to investors and lenders. If you own shares of stock or a bond, you will receive payments in the form of dividends or coupons over a number of years. Most people value funds they already have more highly than funds they will receive some time in the future. For example, you would probably not trade $1,000 you already have for $1,000 you will not receive for one year. The longer you have to wait to receive a payment, the less value it will have for you. One thousand dollars you will not receive for two years is worth less to you than $1,000 you will receive after one year. The value you give today to money you will receive in the future is called the future payment's **present value**. The present value of $1,000 you will receive in one year will be less than $1,000.

Present value The value in today's dollars of funds to be paid or received in the future.

Why is the $1,000 you will not receive for one year less valuable to you than the $1,000 you already have? The most important reason is that if you have $1,000 today, you can use that $1,000 today. You can buy goods and services with the money and receive enjoyment from them. The $1,000 you receive in one year does not have direct use to you now.

Also, prices will likely rise during the year you are waiting to receive your $1,000. So, when you finally do receive the $1,000 in one year, you will not be able to buy as much with it as you could with $1,000 today. Finally, there is some risk that you will not receive the $1,000 in one year. The risk may be very great if an unreliable friend borrows $1,000 from you and vaguely promises to pay you back in one year. The risk may be very small if you lend money to the federal government by buying a U.S. Treasury bond. In either case, though, there is at least some risk that you will not receive the funds promised.

When someone lends money, the lender expects to be paid back both the amount of the loan and some additional interest. Say that you decide that you are willing to lend your $1,000 today if you are paid back $1,100 one year from now. In this case, you are charging $100/$1,000 = 0.10, or 10 percent interest on the funds you have loaned. Economists would say that you value $1,000 today as equivalent to the $1,100 to be received one year in the future.

Notice that $1,100 can be written as $1,000(1 + 0.10)$. That is, the value of money received in the future is equal to the value of money in the present multiplied by 1 plus the interest rate, with the interest rate expressed as a decimal. Or:

$$\$1,100 = \$1,000(1 + 0.10).$$

Notice, also, that if we divide both sides by $(1 + 0.10)$, we can rewrite this formula as:

$$\$1,000 = \frac{\$1,100}{(1 + 0.10)}.$$

The rewritten formula states that the present value is equal to the future value to be received in one year divided by 1 plus the interest rate. This formula is important because you can use it to convert any amount to be received in one year into its present value. Writing the formula generally, we have:

$$\text{Present value} = \frac{\text{Future value}_1}{(1 + i)}.$$

The present value of funds to be received in one year—Future value$_1$—can be calculated by dividing the amount of those funds to be received by 1 plus the interest rate. With an interest rate of 10 percent, the present value of $1,000,000 to be received one year from now is:

$$\frac{\$1,000,000}{(1 + 0.10)} = \$909,090.91.$$

This formula allows us to calculate the value today of funds that will be received in one year. But financial securities such as stocks and bonds involve promises to pay funds over many years. Therefore, it would be useful if we could expand this formula to calculate the present value of funds to be received more than one year in the future.

This expansion is easy to do. Go back to the original example, where we assumed you were willing to loan out your $1,000 for one year, provided that you received 10 percent interest. Suppose you are asked to lend the funds for two years and that you are promised 10 percent interest per year for each year of the loan. That is, you are lending $1,000, which at 10 percent interest will grow to $1,100 after one year, and you are agreeing to loan that $1,100 out for a second year at 10 percent interest. So, after two years, you will be paid back $1,100(1 + 0.10), or $1,210. Or:

$$\$1,210 = \$1,000(1 + 0.10)(1 + 0.10),$$

or:

$$\$1,210 = \$1,000(1 + 0.10)^2.$$

This formula can also be rewritten as:

$$\$1,000 = \frac{\$1.210}{(1 + 0.10)^2}.$$

To put this formula in words, the $1,210 you receive two years from now has a present value equal to $1,210 divided by the quantity 1 plus the interest rate squared. If you agree to lend out your $1,000 for three years at 10 percent interest, you will receive:

$$\$1,331 = \$1,000(1 + 0.10)^3.$$

Notice, again, that:

$$\$1,000 = \frac{\$1,331}{(1 + 0.10)^3}.$$

You can probably see a pattern here. We can generalize the concept to say that the present value of funds to be received n years in the future—whether n is 1, 20, or 85 does not matter—equals the amount of the funds to be received divided by the quantity 1 plus the interest rate raised to the nth power. For instance, with an interest rate of 10 percent, the value of $1,000,000 to be received 25 years in the future is:

$$\text{Present value} = \frac{\$1,000,000}{(1 + 0.10)^{25}} = \$92,296.$$

Or, more generally:

$$\text{Present value} = \frac{\text{Future value}_n}{(1 + i)^n}$$

where Future value$_n$ represents funds that will be received in n years.

Solved Problem 8A.1

MyEconLab Interactive Animation

How to Receive Your Contest Winnings

Suppose you win a contest and are given the choice of the following prizes:

> **Prize 1:** $50,000 to be received right away, with four additional payments of $50,000 to be received each year for the next four years
> **Prize 2:** $175,000 to be received right away

Explain which prize you would choose and the basis for your decision.

Solving the Problem

Step 1: Review the material. This problem involves applying the concept of present value, so you may want to review the section "Using Present Value to Make Investment Decisions" which begins on page 261.

Step 2: Explain the basis for choosing the prize. Unless you need cash immediately, you should choose the prize with the highest present value.

Step 3: Calculate the present value of each prize. Prize 2 consists of one payment of $175,000 received right away, so its present value is $175,000. Prize 1 consists of five payments spread out over time. To find the present value of the prize, we must find the present value of each of these payments and add them together. To calculate present value, we must use an interest rate. Let's assume an interest rate of 10 percent. In that case, the present value of Prize 1 is:

$$\$50,000 + \frac{\$50,000}{(1 + 0.10)} + \frac{\$50,000}{(1 + 0.10)^2} + \frac{\$50,000}{(1 + 0.10)^3} + \frac{\$50,000}{(1 + 0.10)^4}$$

$$= \$50,000 + \$45,454.55 + \$41,322.31 + \$37,565.74 + \$34,150.67$$

$$= \$208,493.$$

Step 4: State your conclusion. Prize 1 has the greater present value, so you should choose it rather than Prize 2.

Your Turn: For more practice, do related problems 8A.6, 8A.7, 8A.8, and 8A.9 on page 268 at the end of this appendix.

MyEconLab Study Plan

Using Present Value to Calculate Bond Prices

Anyone who buys stocks or bonds is really buying a promise to receive certain payments—dividends in the case of stocks or coupons in the case of bonds. The price investors are willing to pay for a financial asset should be equal to the value of the payments they will receive as a result of owning the asset. Because most of the coupon or dividend payments will be received in the future, it is their present value that matters. Put another way, we have the following important idea: *The price of a financial asset should be equal to the present value of the payments to be received from owning that asset.*

Let's consider an example. Suppose that in 1986, General Electric issued a bond with an $80 coupon that will mature in 2016. It is now 2014, and that bond has been bought and sold by investors many times. You are considering buying it. If you buy the bond, you will receive two years of coupon payments plus a final payment of the bond's principal, or face value, of $1,000. Suppose, once again, that you need an interest rate of 10 percent to invest your funds. If the bond has a coupon of $80, the present value of the payments you receive from owning the bond—and, therefore, the present value of the bond—will be:

$$\text{Present value} = \frac{\$80}{(1 + 0.10)} + \frac{\$80}{(1 + 0.10)^2} + \frac{\$1,000}{(1 + 0.10)^2} = \$965.29.$$

That is, the present value of the bond will equal the present value of the three payments you will receive during the two years you own the bond. You should, therefore, be willing to pay $965.29 to own this bond and have the right to receive these payments from GE. This process of calculating present values of future payments is used to determine bond prices, with one qualification: The relevant interest rate used by investors in the bond market to calculate the present value and, therefore, the price of an existing bond is usually the coupon rate on comparable newly issued bonds. Therefore, the general formula for the price of a bond is:

$$\text{Bond price} = \frac{\text{Coupon}_1}{(1 + i)} + \frac{\text{Coupon}_2}{(1 + i)^2} + \cdots + \frac{\text{Coupon}_n}{(1 + i)^n} + \frac{\text{Face value}}{(1 + i)^n},$$

where Coupon_1 is the coupon payment to be received after one year, Coupon_2 is the coupon payment to be received after two years, up to Coupon_n, which is the coupon payment received in the year the bond matures. The ellipsis takes the place of the coupon payments—if any—received between the second year and the year when the bond matures. Face value is the amount that will be received when the bond matures. The interest rate on comparable newly issued bonds is i.   MyEconLab Concept Check

Using Present Value to Calculate Stock Prices

When you own a firm's stock, you are legally entitled to your share of the firm's profits. Remember that the profits a firm pays out to its shareholders are referred to as *dividends*. The price of a share of stock should be equal to the present value of the dividends investors expect to receive as a result of owning that stock. Therefore, the general formula for the price of a stock is:

$$\text{Stock price} = \frac{\text{Dividend}_1}{(1 + i)} + \frac{\text{Dividend}_2}{(1 + i)^2} + \cdots$$

Notice that this formula looks very similar to the one we used to calculate the price of a bond, with a couple of important differences. First, unlike a bond, a share of stock has no maturity date, so we have to calculate the present value of an infinite number of dividend payments. At first, it may seem that the stock's price must be infinite as well, but remember that dollars you don't receive for many years are worth very little today. For instance, a dividend payment of $10 that will be received 40 years in the future is worth only a little more than $0.20 today at a 10 percent interest rate. The second difference between the stock price formula and the bond price formula is that the coupon payments you receive from owning the bond are known with certainty—they are set when the bond is issued and cannot be changed—you don't know for sure what the dividend payments from owning a stock will be. How large a dividend payment you will receive depends on how profitable the company will be in the future.

Although it is possible to forecast the future profitability of a company, this cannot be done with perfect accuracy. To emphasize this point, some economists rewrite the basic stock price formula by adding a superscript e to each dividend term to emphasize that these are *expected* dividend payments. Because the future profitability of companies is often very difficult to forecast, it is not surprising that differences of opinion exist over what the price of a particular stock should be. Some investors will be very optimistic about the future profitability of a company and will, therefore, believe that the company's stock should have a high price. Other investors might be very pessimistic and believe that the company's stock should have a low price.   MyEconLab Concept Check

A Simple Formula for Calculating Stock Prices

It is possible to simplify the formula for determining the price of a stock, if we assume that dividends will grow at a constant rate:

$$\text{Stock price} = \frac{\text{Dividend}}{(i - \text{Growth rate})}.$$

In this equation, Dividend is the dividend expected to be received one year from now, and Growth rate is the rate at which those dividends are expected to grow. If a company pays a dividend of $1 per share to be received one year from now and Growth rate is 10 percent, the company is expected to pay a dividend of $1.10 the following year, $1.21 the year after that, and so on.

Now suppose that IBM will pay a dividend of $5 per share at the end of year, the consensus of investors is that these dividends will increase at a rate of 5 percent per year for the indefinite future, and the interest rate is 10 percent. Then the price of IBM's stock should be:

$$\text{Stock price} = \frac{\$5.00}{(0.10 - 0.05)} = \$100.00.$$

Particularly during the years 1999 and 2000, there was much discussion of whether the high prices of many Internet stocks—such as the stock of Amazon.com—were justified, given that many of these companies had not made any profit yet and so had not paid any dividends. Is there any way that a rational investor would pay a high price for the stock of a company currently not earning profits? The formula for determining stock prices shows that it is possible, provided that the investor's assumptions are optimistic enough! For example, during 1999, one stock analyst predicted that Amazon.com would soon be earning $10 per share of stock. That is, Amazon.com's total earnings divided by the number of shares of its stock outstanding would be $10. Suppose Amazon.com pays out that $10 in dividends and that the $10 will grow rapidly over the years, by, say, 7 percent per year. Then the formula indicates that the price of Amazon.com stock should be:

$$\text{Stock price} = \frac{\$10.00}{(0.10 - 0.07)} = \$333.33.$$

If you are sufficiently optimistic about the future prospects of a company, a high stock price can be justified even if the company is not currently earning a profit. But investors in stocks must be careful. Suppose investors decide that growth prospects for Amazon are only 4 percent per year instead of 7 percent because the firm turns out not to be as profitable as initially believed. Then our formula indicates that the price of Amazon.com stock should be:

$$\text{Stock price} = \frac{\$10.00}{(0.10 - 0.04)} = \$166.67.$$

This price is only half the price determined assuming a more optimistic growth rate. Hence investors use information about a firm's profitability and growth prospects to determine what the firm is worth.   MyEconLab Concept Check

Going Deeper into Financial Statements

Corporations disclose substantial information about their business operations and financial position to actual and potential investors. Some of this information meets the demands of participants in financial markets and of information-collection agencies, such as Moody's Investors Service, which develops credit ratings that help investors judge how risky corporate bonds are. Other information meets the reporting requirements of the U.S. Securities and Exchange Commission.

Key sources of information about a corporation's profitability and financial position are its principal financial statements—the *income statement* and the *balance sheet*. These important information sources were first introduced in the chapter. In the following section we go into more detail, using recent data for Facebook as an example.

Analyzing Income Statements

As discussed in the chapter, a firm's income statement summarizes its revenues, costs, and profit over a period of time. Figure 8A.1 shows Facebook's income statement for 2012.

Facebook's income statement presents the results of the company's operations during the year. Listed first are the revenues it earned, largely from selling advertising on its Web site, from January 1, 2012, to December 31, 2012: $5,089 million. Listed next are Facebook's operating expenses, the most important of which is its *cost of revenue—* which is commonly known as *cost of sales* or *cost of goods sold*: $1,364 million. Cost of revenue is the direct cost of producing the products sold, including in this case the salaries of the computer programmers Facebook hires to write the software for its Web site. Facebook also has substantial costs for researching and developing its products ($1,399 million) and for advertising and marketing them ($896 million). General and administrative expenses ($892 million) include costs such as the salaries of top managers.

The difference between a firm's revenue and its costs is its profit. Profit shows up in several forms on an income statement. A firm's *operating income* is the difference between its revenue and its operating expenses. Most corporations, including Facebook, also have interest expenses and income from investments, such as government and corporate bonds. In this case, Facebook paid $44 million more in interest expenses than it earned on its investments, so its *income before taxes* was $494 million. The federal government taxes the profits of corporations. During 2012, Facebook paid $441 million in taxes. *Net income* after taxes was $53 million. That this level of profits is low considering the price of Facebook's stock is another indication that investors were expecting Facebook's profits to

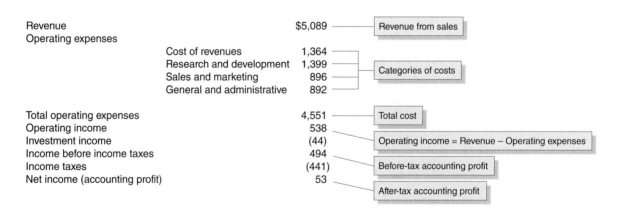

Revenue		$5,089	Revenue from sales
Operating expenses			
	Cost of revenues	1,364	
	Research and development	1,399	Categories of costs
	Sales and marketing	896	
	General and administrative	892	
Total operating expenses		4,551	Total cost
Operating income		538	
Investment income		(44)	Operating income = Revenue − Operating expenses
Income before income taxes		494	
Income taxes		(441)	Before-tax accounting profit
Net income (accounting profit)		53	After-tax accounting profit

Note: All numbers are in millions of dollars.

Figure 8A.1 **Facebook's Income Statement for 2012**   MyEconLab Real-time data

Facebook's income statement shows the company's revenue, costs, and profit for 2012. The difference between its revenue ($5,089 million) and its operating expenses ($4,551 million) is its operating income ($538 million). Most corporations also have interest expenses and income from investments, such as government and corporate bonds. In this case, Facebook paid $44 million more in interest expenses than it

earned on its investments, so its *income before taxes* was $494 million. After paying taxes of $441 million, Facebook was left with a net income, or accounting profit, of $53 million for the year.

Note: Negative values are shown in parentheses.

Source: Facebook 2012 10-K Annual Report. SEC EDGAR Web site www.sec.gov/edgar.shtml.

be much larger in the future. The net income that firms report on their income statements is referred to as their after-tax *accounting profit*.

MyEconLab Concept Check

Analyzing Balance Sheets

As discussed in the chapter, while a firm's income statement reports the firm's activities for a period of time, a firm's balance sheet summarizes its financial position on a particular day, usually the end of a quarter or year. To understand how a balance sheet is organized, first recall that an asset is anything of value that the firm owns, and a liability is a debt or an obligation that the firm owes. Subtracting the value of a firm's liabilities from the value of its assets leaves its *net worth*. Because a corporation's stockholders are its owners, net worth is often listed as **stockholders' equity** on a balance sheet. Using these definitions, we can state the balance sheet equation (also called the basic accounting equation) as follows:

$$\text{Assets} - \text{Liabilities} = \text{Stockholders' Equity,}$$

or:

$$\text{Assets} = \text{Liabilities} + \text{Stockholders' Equity.}$$

This equation tells us that the value of a firm's assets must equal the value of its liabilities plus the value of stockholders' equity. An important accounting rule dating back to the beginning of modern bookkeeping in fifteenth-century Italy holds that balance sheets should list assets on the left side and liabilities and net worth, or stockholders' equity, on the right side. Notice that this means that *the value of the left side of the balance sheet must always equal the value of the right side.* Figure 8A.2 shows Facebook's balance sheet as of December 31, 2012.

A couple of the entries on the asset side of the balance sheet may be unfamiliar: *Current assets* are assets that the firm could convert into cash quickly, such as the balance in its checking account or its accounts receivable, which is money currently owed to the firm for products that have been delivered but not yet paid for. *Goodwill* represents the difference between the purchase price of a company and the market value of its assets. It represents the ability of a business to earn an economic profit from its assets. For example, if you buy a restaurant that is located on a busy intersection and you employ a chef with a reputation for preparing delicious food, you may pay more than the market value of the tables, chairs, ovens, and other assets. This additional amount you pay will be entered on the asset side of your balance sheet as goodwill.

Current liabilities are short-term debts such as accounts payable, which is money owed to suppliers for goods received but not yet paid for, or bank loans that will be paid back in less than one year. Long-term bank loans and the value of outstanding corporate bonds are *long-term liabilities*.

Stockholders' equity The difference between the value of a corporation's assets and the value of its liabilities; also known as *net worth*.

MyEconLab Study Plan

Assets		Liabilities and Stockholders' Equity	
Current assets	$11,267	Current liabilities	$1,052
Property and equipment	2,391	Long-term liabilities	2,296
Goodwill	1,388	Total liabilities	3,348
Other long-term assets	57	Stockholders' equity	11,755
Total assets	$15,103	Total liabilities and stockholders' equity	$15,103

Note: All values are in millions of dollars.

Figure 8A.2

Facebook's Balance Sheet as of December 31, 2012

Corporations list their assets on the left of their balance sheets and their liabilities on the right. The difference between the value of a firm's assets and the value of its liabilities equals the net worth of the firm, or stockholders' equity. Stockholders' equity is listed on the right side of the balance sheet. Therefore, the value of the left side of the balance sheet must always equal the value of the right side.

Source: Facebook 2012 10-K Annual Report. SEC EDGAR Web site www.sec.gov/edgar.shtml.

Key Terms

Present value, p. 261   Stockholders' equity, p. 267

 Tools to Analyze Firms' Financial Information, pages 261–267

8A LEARNING OBJECTIVE: Understand the concept of present value and the information contained on a firm's income statement and balance sheet.

MyEconLab   Visit **www.myeconlab.com** to complete these exercises online and get instant feedback.

Review Questions

8A.1 Why is money you receive at some future date worth less to you than money you receive today? If the interest rate rises, what effect does this have on the present value of payments you receive in the future?

8A.2 Give the formula for calculating the present value of a bond that will pay a coupon of $100 per year for 10 years and that has a face value of $1,000.

8A.3 Compare the formula for calculating the present value of the payments you will receive from owning a bond to the formula for calculating the present value of the payments you will receive from owning a stock. What are the key similarities? What are the key differences?

8A.4 How is operating income calculated? How does operating income differ from net income? How does net income differ from accounting profit?

8A.5 What is the key difference between a firm's income statement and its balance sheet? What is listed on the left side of a balance sheet? What is listed on the right side?

Problems and Applications

8A.6 [Related to Solved Problem 8A.1 **on page 263**] If the interest rate is 10 percent, what is the present value of a bond that matures in two years, pays $85 one year from now, and pays $1,085 two years from now?

8A.7 [Related to Solved Problem 8A.1 **on page 263**] Before the 2013 season, the Los Angeles Angels signed outfielder Josh Hamilton to a contract that would pay him an immediate $10 million signing bonus and the following amounts: $15 million for the 2013 season, $15 million for the 2014 season, $23 million for the 2015 season, $30 million for the 2016 season, and $30 million for the 2017 season. The contract also specified that $2 million would be given to a charity. Assume that Hamilton receives each of his five seasonal salaries as a lump-sum payment at the end of the season.

   a. Some newspaper reports described Hamilton as having signed a $125 million contract with the Angels. Do you agree that $125 million was the value of this contract? Briefly explain.

   b. What was the present value of Hamilton's contract at the time he signed it (assuming an interest rate of 10 percent)? For simplicity, you can ignore the $2 million given to charity.

   c. If you use an interest rate of 5 percent, what was the present value of Hamilton's contract?

   Source: Drew Silva, "Breaking Down Josh Hamilton's Five-Year, $125M Contract," hardballtalk.nbcsports.com, December 15, 2012.

8A.8 [Related to Solved Problem 8A.1 **on page 263**] A winner of the Pennsylvania Lottery was given the choice of receiving $18 million at once or $1,440,000 per year for 25 years.

   a. If the winner had opted for the 25 annual payments, how much in total would she have received?

   b. At an interest rate of 10 percent, what would be the present value of the 25 payments?

   c. At an interest rate of 5 percent, what would be the present value of the 25 payments?

   d. What interest rate would make the present value of the 25 payments equal to the one payment of $18 million? (This question is difficult and requires the use of a financial calculator or a spreadsheet. *Hint:* If you are familiar with the Excel spreadsheet program, use the RATE function. You can answer parts (b) and (c) by using the Excel PV [Present Value] function.)

8A.9 [Related to Solved Problem 8A.1 **on page 263**] Before the start of the 2000 baseball season, the New York Mets decided they didn't want Bobby Bonilla playing for them any longer. But Bonilla had a contract with the Mets for the 2000 season that would have obliged the Mets to pay him $5.9 million. When the Mets released Bonilla, he agreed to take the following payments in lieu of the $5.9 million the Mets would have paid him in the year 2000: He would receive 25 equal payments of $1,193,248.20 each July 1 from 2011 to 2035. If you were Bobby Bonilla, which would you rather have had, the lump-sum $5.9 million in 2000 or the 25 payments beginning in 2011? Explain the basis for your decision.

   Source: Mike Sielski, "There's No Accounting for This," *Wall Street Journal*, July 1, 2010.

8A.10 Suppose that eLake, an online auction site, is paying a dividend of $2 per share. You expect this dividend to grow 2 percent per year, and the interest rate is 10 percent. What is the most you would be willing to pay for a share of stock in eLake? If the interest rate is 5 percent, what is the most you would be willing to pay? When interest rates in the economy decline, would you expect stock prices in general to rise or fall? Briefly explain.

8A.11 Suppose you buy the bond of a large corporation at a time when the inflation rate is very low. If the inflation rate increases during the time you hold the bond, what is likely to happen to the price of the bond?

8A.12 Use the information in the following table for calendar year 2012 to prepare an income statement for McDonald's Corporation. Be sure to include entries for operating income and net income.

Revenue from company restaurants	$18,603 million
Revenue from franchised restaurants	8,965 million
Cost of operating company-owned restaurants	15,224 million
Income taxes	2,614 million
Interest expense	517 million
General and administrative cost	2,455 million
Cost of restaurant leases	1,527 million

Source: McDonalds Corp. 2012 10-K Annual Report. SEC EDGAR Web site, www.sec.gov/edgar.shtml.

8A.13 Use the information in the following table on the financial situation of Starbucks Corporation as of December 31, 2012, to prepare a balance sheet for the firm. Be sure to include an entry for stockholders' equity.

Current assets	$4,220 million
Current liabilities	2,210 million
Property and equipment	2,659 million
Long-term liabilities	895 million
Goodwill	399 million
Other assets	962 million

Source: Starbucks Corp. (2012) 10-K Annual Report. SEC EDGAR Web site (www.sec.gov/edgar.shtml).

8A.14 The *current ratio* is equal to a firm's current assets divided by its current liabilities. Use the information in Figure 8A.2 on page 267 to calculate Facebook's current ratio on December 31, 2012. Investors generally prefer that a firm's current ratio be greater than 1.5. What problems might a firm encounter if the value of its current assets is low relative to the value of its current liabilities?

Comparative Advantage and the Gains from International Trade

Chapter Outline and Learning Objectives

Saving Jobs in the U.S. Tire Industry?

Between 2004 and 2008, Chinese tire companies tripled their exports to the United States. In response, in fall 2009, President Barack Obama announced that importers of Chinese tires used on cars and light trucks would have to pay the U.S. government a tariff equal to 35 percent of the tires' value. The purpose of the tariff was to protect jobs in the U.S. tire industry. In fall 2012, in a debate during his reelection campaign, President Obama argued that the tariff had served its purpose:

> We had a tire case in which … [China was] flooding us with cheap … tires …. And we put a stop to it and as a consequence saved jobs throughout America. … [Opponents] criticized me for being too tough in that tire case; said this wouldn't be good for American workers and that it would be protectionist. But I tell you, those workers don't feel that way.

Economists Gary Clyde Hufbauer and Sean Lowry of the Peterson Institute for International Economics believe the tire tariffs may have saved as many as 1,200 jobs in U.S. tire factories. But was the overall effect of the tariff on Chinese tires favorable to the U.S. economy? At the time it went into effect, owners of U.S. firms that sell Chinese tires claimed that the tariff would cause them losses. Bill Trimarco, the CEO of Hercules Tire & Rubber, located in Findlay, Ohio, argued: "This is an anti–small business policy. A company like Goodyear won't get hit, but a lot of small businesses will be hard hit." Similarly, John Everett, owner of Cybert Tire & Car Care in New York City, noted: "This is a China tire, it costs me $69 today. Before it cost $39. It all gets passed to the customer."

Other businesspeople worried that the Chinese government might retaliate by raising tariffs on some imports from the United States. In fact, China did raise tariffs on some U.S. goods, including broiler chickens, causing lost sales and profits to those U.S. firms. Consumer groups also protested that consumers would suffer because the tariff raised the prices they paid for tires.

The tariff was enacted for a period of three years. When the three years had passed, the Obama administration allowed the tariff to expire without attempting to extend it. By 2013, imports of Chinese tires were rising rapidly to their pre-tariff levels.

Are tariffs and other attempts to protect U.S. firms from foreign competition good ideas? In this chapter, we will analyze this and other important questions related to international trade.

Sources: "Transcript of Final 2012 Presidential Debate, Part 2," cbsnews.com, October 22, 2012; Gary Clyde Hufbauer and Sean Lowry, "US Tire Tariffs: Saving Few Jobs at High Cost," Peterson Institute for International Economics, Policy Brief Number PB12-9, April 2012; Diana Ransom, "Burnt Rubber: Tire Firms Decry New Tariff," *Wall Street Journal*, September 30, 2009; and John Bussey, "Get-Tough Policy on Chinese Tires Falls Flat," *Wall Street Journal*, January 20, 2012.

Economics in Your Life

Have You Heard of the Tariff on Chinese Tires?

Politicians often support restrictions on trade because they want to convince people to vote for them. The workers in the industries these restrictions protect are likely to vote for the politicians because they believe that the restrictions will save their jobs. But most people do *not* work in industries that are protected from foreign competition by trade restrictions. Many people also have to pay higher prices for products, such as tires, that have tariffs imposed on them. How, then, did workers in the tire industry convince the federal government to impose a tariff on imports of Chinese tires, and why have so few people heard of this tariff? As you read this chapter, try to answer these questions. You can check your answers against those we provide on **page 295** at the end of this chapter.

Trade is simply the act of buying or selling. Is there a difference between trade that takes place within a country and international trade? Within the United States, domestic trade makes it possible for consumers in Ohio to eat salmon caught in Alaska and for consumers in Montana to drive cars built in Michigan or Kentucky. Similarly, international trade makes it possible for consumers in the United States to drink wine from France and use Blu-ray players from Japan. One significant difference between domestic trade and international trade is that international trade is more controversial. At one time, nearly all the televisions, shoes, clothing, and toys bought in the United States were also produced there. Today, firms in other countries produce most of these goods. This shift has benefited U.S. consumers because foreign-made goods have lower prices or higher quality than the U.S.-made goods they have replaced. At the same time, though, many U.S. firms that produced these goods have gone out of business, and their workers have had to find other jobs. Not surprisingly, opinion polls show that many Americans favor reducing international trade because they believe doing so will preserve jobs in the United States. But is this belief accurate?

We can use the tools of demand and supply to analyze markets for internationally traded goods and services. We have seen that trade in general—whether within a country or between countries—is based on the principle of comparative advantage (see Chapter 2). In this chapter, we look more closely at the role of comparative advantage in international trade. We also use the concepts of consumer surplus, producer surplus, and deadweight loss (see Chapter 4) to analyze government policies that interfere with trade. With this background, we can return to the political debate over whether the United States benefits from international trade. We begin by looking at how large a role international trade plays in the U.S. economy.

The United States in the International Economy

9.1 LEARNING OBJECTIVE

Discuss the role of international trade in the U.S. economy.

International trade has grown tremendously over the past 50 years. The increase in trade is the result of the decreasing costs of shipping products around the world, the spread of inexpensive and reliable communications, and changes in government policies. Firms can use large container ships to send their products across oceans at low cost. Businesspeople today can travel to Europe or Asia, using fast, inexpensive, and reliable air transportation. The Internet, cellphones, and text messaging allow managers to communicate instantaneously and at a very low cost with customers and suppliers around the world. These and other improvements in transportation and communication have created an integrated global marketplace that earlier generations of businesspeople could only dream of.

Tariff A tax imposed by a government on imports.

Imports Goods and services bought domestically but produced in other countries.

Over the past 50 years, many governments have changed policies to facilitate international trade. For example, tariff rates have fallen. A **tariff** is a tax imposed by a government on *imports* into a country. **Imports** are goods and services bought domestically but produced in other countries. In the 1930s, the United States charged an average tariff rate above 50 percent. Today, the rate is less than 1.5 percent. In North America, most tariffs between Canada, Mexico, and the United States were eliminated following the passage of the North American Free Trade Agreement (NAFTA) in 1994. Twenty-eight countries in Europe have formed the European Union, which has eliminated all tariffs among member countries, greatly increasing both imports and **exports**, which are goods and services produced domestically but sold in other countries.

Exports Goods and services produced domestically but sold in other countries.

The Importance of Trade to the U.S. Economy

U.S. consumers buy increasing quantities of goods and services produced in other countries. At the same time, U.S. businesses sell increasing quantities of goods and services to consumers in other countries. Figure 9.1 shows that since 1970, both exports and imports have been steadily increasing as a fraction of U.S. gross domestic product (GDP). Recall that GDP is the value of all the final goods and services produced in a country

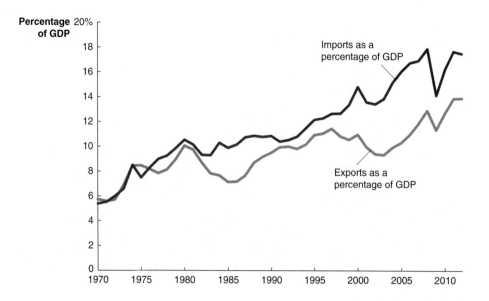

MyEconLab Real-time data

Figure 9.1

International Trade Is of Increasing Importance to the United States

Exports and imports of goods and services as a percentage of total production—measured by GDP—show the importance of international trade to an economy. Since 1970, both imports and exports have been steadily rising as a fraction of U.S. GDP.
Source: U.S. Department of Commerce, Bureau of Economic Analysis.

during a year. In 1970, exports and imports were both less than 6 percent of U.S. GDP. In 2012, exports were about 14 percent of GDP, and imports were about 18 percent.

Not all sectors of the U.S. economy are affected equally by international trade. For example, although it's difficult to import or export some services, such as haircuts and appendectomies, a large percentage of U.S. agricultural production is exported. Each year, the United States exports about 50 percent of its wheat and rice crops and 20 percent of its corn crop.

Many U.S. manufacturing industries also depend on trade. About 20 percent of U.S. manufacturing jobs depend directly or indirectly on exports. In some industries, such as pharmaceutical drugs, the products are directly exported. In other industries, such as steel, the products are used to make other products, such as bulldozers or machine tools, that are then exported. In all, about two-thirds of U.S. manufacturing industries depend on exports for at least 10 percent of jobs.   MyEconLab Concept Check

Making the Connection
MyEconLab Video

Goodyear and the Tire Tariff

Goodyear Tire & Rubber Company, headquartered in Akron, Ohio, has been a leading U.S. manufacturing firm for more than a century. If you watch football or other events, you have probably seen the Goodyear blimp hovering in the sky. Although often thought of as a symbol of U.S. industry, Goodyear is in fact a global company with 52 manufacturing plants in 22 countries. As the following figure shows, today fewer than 40 percent of its tire sales occur in the United States and Canada, although more than half did as recently as 2000.

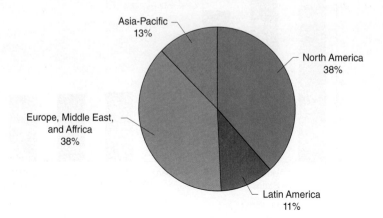

So when President Obama announced a 35 percent tariff on imports of Chinese tires in 2009, it was not necessarily good news for Goodyear for two key reasons. First, like many markets, tires are *differentiated*, meaning that many different types of tires are produced. Chinese firms concentrate primarily on producing inexpensive tires that consumers buy as replacement tires. Goodyear's North American production, sold under its Goodyear and Dunlop brands, sells more expensive tires that car manufacturers like General Motors and Ford buy to install on new cars. After the tariff had been in place for more than two years, a spokesman for Goodyear said: "The tariffs didn't have any material impact on our North American business. The stuff coming in from China is primarily low end. We got out of that market years ago." Second, Goodyear operates factories in China and some of the tires they produced there were exported to the United States and were subject to the tariff.

The Tire Industry Association, which represents both tire manufacturers and retailers who sell tires, had opposed the tariff. A spokesman for this association said the tariff "really hurt a lot of people in the industry—smaller businesses that geared up to bring these tires in from China." In addition, some manufacturers moved production from China to other low-wage countries, such as Mexico and Indonesia, whose exports to the United States were not subject to the tariff.

At the beginning of 2013, with the tire tariff having expired, Goodyear's profits rose more than 50 percent compared with the previous year, despite increases in imports of Chinese tires. Later in this chapter, we will consider further the effects of the tire tariff on the U.S. economy.

Sources: Jeff Bennett, "Goodyear Posts First-Quarter Profit," *Wall Street Journal,* April 26, 2013; John Bussey, "Get-Tough Policy on Chinese Tires Falls Flat," *Wall Street Journal,* January 20, 2012; Edmund L. Andrews, "U.S. Adds Tariffs on Chinese Tires," *New York Times,* September 12, 2009; and Goodyear Tire & Rubber Company, *Annual Report, 2012.*

MyEconLab Study Plan

Your Turn: Test your understanding by doing related problem 1.7 on page 296 at the end of this chapter.

U.S. International Trade in a World Context

The United States is the second largest exporter in the world, just behind China, as Figure 9.2 illustrates. Six of the other seven leading exporting countries are also high-income countries. Although China is still a relatively low-income country, the rapid growth of the Chinese economy over the past 35 years has resulted in its becoming the largest exporter. Three of the top exporting countries are in East Asia, four are in Western Europe, and one is in North America.

MyEconLab Animation

Figure 9.2

The Eight Leading Exporting Countries, 2012

China is the leading exporting country, accounting for 9.3 percent of total world exports. The United States is second, with a 9.2 percent share. The values are the shares of total world exports of merchandise and commercial services.
Source: World Trade Organization, *International Trade Statistics,* 2012.

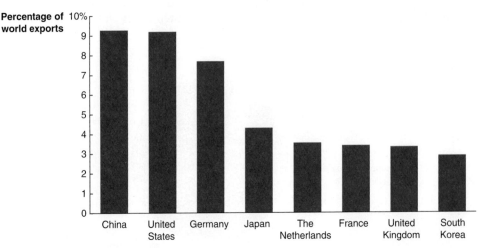

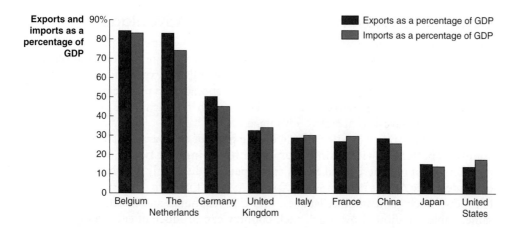

MyEconLab Real-time data

Figure 9.3

International Trade As a Percentage of GDP

International trade is still less important to the United States than it is to most other countries.
Source: Organization for Economic Cooperation and Development, *Country Statistical Profiles.*

Figure 9.3 shows that international trade is less important to the United States than it is to many other countries, with imports and exports being lower percentages of GDP. In some smaller countries, such as Belgium and the Netherlands, imports and exports make up more than half of GDP. In the larger European economies, imports and exports make up one-quarter to one-half of GDP.   MyEconLab Concept Check

MyEconLab Study Plan

Comparative Advantage in International Trade

9.2 LEARNING OBJECTIVE

Understand the difference between comparative advantage and absolute advantage in international trade.

Why have businesses around the world increasingly looked for markets in other countries? Why have consumers increasingly purchased goods and services made in other countries? People trade for one reason: Trade makes them better off. Whenever a buyer and seller agree to a sale, they must both believe they are better off; otherwise, there would be no sale. This outcome must hold whether the buyer and seller live in the same city or in different countries. As we will see, governments are more likely to interfere with international trade than they are with domestic trade, but the reasons for the interference are more political than economic.

A Brief Review of Comparative Advantage

Recall that **comparative advantage** is the ability of an individual, a firm, or a country to produce a good or service at a lower opportunity cost than competitors. **Opportunity cost** is the highest-valued alternative that must be given up to engage in an activity. People, firms, and countries specialize in economic activities in which they have a comparative advantage. In trading, we benefit from the comparative advantage of other people (or firms or countries), and they benefit from our comparative advantage.

Comparative advantage The ability of an individual, a firm, or a country to produce a good or service at a lower opportunity cost than competitors.

Opportunity cost The highest-valued alternative that must be given up to engage in an activity.

A good way to think of comparative advantage is to recall the example of you and your neighbor picking fruit (see Chapter 2). Your neighbor is better at picking both apples and cherries than you are. Why, then, doesn't your neighbor pick both types of fruit? Because the opportunity cost to your neighbor of picking her own apples is very high: She is a particularly skilled cherry picker, and every hour spent picking apples is an hour taken away from picking cherries. You can pick apples at a much lower opportunity cost than your neighbor, so you have a comparative advantage in picking apples. Your neighbor can pick cherries at a much lower opportunity cost than you can, so she has a comparative advantage in picking cherries. Your neighbor is better off specializing in picking cherries, and you are better off specializing in picking apples. You can then trade some of your apples for some of your neighbor's cherries, and both of you will end up with more of each fruit.   MyEconLab Concept Check

Comparative Advantage and Absolute Advantage

The principle of comparative advantage can explain why people pursue different occupations. It can also explain why countries produce different goods and services. International trade involves many countries importing and exporting many different goods and services. Countries are better off if they specialize in producing the goods for which they have a comparative advantage. They can then trade for the goods for which other countries have a comparative advantage.

We can illustrate why specializing on the basis of comparative advantage makes countries better off with a simple example involving just two countries and two products. Suppose the United States and Japan produce only cellphones and tablet computers, like Apple's iPad or Sony's Xperia. Assume that each country uses only labor to produce each good and that Japanese and U.S. cellphones and tablets are exactly the same. Table 9.1 shows how much each country can produce of each good with one hour of labor.

Notice that Japanese workers are more productive than U.S. workers in making both goods. In one hour, Japanese workers can make six times as many cellphones and one and one-half times as many tablets as U.S. workers. Japan has an *absolute advantage* over the United States in producing both goods. **Absolute advantage** is the ability to produce more of a good or service than competitors when using the same amount of resources. In this case, Japan can produce more of both goods using the same amount of labor as the United States.

It might seem at first that Japan has nothing to gain from trading with the United States because it has an absolute advantage in producing both goods. However, Japan should specialize and produce only cellphones and obtain the tablets it needs by exporting cellphones to the United States in exchange for tablets. The reason Japan benefits from trade is that although it has an *absolute advantage* in the production of both goods, it has a *comparative advantage* only in the production of cellphones. The United States has a comparative advantage in the production of tablets.

If it seems contrary to common sense that Japan should import tablets from the United States even though Japan can produce more of them per hour of labor, think about the opportunity cost to each country of producing each good. If Japan wants to produce more tablets, it has to switch labor away from cellphone production. Every hour of labor switched from producing cellphones to producing tablets increases tablet production by 6 and reduces cellphone production by 12. Japan has to give up 12 cellphones for every 6 tablets it produces. Therefore, the opportunity cost to Japan of producing one more tablet is 12/6, or 2 cellphones.

If the United States switches one hour of labor from cellphones to tablets, production of cellphones falls by 2 and production of tablets rises by 4. Therefore, the opportunity cost to the United States of producing one more tablet is 2/4, or 0.5 cellphone. The United States has a lower opportunity cost of producing tablets and, therefore, has a comparative advantage in making this product. By similar reasoning, we can see that Japan has a comparative advantage in producing cellphones. Table 9.2 summarizes the opportunity cost each country faces in producing these goods.

MyEconLab Concept Check

Absolute advantage The ability to produce more of a good or service than competitors when using the same amount of resources.

Table 9.1		Output per Hour of Work	
An Example of Japanese Workers Being More Productive Than American Workers		Cellphones	Tablets
	Japan	12	6
	United States	2	4

	Opportunity Costs	
	Cellphones	Tablets
Japan	0.5 tablet	2 cellphones
United States	2 tablets	0.5 cellphone

Table 9.2

The Opportunity Costs of Producing Cellphones and Tablets

The table shows the opportunity cost each country faces in producing cellphones and tablets. For example, the entry in the first row and second column shows that Japan must give up 2 cellphones for every tablet it produces.

9.3 LEARNING OBJECTIVE

Explain how countries gain from international trade.

Autarky A situation in which a country does not trade with other countries.

Terms of trade The ratio at which a country can trade its exports for imports from other countries.

How Countries Gain from International Trade

Can Japan really gain from producing only cellphones and trading with the United States for tablets? To see that it can, assume at first that Japan and the United States do not trade with each other. A situation in which a country does not trade with other countries is called **autarky**. Assume that in autarky, each country has 1,000 hours of labor available to produce the two goods, and each country produces the quantities of the two goods shown in Table 9.3. Because there is no trade, these quantities also represent consumption of the two goods in each country.

Increasing Consumption through Trade

Suppose now that Japan and the United States begin to trade with each other. The **terms of trade** is the ratio at which a country can trade its exports for imports from other countries. For simplicity, let's assume that the terms of trade end up with Japan and the United States being willing to trade one cellphone for one tablet.

Once trade has begun, the United States and Japan can exchange tablets for cellphones or cellphones for tablets. For example, if Japan specializes by using all 1,000 available hours of labor to produce cellphones, it will be able to produce 12,000 cellphones. It then could export 1,500 cellphones to the United States in exchange for 1,500 tablets. (Remember that we are assuming that the terms of trade are one cellphone for one tablet.) Japan ends up with 10,500 cellphones and 1,500 tablets. Compared with the situation before trade, Japan has the same number of tablets but 1,500 more cellphones. If the United States specializes in producing tablets, it will be able to produce 4,000 tablets. It could then export 1,500 tablets to Japan in exchange for 1,500 cellphones. The United States ends up with 2,500 tablets and 1,500 cellphones. Compared with the situation before trade, the United States has the same number of cellphones but 1,500 more tablets. Trade has allowed both countries to increase the quantities of goods consumed. Table 9.4 summarizes the gains from trade for the United States and Japan.

By trading, Japan and the United States are able to consume more than they could without trade. This outcome is possible because world production of both goods increases after trade. (In this example, our "world" consists of just the United States and Japan.)

Why does total production of cellphones and tablets increase when the United States specializes in producing tablets and Japan specializes in producing cellphones? A domestic analogy helps to answer this question: If a company shifts production from an old factory to a more efficient modern factory, its output will increase. The same thing happens in our example. Producing tablets in Japan and cellphones in the United States is inefficient. Shifting production to the more efficient country—the one with the comparative advantage—increases total production. The key point is: *Countries gain from specializing in producing goods in which they have a comparative advantage and trading for goods in which other countries have a comparative advantage.* MyEconLab Concept Check

	Production and Consumption	
	Cellphones	Tablets
Japan	9,000	1,500
United States	1,500	1,000

Table 9.3

Production without Trade

Table 9.4

Gains from Trade for Japan and the United States

Without Trade

Production and Consumption

	Cellphones	Tablets
Japan	9,000	1,500
United States	1,500	1,000

With Trade

	Production with Trade		Trade		Consumption with Trade	
	Cellphones	Tablets	Cellphones	Tablets	Cellphones	Tablets
Japan	12,000	0	**Export** 1,500	**Import** 1,500	10,500	1,500
United States	0	4,000	**Import** 1,500	**Export** 1,500	1,500	2,500

With trade, the United States and Japan specialize in the good they have a comparative advantage in producing . . .

. . . and export some of that good in exchange for the good the other country has a comparative advantage in producing.

Gains from Trade

Increased Consumption

Japan	1,500 Cellphones
United States	1,500 Tablets

The increased consumption made possible by trade represents the gains from trade.

Solved Problem 9.3

MyEconLab Interactive Animation

The Gains from Trade

The first discussion of comparative advantage appears in *On the Principles of Political Economy and Taxation*, a book written by the British economist David Ricardo in 1817. Ricardo provided a famous example of the gains from trade, using wine and cloth production in Portugal and England. The following table is adapted from Ricardo's example, with cloth measured in sheets and wine measured in kegs:

	Output per Year of Labor	
	Cloth	Wine
Portugal	100	150
England	90	60

a. Explain which country has an absolute advantage in the production of each good.

b. Explain which country has a comparative advantage in the production of each good.

c. Suppose that Portugal and England currently do not trade with each other. Each country has 1,000 workers, so each has 1,000 years of labor time to use in producing cloth and wine, and the countries are currently producing the amounts of each good shown in the following table:

	Cloth	Wine
Portugal	18,000	123,000
England	63,000	18,000

Show that Portugal and England can both gain from trade. Assume that the terms of trade are that one sheet of cloth can be traded for one keg of wine.

Solving the Problem

Step 1: **Review the chapter material.** This problem is about absolute and comparative advantage and the gains from trade, so you may want to review the sections "Comparative Advantage in International Trade," which begins on page 275, and "How Countries Gain from International Trade," which begins on page 277.

Step 2: **Answer part (a) by determining which country has an absolute advantage.** Remember that a country has an absolute advantage over another country when it can produce more of a good using the same resources. The first table in the problem shows that Portugal can produce more cloth *and* more wine with one year's worth of labor than can England. Therefore, Portugal has an absolute advantage in the production of both goods, and England does not have an absolute advantage in the production of either good.

Step 3: **Answer part (b) by determining which country has a comparative advantage.** A country has a comparative advantage when it can produce a good at a lower opportunity cost. To produce 100 sheets of cloth, Portugal must give up producing 150 kegs of wine. Therefore, Portugal's opportunity cost of producing 1 sheet of cloth is 150/100, or 1.5 kegs of wine. England has to give up producing 60 kegs of wine to produce 90 sheets of cloth, so its opportunity cost of producing 1 sheet of cloth is 60/90, or 0.67 keg of wine. The opportunity costs of producing wine can be calculated in the same way. The following table shows the opportunity cost to Portugal and England of producing each good.

| | Opportunity Costs | |
	Cloth	Wine
Portugal	1.5 kegs of wine	0.67 sheet of cloth
England	0.67 keg of wine	1.5 sheets of cloth

Portugal has a comparative advantage in wine because its opportunity cost is lower. England has a comparative advantage in cloth because its opportunity cost is lower.

Step 4: **Answer part (c) by showing that both countries can benefit from trade.** By now it should be clear that both countries will be better off if they specialize in producing the good for which they have a comparative advantage and trade for the other good. The following table is very similar to Table 9.4 and shows one example of trade making both countries better off. (To test your understanding, construct another example.)

Without Trade

| | Production and Consumption | |
	Cloth	Wine
Portugal	18,000	123,000
England	63,000	18,000

With Trade

| | Production with Trade | | Trade | | Consumption with Trade | |
	Cloth	Wine	Cloth	Wine	Cloth	Wine
Portugal	0	150,000	Import 18,000	Export 18,000	18,000	132,000
England	90,000	0	Export 18,000	Import 18,000	72,000	18,000

Gains from Trade

	Increased Consumption
Portugal	9,000 wine
England	9,000 cloth

Your Turn: For more practice, do related problems 3.5 and 3.6 on page 298 at the end of this chapter.

MyEconLab Study Plan

Why Don't We See Complete Specialization?

In our example of two countries producing only two products, each country specializes in producing one of the goods. In the real world, many goods and services are produced in more than one country. For example, the United States, Japan, Germany, Canada, Mexico, India, China, and other countries produce automobiles. We do not see complete specialization in the real world for three main reasons:

- *Not all goods and services are traded internationally.* Even if, for example, Japan had a comparative advantage in the production of medical services, it would be difficult for Japan to specialize in producing medical services and then export them. There is no easy way for U.S. patients who need appendectomies to receive them from surgeons in Japan.

- *Production of most goods involves increasing opportunity costs.* Recall that production of most goods involves increasing opportunity costs (see Chapter 2). In our example, if the United States devotes more workers to producing tablets, the opportunity cost of producing more tablets will increase. At some point, the opportunity cost of producing tablets in the United States may rise to the level of the opportunity cost of producing tablets in Japan. When that happens, international trade will no longer push the United States further toward specialization. The same will be true of Japan: The increasing opportunity cost of producing cellphones will cause Japan to stop short of complete specialization.

- *Tastes for products differ.* Most products are *differentiated*. Cellphones, tablets, cars, and televisions—to name just a few products—come with a wide variety of features. When buying automobiles, some people look for reliability and fuel efficiency, others look for room to carry seven passengers, and still others want styling and high performance. So, some car buyers prefer Toyota Prius hybrids, some prefer Chevy Suburbans, and others prefer BMWs. As a result, Japan, the United States, and Germany may each have a comparative advantage in producing different types of automobiles. MyEconLab Concept Check

Does Anyone Lose as a Result of International Trade?

In our cellphone and tablet example, consumption increases in both the United States and Japan as a result of trade. Everyone gains, and no one loses. Or do they? In our

---

Don't Let This Happen to You

Remember That Trade Creates Both Winners and Losers

The following statement is from a Federal Reserve publication: "Trade is a win–win situation for all countries that participate." People sometimes interpret statements like this to mean that there are no losers from international trade. But notice that the statement refers to *countries*, not individuals. When countries participate in trade, they make their consumers better off by increasing the quantity of goods and services available to them. As we have seen, however, expanding trade eliminates the jobs of workers employed at companies that are less efficient than foreign companies. Trade also creates new jobs at companies that export products to foreign markets. It may be difficult, though, for workers who lose their jobs because of trade to easily find others. That is why in the United States the federal government uses the Trade Adjustment Assistance program to provide funds for workers who have lost their jobs due to international trade. Qualified unemployed workers can use these funds to pay for retraining, searching for new jobs, or relocating to areas where new jobs are available. This program—and similar programs in other countries—recognizes that there are losers from international trade as well as winners.

Source: Federal Reserve Bank of Dallas, "International Trade and the Economy," www.dallasfed.org/educate/everyday/ev7.html.

MyEconLab Study Plan

Your Turn: Test your understanding by doing related problem 3.12 on page 298 at the end of this chapter.

example, we referred repeatedly to "Japan" or the "United States" producing cellphones or tablets. But countries do not produce goods—firms do. In a world without trade, there would be cellphone and tablet firms in both Japan and the United States. In a world with trade, there would be only Japanese cellphone firms and U.S. tablet firms. Japanese tablet firms and U.S. cellphone firms would close. Overall, total employment would not change, and production would increase as a result of trade. Nevertheless, the owners of Japanese tablet firms, the owners of U.S. cellphone firms, and the people who work for them are worse off as a result of trade. The losers from trade are likely to do their best to convince the Japanese and U.S. governments to interfere with trade by barring imports of the competing products from the other country or by imposing high tariffs on them. MyEconLab Concept Check

Where Does Comparative Advantage Come From?

Among the main sources of comparative advantage are the following:

- *Climate and natural resources.* This source of comparative advantage is the most obvious. Because of geology, Saudi Arabia has a comparative advantage in the production of oil. Because of climate and soil conditions, Costa Rica has a comparative advantage in the production of bananas, and the United States has a comparative advantage in the production of wheat.

- *Relative abundance of labor and capital.* Some countries, such as the United States, have many highly skilled workers and a great deal of machinery. Other countries, such as China, have many unskilled workers and relatively little machinery. As a result, the United States has a comparative advantage in the production of goods that require highly skilled workers or sophisticated machinery to make, such as aircraft and computer software. China has a comparative advantage in the production of goods, such as tools, clothing, and children's toys, that require unskilled workers and small amounts of simple machinery.

- *Technology.* Broadly defined, *technology* is the process firms use to turn inputs into goods and services. At any given time, firms in different countries do not all have access to the same technologies. In part, this difference is the result of past investments countries have made in supporting higher education or in providing support for research and development. Some countries are strong in *product technologies*, which involve the ability to develop new products. For example, firms in the United States have pioneered the development of such products as radios, televisions, digital computers, airliners, medical equipment, and many prescription drugs. Other countries are strong in *process technologies*, which involve the ability to improve the processes used to make existing products. For example, Japanese-based firms, such as Toyota and Honda, have succeeded by greatly improving the processes for designing and manufacturing automobiles.

- *External economies.* It is difficult to explain the location of some industries on the basis of climate, natural resources, the relative abundance of labor and capital, or technology. For example, why does southern California have a comparative advantage in making movies or Switzerland in making watches or New York in providing financial services? The answer is that once an industry becomes established in an area, firms located in that area gain advantages over firms located elsewhere. The advantages include the availability of skilled workers, the opportunity to interact with other firms in the same industry, and proximity to suppliers. These advantages result in lower costs to firms located in the area. Because these lower costs result from increases in the size of the industry in an area, economists refer to them as **external economies**. MyEconLab Concept Check

External economies Reductions in a firm's costs that result from an increase in the size of an industry.

Financial firms benefit from the external economies of being located in New York City.

Making the Connection
MyEconLab Video

Leaving New York City Is Risky for Financial Firms

The name "Wall Street" is shorthand for the whole U.S. financial system of banks, brokerage houses, and other financial firms. Wall Street is also, of course, an actual street in the New York City borough of Manhattan. The New York Stock Exchange is located on Wall Street, and many financial firms have their headquarters in Manhattan. There are also a lot of financial firms located outside Manhattan, but many of the largest firms believe that there are advantages to being located close to Wall Street. For instance, in 1997, UBS, a large Swiss bank, moved its North American headquarters from Manhattan to Stamford, Connecticut, where it built the largest facility for trading financial securities in the world. By 2011, UBS had begun moving many of its bankers back to Manhattan and was expected to occupy more than 1 million square feet of the 3 World Trade Center building once construction was complete.

Other financial firms have also moved some operations out of Manhattan only to move them back. As one manager of a new hedge fund put it: "There were enough roadblocks to establishing a new fund that I didn't want to create another" by not being in Manhattan. He was hardly alone: In recent years more than 90 percent of new hedge funds have been located in Manhattan.

The original concentration of financial firms in Manhattan was something of a historical accident. In colonial times and up through the early nineteenth century, Philadelphia and Boston were at least close rivals to New York City as business and financial centers. In fact, Philadelphia had a larger population than New York City and was the headquarters of the federal government's first two central banks. New York City received a boost in its rivalry with other cities when the Erie Canal was completed in upstate New York in 1825. The canal resulted in crops and other raw materials being shipped to New York City rather than to other ports. This inflow led to the development of banking, insurance, and other financial firms. Coupled with the gradual increase in trading on the New York Stock Exchange, the increase in business resulting from the completion of the canal established New York City as the leading financial center in the country.

But the Erie Canal has long since ceased to operate, and most stock trading takes place electronically rather than on the floor of the New York Stock Exchange. So, why has New York continued to see a high concentration of financial firms, with some firms that temporarily left deciding to return? The answer is that financial firms benefit from the external economies of being located in New York City. Even in the Internet age, many financial deals are still conducted face-to-face, so not having a physical presence in Manhattan puts a firm at a disadvantage. Many people pursuing careers in finance also want to be physically located in Manhattan because that is where most of the highest-paying financial jobs are. Firms that have moved out of Manhattan have had more difficulty attracting and retaining the most productive workers. In addition, Manhattan also has a large concentration of firms that provide support services, such as software programming for running financial firms' computer systems.

Large financial firms located outside Manhattan, particularly those that heavily trade securities or attempt to make deals that involve mergers between firms, may have higher costs than firms located in Manhattan. Having many financial firms originally located in Manhattan was a historical accident, but external economies gave the area a comparative advantage in providing financial services once the industry began to grow there.

Sources: Juliet Chung, "Hedge Funds' Manhattan Migration," *Wall Street Journal*, January 14, 2012; Brett Philbin, "UBS Shifts Staff to New York," *Wall Street Journal*, July 13, 2011; and Charles V. Bagli, "Regretting Move, Bank May Return to Manhattan," *New York Times*, June 8, 2011.

MyEconLab Study Plan

Your Turn: Test your understanding by doing related problem 3.13 on page 299 at the end of this chapter.

Comparative Advantage over Time: The Rise and Fall—and Rise—of the U.S. Consumer Electronics Industry

A country may develop a comparative advantage in the production of a good, and then, as time passes and circumstances change, the country may lose its comparative advantage in producing that good and develop a comparative advantage in producing other goods. For several decades, the United States had a comparative advantage in the production of consumer electronic goods, such as televisions, radios, and stereos. The comparative advantage of the United States in these products was based on having developed most of the underlying technology, having the most modern factories, and having a skilled and experienced workforce. Gradually, however, other countries, particularly Japan, gained access to the technology, built modern factories, and developed skilled workforces. As mentioned earlier, Japanese firms have excelled in process technologies, which involve the ability to improve the processes used to make existing products. By the 1970s and 1980s, Japanese firms were able to produce many consumer electronic goods more cheaply and with higher quality than could U.S. firms. Japanese firms Sony, Panasonic, and Pioneer replaced U.S. firms Magnavox, Zenith, and RCA as world leaders in consumer electronics.

By the mid-2000s, however, as the technology underlying consumer electronics had evolved, comparative advantage had shifted again, and several U.S. firms had surged ahead of their Japanese competitors. For example, Apple had developed the iPod, iPhone, and iPad; Linksys, a division of Cisco Systems, took the lead in home wireless networking technology; and TiVo pioneered the digital video recorder (DVR). As pictures and music converted to digital data, process technologies became less important than the ability to design and develop new products. These new consumer electronic products required skills similar to those in computer design and software writing, where the United States had long maintained a comparative advantage. Although for the most part these firms did not manufacture within the United States the products they designed and marketed, even that appeared to be changing as Apple announced in 2013 that its redesigned Mac Pro computer would be assembled in the United States.

Once a country has lost its comparative advantage in producing a good, its income will be higher and its economy will be more efficient if it switches from producing the good to importing it, as the United States did when it switched from producing televisions to importing them. As we will see in the next section, however, there is often political pressure on governments to attempt to preserve industries that have lost their comparative advantage.   MyEconLab Concept Check

MyEconLab Study Plan

Government Policies That Restrict International Trade

Free trade, or trade between countries that is without government restrictions, makes consumers better off. We can expand on this idea by using the concepts of consumer surplus and producer surplus (see Chapter 4). Figure 9.4 shows the market in the United States for the biofuel ethanol, which can be used as a substitute for gasoline. The figure shows the situation of autarky, where the United States does not trade with other countries. The equilibrium price of ethanol is $2.00 per gallon, and the equilibrium quantity is 6.0 billion gallons per year. The blue area represents consumer surplus, and the red area represents producer surplus.

Now suppose that the United States begins importing ethanol from Brazil and other countries that produce ethanol for $1.00 per gallon. Because the world market for ethanol is large, we will assume that the United States can buy as much ethanol as it wants without causing the *world price* of $1.00 per gallon to rise. Therefore, once imports of ethanol are permitted into the United States, U.S. firms will not be able to sell ethanol at prices higher than the world price of $1.00, and the U.S. price will become equal to the world price.

9.4 LEARNING OBJECTIVE

Analyze the economic effects of government policies that restrict international trade.

Free trade Trade between countries that is without government restrictions.

Figure 9.4

The U.S. Market for Ethanol under Autarky

This figure shows the market for ethanol in the United States, assuming autarky, where the United States does not trade with other countries. The equilibrium price of ethanol is $2.00 per gallon, and the equilibrium quantity is 6.0 billion gallons per year. The blue area represents consumer surplus, and the red area represents producer surplus.

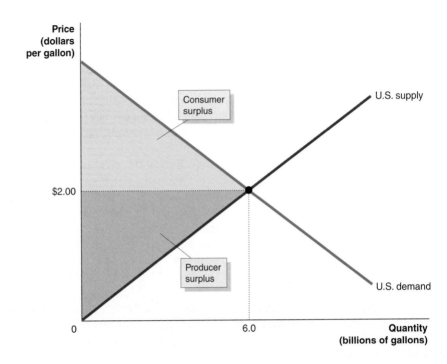

Figure 9.5 shows the result of allowing imports of ethanol into the United States. With the price lowered from $2.00 to $1.00, U.S. consumers increase their purchases from 6.0 billion gallons to 9.0 billion gallons. Equilibrium moves from point *F* to point *G*. In the new equilibrium, U.S. producers have reduced the quantity of ethanol they supply from 6.0 billion gallons to 3.0 billion gallons. Imports will equal 6.0 billion gallons, which is the difference between U.S. consumption and U.S. production.

Under autarky, consumer surplus would be area *A* in Figure 9.5. With imports, the reduction in price increases consumer surplus, so it is now equal to the sum of areas *A*,

Figure 9.5

The Effect of Imports on the U.S. Ethanol Market

When imports are allowed into the United States, the price of ethanol falls from $2.00 to $1.00. U.S. consumers increase their purchases from 6.0 billion gallons to 9.0 billion gallons. Equilibrium moves from point *F* to point *G*. U.S. producers reduce the quantity of ethanol they supply from 6.0 billion gallons to 3.0 billion gallons. Imports equal 6.0 billion gallons, which is the difference between U.S. consumption and U.S. production. Consumer surplus equals the sum of areas *A*, *B*, *C*, and *D*. Producer surplus equals the area *E*.

	Under Autarky	With Imports
Consumer Surplus	*A*	*A + B + C + D*
Producer Surplus	*B + E*	*E*
Economic Surplus	*A + B + E*	*A + B + C + D + E*

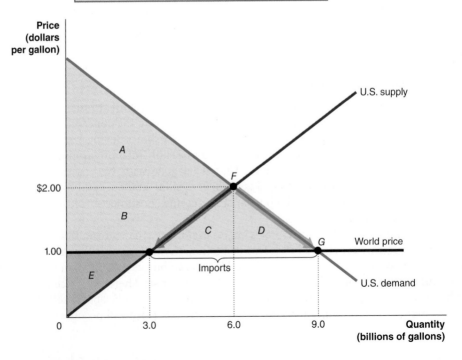

B, C, and D. Although the lower price increases consumer surplus, it reduces producer surplus. Under autarky, producer surplus was equal to the sum of areas B and E. With imports, it is equal to only area E. Recall that economic surplus equals the sum of consumer surplus and producer surplus. Moving from autarky to allowing imports increases economic surplus in the United States by an amount equal to the sum of areas C and D.

We can conclude that international trade helps consumers but hurts firms that are less efficient than foreign competitors. As a result, these firms and their workers are often strong supporters of government policies that restrict trade. These policies usually take one of two forms: *tariffs* or *quotas* and *voluntary export restraints*.

Tariffs

The most common interferences with trade are *tariffs*, which are taxes imposed by a government on goods imported into the country. Like any other tax, a tariff increases the cost of selling a good. Figure 9.6 shows the effect of a tariff of $0.50 per gallon on ethanol imports into the United States. The $0.50 tariff raises the price of ethanol in the United States from the world price of $1.00 per gallon to $1.50 per gallon. At this higher price, U.S. ethanol producers increase the quantity they supply from 3.0 billion gallons to 4.5 billion gallons. U.S. consumers, though, cut back their purchases of ethanol from 9.0 billion gallons to 7.5 billion gallons. Imports decline from 6.0 billion gallons (9.0 billion − 3.0 billion) to 3.0 billion gallons (7.5 billion − 4.5 billion). Equilibrium moves from point G to point H.

By raising the price of ethanol from $1.00 to $1.50, the tariff reduces consumer surplus by the sum of areas A, T, C, and D. Area A is the increase in producer surplus from the higher price. The government collects tariff revenue equal to the tariff of $0.50 per gallon multiplied by the 3.0 billion gallons imported. Area T represents the government's tariff revenue. Areas C and D represent losses to U.S. consumers that are not captured by anyone. These areas are deadweight loss and represent the decline in economic efficiency resulting from the ethanol tariff. Area C shows the effect of U.S. consumers being forced to buy from U.S. producers who are less efficient than foreign producers, and area D shows the effect of U.S. consumers buying less ethanol than they would have at the world price. As a result of the tariff, economic surplus has been reduced by the sum of areas C and D.

We can conclude that the tariff succeeds in helping U.S. ethanol producers but hurts U.S. consumers and the efficiency of the U.S. economy.   MyEconLab Concept Check

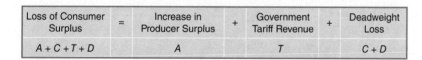

Loss of Consumer Surplus	=	Increase in Producer Surplus	+	Government Tariff Revenue	+	Deadweight Loss
$A + C + T + D$		A		T		$C + D$

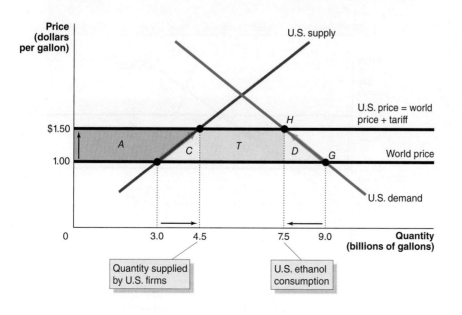

Quantity supplied by U.S. firms

U.S. ethanol consumption

MyEconLab Animation

Figure 9.6

The Effects of a Tariff on Ethanol

Without a tariff on ethanol, U.S. producers will sell 3.0 billion gallons of ethanol, U.S. consumers will purchase 9.0 billion gallons, and imports will be 6.0 billion gallons. The U.S. price will equal the world price of $1.00 per gallon. The $0.50-per-gallon tariff raises the price of ethanol in the United States to $1.50 per gallon, and U.S. producers increase the quantity they supply to 4.5 billion gallons. U.S. consumers reduce their purchases to 7.5 billion gallons. Equilibrium moves from point G to point H. The ethanol tariff causes a loss of consumer surplus equal to the area $A + C + T + D$. The area A is the increase in producer surplus due to the higher price. The area T is the government's tariff revenue. The areas C and D represent deadweight loss.

Quota A numerical limit a government imposes on the quantity of a good that can be imported into the country.

Voluntary export restraint (VER) An agreement negotiated between two countries that places a numerical limit on the quantity of a good that can be imported by one country from the other country.

Quotas and Voluntary Export Restraints

A **quota** is a numerical limit on the quantity of a good that can be imported, and it has an effect similar to that of a tariff. A quota is imposed by the government of the importing country. A **voluntary export restraint (VER)** is an agreement negotiated between two countries that places a numerical limit on the quantity of a good that can be imported by one country from the other country. In the early 1980s, the United States and Japan negotiated a VER that limited the quantity of automobiles the United States would import from Japan. The Japanese government agreed to the VER primarily because it was afraid that if it did not, the United States would impose a tariff or quota on imports of Japanese automobiles. Quotas and VERs have similar economic effects.

The main purpose of most tariffs and quotas is to reduce the foreign competition that domestic firms face. For many years, Congress has imposed a quota on sugar imports to protect U.S. sugar producers. Figure 9.7 shows the actual statistics for the U.S. sugar market in 2012. The effect of a quota is very similar to the effect of a tariff. By limiting imports, a quota forces the domestic price of a good above the world price. In this case, the sugar quota limits sugar imports to 5.8 billion pounds per year (shown by the bracket in Figure 9.7), forcing the U.S. price of sugar up to $0.43 per pound, or $0.16 higher than the world price of $0.27 per pound. The U.S. price is above the world price because the quota keeps foreign sugar producers from selling the additional sugar in the United States that would drive the U.S. price down to the world price. At a price of $0.43 per pound, U.S. producers increase the quantity of sugar they supply from the 7.6 billion pounds they would supply at the world price to 17.3 billion pounds, and U.S. consumers cut back their purchases of sugar from the 25.7 billion pounds they would purchase at the world price to the 23.1 billion pounds they are willing to purchase at the higher U.S. price. If there were no import quota, equilibrium would be at the world price (point *E*), but with the quota equilibrium is at the U.S. price (point *F*).   MyEconLab Concept Check

Measuring the Economic Effect of the Sugar Quota

We can use the concepts of consumer surplus, producer surplus, and deadweight loss to measure the economic impact of the sugar quota. Without a sugar quota, the world price of $0.27 per pound would also be the U.S. price. In Figure 9.7, without a sugar quota, consumer surplus would equal the area above the $0.27 price line and below the demand curve. The sugar quota causes the U.S. price to rise to $0.43 and reduces

MyEconLab Animation

Figure 9.7

The Economic Effect of the U.S. Sugar Quota

Without a sugar quota, U.S. sugar producers would have sold 7.6 billion pounds of sugar, U.S. consumers would have purchased 25.7 billion pounds of sugar, and imports would have been 18.1 billion pounds. The U.S. price would have equaled the world price of $0.27 per pound. Because the sugar quota limits imports to 5.8 billion pounds (the bracket in the graph), the price of sugar in the United States rises to $0.43 per pound, and U.S. producers supply 17.3 billion pounds. U.S. consumers purchase 23.1 billion pounds rather than the 25.7 billion pounds they would purchase at the world price. Without the import quota, equilibrium would be at point *E*; with the quota, equilibrium is at point *F*. The sugar quota causes a loss of consumer surplus equal to the area *A* + *B* + *C* + *D*. The area *A* is the gain to U.S. sugar producers. The area *B* is the gain to foreign sugar producers. The areas *C* and *D* represent deadweight loss. The total loss to U.S. consumers in 2012 was $3.9 billion.

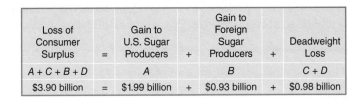

| | | Gain to | | | |
Loss of Consumer Surplus	=	Gain to U.S. Sugar Producers	+	Foreign Sugar Producers	+	Deadweight Loss
A + *C* + *B* + *D*		*A*		*B*		*C* + *D*
$3.90 billion	=	$1.99 billion	+	$0.93 billion	+	$0.98 billion

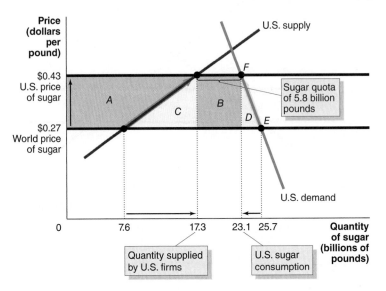

consumer surplus by the area $A + B + C + D$. Without a sugar quota, producer surplus received by U.S. sugar producers would be equal to the area below the $0.27 price line and above the supply curve. The higher U.S. price resulting from the sugar quota increases the producer surplus of U.S. sugar producers by an amount equal to area A.

A foreign producer must have a license from the U.S. government to import sugar under the quota system. Therefore, a foreign sugar producer that is lucky enough to have an import license also benefits from the quota because it is able to sell sugar in the U.S. market at $0.43 per pound instead of $0.27 per pound. Area B is the gain to foreign sugar producers. Areas A and B represent transfers from U.S. consumers of sugar to U.S. and foreign producers of sugar. Areas C and D represent losses to U.S. consumers that are not captured by anyone. These areas are deadweight loss and represent the decline in economic efficiency resulting from the sugar quota. Area C shows the effect of U.S. consumers being forced to buy from U.S. producers that are less efficient than foreign producers, and area D shows the effect of U.S. consumers buying less sugar than they would have at the world price.

Figure 9.7 provides enough information to calculate the dollar value of each of the four areas. The table in the figure shows the results of these calculations. The total loss to consumers from the sugar quota was $3.90 billion in 2012. About 51 percent of the loss to consumers, or $1.99 billion, was gained by U.S. sugar producers as increased producer surplus. About 24 percent, or $0.93 billion, was gained by foreign sugar producers as increased producer surplus, and about 25 percent, or $0.98 billion, was a deadweight loss to the U.S. economy. The U.S. International Trade Commission estimates that eliminating the sugar quota would result in the loss of about 3,000 jobs in the U.S. sugar industry. The cost to U.S. consumers of saving these jobs is equal to $3.9 billion/3,000, or about $1.3 million per job each year. In fact, this cost is an underestimate because eliminating the sugar quota would result in new jobs being created, particularly in the candy industry. Over the years, several U.S. candy companies—including the makers of Life Savers and Star Brite mints—have moved factories to other countries to escape the effects of the sugar quota. Partly as a result of the sugar quota, total employment in U.S. food and beverage firms that use sugar as an input declined from 717,192 in 1997 to 590,669 in 2011.   MyEconLab Concept Check

Solved Problem 9.4

MyEconLab Interactive Animation

Measuring the Economic Effect of a Quota

Suppose that the United States currently both produces and imports apples. The U.S. government then decides to restrict international trade in apples by imposing a quota that allows imports of only 4 million boxes of apples into the United States each year. The figure shows the results of imposing the quota.

Fill in the following table, using the prices, quantities, and letters in the figure:

	Without Quota	With Quota
World price of apples		
U.S. price of apples		
Quantity supplied by U.S. firms		
Quantity demanded by U.S. consumers		
Quantity imported		
Area of consumer surplus		
Area of domestic producer surplus		
Area of deadweight loss		

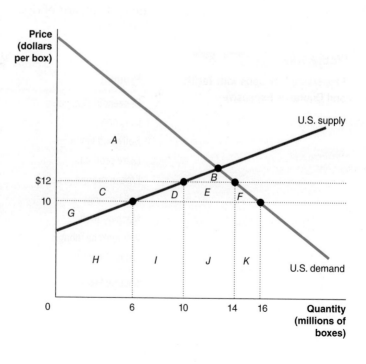

Solving the Problem

Step 1: **Review the chapter material.** This problem is about measuring the economic effects of a quota, so you may want to review the sections "Quotas and Voluntary Export Restraints," and "Measuring the Economic Effect of the Sugar Quota," which begin on page 286.

Step 2: **Fill in the table.** After studying Figure 9.7, you should be able to fill in the table. Remember that consumer surplus is the area below the demand curve and above the market price.

	Without Quota	With Quota
World price of apples	$10	$10
U.S. price of apples	$10	$12
Quantity supplied by U.S. firms	6 million boxes	10 million boxes
Quantity demanded by U.S. consumers	16 million boxes	14 million boxes
Quantity imported	10 million boxes	4 million boxes
Area of consumer surplus	$A + B + C + D + E + F$	$A + B$
Area of domestic producer surplus	G	$G + C$
Area of deadweight loss	No deadweight loss	$D + F$

MyEconLab Study Plan   **Your Turn:** For more practice, do related problem 4.12 on page 300 at the end of this chapter.

The High Cost of Preserving Jobs with Tariffs and Quotas

The sugar quota is not alone in imposing a high cost on U.S. consumers to save jobs at U.S. firms. Table 9.5 shows, for several industries, the costs tariffs and quotas impose on U.S. consumers per year for each job saved.

Many countries besides the United States also use tariffs and quotas to try to protect jobs. Table 9.6 shows the cost to Japanese consumers per year for each job saved as a result of tariffs and quotas in the listed industries. Note the staggering cost of $51 million for each job saved that is imposed on Japanese consumers by their government's restrictions on imports of rice.

Table 9.5

Preserving U.S. Jobs with Tariffs and Quotas Is Expensive

Product	Number of Jobs Saved	Cost to Consumers per Year for Each Job Saved
Benzenoid chemicals	216	$1,376,435
Luggage	226	1,285,078
Softwood lumber	605	1,044,271
Dairy products	2,378	685,323
Frozen orange juice	609	635,103
Ball bearings	146	603,368
Machine tools	1,556	479,452
Women's handbags	773	263,535
Canned tuna	390	257,640

Source: Federal Reserve Bank of Dallas, 2002 *Annual Report*, Exhibit 11.

Product	Cost to Consumers per Year for Each Job Saved
Rice	$51,233,000
Natural gas	27,987,000
Gasoline	6,329,000
Paper	3,813,000
Beef, pork, and poultry	1,933,000
Cosmetics	1,778,000
Radio and TV sets	915,000

Table 9.6

Preserving Japanese Jobs with Tariffs and Quotas Is Also Expensive

"Preserving Japanese Jobs with Tariffs and Quotas Is Also Expensive" by Yoko Sazabami, Shujiro Urata, and Hiroki Kawai from *Measuring the Cost of Protection in Japan.* Copyright © 1995 by the Institute for International Economics. Reprinted by permission.

Just as the sugar quota costs jobs in the candy industry, other tariffs and quotas cost jobs outside the industries immediately affected. For example, in 1991, the United States imposed tariffs on flat-panel displays used in laptop computers. The tariff was good news for U.S. producers of these displays but bad news for companies producing laptop computers. Toshiba, Sharp, and Apple all closed their U.S. laptop production facilities and moved production overseas. In fact, whenever one industry receives tariff or quota protection, other domestic industries lose jobs.   MyEconLab Concept Check

Making the Connection MyEconLab Video

The Effect on the U.S. Economy of the Tariff on Chinese Tires

We saw in the chapter opener that in 2009 the federal government imposed a tariff on imports of tires from China. The United Steelworkers Union, which represents workers in some U.S. tire factories, pushed for the tariff in order to save jobs. As with supporters of other tariffs and quotas who argue that these interferences with trade save jobs, the Steelworkers Union was focusing only on the jobs in tire manufacturing. We have seen that a tariff or quota makes it easier for domestic firms to compete against foreign firms that may have lower costs. More production by domestic firms means more employment at those firms, thereby saving jobs in that industry. But as we have also seen, other industries can see their costs rise as a result of the tariff or quota, causing firms in these industries to raise prices. In fact, the Tire Industry Association, which represents both tire manufacturers and tire retailers, opposed the tariff because it believed higher prices for Chinese tires might cause problems for the U.S. retailers who sold them. In addition, if consumers spend more on a good protected by a tariff, they have less to spend on other goods, thereby potentially reducing production and employment in other industries.

A tariff on tires increased the price of tires U.S. consumers purchased.

Economists Gary Clyde Hufbauer and Sean Lowry of the Petersen Institute for International Economics have estimated the effect of the tire tariff on the U.S. economy. The tariff succeeded in reducing imports of Chinese tires by raising their prices. Some consumers switched from Chinese tires to tires imported from other countries, whose prices were higher than the Chinese tires had been before the tariff. Hufbauer and

Lowry calculate that consumers spent about $800 million more on imported tires as a result of the tariff. In addition, U.S. manufacturers also increased prices as a result of the tariff, causing U.S. consumers to spend nearly $300 million more on U.S.-produced tires. Looking at the trends in employment among U.S. tire manufacturers, Hufbauer and Lowry conclude that the tariff saved at most 1,200 jobs. If the additional $1.1 billion consumers spent on tires as a result of the tariff is divided by the 1,200 jobs saved, the resulting value indicates that it cost U.S. consumers more than $900,000 per year for each job saved in the tire industry.

Because consumers spent more on tires as a result of the tariff, they had less to spend on other goods. Drawing on studies of the relationship between consumer spending and jobs in retailing, Hufbauer and Lowry estimate that the tariff resulted in a decline of 3,731 jobs in retailing. So, the short-run effect of the tariff during the years it was in effect would have been a net *decline* of 2,500 jobs.

This economic analysis indicates that the tire tariff was an expensive and ineffective way to preserve jobs.

Sources: Gary Clyde Hufbauer and Sean Lowry, "US Tire Tariffs: Saving Few Jobs at High Cost," Peterson Institute for International Economics, Policy Brief Number PB12-9, April 2012; Dylan Matthews, "How Obama's Tire Tariffs Have Hurt Consumers," *Washington Post*, October 23, 2013; and John Bussey, "Get-Tough Policy on Chinese Tires Falls Flat," *Wall Street Journal*, January 20, 2012.

MyEconLab Study Plan

Your Turn: Test your understanding by doing related problems 4.14 and 4.15 on page 301 at the end of this chapter.

Gains from Unilateral Elimination of Tariffs and Quotas

Some politicians argue that eliminating U.S. tariffs and quotas would help the U.S. economy only if other countries eliminated their tariffs and quotas in exchange. It is easier to gain political support for reducing or eliminating tariffs or quotas if it is done as part of an agreement with other countries that involves their eliminating some of their tariffs or quotas. But as the example of the sugar quota shows, *the U.S. economy would experience a gain in economic surplus from the elimination of tariffs and quotas even if other countries did not reduce their tariffs and quotas.* MyEconLab Concept Check

Other Barriers to Trade

In addition to tariffs and quotas, governments sometimes erect other barriers to trade. For example, all governments require that imports meet certain health and safety requirements. Sometimes, however, governments use these requirements to shield domestic firms from foreign competition. For example, a government may impose stricter health and safety requirements on imported goods than on goods produced by domestic firms.

Many governments also restrict imports of certain products on national security grounds. The argument is that in time of war, a country should not be dependent on imports of critical war materials. Once again, these restrictions are sometimes used more to protect domestic companies from competition than to protect national security. For example, for years, the U.S. government would buy military uniforms only from U.S. manufacturers, even though uniforms are not a critical war material. MyEconLab Concept Check

MyEconLab Study Plan

9.5 LEARNING OBJECTIVE

Evaluate the arguments over trade policies and globalization.

The Arguments over Trade Policies and Globalization

The argument over whether the U.S. government should regulate international trade has continued since the early days of the country. One particularly controversial attempt to restrict trade took place during the Great Depression of the 1930s. At that time, the United States and other countries attempted to help domestic firms by raising tariffs on foreign imports. The United States started the process by passing the Smoot-Hawley Tariff in 1930, which raised average tariff rates to more than 50 percent. As other countries retaliated by raising their tariffs, international trade collapsed.

By the end of World War II in 1945, government officials in the United States and Europe were looking for a way to reduce tariffs and revive international trade. To help achieve this goal, they set up the General Agreement on Tariffs and Trade (GATT) in 1948. Countries that joined GATT agreed not to impose new tariffs or import quotas. In addition, a series of *multilateral negotiations*, called *trade rounds*, took place, in which countries agreed to reduce tariffs from the very high levels of the 1930s.

In the 1940s, most international trade was in goods, and the GATT agreement covered only goods. In the following decades, trade in services and products incorporating *intellectual property*, such as software programs and movies, grew in importance. Many GATT members pressed for a new agreement that would cover services and intellectual property, as well as goods. A new agreement was negotiated, and in January 1995, the GATT was replaced by the **World Trade Organization (WTO)**, headquartered in Geneva, Switzerland. More than 150 countries are currently members of the WTO.

World Trade Organization (WTO) An international organization that oversees international trade agreements.

Why Do Some People Oppose the World Trade Organization?

During the years immediately after World War II, many low-income, or developing, countries enacted high tariffs and restricted investment by foreign companies. When these policies failed to produce much economic growth, many of these countries decided during the 1980s to become more open to foreign trade and investment. This process became known as **globalization**. Most developing countries joined the WTO and began to follow its policies.

Globalization The process of countries becoming more open to foreign trade and investment.

During the 1990s, opposition to globalization began to increase. Over the years, protests, which have sometimes turned violent, have occurred in cities hosting WTO meetings. Why would attempts to reduce trade barriers with the objective of increasing income around the world cause such a furious reaction? The opposition to the WTO comes from three sources. First, some opponents are specifically against the globalization process that began in the 1980s and became widespread in the 1990s. Second, other opponents have the same motivation as the supporters of tariffs in the 1930s—to erect trade barriers to protect domestic firms from foreign competition. Third, some critics of the WTO support globalization in principle but believe that the WTO favors the interests of the high-income countries at the expense of the low-income countries. Let's look more closely at the sources of opposition to the WTO.

Anti-Globalization Many of those who protest at WTO meetings distrust globalization. Some believe that free trade and foreign investment destroy the distinctive cultures of many countries. As developing countries began to open their economies to imports from the United States and other high-income countries, the imports of food, clothing, movies, and other goods began to replace the equivalent local products. So, a teenager in Thailand might be sitting in a McDonald's restaurant, wearing Levi's jeans and a Ralph Lauren shirt, listening to a song by Lady Gaga on his iPhone, before downloading *World War Z* to his iPad. Globalization has increased the variety of products available to consumers in developing countries, but some people argue that this is too high a price to pay for what they see as damage to local cultures.

Globalization has also allowed multinational corporations to relocate factories from high-income countries to low-income countries. These new factories in Indonesia, Malaysia, Pakistan, and other countries pay much lower wages than are paid in the United States, Europe, and Japan and often do not meet the environmental or safety regulations that are imposed in high-income countries. Some factories use child labor, which is illegal in high-income countries. Some people have argued that firms with factories in developing countries should pay workers wages as high as those paid in high-income countries. They also believe these firms should abide by the health, safety, and environmental regulations that exist in the high-income countries.

The governments of most developing countries have resisted these proposals. They argue that when the currently rich countries were poor, they also lacked environmental or safety standards, and their workers were paid low wages. They argue that it is easier for rich countries to afford high wages and environmental and safety regulations than it is for poor countries. They also point out that many jobs that seem to have very low wages based on the standards of high-income countries are often better than the alternatives available to workers in low-income countries.

Making the Connection
MyEconLab Video

The Unintended Consequences of Banning Goods Made with Child Labor

In many developing countries, such as Indonesia, Thailand, and Peru, children as young as seven or eight years old work ten or more hours a day. Reports of very young workers laboring long hours to produce goods for export have upset many people in high-income countries. In the United States, boycotts have been organized against stores that stock goods made in developing countries with child labor. Many people assume that if child workers in developing countries weren't working in factories making clothing, toys, and other products, they would be in school, as are children in high-income countries.

Would eliminating child labor, such as stitching soccer balls, improve the quality of children's lives?

In fact, children in developing countries usually have few good alternatives to work. Schooling is frequently available for only a few months each year, and even children who attend school rarely do so for more than a few years. Poor families are often unable to afford even the small costs of sending their children to school. Families may rely on the earnings of very young children to survive, as poor families once did in the United States, Europe, and Japan. There is substantial evidence that as incomes begin to rise in poor countries, families rely less on child labor. The United States eventually outlawed child labor, but not until 1938. In developing countries where child labor is common today, jobs producing export goods are usually better paying and less hazardous than the alternatives.

As preparations began in France for the 1998 World Cup, there were protests that Baden Sports—the main supplier of soccer balls—was purchasing the balls from suppliers in Pakistan that used child workers. France decided to ban all use of soccer balls made by child workers. Bowing to this pressure, Baden Sports moved production from Pakistan, where the balls were hand-stitched by child workers, to China, where the balls were machine-stitched by adult workers in factories. There was some criticism of the boycott of hand-stitched soccer balls at the time. In a broad study of child labor, three economists argued:

Of the array of possible employment in which impoverished children might engage, soccer ball stitching is probably one of the most benign.... [In Pakistan] children generally work alongside other family members in the home or in small workshops.... Nor are the children exposed to toxic chemicals, hazardous tools or brutal working conditions. Rather, the only serious criticism concerns the length of the typical child stitcher's work-day and the impact on formal education.

In fact, the alternatives to soccer ball stitching for child workers in Pakistan turned out to be extremely grim. According to Keith Maskus, an economist at the University of Colorado and the World Bank, a "large proportion" of the children who lost their jobs stitching soccer balls ended up begging or in prostitution.

Sources: Tom Wright, "Pakistan Defends Its Soccer Industry," *Wall Street Journal*, April 26, 2010; Drusilla K. Brown, Alan V. Deardorff, and Robert M. Stern, "U.S. Trade and Other Policy Options to Deter Foreign Exploitation of Child Labor," in Magnus Blomstrom and Linda S. Goldberg, eds., *Topics in Empirical International Economics: A Festchrift in Honor of Bob Lispey*, Chicago: University of Chicago Press, 2001; Tomas Larsson, *The Race to the Top: The Real Story of Globalization*,

Washington, DC: Cato Institute, 2001, p. 48; and Eric V. Edmonds and Nina Pavcnik, "Child Labor in the Global Economy," *Journal of Economic Perspectives*, Vol. 19, No. 1, Winter 2005, pp. 199–220.

Your Turn: Test your understanding by doing related problem 5.5 on page 301 at the end of this chapter.

MyEconLab Study Plan

"Old-Fashioned" Protectionism The anti-globalization argument against free trade and the WTO is relatively new. Another argument against free trade, called *protectionism*, has been around for centuries. **Protectionism** is the use of trade barriers to shield domestic firms from foreign competition. For as long as international trade has existed, governments have attempted to restrict it to protect domestic firms. As we saw with the analysis of the sugar quota, protectionism causes losses to consumers and eliminates jobs in the domestic industries that buy the protected product. In addition, by reducing the ability of countries to produce according to comparative advantage, protectionism reduces incomes.

> **Protectionism** The use of trade barriers to shield domestic firms from foreign competition.

Why, then, does protectionism attract support? Protectionism is usually justified on the basis of one of the following arguments:

- *Saving jobs.* Supporters of protectionism argue that free trade reduces employment by driving domestic firms out of business. It is true that when more-efficient foreign firms drive less-efficient domestic firms out of business, jobs are lost, but jobs are also lost when more-efficient domestic firms drive less-efficient domestic firms out of business. These job losses are rarely permanent. In the U.S. economy, jobs are lost and new jobs are created continually. No economic study has ever found a long-term connection between the total number of jobs available and the level of tariff protection for domestic industries. In addition, trade restrictions destroy jobs in some industries at the same time that they preserve jobs in others. The U.S. sugar quota may have saved jobs in the U.S. sugar industry, but it has also destroyed jobs in the U.S. candy industry.

- *Protecting high wages.* Some people worry that firms in high-income countries will have to start paying much lower wages to compete with firms in developing countries. This fear is misplaced, however, because free trade actually raises living standards by increasing economic efficiency. When a country practices protectionism and produces goods and services it could obtain more inexpensively from other countries, it reduces its standard of living. The United States could ban imports of coffee and begin growing it domestically. But doing so would entail a very high opportunity cost because coffee could only be grown in the continental United States in greenhouses and would require large amounts of labor and equipment. The coffee would have to sell for a very high price to cover these costs. Suppose the United States did ban coffee imports: Eliminating the ban at some future time would eliminate the jobs of U.S. coffee workers, but the standard of living in the United States would rise as coffee prices declined and labor, machinery, and other resources were moved out of coffee production and into production of goods and services for which the United States has a comparative advantage.

- *Protecting infant industries.* It is possible that firms in a country may have a comparative advantage in producing a good, but because the country begins production of the good later than other countries, its firms initially have higher costs. In producing some goods and services, substantial "learning by doing" occurs. As workers and firms produce more of the good or service, they gain experience and become more productive. Over time, these firms will have lower costs and can charge lower prices. As the firms in the "infant industry" gain experience, they will be able to compete successfully with foreign producers. Under free trade, however, they may not get a chance. The established foreign producers can sell the product at a lower price and drive domestic producers out of business before they gain enough experience to compete. To economists, the infant industry argument is the most persuasive of the protectionist arguments. It has a significant drawback, however. Tariffs used to protect an infant industry eliminate the need for the firms in the industry to become productive enough to compete with foreign firms. After World War II, the governments of many developing countries used the infant industry argument to justify high tariff rates. Unfortunately, most of their infant industries never grew up, and they continued for years as inefficient drains on their economies.

- *Protecting national security.* As already discussed, a country should not rely on other countries for goods that are critical to its military defense. For example, the United States would probably not want to import all its jet fighter engines from China. The definition of which goods are critical to military defense is a slippery one, however. In fact, it is rare for an industry to ask for protection without raising the issue of national security, even if its products have mainly nonmilitary uses.   MyEconLab Concept Check

Dumping

Dumping Selling a product for a price below its cost of production.

In recent years, the United States has extended protection to some domestic industries by using a provision in the WTO agreement that allows governments to impose tariffs in the case of *dumping*. **Dumping** is selling a product for a price below its cost of production. Using tariffs to offset the effects of dumping is controversial despite being allowed under the WTO agreement.

In practice, it is difficult to determine whether foreign companies are dumping goods because the true production costs of a good are not easy for governments to calculate. As a result, the WTO allows countries to determine that dumping has occurred if a product is exported for a lower price than it sells for on the home market. There is a problem with this approach, however. Often there are good business reasons for a firm to sell a product for different prices to different consumers. For example, the airlines charge business travelers higher ticket prices than leisure travelers. Firms also use "loss leaders"—products that are sold below cost, or even given away free—when introducing a new product or, in the case of retailing, to attract customers who will also buy full-price products. For example, during the holiday season, Wal-Mart sometimes offers toys at prices below what it pays to buy them from manufacturers. It's unclear why these normal business practices should be unacceptable when used in international trade.   MyEconLab Concept Check

Positive versus Normative Analysis (Once Again)

Economists emphasize the burden on the economy imposed by tariffs, quotas, and other government restrictions on free trade. Does it follow that these interferences are bad? Remember the distinction between *positive analysis* and *normative analysis*. Positive analysis concerns what *is*. Normative analysis concerns what *ought to be*. Measuring the effect of the sugar quota on the U.S. economy is an example of positive analysis. Asserting that the sugar quota is bad public policy and should be eliminated is normative analysis. The sugar quota—like all other interferences with trade—makes some people better off and some people worse off, and it reduces total income and consumption. Whether increasing the profits of U.S. sugar companies and the number of workers they employ justifies the costs imposed on consumers and the reduction in economic efficiency is a normative question.

Most economists do not support interferences with trade, such as the sugar quota. Few people become economists if they don't believe that markets should usually be as free as possible. But the opposite view is certainly intellectually respectable. It is possible for someone to understand the costs of tariffs and quotas but still believe that tariffs and quotas are a good idea, perhaps because he or she believes unrestricted free trade would cause too much disruption to the economy.

The success of industries in getting the government to erect barriers to foreign competition depends partly on some members of the public knowing the costs of trade barriers but supporting them anyway. However, two other factors are also at work:

1. The costs tariffs and quotas impose on consumers are large in total but relatively small per person. For example, the sugar quota imposes a total burden of $3.90 billion per year on consumers. Spread across 314 million Americans, the burden is less than $12.50 per person: too little for most people to worry about, even if they know the burden exists.
2. The jobs lost to foreign competition are easy to identify, but the jobs created by foreign trade are less easy to identify.

In other words, the industries that benefit from tariffs and quotas benefit a lot—for example, the sugar quota increases the profits of U.S. sugar producers by almost $2 billion—whereas each consumer loses relatively little. This concentration of benefits and widely spread burdens makes it easy to understand why members of Congress receive strong pressure from some industries to enact tariffs and quotas and relatively little pressure from the general public to reduce them.   MyEconLab Concept Check   MyEconLab Study Plan

Continued from page 271

Economics in Your Life

Have You Heard of the Tariff on Chinese Tires?

At the beginning of the chapter, we asked you to consider how U.S. tire workers convinced the federal government to impose a tariff on Chinese tires and why relatively few people have heard of this tariff. In the chapter, we saw that trade restrictions tend to preserve relatively few jobs in the protected industries, while leading to job losses in other industries and costing consumers billions of dollars per year in higher prices. We have also seen, though, that *per person*, the burden of specific trade restrictions can be small. The sugar quota, for instance, imposes a per-person cost on consumers of only about $12.50 per year. Few people will take the trouble of writing a letter to their member of Congress or otherwise express their views to try to save $12.50 per year. In fact, few people will even spend the time to become aware that a specific trade restriction exists. So, if before you read this chapter you had never heard of the tire tariff, you are certainly not alone.

Conclusion

There are few issues economists agree upon more than the economic benefits of free trade. However, there are few political issues as controversial as government policy toward trade. Many people who would be reluctant to see the government interfere with domestic trade are quite willing to see it interfere with international trade. The damage high tariffs inflicted on the world economy during the 1930s shows what can happen when governments around the world abandon free trade. Whether future episodes of that type can be avoided is by no means certain.

Visit MyEconLab for a news article and analysis related to the concepts in this chapter.

Chapter Summary and Problems

Key Terms

Absolute advantage, p. 276

Autarky, p. 277

Comparative advantage, p. 275

Dumping, p. 294

Exports, p. 272

External economies, p. 281

Free trade, p. 283

Globalization, p. 291

Imports, p. 272

Opportunity cost, p. 275

Protectionism, p. 293

Quota, p. 286

Tariff, p. 272

Terms of trade, p. 277

Voluntary export restraint (VER), p. 286

World Trade Organization (WTO), p. 291

9.1 The United States in the International Economy, pages 272–275

LEARNING OBJECTIVE: Discuss the role of international trade in the U.S. economy.

Summary

International trade has been increasing in recent decades, in part because of reductions in *tariffs* and other barriers to trade. A **tariff** is a tax imposed by a government on imports. The quantity of goods and services the United States imports and exports has been continually increasing. **Imports** are goods and services bought domestically but produced in other countries. **Exports** are goods and services produced domestically and sold to other countries. Today, the United States is the second leading exporting country in the world behind China, and about 20 percent of U.S. manufacturing jobs depend on exports.

 Visit www.myeconlab.com to complete these exercises online and get instant feedback.

Review Questions

1.1 Briefly explain whether the value of U.S. exports is typically larger or smaller than the value of U.S. imports.

1.2 Are imports and exports now a smaller or larger fraction of GDP than they were 40 years ago?

1.3 Briefly explain whether you agree with the following statement: "International trade is more important to the U.S. economy than it is to most other economies."

Problems and Applications

1.4 If the United States were to stop trading goods and services with other countries, which U.S. industries would be likely to see their sales decline the most? Briefly explain.

1.5 Briefly explain whether you agree with the following statement: "Japan has always been much more heavily involved in international trade than are most other nations. In fact, today Japan exports a larger fraction of its GDP than Germany, Great Britain, or the United States."

1.6 Why might a smaller country, such as the Netherlands, be more likely to import and export larger fractions of its GDP than would a larger country, such as China or the United States?

1.7 **[Related to the** Chapter Opener **on page 271 and the** Making the Connection **on page 273]** Goodyear manufactures tires in the United States, so you might expect that the firm would benefit from a tariff on imports of Chinese tires. Yet Goodyear actually opposed the Obama administration's decision to impose the tariff. Briefly explain why Goodyear was not in favor of the tire tariff.

9.2 Comparative Advantage in International Trade, pages 275–277

LEARNING OBJECTIVE: Understand the difference between comparative advantage and absolute advantage in international trade.

Summary

Comparative advantage is the ability of an individual, a firm, or a country to produce a good or service at the lowest **opportunity cost**. **Absolute advantage** is the ability to produce more of a good or service than competitors when using the same amount of resources. Countries trade on the basis of comparative advantage, not on the basis of absolute advantage.

MyEconLab Visit www.myeconlab.com to complete these exercises online and get instant feedback.

Review Questions

2.1 What is the difference between absolute advantage and comparative advantage? Will a country always be an exporter of a good in the production of which it has an absolute advantage? Briefly explain.

2.2 A World Trade Organization (WTO) publication calls comparative advantage "arguably the single most powerful insight in economics." What is comparative advantage? What makes it such a powerful insight?

Source: World Trade Organization, "Understanding the WTO," www .wto.org/english/thewto_e/whatis_e/tif_e/fact3_e.htm.

Problems and Applications

2.3 Why do the goods that countries import and export change over time? Use the concept of comparative advantage in your answer.

2.4 In a newspaper column, Frank Wolak, a professor of economics at Stanford, referred to "the economic forces that lead to most children's toys being developed in the United States and mass-produced in China and other developing countries." What economic forces is he referring to? If a U.S. company develops a toy, why is a Chinese company likely to end up manufacturing the toy?

Source: Frank A. Wolak, "Our Comparative Advantage," *New York Times*, January 19, 2011.

2.5 Briefly explain whether you agree with the following argument: "Unfortunately, Bolivia does not have a comparative advantage with respect to the United States in the production of any good or service." (*Hint:* You do not need any specific information about the economies of Bolivia or the United States to be able to answer this question.)

2.6 The following table shows the hourly output per worker for Greece and Italy measured as quarts of olive oil and pounds of pasta:

	Output per Hour of Work	
	Olive Oil	Pasta
Greece	4	2
Italy	4	8

Calculate the opportunity cost of producing olive oil and pasta in both Greece and Italy.

2.7 Patrick J. Buchanan, a former presidential candidate, argued in his book on the global economy that there is a flaw in David Ricardo's theory of comparative advantage:

> Classical free trade theory fails the test of common sense. According to Ricardo's law of comparative advantage … if America makes better computers and textiles than China does, but our advantage in computers is greater than our advantage in textiles, we should (1) focus on computers, (2) let China make textiles, and (3) trade U.S. computers for Chinese textiles…. The doctrine begs a question. If Americans are more efficient than Chinese in making clothes … why surrender the more efficient American industry? Why shift to a reliance on a Chinese textile industry that will take years to catch up to where American factories are today?

Do you agree with Buchanan's argument? Briefly explain.

Source: Patrick J. Buchanan, *The Great Betrayal: How American Sovereignty and Social Justice Are Being Sacrificed to the Gods of the Global Economy*, Boston: Little, Brown & Company, 1998, p. 66.

2.8 While running for president, Barack Obama made the following statement: "Well, look, people don't want a cheaper T-shirt if they're losing a job in the process." What did Obama mean by the phrase "losing a job in the process"? Using the economic concept of comparative advantage, explain under what circumstances it would make sense for the United States to produce all of the T-shirts purchased in the United States. Do you agree with President Obama's statement? Briefly explain.

Source: James Pethokoukis, "Democratic Debate Spawns Weird Economics," *U.S. News & World Report*, August 8, 2007.

9.3 How Countries Gain from International Trade, pages 277–283

LEARNING OBJECTIVE: Explain how countries gain from international trade.

Summary

Autarky is a situation in which a country does not trade with other countries. The **terms of trade** is the ratio at which a country can trade its exports for imports from other countries. When a country specializes in producing goods for which it has a comparative advantage and trades for the other goods it needs, the country will have a higher level of income and consumption. We do not see complete specialization in production for three reasons: (1) Not all goods and services are traded internationally, (2) production of most goods involves increasing opportunity costs, and (3) tastes for products differ across countries. Although the population of a country as a whole benefits from trade, firms—and their workers—that are unable to compete with lower-cost foreign producers lose. Among the main sources of comparative advantage are climate and natural resources, relative abundance of labor and capital, technology, and external economies. **External economies** are reductions in a firm's costs that result from an increase in the size of an industry. A country may develop a comparative advantage in the production of a good, and then as time passes and circumstances change, the country may lose its comparative advantage in producing that good and develop a comparative advantage in producing other goods.

 MyEconLab　Visit **www.myeconlab.com** to complete these exercises online and get instant feedback.

Review Questions

3.1 Briefly explain how international trade increases a country's consumption.

3.2 What is meant by a country specializing in the production of a good? Is it typical for countries to be completely specialized? Briefly explain.

3.3 What are the main sources of comparative advantage?

3.4 Does everyone gain from international trade? If not, explain which groups lose.

Problems and Applications

3.5 **[Related to** Solved Problem 9.3 **on page 278]** The following table shows the hourly output per worker in two industries in Chile and Argentina:

	Output per Hour of Work	
	Hats	Beer
Chile	8	6
Argentina	1	2

a. Explain which country has an absolute advantage in the production of hats and which country has an absolute advantage in the production of beer.

b. Explain which country has a comparative advantage in the production of hats and which country has a comparative advantage in the production of beer.

c. Suppose that Chile and Argentina currently do not trade with each other. Each has 1,000 hours of labor to use producing hats and beer, and the countries are currently producing the amounts of each good shown in the following table:

	Hats	Beer
Chile	7,200	600
Argentina	600	800

Using this information, give a numerical example of how Chile and Argentina can both gain from trade. Assume that after trading begins, one hat can be exchanged for one barrel of beer.

3.6 **[Related to** Solved Problem 9.3 **on page 278]** A political commentator makes the following statement:

The idea that international trade should be based on the comparative advantage of each country is fine for rich countries like the United States and Japan. Rich countries have educated workers and large quantities of machinery and equipment. These advantages allow them to produce every product more efficiently than poor countries can. Poor countries like Kenya and Bolivia have nothing to gain from international trade based on comparative advantage.

Do you agree with this argument? Briefly explain.

3.7 Briefly explain whether you agree with the following statement: "Most countries exhaust their comparative advantage in producing a good or service before they reach complete specialization."

3.8 Is free trade likely to benefit a large, populous country more than a small country with fewer people? Briefly explain.

3.9 An article in the *New Yorker* magazine states, "the main burden of trade-related job losses and wage declines has fallen on middle- and lower-income Americans. But ... the very people who suffer most from free trade are often, paradoxically, among its biggest beneficiaries." Explain how it is possible that middle- and lower-income Americans are both the biggest losers and at the same time the biggest winners from free trade.

Source: James Surowiecki, "The Free-Trade Paradox," *New Yorker*, May 26, 2008.

3.10 Hal Varian, an economist at the University of California, Berkeley, has made two observations about international trade:

a. Trade allows a country "to produce more with less."

b. There is little doubt who wins [from trade] in the long run: consumers.

Briefly explain whether you agree with either or both of these observations.

Source: Hal R. Varian, "The Mixed Bag of Productivity," *New York Times*, October 23, 2003.

3.11 Imagine that the following graph shows Tanzania's production possibilities frontier for cashew nuts and mangoes. Assume that the output per hour of work is 8 bushels of cashew nuts or 2 bushels of mangoes and that Tanzania has 1,000 hours of labor. Without trade, Tanzania evenly splits its labor hours between cashews and mangoes and produces and consumes at point A.

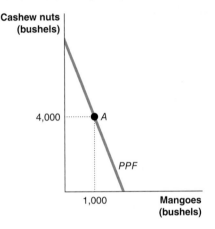

a. Suppose Tanzania opens trade with Kenya, and Kenya's output per hour of work is 1 bushel of cashew nuts or 1 bushel of mangoes. Having the comparative advantage, Tanzania completely specializes in cashew nuts. How many bushels of cashew nuts can Tanzania produce? Denote this point on the graph as point B.

b. Suppose Tanzania keeps 5,000 bushels of cashew nuts and exports the remaining 3,000 bushels. If the terms of trade are 1 bushel of mangoes for 2 bushels of cashew nuts, how many bushels of mangoes will Tanzania get in exchange? Denote on the graph the quantity of cashew nuts and mangoes that Tanzania consumes with trade and label this point as point C. How does point C with trade compare to point A without trade?

c. With trade, is Tanzania producing on its production possibilities frontier? With trade, is Tanzania consuming on its production possibilities frontier?

3.12 **[Related to the** Don't Let This Happen to You **on page 280]** In 2011, President Barack Obama described a trade agreement reached with the government of Colombia as a "'win-win' for both our countries." Is everyone in both countries likely to win from the agreement? Briefly explain.

Source: Kent Klein, "Obama: Free Trade Agreement a 'Win-Win' for US, Colombia," *Voice of America* (voanews.com), accessed April 7, 2011.

3.13 **[Related to the** Making the Connection **on page 282]** Instagram is a smartphone app now owned by Facebook. According to an article that discusses the climate for software firms in the San Francisco Bay Area, the success of Instagram "is a tale about the culture of the Bay Area tech scene, driven by a tightly woven web of entrepreneurs and investors who nurture one another's projects with money, advice and introductions to the right people." What advantages does being located in the Bay Area give to startup software firms? In what circumstances can software firms located elsewhere overcome these advantages? Are the advantages the Bay Area has likely to persist over time?

Source: Somini Sengupta, Nicole Perlroth, and Jenna Wortham, "Behind Instagram's Success, Networking the Old Way," *New York Times*, April 13, 2012.

9.4 **Government Policies That Restrict International Trade, pages 283–290**
LEARNING OBJECTIVE: Analyze the economic effects of government policies that restrict international trade.

Summary

Free trade is trade between countries without government restrictions. Government policies that interfere with trade usually take the form of *tariffs*, *quotas*, or *voluntary export restraints*. A tariff is a tax imposed by a government on imports. A **quota** is a numerical limit imposed by a government on the quantity of a good that can be imported into the country. A **voluntary export restraint (VER)** is an agreement negotiated between two countries that places a numerical limit on the quantity of a good that can be imported by one country from the other country. The federal government's sugar quota costs U.S. consumers $3.9 billion per year, or about $1.3 million per year for each job saved in the sugar industry. Saving jobs by using tariffs and quotas is often very expensive.

MyEconLab   Visit **www.myeconlab.com** to complete these exercises online and get instant feedback.

Review Questions

4.1 What is a tariff? What is a quota? Give an example, other than a quota, of a nontariff barrier to trade.

4.2 Who gains and who loses when a country imposes a tariff or a quota on imports of a good?

Problems and Applications

4.3 Political commentator B. Bruce-Briggs once wrote the following in the *Wall Street Journal*: "This is not to say that the case for international free trade is invalid; it is just irrelevant. It is an 'if only everybody …' argument.… In the real world almost everybody sees benefits in economic nationalism." What do you think he means by "economic nationalism"? Do you agree that a country benefits from free trade only if every other country also practices free trade? Briefly explain.

Source: B. Bruce-Briggs, "The Coming Overthrow of Free Trade," *Wall Street Journal*, February 24, 1983.

4.4 Two U.S. senators made the following argument against allowing free trade: "Fewer and fewer Americans support our government's trade policy. They see a shrinking middle class, lost jobs and exploding trade deficits. Yet supporters of free trade continue to push for more of the same—more job-killing trade agreements." Do you agree with these senators that reducing barriers to trade reduces the number of jobs available to workers in the United States? Briefly explain.

Source: Byron Dorgan and Sherrod Brown, "How Free Trade Hurts," *Washington Post*, December 23, 2006.

4.5 The United States produces beef and also imports beef from other countries.
   a. Draw a graph showing the demand and supply of beef in the United States. Assume that the United States can import as much as it wants at the world price of beef without causing the world price of beef to increase. Be sure to indicate on your graph the quantity of beef imported.
   b. Now show on your graph the effect of the United States imposing a tariff on beef. Be sure to indicate on your graph the quantity of beef sold by U.S. producers before and after the tariff is imposed, the quantity of beef imported before and after the tariff, and the price of beef in the United States before and after the tariff.
   c. Discuss who benefits and who loses when the United States imposes a tariff on beef.

4.6 When Congress was considering a bill to impose quotas on imports of textiles, shoes, and other products, the late Milton Friedman, a Nobel Prize–winning economist, made the following comment: "The consumer will be forced to spend several extra dollars to subsidize the producers [of these goods] by one dollar. A straight handout would be far cheaper." Why would a quota result in consumers paying much more than domestic producers receive? Where do the other dollars go? What does Friedman mean by a "straight handout"? Why would a straight handout be cheaper than a quota?

Source: Milton Friedman, "Free Trade," *Newsweek Magazine*, August 27, 1970.

4.7 A student makes the following argument:

> Tariffs on imports of foreign goods into the United States will cause the foreign companies to add the amount of the tariff to the prices they charge in the United States for those goods. Instead of putting a tariff on imported goods, we should ban importing them. Banning imported goods is better than putting tariffs on them because U.S. producers benefit from the reduced competition, and U.S. consumers don't have to pay the higher prices caused by tariffs.

Briefly explain whether you agree with the student's reasoning.

4.8 Suppose China decides to pay large subsidies to any Chinese company that exports goods or services to the United States. As a result, these companies are able to sell products in the United States at far below their cost of production. In addition, China decides to bar all imports from the United States. The dollars that the United States pays to import Chinese goods are left in banks in China. Will this strategy raise or lower the standard of living in China? Will it raise or lower the standard of living in the United States? Briefly explain. Be sure to provide a definition of "standard of living" in your answer.

4.9 The following graph shows the effect on consumer surplus, producer surplus, government tariff revenue, and economic surplus of a tariff of $1 per unit on imports of plastic combs into the United States. Use the areas denoted in the graph to answer the following questions.

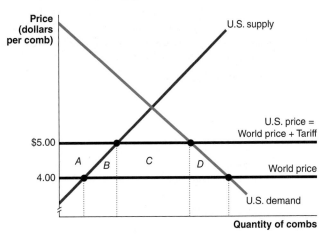

a. Which area shows the losses to U.S. consumers of buying a smaller quantity of combs than they would have if they could have purchased them at the world price?
b. Which area shows the losses to U.S. consumers of having to buy combs from U.S. producers who are less efficient than foreign producers?
c. Which areas show the deadweight loss to the U.S. economy as a result of the tariff on combs?

4.10 The following graph shows the situation after the U.S. government removes a tariff on imports of canned tuna.

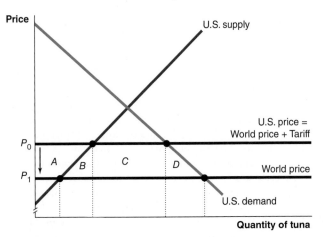

a. Which areas show the gain in consumer surplus?
b. Which area shows the loss in producer surplus?

c. Which area shows the loss in government tariff revenue?
d. Which areas show the gain in economic surplus?

4.11 According to an editorial in the *Washington Post*: "Sugar protectionism is a burden on consumers and a job-killer."
a. In what sense does the United States practice "sugar protectionism"?
b. In what way is sugar protectionism a burden on consumers? In what way is it a job-killer?
c. If sugar protectionism has the bad effects stated in the editorial, why don't Congress and the president eliminate it?

Source: "Sourball," *Washington Post*, March 22, 2010.

4.12 [Related to Solved Problem 9.4 on page 287] Suppose that the United States currently both produces kumquats and imports them. The U.S. government then decides to restrict international trade in kumquats by imposing a quota that allows imports of only 6 million pounds of kumquats into the United States each year. The figure shows the results of imposing the quota.

Fill in the table in the next column using the letters in the figure:

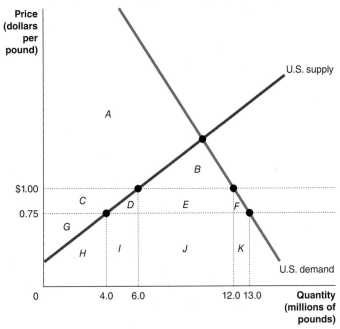

	Without Quota	With Quota
World price of kumquats	_____	_____
U.S. price of kumquats	_____	_____
Quantity supplied by U.S. firms	_____	_____
Quantity demanded	_____	_____
Quantity imported	_____	_____
Area of consumer surplus	_____	_____
Area of domestic producer surplus	_____	_____
Area of deadweight loss	_____	_____

4.13 Suppose the government is considering imposing either a tariff or a quota on canned peaches. Assume that the proposed quota has the same effect on the U.S. price of canned peaches as the proposed tariff. Use the graph to answer the following questions.

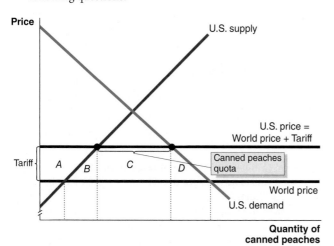

a. If the government imposes a tariff, which area shows the government tariff revenue?

b. If the government imposes a quota, which area shows the gain to foreign producers of canned peaches?

c. As a consumer of peaches, would you prefer the government impose the tariff or the quota? Briefly explain.

4.14 **[Related to the** Making the Connection **on page 289]** An economic analysis of a proposal to impose a quota on steel imports into the United States indicated that the quota would save 3,700 jobs in the steel industry but cost about 35,000 jobs in other U.S. industries. Why would a quota on steel imports cause employment to decline in other industries? Which other industries is a steel quota likely to affect?

Source: Douglas A. Irwin, *Free Trade Under Fire*, Princeton, NJ: Princeton University Press, 2002, p. 82.

4.15 **[Related to the** Making the Connection **on page 289]** According to the analysis by Hufbauer and Lowry, of the additional $1.1 billion consumers spent on tires as a result of the tariff on Chinese tires, the workers whose jobs were saved in the U.S. tire industry received only about $48 million in wages. Wouldn't it have been cheaper for the federal government to have raised taxes on U.S. consumers and given the money to tire workers rather than to have imposed a tariff? If so, why didn't the federal government adopt this alternative policy?

Source: Gary Clyde Hufbauer and Sean Lowry, "US Tire Tariffs: Saving Few Jobs at High Cost," Peterson Institute for International Economics, Policy Brief Number PB12-9, April 2012.

9.5	**The Arguments over Trade Policies and Globalization, pages 290–295**

LEARNING OBJECTIVE: Evaluate the arguments over trade policies and globalization.

Summary

The **World Trade Organization (WTO)** is an international organization that enforces trade agreements among members. The WTO has promoted **globalization**, the process of countries becoming more open to foreign trade and investment. Some critics of the WTO argue that globalization has damaged local cultures around the world. Other critics oppose the WTO because they believe in **protectionism**, which is the use of trade barriers to shield domestic firms from foreign competition. The WTO allows countries to use tariffs in cases of **dumping**, when an imported product is sold for a price below its cost of production. Economists can point out the burden imposed on the economy by tariffs, quotas, and other government interferences with free trade. But whether these policies should be used is a normative decision.

MyEconLab Visit **www.myeconlab.com** to complete these exercises online and get instant feedback.

Review Questions

5.1 What events led to the General Agreement on Tariffs and Trade (GATT)? Why did the WTO eventually replace the GATT?

5.2 What is globalization? Why are some people opposed to globalization?

5.3 What is protectionism? Who benefits and who loses from protectionist policies? What are the main arguments people use to justify protectionism?

5.4 What is dumping? Who benefits and who loses from dumping? What problems arise when anti-dumping laws are implemented?

Problems and Applications

5.5 **[Related to the** Making the Connection **on page 292]** The following excerpt is from a newspaper story on President Bill Clinton's proposal to create a group within the World Trade Organization (WTO) responsible for developing labor standards. The story was published just before a 1999 WTO meeting in Seattle that ended in rioting:

> [President Clinton proposed that] core labor standards ... become "part of every trade agreement. And ultimately I would favor a system in which sanctions would come for violating any provision of a trade agreement...." But the new U.S. stand is sure to meet massive resistance from developing countries, which make up more than 100 of the 135 countries in the WTO. They are not interested in adopting tougher U.S. labor standards.

What did Clinton mean by "core labor standards"? Why would developing countries resist adopting these standards?

Source: Terence Hunt, "Salute to Trade's Benefits Turns into 'Kind of Circus,'" *Associated Press*, December 2, 1999.

5.6 Steven Landsburg, an economist at the University of Rochester, wrote the following in an article in the *New York Times*:

> Free trade is not only about the right of American consumers to buy at the cheapest possible price; it's also about the right of foreign producers to earn a living. Steelworkers in West Virginia struggle hard to make ends meet. So do steelworkers in South Korea. To protect one at the expense of the other, solely because of where they happened to be born, is a moral outrage.

How does the U.S. government protect steelworkers in West Virginia at the expense of steelworkers in South Korea? Is Landsburg making a positive or a normative statement? A few days later, Tom Redburn published an article disagreeing with Landsburg:

> It is not some evil character flaw to care more about the welfare of people nearby than about that of those far away—it's human nature. And it is morally—and economically—defensible.... A society that ignores the consequences of economic disruption on those among its citizens who come out at the short end of the stick is not only heartless, it also undermines its own cohesion and adaptability.

Which of the two arguments do you find most convincing?

Source: Steven E. Landsburg, "Who Cares if the Playing Field Is Level?" *New York Times*, June 13, 2001; and Tom Redburn, "Economic View: Of Politics, Free Markets, and Tending to Society," *New York Times*, June 17, 2001.

5.7 Suppose you are explaining the benefits of free trade and someone states, "I don't understand all the principles of comparative advantage and gains from trade. I just know that if I buy something produced in America, I create a job for an American, and if I buy something produced in Brazil, I create a job for a Brazilian." Do you agree with this statement? When the United States imports products for which it does not have a comparative advantage, does that mean that there are fewer jobs in the United States? In the example with Japan and the United States producing and trading cellphones and tablets, when the United States imports cellphones from Japan, does the number of jobs in the United States decline?

5.8 Every year, the Gallup poll asks a sample of people in the United States whether they believe foreign trade provides "an opportunity for economic growth through increased U.S. exports," or whether they believe foreign trade represents "a threat to the economy from foreign imports." The table shows the responses for two years:

	View of Foreign Trade		
Year	Favorable to Foreign Trade	Unfavorable	State of the U.S. Economy
2008	41%	52%	Deep economic recession
2013	57%	35%	Economic expansion

a. Do you believe that foreign trade helps the economy or hurts it? (Be sure to define what you mean by "helps" or "hurts.")
b. Why might the general public's opinion of foreign trade be substantially different during an economic recession as opposed to during an economic expansion?
c. The poll also showed that while 55 percent of people aged 18 to 29 had a favorable opinion of foreign trade, only 41 percent of people age 65 and over did. Why might younger people have a more favorable view of foreign trade than older people?

Source: Gallup Poll, February 28, 2013, http://www.gallup.com/poll/160748/americans-shift-positive-view-foreign-trade.aspx.

5.9 An article in the *Economist* magazine notes: "One analysis suggests that just getting rid of tariffs could raise Europe's GDP by around 0.4% and America's by a percentage point."
a. Why would getting rid of tariffs be likely to increase the total production of goods and services in Europe and the United States?
b. Why might someone who accepts this analysis still be opposed to eliminating tariffs?

Source: "The Gift That Goes on Giving," *Economist*, December 22, 2012.

5.10 The following appeared in a magazine article that argued against free trade: "The U.S. is currently in a precarious position. In addition to geopolitical threats, we face a severe economic shock. We have already lost trillions of dollars and millions of jobs to foreigners." If a country engages in free trade, is the total number of jobs in the country likely to decline? Briefly explain.

Source: Vladimir Masch, "A Radical Plan to Manage Globalization," *BusinessWeek*, February 14, 2007.

Chapter Outline and **Learning** Objectives

J.C. Penney Learns That Simplifying Prices Isn't Simple

In 2010, the J.C. Penney department store chain had nearly 600 "sales," and it sold almost three-quarters of its products at prices marked down by at least 50 percent. In a sense, however, these sales were illusions because Penney had raised prices before discounting them. They also often required customers to clip coupons to get the sale price. Soon after being named chief executive officer (CEO) of Penney in 2011, Ron Johnson decided to try a new pricing strategy of "everyday low prices" that eliminated most sales and coupons. He argued that the new policy would help consumers by eliminating a confusing pricing system while at the same time cutting Penney's costs because employees would no longer have to continually put new price tags on merchandise. But the new pricing policy backfired. Penney's sales plunged 25 percent in 2012, and Johnson was fired, having been CEO for only 17 months.

What was wrong with Johnson's pricing policy? First, the everyday low prices ended up being higher than the sale prices under the previous pricing policy. Some of Penney's customers noticed the price increases and switched to shopping at Wal-Mart and other department stores. Some economists, though, believe that Johnson ran into an even bigger problem: Although economists generally assume that people have enough information to make optimal buying decisions, this assumption may not always be accurate. For example, many consumers may only have a rough idea of the typical price of a pair of jeans or a shirt. These consumers have difficulty knowing whether everyday low prices really are low. Instead, they wait for sales and use coupons because they believe doing so allows them to buy at lower-than-normal prices. As Alexander Chernev of Northwestern University put it: "J.C. Penney might say its a fair price, but why should consumers trust J.C. Penney?" He argues that consumers "want a great deal," which they believe they get only if a store is having a sale or if they use coupons.

As we will see, we can better understand the failure of Penney's pricing strategy by using insights from *behavioral economics*, which is the study of situations in which people make choices that do not appear to be economically rational. In this chapter, we will examine how consumers make decisions about which products to buy. Firms must understand consumer behavior to determine what strategies are likely to be most effective in selling their products.

Sources: Stephanie Clifford and Catherine Rampell, "Sometimes, We Want Prices to Fool Us," *New York Times*, April 13, 2013; Wendy Liebmann, "What Will We Learn from Ron Johnson's Mistake?" *Forbes*, May 8, 2013; and Brad Tuttle, "The 5 Big Mistakes that Led to Ron Johnson's Ouster at JC Penney," *Time*, April 9, 2013.

Economics in Your Life

Do You Make Rational Decisions?

Economists generally assume that people make decisions in a rational, consistent way. But are people actually as rational as economists assume? Consider the following situation: You bought a concert ticket for $75, which is the most you were willing to pay. While you are in line to enter the concert hall, someone offers you $90 for the ticket. Would you sell the ticket? Would an economist think it is rational to sell the ticket? As you read this chapter, try to answer these questions. You can check your answers against those we provide on **page 328** at the end of this chapter.

W e begin this chapter by exploring how consumers make decisions. We have seen that economists usually assume that people act in a rational, self-interested way. In explaining consumer behavior, economists believe people make choices that will leave them as satisfied as possible, given their *tastes*, their *incomes*, and the *prices* of the goods and services available to them. We will see how downward-sloping demand curves result from the economic model of consumer behavior. We will also explore how in certain situations, knowing which decision is the best one can be difficult. In these cases, economic reasoning provides a powerful tool for consumers to improve their decision making. Finally, we will see that *experimental economics* has shown that factors such as social pressure and notions of fairness can affect consumer behavior. We will look at how businesses take these factors into account when setting prices. In the appendix to this chapter, we extend the analysis by using indifference curves and budget lines to understand consumer behavior.

10.1 LEARNING OBJECTIVE

Define utility and explain how consumers choose goods and services to maximize their utility.

Utility and Consumer Decision Making

We have seen that the model of demand and supply is a powerful tool for analyzing how prices and quantities are determined. We have also seen that, according to the *law of demand*, whenever the price of a good falls, the quantity demanded increases. In this section, we will show how the economic model of consumer behavior leads to the law of demand.

The Economic Model of Consumer Behavior in a Nutshell

Imagine walking through a shopping mall, trying to decide how to spend your clothing budget. If you had an unlimited budget, your decision would be easy: Just buy as much of everything as you want. Given that you have a limited budget, what do you do? Economists assume that consumers act so as to make themselves as well off as possible. Therefore, you should choose the one combination of clothes that makes you as well off as possible from among those combinations that you can afford. Stated more generally, the economic model of consumer behavior predicts that consumers will choose to buy the combination of goods and services that makes them as well off as possible from among all the combinations that their budgets allow them to buy.

Although this prediction may seem obvious and not particularly useful, we will see that it leads to conclusions that are useful—but not obvious.   MyEconLab Concept Check

Utility

Utility The enjoyment or satisfaction people receive from consuming goods and services.

How much satisfaction you receive from consuming a particular combination of goods and services depends on your tastes or preferences. There is an old saying—"There's no accounting for tastes"—and economists don't try to. If you buy a can of Red Bull energy drink instead of a can of Monster Energy, even though Monster Energy has a lower price, you must receive more enjoyment or satisfaction from drinking Red Bull. Economists refer to the enjoyment or satisfaction people receive from consuming goods and services as **utility**. So we can say that the goal of a consumer is to spend available income so as to maximize utility. But utility is a difficult concept to measure because there is no way of knowing exactly how much enjoyment or satisfaction someone receives from consuming a product. Similarly, it is not possible to compare utility across consumers. There is no way of knowing for sure whether Jill receives more or less satisfaction than Jack from drinking a can of Red Bull.

Two hundred years ago, economists hoped to measure utility in units called *utils*. The util would be an objective measure in the same way that temperature is: If it is 75 degrees in New York and 75 degrees in Los Angeles, it is just as warm in both cities. These economists wanted to say that if Jack's utility from drinking a can of Red Bull is 10 utils and Jill's utility is 5 utils, then Jack receives exactly twice the satisfaction from drinking a can of Red Bull as Jill does. In fact, it is *not* possible to measure utility across people. It turns out that none of the important conclusions of the economic model of consumer behavior depend on utility being directly measurable (a point we demonstrate in the appendix to this chapter). Nevertheless, the economic model of consumer behavior is easier to understand if we assume that utility is something directly measurable, like temperature.   MyEconLab Concept Check

The Principle of Diminishing Marginal Utility

To make the model of consumer behavior more concrete, let's see how a consumer makes decisions in a case involving just two products: pizza and Coke. To begin, consider how the utility you receive from consuming a good changes with the quantity of the good you consume. Suppose that you have just arrived at a Super Bowl party where the hosts are serving pizza and you are very hungry. In this situation, you are likely to receive quite a lot of enjoyment, or utility, from consuming the first slice of pizza. Suppose this satisfaction is measurable and is equal to 20 units of utility, or utils. After eating the first slice, you decide to have a second slice. Because you are no longer as hungry, the satisfaction you receive from eating the second slice of pizza is less than the satisfaction you received from eating the first slice. Consuming the second slice increases your utility by only an *additional* 16 utils, which raises your *total* utility from eating the 2 slices to 36 utils. If you continue eating slices, each additional slice gives you less and less additional satisfaction.

The table in Figure 10.1 shows the relationship between the number of slices of pizza you consume while watching the Super Bowl and the amount of utility you receive. The second column in the table shows the total utility you receive from eating a particular number of slices. The third column shows the additional utility, or **marginal utility (*MU*)**, you receive from consuming one additional slice. (Remember that in economics, *marginal* means *additional*.) For example, as you increase your consumption from 2 slices to 3 slices, your total utility increases from 36 to 46, so your marginal utility from consuming the third slice is 10 utils. As the table shows, by the time you eat the fifth slice of pizza that evening, your marginal utility is very low: only 2 utils. If you were to eat a sixth slice, you would become slightly ill, and your marginal utility would actually be a *negative* 3 utils.

Figure 10.1 also plots the numbers from the table as graphs. Panel (a) shows how your total utility rises as you eat the first 5 slices of pizza and then falls as you eat the sixth slice. Panel (b) shows how your marginal utility declines with each additional slice you eat and finally becomes negative when you eat the sixth slice. The height of the marginal utility line at any quantity of pizza in panel (b) represents the change in utility as a result of consuming that additional slice. For example, the change in utility as a result of consuming 4 slices instead of 3 is 6 utils, so the height of the marginal utility line in panel (b) for the fourth slice is 6 utils.

The relationship illustrated in Figure 10.1 between consuming additional units of a product during a period of time and the marginal utility received from consuming each additional unit is called the **law of diminishing marginal utility**. For nearly every good or service, the more you consume during a period of time, the less you increase your total satisfaction from each additional unit you consume.   MyEconLab Concept Check

The Rule of Equal Marginal Utility per Dollar Spent

The key challenge for consumers is to decide how to allocate their limited incomes among all the products they wish to buy. Every consumer has to make trade-offs: If you have $100 to spend on entertainment for the month, then the more movies you rent or buy online, the fewer movies you can see in the theater. Economists refer to the limited amount of income you have available to spend on goods and services as your **budget constraint**. The principle of diminishing marginal utility helps us understand how consumers can best spend their limited incomes on the products available to them.

Suppose you attend a Super Bowl party at a restaurant, and you have $10 to spend on refreshments. Pizza is selling for $2 per slice, and Coke is selling for $1 per cup. Table 10.1 on page 309 shows the relationship between the amount of pizza you eat, the

Marginal utility (*MU*) The change in total utility a person receives from consuming one additional unit of a good or service.

Law of diminishing marginal utility The principle that consumers experience diminishing additional satisfaction as they consume more of a good or service during a given period of time.

Budget constraint The limited amount of income available to consumers to spend on goods and services.

Figure 10.1

Total and Marginal Utility from Eating Pizza on Super Bowl Sunday

The table shows that for the first 5 slices of pizza, the more you eat, the more your total satisfaction, or utility, increases. If you eat a sixth slice, you start to feel ill from eating too much pizza, and your total utility falls. Each additional slice increases your utility by less than the previous slice, so your marginal utility from each slice is less than the one before. Panel (a) shows your total utility rising as you eat the first 5 slices and falling with the sixth slice. Panel (b) shows your marginal utility falling with each additional slice you eat and becoming negative with the sixth slice. The height of the marginal utility line at any quantity of pizza in panel (b) represents the change in utility as a result of consuming that additional slice. For example, the change in utility as a result of consuming 4 slices instead of 3 is 6 utils, so the height of the marginal utility line in panel (b) for the fourth slice is 6 utils.

Number of Slices	Total Utility from Eating Pizza	Marginal Utility from the Last Slice Eaten
0	0	—
1	20	20
2	36	16
3	46	10
4	52	6
5	54	2
6	51	−3

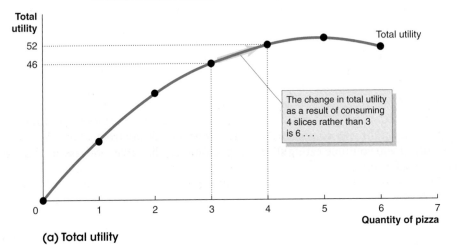

(a) Total utility

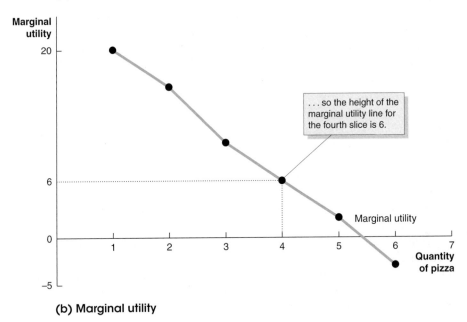

(b) Marginal utility

amount of Coke you drink, and the amount of satisfaction, or utility, you receive. The values for pizza are repeated from the table in Figure 10.1. The values for Coke also follow the principle of diminishing marginal utility.

How many slices of pizza and how many cups of Coke should you buy if you want to maximize your utility? If you did not have a budget constraint, you would buy 5 slices of pizza and 5 cups of Coke because that would give you total utility of 107 (= 54 + 53), which is the maximum utility you can achieve. Eating another slice of pizza or drinking another cup of Coke during the evening would lower your utility. Unfortunately, you do have a budget constraint: You have only $10 to spend. To buy 5 slices of pizza (at $2 per slice) and 5 cups of Coke (at $1 per cup), you would need $15.

Table 10.1

Total Utility and Marginal Utility from Eating Pizza and Drinking Coke

Number of Slices of Pizza	Total Utility from Eating Pizza	Marginal Utility from the Last Slice	Number of Cups of Coke	Total Utility from Drinking Coke	Marginal Utility from the Last Cup
0	0	—	0	0	—
1	20	20	1	20	20
2	36	16	2	35	15
3	46	10	3	45	10
4	52	6	4	50	5
5	54	2	5	53	3
6	51	−3	6	52	−1

To select the best way to spend your $10, remember this key economic principle: *Optimal decisions are made at the margin.* That is, most of the time economic decision makers—consumers, firms, and the government—are faced with decisions about whether to do a little more of one thing or a little more of an alternative. In this case, you are choosing to consume a little more pizza or a little more Coke. Tesla chooses whether to manufacture more sedans or more SUVs in its California factory. Congress and the president choose whether to spend more for research on heart disease or more for preschool programs. Everyone faces a budget constraint and everyone faces trade-offs.

The key to making the best consumption decision is to maximize utility by following the *rule of equal marginal utility per dollar spent*. As you decide how to spend your income, you should buy pizza and Coke up to the point where the last slice of pizza and the last cup of Coke purchased give you equal increases in utility *per dollar*. By doing this, you will have maximized your total utility, given your budget constraint.

It is important to remember that to follow this rule, you must equalize your marginal utility per dollar spent, *not* your marginal utility from each good. Buying season tickets for your favorite National Football League (NFL) team or for the symphony or buying a BMW may give you a lot more satisfaction than drinking a cup of Coke, but the NFL tickets may well give you less satisfaction *per dollar spent*. To decide how many slices of pizza and cups of Coke to buy, you must convert the values for marginal utility in Table 10.1 into marginal utility per dollar. You can do this by dividing marginal utility by the price of each good, as shown in Table 10.2.

In column (3), we calculate marginal utility per dollar spent on pizza. Because the price of pizza is $2 per slice, the marginal utility per dollar from eating 1 slice of pizza equals 20 divided by $2, or 10 utils per dollar. Similarly, we show in column (6) that because the price of Coke is $1 per cup, the marginal utility per dollar from drinking 1 cup of Coke equals 20 divided by $1, or 20 utils per dollar. To maximize the total utility you

Table 10.2

Converting Marginal Utility to Marginal Utility per Dollar

(1) Slices of Pizza	(2) Marginal Utility (MU_{Pizza})	(3) Marginal Utility per Dollar $\left(\dfrac{MU_{Pizza}}{P_{Pizza}}\right)$	(4) Cups of Coke	(5) Marginal Utility (MU_{Coke})	(6) Marginal Utility per Dollar $\left(\dfrac{MU_{Coke}}{P_{Coke}}\right)$
1	20	10	1	20	20
2	16	8	2	15	15
3	10	5	3	10	10
4	6	3	4	5	5
5	2	1	5	3	3
6	−3	−1.5	6	−1	−1

Table 10.3

Equalizing Marginal Utility per Dollar Spent

Combinations of Pizza and Coke with Equal Marginal Utilities per Dollar	Marginal Utility per Dollar (MU/P)	Total Spending	Total Utility
1 slice of pizza and 3 cups of Coke	10	$2 + $3 = $5	20 + 45 = 65
3 slices of pizza and 4 cups of Coke	5	$6 + $4 = $10	46 + 50 = 96
4 slices of pizza and 5 cups of Coke	3	$8 + $5 = $13	52 + 53 = 105

receive, you must make sure that the utility per dollar of pizza for the last slice of pizza is equal to the utility per dollar of Coke for the last cup of Coke. Table 10.2 shows that there are three combinations of slices of pizza and cups of Coke where marginal utility per dollar is equalized. Table 10.3 lists the combinations, the total amount of money needed to buy each combination, and the total utility received from consuming each combination.

Looking at the bottom row of the table, if you buy 4 slices of pizza, the last slice gives you 3 utils per dollar. If you buy 5 cups of Coke, the last cup also gives you 3 utils per dollar, so you have equalized your marginal utility per dollar. Unfortunately, as the third column in the table shows, to buy 4 slices and 5 cups, you would need $13, and you have only $10. The top row of the table shows that you could also equalize your marginal utility per dollar by buying 1 slice and 3 cups, but that would cost just $5, leaving you with $5 not spent. As the middle row shows, only when you buy 3 slices and 4 cups have you equalized your marginal utility per dollar and spent neither more nor less than the $10 available.

We can summarize the two conditions for maximizing utility:

1. $\dfrac{MU_{Pizza}}{P_{Pizza}} = \dfrac{MU_{Coke}}{P_{Coke}}$

2. Spending on pizza + Spending on Coke = Amount available to be spent

The first condition states that the marginal utility per dollar spent must be the same for both goods. The second condition is the budget constraint, which states that total spending on both goods must equal the amount available to be spent. Of course, these conditions for maximizing utility apply not just to pizza and Coke but to any two pairs of goods.

MyEconLab Concept Check

Solved Problem 10.1

MyEconLab Interactive Animation

Finding the Optimal Level of Consumption

The following table shows Lee's utility from consuming ice cream cones and cans of Lime Fizz soda:

Number of Ice Cream Cones	Total Utility from Ice Cream Cones	Marginal Utility from Last Cone	Number of Cans of Lime Fizz	Total Utility from Cans of Lime Fizz	Marginal Utility from Last Can
0	0	—	0	0	—
1	30	30	1	40	40
2	55	25	2	75	35
3	75	20	3	101	26
4	90	15	4	119	18
5	100	10	5	134	15
6	105	5	6	141	7

a. Ed inspects this table and concludes, "Lee's optimal choice would be to consume 4 ice cream cones and 5 cans of Lime Fizz because with that combination, his marginal utility from ice cream cones is equal to his marginal utility from Lime Fizz." Do you agree with Ed's reasoning? Briefly explain.

b. Suppose that Lee has an unlimited budget to spend on ice cream cones and cans of Lime Fizz. Under these circumstances, how many ice cream cones and how many cans of Lime Fizz will he consume? (Assume that Lee cannot consume more than 6 ice cream cones or 6 cans of Lime Fizz.)

c. Suppose that Lee has $7 per week to spend on ice cream cones and cans of Lime Fizz. The price of an ice cream cone is $2, and the price of a can of Lime Fizz is $1. If Lee wants to maximize his utility, how many ice cream cones and how many cans of Lime Fizz should he buy?

Solving the Problem

Step 1: Review the chapter material. This problem involves finding the optimal consumption of two goods, so you may want to review the section "The Rule of Equal Marginal Utility per Dollar Spent," which begins on page 307.

Step 2: Answer part (a) by analyzing Ed's reasoning. Ed's reasoning is incorrect. To maximize utility, Lee needs to equalize marginal utility *per dollar* for the two goods.

Step 3: Answer part (b) by determining how Lee would maximize utility with an unlimited budget. With an unlimited budget, consumers maximize utility by continuing to buy each good as long as their utility is increasing. In this case, Lee will maximize utility by buying 6 ice cream cones and 6 cans of Lime Fizz, given that we are assuming he cannot buy more than 6 units of either good.

Step 4: Answer part (c) by determining Lee's optimal combination of ice cream cones and cans of Lime Fizz. Lee will maximize his utility if he spends his $7 per week so that the marginal utility of ice cream cones divided by the price of ice cream cones is equal to the marginal utility of Lime Fizz divided by the price of Lime Fizz. We can use the following table to solve this part of the problem:

	Ice Cream Cones		Cans of Lime Fizz	
Quantity	MU	$\frac{MU}{P}$	MU	$\frac{MU}{P}$
1	30	15	40	40
2	25	12.5	35	35
3	20	10	26	26
4	15	7.5	18	18
5	10	5	15	15
6	5	2.5	7	7

Lee will maximize his utility by buying 1 ice cream cone and 5 cans of Lime Fizz. At this combination, the marginal utility of each good divided by its price equals 15. He has also spent all of his $7.

Your Turn: For more practice, do related problems 1.8 and 1.9 on pages 331 at the end of this chapter.

MyEconLab Study Plan

What If the Rule of Equal Marginal Utility per Dollar Does Not Hold?

The idea of getting the maximum utility by equalizing the ratio of marginal utility to price for the goods you are buying can be difficult to grasp, so it is worth thinking about in another way. Suppose that instead of buying 3 slices of pizza and 4 cups of Coke, you buy 4 slices and 2 cups. This combination costs $10, so you would meet your budget constraint by spending all the money available to you, but would you

Don't Let This Happen to You

Equalize Marginal Utilities *per Dollar*

Harry likes to read e-books and watch movies on his tablet. The information in the following table gives Harry's utility from buying books and movies:

Harry's Utility from Buying Books and Movies

Quantity of Books	Total Utility from Books	Marginal Utility from Last Book	Quantity of Movies	Total Utility from Movies	Marginal Utility from Last Movie
0	0	—	0	0	—
1	50	50	1	60	60
2	85	35	2	105	45
3	110	25	3	145	40
4	130	20	4	175	30
5	140	10	5	195	20
6	145	5	6	210	15

Can you determine from this information the optimal combination of books and movies for Harry? It is very tempting to say that Harry should buy 4 books and 5 movies because his marginal utility from books is equal to his marginal utility from movies with that combination. In fact, we can't be sure this is the best combination because we are lacking some critical information: Harry's budget constraint—how much he has available to spend on books and movies—and the prices of books and movies.

Let's say that Harry has $100 to spend this month, the price of an e-book is $10, and the price of an online movie is $20. Using the information from the first table, we can now calculate Harry's marginal utility per dollar for both goods, as shown in the following table:

Harry's Marginal Utility and Marginal Utility per Dollar from Buying Books and Movies

Quantity of Books	Marginal Utility from Last Book (MU_{Books})	Marginal Utility per Dollar $\left(\frac{MU_{Books}}{P_{Books}}\right)$	Quantity of Movies	Marginal Utility from Last Movie (MU_{Movies})	Marginal Utility per Dollar $\left(\frac{MU_{Movies}}{P_{Movies}}\right)$
1	50	5	1	60	3
2	35	3.5	2	45	2.25
3	25	2.5	3	40	2
4	20	2	4	30	1.5
5	10	1	5	20	1
6	5	0.5	6	15	0.75

Harry's marginal utility per dollar is the same for two combinations of books and movies, as shown in the following table:

Combinations of Books and Movies with Equal Marginal Utilities per Dollar	Marginal Utility per Dollar (MU/P)	Total Spending	Total Utility
5 books and 5 movies	1	$50 + $100 = $150	140 + 195 = 335
4 books and 3 movies	2	$40 + $60 = $100	130 + 145 = 275

Unfortunately, 5 books and 5 movies would cost Harry $150, and he has only $100. The best Harry can do is to buy 4 books and 3 movies. This combination provides him with the maximum amount of utility attainable, given his budget constraint.

The key point is the same as in Solved Problem 10.1: Consumers maximize their utility when they equalize marginal utility *per dollar* for every good they buy, *not* when they equalize marginal utility.

MyEconLab Study Plan

Your Turn: Test your understanding by doing related problem 1.11 on page 331 at the end of this chapter.

have gotten the maximum amount of utility? No, you wouldn't have. From the information in Table 10.2 on page 309, we can list the additional utility per dollar you are getting from the last slice and the last cup and the total utility from consuming 4 slices and 2 cups:

Marginal utility per dollar for the fourth slice of pizza = 3 utils per dollar

Marginal utility per dollar for the second cup of Coke = 15 utils per dollar

Total utility from 4 slices of pizza and 2 cups of Coke = 87 utils

Obviously, the marginal utilities per dollar are not equal. The last cup of Coke gave you considerably more satisfaction per dollar than did the last slice of pizza. You could raise your total utility by buying less pizza and more Coke. Buying 1 less slice of pizza frees up $2 that will allow you to buy 2 more cups of Coke. Eating 1 less slice of pizza reduces your utility by 6 utils, but drinking 2 additional cups of Coke raises your utility by 15 utils (make sure you see this), for a net increase of 9. You end up equalizing your marginal utility per dollar (5 utils per dollar for both the last slice and the last cup) and raising your total utility from 87 to 96 utils. MyEconLab Concept Check

The Income Effect and Substitution Effect of a Price Change

We can use the rule of equal marginal utility per dollar to analyze how consumers adjust their buying decisions when a price changes. Suppose you are back at the restaurant for the Super Bowl party, but this time the price of pizza is $1.50 per slice, rather than $2. You still have $10 to spend on pizza and Coke.

When the price of pizza was $2 per slice and the price of Coke was $1 per cup, your optimal choice was to consume 3 slices of pizza and 4 cups of Coke. The fall in the price of pizza to $1.50 per slice has two effects on the quantity of pizza you consume: the *income effect* and the *substitution effect*. First, consider the income effect. When the price of a good falls, you have more purchasing power. In our example, 3 slices of pizza and 4 cups of Coke now cost a total of only $8.50 instead of $10.00. An increase in purchasing power is essentially the same thing as an increase in income. The change in the quantity of pizza you will demand because of this increase in purchasing power—holding all other factors constant—is the **income effect** of the price change. Recall that if a product is a *normal good*, a consumer increases the quantity demanded as the consumer's income rises, but if a product is an *inferior good*, a consumer decreases the quantity demanded as the consumer's income rises (see Chapter 3). So, if we assume that pizza is a normal good for you, the income effect of a fall in price causes you to consume more pizza. If pizza were an inferior good for you, the income effect of a fall in the price would have caused you to consume less pizza.

The second effect of the price change is the substitution effect. When the price of pizza falls, pizza becomes cheaper *relative* to Coke, and the marginal utility per dollar for each slice of pizza you consume increases. If we hold constant the effect of the price change on your purchasing power and just focus on the effect of the price being lower relative to the price of the other good, we have isolated the **substitution effect** of the price change. The lower price of pizza relative to the price of Coke has lowered the *opportunity cost* to you of consuming pizza because now you have to give up less Coke to consume the same quantity of pizza. Therefore, the substitution effect from the fall in the price of pizza relative to the price of Coke causes you to eat more pizza and drink less Coke. In this case, both the income effect and the substitution effect of the fall in price cause you to eat more pizza. If the price of pizza had risen, both the income effect and the substitution effect would have caused you to eat less pizza. Table 10.4 summarizes the effect of a price change on the quantity demanded.

We can use Table 10.5 to determine the effect of the fall in the price of pizza on your optimal consumption. Table 10.5 has the same information as Table 10.2, with one

Income effect The change in the quantity demanded of a good that results from the effect of a change in price on consumer purchasing power, holding all other factors constant.

Substitution effect The change in the quantity demanded of a good that results from a change in price making the good more or less expensive relative to other goods, holding constant the effect of the price change on consumer purchasing power.

Table 10.4

Income Effect and Substitution Effect of a Price Change

When price ...	consumer purchasing power ...	The income effect causes quantity demanded to ...	The substitution effect causes the opportunity cost of consuming a good to ...
decreases,	increases.	increase, if a normal good, and decrease, if an inferior good.	decrease when the price decreases, which causes the quantity of the good demanded to increase.
increases,	decreases.	decrease, if a normal good, and increase, if an inferior good.	increase when the price increases, which causes the quantity of the good demanded to decrease.

change: The marginal utility per dollar from eating pizza has been changed to reflect the new lower price of $1.50 per slice. Examining the table, we can see that the fall in the price of pizza will result in you eating 1 more slice of pizza, so your optimal consumption now becomes 4 slices of pizza and 4 cups of Coke. You will be spending all of your $10, and the last dollar you spend on pizza will provide you with about the same marginal utility per dollar as the last dollar you spend on Coke. You will not be receiving exactly the same marginal utility per dollar spent on the two products. As Table 10.5 shows, the last slice of pizza gives you 4 utils per dollar, and the last cup of Coke gives you 5 utils per dollar. But this is as close as you can come to equalizing marginal utility per dollar for the two products, unless you can buy a fraction of a slice of pizza or a fraction of a cup of Coke.

MyEconLab Study Plan

MyEconLab Concept Check

10.2 LEARNING OBJECTIVE

Use the concept of utility to explain the law of demand.

Where Demand Curves Come From

According to the *law of demand*, whenever the price of a product falls, the quantity demanded increases (see Chapter 3). Now that we have covered the concepts of total utility, marginal utility, and the budget constraint, we can look more closely at why the law of demand holds.

In our example of optimal consumption of pizza and Coke at the Super Bowl party, we found the following:

$$\text{Price of pizza} = \$2 \text{ per slice} \rightarrow \text{Quantity of pizza demanded} = 3 \text{ slices}$$
$$\text{Price of pizza} = \$1.50 \text{ per slice} \rightarrow \text{Quantity of pizza demanded} = 4 \text{ slices}$$

Table 10.5

Adjusting Optimal Consumption to a Lower Price of Pizza

Number of Slices of Pizza	Marginal Utility from Last Slice (MU_{Pizza})	Marginal Utility per Dollar $\left(\dfrac{MU_{Pizza}}{P_{Pizza}}\right)$	Number of Cups of Coke	Marginal Utility from Last Cup (MU_{Coke})	Marginal Utility per Dollar $\left(\dfrac{MU_{Coke}}{P_{Coke}}\right)$
1	20	13.33	1	20	20
2	16	10.67	2	15	15
3	10	6.67	3	10	10
4	6	4	4	5	5
5	2	1.33	5	3	3
6	−3	—	6	−1	—

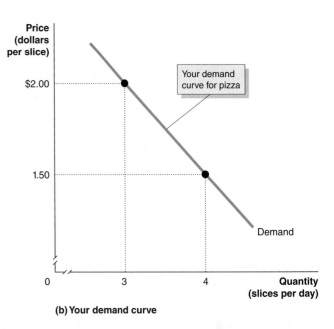

Figure 10.2 **Deriving the Demand Curve for Pizza**

A consumer responds optimally to a fall in the price of a product by consuming more of that product. In panel (a), the price of pizza falls from $2 per slice to $1.50, and the optimal quantity of slices consumed rises from 3 to 4. When we graph this result in panel (b), we have the consumer's demand curve.

In panel (a) of Figure 10.2, we plot the two points showing the optimal number of slices of pizza you choose to consume at each price. In panel (b), we draw a line connecting the two points. This downward-sloping line represents your demand curve for pizza. We could find more points on the line by changing the price of pizza and using the information in Table 10.2 to find the new optimal number of slices of pizza you would demand at each price.

To this point in the chapter, we have been looking at an individual demand curve. Economists, though, are typically interested in market demand curves. We can construct the market demand curve from the individual demand curves for all the consumers in the market. To keep things simple, let's assume that there are only three consumers in the market for pizza: you, David, and Lori. The table in Figure 10.3 shows the individual demand schedules for the three consumers. Because consumers differ in their incomes and their preferences for products, we would not expect every consumer to demand the same quantity of a given product at each price. The final column gives the market demand, which is simply the sum of the quantities demanded by each of the three consumers at each price. For example, at a price of $1.50 per slice, your quantity demanded is 4 slices, David's is 6 slices, and Lori's is 5 slices. So, at a price of $1.50, a quantity of 15 slices is demanded in the market. The graphs in the figure show that we can obtain the market demand curve by adding horizontally the individual demand curves.

Remember that according to the law of demand, market demand curves always slope downward. We now know that this result holds because the income and substitution effects of a decrease in price cause consumers to increase the quantity of the good they demand. There is a complicating factor, however. As we discussed earlier, only for normal goods will the income effect result in consumers increasing the quantity of the good they demand when the price falls. If the good is an inferior good, the income effect leads consumers to *decrease* the quantity of the good they demand. The substitution effect, on the other hand, results in consumers increasing the quantity they demand of both normal and inferior goods when the price falls. So, when the price of an inferior good falls, the income effect and substitution effect work in opposite directions: The income effect causes consumers to decrease the quantity of the good they demand, while the substitution effect causes consumers to increase the quantity of the good they demand. Is it possible, then, that consumers might actually buy less of a good when the price falls? If they did, the demand curve would be upward sloping. MyEconLab Concept Check

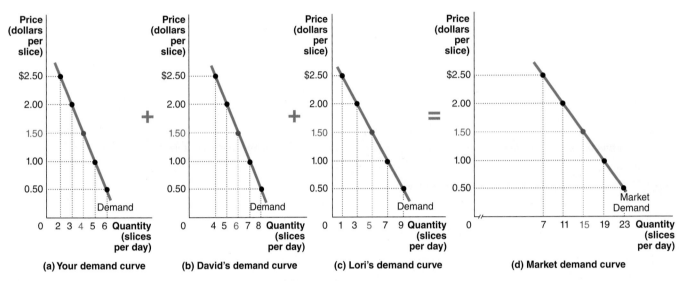

Quantity (slices per day)				
Price (dollars per slice)	You	David	Lori	Market
$2.50	2	4	1	7
2.00	3	5	3	11
1.50	4	6	5	15
1.00	5	7	7	19
0.50	6	8	9	23

(a) Your demand curve   +   (b) David's demand curve   +   (c) Lori's demand curve   =   (d) Market demand curve

MyEconLab Animation

Figure 10.3 Deriving the Market Demand Curve from Individual Demand Curves

The table shows that the total quantity demanded in a market is the sum of the quantities demanded by each buyer. We can find the market demand curve by adding horizontally the individual demand curves in panels (a), (b), and (c). For instance, at a price of $1.50, your quantity demanded is 4 slices, David's is 6 slices, and Lori's is 5 slices. Therefore, panel (d) shows that a price of $1.50 and a quantity demanded of 15 is a point on the market demand curve.

Rice is a Giffen good in poor parts of China.

Making the Connection
MyEconLab Video

Are There Any Upward-Sloping Demand Curves in the Real World?

For a demand curve to be upward sloping, the good would have to be an inferior good and the income effect would have to be larger than the substitution effect. Economists have understood the conditions for an upward-sloping demand curve since the possibility was first discussed by the British economist Alfred Marshall in the 1890s. Marshall wrote that his friend, Sir Robert Giffen, had told him that when the price of bread rose, very poor people in British cities would actually buy more bread rather than less. Since that time, goods with upward-sloping demand curves have been referred to as *Giffen goods*.

For more than a century, finding an actual Giffen good proved impossible. A close examination of the data showed that Giffen had been mistaken and that poor people in British cities bought less bread when prices rose, so their demand curves were downward sloping. Other possible candidates for being Giffen goods were also found to actually have downward-sloping demand curves. Finally, in 2006, Robert Jensen of Brown University and Nolan Miller of Harvard discovered two Giffen goods. They reasoned that to be a Giffen good, with an income effect larger than its substitution effect, a good must be inferior and make up a very large portion of consumers' budgets. Jensen and Miller knew that very poor people in the Hunan region of China spent most of their incomes on rice, while in the Gansu province, very poor people spent most of their income on wheat-based foods, such as buns and noodles. In both places, poor people ate meat when their incomes made it possible because they preferred the taste of meat, even though it did not supply as many calories as the rice or wheat they could purchase for the same price.

Jensen and Miller carried out the following experiment: In Hunan, for a five-month period, they gave a selected number of poor families coupons that would allow them to buy rice at a lower price. Families could not use the coupons for any other purpose. In Gansu, they gave a selected number of poor families coupons to buy wheat at a lower price. Jensen and Miller then observed the purchases of the families during the time they received the coupons and during the period immediately thereafter. In Hunan, during the months they received the coupons, the families bought less rice and more meat, and in Gansu, they bought less wheat and more meat. Because in Hunan, families bought less rice when the price was lower, their demand curves for rice were upward sloping. Similarly, in Gansu, families bought less wheat when the price was lower, so their demand curves for wheat were upward sloping. After more than a century of searching, economists had finally discovered examples of a Giffen good.

Source: Robert T. Jensen and Nolan H. Miller, "Giffen Behavior and Subsistence Consumption," *American Economic Review*, Vol. 98, No. 4, September 2008, pp. 1553–1577.

Your Turn: Test your understanding by doing related problem 2.9 on page 332 at the end of this chapter.

MyEconLab Study Plan

Social Influences on Decision Making

10.3 LEARNING OBJECTIVE

Explain how social influences can affect consumption choices.

Sociologists and anthropologists have argued that social factors such as culture, customs, and religion are very important in explaining the choices people make. Economists have traditionally seen such factors as being relatively unimportant, if they take them into consideration at all. Recently, however, some economists have begun to study how social factors influence consumer choice.

For example, people seem to receive more utility from consuming goods they believe are popular. As the economists Gary Becker and Kevin Murphy put it:

The utility from drugs, crime, going bowling, owning a Rolex watch, voting Democratic, dressing informally at work, or keeping a neat lawn depends on whether friends and neighbors take drugs, commit crimes, go bowling, own Rolex watches, vote Democratic, dress informally, or keep their lawns neat.

This reasoning can help explain why one restaurant is packed, while another restaurant that serves essentially the same food and has similar décor has many fewer customers. Consumers decide which restaurant to go to not only on the basis of food and décor but also on the basis of the restaurant's popularity. People receive utility from being seen eating at a popular restaurant because they believe it makes them appear knowledgeable and fashionable. Whenever consumption takes place publicly, some consumers base their purchasing decisions on what other consumers are buying. Examples of public consumption include eating in restaurants, attending sporting events, wearing clothes or jewelry, and driving cars. In all these cases, the decision to buy a product depends partly on the characteristics of the product and partly on how many other people are buying the product.

The Effects of Celebrity Endorsements

In many cases, it is not just the number of people who use a product that makes it desirable but the types of people who use it. If consumers believe that media stars or professional athletes use a product, demand for the product will often increase. For example, New England Patriots quarterback Tom Brady is one of the biggest stars in the National Football League, so it may not be surprising that companies have lined up to have him endorse their products. His endorsements include Glaceau Smartwater, Stetson cologne, Movado watches, Under Armour sportswear, and Audi automobiles. Brady makes at least $4 million per year from his endorsements.

Tom Brady is a great football player, but should consumers care what products he uses? There seems little doubt that consumers care what products Brady uses, but why do they care? It might be that they believe Brady has better information than they do about the products he endorses. The average football fan might believe that if Brady endorses Under Armour sportswear, maybe Under Armour makes better sportswear. It seems more likely, however, that people buy products associated with Tom Brady or other celebrities because using these products makes them feel closer to the celebrity endorser or because it makes them appear to be fashionable.   MyEconLab Concept Check

Network Externalities

Network externality A situation in which the usefulness of a product increases with the number of consumers who use it.

Technology can play a role in explaining why consumers buy products that many other consumers are already buying. There is a **network externality** in the consumption of a product if the usefulness of the product increases with the number of consumers who use it. For example, if you owned the only phone in the world, it would not be very useful. The usefulness of phones increases as the number of people who own them increases. Similarly, your willingness to buy an Apple iPad depends in part on the number of other people who own iPads. The more people who own iPads, the more applications, or apps, other firms will produce for the iPad, and the more novels, textbooks, newspapers, and magazines publishers will make available for downloading to the iPad, and, therefore, the more useful an iPad is to you.

Some economists have suggested the possibility that network externalities may have a significant downside because they might result in consumers buying products that contain inferior technologies. This outcome could occur because network externalities can create significant *switching costs* related to changing products: When a product becomes established, consumers may find it too costly to switch to a new product that contains a better technology. The selection of products may be *path dependent*: Because of switching costs, the technology that was first available may have advantages over better technologies that were developed later. In other words, the path along which the economy has developed in the past is important.

One example of path dependence and the use of an inferior technology is the QWERTY order of the letters along the top row of most computer keyboards. This order became widely used when manual typewriters were developed in the late nineteenth century. The metal keys on manual typewriters would stick together if a user typed too fast, so the QWERTY keyboard was designed to slow down typists and minimize the problem of the keys sticking together. With computers, the problem that QWERTY was developed to solve no longer exists, so keyboards could be changed to have letters in a more efficient layout. But because the overwhelming majority of people have learned to use keyboards with the QWERTY layout, there might be significant costs to them if they had to switch, even if a new layout ultimately made them faster typists.

Other products that supposedly embodied inferior technologies are VHS video recorders—supposedly inferior to Sony Betamax recorders—and the Windows computer operating system—supposedly inferior to the Macintosh operating system. Some economists have argued that because of path dependence and switching costs, network externalities can result in *market failures,* which are situations in which the market fails to produce the efficient level of output (see Chapter 5). If network externalities result in market failure, government intervention in these markets might improve economic efficiency. Many economists are skeptical, however, that network externalities really do lead to consumers being locked into products with inferior technologies. In particular, economists Stan Leibowitz of the University of Texas, Dallas, and Stephen Margolis of North Carolina State University have argued that, in practice, the gains from using a superior technology are larger than the losses due to switching costs. After carefully studying the cases of the QWERTY keyboard, VHS video recorders, and the Windows computer operating system, they have concluded that there is no good evidence that the alternative technologies were actually superior. The implications of network externalities for economic efficiency remain controversial among economists.   MyEconLab Concept Check

Does Fairness Matter?

If people were only interested in making themselves as well off as possible in a material sense, they would not be concerned with fairness. There is a great deal of evidence, however, that people like to be treated fairly and that they usually attempt to treat others fairly, even if doing so makes them worse off financially. Tipping servers in restaurants is an example. In the United States, diners in restaurants typically add 15 to 20 percent to their food bills as tips to their servers. Tips are not *required*, but most people see it as very unfair not to tip, unless the service has been exceptionally bad. You could argue that people leave tips not to be fair but because they are afraid that if they don't leave a tip, the next time they visit the restaurant they will receive poor service. Studies have shown, however, that most people leave tips at restaurants even while on vacation or in other circumstances where they are unlikely to visit the restaurant again.

There are many other examples where people willingly part with money when they are not required to do so and when they receive nothing material in return. The most obvious example is making donations to charity. Apparently, donating money to charity or leaving tips in restaurants that they will never visit again gives people more utility than they would receive from keeping the money and spending it on themselves.

A Test of Fairness in the Economic Laboratory: The Ultimatum Game Experiment
Economists have used experiments to understand the role that fairness plays in consumer decision making. *Experimental economics* has been widely used during the past two decades, and a number of experimental economics laboratories exist in the United States and Europe. Economists Maurice Allais, Reinhard Selten, and Vernon Smith were awarded the Nobel Prize in Economics in part because of their contributions to experimental economics. Experiments make it possible to focus on a single aspect of consumer behavior. The *ultimatum game*, first popularized by Werner Güth of the Max Planck Institute of Economics in Germany, is an experiment that tests whether fairness is important in consumer decision making. Various economists have conducted the ultimatum game experiment under slightly different conditions, but with generally the same result. In this game, a group of volunteers—often college students—are divided into pairs. One member of each pair is the "allocator," and the other member of the pair is the "recipient."

Each pair is given an amount of money, say $20. The allocator decides how much of the $20 each member of the pair will get. There are no restrictions on how the allocator divides up the money. He or she could keep it all, give it all to the recipient, or anything in between. The recipient must then decide whether to accept the allocation or reject it. If the recipient decides to accept the allocation, each member of the pair gets to keep his or her share. If the recipient decides to reject the allocation, both members of the pair receive nothing.

If neither the allocator nor the recipient cares about fairness, optimal play in the ultimatum game is straightforward: The allocator should propose a division of the money in which the allocator receives $19.99 and the recipient receives $0.01. The allocator has maximized his or her gain. The recipient should accept the division because the alternative is to reject the division and receive nothing at all: Even a penny is better than nothing.

In fact, when the ultimatum game experiment is carried out, both allocators and recipients act as if fairness is important. Allocators usually offer recipients at least a 40 percent share of the money, and recipients almost always reject offers of less than a 10 percent share. Why do allocators offer recipients more than a negligible amount? It might be that allocators do not care about fairness but fear that recipients do care and will reject offers they consider unfair. This possibility was tested in an experiment known as the *dictator game* carried out by Daniel Kahneman (a psychologist who shared the Nobel Prize in Economics), Jack Knetsch, and Richard Thaler, using students at Cornell University. In this experiment, the allocators were given only two possible divisions of $20: either $18 for themselves and $2 for the recipient or an even division of $10 for themselves and $10 for the recipient. One important difference from the ultimatum game was that *the recipient was not allowed to reject the division*. Of the 161 allocators, 122 chose the even division of the $20. Because there was no possibility of the $18/$2 split being rejected, the allocators must have chosen the even split because they valued acting fairly.

Why would recipients in the ultimatum game ever reject any division of the money in which they receive even a very small amount, given that even a small amount of money is better than nothing? Apparently, most people value fairness enough that they will refuse to participate in transactions they consider unfair, even if they are worse off financially as a result.

Are the Results of Economic Experiments Reliable? Because economists have conducted the ultimatum game and the dictator game many times in different countries using different groups of people, most economists believe that the results of the game provide strong evidence that people value fairness. Recently, however, some economists have begun to question this conclusion. To begin with, the experimental situation is artificial, so results obtained from experiments may not hold up in the real world. Although allocators in the dictatorship game give money to the other player, whose identity is not known to the allocator, in the real world, people rarely just hand money to strangers. So, it is possible that the fairness observed in the experiments may be the result of people wanting to avoid appearing selfish rather than people valuing fairness. For instance, in the ultimatum game, anyone who kept $19.99 and gave the other person only $0.01 might be afraid of appearing selfish in the eyes of the economist conducting the experiment. Particularly because the dollar amounts involved in the experiment are small, wanting to please the person conducting the experiment may be the main motive behind the choices made.

John List of the University of Chicago has carried out variations of the dictator game. When he gave every player $5 and followed the usual procedure of having half the players act as dictators in dividing up the $5, he found the usual result, with 71 percent of dictators allocating some money to the other player. But when he gave the dictator the choice of either giving money to the other player or *taking* up to $5 from the other player, only 10 percent of dictators gave the other player any money, and more than half the dictators took money from the other player. When List asked players to work for 30 minutes at a simple task to earn the $5 before playing the game, two-thirds of the dictators neither gave anything nor took anything from the other player. This last result may indicate that the source of the money being allocated matters.

List's results do not completely reverse the usual interpretation of the results of the ultimatum and dictator games. They do show, however, that the results of those games are not as clear-cut as many economists had thought. They also show that the details of an economic experiment can have a significant effect on its results.

Business Implications of Fairness If consumers value fairness, how does this affect firms? One consequence is that firms will sometimes not raise prices of goods and services, even when there is a large increase in demand, because they are afraid their customers will consider the price increases unfair and may buy elsewhere.

Consider three examples where it seems that businesses could increase their profits by raising prices. In 2011, the dance rock band LCD played a concert at New York's Madison Square Garden. The tickets were priced at $50 each. Demand for the tickets was so large, however, that tickets sold online for as much as $2,500 each. Why didn't the band, or the concert promoter, charge more than $50 for the tickets? Each year, many more people would like to buy tickets to see the Super Bowl than there are tickets for them to buy at the price the National Football League (NFL) charges. Why doesn't the NFL raise prices? The restaurant Next opened in Chicago in 2011. Rather than use normal pricing, the restaurant sold tickets that entitled the buyer to a dinner, including drinks and tip. The restaurant sold the tickets for $45 to $75, depending on the dinner chosen. The tickets were resold online for prices from $500 to $3,000. Why didn't Next increase its ticket prices?

In each of these cases, it appears that a firm could increase its profits by raising prices. The seller would be selling the same quantity—of seats at a concert or in a football stadium or meals in a restaurant—at a higher price, so profits should increase. Economists have provided two explanations for why firms sometimes do not raise prices in these situations. Gary Becker, who was awarded the Nobel Prize in Economics, has suggested that the products involved—concerts, football games, or restaurant meals—are all products that buyers consume together with other buyers. In those situations, the amount consumers wish to buy may be related to how much of the product other people are consuming. People like to consume, and be seen consuming, a popular product—ones where the quantity demanded appears to be much greater than the quantity supplied. If rock bands, the NFL, and popular restaurants increased their prices enough to equate the quantity of tickets demanded with the quantity supplied, they might find that they had also eliminated their popularity.

Daniel Kahneman, Jack Knetsch, and Richard Thaler have offered another explanation for why firms don't always raise prices when doing so would seem to increase their profits. In surveys of consumers, these researchers found that most people considered it fair for firms to raise their prices following an increase in costs but unfair to raise prices following an increase in demand. For example, Kahneman, Knetsch, and Thaler conducted a survey in which people were asked their opinion of the following situation: "A hardware store has been selling snow shovels for $15. The morning after a large snowstorm, the store raises the price to $20." Eighty-two percent of those surveyed responded that they considered the hardware store's actions to be unfair. Kahneman, Knetsch, and Thaler have concluded that firms may sometimes not raise their prices even when the quantity demanded of their product is greater than the quantity supplied out of fear that, in the long run, they will lose customers who believe the price increases were unfair.

In analyzing the pricing of Super Bowl tickets, economist Alan Krueger of Princeton University provided some support for Kahneman, Knetsch, and Thaler's explanation of why companies do not always raise prices when the quantity demanded is greater than the quantity supplied. In 2013, the NFL charged $1,250 for the best seats at the Super Bowl and $850 for most of the rest. Many of these tickets were resold online for as much as $5,000 each. Krueger decided to survey football fans attending the game to see if their views could help explain why the NFL didn't charge higher prices for the tickets. When asked whether it would "be fair for the NFL to raise the [price of tickets] to $1,500 if that is still less than the amount most people are willing to pay for tickets," 92 percent of the fans surveyed answered "no." Even 83 percent of the fans who had paid more than $1,500 for their tickets answered "no." Krueger concluded that whatever the NFL might gain in the short run from raising ticket prices, it would more than lose in the long run by alienating football fans.

These explanations for why firms don't always raise prices to a level that would equate the quantity demanded with the quantity supplied share the same basic idea: Sometimes firms will give up some profits in the short run to keep their customers happy and increase their profits in the long run. MyEconLab Concept Check

---

Making the Connection
MyEconLab Video

What's Up with "Fuel Surcharges"?

Ordinarily, when firms present their customers with a bill, they don't itemize the costs of producing the good or service: Restaurants don't list on their menus the costs of the lettuce and tomatoes in a salad, and automobile companies don't list on their window price stickers the prices they paid their suppliers for the transmission or the tires. As oil prices began to rise in 2008, however, a number of companies began adding a line for "fuel surcharge" to their bills. For instance, Waste Management, the largest waste removal firm in the United States, includes a line for a fuel surcharge on its bills even though it doesn't itemize any other costs. The same is true for FedEx and UPS. Most major airlines do so as well. For example, in mid-2013, most airline flights from New York to London included a fuel surcharge of at least $450.

An article in the *Wall Street Journal* noted that although airlines often raise their fuel surcharges when oil—and jet fuel—prices increase, they rarely cut the charges when oil prices fall. The mystery of why airline tickets prices often don't fall when oil prices fall can be solved by considering why the airlines started itemizing a fuel surcharge to begin with. As the research of Kahneman, Knetsch, and Thaler has shown, consumers see it as fair for firms to raise prices after an increase in costs. By explicitly including a fuel surcharge in their prices, the airlines—and other firms that followed this practice—were able to increase prices without consumers seeing the increases as being unfair.

We know, though, that the prices of airline tickets and other goods and services are determined by the interaction of demand and supply. A decline in oil prices can reduce the airlines' costs, thereby shifting the supply curve for airline tickets to the right. As the U.S. economy recovered from the recession of 2007–2009, the demand for airline tickets increased, shifting the demand curve to the right. If these two factors roughly balance out, the price of airline tickets will not decline as oil prices decline. The figure illustrates this point by showing the price of tickets remaining at P_1 despite the shifts in the demand and supply curves.

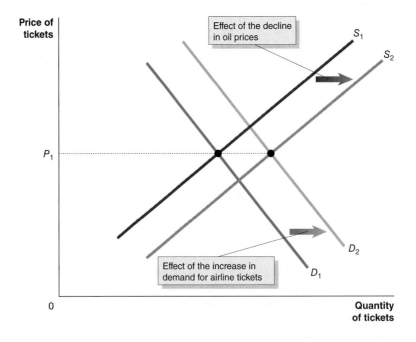

Prices are determined by *all* the factors that affect demand and supply. Airlines and other firms began identifying fuel costs in their prices only because they know that doing so makes consumers believe that the price increases are fair.

Source: Joe Sharkey, "Fuel Surcharges Push Up International Airfares," *Wall Street Journal*, February 18, 2013; Timothy W. Martin and Jennifer Levitz, "Oil Falls, but Surcharges Stay Aloft," *Wall Street Journal*, August 11, 2011; and Daniel Kahneman, Jack Knetsch, and Richard Thaler, "Fairness as a Constraint on Profit Seeking: Entitlements in the Market," *American Economic Review*, Vol. 76, No. 4, September 1986, pp. 728–741.

MyEconLab Study Plan   **Your Turn:** Test your understanding by doing related problems 3.8 and 3.9 on page 333 at the end of this chapter.

Behavioral Economics: Do People Make Their Choices Rationally?

When economists say that consumers and firms are behaving "rationally," they mean that consumers and firms are taking actions that are appropriate to reach their goals, given the information available to them. In recent years, some economists have begun studying situations in which people do not appear to be making choices that are economically rational. This new area of economics is called **behavioral economics**. Why might consumers or businesses not act rationally? The most obvious reason would be that they do not realize that their actions are inconsistent with their goals. One of the objectives of economics is to suggest ways to make better decisions. In this section, we discuss ways in which people can improve their decisions by avoiding some common pitfalls. We also use ideas from behavioral economics to analyze how consumers make decisions when shopping.

10.4 LEARNING OBJECTIVE

Describe the behavioral economics approach to understanding decision making.

Behavioral economics The study of situations in which people make choices that do not appear to be economically rational.

Pitfalls in Decision Making

Consumers commonly commit the following three mistakes when making decisions:

1. They take into account monetary costs but ignore nonmonetary opportunity costs.
2. They fail to ignore sunk costs.
3. They are unrealistic about their future behavior.

Ignoring Nonmonetary Opportunity Costs Remember that the **opportunity cost** of any activity is the highest-valued alternative that must be given up to engage in that activity. For example, if you own something you could sell, using it yourself involves an opportunity cost. It is often difficult for people to think of opportunity costs in these terms.

Consider the following example: The NFL ran a lottery that allowed the winners to purchase Super Bowl tickets at their face value, which was either $325 or $400, depending on where in the stadium the seats were located. Economist Alan Krueger of Princeton surveyed the lottery winners, asking them two questions:

Question 1: If you had not won the lottery, would you have been willing to pay $3,000 for your ticket?
Question 2: If after winning your ticket (and before arriving in Florida for the Super Bowl) someone had offered you $3,000 for your ticket, would you have sold it?

For the first question, 94 percent answered that they would not have paid $3,000 for a ticket. For the second question, 92 percent answered that they would not have sold their ticket for $3,000. But these answers are contradictory! If someone offers you $3,000 for your ticket, then by using the ticket rather than selling it, you incur an opportunity cost of $3,000. There really is a $3,000 cost involved in using that ticket, even though you do not pay $3,000 in cash. The two alternatives—either paying $3,000 or not receiving $3,000—amount to exactly the same thing.

If the ticket is really not worth $3,000 to you, you should sell it. If it is worth $3,000 to you, you should be willing to pay $3,000 in cash to buy it. Not being willing to sell a ticket you already own for $3,000 while at the same time not being willing to buy a ticket for $3,000 if you didn't already own one is inconsistent behavior. The inconsistency comes from a failure to take into account nonmonetary opportunity costs. Behavioral economists believe this inconsistency is caused by the **endowment effect**, which is the tendency of people to be unwilling to sell a good they already own even if they are offered a price that is greater than the price they would be willing to pay to buy the good if they didn't already own it.

The failure to take into account opportunity costs is a very common error in decision making. Suppose, for example, that a friend is in a hurry to have his room

Opportunity cost The highest-valued alternative that must be given up to engage in an activity.

Endowment effect The tendency of people to be unwilling to sell a good they already own even if they are offered a price that is greater than the price they would be willing to pay to buy the good if they didn't already own it.

cleaned—it's the Friday before parents' weekend—and he offers you $50 to do it for him. You turn him down and spend the time cleaning your own room, even though you know somebody down the hall who would be willing to clean your room for $20. Leave aside complicating details—the guy who asked you to clean his room is a real slob, or you don't want the person who offered to clean your room for $20 to go through your stuff—and you should see the point we are making. The opportunity cost of cleaning your own room is $50—the amount your friend offered to pay you to clean his room. It is inconsistent to turn down an offer from someone else to clean your room for $20 when you are doing it for yourself at a cost of $50. The key point here is this: *Nonmonetary opportunity costs are just as real as monetary costs, and people should take them into account when making decisions.*

There are many examples of businesses taking advantage of the tendency of consumers to ignore nonmonetary costs. For example, some firms sell products with mail-in rebates. Rather than have a mail-in rebate of $10, why not just cut the price by $10? Companies are relying on the fact that not mailing in a rebate form once you have already paid for a product is a nonmonetary opportunity cost rather than a direct monetary cost. In fact, only a small percentage of customers actually mail in rebates.

Sunk cost A cost that has already been paid and cannot be recovered.

Failing to Ignore Sunk Costs A **sunk cost** is a cost that has already been paid and cannot be recovered. Once you have paid money and can't get it back, you should ignore that money in any later decisions you make. Consider the following two situations:

Situation 1: You bought a ticket to a play for $75. The ticket is nonrefundable and must be used on Tuesday night, which is the only night the play will be performed. On Monday, a friend calls and invites you to a local comedy club to see a comedian you both like who is appearing only on Tuesday night. Your friend offers to pay the cost of going to the club.

Situation 2: It's Monday night, and you are about to buy a ticket for the Tuesday night performance of the same play as in situation 1. As you are leaving to buy the ticket, your friend calls and invites you to the comedy club.

Would your decision to go to the play or the comedy club be different in situation 1 than in situation 2? Most people would say that in situation 1, they would go to the play because otherwise they would lose the $75 they had paid for the ticket. In fact, the $75 is "lost" no matter what you do because the ticket is nonrefundable. The only real issue for you to decide is whether you would prefer to see the play or prefer to go with your friend to the comedy club. If you would prefer to go to the club, the fact that you have already paid $75 for the ticket to the play is irrelevant. Your decision should be the same in situation 1 as in situation 2.

Psychologists Daniel Kahneman and Amos Tversky explored the tendency of consumers to not ignore sunk costs by asking two samples of people the following questions:

Question 1: One sample of people was asked: "Imagine that you have decided to see a play and have paid the admission price of $10 per ticket. As you enter the theater, you discover that you have lost the ticket. The seat was not marked, and the ticket cannot be recovered. Would you pay $10 for another ticket?" Of those asked, 46 percent answered "yes," and 54 percent answered "no."

Question 2: A different sample of people was asked: "Imagine that you have decided to see a play where admission is $10 per ticket. As you enter the theater, you discover that you have lost a $10 bill. Would you still pay $10 for a ticket to the play?" Of those asked, 88 percent answered "yes," and 12 percent answered "no."

The situations presented in the two questions are actually the same and should have received the same fraction of yes and no responses. Many people, though, have trouble seeing that in question 1, when deciding whether to see the play, they should ignore the $10 already paid for a ticket because it is a sunk cost.

Would you give up being a surgeon to start your own blog?

Making the Connection
MyEconLab Video

A Blogger Who Understands the Importance of Ignoring Sunk Costs

In recent years, many people have started blogs—or "Web logs"—where they record their thoughts on politics, sports, their favorite hobbies, or anything else that interests them. Some bloggers can spend hours a day writing up their latest ideas and providing links to relevant material on the Web. A few blogs become so successful that they attract paid advertising and earn their owners a good income. Arnold Kim began blogging about Apple products in 2000 during his fourth year of medical school. He continued blogging on his site, MacRumors.com, over the next eight years, while pursuing a medical career as a nephrologist—a doctor who treats kidney problems.

By 2008, Kim's site had become very successful, attracting 4.4 million people and more than 40 million page views each month. He was earning more than $100,000 per year from paid advertising by companies such as Verizon, Audible.com, and CDW. But the tasks of compiling rumors about new Apple products, keeping an Apple buying guide up to date, and monitoring multiple discussion boards on the site became more than he could handle as a part-time job. Kim enjoyed working on the Web site and believed that ultimately it could earn him more than he was earning as a doctor. Still, he hesitated to abandon his medical career because he had invested nearly $200,000 in his education.

But the $200,000, as well as the years he had spent in medical school, completing a residency in internal medicine, and completing a fellowship in nephrology, were sunk costs. Kim realized that he needed to ignore these sunk costs in order to make a rational decision about whether to continue in medicine or to become a full-time blogger. After calculating that he would make more from his Web site than from his medical career—and taking into account that by working from home he could spend more time with his young daughter—he decided to blog full time. He was quoted as saying, "on paper it was an easy decision." Despite competition from new blogs, MacRumors continued to do well, being viewed by 5 million people per month in mid-2013, and Kim's income had risen above what he would have made as a doctor.

Knowing that it is rational to ignore sunk costs can be important in making key decisions in life.

Sources: Brian X. Chen, "Arnold Kim Celebrates 10 Years as Apple Rumor King," www.wired.com, February 23, 2010; Brian Stelter, "My Son, the Blogger: An M.D. Trades Medicine for Apple Rumors," *New York Times*, July 21, 2008; Dan Frommer, "Nephrologist to Mac Blogger: The Unlikely Career Path of MacRumors' Arnold Kim," www.businessinsider.com, July 13, 2008; and "Macrumors Traffic," www.quantcast.com, June 13, 2013.

Your Turn: Test your understanding by doing related problems 4.9, 4.10, and 4.11 on page 334 at the end of this chapter.

MyEconLab Study Plan

Being Unrealistic about Future Behavior Studies have shown that a majority of adults in the United States are overweight. Why do many people choose to eat too much? One possibility is that they receive more utility from eating high-calorie foods than they would from being thin. A more likely explanation, however, is that many people eat a lot today because they expect to eat less tomorrow. But they never do eat less, and so they end up overweight. (Of course, some people also suffer from medical problems that lead to weight gain.) Similarly, some people continue smoking today because they expect to be able to give it up sometime in the future. Unfortunately, for many people that time never comes, and they suffer the health consequences of years of smoking. In both these cases, people are overvaluing the utility from current choices—eating chocolate cake or smoking—and undervaluing the utility to be received in the future from being thin or not getting lung cancer.

Economists who have studied this question argue that many people have preferences that are not consistent over time. In the long run, you would like to be thin or give up smoking or achieve some other goal, but each day, you make decisions (such as to eat too much or smoke) that are not consistent with this long-run goal. If you are unrealistic about your future behavior, you underestimate the costs of choices—such as overeating or smoking—that you make today. A key way of avoiding this problem is to be realistic about your future behavior.

Taking into account nonmonetary opportunity costs, ignoring sunk costs, and being more realistic about future behavior are three ways in which consumers are able to improve the decisions they make.   MyEconLab Concept Check

The Behavioral Economics of Shopping

Earlier in this chapter, we analyzed how consumers can choose the products they buy so as to maximize utility. In this section, we briefly consider problems consumers may encounter that keep them from making optimal consumption choices.

In discussing how consumers maximize utility, we used simple examples where people were choosing the optimal quantity of two goods subject to a budget constraint. Consider, though, a typical trip to the supermarket. Someone shopping for a family of four might end up buying 25 or more products. A consumer in that situation is unlikely to equate the ratios of the marginal utilities to the prices for all these products when deciding the quantities to buy. Does it matter that consumers often do not make optimal consumption choices? Economists are divided in their answers to this question. Many economists make two points in arguing that the answer to the question is "no": (1) The assumptions in most scientific models are not literally correct. In the model of consumer choice, for example, unrealistic assumptions are necessary to simplify a complex reality by focusing on the most important factors involved in decision making; and (2) models are best judged by the success of their predictions rather than by the realism of their assumptions. Predictions based on the model of consumer choice have been successful in predicting many types of consumer behavior.

Rules of Thumb Behavioral economists argue that it *does* matter that consumers usually do not make optimal consumption choices. These economists believe that there are benefits to analyzing *how* consumers actually make decisions. The model we have used in this chapter assumes that when people shop they have full information on the prices of products, including information on differences in prices across stores. The model also assumes that people can make complicated calculations such as computing the ratios of marginal utilities to prices across many products. In fact, people often make choices on the basis of only limited information and without the time or capacity to calculate their optimal choices. As a result, rather than making optimal choices, people often use *rules of thumb*, which are guides to decision making that may not produce optimal choices. For example, a consumer may decide that a particular supermarket has the lowest prices for the products the consumer buys, without continually checking whether this assumption is correct. If a new supermarket opens with lower prices, the consumer, at least for a period, may continue shopping at the old supermarket, even though doing so is no longer optimal.

Anchoring How do shoppers decide whether the price of a product is high or low? Behavioral economists use the word *anchoring* to describe one aspect of how consumers evaluate prices. If people are uncertain about a value, such as a price, they often relate—or anchor—that value to some other known value, even if the second value is irrelevant. Psychologists Amos Tversky and Daniel Kahnemann carried out an experiment to illustrate the effects of anchoring. They constructed a wheel that when spun always stopped on a value of either 10 or 65. They spun the wheel for different participants in the experiment and then asked them: "What is your best guess of the percentage of African nations in the United Nations?" When the wheel stopped on a value of 10, the average answer of the participants was 25 percent. When the wheel stopped on 65, the average answer was 45 percent. Even though the value from the spin of the wheel had no relevance to the question being asked, the value anchored the participants' responses. In another experiment, conducted by Brian Wansink of Cornell University, Robert Kent of the University of Delaware, and Stephen Hoch of the University of Pennsylvania, three supermarkets offered cans of Campbell soup for sale at a 12-percent reduction in price. On one day during the sale, a display sign said "Limit of 12 per person"; on another day, a display sign said "No limit per person." On the day when the sign limited sales, the supermarkets sold an average of 7 cans per person. On the day when the sign said there was no limit on sales, the supermarkets sold 3.3 cans per person. The number 12 on the sign had anchored the shoppers' decisions on how many cans to buy.

Consumers often lack the information to evaluate whether the price of a good is "high" or "low." Stores can take advantage of this lack of information to anchor consumers' estimates by marking a high "regular price" on a product, which makes the discounted "sale price" appear to be a bargain even if the product is very rarely offered for sale at the regular price.   MyEconLab Concept Check

Making the Connection
MyEconLab Video

J.C. Penney Meets Behavioral Economics

We saw at the beginning of this chapter that Ron Johnson, after a very successful career as the head of Apple's retail stores, was recruited to become the CEO of the J.C. Penney department store chain. Johnson instituted a new pricing strategy of offering goods at "everyday low prices" and rarely discounting prices below those levels. The new strategy turned out to be a failure as Penney's revenue declined. Johnson was fired as CEO after only 17 months.

The J.C. Penney strategy of "everyday low prices" backfired.

Ideas from behavioral economics can help explain what went wrong. First, Johnson assumed that consumers would understand that the everyday low prices really were low, at least compared with the very high regular prices that Penney had previously based its sales on. In fact, though, there is substantial evidence that some consumers are not well aware of prices even for goods they buy regularly. One study of supermarket shoppers asked people the prices of goods they had just placed in their shopping carts. Fewer than half of the shoppers could accurately recall the prices and a quarter couldn't even offer a guess, even though they had placed the goods in their carts less than a minute earlier. Another study asked people who were about to enter a department store questions about the prices of goods they frequently purchased. Only about one-third could give accurate answers. When asked to evaluate whether a specific price of a good they frequently purchased was high or low, about 15 percent of people identified prices that were actually high as being good deals and prices that were actually low as being bad deals.

Studies of retail sales show that consumers purchase a significant fraction of goods at discount prices. For example, a study of checkout scanner data from nine supermarkets showed that while liquid laundry detergent was offered at discount prices only about a quarter of the time, nearly half of detergent was purchased at the sale prices. That consumers respond so strongly to sales is not good news for a strategy that replaces sales with fixed prices.

Why do consumers respond to sales? Why wasn't Penney able to convince consumers that everyday low prices really were low? One possibility is that by displaying both a high "regular price" and a low "sale price," sales provide consumers with an "anchor" or reference point to interpret the prices being offered. A sale price seems low if offered as a markdown from a higher regular price, even if—because of sales and the use of coupons—few people ever buy the good at the regular price. Without the anchor of the regular price, consumers can have difficulty deciding whether an everyday low price is actually low, particularly because some consumers enter a store with little idea of what typical prices are. As the Northwestern professor quoted in the chapter opener put it: "J.C. Penney might say it's a fair price, but why should consumers trust J.C. Penney?"

By largely eliminating sales, Johnson disregarded some of the insights of behavioral economics. As a result, Penney suffered losses and Johnson lost his job.

Sources: Stephanie Clifford and Catherine Rampell, "Sometimes, We Want Prices to Fool Us," *New York Times*, April 13, 2013; Daniel Kahneman, *Thinking, Fast and Slow*, New York: Farrar, Strauss and Giroux, 2011; Julio Rotemberg, "Behavioral Aspects of Price Setting, and Their Policy Implications," National Bureau of Economic Research, Working Paper 13754, January 2008; Marc Vanhuele and Xavier Drèze, "Measuring the Price Knowledge Shoppers Bring to the Store," *Journal of Marketing*, Vol. 66, No. 4, October 2002, pp. 72–85; Peter R. Dickson and Alan G. Sawyer, "The Price Knowledge and Search of Supermarket Shoppers," *Journal of Marketing*, Vol. 54, No. 3, July 1990, pp. 42–53; and Igal Hendel and Aviv Nevo, "Measuring the Implications of Sales and Consumer Inventory Behavior," *Econometrica*, Vol. 74, No. 6, November 2006, pp. 1637–1673.

MyEconLab Study Plan

Your Turn: Test your understanding by doing related problem 4.15 on page 334 at the end of this chapter.

Continued from page 305

Economics in Your Life

Do You Make Rational Decisions?

At the beginning of this chapter, we asked you to consider a situation in which you had paid $75 for a concert ticket, which is the most you would be willing to pay. Just before you enter the concert hall, someone offers you $90 for the ticket. We posed two questions: Would you sell the ticket? and Would an economist think it is rational to sell the ticket? If you answered that you would sell, then your answer is rational in the sense in which economists use the term. The cost of going to see the concert is what you have to give up for the ticket. Initially, the cost was just $75—the dollar price of the ticket. This amount was also the most you were willing to pay. However, once someone offers you $90 for the ticket, the cost of seeing the concert rises to $90. The reason the cost of the concert is now $90 is that once you turn down an offer of $90 for the ticket, you have incurred a nonmonetary opportunity cost of $90 if you use the ticket yourself. The endowment effect explains why some people would not sell the ticket. People seem to value something that they own more than something that they do not own. Therefore, a concert ticket you already own may be worth more to you than a concert ticket you have yet to purchase. Behavioral economists study situations like this where people make choices that do not appear to be economically rational.

Conclusion

In a market system, consumers are in the driver's seat. Goods are produced only if consumers want them to be. Therefore, how consumers make their decisions is an important area for economists to study. Economists expect that consumers will spend their incomes so that the last dollar spent on each good provides them with equal additional amounts of satisfaction, or utility. In practice, there are significant social influences on consumer decision making, particularly when a good or service is consumed in public. Fairness also seems to be an important consideration for most consumers. Finally, many consumers could improve the decisions they make if they would take into account nonmonetary opportunity costs and ignore sunk costs.

In this chapter, we studied consumers' choices. In the next several chapters, we will study firms' choices.

Visit MyEconLab for a news article and analysis related to the concepts in this chapter.

Chapter Summary and Problems

Key Terms

Behavioral economics, p. 323

Budget constraint, p. 307

Endowment effect, p. 323

Income effect, p. 313

Law of diminishing marginal utility, p. 307

Marginal utility (*MU*), p. 307

Network externality, p. 318

Opportunity cost, p. 323

Substitution effect, p. 313

Sunk cost, p. 324

Utility, p. 306

 Utility and Consumer Decision Making, pages 306–314

LEARNING OBJECTIVE: Define utility and explain how consumers choose goods and services to maximize their utility.

Summary

Utility is the enjoyment or satisfaction that people receive from consuming goods and services. The goal of a consumer is to spend available income so as to maximize utility. **Marginal utility** is the change in total utility a person receives from consuming one additional unit of a good or service. The **law of diminishing marginal utility** states that consumers receive diminishing additional satisfaction as they consume more of a good or service during a given period of time. The **budget constraint** is the amount of income consumers have available to spend on goods and services. To maximize utility, consumers should make sure they spend their income so that the last dollar spent on each product gives them the same marginal utility. The **income effect** is the change in the quantity demanded of a good that results from the effect of a change in the price on consumer purchasing power. The **substitution effect** is the change in the quantity demanded of a good that results from a change in price making the good more or less expensive relative to other goods, holding constant the effect of the price change on consumer purchasing power.

MyEconLab   Visit **www.myeconlab.com** to complete these exercises online and get instant feedback.

Review Questions

1.1 What is the economic definition of *utility*? Is it possible to measure utility?

1.2 What is the definition of *marginal utility*? What is the law of diminishing marginal utility? Why is marginal utility more useful than total utility in consumer decision making?

1.3 What is meant by a consumer's *budget constraint*? What is the rule of equal marginal utility per dollar spent?

1.4 How does a change in the price of a product cause both a substitution effect and an income effect?

Problems and Applications

1.5 Does the law of diminishing marginal utility hold true in every situation? Is it possible to think of goods for which consuming additional units, at least initially, will result in increasing marginal utility?

1.6 If consumers should allocate their income so that the last dollar spent on every product gives them the same amount of additional utility, how should they decide the amount of their income to save?

1.7 You have six hours to study for two exams tomorrow. The following table shows the relationship between hours of study and test scores:

Economics		Psychology	
Hours	**Score**	**Hours**	**Score**
0	54	0	54
1	62	1	60
2	69	2	65
3	75	3	69
4	80	4	72
5	84	5	74
6	87	6	75

a. Use the rule for determining optimal purchases to decide how many hours you should study each subject. Treat each point on an exam as 1 unit of utility and assume that you consider an extra point on an economics exam to have the same value as an extra point on a psychology exam.

b. Now suppose that you are a psychology major and that you value each point you earn on a psychology exam as being worth three times as much as each point you earn on an economics exam. Now how many hours should you study each subject?

1.8 [**Related to** Solved Problem 10.1 **on page 310**] Joe has $16 to spend on Twinkies and Ho-Hos. Twinkies have a price of $1 per pack, and Ho-Hos have a price of $2 per pack. Use the information in these graphs to determine the number of Twinkies and Ho-Hos packs Joe should buy to maximize his utility. Briefly explain your reasoning.

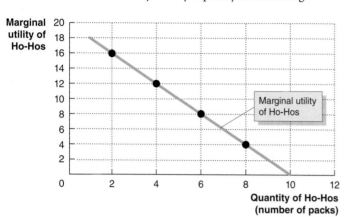

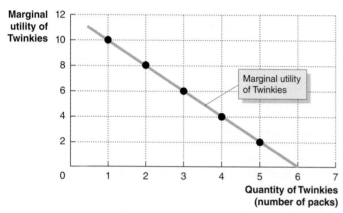

1.9 [**Related to** Solved Problem 10.1 **on page 310**] Joe has $55 to spend on apples and oranges. Given the information in the following table, is Joe maximizing utility? Briefly explain.

	Price	Quantity	Total Utility	Marginal Utility of Last Unit
Apples	$0.50	50	1,000	20
Oranges	$0.75	40	500	30

1.10 Suppose the price of a bag of Frito's corn chips declines from $0.89 to $0.79. Which is likely to be larger: the income effect or the substitution effect? Briefly explain.

1.11 [**Related to the** Don't Let This Happen to You **on page 312**] Mary is buying corn chips and soda. She has 4 bags of corn chips and 5 bottles of soda in her shopping cart. The marginal utility of the fourth bag of corn chips is 10, and the marginal utility of the fifth bottle of soda is also 10. Is Mary maximizing utility? Briefly explain.

1.12 When the price of pizza falls in the Super Bowl example on pages 313–314, both the income effect and the substitution effect cause you to want to consume more pizza. If pizza were an inferior good, how would the analysis be changed? In this case, is it possible that a lower price for pizza might lead you to buy less pizza? Briefly explain.

10.2 ## Where Demand Curves Come From, pages 314–317

LEARNING OBJECTIVE: Use the concept of utility to explain the law of demand.

Summary

When the price of a good falls, the ratio of the marginal utility to price rises. This change leads consumers to buy more of that good. As a result, whenever the price of a product falls, the quantity demanded increases. We saw in Chapter 1 that this relationship is known as the *law of demand*. The market demand curve can be constructed from the individual demand curves for all the consumers in the market.

Review Questions

2.1 Explain how a downward-sloping demand curve results from consumers adjusting their consumption choices to changes in price.

2.2 How is the market demand curve derived from consumers' individual demand curves?

2.3 What would need to be true for a demand curve to be upward sloping?

Problems and Applications

2.4 Considering only the income effect, if the price of an inferior good declines, would a consumer want to buy a larger quantity or a smaller quantity of the good? Does your answer mean that the demand curves for inferior goods should slope upward? Briefly explain.

2.5 The chapter states that "when the price of an inferior good falls, the income effect and substitution effect work in opposite directions." Explain what this statement means.

2.6 Suppose the market for ice cream cones is made up of three consumers: Tiago, Terrell, and Tim. Use the information in the following table to construct the market demand curve for ice cream cones. Show the information in a table and in a graph.

Price	Tiago Quantity Demanded (cones per week)	Terrell Quantity Demanded (cones per week)	Tim Quantity Demanded (cones per week)
$1.75	2	1	0
1.50	4	3	2
1.25	6	4	3
1.00	7	6	4
0.75	9	7	5

2.7 Suppose the wage you are being paid per hour doubles from $15 to $30. Would you decide to work more hours or fewer hours? Is there an income and substitution effect involved in your decision about how many hours you choose to work? If so, what is being substituted for what?

2.8 Consider two goods: pizza and Coke. Along an individual's demand curve for pizza, as the price of pizza falls, does the marginal utility per dollar spent on pizza always equal the marginal utility per dollar spent on Coke? In other words, does the rule of equal marginal utility per dollar spent hold as the price changes and you move up or down the demand curve? How can the rule hold given that the price of pizza changes along the demand curve? If you need help to answer this problem, look back at the discussion of Figure 10.2 on deriving the demand curve for pizza.

2.9 **[Related to** the Making the Connection **on page 316]** In studying the consumption of very poor families in China, Robert Jensen and Nolan Miller found that in both Hunan and Gansu "Giffen behavior is most likely to be found among a range of households that are poor (but not too poor or too rich)."
   a. What do Jensen and Miller mean by "Giffen behavior"?
   b. Why would the poorest of the poor be less likely than people with slightly higher incomes to exhibit this behavior?
   c. Why must a good make up a very large portion of consumers' budgets to be a Giffen good?
   Source: Robert T. Jensen and Nolan H. Miller, "Giffen Behavior and Subsistence Consumption," *American Economic Review*, Vol. 98, No. 4, September 2008, p. 1569.

10.3 Social Influences on Decision Making, pages 317–322

LEARNING OBJECTIVE: Explain how social influences can affect consumption choices.

Summary

Social factors can have an effect on consumption. For example, the amount of utility people receive from consuming a good often depends on how many other people they know who also consume the good. There is a **network externality** in the consumption of a product if the usefulness of the product increases with the number of consumers who use it. There is evidence that people like to be treated fairly and that they usually attempt to treat others fairly, even if doing so makes them worse off financially. This result has been demonstrated in laboratory experiments, such as the ultimatum game. When firms set prices, they take into account consumers' preference for fairness. For example, hardware stores often do not increase the price of snow shovels to take advantage of a temporary increase in demand following a snowstorm.

MyEconLab   Visit www.myeconlab.com to complete these exercises online and get instant feedback.

Review Questions

3.1 In which of the following situations are social influences on consumer decision making likely to be greater: choosing a restaurant for dinner or choosing a brand of toothpaste to buy? Briefly explain.

3.2 What are network externalities? For what types of products are network externalities likely to be important? What is path dependence?

3.3 How does the fact that consumers apparently value fairness affect the pricing decisions that businesses make?

Problems and Applications

3.4 Which of the following products are most likely to have significant network externalities? Briefly explain.
   a. Tablet computers
   b. Dog food
   c. Board games
   d. LCD televisions
   e. 3D televisions

3.5 Speaking about a trip to Switzerland, economist Daniel Hamermesh noted in an article in the *New York Times* that electrical outlets in Switzerland use an unusual three-prong plug. Adapters for that type of plug are not typically included in adapter sets, so he and his wife weren't able to plug their computers into their hotel's outlets. Hamermesh wondered: "Why does Switzerland renounce the network externalities that would come with using standard European plugs with their standard 220-volt electricity?" How is Switzerland "renouncing network externalities" by not using standard European plugs?
   Source: Daniel Hamermesh, "If Switzerland Would Only Change Its Plugs," *New York Times*, September 23, 2008.

3.6 In an opinion survey, Snoopy was found to be the most appealing celebrity endorser. The beagle from the popular *Peanuts* comic strip appeared in commercials for the insurance company MetLife. What advantages and disadvantages are there in using Snoopy, rather than a real person, to endorse a product?
   Source: Jeff Bercovici, "America's Most Loved Spokespersons," *Forbes*, March 14, 2011.

3.7 Las Vegas is one of the most popular tourist destinations in the United States. In November 2008, the Rio Hotel and Casino in Las Vegas dropped the price of its breakfast buffet to $5.99 for local residents, while keeping the regular price of $14.99 for nonlocals. When setting the price for a meal, why would it matter to the restaurant if the customer is a local resident?

Source: *Las Vegas Advisor*, November 2008.

3.8 **[Related to the** Making the Connection **on page 321]** An article in the *New York Times* notes that classic rock star Tom Petty likes to perform in smaller venues that don't have as many seats as large venues such as Madison Square Garden in New York. According to the article, Petty insists that tickets to his concert be sold "below market price." The author of the article wondered why "Petty and his promoter would price tickets so low when there were clearly people willing to pay much, much more."

a. How does the author know that the prices for Petty's concert tickets are below the market price?

b. Why might Petty and his manager want tickets to have prices below the market price?

Source: Adam Davidson, "How Much Is Michael Bolton Worth to You?" *New York Times*, June 4, 2013.

3.9 **[Related to the** Making the Connection **on page 321]** Suppose that *Amazing Spider-Man 2* comes out, and hundreds of people arrive at a theater and discover that the movie is already sold out. Meanwhile, the theater is also showing a boring movie in its third week of release in a mostly empty theater. Why would the theater charge the same price of $7.50 for a ticket to either movie, when the quantity of tickets demanded is much greater than the quantity supplied for one movie, and the quantity of tickets demanded is much less than the quantity supplied for the other?

10.4 **Behavioral Economics: Do People Make Their Choices Rationally? pages 323–328**

LEARNING OBJECTIVE: Describe the behavioral economics approach to understanding decision making.

Summary

Behavioral economics is the study of situations in which people act in ways that are not economically rational. **Opportunity cost** is the highest-valued alternative that must be given up to engage in an activity. People would improve their decision making if they took into account nonmonetary opportunity costs. People sometimes ignore nonmonetary opportunity costs because of the **endowment effect**—the tendency of people to be unwilling to sell something they already own even if they are offered a price that is greater than the price they would be willing to pay to buy the good if they didn't already own it. People would also improve their decision making if they ignored *sunk costs*. A **sunk cost** is a cost that has already been paid and cannot be recovered. Finally, people would improve their decision making if they were more realistic about their future behavior. Behavioral economics gives insights into consumer behavior that can guide business strategies.

 Visit **www.myeconlab.com** to complete these exercises online and get instant feedback.

Review Questions

4.1 What does it mean to be economically rational?

4.2 Define *behavioral economics*. What are the three common mistakes that consumers often make? Give an example of each mistake.

4.3 Does using rules of thumb increase or decrease the likelihood of a consumer making an optimal choice? Briefly explain.

4.4 What is anchoring? How might a firm use anchoring to influence consumer choices so as to increase sales?

Problems and Applications

4.5 Suppose your little brother tells you on Tuesday that one of his friends offered him $80 for his Prince Fielder rookie baseball card, but your brother decides not to sell the card.

On Wednesday, your brother loses the card. Your parents feel sorry for him and give him $80 to make up the loss. Instead of buying another Prince Fielder card with the money (which we will assume he could have done), your brother uses the money to buy movies online. Explain your brother's actions by using the concepts in this chapter.

4.6 Richard Thaler, an economist at the University of Chicago, is the person who first used the term *endowment effect* to describe placing a higher value on something already owned than would be placed on the object if not currently owned. According to an article in the *Economist*:

> Dr. Thaler, who recently had some expensive bottles of wine stolen, observes that he is "now confronted with precisely one of my own experiments: these are bottles I wasn't planning to sell and now I'm going to get a cheque from an insurance company and most of these bottles I will not buy. I'm a good enough economist to know there's a bit of an inconsistency there."

Based on Thaler's statement, how do his stolen bottles of wine illustrate the endowment effect, and why does he make the statement: "I'm a good enough economist to know there's a bit of an inconsistency there"?

Source: "It's Mine, I Tell You," *Economist*, June 19, 2008.

4.7 Suppose that you are a big fan of the Harry Potter books. You would love to own a copy of the very first printing of the first book, but unfortunately you can't find it for sale for less than $5,000. You are willing to pay at most $200 for a copy, but can't find one at that price until one day in a used bookstore you see a copy selling for $10, which you immediately buy. Are you being irrational if you keep the copy rather than sell it?

4.8 Someone who owns a townhouse wrote to a real estate advice columnist to ask whether he should sell his townhouse or wait and sell it in the future when he hoped that prices would be higher. The columnist replied: "Ask yourself: Would you buy this townhouse today as an investment? Because every day you don't sell it, you're buying it." Do you agree with the columnist? In what sense are you buying something if you don't sell it? Should the owner's decision about whether to sell depend on what price he originally paid for the townhouse?

Source: Edith Lane, "Contract Exclusion OK?" (Allentown, PA) *Morning Call*, May 22, 2011.

4.9 **[Related to the** Making the Connection **on page 325]** Rob Neyer is a baseball writer for sbnation.com. He has described attending a Red Sox game at Fenway Park in Boston and having a seat in the sun on a hot, humid day: "Granted, I could have moved under the overhang and enjoyed today's contest from a nice, cool, shady seat. But when you paid forty-five dollars for a ticket in the fourth row, it's tough to move back to the twenty-fourth [row]." Briefly evaluate Neyer's reasoning.

Source: Rob Neyer, *Feeding the Green Monster*, New York: iPublish. com, 2001, p. 50.

4.10 **[Related to the** Making the Connection **on page 325]** After owning a used car for two years, you start having problems with it. You take it to the shop, and a mechanic tells you that repairs will cost $4,000. What factors will you take into account in deciding whether to have the repairs done or to junk the car and buy another one? Will the price you paid for the car be one of those factors? Briefly explain.

4.11 **[Related to the** Making the Connection **on page 325]** The following excerpt is from a letter sent to a financial advice columnist: "My wife and I are trying to decide how to invest a $250,000 windfall. She wants to pay off our $114,000 mortgage, but I'm not eager to do that because we refinanced only nine months ago, paying $3,000 in fees and costs." Briefly discuss what effect the $3,000 refinancing cost should have on this couple's investment decision.

Source: Liz Pulliam, *Los Angeles Times* advice column, March 24, 2004.

4.12 Briefly explain whether you agree with the following statement: "If people were more realistic about their future behavior, the demand curve for potato chips would shift to the left."

4.13 In an article in the *Quarterly Journal of Economics*, Ted O'Donoghue and Matthew Rabin make the following observation: "People have self-control problems caused by a tendency to pursue immediate gratification in a way that their 'long-run selves' do not appreciate." What do they mean by a person's "long-run self"? Give two examples of people pursuing immediate gratification that their long-run selves would not appreciate.

Source: Ted O'Donoghue and Matthew Rabin, "Choice and Procrastination," *Quarterly Journal of Economics*, February 2001, pp. 125–126.

4.14 Data from health clubs show that members who choose a contract with a flat monthly fee of more than $70 attend, on average, 4.8 times per month. They pay a price per expected visit of more than $14, even though a $10-per-visit fee is also available. Why would these consumers choose a monthly contract when they lose money on it?

4.15 **[Related to the** Making the Connection **on page 327]** The *Economist* magazine offered the following two options for subscribing:

1. $56 per year for an online-only subscription
2. $125 per year for print plus online access subscription

A large majority of subscribers chose option 1. But the magazine would have preferred to sell more $125 subscriptions because it can charge higher rates to advertisers in the print magazine than it can online. The magazine decided to rely on insights from behavioral economics to try to increase the number of people choosing the $125 subscriptions. It began offering the following three options:

1. $56 per year for an online-only subscription
2. $125 print plus online access subscription
3. $125 print-only subscription

A large majority of subscribers now chose option 2 rather than option 1. What insights from behavioral economics that were discussed in this chapter can help explain this result?

Source: Mukul Patki, "5 Behavioral Economics Principles Marketers Can't Afford to Ignore," *Forbes*, March 1, 2013.

4.16 **[Related to the** Chapter Opener **on page 305]** An article in the *New York Times* about J.C. Penney's pricing strategy under former CEO Ron Johnson observes: "Penney had pulled up the anchor, only to see many of its customers sail away."

a. In behavioral economics, what is an "anchor"?
b. In what sense did J.C. Penney "pull up the anchor"?
c. Why did Penney follow this strategy and what was the result?

Source: Stephanie Clifford and Katherine Rampell, "Sometimes We Want Prices to Fool Us," *New York Times*, April 13, 2013.

Appendix

Using Indifference Curves and Budget Lines to Understand Consumer Behavior

LEARNING OBJECTIVE

Use indifference curves and budget lines to understand consumer behavior.

Consumer Preferences

In this chapter, we analyzed consumer behavior using the assumption that satisfaction, or *utility*, is measurable in utils. Although this assumption made our analysis easier to understand, it is unrealistic. In this appendix, we use the more realistic assumption that consumers are able to *rank* different combinations of goods and services in terms of how much utility they provide. For example, a consumer is able to determine whether he or she prefers 2 slices of pizza and 1 can of Coke or 1 slice of pizza and 2 cans of Coke, even if the consumer is unsure exactly how much utility he or she would receive from consuming these goods. This approach has the advantage of allowing us to actually draw a map of a consumer's preferences.

To begin with, suppose that a consumer is presented with the following alternatives, or *consumption bundles*:

Consumption Bundle A	Consumption Bundle B
2 slices of pizza and 1 can of Coke	1 slice of pizza and 2 cans of Coke

We assume that the consumer will always be able to decide which of the following is true:

- The consumer prefers bundle A to bundle B.
- The consumer prefers bundle B to bundle A.
- The consumer is indifferent between bundle A and bundle B. That is, the consumer would be equally happy to receive either bundle, so we can say the consumer receives equal utility from the two bundles.

For consistency, we also assume that the consumer's preferences are *transitive*. For example, if a consumer prefers pepperoni pizza to mushroom pizza and prefers mushroom pizza to anchovy pizza, the consumer must prefer pepperoni pizza to anchovy pizza.

Indifference Curves

Given the assumptions in the preceding section, we can draw a map of a consumer's preferences by using indifference curves. An **indifference curve** shows combinations of consumption bundles that give the consumer the same utility. In reality, consumers choose among consumption bundles containing many goods and services, but to make the discussion easier to follow, we will assume that only two goods are involved. Nothing important would change if we expanded the discussion to include many goods instead of just two.

The table in Figure 10A.1 gives Dave's preferences for pizza and Coke. The graph plots the information from the table. Every possible combination of pizza and Coke will have an indifference curve passing through it, although in the figure we have shown only four of Dave's indifference curves. Dave is indifferent among all the consumption bundles that are on the same indifference curve. So, he is indifferent among bundles E, B, and F because they all lie on indifference curve I_3. Even though Dave has 4 fewer cans of Coke with bundle B than with bundle E, the additional slice of pizza he has in bundle B results in his having the same amount of utility at both points.

Indifference curve A curve that shows the combinations of consumption bundles that give the consumer the same utility.

Figure 10A.1

Plotting Dave's Preferences for Pizza and Coke

Every possible combination of pizza and Coke will have an indifference curve passing through it, although in the graph we show just four of Dave's indifference curves. Dave is indifferent among all the consumption bundles that are on the same indifference curve. So, he is indifferent among bundles *E*, *B*, and *F* because they all lie on indifference curve I_3. Moving to the upper right in the graph increases the quantities of both goods available for Dave to consume. Therefore, the further to the upper right the indifference curve is, the greater the utility Dave receives.

Consumption Bundle	Slices of Pizza	Cans of Coke
A	1	2
B	3	4
C	4	5
D	1	6
E	2	8
F	5	2

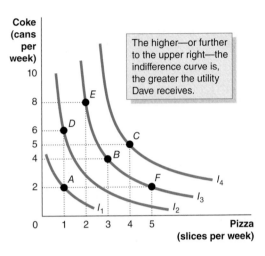

The higher—or further to the upper right—the indifference curve is, the greater the utility Dave receives.

Even without looking at Dave's indifference curves, we know he will prefer consumption bundle *D* to consumption bundle *A* because in *D* he receives the same quantity of pizza as in *A* but 4 additional cans of Coke. But we need to know Dave's preferences, as shown by his indifference curves, to know how he will rank bundle *B* and bundle *D*. Bundle *D* contains more Coke but less pizza than bundle *B*, so Dave's ranking will depend on how much pizza he would be willing to give up to receive more Coke. The higher the indifference curve—that is, the further to the upper right on the graph—the greater the amounts of both goods that are available for Dave to consume and the greater his utility. In other words, Dave receives more utility from the consumption bundles on indifference curve I_2 than from the consumption bundles on indifference curve I_1, more utility from the bundles on I_3 than from the bundles on I_2, and so on. MyEconLab Concept Check

The Slope of an Indifference Curve

Remember that the slope of a curve is the ratio of the change in the variable on the vertical axis to the change in the variable on the horizontal axis. Along an indifference curve, the slope tells us the rate at which the consumer is willing to trade off one product for another while keeping the consumer's utility constant. Economists call this rate the **marginal rate of substitution (*MRS*)**.

Marginal rate of substitution (*MRS*) The rate at which a consumer would be willing to trade off one good for another.

We expect that the *MRS* will change as we move down an indifference curve. In Figure 10A.1, at a point like *E* on indifference curve I_3, Dave's indifference curve is relatively steep. As we move down the curve, it becomes less steep, until it becomes relatively flat at a point like *F*. This is the usual shape of indifference curves: They are bowed in, or convex. A consumption bundle like *E* contains a lot of Coke and not much pizza. We would expect that Dave could give up a significant quantity of Coke for a smaller quantity of additional pizza and still have the same level of utility. Therefore, the *MRS* will be high. As we move down the indifference curve, Dave moves to bundles, like *B* and *F*, that have more pizza and less Coke. At those points, Dave is willing to trade less Coke for pizza, and the *MRS* declines. MyEconLab Concept Check

Can Indifference Curves Ever Cross?

Remember that we assume that consumers have transitive preferences. That is, if Dave prefers consumption bundle *X* to consumption bundle *Y* and he prefers consumption bundle *Y* to consumption bundle *Z*, he must prefer bundle *X* to bundle *Z*. If indifference curves cross, this assumption is violated. To understand why, look at Figure 10A.2, which shows two of Dave's indifference curves crossing.

Because bundle *X* and bundle *Z* are both on indifference curve I_1, Dave must be indifferent between them. Similarly, because bundle *X* and bundle *Y* are on indifference curve I_2, Dave must be indifferent between them. The assumption of transitivity means that Dave should also be indifferent between bundle *Z* and bundle *Y*. We know he won't be however, because bundle *Y* contains more pizza and more Coke than bundle *Z*. So,

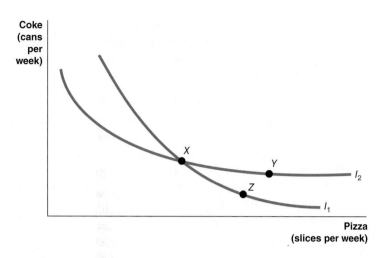

Dave will definitely prefer bundle *Y* to bundle *Z*, which violates the assumption of transitivity. Therefore, none of Dave's indifference curves can cross. MyEconLab Concept Check

The Budget Constraint

Remember that a consumer's *budget constraint* is the amount of income he or she has available to spend on goods and services. Suppose that Dave has $10 per week to spend on pizza and Coke. The table in Figure 10A.3 shows the combinations that he can afford to buy if the price of pizza is $2 per slice and the price of Coke is $1 per can. As you can

MyEconLab Animation

Figure 10A.2

Indifference Curves Cannot Cross

Because bundle *X* and bundle *Z* are both on indifference curve I_1, Dave must be indifferent between them. Similarly, because bundle *X* and bundle *Y* are on indifference curve I_2, Dave must be indifferent between them. The assumption of transitivity means that Dave should also be indifferent between bundle *Z* and bundle *Y*. We know he won't be however, because bundle *Y* contains more pizza and more Coke than bundle *Z*. So, Dave will definitely prefer bundle *Y* to bundle *Z*, which violates the assumption of transitivity. Therefore, none of Dave's indifference curves can cross.

Combinations of Pizza and Coke Dave Can Buy with $10			
Consumption Bundle	Slices of Pizza	Cans of Coke	Total Spending
G	0	10	$10.00
H	1	8	10.00
I	2	6	10.00
J	3	4	10.00
K	4	2	10.00
L	5	0	10.00

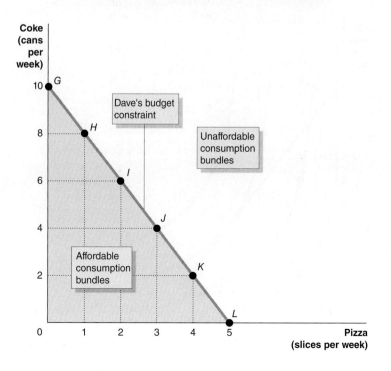

MyEconLab Animation

Figure 10A.3

Dave's Budget Constraint

Dave's budget constraint shows the combinations of slices of pizza and cans of Coke he can buy with $10. The price of Coke is $1 per can, so if he spends all of his $10 on Coke, he can buy 10 cans (bundle *G*). The price of pizza is $2 per slice, so if he spends all of his $10 on pizza, he can buy 5 slices (bundle *L*). As he moves down his budget constraint from bundle *G*, he gives up 2 cans of Coke for every slice of pizza he buys. Any consumption bundles along the line or inside the line are affordable. Any bundles that lie outside the line are unaffordable.

see, all the points lie on a straight line. This line represents Dave's budget constraint. The line intersects the vertical axis at the maximum number of cans of Coke Dave can afford to buy with $10, which is consumption bundle *G*. The line intersects the horizontal axis at the maximum number of slices of pizza Dave can afford to buy with $10, which is consumption bundle *L*. As he moves down his budget constraint from bundle *G*, he gives up 2 cans of Coke for every slice of pizza he buys.

Any consumption bundle along the line or inside the line is *affordable* for Dave because he has the income to buy those combinations of pizza and Coke. Any bundle that lies outside the line is *unaffordable* because those bundles cost more than the income Dave has available to spend.

The slope of the budget constraint is constant because the budget constraint is a straight line. The slope of the line equals the change in the number of cans of Coke divided by the change in the number of slices of pizza. In this case, moving down the budget constraint from one point to another point, the change in the number of cans of Coke equals −2, and the change in the number of slices of pizza equals 1, so the slope equals −2/1, or −2. Notice that with the price of pizza equal to $2 per slice and the price of Coke equal to $1 per can, the slope of the budget constraint is equal to the ratio of the price of pizza to the price of Coke (multiplied by −1). In fact, this result will always hold: *The slope of the budget constraint is equal to the ratio of the price of the good on the horizontal axis divided by the price of the good on the vertical axis multiplied by −1.*

MyEconLab Concept Check

Choosing the Optimal Consumption of Pizza and Coke

Dave would like to be on the highest possible indifference curve because higher indifference curves represent more pizza and more Coke. But Dave can only buy the bundles that lie on or inside his budget constraint. In other words, *to maximize utility, a consumer needs to be on the highest indifference curve, given his budget constraint.*

Figure 10A.4 plots the consumption bundles from Figure 10A.1 along with the budget constraint from Figure 10A.3. The figure also shows the indifference curves that pass through each consumption bundle. In Figure 10A.4, the highest indifference curve shown is I_4. Unfortunately, Dave lacks the income to purchase consumption bundles—such as *C*—that lie on I_4. He has the income to purchase bundles such as *A* and *D*, but

Figure 10A.4

Finding Optimal Consumption

Dave would like to be on the highest possible indifference curve, but he cannot reach indifference curves such as I_4 that are outside his budget constraint. Dave's optimal combination of slices of pizza and cans of Coke is at point *B*, where his budget constraint just touches—or is *tangent* to—the highest indifference curve he can reach. At point *B*, he buys 3 slices of pizza and 4 cans of Coke.

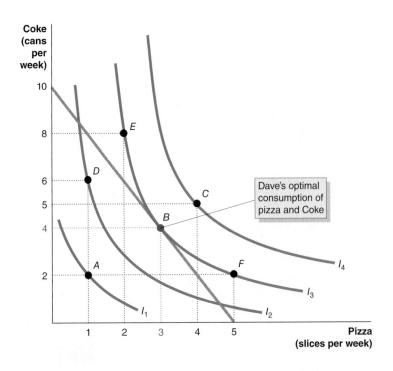

he can do better. If he consumes bundle *B*, he will be on the highest indifference curve he can reach, given his budget constraint of $10. The resulting combination of 3 slices of pizza and 4 cans of Coke represents Dave's optimal consumption of pizza and Coke, given his preferences and his budget constraint. Notice that at point *B*, Dave's budget constraint just touches—or is *tangent* to—I_3. In fact, bundle *B* is the only bundle on I_3 that Dave is able to purchase for $10.

Making	**Dell Determines the Optimal**
the	**Mix of Products**
Connection	

Consumers have different preferences, which helps explain why many firms offer products with a variety of characteristics. For example, Dell sells laptop computers with different screen sizes, processor speeds, hard drive sizes, graphics cards, and so on. We can use the model of consumer choice to analyze a simplified version of the situation Dell faces in deciding which features to offer consumers.

Assume that consumers have $500 each to spend on laptops and that they are concerned with only two laptop characteristics: screen size and processor speed. Because larger screens and faster processors increase Dell's cost of producing laptops, consumers face a trade-off: The larger the screen, the slower the processor speed. Consumers in panel (a) of the figure prefer screen size to processor speed. For this group, the point of tangency between a typical consumer's indifference curve and the budget constraint shows an optimal choice of a 17-inch screen and a 2.0-gigahertz processor. Consumers in panel (b) prefer processor speed to screen size. For this group, the point of tangency between a typical consumer's indifference curve and the budget constraint shows an optimal choice of a 13-inch screen and 3.4-gigahertz processor.

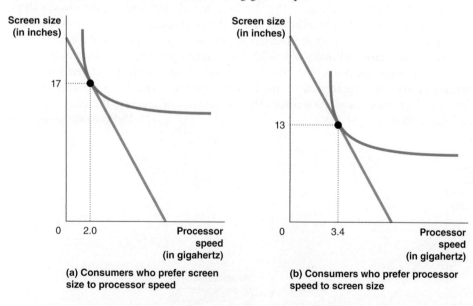

(a) Consumers who prefer screen size to processor speed

(b) Consumers who prefer processor speed to screen size

Companies such as Dell use surveys and other means to gather information about consumer preferences. With knowledge of consumers' preferences and data on the costs of producing different laptop components, Dell can determine the mix of components to offer consumers.

Your Turn: Test your understanding by doing related problem 10A.8 on page 347 at the end of this appendix.

MyEconLab Study Plan

Deriving the Demand Curve

Suppose the price of pizza falls from $2 per slice to $1 per slice. How will this change affect Dave's decision about which combination of pizza and Coke is optimal? First, notice what happens to Dave's budget constraint when the price of pizza falls. As Figure 10A.5 shows, when the price of pizza is $2 per slice, the maximum number of slices Dave can buy is 5. After the price of pizza falls to $1 per slice, Dave can buy a maximum of 10 slices. His budget constraint rotates outward from point *A* to point *B* to represent this. (Notice that the fall in the price of pizza does not affect the maximum number of cans of Coke Dave can buy with his $10.)

When his budget constraint rotates outward, Dave is able to purchase consumption bundles that were previously unaffordable. Panel (a) of Figure 10A.6 shows that the combination of 3 slices of pizza and 4 cans of Coke was optimal when the price of pizza was $2 per slice, but the combination of 7 slices of pizza and 3 cans of Coke is optimal when the price of pizza falls to $1. The lower price of pizza causes Dave to consume more pizza and less Coke and to end up on a higher indifference curve.

The change in Dave's optimal consumption of pizza as the price changes explains why demand curves slope downward. Dave adjusted his consumption of pizza as follows:

Price of pizza = $2 per slice → Quantity of pizza demanded = 3 slices

Price of pizza = $1 per slice → Quantity of pizza demanded = 7 slices

In panel (b) of Figure 10A.6, we plot the two points of optimal consumption and draw a line to connect the points. This downward-sloping line is Dave's demand curve for pizza. We could find more points on the demand curve by changing the price of pizza and finding the new optimal number of slices of pizza Dave would demand.

Remember that according to the law of demand, demand curves always slope downward. We have just shown that the law of demand results from the optimal adjustment by consumers to changes in prices. A fall in the price of a good will rotate *outward* the budget constraint and make it possible for a consumer to reach higher indifference curves. As a result, the consumer will increase the quantity of the good demanded. An increase in price will rotate *inward* the budget constraint and force the consumer to a lower indifference curve. As a result, the consumer will decrease the quantity of the good demanded. MyEconLab Concept Check

MyEconLab Animation

Figure 10A.5

How a Price Decrease Affects the Budget Constraint

A fall in the price of pizza from $2 per slice to $1 per slice increases the maximum number of slices Dave can buy with $10 from 5 to 10. The budget constraint rotates outward from point *A* to point *B* to show the effect of the price decrease.

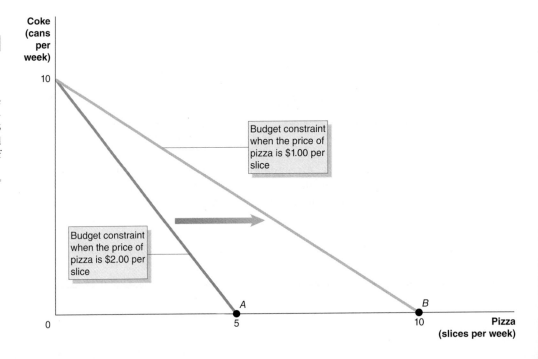

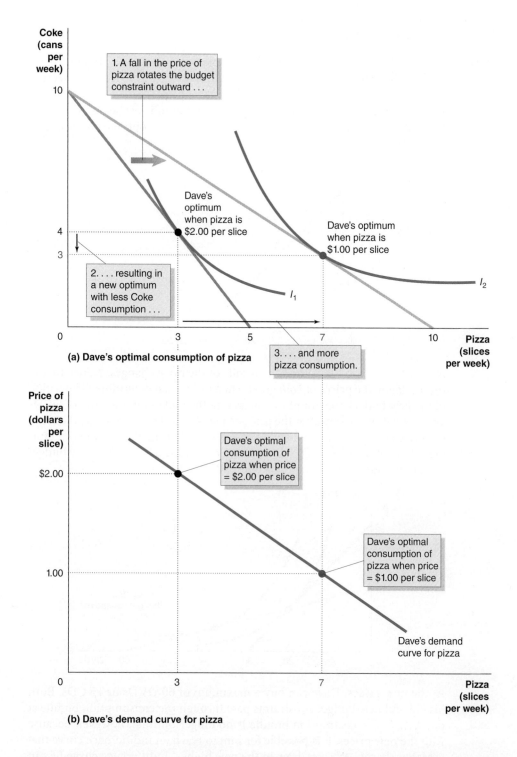

MyEconLab Animation

Figure 10A.6

How a Price Change Affects Optimal Consumption

In panel (a), a fall in the price of pizza results in Dave's consuming less Coke and more pizza.

1. A fall in the price of pizza rotates the budget constraint outward because Dave can now buy more pizza with his $10.
2. In the new optimum on indifference curve I_2, Dave changes the quantities he consumes of both goods. His consumption of Coke falls from 4 cans to 3 cans.
3. In the new optimum, Dave's consumption of pizza increases from 3 slices to 7 slices.

In panel (b), Dave responds optimally to the fall in the price of pizza from $2 per slice to $1 per slice, by increasing the quantity of slices he consumes from 3 slices to 7 slices. When we graph this result, we have Dave's demand curve for pizza.

Solved Problem 10A.1

When Does a Price Change Make a Consumer Better Off?

Dave has $300 to spend each month on DVDs and CDs. DVDs and CDs both currently have a price of $10, and Dave is maximizing his utility by buying 20 DVDs and 10 CDs. Suppose Dave still has $300 to spend, but the price of a CD

rises to $20, while the price of a DVD drops to $5. Is Dave better or worse off than he was before the price change? Use a budget constraint–indifference curve graph to illustrate your answer.

Solving the Problem

Step 1: **Review the chapter material.** This problem concerns the effect of price changes on optimal consumption, so you may want to review the section "Deriving the Demand Curve," which begins on page 340.

Step 2: **Solve the problem by drawing the appropriate graph.** We begin by drawing the budget constraint, indifference curve, and point of optimal consumption for the original prices:

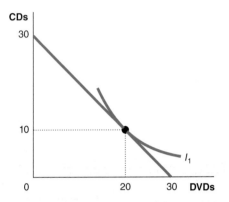

Now draw a graph that shows the results of the price changes. Notice that in this problem, the prices of *both* goods change. You can determine the position of the new budget constraint by calculating the maximum quantity of DVDs and CDs Dave can buy after the price changes. You should also note that after the price changes, Dave can still buy his original optimal consumption bundle—20 DVDs and 10 CDs—by spending all of his $300, so his new budget constraint must pass through this point.

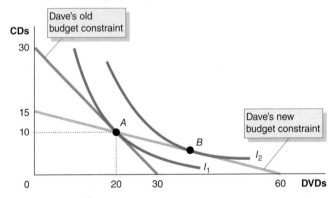

At the new prices, Dave can buy a maximum of 60 DVDs or 15 CDs. Both his old and new budget constraints pass through the consumption bundle at point A. This consumption bundle is no longer optimal, however, because with the new prices, it is possible for him to reach an indifference curve that is higher than I_1. We can draw in the new highest indifference curve he can reach—I_2—and show the new optimal consumption bundle—point B.

Because Dave can now reach a higher indifference curve, we can conclude that he is better off as a result of the price change.

MyEconLab Study Plan   **Your Turn:** For more practice, do related problem 10A.10 on page 347 at the end of this appendix.

The Income Effect and the Substitution Effect of a Price Change

We saw in this chapter that a price change has two effects on the quantity of a good consumed: the *income effect* and the *substitution effect*. The income effect is the change in the quantity demanded of a good that results from the effect of a change in price on consumer purchasing power, holding all other factors constant. The substitution effect is the change in the quantity demanded of a good that results from a change in price making the good more or less expensive relative to other goods, holding constant the effect of the price change on consumer purchasing power. We can use indifference curves and budget constraints to analyze these two effects more exactly.

Figure 10A.7 illustrates the same situation as in Figure 10A.6: The price of pizza has fallen from $2 per slice to $1 per slice, and Dave's budget constraint has rotated outward. As before, Dave's optimal consumption of pizza increases from 3 slices per week (point *A* in Figure 10A.7) to 7 slices per week (point *C*). We can think of this movement from point *A* to point *C* as taking place in two steps: The movement from point *A* to point *B* represents the substitution effect, and the movement from point *B* to point *C* represents the income effect. To isolate the substitution effect, we have to hold constant the effect of the price change on Dave's income. We do this by changing the price of pizza relative to the price of Coke *but at the same time holding his utility constant by keeping Dave on the same indifference curve*. In Figure 10A.7, in moving from point *A* to point *B*, Dave remains on indifference curve I_1. Point *A* is a point of tangency between I_1 and Dave's original budget constraint. Point *B* is a point of tangency between I_1 and a new, *hypothetical* budget constraint that has a slope equal to the new ratio of the price of pizza to the price of Coke. At point *B*, Dave has increased his consumption of pizza from 3 slices to 5 slices. Because we are still on indifference curve I_1, we know that this increase is Dave's response only to the change in the relative price of pizza and, therefore, that the increase represents the substitution effect of the fall in the price of pizza.

At point *B*, Dave has not spent all his income. Remember that the fall in the price of pizza has increased Dave's purchasing power. In Figure 10A.7, we illustrate the additional pizza Dave consumes because of the income effect of increased purchasing power by the movement from point *B* to point *C*. Notice that in moving from point *B* to point *C*, the price of pizza relative to the price of Coke is constant because the slope of

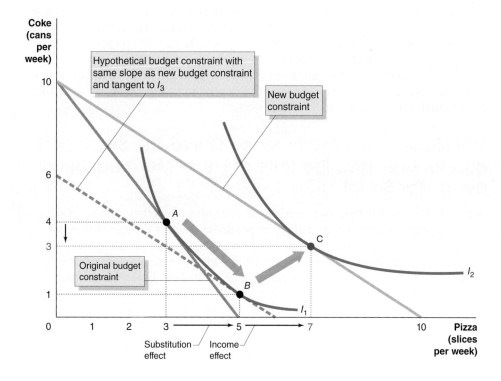

MyEconLab Animation

Figure 10A.7

Income and Substitution Effects of a Price Change

Following a decline in the price of pizza, Dave's optimal consumption of pizza increases from 3 slices per week (point *A*) to 7 slices per week (point *C*). We can think of this movement from point *A* to point *C* as taking place in two steps: The movement from point *A* to point *B* along indifference curve I_1 represents the substitution effect, and the movement from point *B* to point *C* represents the income effect. Dave increases his consumption of pizza from 3 slices per week to 5 slices per week because of the substitution effect of a fall in the price of pizza and from 5 slices per week to 7 slices per week because of the income effect.

MyEconLab Animation

Figure 10A.8

How a Change in Income Affects the Budget Constraint

When the income Dave has to spend on pizza and Coke increases from $10 to $20, his budget constraint shifts outward. With $10, Dave could buy a maximum of 5 slices of pizza or 10 cans of Coke. With $20, he can buy a maximum of 10 slices of pizza or 20 cans of Coke.

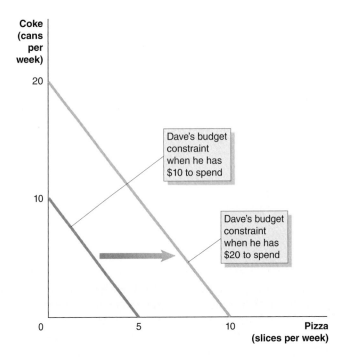

the new budget constraint is the same as the slope of the hypothetical budget constraint that is tangent to I_3 at point *B*.

We can conclude that Dave increases his consumption of pizza from 3 slices per week to 5 slices per week because of the substitution effect of a fall in the price of pizza and from 5 slices per week to 7 slices per week because of the income effect. Recall from our discussion of income and substitution effects in this chapter that the income effect of a price decline causes consumers to buy more of a normal good and less of an inferior good. Because the income effect causes Dave to increase his consumption of pizza, pizza must be a normal good for him. MyEconLab Concept Check

How a Change in Income Affects Optimal Consumption

Suppose that the price of pizza remains at $2 per slice, but the income Dave has to spend on pizza and Coke increases from $10 to $20. Figure 10A.8 shows how this change affects his budget constraint. With an income of $10, Dave could buy a maximum of 5 slices of pizza or 10 cans of Coke. With an income of $20, he can buy 10 slices of pizza or 20 cans of Coke. The additional income allows Dave to increase his consumption of both pizza and Coke and to move to a higher indifference curve. Figure 10A.9 shows Dave's new optimum. Dave is able to increase his consumption of pizza from 3 to 7 slices per week and his consumption of Coke from 4 to 6 cans per week. MyEconLab Concept Check

The Slope of the Indifference Curve, the Slope of the Budget Line, and the Rule of Equal Marginal Utility per Dollar Spent

In this chapter, we saw that consumers maximize utility when they consume each good up to the point where the marginal utility per dollar spent is the same for every good. This condition seems different from the one we stated earlier in this appendix that to maximize utility, a consumer needs to be on the highest indifference curve, given his budget constraint. In fact, the two conditions are equivalent. To see this, begin by looking at Figure 10A.10, which again combines Dave's indifference curve and budget constraint. Remember that at the point of optimal consumption, the indifference curve and the budget constraint are tangent, so they have the same slope. Therefore, *at the point of optimal consumption, the marginal rate of substitution (MRS) is equal to the ratio of the price of the product on the horizontal axis to the price of the product on the vertical axis.*

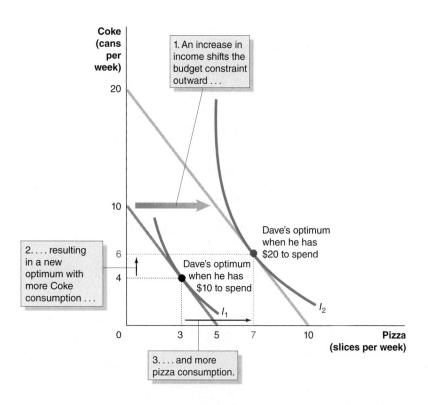

Figure 10A.9

How a Change in Income Affects Optimal Consumption

An increase in income leads Dave to consume more Coke and more pizza.

1. An increase in income shifts Dave's budget constraint outward because he can now buy more of both goods.
2. In the new optimum on indifference curve I_2, Dave changes the quantities he consumes of both goods. His consumption of Coke increases from 4 to 6 cans.
3. In the new optimum, Dave's consumption of pizza increases from 3 to 7 slices.

The slope of the indifference curve tells us the rate at which a consumer is *willing* to trade off one good for the other. The slope of the budget constraint tells us the rate at which a consumer is *able* to trade off one good for the other. Only at the point of optimal consumption is the rate at which a consumer is willing to trade off one good for the other equal to the rate at which the consumer can trade off one good for the other.

The Rule of Equal Marginal Utility per Dollar Spent Revisited

Recall from this chapter the *rule of equal marginal utility per dollar*, which states that to maximize utility, consumers should spend their income so that the last dollar spent on each product gives them the same marginal utility. We can use our indifference curve

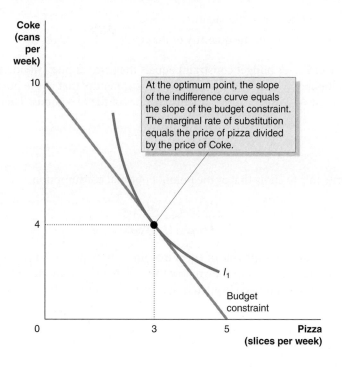

Figure 10A.10

At the Optimum Point, the Slopes of the Indifference Curve and Budget Constraint Are the Same

At the point of optimal consumption, the marginal rate of substitution is equal to the ratio of the price of the product on the horizontal axis to the price of the product on the vertical axis.

and budget constraint analysis to see why this rule holds. When we move from one point on an indifference curve to another, we end up with more of one product and less of the other product but the same amount of utility. For example, as Dave moves down an indifference curve, he consumes less Coke and more pizza, but he has the same amount of utility.

Remember that marginal utility (*MU*) tells us how much additional utility a consumer gains (or loses) from consuming more (or less) of a good. So when Dave consumes less Coke by moving down an indifference curve, he loses utility equal to:

$$-\text{Change in the quantity of Coke} \times MU_{Coke}$$

but he consumes more pizza, so he gains utility equal to:

$$\text{Change in the quantity of Pizza} \times MU_{Pizza}.$$

We know that the gain in utility from the additional pizza is equal to the loss from the smaller quantity of Coke because Dave's total utility remains the same along an indifference curve. Therefore, we can write:

$$-(\text{Change in the quantity of Coke} \times MU_{Coke}) = (\text{Change in the quantity of pizza} \times MU_{Pizza}).$$

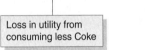

Loss in utility from consuming less Coke

Gain in utility from consuming more pizza

If we rearrange terms, we have:

$$\frac{-\text{Change in the quantity of Coke}}{\text{Change in the quantity of Pizza}} = \frac{MU_{Pizza}}{MU_{Coke}}.$$

Because the expression:

$$\frac{-\text{Change in the quantity of Coke}}{\text{Change in the quantity of Pizza}}$$

is the slope of the indifference curve, it is equal to the *MRS* (multiplied by –1). So, we can write:

$$\frac{-\text{Change in the quantity of Coke}}{\text{Change in the quantity of Pizza}} = MRS = \frac{MU_{Pizza}}{MU_{Coke}}.$$

The slope of Dave's budget constraint equals the price of pizza divided by the price of Coke (multiplied by –1). We saw earlier in this appendix that at the point of optimal consumption, the *MRS* equals the ratio of the prices of the two goods. Therefore:

$$\frac{MU_{Pizza}}{MU_{Coke}} = \frac{P_{Pizza}}{P_{Coke}}.$$

We can rewrite this to show that at the point of optimal consumption:

$$\frac{MU_{Pizza}}{P_{Pizza}} = \frac{MU_{Coke}}{P_{Coke}}.$$

This last expression is the rule of equal marginal utility per dollar that we first developed in this chapter. So we have shown how this rule follows from the indifference curve and budget constraint approach to analyzing consumer choice.   MyEconLab Concept Check

Key Terms

Indifference curve, p. 335

Marginal rate of substitution (*MRS*), p. 336

10.A **Using Indifference Curves and Budget Lines to Understand Consumer Behavior, pages 335–346**

LEARNING OBJECTIVE: Use indifference curves and budget lines to understand consumer behavior.

MyEconLab   Visit **www.myeconlab.com** to complete these exercises online and get instant feedback.

Review Questions

10A.1 What are the two assumptions economists make about consumer preferences?

10A.2 What is an indifference curve? What is a budget constraint?

10A.3 How do consumers choose the optimal consumption bundle?

Problems and Applications

10A.4 Jacob receives an allowance of $5 per week. He spends all his allowance on ice cream cones and cans of Lemon Fizz soda.

a. If the price of ice cream cones is $0.50 per cone and the price of cans of Lemon Fizz is $1 per can, draw a graph showing Jacob's budget constraint. Be sure to indicate on the graph the maximum number of ice cream cones and the maximum number of cans of Lemon Fizz that Jacob can buy.

b. Jacob buys 8 ice cream cones and 1 can of Lemon Fizz. Draw an indifference curve representing Jacob's choice, assuming that he has chosen the optimal combination.

c. Suppose that the price of ice cream cones rises to $1 per cone. Draw Jacob's new budget constraint and his new optimal consumption of ice cream cones and cans of Lemon Fizz.

10A.5 Suppose that Jacob's allowance in problem 10A.4 climbs from $5 to $10 per week.

a. Show how the increased allowance alters Jacob's budget constraint.

b. Draw a set of indifference curves showing how Jacob's choice of ice cream cones and cans of Lemon Fizz changes when his allowance increases. Assume that both goods are normal.

c. Draw a set of indifference curves showing how Jacob's choice of ice cream cones and cans of Lemon Fizz changes when his allowance increases. Assume that Lemon Fizz is a normal good but ice cream is an inferior good.

10A.6 Suppose that Calvin considers Pepsi and Coke to be perfect substitutes. They taste the same to him, and he gets exactly the same amount of enjoyment from drinking a can of Pepsi or a can of Coke.

a. Will Calvin's indifference curves showing his trade-off between Pepsi and Coke have the same curvature as the indifference curves drawn in the figures in this appendix? Briefly explain.

b. How will Calvin decide whether to buy Pepsi or Coke?

10A.7 In the following budget constraint–indifference curve graph, Nikki has $200 to spend on blouses and skirts.

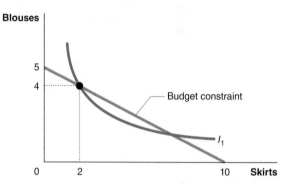

a. What is the price of blouses? What is the price of skirts?

b. Is Nikki making the optimum choice if she buys 4 blouses and 2 skirts? Explain how you know this.

10A.8 **[Related to the** Making the Connection **on page 339]** Marilou and Hunter both purchase milk and doughnuts at the same Quik Mart. They have different tastes for milk and doughnuts and different incomes. They both buy some milk and some doughnuts, but they buy considerably different quantities of the two goods. Can we conclude that their marginal rate of substitution between milk and doughnuts is the same? Draw a graph showing their budget constraints and indifference curves and explain.

10A.9 Sunsweet decides that prune juice has a bad image, so it launches a slick advertising campaign to convince young people that prune juice is very hip. The company hires Eminem, Jay-Z, and Trick Daddy to endorse its product. The campaign works! Prune juice sales soar, even though Sunsweet hasn't cut the price. Draw a budget constraint and indifference curve diagram with Sunsweet prune juice on one axis and other drinks on the other axis and show how the celebrity endorsements have changed things.

10A.10 **[Related to** Solved Problem 10A.1 **on page 341]** Dave has $300 to spend each month on DVDs and CDs. DVDs and CDs both currently have a price of $10, and Dave is maximizing his utility by buying 20 DVDs and 10 CDs.

Suppose Dave still has $300 to spend, but the price of a DVD rises to $12, while the price of a CD drops to $6. Is Dave better or worse off than he was before the price change? Use a budget constraint–indifference curve graph to illustrate your answer.

10A.11 The following graph illustrates the combination of apples and oranges (point *A*) that maximizes Yolanda's total utility, given her budget. Suppose the price of oranges doubles, while the price of apples and Yolanda's income both stay the same.

a. Draw a new budget constraint to reflect the increase in the price of oranges.
b. Based on the assumptions regarding consumer preferences listed at the beginning of this appendix, sketch in a new indifference curve to reflect the new optimal combination of apples and oranges now that the price of oranges has doubled.
c. Are there any circumstances in which the new optimal combination of apples and oranges will include a larger quantity of oranges (compared to the original combination)? Briefly explain.

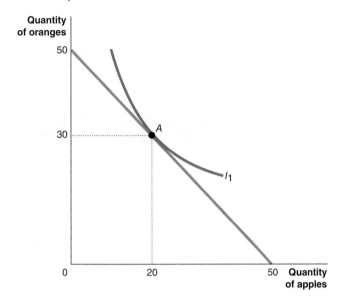

CHAPTER
11

Technology, Production, and Costs

Chapter Outline and Learning Objectives

Fracking, Marginal Costs, and Energy Prices

Technological change helps firms create new products and lower the costs of making existing products. As a firm's costs change, how does the firm adjust the price it charges consumers? In recent years, important technological changes have affected the oil industry. For example, oil companies had avoided drilling for oil in shale rock formations such as the Bakken field in North Dakota and Montana because of the high cost. Recent changes in techniques and equipment have lowered the cost of drilling, making producing oil from shale rock formations profitable.

In 2012, the United States experienced the largest increase in oil production in its history. Similar increases occurred in 2013 and were expected for many years to follow. Production of natural gas has also been rapidly increasing. The U.S. Energy Information Administration predicts that by 2025, the United States will be a net exporter of oil for the first time since the 1960s. The increases in oil and gas production are due in large part to a new technology, hydraulic fracturing ("fracking"). Fracking involves injecting a mixture of water, sand, and chemicals into rock formations at high pressure to release oil and natural gas. Fracking remains controversial with some environmentalists who argue that it has the potential to pollute ground water supplies if carried out improperly. But will new production from U.S. shale oil fields reduce the price of oil in the world oil market?

As we will see, the price of a good sold in a competitive market is determined by the marginal cost of producing the good. Recall that marginal cost is the additional cost of producing one more unit of a good or service (see Chapter 4). In the world oil market, oil is supplied up to the point where the marginal cost of the last barrel just equals the price buyers are willing to pay for that last barrel. Oil produced in North Dakota, Montana, Saudi Arabia, and other relatively low-cost areas is not sufficient to meet all of world demand. In this sense, the last barrel of oil sold is produced in the North Sea, the Arctic, and other areas where production costs are much higher. As Pierre Sigonney, an oil economist for the French oil company Total SA put it: "Costs are still at a very high level because of the complexity of marginal fields...."

In this chapter, we will analyze the basic cost concepts involved in production and see how they affect the operations of firms.

Sources: James Herron, "Oil Price Likely to Stay Buoyed by Marginal Costs," *Wall Street Journal*, May 22, 2012; Richard Mably, "Shale Oil Can't Stop Crude Topping $150 by 2020-Bernstein," *Reuters*, September 11, 2012; and James Herron, "Energy Journal: Big Oil, Big Data," *Wall Street Journal*, June 13, 2013.

Economics in Your Life

Using Cost Concepts in Your Own Business

Suppose that you have the opportunity to open a store that sells recliners. You learn that you can purchase recliners from the manufacturer for $300 each. Bob's Big Chairs is an existing store that is the same size your new store will be. Bob's sells the same recliners you plan to sell and also buys them from the manufacturer for $300 each. Your plan is to sell the recliners for a price of $500. After studying how Bob's is operated, you find that Bob's is selling more recliners per month than you expect to be able to sell and that it is selling them for $450. You wonder how Bob's makes a profit at the lower price. Are there any reasons to expect that because Bob's sells more recliners per month, its costs will be lower than your store's costs? As you read this chapter, see if you can answer this question. You can check your answer against the one we provide on **page 370** at the end of this chapter.

W e have looked behind the demand curve to better understand consumer decision making (see Chapter 10). In this chapter, we look behind the supply curve to better understand firm decision making. Earlier chapters showed that supply curves are upward sloping because marginal cost increases as firms increase the quantity of a good that they supply. In this chapter, we look more closely at why this is true. In the appendix to this chapter, we extend the analysis by using isoquants and isocost lines to understand the relationship between production and costs. Once we have a good understanding of production and cost, we can proceed in the following chapters to understand how firms decide what level of output to produce and what price to charge.

11.1 LEARNING OBJECTIVE

Define technology and give examples of technological change.

Technology The processes a firm uses to turn inputs into outputs of goods and services.

Technological change A change in the ability of a firm to produce a given level of output with a given quantity of inputs.

Technology: An Economic Definition

The basic activity of a firm is to use *inputs*, such as workers, machines, and natural resources, to produce *outputs* of goods and services. A pizza parlor, for example, uses inputs such as pizza dough, pizza sauce, cooks, and ovens to produce pizza. A firm's **technology** is the processes it uses to turn inputs into outputs of goods and services. Notice that this economic definition of technology is broader than the everyday definition. When we use the word *technology* in everyday language, we usually refer only to the development of new products. In the economic sense, a firm's technology depends on many factors, such as the skills of its managers, the training of its workers, and the speed and efficiency of its machinery and equipment. The technology of pizza production, for example, includes not only the capacity of the pizza ovens and how quickly they bake the pizza but also how quickly the cooks can prepare the pizza for baking, how well the firm's manager motivates the workers, and how well the manager has arranged the facilities to allow the cooks to quickly prepare the pizzas and get them in the ovens.

Whenever a firm experiences positive **technological change**, it is able to produce more output using the same inputs or the same output using fewer inputs. Positive technological change can come from many sources. A firm's managers may rearrange the factory floor or the layout of a retail store in order to increase production and sales. The firm's workers may go through a training program. The firm may install faster or more reliable machinery or equipment. It is also possible for a firm to experience negative technological change. If a firm, for example, hires less-skilled workers or if a hurricane damages its facilities, the quantity of output it can produce from a given quantity of inputs may decline. MyEconLab Concept Check

Making the Connection
MyEconLab Video

Improving Inventory Control at Wal-Mart

Inventories are goods that have been produced but not yet sold. For a retailer such as Wal-Mart, inventories at any point in time include the goods on the store shelves as well as goods in warehouses. Inventories are an input into Wal-Mart's output of goods sold to consumers. Having money tied up in holding inventories is costly, so firms have an incentive to hold as few inventories as possible and to *turn over* their inventories as rapidly as possible by ensuring that goods do not remain on the shelves long. Holding too few inventories, however, results in *stockouts*—that is, sales being lost because the goods consumers want to buy are not on the shelves.

Improvements in inventory control meet the economic definition of positive technological change because they allow firms to produce the same output with fewer inputs. In recent years, many firms have adopted *just-in-time* inventory systems in which firms accept shipments from suppliers as close as possible to the time the goods will be needed. The just-in-time system was pioneered by Toyota, which used it to reduce the inventories of parts in its automobile assembly plants. Wal-Mart has been a pioneer in using similar inventory control systems in its stores.

Wal-Mart actively manages its *supply chain*, which stretches from the manufacturers of the goods it sells to its retail stores. Entrepreneur Sam Walton, the company founder, built a series of distribution centers spread across the country to supply goods to the retail stores. As goods are sold in the stores, the *point-of-sale* information is sent electronically to the firm's distribution centers to help managers determine what products will be shipped to each store. Depending on a store's location relative to a distribution center, managers can use Wal-Mart's trucks to ship goods overnight. This distribution system allows Wal-Mart to minimize its inventory holdings without running the risk of many stockouts occurring. Because Wal-Mart sells 15 percent to 25 percent of all the toothpaste, disposable diapers, dog food, and many other products sold in the United States, it has been able to involve many manufacturers closely in its supply chain. For example, a company such as Procter & Gamble, which is one of the world's largest manufacturers of toothpaste, laundry detergent, toilet paper, and other products, receives Wal-Mart's point-of-sale and inventory information electronically. Procter & Gamble uses that information to help determine its production schedules and the quantities it should ship to Wal-Mart's distribution centers.

Better inventory controls have helped Wal-Mart and other firms to reduce their costs.

Technological change has been a key to Wal-Mart's becoming one of the largest firms in the world, with 2.2 million employees and revenue of nearly $470 billion in 2013, but to maintain its position Wal-Mart needs to improve its performance in online retailing. Amazon has taken a substantial lead over Wal-Mart in online retailing in part because of Amazon's network of warehouses, some of which use robots to retrieve goods from shelves and box them for shipment. Wal-Mart is attempting to catch up by shipping some goods to online buyers from its retail stores rather than from dedicated warehouses. Because two-thirds of the U.S. population lives within five miles of a Wal-Mart store, the company believes that it can reduce shipping costs by filling online orders from store inventories.

It remains to be seen whether Wal-Mart can reproduce its great success in brick-and-mortar retailing as it tries to catch up with Amazon in online retailing.

Source: Shelly Banjo, "Wal-Mart's E-Stumble with Amazon," *Wall Street Journal*, June 19, 2013.

Your Turn: Test your understanding by doing related problem 1.5 on page 372 at the end of this chapter.

MyEconLab Study Plan

The Short Run and the Long Run in Economics

When firms analyze the relationship between their level of production and their costs, they separate the time period involved into the short run and the long run. In the **short run**, at least one of the firm's inputs is fixed. In particular, in the short run, the firm's technology and the size of its physical plant—its factory, store, or office—are both fixed, while the number of workers the firm hires is variable. In the **long run**, the firm is able to vary all its inputs and can adopt new technology and increase or decrease the size of its physical plant. Of course, the actual length of calendar time in the short run will be different from firm to firm. A pizza parlor may be able to increase its physical plant by adding another pizza oven and some tables and chairs in just a few weeks. General Motors, in contrast, may take more than a year to increase the capacity of one of its automobile assembly plants by installing new equipment.

The Difference between Fixed Costs and Variable Costs

Total cost is the cost of all the inputs a firm uses in production. We have just seen that in the short run, some inputs are fixed and others are variable. The costs of the fixed inputs are called *fixed costs*, and the costs of the variable inputs are called *variable costs*. We can also think of **variable costs** as the costs that change as output changes. Similarly, **fixed costs** are costs that remain constant as output changes. A typical firm's variable costs include its labor costs, raw material costs, and costs of electricity and other utilities. Typical fixed costs include lease payments for factory or retail space, payments for

11.2 LEARNING OBJECTIVE

Distinguish between the economic short run and the economic long run.

Short run The period of time during which at least one of a firm's inputs is fixed.

Long run The period of time in which a firm can vary all its inputs, adopt new technology, and increase or decrease the size of its physical plant.

Total cost The cost of all the inputs a firm uses in production.

Variable costs Costs that change as output changes.

Fixed costs Costs that remain constant as output changes.

fire insurance, and payments for online and television advertising. All of a firm's costs are either fixed or variable, so we can state the following: MyEconLab Concept Check

$$Total\ cost = Fixed\ cost + Variable\ cost$$

or, using symbols:

$$TC = FC + VC.$$

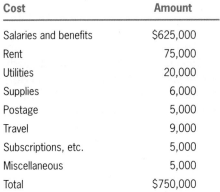

The wages of this worker are a variable cost to the publisher who employs him.

Making the Connection
MyEconLab Video

Fixed Costs in the Publishing Industry

An editor at Cambridge University Press gives the following estimates of the annual fixed cost for a medium-size academic book publisher:

Cost	Amount
Salaries and benefits	$625,000
Rent	75,000
Utilities	20,000
Supplies	6,000
Postage	5,000
Travel	9,000
Subscriptions, etc.	5,000
Miscellaneous	5,000
Total	$750,000

Academic book publishers hire editors, designers, and production and marketing managers who help prepare books for publication. Because these employees work on several books simultaneously, the number of people the company hires does not go up and down with the quantity of books the company publishes during any particular year. Publishing companies therefore consider the salaries and benefits of people in these job categories to be fixed costs.

In contrast, for a company that *prints* books, the quantity of workers varies with the quantity of books printed. The wages and benefits of the workers operating the printing presses, for example, would be a variable cost.

The other costs listed in the table are typical of fixed costs at many firms.

Source: *Handbook for Academic Authors*, 5th edition by Beth Lucy. Copyright © 2010 by Cambridge University Press. Reprinted by permission.

MyEconLab Study Plan

Your Turn: Test your understanding by doing related problems 2.6, 2.7, and 2.8 on page 373 at the end of this chapter.

Implicit Costs Versus Explicit Costs

Opportunity cost The highest-valued alternative that must be given up to engage in an activity.

Explicit cost A cost that involves spending money.

Implicit cost A nonmonetary opportunity cost.

Remember that economists always measure cost as **opportunity cost**, which is the highest-valued alternative that must be given up to engage in an activity. Costs are either *explicit* or *implicit* (see Chapter 8). When a firm spends money, it incurs an **explicit cost**. When a firm experiences a nonmonetary opportunity cost, it incurs an **implicit cost**.

For example, suppose that Jill Johnson owns a pizza restaurant. In operating her restaurant, Jill has explicit costs, such as the wages she pays her workers and the payments she makes for rent and electricity. But some of Jill's most important costs are implicit. Before opening her own restaurant, Jill earned a salary of $30,000 per year managing a restaurant for someone else. To start her restaurant, Jill quit her job, withdrew $50,000 from her bank account—where it earned her interest of $3,000 per year—and used the funds to equip her restaurant with tables, chairs, a cash register, and other equipment. To open

Pizza dough, tomato sauce, and other ingredients	$20,000	
Wages	48,000	
Interest payments on loan to buy pizza ovens	10,000	
Electricity	6,000	
Lease payment for store	24,000	
Forgone salary	30,000	
Forgone interest	3,000	
Economic depreciation	10,000	
Total	$151,000	

Table 11.1

Jill Johnson's Costs per Year

her own business, Jill had to give up the $30,000 salary and the $3,000 in interest. This $33,000 is an implicit cost because it does not represent payments that Jill has to make. Nevertheless, giving up this $33,000 per year is a real cost to Jill. In addition, during the course of the year, the $50,000 worth of tables, chairs, and other physical capital in Jill's store will lose some of its value due partly to wear and tear and partly to better furniture, cash registers, and so forth, becoming available. *Economic depreciation* is the difference between what Jill paid for her capital at the beginning of the year and what she would receive if she sold the capital at the end of the year. If Jill could sell the capital for $40,000 at the end of the year, the $10,000 in economic depreciation represents another implicit cost. (Note that the whole $50,000 she spent on the capital is not a cost because she still has the equipment at the end of the year, although it is now worth only $40,000.)

Table 11.1 lists Jill's costs. The entries in red are explicit costs, and the entries in blue are implicit costs. The rules of accounting generally require that only explicit costs be used for purposes of keeping the company's financial records and for paying taxes (see Chapter 8). Therefore, explicit costs are sometimes called *accounting costs*. *Economic costs* include both accounting costs and implicit costs. MyEconLab Concept Check

The Production Function

Let's look at the relationship in the short run between Jill Johnson's level of production and her costs. We can simplify the situation in Table 11.1 by assuming that Jill uses only labor—workers—and one type of capital—pizza ovens—to produce a single good: pizzas. Many firms use more than two inputs and produce more than one good, but it is easier to understand the relationship between output and cost by focusing on the case of a firm using only two inputs and producing only one good. In the short run, Jill doesn't have time to build a larger restaurant, install additional pizza ovens, or redesign the layout of her restaurant. So, in the short run, she can increase or decrease the quantity of pizzas she produces only by increasing or decreasing the number of workers she employs.

The first three columns of Table 11.2 show the relationship between the quantity of workers and ovens Jill uses per week and the quantity of pizzas she can produce. The

Table 11.2 **Short-Run Production and Cost at Jill Johnson's Restaurant**

Quantity of Workers	Quantity of Pizza Ovens	Quantity of Pizzas per Week	Cost of Pizza Ovens (Fixed Cost)	Cost of Workers (Variable Cost)	Total Cost of Pizzas per Week	Cost per Pizza (Average Total Cost)
0	2	0	$800	$0	$800	—
1	2	200	800	650	1,450	$7.25
2	2	450	800	1,300	2,100	4.67
3	2	550	800	1,950	2,750	5.00
4	2	600	800	2,600	3,400	5.67
5	2	625	800	3,250	4,050	6.48
6	2	640	800	3,900	4,700	7.34

Production function The relationship between the inputs employed by a firm and the maximum output it can produce with those inputs.

relationship between the inputs employed by a firm and the maximum output it can produce with those inputs is called the firm's **production function**. Because a firm's technology is the processes it uses to turn inputs into output, the production function represents the firm's technology. The first three columns of Table 11.2 show Jill's *short-run* production function because we are assuming that the time period is too short for Jill to increase or decrease the quantity of ovens she is using. MyEconLab Concept Check

A First Look at the Relationship between Production and Cost

Table 11.2 shows Jill Johnson's costs. We can determine the total cost of producing a given quantity of pizzas if we know how many workers and ovens are required to produce that quantity of pizzas and how much Jill has to pay for those workers and ovens. Suppose Jill has taken out a bank loan to buy two pizza ovens. The cost of the loan is $800 per week. Therefore, her fixed costs are $800 per week. If Jill pays $650 per week to each worker, her variable costs depend on how many workers she hires. In the short run, Jill can increase the quantity of pizzas she produces only by hiring more workers. Table 11.2 shows that if she hires 1 worker, she produces 200 pizzas during the week; if she hires 2 workers, she produces 450 pizzas; and so on. For a particular week, Jill's total cost of producing pizzas is equal to the $800 she pays on the loan for the ovens plus the amount she pays to hire workers. If Jill decides to hire 4 workers and produce 600 pizzas, her total cost is $3,400: $800 to lease the ovens and $2,600 to hire the workers. Her cost per pizza is equal to her total cost of producing pizzas divided by the quantity of pizzas produced. If she produces 600 pizzas at a total cost of $3,400, her cost per pizza, or *average total cost*, is $3,400/600 = $5.67. A firm's **average total cost** is always equal to its total cost divided by the quantity of output produced.

Average total cost Total cost divided by the quantity of output produced.

Panel (a) of Figure 11.1 uses the numbers in the next-to-last column of Table 11.2 to graph Jill's total cost. Panel (b) uses the numbers in the last column to graph her average

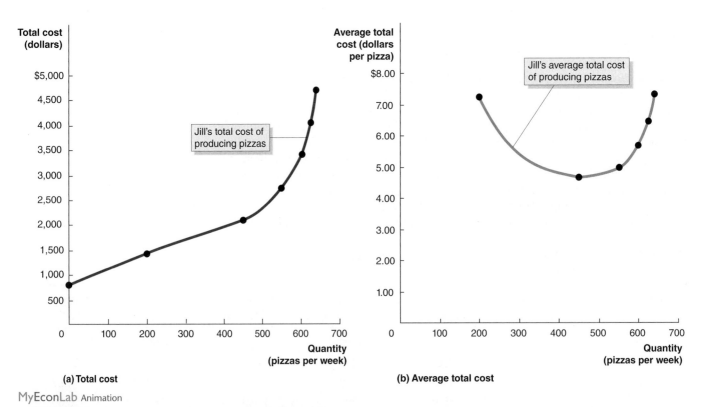

(a) Total cost

(b) Average total cost

MyEconLab Animation

Figure 11.1 **Graphing Total Cost and Average Total Cost at Jill Johnson's Restaurant**

We can use the information from Table 11.2 to graph the relationship between the quantity of pizzas Jill produces and her total cost and average total cost. Panel (a) shows that total cost increases as the level of production increases.

Panel (b) shows that her average total cost is roughly U shaped: As production increases from low levels, average total cost falls, before rising at higher levels of production.

total cost. Notice in panel (b) that Jill's average cost curve has a roughly U shape. As production increases from low levels, average total cost falls. Average total cost then becomes fairly flat, before rising at higher levels of production. To understand why average total cost curve has this U shape, we first need to look more closely at the technology of producing pizzas, as shown by the production function for Jill's restaurant. Then we need to look at how this technology determines the relationship between production and cost.   MyEconLab Concept Check

MyEconLab Study Plan

The Marginal Product of Labor and the Average Product of Labor

11.3 LEARNING OBJECTIVE

Understand the relationship between the marginal product of labor and the average product of labor.

To better understand the choices Jill faces, given the technology available to her, think first about what happens if she hires only one worker. That one worker will have to perform several different activities, including taking orders from customers, baking the pizzas, bringing the pizzas to the customers' tables, and ringing up sales on the cash register. If Jill hires two workers, some of these activities can be divided up: One worker could take the orders and ring up the sales, and one worker could bake the pizzas. With such a division of tasks, Jill will find that hiring two workers actually allows her to produce more than twice as many pizzas as she could produce with just one worker.

The additional output a firm produces as a result of hiring one more worker is called the **marginal product of labor**. We can calculate the marginal product of labor by determining how much total output increases as each additional worker is hired, which we do for Jill's restaurant in Table 11.3.

When Jill hires only 1 worker, she increases output from 0 pizzas to 200 pizzas per week. So, the marginal product of labor for the first worker is 200 pizzas. When she hires 2 workers, she produces 450 pizzas per week. Hiring the second worker increases her output by 250 pizzas per week. For the second worker, the marginal product of labor rises to 250 pizzas. This increase in marginal product results from the *division of labor* and from *specialization*. By dividing the tasks to be performed—the division of labor—Jill reduces the time workers lose moving from one activity to the next. She also allows them to become more specialized at their tasks. For example, a worker who concentrates on baking pizzas will become skilled at doing so quickly and efficiently.

Marginal product of labor The additional output a firm produces as a result of hiring one more worker.

The Law of Diminishing Returns

In the short run, the quantity of pizza ovens Jill leases is fixed, so as she hires more workers, the marginal product of labor eventually begins to decline. At some point, Jill uses up all the gains from the division of labor and from specialization and starts to experience the effects of the **law of diminishing returns**. This law states that adding more of a variable input, such as labor, to the same amount of a fixed input, such as capital, will eventually cause the marginal product of the variable input to decline. For Jill, the marginal product of labor begins to decline when she hires the third worker. Hiring three workers raises the quantity of pizzas she produces from 450 per week to 550. But the increase in the quantity of pizzas—100—is less than the increase when she hired the second worker—250—so the marginal product of labor has declined.

Law of diminishing returns The principle that, at some point, adding more of a variable input, such as labor, to the same amount of a fixed input, such as capital, will cause the marginal product of the variable input to decline.

Table 11.3

The Marginal Product of Labor at Jill Johnson's Restaurant

Quantity of Workers	Quantity of Pizza Ovens	Quantity of Pizzas	Marginal Product of Labor
0	2	0	—
1	2	200	200
2	2	450	250
3	2	550	100
4	2	600	50
5	2	625	25
6	2	640	15

If Jill kept adding more and more workers to the same quantity of pizza ovens, workers would eventually begin to get in each other's way, and the marginal product of labor would actually become negative. When the marginal product is negative, the level of total output declines. No firm would actually hire so many workers as to experience a negative marginal product of labor and falling total output.   MyEconLab Concept Check

Graphing Production

Panel (a) in Figure 11.2 shows the relationship between the quantity of workers Jill hires and her total output of pizzas, using the numbers from Table 11.3. Panel (b) shows the marginal product of labor. In panel (a), output increases as more workers are hired, but the increase in output does not occur at a constant rate. Because of specialization and the division of labor, output at first increases at an increasing rate, with each additional worker hired causing production to increase by a *larger* amount than did the hiring of the previous worker. But after the second worker has been hired, hiring more workers while

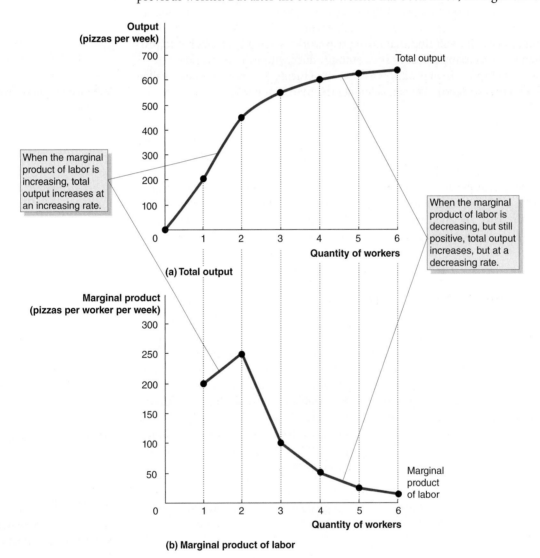

(a) Total output

When the marginal product of labor is increasing, total output increases at an increasing rate.

When the marginal product of labor is decreasing, but still positive, total output increases, but at a decreasing rate.

(b) Marginal product of labor

MyEconLab Animation

Figure 11.2   Total Output and the Marginal Product of Labor

In panel (a), output increases as more workers are hired, but the increase in output does not occur at a constant rate. Because of specialization and the division of labor, output at first increases at an increasing rate, with each additional worker hired causing production to increase by a *greater* amount than did the hiring of the previous worker. When the point of diminishing returns is reached, production increases at a decreasing rate. Each additional worker

Jill hires after the second worker causes production to increase by a *smaller* amount than did the hiring of the previous worker. In panel (b), the *marginal product of labor* is the additional output produced as a result of hiring one more worker. The marginal product of labor rises initially because of the effects of specialization and division of labor, and then falls because of the effects of diminishing returns.

keeping the quantity of ovens constant results in diminishing returns. When the point of diminishing returns is reached, production increases at a decreasing rate. Each additional worker Jill hires after the second worker causes production to increase by a *smaller* amount than did the hiring of the previous worker. In panel (b), the marginal product of labor curve rises initially because of the effects of specialization and the division of labor, and then falls because of the effects of diminishing returns.   MyEconLab Concept Check

The gains from division of labor and specialization are as important to firms today as they were in the eighteenth century, when Adam Smith first discussed them.

Making the Connection
MyEconLab Video

Adam Smith's Famous Account of the Division of Labor in a Pin Factory

The Wealth of Nations, written in Scotland by Adam Smith in 1776, is the first book to have discussed some of the key ideas of economics. Smith considered the concept of the division of labor important enough to discuss in the first chapter of the book. He illustrated the concept using an example of a pin factory. The following is an excerpt from his account of how pin making was divided into a series of tasks:

> One man draws out the wire, another straightens it, a third cuts it, a fourth points it, a fifth grinds it at the top for receiving the head; to make the head requires two or three distinct operations; to put it on is a ... [distinct operation], to whiten the pins is another; it is even a trade by itself to put them into the paper; and the important business of making a pin is, in this manner, divided into eighteen distinct operations.

Because the labor of pin making was divided up in this way, an average worker was able to produce about 4,800 pins per day. Smith estimated that a single worker using the pin-making machinery by himself would make only about 20 pins per day. This lesson from more than 235 years ago, showing the tremendous gains from the division of labor and specialization, remains relevant to most business situations today.

Source: Adam Smith, *An Inquiry into the Nature and Causes of the Wealth of Nations*, Vol. I, Oxford, UK: Oxford University Press, 1976. original edition, 1776, pp. 14–15.

Your Turn: Test your understanding by doing related problem 3.7 on page 374 at the end of this chapter.

MyEconLab Study Plan

The Relationship between Marginal Product and Average Product

The marginal product of labor tells us how much total output changes as the quantity of workers hired changes. We can also calculate the average quantity of pizzas workers produce. The **average product of labor** is the total output produced by a firm divided by the quantity of workers. For example, using the numbers in Table 11.3 on page 357, if Jill hires 4 workers to produce 600 pizzas, the average product of labor is 600/4 = 150.

Average product of labor The total output produced by a firm divided by the quantity of workers.

We can state the relationship between the marginal and average products of labor this way: *The average product of labor is the average of the marginal products of labor.* For example, the numbers from Table 11.3 show that the marginal product of the first worker Jill hires is 200, the marginal product of the second worker is 250, and the marginal product of the third worker is 100. Therefore, the average product of labor for three workers is 183.3:

$$183.3 = (200 + 250 + 100) / 3$$

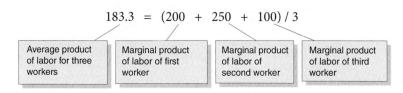

| Average product of labor for three workers | Marginal product of labor of first worker | Marginal product of labor of second worker | Marginal product of labor of third worker |

By taking the average of the marginal products of the first three workers, we have the average product of the three workers.

Whenever the marginal product of labor is greater than the average product of labor, the average product of labor must be increasing. This statement is true for the same reason that a person 6 feet, 2 inches tall entering a room where the average height is 5 feet, 9 inches raises the average height of people in the room. Whenever the marginal product of labor is less than the average product of labor, the average product of labor must be decreasing. The marginal product of labor equals the average product of labor at the quantity of workers for which the average product of labor is at its maximum.   MyEconLab Concept Check

An Example of Marginal and Average Values: College Grades

The relationship between the marginal product of labor and the average product of labor is the same as the relationship between the marginal and average values of any variable. To see this point more clearly, think about the familiar relationship between a student's grade point average (GPA) in one semester and his overall, or cumulative, GPA. The table in Figure 11.3 shows Paul's college grades for each semester, beginning

MyEconLab Animation

Figure 11.3

Marginal and Average GPAs

The relationship between marginal and average values for a variable can be illustrated using GPAs. We can calculate the GPA Paul earns in a particular semester (his "marginal GPA"), and we can calculate his cumulative GPA for all the semesters he has completed so far (his "average GPA"). Paul's GPA is only 1.50 in the fall semester of his first year. In each following semester through the fall of his junior year, his GPA for the semester increases—raising his cumulative GPA. In Paul's junior year, even though his semester GPA declines from fall to spring, his cumulative GPA rises. Only in the fall of his senior year, when his semester GPA drops below his cumulative GPA, does his cumulative GPA decline.

	Semester GPA (marginal GPA)	Cumulative GPA (average GPA)
Freshman year		
Fall	1.50	1.50
Spring	2.00	1.75
Sophomore year		
Fall	2.20	1.90
Spring	3.00	2.18
Junior year		
Fall	3.20	2.38
Spring	3.00	2.48
Senior year		
Fall	2.40	2.47
Spring	2.00	2.41

Average GPA continues to rise, although marginal GPA falls.

With the marginal GPA below the average, the average GPA falls.

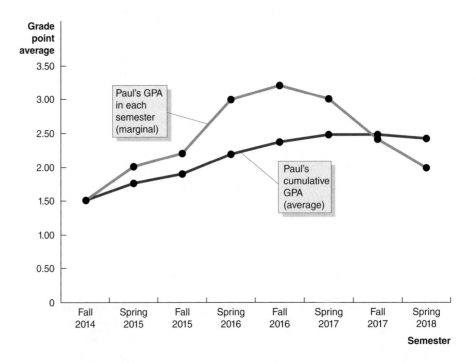

with fall 2014. The graph in Figure 11.3 plots the grades from the table. Just as each additional worker hired adds to a firm's total production, each additional semester adds to Paul's total grade points. We can calculate what hiring each individual worker adds to total production (marginal product), and we can calculate the average production of the workers hired so far (average product).

Similarly, we can calculate the GPA Paul earns in a particular semester (his "marginal GPA") and we can calculate his cumulative GPA for all the semesters he has completed so far (his "average GPA"). As the table shows, Paul gets off to a weak start in the fall semester of his first year, earning only a 1.50 GPA. In each subsequent semester through the fall of his junior year, his GPA for the semester increases from the previous semester—raising his cumulative GPA. As the graph shows, however, his cumulative GPA does not increase as rapidly as his semester-by-semester GPA because his cumulative GPA is held back by the low GPAs of his first few semesters. Notice that in Paul's junior year, even though his semester GPA declines from fall to spring, his cumulative GPA rises. Only in the fall of his senior year, when his semester GPA drops below his cumulative GPA, does his cumulative GPA decline.   MyEconLab Concept Check

MyEconLab Study Plan

The Relationship between Short-Run Production and Short-Run Cost

11.4 LEARNING OBJECTIVE

Explain and illustrate the relationship between marginal cost and average total cost.

We have seen that technology determines the values of the marginal product of labor and the average product of labor. In turn, the marginal and average products of labor affect the firm's costs. Keep in mind that the relationships we are discussing are *short-run* relationships: We are assuming that the time period is too short for the firm to change its technology or the size of its physical plant.

The average total cost curve in panel (b) of Figure 11.1 on page 356 for Jill Johnson's restaurant has a U shape. As we will soon see, the U shape of the average total cost curve is determined by the shape of the curve that shows the relationship between *marginal cost* and the level of production.

Marginal Cost

One of the key ideas in economics is that optimal decisions are made at the margin (see Chapter 1). Consumers, firms, and government officials usually make decisions about doing a little more or a little less. As Jill Johnson considers whether to hire additional workers to produce additional pizzas, she needs to consider how much she will add to her total cost by producing the additional pizzas. **Marginal cost** is the change in a firm's total cost from producing one more unit of a good or service. We can calculate marginal cost for a particular increase in output by dividing the change in total cost by the change in output. We can express this idea mathematically (remember that the Greek letter delta, Δ, means, "change in"):

Marginal cost The change in a firm's total cost from producing one more unit of a good or service.

$$MC = \frac{\Delta TC}{\Delta Q}.$$

In the table in Figure 11.4, we use this equation to calculate Jill's marginal cost of producing pizzas. The other values in the table are from Table 11.2 on page 355 and Table 11.3 on page 357.   MyEconLab Concept Check

Why Are the Marginal and Average Cost Curves U Shaped?

Notice in the graph in Figure 11.4 that Jill's marginal cost of producing pizzas declines at first and then increases, giving the marginal cost curve a U shape. The table in Figure 11.4 also shows the marginal product of labor. This table helps us understand the important relationship between the marginal product of labor and the marginal cost of production: The marginal product of labor is *rising* for the first two workers, but the marginal cost of the pizzas produced by these workers is *falling*. The marginal product of labor is *falling* for the last four workers, but the marginal cost of pizzas produced by

Figure 11.4

Jill Johnson's Marginal Cost and Average Total Cost of Producing Pizzas

We can use the information in the table to calculate Jill's marginal cost and average total cost of producing pizzas. For the first two workers hired, the marginal product of labor is increasing, which causes the marginal cost of production to fall. For the last four workers hired, the marginal product of labor is falling, which causes the marginal cost of production to increase. Therefore, the marginal cost curve falls and then rises—that is, has a U shape—because the marginal product of labor rises and then falls. As long as marginal cost is below average total cost, average total cost will be falling. When marginal cost is above average total cost, average total cost will be rising. The relationship between marginal cost and average total cost explains why the average total cost curve also has a U shape.

Quantity of Workers	Quantity of Pizzas	Marginal Product of Labor	Total Cost of Pizzas	Marginal Cost of Pizzas	Average Total Cost of Pizzas
0	0	—	$800	—	—
1	200	200	1,450	$3.25	$7.25
2	450	250	2,100	2.60	4.67
3	550	100	2,750	6.50	5.00
4	600	50	3,400	13.00	5.67
5	625	25	4,050	26.00	6.48
6	640	15	4,700	43.33	7.34

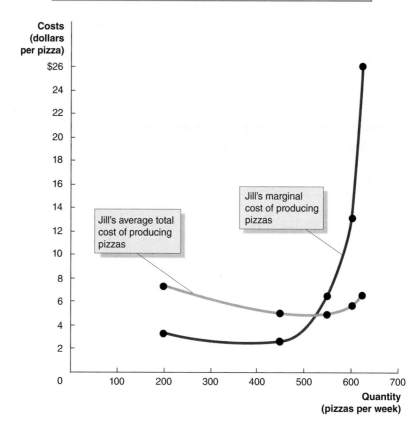

these workers is *rising*. We can generalize this point: *When the marginal product of labor is rising, the marginal cost of output is falling. When the marginal product of labor is falling, the marginal cost of output is rising.*

One way to understand the relationship between the marginal product of labor and the marginal cost of output is to notice that the only additional cost to Jill from producing more pizzas is the additional wages she pays to hire more workers. She pays each new worker the same $650 per week. So the marginal cost of the additional pizzas each worker makes depends on that worker's additional output, or marginal product. As long as the additional output from each new worker is rising, the marginal cost of that output is falling. When the additional output from each new worker is falling, the marginal cost of that output is rising. *We can conclude that the marginal cost of output falls and then rises—forming a U shape—because the marginal product of labor rises and then falls.*

The relationship between marginal cost and average total cost follows the usual relationship between marginal and average values. As long as marginal cost is below average total cost, average total cost falls. When marginal cost is above average total cost, average total cost rises. Marginal cost equals average total cost when average total cost is at its lowest point. Therefore, the average total cost curve has a U shape because the marginal cost curve has a U shape.

Solved Problem 11.4

Calculating Marginal Cost and Average Cost

Santiago Delgado owns a copier store. He leases two copy machines for which he pays $12.50 each per day. He cannot increase the number of machines he leases without giving the office machine company six weeks' notice. He can hire as many workers as he wants, at a cost of $50 per day per worker. These are the only two inputs he uses to produce copies.

a. Fill in the remaining columns in the table by using the definitions of costs.
b. Draw the average total cost curve and marginal cost curve for Santiago's store. Do these curves have the expected shape? Briefly explain.

Quantity of Workers	Quantity of Copies per Day	Fixed Cost	Variable Cost	Total Cost	Average Total Cost	Marginal Cost
0	0					
1	625					
2	1,325					
3	2,200					
4	2,600					
5	2,900					
6	3,100					

Solving the Problem

Step 1: **Review the chapter material.** This problem requires you to understand definitions of costs, so you may want to review the section "The Difference between Fixed Costs and Variable Costs" on page 353, and the section "Why Are the Marginal and Average Cost Curves U Shaped?" which begins on page 361.

Step 2: **Answer part (a) by using the definitions of costs.** Santiago's fixed cost is the amount he pays to lease the copy machines. He uses two copy machines and pays $12.50 each to lease them, so his fixed cost is $25. Santiago's variable cost is the amount he pays to hire workers. He pays $50 per worker per day. His total cost is the sum of his fixed cost and his variable cost. His average total cost is his total cost divided by the quantity of copies he produces that day. His marginal cost is the change in total cost divided by the change in output. So, for example, his marginal cost of producing 1,325 copies per day, rather than 625 copies, is:

$$MC = (\$125 - \$75)/(1,325 - 625) = \$0.07.$$

Quantity of Workers	Quantity of Copies per Day	Fixed Cost	Variable Cost	Total Cost	Average Total Cost	Marginal Cost
0	0	$25	$0	$25	—	—
1	625	25	50	75	$0.12	$0.08
2	1,325	25	100	125	0.09	0.07
3	2,200	25	150	175	0.08	0.06
4	2,600	25	200	225	0.09	0.13
5	2,900	25	250	275	0.09	0.17
6	3,100	25	300	325	0.10	0.25

Step 3: **Answer part (b) by drawing the average total cost and marginal cost curves for Santiago's store and by explaining whether they have the usual shape.** You can use the numbers from the table to draw your graph:

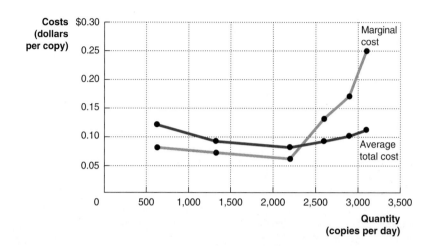

We expect average total cost and marginal cost curves to have a U shape, which Santiago's cost curves do. Both cost curves fall and then rise in the same way as the cost curves in Figure 11.4 on page 362.

MyEconLab Study Plan

Your Turn: For more practice, do related problem 4.7 on page 375 at the end of this chapter.

11.5 LEARNING OBJECTIVE

Graph average total cost, average variable cost, average fixed cost, and marginal cost.

Average fixed cost Fixed cost divided by the quantity of output produced.

Average variable cost Variable cost divided by the quantity of output produced.

Graphing Cost Curves

We have seen that we calculate average total cost by dividing total cost by the quantity of output produced. Similarly, we can calculate **average fixed cost** by dividing fixed cost by the quantity of output produced. And we can calculate **average variable cost** by dividing variable cost by the quantity of output produced. Or, mathematically, with Q being the level of output, we have:

$$\text{Average total cost} = ATC = \frac{TC}{Q}$$

$$\text{Average fixed cost} = AFC = \frac{FC}{Q}$$

$$\text{Average variable cost} = AVC = \frac{VC}{Q}$$

Finally, notice that average total cost is the sum of average fixed cost plus average variable cost:

$$ATC = AFC + AVC.$$

The only fixed cost Jill incurs in operating her restaurant is the $800 per week she pays on the bank loan for her pizza ovens. Her variable costs are the wages she pays her workers. The table and graph in Figure 11.5 show Jill's costs.

We will use graphs like the one in Figure 11.5 in the next several chapters to analyze how firms decide the level of output to produce and the price to charge. Before going further, be sure you understand the following three key facts about Figure 11.5:

1. The marginal cost (*MC*), average total cost (*ATC*), and average variable cost (*AVC*) curves are all U shaped, and the marginal cost curve intersects both the

Quantity of Workers	Quantity of Ovens	Quantity of Pizzas	Cost of Ovens (fixed cost)	Cost of Workers (variable cost)	Total Cost of Pizzas	ATC	AFC	AVC	MC
0	2	0	$800	$0	$800	–	–	–	–
1	2	200	800	650	1,450	$7.25	$4.00	$3.25	$3.25
2	2	450	800	1,300	2,100	4.67	1.78	2.89	2.60
3	2	550	800	1,950	2,750	5.00	1.45	3.54	6.50
4	2	600	800	2,600	3,400	5.67	1.33	4.33	13.00
5	2	625	800	3,250	4,050	6.48	1.28	5.20	26.00
6	2	640	800	3,900	4,700	7.34	1.25	6.09	43.33

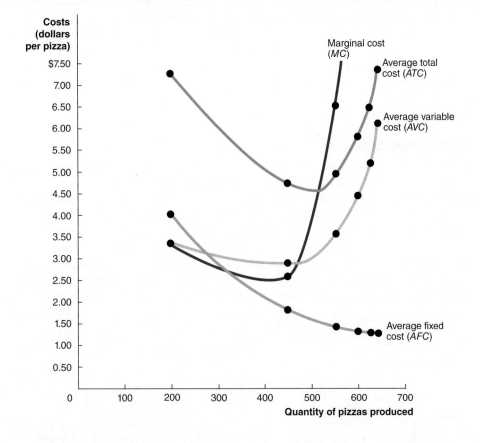

MyEconLab Animation

Figure 11.5

Costs at Jill Johnson's Restaurant

Jill's costs of making pizzas are shown in the table and plotted in the graph. Notice three important facts about the graph: (1) The marginal cost (MC), average total cost (ATC), and average variable cost (AVC) curves are all U shaped, and the marginal cost curve intersects both the average variable cost curve and the average total cost curve at their minimum points. (2) As output increases, average fixed cost (AFC) gets smaller and smaller. (3) As output increases, the difference between average total cost and average variable cost decreases. Make sure you can explain why each of these three facts is true. You should spend time becoming familiar with this graph because it is one of the most important graphs in microeconomics.

average variable cost curve and the average total cost curve at their minimum points. When marginal cost is less than either average variable cost or average total cost, it causes them to decrease. When marginal cost is above average variable cost or average total cost, it causes them to increase. Therefore, when marginal cost equals average variable cost or average total cost, they must be at their minimum points.

2. As output increases, average fixed cost gets smaller and smaller. This result occurs because in calculating average fixed cost, we are dividing something that gets larger and larger—output—into something that remains constant—fixed cost. Firms often refer to this process of lowering average fixed cost by selling more output as "spreading the overhead" (where "overhead" refers to fixed costs).

3. As output increases, the difference between average total cost and average variable cost decreases. This result occurs because the difference between average total cost and average variable cost is average fixed cost, which gets smaller as output increases.

MyEconLab Concept Check   MyEconLab Study Plan

Costs in the Long Run

The distinction between fixed cost and variable cost that we just discussed applies to the short run but *not* to the long run. For example, in the short run, Jill Johnson has fixed costs of $800 per week because she signed a loan agreement with a bank when she bought her pizza ovens. In the long run, the cost of purchasing more pizza ovens becomes variable because Jill can choose whether to expand her business by buying more ovens. The same would be true of any other fixed costs a company like Jill's might have. Once a company has purchased a fire insurance policy, the cost of the policy is fixed. But when the policy expires, the company must decide whether to renew it, and the cost becomes variable. The important point here is this: *In the long run, all costs are variable. There are no fixed costs in the long run.* In other words, in the long run, total cost equals variable cost, and average total cost equals average variable cost.

Managers of successful firms simultaneously consider how they can most profitably run their current store, factory, or office and also whether in the long run they would be more profitable if they became larger or, possibly, smaller. Jill must consider how to run her current restaurant, which has only two pizza ovens, and she must also plan what to do when her current bank loan is paid off and the lease on her store ends. Should she buy more pizza ovens? Should she lease a larger restaurant?

Economies of Scale

Long-run average cost curve A curve that shows the lowest cost at which a firm is able to produce a given quantity of output in the long run, when no inputs are fixed.

Economies of scale The situation when a firm's long-run average costs fall as it increases the quantity of output it produces.

Short-run average cost curves represent the costs a firm faces when some input, such as the quantity of machines it uses, is fixed. The **long-run average cost curve** shows the lowest cost at which a firm is able to produce a given quantity of output in the long run, when no inputs are fixed. A firm may experience **economies of scale**, which means the firm's long-run average costs fall as it increases the quantity of output it produces. We can see the effects of economies of scale in Figure 11.6, which shows the relationship between short-run and long-run average cost curves. Managers can use long-run average cost curves for planning because they show the effect on cost of expanding output by, for example, building a larger factory or restaurant. MyEconLab Concept Check

Figure 11.6

The Relationship between Short-Run Average Cost and Long-Run Average Cost

If a small car company expects to sell only 20,000 cars per year, it will be able to produce cars at the lowest average cost of $52,000 per car if it builds the small factory represented by the *ATC* curve on the left of the figure. A larger factory will be able to produce 200,000 cars per year at a lower cost of $27,000 per car. An automobile factory producing 200,000 cars per year and a factory producing 400,000 cars per year will experience constant returns to scale and have the same average cost. An automobile factory assembling 200,000 cars per year will have reached minimum efficient scale. Very large automobile factories will experience diseconomies of scale, and their average costs will rise as production increases beyond 400,000 cars per year.

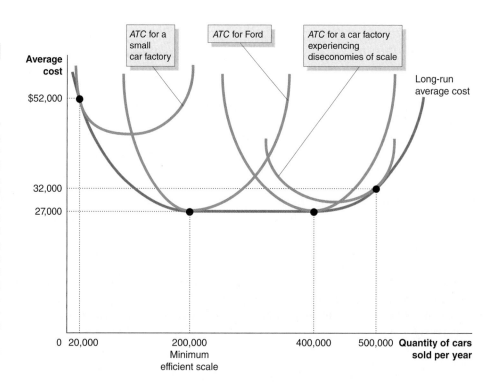

Long-Run Average Cost Curves for Automobile Factories

Figure 11.6 shows long-run average cost in the automobile industry. If a small company, such as Tesla Motors, expects to sell only 20,000 cars per year, then it will be able to assemble cars at the lowest average cost of $52,000 per car if it builds a small factory, as represented by the *ATC* curve on the left of the figure. A much larger factory, such as those operated by Ford, General Motors, or Toyota, will be able to produce 200,000 cars per year at a lower average cost of $27,000 per car. This decline in average cost from $52,000 to $27,000 represents the economies of scale that exist in manufacturing automobiles. Why would the larger automobile factory have lower average costs? One important reason is that a company like Ford is producing 10 times as many cars per year in one of its factories as Tesla produces in its factory but might need only 6 times as many workers. This saving in labor cost would reduce Ford's average cost of selling cars.

In general, firms may experience economies of scale for several reasons. First, as in the case of automobile production, the firm's technology may make it possible to increase production with a smaller proportional increase in at least one input. Second, both workers and managers can become more specialized, enabling them to become more productive, as output expands. Third, large firms, like Ford, Wal-Mart, or Apple, may be able to purchase inputs at lower costs than smaller competitors. In fact, as Apple and Wal-Mart expanded, their bargaining power with their suppliers increased, and their average costs fell. Finally, as a firm expands, it may be able to borrow money at a lower interest rate, thereby lowering its costs.

Economies of scale do not continue forever. The long-run average cost curve in most industries has a flat segment that often stretches over a substantial range of output. As Figure 11.6 shows, an automobile factory producing 200,000 cars per year and a factory producing 400,000 cars per year have the same average cost. Over this range of output, firms in the industry experience **constant returns to scale**. As these firms increase their output, they increase their inputs, such as the size of the factory and the quantity of workers, proportionally. The level of output at which all economies of scale are exhausted is known as **minimum efficient scale**. An automobile factory producing 200,000 cars per year has reached minimum efficient scale.

Very large automobile factories experience increasing average costs as managers begin to have difficulty coordinating the operation of the factory. Figure 11.6 shows that for production above 400,000 cars per year, firms in the industry experience **diseconomies of scale**. For instance, Toyota found that as it expanded production at its Georgetown, Kentucky, plant and its plants in China, its managers had difficulty keeping average cost from rising. According to the president of Toyota's Georgetown plant: "Demand for … high volumes saps your energy. Over a period of time, it eroded our focus … [and] thinned out the expertise and knowledge we painstakingly built up over the years." One analysis of the problems Toyota faced in expanding production concluded: "It is the kind of paradox many highly successful companies face: Getting bigger doesn't always mean getting better." MyEconLab Concept Check

Constant returns to scale The situation in which a firm's long-run average costs remain unchanged as it increases output.

Minimum efficient scale The level of output at which all economies of scale are exhausted.

Diseconomies of scale The situation in which a firm's long-run average costs rise as the firm increases output.

Solved Problem 11.6

MyEconLab Interactive Animation

Using Long-Run Average Cost Curves to Understand Business Strategy

The officials in charge of the port of Rotterdam in the Netherlands decided to expand its capacity from 9.7 million containers processed per year to 18.2 million containers processed per year. An article in the *Wall Street Journal* described the port as attempting to "provide economies of scale to shippers." Shippers using the port expected that the fees charged to process their containers would decline following the expansion.

a. What does it mean to say that expanding the size of the port will "provide economies of scale to shippers"?

b. Use a long-run average cost curve to explain why the expansion of the port might result in lower fees to shippers.

Solving the Problem

Step 1: **Review the chapter material.** This problem is about the long-run average cost curve, so you may want to review the material in the section "Costs in the Long Run," which begins on page 366.

Step 2: **Answer part (a) by explaining what it means for the port to "provide economies of scale to shippers."** If by expanding, the port of Rotterdam will lower its average cost of processing a shipping container, then the port was operating at less than minimum efficient scale. In that case, the expansion of the port would provide economies of scale to shippers by lowering the average cost of processing a container.

Step 3: **Draw a long-run average cost graph for the port.** The problem provides us with enough information to draw the following graph:

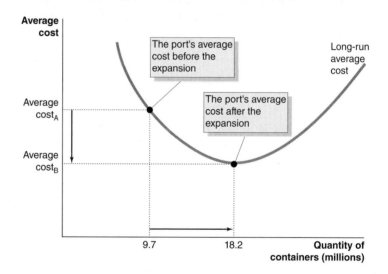

Step 4: **Use your graph to explain why the expansion of the port might result in lower fees to shippers.** Before the expansion, the port was below minimum efficient scale and was processing 9.7 million containers per year, at an average cost of Average cost$_A$. By expanding, the port can move to the minimum efficient scale of 18.2 million containers per year, and average cost falls to Average cost$_B$. (We can't be sure whether the expansion will actually take the port to minimum efficient scale, but it seems likely that the engineers and economists advising the port's managers would suggest an expansion that would raise capacity to that level.) With lower costs, the port may reduce the fees that it charges shippers, which is what shippers were expecting.

Source: John W. Miller, "For Port Expansion, It's Full Speed Ahead," *Wall Street Journal*, October 26, 2010.

MyEconLab Study Plan

Your Turn: For more practice, do related problems 6.7, 6.8, 6.9, and 6.10 on pages 377–378 at the end of this chapter.

Over time, most firms in an industry will build factories or stores that are at least as large as the minimum efficient scale but not so large that diseconomies of scale occur. For example, in the automobile industry, most factories will produce between 200,000 and 400,000 cars per year. However, firms often do not know the exact shape of their long-run average cost curves. As a result, they may mistakenly build factories or stores that are either too large or too small.

Making the Connection MyEconLab Video	**The Colossal River Rouge: Diseconomies of Scale at Ford Motor Company**

When Henry Ford started the Ford Motor Company in 1903, automobile companies produced cars in small workshops, using highly skilled workers. Ford introduced two new ideas to the automobile industry that allowed him to take advantage of economies of scale. First, Ford used identical—or, interchangeable—parts so that unskilled workers could assemble the cars. Second, instead of having groups of workers moving from one stationary automobile to the next, he had the workers remain stationary, while the automobiles moved along an assembly line. Ford built a large factory at Highland Park, outside Detroit, where he used these ideas to produce the famous Model T at an average cost well below what his competitors could match using older production methods in smaller factories.

Was Ford's River Rouge plant too big?

Ford believed that he could produce automobiles at an even lower average cost by building a still larger plant along the River Rouge in Dearborn, Michigan. Unfortunately, Ford's River Rouge plant was too large and suffered from diseconomies of scale. Ford's managers had great difficulty coordinating the production of automobiles in such a large plant. The following description of the River Rouge plant comes from a biography of Ford by Allan Nevins and Frank Ernest Hill:

> A total of 93 separate structures stood on the [River Rouge] site .... Railroad trackage covered 93 miles, conveyors 27 [miles]. About 75,000 men worked in the great plant. A force of 5000 did nothing but keep it clean, wearing out 5000 mops and 3000 brooms a month, and using 86 tons of soap on the floors, walls, and 330 acres of windows. The Rouge was an industrial city, immense, concentrated, packed with power .... By its very massiveness and complexity, it denied men at the top contact with and understanding of those beneath, and gave those beneath a sense of being lost in inexorable immensity and power.

Beginning in 1927, Ford produced the Model A—its only car model at that time—at the River Rouge plant. Ford failed to achieve economies of scale and actually *lost money* on each of the four Model A body styles.

Ford could not raise the price of the Model A to make it profitable because at a higher price, the car could not compete with similar models produced by competitors such as General Motors and Chrysler. He eventually reduced the cost of making the Model A by constructing smaller factories spread out across the country. These smaller factories produced the Model A at a lower average cost than was possible at the River Rouge plant.

Source: Allan Nevins and Frank Ernest Hill, *Ford: Expansion and Challenge, 1915–1933*, New York: Scribner, 1957, pp. 293, 295.

Your Turn: Test your understanding by doing related problem 6.11 on page 378 at the end of this chapter.

MyEconLab Study Plan

Don't Let This Happen to You

Don't Confuse Diminishing Returns with Diseconomies of Scale

The concepts of diminishing returns and diseconomies of scale may seem similar, but they are actually unrelated. Diminishing returns applies only to the short run, when at least one of the firm's inputs, such as the quantity of machinery it uses, is fixed. The law of diminishing returns tells us that in the short run, hiring more workers will, at some point, result in less additional output. Diminishing returns explains why marginal cost curves

eventually slope upward. Diseconomies of scale apply only in the long run, when the firm is free to vary all its inputs, can adopt new technology, and can vary the amount of machinery it uses and the size of its facility. Diseconomies of scale explain why long-run average cost curves eventually slope upward.

MyEconLab Study Plan

Your Turn: Test your understanding by doing related problem 6.13 on page 378 at the end of this chapter.

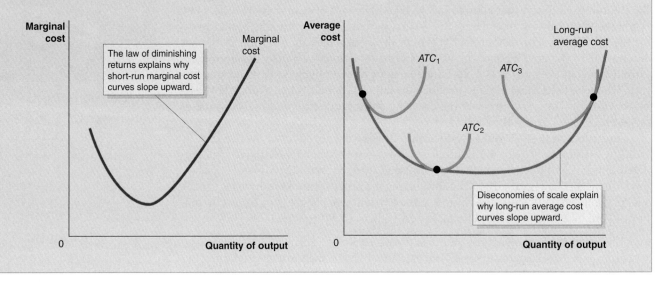

Continued from page 351

Economics in Your Life

Using Cost Concepts in Your Own Business

At the beginning of the chapter, we asked you to suppose that you are about to open a store to sell recliners. Both you and a competing store, Bob's Big Chairs, can buy recliners from the manufacturer for $300 each. But because Bob's sells more recliners per month than you expect to be able to sell, his costs per recliner are lower than yours. We asked you to think about why this might be true. In this chapter, we have seen that firms often experience declining average costs as the quantity they sell increases. A key reason Bob's average costs might be lower than yours has to do with fixed costs. Because your store is the same size as Bob's store, you may be paying about the same amount to lease the store space. You may also be paying about the same amounts for utilities, insurance, and advertising. All these are fixed costs because they do not change as the quantity of recliners you sell changes. Because Bob's fixed costs are the same as yours, but he is selling more recliners, his average fixed costs are lower than yours, and, therefore, so are his average total costs. With lower average total costs, he can sell his recliners for a lower price than you do and still make a profit.

Conclusion

In this chapter, we discussed the relationship between a firm's technology, production, and costs. In the discussion, we encountered a number of definitions of costs. Because we will use these definitions in later chapters, it is useful to bring them together in Table 11.4 for you to review.

We have seen the important relationship between a firm's level of production and its costs. This information is vital to all firms as they attempt to decide the optimal level of production and the optimal prices to charge for their products. We will explore this point further in the next chapter.

Visit MyEconLab for a news article and analysis related to the concepts in this chapter.

Term	Definition	Symbols and Equations
Total cost	The cost of all the inputs used by a firm, or fixed cost plus variable cost	TC
Fixed costs	Costs that remain constant as a firm's level of output changes	FC
Variable costs	Costs that change as a firm's level of output changes	VC
Marginal cost	An increase in total cost resulting from producing another unit of output	$MC = \dfrac{\Delta TC}{\Delta Q}$
Average total cost	Total cost divided by the quantity of output produced	$ATC = \dfrac{TC}{Q}$
Average fixed cost	Fixed cost divided by the quantity of output produced	$AFC = \dfrac{FC}{Q}$
Average variable cost	Variable cost divided by the quantity of output produced	$AVC = \dfrac{VC}{Q}$
Implicit cost	A nonmonetary opportunity cost	—
Explicit cost	A cost that involves spending money	—

Table 11.4

A Summary of Definitions of Cost

Chapter Summary and Problems

Key Terms

Average fixed cost, p. 364

Average product of labor, p. 359

Average total cost, p. 356

Average variable cost, p. 364

Constant returns to scale, p. 367

Diseconomies of scale, p. 367

Economies of scale, p. 366

Explicit cost, p. 354

Fixed costs, p. 353

Implicit cost, p. 354

Law of diminishing returns, p. 357

Long run, p. 353

Long-run average cost curve, p. 366

Marginal cost, p. 361

Marginal product of labor, p. 357

Minimum efficient scale, p. 367

Opportunity cost, p. 354

Production function, p. 356

Short run, p. 353

Technological change, p. 352

Technology, p. 352

Total cost, p. 353

Variable costs, p. 353

Technology: An Economic Definition, pages 352–353

LEARNING OBJECTIVE: Define technology and give examples of technological change.

Summary

The basic activity of a firm is to use inputs, such as workers, machines, and natural resources, to produce goods and services. The firm's **technology** is the processes it uses to turn inputs into goods and services. **Technological change** refers to a change in the ability of a firm to produce a given level of output with a given quantity of inputs.

MyEconLab   Visit **www.myeconlab.com** to complete these exercises online and get instant feedback.

Review Questions

1.1 What is the difference between technology and technological change?

1.2 Is it possible for technological change to be negative? If so, give an example.

Problems and Applications

1.3 Briefly explain whether you agree with the following observation: "Technological change refers only to the introduction of new products, so it is not relevant to the operations of most firms."

1.4 Which of the following are examples of a firm experiencing positive technological change?
   a. A fall in oil prices leads United Airlines to lower its ticket prices.
   b. A training program makes a firm's workers more productive.
   c. An exercise program makes a firm's workers more healthy and productive.
   d. A firm cuts its workforce and is able to maintain its initial level of output.
   e. A firm rearranges the layout of its factory and finds that by using its initial set of inputs, it can produce exactly as much as before.

1.5 **[Related to the** Making the Connection **on page 352]** The 7-Eleven chain of convenience stores in Japan reorganized the timing of truck deliveries of food to their stores, as well as the routes the trucks traveled. This reorganization led to a sharp reduction in the number of trucks the company had to use, while increasing the amount of fresh food on store shelves. Someone discussing 7-Eleven's new system argues: "This is not an example of technological change because it did not require the use of new machinery or equipment." Briefly explain whether you agree with this argument.

The Short Run and the Long Run in Economics, pages 353–357

LEARNING OBJECTIVE: Distinguish between the economic short run and the economic long run.

Summary

In the **short run**, a firm's technology and the size of its factory, store, or office are fixed. In the **long run**, a firm is able to adopt new technology and to increase or decrease the size of its physical plant. **Total cost** is the cost of all the inputs a firm uses in production. **Variable costs** are costs that change as output changes. **Fixed costs** are costs that remain constant as output changes. **Opportunity cost** is the highest-valued alternative that must be given up to engage in an activity. An **explicit cost** is a cost that involves spending money. An **implicit cost** is a nonmonetary opportunity cost. The relationship between the inputs employed by a firm and the maximum output it can produce with those inputs is called the firm's **production function**.

MyEconLab   Visit **www.myeconlab.com** to complete these exercises online and get instant feedback.

Review Questions

2.1 What is the difference between the short run and the long run? Is the amount of time that separates the short run from the long run the same for every firm?

2.2 Distinguish between a firm's fixed costs and variable costs and give an example of each.

2.3 What are implicit costs? How are they different from explicit costs?

2.4 What is the production function? What does the short-run production function hold constant?

Problems and Applications

2.5 An article in *Forbes* discussed an estimate that the cost of materials in Apple's iPhone 5 with 64 gigabytes of memory was $230. Apple was selling the iPhone 5 for $849 (most phone carriers made payments to Apple that reduced the price to consumers to $399). Can we conclude from this information that Apple is making a profit of about $619 per iPhone? Briefly explain.

Source: John Gaudiosi, "Research Teardown Details Why the New iPhone 5 Only Costs Apple $207 to Make," *Forbes*, September 19, 2012.

2.6 [Related to the Making the Connection **on page 354**] Many firms consider their wage costs to be variable costs. Why, then, do publishers usually consider their wage and salary costs to be fixed costs? Are the costs of utilities always fixed, are they always variable, or can they be both? Briefly explain.

2.7 [Related to the Making the Connection **on page 354**] For Jill Johnson's pizza restaurant, explain whether each of the following is a fixed cost or a variable cost:
   a. The payment she makes on her fire insurance policy
   b. The payment she makes to buy pizza dough
   c. The wages she pays her workers
   d. The lease payment she makes to the landlord who owns the building where her store is located
   e. The $300-per-month payment she makes to her local newspaper for running her weekly advertisements

2.8 [Related to the Making the Connection **on page 354**] The *Statistical Abstract of the United States* was published for many years by the U.S. Census Bureau. The *Abstract* provided a summary of business, economic, social, and political statistics. It was available for free online, and a printed copy could also be purchased from the U.S. Government Printing Office for $39. Because government documents are not copyrighted, anyone could print and sell copies of the *Statistical Abstract*. Each year, typically one or two companies would print and sell copies for a significantly lower price than the Government Printing Office did. The copies of the *Statistical Abstract* that these companies sold were usually identical to those sold by the government, except for having different covers. How could these companies have sold the same book for a lower price than the government did and still have covered their costs?

2.9 Suppose that Bill owns an automobile collision repair shop. The following table shows how the quantity of cars Bill can repair per month depends on the number of workers he hires. Assume that he pays each worker $4,000 per month and his fixed cost is $6,000 per month. Using the information provided, complete the table.

Quantity of Workers	Quantity of Cars per Month	Fixed Cost	Variable Cost	Total Cost	Average Total Cost
0	0	$6,000			—
1	20				
2	30				
3	40				
4	50				
5	55				

2.10 In 2008, Clay Bennett, the owner of the then Seattle Supersonics NBA basketball team (now the Oklahoma City Thunder), estimated that if the team remained in Seattle, he would suffer a loss of about $63 million over the following two seasons. If the team were allowed to move to Oklahoma City, he estimated that he would earn a profit of $19 million. What was the opportunity cost to Bennett of his team playing in Seattle rather than in Oklahoma City? Briefly explain.

Source: Jim Brunner, "New Details Emerge from Sonics Owner's Combative Deposition," *Seattle Times*, June 7, 2008.

2.11 Suppose Jill Johnson operates her pizza restaurant in a building she owns in the center of the city. Similar buildings in the neighborhood rent for $4,000 per month. Jill is considering selling her building and renting space in the suburbs for $3,000 per month, but she decides not to make the move. She reasons: "I would like to have a restaurant in the suburbs, but I pay no rent for my restaurant now, and I don't want to see my costs rise by $3,000 per month." Evaluate Jill's reasoning.

2.12 When the DuPont chemical company first attempted to enter the paint business, it was not successful. According to a company report, in one year it "lost nearly $500,000 in actual cash in addition to an expected return on investment of nearly $500,000, which made a total loss of income to the company of nearly a million." Why did this report include as part of the company's loss the amount it had expected to earn—but didn't—on its investment in manufacturing paint?

Source: Alfred D. Chandler, Jr., Thomas K. McCraw, and Richard Tedlow, *Management Past and Present*, Cincinnati, OH: South-Western, 2000.

11.3 **The Marginal Product of Labor and the Average Product of Labor, pages 357–361**
LEARNING OBJECTIVE: Understand the relationship between the marginal product of labor and the average product of labor.

Summary

The **marginal product of labor** is the additional output produced by a firm as a result of hiring one more worker. Specialization and division of labor cause the marginal product of labor to rise for the first few workers hired. Eventually, the **law of diminishing returns** causes the marginal product of labor to decline. The **average product of labor** is the total amount of output produced by a firm divided by the quantity of workers hired. When the marginal product of labor is greater than the average product of labor, the average product of labor increases. When the marginal product of labor is less than the average product of labor, the average product of labor decreases.

Review Questions

3.1 Draw a graph that shows the usual relationship between the marginal product of labor and the average product of labor. Why do the marginal product of labor and the average product of labor curves have the shapes you drew?

3.2 How do specialization and division of labor typically affect the marginal product of labor?

3.3 What is the law of diminishing returns? Does it apply in the long run?

Problems and Applications

3.4 Fill in the missing values in the following table:

Quantity of Workers	Total Output	Marginal Product of Labor	Average Product of Labor
0	0		
1	400		
2	900		
3	1,500		
4	1,900		
5	2,200		
6	2,400		
7	2,300		

3.5 Use the numbers from problem 3.4 to draw one graph that shows how total output increases with the quantity of workers hired and a second graph that shows the marginal product of labor and the average product of labor.

3.6 A student looks at the numbers in Table 11.3 on page 357 and draws this conclusion:

The marginal product of labor is increasing for the first two workers hired, and then it declines for the next four workers. I guess each of the first two workers must have been hard workers. Then Jill must have had to settle for increasingly bad workers.

Do you agree with the student's analysis? Briefly explain.

3.7 **[Related to the** Making the Connection **on page 359]** Briefly explain whether you agree with the following argument:

Adam Smith's idea of the gains to firms from the division of labor makes a lot of sense when the good being manufactured is something complex like automobiles or computers, but it doesn't apply in the manufacturing of less complex goods or in other sectors of the economy, such as retail sales.

3.8 Sally looks at her college transcript and says to you, "How is this possible? My grade point average for this semester's courses is higher than my grade point average for last semester's courses, but my cumulative grade point average still went down from last semester to this semester." Explain to Sally how this is possible.

3.9 Is it possible for a firm to experience a technological change that would increase the marginal product of labor while leaving the average product of labor unchanged? Explain.

3.10 The following table shows the quantity of workers and total output for a local pizza parlor. Answer the following questions based on this table:

Quantity of Workers	Total Output
0	0
1	5
2	—
3	19
4	24
5	28
6	26

  a. When the owner hires 4 workers, what is average product of labor?

  b. What is the marginal product of the fifth worker?

  c. If the marginal product of the second worker is 6, what is the total number of pizzas produced when 2 workers are hired?

  d. Assuming the marginal product of the second worker is 6, with which worker hired does the law of diminishing returns set in?

11.4 ## The Relationship between Short-Run Production and Short-Run Cost, pages 361–364

LEARNING OBJECTIVE: Explain and illustrate the relationship between marginal cost and average total cost.

Summary

The **marginal cost** of production is the increase in total cost resulting from producing another unit of output. The marginal cost curve has a U shape because when the marginal product of labor is rising, the marginal cost of output is falling, and when the marginal product of labor is falling, the marginal cost of output is rising. When marginal cost is less than average total cost, average total cost falls. When marginal cost is greater than average total cost, average total cost rises. Therefore, the average total cost curve also has a U shape.

Review Questions

4.1 What is the difference between the average cost of production and marginal cost of production?

4.2 If the marginal product of labor is rising, is the marginal cost of production rising or falling? Briefly explain.

4.3 Explain why the marginal cost curve intersects the average total cost curve at the level of output where average total cost is at a minimum.

Problems and Applications

4.4 **[Related to the** Chapter opener **on page 351]** Older oil wells that produce fewer than 10 barrels of oil a day are called "stripper" wells. Suppose that you and a partner own a stripper well that can produce eight barrels of oil per day and you estimate that the marginal cost of producing another barrel of oil is $80. In making your calculation, you take into account the cost of labor, materials, and other inputs that increase when you produce more oil. Your partner looks over your calculation of marginal cost and says: "You forgot about that bank loan we received two years ago. If we take into account the amount we pay on that loan, it adds $10 per barrel to our marginal cost of production." Briefly explain whether you should agree with your partner's analysis.

4.5 Is it possible for average total cost to be decreasing over a range of output where marginal cost is increasing? Briefly explain.

4.6 Suppose a firm has no fixed costs, so all its costs are variable, even in the short run.
  a. If the firm's marginal costs are continually increasing (that is, marginal cost is increasing from the first unit of output produced), will the firm's average total cost curve have a U shape?
  b. If the firm's marginal costs are $5 at every level of output, what shape will the firm's average total cost have?

4.7 **[Related to** Solved Problem 11.4 **on page 363]** Santiago Delgado owns a copier store. He leases two copy machines for which he pays $20 each per day. He cannot increase the number of machines he leases without giving the office machine company six weeks' notice. He can hire as many workers as he wants, at a cost of $40 per day per worker. These are the only two inputs he uses to produce copies.
  a. Fill in the remaining columns in the following table.
  b. Draw the average total cost curve and marginal cost curve for Santiago's store. Do these curves have the expected shape? Briefly explain.

Quantity of Workers	Quantity of Copies per Day	Fixed Cost	Variable Cost	Total Cost	Average Total Cost	Marginal Cost
0	0					
1	600					
2	1,100					
3	1,500					
4	1,800					
5	2,000					
6	2,100					

4.8 Is Jill Johnson correct when she says the following: "I am currently producing 10,000 pizzas per month at a total cost of $50,000.00. If I produce 10,001 pizzas, my total cost will rise to $50,011.00. Therefore, my marginal cost of producing pizzas must be increasing." Draw a graph to illustrate your answer.

4.9 Is Jill Johnson correct when she says the following: "I am currently producing 20,000 pizzas per month at a total cost of $75,000. If I produce 20,001 pizzas, my total cost will rise to $75,002. Therefore, my marginal cost of producing pizzas must be increasing." Illustrate your answer with a graph.

4.10 (This problem is somewhat advanced.) Using symbols, we can write that the marginal product of labor is equal to $\Delta Q/\Delta L$. Marginal cost is equal to $\Delta TC/\Delta Q$. Because fixed costs by definition don't change, marginal cost is also equal to $\Delta VC/\Delta Q$. If Jill Johnson's only variable cost (VC) is labor cost, then her variable cost equals the wage multiplied by the quantity of workers hired, or wL.
  a. If the wage Jill pays is constant, then what is ΔVC in terms of w and L?
  b. Use your answer to part (a) and the expressions given for the marginal product of labor and the marginal cost of output to find an expression for marginal cost, $\Delta TC/\Delta Q$, in terms of the wage, w, and the marginal product of labor, $\Delta Q/\Delta L$.
  c. Use your answer to part (b) to determine Jill's marginal cost of producing pizzas if the wage is $750 per week and the marginal product of labor is 150 pizzas. If the wage falls to $600 per week and the marginal product of labor is unchanged, what happens to Jill's marginal cost? If the wage is unchanged at $750 per week and the marginal product of labor rises to 250 pizzas, what happens to Jill's marginal cost?

<table>
<tr><td>**11.5**</td><td>

Graphing Cost Curves, pages 364–365

LEARNING OBJECTIVE: Graph average total cost, average variable cost, average fixed cost, and marginal cost.

</td></tr>
</table>

Summary

Average fixed cost is equal to fixed cost divided by the level of output. **Average variable cost** is equal to variable cost divided by the level of output. Figure 11.5 on page 365 shows the relationship among marginal cost, average total cost, average variable cost, and average fixed cost. It is one of the most important graphs in microeconomics.

Review Questions

5.1 Where does the marginal cost curve intersect the average variable cost curve and the average total cost curve?

5.2 As the level of output increases, what happens to the difference between the value of average total cost and average variable cost?

Problems and Applications

5.3 Suppose the total cost of producing 10,000 tennis balls is $30,000 and the fixed cost is $10,000.
  a. What is the variable cost?
  b. When output is 10,000, what are the average variable cost and the average fixed cost?
  c. Assume that the cost curves have the usual shape. Is the dollar difference between the average total cost and the average variable cost greater when the output is 10,000 tennis balls or when the output is 30,000 tennis balls? Explain.

5.4 One description of the costs of operating a railroad makes the following observation: "The fixed … expenses which attach to the operation of railroads … are in the nature of a tax upon the business of the road; the smaller the [amount of] business, the larger the tax." Briefly explain why fixed costs are like a tax. In what sense is this tax smaller when the amount of business is larger?
  Source: Alfred D. Chandler, Jr., Thomas K. McCraw, and Richard Tedlow, *Management Past and Present*, Cincinnati, OH: South-Western, 2000, p. 2–27.

5.5 In the ancient world, a book could be produced either on a scroll or as a codex, which was made of folded sheets glued together, something like a modern book. One scholar has estimated the following variable costs (in Greek drachmas) of the two methods:

	Scroll	Codex
Cost of writing (wage of a scribe)	11.33 drachmas	11.33 drachmas
Cost of paper	16.50 drachmas	9.25 drachmas

Another scholar points out that a significant fixed cost was involved in producing a codex:

> In order to copy a codex … the amount of text and the layout of each page had to be carefully calculated in advance to determine the exact number of sheets … needed. No doubt, this is more time-consuming and calls for more experimentation than the production of a scroll would. But for the next copy, these calculations would be used again.

  a. Suppose that the fixed cost of preparing a codex was 58 drachmas and that there was no similar fixed cost for a scroll. Would an ancient book publisher who intended to sell 5 copies of a book be likely to publish it as a scroll or as a codex? What if he intended to sell 10 copies? Briefly explain.
  b. Although most books were published as scrolls in the first century A.D., by the third century, most were published as codices. Considering only the factors mentioned in this problem, explain why this change may have taken place.
  Sources: T. C. Skeat, "The Length of the Standard Papyrus Roll and the Cost-Advantage of the Codex," *Zeitschrift fur Pspyrologie and Epigraphik*, Germany: Rudolph Habelt, 1982, p. 175; and David Trobisch, *The First Edition of the New Testament*, New York: Oxford University Press, 2000, p. 73.

5.6 Recently some colleges and private companies have launched free online courses that can be taken by anyone with an Internet connection. The most successful of these "massive open online courses" (MOOCs) have attracted tens of thousands of students. An article in the *Economist* magazine discussing MOOCs observed: "Though marginal costs are low, designing enticing online material is costly." Why would the marginal costs of offering a MOOC be low? What is the relationship between the marginal costs, average fixed costs, and average total costs of offering a MOOC? Draw a graph to illustrate your answer.
  Source: "Learning New Lessons," *Economist*, December 22, 2012.

5.7 Use the information in the graph to find the values for the following at an output level of 1,000.

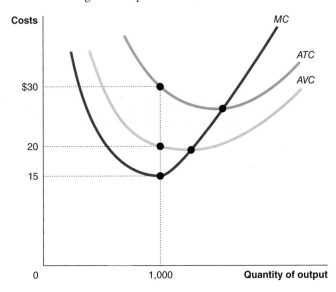

  a. Marginal cost
  b. Total cost
  c. Variable cost
  d. Fixed cost

5.8 List the errors in the following graph. Carefully explain why the curves drawn this way are wrong. In other words, why can't these curves be as they are shown in the graph?

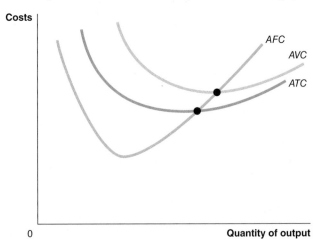

5.9 Explain how the events listed in a. through d. would affect the following costs at Southwest Airlines:
  1. Marginal cost
  2. Average variable cost
  3. Average fixed cost

4. Average total cost
   a. Southwest signs a new contract with the Transport Workers Union that requires the airline to increase wages for its flight attendants.
   b. The federal government starts to levy a $20-per-passenger carbon emissions tax on all commercial air travel.
   c. Southwest decides on an across-the-board 10 percent cut in executive salaries.
   d. Southwest decides to double its television advertising budget.

  11.6 ## Costs in the Long Run, pages 366–370

LEARNING OBJECTIVE: Understand how firms use the long-run average cost curve in their planning.

Summary

The **long-run average cost curve** shows the lowest cost at which a firm is able to produce a given level of output in the long run. For many firms, the long-run average cost curve falls as output expands because of **economies of scale. Minimum efficient scale** is the level of output at which all economies of scale have been exhausted. After economies of scale have been exhausted, firms experience **constant returns to scale**, where their long-run average cost curve is flat. At high levels of output, the long-run average cost curve turns up as the firm experiences **diseconomies of scale**.

MyEconLab   Visit www.myeconlab.com to complete these exercises online and get instant feedback.

Review Questions

6.1 What is the difference between total cost and variable cost in the long run?

6.2 What is minimum efficient scale? What is likely to happen in the long run to firms that do not reach minimum efficient scale?

6.3 What are economies of scale? What are four reasons that firms may experience economies of scale?

6.4 What are diseconomies of scale? What is the main reason that a firm eventually encounters diseconomies of scale as it keeps increasing the size of its store or factory?

6.5 Why can short-run average cost never be less than long-run average cost for a given level of output?

Problems and Applications

6.6 Factories for producing computer chips are called "fabs." As the semiconductors used in computer chips have become smaller and smaller, the machines necessary to make them have become more and more expensive. According to an article in the *Economist* magazine:

> To reach the economies of scale needed to make such investments pay, chipmakers must build bigger fabs .... In 1966 a new fab cost $14 million. By 1995 the price had risen to $1.5 billion. Today, says Intel, the cost of a leading-edge fab exceeds $6 billion.

Why would the rising costs of chipmaking machines lead chipmaking companies, such as Intel, to build larger factories?
Source: "The Semiconductor Industry," *Economist*, April 2, 2009.

6.7 **[Related to** Solved Problem 11.6 **on page 367]** Suppose that Jill Johnson has to choose between building a smaller restaurant and a larger restaurant. In the following graph, the relationship between costs and output for the smaller restaurant is represented by the curve ATC_1, and the relationship between costs and output for the larger restaurant is represented by the curve ATC_2.

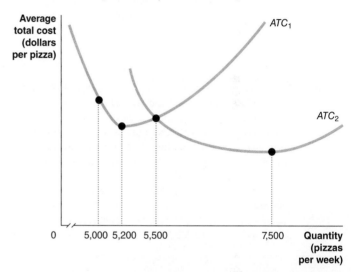

a. If Jill expects to produce 5,100 pizzas per week, should she build a smaller restaurant or a larger restaurant? Briefly explain.

b. If Jill expects to produce 6,000 pizzas per week, should she build a smaller restaurant or a larger restaurant? Briefly explain.

c. A student asks, "If the average cost of producing pizzas is lower in the larger restaurant when Jill produces 7,500 pizzas per week, why isn't it also lower when Jill produces 5,200 pizzas per week?" Give a brief answer to the student's question.

6.8 **[Related to** Solved Problem 11.6 **on page 367]** An article in the *Wall Street Journal* discussed the purchase of the small Zipcar rental car firm by the much larger Avis. The article predicted that the purchase would be successful because of the "efficiencies gained by putting the two companies together." The article also observed: "On its own, Zipcar is too small to achieve economies of scale."

a. What economies of scale may exist in the rental car industry? Why would a rental car firm that is too small be unable to achieve these economies of scale?

b. What does the article mean by "efficiencies" that might be gained by putting the two companies together?

c. If Avis had already achieved minimum efficient scale before buying Zipcar, would the combined companies still be more efficient than if they operated separately? Briefly explain.
Source: Rolfe Winkler, "Avis Puts Some Zip in Its Weekend," *Wall Street Journal*, January 2, 2013.

6.9 [Related to Solved Problem 11.6 **on page 367**] An account of the difficulties of Japanese mobile phone manufacturers argues that these firms made a mistake by concentrating on selling in high-income countries while making little effort to sell in low-income countries:

> The main growth in the wireless industry overall is in emerging markets, which need cheap phones. The world's top three makers—Nokia, Samsung and Motorola—focus on this segment .... Japanese firms are caught in a vicious circle: because they are not selling to poor countries, their volume stays low, which keeps prices high, which makes selling to poor countries infeasible.

Why would the price of Japanese mobile phones be high because Japanese firms are producing these phones in low volumes? Use a graph like Figure 11.6 on page 366 to illustrate your answer.

Source: "Dropped Call: Why Japan Lost the Mobile-Phone Wars," *Economist*, March 7, 2008.

6.10 [Related to Solved Problem 11.6 **on page 367**] At one point, Time Warner and the Walt Disney Company discussed merging their news operations. Time Warner owns Cable News Network (CNN) and Disney owns ABC News. After analyzing the situation, the companies decided that a combined news operation would have higher average costs than either CNN or ABC News had separately. Use a long-run average cost curve graph to illustrate why the companies did not merge their news operations.

Source: Martin Peers and Joe Flint, "AOL Calls Off CNN–ABC Deal, Seeing Operating Difficulties," *Wall Street Journal*, February 14, 2003.

6.11 [Related to the Making the Connection **on page 369**] Suppose that Henry Ford had continued to experience economies of scale, no matter how large an automobile factory he built. Discuss what the implications of this would have been for the automobile industry.

6.12 [Related to the Chapter Opener **on page 351**] Suppose that the economies of scale in using fracking methods in drilling for oil are greater than when using conventional drilling methods. What would the likely consequences be for the number of firms drilling for oil in the United States?

6.13 [Related to the Don't Let This Happen to You **on page 370**] Explain whether you agree with the following statement: "Henry Ford expected to be able to produce cars at a lower average cost at his River Rouge plant. Unfortunately, because of diminishing returns, his costs were actually higher."

6.14 In 2012, then Barnes & Noble CEO William Lynch predicted that although the firm was suffering losses in selling its Nook tablet, "the Nook business will scale in fiscal 2013, reducing losses from last year."

a. What did Lynch mean that "the Nook business will scale"?

b. Why would the Nook business scaling reduce the firm's losses?

c. In 2013, Barnes & Noble's losses from selling the Nook increased and Lynch resigned as CEO. Can we conclude that the Nook business didn't scale? Briefly explain.

Source: Jeffrey A. Trachtenberg "Nook Loses Ground in Tablet War," *Wall Street Journal*, January 3, 2013.

Appendix

Using Isoquants and Isocost Lines to Understand Production and Cost

LEARNING OBJECTIVE

Use isoquants and isocost lines to understand production and cost.

Isoquants

In this chapter, we studied the important relationship between a firm's level of production and its costs. In this appendix, we will look more closely at how firms choose the combination of inputs to produce a given level of output. Firms usually have a choice about how they will produce their output. For example, Jill Johnson is able to produce 5,000 pizzas per week by using 10 workers and 2 ovens or by using 6 workers and 3 ovens. We will see that firms search for the *cost-minimizing* combination of inputs that will allow them to produce a given level of output. The cost-minimizing combination of inputs depends on two factors: technology—which determines how much output a firm receives from employing a given quantity of inputs—and input prices—which determine the total cost of each combination of inputs.

An Isoquant Graph

We begin by graphing the levels of output that Jill can produce using different combinations of two inputs: labor—the quantity of workers she hires per week—and capital—the quantity of ovens she uses per week. In reality, of course, Jill uses more than just these two inputs to produce pizzas, but nothing important would change if we expanded the discussion to include many inputs instead of just two. Figure 11A.1 measures the quantity of capital along the vertical axis and the quantity of labor along the horizontal axis. The curves in the graph are **isoquants**, which show all the combinations of two inputs, in this case capital and labor, that will produce the same level of output.

The isoquant labeled $Q = 5,000$ shows all the combinations of workers and ovens that enable Jill to produce that quantity of pizzas per week. For example, at point A, she produces 5,000 pizzas using 6 workers and 3 ovens, and at point B, she produces the same output using 10 workers and 2 ovens. With more workers and ovens, she can move to a higher isoquant. For example, with 12 workers and 4 ovens, she can produce at point C on the isoquant $Q = 10,000$. With even more workers and ovens, she could move to the isoquant $Q = 13,000$. The higher the isoquant—that is, the further to the upper right on the graph—the more output the firm produces. Although we have shown only three isoquants in this graph, there is, in fact, an isoquant for every level of output. MyEconLab Concept Check

Isoquant A curve that shows all the combinations of two inputs, such as capital and labor, that will produce the same level of output.

MyEconLab Animation

Figure 11A.1

Isoquants

Isoquants show all the combinations of two inputs, in this case capital and labor, that will produce the same level of output. For example, the isoquant labeled $Q = 5,000$ shows all the combinations of ovens and workers that enable Jill to produce that quantity of pizzas per week. At point A, she produces 5,000 pizzas using 3 ovens and 6 workers, and at point B, she produces the same output using 2 ovens and 10 workers. With more ovens and workers, she can move to a higher isoquant. For example, with 4 ovens and 12 workers, she can produce at point C on the isoquant $Q = 10,000$. With even more ovens and workers, she could move to the isoquant $Q = 13,000$.

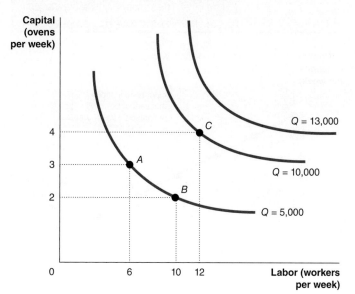

The Slope of an Isoquant

Marginal rate of technical substitution (*MRTS*) The rate at which a firm is able to substitute one input for another while keeping the level of output constant.

Remember that the slope of a curve is the ratio of the change in the variable on the vertical axis to the change in the variable on the horizontal axis. Along an isoquant, the slope tells us the rate at which a firm is able to substitute one input for another while keeping the level of output constant. This rate is called the **marginal rate of technical substitution (*MRTS*)**.

We expect that the *MRTS* will change as we move down an isoquant. In Figure 11A.1, at a point like A on isoquant Q = 5,000, the isoquant is relatively steep. As we move down the curve, it becomes less steep at a point like B. This shape is the usual one for isoquants: They are bowed in, or convex. The reason isoquants have this shape is that as we move down the curve, we continue to substitute labor for capital. As the firm produces the same quantity of output using less capital, the additional labor it needs increases because of diminishing returns. Remember from the chapter that, as a consequence of diminishing returns, for a given decline in capital, increasing amounts of labor are necessary to produce the same level of output. Because the *MRTS* is equal to the change in capital divided by the change in labor, it will become smaller (in absolute value) as we move down an isoquant. MyEconLab Concept Check

Isocost Lines

A firm wants to produce a given quantity of output at the lowest possible cost. We can show the relationship between the quantity of inputs used and the firm's total cost by using an *isocost* line. An **isocost line** shows all the combinations of two inputs, such as capital and labor, that have the same total cost.

Isocost line All the combinations of two inputs, such as capital and labor, that have the same total cost.

Graphing the Isocost Line

Suppose that Jill has $6,000 per week to spend on capital and labor. Suppose, to simplify the analysis, that Jill can rent pizza ovens by the week. The table in Figure 11A.2 shows the combinations of capital and labor available to her if the rental price of ovens is $1,000

MyEconLab Animation

Figure 11A.2

An Isocost Line

The isocost line shows the combinations of inputs with a total cost of $6,000. The rental price of ovens is $1,000 per week, so if Jill spends the whole $6,000 on ovens, she can rent 6 ovens (point A). The wage rate is $500 per week, so if Jill spends the whole $6,000 on workers, she can hire 12 workers (point G). As she moves down the isocost line, she gives up renting 1 oven for every 2 workers she hires. Any combination of inputs along the line or inside the line can be purchased with $6,000. Any combination that lies outside the line cannot be purchased with $6,000.

	Combinations of Workers and Ovens with a Total Cost of $6,000		
Point	Ovens	Workers	Total Cost
A	6	0	(6 x $1,000) + (0 x $500) = $6,000
B	5	2	(5 x $1,000) + (2 x $500) = $6,000
C	4	4	(4 x $1,000) + (4 x $500) = $6,000
D	3	6	(3 x $1,000) + (6 x $500) = $6,000
E	2	8	(2 x $1,000) + (8 x $500) = $6,000
F	1	10	(1 x $1,000) + (10 x $500) = $6,000
G	0	12	(0 x $1,000) + (12 x $500) = $6,000

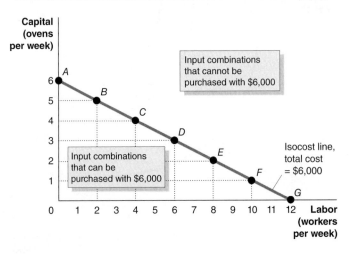

per week and the wage rate is $500 per week. The graph uses the data in the table to construct an isocost line. The isocost line intersects the vertical axis at the maximum number of ovens Jill can rent per week, which is shown by point *A*. The line intersects the horizontal axis at the maximum number of workers Jill can hire per week, which is point *G*. As Jill moves down the isocost line from point *A*, she gives up renting 1 oven for every 2 workers she hires. Any combination of inputs along the line or inside the line can be purchased with $6,000. Any combination that lies outside the line cannot be purchased because it would have a total cost to Jill of more than $6,000.   MyEconLab Concept Check

The Slope and Position of the Isocost Line

The slope of the isocost line is constant and equals the change in the quantity of ovens divided by the change in the quantity of workers. In this case, in moving from any point on the isocost line to any other point, the change in the quantity of ovens equals –1, and the change in the quantity of workers equals 2, so the slope equals –1/2. Notice that with a rental price of ovens of $1,000 per week and a wage rate for labor of $500 per week, the slope of the isocost line is equal to the ratio of the wage rate divided by the rental price of capital, multiplied by –1, or –$500/$1,000 = –1/2. In fact, this result will always hold, whatever inputs are involved and whatever their prices may be: *The slope of the isocost line is equal to the ratio of the price of the input on the horizontal axis divided by the price of the input on the vertical axis multiplied by –1.*

The position of the isocost line depends on the level of total cost. Higher levels of total cost shift the isocost line outward, and lower levels of total cost shift the isocost line inward. This can be seen in Figure 11A.3, which shows isocost lines for total costs of $3,000, $6,000, and $9,000. We have shown only three isocost lines in the graph, but there is, in fact, a different isocost line for each level of total cost.   MyEconLab Concept Check

Choosing the Cost-Minimizing Combination of Capital and Labor

Suppose Jill wants to produce 5,000 pizzas per week. Figure 11A.1 shows that there are many combinations of ovens and workers that will allow Jill to produce this level of output. There is only one combination of ovens and workers, however, that will allow her to produce 5,000 pizzas *at the lowest total cost*. Figure 11A.4 shows the isoquant $Q = 5,000$ along with three isocost lines. Point *B* is the lowest-cost combination of inputs shown in the graph, but this combination of 1 oven and 4 workers will produce fewer than the 5,000 pizzas needed. Points *C* and *D* are combinations of ovens and workers that will produce 5,000 pizzas, but their total cost is $9,000. The combination of 3 ovens and 6 workers at point *A* produces 5,000 pizzas at the lowest total cost of $6,000.

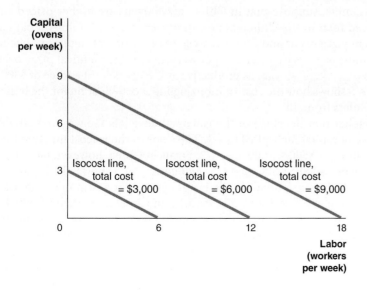

MyEconLab Animation

Figure 11A.3

The Position of the Isocost Line

The position of the isocost line depends on the level of total cost. As total cost increases from $3,000 to $6,000 to $9,000 per week, the isocost line shifts outward. For each isocost line shown, the rental price of ovens is $1,000 per week, and the wage rate is $500 per week.

Figure 11A.4

Choosing Capital and Labor to Minimize Total Cost

Jill wants to produce 5,000 pizzas per week at the lowest total cost. Point *B* is the lowest-cost combination of inputs shown in the graph, but this combination of 1 oven and 4 workers will produce fewer than the 5,000 pizzas needed. Points *C* and *D* are combinations of ovens and workers that will produce 5,000 pizzas, but their total cost is $9,000. The combination of 3 ovens and 6 workers at point *A* produces 5,000 pizzas at the lowest total cost of $6,000.

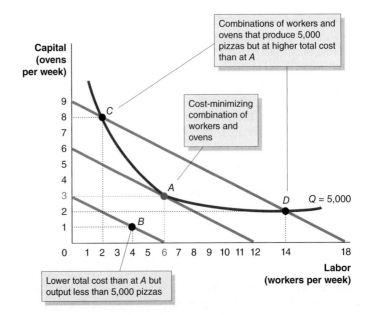

Figure 11A.4 shows that moving to an isocost line with a total cost of less than $6,000 would mean producing fewer than 5,000 pizzas. Being at any point along the isoquant $Q = 5,000$ other than point *A* would increase total cost above $6,000. In fact, the combination of inputs at point *A* is the only one on isoquant $Q = 5,000$ that has a total cost of $6,000. All other input combinations on this isoquant have higher total costs. Notice also that at point *A*, the isoquant and the isocost lines are tangent, so the slope of the isoquant is equal to the slope of the isocost line at that point.

Different Input Price Ratios Lead to Different Input Choices

Jill's cost-minimizing choice of 3 ovens and 6 workers is determined jointly by the technology available to her—as represented by her firm's isoquants—and by input prices—as represented by her firm's isocost lines. If the technology of making pizzas changes, perhaps because new ovens are developed, her isoquants will be affected, and her choice of inputs may change. If her isoquants remain unchanged but input prices change, then her choice of inputs may also change. This fact can explain why firms in different countries that face different input prices may produce the same good using different combinations of capital and labor, even though they have the same technology available.

For example, suppose that in China, pizza ovens are higher priced and labor is lower priced than in the United States. In our example, Jill Johnson pays $1,000 per week to rent pizza ovens and $500 per week to hire workers. Suppose a businessperson in China must pay a price of $1,500 per week to rent the identical pizza ovens but can hire Chinese workers who are as productive as U.S. workers at a wage of $300 per week. Figure 11A.5 shows how the cost-minimizing input combination for the businessperson in China differs from Jill's.

Remember that the slope of the isocost line equals the wage rate divided by the rental price of capital multiplied by –1. The slope of the isocost line that Jill and other U.S. firms face is –$500/$1,000, or –1/2. Firms in China, however, face an isocost line with a slope of –$300/$1,500, or –1/5. As Figure 11A.5 shows, the input combination at point *A*, which was optimal for Jill, is not optimal for a firm in China. Using the input combination at point *A* would cost a firm in China more than $6,000. Instead, the Chinese isocost line is tangent to the isoquant at point *B*, where the input combination is 2 ovens and 10 workers. This result makes sense: Because ovens cost more in China, but workers cost less, a Chinese firm will use fewer ovens and more workers than a U.S. firm, even if it has the same technology as the U.S. firm.

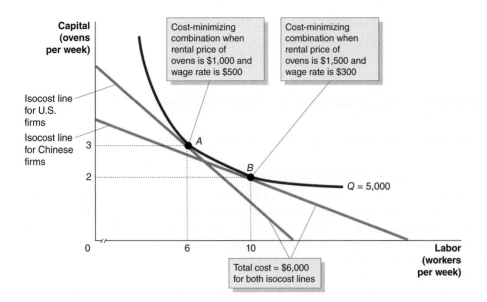

MyEconLab Animation

Figure 11A.5

Changing Input Prices Affects the Cost-Minimizing Input Choice

As the graph shows, the input combination at point *A*, which was optimal for Jill, is not optimal for a businessperson in China. Using the input combination at point *A* would cost businesspeople in China more than $6,000. Instead, the Chinese isocost line is tangent to the isoquant at point *B*, where the input combination is 2 ovens and 10 workers. Because ovens cost more in China but workers cost less, a Chinese firm will use fewer ovens and more workers than a U.S. firm, even if it has the same technology as the U.S. firm.

Making the Connection

The Changing Input Mix in Walt Disney Film Animation

The inputs used to make feature-length animated films have changed dramatically in the past 15 years. Prior to the early 1990s, the Walt Disney Company dominated the market for animated films. Disney's films were produced using hundreds of animators drawing most of the film by hand. Each film would contain as many as 170,000 individual drawings. Then, two developments dramatically affected how animated films are produced. First, in 1994, Disney had a huge hit with *The Lion King*, which cost only $50 million to produce but earned the company more than $1 billion in profit. As a result of this success, Disney and other film studios began to produce more animated films, increasing the demand for animators and more than doubling their salaries. The second development came in 1995, when Pixar Animation Studios released the film *Toy Story*. This was the first successful feature-length film produced using computers, with no hand-drawn animation. In the following years, technological advance continued to reduce the cost of the computers and software necessary to produce an animated film.

As a result of these two developments, the price of capital—computers and software—fell relative to the price of labor—animators. As the figure shows, the change in the price of computers relative to animators changed the slope of the isocost line and resulted in film studios now producing animated films using many more computers and many fewer animators than in the early 1990s. In 2006, Disney bought Pixar, and within a few years, all the major film studios had converted to computer animation, now

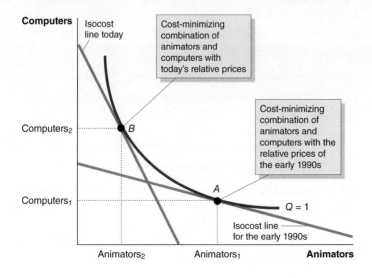

referred to as CGI animation, although a few hand-drawn films, such as Disney's film *Winnie the Pooh* released in 2011, continued to be produced.

Sources: "Magic Restored," *Economist*, April 17, 2008; and Laura M. Holson, "Disney Moves Away from Hand-Drawn Animation," *New York Times*, September 18, 2005.

MyEconLab Study Plan

Your Turn: Test your understanding by doing related problem 11A.6 on page 388 at the end of this appendix.

Another Look at Cost Minimization

We know that consumers maximize utility when they consume each good up to the point where the marginal utility per dollar spent is the same for every good. We can derive a very similar cost-minimization rule for firms. Remember that at the point of cost minimization, the isoquant and the isocost line are tangent, so they have the same slope. Therefore, *at the point of cost minimization, the marginal rate of technical substitution* (MRTS) *is equal to the wage rate divided by the rental price of capital.*

The slope of the isoquant tells us the rate at which a firm is able to substitute labor for capital, *keeping the level of output constant*. The slope of the isocost line tells us the rate at which a firm is able to substitute labor for capital, *given current input prices*. Only at the point of cost minimization are these two rates the same.

When we move from one point on an isoquant to another, we end up using more of one input and less of the other input, but the level of output remains the same. For example, as Jill moves down an isoquant, she uses fewer ovens and more workers but produces the same quantity of pizzas. In this chapter, we defined the *marginal product of labor* (MP_L) as the additional output produced by a firm as a result of hiring one more worker. Similarly, we can define the *marginal product of capital* (MP_K) as the additional output produced by a firm as a result of using one more machine. So, when Jill uses fewer ovens by moving down an isoquant, she loses output equal to:

$$-\text{Change in the quantity of ovens} \times MP_K.$$

But she uses more workers, so she gains output equal to:

$$\text{Change in the quantity of workers} \times MP_L.$$

We know that the gain in output from the additional workers is equal to the loss from the smaller quantity of ovens because total output remains the same along an isoquant. Therefore, we can write:

$$-\text{Change in the quantity of ovens} \times MP_K = \text{Change in the quantity of workers} \times MP_L.$$

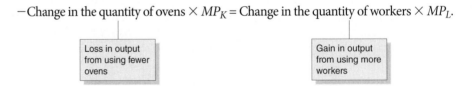

Loss in output from using fewer ovens

Gain in output from using more workers

If we rearrange terms, we have the following:

$$\frac{-\text{Change in the quantity of ovens}}{\text{Change in the quantity of workers}} = \frac{MP_L}{MP_K}.$$

Because

$$\frac{-\text{Change in the quantity of ovens}}{\text{Change in the quantity of workers}}$$

is the slope of the isoquant, it is equal to the marginal rate of technical substitution (multiplied by negative 1). So, we can write:

$$\frac{-\text{Change in the quantity of ovens}}{\text{Change in the quantity of workers}} = MRTS = \frac{MP_L}{MP_K}.$$

The slope of the isocost line equals the wage rate (w) divided by the rental price of capital (r). We saw earlier in this appendix that at the point of cost minimization, the *MRTS* equals the ratio of the prices of the two inputs. Therefore:

$$\frac{MP_L}{MP_K} = \frac{w}{r}.$$

We can rewrite this to show that at the point of cost minimization:

$$\frac{MP_L}{w} = \frac{MP_K}{r}.$$

This last expression tells us that to minimize cost for a given level of output, a firm should hire inputs up to the point where the last dollar spent on each input results in the same increase in output. If this equality did not hold, a firm could lower its costs by using more of one input and less of the other. For example, if the left side of the equation were greater than the right side, a firm could rent fewer ovens, hire more workers, and produce the same output at lower cost. MyEconLab Concept Check

Solved Problem 11A.1

MyEconLab Interactive Animation

Determining the Optimal Combination of Inputs

Consider the information in the following table for Jill Johnson's restaurant.

Marginal product of capital	3,000 pizzas per oven
Marginal product of labor	1,200 pizzas per worker
Wage rate	$300 per week
Rental price of ovens	$600 per week

Briefly explain whether Jill is minimizing costs. If she is not minimizing costs, explain whether she should rent more ovens and hire fewer workers or rent fewer ovens and hire more workers.

Solving the Problem

Step 1: Review the chapter material. This problem is about determining the optimal choice of inputs by comparing the ratios of the marginal products of inputs to their prices, so you may want to review the section "Another Look at Cost Minimization," which begins on page 384.

Step 2: Compute the ratios of marginal product to input price to determine whether Jill is minimizing costs. If Jill is minimizing costs, the following relationship should hold:

$$\frac{MP_L}{w} = \frac{MP_K}{r}.$$

In this case, we have

$$MP_L = 1,200$$
$$MP_K = 3,000$$
$$w = \$300$$
$$r = \$600.$$

So

$$\frac{MP_L}{w} = \frac{1,200}{\$300} = 4 \text{ pizzas per dollar, and } \frac{MP_K}{r} = \frac{3,000}{\$600} = 5 \text{ pizzas per dollar.}$$

Because the two ratios are not equal, Jill is not minimizing cost.

Step 3: Determine how Jill should change the mix of inputs she uses. Jill produces more pizzas per dollar from the last oven than from the last worker. This indicates that she has too many workers and too few ovens. Therefore, to minimize cost, Jill should use more ovens and hire fewer workers.

MyEconLab Study Plan

Your Turn: For more practice, do related problems 11A.7 and 11A.8 on page 388 at the end of this appendix.

Did new rules keep the Kansas City Chiefs from paying Eric Fisher too much?

Making the Connection

Do National Football League Teams Behave Efficiently?

In the National Football League (NFL), the "salary cap" is the maximum amount each team can spend in a year on salaries for football players. Each year's salary cap results from negotiations between the league and the union representing the players. To achieve efficiency, an NFL team should distribute salaries among players so as to maximize the level of output—in this case, winning football games—given the constant level of cost represented by the salary cap. (Notice that maximizing the level of output for a given level of cost is equivalent to minimizing cost for a given level of output. To see why, think about the situation in which an isocost line is tangent to an isoquant. At the point of tangency, the firm has simultaneously minimized the cost of producing the level of output represented by the isoquant and maximized the output produced at the level of cost represented by the isocost line.)

In distributing the fixed amount of salary payments available, teams should equalize the ratios of the marginal productivity of players, as represented by their contribution to winning games, to the salaries players receive. Just as a firm may not use a machine that has a very high marginal product if its rental price is very high, a football team may not want to hire a superstar player if the salary the team would need to pay is too high.

Economists Cade Massey, of the University of Pennsylvania, and Richard Thaler, of the University of Chicago, have analyzed whether NFL teams distribute their salaries efficiently. NFL teams obtain their players either by signing free agents—who are players whose contracts with other teams have expired—or by signing players chosen in the annual draft of eligible college players. The college draft consists of seven rounds, with the teams with the worst records the previous year choosing first. Massey and Thaler find that, in fact, NFL teams do not allocate salaries efficiently. In particular, the players chosen with the first few picks of the first round of the draft tend to be paid salaries that are much higher relative to their marginal products than are players taken later in the first round. A typical team with a high draft pick would increase its ability to win football games at the constant cost represented by the salary cap if it traded for lower draft picks, providing it could find another team willing to make the trade. Why do NFL teams apparently make the error of not efficiently distributing salaries? Massey and Thaler argue that general managers of NFL teams tend to be overconfident in their ability to forecast how well a college player is likely to perform in the NFL.

General managers of NFL teams are not alone in suffering from overconfidence. Studies have shown that, in general, people tend to overestimate their ability to forecast an uncertain outcome. Because NFL teams tend to overestimate the future marginal productivity of high draft picks, they pay them salaries that are inefficiently high compared to salaries other draft picks receive. NFL teams were aware that they were probably overpaying high draft picks. In 2011, they negotiated a new contract with the NFL Players Union that limited the salaries that drafted players could receive.

This example shows that the concepts developed in this chapter provide powerful tools for analyzing whether firms are operating efficiently.

Source: Cade Massey and Richard Thaler, "The Loser's Curse: Overconfidence vs. Market Efficiency in the National Football League draft," National Bureau of Economic Research Working Paper 11270, April 8, 2010.

MyEconLab Study Plan

Your Turn: Test your understanding by doing related problem 11A.14 on page 389 at the end of this appendix.

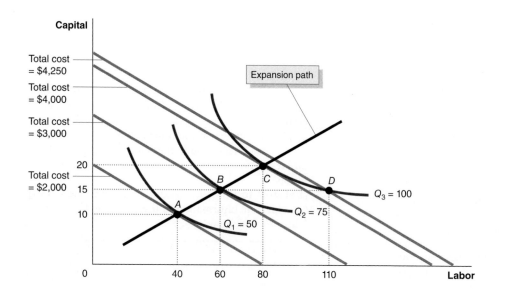

MyEconLab Animation

Figure 11A.6

The Expansion Path

The tangency points *A*, *B*, and *C* lie along the firm's expansion path, which is a curve that shows the cost-minimizing combination of inputs for every level of output. In the short run, when the quantity of machines is fixed, the firm can expand output from 75 bookcases per day to 100 bookcases per day at the lowest cost only by moving from point *B* to point *D* and increasing the number of workers from 60 to 110. In the long run, when it can increase the quantity of machines it uses, the firm can move from point *D* to point *C*, thereby reducing its total costs of producing 100 bookcases per day from $4,250 to $4,000.

The Expansion Path

We can use isoquants and isocost lines to examine what happens as a firm expands its level of output. Figure 11A.6 shows three isoquants for a firm that produces bookcases. The isocost lines are drawn under the assumption that the machines used in producing bookcases can be rented for $100 per day and the wage rate is $25 per day. The point where each isoquant is tangent to an isocost line determines the cost-minimizing combination of capital and labor for producing that level of output. For example, 10 machines and 40 workers is the cost-minimizing combination of inputs for producing 50 bookcases per day. The cost-minimizing points *A*, *B*, and *C* lie along the firm's **expansion path**, which is a curve that shows the cost-minimizing combination of inputs for every level of output.

An important point to note is that the expansion path represents the least-cost combination of inputs to produce a given level of output *in the long run*, when the firm is able to vary the levels of all of its inputs. We know, though, that in the short run, at least one input is fixed. We can use Figure 11A.6 to show that as the firm expands in the short run, its costs will be higher than in the long run. Suppose that the firm is currently at point *B*, using 15 machines and 60 workers to produce 75 bookcases per day. The firm wants to expand its output to 100 bookcases per day, but in the short run, it is unable to increase the quantity of machines it uses. Therefore, to expand output, it must hire more workers. The figure shows that in the short run, to produce 100 bookcases per day using 15 machines, the lowest costs it can attain are at point *D*, where it employs 110 workers. With a rental price of machines of $100 per day and a wage rate of $25 per day, in the short run, the firm will have total costs of $4,250 to produce 100 bookcases per day. In the long run, though, the firm can increase the number of machines it uses from 15 to 20 and reduce the number of workers from 110 to 80. This change allows it to move from point *D* to point *C* on its expansion path and to lower its total costs of producing 100 bookcases per day from $4,250 to $4,000. The firm's minimum total costs of production are lower in the long run than in the short run.   MyEconLab Concept Check

Expansion path A curve that shows a firm's cost-minimizing combination of inputs for every level of output.

MyEconLab Study Plan

Key Terms

11A | Using Isoquants and Isocost Lines to Understand Production and Cost, pages 379–387

LEARNING OBJECTIVE: Use isoquants and isocost lines to understand production and cost.

MyEconLab   Visit **www.myeconlab.com** to complete these exercises online and get instant feedback.

Review Questions

11A.1 What is an isoquant? What is the slope of an isoquant?

11A.2 What is an isocost line? What is the slope of an isocost line?

11A.3 How do firms choose the optimal combination of inputs?

Problems and Applications

11A.4 Draw an isoquant–isocost line graph to illustrate the following situation: Jill Johnson can rent pizza ovens for $400 per week and hire workers for $200 per week. She is currently using 5 ovens and 10 workers to produce 20,000 pizzas per week and has total costs of $4,000. Make sure to label your graph to show the cost-minimizing input combination and the maximum quantity of labor and capital she can use with total costs of $4,000.

11A.5 Use the following graph to answer the questions.

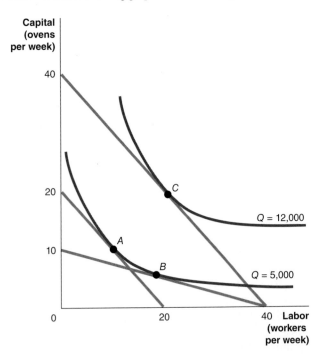

a. If the wage rate and the rental price of ovens are both $100 and total cost is $2,000, is the cost-minimizing point *A*, *B*, or *C*? Briefly explain.

b. If the wage rate is $25, the rental price of ovens is $100, and total cost is $1,000, is the cost-minimizing point *A*, *B*, or *C*? Briefly explain.

c. If the wage rate and the rental price of ovens are both $100 and total cost is $4,000, is the cost-minimizing point *A*, *B*, or *C*? Briefly explain.

11A.6 **[Related to the** Making the Connection **on page 383]** During the eighteenth century, the American colonies had much more land per farmer than did Europe. As a result, the price of labor in the colonies was much higher relative to the price of land than it was in Europe. Assume that Europe and the colonies had access to the same technology for producing food. Use an isoquant–isocost line graph to illustrate why the combination of land and labor used in producing food in the colonies would have been different from the combination used to produce food in Europe.

11A.7 **[Related to** Solved Problem 11A.1 **on page 385]** Consider the information in the following table for Jill Johnson's restaurant:

Marginal product of capital	4,000
Marginal product of labor	100
Wage rate	$10
Rental price of pizza ovens	$500

Briefly explain whether Jill is minimizing costs. If she is not minimizing costs, explain whether she should rent more ovens and hire fewer workers or rent fewer ovens and hire more workers.

11A.8 **[Related to** Solved Problem 11A.1 **on page 385]** Draw an isoquant–isocost line graph to illustrate the following situation: Jill Johnson can rent pizza ovens for $200 per week and hire workers for $100 per week. Currently, she is using 5 ovens and 10 workers to produce 20,000 pizzas per week and has total costs of $2,000. Jill's marginal rate of technical substitution (*MRTS*) equals −1. Explain why this means that she's not minimizing costs and what she could do to minimize costs.

11A.9 Draw an isoquant–isocost line graph to illustrate the following situation and the change that occurs: Jill Johnson can rent pizza ovens for $2,000 per week and hire workers for $1,000 per week. Currently, she is using 5 ovens and 10 workers to produce 20,000 pizzas per week and has total costs of $20,000. Then Jill reorganizes the way things are done in her business and achieves positive technological change.

11A.10 Use the following graph to answer the following questions about Jill Johnson's isoquant curve.

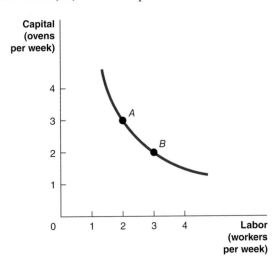

a. Which combination of inputs yields more output: combination *A* (3 ovens and 2 workers) or combination *B* (2 ovens and 3 workers)?

b. What will determine whether Jill selects *A*, *B*, or some other point along this isoquant curve?

c. Is the marginal rate of technical substitution (*MRTS*) greater at point *A* or point *B*?

11A.11 Draw an isoquant–isocost line graph to illustrate the following situation: Jill Johnson can rent pizza ovens for $2,000 per week and hire workers for $1,000 per week. She can minimize the cost of producing 20,000 pizzas per week by using 5 ovens and 10 workers, at a total cost of $20,000. She can minimize the cost of producing 45,000 pizzas per week by using 10 ovens and 20 workers, at a total cost of $40,000. She can minimize the cost of producing 60,000 pizzas per week by using 15 ovens and 30 workers, at a total cost of $60,000. Draw Jill's long-run average cost curve and discuss its economies of scale and diseconomies of scale.

11A.12 In Brazil, a grove of oranges is picked using 20 workers, ladders, and baskets. In Florida, a grove of oranges is picked using 1 worker and a machine that shakes the oranges off the trees and scoops up the fallen oranges. Using an isoquant–isocost line graph, illustrate why these two different methods are used to pick the same number of oranges per day in these two locations.

11A.13 Jill Johnson is minimizing the costs of producing pizzas. The rental price of one of her ovens is $2,000 per week, and the wage rate is $600 per week. The marginal product of capital in her business is 12,000 pizzas. What must be the marginal product of her workers?

11A.14 **[Related to the** Making the Connection **on page 386]** If Cade Massey and Richard Thaler are correct, should the team that has the first pick in the draft keep the pick or trade it to another team for a lower pick? Briefly explain. Does the 2011 agreement that limits the salaries of drafted players affect your answer?

11A.15 Swift Ellis, Inc. manufactures running shoes. The following graph illustrates the combination of capital and labor (point *A*) that minimizes the firm's cost of producing 5,000 pairs of shoes. Suppose both the wage rate and the rental price of machinery doubles.

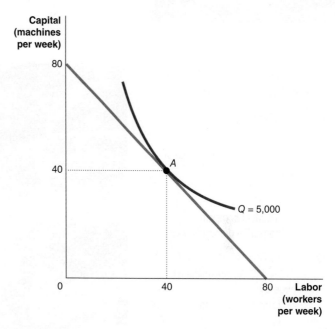

a. Draw a new isocost line to reflect this change in the wage rate and rental price of machinery.

b. Draw a new isoquant to show the combination of capital and labor that minimizes total cost given the increase in input prices. Label this combination point *B*.

c. Comparing point *A* to point *B*, can we be sure that at point *B* the firm will be using more or less labor? More or less capital? Briefly explain.

Firms in Perfectly Competitive Markets

Chapter Outline and Learning Objectives

Perfect Competition in Farmers' Markets

In recent years, the demand for healthier foods has increased. For example, sales of organically grown food have increased at a rate of 20 percent per year. Because farmers' markets typically offer a wide selection of organically grown food, many people have begun buying their fruits and vegetables there. At these markets, local farmers come together at a fairground, a city plaza, or some other open space to sell their products directly to consumers. Many customers are like Tracy Stuntz, who shops at a farmers' market in Fresno, California: "My husband and I prefer to eat … organically …. The farmer's market has … produce you don't see [in] other places." Farmers hope that by selling in farmers' markets they can receive higher prices from consumers than they would receive from selling their produce to supermarkets.

In the United States, higher prices and higher profits led to a dramatic increase in the number of farmers' markets, from 1,774 in 1994 to 7,864 in 2012. More markets, though, means more competition for farmers selling their produce. The competition has forced down prices and reduced farmers' profits. As one farmer explained: "You have a certain amount of demand, and the more you spread out the demand, you're making less." Many farmers have found that the profits they earn from selling their produce in farmers' markets are no longer higher than what they earn selling to supermarkets.

The process of new firms entering a profitable market and driving down prices and profits is not unique to agriculture. Throughout the economy, entrepreneurs are continually introducing new products or new ways of selling products, which—when successful—enable them to earn economic profits in the short run. But in the long run, competition among firms forces prices to the level where they just cover the costs of production. This process of competition is at the heart of the market system and is the focus of this chapter.

Sources: Tracie Cone, "USDA: Number of Farmers Markets Up Due to Demand," *Associated Press*, August 3, 2012; Katie Zezima, "As Farmers' Markets Go Mainstream, Some Fear a Glut," *New York Times*, August 20, 2011; and United States Department of Agriculture, *Farmers Market Growth: 1994–2012*, August 3, 2012.

Economics in Your Life

Are You an Entrepreneur?

Were you an entrepreneur during your high school years? Perhaps you didn't have your own store, but you may have worked as a babysitter, or perhaps you mowed lawns for families in your neighborhood. While you may not think of these jobs as being small businesses, that is exactly what they are. How did you decide what price to charge for your services? You may have wanted to charge $25 per hour to babysit or mow lawns, but you probably charged much less. As you read the chapter, think about the competitive situation you faced as a teenage entrepreneur and try to determine why the prices received by most people who babysit and mow lawns are so low. You can check your answers against those we provide on **page 415** at the end of this chapter.

Farmers' markets are an example of a *perfectly competitive* industry. Firms in perfectly competitive industries are unable to control the prices of the products they sell and are unable to earn an economic profit in the long run for two main reasons: Firms in these industries sell identical products, and it is easy for new firms to enter these industries. Studying how perfectly competitive industries operate is the best way to understand how markets answer the fundamental economic questions discussed in Chapter 1:

- What goods and services will be produced?
- How will the goods and services be produced?
- Who will receive the goods and services produced?

In fact, though, most industries are not perfectly competitive. In most industries, firms do *not* produce identical products, and in some industries, it may be difficult for new firms to enter. There are thousands of industries in the United States. Although in some ways each industry is unique, industries share enough similarities that economists group them into four market structures. In particular, any industry has three key characteristics:

1. The number of firms in the industry
2. The similarity of the good or service produced by the firms in the industry
3. The ease with which new firms can enter the industry

Economists use these characteristics to classify industries into the four market structures listed in Table 12.1.

Many industries, including restaurants, clothing stores, and other retailers, have a large number of firms selling products that are differentiated, rather than identical, and fall into the category of *monopolistic competition*. Some industries, such as computers and automobiles, have only a few firms and are *oligopolies*. Finally, a few industries, such as the delivery of first-class mail by the U.S. Postal Service, have only one firm and are *monopolies*. After discussing perfect competition in this chapter, we will devote a chapter to each of these other market structures.

Table 12.1

The Four Market Structures

	Market Structure			
Characteristic	Perfect Competition	Monopolistic Competition	Oligopoly	Monopoly
Number of firms	Many	Many	Few	One
Type of product	Identical	Differentiated	Identical or differentiated	Unique
Ease of entry	High	High	Low	Entry blocked
Examples of industries	• Growing wheat • Growing apples	• Clothing stores • Restaurants	• Manufacturing computers • Manufacturing automobiles	• First-class mail delivery • Tap water

Perfectly Competitive Markets

Why are firms in a **perfectly competitive market** unable to control the prices of the goods they sell, and why are the owners of these firms unable to earn economic profits in the long run? We can begin our analysis by listing the three conditions that make a market perfectly competitive:

1. There must be many buyers and many firms, all of which are small relative to the market.
2. All firms in the market must sell identical products.
3. There must be no barriers to new firms entering the market.

All three of these conditions hold in markets for agricultural products. For example, no single consumer or producer of apples buys or sells more than a tiny fraction of the total apple crop. The apples sold by each apple grower are identical, and there are no barriers to a new firm entering the apple market by purchasing land and planting apple trees. As we will see, it is the existence of many firms, all selling the same good, that keeps any single apple farmer from affecting the price of apples.

Although the market for apples meets the conditions for perfect competition, the markets for most goods and services do not. In particular, the second and third conditions are very restrictive. In most markets that have many buyers and sellers, firms do not sell identical products. For example, not all restaurant meals are the same, nor is all women's clothing the same. In later chapters, we will explore the common situation of monopolistic competition where many firms are selling similar but not identical products, and we will analyze industries that are oligopolies or monopolies, where it is difficult for new firms to enter. In this chapter, we concentrate on perfectly competitive markets so we can use them as a benchmark to analyze how firms behave when they face the maximum possible competition.

A Perfectly Competitive Firm Cannot Affect the Market Price

Prices in perfectly competitive markets are determined by the interaction of demand and supply for the good or service. The actions of any single consumer or any single firm have no effect on the market price. Consumers and firms have to accept the market price if they want to buy and sell in a perfectly competitive market.

Because a firm in a perfectly competitive market is very small relative to the market and because it is selling exactly the same product as every other firm, it can sell as much as it wants without having to lower its price. If a perfectly competitive firm tries to raise its price, it won't sell anything at all because consumers will switch to buying the product from the firm's competitors. Therefore, the firm will be a **price taker** and will have to charge the same price as every other firm in the market. Although we don't usually think of firms as being too small to affect the market price, consumers are often in the position of being price takers. For instance, suppose your local supermarket is selling bread for $2.50 per loaf. You can load up your shopping cart with 10 loaves of bread, and the supermarket will gladly sell them all to you for $2.50 per loaf. But if you go to the cashier and offer to buy the bread for $2.49 per loaf, he or she will not sell it to you at that price. As a buyer, you are too small relative to the bread market to have any effect on the equilibrium price. Whether you leave the supermarket and buy no bread or you buy 10 loaves, you are unable to change the market price of bread by even 1 cent.

The situation you face as a bread buyer is the same one a wheat farmer faces as a wheat seller. In 2013, about 150,000 farmers grew wheat in the United States. The market price of wheat is determined not by any individual wheat farmer but by the interaction of all the buyers and all the sellers in the wheat market. If any one wheat farmer has the best crop the farmer has ever had, or if any one wheat farmer stops growing wheat altogether, the market price of wheat will not be affected *because the market supply curve for wheat will not shift enough to change the equilibrium price by even 1 cent.* MyEconLab Concept Check

12.1 LEARNING OBJECTIVE

Explain what a perfectly competitive market is and why a perfect competitor faces a horizontal demand curve.

Perfectly competitive market A market that meets the conditions of (1) many buyers and sellers, (2) all firms selling identical products, and (3) no barriers to new firms entering the market.

Price taker A buyer or seller that is unable to affect the market price.

Figure 12.1

A Perfectly Competitive Firm Faces a Horizontal Demand Curve

A firm in a perfectly competitive market is selling exactly the same product as many other firms. Therefore, it can sell as much as it wants at the current market price, but it cannot sell anything at all if it raises the price by even 1 cent. As a result, the demand curve for a perfectly competitive firm's output is a horizontal line. In the figure, whether the wheat farmer sells 6,000 bushels per year or 15,000 bushels has no effect on the market price of $7.

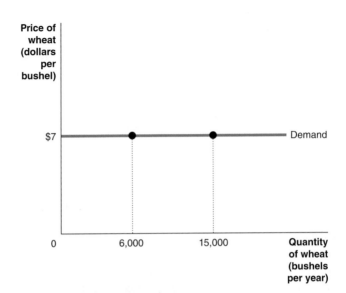

The Demand Curve for the Output of a Perfectly Competitive Firm

Suppose Bill Parker grows wheat on a 250-acre farm in Washington State. Farmer Parker is selling wheat in a perfectly competitive market, so he is a price taker. Because he can sell as much wheat as he chooses at the market price—but can't sell any wheat at all at a higher price—the demand curve for his wheat has an unusual shape: It is horizontal, as shown in Figure 12.1. With a horizontal demand curve, Farmer Parker must accept the market price, which in this case is $7 per bushel. Whether Farmer Parker sells 6,000 bushels per year or 15,000 has no effect on the market price.

The demand curve for Farmer Parker's wheat is very different from the market demand curve for wheat. Panel (a) of Figure 12.2 shows the market for wheat. The demand curve in panel (a) is the *market demand curve for wheat* and has the normal downward slope we are familiar with from the market demand curves in Chapter 3. Panel (b) of Figure 12.2 shows the demand curve for Farmer Parker's wheat, which is a horizontal line. By viewing these graphs side by side, you can see that the price Farmer Parker receives for his wheat in panel (b) is determined by the interaction of

Don't Let This Happen to You

Don't Confuse the Demand Curve for Farmer Parker's Wheat with the Market Demand Curve for Wheat

The demand curve for wheat has the normal downward-sloping shape. If the price of wheat goes up, the quantity of wheat demanded goes down, and if the price of wheat goes down, the quantity of wheat demanded goes up. But the demand curve for the output of a single wheat farmer is *not* downward sloping: It is a horizontal line. If an individual wheat farmer tries to increase the price he charges for his wheat, the quantity demanded falls to zero because buyers will purchase from one of the other 150,000 wheat farmers. But any one farmer can sell as much wheat as the farmer can produce without needing to cut the price. Both of these features of this market hold because each

wheat farmer is very small relative to the overall market for wheat.

When we draw graphs of the wheat market, we usually show the market equilibrium quantity in millions or billions of bushels. When we draw graphs of the demand for wheat produced by one farmer, we usually show the quantity produced in smaller units, such as thousands of bushels. It is important to remember this difference in scale when interpreting these graphs.

Finally, it is not just wheat farmers who have horizontal demand curves for their products; any firm in a perfectly competitive market faces a horizontal demand curve.

Your Turn: Test your understanding by doing related problem 1.6 on page 416 at the end of this chapter.

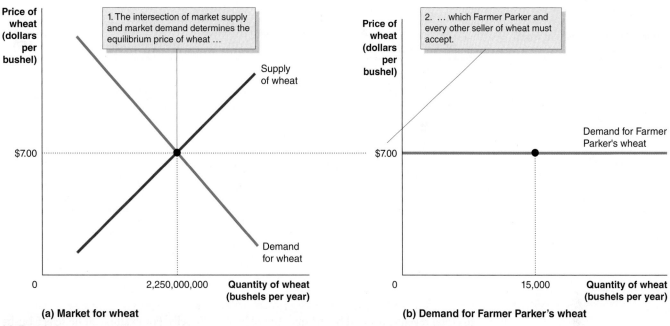

Figure 12.2   The Market Demand for Wheat versus the Demand for One Farmer's Wheat

In a perfectly competitive market, price is determined by the intersection of market demand and market supply. In panel (a), the demand and supply curves for wheat intersect at a price of $7 per bushel. An individual wheat farmer like Farmer Parker cannot affect the market price for wheat. Therefore, as panel (b) shows, the demand curve for Farmer Parker's wheat is a horizontal line. To understand this figure, it is important to notice that the scales on the horizontal axes in the two panels are very different. In panel (a), the equilibrium quantity of wheat is 2.25 *billion* bushels, and in panel (b), Farmer Parker is producing only 15,000 bushels of wheat.

all sellers and all buyers of wheat in the wheat market in panel (a). Notice, however, that the scales on the horizontal axes in the two panels are very different. In panel (a), the equilibrium quantity of wheat is 2.25 *billion* bushels. In panel (b), Farmer Parker is producing only 15,000 bushels, or less than 0.001 percent of market output. We need to use different scales in the two panels so we can display both of them on one page. Keep in mind this key point: Farmer Parker's output of wheat is very small relative to the total market output.

MyEconLab Concept Check

How a Firm Maximizes Profit in a Perfectly Competitive Market

We have seen that Farmer Parker cannot control the price of his wheat. In this situation, how does he decide how much wheat to produce? We assume that Farmer Parker's objective is to maximize profit. This assumption is reasonable for most firms, most of the time. Remember that **profit** is the difference between total revenue (TR) and total cost (TC):

$$\text{Profit} = TR - TC.$$

To maximize his profit, Farmer Parker should produce the quantity of wheat where the difference between the total revenue he receives and his total cost is as large as possible.

Revenue for a Firm in a Perfectly Competitive Market

To understand how Farmer Parker maximizes profit, let's first consider his revenue. To keep the numbers simple, we will assume that he owns a very small farm and produces at most 10 bushels of wheat per year. Table 12.2 shows the revenue Farmer Parker will earn from selling various quantities of wheat if the market price for wheat is $7.

The third column in Table 12.2 shows that Farmer Parker's *total revenue* rises by $7 for every additional bushel he sells because he can sell as many bushels as he wants at the market price of $7 per bushel. The fourth and fifth columns in the table show Farmer Parker's *average revenue* and *marginal revenue* from selling wheat. His **average revenue (AR)** equals

---

MyEconLab Study Plan

12.2 LEARNING OBJECTIVE

Explain how a firm maximizes profit in a perfectly competitive market.

Profit Total revenue minus total cost.

Average revenue (AR) Total revenue divided by the quantity of the product sold.

	(1) Number of Bushels (Q)	(2) Market Price (per bushel) (P)	(3) Total Revenue (TR)	(4) Average Revenue (AR)	(5) Marginal Revenue (MR)
Table 12.2	0	$7	$0	—	—
Farmer Parker's Revenue from Wheat Farming	1	7	7	$7	$7
	2	7	14	7	7
	3	7	21	7	7
	4	7	28	7	7
	5	7	35	7	7
	6	7	42	7	7
	7	7	49	7	7
	8	7	56	7	7
	9	7	63	7	7
	10	7	70	7	7

his total revenue divided by the quantity of bushels he sells. For example, if he sells 5 bushels for a total of $35, his average revenue is $35/5 = $7. Notice that his average revenue is also equal to the market price of $7. In fact, for any level of output, a firm's average revenue is always equal to the market price. This equality holds because total revenue equals price times quantity ($TR = P \times Q$), and average revenue equals total revenue divided by quantity ($AR = TR/Q$). So, $AR = TR/Q = (P \times Q)/Q = P$.

Farmer Parker's **marginal revenue** (**MR**) is the change in his total revenue from selling one more bushel:

Marginal revenue (MR) The change in total revenue from selling one more unit of a product.

$$\text{Marginal revenue} = \frac{\text{Change in total revenue}}{\text{Change in quantity}}, \text{ or } MR = \frac{\Delta TR}{\Delta Q}.$$

Each additional bushel Farmer Parker sells always adds $7 to his total revenue, so his marginal revenue is $7. Farmer Parker's marginal revenue is $7 per bushel because he is selling wheat in a perfectly competitive market and can sell as much as he wants at the market price. In fact, Farmer Parker's marginal revenue and average revenue are both equal to the market price. This is an important point: *For a firm in a perfectly competitive market, price is equal to both average revenue and marginal revenue.*

MyEconLab Concept Check

Determining the Profit-Maximizing Level of Output

To determine how Farmer Parker can maximize profit, we have to consider his costs as well as his revenue. A wheat farmer has many costs, including the cost of seed and fertilizer, as well as the wages of farm workers. In Table 12.3, we bring together the revenue data from Table 12.2 with cost data for Farmer Parker's farm. Recall that a firm's *marginal cost* is the increase in total cost resulting from producing another unit of output.

We calculate profit in the fourth column by subtracting total cost in the third column from total revenue in the second column. The fourth column shows that as long as Farmer Parker produces between 3 and 9 bushels of wheat, he will earn a profit. His maximum profit is $13.50, which he will earn by producing 7 bushels of wheat. Because Farmer Parker wants to maximize his profit, we would expect him to produce 7 bushels of wheat. Producing more than 7 bushels reduces his profit. For example, if he produces 8 bushels of wheat, his profit will decline from $13.50 to $11.50. The values for marginal cost given in the last column of the table help us understand why Farmer Parker's profits will decline if he produces more than 7 bushels of wheat: After the seventh bushel of wheat, rising marginal cost causes Farmer Parker's profits to decline.

In fact, comparing the marginal cost and marginal revenue at each level of output is an alternative method of calculating Farmer Parker's profit. We illustrate the two

Table 12.3

Farmer Parker's Profit from Wheat Farming

(1) Quantity (bushels) (Q)	(2) Total Revenue (TR)	(3) Total Cost (TC)	(4) Profit ($TR - TC$)	(5) Marginal Revenue (MR)	(6) Marginal Cost (MC)
0	$0.00	$10.00	−$10.00	—	—
1	7.00	14.00	−7.00	$7.00	$4.00
2	14.00	16.50	−2.50	7.00	2.50
3	21.00	18.50	2.50	7.00	2.00
4	28.00	21.00	7.00	7.00	2.50
5	35.00	24.50	10.50	7.00	3.50
6	42.00	29.00	13.00	7.00	4.50
7	49.00	35.50	13.50	7.00	6.50
8	56.00	44.50	11.50	7.00	9.00
9	63.00	56.50	6.50	7.00	12.00
10	70.00	72.00	−2.00	7.00	15.50

methods of calculating profit in Figure 12.3. We show the total revenue and total cost approach in panel (a) and the marginal revenue and marginal cost approach in panel (b). Total revenue is a straight line on the graph in panel (a) because total revenue increases at a constant rate of $7 for each additional bushel sold. Farmer Parker's profit is maximized when the vertical distance between the line representing total revenue and the total cost curve is as large as possible. Just as we saw in Table 12.3, his maximum profit occurs at an output of 7 bushels.

The last two columns of Table 12.3 show the marginal revenue (MR) Farmer Parker receives from selling another bushel of wheat and his marginal cost (MC) of producing another bushel of wheat. Panel (b) of Figure 12.3 is a graph of Farmer Parker's marginal revenue and marginal cost. Because marginal revenue is always equal to $7, it is

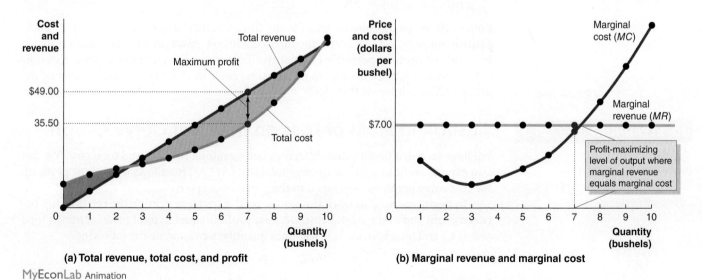

(a) Total revenue, total cost, and profit   (b) Marginal revenue and marginal cost

MyEconLab Animation

Figure 12.3   **The Profit-Maximizing Level of Output**

In panel (a), Farmer Parker maximizes his profit where the vertical distance between total revenue and total cost is the largest, which occurs at an output of 7 bushels. Panel (b) shows that Farmer Parker's marginal revenue (MR) is equal to a constant $7 per bushel. Farmer Parker maximizes profit by producing wheat up to the point where the marginal revenue of the last bushel produced is equal to its marginal cost, or $MR = MC$. In this case, at no level of output

does marginal revenue exactly equal marginal cost. The closest Farmer Parker can come is to produce 7 bushels of wheat. He will not want to continue to produce once marginal cost is greater than marginal revenue because that would reduce his profits. Panels (a) and (b) show alternative ways of thinking about how Farmer Parker can determine the profit-maximizing quantity of wheat to produce.

a horizontal line at the market price. We have already seen that the demand curve for a perfectly competitive firm is also a horizontal line at the market price. *Therefore, the marginal revenue curve for a perfectly competitive firm is the same as its demand curve.* Farmer Parker's marginal cost of producing wheat first falls and then rises, following the usual pattern we discussed in the previous chapter.

We know from panel (a) that profit is at a maximum at 7 bushels of wheat. In panel (b), profit is also at a maximum at 7 bushels of wheat. To understand why profit is maximized at the level of output where marginal revenue equals marginal cost, remember a key economic principle: *Optimal decisions are made at the margin.* Firms use this principle to decide the quantity of a good to produce. For example, in deciding how much wheat to produce, Farmer Parker needs to compare the marginal revenue he earns from selling another bushel of wheat to the marginal cost of producing that bushel. The difference between the marginal revenue and the marginal cost is the additional profit (or loss) from producing one more bushel. As long as marginal revenue is greater than marginal cost, Farmer Parker's profits are increasing, and he will want to expand production. For example, he will not stop producing at 6 bushels of wheat because producing and selling the seventh bushel adds $7.00 to his revenue but only $6.50 to his cost, so his profit increases by $0.50. He wants to continue producing until the marginal revenue he receives from selling another bushel is equal to the marginal cost of producing it. At that level of output, he will make no *additional* profit by selling another bushel, so he will have maximized his profit.

By inspecting Table 12.3 on page 397, we can see that there is no level of output at which marginal revenue exactly equals marginal cost. The closest Farmer Parker can come is to produce 7 bushels of wheat. He will not want to produce additional wheat once marginal cost is greater than marginal revenue because that would reduce his profits. For example, the eighth bushel of wheat adds $9.00 to his cost but only $7.00 to his revenue, so producing the eighth bushel *reduces* his profit by $2.00.

From the information in Table 12.3 and Figure 12.3, we can draw the following conclusions:

1. The profit-maximizing level of output is where the difference between total revenue and total cost is the greatest.

2. The profit-maximizing level of output is also where marginal revenue equals marginal cost, or $MR = MC$.

Both of these conclusions are true for any firm, whether or not it is in a perfectly competitive industry. We can draw one other conclusion about profit maximization that is true only of firms in perfectly competitive industries: For a firm in a perfectly competitive industry, price is equal to marginal revenue, or $P = MR$. So we can restate the $MR = MC$ condition as $P = MC$.

MyEconLab Study Plan   MyEconLab Concept Check

12.3 LEARNING OBJECTIVE

Illustrating Profit or Loss on the Cost Curve Graph

Use graphs to show a firm's profit or loss.

We have seen that profit is the difference between total revenue and total cost. We can also express profit in terms of *average total cost* (*ATC*). This allows us to show profit on the cost curve graph we developed in the previous chapter.

To begin, we need to work through several steps to determine the relationship between profit and average total cost. Because profit is equal to total revenue minus total cost (*TC*) and total revenue is price times quantity, we can write the following:

$$\text{Profit} = (P \times Q) - TC.$$

If we divide both sides of this equation by Q, we have

$$\frac{\text{Profit}}{Q} = \frac{(P \times Q)}{Q} - \frac{TC}{Q}$$

or

$$\frac{\text{Profit}}{Q} = P - ATC,$$

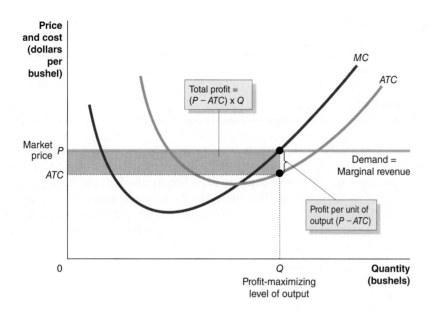

MyEconLab Animation

Figure 12.4

The Area of Maximum Profit

A firm maximizes profit at the level of output at which marginal revenue equals marginal cost. The difference between price and average total cost equals profit per unit of output. Total profit equals profit per unit multiplied by the number of units produced. Total profit is represented by the area of the green-shaded rectangle, which has a height equal to $(P − ATC)$ and a width equal to Q.

because TC/Q equals ATC. This equation tells us that profit per unit (or average profit) equals price minus average total cost. Finally, we obtain the equation for the relationship between total profit and average total cost by multiplying by Q:

$$\text{Profit} = (P − ATC) \times Q.$$

This equation tells us that a firm's total profit is equal to the difference between price and average total cost multiplied by the quantity produced.

Showing a Profit on the Graph

Figure 12.4 shows the relationship between a firm's average total cost and its marginal cost that we discussed in the previous chapter. In this figure, we also show the firm's marginal revenue curve (which is the same as its demand curve) and the area representing total profit. Using the relationship between profit and average total cost that we just determined, we can say that the area representing total profit has a height equal to $(P − ATC)$ and a base equal to Q. This area is shown by the green-shaded rectangle.   MyEconLab Concept Check

Solved Problem 12.3

MyEconLab Interactive Animation

Determining Profit-Maximizing Price and Quantity

Suppose that Andy sells basketballs in the perfectly competitive basketball market. His output per day and his costs are as follows:

Output per Day	Total Cost
0	$10.00
1	20.50
2	24.50
3	28.50
4	34.00
5	43.00
6	55.50
7	72.00
8	93.00
9	119.00

a. Suppose the current equilibrium price in the basketball market is $12.50. To maximize profit, how many basketballs will Andy produce, what price will he charge, and how much profit (or loss) will he make? Draw a graph to illustrate your answer. Your graph should be labeled clearly and should include Andy's demand, ATC, AVC, MC, and MR curves; the price he is charging; the quantity he is producing; and the area representing his profit (or loss).

b. Suppose the equilibrium price of basketballs falls to $6.00. Now how many basketballs will Andy produce, what price will he charge, and how much profit (or loss) will he make? Draw a graph to illustrate this situation, using the instructions in part (a).

Solving the Problem

Step 1:   Review the chapter material. This problem is about using cost curve graphs to analyze perfectly competitive firms, so you may want to review the section "Illustrating Profit or Loss on the Cost Curve Graph," which begins on page 398.

Step 2:   Calculate Andy's marginal cost, average total cost, and average variable cost. To maximize profit, Andy will produce the level of output where marginal revenue is equal to marginal cost. We can calculate marginal cost from the information given in the following table. We can also calculate average total cost and average variable cost in order to draw the required graph. Average total cost (ATC) equals total cost (TC) divided by the level of output (Q). Average variable cost (AVC) equals variable cost (VC) divided by output (Q). To calculate variable cost, recall that total cost equals variable cost plus fixed cost. When output equals zero, total cost equals fixed cost. In this case, fixed cost equals $10.00.

Output per Day (Q)	Total Cost (TC)	Fixed Cost (FC)	Variable Cost (VC)	Average Total Cost (ATC)	Average Variable Cost (AVC)	Marginal Cost (MC)
0	$10.00	$10.00	$0.00	—	—	—
1	20.50	10.00	10.50	$20.50	$10.50	$10.50
2	24.50	10.00	14.50	12.25	7.25	4.00
3	28.00	10.00	18.00	9.33	6.00	3.50
4	34.00	10.00	24.00	8.50	6.00	6.00
5	43.00	10.00	33.00	8.60	6.60	9.00
6	55.50	10.00	45.50	9.25	7.58	12.50
7	72.00	10.00	62.00	10.29	8.86	16.50
8	93.00	10.00	83.00	11.63	10.38	21.00
9	119.00	10.00	109.00	13.22	12.11	26.00

Step 3:   Use the information from the table in Step 2 to calculate how many basketballs Andy will produce, what price he will charge, and how much profit he will earn if the market price of basketballs is $12.50. Andy's marginal revenue is equal to the market price of $12.50. Marginal revenue equals marginal cost when Andy produces 6 basketballs per day. So, Andy will produce 6 basketballs per day and charge a price of $12.50 per basketball. Andy's profit is equal to his total revenue minus his total costs. His total revenue equals the 6 basketballs he sells multiplied by the $12.50 price, or $75.00. So, his profit equals: $75.00 − $55.50 = $19.50.

Step 4:   Use the information from the table in Step 2 to illustrate your answer to part (a) with a graph.

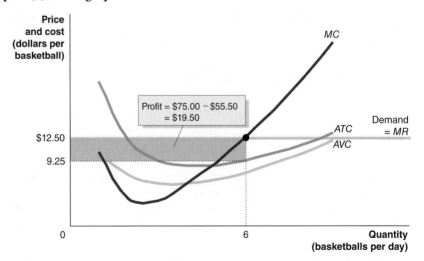

Step 5: **Calculate how many basketballs Andy will produce, what price he will charge, and how much profit he will earn when the market price of basketballs is $6.00.** Referring to the table in Step 2, we can see that marginal revenue equals marginal cost when Andy produces 4 basketballs per day. He charges the market price of $6.00 per basketball. His total revenue is only $24.00, while his total costs are $34.00, so he will have a loss of $10.00. (Can we be sure that Andy will continue to produce even though he is operating at a loss? We answer this question in the next section.)

Step 6: **Illustrate your answer to part (b) with a graph.**

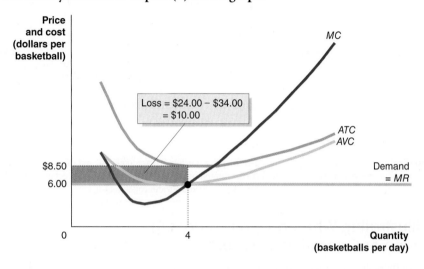

Your Turn: For more practice, do related problems 3.3 and 3.4 on pages 417–418 at the end of this chapter.

MyEconLab Study Plan

Don't Let This Happen to You

Remember That Firms Maximize Their Total Profit, Not Their Profit per Unit

A student examines the following graph and argues: "I believe that a firm will want to produce at Q_1, not Q_2. At Q_1, the distance between price and average total cost is the greatest. So at Q_1, the firm will be maximizing its profit per unit." Briefly explain whether you agree with the student's argument.

The student's argument is incorrect because firms are interested in maximizing their *total* profit, not their profit per unit. We know that profit is not maximized at Q_1 because at that level of output, marginal revenue is greater than marginal cost. A firm can always increase its profit by producing any unit that adds more to its revenue than it does to its costs. Only when the firm has expanded production to Q_2 will it have produced every unit for which marginal revenue is greater than marginal cost. At that level of output, it will have maximized profit.

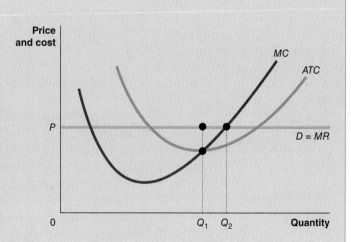

MyEconLab Study Plan

Your Turn: Test your understanding by doing related problem 3.5 on page 418 at the end of this chapter.

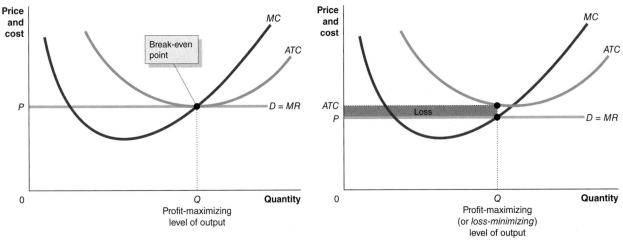

(a) A firm breaking even

(b) A firm experiencing a loss

MyEconLab Animation

Figure 12.5 **A Firm Breaking Even and a Firm Experiencing a Loss**

In panel (a), price equals average total cost, and the firm breaks even because its total revenue will be equal to its total cost. In this situation, the firm makes zero economic profit.

In panel (b), price is below average total cost, and the firm experiences a loss. The loss is represented by the area of the red-shaded rectangle, which has a height equal to $(ATC - P)$ and a width equal to Q.

Illustrating When a Firm Is Breaking Even or Operating at a Loss

We have already seen that to maximize profit, a firm produces the level of output where marginal revenue equals marginal cost. But will the firm actually make a profit at that level of output? It depends on the relationship of price to average total cost. There are three possibilities:

1. $P > ATC$, which means the firm makes a profit.
2. $P = ATC$, which means the firm *breaks even* (its total cost equals its total revenue).
3. $P < ATC$, which means the firm experiences a loss.

Figure 12.4 on page 399 shows the first possibility, where the firm makes a profit. Panels (a) and (b) of Figure 12.5 show the situations where a firm breaks even or suffers a loss. In panel (a) of Figure 12.5, at the level of output at which $MR = MC$, price is equal to average total cost. Therefore, total revenue is equal to total cost, and the firm will break even, making zero economic profit. In panel (b), at the level of output at which $MR = MC$, price is less than average total cost. Therefore, total revenue is less than total cost, and the firm suffers a loss. In this case, maximizing profit amounts to *minimizing* loss.   MyEconLab Concept Check

Making the Connection

MyEconLab Video

Losing Money in the Solar Panel Industry

In a market system, a good or service becomes available to consumers only if an entrepreneur brings the product to market. Thousands of new businesses open every week in the United States. Each new business represents an entrepreneur risking his or her funds to earn a profit. Of course, there are no guarantees of success, and many new businesses experience losses rather than earn the profits their owners hoped for.

By the mid-2000s, high oil prices and concern over the pollution caused by burning fossil fuels made more people become interested in solar energy. Technological advances reduced the cost of solar photovoltaic cells used in solar panels. In addition, households installing a solar energy system could receive a federal tax credit equal to 30 percent of the cost of the system. For several years, falling costs and increased demand led entrepreneurs in the United States to start new firms manufacturing solar panels. By 2009, though, large imports of solar panels produced by Chinese firms were driving down the market price. As panel (a) in the following figure shows, the price of solar panels, measured as dollars per watt of power produced, declined by three quarters, from $2.00 per watt in 2009 to $0.50 per watt in 2013.

Panel (b) shows the situation a typical U.S. firm producing solar panels faced. The price of $0.50 was below these firms' average total cost of producing solar panels, so the firms began to suffer losses. U.S. firms argued that Chinese firms were able to sell at low prices because they were receiving subsidies from the Chinese government, which are not allowed under international trade agreements. The U.S. government imposed a tariff of 30 percent on imports of solar panels from China. Most environmentalists opposed the tariff, arguing that if it resulted in higher prices for solar panels, fewer people would convert their homes to use solar power to generate electricity. Some U.S. firms also opposed the tariff because they use solar panels in products they export, which meant the tariff would raise their production costs. In 2013, however, the tariff did not seem to be having much effect on the U.S. market because Chinese imports were largely replaced by imports from Taiwan and South Korea. One energy analyst argued: "The economics of today, and supply and demand of today, aren't going to change because of [the tariff]."

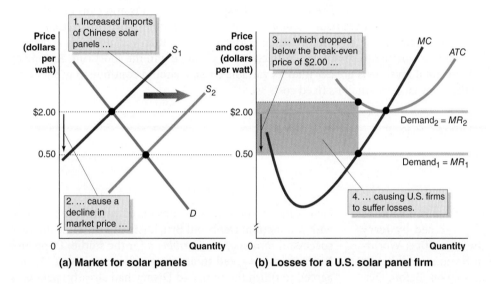

(a) Market for solar panels   (b) Losses for a U.S. solar panel firm

Why didn't the U.S. firms producing solar panels just raise the price they charged to the level they needed to break even? We have already seen that any firm that tries to raise the price of its product above the market price loses customers to competing firms. What will happen to the U.S. solar panel industry in the long run is unclear, but by 2013 a number of U.S. solar panel firms had gone out of business. The entrepreneurs who had started those businesses lost most of their investments.

Sources: Keith Bradsher, "U.S. and Europe Prepare to Settle Chinese Solar Panel Cases," *New York Times*, May 20, 2013; "Chinese Solar Imports Drop but Prices Continue to Fall," cleantechnica.com, January 22, 2013; and Diane Cardwell, "Solar Tariffs Upheld, but May Not Help in U.S.," *New York Times*, November 7, 2012.

Your Turn: Test your understanding by doing related problem 3.7 on page 418 at the end of this chapter.

MyEconLab Study Plan

Deciding Whether to Produce or to Shut Down in the Short Run

In panel (b) of Figure 12.5 on page 402, we assumed that the firm would continue to produce even though it was operating at a loss. In the short run, a firm experiencing a loss has two choices:

1. Continue to produce

2. Stop production by shutting down temporarily

12.4 LEARNING OBJECTIVE

Explain why firms may shut down temporarily.

In many cases, a firm experiencing a loss will consider stopping production temporarily. Even during a temporary shutdown, however, a firm must still pay its fixed costs. For example, if the firm has signed a lease for its building, the landlord will expect to receive a monthly rent payment, even if the firm is not producing anything that month. Therefore, if a firm does not produce, it will suffer a loss equal to its fixed costs. This loss is the maximum the firm will accept. The firm will shut down if producing would cause it to lose an amount greater than its fixed costs.

A firm can reduce its loss below the amount of its total fixed cost by continuing to produce, provided that the total revenue it receives is greater than its variable cost. A firm can use the revenue over and above variable cost to cover part of its fixed cost. In this case, a firm will have a smaller loss by continuing to produce than if it shuts down.

In analyzing the firm's decision to shut down, we are assuming that its fixed costs are *sunk costs*. Remember that a **sunk cost** is a cost that has already been paid and cannot be recovered. We assume, as is usually the case, that the firm cannot recover its fixed costs by shutting down. For example, if a farmer has taken out a loan to buy land, the farmer is legally required to make the monthly loan payment whether he grows any wheat that season or not. The farmer has to spend those funds and cannot get them back, *so the farmer should treat his sunk costs as irrelevant to his short-run decision making*. For any firm, whether total revenue is greater or less than *variable costs* is the key to deciding whether to shut down or to continue producing in the short run. As long as a firm's total revenue is greater than its variable costs, it should continue to produce no matter how large or small its fixed costs are.

Sunk cost A cost that has already been paid and cannot be recovered.

Solved Problem 12.4

MyEconLab Interactive Animation

When to Pull the Plug on a Movie

In the summer of 2013, Walt Disney released *The Lone Ranger*, starring Johnny Depp and produced by Jerry Bruckheimer. The film bombed at the box office: Worldwide, it earned about $245 million in revenue, well below the $375 million it cost to produce and market. Before Disney completed the film, executives became concerned that it might not be successful. They were disappointed in the early work on the film and temporarily stopped production. According to media reports, Disney executives took several

factors into account as they considered whether to continue with production: Depp and Bruckheimer had made the very successful *Pirates of the Caribbean* for the studio; Depp and Bruckheimer agreed to accept smaller salaries if Disney agreed to finish the film; and Disney had already spent tens of millions of dollars on the film. How should Disney have decided whether to finish *The Lone Ranger* and release it to theaters? What role should the money Disney executives had already spent on the film have played in their decision?

Solving the Problem

Step 1: **Review the chapter material.** This problem is about the role of sunk costs in business decision making, so you may want to review the section "Deciding Whether to Produce or to Shut Down in the Short Run," which begins on page 403.

Step 2: **Use the concept of sunk costs to analyze Disney's decision about whether to finish the film.** In this case, Disney was not considering whether to shut down the company but whether to shut down production of this particular film. Disney had already invested millions of dollars in *The Lone Ranger* at the time they were considering whether to finish the film. It is tempting to argue that unless Disney completed the film, these millions of dollars would be lost. It is important to see, however, that the millions were a sunk cost: Whether Disney shut down the film or finished it and released it to theaters, the company would not be able to get back what it had already invested. Therefore, the millions were irrelevant to Disney's decision. Instead, Disney should have made the decision based on comparing the additional cost of completing and releasing the film to the revenue the film was expected to earn. In other words, Disney should have completed the film if marginal revenue was expected to be greater than marginal cost, and it should have shut down the film if marginal cost was expected to be greater than marginal revenue.

Although Disney knew the marginal cost of completing and releasing the film, it had to estimate the marginal revenue based on its forecasts of ticket sales and later sales of DVDs and streaming video. Disney decided to finish the film. The additional cost to complete the film was more than $300 million, but it earned only about $245 million at the box office. With hindsight, Disney made the wrong decision, but on the basis of the past success of the *Pirates of the Caribbean* films Depp and Bruckheimer made together, Disney overestimated ticket sales.

Sources: Lucas Shaw, "'Lone Ranger' Fallout: Jerry Bruckheimer May Lose Final Cut on 'Pirates 5,'" Reuters, August 7, 2013; Brooks Barnes, "Masked Lawman Stumbles at the Gate," *New York Times*, July 7, 2013; and Mike Fleming, Jr., "Shocker! Disney Halts 'Lone Ranger' with Johnny Depp and Gore Verbinski," www.dealince.com, August 12, 2011.

Your Turn: Test your understanding by doing related problems 4.8 and 4.9 on page 419 at the end of this chapter.

MyEconLab Study Plan

One option not available to a firm with losses in a perfectly competitive market is to raise its price. If the firm did raise its price, it would lose all its customers, and its sales would drop to zero. For example, during the past 15 years, the price of wheat has typically been high enough for a typical wheat farmer in the United States to at least break even. But in 2004, the price of wheat was $3.16 per bushel. At that price, the typical U.S. wheat farmer lost $9,500. At a price of about $4.25 per bushel, the typical wheat farmer would have broken even. But any wheat farmer who tried to raise his price to $4.25 per bushel would have seen his sales quickly disappear because buyers could purchase all the wheat they wanted at $3.16 per bushel from the thousands of other wheat farmers.

The Supply Curve of a Firm in the Short Run

Remember that the supply curve for a firm tells us how many units of a product the firm is willing to sell at any given price. Notice that the marginal cost curve for a firm in a perfectly competitive market tells us the same thing. The firm will produce at the level of output where $MR = MC$. Because price equals marginal revenue for a firm in a perfectly competitive market, the firm will produce where $P = MC$. For any given price, we can determine from the marginal cost curve the quantity of output the firm will supply. *Therefore, a perfectly competitive firm's marginal cost curve is also its supply curve.* There is, however, an important qualification to this fact. We have seen that if a firm is experiencing a loss, it will shut down if its total revenue is less than its variable cost:

$$\text{Total revenue} < \text{Variable cost,}$$

or, in symbols:

$$(P \times Q) < VC.$$

If we divide both sides by Q, we have the result that the firm will shut down if

$$P < AVC.$$

If the price drops below average variable cost, the firm will have a smaller loss if it shuts down and produces no output. *So, the firm's marginal cost curve is its supply curve only for prices at or above average variable cost.*

Recall that the marginal cost curve intersects the average variable cost where the average variable cost curve is at its minimum point. Therefore, as shown in Figure 12.6, the firm's supply curve is its marginal cost curve above the minimum point of the average variable cost curve. For prices below minimum average variable cost (P_{MIN}), the firm will shut down, and its output will drop to zero. The minimum point on the average variable cost curve is called

Figure 12.6

The Firm's Short-Run Supply Curve

Because price equals marginal revenue for a firm in a perfectly competitive market, the firm will produce where $P = MC$. For any given price, we can determine the quantity of output the firm will supply from the marginal cost curve, so the marginal cost curve is the firm's supply curve. But the firm will shut down if the price falls below average variable cost. The marginal cost curve crosses the average variable cost at the firm's shutdown point at the output level Q_{SD}. For prices below P_{MIN}, the supply curve is a vertical line along the price axis, which shows that the firm will supply zero output at those prices. The red line is the firm's short-run supply curve.

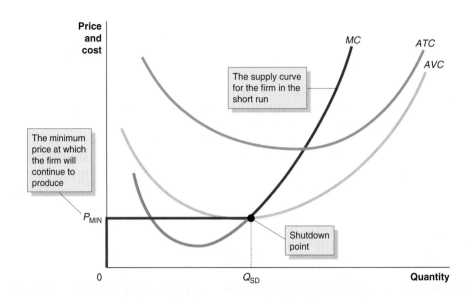

Shutdown point The minimum point on a firm's average variable cost curve; if the price falls below this point, the firm shuts down production in the short run.

the **shutdown point**, and it occurs at the output level Q_{SD}. The dark red line in Figure 12.6 shows the supply curve for the firm in the short run.

The Market Supply Curve in a Perfectly Competitive Industry

The market demand curve is determined by adding up the quantity demanded by each consumer in the market at each price (see Chapter 10). Similarly, the market supply curve is determined by adding up the quantity supplied by each firm in the market at each price. Each firm's marginal cost curve tells us how much that firm will supply at each price. So, the market supply curve can be derived directly from the marginal cost curves of the firms in the market. Panel (a) of Figure 12.7 shows the marginal cost

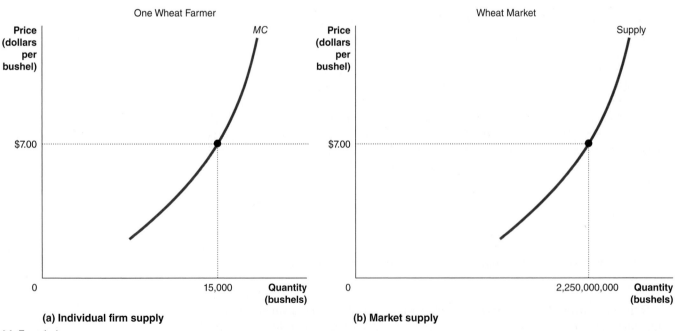

(a) Individual firm supply

(b) Market supply

Figure 12.7 **Firm Supply and Market Supply**

We can derive the market supply curve by adding up the quantity that each firm in the market is willing to supply at each price. In panel (a), one wheat farmer is willing to supply 15,000 bushels of wheat at a price of $7 per bushel. If every wheat farmer supplies the same amount of wheat at this price and if there are 150,000 wheat farmers, the total amount of wheat supplied at a price of $7 will equal

15,000 bushels per farmer × 150,000 farmers = 2.25 billion bushels of wheat. This amount is one point on the market supply curve for wheat shown in panel (b). We can find the other points on the market supply curve by determining how much wheat each farmer is willing to supply at each price.

curve for one wheat farmer. At a price of $7, this wheat farmer supplies 15,000 bushels of wheat. If every wheat farmer supplies the same amount of wheat at this price and if there are 150,000 wheat farmers, the total amount of wheat supplied at a price of $7 will be

15,000 bushels per farmer × 150,000 farms = 2.25 billion bushels of wheat.

Panel (b) shows a price of $7 and a quantity of 2.25 billion bushels as a point on the market supply curve for wheat. In reality, of course, not all wheat farms are alike. Some wheat farms supply more at the market price than the typical farm; other wheat farms supply less. The key point is that we can derive the market supply curve by adding up the quantity that each firm in the market is willing and able to supply at each price. MyEconLab Concept Check

MyEconLab Study Plan

"If Everyone Can Do It, You Can't Make Money at It": The Entry and Exit of Firms in the Long Run

12.5 LEARNING OBJECTIVE

Explain how entry and exit ensure that perfectly competitive firms earn zero economic profit in the long run.

In the long run, unless a firm can cover all its costs, it will shut down and exit the industry. In a market system, firms continually enter and exit industries. In this section, we will see how profits and losses provide signals to firms that lead to entry and exit.

Economic Profit and the Entry or Exit Decision

To begin, let's look more closely at how economists characterize the profits earned by the owners of a firm. Suppose Sacha Gillette decides to start her own business. After considering her skills and interests and preparing a business plan, she decides to start an organic vegetable farm rather than a restaurant or clothing boutique. After 10 years of effort, Sacha has saved $100,000, and she is able to borrow another $900,000 from a bank. With these funds, she has bought the land and farm equipment necessary to start her farm. She intends to sell the carrots she grows in a local farmer's market. When someone invests her own funds in her firm, the opportunity cost to the firm is the return the funds would have earned in their best alternative use (see Chapter 11). If Farmer Gillette could have earned a 10 percent return on her $100,000 in savings in their best alternative use—which might have been, for example, to buy a small restaurant—then her carrot business incurs a $10,000 opportunity cost. We can also think of this $10,000 as being the minimum amount that Farmer Gillette needs to earn on her $100,000 investment in her farm to remain in the industry in the long run.

Table 12.4 lists Farmer Gillette's costs. In addition to her explicit costs, we assume that she has two implicit costs: the $10,000 that represents the opportunity cost of the funds she invested in her farm and the $30,000 salary she could have earned managing someone else's farm instead of her own. Her total costs are $125,000. If the market price of carrots is $15 per box and Farmer Gillette sells 10,000 boxes, her total revenue will be $150,000, and her economic profit will be $25,000 (total revenue of $150,000 minus total costs of $125,000). Recall that **economic profit** equals a firm's revenues minus all its costs, implicit and explicit. So, Farmer Gillette is covering the $10,000 opportunity cost of the funds invested in her firm, and she is also earning an additional $25,000 in economic profit.

Economic profit A firm's revenues minus all its costs, implicit and explicit.

Explicit Costs	
Water	$10,000
Wages	$15,000
Fertilizer	$10,000
Electricity	$5,000
Payment on bank loan	$45,000
Implicit Costs	
Forgone salary	$30,000
Opportunity cost of the $100,000 she has invested in her farm	$10,000
Total cost	**$125,000**

Table 12.4

Farmer Gillette's Costs per Year

Economic Profit Leads to Entry of New Firms Unfortunately, Farmer Gillette is unlikely to earn an economic profit for very long. Suppose other farmers are just breaking even by selling their carrots to supermarkets. In that case, they will have an incentive to switch to selling at farmers' markets so they can begin earning an economic profit. As we saw in the chapter opener, in recent years many small farmers have begun to sell their produce in farmers' markets in the hope of earning higher profits. Remember that the more firms there are in an industry, the farther to the right the market supply curve is. Panel (a) of Figure 12.8 shows that as more farmers begin selling carrots in farmers' markets, the market supply curve shifts to the right. Farmers will continue entering the market until the market supply curve has shifted from S_1 to S_2.

With the supply curve at S_2, the market price will fall to $10 per box. Panel (b) shows the effect on Farmer Gillette, whom we assume has the same costs as other carrot farmers. As the market price falls from $15 to $10 per box, Farmer Gillette's demand curve shifts down, from D_1 to D_2. In the new equilibrium, Farmer Gillette is selling 8,000 boxes, at a price of $10 per box. She and the other carrot farmers are no longer earning any economic profit. They are just breaking even, and the return on their investment is just covering the opportunity cost of these funds. New farmers will stop entering the market because the rate of return from selling carrots in farmers' markets is now no better than they can earn by selling them elsewhere.

Will Farmer Gillette continue to sell carrots at farmers' markets even though she is just breaking even? She will because selling carrots at farmers' markets earns her as high a return on her investment as she could earn elsewhere. It may seem strange that new firms will continue to enter a market until all economic profits are eliminated and that established firms remain in a market despite not earning any economic profit. But it seems strange only because we are used to thinking in terms of accounting profit rather than *economic* profit. Remember that accounting rules generally require that only explicit costs be included on a firm's financial statements. The opportunity cost of the funds Farmer Gillette invested in her farm—$10,000—and her forgone salary—$30,000—are

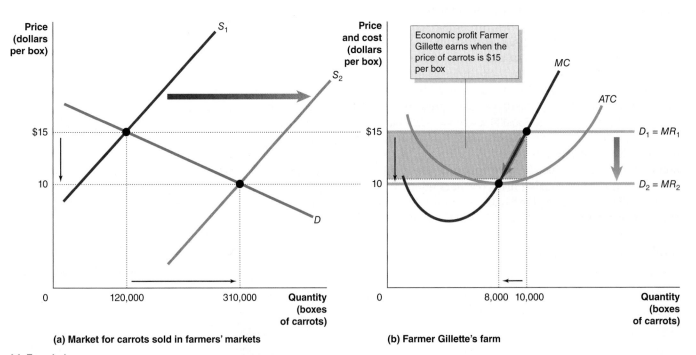

(a) Market for carrots sold in farmers' markets

(b) Farmer Gillette's farm

MyEconLab Animation

Figure 12.8 **The Effect of Entry on Economic Profit**

Initially, Farmer Gillette and other farmers selling carrots in farmers' markets are able to charge $15 per box and earn an economic profit. Farmer Gillette's economic profit is represented by the area of the green box in panel (b). Panel (a) shows that as other farmers begin to sell carrots in farmers' markets, the market supply curve shifts to the right, from S_1 to S_2, and the market price drops to $10 per box.

Panel (b) shows that the falling price causes Farmer Gillette's demand curve to shift down from D_1 to D_2, and she reduces her output from 10,000 boxes to 8,000. At the new market price of $10 per box, carrot growers are just breaking even: Their total revenue is equal to their total cost, and their economic profit is zero. Notice the difference in scale between the graphs in panels (a) and (b).

economic costs, but neither of them is an accounting cost. So, although an accountant would see Farmer Gillette as earning a profit of $40,000, an economist would see her as just breaking even. Farmer Gillette must pay attention to her accounting profit when preparing her financial statements and when paying her income tax. But because economic profit takes into account all her costs, it gives a more accurate indication of the financial health of her farm.

Economic Losses Lead to Exit of Firms Suppose some consumers decide that there are no important benefits from locally grown produce sold at farmers' markets, and they switch back to buying their produce in supermarkets. Panel (a) of Figure 12.9 shows that the demand curve for carrots sold in farmers' markets will shift to the left, from D_1 to D_2, and the market price will fall from $10 per box to $7. Panel (b) shows that as the price falls, a farmer, like Sacha Gillette, will move down her marginal cost curve to a lower level of output. At the lower level of output and lower price, she will be suffering an **economic loss** because she will not cover all her costs. As long as price is above average variable cost, she will continue to produce in the short run, even when suffering losses. But in the long run, firms will exit an industry if they are unable to cover all their costs. In this case, some farmers will switch back to selling carrots to supermarkets rather than selling them in farmers' markets.

> **Economic loss** The situation in which a firm's total revenue is less than its total cost, including all implicit costs.

Panel (c) of Figure 12.9 shows that as firms exit from selling at farmers' markets, the market supply curve shifts to the left. Firms will continue to exit, and the supply curve will continue to shift to the left until the price has risen back to $10 and the market supply curve is at S_2. Panel (d) shows that when the price is back to $10, the remaining firms in the industry will be breaking even.   MyEconLab Concept Check

Long-Run Equilibrium in a Perfectly Competitive Market

We have seen that economic profits attract firms to enter an industry. The entry of firms forces down the market price until a typical firm is breaking even. Economic losses cause firms to exit an industry. The exit of firms forces up the equilibrium market price until the typical firm is breaking even. In **long-run competitive equilibrium**, entry and exit have resulted in the typical firm breaking even. In the long run, firms can also vary their scale by becoming larger or smaller (see Chapter 11). The *long-run average cost curve* shows the lowest cost at which a firm is able to produce a given quantity of output in the long run. So, we would expect that in the long run, competition drives the market price to the minimum point on the typical firm's long-run average cost curve.

> **Long-run competitive equilibrium** The situation in which the entry and exit of firms has resulted in the typical firm breaking even.

The long run in selling produce in farmers' markets appears to be several years, which is the amount of time it takes for new farmers' markets to be organized and for farmers to make the investment necessary to sell directly to consumers. As we discussed in the chapter opener, the number of farmers' markets operating in the United States had increased from 1,774 in 2005 to 7,864 in 2012. But some farmers have begun to exit the market because the prices they were receiving were lower than they could get by selling their produce elsewhere. In Oregon, 32 of 62 farmers' markets that had opened in recent years have since closed.

Firms in perfectly competitive markets are in a constant struggle to stay one step ahead of their competitors. They are always looking for new ways to provide a product, such as selling carrots in farmers' markets. It is possible for firms to find ways to earn an economic profit for a while, but competition typically eliminates those profits in just a few years. This observation is not restricted to agriculture. In any perfectly competitive market, an opportunity to make economic profits never lasts long. As Sharon Oster, an economist at Yale University, has put it: "If everyone can do it, you can't make money at it."   MyEconLab Concept Check

The Long-Run Supply Curve in a Perfectly Competitive Market

If a typical farmer selling carrots in a farmers' market breaks even at a price of $10 per box, in the long run the market price will always return to this level. If an increase in demand causes the market price to rise above $10, farmers will be earning economic profits. These profits will attract additional farmers into the market, and the market supply curve will shift to the right until the price is back to $10.

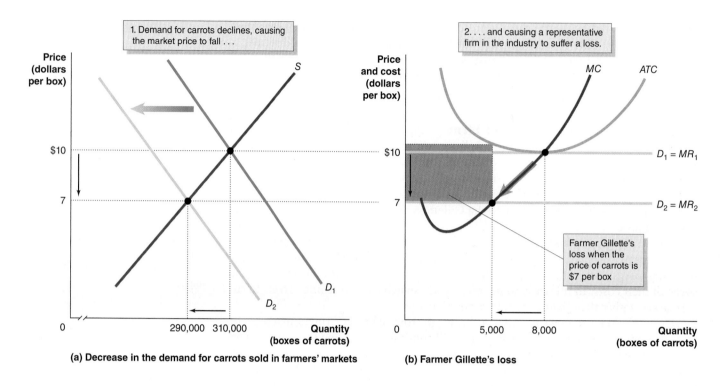

(a) Decrease in the demand for carrots sold in farmers' markets

(b) Farmer Gillette's loss

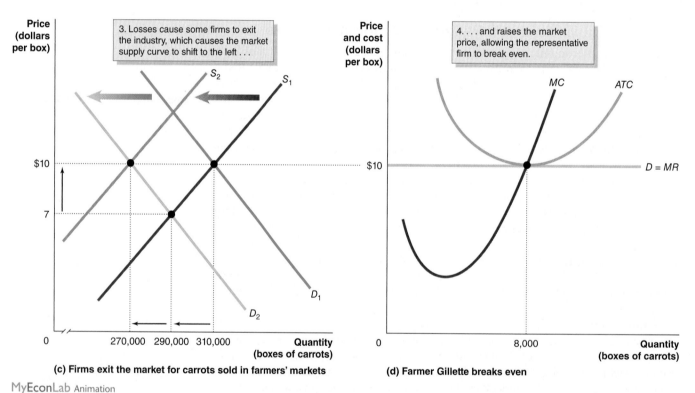

(c) Firms exit the market for carrots sold in farmers' markets

(d) Farmer Gillette breaks even

MyEconLab Animation

Figure 12.9   The Effect of Exit on Economic Losses

When the price of carrots is $10 per box, Farmer Gillette and other farmers are breaking even. A total quantity of 310,000 boxes is sold in the market. Farmer Gillette sells 8,000 boxes. Panel (a) shows a decline in the demand for carrots sold in farmers' markets from D_1 to D_2 that reduces the market price to $7 per box. Panel (b) shows that the falling price causes Farmer Gillette's demand curve to shift down from D_1 to D_2 and her output to fall from 8,000 to 5,000 boxes. At a market price of $7 per box,

farmers have economic losses, represented by the area of the red box. As a result, some farmers will exit the market, which shifts the market supply curve to the left. Panel (c) shows that exit continues until the supply curve has shifted from S_1 to S_2 and the market price has risen from $7 back to $10. Panel (d) shows that with the price back at $10, Farmer Gillette will break even. In the new market equilibrium in panel (c), total sales of carrots in farmers' markets have fallen from 310,000 to 270,000 boxes.

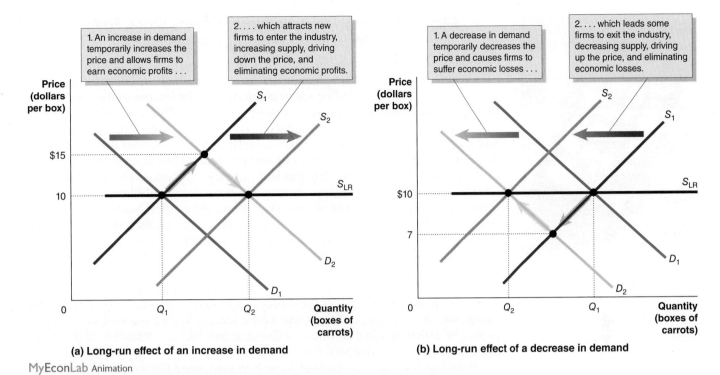

(a) Long-run effect of an increase in demand

(b) Long-run effect of a decrease in demand

MyEconLab Animation

Figure 12.10   **The Long-Run Supply Curve in a Perfectly Competitive Industry**

Panel (a) shows that an increase in demand for carrots sold in farmers' markets will lead to a temporary increase in price from $10 to $15 per box, as the market demand curve shifts to the right, from D_1 to D_2. The entry of new firms shifts the market supply curve to the right, from S_1 to S_2, which will cause the price to fall back to its long-run level of $10. Panel (b) shows that a decrease in demand will lead to a temporary decrease in price from $10 to $7 per box, as the market demand curve shifts to the left, from D_1 to D_2. The exit of firms shifts the market supply curve to the left, from S_1 to S_2, which causes the price to rise back to its long-run level of $10. The long-run supply curve (S_{LR}) shows the relationship between market price and the quantity supplied in the long run. In this case, the long-run supply curve is a horizontal line.

Panel (a) in Figure 12.10 illustrates the long-run effect of an increase in demand. An increase in demand from D_1 to D_2 causes the market price to temporarily rise from $10 per box to $15. At this price, farmers are making economic profits selling carrots at farmers' markets, but these profits attract the entry of new farmers. The result is an increase in supply from S_1 to S_2, which forces the price back down to $10 per box and eliminates the economic profits.

Similarly, if a decrease in demand causes the market price to fall below $10, farmers will experience economic losses. These losses will cause some farmers to exit the market, the supply curve will shift to the left, and the price will return to $10. Panel (b) in Figure 12.10 illustrates the long-run effect of a decrease in demand. A decrease in demand from D_1 to D_2 causes the market price to fall temporarily from $10 per box to $7. At this price, farmers are suffering economic losses, but these losses cause some farmers to exit the market for selling carrots in farmers' markets. The result is a decrease in supply from S_1 to S_2, which forces the price back up to $10 per box and eliminates the losses.

The **long-run supply curve** shows the relationship in the long run between market price and the quantity supplied. In the long run, the price will be $10 per box, no matter how many boxes of carrots are produced. So, as Figure 12.10 shows, the long-run supply curve (S_{LR}) is a horizontal line at a price of $10. Remember that the price returns to $10 in the long run because at this price a typical firm in the industry just breaks even. The typical firm breaks even because $10 is at the minimum point on the firm's average total cost curve. We can draw the important conclusion that *in the long run, a perfectly competitive market will supply whatever amount of a good consumers demand at a price determined by the minimum point on the typical firm's average total cost curve.*

Because the position of the long-run supply curve is determined by the minimum point on the typical firm's average total cost curve, anything that raises or lowers the costs of the typical firm in the long run will cause the long-run supply curve to shift. For example, if a new disease infects carrots and the costs of treating the disease adds $2 per box to every farmer's cost of producing carrots, the long-run supply curve will shift up by $2.   MyEconLab Concept Check

Long-run supply curve A curve that shows the relationship in the long run between market price and the quantity supplied.

Economic profits are rapidly competed away in the iTunes apps store.

Making the Connection
MyEconLab Video

In the Apple iPhone Apps Store, Easy Entry Makes the Long Run Pretty Short

Apple introduced the first version of the iPhone in June 2007. Although popular, the original iPhone had some drawbacks, including a slow connection to the Internet and an inability to run any applications except those written by Apple. The iPhone 3G, released in July 2008, could connect to the Internet more quickly and easily, had a faster processor, and had a larger capacity. Perhaps more importantly, Apple announced that a section of its immensely popular iTunes music and video store would be devoted to applications (or "apps") for the iPhone 3G. Independent software programmers would write these iPhone apps. Apple would approve the apps and make them available in the iTunes app store in exchange for receiving 30 percent of the purchase price. Major software companies, as well as individuals writing their first software programs, have posted games, calendars, dictionaries, and many other types of apps to the iTunes store.

Apple sold more than 3 million iPhones within a month of launching the iPhone 3G. Demand for apps from the iTunes store soared along with sales of the iPhone. Ethan Nicholas, who was a programmer at Sun Microsystems but had never written a game before, decided to teach himself the coding language used in iPhone apps. His game, iShoot, with an initial price of $4.99, was a great success. Within one week of posting to iTunes, enough people had downloaded iShoot to earn Nicholas $200,000. At the end of five months, he had earned $800,000.

But could Nicholas's success last? As we have seen, when firms earn economic profits in a market, other firms have a strong economic incentive to enter that market. This is exactly what happened with iPhone apps, and by April 2009, more than 25,000 apps were available in the iTunes store. The cost of entering this market was very small. Anyone with the programming skills and the available time could write an app and have it posted in the store. As a result of this enhanced competition, the ability to get rich quick with a killer app was quickly fading. As an article in the *New York Times* put it: "The chances of hitting the iPhone jackpot keep getting slimmer: the Apple store is already crowded with look-alike games ... and fresh inventory keeps arriving daily. Many of the simple but clever concepts that sell briskly ... are already taken."

To try to maintain sales, Ethan Nicholas was forced to drop the price of iShoot from $4.99 in October 2008 to $2.99 in April 2009 to $1.99 in May 2009, and finally to $0.99 in September 2010. His profits from the game continued to decline. In a competitive market, earning an economic profit in the long run is extremely difficult. And the ease of entering the market for iPhone apps has made the long run pretty short.

Sources: Jenna Wortham, "The iPhone Gold Rush," *New York Times*, April 5, 2009; and Bruce X. Chen, "Coder's Half-Million-Dollar Baby Proves iPhone Gold Rush Is Still On," wired.com, February 12, 2009.

MyEconLab Study Plan

Your Turn: Test your understanding by doing related problem 5.9 on page 420 at the end of this chapter.

Increasing-Cost and Decreasing-Cost Industries

Any industry in which the typical firm's average costs do not change as the industry expands production will have a horizontal long-run supply curve, like the one in Figure 12.10. These industries, the carrot industry, for example, are called *constant-cost industries*. It's possible, however, for the typical firm's average costs to change as an industry expands.

For example, if an input used in producing a good is available in only limited quantities, the cost of the input will rise as the industry expands. If only a limited amount of land is available on which to grow the grapes to make a certain variety of wine, an increase in demand for wine made from these grapes will result in competition for the land and will drive up its price. As a result, more of the wine will be produced in the long run only if the price rises to cover the typical firm's higher average costs. In this case, the long-run supply curve will slope upward. Industries with upward-sloping long-run supply curves are called *increasing-cost industries*.

Finally, in some cases, the typical firm's costs may fall as the industry expands. Suppose that someone invents a new microwave oven that uses as an input a specialized memory chip that is currently produced only in small quantities. If demand for the microwave increases, firms that produce microwaves will increase their orders for the memory chip. If there are *economies of scale* in producing a good, its average cost will decline as output increases (see Chapter 11). If there are economies of scale in producing this memory chip, the average cost of producing it will fall, and competition will result in its price falling as well. This price decline, in turn, will lower the average cost of producing the new microwave. In the long run, competition will force the price of the microwave to fall to the level of the typical firm's new lower average cost. In this case, the long-run supply curve will slope downward. Industries with downward-sloping long-run supply curves are called *decreasing-cost industries*.   MyEconLab Concept Check

MyEconLab Study Plan

Perfect Competition and Efficiency

12.6 LEARNING OBJECTIVE

Explain how perfect competition leads to economic efficiency.

Notice how powerful consumers are in a market system. If consumers want more locally grown carrots, the market will supply them. More carrots are supplied not because a government bureaucrat in Washington, DC, or an official in a carrot growers' association gives orders. The additional carrots are produced because an increase in demand results in higher prices and a higher profit from selling at farmers' markets. Carrot growers, trying to get the highest possible return on their investments, begin to switch from selling to supermarkets to selling at farmers' markets. If consumers lose their taste for locally grown carrots and demand falls, the process works in reverse.

Productive Efficiency

In a market system, consumers get as many carrots as they want, produced at the lowest average cost possible. The forces of competition will drive the market price to the typical firm's minimum average cost. **Productive efficiency** refers to the situation in which a good or service is produced at the lowest possible cost. As we have seen, perfect competition results in productive efficiency.

Productive efficiency The situation in which a good or service is produced at the lowest possible cost.

The managers of every firm strive to earn an economic profit by reducing costs. But in a perfectly competitive market, other firms quickly copy ways of reducing costs. Therefore, in the long run, only the consumer benefits from cost reductions. MyEconLab Concept Check

Solved Problem 12.6

MyEconLab Interactive Animation

How Productive Efficiency Benefits Consumers

Financial writer Michael Lewis once remarked: "The sad truth, for investors, seems to be that most of the benefits of new technologies are passed right through to consumers free of charge."

a. What do you think Lewis means by the benefits of new technology being "passed right through to consumers free of charge"? Use a graph like Figure 12.8 on page 408 to illustrate your answer.
b. Explain why this result is a "sad truth" for investors.

Solving the Problem

Step 1: **Review the chapter material.** This problem is about perfect competition and efficiency, so you may want to review the section "Perfect Competition and Efficiency," which begins above.

Step 2: **Use the concepts from this chapter to explain what Lewis means.** By "new technologies," Lewis means new products—such as smartphones or LED television sets—or lower-cost ways of producing existing products. In either case, new technologies will allow firms to earn economic profits for a while, but these profits will lead new firms to enter the market in the long run.

Step 3: **Use a graph like Figure 12.8 on page 408 to illustrate why the benefits of new technologies are "passed right through to consumers free of charge."** Figure 12.8 shows the situation in which a firm is making economic profits in the short run but has these profits eliminated by entry in the long run. We can draw a similar graph to analyze what happens in the long run in the market for LED televisions.

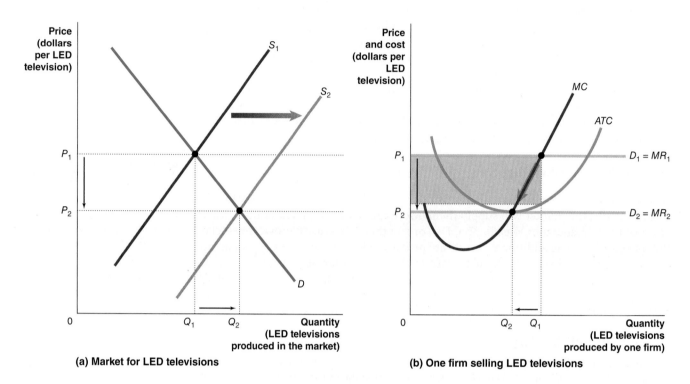

(a) Market for LED televisions

(b) One firm selling LED televisions

When LED televisions were first introduced, prices were high, and only a few firms were in the market. Panel (a) shows that the initial equilibrium price in the market for LED televisions is P_1. Panel (b) shows that at this price, the typical firm in the industry is earning an economic profit, which is shown by the green-shaded box. The economic profit attracts new firms into the industry. This entry shifts the market supply curve from S_1 to S_2 in panel (a) and lowers the equilibrium price from P_1 to P_2. Panel (b) shows that at the new market price, P_2, the typical firm is breaking even. Therefore, LED televisions are being produced at the lowest possible cost, and productive efficiency is achieved. Consumers receive the new technology "free of charge" in the sense that they only have to pay a price equal to the lowest possible cost of production.

Step 4: **Answer part (b) by explaining why the result in part (a) is a "sad truth" for investors.** We have seen in answering part (a) that in the long run, firms only break even on their investment in producing high-technology goods. That result implies that investors in these firms are also unlikely to earn an economic profit in the long run.

Extra Credit: Lewis is using a key result from this chapter: In the long run, the entry of new firms competes away economic profits. We should notice that, strictly speaking, the high-technology industries Lewis is discussing are not perfectly competitive. Smartphones or LED televisions, for instance, are not identical, and each smartphone company produces a quantity large enough to affect the market price. However, as we will see in the next chapter, these deviations from perfect competition do not change the important conclusion that the entry of new firms benefits consumers by forcing prices down to the level of average cost. In fact, the price of LED televisions dropped by more than 35 percent within three years of their first becoming widely available.

Source: Michael Lewis, "In Defense of the Boom," *New York Times*, October 27, 2002.

MyEconLab Study Plan   **Your Turn:** For more practice, do related problems 6.6, 6.7, and 6.8 on pages 421–422 at the end of this chapter.

Allocative Efficiency

Not only do perfectly competitive firms produce goods and services at the lowest possible cost, they also produce the goods and services that consumers value most. Firms will produce a good up to the point where the marginal cost of producing another unit is equal to the marginal benefit consumers receive from consuming that unit. In other words, firms will supply all those goods that provide consumers with a marginal benefit at least as great as the marginal cost of producing them. This result holds because:

1. The price of a good represents the marginal benefit consumers receive from consuming the last unit of the good sold.
2. Perfectly competitive firms produce up to the point where the price of the good equals the marginal cost of producing the last unit.
3. Therefore, firms produce up to the point where the last unit provides a marginal benefit to consumers equal to the marginal cost of producing it.

These statements are another way of saying that entrepreneurs in a market system efficiently *allocate* labor, machinery, and other inputs to produce the goods and services that best satisfy consumer wants. In this way, perfect competition achieves **allocative efficiency**. As we will explore in the next few chapters, many goods and services sold in the U.S. economy are not produced in perfectly competitive markets. Nevertheless, productive efficiency and allocative efficiency are useful benchmarks against which to compare the actual performance of the economy.   MyEconLab Concept Check

Allocative efficiency A state of the economy in which production represents consumer preferences; in particular, every good or service is produced up to the point where the last unit provides a marginal benefit to consumers equal to the marginal cost of producing it.

MyEconLab Study Plan

Continued from page 391

Economics in Your Life

Are You an Entrepreneur?

At the beginning of the chapter, we asked you to think about why you can charge only a relatively low price for performing services such as babysitting or lawn mowing. In the chapter, we saw that firms selling products in competitive markets can't charge prices higher than those being charged by competing firms. The market for babysitting and lawn mowing is very competitive because in most neighborhoods there are many teenagers willing to supply these services. The price you can charge for babysitting may not be worth your time when you are 20 but is enough to cover the opportunity cost of a 14-year-old eager to enter the market. In other words, the ease of entry into babysitting and lawn mowing is high. So, in your career as a teenage entrepreneur, you may have become familiar with one of the lessons of this chapter: A firm in a competitive market has no control over price.

Conclusion

The competitive forces of the market impose relentless pressure on firms to produce new and better goods and services at the lowest possible cost. Firms that fail to adequately anticipate changes in consumer tastes or that fail to adopt the latest and most efficient technology do not survive in the long run. In the nineteenth century, the biologist Charles Darwin developed a theory of evolution based on the idea of the "survival of the fittest." Only those plants and animals that are best able to adapt to the demands of their environment are able to survive. Darwin first realized the important role that the struggle for existence plays in the natural world after reading early nineteenth-century economists' descriptions of the role it plays in the economic world. Just as "survival of the fittest" is the rule in nature, so it is in the economic world.

At the start of this chapter, we saw that there are four market structures: perfect competition, monopolistic competition, oligopoly, and monopoly. Now that we have studied perfect competition, in the following chapters we move on to the other three market structures.

Visit MyEconLab for a news article and analysis related to the concepts in this chapter.

Chapter Summary and Problems

Key Terms

Allocative efficiency, p. 415

Average revenue (*AR*), p. 395

Economic loss, p. 409

Economic profit, p. 407

Long-run competitive equilibrium, p. 409

Long-run supply curve, p. 411

Marginal revenue (*MR*), p. 396

Perfectly competitive market, p. 393

Price taker, p. 393

Productive efficiency, p. 413

Profit, p. 395

Shutdown point, p. 406

Sunk cost, p. 404

 Perfectly Competitive Markets, pages 393–395

LEARNING OBJECTIVE: Explain what a perfectly competitive market is and why a perfect competitor faces a horizontal demand curve.

Summary

A **perfectly competitive market** must have many buyers and sellers, firms must be producing identical products, and there must be no barriers to new firms entering the market. The demand curve for a good or service produced in a perfectly competitive market is downward sloping, but the demand curve for the output of one firm in a perfectly competitive market is a horizontal line at the market price. Firms in perfectly competitive markets are **price takers**, and their sales drop to zero if they attempt to charge more than the market price.

MyEconLab   Visit www.myeconlab.com to complete these exercises online and get instant feedback.

Review Questions

1.1 What are the three conditions for a market to be perfectly competitive?

1.2 What is a price taker? When are firms likely to be price takers?

1.3 Draw a graph showing the market demand and supply curves for corn and the demand curve for the corn produced by one corn farmer. Be sure to indicate the market price and the price the corn farmer receives.

Problems and Applications

1.4 Explain whether each of the following is a perfectly competitive market. For each market that is not perfectly competitive, explain why it is not.
   a. Corn farming
   b. Coffee shops
   c. Automobile manufacturing
   d. New home construction

1.5 Why are consumers usually price takers when they buy most goods and services, while relatively few firms are price takers?

1.6 **[Related to the** Don't Let This Happen to You **on page 394]** Explain whether you agree with the following remark:

> According to the model of perfectly competitive markets, the demand curve for wheat should be a horizontal line. But this can't be true: When the price of wheat rises, the quantity of wheat demanded falls, and when the price of wheat falls, the quantity of wheat demanded rises. Therefore, the demand curve for wheat is not a horizontal line.

1.7 The financial writer Andrew Tobias described an incident that occurred when he was a student at the Harvard Business School: Each student in the class was given large amounts of information about a particular firm and asked to determine a pricing strategy for the firm. Most of the students spent hours preparing their answers and came to class carrying many sheets of paper with their calculations. Tobias came up with the correct answer after just a few minutes and without having made any calculations. When his professor called on him in class for an answer, Tobias stated: "The case said the XYZ Company was in a very competitive industry ... and the case said that the company had all the business it could handle." Given this information, what price do you think Tobias argued the company should charge? Briefly explain. (Tobias says the class greeted his answer with "thunderous applause.")

Source: Andrew Tobias, *The Only Investment Guide You'll Ever Need*, Houghton Mifflin Harcourt, 2010, pp. 7–8.

 How a Firm Maximizes Profit in a Perfectly Competitive Market, pages 395–398

LEARNING OBJECTIVE: Explain how a firm maximizes profit in a perfectly competitive market.

Summary

Profit is the difference between total revenue (*TR*) and total cost (*TC*). **Average revenue (*AR*)** is total revenue divided by the quantity of the product sold. A firm maximizes profit by producing the level of output where the difference between revenue and cost is the greatest. This is the same level of output where marginal revenue is equal to marginal cost. **Marginal revenue (*MR*)** is the change in total revenue from selling one more unit.

MyEconLab   Visit www.myeconlab.com to complete these exercises online and get instant feedback.

Review Questions

2.1 Explain why it is true that for a firm in a perfectly competitive market, $P = MR = AR$.

2.2 Explain why at the level of output where the difference between TR and TC is at its maximum positive value, MR must equal MC.

2.3 Explain why it is true that for a firm in a perfectly competitive market, the profit-maximizing condition $MR = MC$ is equivalent to the condition $P = MC$.

Problems and Applications

2.4 A student argues: "To maximize profit, a firm should produce the quantity where the difference between marginal revenue and marginal cost is the greatest. If a firm produces more than this quantity, then the profit made on each additional unit will be falling." Briefly explain whether you agree with this reasoning.

2.5 Why don't firms maximize revenue rather than profit? Briefly explain whether a firm that maximized revenue would be likely to produce a smaller or larger quantity than if it were maximizing profit.

2.6 Refer to Table 12.3 on page 397. Suppose the price of wheat falls to $5.50 per bushel. How many bushels of wheat will Farmer Parker produce, and how much profit will he make? Briefly explain.

2.7 Refer to Table 12.3 on page 397. Suppose that the marginal cost of wheat is $0.50 higher for every bushel of wheat produced. For example, the marginal cost of producing the eighth bushel of wheat is now $9.50. Assume that the price of wheat remains $7 per bushel. Will this increase in marginal cost change the profit-maximizing level of production for Farmer Parker? Briefly explain. How much profit will Farmer Parker make now?

2.8 In Table 12.3 on page 397, what are Farmer Parker's fixed costs? Suppose that his fixed costs increase by $10. Will this increase in fixed costs change the profit-maximizing level of production for Farmer Parker? Briefly explain. How much profit will Farmer Parker make now?

12.3 | Illustrating Profit or Loss on the Cost Curve Graph, pages 398–403

LEARNING OBJECTIVE: Use graphs to show a firm's profit or loss.

Summary

From the definitions of profit and average total cost, we can develop the following expression for the relationship between total profit and average total cost: Profit $= (P - ATC) \times Q$. Using this expression, we can determine the area showing profit or loss on a cost curve graph: The area of profit or loss is a rectangle with a height equal to price minus average total cost (for profit) or average total cost minus price (for loss) and a base equal to the quantity of output.

MyEconLab   Visit **www.myeconlab.com** to complete these exercises online and get instant feedback.

Output per Day	Total Cost
0	$1.00
1	2.50
2	3.50
3	4.20
4	4.50
5	5.20
6	6.80
7	8.70
8	10.70
9	13.00

Review Questions

3.1 Draw a graph showing a firm that is making a profit in a perfectly competitive market. Be sure your graph includes the firm's demand curve, marginal revenue curve, marginal cost curve, average total cost curve, and average variable cost curve, and make sure to indicate the area representing the firm's profit.

3.2 Draw a graph showing a firm that is operating at a loss in a perfectly competitive market. Be sure your graph includes the firm's demand curve, marginal revenue curve, marginal cost curve, average total cost curve, and average variable cost curve, and make sure to indicate the area representing the firm's loss.

Problems and Applications

3.3 [Related to Solved Problem 12.3 on page 399] Frances sells earrings in the perfectly competitive earrings market. Her output per day and her costs are as follows:

a. If the current equilibrium price in the earring market is $1.80, how many earrings will Frances produce, what price will she charge, and how much profit (or loss) will she make? Draw a graph to illustrate your answer. Your graph should be clearly labeled and should include Frances's demand, ATC, AVC, MC, and MR curves; the price she is charging; the quantity she is producing; and the area representing her profit (or loss).

b. Suppose the equilibrium price of earrings falls to $1.00. Now how many earrings will Frances produce, what price will she charge, and how much profit (or loss) will she make? Show your work. Draw a graph to illustrate this situation, using the instructions in part (a).

c. Suppose the equilibrium price of earrings falls to $0.25. Now how many earrings will Frances produce, what price will she charge, and how much profit (or loss) will she make?

3.4 [Related to Solved Problem 12.3 on page 399] Review Solved Problem 12.3 and then answer the following: Suppose the equilibrium price of basketballs falls to $2.50. Now how many basketballs will Andy produce? What price will he charge? How much profit (or loss) will he make?

3.5 **[Related to the** Don't Let This Happen to You **on page 401]** A student examines the following graph and argues: "I believe that a firm will want to produce at Q_1, not at Q_2. At Q_1, the distance between price and marginal cost is the greatest. Therefore, at Q_1, the firm will be maximizing its profit." Briefly explain whether you agree with the student's argument.

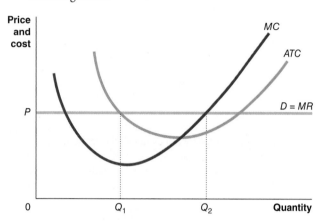

3.6 A newspaper article discussed the financial results for Texas Instruments Inc., a semiconductor manufacturer, during the first quarter of 2013. "First quarter profit jumped 37 percent to $362 million, or 32 cents per share, but revenue declined 6.8 percent to $2.89 billion from a year earlier." How is it possible for Texas Instruments' revenue to decrease but its profit to increase? Doesn't Texas Instruments have to maximize its revenue to maximize its profit?

Source: Sheryl Jean, "TI Narrows its 2nd-Quarter Projections," *The Dallas Morning News*, June 11, 2013.

3.7 **[Related to the** Making the Connection **on page 402]** Suppose that the price of oil doubles, raising the cost of

home-heating oil and electricity. What effect would this development have on U.S. firms manufacturing solar panels? Illustrate your answer with two graphs: one showing the situation in the market for solar panels and another graph showing the situation for a representative firm in the industry. Be sure your graph for the industry shows any shifts in the market demand and supply curve and any changes in the equilibrium market price. Be sure that your graph for the representative firm includes the firm's demand curve, marginal revenue curve, marginal cost curve, and average total cost curve.

3.8 The following graph represents the situation of Marguerite's Caps, a firm selling caps in the perfectly competitive cap industry:

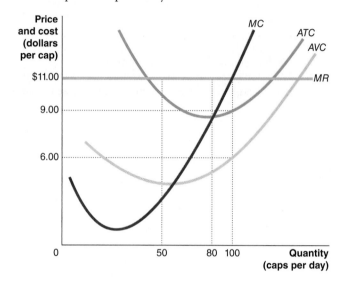

a. How much output should Marguerite produce to maximize her profits?
b. How much profit will she earn?
c. Suppose Marguerite decides to shut down. What would her loss be?

12.4 **Deciding Whether to Produce or to Shut Down in the Short Run, pages 403–407**
LEARNING OBJECTIVE: Explain why firms may shut down temporarily.

Summary

In deciding whether to shut down or produce in the short run, a firm should ignore its *sunk costs*. A **sunk cost** is a cost that has already been paid and that cannot be recovered. In the short run, a firm continues to produce as long as its price is at least equal to its average variable cost. A perfectly competitive firm's **shutdown point** is the minimum point on the firm's average variable cost curve. If price falls below average variable cost, the firm shuts down in the short run. For prices above the shutdown point, a perfectly competitive firm's marginal cost curve is also its supply curve.

 Visit **www.myeconlab.com** to complete these exercises online and get instant feedback.

Review Questions

4.1 What is the difference between a firm's shutdown points in the short run and in the long run? Why are firms willing to accept losses in the short run but not in the long run?

4.2 What is the relationship between a perfectly competitive firm's marginal cost curve and its supply curve?

4.3 How is the market supply curve derived from the supply curves of individual firms?

Problems and Applications

4.4 Edward Scahill produces table lamps in the perfectly competitive desk lamp market.
a. Fill in the missing values in the following table:

Output per Week	Total Cost	AFC	AVC	ATC	MC
0	$100				
1	150				
2	175				
3	190				
4	210				
5	240				
6	280				
7	330				
8	390				
9	460				
10	540				

  b. Suppose the equilibrium price in the desk lamp market is $50. How many table lamps should Scahill produce, and how much profit will he make?

  c. If next week the equilibrium price of desk lamps drops to $30, should Scahill shut down? Explain.

4.5 Matthew Rafferty produces hiking boots in the perfectly competitive hiking boot market.

  a. Fill in the missing values in the following table:

Output per Week	Total Cost	AFC	AVC	ATC	MC
0	$100.00				
1	155.70				
2	205.60				
3	253.90				
4	304.80				
5	362.50				
6	431.20				
7	515.10				
8	618.40				
9	745.30				
10	900.00				

  b. Suppose the equilibrium price in the hiking boot market is $100. How many boots should Rafferty produce, what price should he charge, and how much profit will he make?

  c. If next week the equilibrium price of boots drops to $65, how many boots should Rafferty produce, what price should he charge, and how much profit (or loss) will he make?

  d. If the equilibrium price of boots falls to $50, how many boots should Rafferty produce, what price should he charge, and how much profit (or loss) will he make?

4.6 The following graph represents the situation of a perfectly competitive firm. Indicate on the graph the areas that represent the following:

  a. Total cost

  b. Total revenue

  c. Variable cost

  d. Profit or loss

Briefly explain whether the firm will continue to produce in the short run.

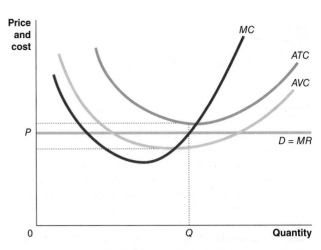

4.7 Look again at the *Making the Connection* on page 402 that discusses the U.S. solar panel industry. According to an article in the *New York Times*, interest payments on bank loans make up more than half the costs of a typical solar panel manufacturer. The owner of a firm that imports solar panels made this observation about solar panel manufacturers: "So as long as companies can cover their variable costs and earn at least some revenue to put toward interest payments, they will continue to operate even at a loss."

  a. Are the interest payments these firms make a variable cost or a fixed cost? Briefly explain.

  b. Does the quotation accurately describe the behavior of solar panel manufacturers in the short run? Does it accurately describe their behavior in the long run? Briefly explain.

Source: Diane Cardwell, "Solar Tariffs Upheld, but May Not Help in U.S.," *New York Times*, November 7, 2012.

4.8 **[Related to** Solved Problem 12.4 **on page 404]** Suppose you decide to open a copy store. You rent store space (signing a one-year lease to do so), and you take out a loan at a local bank and use the money to purchase 10 copiers. Six months later, a large chain opens a copy store two blocks away from yours. As a result, the revenue you receive from your copy store, while sufficient to cover the wages of your employees and the costs of paper and utilities, doesn't cover all your rent and the interest and repayment costs on the loan you took out to purchase the copiers. Should you continue operating your business?

4.9 **[Related to** Solved Problem 12.4 **on page 404]** According to an article in the *Wall Street Journal*, in 2007 the insurance company AXA Equitable signed a long-term lease on 2 million square feet of office space in a skyscraper on Sixth Avenue in Manhattan in New York City. In 2013, AXA decided that it only needed 1.7 million square feet of office space, so it subleased 300,000 square feet of space to several other firms. Although AXA is paying a rent of $88 per square foot on all 2 million square feet it is leasing, it is only receiving $40 per square foot from the firms it is subleasing the 300,000 square feet to. Briefly explain why AXA's actions might make economic sense in the short run. Would these actions make sense in the long run? Briefly explain.

Source: Molly Hensley-Clancy, "A Slump on Sixth Avenue," *Wall Street Journal*, June 16, 2013.

12.5 "If Everyone Can Do It, You Can't Make Money at It": The Entry and Exit of Firms in the Long Run, pages 407–413

LEARNING OBJECTIVE: Explain how entry and exit ensure that perfectly competitive firms earn zero economic profit in the long run.

Summary

Economic profit is a firm's revenue minus all its costs, implicit and explicit. **Economic loss** is the situation in which a firm's total revenue is less than its total cost, including all implicit costs. If firms make economic profits in the short run, new firms enter the industry until the market price has fallen enough to wipe out the profits. If firms make economic losses, firms exit the industry until the market price has risen enough to wipe out the losses. **Long-run competitive equilibrium** is the situation in which the entry and exit of firms has resulted in the typical firm breaking even. The **long-run supply curve** shows the relationship between market price and the quantity supplied.

MyEconLab   Visit www.myeconlab.com to complete these exercises online and get instant feedback.

Review Questions

5.1 When are firms likely to enter an industry? When are they likely to exit an industry?

5.2 Would a firm earning zero economic profit continue to produce, even in the long run?

5.3 Discuss the shape of the long-run supply curve in a perfectly competitive market. Suppose that a perfectly competitive market is initially at long-run equilibrium and then there is a permanent decrease in the demand for the product. Draw a graph showing how the market adjusts in the long run.

Problems and Applications

5.4 Suppose an assistant professor of economics is earning a salary of $75,000 per year. One day she quits her job, sells $100,000 worth of bonds that had been earning 3 percent per year, and uses the funds to open a bookstore. At the end of the year, she shows an accounting profit of $80,000 on her income tax return. What is her economic profit?

5.5 Why does the entry of firms into an industry decrease the economic profits of the existing firms? Why does the exit of firms from an industry increase the economic profits of the existing firms?

5.6 Briefly explain whether you agree with the following statement: "The products for which demand is the greatest will also be the products that are most profitable to produce."

5.7 In panel (b) of Figure 12.9 on page 410, Sacha Gillette reduces her output from 8,000 to 5,000 boxes of carrots when the price falls to $7. At this price and this output level, she is operating at a loss. Why doesn't she just continue charging the original $10 and continue producing 8,000 boxes of carrots?

5.8 For a given decrease in demand, will more firms exit a constant-cost industry or an increasing-cost industry? Briefly explain.

5.9 **[Related to the** Making the Connection **on page 412]** Ethan Nicholas developed his first game while still working as a programmer for Sun Microsystems. After his first game was a success, he quit Sun to form his own company—with himself as the only employee. How did Nicholas's quitting Sun to work full time for himself affect the cost to him of developing games?

Source: Jenna Wortham, "The iPhone Gold Rush," *New York Times*, April 5, 2009.

5.10 A student in a principles of economics course makes the following remark:

> The economic model of perfectly competitive markets is fine in theory but not very realistic. It predicts that in the long run, a firm in a perfectly competitive market will earn no profits. No firm in the real world would stay in business if it earned zero profits.

Do you agree with this remark?

5.11 In 2011, National Public Radio ran a story about the market for gold. It reported:

> The price of gold in the international market is steadily rising: more than fivefold in the past decade alone. It's currently selling for about $1,500 an ounce, paving the way for a new gold rush. Ten old mines have reopened in remote mountain and desert areas of the American West over the past decade.

a. The new gold rush is not just in the United States. It is also in Australia, Africa, Asia, and elsewhere. If old gold mines still have gold in them, why weren't they being operated before the increase in the price of gold?

b. Assuming the increased demand for gold continues, in the long run, what will the entry of new firms into gold mining do to the price of gold and the economic profits from gold mining?

Sources: Ruxandra Guidi, "Mining Companies on Quest to Cash In on Gold," National Public Radio, July 7, 2011; Jeanne Baron, "Gold Fever Draws African Farmers from Fields," National Public Radio, July 2, 2011; "China Mining Company, Zijin Mining Group to Expand Gold Mines Exploration in Australia," *Mining Exploration News*, August 2, 2011; "Sixteen New Firms to Prospect for Gold in Turkey's Kaz Mountains," *Hurriyet Daily News*, August 22, 2011.

5.12 Suppose that the laptop computer industry is perfectly competitive and that the firms that assemble laptops do not also make the displays, or screens. Suppose that the laptop display industry is also perfectly competitive. Finally, suppose that because the demand for laptop displays is currently relatively small, firms in the laptop display industry have not been able to take advantage of all the economies of scale in laptop display production. Use a graph of the laptop computer market to illustrate the long-run effects on equilibrium price and quantity in the laptop computer market of a substantial and sustained increase in the demand for laptop computers. Use another graph to show the effect on the cost curves of a typical firm in the laptop computer industry. Briefly explain your graphs. Do your graphs indicate that the laptop computer industry is a constant-cost industry, an increasing-cost industry, or a decreasing-cost industry?

5.13 [**Related to the** Chapter Opener **on page 391**] If in the long run vegetable growers who sell in farmers' markets make no greater rate of return on their investment than vegetable growers who sell to supermarkets, why did a significant number of vegetable growers switch from selling to supermarkets to selling in farmers' markets in the first place?

5.14 Suppose that some soybean farmers experience losses over a long period and therefore decide to exit the market. What effect will this exit have on the market supply of soybeans? How will the change in supply affect the market price of soybeans and the ability of farmers remaining in the soybean market to earn a profit?

 12.6 Perfect Competition and Efficiency, pages 413–415

LEARNING OBJECTIVE: Explain how perfect competition leads to economic efficiency.

Summary

Perfect competition results in **productive efficiency**, which means that goods and services are produced at the lowest possible cost. Perfect competition also results in **allocative efficiency**, which means the goods and services are produced up to the point where the last unit provides a marginal benefit to consumers equal to the marginal cost of producing it.

MyEconLab   Visit www.myeconlab.com to complete these exercises online and get instant feedback.

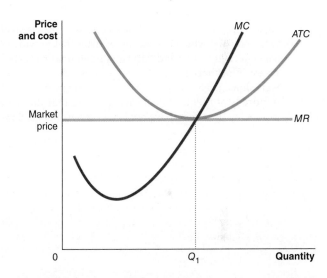

Review Questions

6.1 Why are consumers so powerful in a market system?

6.2 What is meant by allocative efficiency? What is meant by productive efficiency? Briefly discuss the difference between these two concepts.

6.3 How does perfect competition lead to allocative and productive efficiency?

Problems and Applications

6.4 The chapter states, "Firms will supply all those goods that provide consumers with a marginal benefit at least as great as the marginal cost of producing them." A student objects to this statement, arguing, "I doubt that firms will really do this. After all, firms are in business to make a profit; they don't care about what is best for consumers." Evaluate the student's argument.

6.5 The following graph represents the situation of Karl's Kumquats, a kumquat grower.
   a. How much profit is Karl earning?
   b. Does the current situation of Karl's firm illustrate productive efficiency or allocative efficiency? If so, briefly explain how.

6.6 [**Related to** Solved Problem 12.6 **on page 413**] Discuss the following statement: "In a perfectly competitive market, in the long run consumers benefit from reductions in costs, but firms don't." Don't firms also benefit from cost reductions because they are able to earn larger profits?

6.7 [**Related to** Solved Problem 12.6 **on page 413**] Suppose you read the following item in a newspaper article, under the headline "Price Gouging Alleged in Pencil Market":

> Consumer advocacy groups charged at a press conference yesterday that there is widespread price gouging in the sale of pencils. They released a study showing that whereas the average retail price of pencils was $1.00, the average cost of producing pencils was only $0.50. "Pencils can be produced without complicated machinery or highly skilled workers, so there is no justification for companies charging a price that is twice what it costs them to produce the product. Pencils are too

important in the life of every American for us to tolerate this sort of price gouging any longer," said George Grommet, chief spokesperson for the consumer groups. The consumer groups advocate passage of a law that would allow companies selling pencils to charge a price no more than 20 percent greater than their average cost of production.

Do you believe such a law would be advisable in a situation like this? Explain.

6.8 **[Related to** Solved Problem 12.6 **on page 413]** In 2013, Sony announced that it had suffered losses selling televisions for the ninth straight year. Given the strong consumer demand for plasma, LCD, and LED television sets, shouldn't Sony have been able to raise prices to earn a profit? Briefly explain.

Source: Daisuke Wakabayashi, "Investor Pushes Sony to Take Entertainment Unit Public," *Wall Street Journal*, May 14, 2013.

6.9 An article in the *Wall Street Journal* discusses the visual effects industry, which is made up of firms that provide visual effects for films and television programs. The article notes: "Blockbusters … often have thousands of visual effects shots. Even dramas and comedies today can include hundreds of them." But the article notes that the firms producing the effects have not been very profitable. Some firms have declared bankruptcy, and the former general manager of one firm was quoted as saying: "A good year for us was a 5% return." If demand for visual effects is so strong, why is it difficult for the firms that supply them to make an economic profit?

Source: Ben Fritz, "Visual Effects Industry Does a Disappearing Act," *Wall Street Journal*, February 22, 2013.

6.10 Although New York State is second only to Washington State in production of apples, its production has been declining during the past 20 years. The decline has been particularly steep in counties close to New York City. In 1985, there were more than 11,000 acres of apple orchards in Ulster County, which is 75 miles north of New York City. Today, only about 6,000 acres remain. As it became difficult for apple growers in the county to compete with lower-cost producers elsewhere, the resources these entrepreneurs were using to produce apples—particularly land—became more valuable in other uses. Many farmers sold their land to housing developers. Suppose a nutritionist develops a revolutionary new diet that involves eating 10 apples per day. The new diet becomes wildly popular. What effect is the new diet likely to have on the number of apple orchards within 100 miles of New York City? What effect is the diet likely to have on housing prices in New York City?

Starbucks: The Limits to Growth through Product Differentiation

Like many other large firms, Starbucks started small. In 1971, entrepreneurs Gordon Bowker, Gerald Baldwin, and Zev Siegl opened the first Starbucks in Seattle, Washington. Current CEO Howard Schultz joined the company 10 years later. Schultz realized that many consumers wanted a coffeehouse where they could relax, read, chat, and drink higher-quality coffee than was typically served in diners or donut shops. Designing Starbucks coffeehouses to provide this experience was the key to Schultz's success. But it was easy for other coffeehouses to copy the Starbucks approach.

By 2009, fierce competition and a weak economy led Starbucks to close hundreds of stores in the United States and cut prices as it tried to overcome the impression that it was the "home of the $4 coffee." Starbucks became profitable once more in 2010, partly due to expansion of its overseas markets, with sales in Asia exceeding $1 billion in 2013. Starbucks also made its coffeehouses friendlier to customers using smartphones and other mobile devices. The following quote from Schultz shows that he realizes that his company faces a constant challenge to stay ahead of its competitors and satisfy its customers: "I feel it's so important to remind us all of how fleeting success ... can be."

When we discussed the situation of firms in perfectly competitive markets, we saw that these markets share three key characteristics:

1. There are many firms.
2. All firms sell identical products.
3. There are no barriers to new firms entering the industry.

The market Starbucks competes in shares two of these characteristics: There are many coffeehouses, and the barriers to entering the market are very low. But the coffee at Starbucks is not identical to what competing coffeehouses offer. Selling coffee in coffeehouses is not like selling wheat: The products that Starbucks and its competitors sell are *differentiated* rather than identical. So, the coffeehouse market is *monopolistically competitive* rather than perfectly competitive. As we will see, most monopolistically competitive firms are unable to earn economic profits in the long run.

Sources: Annie Gasparro, "Starbucks Shuffles Global Management Team," *Wall Street Journal*, May 2, 2013; Annie Gasparo, "U.S., China Boost Starbucks," *Wall Street Journal*, April 25, 2013; and Claire Cain Miller, "A Changed Starbucks. A Changed C.E.O.," *New York Times*, March 12, 2011.

Economics in Your Life

Opening Your Own Restaurant

After you graduate, you plan to realize your dream of opening your own Italian restaurant. You are confident that many people will enjoy the pasta prepared with your grandmother's secret sauce. Although your hometown already has three Italian restaurants, you are convinced that you can enter this market and make a profit.

You have many choices to make in operating your restaurant. Will it be "family style," with sturdy but inexpensive furniture, where families with small—and noisy!—children will feel welcome, or will it be more elegant, with nice furniture, tablecloths, and candles? Will you offer a full menu or concentrate on pasta dishes that use your grandmother's secret sauce? These and other choices you make will distinguish your restaurant from competitors. What's likely to happen in the restaurant market in your hometown after you open your restaurant? How successful are you likely to be? Try to answer these questions as you read this chapter. You can check your answers against those we provide on **page 441** at the end of this chapter.

Monopolistic competition A market structure in which barriers to entry are low and many firms compete by selling similar, but not identical, products.

M any markets in the U.S. economy are similar to the coffeehouse market: They have many buyers and sellers, and the barriers to entry are low, but the goods and services offered for sale are differentiated rather than identical. Examples of these markets include restaurants, movie theaters, supermarkets, and clothing manufacturing. In fact, the majority of the firms you buy from are competing in **monopolistically competitive** markets.

We have seen how perfect competition benefits consumers and results in economic efficiency. Will these same desirable outcomes also hold for monopolistically competitive markets? This question is important because monopolistically competitive markets are common.

13.1 LEARNING OBJECTIVE

Explain why a monopolistically competitive firm has downward-sloping demand and marginal revenue curves.

Demand and Marginal Revenue for a Firm in a Monopolistically Competitive Market

If the Starbucks coffeehouse located a mile from where you live raises the price of a caffè latte from $3.00 to $3.25, it will lose some, but not all, of its customers. Some customers will switch to buying their coffee at another store, but other customers will be willing to pay the higher price for a variety of reasons: This store may be closer to them, or they may prefer Starbucks caffè lattes to similar coffees at competing stores. Because changing the price affects the quantity of caffè lattes sold, a Starbucks store will face a downward-sloping demand curve rather than the horizontal demand curve that a wheat farmer faces.

The Demand Curve for a Monopolistically Competitive Firm

Figure 13.1 shows how a change in price affects the quantity of caffè lattes Starbucks sells. The increase in the price from $3.00 to $3.25 decreases the quantity of caffè lattes sold from 3,000 per week to 2,400 per week. MyEconLab Concept Check

Marginal Revenue for a Firm with a Downward-Sloping Demand Curve

For a firm in a perfectly competitive market, the demand curve and the marginal revenue curve are the same (see Chapter 12). A perfectly competitive firm faces a horizontal demand curve and does not have to cut the price to sell a larger quantity. A monopolistically competitive firm, on the other hand, must cut the price to sell more, so its marginal revenue curve will slope downward and will be below its demand curve.

The data in Table 13.1 illustrate this point. To keep the numbers simple, let's assume that your local Starbucks coffeehouse is very small and sells at most 10 caffè lattes per week.

MyEconLab Animation

Figure 13.1

The Downward-Sloping Demand for Caffè Lattes at a Starbucks

If a Starbucks increases the price of caffè lattes, it will lose some, but not all, of its customers. In this case, raising the price from $3.00 to $3.25 reduces the quantity of caffè lattes sold from 3,000 to 2,400. Therefore, unlike a perfect competitor, a Starbucks coffeehouse faces a downward-sloping demand curve.

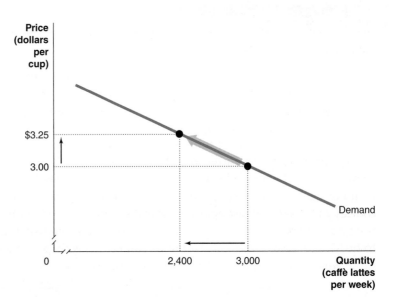

Table 13.1

Demand and Marginal Revenue at a Starbucks

Caffè Lattes Sold per Week (Q)	Price (P)	Total Revenue (TR = P × Q)	Average Revenue $\left(AR = \dfrac{TR}{Q}\right)$	Marginal Revenue $\left(MR = \dfrac{\Delta TR}{\Delta Q}\right)$
0	$6.00	$0.00	—	—
1	5.50	5.50	$5.50	$5.50
2	5.00	10.00	5.00	4.50
3	4.50	13.50	4.50	3.50
4	4.00	16.00	4.00	2.50
5	3.50	17.50	3.50	1.50
6	3.00	18.00	3.00	0.50
7	2.50	17.50	2.50	−0.50
8	2.00	16.00	2.00	−1.50
9	1.50	13.50	1.50	−2.50
10	1.00	10.00	1.00	−3.50

If the local Starbucks charges a price of $6.00 or more, all of its potential customers will buy their coffee somewhere else. If it charges $5.50, it will sell 1 caffè latte per week. For each additional $0.50 this Starbucks reduces the price, it increases the number of caffè lattes it sells by 1. The third column in the table shows how the firm's *total revenue* changes as it sells more caffè lattes. The fourth column shows the firm's revenue per unit, or its *average revenue*. Average revenue is equal to total revenue divided by quantity. Because total revenue equals price multiplied by quantity, dividing by quantity leaves just price. Therefore, *average revenue is always equal to price*. This result will be true for firms selling in any of the four market structures (see Chapter 12).

The last column in Table 13.1 shows the firm's marginal revenue, or the change in total revenue as the firm sells 1 more caffè latte. For a perfectly competitive firm, the additional revenue received from selling 1 more unit is just equal to the price. That will not be true for this Starbucks because to sell another caffè latte, it has to reduce the price. When the firm cuts the price by $0.50, one good thing and one bad thing happen:

- **The good thing.** It sells 1 more caffè latte; we can call this the *output effect*.
- **The bad thing.** It receives $0.50 less for each caffè latte that it could have sold at the higher price; we can call this the *price effect*.

Figure 13.2 illustrates what happens when the firm cuts the price from $3.50 to $3.00. Selling the sixth caffè latte adds the $3.00 price to the firm's revenue; this is the

MyEconLab Animation

Figure 13.2

How a Price Cut Affects a Firm's Revenue

If a local Starbucks reduces the price of a caffè latte from $3.50 to $3.00, the number of caffè lattes it sells per week will increase from 5 to 6. Its marginal revenue from selling the sixth caffè latte will be $0.50, which is equal to the $3.00 additional revenue from selling 1 more caffè latte (the area of the green box) minus the $2.50 loss in revenue from selling the first 5 caffè lattes for $0.50 less each (the area of the red box).

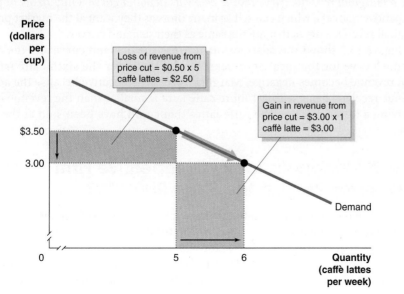

Figure 13.3

The Demand and Marginal Revenue Curves for a Monopolistically Competitive Firm

Any firm that has the ability to affect the price of the product it sells will have a marginal revenue curve that is below its demand curve. We plot the data from Table 13.1 to create the demand and marginal revenue curves. After the sixth caffè latte, marginal revenue becomes negative because the additional revenue received from selling 1 more caffè latte is smaller than the revenue lost from receiving a lower price on the caffè lattes that could have been sold at the original price.

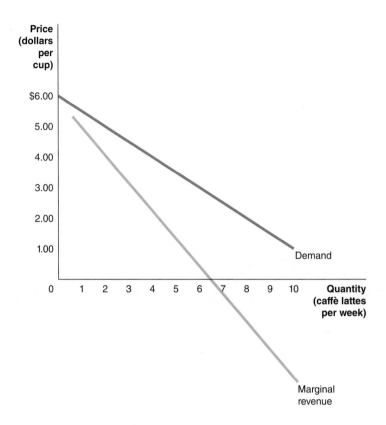

output effect. But this Starbucks now receives a price of $3.00, rather than $3.50, on the first 5 caffè lattes sold; this is the price effect. As a result of the price effect, the firm's revenue on these 5 caffè lattes is $2.50 less than it would have been if the price had remained at $3.50. So, the firm has gained $3.00 in revenue on the sixth caffè latte and lost $2.50 in revenue on the first 5 caffè lattes, for a net change in revenue of $0.50. Marginal revenue is the change in total revenue from selling 1 more unit. Therefore, the marginal revenue of the sixth caffè latte is $0.50. Notice that the marginal revenue of the sixth unit is far below its price of $3.00. In fact, for each additional caffè latte this Starbucks sells, marginal revenue will be less than price. There is an important general point: *Every firm that has the ability to affect the price of the good or service it sells will have a marginal revenue curve that is below its demand curve.* Only firms in perfectly competitive markets, which can sell as many units as they want at the market price, have marginal revenue curves that are the same as their demand curves.

Figure 13.3 shows the relationship between the demand curve and the marginal revenue curve for the local Starbucks. Notice that after the sixth caffè latte, marginal revenue becomes negative. Marginal revenue is negative because the additional revenue received from selling 1 more caffè latte is smaller than the revenue lost from receiving a lower price on the caffè lattes that could have been sold at the original price.

How a Monopolistically Competitive Firm Maximizes Profit in the Short Run

All firms use the same approach to maximize profits: They produce the quantity where marginal revenue is equal to marginal cost. So the local Starbucks will maximize profits by selling the quantity of caffè lattes for which the last caffè latte sold adds the same amount to the firm's revenue as to its costs. Let's look more carefully at how monopolistically competitive firms maximize profits by considering the situation the local Starbucks faces in the short run. Recall that in the short run, at least one factor of production is fixed, and there is not enough time for new firms to enter the market (see Chapter 11). A Starbucks has many costs, including the cost of purchasing the ingredients for its caffè lattes and other coffees, the electricity it uses, and the wages of its employees. Recall that a firm's *marginal cost* is the increase in total cost resulting from producing another unit of output. We have seen that for many firms, the marginal cost curve has a U shape. We will assume that the marginal cost curve for this Starbucks has the usual shape.

We combine the revenue data for this Starbucks from Table 13.1 with cost data to create the table in Figure 13.4. The graphs in Figure 13.4 plot the data from the table. In panel (a), we see how this Starbucks can determine its profit-maximizing quantity and price. As long as the marginal cost of selling 1 more caffè latte is less than the marginal revenue, the firm should sell additional caffè lattes. For example, increasing the quantity of caffè lattes sold from 3 per week to 4 per week increases cost by $1.00 but increases

Caffè Lattes Sold per Week (Q)	Price (P)	Total Revenue (TR)	Marginal Revenue (MR)	Total Cost (TC)	Marginal Cost (MC)	Average Total Cost (ATC)	Profit
0	$6.00	$0.00	—	$5.00	—	—	−$5.00
1	5.50	5.50	$5.50	8.00	$3.00	$8.00	−2.50
2	5.00	10.00	4.50	9.50	1.50	4.75	0.50
3	4.50	13.50	3.50	10.00	0.50	3.33	3.50
4	4.00	16.00	2.50	11.00	1.00	2.75	5.00
5	3.50	17.50	1.50	12.50	1.50	2.50	5.00
6	3.00	18.00	0.50	14.50	2.00	2.42	3.50
7	2.50	17.50	−0.50	17.00	2.50	2.43	0.50
8	2.00	16.00	−1.50	20.00	3.00	2.50	−4.00
9	1.50	13.50	−2.50	23.50	3.50	2.61	−10.00
10	1.00	10.00	−3.50	27.50	4.00	2.75	−17.50

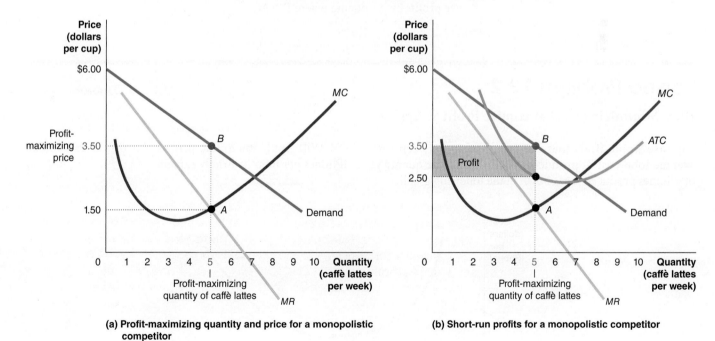

(a) Profit-maximizing quantity and price for a monopolistic competitor

(b) Short-run profits for a monopolistic competitor

MyEconLab Animation

Figure 13.4   **Maximizing Profit in a Monopolistically Competitive Market**

To maximize profit, a Starbucks coffeehouse wants to sell caffè lattes up to the point where the marginal revenue from selling the last caffè latte is just equal to the marginal cost. As the table shows, selling the fifth caffè latte—point A in panel (a)—adds $1.50 to the firm's costs and $1.50 to its revenues. The firm then uses the demand curve to find the price that will lead consumers to buy this quantity of

caffè lattes (point B). In panel (b), the green box represents the firm's profits. The box has a height equal to $1.00, which is the $3.50 price minus the average total cost of $2.50, and it has a base equal to the quantity of 5 caffè lattes. So, for this Starbucks profit equals $1 × 5 = $5.00.

revenue by $2.50. So, the firm's profits are increased by $1.50 as a result of selling the fourth caffè latte.

As this Starbucks sells more caffè lattes, rising marginal cost eventually equals marginal revenue, and the firm sells the profit-maximizing quantity of caffè lattes. Marginal cost equals marginal revenue with the fifth caffè latte, which adds $1.50 to the firm's costs and $1.50 to its revenues—point *A* in panel (a) of Figure 13.4. The demand curve tells us the price at which the firm is able to sell 5 caffè lattes per week. In Figure 13.4, if we draw a vertical line from 5 caffè lattes up to the demand curve, we can see that the price at which the firm can sell 5 caffè lattes per week is $3.50 (point *B*). We can conclude that for this Starbucks, the profit-maximizing quantity is 5 caffè lattes, and the profit-maximizing price is $3.50. If the firm sells more than 5 caffè lattes per week, its profit will fall. For example, selling a sixth caffè latte adds $2.00 to its costs and only $0.50 to its revenues. So, its profit will fall from $5.00 to $3.50.

Panel (b) adds the average total cost curve for Starbucks. The panel shows that the average total cost of selling 5 caffè lattes is $2.50. Recall from Chapter 12 that:

$$\text{Profit} = (P - ATC) \times Q.$$

In this case, profit = ($3.50 − $2.50) × 5 = $5.00. The green rectangle in panel (b) shows the amount of profit. The rectangle has a base equal to Q and a height equal to $(P - ATC)$, so its area equals profit.

Notice that, unlike a perfectly competitive firm, which produces where $P = MC$, a monopolistically competitive firm produces where $P > MC$. In this case, this Starbucks is charging a price of $3.50, although marginal cost is $1.50. For a perfectly competitive firm, price equals marginal revenue, $P = MR$. Therefore, to fulfill the $MR = MC$ condition for profit maximization, a perfectly competitive firm will produce where $P = MC$. $P > MR$ for a monopolistically competitive firm because the firm's marginal revenue curve is below its demand curve. Therefore, a monopolistically competitive firm will maximize profits by producing where $P > MC$.

Solved Problem 13.2

MyEconLab Interactive Animation

Does Minimizing Cost Maximize Profit at Apple?

Suppose Apple finds that the relationship between the average total cost of producing iPhones and the quantity of iPhones produced is as shown in the following graph.

Will Apple maximize profits if it produces 800,000 iPhones per month? Briefly explain.

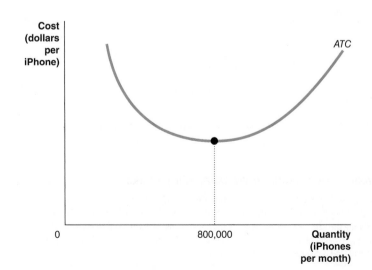

Solving the Problem

Step 1: **Review the chapter material.** This problem is about how monopolistically competitive firms maximize profits, so you may want to review the section "How a Monopolistically Competitive Firm Maximizes Profit in the Short Run," which begins on page 428.

Step 2: **Discuss the relationship between minimizing costs and maximizing profits.** Firms often talk about the steps they take to reduce costs. The graph shows that by producing 800,000 iPhones per month, Apple will minimize its average cost of production. But remember that minimizing cost is not the firm's ultimate goal; the firm's ultimate goal is to maximize profit. Depending on demand, a firm may maximize profit by producing a quantity that is either larger or smaller than the quantity that would minimize average total cost.

Step 3: **Draw a graph that shows Apple maximizing profit at a quantity where average cost is not minimized.** Note that in the graph, average total cost reaches a minimum at a quantity of 800,000, but profit is maximized at a quantity of 600,000.

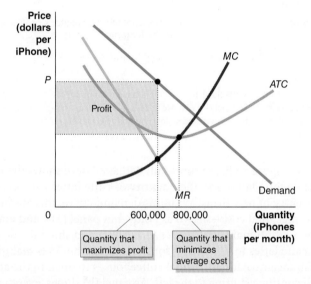

Your Turn: For more practice, do related problem 2.5 on pages 443–444 at the end of this chapter.

MyEconLab Study Plan

What Happens to Profits in the Long Run?

13.3 LEARNING OBJECTIVE

Analyze the situation of a monopolistically competitive firm in the long run.

Remember that a firm makes an economic profit when its total revenue is greater than all of its costs, including the opportunity cost of the funds invested in the firm by its owners. Because cost curves include the owners' opportunity costs, the Starbucks coffeehouse represented in Figure 13.4 on page 429 is making an economic profit. This economic profit gives entrepreneurs an incentive to enter this market and establish new firms. If a Starbucks is earning an economic profit selling caffè lattes, new coffeehouses are likely to open in the same area.

How Does the Entry of New Firms Affect the Profits of Existing Firms?

As new coffeehouses open near a local Starbucks, the firm's demand curve will shift to the left. The demand curve will shift because the Starbucks will sell fewer caffè lattes at each price when there are additional coffeehouses in the area selling similar drinks. The demand curve will also become more elastic because consumers have additional coffeehouses from which to buy coffee, so the Starbucks will lose more sales if it raises its prices. Figure 13.5 shows how the demand curve for the local Starbucks shifts as new firms enter its market.

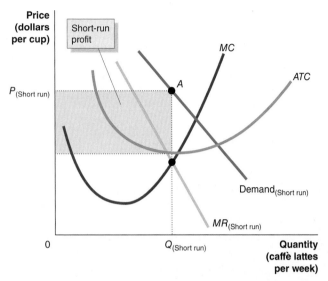

(a) A monopolistic competitor may earn a short-run profit

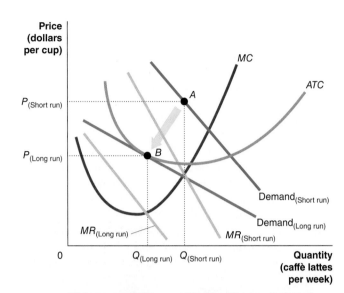

(b) A monopolistic competitor's profits are eliminated in the long run

MyEconLab Animation

Figure 13.5 **How Entry of New Firms Eliminates Profits**

Panel (a) shows that in the short run, the local Starbucks faces the demand and marginal revenue curves labeled "Short run." With this demand curve, Starbucks can charge a price above average total cost (point A) and make a profit, shown by the green rectangle. But this profit attracts new firms to enter the market, which shifts the demand and marginal revenue curves to the curves labeled "Long run" in panel (b). Because price is now equal to average total cost (point B), Starbucks breaks even and no longer earns an economic profit.

In panel (a) of Figure 13.5, the short-run demand curve shows the relationship between the price of caffè lattes and the quantity of caffè lattes this Starbucks sells per week before the entry of new firms. With this demand curve, this Starbucks can charge a price above average total cost—shown as point A in panel (a)—and make a profit. But this profit attracts additional coffeehouses to the area and shifts the demand curve for this Starbucks' caffè lattes to the left. As long as this Starbucks is making an economic profit, there is an incentive for additional coffeehouses to open in the area, and the demand curve will continue shifting to the left. As panel (b) shows, eventually the demand curve will have shifted to the point where it is just touching—or tangent to—the average total cost curve.

In the long run, at the point where the demand curve is tangent to the average total cost curve, price is equal to average total cost (point B), the firm is breaking even, and it no longer earns an economic profit. In the long run, the demand curve is also more elastic because the more coffeehouses there are in the area, the more sales this Starbucks will lose to other coffeehouses if it raises its price.

Don't Let This Happen to You

Don't Confuse Zero Economic Profit with Zero Accounting Profit

Remember that economists count the opportunity cost of the owner's investment in a firm as a cost. Suppose you invest $200,000 opening a pizza parlor, and the return you could earn on those funds each year in a similar investment—such as opening a sandwich shop—is 10 percent. Therefore, the annual opportunity cost of investing the funds in your own business is 10 percent of $200,000, or $20,000. This $20,000 is part of your profit in the accounting sense, and you would have to pay taxes on it. But in an economic sense, the $20,000 is a cost. In long-run equilibrium, we would expect that entry of new firms would keep you from earning more than 10 percent on your investment. So, you would end up breaking even and earning zero economic profit, even though you were earning an accounting profit of $20,000.

MyEconLab Study Plan

Your Turn: Test your understanding by doing related problem 3.6 on page 445 at the end of this chapter.

Of course, it is possible that a monopolistically competitive firm will suffer an economic loss in the short run. As a consequence, the owners of the firm will not be covering the opportunity cost of their investment. We expect that, in the long run, firms will exit an industry if they are suffering economic losses. If firms exit, the demand curve for the output of a remaining firm will shift to the right. This process will continue until the representative firm in the industry is able to charge a price equal to its average total cost and break even. Therefore, in the long run, monopolistically competitive firms will experience neither economic profits nor economic losses. Table 13.2 summarizes the short run and the long run for a monopolistically competitive firm.

MyEconLab Concept Check

Table 13.2   The Short Run and the Long Run for a Monopolistically Competitive Firm

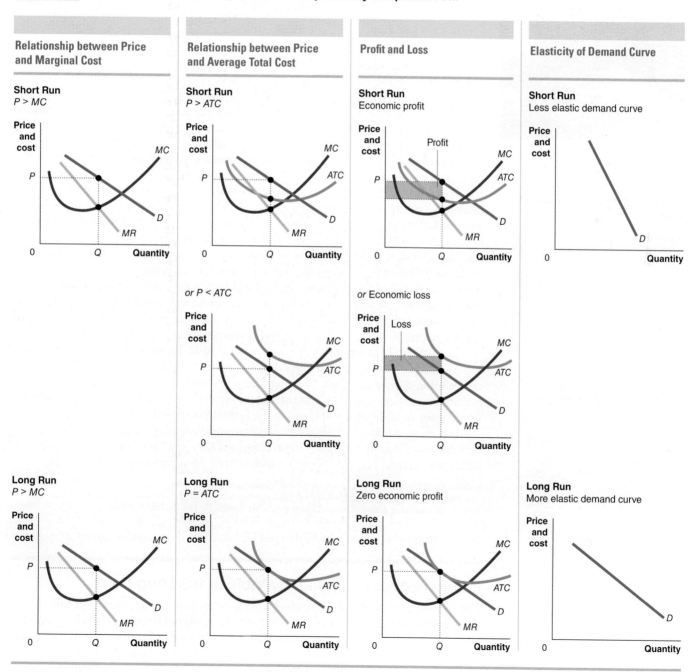

The Rise and Decline and Rise of Starbucks

In the spring of 2009, an article from Bloomberg News summed up the situation that Starbucks was in: "After more than a decade of sensational buzz, Starbucks is struggling nationwide as it faces slowing sales growth and increased competition." The initial success and later struggles of Starbucks are a familiar pattern for firms in monopolistically competitive markets.

When Starbucks began rapidly expanding, CEO Howard Schultz knew that fresh-brewed coffee was widely available in restaurants, diners, and donut shops. He believed, though, that he had a strategy that would differentiate Starbucks from competitors: Starbucks would offer a European espresso bar atmosphere, with large, comfortable chairs, music playing, and groups of friends dropping in and out during the day. From the mid-1990s through the mid-2000s, this strategy worked very well, and Starbucks opened nearly 17,000 stores worldwide. But the profitability of Starbucks attracted competitors. Other nationwide chains, such as Caribou Coffee, Peet's Coffee, and Diedrich Coffee, and regional chains, such as Dunn Brothers Coffee, provided stores with similar atmospheres, as did many individually owned coffeehouses.

Starbucks used innovations such as Wi-Fi to return to profitability after several years of struggling with intense competition from other firms.

In addition, McDonald's and Dunkin' Donuts began competing more directly with Starbucks. Dunkin' Donuts began building more upscale restaurants, and McDonald's began selling espresso-based coffee drinks for prices considerably below those at Starbucks. Schultz was also worried that in opening thousands of coffeehouses worldwide, Starbucks had made the customers' experience less distinctive and easier for competitors to copy.

Beginning in 2010, Schultz managed a remarkable turnaround, with Starbucks' sales and profits increasing. Some of the success was attributable to an expansion in overseas markets, where competition was not as strong as in the United States. By 2013, the firm had sales of more than $1 billion in Asia and plans to open thousands of additional stores in China. But the firm's focus remained on staying one step ahead of its competition in the United States. The revival of Starbucks in the United States was based on several factors: The firm gave customers more freedom to customize drinks; it started a loyalty program that included free refills and other perks for regular customers; it started a mobile payment system that allowed customers to pay with a smartphone; and it provided stores with machines that brewed higher-quality coffees. Stephen Gillett, the firm's chief information officer, improved in-store Wi-Fi so customers could use it without having to go through a logon screen and could get free access to content from sources such as the *Wall Street Journal* and *USA Today*, as well as see exclusive movie trailers. The objective was to keep customers in the store longer so they would buy more coffee. The customer loyalty program, by reducing the average price for frequent customers, helped fight the impression that Starbucks coffee was too expensive to buy a cup every day.

In mid-2013, Starbucks's strategy appeared to be working as its U.S. stores experienced increasing sales while sales at Dunkin' Donuts and McDonald's were flat or declining. Schulz declared: "Anyone who suggested in '08 or '09 that Starbucks was reaching saturation in the U.S. was just flat out wrong," and he announced that Starbucks would open an additional 300 stores in the United States by the end of the year.

In a monopolistically competitive industry, maintaining profits in the long run is very difficult. Only by constantly innovating has Starbucks been able to return to profitability after several years of struggling with intense competition from other firms.

Sources: Annie Gasparro, "Starbucks Shuffles Global Management Team," *Wall Street Journal*, May 2, 2013; Annie Gasparo, "U.S., China Boost Starbucks," *Wall Street Journal*, April 25, 2013; Andrew Harrer, "Starbucks Corporation," Bloomberg News, April 13, 2009; and Janet Adamy, "Dunkin' Donuts Tries to Go Upscale, But Not Too Far," *Wall Street Journal*, April 8, 2006.

MyEconLab Study Plan **Your Turn:** Test your understanding by doing related problem 3.8 on page 445 at the end of this chapter.

Is Zero Economic Profit Inevitable in the Long Run?

The economic analysis of the long run shows the effects of market forces over time. Owners of monopolistically competitive firms, of course, do not have to passively accept this long-run result. The key to earning an economic profit is either to sell a differentiated product or to find a way of producing an existing product at a lower cost. If a monopolistically competitive firm selling a differentiated product is earning a profit, the profit will attract the entry of additional firms, and the entry of those firms will eventually eliminate the firm's profit. If a firm introduces new technology that allows it to sell a good or service at a lower cost, competing firms will eventually duplicate that technology and eliminate the firm's profit. *But this result holds only if the firm stands still and fails to find new ways of differentiating its product or fails to find new ways of lowering the cost of producing its product.* Starbucks had great initial success, had difficulty maintaining its profitability after the entry of new firms, and then found its way back to profitability by introducing new products and improving its customers' experience through a loyalty program and other innovations. Firms continually struggle to find new ways of differentiating their products as they try to stay one step ahead of other firms that are attempting to copy their success.

The owner of a competitive firm is in a position like that of Ebenezer Scrooge in Charles Dickens's *A Christmas Carol*. When the Ghost of Christmas Yet to Come shows Scrooge visions of his own death, he asks the ghost, "Are these the shadows of the things that Will be, or are they shadows of things that May be, only?" The shadow of the end of their profits haunts owners of every firm. Firms try to continue earning profits by reducing costs, by improving their products, by providing exceptional customer service, or by convincing consumers that their products are indeed different from what competitors offer. To stay one step ahead of its competitors, a firm has to offer consumers goods or services that they perceive to have greater *value* than those competing firms offer. Value can take the form of product differentiation that makes the good or service more suited to consumers' preferences, or it can take the form of a lower price. MyEconLab Concept Check

---

Solved Problem 13.3

MyEconLab Interactive Animation

Can It Be Profitable to Be the High-Price Seller?

h.h.gregg is an appliance and electronics retailer with stores in 20 states. As a relatively small firm, it has to pay more for its appliances, televisions, and other goods from manufacturers than does a large chain, such as Best Buy. Because h.h.gregg must pay higher prices to manufacturers, it must charge higher prices to consumers. How is h.h.gregg able to succeed in competition with Best Buy, Wal-Mart, Amazon, and other big retailers, despite charging higher prices?

According to an article in the *Wall Street Journal*: "h.h.gregg's commissioned sales staff is an advantage over

national chains with young, lower-paid hourly workers that tend to stay for shorter periods." h.h.gregg's CEO noted that: "We have sales people that have been with us 10 to 20 years, and customers who come in and ask for them by name."

Use this information to explain how an h.h.gregg store might be more profitable than a similar Best Buy store, despite the fact that the h.h.gregg store charges higher prices. Use a graph for h.h.gregg and a graph for Best Buy to illustrate your answer.

Solving the Problem

Step 1: Review the chapter material. This problem is about how a monopolistically competitive firm maximizes profits and about how firms attempt to earn economic profits in the long run, so you may want to review the section "How a Monopolistically Competitive Firm Maximizes Profit in the Short Run," which begins on page 428, and the section "Is Zero Economic Profit Inevitable in the Long Run?" on page 434.

Step 2: Explain how h.h.gregg can remain profitable despite its high costs. If an h.h.gregg store has higher costs than a comparable Best Buy store, it can have greater profits only if the demand for its goods is higher. According to the *Wall Street Journal* article, h.h.gregg has differentiated itself from the competition, particularly from large chain stores such as Best Buy, by offering better customer service. By having salespeople who are more knowledgeable and more experienced than the salespeople hired by competitors, h.h.gregg has attracted consumers who need help in buying televisions and appliances. The higher demand from these consumers must be enough to offset h.h.gregg's higher costs.

Step 3: Draw graphs to illustrate your argument. For simplicity, the graphs here assume that televisions are the product being sold. Panel (a) shows the situation for h.h.gregg, and panel (b) shows the situation for Best Buy.

The graphs show that the h.h.gregg store has both greater demand and higher costs than the Best Buy store. Because the greater demand more than offsets the higher costs, the h.h.gregg store makes a larger profit.

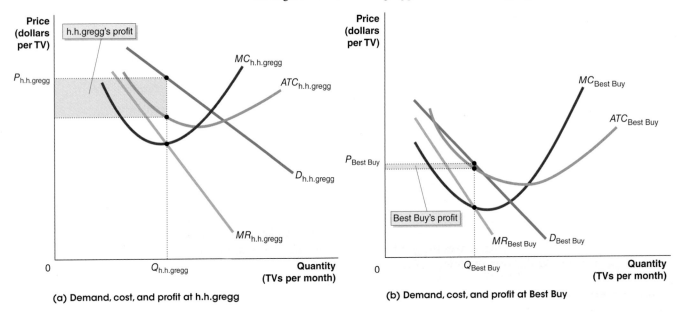

(a) Demand, cost, and profit at h.h.gregg

(b) Demand, cost, and profit at Best Buy

Extra Credit: As we have seen, firms constantly search for means of differentiating themselves from their competitors. Often, differentiation works for a while but then breaks down as competitors copy the strategy. After a number of years of success, by 2013, the competition may have caught up with h.h.gregg, as its sales were declining.

Sources: Debbi Cai, "Hhgregg 4th-Quarter Profit Down 82% on Weaker Same-Store Sales," *Wall Street Journal*, May 20, 2013; Scott Tilghman, "Hhgregg Could Get a Leg Up," *Barron's*, June 2, 2011; and Miguel Bustillo, "Small Electronics Chains Thrive in Downturn," *Wall Street Journal*, May 27, 2009.

MyEconLab Study Plan

Your Turn: For more practice, do related problem 3.9 on pages 445–446 at the end of this chapter.

13.4 LEARNING OBJECTIVE

Compare the efficiency of monopolistic competition and perfect competition.

Comparing Monopolistic Competition and Perfect Competition

We have seen that monopolistic competition and perfect competition share the characteristic that in long-run equilibrium firms earn zero economic profits. As Figure 13.6 shows, however, there are two important differences between long-run equilibrium in the two markets:

- Monopolistically competitive firms charge a price greater than marginal cost.
- Monopolistically competitive firms do not produce at minimum average total cost.

Excess Capacity under Monopolistic Competition

Recall that a firm in a perfectly competitive market faces a perfectly elastic demand curve that is also its marginal revenue curve. Therefore, the firm maximizes profit by producing the quantity where price equals marginal cost. As panel (a) of Figure 13.6 shows, in long-run equilibrium, a perfectly competitive firm produces at the minimum point of its average total cost curve.

Panel (b) of Figure 13.6 shows that the profit-maximizing level of output for a monopolistically competitive firm comes at a level of output where price is greater than marginal cost, and the firm is not at the minimum point of its average total cost curve. A monopolistically competitive firm has *excess capacity*: If it increased its output, it could produce at a lower average total cost.

MyEconLab Concept Check

Is Monopolistic Competition Inefficient?

We previously discussed the difference between productive efficiency and allocative efficiency (see Chapter 12). *Productive efficiency* refers to the situation where a good is

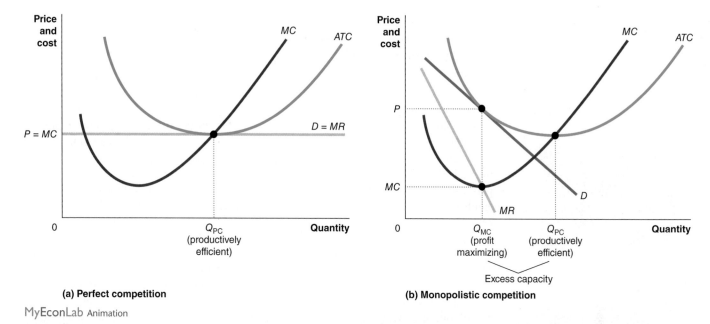

(a) Perfect competition

(b) Monopolistic competition

MyEconLab Animation

Figure 13.6 Comparing Long-Run Equilibrium under Perfect Competition and Monopolistic Competition

In panel (a), a perfectly competitive firm in long-run equilibrium produces at Q_{PC}, where price equals marginal cost, and average total cost is at a minimum. The perfectly competitive firm is both allocatively efficient and productively efficient. In panel (b), a monopolistically competitive firm produces at Q_{MC}, where price is greater than marginal cost, and average total cost is not at a minimum. As a result, the monopolistically competitive firm is neither allocatively efficient nor productively efficient. The monopolistically competitive firm has excess capacity equal to the difference between its profit-maximizing level of output and the productively efficient level of output.

produced at the lowest possible cost. *Allocative efficiency* refers to the situation where every good or service is produced up to the point where the last unit provides a marginal benefit to consumers equal to the marginal cost of producing it. For productive efficiency to hold, firms must produce at the minimum point of average total cost. For allocative efficiency to hold, firms must charge a price equal to marginal cost. In a perfectly competitive market, both productive efficiency and allocative efficiency are achieved, but in a monopolistically competitive market, neither is achieved. Does it matter? Economists have debated whether monopolistically competitive markets being neither productively nor allocatively efficient results in a significant loss of well-being to society in these markets compared with perfectly competitive markets.   MyEconLab Concept Check

How Consumers Benefit from Monopolistic Competition

Looking again at Figure 13.6, you can see that the key difference between the monopolistically competitive firm and the perfectly competitive firm is that the demand curve for the monopolistically competitive firm slopes downward, whereas the demand curve for the perfectly competitive firm is a horizontal line. The demand curve for the monopolistically competitive firm slopes downward because the good or service the firm is selling is differentiated from the goods or services being sold by competing firms. The perfectly competitive firm is selling a good or service identical to those being sold by its competitors. A key point to remember is that *firms differentiate their products to appeal to consumers.* For example, when Starbucks coffeehouses begin offering slower-brewed, higher-quality coffees, when Wal-Mart begins carrying more Blu-ray discs and fewer regular DVDs, when General Mills introduces Apple-Cinnamon Cheerios, or when PepsiCo introduces Diet Wild Cherry Pepsi, they are all attempting to attract and retain consumers through product differentiation. The success of these product differentiation strategies indicates that some consumers find these products preferable to the alternatives. Consumers, therefore, are better off than they would have been had these companies not differentiated their products.

We can conclude that consumers face a trade-off when buying the product of a monopolistically competitive firm: They are paying a price that is greater than marginal cost, and the product is not being produced at minimum average cost, but they benefit from being able to purchase a product that is differentiated and more closely suited to their tastes.   MyEconLab Concept Check

Will NJOY own the e-cigarette market?

Making the Connection
MyEconLab Video

Peter Thiel, e-Cigarettes, and the Monopoly in Monopolistic Competition

The term *monopolistic competition* is a combination of two words with opposite economic meanings: monopoly—meaning an industry with one firm—and competition—meaning an industry with many firms. A true monopoly—like a town's water department delivering tap water to homes—has no competition and is very rare, but the economists who first began using the term monopolistic competition wanted to emphasize that most firms have, in a sense, a *limited* monopoly. If you open a pizza parlor on the corner, yours will be the only pizza parlor on that corner and probably the only pizza parlor on that block and possibly—if you are lucky!—the only pizza parlor in that part of town. The "competition" in monopolistic competition was meant to emphasize that if your firm is a success and you make a profit, new firms will enter the market and your profit is likely to be competed away.

Peter Thiel is a billionaire entrepreneur. He was co-founder of PayPal, the online payment system, and was an early investor in firms such as LinkedIn, Zynga, and Facebook. Thiel has emphasized that the key to starting a successful firm is rarely to provide an existing product at a higher quality or lower price—although Toyota is an example of a firm that succeeded using that approach. Instead, Thiel recommends focusing on the monopoly part of monopolistic competition by coming up with a new product or service or a product or service that meets an existing consumer demand in an entirely new way. Before PayPal, people could pay for Internet services using a credit card or by sending a check. But these ways of paying had drawbacks: In the early days of the Internet, many sellers on eBay and elsewhere didn't have the ability to accept credit cards or wanted to avoid the fees that credit card companies charge sellers. Checks take time to clear through banks, making sellers wait for payment and buyers wait for goods to be shipped. PayPal gave consumers using eBay and other Web sites a new way to pay for purchases.

One columnist summarized Thiel's approach: "He's talking about doing something so creative that you establish a distinct market, niche and identity. You've established a creative monopoly and everybody has to come to you if they want that service, at least for a time." In a course Thiel gave at Stanford University, he argued that an entrepreneur should aim for "owning a market"—at least for a period: "For a company to own its market, it must have some combination of brand, scale cost advantages, network effects, or proprietary technology."

Thiel's latest project is investing in NJOY, a firm that makes e-cigarettes. E-cigarettes look like regular tobacco cigarettes but use a battery to turn a liquid containing nicotine into a vapor. E-cigarettes have a potential advantage over conventional cigarettes in providing nicotine to smokers without the risks of cancer, heart disease, and other health problems. U.S. consumers spend about $100 billion per year on conventional cigarettes, so converting even a small percentage of smokers to e-cigarettes could prove very profitable. But a firm selling e-cigarettes faces a number of problems. The U.S. Food and Drug Administration has stated that further research is necessary to determine whether e-cigarettes may pose health risks to smokers. Some states have banned their sale to minors, and some businesses—including Starbucks—have banned their use.

Time will tell whether NJOY will succeed in owning an important market—at least for a time.

Sources: Mike Esterl, "E-Cigarettes Fire Up Investors, Regulators," *Wall Street Journal*, June 9, 2013; Teresa Novellino, "With Cash, Sean Parker and Peter Thiel Follow NJOY's Vapor Trail," http://upstart.bizjournals.com, June 10, 2013; David Brooks, "The Creative Monopoly," *New York Times*, April 23, 2012; and Blake Masters, "Ten Lessons from Peter Thiel's Class on Startups," *Forbes*, June 7, 2012.

MyEconLab Study Plan

Your Turn: Test your understanding by doing related problem 4.8 on page 447 at the end of this chapter.

13.5 LEARNING OBJECTIVE

Define marketing and explain how firms use marketing to differentiate their products.

How Marketing Differentiates Products

Firms can differentiate their products through **marketing**, which refers to all the activities necessary for a firm to sell a product to a consumer. Marketing includes activities such as determining which product to sell, designing the product, advertising the product, deciding how to distribute the product—for example, in retail stores or through a Web site—and monitoring how changes in consumer tastes are affecting the market for the product. Peter F. Drucker, a leading business strategist, described marketing as follows: "It is the whole business seen from the point of view of its final result, that is, from the consumer's point of view.... True marketing ... does not ask, 'What do we want to sell?' It asks, 'What does the consumer want to buy?' "

For monopolistically competitive firms to earn economic profits and defend those profits from competitors, they must differentiate their products. Firms use two marketing tools to differentiate their products: brand management and advertising.

Brand Management

Once a firm has succeeded in differentiating its product, it must try to maintain that differentiation over time through **brand management**. As we have seen, whenever a firm successfully introduces a new product or a significantly different version of an old product, it earns an economic profit in the short run. But the success of the firm inspires competitors to copy the new or improved product, and, in the long run, the firm's economic profit will be competed away. Firms use brand management to postpone the time when they will no longer be able to earn economic profits.   MyEconLab Concept Check

Advertising

An innovative advertising campaign can make even long-established and familiar products, such as Coke or McDonald's Big Mac hamburgers, seem more desirable than competing products. When a firm advertises a product, it is trying to shift the demand curve for the product to the right and to make it more inelastic. If the firm is successful, it will sell more of the product at every price, and it will be able to increase the price it charges without losing as many customers. Of course, advertising also increases a firm's costs. If the increase in revenue that results from the advertising is greater than the increase in costs, the firm's profits will rise.   MyEconLab Concept Check

Defending a Brand Name

Once a firm has established a successful brand name, it has a strong incentive to defend it. A firm can apply for a *trademark*, which grants legal protection against other firms using its product's name.

One threat to a trademarked name is the possibility that it will become so widely used for a type of product that it will no longer be associated with the product of a specific company. Courts in the United States have ruled that when this happens, a firm is no longer entitled to legal protection of the brand name. For example, "aspirin," "escalator," and "thermos" were originally all brand names of the products of particular firms, but each became so widely used to refer to a type of product that none remains a legally protected brand name. Firms spend substantial amounts of money trying to make sure that this does not happen to them. Coca-Cola, for example, employs people to travel to restaurants around the country and order a "Coke" with their meal. If the restaurant serves Pepsi or some other cola, rather than Coke, Coca-Cola's legal department sends the restaurant a letter reminding the owner that "Coke" is a trademarked name and not a generic name for any cola. Similarly, Xerox Corporation spends money on advertising to remind the public that "Xerox" is not a generic term for making photocopies.

Legally enforcing trademarks can be difficult. Estimates are that each year, U.S. firms lose hundreds of billions of dollars in sales worldwide as a result of unauthorized use of their trademarked brand names. U.S. firms often find it difficult to enforce their trademarks in the courts of some foreign countries, although recent international agreements have increased the legal protections for trademarks.

Firms that sell their products through franchises rather than through company-owned stores encounter the problem that if a franchisee does not run his or her business well, the firm's brand may be damaged. Automobile firms send "roadmen" to visit their dealers to make sure the dealerships are clean and well maintained and that the service departments employ competent mechanics and are well equipped with spare parts. Similarly, McDonald's sends employees from corporate headquarters to visit McDonald's franchises to make sure the bathrooms are clean and the French fries are hot.   MyEconLab Concept Check   MyEconLab Study Plan

Marketing All the activities necessary for a firm to sell a product to a consumer.

Brand management The actions of a firm intended to maintain the differentiation of a product over time.

Figure 13.7

What Makes a Firm Successful?

The factors under a firm's control—the ability to differentiate its product and the ability to produce it at lower cost—combine with the factors beyond its control to determine the firm's profitability.
Source: Adapted from Figure 9.2 in David Besanko, David Dranove, Mark Shanley, and Scott Schaefer, *The Economics of Strategy*, 6th edition, New York: John Wiley & Sons, Inc., 2012, p. 295.

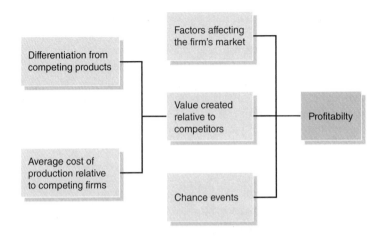

13.6 LEARNING OBJECTIVE

Identify the key factors that determine a firm's success.

What Makes a Firm Successful?

A firm's owners and managers control some of the factors that make a firm successful and allow it to earn economic profits. The most important of these is the firm's ability to differentiate its product or to produce it at a lower average cost than competing firms. A firm that successfully does one or both of these things creates *value* for its customers. Consumers will buy a product if they believe it meets a need not met by competing products or if its price is below that of competitors.

Some factors that affect a firm's profitability are not directly under the firm's control. Certain factors will affect all the firms in a market. For example, rising prices for jet fuel will reduce the profitability of all airlines. When some consumers decided that rather than buy DVDs, they preferred to download or stream movies from Netflix, iTunes, or Amazon, the profitability of all stores selling DVDs was reduced.

Sheer chance also plays a role in business, as it does in all other aspects of life. A struggling McDonald's franchise may see profits increase dramatically after the county unexpectedly decides to build a new road nearby. Many businesses in New York City, including restaurants, hotels, and theaters, experienced a marked drop in customers and profits as a result of the effects of Hurricane Sandy in October 2012. Figure 13.7 illustrates the important point that factors within the firm's control and factors outside the firm's control interact to determine the firm's profitability.

Making the Connection
MyEconLab Video

Is Being the First Firm in the Market a Key to Success?

Some business analysts argue that the first firm to enter a market can have important *first-mover advantages*. By being the first to sell a particular good, a firm may find its name closely associated with the good in the public's mind, as, for instance, Amazon is closely associated with ordering books online or eBay is associated with online auctions. This close association may make it more difficult for new firms to enter the market and compete against the first mover.

Surprisingly, though, recent research has shown that the first firm to enter a market often does *not* have a long-lived advantage over later entrants. Consider, for instance, the market for pens. Until the 1940s, the only pens available were fountain pens that had to be refilled frequently from an ink bottle and used ink that dried slowly and smeared easily. In October 1945, entrepreneur Milton Reynolds introduced the first ballpoint pen, which did not need to be refilled. When it went on sale at Gimbel's department store in New York City, it was an instant success. Although the pen had a price of $12.00—the equivalent of about $155.00 at today's prices—hundreds of thousands were sold, and Milton Reynolds became a millionaire. Unfortunately, it didn't last. Although Reynolds had guaranteed that his pens would write for two years—later raised to five years—in fact, the pens often leaked and frequently stopped writing after only limited use. Sales began to collapse, the flood of pens returned under the company's guarantee wiped out its profits, and within a few years, Reynolds International Pen Company stopped selling pens in the United States. By the late 1960s, firms such as Bic, selling inexpensive—but reliable—ballpoint pens, dominated the market.

Although not first to market, Bic ultimately was more successful than the firm that pioneered ballpoint pens.

What happened to the Reynolds International Pen Company turns out to be more the rule than the exception. For example, Apple's iPod was not the first digital music player to appear on the U.S. market. Both SeaHan's MPMan and Diamond's PMP300 were released in the United States in 1998, three years before the iPod. Similarly, although Hewlett-Packard currently leads the market for laser printers, with a market share of more than 35 percent, it did not invent the laser printer. Xerox invented the laser printer, and IBM sold the first commercial laser printers, although neither firm is important in the market today. Nor was Procter & Gamble the first firm to sell disposable diapers when it introduced Pampers in 1961. Microsoft's Internet Explorer was not the first Web browser: Before Internet Explorer, there was Netscape; before Netscape, there was Mosaic; and before Mosaic, there were several other Web browsers that for a time looked as if they might dominate the market. In all these cases, the firms that were first to introduce a product ultimately lost out to latecomers who did a better job of providing consumers with products that were more reliable, less expensive, more convenient, or otherwise provided greater value.

Sources: Steven P. Schnaars, *Managing Imitation Strategies: How Late Entrants Seize Markets from Pioneers*, New York: The Free Press, 1994; and Gerard J. Tellis and Peter N. Golder, *Will and Vision: How Latecomers Grow to Dominate Markets*, Los Angeles: Figueroa Press, 2002.

Your Turn: Test your understanding by doing related problem 6.5 on pages 448–449 at the end of this chapter.

MyEconLab Study Plan

Continued from page 425

Economics in Your Life

Opening Your Own Restaurant

At the beginning of the chapter, we asked you to think about how successful you are likely to be in opening an Italian restaurant in your hometown. As you learned in this chapter, if your restaurant is successful, other people are likely to open competing restaurants, and all your economic profit will eventually disappear. Your new competitors will sell Italian food, but it won't be exactly like your Italian food—after all, they don't have your grandmother's secret sauce recipe! Each restaurant will have its own ideas on how best to appeal to people who like Italian food. Unless your food is very different from your competitors' food—or your service is much better—in the long run you will be unable to charge prices high enough to allow you to earn an economic profit.

In a monopolistically competitive market, free entry will reduce prices and lead to zero economic profits in the long run. In addition to lowering prices, competition benefits consumers by leading firms to offer somewhat different versions of the same product; for example, two Italian restaurants will rarely be exactly alike.

Conclusion

In this chapter, we have applied many of the ideas about competition we developed in discussing perfect competition to the more common market structure of monopolistic competition. We have seen that these ideas apply to monopolistically competitive markets, just as they do to perfectly competitive markets. At the end of the chapter on perfect competition, we concluded: "The competitive forces of the market impose relentless pressure on firms to produce new and better goods and services at the lowest possible cost. Firms that fail to adequately anticipate changes in consumer tastes or that fail to adopt the latest and most efficient production technology do not survive in the long run." These conclusions are as true for coffeehouses and firms in other monopolistically competitive markets as they are for wheat farmers and carrot growers.

In next two chapters, we discuss the remaining market structures: oligopoly and monopoly.

Visit MyEconLab for a news article and analysis related to the concepts in this chapter.

Chapter Summary and Problems

Key Terms

 ### 13.1 Demand and Marginal Revenue for a Firm in a Monopolistically Competitive Market, pages 426–428

LEARNING OBJECTIVE: Explain why a monopolistically competitive firm has downward-sloping demand and marginal revenue curves.

Summary

A firm competing in a **monopolistically competitive** market sells a differentiated product. Therefore, unlike a firm in a perfectly competitive market, it faces a downward-sloping demand curve. When a monopolistically competitive firm cuts the price of its product, it sells more units but must accept a lower price on the units it could have sold at the higher price. As a result, its marginal revenue curve is downward sloping. Every firm that has the ability to affect the price of the good or service it sells will have a marginal revenue curve that is below its demand curve.

MyEconLab   Visit **www.myeconlab.com** to complete these exercises online and get instant feedback.

Review Questions

1.1 What are the most important differences between perfectly competitive markets and monopolistically competitive markets? Give two examples of products sold in perfectly competitive markets and two examples of products sold in monopolistically competitive markets.

1.2 Why does a local McDonald's face a downward-sloping demand curve for its Quarter Pounders? If McDonald's raises the price of Quarter Pounders above the prices other fast-food restaurants charge for hamburgers, won't it lose all its customers?

1.3 With a downward-sloping demand curve, why is average revenue equal to price? Why is marginal revenue less than price?

Problems and Applications

1.4 In 2013, Purell announced that the new chemical formula for its hand sanitizer was so effective that: "Just 1 squirt of Purell Advanced Hand Sanitizer kills as many germs as two squirts of any other national brand." If Purell succeeds in convincing consumers that its claims are correct, would its demand curve become flatter or steeper? Briefly explain.

Source: http://www.purell.com/purell-advanced.aspx.

1.5 Complete the following table, which shows the demand for snow skiing lessons per day:

Snow Skiing Lessons per Day (Q)	Price (P)	Total Revenue ($TR = P \times Q$)	Average Revenue $\left(AR = \dfrac{TR}{Q} \right)$	Marginal Revenue $\left(MR = \dfrac{\Delta TR}{\Delta Q} \right)$
0	$80.00			
1	75.00			
2	70.00			
3	65.00			
4	60.00			
5	55.00			
6	50.00			
7	45.00			
8	40.00			

1.6 A student makes the following argument:

> When a firm sells another unit of a good, the additional revenue the firm receives is equal to the price: If the price is $10, the additional revenue is also $10. Therefore, this chapter is incorrect when it says that marginal revenue is less than price for a monopolistically competitive firm.

Briefly explain whether you agree with this argument.

1.7 There are many wheat farms in the United States, and there are also more than 7,000 Starbucks coffeehouses. Why, then, does a Starbucks coffeehouse face a downward-sloping demand curve, while a wheat farmer faces a horizontal demand curve?

1.8 Is it possible for marginal revenue to be negative for a firm selling in a perfectly competitive market? Is it possible for marginal revenue to be negative for a firm selling in a monopolistically competitive market? Briefly explain.

1.9 In the following figure, consider the marginal revenue of the eleventh unit sold. When the firm cuts the price from $5.00 to $4.75 to sell the eleventh unit, what area in the graph denotes the output effect, and what is the dollar value of the output effect? What area in the graph denotes the price effect, and what is the dollar value of the price effect? What is the marginal revenue of the eleventh unit?

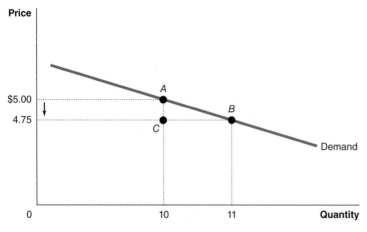

1.10 Sally runs a vegetable stand. She is selling 100 pounds of heirloom tomatoes per week, at a price of $3.75 per pound. If she lowers the price to $3.70, she will sell 101 pounds of heirloom tomatoes. What is the marginal revenue of the 101st pound of heirloom tomatoes?

| **13.2** | How a Monopolistically Competitive Firm Maximizes Profit in the Short Run, pages 428–431 |

LEARNING OBJECTIVE: Explain how a monopolistically competitive firm maximizes profit in the short run.

Summary

A monopolistically competitive firm maximizes profit at the level of output where marginal revenue equals marginal cost. Price equals marginal revenue for a perfectly competitive firm, but price is greater than marginal revenue for a monopolistically competitive firm. Therefore, unlike a perfectly competitive firm, which produces where $P = MC$, a monopolistically competitive firm produces where $P > MC$.

MyEconLab   Visit **www.myeconlab.com** to complete these exercises online and get instant feedback.

Review Questions

2.1 Why doesn't a monopolistically competitive firm produce where $P = MC$, as a perfectly competitive firm does?

2.2 Stephen runs a pet salon. He is currently grooming 125 dogs per week. If instead of grooming 125 dogs, he grooms 126 dogs, he will add $68.50 to his costs and $60.00 to his revenues. What will be the effect on his profit of grooming 126 dogs instead of 125 dogs?

2.3 If Daniel sells 350 Big Macs at a price of $3.25 each, and his average cost of producing 350 Big Macs is $3.00 each, what is his profit?

Problems and Applications

2.4 Maria manages a bakery that specializes in ciabatta bread, and she has the following information on the bakery's demand and costs:

Ciabatta Bread Sold per Hour (Q)	Price (P)	Total Cost (TC)
0	$6.00	$3.00
1	5.50	7.00
2	5.00	10.00
3	4.50	12.50
4	4.00	14.50
5	3.50	16.00
6	3.00	17.00
7	2.50	18.50
8	2.00	21.00

a. To maximize profit, how many loaves of ciabatta bread should Maria sell per hour, what price should she charge, and how much profit will she make?

b. What is the marginal revenue Maria receives from selling the profit-maximizing quantity of ciabatta bread? What is the marginal cost of producing the profit-maximizing quantity of ciabatta bread?

2.5 [Related to Solved Problem 13.2 **on page 430**] Suppose a firm producing table lamps has the following costs:

Quantity	Average Total Cost
1,000	$15.00
2,000	9.75
3,000	8.25
4,000	7.50
5,000	7.75
6,000	8.50
7,000	9.75
8,000	10.50
9,000	12.00

Ben and Jerry are managers at the company, and they have this discussion:

Ben: We should produce 4,000 lamps per month because that will minimize our average costs.

Jerry: But shouldn't we maximize profits rather than minimize costs? To maximize profits, don't we need to take demand into account?

Ben: Don't worry. By minimizing average costs, we will be maximizing profits. Demand will determine how high the price we can charge will be, but it won't affect our profit-maximizing quantity.

Evaluate the discussion between the two managers.

2.6 During the last three months of 2011, the Abercrombie & Fitch clothing chain cut the prices of many of its products. During that period, its profits per item of clothing declined, and its total profits declined by 79 percent. An article discussing Abercrombie's situation had the headline: "Abercrombie Markdowns Cut Profit." Do we have enough information to decide whether Abercrombie's decision to markdown—or cut the prices—of its clothing caused its profit to fall? Is it possible that Abercrombie's decision to cut prices was a profit-maximizing strategy? Briefly explain.

Source: Karen Talley and Mia Lamar, "Abercrombie Markdowns Cut Profit," *Wall Street Journal*, February 16, 2012.

2.7 William Germano previously served as the vice president and publishing director at the Routledge publishing company. He once gave the following description of how a publisher might deal with an unexpected increase in the cost of publishing a book:

> It's often asked why the publisher can't simply raise the price [if costs increase].... It's likely that the editor [is already] ... charging as much as the market will bear .... In other words, you might be willing to pay $50.00 for a ... book on the Brooklyn Bridge, but if ... production costs [increase] by 25 percent, you might think $62.50 is too much to pay, though that would be what the publisher needs to charge. And indeed the publisher may determine that $50.00 is this book's ceiling—the most you would pay before deciding to rent a movie instead.

a. According to what you have learned in this chapter, how do firms adjust the price of a good when there is an increase in cost? Use a graph to illustrate your answer.

b. Does the model of monopolistic competition seem to fit Germano's description? If a publisher does not raise the price of a book following an increase in its production cost, what will be the result?

c. How would the elasticity of demand for published books affect the ability of the publishing company to raise book prices when costs increase?

Source: William Germano, *Getting It Published: A Guide to Scholars and Anyone Else Serious About Serious Books*, 2nd edition, Chicago: University of Chicago Press, 2008, p. 107.

2.8 In 1916, Ford Motor Company produced 500,000 Model T Fords, at a price of $440 each. The company made a profit of $60 million that year. Henry Ford told a newspaper reporter that he intended to reduce the price of the Model T to $360, and he expected to sell 800,000 cars at that price. Ford said, "Less profit on each car, but more cars, more employment of labor, and in the end we get all the total profit we ought to make."

a. Did Ford expect the total revenue he received from selling Model Ts to rise or fall following the price cut?

b. Use the information given above to calculate the price elasticity of demand for Model Ts. Use the midpoint formula to make your calculation. (See Chapter 6, page 174, if you need a refresher on the midpoint formula.)

c. What would the average total cost of producing 800,000 Model Ts have to be for Ford to make as much profit selling 800,000 Model Ts as it made selling 500,000 Model Ts? Is this smaller or larger than the average total cost of producing 500,000 Model Ts?

d. Assume that Ford would make the same total profit when selling 800,000 cars as when selling 500,000 cars. Was Henry Ford correct in saying he would make less profit per car when selling 800,000 cars than when selling 500,000 cars?

2.9 Use the following graph for Elijah's Burgers to answer the questions:

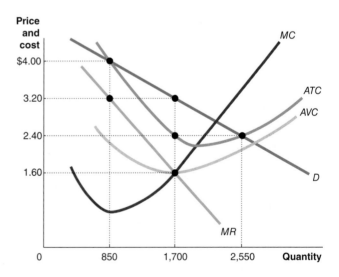

a. If Elijah produces at the profit-maximizing level of output, how much is his total revenue? How much is his total cost? Briefly explain your calculations.

b. How much economic profit is Elijah earning? Briefly explain your calculation.

13.3 **What Happens to Profits in the Long Run? pages 431–436**
LEARNING OBJECTIVE: Analyze the situation of a monopolistically competitive firm in the long run.

Summary

If a monopolistically competitive firm earns an economic profit in the short run, entry of new firms will eliminate the profit in the long run. If a monopolistically competitive firm is suffering an economic loss in the short run, exit of existing firms will eliminate the loss in the long run. Monopolistically competitive firms continually struggle to find new ways of differentiating their products as they try to stay one step ahead of other firms that are attempting to copy their success.

MyEconLab   Visit **www.myeconlab.com** to complete these exercises online and get instant feedback.

Review Questions

3.1 What effect does the entry of new firms have on the economic profits of existing firms?

3.2 Why does the entry of new firms cause the demand curve of an existing firm in a monopolistically competitive market to shift to the left and to become more elastic?

3.3 What is the difference between zero accounting profit and zero economic profit?

3.4 Is it possible for a monopolistically competitive firm to continue to earn an economic profit as new firms enter the market?

Problems and Applications

3.5 Suppose Angelica opens a small store near campus, selling beef brisket sandwiches. Use the graph below, which shows the demand and cost for Angelica's beef brisket sandwiches, to answer the following questions.

a. If Angelica wants to maximize profit, how many beef brisket sandwiches should she sell per day, and what price should she charge? Briefly explain your answer.

b. How much economic profit (or loss) is Angelica making? Briefly explain.

c. Is Angelica likely to continue selling this number of beef brisket sandwiches in the long run? Briefly explain.

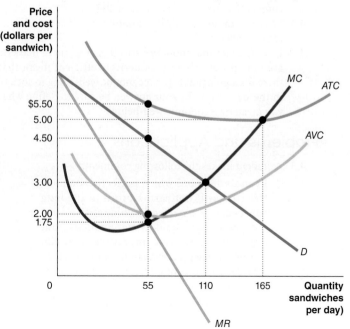

3.6 **[Related to the** Don't Let This Happen to You **on page 432]** A student remarks:

> If firms in a monopolistically competitive industry are earning economic profits, new firms will enter the industry. Eventually, a representative firm will find that its demand curve has shifted to the left, until it is just tangent to its average total cost curve and it is earning zero profit. Because firms are earning zero profit at that point, some firms will leave the industry, and the representative firm will find that its demand curve will shift to the right. In long-run equilibrium, price will be above average total cost by just enough so that each firm is just breaking even.

Briefly explain whether you agree with this analysis.

3.7 A columnist for the *Wall Street Journal* made the following observation: "The [oil] refining business is just too competitive, which is great for consumers, but not shareholders." Briefly explain why the high level of competition in the oil refining industry is good for consumers but bad for the shareholders who own these firms.

Source: James B. Stewart, "Coping with the Inevitable: The Losers in Your Portfolio," *Wall Street Journal*, December 3, 2008.

3.8 **[Related to the** Making the Connection **on page 434]** An article in *Forbes* magazine in 2013 discussed the reasons for the ability of Starbucks to remain profitable despite competition. The author argued the most important reason for the firm's success was "Right market segmentation. The company has stayed with the upper-scale of the coffee market, competing on comfort rather than convenience…."

a. What does the author mean by "market segmentation"?

b. What does the author mean by the "upper-scale" of the coffee market? Why might it be more difficult for other firms to compete with Starbucks in that segment of the coffeehouse market?

Source: Panos Mourdoukoutas, "Starbucks and McDonald's Winning Strategy," *Forbes*, April 25, 2013.

3.9 **[Related to** Solved Problem 13.3 **on page 435]** h.h.gregg has been successful in retailing appliances and electronics by combining high prices with excellent customer service. In late 2008, Saks Fifth Avenue tried a new strategy in retailing luxury clothing. Saks decided to slash prices on designer clothing by 70 percent just before the beginning of the holiday sales season. According to an article in the *Wall Street Journal*, "Saks's risky price-cut strategy was to be one of the first to discount deeply, rather than one of the last." The article continued:

> Saks's maneuver marked an open abandonment of the longstanding unwritten pact between retailers and designers…. Those old rules boiled down to this: Leave the goods at full price at least two months, and don't do markdowns until the very end of the season.

Is Saks's strategy of becoming the low-priced luxury clothing retailer likely to succeed? Contrast Saks's strategy with the strategy of h.h.gregg in terms of how likely the two strategies are to be successful over the long run.

Source: Vanessa O'Connell and Rachel Dodes, "Saks Upends Luxury Market with Strategy to Slash Prices," *Wall Street Journal*, February 9, 2009.

3.10 Michael Korda was, for many years, editor-in-chief at the Simon & Schuster book publishing company. He has written about the many books that have become bestsellers by promising to give readers financial advice that will make them wealthy, by, for example, buying and selling real estate. Korda is skeptical about the usefulness of the advice in these books because "I have yet to meet anybody who got rich by buying a book, though quite a few people got rich by writing one." On the basis of the analysis in this chapter, discuss why it may be very difficult to become rich by following the advice found in a book.

Source: Michael Korda, *Making the List: A Cultural History of the American Bestseller, 1900–1999*, New York: Barnes & Noble Books, 2001, p. 168.

3.11 [Related to the Chapter Opener on page 425] John Quelch, a marketing professor at the Harvard Business School, commented on the situation facing Starbucks: "Starbucks is fundamentally selling an experience, but by no means is coffee the only part of the experience." Why might Starbucks have problems if selling coffee were the only part of the Starbucks "experience"?

Source: Sarah Skidmore, "Starbucks Gives Logo a New Look," *Associated Press*, January 5, 2011.

3.12 In 2011, some Starbucks stores in New York City began putting metal plates over electric outlets to limit the time people using laptop computers could sit at tables. A spokesman for Starbucks stated that individual stores could make the decision whether to cover up power outlets. Why might some Starbucks stores cover up the outlets while others leave them uncovered?

Source: Emily Maltby, "Should Coffee Shop Owners Limit Laptop Usage?" *Wall Street Journal*, August 4, 2011.

3.13 The *Wall Street Journal* reported that Western European brewers such as Heineken, Carlsberg, and Anheuser-Busch InBev are increasing their production and marketing of nonalcoholic beer. The article quotes a Carlsberg executive for new-product development as saying:

> Nonalcoholic beer is a largely unexploited opportunity for big brewers. It is quite a natural move when you see that the overall beer market [in Western Europe is] going down. So, of course, we're battling for market share.

The article further states that "brewers are hoping to capitalize on health consciousness" and that "recent brewing advances are helping improve the taste of nonalcoholic beers."

a. In what sense is nonalcoholic beer an "unexploited opportunity" for big brewers?

b. Are the brewers responding to consumer desires, or are brewers exploiting consumers? Briefly explain.

c. How will the "recent brewing advances" that improve taste affect the market for nonalcoholic beer?

Source: Ilan Brat, "Taking the Buzz out of Beer," *Wall Street Journal*, August 30, 2011.

13.4 Comparing Monopolistic Competition and Perfect Competition, pages 436–438

LEARNING OBJECTIVE: Compare the efficiency of monopolistic competition and perfect competition.

Summary

Perfectly competitive firms produce at a quantity where price equals marginal cost and at minimum average total cost. Perfectly competitive firms achieve both allocative and productive efficiency. Monopolistically competitive firms produce at a quantity where price is greater than marginal cost and above minimum average total cost. Monopolistically competitive firms do not achieve either allocative or productive efficiency. Consumers face a trade-off when buying the product of a monopolistically competitive firm: They are paying a price that is greater than marginal cost, and the product is not being produced at minimum average total cost, but they benefit from being able to purchase a product that is differentiated and more closely suited to their tastes.

MyEconLab   Visit **www.myeconlab.com** to complete these exercises online and get instant feedback.

Review Questions

4.1 What are the differences between the long-run equilibrium of a perfectly competitive firm and the long-run equilibrium of a monopolistically competitive firm?

4.2 Why is a monopolistically competitive firm not productively efficient? In what sense does a monopolistically competitive firm have excess capacity?

4.3 Why is a monopolistically competitive firm not allocatively efficient?

4.4 Does the fact that monopolistically competitive markets are not allocatively or productively efficient mean that there is a significant loss in economic well-being to society in these markets? In your answer, be sure to define what you mean by "economic well-being."

Problems and Applications

4.5 A student makes the following comment:

> I can understand why a perfectly competitive firm will not earn a profit in the long run because a perfectly competitive firm charges a price equal to marginal cost. But a monopolistically competitive firm can charge a price greater than marginal cost, so why can't it continue to earn a profit in the long run?

How would you answer this question?

4.6 Consider the following graph:

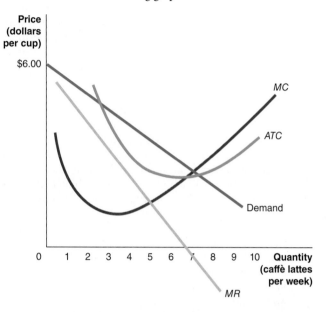

a. Is it possible to say whether this firm is a perfectly competitive firm or a monopolistically competitive firm? If so, explain how you are able to make this determination.
b. Does the graph show a short-run equilibrium or a long-run equilibrium? Briefly explain.
c. What quantity on the graph represents long-run equilibrium if the firm is perfectly competitive?

4.7 Before the fall of Communism, most basic consumer products in Eastern Europe and the Soviet Union were standardized. For example, government-run stores would offer for sale only one type of bar soap or one type of toothpaste. Soviet economists often argued that this system of standardizing basic consumer products avoided the waste associated with the differentiated goods and services produced in Western Europe and the United States. Do you agree with this argument?

4.8 **[Related to the** Making the Connection **on page 438]** According to Peter Thiel: "For a company to own its market, it must have some combination of brand, scale cost advantages, network effects, or proprietary technology." Thiel has invested in the NJOY e-cigarette firm.
a. What does Thiel mean by a company "owning" its market?
b. What information would you need to know to determine whether NJOY owns—or is likely to own in the future—the e-cigarette market?
Source: Blake Masters, "Ten Lessons from Peter Thiel's Class on Startups," *Forbes*, June 7, 2012.

4.9 Consider the following graph:
a. At the profit-maximizing level of output, how much economic profit is this firm earning? Briefly explain.
b. Is this firm allocatively efficient? Is it productively efficient? Briefly explain.

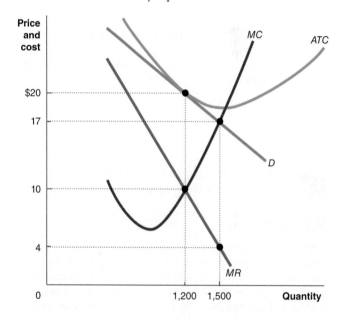

13.5 **How Marketing Differentiates Products, pages 438–439**
LEARNING OBJECTIVE: Define marketing and explain how firms use marketing to differentiate their products.

Summary

Marketing refers to all the activities necessary for a firm to sell a product to a consumer. Firms use two marketing tools to differentiate their products: brand management and advertising. **Brand management** refers to the actions of a firm intended to maintain the differentiation of a product over time. When a firm has established a successful brand name, it has a strong incentive to defend it. A firm can apply for a *trademark*, which grants legal protection against other firms using its product's name.

MyEconLab   Visit **www.myeconlab.com** to complete these exercises online and get instant feedback.

Review Questions

5.1 Define *marketing*. Is marketing just another name for advertising?
5.2 Why are many companies so concerned about brand management?

Problems and Applications

5.3 Draw a graph that shows the effect on a firm's profits when it increases spending on advertising but the increased advertising has *no* effect on the demand for the firm's product.
5.4 A skeptic says: "Marketing research and brand management are unnecessary. If a company wants to find

out what customers want, it should simply look at what they're already buying." Do you agree with this comment? Explain.

5.5 The National Football League (NFL) has a trademark on the name "Super Bowl" for its championship game. Advertisers can use the words Super Bowl in their advertising only if they pay the NFL a fee. Many companies attempt to get around this trademark by using the phrase "the big game" in their advertising. For example, a few days before the Super Bowl, a consumer electronics store might have an advertisement with the phrase "Watch the big game on a new LED TV." In 2006, the National Football League filed for a trademark on the phrase "Big Game," although it eventually withdrew the filing after firms such as Domino's Pizza, Dell, Time Warner Cable, and some universities filed an objection with the U.S. Patent and Trademark Office.

a. Why does the government allow firms to trademark their products?

b. Would consumers gain or lose if the NFL were allowed to trademark the phrase "Big Game"? Briefly explain.

Source: Richard Sandomir, "Not Quite Saying 'Super Bowl,' but Cashing In on It," *New York Times*, February 6, 2010.

5.6 Some companies have done a poor job protecting the images of their products. For example, Hormel's Spam brand name is widely ridiculed and is associated with annoying commercial messages received via e-mail. Think of other cases of companies failing to protect their brand names. What can companies do about the situation now? Should the companies re-brand their products?

5.7 Walgreens, one of the largest drugstore chains in the United States, recently built new flagship stores and expanded and upgraded existing stores. As a newspaper article described it: "More than a drugstore, Walgreens wants customers to be able to grab a smoothie, pick up a prescription, find a bottle of wine for dinner and get a mini makeover—all on their lunch hour." In addition, to take advantage of changes in the pharmacy business as a result of the continued implementation of the Affordable Care Act, Walgreens is expanding its immunization program and increasing the time pharmacists have to assist customers with their health care needs. Briefly discuss Walgreens' strategy in the context of marketing and brand management.

Source: Hadley Malcolm, "A Chi-Chi Pharmacy? Walgreens Goes All Out," *USA Today*, June 14, 2013.

13.6 What Makes a Firm Successful? pages 440–441

LEARNING OBJECTIVE: Identify the key factors that determine a firm's success.

Summary

A firm's owners and managers control some of the factors that determine the profitability of the firm. Other factors affect all the firms in the market or are the result of chance, so they are not under the control of the firm's owners. The interactions between factors the firm controls and factors it does not control determine its profitability.

 Visit **www.myeconlab.com** to complete these exercises online and get instant feedback.

Review Questions

6.1 What are the key factors that determine the profitability of a firm in a monopolistically competitive market?

6.2 How might a monopolistically competitive firm continually earn an economic profit?

Problems and Applications

6.3 According to an article in the *Wall Street Journal*:

> In early January last year, after a disappointing Christmas season and amid worries about competition from discount retailers, Zale Corp. decided to shake things up: The self-proclaimed jeweler to Middle America was going to chase upscale customers.... The move was a disaster. The Irving, Texas, retailer

lost many of its traditional customers without winning the new ones it coveted.

Why would a firm like Zale abandon one market niche for another market niche? We know that in this case the move was not successful. Can you think of other cases where such a move has been successful?

Source: Ann Zimmerman and Kris Hudson, "Chasing Upscale Customers Tarnishes Mass-Market Jeweler," *Wall Street Journal*, June 26, 2006.

6.4 7-Eleven, Inc., operates more than 20,000 convenience stores worldwide. Edward Moneypenny, 7-Eleven's chief financial officer, was asked to name the biggest risk the company faced. He replied, "I would say that the biggest risk that 7-Eleven faces, like all retailers, is competition ... because that is something that you've got to be aware of in this business." In what sense is competition a "risk" to a business? Why would a company in the retail business need to be particularly aware of competition?

Source: Company Report, "CEO Interview: Edward Moneypenny—7-Eleven, Inc.," The Wall Street Transcript Corporation, February 24, 2003.

6.5 [**Related to the** Making the Connection **on page 440**] A firm that is first to market with a new product frequently discovers that there are design flaws or problems with the product that were not anticipated. For example, the ballpoint pens made by the Reynolds International

Pen Company often leaked. What effect do these problems have on the innovating firm, and how do these unexpected problems open up possibilities for other firms to enter the market?

6.6 Wealthy investors often invest in hedge funds. Hedge fund managers use investors' money to buy stocks, bonds, and other investments with the intention of earning high returns. But an article in the *New York Times* notes that: "Even professionals have a problem in evaluating hedge fund performance, because distinguishing skill from luck … is extremely difficult." Is it ever easy to determine whether a firm making an economic profit is doing so because of the skills of the firm's managers or because of luck? Briefly explain.

Source: Jesse Eisinger, "Pruning Hedge Fund Regulation Without Cultivating Better Rules," *New York Times*, September 5, 2012.

CHAPTER 4

Oligopoly: Firms in Less Competitive Markets

Chapter Outline and Learning Objectives

Competition in the Video Game Console Market

Many of the largest corporations in the United States began as small businesses. In 1975, Bill Gates and Paul Allen founded Microsoft Corporation in Albuquerque, New Mexico, with themselves as the only employees. Steve Jobs and Steve Wozniak formed Apple in 1976, working at first out of Jobs's garage in Los Altos, California. They were following in the tradition of William Hewlett and David Packard, who founded what became the Hewlett-Packard (H-P) company in a garage in Palo Alto, California, in the 1930s. Michael Dell started the Dell computer company in 1984 from his dorm room at the University of Texas. When each of these firms was founded, their industries included many more firms than they do now. For example, today in the software and computer industries, fewer than 10 firms account for the great majority of sales.

Although Microsoft is known mainly for its software, it also sells the Xbox video game console. Three firms—Microsoft, Sony, and Nintendo—account for nearly all sales of video game consoles. An industry with only a few firms is an *oligopoly*. In an oligopoly, a firm's profitability depends on its interactions with other firms. In these industries, firms must develop *business strategies*, which involve not just deciding what price to charge and how many units to produce but also how much to advertise, which new technologies to adopt, how to manage relations with suppliers, and which new markets to enter.

In 2007, when Microsoft updated its Xbox video game console and Sony updated its PlayStation console, sales of both consoles and games soared. By 2013, though, many people had abandoned expensive consoles to play games on smartphones or tablets. As Microsoft, Sony, and Nintendo prepared to launch new versions of their game consoles in 2013, they had important choices to make. Sony and Nintendo decided to emphasize improved graphics and other features intended primarily to appeal to game players. Microsoft took another approach by marketing its new Xbox One as an all-in-one system integrated with the owner's television so that "you can jump from TV to movies to music to a game in an instant." Because there are relatively few firms competing in an oligopolistic industry like the video game console industry, firms must continually react to each other's actions or risk a substantial decline in sales. In this chapter, we focus on strategic interactions among firms.

Sources: Ian Sherr and Daisuke Wakabayashi, "Xbox One to Launch at $499, PlayStation 4 at $399," *Wall Street Journal*, June 10, 2013; and Microsoft, *Introducing Xbox One*, www.xbox.com/en-US/xboxone/meet-xbox-one.

Economics in Your Life

Why Can't You Find a Cheap PlayStation 4?

You and your roommates have just moved into a great apartment and decide to treat yourselves to a PlayStation 4 game system—provided that you can find one at a relatively low price. First, you check Amazon and find a price of $399. Then, you check Best Buy, and the price there is also $399. Then, you check Target; $399 again! Finally, you check Wal-Mart, and you find a lower price: $398.95, a whopping discount of $0.05. Why isn't one of these big retailers willing to charge a lower price? What happened to price competition? As you read this chapter, try to answer these questions. You can check your answers against those we provide on **page 469** at the end of this chapter.

I n studying perfectly competitive and monopolistically competitive industries, our analysis focused on how to determine a firm's profit-maximizing price and quantity. We concluded that firms maximize profit by producing where marginal revenue equals marginal cost. To determine marginal revenue and marginal cost, we used graphs that included the firm's demand, marginal revenue, and marginal cost curves. In this chapter, we will study oligopoly, a market structure in which a small number of interdependent firms compete. In analyzing oligopoly, we cannot rely on the same types of graphs we used in analyzing perfect competition and monopolistic competition for two reasons.

First, we need to use economic models that allow us to analyze the more complex business strategies of large oligopoly firms. These strategies involve more than choosing the profit-maximizing price and output. Second, even in determining the profit-maximizing price and output for an oligopoly firm, demand curves and cost curves are not as useful as in the cases of perfect competition and monopolistic competition. We are able to draw the demand curves for competitive firms by assuming that the prices these firms charge have no effect on the prices other firms in their industries charge. This assumption is realistic when each firm is small relative to the market. It is not a realistic assumption, however, for firms that are as large relative to their markets as Microsoft, Sony, or Wal-Mart.

When large firms cut their prices, their rivals in the industry often—but not always—respond by also cutting their prices. Because we don't know for sure how other firms will respond to a price change, we don't know the quantity an oligopolist will sell at a particular price. In other words, it is difficult to know what an oligopolist's demand curve will look like. As we have seen, a firm's marginal revenue curve depends on its demand curve. If we don't know what an oligopolist's demand curve looks like, we also don't know what its marginal revenue curve looks like. Because we don't know marginal revenue, we can't calculate the profit-maximizing level of output and the profit-maximizing price the way we do for competitive firms.

The approach we use to analyze competition among oligopolists is called *game theory*. Game theory can be used to analyze any situation in which groups or individuals interact. In the context of economic analysis, game theory is the study of the decisions of firms in industries where the profits of each firm depend on its interactions with other firms. It has been applied to strategies for nuclear war, international trade negotiations, and political campaigns, among many other examples. In this chapter, we use game theory to analyze the business strategies of large firms.

Oligopoly and Barriers to Entry

14.1 LEARNING OBJECTIVE

Show how barriers to entry explain the existence of oligopolies.

Oligopoly A market structure in which a small number of interdependent firms compete.

An **oligopoly** is an industry with only a few firms. This market structure lies between competitive industries, which have many firms, and monopolies, which have only a single firm. One measure of the extent of competition in an industry is the *concentration ratio*. Every five years, the U.S. Bureau of the Census publishes four-firm concentration ratios that measure the fraction of each industry's sales accounted for by its four largest firms. Most economists believe that a four-firm concentration ratio greater than 40 percent indicates that an industry is an oligopoly.

The concentration ratio has some flaws as a measure of the extent of competition in an industry. For example, concentration ratios do not include the goods and services that foreign firms export to the United States. In addition, concentration ratios are calculated for the national market, even though the competition in some industries, such as restaurants or college bookstores, is mainly local. Finally, competition sometimes exists between firms in different industries. For example, Wal-Mart is included in the discount department store industry but also competes with firms in the supermarket industry and the retail toy store industry. Some economists prefer another measure of competition, known as the *Herfindahl-Hirschman Index* (see Chapter 15).

Retail Trade		Manufacturing	
Industry	Four-Firm Concentration Ratio	Industry	Four-Firm Concentration Ratio
Discount department stores	97%	Cigarettes	98%
Warehouse clubs and supercenters	94%	Beer	90%
College bookstores	75%	Computers	87%
Hobby, toy, and game stores	72%	Aircraft	81%
Radio, television, and other electronic stores	70%	Breakfast cereal	80%
Athletic footwear stores	68%	Dog and cat food	71%
Pharmacies and drugstores	63%	Automobiles	68%

Table 14.1

Examples of Oligopolies in Retail Trade and Manufacturing

Source: U.S. Census Bureau, *Concentration Ratios*, 2007.

Despite their shortcomings, concentration ratios can provide a general idea of the extent of competition in an industry.

Table 14.1 lists examples of oligopolies in manufacturing and retail trade. The Bureau of the Census does not track the video game console industry separately, but in 2013 just three firms—Microsoft, Sony, and Nintendo—accounted for nearly all of worldwide sales, making the industry an oligopoly.

Barriers to Entry

Why do oligopolies exist? Why aren't there many more firms in the computer, discount department store, beer, or video game console industries? Recall that new firms will enter industries when existing firms are earning economic profits. But new firms often have difficulty entering an oligopoly. Anything that keeps new firms from entering an industry in which firms are earning economic profits is called a **barrier to entry**. Three important barriers to entry are economies of scale, ownership of a key input, and government-imposed barriers.

Economies of Scale The most important barrier to entry is **economies of scale**, which exist when a firm's long-run average costs fall as the firm increases output (see Chapter 11). The greater the economies of scale, the smaller the number of firms that will be in the industry. Figure 14.1 illustrates this point.

If economies of scale are relatively unimportant in the industry, the typical firm's long-run average cost curve (*LRAC*) will reach a minimum at a level of output (Q_1 in Figure 14.1) that is a small fraction of total industry sales. The industry will have room for a large number of firms and will be competitive. If economies of scale are significant, the typical firm will not reach the minimum point on its long-run average cost curve (Q_2 in Figure 14.1) until it has produced a large fraction of industry sales. In that case, the industry will have room for only a few firms and will be an oligopoly.

Economies of scale can explain why there is much more competition in the restaurant industry than in the video game console industry. Because very large restaurants do not have significantly lower average costs than smaller restaurants, the restaurant industry has room for many firms. In contrast, a large video game console firm such as Microsoft has much lower average costs than would a small video game console firm, partly because a large firm can spread the high fixed costs of producing consoles—including very large research and development costs—over a much larger quantity of consoles.

Barrier to entry Anything that keeps new firms from entering an industry in which firms are earning economic profits.

Economies of scale The situation when a firm's long-run average costs fall as the firm increases output.

Figure 14.1

Economies of Scale Help Determine the Extent of Competition in an Industry

An industry will be competitive if the minimum point on the typical firm's long-run average cost curve ($LRAC_1$) occurs at a level of output that is a small fraction of total industry sales, such as Q_1. The industry will be an oligopoly if the minimum point comes at a level of output that is a large fraction of industry sales, such as Q_2.

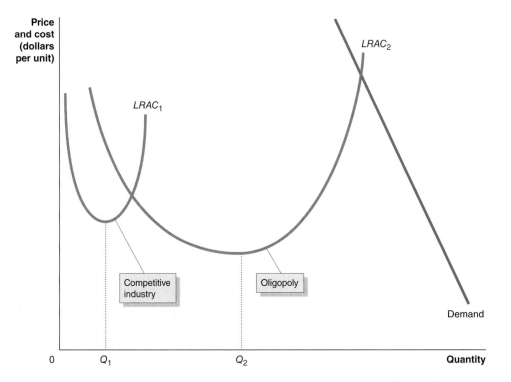

Patent The exclusive right to a product for a period of 20 years from the date the patent is filed with the government.

Ownership of a Key Input If production of a good requires a particular input, then control of that input can be a barrier to entry. For many years, the Aluminum Company of America (Alcoa) controlled most of the world's supply of high-quality bauxite, the mineral needed to produce aluminum. The only way other companies could enter the industry to compete with Alcoa was to recycle aluminum. The De Beers Company of South Africa was able to block competition in the diamond market by controlling the output of most of the world's diamond mines. Until the 1990s, Ocean Spray had very little competition in the market for fresh and frozen cranberries because it controlled almost the entire supply of cranberries. Even today, Ocean Spray controls about 65 percent of the cranberry crop through agreements with 650 cranberry growers.

Government-Imposed Barriers Firms sometimes try to convince the government to impose barriers to entry. Many large firms employ *lobbyists* to convince state legislators and members of Congress to pass laws favorable to the economic interests of the firms. There are tens of thousands of lobbyists in Washington, DC, alone. Top lobbyists command annual salaries of $300,000 or more, which indicates the value firms place on their activities. Examples of government-imposed barriers to entry are patents, licensing requirements, and barriers to international trade.

A **patent** gives a firm the exclusive right to a new product for a period of 20 years from the date the patent is filed with the government. Governments use patents to encourage firms to carry out research and development of new and better products and better ways of producing existing products. Output and living standards increase faster when firms devote resources to research and development, but a firm that spends money to develop a new product may not earn much profit if other firms can copy the product. For example, the pharmaceutical company Merck spends more than $5 billion per year on developing new prescription drugs. If rival companies could freely produce these new drugs as soon as Merck developed them, most of the firm's investment would be wasted. Because Merck can patent a new drug, the firm can charge higher prices during the years the patent is in force and make an economic profit on its successful innovation.

Governments also restrict competition through *occupational licensing*. The United States currently has about 500 occupational licensing laws. For example, doctors and dentists in every state need licenses to practice. The justification for the laws is to protect the public from incompetent practitioners, but by restricting the number of people who can enter the licensed professions, the laws also raise prices. Studies have shown that states that make it harder to earn a dentist's license have prices for dental services that are about 15 percent higher than in other states. Similarly, states that require a license for out-of-state firms to sell contact lenses have higher prices for contact lenses. When state licenses are required for occupations such as hair braiding, which was done several years ago in California, restricting competition is the main result.

Governments also impose barriers to entering some industries by imposing tariffs and quotas on foreign competition. A *tariff* is a tax on imports, and a *quota* limits the quantity of a good that can be imported into a country (see Chapter 9). A quota on foreign sugar imports severely limits competition in the U.S. sugar market. As a result, U.S. sugar companies can charge prices that are much higher than the prices companies outside the United States charge.

In summary, to earn an economic profit, all firms would like to charge a price well above average cost, but earning an economic profit attracts new firms to enter the industry. Eventually, the increased competition forces price down to average total cost, and firms just break even. In an oligopoly, barriers to entry prevent—or at least slow down—entry, which allows firms to earn economic profits over a longer period.   MyEconLab Concept Check   MyEconLab Study Plan

Using Game Theory to Analyze Oligopoly

As we noted at the beginning of the chapter, economists analyze oligopolies by using *game theory*, which was developed during the 1940s by the mathematician John von Neumann and the economist Oskar Morgenstern. **Game theory** is the study of how people make decisions in situations in which attaining their goals depends on their interactions with others. In oligopolies, the interactions among firms are crucial in determining profitability because the firms are large relative to the market.

In all games—whether poker, chess, or Monopoly—the interactions among the players are crucial in determining the outcome. In addition, games share three key characteristics:

1. *Rules* that determine what actions are allowable
2. *Strategies* that players employ to attain their objectives in the game
3. *Payoffs* that are the results of the interactions among the players' strategies

In business situations, the rules of the "game" include not just laws that a firm must obey but also other matters beyond a firm's control—at least in the short run—such as its production function. A **business strategy** is a set of actions that a firm takes to achieve a goal, such as maximizing profit. The *payoffs* are the profits a firm earns as a result of how its strategies interact with the strategies of other firms. The best way to understand the game theory approach is to look at an example.

A Duopoly Game: Price Competition between Two Firms

In this simple example, we use game theory to analyze price competition in a *duopoly*—an oligopoly with two firms. Suppose we assume that Microsoft and Sony are the only two firms producing video game consoles. Let's focus on the pricing decisions the two firms face. We assume the managers of the two firms have to decide whether to charge $499 or $399 for their consoles. Which price will be more profitable depends on the price the other firm charges. The decision regarding what price to charge is an example of a business strategy. In Figure 14.2, we organize the possible outcomes that result from the actions of the two firms into a **payoff matrix**, which is a table that shows the payoffs that each firm earns from every combination of strategies by the firms.

Microsoft's profit is shown in red, and Sony's profit is shown in blue. Each of the four quadrants of the payoff matrix shows the results of different combinations of strategies the two firms use. For example, if Microsoft and Sony both charge $499 for their video game consoles, we are in the upper-left quadrant, which shows that each firm will make a profit of $10 million per month. If Microsoft charges the lower price of $399 while Sony charges $499, Microsoft will gain many of Sony's customers. Microsoft's

14.2 LEARNING OBJECTIVE

Use game theory to analyze the strategies of oligopolistic firms.

Game theory The study of how people make decisions in situations in which attaining their goals depends on their interactions with others; in economics, the study of the decisions of firms in industries where the profits of a firm depend on its interactions with other firms.

Business strategy Actions that a firm takes to achieve a goal, such as maximizing profits.

Payoff matrix A table that shows the payoffs that each firm earns from every combination of strategies by the firms.

Figure 14.2

A Duopoly Game

Sony's profit is shown in blue, and Microsoft's profit is shown in red. Sony and Microsoft would each make a profit of $10 million per month on sales of video game consoles if they both charge $499. However, each firm has an incentive to undercut the other by charging a lower price. If both firms charge $399, they would each make a profit of only $7.5 million per month.

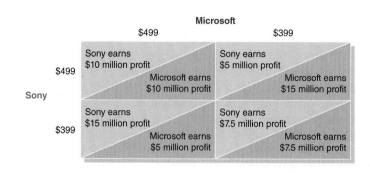

Collusion An agreement among firms to charge the same price or otherwise not to compete.

Dominant strategy A strategy that is the best for a firm, no matter what strategies other firms use.

Nash equilibrium A situation in which each firm chooses the best strategy, given the strategies chosen by other firms.

Cooperative equilibrium An equilibrium in a game in which players cooperate to increase their mutual payoff.

Noncooperative equilibrium An equilibrium in a game in which players do not cooperate but pursue their own self-interest.

Prisoner's dilemma A game in which pursuing dominant strategies results in noncooperation that leaves everyone worse off.

profit will be $15 million, and Sony's profit will be only $5 million. Similarly, if Sony charges $399 while Microsoft charges $499, Microsoft's profit will be only $5 million while Sony's profit will be $15 million. If both firms charge $399, each will earn a profit of $7.5 million per month.

Clearly, the firms will be better off if they both charge $499 for their console. But will they both charge this price? One possibility is that Microsoft's managers and Sony's managers will get together and *collude* by agreeing to charge the higher price. **Collusion** is an agreement among firms to charge the same price or otherwise not to compete. Unfortunately for Microsoft and Sony—but fortunately for their customers—collusion is against the law in the United States. The government can fine companies that collude and send the managers involved to prison.

Microsoft's managers can't legally discuss their pricing decision with Sony's managers, so they have to predict what the other managers will do. Suppose Microsoft's managers are convinced that Sony's managers will charge $499 for their consoles. In this case, Microsoft's managers will definitely charge $399 because doing so will increase Microsoft's profit from $10 million to $15 million. But suppose that, instead, Microsoft's managers are convinced that Sony's managers will charge $399. Then Microsoft's managers also will definitely charge $399 because that will increase their profit from $5 million to $7.5 million. In fact, regardless of which price Sony's managers decide to charge, Microsoft's managers are better off charging $399. So, we know that Microsoft's managers will choose a price of $399 for their consoles.

Now consider the situation from the point of view of Sony's managers. They are in the same position as Microsoft's managers, so we can expect them to make the same decision to charge $399 for their consoles. In this situation, both firms have a *dominant strategy*. A **dominant strategy** is the best strategy for a firm, no matter what strategies other firms use. The result is an equilibrium where both firms charge $399 for their consoles. This situation is an equilibrium because each firm is maximizing profit, *given the price chosen by the other firm*. In other words, neither firm can increase its profit by changing its price, given the price chosen by the other firm. An equilibrium where each firm chooses the best strategy, given the strategies chosen by other firms, is called a **Nash equilibrium**, named after Nobel Laureate John Nash of Princeton University, a pioneer in the development of game theory. MyEconLab Concept Check

Firm Behavior and the Prisoner's Dilemma

Notice that the equilibrium in Figure 14.2 is not very satisfactory for either firm. The firms earn $7.5 million in profit each month by charging $399, but they could have earned $10 million in profit if they both had charged $499. By "cooperating" and charging the higher price, they would have achieved a *cooperative equilibrium*. In a **cooperative equilibrium**, players cooperate to increase their mutual payoff. We have seen, though, that the outcome of this game is likely to be a **noncooperative equilibrium**, in which each firm pursues its own self-interest.

A situation like this one, in which pursuing dominant strategies results in noncooperation that leaves everyone worse off, is called a **prisoner's dilemma**. The game gets its name from the problem two suspects face when arrested for a crime. If the police lack other evidence, they may separate the suspects and offer each a reduced prison sentence

Don't Let This Happen to You

Don't Misunderstand Why Each Firm Ends Up Charging a Price of $399

It is tempting to think that Microsoft and Sony would each charge $399 rather than $499 for their video game consoles because each is afraid that the other firm will charge $399. In fact, fear of being undercut by the other firm charging a lower price is not the key to understanding each firm's pricing strategy. Notice that charging $399 is the most profitable strategy for each firm, no matter which price the other firm decides to charge. For

example, even if Microsoft's managers somehow knew for sure that Sony's managers intended to charge $499, Microsoft would still charge $399 because its profits would be $15 million instead of $10 million. Sony's managers are in the same situation. That is why charging $399 is a dominant strategy for both firms.

MyEconLab Study Plan

Your Turn: Test your understanding by doing related problem 2.10 on page 472 at the end of the chapter.

---

in exchange for confessing to the crime and testifying against the other suspect. Because each suspect has a dominant strategy to confess to the crime, they both will confess and serve a jail term, even though they would have gone free if they both had remained silent.

MyEconLab Concept Check

Solved Problem 14.2

MyEconLab Interactive Animation

Is Same-Day Delivery a Prisoner's Dilemma for Wal-Mart and Amazon?

Online shopping has increased dramatically in the past 15 years. One drawback consumers face when shopping online, though, is the wait to receive a good compared with going to a store and buying it off the shelf. Amazon has been a pioneer in reducing delivery times, including offering a same-day delivery service in several cities. By 2013, to avoid losing customers to Amazon, several other firms, including Wal-Mart, eBay, and Google, were offering same-day delivery in some cities. To achieve same-day delivery, firms were typically hiring people to go to retail stores, buy the products customers had ordered, and deliver the products directly to them. Some retail analysts argued that this process was so costly that the firms were actually losing money on most same-day delivery orders. Failing to offer the service, though, might cause customers to take all of their business—including their profitable orders—to firms that did offer the service.

Suppose Amazon and Wal-Mart are competing with same-day delivery in a particular city. Construct a payoff matrix using the following hypothetical information:

- If neither firm offers same-day delivery, Amazon and Wal-Mart each earn a profit of $7 million per month.

- If both firms offer same-day delivery, Amazon and Wal-Mart each earn a profit of $5 million per month.

- If Amazon offers same-day delivery and Wal-Mart doesn't, Amazon earns a profit of $9 million and Wal-Mart earns a profit of $4 million.

- If Wal-Mart offers same-day delivery and Amazon doesn't, Wal-Mart earns a profit of $9 million and Amazon earns a profit of $4 million.

  a. If Amazon wants to maximize profit, will it offer same-day delivery? Briefly explain.

  b. If Wal-Mart wants to maximize profit, will it offer same-day delivery? Briefly explain.

  c. Is there a Nash equilibrium to this game? If so, what is it?

Solving the Problem

Step 1: **Review the chapter material.** This problem uses payoff matrixes to analyze a business situation, so you may want to review the section "A Duopoly Game: Price Competition between Two Firms," which begins on page 455.

Step 2: **Construct the payoff matrix.**

Wal-Mart

		Don't Offer	Offer
Amazon	**Don't Offer**	Amazon earns $7 million profit / Wal-Mart earns $7 million profit	Amazon earns $4 million profit / Wal-Mart earns $9 million profit
	Offer	Amazon earns $9 million profit / Wal-Mart earns $4 million profit	Amazon earns $5 million profit / Wal-Mart earns $5 million profit

Step 3: **Answer part (a) by showing that Amazon has a dominant strategy of offering same-day delivery.** If Wal-Mart doesn't offer the service, Amazon will make $9 million if it offers the service but only $7 million if it doesn't. If Wal-Mart offers the service, Amazon will make $5 million if it offers the service but only $4 million if it doesn't. Therefore, offering the service is a dominant strategy for Amazon.

Step 4: **Answer part (b) by showing that Wal-Mart has a dominant strategy of offering same-day delivery.** Wal-Mart is in the same position as Amazon, so it also has a dominant strategy of offering the service.

Step 5: **Answer part (c) by showing that there is a Nash equilibrium for this game.** Both firms offering same-day delivery is a Nash equilibrium. Given that Amazon is offering the service, Wal-Mart's best strategy is to offer the service. Given that Wal-Mart is offering the service, Amazon's best strategy is to offer it. Therefore, offering same-day delivery is the optimal decision for both firms, *given the decision by the other firm.*

Extra Credit: This game is another example of the prisoner's dilemma. Amazon and Wal-Mart would be more profitable if they both refrained from offering same-day delivery, thereby saving the high cost of hiring people to deliver individual packages in a short amount of time. Each firm's dominant strategy is to offer the service, however, so they end up in an equilibrium where both offer the service, and their profits are reduced.

MyEconLab Study Plan

Your Turn: For more practice, do related problems 2.11 and 2.12 on page 472 at the end of this chapter.

Making the Connection

MyEconLab Video

Is There a Dominant Strategy for Bidding on eBay?

An auction is a game in which bidders compete to buy a product. The payoff in winning an auction is equal to the difference between the subjective value you place on the product being auctioned and the amount of the winning bid. On the online auction site eBay, more than 100 million people buy and sell more than 360 million items annually.

Many items on eBay are sold in *second-price auctions,* where the winning bidder pays an amount equal to the bid of the second-highest bidder. If the highest bidder for a DVD of *World War Z* bids $12, and the second-highest bidder bids $8, the highest bidder wins the auction and pays $8. It may seem that your best strategy when bidding on eBay is to place a bid well below the subjective value you place on the item in the hope of winning it at a low price. In fact, bidders on eBay have a dominant strategy of entering a bid equal to the maximum value they place on the item. Suppose you are looking for a present for your parents' anniversary. Your parents are Dave Matthews fans, and someone is auctioning a pair of Dave Matthews concert tickets. If the maximum value you place on the tickets is $200, then that should be your bid. To see why, consider the results of strategies of bidding more or less than $200.

There are two possible outcomes of the auction: Either someone else bids more than you do, or you are the highest bidder. First, suppose you bid $200 but someone else bids more than you do. If you had bid less than $200, you would still have lost. If you had bid more than $200, you might have been the highest bidder, but because your bid would be for more than the value you place on the tickets, you would have a negative payoff. Second, suppose you bid $200 and you are the highest bidder. If you had bid less than $200, you would have risked losing the tickets to someone whose bid you would have beaten by bidding $200. You would be worse off than if you had bid $200 and won. If you had bid more than $200, you would not have affected the price you ended up paying—which, remember, is equal to the second-highest bid. Therefore, a strategy of bidding $200—the maximum value you place on the tickets—dominates bidding more or less than $200.

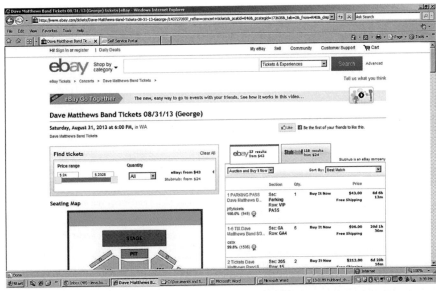

Even though making your first bid your highest bid is a dominant strategy on eBay, many bidders don't use it. After an auction is over, a link leads to a Web page showing all the bids. In many auctions, the same bidder bids several times, showing that the bidder had not understood his or her dominant strategy.

On eBay, bidding the maximum value you place on an item is a dominant strategy.

Your Turn: Test your understanding by doing related problem 2.13 on pages 472–473 at the end of this chapter.

MyEconLab Study Plan

Can Firms Escape the Prisoner's Dilemma?

Although the prisoner's dilemma game seems to show that cooperative behavior always breaks down, we know that people often cooperate to achieve their goals, and firms find ways to cooperate by not competing on price. The reason the basic prisoner's dilemma story is not always applicable in the real world is that it assumes the game will be played only once. Most business situations, however, are repeated over and over. For example, consider the following situation: Suppose that in a small town, the only places to buy a pizza are Domino's and Pizza Hut. We will assume that the managers will charge either $12 or $10 for a large pepperoni pizza. Panel (a) of Figure 14.3 shows the payoff matrix. Examining the matrix shows that each manager has an incentive to charge the lower price. Once again, the firms appear caught in a prisoner's dilemma. But the managers will not play this game only once; each day they will decide again what price they will charge for a pizza. In the language of game theory, the managers are playing a *repeated game*, where the losses from not cooperating are greater than in a game played once, and players can employ *retaliation strategies* against other players who don't cooperate. As a result, firms have a greater incentive to cooperate.

Panel (a) of Figure 14.3 shows that Domino's and Pizza Hut are earning $150 less per day by both charging $10 instead of $12 for the pizza. Every day that passes with both stores charging $10 increases the total amount lost: A year of charging $10 will cause each store to lose more than $50,000 in profit. This lost profit increases the incentive for the store managers to cooperate by *implicitly* colluding. Remember that *explicit* collusion—such as the managers meeting and agreeing to charge $12—is illegal. But if the managers can find a way to signal each other that they will charge $12, they may be within the law.

Suppose that Domino's and Pizza Hut both advertise that they will match the lowest price offered by any competitor—in our simple example, they are each other's only competitor. These advertisements are signals to each other that they intend to charge $12 for a pizza. The signal is clear because each restaurant knows that if it charges $10, the other restaurant will automatically retaliate by also lowering its price to $10. The offer

MyEconLab Animation

Figure 14.3

Changing the Payoff Matrix in a Repeated Game

Domino's and Pizza Hut can change the pay-off matrix for selling pepperoni pizzas by advertising that each will match its competitor's price. This retaliation strategy provides a signal that one restaurant charging a lower price will be met automatically by the other restaurant charging a lower price. In the payoff matrix in panel (a), there is no advertisement about matching prices, and each restaurant benefits if it charges $10 when the other charges $12. In the payoff matrix in panel (b), after advertising that they will match prices, the managers have only two choices: They can charge $12 and receive a profit of $500 per day, or they can charge $10 and receive a profit of $350 per day. The equilibrium shifts from the prisoner's dilemma result of both restaurants charging the low price and receiving low profits to both restaurants charging the high price and receiving high profits.

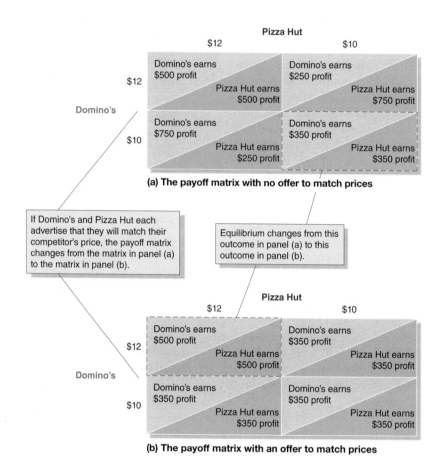

(a) The payoff matrix with no offer to match prices

If Domino's and Pizza Hut each advertise that they will match their competitor's price, the payoff matrix changes from the matrix in panel (a) to the matrix in panel (b).

Equilibrium changes from this outcome in panel (a) to this outcome in panel (b).

(b) The payoff matrix with an offer to match prices

Price leadership A form of implicit collusion in which one firm in an oligopoly announces a price change and the other firms in the industry match the change.

to match prices is a good *enforcement mechanism* because it guarantees that if either restaurant fails to cooperate and charges the lower price, the competing restaurant will automatically punish that restaurant by also charging the lower price. As Figure 14.3 shows, the restaurants have changed the payoff matrix they face.

With the original payoff matrix in panel (a), there are no advertisements about matching prices, and each restaurant makes more profit if it charges $10 when the other charges $12. The advertisements about matching prices changes the payoff matrix to that shown in panel (b). Now the managers can charge $12 and receive a profit of $500 per day, or they can charge $10 and receive a profit of $350 per day. The equilibrium shifts from the prisoner's dilemma result of both managers charging the low price and receiving low profits to a result where both charge the high price and receive the high profit. An advertisement offering to match competitors' prices might seem to benefit consumers, but game theory shows that it actually may hurt consumers by helping to keep prices high.

One form of implicit collusion occurs as a result of **price leadership**, where one firm takes the lead in announcing a price change that other firms in the industry then match. For example, through the 1970s, General Motors (GM) would announce a price change at the beginning of a model year, and Ford and Chrysler would match GM's price change. In some cases, such as in the airline industry, firms have attempted to act as price leaders but failed when other firms in the industry declined to cooperate.

MyEconLab Concept Check

Making the Connection

MyEconLab Video

With Price Collusion, More Is Not Merrier

Coordinating prices is easier in some industries than in others. Fixed costs in the airline industry are very large, and marginal costs are very small. The marginal cost of flying one more passenger from Chicago to New York is no more than a few dollars: the cost of another snack served and a small amount of additional jet fuel. As a result, airlines often engage in last-minute price cutting to fill the remaining empty seats on a flight. Even a low-price ticket will increase marginal revenue more than marginal cost. As with other oligopolies, if all airlines cut prices, industry profits will decline. Airlines therefore continually adjust their prices while at the same time monitoring their rivals' prices and retaliating against them for either cutting prices or failing to go along with price increases.

When JetBlue enters a market, other airlines often cut their ticket prices.

In recent years, mergers in the airline industry have increased the possibility of implicit collusion by reducing the number of airlines flying between two cities. Often only one or two airlines will fly on a particular route. Southwest Airlines and JetBlue, however, have undertaken an aggressive campaign to enter many airports, thereby increasing competition. For example, before Southwest entered Washington, DC's Dulles International Airport in October 2006, United and Continental Airlines were the only major airlines serving the airport. But would increasing the number of airlines on a route from two to three have much effect on the ability of the airlines to engage in price collusion? Austan Goolsbee and Chad Syverson of the University of Chicago studied the effects of Southwest's entering airline markets over an 11-year period. They found that when Southwest begins flying a particular route, ticket prices drop by an average of 29 percent. These price declines indicate that airlines may have been practicing implicit price collusion before Southwest's entry into the market. Perhaps surprisingly, Goolsbee and Syverson found that more than half of the price decline occurred after it became likely that Southwest would enter a market but *before* Southwest actually began flying planes on the route. One possibility is that airlines already in the market lowered prices to keep frequent flyers from switching to Southwest.

JetBlue has had a similar effect on airline fares. For example, when JetBlue entered the Chicago-to-New York market in 2006, United and American, which had previously dominated the route, slashed fares by 65 percent, to $108 for a round-trip ticket. For several years, the airlines had trouble reestablishing the implicit price collusion they had practiced before JetBlue entered: In September 2011, a round-trip ticket from Chicago to New York had a price of $106 on United and American, and $101 dollars on JetBlue.

In the airline industry, it apparently doesn't take much competition to greatly reduce opportunities for price collusion. But does the effect of increased competition continue indefinitely? We might expect that the longer the same firms compete in a market, the more likely they are to eventually reestablish implicit price collusion, particularly if other factors, such as rising costs and increasing demand, put upward pressure on prices. Something like this outcome occurred in the Chicago-to-New York market. Following increases in jet fuel costs and rising demand as the U.S. economy recovered from the 2007–2009 recession, in July 2013 round-trip ticket prices had risen to $321.80 on JetBlue, $327.80 on American, and $343.80 on United.

Sources: Austan Goolsbee and Chad Syverson, "How Do Incumbents Respond to the Threat of Entry? Evidence from the Major Airlines," *Quarterly Journal of Economics*, Vol. 123, No. 4, November 2008, pp. 1611–1633; Julie Johnson, "Rude Welcome Awaits JetBlue," *Chicago Tribune*, November 6, 2006; and route pricing data from www.orbitz.com.

Your Turn: Test your understanding by doing related problems 2.14, 2.15, and 2.16 on page 473 at the end of this chapter.

MyEconLab Study Plan

Cartels: The Case of OPEC

In the United States, firms cannot legally meet to agree on what prices to charge and how much to produce. But suppose they could. Would this be enough to guarantee that their collusion would be successful? The example of the Organization of the Petroleum Exporting Countries (OPEC) indicates that the answer to this question is "no." OPEC

MyEconLab Animation

Figure 14.4

Oil Prices, 1972 to mid-2013

The blue line shows the price of a barrel of oil in each year. The red line measures the price of a barrel of oil in terms of the purchasing power of the dollar in 2013. By reducing oil production, OPEC was able to raise the world price of oil in the mid-1970s and early 1980s. Sustaining high prices has been difficult over the long run, however, because OPEC members often exceed their output quotas.

Source: Federal Reserve Bank of St. Louis.

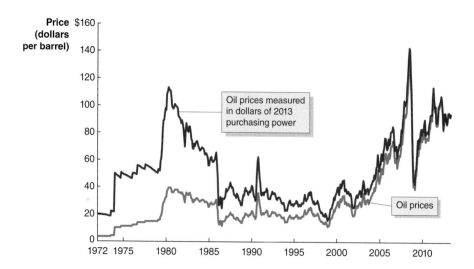

Cartel A group of firms that collude by agreeing to restrict output to increase prices and profits.

has 12 members, including Saudi Arabia, Kuwait, and other Arab countries, as well as Iran, Venezuela, and Nigeria. Together, these countries own more than 75 percent of the world's proven crude oil reserves, although they pump about 35 percent of the total oil sold each year. OPEC operates as a **cartel**, which is a group of firms that collude by agreeing to restrict output to increase prices and profits. The members of OPEC meet periodically and agree on quotas, which are quantities of oil that each country agrees to produce. The quotas are intended to reduce oil production well below the competitive level to force up the price of oil and increase the profits of member countries.

Figure 14.4 shows oil prices from 1972 to mid-2013. The blue line shows the price of a barrel of oil in each year. Prices in general have risen since 1972, which has reduced the amount of goods and services that consumers can purchase with a dollar. The red line corrects for general price increases by measuring oil prices in terms of the dollar's purchasing power in 2013. The figure shows that OPEC succeeded in raising the price of oil during the mid-1970s and early 1980s, although political unrest in the Middle East and other factors also affected the price of oil during these years. Oil prices had been below $3 per barrel in 1972 but rose to more than $39 per barrel in 1980, which was more than $110 measured in dollars of 2013 purchasing power. The figure also shows that OPEC has had difficulty sustaining the high prices of 1980 in later years, although oil prices rose sharply between 2004 and mid-2008, in part due to increasing demand from China and India.

Game theory helps us understand why oil prices have fluctuated. If every member of OPEC cooperates and produces the low output level dictated by its quota, prices will be high, and the cartel will earn large profits. Once the price has been driven up, however, each member has an incentive to stop cooperating and to earn even higher profits by increasing output beyond its quota. But if no country sticks to its quota, total oil output will increase, and profits will decline. In other words, OPEC is caught in a prisoner's dilemma.

If the members of OPEC always exceeded their production quotas, the cartel would have no effect on world oil prices. In fact, the members of OPEC periodically meet and assign new quotas that, at least for a while, enable them to restrict output enough to raise prices. Two factors explain OPEC's occasional success at behaving as a cartel. First, the members of OPEC are participating in a repeated game. As we have seen, this increases the likelihood of a cooperative outcome. Second, Saudi Arabia has far larger oil reserves than any other member of OPEC. Therefore, it has the most to gain from high oil prices and a greater incentive to cooperate. To see this, consider the payoff matrix shown in Figure 14.5. To keep things simple, let's assume that OPEC has only two members: Saudi Arabia and Nigeria. In Figure 14.5, "Low Output" corresponds to cooperating with the OPEC-assigned output quota, and "High Output" corresponds to producing at maximum capacity. The payoff matrix shows the profits received per day by each country.

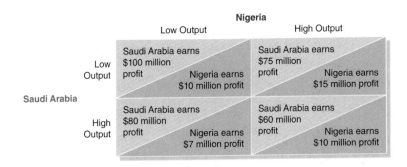

MyEconLab Animation

Figure 14.5

The OPEC Cartel with Unequal Members

Because Saudi Arabia can produce much more oil than Nigeria, its output decisions have a larger effect on the price of oil. In the figure, Low Output corresponds to cooperating with the OPEC-assigned output quota, and High Output corresponds to producing at maximum capacity. Saudi Arabia has a dominant strategy to cooperate and produce a low output. Nigeria, however, has a dominant strategy not to cooperate and instead produce a high output. Therefore, the equilibrium of this game will occur with Saudi Arabia producing a low output and Nigeria producing a high output.

We can see that Saudi Arabia has a strong incentive to cooperate and maintain its low output quota. By keeping output low, Saudi Arabia can by itself significantly raise the world price of oil, increasing its own profits as well as those of other members of OPEC. Therefore, Saudi Arabia has a dominant strategy of cooperating with the quota and producing a low output. Nigeria, however, cannot by itself have much effect on the price of oil. Therefore, Nigeria has a dominant strategy of not cooperating and instead producing a high output. The equilibrium of this game will occur with Saudi Arabia producing a low output and Nigeria producing a high output. In fact, OPEC often operates in just this way. Saudi Arabia will cooperate with the quota, while the other 11 members produce at capacity. Because this is a repeated game, however, Saudi Arabia will occasionally produce more oil than its quota to intentionally drive down the price and retaliate against the other members for not cooperating.   MyEconLab Concept Check

MyEconLab Study Plan

Sequential Games and Business Strategy

We have been analyzing games in which both players move simultaneously. In many business situations, however, one firm will act first, and then other firms will respond. These situations can be analyzed using *sequential games*. We will use sequential games to analyze two business strategies: deterring entry and bargaining between firms. To keep things simple, we consider situations that involve only two firms.

14.3 LEARNING OBJECTIVE

Use sequential games to analyze business strategies.

Deterring Entry

We saw earlier that barriers to entry are a key to firms continuing to earn economic profits. Can firms create barriers to deter new firms from entering an industry? Some recent research in game theory has focused on this question. To take a simple example, suppose that Apple and Dell are the only makers of very thin, light laptop computers. One factor firms consider in pricing a new product is the effect different prices have on the likelihood that competitors will enter the market. A high price might lead to a large profit if other firms do not enter the market, but if a high price attracts entry from other firms, it might actually result in a smaller profit. A low price, by deterring entry, might lead to a larger profit. Assume that managers at Apple have developed a very thin, light laptop before Dell has and are considering what price to charge. To break even by covering the opportunity cost of the funds used, laptops must provide a minimum rate of return of 15 percent on Apple's investment. If Apple has the market for this type of laptop to itself and charges a price of $800, it will earn an economic profit by receiving a return of 20 percent. If Apple charges a price of $1,000 and has the market to itself, it will receive a higher return of 30 percent.

It seems clear that Apple should charge $1,000 for its laptops, but the managers are worried that Dell might also begin selling this type of laptop. If Apple charges $800 and Dell enters the market, Apple and Dell will divide up the market, and both will earn only 5 percent on their investments, which is below the 15 percent return necessary to break even. If Apple charges $1,000 and Dell enters, although the market will still be divided, the higher price means that each firm will earn 16 percent on its investment.

Apple and Dell are playing a sequential game, because Apple makes the first move—deciding what price to charge—and Dell responds. We can analyze a sequential game by

Figure 14.6

The Decision Tree for an Entry Game

Apple earns its highest return if it charges $1,000 for its very thin, light laptop and Dell does not enter the market. But at that price, Dell will enter the market, and Apple will earn only 16 percent. If Apple charges $800, Dell will not enter because Dell will suffer an economic loss by receiving only a 5 percent return on its investment. Therefore, Apple's best decision is to deter Dell's entry by charging $800. Apple will earn an economic profit by receiving a 20 percent return on its investment. Note that the dashes (—) indicate the situation where Dell does not enter the market and so makes no investment and receives no return.

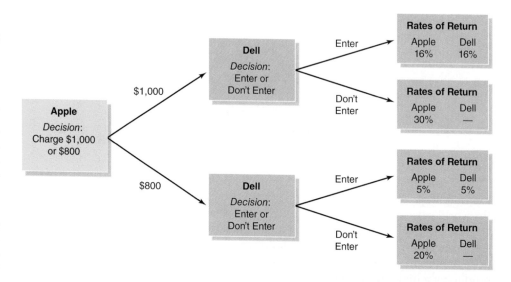

using a *decision tree*, like the one shown in Figure 14.6. The boxes in the figure represent *decision nodes*, which are points where the firms must make the decisions contained in the boxes. At the left, Apple makes the initial decision of what price to charge, and then Dell responds by either entering the market or not. The decisions made are shown beside the arrows. The *terminal nodes*, in green at the right side of the figure, show the resulting rates of return.

Let's start with Apple's initial decision. If Apple charges $1,000, then the arrow directs us to the upper red decision node for Dell. If Dell decides to enter, it will earn a 16 percent rate of return on its investment, which represents an economic profit because it is above the opportunity cost of the funds involved. If Dell doesn't enter, Apple will earn 30 percent, and Dell will not earn anything in this market (indicated by the dash). Apple's managers can conclude that if they charge $1,000 for their laptops, Dell will enter the very thin, light laptop market, and both firms will earn 16 percent on their investments.

If Apple decides to charge $800, then the arrow directs us to the lower red decision node for Dell. If Dell decides to enter, it will earn only a 5 percent rate of return. If it doesn't enter, Apple will earn 20 percent, and Dell will not earn anything in this market. Apple's managers can conclude that if they charge $800, Dell will not enter, and Apple will earn 20 percent on its investment.

This analysis should lead Apple's managers to conclude that they can charge $1,000 and earn 16 percent—because Dell will enter—or they can charge $800 and earn 20 percent by deterring Dell's entry. Using a decision tree helps Apple's managers make the correct choice and charge $800 to deter Dell's entry into this market. Note that our discussion is simplified because we are ignoring other characteristics, apart from price, on which the firms also compete. In practice, Apple charged a relatively high price for its lightweight laptop, the MacBook Air, which caused Dell to enter the market with the lower-priced XPS 15z Ultrabook. Apple's managers believed that the MacBook Air's features would remain attractive to consumers, despite the XPS 15z Ultrabook having a lower price. Time will tell whether Apple made the correct decision by not charging a low enough price to deter Dell's entry. MyEconLab Concept Check

Solved Problem 14.3

MyEconLab Interactive Animation

Is Deterring Entry Always a Good Idea?

Like any other business strategy, deterring entry is a good idea only if it has a higher payoff than alternative strategies. Use the following decision tree to decide whether

Apple should deter Dell from entering the market for very thin, light laptops. Assume that each firm must earn a 15 percent return on its investment to break even.

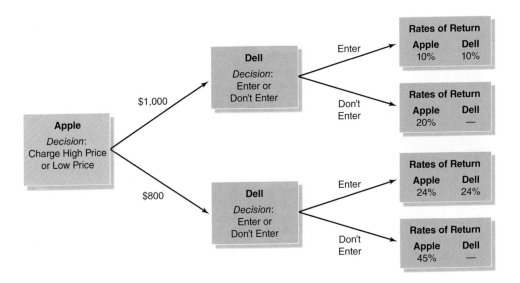

Solving the Problem

Step 1: **Review the chapter material.** This problem is about sequential games, so you may want to review the section "Deterring Entry," which begins on page 463.

Step 2: **Determine how Dell will respond to Apple's decision.** If Apple charges $1,000 for its very thin, light laptops, Dell will not enter the market because the return on its investment represents an economic loss. If Apple charges $800, Dell will enter because it will earn a return that represents an economic profit.

Step 3: **Given how Dell will react, determine which strategy maximizes profits for Apple.** If Apple charges $1,000, it will have deterred Dell's entry, and the rate of return on its investment will be 20 percent. If Apple charges $800, Dell will enter, but because these low prices will substantially increase the market for these laptops, Apple will actually earn a higher return of 24 percent, splitting the market with Dell at a lower price than it would have earned having the whole market to itself at a high price.

Step 4: **State your conclusion.** Like any other business strategy, deterrence is worth pursuing only if the payoff is higher than for other strategies. In this case, expanding the market for very thin, light laptops by charging a lower price has a higher payoff for Apple, even given that Dell will enter the market.

Your Turn: For more practice, do related problem 3.3 on page 474 at the end of this chapter.

MyEconLab Study Plan

Bargaining

The success of many firms depends on how well they bargain with other firms. For example, firms often must bargain with their suppliers over the prices they pay for inputs. Suppose that TruImage is a small firm that has developed software that improves how pictures from digital cameras or smartphones are displayed on computer screens. TruImage currently sells its software only on its Web site and earns a profit of $2 million per year. Dell informs TruImage that it is considering installing the software on every new computer Dell sells. Dell expects to sell more computers at a higher price if it can install TruImage's software on its computers. The two firms begin bargaining over what price Dell will pay TruImage for its software.

The decision tree in Figure 14.7 illustrates this bargaining game. At the left, Dell makes the initial decision about what price to offer TruImage for its software, and then TruImage responds by either accepting or rejecting the contract offer. First, suppose that Dell offers TruImage a contract price of $30 per copy for its software. If TruImage accepts this contract, its profit will be $5 million per year, and Dell will earn $10 million in

MyEconLab Animation

Figure 14.7

The Decision Tree for a Bargaining Game

Dell earns the highest profit if it offers a contract price of $20 per copy and TruImage accepts the contract. TruImage earns the highest profit if Dell offers it a contract of $30 per copy and it accepts the contract. TruImage may attempt to bargain by threatening to reject a $20-per-copy contract. But Dell knows this threat is not credible because once Dell has offered a $20-per-copy contract, TruImage's profits are higher if it accepts the contract than if it rejects it.

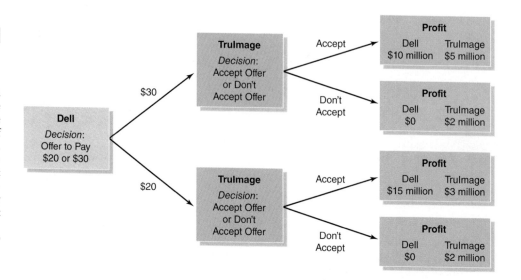

additional profit. If TruImage rejects the contract, its profit will be the $2 million per year it earns selling its software on its Web site, and Dell will earn zero additional profit.

Now, suppose Dell offers TruImage a contract price of $20 per copy. If TruImage accepts this contract, its profit will be $3 million per year, and Dell will earn $15 million in additional profit. If TruImage rejects this contract, its profit will be the $2 million it earns selling its software on its Web site, and Dell will earn zero additional profit. Clearly, for Dell, a contract price of $20 per copy is more profitable, while for TruImage, a contract price of $30 per copy is more profitable.

Suppose TruImage attempts to obtain a favorable outcome from the bargaining by telling Dell that it will reject a $20-per-copy contract price. If Dell believes this threat, then it will offer TruImage a $30-per-copy contract price because Dell is better off with the $10 million profit that will result from TruImage accepting the contract than with the zero profit Dell will earn if TruImage rejects the $20-per-copy contract price. This result is a Nash equilibrium because neither firm can increase its profit by changing its choice—*provided that Dell believes TruImage's threat.* But is TruImage's threat credible? Once Dell has offered TruImage the $20 contract price, TruImage's choices are to accept the contract and earn $3 million or reject the contract and earn only $2 million. Because rejecting the contract reduces TruImage's profit, TruImage's threat to reject the contract is not credible, and Dell should ignore it.

As a result, we would expect Dell to use the strategy of offering TruImage a $20-per-copy contract price and TruImage to use the strategy of accepting the contract. Dell will earn an additional profit of $15 million per year, and TruImage will earn a profit of $3 million per year. This outcome is called a *subgame-perfect equilibrium*. A subgame-perfect equilibrium is a Nash equilibrium in which no player can make himself or herself better off by changing his or her decision at any decision node. In our simple bargaining game, each player has only one decision to make. As we have seen, Dell's profits are highest if it offers the $20-per-copy contract price, and TruImage's profits are highest if it accepts the contract. Typically, in sequential games of this type, there is only one subgame-perfect equilibrium.

Managers use decision trees like those in Figures 14.6 and 14.7 in business planning because they provide a systematic way of thinking through the implications of a strategy and of predicting the reactions of rivals. We can see the benefits of decision trees in the simple examples considered here. In the first example, Apple's managers can conclude that charging a low price is more profitable than charging a high price. In the second example, Dell's managers can conclude that TruImage's threat to reject a $20-per-copy contract is not credible.

MyEconLab Study Plan

MyEconLab Concept Check

The Five Competitive Forces Model

We have seen that the number of competitors in an industry affects a firm's ability to charge a price above average cost and earn an economic profit. The number of firms is not the only determinant of the level of competition in an industry, however. Michael Porter of the Harvard Business School has developed a model that shows how five competitive forces determine the overall level of competition in an industry.

We now look at each of the five competitive forces: (1) competition from existing firms, (2) the threat from potential entrants, (3) competition from substitute goods or services, (4) the bargaining power of buyers, and (5) the bargaining power of suppliers.

14.4 LEARNING OBJECTIVE

Use the five competitive forces model to analyze competition in an industry.

Competition from Existing Firms

We have already seen that competition among firms in an industry can lower prices and profits. Consider another example: Educational Testing Service (ETS) produces the Scholastic Aptitude Test (SAT) and the Graduate Record Exam (GRE). High school students applying to college take the SAT, and college students applying to graduate school take the GRE. In 2013, ETS charged a price of $51 to take the SAT, and it charged $150 to take the GRE. Part of the explanation for this large price difference is that ETS faces competition in the market for tests given to high school students applying to college, where the SAT competes with the ACT Assessment, produced by ACT, Inc. But there is no competition for the GRE. As we saw earlier in this chapter, when there are only a few firms in a market, it is easier for them to implicitly collude and to charge a price close to the monopoly price. In this case, however, competition from a single firm was enough to cause ETS to keep the price of the SAT near the competitive level.

Competition in the form of advertising, better customer service, or longer warranties can also reduce profits by raising costs. For example, online booksellers Amazon.com and BarnesandNoble.com have competed by offering low-cost—or free—shipping, by increasing their customer service staffs, and by building more warehouses to provide faster deliveries. These activities have raised the booksellers' costs and reduced their profits.

MyEconLab Concept Check

The Threat from Potential Entrants

Firms face competition from companies that currently are not in the market but might enter. We have already seen how actions taken to deter entry can reduce profits. In our hypothetical example in the previous section, Apple charged a lower price and earned less profit to deter Dell's entry. Business managers often take actions aimed at deterring entry. Some of these actions include advertising to create product loyalty, introducing new products—such as slightly different cereals or toothpastes—to fill market niches, and setting lower prices to keep profits at a level that makes entry less attractive. In 2013, Google was considering entering the market for video game consoles. Microsoft and Sony have purchased game studios that make games, such as Halo and Uncharted, exclusively for those consoles. Google's game console will have to overcome the substantial entry barrier of not being able to play some of the most popular existing games.

MyEconLab Concept Check

Competition from Substitute Goods or Services

Firms are always vulnerable to competitors introducing a new product that fills a consumer need better than their current product does. Consider the encyclopedia business. For decades, many parents bought expensive and bulky encyclopedias for their children attending high school or college. By the 1990s, computer software companies were offering electronic encyclopedias that sold for a small fraction of the price of printed encyclopedias. Encyclopedia Britannica and the other encyclopedia publishers responded by cutting prices and launching advertising campaigns aimed at showing the superiority of printed encyclopedias. Still, profits continued to decline, and by the end of the 1990s, most printed encyclopedias had disappeared. MyEconLab Concept Check

The Bargaining Power of Buyers

If buyers have enough bargaining power, they can insist on lower prices, higher-quality products, or additional services. Automobile companies, for example, have significant bargaining power in the tire market, which tends to lower tire prices and limit the profitability of tire manufacturers. Some retailers have significant buying power over their suppliers. For instance, Wal-Mart has required many of its suppliers to alter their distribution systems to accommodate Wal-Mart's desire to reduce the inventories it holds in its warehouses. MyEconLab Concept Check

The Bargaining Power of Suppliers

If many firms can supply an input and the input is not specialized, the suppliers are unlikely to have the bargaining power to limit a firm's profit. For instance, suppliers of paper napkins to McDonald's restaurants have very little bargaining power. With only a single or a few suppliers of an input, however, the purchasing firm may face a high price. During the 1930s and 1940s, for example, the Technicolor Company was the only producer of the cameras and film that studios needed to produce color movies. Technicolor charged the studios high prices to use its cameras, and it had the power to insist that only its technicians could operate the cameras. The only alternative for the movie studios was to make black-and-white movies.

As with other competitive forces, the bargaining power of suppliers can change over time. For instance, when IBM chose Microsoft to supply the operating system for its personal computers, Microsoft was a small company with very limited bargaining power. As Microsoft's Windows operating system became standard in more than 90 percent of personal computers, this large market share increased Microsoft's bargaining power. MyEconLab Concept Check

Making the Connection
MyEconLab Video

Can We Predict Which Firms Will Continue to Be Successful?

For years, economists and business strategists believed that market structure was the most important factor in explaining the ability of some firms to continue earning economic profits. For example, most economists argued that during the first few decades after World War II, steel companies in the United States earned economic profits because barriers to entry were high, there were few firms in the industry, and competition among firms was low. In contrast, restaurants were seen as less profitable because barriers to entry were low and the industry was intensely competitive. One problem with this approach to analyzing the profitability of firms is that it does not explain how firms in the same industry can have very different levels of profit.

Today, economists and business strategists put greater emphasis on the characteristics of individual firms and the strategies their managers use to continue to earn economic profits. This approach helps explain why Nucor continues to be a profitable steel company while Bethlehem Steel, at one time the second-largest steel producer in the United States, was forced into bankruptcy. It also explains why Amazon, which began as a small company Jeff Bezos started in Seattle, Washington, with a handful of employees, went on to become the leading online retailer, while many other online retailers that were also started in the 1990s have long since disappeared.

Is it possible to draw general conclusions about which business strategies are likely to be successful in the future? A number of business analysts have tried to identify strategies that have made firms successful and have recommended those strategies to other firms. Although books with these recommendations are often bestsellers, they

Although its business strategy had once been widely admired, Circuit City declared bankruptcy in 2009.

have a mixed record in identifying winning strategies. For instance, in 1982, Thomas J. Peters and Robert H. Waterman, Jr., published *In Search of Excellence: Lessons from America's Best-Run Companies*. The book was favorably reviewed by business magazines and sold more than 3 million copies. Peters and Waterman identified 43 companies that were the best at using eight key strategies to "stay on top of the heap." But just two years after the book was published, an article in *BusinessWeek* pointed out that 14 of the 43 companies were experiencing significant financial difficulties. The article noted: "It comes as a shock that so many companies have fallen from grace so quickly—and it also raises some questions. Were these companies so excellent in the first place?"

In 2002, Jim Collins published *Good to Great: Why Some Companies Make the Leap ... and Others Don't*, with the goal of determining how companies can "achieve enduring greatness." Although this book also sold 3 million copies, not all of the 11 "great companies" it identified were able to remain successful. For instance, Circuit City was forced to file for bankruptcy in 2009, and the Federal National Mortgage Association ("Fannie Mae") avoided bankruptcy only after the federal government largely took it over in 2008.

These two books, and many others like them, provide useful analyses of the business strategies of successful firms. That many of the firms highlighted in these books are unable to sustain their success should not be surprising. Many successful strategies can be copied—and, often, improved on—by competitors. Even in oligopolies, competition can quickly erode profits and even turn a successful firm into an unsuccessful one. It remains difficult to predict which currently successful firms will maintain their success.

Sources: Thomas J. Peters and Robert H. Waterman, Jr., *In Search of Excellence: Lessons from America's Best-Run Companies*, New York: HarperCollins Publishers, 1982; Jim Collins, *Good to Great: Why Some Companies Make the Leap ... and Others Don't*, New York: HarperCollins Publishers, 2001; "Who's Excellent Now?" *BusinessWeek*, November 5, 1984; and Steven D. Leavitt, "From Good to Great ... to Below Average," *New York Times*, July 28, 2008.

Your Turn: Test your understanding by doing related problem 4.5 on page 475 at the end of this chapter.

MyEconLab Study Plan

Continued from page 451

Economics in Your Life

Why Can't You Find a Cheap PlayStation 4?

At the beginning of this chapter, we asked you to consider why the price of the PlayStation 4 game console is almost the same at every large retailer, from Amazon to Wal-Mart. Why don't these retailers seem to compete on price for this type of product? In this chapter, we have seen that if big retailers were engaged in a one-time game of pricing PlayStations, they would be in a prisoner's dilemma and would probably all charge a low price. However, pricing PlayStations is actually a repeated game because the retailers will be selling the game system in competition over a long period of time. In this situation, it is more likely that the retailers will arrive at a cooperative equilibrium, in which they will all charge a high price—a result that is good news for the profits of the retailers but bad news for consumers! This analysis is one of many insights that game theory provides into the business strategies of oligopolists.

Conclusion

Firms are locked in a never-ending struggle to earn economic profits. As we have noted several times, competition erodes economic profits. Even in the oligopolies discussed in this chapter, firms have difficulty earning economic profits in the long run. We have seen that firms attempt to avoid the effects of competition in various ways. For example, they can stake out a secure niche in the market, they can engage in implicit collusion with competing firms, or they can attempt to have the government impose barriers to entry.

Visit MyEconLab for a news article and analysis related to the concepts in this chapter.

Chapter Summary and Problems

Key Terms

Barrier to entry, p. 453

Business strategy, p. 455

Cartel, p. 462

Collusion, p. 456

Cooperative equilibrium, p. 456

Dominant strategy, p. 456

Economies of scale, p. 453

Game theory, p. 455

Nash equilibrium, p. 456

Noncooperative equilibrium, p. 456

Oligopoly, p. 452

Patent, p. 454

Payoff matrix, p. 455

Price leadership, p. 460

Prisoner's dilemma, p. 456

14.1 Oligopoly and Barriers to Entry, pages 452–455

LEARNING OBJECTIVE: Show how barriers to entry explain the existence of oligopolies.

Summary

An **oligopoly** is a market structure in which a small number of interdependent firms compete. **Barriers to entry** keep new firms from entering an industry. The three most important barriers to entry are economies of scale, ownership of a key input, and government barriers. Economies of scale are the most important barrier to entry. **Economies of scale** exist when a firm's long-run average costs fall as it increases output. Government barriers include patents, licensing, and barriers to international trade. A **patent** is the exclusive right to a product for a period of 20 years from the date the patent is filed with the government.

MyEconLab   Visit www.myeconlab.com to complete these exercises online and get instant feedback.

Review Questions

1.1 What is an oligopoly? Give three examples of oligopolistic industries in the United States.

1.2 What do barriers to entry have to do with the extent of competition in an industry? What are the most important barriers to entry?

1.3 Give an example of a government-imposed barrier to entry. Why would a government be willing to erect barriers to firms entering an industry?

1.4 What is a patent? If a patent serves as a barrier to entry, why do governments issue patents?

Problems and Applications

1.5 Michael Porter has argued: "The intensity of competition in an industry is neither a matter of coincidence nor bad luck. Rather, competition in an industry is rooted in its underlying economic structure." What does Porter mean by "economic structure"? What factors besides economic structure might be expected to determine the intensity of competition in an industry?

Source: Michael Porter, *Competitive Strategy: Techniques for Analyzing Industries and Competitors*, New York: The Free Press, 1980, p. 3.

1.6 An article in the *Wall Street Journal* noted that online retailer Amazon was spending $2 billion per year to build additional distribution warehouses and data centers. The article observed that "such investments create a significant barrier to new entrants." Briefly explain the reasoning behind this observation.

Source: Rolfe Winkler, "Amazon's Bargains Don't Come Cheap," *Wall Street Journal*, April 27, 2012.

1.7 Thomas McCraw, at the time a professor at the Harvard Business School, wrote: "Throughout American history, entrepreneurs have tried, sometimes desperately, to create big businesses out of naturally small-scale operations. It has not worked." What advantage would entrepreneurs expect to gain from creating "big businesses"? Why would entrepreneurs fail to create big businesses with "naturally small-scale operations"? Illustrate your answer with a graph showing long-run average costs.

Source: Thomas K. McCraw, ed., *Creating Modern Capitalism*, Cambridge, MA: Harvard University Press, 1997, p. 323.

1.8 The following graph illustrates the average total cost curves for two automobile manufacturing firms: Little Auto and Big Auto. Under which of the following conditions would you expect to see the market composed of firms like Little Auto, and under which conditions would you expect to see the market dominated by firms like Big Auto?

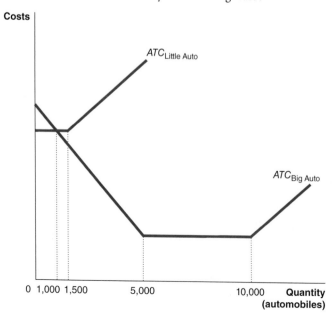

a. When the market demand curve intersects the quantity axis at fewer than 1,000 units

b. When the market demand curve intersects the quantity axis at more than 1,000 units but fewer than 10,000 units

c. When the market demand curve intersects the quantity axis at more than 10,000 units

1.9 Alfred Chandler, who was a professor at the Harvard Business School, once observed: "Imagine the diseconomies of scale—the great increase in unit costs—that would result from placing close to one-fourth of the world's production of shoes, or textiles, or lumber into three factories or mills!" The shoe, textile, and lumber industries are very competitive, with many firms producing each of these products. Briefly explain how Chandler's observation helps explain why these industries are competitive.

Source: Alfred D. Chandler, Jr., "The Emergence of Managerial Capitalism," in Alfred D. Chandler, Jr., and Richard S. Tedlow, *The Coming of Managerial Capitalism*, New York: Irwin, 1985, p. 406.

1.10 A historical account of the development of the cotton textile industry in England argued:

> The cotton textile industry was shaped by ruthless competition. Rapid growth in demand, low barriers to entry, frequent technological innovations, and a high rate of firm bankruptcy all combined to form an environment in which … oligopolistic competition became almost impossible.

Explain how each of the factors described here would contribute to making oligopolistic competition in the cotton textile industry very difficult.

Source: Thomas K. McCraw, ed., *Creating Modern Capitalism*, Cambridge, MA: Harvard University Press, 1997, pp. 61–62.

14.2 **Using Game Theory to Analyze Oligopoly, pages 455–463**
LEARNING OBJECTIVE: Use game theory to analyze the strategies of oligopolistic firms.

Summary

Because an oligopoly has only a few firms, interactions among those firms are particularly important. **Game theory** is the study of how people make decisions in situations in which attaining their goals depends on their interactions with others; in economics, it is the study of the decisions of firms in industries where the profits of each firm depend on its interactions with other firms. A **business strategy** refers to actions taken by a firm to achieve a goal, such as maximizing profit. Oligopoly games can be illustrated with a **payoff matrix**, which is a table that shows the payoffs that each firm earns from every combination of strategies by the firms. One possible outcome in oligopoly is **collusion**, which is an agreement among firms to charge the same price or otherwise not to compete. A **cartel** is a group of firms that collude by agreeing to restrict output to increase prices and profits. In a **cooperative equilibrium**, firms cooperate to increase their mutual payoff. In a **noncooperative equilibrium**, firms do not cooperate but pursue their own self-interest. A **dominant strategy** is a strategy that is the best for a firm, no matter what strategies other firms choose. A **Nash equilibrium** is a situation in which each firm chooses the best strategy, given the strategies chosen by other firms. A situation in which pursuing dominant strategies results in noncooperation that leaves everyone worse off is called a **prisoner's dilemma**. Because many business situations are repeated games, firms may end up implicitly colluding to keep prices high. With **price leadership**, one firm takes the lead in announcing a price change, which is then matched by the other firms in the industry.

 MyEconLab   Visit **www.myeconlab.com** to complete these exercises online and get instant feedback.

Review Questions

2.1 Give brief definitions of the following concepts:
a. Game theory
b. Cooperative equilibrium
c. Noncooperative equilibrium
d. Dominant strategy
e. Nash equilibrium
f. Price leadership

2.2 Why do economists refer to the methodology for analyzing oligopolies as game theory?

2.3 What is the difference between explicit collusion and implicit collusion? Give an example of each.

2.4 What is a prisoner's dilemma game? Is the outcome of the game likely to be different in a repeated game? Briefly explain.

Problems and Applications

2.5 Bob and Tom are two criminals who have been arrested for burglary. The police put Tom and Bob in separate cells. They offer to let Bob go free if he confesses to the crime and testifies against Tom. Bob also is told that he will serve a 15-year sentence if he remains silent while Tom confesses. If Bob confesses and Tom also confesses, they will each serve a 10-year sentence. Separately, the police make the same offer to Tom. Assume that Bob and Tom know that if they both remain silent, the police have only enough evidence to convict them of a lesser crime, and they will both serve 3-year sentences.
a. Use the information provided to write a payoff matrix for Bob and Tom.
b. Does Bob have a dominant strategy? If so, what is it?
c. Does Tom have a dominant strategy? If so, what is it?
d. What sentences do Bob and Tom serve? How might they have avoided this outcome?

2.6 Explain how collusion makes firms better off. Given the incentives to collude, briefly explain why every industry doesn't become a cartel.

2.7 Under "early decision" college admission plans, students apply to a college in the fall and, if they are accepted, they must enroll in that college. Some critics of early decision plans, including some college presidents, argue that the plans put too much pressure on students to decide early in their senior year in high school which college to attend. Some college administrators have proposed abolishing early decision plans, but as one newspaper headline put it: "Applicants Continue to Flock to Early Admission Programs." If many college administrators believe that early decision plans should be abolished, why do their schools continue to use them? Can game theory help analyze this situation?

Source: Jacques Steinberg and Tanya Abrams, "Applicants Continue to Flock to Early Admission Programs," *New York Times*, December 20, 2012.

2.8 Baseball players who hit the most home runs *relative to other players* usually receive the highest pay. Beginning in the mid-1990s, the typical baseball player became significantly stronger and more muscular. As one baseball announcer put it: "The players of 20 years ago look like stick figures compared with the players of today." As a result, the average number of home runs hit each year increased dramatically. Some of the increased strength that baseball players gained came from more weight training and better conditioning and diet. As some players admitted, though, some of the increased strength came from taking steroids and other illegal drugs. Taking steroids can significantly increase the risk of developing cancer and other medical problems.

    a. In these circumstances, are baseball players in a prisoner's dilemma? Carefully explain.

    b. Major League Baseball has begun testing players for steroids and fining and suspending players who are caught using steroids (or other illegal muscle-building drugs). Has this testing made baseball players as a group better off or worse off? Briefly explain.

2.9 For several years, a professor at Johns Hopkins University had been using the following grading scheme for his final exam: He would give an A to the student with the highest score. The grades of the remaining students were then based on what percentage their scores were of the top student's score. In the fall of 2012, the students in the class came up with the idea of boycotting the final exam. They stood in the hallway outside the classroom but did not enter the room to take the exam. After waiting for a time, the professor cancelled the exam and, applying his grading scale, gave everyone in the class an A on the exam. An article in the *New York Times* about this incident observes: "This is an amazing game theory outcome, and not one that economists would likely predict." Do you agree with this observation that game theory indicates the students' strategy was unlikely to work? Briefly explain.

Source: Catherine Rampell, "Gaming the System," *New York Times*, February 14, 2013.

2.10 **[Related to the** Don't Let This Happen to You **on page 457]** A student argues: "The prisoner's dilemma game is unrealistic. Each player's strategy is based on the assumption that the other player won't cooperate. But if each player assumes that the other player *will* cooperate, the 'dilemma'

disappears." Briefly explain whether you agree with this argument.

2.11 **[Related to** Solved Problem 14.2 **on page 457]** Coca-Cola and Pepsi both advertise aggressively, but would they be better off if they didn't? Their commercials are usually not designed to convey new information about their products. Instead, they are designed to capture each other's customers. Construct a payoff matrix using the following hypothetical information:

- If neither firm advertises, Coca-Cola and Pepsi each earn a profit of $750 million per year.
- If both firms advertise, Coca-Cola and Pepsi each earns a profit of $500 million per year.
- If Coca-Cola advertises and Pepsi doesn't, Coca-Cola earns a profit of $900 million and Pepsi earns a profit of $400 million.
- If Pepsi advertises and Coca-Cola doesn't, Pepsi earns a profit of $900 million and Coca-Cola earns a profit of $400 million.

    a. If Coca-Cola wants to maximize profit, will it advertise? Briefly explain.

    b. If Pepsi wants to maximize profit, will it advertise? Briefly explain.

    c. Is there a Nash equilibrium to this advertising game? If so, what is it?

2.12 **[Related to** Solved Problem 14.2 **on page 457]** Radio frequency identification (RFID) tracking tags may ultimately replace bar codes. With this system, a radio signal automatically records the arrival of a product in a warehouse, its shipment to a store, and its purchase by the consumer. Suppose that Wal-Mart and Target are independently deciding whether to stick with bar codes or switch to RFID tags to monitor the flow of products. Because many suppliers sell to both Wal-Mart and Target, it is much less costly for suppliers to use one system or the other rather than to use both. The following payoff matrix shows the profit per year for each company resulting from the interaction of their strategies.

    a. Briefly explain whether Wal-Mart has a dominant strategy.

    b. Briefly explain whether Target has a dominant strategy.

    c. Briefly explain whether there is a Nash equilibrium in this game.

2.13 **[Related to the** Making the Connection **on page 458]** We made the argument that a bidder on an eBay auction has a dominant strategy of bidding only once, with that bid being the maximum the bidder would be willing to pay.

a. Is it possible that a bidder might receive useful information during the auction, particularly from the dollar amounts other bidders are bidding? If so, how does that change a bidder's optimal strategy?

b. Many people recommend the practice of "sniping," or placing your bid at the last second before the auction ends. Is there a connection between sniping and your answer to part (a)?

2.14 **[Related to the** Making the Connection **on page 460]** The following appeared in an article in the *Wall Street Journal*: "Last week, true to discount roots dating to 1971, Southwest [Airlines] launched a summer fare sale on domestic flights, with one-way prices as low as $49. As in the past, major competitors were forced to follow suit." Why would other airlines be "forced" to follow Southwest's fare decrease? Does your answer change if you learn that this fare decrease took place during an economic recession, when incomes and the demand for airline travel were falling? Briefly explain.

Source: Mike Esterl, "Southwest Airlines CEO Flies Uncharted Skies," *Wall Street Journal*, March 25, 2009.

2.15 **[Related to the** Making the Connection **on page 460]** Airlines often find themselves in price wars. Consider the following game: Delta and United are the only two airlines flying the route from Houston to Omaha. Each firm has two strategies: charge a high price or charge a low price.

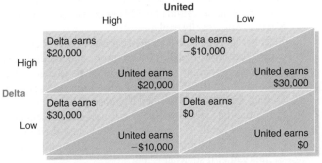

a. What (if any) is the dominant strategy for each firm?
b. Is this game a prisoner's dilemma?
c. How could repeated playing of the game change the strategy each firm uses?

2.16 **[Related to the** Making the Connection **on page 460]** Until the late 1990s, airlines would post proposed changes in ticket prices on computer reservation systems several days before the new ticket prices went into effect. Then the federal government took action to end this practice. Now airlines can post prices on their reservation systems only for tickets that are immediately available for sale. Why would the federal government object to the old system of posting prices before they went into effect?

Source: Scott McCartney, "Airfare Wars Show Why Deals Arrive and Depart," *Wall Street Journal*, March 19, 2002.

2.17 Finding dominant strategies is often a very effective way of analyzing a game. Consider the following game: Microsoft and Apple are the two firms in the market for operating systems. Each firm has two strategies: charge a high price or charge a low price.

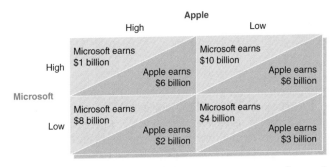

a. What (if any) is the dominant strategy for each firm?
b. Is there a Nash equilibrium? Briefly explain.

2.18 DemandTec is a firm that provides software to retailers, such as department stores, that allow the firms to make better decisions about when to increase or cut prices, based on changes in demand, changes in costs, and other factors. DemandTec and firms selling similar software have allowed smaller retailers to adopt pricing strategies that had long been used by larger retailers, such as Wal-Mart. According to an article in the *Wall Street Journal*, use of this software has reduced the amount of price cutting that retail firms engage in following a fall in demand. Is a decline in price cutting good news for consumers? Good news for the firms involved? Good news for both? Briefly explain.

Source: John Jannarone, "Fashioning a Retail Stock Rally," *Wall Street Journal*, July 8, 2011.

2.19 A newspaper article referred to problems OPEC was having in affecting the world price of oil. The article noted that a key problem was OPEC's "inability to enforce internal production targets." An executive at an oil company was quoted as saying: "Those [OPEC countries] crying about too much oil on the market, they could cut it off if they wanted to."

a. How does OPEC try to affect the world price of oil? What role do "internal production targets" play in its strategy?

b. Explain what the oil executive means by the quoted statement. If countries complaining about too much oil being supplied could cut if off if they wanted to, why don't they?

Source: James Herron, "OPEC Hamstrung by Events Beyond Its Control," *Wall Street Journal*, June 17, 2012.

2.20 Suppose there are four large manufacturers of toilet tissue. The largest of these manufacturers announces that it will raise its prices by 15 percent due to higher paper costs. Within three days, the other three large toilet tissue manufacturers announce similar price hikes. Would this decision to raise prices be evidence of explicit collusion among the four companies? Briefly explain.

2.21 Anheuser-Busch InBev is the foreign-owned company that produces Budweiser, which has a large market share in the U.S. beer industry. According to an article in the *New York Times*, "Anheuser-Busch (InBev) signals to its competitors that if they lower prices, it will start a vicious retail war."

a. What does the article mean by a "retail war"?
b. Why would Anheuser-Busch threaten to start a retail war?

Source: Adam Davidson, "Are We in Danger of a Beer Monopoly?" *New York Times*, February 26, 2013.

14.3 Sequential Games and Business Strategy, pages 463–466

LEARNING OBJECTIVE: Use sequential games to analyze business strategies.

Summary

Recent work in game theory has focused on actions firms can take to deter the entry of new firms into an industry. Deterring entry can be analyzed using a sequential game, where first one firm makes a decision and then another firm reacts to that decision. Sequential games can be illustrated using decision trees.

MyEconLab   Visit **www.myeconlab.com** to complete these exercises online and get instant feedback.

Review Questions

3.1 What is a sequential game?

3.2 How are decision trees used to analyze sequential games?

Problems and Applications

3.3 **[Related to** Solved Problem 14.3 **on page 464]** Bradford is a small town that currently has no fast-food restaurants. McDonald's and Burger King both are considering entering this market. Burger King will wait until McDonald's has made its decision before deciding whether to enter. McDonald's will choose between building a large store and building a small store. Once McDonald's has made its decision about the size of the store it will build, Burger King will decide whether to enter this market. Use the following decision tree to decide the optimal strategy for each company. Does your answer depend on the rate of return that owners of fast-food restaurants must earn on their investments to break even? Briefly explain.

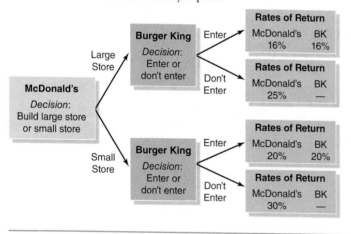

3.4 **[Related to the** Chapter Opener **on page 451]** In June 2013, Microsoft announced that its new Xbox One video game console would have a price of $499. Sony then announced that its new PlayStation 4 video game console would have a price of $399. An article on the event where Microsoft introduced the new console noted that the Microsoft spokesman "started by showing off features like live-television technology and the ability to video-chat through its Skype service." The article goes on to say that not until nearly half way through the presentation did the Microsoft spokesman mention the new games the console could play.

a. Why in announcing a new video game console would Microsoft focus its presentation on features of the console other than its ability to play games?

b. Was it an advantage to Sony that Microsoft announced the price of the Xbox One before Sony announced the price of the PlayStation 4? Briefly explain.

Source: Ian Sherr and Daisuke Wakabayashi, "Xbox One to Launch at $499, PlayStation 4 at $399," *Wall Street Journal*, June 10, 2013.

3.5 Suppose that in the situation shown in Figure 14.7 on page 466, TruImage's profit is $1.5 million if the firm accepts Dell's contract offer of $20 per copy. Now will Dell offer TruImage a contract for $20 per copy or a contract for $30 per copy? Briefly explain.

3.6 Refer to Figure 14.5 on page 463. Consider the entries in the row of the payoff matrix that correspond to Saudi Arabia choosing "low output." Suppose the numbers change so that Nigeria's profit is $15 million when Nigeria chooses "Low Output" and $10 million when it chooses "High Output."

a. Create the payoff matrix for this new situation, assuming that Saudi Arabia and Nigeria choose their output levels simultaneously. Is there a Nash equilibrium to this game? If so, what is it?

b. Draw the decision tree for this situation (using the values from the payoff matrix you created in part (a)), assuming that Saudi Arabia and Nigeria make their decisions sequentially: First, Saudi Arabia chooses its output level, and then Nigeria responds by choosing its output level. Is there a Nash equilibrium in this game? If so, what is it?

c. Compare your answers to parts (a) and (b). Briefly explain the reason for any differences in the outcomes of these two games.

14.4 The Five Competitive Forces Model, pages 467–469

LEARNING OBJECTIVE: Use the five competitive forces model to analyze competition in an industry.

Summary

Michael Porter of the Harvard Business School argues that the state of competition in an industry is determined by five competitive forces: competition from existing firms, the threat from new entrants, competition from substitute goods or services, the bargaining power of buyers, and the bargaining power of suppliers.

MyEconLab   Visit **www.myeconlab.com** to complete these exercises online and get instant feedback.

Review Questions

4.1 Describe the five competitive forces model.

4.2 Does the strength of each of the five competitive forces remain constant over time? Briefly explain.

Problems and Applications

4.3 Michael Porter argued that in many industries, "strategies converge and competition becomes a series of races down identical paths that no one can win." Briefly explain whether firms in these industries will likely earn economic profits.

Source: Michael E. Porter, "What Is Strategy?" *Harvard Business Review*, November–December 1996, p. 64.

4.4 In 2013, Google was developing a video game console. In designing the console, Google considered what types of microchips to use. The company was choosing between chips made by AMD that Microsoft and Sony were using in their game consoles and chips made by ARM that Google was using in its smartphones and tablets. According to an article in the *Wall Street Journal*, game developers had lower costs of development because Microsoft and Sony used the same microchips. But, "If Google used the same chips for its console that it does for mobile devices, which are based on designs made by ARM, that would make extra work for game developers." In this situation, who is likely to have the greater bargaining power, Google or the game developers? That is, is Google's bargaining power a greater threat to the game developers' profits or is the game developers' bargaining power a greater threat to Google's profit?

Source: Ian Sherr, "Challenges Ahead for Google's Game Console," *Wall Street Journal*, June 28, 2013.

4.5 **[Related to the** Making the Connection **on page 468]** In the preface to the 2004 reprint of *In Search of Excellence*, Thomas Peters and Robert Waterman wrote: "Our main detractors point to the decline of some of the companies we featured. They miss the point.... We weren't writing *Forever Excellent*, just as it would be absurd to expect any great athlete not to age." Is the analogy the authors make between great firms and great athletes a good one? Should we expect firms to become less successful as they age, just as athletes do?

Source: Thomas Peters and Robert H. Waterman, Jr., "Authors' Note: Excellence 2003," in *In Search of Excellence: Lessons from America's Best-Run Companies*, New York: HarperCollins, 2004 (original edition 1982).

4.6 In a forum posting on the Web site www.startupnation .com, a contributor made the following comment regarding the advice in the business strategy book *Blue Ocean Strategy*: "The key message for me was don't try to look like, taste like, act like the competition." Briefly explain what this person meant by "look like, taste like, act like the competition." Briefly discuss whether the strategy of "look like, taste like, act like the competition" ever makes sense.

Source: "As a Small Business Owner, What Kind of Book Would You Like to Read?" "Coffee Talk" Forum, www.startupnation.com, April 25, 2007.

4.7 In August 2013, the U.S. Department of Justice blocked a proposed merger between American Airlines and U.S. Airways. If the merger were allowed, American, Delta, United Continental, and Southwest would account for 85 percent of seats on domestic flights. An article discussing the merger observed that: "Such concentration doesn't always dictate the direction of airfares. Discount airlines can still police pricing, even with just 5% to 10% of the seats in a market...."

a. What does the article mean by "discount airlines can still police pricing"?

b. Consider the situation one of the big four airlines would face in a particular market, for example, the Chicago to Houston market. Which of the forces in the five competitive forces model does the threat from discount airlines represent? Briefly explain.

Source: Jack Nicas and Susan Carey, "American-US Airways Merger: Fewer Seats and Higher Fares?" *Wall Street Journal*, August 13, 2013.

4.8 The market for electronic readers consists of relatively few firms, including Amazon, Sony, and Plastic Logic. In an interview, Walter Mossberg of the *Wall Street Journal* asked Rich Archuleta, CEO of Plastic Logic, what price the company would be charging for a new electronic reader that it was developing, aimed at business users. Archuleta declined to give a specific price, saying instead: "The market sets pricing. We don't set pricing." But Plastic Logic is competing in an oligopolistic industry, so shouldn't the firm, not the market, be setting the price? Explain why Archuleta made this statement.

Source: "Plastic Logic Shows New E-Book Reader," *Wall Street Journal*, May 27, 2009.

CHAPTER 15

Monopoly and Antitrust Policy

Chapter Outline and Learning Objectives

A Monopoly on Lobster Dinners in Maine?

A *New York Times* article written from Stonington, Maine, explained that: "Lobsters are flooding the market here." The reporter observed that the huge lobster harvest was not good news for fishermen because "the law of supply and demand has forced the price down to a 40-year low" of $1.35 per pound. Yet shortly after this article appeared, a columnist for *Slate*, an online magazine, had dinner with his father at the only lobster restaurant in Stonington, The Fisherman's Friend. He was surprised that the restaurant charged $20.99 for each dinner.

How could The Fisherman's Friend charge so much for a lobster dinner when the price of lobsters was so low? The answer is that The Fisherman's Friend is the *only* seafood restaurant in Stonington. The reporter and his father couldn't eat at "the competitor next door" because there wasn't one. To eat lobster while staying in Stonington, they had to eat at that restaurant or buy lobsters in a store and cook the lobsters themselves. In other words,

The Fisherman's Friend has a *monopoly* on selling seafood dinners in that town.

Few firms in the United States are monopolies because in a market system whenever a firm earns an economic profit, typically other firms will enter that market. Therefore, it is very difficult for a firm to remain the only provider of a good or service. Only if the gap between the price of lobsters and the price of lobster dinners in Stonington fails to attract a competitor would The Fisherman's Friend be able to maintain its monopoly. Although not common, monopolies are worth studying because they provide a benchmark for how firms behave when they face the minimum possible competition. In this chapter, we will build a model to analyze monopolies.

Sources: Katharine Q. Seelye, "In Maine, More Lobsters Than They Know What to Do With," *New York Times*, July 28, 2012; and Matthew Yglesias, "The Mystery of the Market Price" www.slate.com, August 21, 2012.

Economics in Your Life

Is There a Monopoly in Your Dorm?

You and your roommate Fatma come up with an idea for a business: You will buy rolls, lunch meat, lettuce, and tomatoes and become the sole seller of submarine sandwiches in your school's dormitories on Saturday and Sunday evenings when there are no other food vendors open on campus. You believe that there will be many hungry customers when students return to campus from the library and off-campus events. But you and Fatma must decide on the prices to charge for the subs. Fatma argues that because your business is a monopoly, you can charge prices much higher than what local shops charge for subs during the day—hungry students will have to buy your subs or stay hungry until the following day. You want to make a profit from your business but are not sure if Fatma is right. Is your business a monopoly? Should you charge high prices for your sandwiches? As you read this chapter, try to answer these questions. You can check your answers against those we provide on **page 499** at the end of this chapter.

Although few firms are monopolies, the economic model of monopoly can be quite useful. As we have seen, even though perfectly competitive markets are rare, the competitive market model provides a benchmark for how a firm acts in the most competitive situation possible: when it is in an industry with many firms that all supply the same product. Monopoly provides a benchmark for the other extreme, where a firm is the only one in its market and, therefore, faces no competition from other firms supplying its product. The monopoly model is also useful in analyzing situations in which firms agree to *collude*, or not compete, and act together as if they were a monopoly. As we will discuss in this chapter, collusion is illegal in the United States, but it occasionally happens.

Monopolies pose a dilemma for the government. Should the government allow monopolies to exist? Are there circumstances in which the government should actually promote the existence of monopolies? Should the government regulate the prices monopolies charge? If so, will such price regulation increase economic efficiency? In this chapter, we will explore these public policy issues.

Is Any Firm Ever Really a Monopoly?

15.1 LEARNING OBJECTIVE

Define monopoly.

Monopoly A firm that is the only seller of a good or service that does not have a close substitute.

A **monopoly** is a firm that is the only seller of a good or service that does not have a close substitute. Because substitutes of some kind exist for just about every product, are there actually any monopolies? The answer is "yes," provided that the substitutes are not "close" substitutes. But how do we decide whether a substitute is a close substitute? A narrow definition of monopoly that some economists use is that a firm has a monopoly if it can ignore the actions of all other firms. In other words, if a firm can ignore the prices other firms charge, the firm has a monopoly because other firms must not be producing close substitutes. For example, candles are a substitute for electric lights, but your local electric company can ignore candle prices because however low the price of candles becomes, almost no customers will give up using electric lights and switch to candles. Therefore, your local electric company is clearly a monopoly.

Many economists, however, use a broader definition of *monopoly*. For example, consider again The Fisherman's Friend seafood restaurant in Stonington, Maine, that we discussed in the chapter opener. Does this restaurant have a monopoly? Substitutes for lobster dinners certainly exist. If the price of lobster dinners is too high, people will switch to steak dinners or spaghetti dinners or some other food. People do not have to eat at The Fisherman's Friend or starve. The restaurant is in competition with several other local restaurants. So, The Fisherman's Friend does not meet the narrow definition of a monopoly. Many economists, however, would still argue that it is useful to think of the restaurant as having a monopoly.

Although steak and spaghetti are substitutes for lobster, competition from firms selling them is not enough to keep The Fisherman's Friend from earning an economic profit. We have seen that when firms earn economic profits, we can expect new firms to enter the industry, and in the long run, the economic profits are competed away (see Chapter 12). The Fisherman's Friend's profits will not be competed away as long as it is the *only* seller of lobster dinners. The *Slate* reporter mentioned in the chapter opener noted that: "Stonington is a great place to visit. But it's also a very small town." So it's possible that no other seafood restaurants will choose to open in the town. In that case, using the broader definition of monopoly, The Fisherman's Friend has a monopoly because there are no other firms selling a substitute close enough that its economic profits are competed away in the long run. MyEconLab Concept Check

Making the Connection	Is Google a Monopoly?

MyEconLab Video

As we will discuss later in this chapter, the federal government can take legal action against a firm under *antitrust laws* if the government believes that the firm has created a monopoly. The U.S. Federal Trade Commission (FTC) spent two years beginning in 2011 investigating whether Google had violated antitrust laws before concluding that it hadn't. The European Union, which is an organization of 28 European countries, has similar rules against firms forming monopolies. The European Commission enforces these rules. In early

2011, Microsoft filed a complaint with the European Commission that Google was using its dominant position as an Internet search engine to exclude competitors. In 2013, Google reached a settlement with the European Commission in which the firm agreed to clearly label any search results that directed users to sites that Google owns. Still, many critics argued that both the FTC and the European Commission should take further actions against some of Google's practices.

But is Google a monopoly? Clearly, Google is not the only Internet search option available. Yahoo! has for a number of years operated a search engine, Microsoft operates the Bing search engine, and there are a number of smaller search engines. Critics point out, though, that Google has a dominant market share of 70 percent in the United States and 90 percent in Europe. Can the other search engines effectively compete with Google? Microsoft argues that Google has taken steps to create an effective monopoly:

Google has a dominant market share in the United States and in Europe. Can other search engines effectively compete?

> [Google] understands as well as anyone that search engines depend upon the openness of the Web in order to function properly.... Unfortunately, Google has engaged in a broadening pattern of walling off access to content and data that competitors need to provide search results to consumers and to attract advertisers.

Microsoft was particularly concerned that Google was limiting the access of other search engines to YouTube, which Google owns: "Without proper access to YouTube, Bing and other search engines cannot stand with Google on an equal footing in returning search results with links to YouTube videos and that, of course, drives more users away from competitors and to Google." Microsoft also complained that Google was limiting the access of other search engines to many of the books that Google had scanned and made available on the Web.

Google, naturally, takes a different view of its position. The company argues that its dominant market share is due to the higher quality of its search engine, not any attempts the company has made to reduce the access of other search engines to online content. In a response to the FTC investigation, Google noted: "We want [users of search engines] to stay with us because we're innovating and making our products better—not because [they are] locked in."

As we have seen, many economists consider a firm to have a monopoly if other firms are unable to compete away its profit in the long run. Some economists argue that rapid technological advances affecting search engines and other aspects of the Internet make it unlikely that Google would be able to maintain its current level of profitability indefinitely. The debate over whether other search engines can compete with Google or whether it is effectively a monopoly is likely to continue.

Sources: Vanessa Mock, "Google's Grand Bargain," *Wall Street Journal*, April 18, 2013; Miguel Helft, "Google Confirms F.T.C. Antitrust Inquiry," *New York Times*, June 24, 2011; Amit Singhal, "Supporting Choice, Ensuring Economic Opportunity," www.googleblog.blogspot.com, June 24, 2011; David Goldman, "Microsoft Accuses Google of Antitrust Violations," www.money.cnn.com, March 31, 2011; and Brad Smith, "Adding Our Voice to Concerns about Search in Europe," www.blogs.technet.com, March 31, 2011.

Your Turn: Test your understanding by doing related problems 1.6 and 1.7 on page 500 at the end of this chapter.

MyEconLab Study Plan

Where Do Monopolies Come From?

15.2 LEARNING OBJECTIVE

Explain the four main reasons monopolies arise.

Because monopolies do not face competition, every firm would like to have a monopoly. But to have a monopoly, barriers to entering the market must be so high that no other firms can enter. *Barriers to entry* may be high enough to keep out competing firms for four main reasons:

1. Government action blocks the entry of more than one firm into a market.
2. One firm has control of a key resource necessary to produce a good.
3. There are important *network externalities* in supplying the good or service.
4. Economies of scale are so large that one firm has a *natural monopoly*.

Government Action Blocks Entry

As we will discuss later in this chapter, governments ordinarily try to promote competition in markets, but sometimes governments take action to block entry into a market. In the United States, governments block entry in two main ways:

1. By granting a *patent*, *copyright*, or *trademark* to an individual or a firm, giving it the exclusive right to produce a product
2. By granting a firm a *public franchise*, making it the exclusive legal provider of a good or service

Patent The exclusive right to a product for a period of 20 years from the date the patent is filed with the government.

Patents, Copyrights, and Trademarks The U.S. government grants patents to firms that develop new products or new ways of making existing products. A **patent** gives a firm the exclusive right to a new product for a period of 20 years from the date the patent is filed with the government. Because Microsoft has a patent on the Windows operating system, other firms cannot sell their versions of Windows. The government grants patents to encourage firms to spend money on the research and development necessary to create new products. If other firms could have freely copied Windows, Microsoft would have been unlikely to spend the money necessary to develop it. Sometimes a firm is able to maintain a monopoly in the production of a good without patent protection, provided that it can keep secret how the product is made.

Patent protection is of vital importance to pharmaceutical firms as they develop new prescription drugs. Pharmaceutical firms start research and development work on a new prescription drug an average of 12 years before the drug is available for sale. A firm applies for a patent about 10 years before it begins to sell the product. The average 10-year delay between the government granting a patent and the firm actually selling the drug is due to the federal Food and Drug Administration's requirements that the firm demonstrate that the drug is both safe and effective. Therefore, during the period before the drug can be sold, the firm will have significant costs to develop and test the drug. If the drug does not successfully make it to market, the firm will have a substantial loss.

Once a drug is available for sale, the profits the firm earns from the drug will increase throughout the period of patent protection—which is usually about 10 years—as the drug becomes more widely known to doctors and patients. After the patent has expired, other firms are free to legally produce chemically identical drugs called *generic drugs*. Gradually, competition from generic drugs will eliminate the profits the original firm had been earning. For example, when patent protection expired for Glucophage, a diabetes drug manufactured by Bristol-Myers Squibb, sales of the drug declined by more than $1.5 billion in the first year due to competition from 12 generic versions of the drug produced by other firms. When the patent expired on Prozac, an antidepressant drug manufactured by Eli Lilly, sales dropped by more than 80 percent. Most economic profits from selling a prescription drug are eliminated 20 years after the drug is first offered for sale.

A *trademark* grants a firm legal protection against other firms using its product's name. Trademarks are also referred to as *brand names*. The U.S. Patent and Trademark Office defines a trademark as "any word, name, symbol, device, or any combination, used or intended to be used to identify and distinguish the goods/services of one seller or provider from those of others, and to indicate the source of the goods/services." Firms often vigorously defend their trademarks, including by filing lawsuits against other firms for selling goods that infringe on their trademarks. For example, Christian Louboutin filed a lawsuit against Yves Saint Laurent claiming that Yves Saint Laurent had infringed on Louboutin's trademark on women's shoes with red soles.

Making the Connection
MyEconLab Video

Does Hasbro Have a Monopoly on Monopoly?

To receive a copyright, patent, or trademark, a work has to be substantially new. Once a work no longer has legal protection, it is in the *public domain* and available to be freely used. It wouldn't be possible, for example, to make small changes to Mark Twain's novel *Huckle-berry Finn* and then claim copyright on the book because it has been in the public domain for decades. (If you drew new illustrations for the book, however, it would be possible to copyright those illustrations independently of the text of the book.)

Hasbro is the multinational American company that owns Monopoly, one of the world's most popular board games. The company estimates that more than 275 million copies of the game have been sold, and it is available in 43 languages. According to Hasbro, Charles Darrow invented the game in the 1930s. After selling many homemade copies, Darrow sold the game to Parker Brothers. In 1935, the U.S. Patent and Trademark Office issued Parker Brothers a trademark on the use of the name Monopoly for a board game. Hasbro bought Parker Brothers in 1991. Trademarks, unlike patents and copyrights, never expire, so Hasbro continues to have a trademark on the name Monopoly.

Hasbro's trademark on its Monopoly game prevents other companies from creating and selling similar games using the same title. In 2013, Hasbro displayed its new cat token at a toy fair.

Economics professor Ralph Anspach of California State University, San Francisco, received an unexpected lesson in the law of trademarks when he decided in the 1970s to sell a game about competition that he titled Anti-Monopoly. The game was a hit, selling 200,000 copies the first year. Parker Brothers sued Anspach, though, on the grounds that his game infringed on their Monopoly trademark. In the course of defending the lawsuit, Anspach believed he had uncovered evidence that in 1904 a woman named Elizabeth Magie had developed The Landlord's Game, which was very similar to Monopoly. The game was never trademarked and was played for years on the east coast. According to Anspach, Darrow became aware of The Landlord's Game in the mid-1930s, made a few changes to it, and sold it to Parker Brothers in 1935. A federal appeals court largely agreed with Anspach that given the history of the game, the name Monopoly was in the public domain and so couldn't be trademarked. Congress later amended the law, though, in a way that reinstated Parker Brothers' trademark. Eventually, Anspach and Hasbro worked out a settlement under which Anspach was allowed to sell his Anti-Monopoly game under a license from Hasbro.

Losing the trademark on its Monopoly game would have cost Hasbro millions of dollars per year because other companies could have begun to market similar games using the same title. The long legal fight the company had with Professor Anspach illustrates that companies consider it critical to retain exclusive control over their products.

Sources: Mary Pilon, "How a Fight Over a Board Game Monopolized an Economist's Life," *Wall Street Journal*, October 20, 2009; Ralph Anspach, *The Billion Dollar Monopoly® Swindle*, 2nd ed., Bloomington, IN: Xlibris, 2007; and Rachel Doepker, "Monopoly Patented," Business Reference Services, Library of Congress, www.loc.gov/rr/business/businesshistory/December/monopoly.html.

Your Turn: Test your understanding by doing related problem 2.10 on page 501 at the end of this chapter.

MyEconLab Study Plan

Just as the government grants a new product patent or trademark protection, it grants books, films, and pieces of music **copyright** protection. U.S. law grants the creator of a book, film, or piece of music the exclusive right to use the creation during the creator's lifetime. The creator's heirs retain this exclusive right for 70 years after the creator's death. In effect, copyrights create monopolies for the copyrighted items. Without copyrights, individuals and firms would be less likely to invest in creating new books, films, and software.

Copyright A government-granted exclusive right to produce and sell a creation.

Public Franchises In some cases, the government grants a firm a **public franchise** that allows it to be the only legal provider of a good or service. For example, state and local governments often designate one company as the sole provider of electricity, natural gas, or water.

Public franchise A government designation that a firm is the only legal provider of a good or service.

Occasionally, a government may decide to provide certain services directly to consumers through a *public enterprise*. This is much more common in Europe than in the United States. For example, the governments in most European countries own the railroad systems. In the United States, many city governments provide water and sewage service rather than rely on private firms. MyEconLab Concept Check

Control of a Key Resource

Another way for a firm to become a monopoly is by controlling a key resource. This happens infrequently because most resources, including raw materials such as oil or iron ore, are widely available from a variety of suppliers. There are, however, a few prominent examples of monopolies based on control of a key resource, such as the Aluminum Company of America (Alcoa) and the International Nickel Company of Canada.

For many years until the 1940s, Alcoa either owned or had long-term contracts to buy nearly all of the available bauxite, the mineral needed to produce aluminum. Without access to bauxite, competing firms had to use recycled aluminum, which limited the amount of aluminum they could produce. Similarly, the International Nickel Company of Canada controlled more than 90 percent of available nickel supplies. Competition in the nickel market increased when the Petsamo nickel fields in northern Russia were developed after World War II.

In the United States, a key resource for a professional sports team is a large stadium. The teams that make up the major professional sports leagues—Major League Baseball, the National Football League, and the National Basketball Association—usually either own or have long-term leases with the stadiums in major cities. Control of these stadiums is a major barrier to new professional baseball, football, or basketball leagues forming. MyEconLab Concept Check

Making the Connection

MyEconLab Video

Are Diamond Profits Forever? The De Beers Diamond Monopoly

The most famous monopoly based on control of a raw material is the De Beers diamond mining and marketing company of South Africa. Before the 1860s, diamonds were extremely rare. Only a few pounds of diamonds were produced each year, primarily from Brazil and India. Then in 1870, enormous deposits of diamonds were discovered along the Orange River in South Africa. It became possible to produce thousands of pounds of diamonds per year, and the owners of the new mines feared that the price of diamonds would plummet. To avoid financial disaster, the mine owners decided in 1888 to merge and form De Beers Consolidated Mines, Ltd.

De Beers became one of the most profitable and longest-lived monopolies in history. The company carefully controlled the supply of diamonds to keep prices high. As new diamond deposits were discovered in Russia and Zaire, De Beers was able to maintain prices by buying most of the new supplies.

Because diamonds are rarely destroyed, De Beers has always worried about competition from the resale of stones. Heavily promoting diamond engagement and wedding rings with the slogan "A Diamond Is Forever" was a way around this problem. Because engagement and wedding rings have great sentimental value, they are seldom resold, even by the heirs of the original recipients. De Beers advertising has been successful even in some countries, such as Japan, that have had no custom of giving diamond engagement rings. As the populations in De Beers's key markets age, its advertising in recent years has focused on middle-aged men presenting diamond rings to their wives as symbols of financial success and continuing love and on professional women buying "right-hand rings" for themselves.

Over the years, competition has gradually increased in the diamond business. By 2000, De Beers directly controlled only about 40 percent of world diamond production. The company became concerned about how much it was spending to buy diamonds from other sources to keep them off the market. It decided to abandon its strategy of attempting to control the worldwide supply of diamonds and to concentrate instead on differentiating its diamonds by relying on its name recognition. Each De Beers diamond is now marked with a microscopic brand—a "Forevermark"—to reassure consumers of its high quality. Other firms, such as BHP Billiton, which owns mines in northern Canada, have followed

De Beers promoted the sentimental value of diamonds as a way to maintain its position in the diamond market.

suit by branding their diamonds. Whether consumers will pay attention to brands on diamonds remains to be seen, although through 2013, the branding strategy had helped De Beers to maintain about a 35 to 40 percent share of the diamond market.

Sources: Alex MacDonald, "De Beers Brings Oppenheimer Era to End," *Wall Street Journal*, October 3, 2012; William J. Holstein, "De Beers Reworks Its Image as Rivals Multiply," *New York Times*, December 12, 2008; Edward Jay Epstein, "Have You Ever Tried to Sell a Diamond?" *Atlantic Monthly*, February 1982; and Donna J. Bergenstock, Mary E. Deily, and Larry W. Taylor, "A Cartel's Response to Cheating: An Empirical Investigation of the De Beers Diamond Empire," *Southern Economic Journal*, Vol. 73, No. 1, July 2006, pp. 173–189.

Your Turn: Test your understanding by doing related problem 2.11 on page 501 at the end of this chapter.

MyEconLab Study Plan

Network Externalities

There are **network externalities** in the consumption of a product if its usefulness increases with the number of people who use it. If you owned the only HD television in the world, for example, it would not be very valuable because firms would not have an incentive to develop HD programming. The more HD televisions there are in use, the more valuable they become to consumers.

Some economists argue that network externalities can serve as barriers to entry. For example, in the early 1980s, Microsoft gained an advantage over other software companies by developing MS-DOS, the operating system for the first IBM personal computers. Because IBM sold more computers than any other company, software developers wrote many application programs for MS-DOS. The more people who used MS-DOS–based programs, the greater the value to a consumer of using an MS-DOS–based program. By the 1990s, Microsoft had replaced MS-DOS with Windows. Today, Windows has an 85 percent share in the market for personal computer operating systems, with Apple's operating system having a 10 percent share, and other operating systems, including the open-source Linux system, having shares of about 1 percent or less. If another firm introduced a new operating system, some economists argue that relatively few people would use it initially, and few applications would run on it, which would limit the operating system's value to other consumers.

eBay was the first Internet site to attract a significant number of people to its online auctions. Once a large number of people began to use eBay to buy and sell collectibles, antiques, and many other products, it became a more valuable place to buy and sell. Yahoo .com, Amazon.com, and other Internet sites eventually started online auctions, but they had difficulty attracting buyers and sellers. On eBay, a buyer expects to find more sellers, and a seller expects to find more potential buyers than on Amazon or other auction sites.

As these examples show, from a firm's point of view, network externalities can set off a *virtuous cycle*: If a firm can attract enough customers initially, it can attract additional customers because the value of its product has been increased by more people using it, which attracts even more customers, and so on. With products such as computer operating systems and online auctions, it might be difficult for new firms to enter the market and compete away the profit being earned by the first firm in the market.

Economists engage in considerable debate, however, about the extent to which network externalities are important barriers to entry in the business world. Some economists argue that Microsoft and eBay have dominant positions primarily because they are efficient in offering products that satisfy consumer preferences rather than because of the effects of network externalities. In this view, the advantages existing firms gain from network externalities would not be enough to protect them from competing firms offering better products. For example, many people have switched from computers to tablets and smartphones that run on Apple's iOS or Google's Android operating system, making Microsoft's domination of computer operating systems less important. MyEconLab Concept Check

Network externalities A situation in which the usefulness of a product increases with the number of consumers who use it.

Natural Monopoly

Economies of scale exist when a firm's long-run average costs fall as it increases the quantity of output it produces (see Chapter 11). A **natural monopoly** occurs when economies of scale are so large that one firm can supply the entire market at a lower

Natural monopoly A situation in which economies of scale are so large that one firm can supply the entire market at a lower average total cost than can two or more firms.

MyEconLab Animation

Figure 15.1

Average Total Cost Curve for a Natural Monopoly

With a natural monopoly, the average total cost curve is still falling when it crosses the demand curve (point *A*). If only one firm is producing electric power in the market, and it produces where the average cost curve intersects the demand curve, average total cost will equal $0.04 per kilowatt-hour of electricity produced. If the market is divided between two firms, each producing 15 billion kilowatt-hours, the average cost of producing electricity rises to $0.06 per kilowatt-hour (point *B*). In this case, if one firm expands production, it can move down the average total cost curve, lower its price, and drive the other firm out of business.

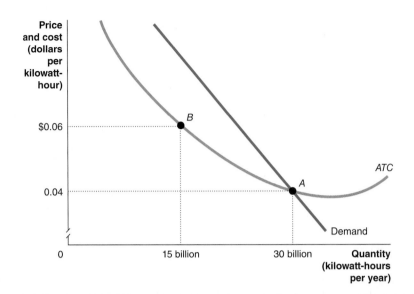

average total cost than can two or more firms. In that case, there is "room" in the market for only one firm.

Figure 15.1 shows the average total cost curve for a firm producing electricity and the total demand for electricity in the firm's market. Notice that the average total cost curve is still falling when it crosses the demand curve at point *A*. If the firm is a monopoly and produces 30 billion kilowatt-hours of electricity per year, its average total cost of production will be $0.04 per kilowatt-hour. Suppose instead that two firms are in the market, each producing half of the market output, or 15 billion kilowatt-hours per year. Assume that each firm has the same average total cost curve. The figure shows that producing 15 billion kilowatt-hours would move each firm back up its average cost curve so that the average cost of producing electricity would rise to $0.06 per kilowatt-hour (point *B*). In this case, if one of the firms expands production, it will move down the average total cost curve. With lower average costs, it will be able to offer electricity at a lower price than the other firm can offer. Eventually, the other firm will be driven out of business, and the remaining firm will have a monopoly. Because a monopoly would develop automatically—or *naturally*—in this market, it is a natural monopoly.

Natural monopolies are most likely to occur in markets where fixed costs are very large relative to variable costs. For example, a firm that produces electricity must make a substantial investment in machinery and equipment necessary to generate the electricity and in the wires and cables necessary to distribute it. Once the initial investment has been made, however, the marginal cost of producing another kilowatt-hour of electricity is relatively small. MyEconLab Concept Check

Solved Problem 15.2

MyEconLab Interactive Animation

Can a Seafood Restaurant Be a Natural Monopoly?

We saw in the chapter opener that there is only one seafood restaurant in the town of Stonington, Maine. While eating at the restaurant, a principles of economics student visiting Stonington makes the following observation: "This restaurant must be a natural monopoly. We can reach this conclusion because it is making a large profit by selling lobster dinners for high prices even though the price of live lobsters has fallen to very low levels. If the restaurant wasn't a natural monopoly, other restaurants would open in Stonington and compete away this restaurant's profit." Briefly explain whether you agree with the student's observation. Does the amount of time the restaurant has been earning a large profit on lobster dinners matter for your answer? Include a graph in your answer showing the demand for this restaurant's meals and its cost curves.

Solving the Problem

Step 1:   Review the chapter material. This problem is about natural monopoly, so you may want to review the section "Natural Monopoly," which begins on page 483.

Step 2:   Begin your answer by explaining what must be true for the restaurant to be a natural monopoly. We know for a firm to be a natural monopoly, its average total cost curve should still be declining when it crosses the firm's demand curve. If the market for lobster dinners in Stonington were a natural monopoly, then if there were two seafood restaurants in Stonington, the average cost of supplying lobster dinners would be higher than if only one restaurant were in the market. So, we would expect one restaurant to expand, thereby moving down its average total cost curve, lowering its price of lobster dinners, and driving the other restaurant out of business.

Step 3:   Explain whether it is likely that the seafood restaurant in Stonington is a natural monopoly and draw a graph to illustrate your answer. Restaurants are not usually natural monopolies. Most towns have at least several restaurants in each category—seafood, Italian, Chinese, and so on—which would not be true if the restaurants were natural monopolies. It is possible, though, that in a very small town, demand for seafood dinners might be limited enough that the demand curve intersects the average total cost at a quantity where the average total cost curve is still falling. The following graph illustrates this situation.

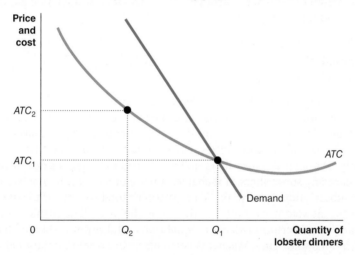

As shown in the graph, the market for seafood dinners in Stonington is a natural monopoly because if one restaurant can supply Q_1 dinners at an average total cost of ATC_1, then dividing the business equally between two restaurants each supplying Q_2 dinners would raise average total cost to ATC_2.

Step 4:   Complete your answer by explaining whether the amount of time the restaurant has been earning a large profit on lobster dinners matters to your answer. The chapter opener indicates that the large profit earned by The Fisherman's Friend was largely due to low prices for lobsters following a record harvest. It can take time for potential competitors to decide whether it would be profitable to enter an industry. The longer the restaurant continues to operate without significant competition, the more likely it is that the firm actually is a natural monopoly in the small Stonington market.

Extra Credit: Keep in mind that competition is not good for its own sake. It is good because it can lead to lower costs, lower prices, and better products. In certain markets, however, cost conditions are such that competition is likely to lead to higher costs and higher prices. These markets are natural monopolies that are best served by one firm. The market for restaurant meals is rarely a natural monopoly, but the market for seafood in tiny Stonington, Maine, might be an example.

Your Turn: For more practice, do related problem 2.13 on page 501 at the end of this chapter.   MyEconLab Study Plan

How Does a Monopoly Choose Price and Output?

Like every other firm, a monopoly maximizes profit by producing where marginal revenue equals marginal cost. A monopoly differs from other firms in that *a monopoly's demand curve is the same as the market demand curve for the product*. When discussing perfect competition, we emphasized that the market demand curve for wheat was very different from the demand curve for the wheat produced by any one farmer (see Chapter 12). If, however, one farmer had a monopoly on wheat production, the two demand curves would be exactly the same.

Marginal Revenue Once Again

Recall that firms in perfectly competitive markets—such as a farmer in the wheat market—face horizontal demand curves (see Chapter 12). These firms are *price takers*. All other firms, including monopolies, are *price makers*. If price makers raise their prices, they will lose some, but not all, of their customers. Therefore, they face both a downward-sloping demand curve and a downward-sloping marginal revenue curve. Let's review why a firm's marginal revenue curve slopes downward if its demand curve slopes downward.

Remember that when a firm cuts the price of a product, one good thing happens, and one bad thing happens:

- *The good thing.* It sells more units of the product.
- *The bad thing.* It receives less revenue from each unit than it would have received at the higher price.

For example, consider the table in Figure 15.2, which shows information on the market for Time Warner Cable's basic cable package. To operate a cable system in a city, firms typically need a license from the city government. Time Warner is the only cable television available in some cities. For simplicity, we assume that a particular market has only 10 potential subscribers. If Time Warner charges a price of $60 per month, it won't have any subscribers. If it charges a price of $57, it sells 1 subscription. At $54, it sells 2 subscriptions, and so on. Time Warner's total revenue is equal to the number of subscriptions sold per month multiplied by the price. The firm's average revenue—or revenue per subscription sold—is equal to its total revenue divided by the quantity of subscriptions sold. Time Warner is particularly interested in marginal revenue because marginal revenue tells the firm how much its revenue will increase if it cuts the price to sell one more subscription.

Notice that Time Warner's marginal revenue is less than the price for every subscription sold after the first subscription. To see why, think about what happens if Time Warner cuts the price of its basic cable package from $42 to $39, which increases its subscriptions sold from 6 to 7. Time Warner increases its revenue by the $39 it receives for the seventh subscription. But it also loses revenue of $3 per subscription on the first 6 subscriptions because it could have sold them at the old price of $42. So, its marginal revenue on the seventh subscription is $39 − $18 = $21, which is the value shown in the table. The graph in Figure 15.2 plots Time Warner's demand and marginal revenue curves, based on the information in the table. MyEconLab Concept Check

Profit Maximization for a Monopolist

Figure 15.3 on page 488 shows how Time Warner combines the information on demand and marginal revenue with information on average and marginal costs to decide how many subscriptions to sell and what price to charge. We assume that the firm's marginal cost and average total cost curves have the usual U shapes we encountered in previous chapters (see Chapters 11 and 12). In panel (a), we see how Time Warner can calculate its profit-maximizing quantity and price. As long as the marginal cost of selling one more subscription is less than the marginal revenue, the firm should sell additional subscriptions because it is adding to its profits. As Time Warner sells more cable subscriptions,

MyEconLab Animation

Subscribers per Month (Q)	Price (P)	Total Revenue (TR = P × Q)	Average Revenue (AR = TR/Q)	Marginal Revenue (MR = ΔTR/ΔQ)
0	$60	$0	–	–
1	57	57	$57	$57
2	54	108	54	51
3	51	153	51	45
4	48	192	48	39
5	45	225	45	33
6	42	252	42	27
7	39	273	39	21
8	36	288	36	15
9	33	297	33	9
10	30	300	30	3

Figure 15.2

Calculating a Monopoly's Revenue

Time Warner Cable faces a downward-sloping demand curve for subscriptions to basic cable. To sell more subscriptions, it must cut the price. When this happens, it gains revenue from selling more subscriptions but loses revenue from selling at a lower price the subscriptions that it could have sold at a higher price. The firm's marginal revenue is the change in revenue from selling another subscription. We can calculate marginal revenue by subtracting the revenue lost as a result of a price cut from the revenue gained. The table shows that Time Warner's marginal revenue is less than the price for every subscription sold after the first subscription. Therefore, Time Warner's marginal revenue curve will be below its demand curve.

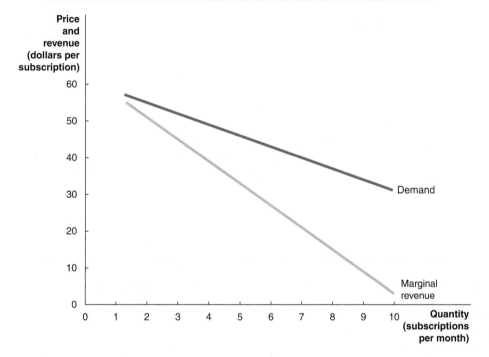

rising marginal cost will eventually equal marginal revenue, and the firm will be selling the profit-maximizing quantity of subscriptions. Time Warner maximizes profit with the sixth subscription, which adds $27 to the firm's costs and $27 to its revenues—point *A* in panel (a) of Figure 15.3. The demand curve tells us that Time Warner can sell 6 subscriptions for a price of $42 per month. We can conclude that Time Warner's profit-maximizing quantity of subscriptions is 6, and its profit-maximizing price is $42.

Panel (b) shows that the average total cost of 6 subscriptions is $30 and that Time Warner can sell 6 subscriptions at a price of $42 per month (point *B* on the demand curve). Time Warner is making a profit of $12 per subscription—the price of $42 minus the average cost of $30. Its total profit is $72 (= 6 subscriptions × $12 profit per subscription), which is shown by the area of the green-shaded rectangle in the figure. We could also have calculated Time Warner's total profit as the difference between its total revenue and its total cost. Its total revenue from selling 6 subscriptions is $252. Its total cost equals its average total cost multiplied by the number of subscriptions sold, or $30 × 6 = $180. So, its profit is $252 − $180 = $72.

It's important to note that even though Time Warner is earning an economic profit, new firms will *not* enter the market unless they can obtain licenses from the city. If it holds the only license, Time Warner has a monopoly and will not face competition from other cable operators. Therefore, if other factors remain unchanged, Time Warner will be able to continue to earn an economic profit, even in the long run.   MyEconLab Concept Check

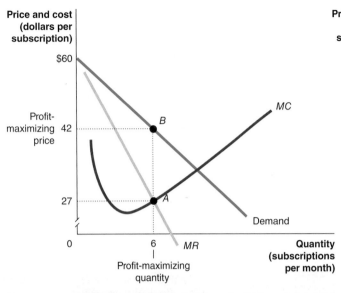

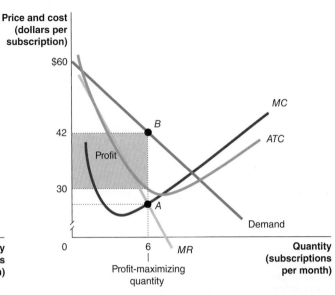

(a) Profit-maximizing quantity and price for a monopolist

(b) Profit for a monopolist

MyEconLab Animation

Figure 15.3 **Profit-Maximizing Price and Output for a Monopoly**

Panel (a) shows that to maximize profit, Time Warner should sell subscriptions up to the point where the marginal revenue from selling the last subscription equals its marginal cost (point A). In this case, both the marginal revenue from selling the sixth subscription and the marginal cost are $27. Time Warner maximizes profit by selling 6 subscriptions per month and charging a price of $42 (point B).

In panel (b), the green rectangle represents Time Warner's profit. The rectangle has a height equal to $12, which is the price of $42 minus the average total cost of $30, and a base equal to the quantity of 6 cable subscriptions. Time Warner's profit therefore equals $12 × 6 = $72.

Solved Problem 15.3

MyEconLab Interactive Animation

Finding the Profit-Maximizing Price and Output for a Cable Monopoly

Suppose that Comcast has a cable monopoly in Philadelphia. The following table gives Comcast's demand and costs per month for subscriptions to basic cable (for simplicity, we once again keep the number of subscribers artificially small):

Price	Quantity	Total Revenue	Marginal Revenue $\left(MR = \dfrac{\Delta TR}{\Delta Q} \right)$	Total Cost	Marginal Cost $\left(MC = \dfrac{\Delta TC}{\Delta Q} \right)$
$27	3			$56	
26	4			73	
25	5			91	
24	6			110	
23	7			130	
22	8			151	

a. Fill in the missing values in the table.
b. If Comcast wants to maximize profit, what price should it charge, and how many cable subscriptions per month should it sell? How much profit will Comcast make? Briefly explain.

c. Suppose the local government imposes a $25-per-month tax on cable companies. Now what price should Comcast charge, how many subscriptions should it sell, and what will its profit be?

Solving the Problem

Step 1: **Review the chapter material.** This problem is about finding the profit-maximizing quantity and price for a monopolist, so you may want to review the section "Profit Maximization for a Monopolist," which begins on page 486.

Step 2: **Answer part (a) by filling in the missing values in the table.** Remember that to calculate marginal revenue and marginal cost, you must divide the change in total revenue or total cost by the change in quantity.

We don't have enough information from the table to fill in the values for marginal revenue and marginal cost in the first row.

Price	Quantity	Total Revenue	Marginal Revenue $\left(MR = \dfrac{\Delta TR}{\Delta Q} \right)$	Total Cost	Marginal Cost $\left(MC = \dfrac{\Delta TC}{\Delta Q} \right)$
$27	3	$81	—	$56	—
26	4	104	$23	73	$17
25	5	125	21	91	18
24	6	144	19	110	19
23	7	161	17	130	20
22	8	176	15	151	21

Step 3: **Answer part (b) by determining the profit-maximizing quantity and price.** We know that Comcast will maximize profit by selling subscriptions up to the point where marginal cost equals marginal revenue. In this case, that means selling 6 subscriptions per month. From the information in the first two columns, we know Comcast can sell 6 subscriptions at a price of $24 each. Comcast's profit is equal to the difference between its total revenue and its total cost: Profit = $144 − $110 = $34 per month.

Step 4: **Answer part (c) by analyzing the effect of the tax.** This tax is a fixed cost to Comcast because it is a flat $25 no matter how many subscriptions it sells. Because the tax doesn't affect Comcast's marginal revenue or marginal cost, the profit-maximizing level of output has not changed. So, Comcast will still sell 6 subscriptions per month at a price of $24, but its profit will fall by the amount of the tax, from $34 per month to $9 per month.

Your Turn: For more practice, do related problems 3.4 and 3.5 on pages 501–502 at the end of this chapter.

MyEconLab Study Plan

Don't Let This Happen to You

Don't Assume That Charging a Higher Price Is Always More Profitable for a Monopolist

In answering part (c) of Solved Problem 15.3, it's tempting to argue that Comcast should increase its price to make up for the tax. After all, Comcast is a monopolist, so why can't it just pass along the tax to its customers? The reason it can't is that Comcast, like any other monopolist, must pay attention to demand. Comcast is not interested in charging high prices for the sake of charging high prices; it is interested in maximizing profit. Charging a price of $1,000 for a basic cable subscription sounds nice, but if no one will buy at that price, Comcast would hardly be maximizing profit.

To look at it another way, before the tax is imposed, Comcast has already determined that $24 is the price that will maximize its profit. After the tax is imposed, it must determine whether $24 is still the profit-maximizing price. Because the tax has not affected Comcast's marginal revenue or marginal cost (or had any effect on consumer demand), $24 is still the profit-maximizing price, and Comcast should continue to charge it. The tax reduces Comcast's profit but doesn't cause it to increase the price of cable subscriptions.

MyEconLab Study Plan

Your Turn: Test your understanding by doing related problem 3.8 on page 502 at the end of this chapter.

15.4 LEARNING OBJECTIVE

Use a graph to illustrate how a monopoly affects economic efficiency.

Does Monopoly Reduce Economic Efficiency?

We have seen that a perfectly competitive market is economically efficient (see Chapter 12). How would economic efficiency be affected if instead of being perfectly competitive, a market were a monopoly? *Economic surplus* provides a way of characterizing the economic efficiency in a market. *Equilibrium in a perfectly competitive market results in the greatest amount of economic surplus, or total benefit to society, from the production of a good or service* (see Chapter 4). What happens to economic surplus under a monopoly? We can begin the analysis by considering the hypothetical case of what would happen if the market for smartphones begins as perfectly competitive and then becomes a monopoly.

Comparing Monopoly and Perfect Competition

Panel (a) in Figure 15.4 illustrates the situation if the market for smartphones is perfectly competitive. Price and quantity are determined by the intersection of the demand and supply curves. Remember that none of the individual firms in a perfectly competitive industry has any control over price. Each firm must accept the price determined by the market. Panel (b) shows what happens if the smartphone market becomes a monopoly. We know that the monopoly will maximize profit by producing where marginal revenue equals marginal cost. To do this, the monopoly reduces the quantity of smartphones that would have been produced if the industry were perfectly competitive and increases the price. Panel (b) illustrates an important conclusion: *A monopoly will produce less and charge a higher price than would a perfectly competitive industry producing the same good.*

MyEconLab Concept Check

Measuring the Efficiency Losses from Monopoly

Figure 15.5 uses panel (b) from Figure 15.4 to illustrate how monopoly affects consumers, producers, and the efficiency of the economy. Recall that *consumer surplus* measures the net benefit received by consumers from purchasing a good or service (see

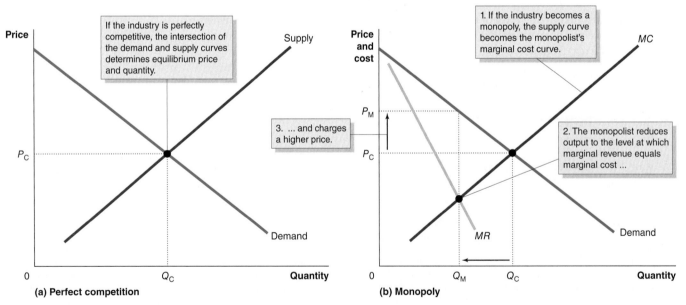

MyEconLab Animation

Figure 15.4 **What Happens If a Perfectly Competitive Industry Becomes a Monopoly?**

In panel (a), the market for smartphones is perfectly competitive, and price and quantity are determined by the intersection of the demand and supply curves. In panel (b), the perfectly competitive smartphone market becomes a monopoly. As a result:

1. The industry supply curve becomes the monopolist's marginal cost curve.
2. The monopolist reduces output to where marginal revenue equals marginal cost, Q_M.
3. The monopolist raises the price from P_C to P_M.

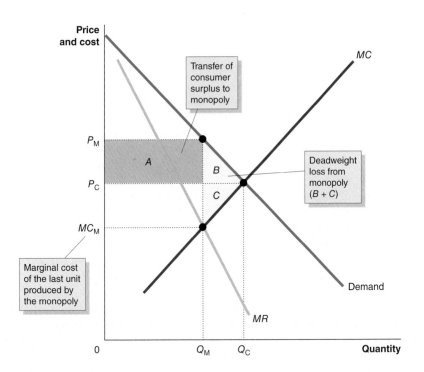

MyEconLab Animation

Figure 15.5

The Inefficiency of Monopoly

A monopoly charges a higher price, P_M, and produces a smaller quantity, Q_M, than a perfectly competitive industry, which charges price P_C and produces Q_C. The higher price reduces consumer surplus by the area equal to the rectangle A and the triangle B. Some of the reduction in consumer surplus is captured by the monopoly as producer surplus, and some becomes deadweight loss, which is the area equal to triangles B and C.

Chapter 4). We measure consumer surplus as the area below the demand curve and above the market price. The higher the price, the smaller the consumer surplus. Because a monopoly raises the market price, it reduces consumer surplus. In Figure 15.5, the loss of consumer surplus is equal to rectangle A plus triangle B. Remember that *producer surplus* measures the net benefit to producers from selling a good or service. We measure producer surplus as the area above the supply curve and below the market price. The increase in price due to monopoly increases producer surplus by an amount equal to rectangle A and reduces it by an amount equal to triangle C. Because rectangle A is larger than triangle C, we know that a monopoly increases producer surplus compared with perfect competition.

Economic surplus is equal to the sum of consumer surplus plus producer surplus. By increasing price and reducing the quantity produced, the monopolist has reduced economic surplus by an amount equal to the areas of triangles B and C. This reduction in economic surplus is called *deadweight loss* and represents the loss of economic efficiency due to monopoly.

The best way to understand how a monopoly causes a loss of economic efficiency is to recall that price is equal to marginal cost in a perfectly competitive market. As a result, a consumer in a perfectly competitive market is always able to buy a good if she is willing to pay a price equal to the marginal cost of producing it. As Figure 15.5 shows, the monopolist stops producing smartphones at a point where the price is well above marginal cost. Consumers are unable to buy some smartphones for which they would be willing to pay a price greater than the marginal cost of producing them. Why doesn't the monopolist produce these additional smartphones? Because the monopolist's profit is greater if it restricts output and forces up the price. A monopoly produces the profit-maximizing level of output but fails to produce the efficient level of output from the point of view of society.

We can summarize the effects of monopoly as follows:

1. Monopoly causes a reduction in consumer surplus.

2. Monopoly causes an increase in producer surplus.

3. Monopoly causes a deadweight loss, which represents a reduction in economic efficiency.

MyEconLab Concept Check

Market power The ability of a firm to charge a price greater than marginal cost.

How Large Are the Efficiency Losses Due to Monopoly?

We know that there are relatively few monopolies, so the loss of economic efficiency due to monopoly must be small. Many firms, though, have **market power**, which is the ability of a firm to charge a price greater than marginal cost. The analysis we just completed shows that some loss of economic efficiency will occur whenever a firm has market power and can charge a price greater than marginal cost, even if the firm is not a monopoly. The only firms that do *not* have market power are firms in perfectly competitive markets, which must charge a price equal to marginal cost. Because few markets are perfectly competitive, *some loss of economic efficiency occurs in the market for nearly every good or service.*

Is the total loss of economic efficiency due to market power large or small? It is possible to put a dollar value on the loss of economic efficiency by estimating for every industry the size of the deadweight loss triangle, as in Figure 15.5. The first economist to do this was Arnold Harberger of the University of California, Los Angeles. His estimates—largely confirmed by later researchers—indicated that the total loss of economic efficiency in the U.S. economy due to market power is relatively small. According to his estimates, if every industry in the economy were perfectly competitive, so that price were equal to marginal cost in every market, the gain in economic efficiency would equal less than 1 percent of the value of total production in the United States, or about $500 per person.

The loss of economic efficiency is this small primarily because true monopolies are very rare. In most industries, competition keeps price much closer to marginal cost than would be the case in a monopoly. The closer price is to marginal cost, the smaller the size of the deadweight loss.

MyEconLab Concept Check

Market Power and Technological Change

Some economists have raised the possibility that the economy may actually benefit from firms having market power. This argument is most closely identified with Joseph Schumpeter, an Austrian economist who spent many years as a professor of economics at Harvard. Schumpeter argued that economic progress depends on technological change in the form of new products. For example, the replacement of horse-drawn carriages by automobiles, the replacement of ice boxes by refrigerators, and the replacement of mechanical calculators by electronic computers all represent technological changes that significantly raised living standards. In Schumpeter's view, new products unleash a "gale of creative destruction" that drives older products—and, often, the firms that produced them—out of the market. Schumpeter was not concerned that firms with market power would charge higher prices than perfectly competitive firms:

> It is not that kind of [price] competition which counts but the competition from the new commodity, the new technology, the new source of supply, the new type of organization … competition which commands a decisive cost or quality advantage and which strikes not at the margins of the profits and outputs of the existing firms but at their foundations and their very lives.

Economists who support Schumpeter's view argue that the introduction of new products requires firms to spend funds on research and development. It is possible for firms to raise this money by borrowing from investors or banks. But investors and banks are usually skeptical of ideas for new products that have not yet passed the test of consumer acceptance in the market. As a result, firms are often forced to rely on their profits to finance the research and development needed for new products. Because firms with market power are more likely to earn economic profits than are perfectly competitive firms, they are also more likely to carry out research and development and introduce new products. In this view, the higher prices firms with market power charge are unimportant compared with the benefits from the new products these firms introduce to the market.

Some economists disagree with Schumpeter's views. These economists point to the number of new products developed by smaller firms, including, for example, Steve Jobs and Steve Wozniak inventing the first Apple computer in Jobs's garage, and Larry Page and Sergey Brin inventing the Google search engine as graduate students at Stanford. As we will see in the next section, government policymakers continue to struggle with the issue of whether, on balance, large firms with market power are good or bad for the economy. MyEconLab Concept Check

MyEconLab Study Plan

Government Policy toward Monopoly

15.5 LEARNING OBJECTIVE

Discuss government policies toward monopoly.

Because monopolies reduce consumer surplus and economic efficiency, most governments have policies that regulate their behavior. **Collusion** refers to an agreement among firms to charge the same price or otherwise not to compete (see Chapter 14). In the United States, *antitrust laws* are designed to prevent monopolies and collusion. Governments also regulate firms that are natural monopolies, often by controlling the prices they charge.

Collusion An agreement among firms to charge the same price or otherwise not to compete.

Antitrust Laws and Antitrust Enforcement

The first important law regulating monopolies in the United States was the Sherman Act, which Congress passed in 1890 to promote competition and prevent the formation of monopolies. Section 1 of the Sherman Act outlaws "every contract, combination in the form of trust or otherwise, or conspiracy in restraint of trade." Section 2 states that "every person who shall monopolize, or attempt to monopolize, or combine or conspire with any other person or persons, to monopolize any part of the trade or commerce … shall be deemed guilty of a felony."

The Sherman Act targeted firms in several industries that had combined together during the 1870s and 1880s to form "trusts." In a trust, the firms were operated independently but gave voting control to a board of trustees. The board enforced collusive agreements for the firms to charge the same price and not to compete for each other's customers. The most notorious of the trusts was the Standard Oil Trust, organized by John D. Rockefeller. In the years following passage of the Sherman Act, business trusts disappeared, but the term **antitrust laws** has lived on to refer to the laws aimed at eliminating collusion and promoting competition among firms.

Antitrust laws Laws aimed at eliminating collusion and promoting competition among firms.

The Sherman Act prohibited trusts and collusive agreements, but it left several loopholes. For example, it was not clear whether it would be legal for two or more firms to merge to form a new, larger firm that would have substantial market power. A series of Supreme Court decisions interpreted the Sherman Act narrowly, and the result was a wave of mergers at the turn of the twentieth century. Included in these mergers was U.S. Steel Corporation, which was formed from dozens of smaller companies. U.S. Steel, organized by J. P. Morgan, was the first billion-dollar corporation, and it controlled two-thirds of steel production in the United States. The Sherman Act also left unclear whether any business practices short of outright collusion were illegal.

To address the loopholes in the Sherman Act, in 1914 Congress passed the Clayton Act and the Federal Trade Commission Act. Under the Clayton Act, a merger was illegal if its effect was "substantially to lessen competition, or to tend to create a monopoly." The Federal Trade Commission Act set up the Federal Trade Commission (FTC), which was given the power to police unfair business practices. The FTC has brought lawsuits against firms employing a variety of business practices, including deceptive advertising. In setting up the FTC, Congress divided the authority to police mergers. Currently, both the Antitrust Division of the U.S. Department of Justice and the FTC are responsible for merger policy. Table 15.1 lists the most important U.S. antitrust laws and the purpose of each. MyEconLab Concept Check

Table 15.1	Law	Date Enacted	Purpose
Important U.S. Antitrust Laws	Sherman Act	1890	Prohibited "restraint of trade," including price fixing and collusion. Also outlawed monopolization.
	Clayton Act	1914	Prohibited firms from buying stock in competitors and from having directors serve on the boards of competing firms.
	Federal Trade Commission Act	1914	Established the Federal Trade Commission (FTC) to help administer antitrust laws.
	Robinson–Patman Act	1936	Prohibited firms from charging buyers different prices if the result would reduce competition.
	Cellar–Kefauver Act	1950	Toughened restrictions on mergers by prohibiting any mergers that would reduce competition.

Making the Connection
MyEconLab Video

Did Apple try to artificially restrict competition to raise prices of e-books?

Did Apple Violate the Law in Pricing e-Books?

People who buy e-books got some bad news in 2010 when Apple introduced the iPad: The prices of new books and best sellers increased from $9.99 to $12.99 or $14.99. The price increases were not just for books sold in Apple's iBookstore but also for books Amazon was selling for its Kindle. Why did this big jump in prices happen? The U.S. Justice Department had a straightforward answer: Apple had organized an agreement with five large book publishers to raise the prices of e-books. As one Justice Department lawyer put it, Apple had directed "an old-fashioned, straight-forward price-fixing agreement." Accordingly, the Justice Department sued Apple for violating antitrust laws. The lawsuit was a civil action, meaning that the Justice Department was not pursuing criminal charges against Apple executives.

When Amazon introduced its Kindle e-reader in 2007, it priced most new books and best sellers at $9.99, even though this price was less than the price the publishers were charging Amazon for the books. Amazon believed that by selling e-books at a loss, it would increase sales of the Kindle. Most publishers were unhappy with Amazon's low e-book prices, however, because they believed the prices reduced sales of hardcover copies of best sellers on which the publishers made a larger profit. According to the Justice Department, Apple took advantage of the publishers' unhappiness to propose an "agency pricing model." Under this model, the publishers would set the retail price of e-books, and Apple would keep 30 percent of the price of every e-book it sold.

In addition, Apple negotiated a clause in its contracts with the publishers that allowed Apple to match the retail prices of other e-book sellers. By invoking this clause, Apple would be able to sell e-books for $9.99 if Amazon continued to do so. The publishers then insisted that Amazon switch to an agency pricing model. If Amazon failed to switch, the publishers said they would not allow Amazon to sell e-versions of their books until months after the hardcover editions were first published, which would give Apple a huge advantage in the e-book market. Faced with this situation, Amazon also adopted the agency pricing model, and the publishers were able to raise the prices of most new books to $12.99 or $14.99.

At the trial, Apple argued that it had not attempted to organize a price-fixing agreement with the publishers. Instead, Apple had simply proposed a pricing model similar to the one they were already using for songs in their iTunes store. As Apple's executive in charge of negotiating with the publishers put it: "I didn't raise prices. The publishers set the prices." Representatives of the publishers also testified during the trial that they had not conspired with Apple or with each other to fix the prices of e-books.

In the end, the judge in charge of the case decided that Apple had conspired with the publishers to raise e-book prices. Following the decision, the Justice Department proposed that the judge bar Apple from entering agency pricing contracts with publishers for a period of five years. The Justice Department also proposed that it be given oversight of pricing of music, television shows, and movies in Apple's iTunes online store. Apple appealed the judge's decision and continued to maintain that it had not violated the law.

The lawsuit the Justice Department brought against Apple is an example of attempts by the government to keep firms from artificially restricting competition to raise prices. As we have seen, higher prices reduce consumer surplus and economic efficiency.

Sources: Chad Bray, "Apple's E-Book Damages Trial Set to Begin in May," *Wall Street Journal*, August 15, 2013; Bob Van Voris, "Apple Awaits e-Book Decision with State, Private Suits in Wings," *Bloomberg BusinessWeek*, June 22, 2013; Joe Palazzolo and Chad Bray, "Apple's Civil Antitrust Trial: The Highlights," *Wall Street Journal*, June 20, 2013; and Julie Bosman, "Publishers Tell of Disputes with Apple on e-Book Prices," *New York Times*, June 5, 2013.

Your Turn: Test your understanding by doing related problem 5.12 on page 505 at the end of this chapter.

MyEconLab Study Plan

Mergers: The Trade-off between Market Power and Efficiency

The federal government regulates business mergers because if firms gain market power by merging, they may use that market power to raise prices and reduce output. As a result, the government is most concerned with **horizontal mergers**, or mergers between firms in the same industry. Two airlines or two candy manufacturers merging are examples of a horizontal merger. Horizontal mergers are more likely to increase market power than **vertical mergers**, which are mergers between firms at different stages of the production of a good. An example of a vertical merger would be a merger between a company making soft drinks and a company making aluminum cans.

Two factors can complicate regulating horizontal mergers. First, the "market" that firms are in is not always clear. For example, if Hershey Foods wants to merge with Mars, Inc., maker of M&Ms, Snickers, and other candies, what is the relevant market? If the government looks just at the candy market, the newly merged company would have more than 70 percent of the market, a level at which the government would likely oppose the merger. What if the government looks at the broader market for snacks? In this market, Hershey and Mars compete with makers of potato chips, pretzels, and peanuts—and perhaps even producers of fresh fruit. Of course, if the government looked at the very broad market for food, then both Hershey and Mars have very small market shares, and there would be no reason to oppose their merger. In practice, the government defines the relevant market on the basis of whether there are close substitutes for the products being made by the merging firms. In this case, potato chips and the other snack foods mentioned are not close substitutes for candy. So, the government would consider the candy market to be the relevant market and would oppose the merger, on the grounds that the new firm would have too much market power.

The second factor that complicates merger policy is the possibility that the newly merged firm might be more efficient than the merging firms were individually. For example, one firm might have an excellent product but a poor distribution system for getting the product into the hands of consumers. A competing firm might have built a great distribution system but have an inferior product. Allowing these firms to merge might be good for both the firms and consumers. Or, two competing firms might each have an extensive system of warehouses that are only half full, but if the firms merged, they could consolidate their warehouses and significantly reduce their average costs.

Most of the mergers that come under scrutiny by the Department of Justice and the FTC are between large firms. For simplicity, though, let's consider a case in which all

Horizontal merger A merger between firms in the same industry.

Vertical merger A merger between firms at different stages of production of a good.

MyEconLab Animation

Figure 15.6

A Merger That Makes Consumers Better Off

This figure shows the result of all the firms in a perfectly competitive industry merging to form a monopoly. If the merger does not affect costs, the result is the same as in Figure 15.5 on page 491: Price rises from P_C to P_M, quantity falls from Q_C to Q_M, consumer surplus declines, and a loss of economic efficiency results. If, however, the monopoly has lower costs than the perfectly competitive firms, as shown by the marginal cost curve shifting to MC after the merger, it is possible that the price of the good will actually decline from P_C to P_{Merge} and that output will increase from Q_C to Q_{Merge} following the merger.

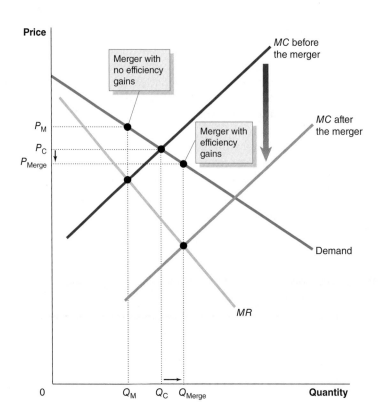

the firms in a perfectly competitive industry want to merge to form a monopoly. As we saw in Figure 15.5, as a result of this merger, prices will rise and output will fall, leading to a decline in consumer surplus and economic efficiency. But what if the larger, newly merged firm actually is more efficient than the smaller firms were? Figure 15.6 shows a possible result.

If the merger doesn't affect costs, we get the same result as in Figure 15.5: Price rises from P_C to P_M, quantity falls from Q_C to Q_M, consumer surplus declines, and a loss of economic efficiency results. If the monopoly has lower costs than the competitive firms, it is possible for price to decline and quantity to increase. In Figure 15.6, note that after the merger MR crosses MC at the new profit-maximizing quantity, Q_{Merge}. The demand curve shows that the monopolist can sell this quantity of the good at a price of P_{Merge}. Therefore, the price declines after the merger from P_C to P_{Merge}, and the quantity increases from Q_C to Q_{Merge}. We have the following seemingly paradoxical result: *The newly merged firm has a great deal of market power, but consumers are better off and economic efficiency is increased because the firm is more efficient.* Of course, sometimes a merged firm will be more efficient and have lower costs, and other times it won't. Even if a merged firm is more efficient and has lower costs, the lower costs may not offset the increased market power of the firm enough to increase consumer surplus and economic efficiency.

As you might expect, whenever large firms propose a merger, they claim that the newly merged firm will be more efficient and have lower costs. They realize that without these claims, the Department of Justice and the FTC, along with the court system, are unlikely to approve the merger.   MyEconLab Concept Check

The Department of Justice and FTC Merger Guidelines

For many years after the passage of the Sherman Act in 1890, lawyers from the Department of Justice enforced the antitrust laws. The lawyers rarely considered economic arguments, such as the possibility that consumers might be made better off by a merger if economic efficiency were significantly improved. This situation began to change in 1965, when Donald Turner became the first Ph.D. economist to head the Antitrust Division of the Department of Justice. Under Turner and his successors, economic analysis shaped antitrust policy. In 1973, the Economics Section of the Antitrust Division was established and staffed with economists who evaluate the economic consequences of proposed mergers.

Economists played a major role in the development of merger guidelines by the Department of Justice and the FTC in 1982. The guidelines made it easier for firms considering a merger to understand whether the government was likely to allow the merger or to oppose it. The guidelines were modified in 2010 and have three main parts:

1. Market definition
2. Measure of concentration
3. Merger standards

Market Definition A market consists of all firms making products that consumers view as close substitutes. Economists can identify close substitutes by looking at the effect of a price increase. If the definition of a market is too narrow, a price increase will cause firms to experience a significant decline in sales—and profits—as consumers switch to buying close substitutes.

Identifying the relevant market involved in a proposed merger begins with a narrow definition of the industry. For a hypothetical merger of Hershey Foods and Mars, Inc., economists might start with the candy industry. If all firms in the candy industry increased price by 5 percent, would their profits increase or decrease? If profits would increase, the market is defined as being just these firms. If profits would decrease, economists would try a broader definition—say, by adding in potato chips and other snacks. Would a price increase of 5 percent by all firms in the broader market raise profits? If profits increase, the relevant market has been identified. If profits decrease, economists consider a broader definition. Economists continue the process until a market has been identified.

Measure of Concentration A market is *concentrated* if a relatively small number of firms have a large share of total sales in the market. A merger between firms in a market that is already highly concentrated is very likely to increase market power. A merger between firms in an industry that has a very low concentration is unlikely to increase market power and can be ignored. The guidelines use the *Herfindahl-Hirschman Index (HHI)* of concentration, which squares the market shares of each firm in the industry and adds up the values of the squares. The following are some examples of calculating HHI:

- 1 firm, with 100 percent market share (a monopoly):

$$HHI = 100^2 = 10,000.$$

- 2 firms, each with a 50 percent market share:

$$HHI = 50^2 + 50^2 = 5,000.$$

- 4 firms, with market shares of 30 percent, 30 percent, 20 percent, and 20 percent:

$$HHI = 30^2 + 30^2 + 20^2 + 20^2 = 2,600.$$

- 10 firms, each with a 10 percent market share:

$$HHI = 10 \times (10)^2 = 1,000.$$

Merger Standards The Department of Justice and the FTC use the HHI calculation for a market to evaluate proposed horizontal mergers according to these standards:

- *Postmerger HHI below 1,500.* These markets are not concentrated, so mergers in them are not challenged.
- *Postmerger HHI between 1,500 and 2,500.* These markets are moderately concentrated. Mergers that raise the HHI by fewer than 100 points probably will not be challenged. Mergers that raise the HHI by more than 100 points may be challenged.

- *Postmerger HHI above 2,500.* These markets are highly concentrated. Mergers that increase the HHI by fewer than 100 points will not be challenged. Mergers that increase the HHI by 100 to 200 points may be challenged. Mergers that increase the HHI by more than 200 points will likely be challenged.

Increases in economic efficiency will be taken into account and can lead to approval of a merger that otherwise would be opposed, but the burden of showing that the efficiencies exist lies with the merging firms:

> The merging firms must substantiate efficiency claims so that the [Department of Justice and the FTC] can verify by reasonable means the likelihood and magnitude of each asserted efficiency.... Efficiency claims will not be considered if they are vague or speculative or otherwise cannot be verified by reasonable means.

MyEconLab Concept Check

Regulating Natural Monopolies

If a firm is a natural monopoly, competition from other firms will not play its usual role of forcing price down to the level where the company earns zero economic profit. As a result, local or state *regulatory commissions* usually set the prices for natural monopolies, such as firms selling natural gas or electricity. What price should these commissions set? Economic efficiency requires the last unit of a good or service produced to provide an additional benefit to consumers equal to the additional cost of producing it (see Chapter 11). We can measure the additional benefit consumers receive from the last unit by the price of the product, and we can measure the additional cost to the monopoly of producing the last unit by marginal cost. Therefore, to achieve economic efficiency, regulators should require that the monopoly charge a price equal to its marginal cost. There is, however, an important drawback to doing so, as illustrated in Figure 15.7, which shows the situation of a typical regulated natural monopoly.

Remember that with a natural monopoly, the average total cost curve is still falling when it crosses the demand curve. If unregulated, the monopoly will charge a price equal to P_M and produce Q_M. To achieve economic efficiency, regulators should require the monopoly to charge a price equal to P_E. The monopoly will then produce Q_E. But here is the drawback: P_E is less than average total cost, so the monopoly will be suffering a loss, shown by the area of the red-shaded rectangle. In the long run, the owners of the monopoly will not continue in business if they are experiencing losses. Realizing this, most regulators will set the regulated price, P_R, equal to the level of average total cost at which the demand curve intersects the *ATC*

MyEconLab Animation

Figure 15.7

Regulating a Natural Monopoly

A natural monopoly that is not subject to government regulation will charge a price equal to P_M and produce Q_M. If government regulators want to achieve economic efficiency, they will set the regulated price equal to P_E, and the monopoly will produce Q_E. Unfortunately, P_E is below average total cost, and the monopoly will suffer a loss, shown by the red rectangle. Because the monopoly will not continue to produce in the long run if it suffers a loss, government regulators set a price equal to average total cost, which is P_R in the figure. The resulting production, Q_R, will be below the efficient level.

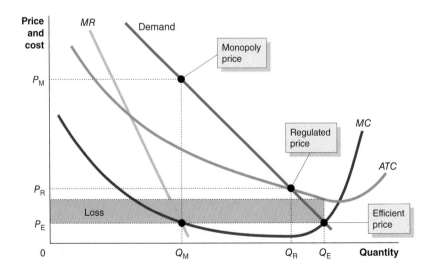

curve. At that price, the owners of the monopoly are able to break even on their investment by producing the quantity Q_R, although this quantity is below the efficient quantity, Q_E.

MyEconLab Concept Check MyEconLab Study Plan

Continued from page 477

Economics in Your Life

Is There a Monopoly in Your Dorm?

At the beginning of the chapter, we asked if the submarine sandwich business you and your roommate, Fatma, start in your dorm was a monopoly, and if you should charge high prices for the subs to increase your profit. In this chapter, we have seen that a monopoly is a firm that is the only seller of a good or service that does not have a close substitute. Even though you and Fatma would be the only sellers of submarine sandwiches on campus during the evening hours of Saturdays and Sundays, there could be other options for hungry students. For example, students could buy food from nearby off-campus stores, have it delivered to campus from those stores, or buy from vendors open earlier in the day. Most goods have substitutes, and you and Fatma should realize that for many students pizza and hamburgers are good substitutes for subs. High prices are likely to lead many of your customers to search for these substitutes.

Conclusion

The more intense the level of competition among firms, the better a market works. In this chapter, we have seen that, compared with perfect competition, in a monopoly, the price of a good or service is higher, output is lower, and consumer surplus and economic efficiency are reduced. Fortunately, true monopolies are rare. Even though most firms resemble monopolies in being able to charge a price above marginal cost, most markets have enough competition to keep the efficiency losses from market power low.

Visit MyEconLab for a news article and analysis related to the concepts in this chapter.

Chapter Summary and Problems

Key Terms

Antitrust laws, p. 493

Collusion, p. 493

Copyright, p. 481

Horizontal merger, p. 495

Market power, p. 492

Monopoly, p. 478

Natural monopoly, p. 483

Network externalities, p. 483

Patent, p. 480

Public franchise, p. 481

Vertical merger, p. 495

15.1 | **Is Any Firm Ever Really a Monopoly? pages 478–479**
LEARNING OBJECTIVE: Define monopoly.

Summary

A **monopoly** exists only in the rare situation in which a firm is producing a good or service for which there are no close substitutes. A narrow definition of monopoly that some economists use is that a firm has a monopoly if it can ignore the actions of all other firms. Many economists favor a broader definition of monopoly. Under the broader definition, a firm has a monopoly if no other firms are selling a substitute close enough that the firm's economic profit is competed away in the long run.

MyEconLab   Visit www.myeconlab.com to complete these exercises online and get instant feedback.

Review Questions

1.1 What is a monopoly? Can a firm be a monopoly if close substitutes for its product exist?

1.2 If you own the only hardware store in a small town, do you have a monopoly?

Problems and Applications

1.3 The great baseball player Ty Cobb was known for being very thrifty. Near the end of his life, he was interviewed by a reporter who was surprised to find that Cobb used candles, rather than electricity, to light his home. From Ty Cobb's point of view, was the local electric company a monopoly?

1.4 Some observers say that changes in the past few years have eroded the monopoly power of local cable television companies, even if no other cable firms have entered their markets. What are these changes? Do these "monopoly" firms still have monopoly power?

1.5 Are there any products for which there are no substitutes? Are these the only products for which it would be possible to have a monopoly? Briefly explain.

1.6 **[Related to the** Making the Connection **on page 478]** A newspaper article has the headline "Google Says It's Actually Quite Small." According to the article:

> Google rejects the idea that it's in the search advertising business, an industry in which it holds more than a 70 percent share of revenue. Instead, the company says its competition is all advertising, a category broad enough to include newspaper, radio and highway billboards.

Why does Google care whether people think it is large or small? Do highway billboards actually provide competition for Google? Briefly explain.

Source: Jeff Horwitz, "Google Says It's Actually Quite Small," *Washington Post*, June 7, 2009.

1.7 **[Related to the** Making the Connection **on page 478]** Why is access to YouTube by other search engines such as Yahoo and Bing relevant to the question of whether Google has a monopoly in the Internet search engine market?

15.2 | **Where Do Monopolies Come From? pages 479–485**
LEARNING OBJECTIVE: Explain the four main reasons monopolies arise.

Summary

To have a monopoly, barriers to entering the market must be so high that no other firms can enter. Barriers to entry may be high enough to keep out competing firms for four main reasons: (1) A government blocks the entry of more than one firm into a market by issuing a **patent**, which is the exclusive right to make a product for 20 years, a **copyright**, which is the exclusive right to produce and sell a creation, or a *trademark*, which grants a firm legal protection against other firms using its product's name, or by giving a firm a **public franchise**, which is the right to be the only legal provider of a good or service; (2) one firm has control of a key raw material necessary to produce a good; (3) there are important *network externalities* in supplying the good or service; or (4) economies of scale are so large

that one firm has a *natural monopoly*. **Network externalities** refer to the situation where the usefulness of a product increases with the number of consumers who use it. A **natural monopoly** is a situation in which economies of scale are so large that one firm can supply the entire market at a lower average cost than can two or more firms.

MyEconLab   Visit www.myeconlab.com to complete these exercises online and get instant feedback.

Review Questions

2.1 What are the four most important ways a firm becomes a monopoly?

2.2 If patents, copyrights, and trademarks reduce competition, why does the federal government grant them?

2.3 What is a public franchise? Are all public franchises natural monopolies?

2.4 What is "natural" about a natural monopoly?

Problems and Applications

2.5 The U.S. Postal Service (USPS) is a monopoly because the federal government has blocked entry into the market for delivering first-class mail. Is the USPS also a natural monopoly? How can we tell? What would happen if the law preventing competition in this market were removed?

2.6 Patents are granted for 20 years, but pharmaceutical companies can't use their patent-guaranteed monopoly powers for anywhere near this long because it takes several years to acquire approval of drugs from the Food and Drug Administration (FDA). Should the life of drug patents be extended to 20 years *after* FDA approval? What would be the costs and benefits of such an extension?

2.7 Under U.S. copyright law, authors have the exclusive right to their writings during their lifetimes—unless they sell this right, as most authors do to their publishers—and their heirs retain this exclusive right for 70 years after their death. The historian Thomas Macaulay once described the copyright law as "a tax on readers to give a bounty to authors." In what sense does the existence of the copyright law impose a tax on readers? What "bounty" do copyright laws give authors? Discuss whether the government would be doing readers a favor by abolishing the copyright law.

Source: Thomas Mallon, *Stolen Words: The Classic Book on Plagiarism*, Boston: Houghton Mifflin Harcourt, 2001 (original ed. 1989), p. 59.

2.8 If firms incurred no cost in developing new technologies and new products, would there be any need for patents? Briefly explain.

2.9 The German company Koenig & Bauer has 90 percent of the world market for presses that print currency. Discuss the factors that would make it difficult for new companies to enter this market.

2.10 **[Related to the** Making the Connection **on page 480]** Why should it matter legally whether Professor Anspach is correct that Hasbro's Monopoly game closely resembles a game that had been played for decades before Charles

Darrow claimed to have invented it? Does it matter economically? Briefly explain.

2.11 **[Related to the** Making the Connection **on page 482]** Why was De Beers worried that people might resell their old diamonds? How did De Beers attempt to convince consumers that previously owned diamonds were not good substitutes for new diamonds? How did De Beers's strategy affect the demand curve for new diamonds? How did De Beers's strategy affect its profit?

2.12 In China, the government owns many more firms than in the United States. A former Chinese government official argued that a number of government-run industries such as oil refining were natural monopolies. Is it likely that oil refining is a natural monopoly? How would you be able to tell?

Source: Shen Hong, "Former State Assets Regulator: SOE Monopolies 'Natural'," *Wall Street Journal*, January 4, 2012.

2.13 **[Related to** Solved Problem 15.2 **on page 484]** Suppose that the quantity demanded per day for a product is 90 when the price is $35. The following table shows costs for a firm with a monopoly in this market:

Quantity (per day)	Total Cost
30	$1,200
40	1,400
50	2,250
60	3,000

Briefly explain whether this firm has a natural monopoly.

2.14 As noted in this chapter, many generic versions of the diabetes drug Glucophage were introduced within the first year of Glucophage's patent expiration. Recently, the U.S. Supreme Court ruled that patients who become ill taking generic drugs cannot sue the manufacturer of those drugs, even though: "People who are hurt by a brand-name drug can sue the drug maker for damages." How might the Supreme Court's decision affect the willingness of pharmaceutical firms to invest in research and development on new drugs?

Source: David G. Savage, "Supreme Court Rules Drug Makers Can't Be Sued over Defects," *Los Angeles Times*, June 25, 2013.

15.3 ## How Does a Monopoly Choose Price and Output? pages 486–489

LEARNING OBJECTIVE: Explain how a monopoly chooses price and output.

Summary

Monopolists face downward-sloping demand and marginal revenue curves and, like all other firms, maximize profit by producing where marginal revenue equals marginal cost. Unlike a perfect competitor, a monopolist that earns an economic profit does not face the entry of new firms into the market. Therefore, a monopolist can earn an economic profit even in the long run.

 MyEconLab   Visit **www.myeconlab.com** to complete these exercises online and get instant feedback.

Review Questions

3.1 What is the relationship between a monopolist's demand and the market demand curve? What is the

relationship between a monopolist's demand curve and its marginal revenue curve?

3.2 In what sense is a monopolist a *price maker*? Will charging the highest possible price always maximize a monopolist's profit? Briefly explain.

3.3 Draw a graph that shows a monopolist earning a profit. Be sure your graph includes the monopolist's demand, marginal revenue, average total cost, and marginal cost curves. Be sure to indicate the profit-maximizing level of output and price.

Problems and Applications

3.4 **[Related to** Solved Problem 15.3 **on page 488]** Ed Scahill has acquired a monopoly on the production of baseballs (don't ask how) and faces the demand and cost situation shown in the following table:

Price	Quantity (per week)	Total Revenue	Marginal Revenue	Total Cost	Marginal Cost
$20	15,000			$330,000	
19	20,000			365,000	
18	25,000			405,000	
17	30,000			450,000	
16	35,000			500,000	
15	40,000			555,000	

    a. Fill in the remaining values in the table.

    b. If Scahill wants to maximize profit, what price should he charge, and how many baseballs should he sell? How much profit (or loss) will he make? Draw a graph to illustrate your answer. Your graph should be clearly labeled and should include Scahill's demand, *ATC*, *AVC*, *AFC*, *MC*, and *MR* curves, the price he is charging, the quantity he is producing, and the area representing his profit (or loss).

    c. Suppose the government imposes a tax of $50,000 per week on baseball production. Now what price should Scahill charge, how many baseballs should he sell, and what will his profit (or loss) be?

    d. Suppose that the government raises the tax in part (c) to $70,000. Now what price should Scahill charge, how many baseballs should he sell, and what will his profit (or loss) be? Will his decision on what price to charge and how much to produce be different in the short run than in the long run? Briefly explain.

3.5 **[Related to** Solved Problem 15.3 **on page 488]** Use the information in Solved Problem 15.3 to answer the following questions.

    a. What will Comcast do if the tax is $36.00 per month instead of $25.00? (*Hint:* Will its decision be different in the long run than in the short run?)

    b. Suppose that the flat per-month tax is replaced with a tax on the firm of $25.00 per cable subscriber. Now how many subscriptions should Comcast sell if it wants to maximize profit? What price should it charge? What is its profit? (Assume that Comcast will sell only the quantities listed in the table.)

3.6 Before inexpensive pocket calculators were developed, many science and engineering students used slide rules to make numerical calculations. Slide rules are no longer produced, which means nothing prevents you from establishing a monopoly in the slide rule market. Draw a graph showing the situation your slide rule firm would be in. Be sure to include on your graph your demand, marginal revenue, average total cost, and marginal cost curves. Indicate the price you would charge and the quantity you would produce. Are you likely to make a profit or a loss? Show this area on your graph.

3.7 Does a monopolist have a supply curve? Briefly explain. (*Hint:* Look again at the definition of a supply curve in Chapter 3 on page 78 and consider whether this definition applies to a monopolist.)

3.8 **[Related to the** Don't Let This Happen to You **on page 489]** A student argues: "If a monopolist finds a way of producing a good at lower cost, he will not lower his price. Because he is a monopolist, he will keep the price and the quantity the same and just increase his profit." Do you agree? Use a graph to illustrate your answer.

3.9 When homebuilders construct a new housing development, they usually sell to a single cable television company the rights to lay cable. As a result, anyone buying a home in that development is not able to choose between competing cable companies. Some cities have begun to ban such exclusive agreements. Williams Township, Pennsylvania, decided to allow any cable company to lay cable in the utility trenches of new housing developments. The head of the township board of supervisors argued: "What I would like to see and do is give the consumers a choice. If there's no choice, then the price [of cable] is at the whim of the provider." In a situation in which the consumers in a housing development have only one cable company available, is the price really at the whim of the company? Would a company in this situation be likely to charge, say, $500 per month for basic cable services? Briefly explain why or why not.

    Source: Sam Kennedy, "Williams Township May Ban Exclusive Cable Provider Pacts," (Allentown, PA), *Morning Call* November 5, 2004.

3.10 Will a monopoly that maximizes profit also be maximizing revenue? Will it be maximizing production? Briefly explain.

15.4 | **Does Monopoly Reduce Economic Efficiency? pages 490–493**
LEARNING OBJECTIVE: Use a graph to illustrate how a monopoly affects economic efficiency.

Summary

Compared with a perfectly competitive industry, a monopoly charges a higher price and produces less, which reduces consumer surplus and economic efficiency. Some loss of economic efficiency will occur whenever firms have **market power** and can charge a price greater than marginal cost. The total loss of economic efficiency in the U.S. economy due to market power is small, however, because true monopolies are very rare. In most industries, competition will keep price much closer to marginal cost than would be the case in a monopoly.

MyEconLab   Visit **www.myeconlab.com** to complete these exercises online and get instant feedback.

Review Questions

4.1 Suppose that a perfectly competitive industry becomes a monopoly. Describe the effects of this change on consumer surplus, producer surplus, and deadweight loss.

4.2 Explain why market power leads to a deadweight loss. Is the total deadweight loss from market power for the economy large or small?

Problems and Applications

4.3 Review Figure 15.5 on page 491 on the inefficiency of monopoly. Will the deadweight loss due to monopoly be larger if the demand is elastic or if it is inelastic? Briefly explain.

4.4 Economist Harvey Leibenstein argued that the loss of economic efficiency in industries that are not perfectly competitive has been understated. He argued that when competition is weak, firms are under less pressure to adopt the best techniques or to hold down their costs. He referred to this effect as "x-inefficiency." If x-inefficiency causes a firm's marginal costs to rise, use a graph to show that the deadweight loss in Figure 15.5 understates the true deadweight loss caused by a monopoly.

4.5 Most cities own the water system that provides water to homes and businesses. Some cities charge a flat monthly fee, while other cities charge by the gallon. Which method of pricing is more likely to result in economic efficiency in the water market? Be sure to refer to the definition of *economic efficiency* in your answer. Why do you think the same method of pricing isn't used by all cities?

4.6 Review the concept of externalities from Chapter 5, page 138. If a market is a monopoly, will a negative externality in production always lead to production beyond the level of economic efficiency? Use a graph to illustrate your answer.

4.7 **[Related to the** Chapter Opener **on page 477]** Suppose a second seafood restaurant opens in Stonington, Maine. Will consumer surplus and economic efficiency necessarily increase? Briefly explain.

4.8 Suppose that the city has given Jorge a monopoly selling baseball caps at the local minor league stadium. Use the following graph to answer the questions:

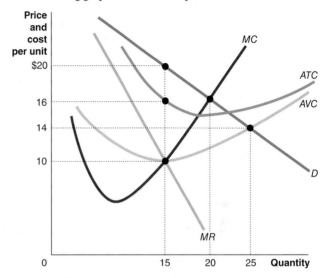

a. What quantity will Jorge produce, and what price will he charge?

b. How much profit will he earn?

c. Review the definition of allocatively efficiency. If Jorge produced at the allocatively efficient level of output, what quantity would he produce?

d. How much deadweight loss did Jorge create by acting like a monopolist rather than a perfect competitor? (Assume that the marginal cost curve is linear (a straight line) between the two relevant points.)

15.5 ## Government Policy toward Monopoly, pages 493–499

LEARNING OBJECTIVE: Discuss government policies toward monopoly.

Summary

Because monopolies reduce consumer surplus and economic efficiency, governments often regulate monopolies. Firms that are not monopolies have an incentive to avoid competition by **colluding**, or agreeing to charge the same price or otherwise not to compete. In the United States, **antitrust laws** are aimed at deterring monopoly, eliminating collusion, and promoting competition among firms. The Antitrust Division of the U.S. Department of Justice and the Federal Trade Commission share responsibility for enforcing the antitrust laws, including regulating mergers between firms. A **horizontal merger** is a merger between firms in the same industry. A **vertical merger** is a merger between firms at different stages of production of a good. Local governments often regulate the prices charged by natural monopolies.

MyEconLab   Visit **www.myeconlab.com** to complete these exercises online and get instant feedback.

Review Questions

5.1 What is the purpose of the antitrust laws? Who is in charge of enforcing these laws?

5.2 What is the difference between a horizontal merger and a vertical merger? Which type of merger is more likely to increase the market power of a newly merged firm?

5.3 Why would it be economically efficient to require a natural monopoly to charge a price equal to marginal cost? Why do most regulatory agencies require natural monopolies to charge a price equal to average cost instead?

Problems and Applications

5.4 Use the following graph for a monopoly to answer the questions:

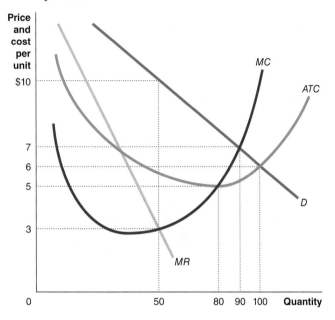

a. What quantity will the monopoly produce and what price will the monopoly charge?

b. Suppose the monopoly is regulated. If the regulatory agency wants to achieve economic efficiency, what price should it require the monopoly to charge? How much output will the monopoly produce at this price? Will the monopoly make a profit if it charges this price? Briefly explain.

5.5 Use the following graph of a monopoly to answer the questions:

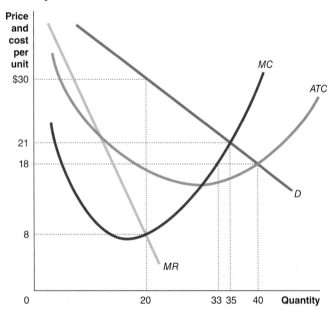

a. What quantity will the monopoly produce, and what price will the monopoly charge?

b. Suppose the government decides to regulate this monopoly and imposes a price ceiling of $18 (in other

words, the monopoly can charge less than $18 but can't charge more). Now what quantity will the monopoly produce, and what price will the monopoly charge? Will every consumer who is willing to pay this price be able to buy the product? Briefly explain.

5.6 In Pennsylvania, wine and liquor can only be purchased from "state stores," which are stores that are owned and operated by the state government. According to an analysis by Katja Seim of the University of Pennsylvania and Joel Waldfogel of the University of Minnesota, if the state of Pennsylvania were to allow unlimited entry of private liquor stores, the number of stores would increase by 2.5 times and consumer surplus would increase by 9 percent. Are these results sufficient to decide whether the state of Pennsylvania should abolish the system of state stores and allow free entry of private stores? In your answer, discuss the distinction between positive and normative analysis.

Source: Katja Seim and Joel Waldfogel, "Public Monopoly and Economic Efficiency: Evidence from the Pennsylvania Liquor Control Board's Entry Decisions," *American Economic Review*, Vol. 103, No. 2, April 2013, pp. 811–862.

5.7 Consider the natural monopoly shown in Figure 15.7 on page 498. Assume that the government regulatory agency sets the regulated price, P_R, at the level of average total cost at which the demand curve intersects the *ATC* curve. If the firm knows that it will always be able to charge a price equal to its average total cost, does it have an incentive to reduce its average cost? Briefly explain.

5.8 Draw a graph like Figure 15.6 on page 496 that shows a merger lowering costs. On your graph, show producer surplus and consumer surplus before a merger and consumer surplus and producer surplus after a merger.

5.9 Look again at the section "The Department of Justice and FTC Merger Guidelines," which begins on page 496. Evaluate the following situations.

a. A market initially has 20 firms, each with a 5 percent market share. Of the firms, 4 propose to merge, leaving a total of 17 firms in the industry. Are the Department of Justice and the Federal Trade Commission likely to oppose the merger? Briefly explain.

b. A market initially has 5 firms, each with a 20 percent market share. Of the firms, 2 propose to merge, leaving a total of 4 firms in the industry. Are the Department of Justice and the Federal Trade Commission likely to oppose the merger? Briefly explain.

5.10 In October 2008, Delta Air Lines completed its acquisition of Northwest Airlines. The newly merged company is the largest airline in the world. The following statement regarding the merger is from a Justice Department press release:

> After a thorough, six-month investigation, during which the [Antitrust] Division obtained extensive information from a wide range of market participants—including the companies, other airlines, corporate customers and travel agents—the Division has determined that the proposed merger between Delta and Northwest is likely to produce substantial and credible efficiencies that will benefit U.S. consumers and is not likely to substantially lessen competition.

What does the Justice Department mean by "substantial and credible efficiencies," and how might they benefit U.S. consumers? Why would a merger between two large airlines not be "likely to substantially lessen competition"?

Sources: Andrew Ross Sorkin, "Regulators Approve Delta–Northwest Merger," *New York Times*, October 30, 2008; and Department of Justice, "Statement of the Department of Justice's Antitrust Division on Its Decision to Close Its Investigation of the Merger of Delta Air Lines Inc. and Northwest Airlines Corporation," October 29, 2008.

5.11 The following table shows the market shares during the first three months of 2013 for companies in the U.S. personal computer (PC) market, which includes desk-based PCs and mobile PCs, such as mini-notebooks, but not tablet computers, such as the iPad:

Company	Market Share
Hewlett-Packard	25%
Dell	22
Apple	10
Toshiba	9
Lenovo	9
Other	25

Use the information in the section "The Department of Justice and FTC Merger Guidelines," which begins on page 496, to predict whether the Department of Justice and the Federal Trade Commission would be likely to oppose a merger between any of the five firms listed in the table. Assume that "Other" in the table consists of five firms, each of which has a 5 percent share of the market.

Source: Eric Slivka, "Apple's U.S. Mac Shipments Fall 7.5% as Overall PC Market Plunges 14% Year-Over-Year," www.macrumors.com, April 10, 2013.

5.12 **[Related to the** Making the Connection **on page 494]** After a federal court judge had found Apple guilty of conspiring with book publishers to raise e-book prices, the Department of Justice recommended that the judge order Apple not to sign agency pricing model contracts with publishers for five years. The publishers objected to the recommendation, arguing that the recommendation would "effectively punish the [publishers] by prohibiting agreements with Apple using an agency model."
a. What is an agency pricing model?
b. Why would the Department of Justice want to keep Apple from signing agency pricing model contracts with publishers? Why would the publishers want to continue signing such contracts?

Source: Chad Bray, "Publishers Object to E-Book Plan for Apple," *Wall Street Journal*, August 7, 2013.

CHAPTER
16

Pricing Strategy

Chapter Outline and Learning Objectives

Getting into Walt Disney World: One Price Does Not Fit All

When you visit Walt Disney World's Magic Kingdom in Florida, your age, home address, and occupation can determine how much you pay for admission. In 2013, the price for a one-day ticket for an adult was $101.18. The same ticket for a child, aged three to nine, was $94.79. Children under three were free. Students at the University of Central Florida paid $65. Active members of the military paid $98, and were charged $82 for their children aged three to nine. Why does Disney charge so many different prices for the same product?

In previous chapters, we assumed that firms charge all consumers the same price for a given product. In reality, many firms charge customers different prices, based on differences in their willingness to pay for the product. Firms often face complicated pricing problems. For example, the Walt Disney Company faces the problem of determining the profit-maximizing prices to charge different groups of consumers for admission to its Disneyland and Walt Disney World theme parks.

In the early 1950s, most amusement parks were collections of unrelated rides, such as roller coasters and Ferris wheels. Walt Disney believed that a theme park, with attractions that emphasized storytelling over thrills, would be more appealing to families than were amusement parks. Disney hired an economist to evaluate the feasibility of such a park. Managers of existing parks gave this advice to the economist: "Tell your boss . . . to stick to what he knows and leave the amusement business to people who know it." Eventually, Disney convinced the ABC television network to provide funding in exchange for his providing them with a weekly television program.

When Disneyland opened in 1955, Disney charged a low price—$1 for adults and $0.50 for children—for admission into the park and charged for tickets to the rides. This system of separate charges for admission and for rides continued until the early 1980s. Today, the Walt Disney Company charges a high price for admission to its theme parks, but once a customer is in the park, the rides are free. In this chapter, we will study some common pricing strategies, and we will see how Disney and other firms use these strategies to increase their profits.

Sources: Disney World prices from www.mousesavers. com, June 27, 2013; Harrison Price, *Walt's Revolution! By the Numbers*, Ripley Entertainment, Inc., 2004, p. 31; and Bruce Gordon and David Mumford, *Disneyland: The Nickel Tour*, Santa Clarita, CA: Camphor Tree Publishers, 2000, pp. 174–175.

Economics in Your Life

Why So Many Prices to See a Movie?

How much do you, as a student, pay to get into a movie theater? Would your parents pay the same amount? What about your grandparents? How about your little brother or sister? Is the price the same in the evening as in the afternoon? Why do you suppose movie theaters charge different prices to different groups of consumers?

If you buy popcorn at the movie theater, you pay the same price as everyone else. Why do you suppose people in certain age groups get a discount on movie admission but not on popcorn? As you read this chapter, try to answer these questions. You can check your answers against those we provide on **page 524** at the end of this chapter.

I n previous chapters, we saw that entrepreneurs continually seek out economic profit. Using pricing strategies is one way firms can attempt to increase their economic profit. One of these strategies, called *price discrimination*, involves firms setting different prices for the same good or service, as Disney does when setting admission prices at Walt Disney World. In this chapter, we will see how a firm can increase its profit by charging a higher price to consumers who value the good more and a lower price to consumers who value the good less.

We will also analyze the widely used strategies of *odd pricing* and *cost-plus pricing*. Finally, we will analyze situations in which firms are able to charge consumers one price for the right to buy a good and a second price for each unit of the good purchased. Disney's old pricing scheme of charging for admission to Disney World and also charging for each ride is an example of a strategy economists call a *two-part tariff*.

16.1 LEARNING OBJECTIVE

Define the law of one price and explain the role of arbitrage.

Pricing Strategy, the Law of One Price, and Arbitrage

We saw in the chapter opener that sometimes firms can charge different prices for the same good. In fact, many firms rely on economic analysis to practice *price discrimination* by charging higher prices to some customers and lower prices to others. Some firms practice a sophisticated form of price discrimination in which they use technology to gather information on the preferences of consumers and their responsiveness to changes in prices. Managers use the information to rapidly adjust the prices of their goods and services. This practice of rapidly adjusting prices, called *yield management*, has been particularly important to airlines and hotels. There are limits, though, to the ability of firms to charge different prices for the same product. The key limit is the possibility in some circumstances that consumers who can buy a good at a low price will resell it to consumers who would otherwise have to buy at a high price.

Arbitrage

According to the *law of one price*, identical products should sell for the same price everywhere. Let's explore why the law of one price usually holds true. Suppose that an Apple iPad sells for $499 in stores in Atlanta and for $429 in stores in San Francisco. Anyone who lives in San Francisco could buy iPads for $429 and resell them for $499 in Atlanta. They could sell them on eBay or Craigslist or ship them to someone they know in Atlanta who could sell them in local flea markets. Buying a product in one market at a low price and reselling it in another market at a high price is called *arbitrage*. The profits received from engaging in arbitrage are called *arbitrage profits*.

As people take advantage of the price difference to earn arbitrage profits, the supply of iPads in Atlanta will increase and the price of iPads in Atlanta will decline. At the same time, the supply of iPads in San Francisco will decrease and the price of iPads in San Francisco will rise. Eventually, the arbitrage process will eliminate most, but not all, of the price difference. Some price difference will remain because sellers must pay to list iPads on eBay or to ship them to Atlanta. The costs of carrying out a transaction—by, for example, listing items on eBay and shipping them across the country—are called **transactions costs**. The law of one price holds exactly *only if transactions costs are zero*. As we will soon see, in cases in which it is impossible to resell a product, the law of one price will not hold, and firms will be able to practice price discrimination. Apart from this important qualification, we expect that arbitrage will result in a product selling for the same price everywhere. MyEconLab Concept Check

Transactions costs The costs in time and other resources that parties incur in the process of agreeing to and carrying out an exchange of goods or services.

Solved Problem 16.1

MyEconLab Interactive Animation

Is Arbitrage Just a Rip-Off?

People are often suspicious of arbitrage. Buying something at a low price and reselling it at a high price exploits the person buying at the high price. Or does it? Is this view correct? If so, do the auctions on eBay serve any useful economic purpose?

Solving the Problem

Step 1: **Review the chapter material.** This problem is about arbitrage, so you may want to review the section "Arbitrage" on page 508. If necessary, also review the discussion of the benefits from trade in earlier chapters (see Chapters 2 and 9).

Step 2: **Use the discussion of arbitrage and the discussion in earlier chapters of the benefits from trade to answer the questions.** Many of the goods on eBay have been bought at low prices and are being resold at higher prices. In fact, some people supplement their incomes by buying collectibles and other goods at garage sales and reselling them on eBay. Does eBay serve a useful economic purpose? Economists would say that it does. Consider the case of Lou, who buys collectible movie posters and resells them on eBay. Suppose Lou buys a *Guardians of the Galaxy* poster at a garage sale for $30 and resells it on eBay for $60. Both the person who sold to Lou at the garage sale and the person who bought from him on eBay must have been made better off by the deals *or they would not have made them*. Lou has performed the useful service of locating the poster and making it available for sale on eBay. In carrying out this service, Lou has incurred costs, including the opportunity cost of his time spent searching garage sales, the opportunity cost of the funds he has tied up in posters he has purchased but not yet sold, and the cost of the fees eBay charges him. It is easy to sell goods on eBay, so over time, competition among Lou and other movie poster dealers should cause the difference between the prices of posters sold at garage sales and the prices on eBay to shrink until they are equal to the dealers' costs of reselling the posters, including the opportunity cost of their time.

Your Turn: For more practice, do related problems 1.5 and 1.6 on page 526 at the end of this chapter.

MyEconLab Study Plan

Why Don't All Firms Charge the Same Price?

The law of one price may appear to be violated even where transactions costs are zero and a product can be resold. For example, different Web sites may sell what seem to be identical products for different prices. We can resolve this apparent contradiction if we look more closely at what "product" an Internet Web site—or another business—actually offers for sale.

Suppose you want to buy a copy of the Blu-ray disc for *The Amazing Spider-Man 2*. You use Google, Pricegrabber.com, or some other search engine to compare prices at various Web sites. You get the results shown in Table 16.1.

Because they have the lowest prices, would you automatically buy from one of the last two sites listed rather than from Amazon.com or Wal-Mart.com? We can think about why you might not. Consider what these sites offer for sale. Amazon.com is not just offering *The Amazing Spider-Man 2*; it is offering *The Amazing Spider-Man 2* delivered

Product: *The Amazing Spider-Man 2* Blu-ray Disc

Company	Price
Amazon.com	$24.99
Wal-Mart.com	24.98
WaitForeverForYourOrder.com	22.50
JustStartedinBusinessLastWednesday.com	21.25

quickly to your home, well packaged so it's not damaged in the mail, and charged to your credit card using a secure method that keeps your credit card number safe from computer hackers. As we have discussed, firms differentiate the products they sell in many ways (see Chapter 13). One way is by providing faster and more reliable delivery than competitors.

Amazon.com and Wal-Mart.com have built reputations for fast and reliable service. New Internet sellers who lack that reputation will have to differentiate their products on the basis of price, as the two fictitious firms listed in the table have done. So, the difference in the prices of products offered on Web sites does *not* violate the law of one price. A Blu-ray disc Amazon.com offers for sale is not the same product as a Blu-ray disc JustStartedinBusinessLastWednesday.com offers for sale.

MyEconLab Study Plan — left margin

MyEconLab Concept Check

16.2 LEARNING OBJECTIVE

Explain how a firm can increase its profits through price discrimination.

Price discrimination Charging different prices to different customers for the same product when the price differences are not due to differences in cost.

Price Discrimination: Charging Different Prices for the Same Product

We saw at the beginning of this chapter that the Walt Disney Company charges different prices for the same product: admission to Disney World. Charging different prices to different customers for the same good or service when the price differences are not due to differences in cost is called **price discrimination**. But doesn't price discrimination contradict the law of one price? Why doesn't the possibility of arbitrage profits lead people to buy at the low price and resell at the high price?

Don't Let This Happen to You

Don't Confuse Price Discrimination with Other Types of Discrimination

Don't confuse price discrimination with discrimination based on race or gender. Discriminating on the basis of arbitrary characteristics, such as race or gender, is illegal under the civil rights laws. Price discrimination is legal because it involves charging people different prices on the basis of their willingness to pay rather than on the basis of arbitrary characteristics. There is a gray area, however, when companies charge different prices on the basis of gender. For example, insurance companies usually charge women lower prices than men for automobile insurance. The courts have ruled that this is not

illegal discrimination under the civil rights laws because women, on average, have better driving records than men. Because the costs of insuring men are higher than the costs of insuring women, insurance companies are allowed to charge men higher prices. Notice that this is not actually price discrimination as we have defined it here. Price discrimination involves charging different prices for the same product *where the price differences are not due to differences in cost*.

MyEconLab Study Plan

Your Turn: Test your understanding by doing related problem 2.10 on page 527 at the end of this chapter.

The Requirements for Successful Price Discrimination

A successful strategy of price discrimination has three requirements:

1. A firm must possess market power.

2. Some consumers must have a greater willingness to pay for the product than other consumers, and the firm must be able to know which consumers have a greater willingness to pay.

3. The firm must be able to divide up—or *segment*—the market for the product so that consumers who buy the product at a low price are not able to resell it at a high price. In other words, price discrimination will not work if arbitrage is possible.

A firm selling in a perfectly competitive market cannot practice price discrimination because it can only charge the market price. Because most firms do not sell in perfectly competitive markets, they have market power and can set the price of the good they sell. Many firms may also be able to determine that some consumers have a greater willingness to pay for a product than others. However, the third requirement—that markets be segmented so that consumers buying at a low price will not be able to resell the product—can be difficult to fulfill. For example, some people really love Big Macs and would be willing to pay $10 rather than do without one. Other people would not be willing to pay a penny more than $1 for a Big Mac. Even if McDonald's could identify differences in the willingness of consumers to pay for Big Macs, it would not be able to charge them different prices. Suppose McDonald's knows that Joe is willing to pay $10, whereas Jill will pay only $1. If McDonald's tries to charge Joe $10, he will just have Jill buy a Big Mac for him.

Only firms that can keep consumers from reselling a product are able to practice price discrimination. Because buyers cannot resell the product, the law of one price does not hold. For example, movie theaters know that many people are willing to pay more to see a movie in the evening than during the afternoon. As a result, theaters usually charge higher prices for tickets to evening showings than for tickets to afternoon showings. They keep these markets separate by making the tickets to afternoon showings a different color or by having the time printed on them and by having a ticket taker examine the tickets. That practice makes it difficult for someone to buy a lower-priced ticket in the afternoon and use the ticket to gain admission to an evening showing.

Figure 16.1 illustrates how the owners of movie theaters use price discrimination to increase their profits. The marginal cost to the movie theater owner from another person attending a showing is very small: a little more wear on a theater seat and a few more kernels of popcorn to be swept from the floor. In previous chapters, we assumed that the marginal cost curve has a U shape. In Figure 16.1, we assume for simplicity that marginal cost is a constant $0.50, shown as a horizontal line. Panel (a) shows the demand for afternoon showings. In this segment of its market, the theater should maximize profit by selling the quantity of tickets for which marginal revenue equals marginal cost, or 450 tickets. We know from the demand curve that the theater can sell 450 tickets at a price of $7.25 per ticket. Panel (b) shows the demand for evening showings. Notice that charging $7.25 per ticket would *not* be profit maximizing in this market. At a price of $7.25, the theater sells 850 tickets, which is 225 more tickets than the profit-maximizing quantity of 625. By charging $7.25 for tickets to afternoon showings and $9.75 for tickets to evening showings, the theater has maximized profit.

Figure 16.1 also illustrates another important point about price discrimination: When firms can practice price discrimination, they will charge customers who are less sensitive to price—those whose demand for the product is *less elastic*—a higher price and charge customers who are more sensitive to price—those whose demand is *more elastic*—a lower price. In this case, the demand for tickets to evening showings is less elastic, so the price charged is higher, and the demand for tickets to afternoon showings is more elastic, so the price charged is lower. MyEconLab Concept Check

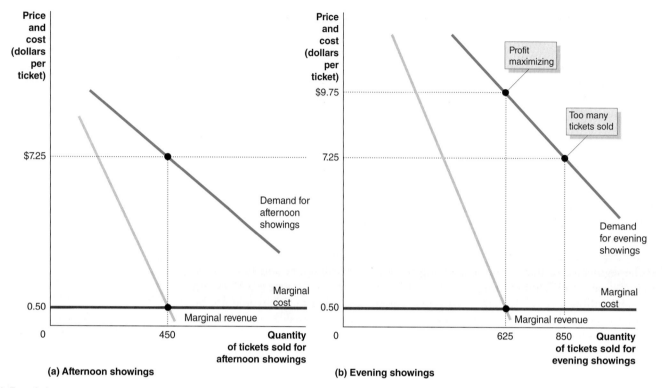

Figure 16.1 Price Discrimination by a Movie Theater

Fewer people want to go to the movies in the afternoon than in the evening. In panel (a), the profit-maximizing price for a ticket to an afternoon showing is $7.25. Charging this same price for evening showings would not be profit maximizing, as panel (b) shows. At a price of $7.25, the theater would sell 850 tickets to evening showings, which is more than the profit-maximizing number of 625 tickets. To maximize profit, the theater should charge $9.75 for tickets to evening showings.

Solved Problem 16.2

How Apple Uses Price Discrimination to Increase Profits

During the summer of 2013, Apple was selling MacBook Pro laptop computers with 13-inch retina displays on its Web site and in its retail stores for $1,499. But college students and faculty members could buy the same laptop from Apple for $1,399. Why would Apple charge different prices for the same laptop, depending on whether the buyer is an education customer? Draw two graphs to illustrate your answers: one for the general public and one for education customers.

Solving the Problem

Step 1: Review the chapter material. This problem is about using price discrimination to increase profits, so you may want to review the section "Price Discrimination: Charging Different Prices for the Same Product," which begins on page 510.

Step 2: Explain why charging different prices to education customers and other customers will increase Apple's profit. It makes sense for Apple to charge different prices if education customers have a different price elasticity of demand than do other customers. In that case, Apple will charge the market segment with the less elastic demand a higher price and the market segment with the more elastic demand a lower price. Because Apple is charging education customers the lower price, they must have a more elastic demand than do other customers.

Step 3: Draw a graph to illustrate your answer. Your graphs should look like the following ones, where we have chosen hypothetical quantities to illustrate the ideas. As in the case of movie theaters, you can assume for simplicity that marginal cost is constant; in the graph we assume that marginal cost is $400.

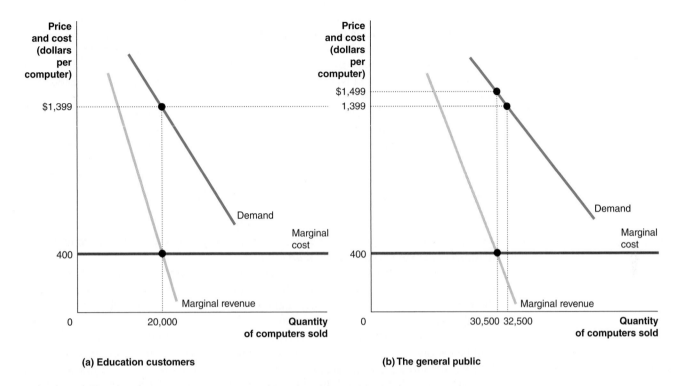

(a) Education customers   **(b) The general public**

Panel (a) shows that in the education customers segment of the market, marginal revenue equals marginal cost at 20,000 laptops sold. Therefore, Apple should charge a price of $1,399 to maximize profits. But if Apple also charges $1,399 in the general public segment of the market, shown in panel (b), it will sell 32,500 laptops, which is more than the profit-maximizing quantity. By charging $1,499 to the general public, Apple will sell 30,500 laptops, the profit-maximizing quantity. We have shown that Apple maximizes its profits by charging education customers a lower price than it charges the general public. Notice that although the demand curve in panel (a) is more elastic, it is also steeper. This reminds us of the important point that elasticity is different from slope (see Chapter 6).

Your Turn: For more practice, do problems 2.11, 2.12, and 2.13 on pages 527–528 at the end of this chapter.

MyEconLab Study Plan

Airlines: The Kings of Price Discrimination

Airline seats are a perishable product. Once a plane has taken off from Chicago for Los Angeles, any seat that has not been sold on that particular flight will never be sold. In addition, the marginal cost of flying one additional passenger is low. As a result, airlines have a strong incentive to manage prices to fill as many seats as possible on each flight.

Airlines divide their customers into two main categories: business travelers and leisure travelers. Business travelers often have inflexible schedules, can't commit until the last minute to travel on a particular day, and, most importantly, are not very sensitive to changes in price. The opposite is true for leisure travelers: They are flexible about when they travel, willing to buy their tickets well in advance, and sensitive to changes in price. Based on what we discussed earlier in this chapter, you can see that airlines will maximize profits by charging business travelers higher ticket prices than leisure travelers, but they need to determine who is a business traveler and who is a leisure traveler. Some airlines do this by requiring people who want to buy a ticket at the leisure price to buy 14 days in advance and to stay at their destination over a Saturday night. Anyone unable to meet these requirements must pay a much higher price. Business travelers end up paying the higher ticket price because they often cannot make their plans 14 days in advance of their flight and don't want to stay over a weekend. The gap between leisure fares and business fares is often substantial. For example, in mid-2013, the price of a leisure-fare ticket between New York and San Francisco on U.S. Airways was $460. The price of a business-fare ticket was $1,016.

The airlines go well beyond a single leisure fare and a single business fare in their pricing strategies. Although they ordinarily charge high prices for tickets sold only a few days in advance, airlines are willing to reduce prices for seats that they doubt they will be able to sell at current prices. Since the late 1980s, airlines have employed economists and mathematicians to construct computer models of the market for airline tickets. To calculate a suggested price each day for each seat, these models take into account factors that affect the demand for tickets, such as the season of the year, the length of the route, the day of the week, and whether the flight typically attracts primarily business or leisure travelers. This practice of continually adjusting prices to take into account fluctuations in demand is called *yield management*.

Since the late 1990s, Internet sites such as Priceline.com have helped the airlines to implement yield management. On Priceline.com, buyers commit to paying a price of their choosing for a ticket on a particular day and agree that they will fly at any time on that day. This gives airlines the opportunity to fill seats that otherwise would have gone empty, particularly on late-night or early-morning flights, even though the price may be well below the normal leisure fare. In 2001, several airlines came together to form the Internet site Orbitz, which became another means of filling seats at discount prices. In fact, the chance that you paid the same price for your airline ticket as the person sitting next to you has become quite small. Figure 16.2 shows an actual United Air Lines flight from Chicago to Los Angeles. The 33 passengers on the flight paid 27 different prices for their tickets, including one passenger who used frequent flyer miles to obtain a free ticket.

MyEconLab Concept Check

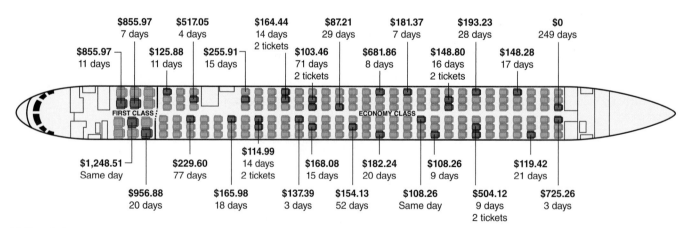

MyEconLab Animation

Figure 16.2 **33 Customers and 27 Different Prices**

To fill as many seats on a flight as possible, airlines charge many different ticket prices. The 33 passengers on this United Air Lines flight from Chicago to Los Angeles paid 27 different prices for their tickets, including one passenger who used frequent flyer miles to obtain a free ticket. The first number in the figure is the price paid for the ticket; the second number is the number of days in advance that the customer purchased the ticket.

Source: "So, How Much Did You Pay for Your Ticket," by Matthew L. Wald. *The New York Times*, April 12, 1998. Copyright © 1998 by The New York Times Company. All rights reserved. Used by permission and protected by the copyright laws of the United States. The printing, copying, redistribution, or retransmission of the Material without express written permission is prohibited.

How Colleges Use Yield Management

Traditionally, colleges have based financial aid decisions only on the incomes of prospective students. In recent years, however, many colleges have started using yield management techniques, first developed for the airlines, to determine the amount of financial aid they offer different students. Colleges typically use a name such as *financial aid engineering* or *student enrollment management* rather than yield management to describe what they are doing. There is an important difference between the airlines and colleges: Colleges are interested not just in maximizing the revenue they receive from student tuition but also in increasing the academic quality of the students who enroll. As one newspaper article puts it, many colleges will "offer merit scholarships to attract smart students whose grades and test scores will increase their academic profile."

Some colleges use yield management techniques to determine financial aid.

The "price" a college charges equals the full tuition minus any financial aid it provides students. When colleges use yield management techniques, they increase financial aid offers to students who are likely to be more price sensitive, and they reduce financial aid offers to students who are likely to be less price sensitive. As Stanford economist Caroline Hoxby puts it: "Universities are trying to find the people whose decisions will be changed by these [financial aid] grants." Some of the factors colleges use to judge how sensitive students are likely to be to price include whether they applied for early admission, whether they came for an on-campus interview, their intended major, their home state, and the level of their family's income. William F. Elliott, vice president for enrollment management at Carnegie Mellon University, advises: "If finances are a concern, you shouldn't be applying any place [for] early decision" because you are less likely to receive a large financial aid offer.

Many students (and their parents) are critical of colleges that use yield management techniques in allocating financial aid. Some colleges, such as those in the Ivy League, have large enough endowments to meet all of their students' financial aid needs, so they don't practice yield management. Less well-endowed colleges defend the practice on the grounds that it allows them to recruit the best students at a lower cost in financial aid.

Sources: Paul Sullivan, "College Admission Roulette: Ask for Financial Aid, or Not?" *New York Times*, March 1, 2013; Jacques Steinberg, "Early Signs That College Yields Did Not Change Dramatically," *New York Times*, May 8, 2009; and Jane J. Kim and Anjali Athavaley, "Colleges Seek to Address Affordability," *Wall Street Journal*, May 3, 2007; Albert B. Crenshaw, "Price Wars on Campus: Colleges Use Discounts to Draw Best Mix of Top Students, Paying Customers," *Washington Post*, October 15, 2002 .

Your Turn: Test your understanding by doing related problem 2.14 on page 528 at the end of this chapter.

MyEconLab Study Plan

Perfect Price Discrimination

If a firm knew every consumer's willingness to pay—and could keep consumers who bought a product at a low price from reselling it—the firm could charge every consumer a different price. In this case of *perfect price discrimination*—also known as *first-degree price discrimination*—each consumer would have to pay a price equal to the consumer's willingness to pay and, therefore, would receive no consumer surplus. To see why, remember that consumer surplus is the difference between the highest price a consumer is willing to pay for a product and the price the consumer actually pays (see Chapter 4). But if the price the consumer pays is the maximum the consumer would be willing to pay, there is no consumer surplus.

Figure 16.3 shows the effects of perfect price discrimination. To simplify the discussion, we assume that the firm is a monopoly and that it has constant marginal and average total costs. Panel (a) shows the case of a monopolist who cannot practice

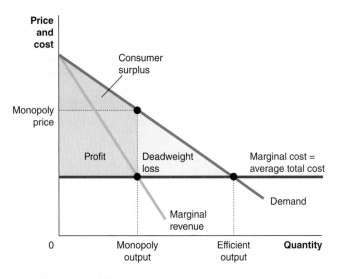

(a) A monopolist who cannot practice price discrimination

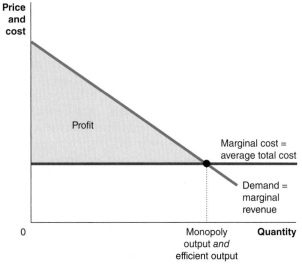

(b) A monopolist practicing perfect price discrimination

MyEconLab Animation

Figure 16.3 **Perfect Price Discrimination**

Panel (a) shows the case of a monopolist who cannot practice price discrimination and, therefore, can charge only a single price for its product. The graph shows that to maximize profit, the monopolist will produce the level of output where marginal revenue equals marginal cost. The resulting profit is shown by the area of the green rectangle. Given the monopoly price, the amount of consumer surplus in this market is shown by the area of the blue triangle. The economically efficient level of output occurs where price equals marginal cost. Because the monopolist stops production at a level of output where price is above marginal cost, there is a deadweight loss equal to the area of the yellow triangle. In panel (b), the monopolist is able to practice perfect price discrimination by charging a different price to each consumer. The result is to convert both the consumer surplus *and* the deadweight loss from panel (a) into profit.

price discrimination and, therefore, can charge only a single price for its product (see Chapter 15). The monopolist maximizes profit by producing the level of output where marginal revenue equals marginal cost. Recall that the economically efficient level of output occurs where price is equal to marginal cost, which is the level of output in a perfectly competitive market. Because the monopolist produces where price is greater than marginal cost, it causes a loss of economic efficiency equal to the area of the deadweight loss triangle in the figure.

Panel (b) shows the situation of a monopolist practicing perfect price discrimination. Because the firm can charge each consumer the maximum each consumer is willing to pay, its marginal revenue from selling one more unit is equal to the price of that unit. Therefore, the monopolist's marginal revenue curve becomes equal to its demand curve, and the firm will continue to produce up to the point where price is equal to marginal cost. It may seem like a paradox, but the ability to practice perfect price discrimination causes the monopolist to produce the efficient level of output. By doing so, the monopolist converts the consumer surplus *and* the deadweight loss in panel (a) into profits. In both panel (a) and panel (b), the profit shown is also producer surplus.

Even though the result in panel (b) is more economically efficient than the result in panel (a), consumers clearly are worse off because the amount of consumer surplus has been reduced to zero. We probably will never see a case of perfect price discrimination in the real world because firms typically do not know how much each consumer is willing to pay and, therefore, cannot charge each consumer a different price. Still, this extreme case helps us to see the two key results of price discrimination:

1. Profits increase.

2. Consumer surplus decreases.

Perfect price discrimination improves economic efficiency. Can we also say that this will be the case if price discrimination is less than perfect? Often, less-than-perfect price discrimination will improve economic efficiency. But under certain circumstances, it may actually reduce economic efficiency, so we can't draw a general conclusion. MyEconLab Concept Check

Price Discrimination across Time

Firms are sometimes able to engage in price discrimination over time. With this strategy, firms charge a higher price for a product when it is first introduced and a lower price later. Some consumers are *early adopters* who will pay a high price to be among the first to own certain new products. This pattern helps explain why DVD players, Blu-ray players, digital cameras, and flat-screen plasma televisions all sold for very high prices when they were first introduced. After the demand of the early adopters was satisfied, the companies reduced prices to attract more price-sensitive customers. For example, the price of DVD players dropped by 95 percent within five years of their introduction. Some of the price reductions over time for these products were also due to falling costs, as companies took advantage of economies of scale, but some represented price discrimination across time.

Book publishers routinely use price discrimination across time to increase profits. Hardcover editions of novels have much higher prices and are published months before paperback editions. For example, the hardcover edition of John Grisham's novel *The Racketeer* was published in October 2012 at a price of $28.95. The paperback edition was published in August 2013 for $9.99. Although this difference in price might seem to reflect the higher costs of producing hardcover books, in fact, it does not. The marginal cost of printing another copy of the hardcover edition is about $1.50. The marginal cost of printing another copy of the paperback edition is only slightly less, about $1.25. So, the difference in price between the hardcover and paperback editions is explained primarily by differences in demand. John Grisham's most devoted fans want to read his next book at the earliest possible moment and are not very sensitive to price. Many casual readers are also interested in Grisham's books but will read something else if the price of Grisham's latest book is too high.

As Figure 16.4 shows, a publisher will maximize profit by segmenting the market—in this case, across time—and by charging a higher price to the less elastic market segment and a lower price to the more elastic segment. (This example is similar to our earlier analysis of movie tickets in Figure 16.1 on page 512.) If the publisher had skipped the hardcover and issued only the paperback version at a price of $9.99 when the book was first published in October, its revenue would have dropped by the number of readers who bought the hardcover edition multiplied by the difference in price between the hardcover and paperback editions, or $500,000 \times (\$28.95 - \$9.99) = \$9,480,000$. MyEconLab Concept Check

Can Price Discrimination Be Illegal?

When discussing monopoly, we saw that Congress has passed *antitrust laws* to promote competition. Price discrimination may be illegal if its effect is to reduce competition in an industry (see Chapter 15). In 1936, Congress passed the Robinson–Patman Act, which outlawed price discrimination that reduced competition. The act also contained language that could be interpreted as making illegal *all* price discrimination not based on differences in cost. In the 1960s, the Federal Trade Commission sued Borden, Inc., under this act because Borden was selling the same evaporated milk for two different prices. Cans with the Borden label were sold for a high price, and cans the company sold to supermarkets to be repackaged as the supermarkets' private brands were sold for a much lower price. The courts ultimately ruled that Borden had not violated the law because the price differences increased, rather than reduced, competition in the market for evaporated milk. In recent years, the courts have interpreted the Robinson–Patman Act narrowly, allowing firms to use the types of price discrimination described in this chapter. MyEconLab Concept Check

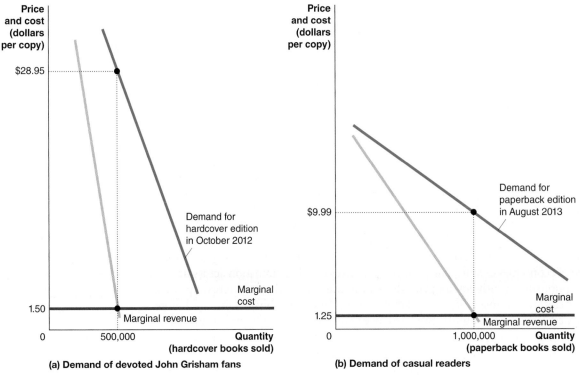

Price
and cost
(dollars
per copy)

$28.95

Demand for
hardcover edition
in October 2012

Marginal
cost

1.50

Marginal revenue

0   500,000   **Quantity
(hardcover books sold)**

(a) Demand of devoted John Grisham fans

Price
and cost
(dollars
per copy)

$9.99

Demand for
paperback edition
in August 2013

Marginal
cost

1.25

Marginal revenue

0   1,000,000   **Quantity
(paperback books sold)**

(b) Demand of casual readers

MyEconLab Animation

Figure 16.4   **Price Discrimination across Time**

Publishers issue most novels in hardcover editions at high prices to satisfy the demand of the novelists' most devoted fans. Later, publishers issue paperback editions
at much lower prices to capture sales from casual readers. In panel (a), with a marginal cost of $1.50 per copy for a hardcover edition, the profit-maximizing level of

output is 500,000 copies, which can be sold at a price of $28.95. In panel (b), the
more elastic demand of casual readers and the slightly lower marginal cost result
in a profit-maximizing output of 1,000,000 for the paperback edition, which can
be sold at a price of $9.99.

Making	The Internet Leaves You Open to Price
the	**Discrimination**
Connection	
MyEconLab Video	

Making
the
Connection
MyEconLab Video

**The Internet Leaves You Open to Price
Discrimination**

Have you ever used Google or Pricegrabber.com to search
for the best price for a book, a computer, or an airline ticket?
Although the Internet can help you compare prices among dif-
ferent Web sites, it can also be a way for some sellers to price discriminate. When you
log on to a Web site, its servers can gather important information about you, including your location—which can be determined from the address of your Internet Service
Provider (ISP)—and your browsing history. If the site already has your e-mail address,
it may be able to use an Internet data firm to learn facts about you, including your age,
race, gender, and income.

Reporters for the *Wall Street Journal* performed an experiment by logging on
to the Web site of Staples, the office supply store, from computers in many different
zip codes. They found that the Staples Web site displayed different prices for several
items based on the zip code of the person who logged on to the site. For example,
some people saw a price of $15.79 for a Swingline stapler, while other people saw a
price of $14.29 for the same stapler. Similarly, some people saw a price of $28.49 for
a 12-pack of Bic roller ball pens, while other people saw a price of $25.99. From the
analysis in this chapter, we know that Staples was attempting to use the information
it had gathered to estimate the price elasticities of demand of people shopping on its
site. Those people Staples believed to have a low price elasticity of demand would
see the high price for goods, and those Staples believed to have a high price elasticity
of demand would see the low price. Staples managers declined to explain their pricing strategy, so the reporters did a statistical analysis of the characteristics of the zip

codes. The most important characteristic turned out to be whether a zip code was within 20 miles of an OfficeMax or Office Depot store, which are Staples's main competitors. People living in zip codes close to a rival store were likely to see the low price, and people in zip codes far away from a rival store were likely to see the high price.

A number of firms in addition to Staples use this pricing strategy. Is the strategy an effective way of increasing profits? In the case of Staples, the firm was able to gather only limited information on potential buyers, so it was unable to effectively price discriminate. For example, the *Wall Street Journal* reporters found that the zip codes seeing the higher-priced stapler had lower average income than the zip codes seeing the lower-priced stapler, even though people with lower incomes might be expected to be more sensitive to price. More generally, Web sites using personal information to price discriminate run the risk of upsetting consumers. For instance, when told of Staples's price strategy, one person who had used the firm's Web site asked: "How can they get away with that?" For a brief time, Amazon varied prices on its site depending on a shopper's buying history. One customer saw a DVD price of $26.24 when he first logged on to the site. After deleting the "cookies" in his browser, so that he appeared to Amazon's servers to be a new customer, the price of the DVD dropped to $22.74. Widespread complaints about this pricing strategy caused Amazon to quickly drop it.

As Web sites become more sophisticated in gathering information about shoppers, they will have a greater ability to price discriminate. Whether negative reactions from consumers will cause sites to avoid this pricing strategy remains to be seen.

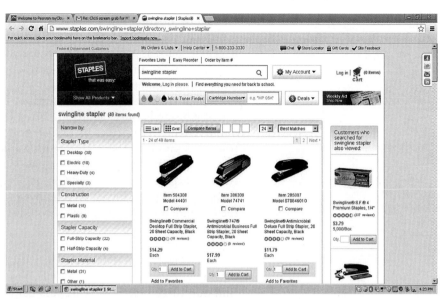

The price of this stapler may change depending on the consumer's zip code.

Sources: Jennifer Valentino-Devries, Jeremy Singer-Vine, and Ashkan Soltani, "Websites Vary Prices, Deals Based on Users' Information," *Wall Street Journal*, December 24, 2012; Jennifer Valentino-Devries and Jeremy Singer-Vine, "They Know What You're Shopping For," *Wall Street Journal*, December 7, 2012; and Anita Ramasastry, "Web Sites Change Prices Based on Customers' Habits," www.cnn.com, June 24, 2005.

Your Turn: Test your understanding by doing related problem 2.16 on pages 528–529 at the end of this chapter.

MyEconLab Study Plan

Other Pricing Strategies

16.3 LEARNING OBJECTIVE

Explain how some firms increase their profits by using odd pricing, cost-plus pricing, and two-part tariffs.

In addition to price discrimination, firms use many other pricing strategies, depending on the nature of their products, the level of competition in their markets, and the characteristics of their customers. In this section, we consider three important strategies: odd pricing, cost-plus pricing, and two-part tariffs.

Odd Pricing: Why Is the Price $2.99 Instead of $3.00?

Many firms use *odd pricing*—for example, charging $4.95 instead of $5.00, or $199 instead of $200. Surveys show that 80 percent to 90 percent of the products sold in supermarkets have prices ending in "9" or "5" rather than "0." Odd pricing has a long history. In the early nineteenth century, most goods in the United States were sold in general stores and did not have fixed prices. Instead, prices were often determined by haggling, much as prices of new cars are often determined today by haggling on dealers' lots. Later in the nineteenth century, when most products began to sell for a fixed price, odd pricing became popular.

There are different explanations for the origin of odd pricing. One explanation is that it began because goods imported from Great Britain had a reputation for high quality. When the prices of British goods in British currency—the pound—were translated into U.S. dollars, the result was an odd price. Because customers connected odd prices with high-quality goods, even sellers of domestic goods charged odd prices. Another explanation is that odd pricing began as an attempt to guard against employee theft. An odd price forced an employee to give the customer change, which reduced the likelihood that the employee would simply pocket the customer's money without recording the sale.

Whatever the origins of odd pricing, why do firms still use it today? The most obvious answer is that an odd price, say $9.99, seems somehow significantly—more than a penny—cheaper than $10.00. But do consumers really have this illusion? To find out, three market researchers conducted a study. We have seen that demand curves can be estimated statistically (see Chapter 3). If consumers have the illusion that $9.99 is significantly cheaper than $10.00, they will demand a greater quantity of goods at $9.99—and other odd prices—than the estimated demand curve predicts. The researchers surveyed consumers about their willingness to purchase six different products—ranging from a block of cheese to an electric blender—at a series of prices. Ten of the prices were either odd cent prices—99 cents or 95 cents—or odd dollar prices—$95 or $99. Nine of these 10 odd prices resulted in an odd-price effect, with the quantity demanded being greater than predicted using the estimated demand curve. The study was not conclusive because it relied on surveys rather than on observing actual purchasing behavior and because it used only a small group of products, but the study does provide some evidence that using odd prices makes economic sense.

Another study carried out in the 1990s used mail-order catalogs for women's clothing. With the cooperation of the clothing firm, some women were mailed catalogs with even dollar prices and other women received catalogs with prices ending in 99 cents. The women receiving the catalogs with prices ending in 99 cents bought 8 percent more clothes than the women receiving catalogs with even dollar prices.

Many firms have begun to use sales strategies that rely on insights from *behavioral economics*, which is the study of situations in which people make choices that do not appear to be economically rational (see Chapter 10). Odd pricing is an old strategy that is consistent with the modern analysis of behavioral economics.   MyEconLab Concept Check

Why Do McDonald's and Other Firms Use Cost-Plus Pricing?

Many firms use *cost-plus pricing*, which involves adding a percentage *markup* to average total cost. With this pricing strategy, the firm first calculates average total cost at a particular level of production, usually equal to the firm's expected sales. The firm then applies a percentage markup, say 30 percent, to the estimated average total cost to arrive at the price. For example, if average total cost is $100 and the percentage markup is 30 percent, the price will be $130. For a firm selling multiple products, the markup is intended to cover all costs, including those that the firm cannot assign to any particular product. Most firms have costs that are difficult to assign to one particular product. For example, the work performed by the employees in the accounting and finance departments at McDonald's applies to all of McDonald's products and can't be assigned directly to Big Macs or Happy Meals.   MyEconLab Concept Check

Making the Connection
MyEconLab Video

Cost-Plus Pricing in the Publishing Industry

Book publishing companies incur substantial costs for editing, designing, marketing, and warehousing books. These costs are difficult to assign directly to any particular book. Most publishers arrive at a price for a book by applying a markup to their production costs, which are usually divided into plant costs and manufacturing costs. Plant costs include typesetting the manuscript and preparing graphics or artwork for printing. Manufacturing costs include the costs of printing, paper, and binding the book.

Consider the following example for the hypothetical new book by Adam Smith, *How to Succeed at Economics without Really Trying*. We will assume that the book is 250 pages long, the publisher expects to sell 5,000 copies, and plant and manufacturing costs are as given in the following table:

Plant Costs		
	Typesetting	$3,500
	Other plant costs	2,000
Manufacturing Costs		
	Printing	$5,750
	Paper	6,250
	Binding	5,000
Total Production Cost		
		$22,500

With total production cost of $22,500 and production of 5,000 books, the per-unit production cost is $22,500/5,000 = $4.50. Many publishers multiply the unit production cost number by 7 or 8 to arrive at the retail price they will charge customers in bookstores. In this case, multiplying by 7 results in a price of $31.50 for the book. The markup seems quite high, but publishers typically sell books to bookstores at a 40 percent discount. Although a customer in a bookstore will pay $31.50 for the book—or less, of course, if it is purchased from a bookseller that discounts the retail price—the publisher receives only $18.90. The difference between the $18.90 received from the bookstore and the $4.50 production cost equals the cost of editing, marketing, warehousing, paying a royalty to the author of the book, and all other costs, including the opportunity cost of the investment in the firm by its owners, plus any economic profit the owners receive.

Source: Beth Luey, *Handbook for Academic Authors*, 5th ed., New York: Cambridge University Press, 2010.

Your Turn: Test your understanding by doing related problem 3.8 on page 530 at the end of this chapter.

MyEconLab Study Plan

We have seen that firms maximize profit by producing the quantity where marginal revenue equals marginal cost and charging a price that will cause consumers to buy that quantity. The cost-plus approach doesn't appear to maximize profit unless the cost-plus price turns out to be the same as the price that will cause the marginal revenue earned on the last unit to equal the unit's marginal cost. Economists have two views of cost-plus pricing. One is that cost-plus pricing is simply a mistake that firms should avoid. The other view is that cost-plus pricing is a good way to come close to the profit-maximizing price when either marginal revenue or marginal cost is difficult to calculate.

Small firms often like cost-plus pricing because it is easy to use. Unfortunately, these firms can fall into the trap of mechanically applying a cost-plus pricing rule, which may result in charging prices that do not maximize profit. The most obvious problems with cost-plus pricing are that it ignores demand and focuses on average total cost rather than marginal cost. If a firm's marginal cost is significantly different from its average total cost at its current level of production, cost-plus pricing is unlikely to maximize profit.

Despite these problems, cost-plus pricing is used by some large firms that have the knowledge and resources to devise a better method of pricing if cost-plus pricing fails to maximize profit. Economists conclude that using cost-plus pricing may be the best way to determine the optimal price in two situations:

1. When marginal cost and average total cost are roughly equal

2. When a firm has difficulty estimating its demand curve

In fact, most large firms that use cost-plus pricing do not just mechanically apply a markup to their estimate of average total cost. Instead, they adjust the markup to reflect their best estimate of current demand. A large firm is likely to have a pricing policy committee that adjusts prices based on the current state of competition in the industry and the current state of the economy. If competition is strong in a weak economy, the pricing committee may decide to set price significantly below the cost-plus price.

In general, firms that take demand into account will charge lower markups on products that are more price elastic and higher markups on products that are less elastic. Supermarkets, where cost-plus pricing is widely used, have markups in the 5 to 10 percent range for products with more elastic demand, such as soft drinks and breakfast cereals, and markups in the 50 percent range for products with less elastic demand, such as fresh fruits and vegetables.

Why Do Some Firms Use Two-Part Tariffs?

Some firms require consumers to pay an initial fee for the right to buy their product and an additional fee for each unit of the product purchased. For example, many golf and tennis clubs require members to buy an annual membership in addition to paying a fee each time they use the golf course or tennis court. Sam's Club requires consumers to pay a membership fee before shopping at its stores. Cellphone companies sometimes charge a monthly fee and then have a per-minute charge after a certain number of minutes have been used. Economists call this pricing strategy a **two-part tariff**.

Two-part tariff A situation in which consumers pay one price (or tariff) for the right to buy as much of a related good as they want at a second price.

The Walt Disney Company is in a position to use a two-part tariff by charging consumers for admission to Walt Disney World or Disneyland and also charging them to use the rides in the parks. As mentioned at the beginning of this chapter, at one time, the admission price to Disneyland was low, but people had to purchase tickets to go on the rides. Today, you must pay a high price for admission to Disneyland or Disney World, but the rides are free once you're in the park. Figure 16.5 helps us understand which of these pricing strategies is more profitable for Disney. The numbers in the figure are simplified to make the calculations easier.

Once visitors are inside the park, Disney is in the position of a monopolist: No other firm is operating rides in Disney World. So, we can draw panel (a) in Figure 16.5 to represent the market for rides at Disney World. This graph looks like the standard monopoly graph (see Chapter 15). (Note that the marginal cost of another rider is quite low. We assume that it is a constant $2 and equal to the average total cost.) It seems obvious—but it will turn out to be wrong!—that Disney should determine the profit-maximizing quantity of ride tickets by setting marginal revenue equal to marginal cost. In this case, the result would be 20,000 ride tickets sold per day at a price of $26 per ride. Disney's profit from selling *ride tickets* is shown by the area of rectangle *B*. The area equals the difference between the $26 price and the average total cost of $2, multiplied by the 20,000 tickets sold, or ($26 − $2) × 20,000 = $480,000. Disney also has a second source of profit from selling *admission tickets* to the park. Given the $26 price for ride tickets, what price would Disney be able to charge for admission tickets?

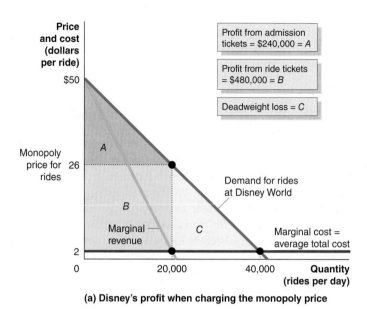

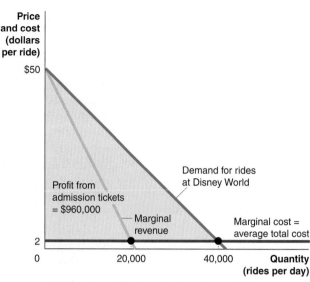

Figure 16.5 A Two-Part Tariff at Disney World

In panel (a), Disney charges the monopoly price of $26 per ride ticket and sells 20,000 ride tickets. Its profit from *ride tickets* is shown by the area of rectangle *B*, or $480,000. If Disney is in the position of knowing every consumer's willingness to pay, it can also charge a price for *admission tickets* that would result in the total amount paid for admission tickets being equal to total consumer surplus from the rides. Total consumer surplus from the rides equals the area of the triangle, *A*, or $240,000. So, when charging the monopoly price, Disney's total profit equals $480,000 + $240,000 or $720,000. In panel (b), Disney charges the perfectly competitive price of $2, which results in a quantity of 40,000 ride tickets sold. At the lower ride ticket price, Disney can charge a higher price for admission tickets, which will increase its total profits from operating the park to the area of the green triangle, or $960,000.

Let's assume the following for simplicity: The only reason people want admission to Disney World is to go on the rides, all consumers have the same individual demand curve for rides, and Disney knows what this demand curve is. This last assumption allows Disney to practice perfect price discrimination. More realistic assumptions would make the outcome of the analysis somewhat different but would not affect the main point of how Disney uses a two-part tariff to increase its profits. With these assumptions, we can use the concept of consumer surplus to calculate the maximum total amount consumers would be willing to pay for admission. Remember that consumer surplus is equal to the area below the demand curve and above the price line, shown by the the area of triangle *A* in panel (a). Consumers would not be willing to pay more for admission to the park than the consumer surplus they receive from the rides. In panel (a) of Figure 16.5, the total consumer surplus when Disney charges a price of $26 per ride is $240,000. (This number is easy to calculate if you remember that the formula for the area of a triangle is ½ × base × height, or ½ × 20,000 × $24.) Disney can set the price of admission tickets so that the *total* amount spent by buyers would be $240,000. In other words, Disney can set the price of admission to capture the entire consumer surplus from the rides. So, Disney's total profit from Disney World would be the $240,000 it receives from admission tickets plus the $480,000 in profit from the rides, or $720,000 per day.

Is this the most profit Disney can earn from selling admission tickets and ride tickets? The answer is "no." The key to understanding why is to notice that *the lower the price Disney charges for ride tickets, the higher the price it can charge for admission tickets.* Lower-priced ride tickets increase consumer surplus from the rides and, therefore, increase the willingness of buyers to pay a higher price for admission tickets. In panel (b) of Figure 16.5, we assume that Disney acts as it would in a perfectly competitive market and charges a price for ride tickets that is equal to marginal cost, or $2. Charging this price increases consumer surplus—*and* the maximum total amount that Disney can charge for admission tickets—from $240,000 to $960,000. (Once again, we use the

	Monopoly Price for Rides	Competitive Price for Rides
Profits from admission tickets	$240,000	$960,000
Profits from ride tickets	480,000	0
Total profit	720,000	960,000

formula for the area of a triangle to calculate the area of the green triangle in panel (b): $\frac{1}{2} \times 40,000 \times 48 = \$960,000$.) Disney's profits from the rides will decline to zero because it is now charging a price equal to average total cost, *but its total profit from Disney World will rise from $720,000 to $960,000 per day.* Table 16.2 summarizes this result.

What is the source of Disney's increased profit from charging a price equal to marginal cost? Disney has converted what was deadweight loss when the monopoly price was charged—the area of triangle C in panel (a)—into consumer surplus. Disney then turns this consumer surplus into profit by increasing the price of admission tickets.

It is important to note the following about the outcome of a firm using an optimal two-part tariff:

1. Because price equals marginal cost at the level of output supplied, the outcome is economically efficient.

2. All consumer surplus is transformed into profit.

Notice that, in effect, Disney is practicing perfect price discrimination. As we noted in our discussion of perfect price discrimination on page 515, Disney's use of a two-part tariff has increased the amount of the product—in this case, rides at Disney World—consumers are able to purchase but has eliminated consumer surplus. Although it may seem paradoxical, consumer surplus was actually higher when consumers were being charged the monopoly price for the rides. The solution to the paradox is that although consumers pay a lower price for the rides when Disney employs a two-part tariff, the overall amount they pay to be at Disney World increases.

Disney actually does follow the profit-maximizing strategy of charging a high price for admission to the park and a very low price—zero—for the rides. It seems that Disney could increase its profits by raising the price for the rides from zero to the marginal cost of the rides. But the marginal cost is so low that it would not be worth the expense of printing ride tickets and hiring additional workers to sell the tickets and collect them at each ride. Finally, note that in practice Disney can't convert all consumer surplus into profit because (1) the demand curves of customers are not all the same, and (2) Disney does not know precisely what these demand curves are.

MyEconLab Study Plan

MyEconLab Concept Check

Continued from page 507

Economics in Your Life

Why So Many Prices to See a Movie?

At the beginning of the chapter, we asked you to think about what you pay for a movie ticket and what people in other age groups pay. A movie theater will try to charge different prices to different consumers, based on their willingness to pay. If you have two otherwise identical people, one a student and one not, you might assume that the student has less income, and therefore a lower willingness to pay, than the nonstudent, and the movie theater would like to charge the student a lower price. The movie theater employee can ask to see a student ID to ensure that the theater is giving the discount to a student.

But why don't theaters practice price discrimination at the concession stand? It is likely that a student will also have a lower willingness to pay for popcorn, and the theater can check for a student ID at the time of purchase, but unlike with the entry ticket, the theater would have a hard time preventing the student from giving the popcorn to a nonstudent once inside the theater. Because it is easier to limit resale in movie admissions, we often see different prices for different groups. Because it is difficult to limit resale of popcorn and other movie concessions, everyone will typically pay the same price.

Conclusion

Firms in perfectly competitive industries must sell their products at the market price. For firms in other industries—which means, of course, the vast majority of firms—pricing is an important part of the strategy used to maximize profits. We have seen in this chapter, for example, that if firms can successfully segment their customers into different groups on the basis of the customers' willingness to pay, the firms can increase their profits by charging different segments different prices.

Visit MyEconLab for a news article and analysis related to the concepts in this chapter.

Chapter Summary and Problems

Key Terms

Price discrimination, p. 510   Transactions costs, p. 508   Two-part tariff, p. 522

 16.1 Pricing Strategy, the Law of One Price, and Arbitrage, pages 508–510
LEARNING OBJECTIVE: Define the law of one price and explain the role of arbitrage.

Summary

According to the *law of one price*, identical products should sell for the same price everywhere. If a product sells for different prices, it will be possible to make a profit through *arbitrage*: buying a product at a low price and reselling it at a high price. The law of one price will hold as long as arbitrage is possible. Arbitrage is sometimes blocked by high **transactions costs**, which are the costs in time and other resources incurred to carry out an exchange or because the product cannot be resold. Another apparent exception to the law of one price occurs when companies offset the higher price they charge for a product by providing superior or more reliable service to customers.

MyEconLab   Visit **www.myeconlab.com** to complete these exercises online and get instant feedback.

Review Questions

1.1 What is the law of one price? What is arbitrage?

1.2 Does a product always have to sell for the same price everywhere? Briefly explain.

Problems and Applications

1.3 A newspaper article contains the following description of New York consumers avoiding the state's 8.375 percent sales tax by shopping in New Jersey:

> For years, shoppers from New York City have played a game of retail arbitrage, traveling to the many malls in northern New Jersey, a state where there is no tax on clothing and shoes.

Does this article use the word arbitrage as it is used in this chapter? Briefly explain.

Source: Ken Belson and Nate Schweber, "Sales Tax Cut in City May Dim Allure of Stores Across Hudson," *New York Times*, January 18, 2007.

1.4 The following table contains the actual prices four Web sites charged for a Blu-ray disc of the movie *X-Men: First Class*:

Amazon	$24.99
Wal-Mart	24.96
OrlandsBricks	21.58
ranch_records	17.75

On Google's price comparison Web site, which allows customers to rate the seller, Amazon had been rated by 6,233 people, Wal-Mart had been rated by 835 people, ranch_records had been rated by 153 people, and OrlandsBricks had not been rated by anyone. Briefly explain whether the information in this table contradicts the law of one price.

1.5 **[Related to** Solved Problem 16.1 **on page 509]** Suppose California has many apple trees, and the price of apples there is low. Nevada has few apple trees, and the price of apples there is high. Abner buys low-priced California apples and ships them to Nevada, where he resells them at a high price. Is Abner exploiting Nevada consumers by doing this? Is Abner likely to earn an economic profit in the long run? Briefly explain.

1.6 **[Related to** Solved Problem 16.1 **on page 509]** Suspicions about arbitrage have a long history. For example, Valerian of Cimiez, a Catholic bishop who lived during the fifth century, wrote: "When something is bought cheaply only so it can be retailed dearly, doing business always means cheating." What might Valerian think of eBay? Do you agree with his conclusion? Briefly explain.

Source: Michael McCormick, *The Origins of the European Economy: Communications and Commerce*, A.D. 300–900, New York: Cambridge University Press, 2001, p. 85.

 16.2 Price Discrimination: Charging Different Prices for the Same Product, pages 510–519
LEARNING OBJECTIVE: Explain how a firm can increase its profits through price discrimination.

Summary

Price discrimination occurs if a firm charges different prices for the same product when the price differences are not due to differences in cost. Three requirements must be met for a firm to successfully practice price discrimination: (1) A firm must possess market power; (2) some consumers must have a greater willingness to pay for the product than other consumers, and firms must be able to know what consumers are willing to pay; and (3) firms must be able to divide up—or segment—the market for the product so that consumers who buy the product at a low price cannot resell it at a high price. In the case of *perfect price discrimination*, each consumer pays a price equal to the consumer's willingness to pay.

MyEconLab   Visit **www.myeconlab.com** to complete these exercises online and get instant feedback.

Review Questions

2.1 What is price discrimination? Under what circumstances can a firm successfully practice price discrimination?

2.2 In 2013, the Rock and Roll Hall of Fame and Museum charged adults $22 for admission. Seniors (65 years and older) and military personnel were charged $17, and children between 9 and 12 years old were charged $13. Use the admission fees to rank these groups based on their elasticities of demand from highest to lowest.

Source: www.rockhall.com.

2.3 What is yield management? Give an example of a firm using yield management to increase profits.

2.4 What is perfect price discrimination? Is it likely to ever occur? Explain. Is perfect price discrimination economically efficient? Explain.

2.5 Is it possible to practice price discrimination across time? Briefly explain.

Problems and Applications

2.6 According to an article in the *Wall Street Journal*:

> Airlines have increased restrictions on cheap fares by raising overnight requirements, upping what had commonly been only a one-night stay requirement to two and three nights. The overnights can be weeknights, so those tickets aren't as onerous as Saturday-night stay tickets. But the three-night requirement does limit the utility of discounted fares for road warriors.

What is a "road warrior"? Why would a company put restrictions on a service that make the service less desirable to some of its customers?

Source: Scott McCartney, "Airlines Revive Minimum Stays on Cheap Fares," *Wall Street Journal*, August 19, 2008.

2.7 A newspaper article provides advice to airline travelers: "The ideal time to book domestic travel last year was 21 to 35 days before departure and within three months before departure for international travel." Why would airlines offer their lowest prices so far in advance of the day of the flight? Wouldn't the airlines be better off discounting only

just before the day of the flight when they know how many empty seats they have left to fill?

Source: Scott McCartney, "The Best Places to Fly This Summer," *Wall Street Journal*, May 1, 2013.

2.8 Political columnist Michael Kinsley wrote: "The infuriating [airline] rules about Saturday night stayovers and so on are a crude alternative to administering truth serum and asking, 'So how much are you really willing to pay?'" Would a truth serum—or some other way of knowing how much people would be willing to pay for an airline ticket—really be all the airlines need in order to practice price discrimination? Briefly explain.

Source: Michael Kinsley, "Consuming Gets More Complicated," *Slate*, November 21, 2001.

2.9 Journalist Timothy Noah discovered that when he called up the *New York Times* and threatened to end his subscription, he was offered a 50 percent discount on the regular subscription price. He became convinced that anyone who called up and threatened to end his or her subscription would be offered the same discount. Briefly explain whether the *New York Times* is practicing price discrimination.

Source: Timothy Noah, "Wise Up, Print Addicts!" www.slate.com, November 17, 2010.

2.10 **[Related to the** Don't Let This Happen to You **on page 510]** A state law in California makes it illegal for businesses to charge men and women different prices for dry cleaning, laundry, tailoring, or hair grooming. The state legislator who introduced the law did so after a dry cleaner charged her more to have her shirts dry cleaned than to have her husband's shirts dry cleaned. According to a newspaper article, the owner of the dry cleaner told the legislator that his costs for cleaning women's shirts were higher because he had to iron them by hand rather than use an automatic press. The law proved difficult to enforce, with many dry cleaners continuing to ignore it years after it was passed.

a. Was the dry cleaner practicing price discrimination, as defined in this chapter? Briefly explain.

b. Do you support laws like this one? Briefly explain.

Source: Veronique de Turenne, "Santa Monica Sues Nine Dry Cleaners under Gender Discrimination Law," *Los Angeles Times*, May 13, 2008; and Harry Brooks, "Law Mandates Equality in Dry Cleaning, Hair Styling," *North County (California) Times*, October 7, 2001.

2.11 **[Related to** Solved Problem 16.2 **on page 512]** Use the graphs on the next page to answer the questions.

a. If this firm wants to maximize profits, what price will it charge in Market 1, and what quantity will it sell?

b. If this firm wants to maximize profits, what price will it charge in Market 2, and what quantity will it sell?

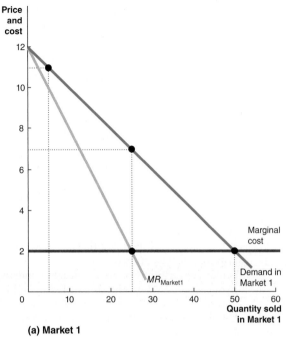

(a) Market 1

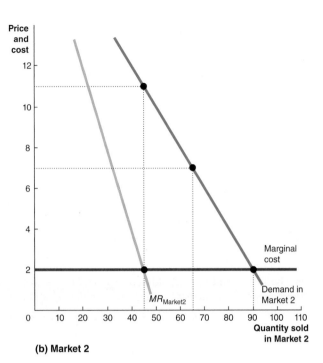

(b) Market 2

2.12 **[Related to** Solved Problem 16.2 **on page 512]** In mid-2013, Apple was offering a $100 discount to students on MacBook Pro laptops but only $50 on MacBook Air laptops. The MacBook Air is a very thin, light laptop that is particularly aimed at businesspeople who travel frequently. Why would Apple cut the price more for MacBook Pros than for MacBook Airs?

2.13 **[Related to** Solved Problem 16.2 **on page 512]** In addition to discounting the price of computers purchased by students and faculty, Apple sells certain computer models only to schools and universities. According to a discussion on the MacRumors blog:

> Apple has quietly launched a lower cost $999 iMac for educational institutions this morning. The new low-end model is labeled "Education only" and is not available for individuals.... Apple, in the past, has also offered special education only models for institutions ... [and] has adjusted the hardware down in order to fit the sub-$1000 price point.

Is Apple engaging in price discrimination in following this policy? If so, why does it prepare special models for educational institutions rather than cutting the prices of existing models purchased by educational buyers? If this is not an example of price discrimination, why doesn't Apple offer these computers to the general public?

Source: "Apple Launches $999 iMac for Educational Institutions," by Arnold Kim. From www.macrumors.com, August 8, 2011. Reprinted with permission.

2.14 **[Related to the** Making the Connection **on page 515]** Assume that the marginal cost of admitting one more student is constant for every university. Also assume that at every university, the demand for places in the freshman class is downward sloping. Now, suppose that the public becomes upset that universities charge different prices to different students. Responding to these concerns, the federal government requires universities to charge the same price to each student. In this situation, who will gain, and who will lose?

2.15 **[Related to the** Chapter Opener **on page 507]** Walt Disney World charges residents of Florida lower prices for various theme park ticket packages than it charges non-Florida residents. For example, in 2013 an adult Florida resident was charged $190.64 for a three-day "Magic Your Way" package that included lodging at a Disney Resort hotel and a ticket to one theme park per day. The price of the same package for a non-Florida resident was $326.96.

  a. What is Disney assuming about the willingness to pay of Florida residents? Why might it make this assumption?

  b. How might Disney keep Florida residents from buying Walt Disney World tickets at discounted prices and reselling them to non-Florida residents at higher prices?

  c. Disney offers discount tickets to students at universities located in Florida, but does not offer discount tickets to students at most universities in other states. Briefly explain Disney's strategy. Would you expect the discount Disney offers to students at Florida universities to be higher or lower than the discount it offers to other residents of Florida? Briefly explain.

Source: Disney prices from allears.net, June 23, 2013.

2.16 **[Related to the** Making the Connection **on page 518]** Many supermarkets provide regular shoppers with "loyalty cards" that the shoppers swipe each time they checkout. By swiping the card, the shopper receives reduced prices on a few goods and the supermarket compiles information on all the shoppers' purchases. Recently, some supermarkets have switched from giving the same price reductions to all shoppers to giving shoppers differing price reductions depending on their shopping history. A manager at one company that uses this approach said: "It comes down to understanding elasticity at a household level."

a. Is the use of loyalty cards that provide the same price discounts for every shopper who uses them a form of price discrimination? Briefly explain.

b. Why would making price discounts depend on a shopper's buying history involve "elasticity at a household level"? What information from a shopper's buying history would be relevant in predicting the shopper's response to a price discount?

Source: Stephanie Clifford, "Shopper Alert: Price May Drop for You Alone," *New York Times*, August 9, 2012.

2.17 One company sells underpads that can be used on the beds of people who are ill or the sleeping area for dogs that are being house trained. The packages for dogs are different and have a different brand name than the packages for people, but the pads in the packages are identical. Recently on Amazon, the company was selling the pads for dogs at a price that was 11 percent higher than the price they charged for the pads for people.

a. How is the company able to price discriminate in this situation?

b. Why would the company sell the pads for dogs at a higher price than the pads for people?

2.18 General Mills periodically puts $1 coupons in Sunday newspapers and online for large boxes of its Cheerios breakfast cereal. Why doesn't General Mills just charge $1 less for Cheerios instead of using coupons? Is issuing coupons a form of price discrimination? Briefly explain.

2.19 Yasiel has a monopoly on sales of pizzas in the small town of North Key Largo, Florida. Use the following information on the demand for Yasiel's pizzas to answer the questions:

Price	Quantity Demanded
$30	0
25	1
20	2
15	3
10	4
5	5
0	6

a. If Yasiel can produce pizzas at a constant cost of $5 per pizza, how many pizzas does he produce, what price does he charge, and how much profit does he make?

b. If Yasiel is able to engage in perfect price discrimination, what is his total revenue for 3 units? What is the marginal revenue of the third unit?

c. If Yasiel is able to engage in perfect price discrimination, how many pizzas does he produce and how much profit does he make?

d. Draw a graph showing producer surplus, consumer surplus, and deadweight loss if Yasiel does not price discriminate. Draw a second graph showing producer surplus, consumer surplus, and deadweight loss if he practices perfect price discrimination.

16.3 | **Other Pricing Strategies, pages 519–524**

LEARNING OBJECTIVE: Explain how some firms increase their profits by using odd pricing, cost-plus pricing, and two-part tariffs.

Summary

In addition to price discrimination, firms use *odd pricing*, *cost-plus pricing*, and *two-part tariffs* as pricing strategies. Firms use *odd pricing*—for example, charging $1.99 rather than $2.00—because consumers tend to buy more at odd prices than would be predicted from estimated demand curves. With *cost-plus pricing*, firms set the price for a product by adding a percentage markup to average total cost. Using cost-plus pricing may be a good way to come close to the profit-maximizing price when marginal revenue or marginal cost is difficult to measure. Some firms can require consumers to pay an initial fee for the right to buy their product and an additional fee for each unit of the product purchased. Economists refer to this situation as a **two-part tariff**. Sam's Club, cellphone companies, and many golf and tennis clubs use two-part tariffs in pricing their products.

MyEconLab   Visit **www.myeconlab.com** to complete these exercises online and get instant feedback.

Review Questions

3.1 What is odd pricing?

3.2 What is cost-plus pricing? Is using cost-plus pricing consistent with a firm maximizing profit? How does the elasticity of demand affect the percentage price markup that firms use?

3.3 Give an example of a firm using a two-part tariff as part of its pricing strategy.

Problems and Applications

3.4 One leading explanation for odd pricing is that it allows firms to trick buyers into thinking they are paying less than they really are. If this explanation is correct, in what types of markets and among what groups of consumers would you be most likely to find odd pricing? Should the government ban this practice and force companies to round up their prices to the nearest dollar?

3.5 According to an article in the *Wall Street Journal*, McDonald's and Burger King have much larger markups on French fries and sodas than on hamburgers. Is it likely that the companies believe that the demand for French fries and sodas is more elastic or less elastic than the demand for hamburgers? Briefly explain.

Source: Diana Ransom, "Can They Really Make Money Off the Dollar Menu?" *Wall Street Journal*, May 21, 2009.

3.6 According to an article in the *Wall Street Journal*, most restaurants in New York City price wine at a 300 percent markup over the price the restaurants pay for the wine. The restaurants use a much smaller markup on the food they serve. What might explain the difference in the markups?

Source: Lettie Teague, "Highs and (Rare) Lows in Restaurant Wine Prices," *Wall Street Journal*, June 21, 2013.

3.7 An article in the *Wall Street Journal* gave the following explanation of how products were traditionally priced at Parker-Hannifin Corporation:

> For as long as anyone at the 89-year-old company could recall, Parker used the same simple formula to determine prices of its 800,000 parts—from heat-resistant seals for jet engines to steel valves that hoist buckets on cherry pickers. Company managers would calculate how much it cost to make and deliver each product and add a flat percentage on top, usually aiming for about 35%. Many managers liked the method because it was straightforward.

Is it likely that this system of pricing maximized the firm's profit? Briefly explain.

Source: Timothy Aeppel, "Seeking Perfect Prices, CEO Tears Up the Rules," *Wall Street Journal*, March 27, 2007.

3.8 **[Related to the** Making the Connection **on page 521]** Would you expect a publishing company to use a strict cost-plus pricing system for all its books? How might you find some indication about whether a publishing company actually was using cost-plus pricing for all its books?

3.9 Some professional sports teams charge fans a one-time lump sum for a personal seat license. The personal seat license allows a fan the right to buy season tickets each year. No one without a personal seat license can buy season tickets. After the original purchase from the team, the personal seat licenses usually can be bought and sold by fans—whoever owns the seat license in a given year can buy season tickets—but the team does not earn any additional revenue from this buying and selling. Suppose a new sports stadium has been built, and the team is trying to decide on the price to charge for season tickets.
   a. Will the team make more profit from the combination of selling personal seat licenses and season tickets if it keeps the prices of the season tickets low or if it charges the monopoly price? Briefly explain.
   b. After the first year, is the team's strategy for pricing season tickets likely to change?

   c. Will it make a difference in the team's pricing strategy for season tickets if all the personal seat licenses are sold in the first year?

3.10 During the nineteenth century, the U.S. Congress encouraged railroad companies to build transcontinental railways across the Great Plains by giving them land grants. At that time, the federal government owned most of the land on the Great Plains. The land grants consisted of the land on which the railway was built and alternating sections of 1 square mile each on either side of the railway to a distance of 6 to 40 miles, depending on the location. The railroad companies were free to sell this land to farmers or anyone else who wanted to buy it. The process of selling the land took decades. Some economic historians have argued that the railroad companies charged lower prices to ship freight because they owned so much land along the tracks. Briefly explain the reasoning of these economic historians.

3.11 **[Related to the** Chapter Opener **on page 507]** If you visited Disneyland between 1955 and 1982, you could not go on most rides without buying a ticket for the ride—in addition to the ticket necessary to enter the park. Explain why this pricing strategy earned Disney a lower profit than the current strategy of requiring visitors to purchase a ticket to enter the park but not requiring an additional ticket to be purchased for each ride.

3.12 Thomas Kinnaman, an economist at Bucknell University, has analyzed the pricing of garbage collection:

> Setting the appropriate fee for garbage collection can be tricky when there are both fixed and marginal costs of garbage collection…. A curbside price set equal to the average total cost of collection would have high garbage generators partially subsidizing the fixed costs of low garbage generators. For example, if the time that a truck idles outside a one-can household and a two-can household is the same, and the fees are set to cover the total cost of garbage collection, then the two-can household paying twice that of the one-can household has subsidized a portion of the collection costs of the one-can household.

Briefly explain how a city might solve this pricing problem by using a two-part tariff in setting the garbage collection fees it charges households.

Source: Thomas C. Kinnaman, "Examining the Justification for Residential Recycling," *Journal of Economic Perspectives*, Vol. 20, No. 4, Fall 2006.

The Markets for Labor and Other Factors of Production

Chapter Outline and Learning Objectives

Who Is Zach Greinke and Why Is He Being Paid $147 Million?

Few businesses generate as much passion as sports teams. Sports fans admire the skills of star athletes, but many people question why they are paid high salaries "just for playing a game." Some fans also get frustrated when their teams lose star players to wealthier teams that can afford to sign players to long-term contracts for large salaries. Zack Greinke is a star baseball pitcher who won the Cy Young Award in 2009 as the best pitcher in the American League. Yet in 2013, Greinke was playing for the fourth team since he started his major league career in 2004 with the Kansas City Royals. The Royals couldn't afford to sign Greinke to a long-term contract and traded him to the Milwaukee Brewers in 2010, who in turn traded him to the Los Angeles Angels in 2012. Following the 2012 season, Greinke became a free agent and was eligible to sign with any team. The Los Angeles Dodgers signed Greinke to a contract that will pay him $147 million over six years—making him one of the highest paid players in history.

In 2013, the Dodgers sold the rights to televise their games to Time Warner Cable for more than $6 *billion* over a 25-year period. Because of the high revenues the Dodgers generate from ticket sales, cable television, and broadcast television and radio, they can afford to pay more for players than teams such as the Milwaukee Brewers and Kansas City Royals that play in smaller cities.

Throughout this book we have been using a demand and supply model to analyze the markets for goods and services. We will use some of the same concepts in this chapter to analyze the markets for labor and other factors of production. But there are important differences between the markets for factors of production and the markets for goods and services. The most obvious difference is that in factor markets, firms are demanders and households are suppliers.

Another difference between the labor market and the markets for goods and services is that concepts of fairness arise more frequently in labor markets. When an athlete signs a contract for millions of dollars, people often wonder: "Why should someone playing a game get paid so much more than teachers, nurses, and other people doing more important jobs?" Because people typically earn most of their income from wages and salaries, they often view the labor market as the most important market in which they participate.

Sources: Jonah Keri, "Pondering Zack Greinke's $147 Million Deal," www.grantland.com, December 10, 2012; and Bill Shaikin, "Dodgers to Keep More than $6 Billion from TV Contract in Tentative Pact," *Los Angeles Times*, June 13, 2013.

Economics in Your Life

How Can You Convince Your Boss to Give You a Raise?

Imagine that you have worked for a local sandwich shop for over a year and are preparing to ask for a raise. You might tell the manager that you are a good employee, with a good attitude and work ethic. You might also explain that you have learned more about your job and are now able to make sandwiches more quickly, track inventory more accurately, and work the cash register more effectively than when you were first hired. Will this be enough to convince your manager to give you a raise? How can you convince your manager that you are worth a higher wage than you are currently being paid? As you read this chapter, try to answer these questions. You can check your answers against those we provide on **page 559** at the end of this chapter.

Factors of production Labor, capital, natural resources, and other inputs used to produce goods and services.

Firms use **factors of production**—such as labor, capital, and natural resources—to produce goods and services. For example, the Los Angeles Dodgers use labor (baseball players), capital (Dodger Stadium), and natural resources (the land on which Dodger Stadium sits) to produce baseball games. In this chapter, we will explore how firms choose the profit-maximizing quantity of labor and other factors of production. The interaction between firms' demand for labor and households' supply of labor determines the equilibrium wage rate.

Because there are many different types of labor, there are many different labor markets. The equilibrium wage in the market for baseball players is much higher than the equilibrium wage in the market for college professors. We will analyze why. We will also analyze how factors such as discrimination, unions, and compensation for dangerous or unpleasant jobs help explain differences in wages. We will then look at *personnel economics*, which is concerned with how firms can use economic analysis to design their employee compensation plans. Finally, we will analyze the markets for other factors of production.

Explain how firms choose the profit-maximizing quantity of labor to employ.

Derived demand The demand for a factor of production; it depends on the demand for the good the factor produces.

The Demand for Labor

Until now, we have concentrated on consumer demand for final goods and services. The demand for labor is different from the demand for final goods and services because it is a *derived demand*. A **derived demand** for a factor of production depends on the demand for the good the factor produces. You demand an Apple iPhone because of the utility you receive from making phone calls, texting, posting to Facebook, playing games, and listening to music. Apple's demand for the labor to make iPhones is derived from the underlying consumer demand for iPhones. As a result, we can say that Apple's demand for labor depends primarily on two factors:

1. The additional iPhones Apple can produce if it hires one more worker
2. The additional revenue Apple receives from selling the additional iPhones

(In fact, Apple's suppliers, rather than Apple itself, manufacture the iPhone. For simplicity, we are assuming here that Apple does the manufacturing.)

The Marginal Revenue Product of Labor

Let's consider an example. To keep the main point clear, we'll assume that in the short run, Apple can increase production of iPhones only by increasing the quantity of labor it employs. The table in Figure 17.1 shows the relationship between the quantity of workers Apple hires, the quantity of iPhones it produces, the additional revenue from selling the additional iPhones, and the additional profit from hiring each additional worker.

Marginal product of labor The additional output a firm produces as a result of hiring one more worker.

For simplicity, we are keeping the scale of Apple's factory very small. We will also assume that Apple is a perfect competitor both in the market for selling cellphones and in the market for hiring labor. As a result, Apple is a *price taker* in both markets. Although this assumption is not realistic, the basic analysis would not change if we assumed that Apple can affect the price of cellphones and the wage paid to workers. Suppose that Apple can sell as many iPhones as it wants at a price of $200 and can hire as many workers as it wants at a wage of $600 per week. Remember that the additional output a firm produces as a result of hiring one more worker is called the **marginal product of labor** (see Chapter 11). In the table in Figure 17.1, we calculate the marginal product of labor as the change in total output as each additional worker is hired. Because of *the law of diminishing returns*, the marginal product of labor declines as a firm hires more workers.

When deciding how many workers to hire, a firm is not interested in how much *output* will increase as it hires another worker but in how much *revenue* will increase as it hires another worker. In other words, what matters is how much the firm's revenue will rise when it sells the additional output it can produce by hiring one more worker.

MyEconLab Animation

Number of Workers	Output of iPhones per Week	Marginal Product of Labor (iPhones per week)	Product Price	Marginal Revenue Product of Labor (dollars per week)	Wage (dollars per week)	Additional Profit from Hiring One More Worker (dollars per week)
L	Q	MP	P	MRP = P x MP	W	MRP − W
0	0	—	$200	—	$600	—
1	6	6	200	$1,200	600	$600
2	11	5	200	1,000	600	400
3	15	4	200	800	600	200
4	18	3	200	600	600	0
5	20	2	200	400	600	−200
6	21	1	200	200	600	−400

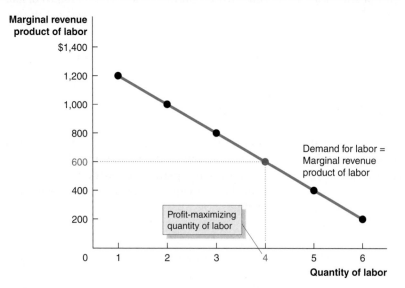

Figure 17.1

The Marginal Revenue Product of Labor and the Demand for Labor

The marginal revenue product of labor equals the marginal product of labor multiplied by the price of the good. The marginal revenue product curve slopes downward because diminishing returns cause the marginal product of labor to decline as more workers are hired. A firm maximizes profits by hiring workers up to the point where the wage equals the marginal revenue product of labor. The marginal revenue product of labor curve is the firm's demand curve for labor because it tells the firm the profit-maximizing quantity of workers to hire at each wage. For example, using the demand curve shown in this figure, if the wage is $600, the firm will hire 4 workers.

We can calculate this amount, which is called the **marginal revenue product of labor** (*MRP*), by multiplying the additional output produced by the product price. For example, consider what happens if Apple increases the number of workers hired from 2 to 3. The table in Figure 17.1 shows that hiring the third worker allows Apple to increase its weekly output of iPhones from 11 to 15, so the marginal product of labor is 4 iPhones. The price of the iPhones is $200, so the marginal revenue product of the third worker is 4 × $200 or $800. In other words, Apple adds $800 to its revenue as a result of hiring the third worker. In the graph, we plot the values of the marginal revenue product of labor at each quantity of labor.

To decide how many workers to hire, Apple must compare the additional revenue it earns from hiring another worker to the increase in its costs from paying that worker. The difference between the additional revenue and the additional cost is the additional profit (or loss) from hiring one more worker. This additional profit is shown in the last column of the table in Figure 17.1 and is calculated by subtracting the wage from the marginal revenue product of labor. As long as the marginal revenue product of labor is greater than the wage, Apple's profits are increasing, and it should continue to hire more workers. When the marginal revenue product of labor is less than the wage, Apple's profits are falling, and it should hire fewer workers. When the marginal revenue product of labor is equal to the wage, Apple has maximized its profits by hiring the optimal number of workers. The values in the table show that Apple should hire 4 workers. If Apple hires a fifth worker, the marginal revenue product of $400 will be less than the wage of $600, and its profits will fall by $200. Table 17.1 summarizes the relationship between the marginal revenue product of labor and the wage.

Marginal revenue product of labor (*MRP*) The change in a firm's revenue as a result of hiring one more worker.

Table 17.1	When …	the firm …
The Relationship between the Marginal Revenue Product of Labor and the Wage	$MRP > W$,	should hire more workers to increase profits.
	$MRP < W$,	should hire fewer workers to increase profits.
	$MRP = W$,	is hiring the optimal number of workers and is maximizing profits.

We can see from Figure 17.1 that if Apple has to pay a wage of $600 per week, it should hire 4 workers. If the wage rises to $1,000, then applying the rule that profits are maximized where the marginal revenue product of labor equals the wage, Apple should hire only 2 workers. Similarly, if the wage falls to $400 per week, Apple should hire 5 workers. In fact, the marginal revenue product curve tells a firm how many workers it should hire at any wage rate. In other words, *the marginal revenue product of labor curve is the demand curve for labor.*

MyEconLab Concept Check

Solved Problem 17.1

MyEconLab Interactive Animation

Hiring Decisions by a Firm That Is a Price Maker

We have assumed that Apple can sell as many iPhones as it wants without having to cut the price. A firm in a perfectly competitive market is in this situation. These firms are *price takers*. Suppose instead that a firm has market power and is a *price maker*, so that to increase sales, it must reduce the price.

Assume that Apple faces the situation shown in the following table. Fill in the blanks and then determine the profit-maximizing quantity of workers for Apple to hire. Briefly explain why hiring this quantity of workers is profit maximizing.

(1) Quantity of Labor	(2) Output of iPhones per Week	(3) Marginal Product of Labor	(4) Product Price	(5) Total Revenue	(6) Marginal Revenue Product of Labor	(7) Wage	(8) Additional Profit from Hiring One Additional Worker
0	0	—	$200		—	$500	—
1	6	6	180			500	
2	11	5	160			500	
3	15	4	140			500	
4	18	3	120			500	
5	20	2	100			500	
6	21	1	80			500	

Solving the Problem

Step 1: **Review the chapter material.** This problem is about determining the profit-maximizing quantity of labor for a firm to hire, so you may want to review the section "The Demand for Labor," which begins on page 534.

Step 2: **Fill in the blanks in the table.** As Apple hires more workers, it sells more iPhones and earns more revenue. You can calculate how revenue increases by multiplying the quantity of iPhones produced—shown in column (2)—by the price—shown in column (4). Then you can calculate the marginal revenue product of labor as the change in revenue as each additional worker is hired. (Notice that in this case, marginal revenue product is *not* calculated by multiplying the marginal product by the product price. Because Apple is a price maker, its marginal revenue from selling additional iPhones is less than the price of iPhones.) Finally, you can calculate the additional profit from hiring one more worker by subtracting the wage—shown in column (7)—from each worker's marginal revenue product.

(1) Quantity of Labor	(2) Output of iPhones per Week	(3) Marginal Product of Labor	(4) Product Price	(5) Total Revenue	(6) Marginal Revenue Product of Labor	(7) Wage	(8) Additional Profit from Hiring One Additional Worker
0	0	—	$200	$0	—	$500	—
1	6	6	180	1,080	$1,080	500	$580
2	11	5	160	1,760	680	500	180
3	15	4	140	2,100	340	500	−160
4	18	3	120	2,160	60	500	−440
5	20	2	100	2,000	−160	500	−660
6	21	1	80	1,680	−320	500	−820

Step 3: **Use the information in the table to determine the profit-maximizing quantity of workers to hire.** To determine the profit-maximizing quantity of workers to hire, you need to compare the marginal revenue product of labor with the wage. Column (8) makes this comparison by subtracting the wage from the marginal revenue product. As long as the values in column (8) are positive, the firm should continue to hire workers. The marginal revenue product of the second worker is $680, and the wage is $500, so column (8) shows that hiring the second worker will add $180 to Apple's profits. The marginal revenue product of the third worker is $340, and the wage is $500, so hiring the third worker would reduce Apple's profits by $160. Therefore, Apple will maximize profits by hiring 2 workers.

Your Turn: For more practice, do related problem 1.6 on page 560 at the end of this chapter.   MyEconLab Study Plan

The Market Demand Curve for Labor

We can determine the market demand curve for labor in the same way we determine the market demand curve for a good—by adding up the quantity of the good demanded by each consumer at each price (see Chapter 10). Similarly, we find the market demand curve for labor by adding up the quantity of labor demanded by each firm at each wage, holding constant all other variables that might affect the willingness of firms to hire workers.

MyEconLab Concept Check

Factors That Shift the Market Demand Curve for Labor

In constructing the demand curve for labor, we held constant all variables—except for the wage—that would affect the willingness of firms to demand labor. An increase or a decrease in the wage causes *an increase or a decrease in the quantity of labor demanded*, which we show by a movement along the demand curve. If any variable other than the wage changes, the result is *an increase or a decrease in the demand for labor*, which we show by a shift of the demand curve. The following are the five most important variables that cause the labor demand curve to shift:

1. *Increases in human capital.* **Human capital** represents the accumulated training and skills that workers possess. For example, a worker with a college education generally has more skills and is more productive than a worker who has only a high school diploma. If workers become more educated and are therefore able to produce more output per day, the demand for their services will increase, shifting the labor demand curve to the right.

2. *Changes in technology.* As new and better machinery and equipment are developed, workers become more productive. This effect causes the labor demand curve to shift to the right over time.

3. *Changes in the price of the product.* The marginal revenue product of labor depends on the price a firm receives for its output. A higher price increases the marginal revenue product and shifts the labor demand curve to the right. A lower price shifts the labor demand curve to the left.

4. *Changes in the quantity of other inputs.* Workers are able to produce more if they have more machinery and other inputs available to them. The marginal product of labor in the United States is higher than the marginal product of labor in most other countries in large part because U.S. firms provide workers with more machinery and equipment. Over time, workers in the United States have had increasing amounts of other inputs available to them, which has increased their productivity and caused the labor demand curve to shift to the right.

5. *Changes in the number of firms in the market.* If new firms enter the market, the labor demand curve will shift to the right. If firms exit the market, the demand for labor will shift to the left. The result is similar to the effect that increasing or decreasing the number of consumers in a market has on the demand for a good. MyEconLab Concept Check

Human capital The accumulated training and skills that workers possess.

MyEconLab Study Plan

17.2 LEARNING OBJECTIVE

Explain how people choose the quantity of labor to supply.

The Supply of Labor

Having discussed the demand for labor, we can now consider the supply of labor. Of the many trade-offs each of us faces in life, one of the most important is how to divide up the 24 hours in a day between labor and leisure. Every hour spent posting to Facebook, walking on the beach, or in other forms of leisure is one hour less spent working. Because in devoting an hour to leisure we give up an hour's earnings from working, the *opportunity cost* of leisure is the wage. The higher the wage we could earn working, the higher the opportunity cost of leisure. Therefore, as the wage increases, we tend to take less leisure and work more. As Figure 17.2 shows, the result is that the labor supply curve for most people is upward sloping.

MyEconLab Animation

Figure 17.2

The Labor Supply Curve

As the wage increases, the opportunity cost of leisure increases, causing individuals to supply a greater quantity of labor. Therefore, the labor supply curve is upward sloping.

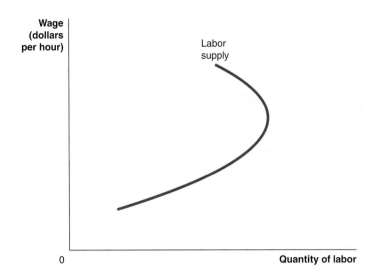

MyEconLab Animation

Figure 17.3

A Backward-Bending Labor Supply Curve

As the wage rises, a greater quantity of labor is usually supplied. As the wage rises above a certain level, the individual is able to afford more leisure even though the opportunity cost of leisure is higher. The result may be that an increase in the wage leads to a smaller quantity of labor supplied.

Although we normally expect the labor supply curve for an individual to be upward sloping, it is possible that at very high wage levels, the labor supply curve of an individual might be *backward bending*, so that higher wages actually result in a *smaller* quantity of labor supplied, as shown in Figure 17.3. To understand why, recall the definitions of the *substitution effect* and the *income effect* (see Chapters 3 and 10). The substitution effect of a price change refers to the fact that an increase in price makes a good more expensive *relative* to other goods. In the case of a wage change, the substitution effect refers to the fact that an increase in the wage raises the opportunity cost of leisure and causes a worker to devote *more* time to working and less time to leisure.

The income effect of a price change refers to the change in the quantity demanded of a good that results from changes in consumer purchasing power as the price changes. An increase in the wage will clearly increase a consumer's purchasing power for any given number of hours worked. For a normal good, the income effect leads to a larger quantity demanded. Because leisure is a normal good, the income effect of a wage increase will cause a worker to devote *less* time to working and more time to leisure. So, the substitution effect of a wage increase causes a worker to supply a larger quantity of labor, but the income effect causes a worker to supply a smaller quantity of labor. Whether a worker supplies more or less labor following a wage increase depends on whether the substitution effect is larger than the income effect. Figure 17.3 shows the typical case of the substitution effect being larger than the income effect at low levels of wages—so the worker supplies a larger quantity of labor as the wage rises—and the income effect being larger than the substitution effect at high levels of wages—so the worker supplies a smaller quantity of labor as the wage rises. For example, suppose an attorney has become quite successful and can charge clients very high fees. Or suppose a rock band has become very popular and receives a large payment for every performance. In these cases, there is a high opportunity cost for the lawyer to turn down another client to take a longer vacation or for the band to turn down another concert. But because their incomes are already very high, they may decide to give up additional income for more leisure. In this case, for the lawyer or the rock band, the income effect is larger than the substitution effect, and a higher wage causes them to supply *less* labor.

The Market Supply Curve of Labor

We can determine the market supply curve of labor in the same way we determine a market supply curve of a good. We find the market supply curve of a good by adding up the quantity of the good supplied by each firm at each price (see Chapter 12). Similarly, we find the market supply curve of labor by adding up the quantity of labor supplied by each worker at each wage, holding constant all other variables that might affect the willingness of workers to supply labor. MyEconLab Concept Check

Factors That Shift the Market Supply Curve of Labor

In constructing the market supply curve of labor, we hold constant all other variables that would affect the willingness of workers to supply labor, except the wage. If any of these other variables change, the market supply curve will shift. The following are the three most important variables that cause the market supply curve of labor to shift:

1. *Increasing population.* As the population grows due to the number of births exceeding the number of deaths and due to immigration, the supply curve of labor shifts to the right. The effects of immigration on labor supply are largest in the markets for unskilled workers. In some large cities in the United States, for example, the majority of taxi drivers and workers in hotels and restaurants are immigrants. Some supporters of reducing immigration argue that wages in these jobs have been depressed by the increased supply of labor from immigrants.

2. *Changing demographics. Demographics* refers to the composition of the population. The more people who are between the ages of 16 and 65, the greater the quantity of labor supplied. During the 1970s and 1980s, the U.S. labor force grew particularly rapidly as members of the Baby Boom generation—born between 1946 and 1964—first began working. In contrast, a low birthrate in Japan has resulted in an aging population. The number of working-age people in Japan actually began to decline during the 1990s, causing the labor supply curve to shift to the left.

   A related demographic issue is the changing role of women in the labor force. In 1900, only 21 percent of women in the United States were in the labor force. By 1950, this figure had risen to 30 percent, and today it is 60 percent. This increase in the *labor force participation* of women has significantly increased the supply of labor in the United States.

3. *Changing alternatives.* The labor supply in any particular labor market depends, in part, on the opportunities available in other labor markets. For example, the problems in the financial services industry that began in 2007 reduced the opportunities for investment bankers, stockbrokers, and other financial workers. Many workers left this industry—causing the labor supply curve to shift to the left—and entered other markets, causing the labor supply curves to shift to the right in those markets. People who have lost jobs or who have low incomes are eligible for unemployment insurance and other payments from the government. The more generous these payments are, the less pressure unemployed workers have to quickly find another job. In many European countries, it is much easier than in the United States for unemployed workers to re-place a larger fraction of their wage income with government payments. Many economists believe generous unemployment benefits help explain the higher unemployment rates experienced in some European countries. MyEconLab Concept Check

MyEconLab Study Plan

17.3 LEARNING OBJECTIVE

Explain how equilibrium wages are determined in labor markets.

Equilibrium in the Labor Market

In Figure 17.4, we bring together labor demand and labor supply to determine equilibrium in the labor market. We can use demand and supply to analyze changes in the equilibrium wage and the level of employment for the entire labor market, and we can also use it to analyze markets for different types of labor, such as baseball players or college professors.

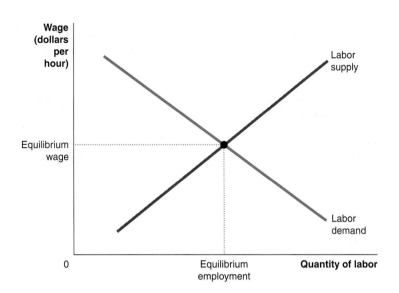

MyEconLab Animation

Figure 17.4

Equilibrium in the Labor Market

As in other markets, equilibrium in the labor market occurs where the demand curve for labor and the supply curve of labor intersect.

The Effect on Equilibrium Wages of a Shift in Labor Demand

In many labor markets, increases over time in labor productivity will cause the demand for labor to increase. As Figure 17.5 shows, if labor supply is unchanged, an increase in labor demand will increase both the equilibrium wage and the number of workers employed.   MyEconLab Concept Check

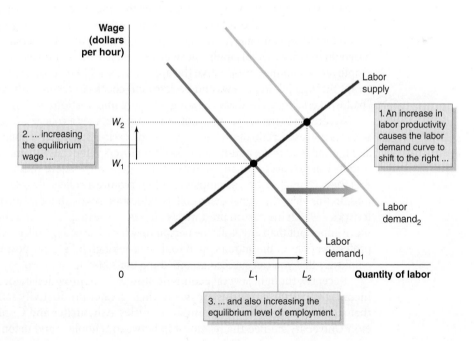

MyEconLab Animation

Figure 17.5 **The Effect of an Increase in Labor Demand**

Increases in labor demand will cause the equilibrium wage and the equilibrium level of employment to rise:

1. If the productivity of workers rises, the marginal revenue product increases, causing the labor demand curve to shift to the right.

2. The equilibrium wage rises from W_1 to W_2.
3. The equilibrium level of employment rises from L_1 to L_2.

<table>
<tr><td>Making
the
Connection
MyEconLab Video</td><td>**Will Your Future Income Depend on Which Courses You Take in College?**</td></tr>
</table>

Most people realize the value of a college education. As the following chart shows, in 2013, full-time workers aged 25 and over with a college degree earned more per week than other workers; for example, they earned 2.5 times as much as high school dropouts.

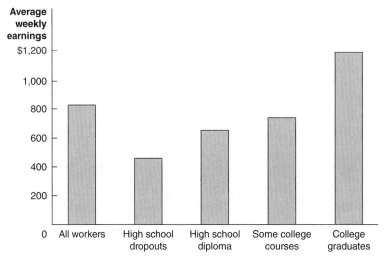

Source: U.S. Bureau of Labor Statistics, "Usual Weekly Earnings of Wage and Salary Workers," April 18, 2013.

Why do college graduates earn more than others? The obvious answer would seem to be that a college education provides skills that increase productivity. Some economists, though, advocate an alternative explanation, known as the *signaling hypothesis*, first proposed by Nobel Laureate A. Michael Spence of New York University. This hypothesis is based on the idea that job applicants will always have more information than will potential employers about how productive the applicants are likely to be. Although employers attempt through job interviews and background checks to distinguish "good workers" from "bad workers," they are always looking for more information.

According to the signaling hypothesis, employers see a college education as a signal that workers possess certain desirable characteristics: self-discipline, the ability to meet deadlines, and the ability to make a sustained effort. Employers value these characteristics because they usually lead to success in any activity. People generally believe that college graduates possess these characteristics, so employers often require a college degree for their best-paying jobs. In this view, the signal that a college education sends about a person's inherent characteristics—which the person presumably already possessed *before* entering college—is much more important than any skills the person may have learned in college. Or, as a college math professor of one of the authors put it (only half-jokingly): "The purpose of college is to show employers that you can succeed at something that's boring and hard."

Recently, though, several economic studies have provided evidence that the higher incomes of college graduates are due to their greater productivity rather than the signal that a college degree sends to employers. Orley Ashenfelter and Cecilia Rouse of Princeton University studied the relationship between schooling and income among 700 pairs of identical twins. Identical twins have identical genes, so differences in their inherent abilities should be relatively small. Therefore, if they have different numbers of years in school, differences in their earnings should be mainly due to the effect of schooling on their productivity. Ashenfelter and Rouse found that identical twins had returns of about 9 percent per additional year of schooling, enough to account for most of the gap in income between high school graduates and college graduates.

Daniel Hamermesh and Stephen G. Donald of the University of Texas studied the determinants of the earnings of college graduates 5 to 25 years after graduation. They collected extensive information on each person in their study, including the person's SAT scores, rank in high school graduating class, grades in every college course taken, and college major. Hamermesh and Donald discovered that, holding constant all other factors, business and engineering majors earned more than graduates with other majors. They also discovered that taking science and math courses has a large effect on future earnings: "A student who takes 15 credits of upper-division science and math courses and obtains a B average in them will earn about 10% more than an otherwise identical student in the same major ... who takes no upper-division classes in these areas." This result held even after adjusting for a student's SAT score. The study by Hamermesh and Donald contradicts the signaling hypothesis because if that hypothesis is correct, the choice of courses taken in college should be of minor importance compared with the signal workers send to employers just by having completed college.

Sources: Orley Ashenfelter and Cecilia Rouse, "Income, Schooling, and Ability: Evidence from a New Sample of Identical Twins," *Quarterly Journal of Economics*, Vol. 113, No. 1, February 1998, pp. 253–284; and Daniel S. Hamermesh and Stephen G. Donald, "The Effect of College Curriculum on Earnings: An Affinity Identifier for Non-Ignorable Non-Response Bias," *Journal of Econometrics*, Vol. 144, No. 2, June 2008, pp. 479–491.

Your Turn: Test your understanding by doing related problem 3.3 on page 561 at the end of this chapter.

MyEconLab Study Plan

The Effect on Equilibrium Wages of a Shift in Labor Supply

What is the effect on the equilibrium wage of an increase in labor supply due to population growth? As Figure 17.6 shows, if labor demand is unchanged, an increase in labor supply will decrease the equilibrium wage but increase the number of workers employed.

Whether the wage rises in a market depends on whether demand increases faster than supply. For example, as Facebook, Twitter, Pinterest, and other social networking sites became increasingly popular, the demand for software engineers in California's Silicon Valley began to increase faster than the supply of new engineers graduating from college. Starting salaries for new graduates had increased from about $80,000 in 2009 to as much as $150,000 in 2013. To keep their engineers from jumping to other employers, Google, Tagged, and other firms had to give their existing employees across-the-board raises. Start-up firms found that the salaries they needed to pay were raising their costs to levels that made it difficult to compete. If these escalating salaries lead more students to graduate with degrees in software engineering, the increased labor supply could eventually bring down salaries.

MyEconLab Concept Check

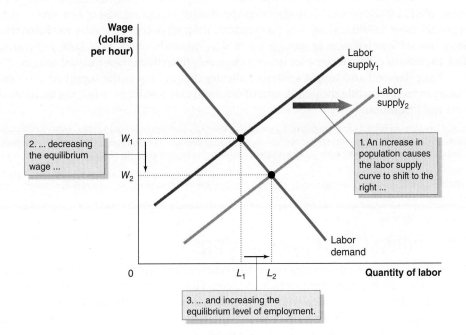

MyEconLab Animation

Figure 17.6

The Effect of an Increase in Labor Supply

Increases in labor supply will cause the equilibrium wage to fall but the equilibrium level of employment to rise:

1. As population increases, the labor supply curve shifts to the right.
2. The equilibrium wage falls from W_1 to W_2.
3. The equilibrium level of employment increases from L_1 to L_2.

<table>
<tr><td>Making
the
Connection
MyEconLab Video</td><td>**Veterinarians Fall Victim
to Demand and Supply**</td></tr>
</table>

A rapid increase in demand and a slow increase in supply has driven up the salaries of software engineers. Veterinarians have been hurt, rather than helped, by changes in demand and supply in recent years. Schools of veterinary medicine in the United States have continued to turn out about 2,500 new veterinarians each year, while demand for the most important veterinary specialty—small animal medicine—has been declining. Over the long run, as more women have entered the workforce, some families have had greater difficulty caring for pets that may have to be left home alone during the day. The decline in incomes and employment during the 2007–2009 recession and the slow recovery that followed have also left many families looking for ways to cut back spending. As a result, the number of dogs and cats in the United States has declined, thereby reducing the demand for small animal vets.

The following figure shows that increases in the supply of small animal vets combined with a decrease in the demand for their services caused the equilibrium annual income of these vets to decline from $139,000 in 2003 to $121,000 in 2013 (both values are measured in dollars of 2013 purchasing power) at the same time that the number of small animal vets increased from 42,000 to 47,000.

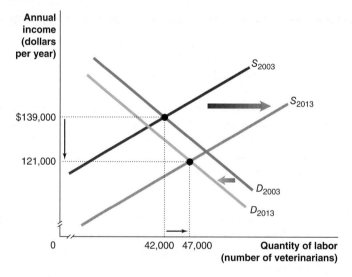

The situation for new vets is worse than the graph indicates. Although an annual income of $121,000 may sound comfortable, the average annual income of *new* vets in 2013 was only about $46,000. Many new vets graduate from schools of veterinary medicine with large student loan balances as average out-of-state tuition has risen to $63,000 per year. In fact, the ratio of debt to income for new vets is double the ratio for new medical doctors.

Basic demand and supply analysis indicates that as long as the supply of vets continues to increase while the population of dogs and cats continues to fall, the incomes of vets will be declining.

Sources: David Segal, "High Debt and Falling Demand Trap New Vets," *New York Times*, February 23, 2013; American Veterinary Medical Association, *Veterinary Market Statistics*, various issues; and Committee to Assess the Current and Future Workforce Needs in Veterinary Medicine, *Workforce Needs in Veterinary Medicine*, Washington, D.C.: The National Academies Press, 2013.

MyEconLab Study Plan   **Your Turn:** Test your understanding by doing related problem 3.8 on page 562 at the end of this chapter.

17.4 LEARNING OBJECTIVE

Use demand and supply analysis to explain how compensating differentials, discrimination, and labor unions cause wages to differ.

Explaining Differences in Wages

A key conclusion of our discussion of the labor market is that the equilibrium wage equals the marginal revenue product of labor. The more productive workers are and the higher the price for which workers' output can be sold, the higher the wages workers will receive. At the beginning of this chapter, we raised the question of why Major League Baseball players are paid so much more than most other workers. We are now

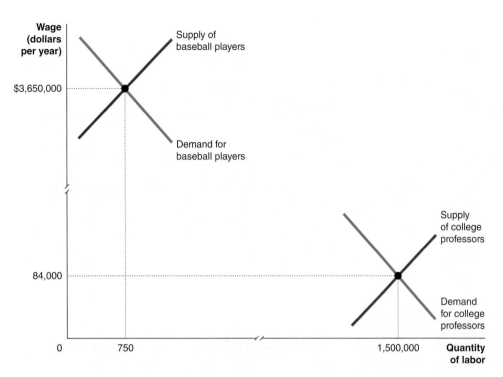

MyEconLab Animation

Figure 17.7

Baseball Players Are Paid More Than College Professors

The marginal revenue product of baseball players is very high, and the supply of people with the ability to play Major League Baseball is low. The result is that the 750 Major League Baseball players receive an average wage of $3,650,000. The marginal revenue product of college professors is much lower, and the supply of people with the ability to be college professors is much higher. The result is that the 1.5 million college professors in the United States receive an average wage of $84,000, far below the average wage of baseball players.

ready to use demand and supply analysis to answer this question. Figure 17.7 shows the demand and supply curves for Major League Baseball players and the demand and supply curves for college professors.

Consider the marginal revenue product of baseball players, which is the additional revenue a team owner will receive from hiring one more player. Baseball players are hired to produce baseball games that are then sold to fans, who pay admission to baseball stadiums, and to radio and television stations and to cable systems that broadcast the games. Because a Major League Baseball team can sell each baseball game for a large amount, the marginal revenue product of baseball players is high. The supply of people with the ability to play Major League Baseball is also very limited. As a result, the average annual salary of the 750 Major League Baseball players was $3,650,000 in 2013.

The marginal revenue product of college professors is much lower than for baseball players. College professors are hired to produce college educations that are sold to students and their parents. Although one year's college tuition is quite high at many colleges, hiring one more professor allows a college to admit at most a few more students. So, the marginal revenue product of a college professor is much lower than the marginal revenue product of a baseball player. There are also many more people who possess the skills to be a college professor than possess the skills to be a Major League Baseball player. As a result, the average annual salary of the country's 1.5 million college professors was about $84,000 in 2013.

This discussion still leaves unanswered the question raised at the beginning of this chapter: Why are the Los Angeles Dodgers willing to pay Zack Greinke more than the Kansas City Royals or Milwaukee Brewers, two of his previous teams, were? Greinke's marginal product—which we can think of as the extra games a team will win by employing him—should be about the same in Los Angeles as in Kansas City or Milwaukee. But his *marginal revenue product* will be higher in Los Angeles. Because the Dodgers play in the second largest metropolitan area in the United States, the number of Dodgers fans is much greater than the number of Kansas City or Milwaukee fans, so winning additional games will result in a greater increase in attendance at Dodgers games than it would at Royals or Brewers games. It will also result in a greater increase in viewers for Dodgers games on television. Therefore, the Dodgers are able to sell the extra wins that Greinke produces for much more than the Royals or Brewers can. This difference explains why the Dodgers were willing to pay Greinke much more than the Royals or Brewers were.

Don't Let This Happen to You

Remember That Prices and Wages Are Determined at the Margin

You have probably heard some variation of the following remark: "We could live without baseball, but we can't live without the trash being hauled away. In a more rational world, trash collectors would be paid more than baseball players." This remark seems logical: The total value to society of having the trash hauled away certainly is greater than the total value of baseball games. But wages—like prices—do not depend on total value but on *marginal* value. The *additional* baseball games the Los Angeles Dodgers expect to win by signing Zack Greinke will result in millions of dollars in increased revenue. The supply of people with the ability to play Major League Baseball is very limited. The supply of people with the ability to be trash haulers is much greater. If a trash-hauling firm hires another worker, the *additional* trash-hauling services it can now offer will bring in a relatively small amount of revenue. The *total* value of baseball games and the *total* value of trash hauling

are not relevant in determining the relative salaries of baseball players and trash collectors.

This point is related to the diamond and water paradox first noted by Adam Smith. On the one hand, water is very valuable—we literally couldn't live without it—but its price is very low. On the other hand, apart from a few industrial purposes, diamonds are used only for jewelry, yet their price is quite high. We resolve the paradox by noting that the price of water is low because the supply is very large and the additional benefit consumers receive from the last gallon purchased is low. The price of diamonds is high because the supply is very small, and the additional benefit consumers receive from the last diamond purchased is high.

MyEconLab Study Plan

Your Turn: Test your understanding by doing related problem 4.7 on page 562 at the end of this chapter.

Why does Brad Pitt earn more today relative to the typical actor than stars did in the 1940s?

Making the Connection MyEconLab Video

Technology and the Earnings of "Superstars"

The gap between Zack Greinke's salary and the salary of the lowest-paid baseball players is much greater than the gap between the salaries paid during the 1950s and 1960s to top players such as Mickey Mantle and Willie Mays and the salaries of the lowest-paid players. Similarly, the gap between the $30 million Brad Pitt is paid to star in a movie and the salary paid to an actor in a minor role is much greater than the gap between the salaries paid during the 1930s and 1940s to stars such as Clark Gable and Cary Grant and the salaries paid to bit players. In fact, in most areas of sports and entertainment, the highest-paid performers—the "superstars"—now have much higher incomes relative to other members of their professions than was true a few decades ago.

The increase in the relative incomes of superstars is mainly due to technological advances. The spread of cable television has increased the number of potential viewers of Dodgers games, but many of those viewers will watch only if the Dodgers are winning. This increases the value to the Dodgers of winning games and, therefore, increases Greinke's marginal revenue product and the salary he can earn.

With Blu-ray discs, DVDs, Internet streaming video, and pay-per-view cable, the value to movie studios of producing a hit movie has greatly risen. Not surprisingly, movie studios have also increased their willingness to pay large salaries to stars such as Brad Pitt and Leonardo DiCaprio because they think these superstars will significantly increase the chances that a film will be successful.

This process has been going on for a long time. For instance, before the invention of the motion picture, anyone who wanted to see a play had to attend the theater and see a live performance. Limits on the number of people who could see the best actors and actresses perform created an opportunity for many more people to succeed in the acting profession, and the gap between the salaries earned by the best actors and the salaries earned by average actors was relatively small. Today, when a hit movie starring Brad Pitt is available on DVD or for downloading, millions of people will buy or rent it, and they will not be forced to spend money to see a less popular actor, as their great-great-grandparents might have been.

Your Turn: Test your understanding by doing related problems 4.10 and 4.11 on page 563 at the end of this chapter.

MyEconLab Study Plan

Differences in marginal revenue products are the most important factor in explaining differences in wages, but they are not the whole story. To provide a more complete explanation for differences in wages, we must take into account three important aspects of labor markets: compensating differentials, discrimination, and labor unions.

Compensating Differentials

Suppose Paul runs a pizza parlor and acquires a reputation for being a bad boss who yells at his workers and is generally unpleasant. Two blocks away, Brendan also runs a pizza parlor, but he is always very polite to his workers. We would expect in these circumstances that Paul will have to pay a higher wage than Brendan to attract and retain workers. Higher wages that compensate workers for unpleasant aspects of a job are called **compensating differentials**.

Compensating differentials Higher wages that compensate workers for unpleasant aspects of a job.

If working in a dynamite factory requires the same degree of training and education as working in a semiconductor factory but is much more dangerous, a larger number of workers will want to work making semiconductors than will want to work making dynamite. As a consequence, the wages of dynamite workers will be higher than the wages of semiconductor workers. We can think of the difference in wages as being the price of risk. As each worker decides on his or her willingness to assume risk and decides how much higher the wage must be to compensate for assuming more risk, wages will adjust so that dynamite factories will pay wages that are just high enough to compensate workers who choose to work there for the extra risk they assume. Only when workers in dynamite factories have been fully compensated with higher wages for the additional risk they assume will dynamite companies be able to attract enough workers.

One surprising implication of compensating differentials is that *laws protecting the health and safety of workers may not make workers better off*. To see this point, suppose that dynamite factories pay wages of $25 per hour and semiconductor factories pay wages of $20 per hour, with the $5 difference in wages being a compensating differential for the greater risk of working in a dynamite factory. Suppose that the government passes a law regulating the manufacture of dynamite in order to improve safety in dynamite factories. As a result of this law, dynamite factories are no longer any more dangerous than semiconductor factories. Once this change occurs, the wages in dynamite factories will decline to $20 per hour, the same as in semiconductor factories. Are workers in dynamite factories any better or worse off? Before the law was passed, their wages were $25 per hour, but $5 per hour was a compensating differential for the extra risk they were exposed to. Now their wages are only $20 per hour, but the extra risk has been eliminated. The conclusion seems to be that dynamite workers are no better off as a result of the safety legislation.

This conclusion is true, though, only if the compensating differential actually does compensate workers fully for the additional risk. Nobel Laureate George Akerlof of the University of California, Berkeley, and William Dickens of the Brookings Institution have argued that the psychological principle known as *cognitive dissonance* might cause workers to underestimate the true risk of their jobs. According to this principle, people prefer to think of themselves as intelligent and rational and tend to reject evidence that seems to contradict this image. Because working in a very hazardous job may seem irrational, workers in such jobs may refuse to believe that the jobs really are hazardous. Akerlof and Dickens present evidence that workers in chemical plants producing benzene and workers in nuclear power plants underestimate the hazards of their jobs. If Akerlof and Dickens are correct, the wages of these workers will not be high enough to compensate them fully for the risk they have assumed. So, in this situation, safety legislation may make workers better off. MyEconLab Concept Check

Discrimination

Economic discrimination Paying a person a lower wage or excluding a person from an occupation on the basis of an irrelevant characteristic such as race or gender.

Table 17.2 shows that in the United States, white males on average earn more than other groups. One possible explanation for this fact is **economic discrimination**, which involves paying a person a lower wage or excluding a person from an occupation on the basis of an irrelevant characteristic such as race or gender.

If employers discriminated by hiring only white males for high-paying jobs or by paying white males higher wages than other groups working the same jobs, white males would have higher earnings, as Table 17.2 shows. However, excluding groups from certain jobs or paying one group more than another has been illegal in the United States since the passage of the Equal Pay Act of 1963 and the Civil Rights Act of 1964. Nevertheless, it is possible that employers are ignoring the law and practicing economic discrimination.

Most economists believe that only part of the gap between the wages of white males and the wages of other groups is due to discrimination. Instead, some of the gap is explained by three main factors:

1. Differences in education
2. Differences in experience
3. Differing preferences for jobs MyEconLab Concept Check

Differences in Education Some of the difference between the incomes of white workers and the incomes of black workers can be explained by differences in education. Historically, African Americans have had less schooling than have whites. Although the gap has closed significantly over the years, 88 percent of adult white males in 2012 had graduated from high school as opposed to 84 percent of adult African-American males. Thirty-two percent of white males had graduated from college as opposed to 19 percent of African-American males. These statistics understate the true gap in education between blacks and whites because many blacks receive a substandard education in inner-city schools. Not surprisingly, studies have shown that differing levels of education can account for a significant part of the gap between the earnings of white and black males. Some of the difference in educational levels between blacks and whites may itself reflect past and current discrimination by governments in failing to provide equal educational opportunities.

Differences in Experience Women are much more likely than men to leave their jobs for a period of time after having a child. Women with several children will sometimes have several interruptions in their careers. Some women leave the workforce for several years until their children are of school age. As a result, on average, women

Table 17.2	Group	Annual Earnings
Why Do White Males Earn More Than Other Groups?	White males	$56,247
	White females	42,171
	Black males	39,816
	Black females	35,090
	Hispanic males	32,516
	Hispanic females	29,508

Note: The values are median annual earnings for persons who worked full time, year-round in 2012. Persons of Hispanic origin can be of any race.
Source: U.S. Bureau of the Census, Table PINC-01, "Current Population Survey," *2013 Annual Social and Economic Supplement.*

with children have less workforce experience than do men of the same age. Because workers with greater experience are, on average, more productive, the difference in levels of experience helps to explain some of the difference in earnings between men and women. Providing some support for this explanation is the fact that, on average, married women earn about 25 percent less than married men, but women who have never been married—and whose careers are less likely to have been interrupted—earn only about 9 percent less than men who have never been married.

Differing Preferences for Jobs Significant differences exist between the types of jobs held by women and men. Women represent 90 percent or more of the people employed in some relatively low-paying jobs, such as preschool teachers, dental assistants, and childcare workers, while men represent more than 90 percent of the people employed in some relatively high-paying jobs, such as airline pilots, engineering managers, and electricians. Although the overrepresentation of women in low-paying jobs and men in high-paying jobs may be due, in part, to discrimination, it is also likely to reflect differences in job preferences between men and women. For example, because many women interrupt their careers—at least briefly—when their children are born, they are more likely to take jobs where work experience is less important. More women may also be likely to take jobs, such as teaching, that allow them to be home in the afternoons when their children return from school.

Solved Problem 17.4

MyEconLab Interactive Animation

Is Passing "Comparable Worth" Legislation a Good Way to Close the Gap between Men's and Women's Pay?

As we have seen, because of either discrimination or differing preferences, certain jobs are filled primarily by men, and other jobs are filled primarily by women. On average, the "men's jobs" have higher wages than the "women's jobs." Some commentators have argued that many "men's jobs" are more highly paid than "women's jobs," despite the jobs being comparable in terms of the education and skills required and the working conditions involved. These commentators have argued that the earnings gap between men and women could be closed at least partially if the government required employers to pay the same wages for jobs that have *comparable worth*. Many economists are skeptical of these proposals

because they believe allowing markets to determine wages results in a more efficient outcome.

Suppose that electricians are currently being paid a market equilibrium wage of $800 per week, and dental assistants are being paid a market equilibrium wage of $500 per week. Comparable-worth legislation is passed, and a study finds that an electrician and a dental assistant have comparable jobs, so employers will now be required to pay workers in both jobs $650 per week. Analyze the effects of this requirement on the market for electricians and on the market for dental assistants. Be sure to use demand and supply graphs.

Solving the Problem

Step 1: Review the chapter material. This problem is about economic discrimination, so you may want to review the section "Discrimination," which begins on page 548.

Step 2: Draw the graphs. When the government sets the price in a market, the result is a surplus or a shortage, depending on whether the government-mandated price is above or below the competitive market equilibrium (see Chapter 4). A wage of $650 per week is below the market wage for electricians and above the market wage for dental assistants. Therefore, we expect the requirement to result in a shortage of electricians and a surplus of dental assistants.

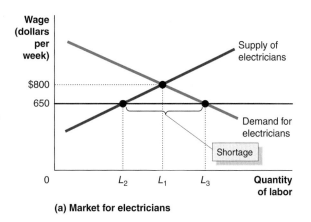

(a) Market for electricians

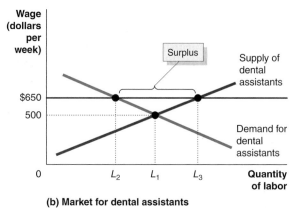

(b) Market for dental assistants

In panel (a), without comparable-worth legislation, the equilibrium wage for electricians is $800, and the equilibrium quantity of electricians hired is L_1. Setting the wage for electricians below equilibrium at $650 reduces the quantity of labor supplied in this occupation from L_1 to L_2 but increases the quantity of labor demanded by employers from L_1 to L_3. The result is a shortage of electricians equal to $L_3 - L_2$, as shown by the bracket in the graph.

In panel (b), without comparable-worth legislation, the equilibrium wage for dental assistants is $500, and the equilibrium quantity of dental assistants hired is L_1. Setting the wage for dental assistants above equilibrium at $650 increases the quantity of labor supplied in this occupation from L_1 to L_3 but reduces the quantity of labor demanded by employers from L_1 to L_2. The result is a surplus of dental assistants equal to $L_3 - L_2$, as shown by the bracket in the graph.

Extra Credit: Most economists are skeptical of government attempts to set wages and prices, as comparable-worth legislation would require. Supporters of comparable-worth legislation, by contrast, see differences between men's and women's wages as being mainly due to discrimination and see government legislation as a solution.

MyEconLab Study Plan

Your Turn: For more practice, do related problems 4.17 and 4.18 on page 564 at the end of this chapter.

The Difficulty of Measuring Discrimination When two people are paid different wages, discrimination may be the explanation. But differences in productivity or preferences may also be an explanation. Labor economists have attempted to measure what part of differences in wages between black workers and white workers and between men and women is due to discrimination and what part is due to other factors. Unfortunately, it is difficult to precisely measure differences in productivity or in worker preferences. As a result, we can't know exactly the extent of economic discrimination in the United States today.

Making the Connection

MyEconLab Video

Does Greg Have an Easier Time Finding a Job Than Jamal?

One difficulty in accurately measuring economic discrimination is that two workers may not only differ in race and gender but also in characteristics that employers expect will affect the workers' productivity. If Worker A is hired instead of Worker B, is it because A is a white male, while B is a black female, or is it because of A's and B's other characteristics?

Marianne Bertrand of the University of Chicago and Sendhil Mullainathan of Harvard found an ingenious way of gaining insight into the extent of economic discrimination. They responded to help wanted ads in newspapers by sending identical résumés, with the exception that half of the résumés were assigned an African-American–sounding name and half were assigned a white-sounding name. In other words, the characteristics of these fictitious people were the same, except for their names. In the absence of discrimination, résumés with African-American–sounding names, such as Jamal Jones, should have been as likely to get job interviews as the identical résumés with white-sounding names, such as Greg Baker. Bertrand and Mullainathan sent out more than 5,000 résumés to many different employers who were advertising for jobs in sales, administrative support, clerical services, and customer services. They found that employers were 50 percent more likely to interview workers with white-sounding names than workers with African-American–sounding names.

Some economists have questioned whether the study by Bertrand and Mullainathan, as well as other similar studies, actually do show that employers discriminate. They argue that employers may believe that the typical white job applicant and the typical black job applicant have different characteristics, apart from those included in the résumés, that may affect their productivity. If so, the employers may be responding to these differences in productivity rather than solely to the job applicant's race. Because Bertrand and Mullainathan based their artificial résumés on actual résumés, however, the artificial résumés probably include all the characteristics that actual job applicants think are relevant. Bertrand and Mullainathan believe that the results of their experiment show that "differential treatment by race … appears to still be prominent in the U.S. labor market."

Does having an African-American-sounding name make it more difficult to find a job?

Sources: Marianne Bertrand and Sendhil Mullainathan, "Are Emily and Greg More Employable Than Lakisha and Jamal? A Field Experiment on Labor Market Discrimination," *American Economic Review*, Vol. 94, No. 4, September 2004, pp. 991–1013; and David Neumark, "Detecting Discrimination in Audit and Correspondence Studies," *Journal of Human Resources*, Vol. 47, No. 4, Fall 2012, pp. 1128–1157.

Your Turn: Test your understanding by doing related problem 4.19 on page 564 at the end of this chapter.

MyEconLab Study Plan

Does It Pay to Discriminate? Many economists believe that in the long run, markets can undermine economic discrimination. One reason is that *employers who discriminate pay an economic penalty.* To see why, let's consider a simplified example. Suppose that men and women are equally qualified to be airline pilots and that, initially, airlines do not discriminate. In Figure 17.8, we divide the airlines into two groups: "A" airlines and "B" airlines. If neither group of airlines discriminates, we would expect them to pay an equal wage of $1,100 per week to both men and women pilots. Now suppose that "A" airlines decide to discriminate and to fire all their women pilots. This action will reduce the supply of pilots to these airlines and, as shown in panel (a), will force up the wage from $1,100 to $1,300 per week. At the same time, as women fired from the jobs with "A" airlines apply for jobs with "B" airlines, the supply of pilots to "B" airlines will increase, and the equilibrium wage will fall from $1,100 to $900 per week. All the women pilots will end up being employed at the nondiscriminating airlines and will be paid a lower wage than the men who are employed by the discriminating airlines.

But this situation cannot persist for two reasons. First, male pilots employed by "B" airlines will also receive the lower wage. This lower wage gives them an incentive to quit their jobs at "B" airlines and apply at "A" airlines, which will shift the labor supply curve for "B" airlines to the left and the labor supply curve for "A" airlines to the right. Second, "A" airlines are paying $1,300 per week to hire pilots who are no more productive than the pilots being paid $900 per week by "B" airlines. As a result, "B" airlines will have lower costs and will be able to charge lower prices. Eventually, high-price "A" airlines will lose their customers to low-price "B" airlines and will be driven out of business. The

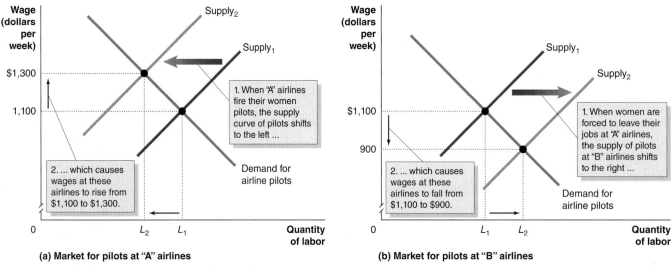

MyEconLab Animation

Figure 17.8 **Discrimination and Wages**

In this hypothetical example, we assume that initially neither "A" airlines nor "B" airlines discriminate. As a result, men and women pilots receive the same wage of $1,100 per week at both groups of airlines. We then assume that "A" airlines discriminate by firing all their women pilots. Panel (a) shows that discrimination reduces the supply of pilots to "A" airlines and raises the wage paid by these airlines from $1,100 to $1,300. Panel (b) shows that discrimination increases the supply of pilots to "B" airlines and lowers the wage paid by these airlines from $1,100 to $900. All the women pilots will end up being employed at the nondiscriminating airlines and will be paid a lower wage than the men who are employed by the discriminating airlines.

market will have imposed an economic penalty on the discriminating airlines. So, discrimination will not persist, and the wages of men and women pilots will become equal.

Can we conclude from this analysis that competition in markets will eliminate all economic discrimination? Unfortunately, this optimistic conclusion is not completely accurate. We know that until the Civil Rights Act of 1964 was passed, many firms in the United States refused to hire black workers. Even though this practice had persisted for decades, nondiscriminating competitors did not drive these firms out of business. Why not? There were three important factors:

1. *Worker discrimination.* In some cases, white workers refused to work alongside black workers. As a result, some industries—such as the important cotton textile industry in the South—were all white. Because of discrimination by white workers, an entrepreneur who wanted to use low-cost black labor might need to hire an all-black workforce. Some entrepreneurs tried this approach, but because black workers had been excluded from these industries, they often lacked the skills and experience to form an effective workforce.

2. *Customer discrimination.* Some white consumers were unwilling to buy from companies in certain industries if they employed black workers. This discrimination was not a significant barrier in manufacturing industries, where customers would not know the race of the workers producing the good. It was, however, a problem for firms in industries in which workers came into direct contact with the public.

3. *Negative feedback loops.* Our analysis in Figure 17.8 assumed that men and women pilots were equally qualified. However, if discrimination makes it difficult for a member of a group to find employment in a particular occupation, his or her incentive to be trained to enter that occupation is reduced. Consider the legal profession as an example. In 1952, future Supreme Court Justice Sandra Day O'Connor graduated third in her class at Stanford University Law School and was an editor of the *Stanford Law Review*, but for some time she was unable to get a job as a lawyer because in those years, many law firms would not hire women. Given such bleak job prospects, it's not surprising that relatively few women entered law school. As a

result, a law firm that did not discriminate would have been unable to hire women lawyers at a lower salary and use this cost advantage to drive discriminating law firms out of business. Notice the difference between this situation and the airline example discussed earlier. In this situation, an unfortunate feedback loop was in place: Few women prepared to become lawyers because many law firms discriminated against women, and nondiscriminating law firms were unable to drive discriminating law firms out of business because there were too few women lawyers available.

Most economists agree that the market imposes an economic penalty on firms that discriminate, but because of the factors just discussed, it may take the market a very long time to eliminate discrimination entirely. The passage of the Civil Rights Act of 1964, which outlawed hiring discrimination on the basis of race and sex, greatly sped up the process of reducing economic discrimination in the United States.

Labor Unions

Workers' wages can differ depending on whether the workers are members of **labor unions**, which are organizations of employees that have the legal right to bargain with employers about wages and working conditions. If a union is unable to reach an agreement with a company, it has the legal right to call a *strike*, which means its members refuse to work until a satisfactory agreement has been reached. As Figure 17.9 shows, a smaller fraction of the U.S. labor force is unionized than in most other high-income countries.

As Table 17.3 shows, in the United States, workers who are in unions receive higher wages than workers who are not in unions. Do union members earn more than nonunion members because they are in unions? The answer might seem to be "yes," but many union workers are in industries, such as automobile manufacturing, in which their marginal revenue products are high, so their wages would be high even if they were not unionized. Economists who have attempted to estimate statistically the effect of unionization on wages have concluded that being in a union increases a worker's wages about 10 percent, holding constant other factors, such as the industry the worker is in. A related question is whether unions raise the total amount of wages received by all workers, whether unionized or not. Because the share of national income received by workers has remained roughly constant over many years, most economists do not believe that unions have raised the total amount of wages received by workers.

MyEconLab Concept Check

Labor union An organization of employees that has a legal right to bargain with employers about wages and working conditions.

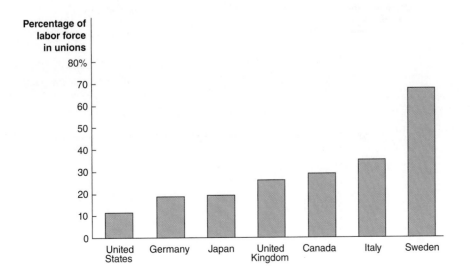

MyEconLab Animation

Figure 17.9

The United States Is Less Unionized Than Most Other High-Income Countries

The percentage of the labor force belonging to unions is lower in the United States than in most other high-income countries.
Source: Organization for Economic Cooperation and Development.

Table 17.3

Union Workers Earn More Than Nonunion Workers

MyEconLab Study Plan

	Average Weekly Earnings
Union workers	$943
Nonunion workers	742

Note: "Union workers" includes union members as well as workers who are represented by unions but who are not members of them.
Source: U.S. Bureau of Labor Statistics, *Union Members Summary*, January 23, 2013.

17.5 LEARNING OBJECTIVE

Discuss the role personnel economics can play in helping firms deal with human resources issues.

Personnel economics The application of economic analysis to human resources issues.

Personnel Economics

Traditionally, labor economists have focused on issues such as the effects of labor unions on wages or the determinants of changes in average wages over time. They have spent less time analyzing *human resources issues*, which address how firms hire, train, and promote workers and set their wages and benefits. In recent years, some labor economists, including Edward Lazear of Stanford University and William Neilson of the University of Tennessee, have begun exploring the application of economic analysis to human resources issues. This new focus has become known as *personnel economics*.

Personnel economics analyzes the link between differences among jobs and differences in the way workers are paid. Jobs have different skill requirements, require more or less interaction with other workers, have to be performed in more or less unpleasant environments, and so on. Firms need to design compensation policies that take into account these differences. Personnel economics also analyzes policies related to other human resources issues, such as promotions, training, and pensions. In this brief overview, we look only at compensation policies.

Should Workers' Pay Depend on How Much They Work or on How Much They Produce?

One issue personnel economics addresses is when workers should receive *straight-time pay*—a certain wage per hour or salary per week or month—and when they should receive *commission* or *piece-rate pay*—a wage based on how much output they produce.

Suppose that Anne owns a car dealership and is trying to decide whether to pay her salespeople a salary of $800 per week or a commission of $200 on each car they sell. Figure 17.10 compares the compensation a salesperson would receive under the two systems, according to the number of cars the salesperson sells.

MyEconLab Animation

Figure 17.10

Paying Car Salespeople by Salary or by Commission

This figure compares the compensation a car salesperson receives if she is on a straight salary of $800 per week and if she receives a commission of $200 for each car she sells. With a straight salary, she receives $800 per week, no matter how many cars she sells. This outcome is shown by the horizontal line in the figure. If she receives a commission of $200 per car, her compensation will increase with every car she sells. This outcome is shown by the upward-sloping line. If she sells fewer than 4 cars per week, she would be better off with the $800 salary. If she sells more than 4 cars per week, she would be better off with the $200-per-car commission.

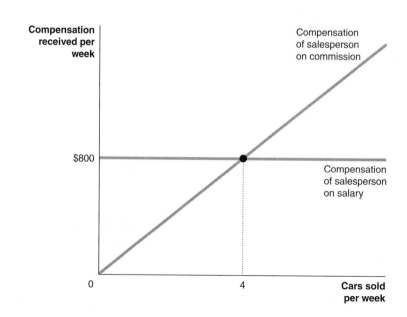

With a straight salary, the salesperson receives $800 per week, no matter how many cars she sells. This outcome is shown by the horizontal line in Figure 17.10. If she receives a commission of $200 per car, her compensation will increase with every car she sells. This outcome is shown by the upward-sloping line. A salesperson who sells fewer than 4 cars per week would earn more by receiving a straight salary of $800 per week. A salesperson who sells more than 4 cars per week would be better off receiving the $200-per-car commission. We can identify two advantages Anne would receive from paying her salespeople commissions rather than salaries: She would attract and retain the most productive employees, and she would provide an incentive to her employees to sell more cars.

Suppose that other car dealerships are all paying salaries of $800 per week. If Anne pays her employees on commission, any of her employees who are unable to sell at least 4 cars per week can improve their pay by going to work for one of her competitors. And any salespeople at Anne's competitors who can sell more than 4 cars per week can raise their pay by quitting and coming to work for Anne. Over time, Anne will find her least productive employees leaving, while she is able to hire new employees who are more productive.

Paying a commission also increases the incentive Anne's salespeople have to sell more cars. If Anne paid a salary, her employees would receive the same amount no matter how few cars they sold. An employee on salary might decide on a particularly hot or cold day that it was less trouble to stay inside the building than to go out on the car lot to greet potential customers. An employee on commission would know that the additional effort expended on selling more cars would be rewarded with additional compensation.

MyEconLab Concept Check

Making the Connection
MyEconLab Video

Raising Pay, Productivity, and Profits at Safelite AutoGlass

Safelite Group, headquartered in Columbus, Ohio, is the parent company of Safelite AutoGlass, the nation's largest installer of auto glass, with 600 repair shops. In the mid-1990s, Safelite shifted from paying its glass installers hourly wages to paying them on the basis of how many windows they installed. Safelite already had in place a computer system that allowed it to easily track how many windows each worker installed per day. To make sure quality did not suffer, Safelite added a rule that if a workmanship-related defect occurred with an installed windshield, the worker would have to install a new windshield and would not be paid for the additional work.

Edward Lazear analyzed data provided by the firm and discovered that under the new piece-rate system, the number of windows installed per worker jumped 44 percent. Lazear estimated that half of this increase was due to increased productivity from workers who continued with the company and half was due to new hires being more productive than the workers they replaced who had left the company. Worker pay rose on average by about 9.9 percent. Ninety-two percent of workers experienced a pay increase, and one-quarter received an increase of at least 28 percent. Safelite's profit also increased as the cost to the company per window installed fell from $44.43 under the hourly wage system to $35.24 under the piece-rate system.

Sociologists sometimes question whether worker productivity can be increased through the use of monetary incentives. The experience of Safelite AutoGlass provides a clear example of workers reacting favorably to the opportunity to increase output in exchange for higher compensation.

A piece-rate system at Safelite AutoGlass led to increased worker wages and firm profits.

Source: Edward P. Lazear, "Performance Pay and Productivity," *American Economic Review*, Vol. 90, No. 5, December 2000, pp. 1346–1361.

Your Turn: Test your understanding by doing related problem 5.8 on page 565 at the end of this chapter.

MyEconLab Study Plan

Other Considerations in Setting Compensation Systems

The discussion so far indicates that companies will find it more profitable to use a commission or piece-rate system of compensation rather than a salary system. In fact, many firms continue to pay their workers salaries, which means they are paying their workers on the basis of how long they work rather than on the basis of how much they produce. Firms may choose a salary system for several good reasons:

- *Difficulty measuring output.* Often firms have difficulty attributing output to any particular worker. For example, an engineering firm may carry out a project using teams of workers whose individual contributions are difficult to distinguish. On assembly lines, such as those used in the automobile industry, the amount produced by each worker is determined by the speed of the line, which is set by managers rather than by workers. Managers at many firms perform such a wide variety of tasks that measuring their output would be costly, if it could be done at all.

- *Concerns about quality.* If workers are paid on the basis of the number of units produced, they may become less concerned about quality. An office assistant who is paid on the basis of the quantity of letters typed may become careless about how many typos the letters contain. In some cases, there are ways around this problem; for example, the assistant may be required to correct the mistakes on his or her own time, without pay.

- *Worker dislike of risk.* Piece-rate or commission systems of compensation increase the risk to workers because sometimes output declines for reasons not connected to the worker's effort. For example, if there is a very snowy winter, few customers may show up at Anne's auto dealership. Through no fault of their own, her salespeople may have great difficulty selling any cars. If they are paid a salary, their income will not be affected, but if they are on commission, their incomes may drop to low levels. The flip side of this is that by paying salaries, Anne assumes a greater risk. During a snowy winter, her payroll expenses will remain high even though her sales are low. With a commission system of compensation, her payroll expenses will decline along with her sales. But owners of firms are typically better able to bear risk than are workers. As a result, some firms may find that workers who would earn more under a commission system will prefer to receive a salary to reduce their risk. In these situations, paying a lower salary may reduce the firm's payroll expenses compared with what they would have been under a commission or piece-rate system.

Personnel economics is a relatively new field, but it holds great potential for helping firms deal more efficiently with human resources issues.   MyEconLab Concept Check

MyEconLab Study Plan

17.6 LEARNING OBJECTIVE

Show how equilibrium prices are determined in the markets for capital and natural resources.

The Markets for Capital and Natural Resources

The approach we have used to analyze the market for labor can also be used to analyze the markets for other factors of production. We have seen that the demand for labor is determined by the marginal revenue product of labor because the value to a firm of hiring another worker equals the increase in the firm's revenue from selling the additional output it can produce by hiring the worker. The demand for capital and natural resources is determined in a similar way.

The Market for Capital

Physical capital includes machines, equipment, and buildings. Firms sometimes buy capital, but we will focus on situations in which firms rent capital. A chocolate manufacturer renting a warehouse and an airline leasing a plane are examples of firms renting capital. Like the demand for labor, the demand for capital is a derived demand. When a firm is considering increasing its capital by, for example, employing another machine, the value it receives equals the increase in the firm's revenue from selling the additional

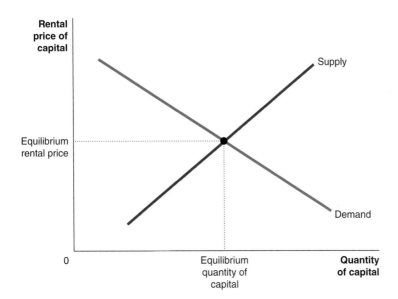

MyEconLab Animation

Figure 17.11

Equilibrium in the Market for Capital

The rental price of capital is determined by demand and supply in the market for capital. In equilibrium, the rental price of capital is equal to the marginal revenue product of capital.

output it can produce by employing the machine. The *marginal revenue product of capital* is the change in the firm's revenue as a result of employing one more unit of capital, such as a machine. We have seen that the marginal revenue product of labor curve is the demand curve for labor. Similarly, the marginal revenue product of capital curve is the demand curve for capital.

Firms producing capital goods face increasing marginal costs, so the supply curve of capital goods is upward sloping. Figure 17.11 shows equilibrium in the market for capital. In equilibrium, suppliers of capital receive a rental price equal to the marginal revenue product of capital, just as suppliers of labor receive a wage equal to the marginal revenue product of labor. MyEconLab Concept Check

The Market for Natural Resources

The market for natural resources can be analyzed in the same way as the markets for labor and capital. When a firm is considering employing more natural resources, the value it receives equals the increase in the firm's revenue from selling the additional output it can produce by buying the natural resources. So, the demand for natural resources is also a derived demand. The *marginal revenue product of natural resources* is the change in a firm's revenue as a result of employing one more unit of natural resources, such as a barrel of oil. The marginal revenue product of natural resources curve is also the demand curve for natural resources.

Although the total quantity of most natural resources is ultimately fixed—as the humorist Will Rogers once remarked: "Buy land. They ain't making any more of it"—in many cases, the quantity supplied still responds to the price. For example, although the total quantity of oil deposits in the world is fixed, an increase in the price of oil will result in an increase in the quantity of oil supplied during a particular period. The result, as shown in panel (a) of Figure 17.12, is an upward-sloping supply curve. In some cases, however, the quantity of a natural resource that will be supplied is fixed and will not change as the price changes. The land available at a busy intersection is fixed, for example. In panel (b) of Figure 17.12, we illustrate this situation with a supply curve that is a vertical line, or perfectly inelastic. The owner of a factor of production that is in fixed supply receives an **economic rent** (or a **pure rent**). In this case, the price of the factor is determined only by demand. For example, if a new highway diverts much of the traffic from a previously busy intersection, the demand for the land will decline, and the price of the land will fall, but the quantity of the land will not change. MyEconLab Concept Check

Economic rent (or **pure rent**) The price of a factor of production that is in fixed supply.

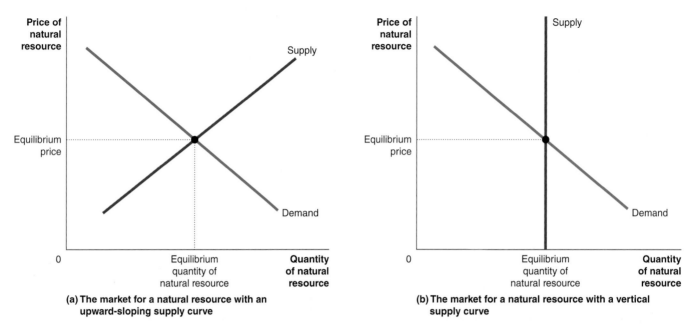

MyEconLab Animation

Figure 17.12   **Equilibrium in the Market for Natural Resources**

In panel (a), the supply curve of a natural resource is upward sloping. The price of the natural resource is determined by the interaction of demand and supply. In panel (b), the supply curve of the natural resource is a vertical line, indicating that

the quantity supplied does not respond to changes in price. In this case, the price of the natural resource is determined only by demand. The price of a factor of production with a vertical supply curve is called an *economic rent,* or a *pure rent.*

Monopsony

Monopsony The situation in which a firm is sole buyer of a factor of production.

We have analyzed the case of *monopoly*, where a firm is the sole *seller* of a good or service (see Chapter 15). What happens if a firm is the sole *buyer* of a factor of production? This case, which is called **monopsony**, is comparatively rare. An example is a firm in an isolated town—perhaps a lumber mill in a small town in Washington or Oregon—that is the sole employer of labor in that location. In the nineteenth and early twentieth centuries, some coal mining firms were the sole employers in certain small towns in West Virginia, and some pineapple plantations were the sole employers on certain small islands in Hawaii. In these cases, not only would the firm own the mill, mine, or plantation, but it would also own the stores and other businesses in the town. Workers would have the choice of working for the sole employer in the town or moving to another town.

We know that a firm with a monopoly in an output market takes advantage of its market power to reduce the quantity supplied to force up the market price and increase its profits. A firm that has a monopsony in a factor market would employ a similar strategy: It would restrict the quantity of the factor demanded to force down the price of the factor and increase profits. A firm with a monopsony in a labor market will hire fewer workers and pay lower wages than would be the case in a competitive market. Because fewer workers are hired than would be hired in a competitive market, monopsony results in a deadweight loss. Monopoly and monopsony have similar effects on the economy: In both cases, a firm's market power results in a lower equilibrium quantity, a deadweight loss, and a reduction in economic efficiency compared with a competitive market.

In some cases, monopsony in labor markets is offset by worker membership in a labor union. A notable example of this is professional sports. For instance, Major League Baseball effectively has a monopsony on employing professional baseball players. (Although independent baseball leagues exist, none of the best players play for these teams, and the teams pay salaries that are a small fraction of those paid by Major League Baseball teams.) The monopsony power of the owners of Major League Baseball teams is offset by the power of the Major League Baseball Players Association, the union that represents baseball players. Bargaining between the representatives of Major League Baseball and the players' union has resulted in baseball players being paid something close to what they would be receiving in a competitive market. MyEconLab Concept Check

The Marginal Productivity Theory of Income Distribution

We have seen that in equilibrium each factor of production receives a price equal to its marginal revenue product. We can use this fact to explain the distribution of income. Marginal revenue product represents the value of a factor's marginal contribution to producing goods and services. Therefore, individuals will receive income equal to the marginal contributions to production from the factors of production they own, including their labor. The more factors of production an individual owns and the more productive those factors are, the higher the individual's income will be. This approach to explaining the distribution of income is called the **marginal productivity theory of income distribution**. The theory was developed by John Bates Clark, who taught at Columbia University in the late nineteenth and early twentieth centuries. MyEconLab Concept Check

Marginal productivity theory of income distribution The theory that the distribution of income is determined by the marginal productivity of the factors of production that individuals own.

MyEconLab Study Plan

Continued from page 533

Economics in Your Life

How Can You Convince Your Boss to Give You a Raise?

At the beginning of this chapter, we asked you to imagine that you work at a local sandwich shop and that you plan to ask your manager for a raise. One way to show the manager your worth is to demonstrate how many dollars your work earns for the sandwich shop: your marginal revenue product. You could certainly suggest that as you have become better at your job and have gained new skills, you have become a more productive employee. But more importantly, you could say that your productivity results in increased revenue for the sandwich shop. By showing how your employment contributes to higher revenue and profit, you may be able to convince your manager to give you a raise.

Conclusion

In this chapter, we used the demand and supply model to explain why wages differ among workers. The demand for workers depends on their productivity and on the prices firms receive for the output the workers produce. The supply of workers to an occupation depends on the wages and working conditions offered by employers and on the skills required. The demand and supply for labor can also help us analyze issues such as economic discrimination and the effect of labor unions.

Visit MyEconLab for a news article and analysis related to the concepts in this chapter.

Chapter Summary and Problems

Key Terms

Compensating differentials, p. 547

Derived demand, p. 534

Economic discrimination, p. 548

Economic rent (or pure rent), p. 557

Factors of production, p. 534

Human capital, p. 538

Labor union, p. 553

Marginal product of labor, p. 534

Marginal productivity theory of income distribution, p. 559

Marginal revenue product of labor (*MRP*), p. 535

Monopsony, p. 558

Personnel economics, p. 554

17.1 The Demand for Labor, pages 534–538

LEARNING OBJECTIVE: Explain how firms choose the profit-maximizing quantity of labor to employ.

Summary

The demand for labor is a **derived demand** because it depends on the demand consumers have for goods and services. The additional output produced by a firm as a result of hiring another worker is called the **marginal product of labor**. The amount by which a firm's revenue will increase as a result of hiring one more worker is called the **marginal revenue product of labor (*MRP*)**. A firm's marginal revenue product of labor curve is its demand curve for labor. Firms maximize profit by hiring workers up to the point where the wage is equal to the marginal revenue product of labor. We find the market demand curve for labor by adding up the quantity of labor demanded by each firm at each wage, holding constant all other variables that might affect the willingness of firms to hire workers. The most important variables that shift the labor demand curve are changes in human capital, technology, the price of the product, the quantity of other inputs, and the number of firms in the market. **Human capital** is the accumulated training and skills that workers possess.

 Visit www.myeconlab.com to complete these exercises online and get instant feedback.

Review Questions

1.1 In what sense is the demand for labor a derived demand?

1.2 What is the difference between the marginal product of labor and the marginal revenue product of labor?

1.3 Why is the demand curve for labor downward sloping?

1.4 What are the five most important variables that cause the market demand curve for labor to shift?

Problems and Applications

1.5 Frank Gunter owns an apple orchard. He employs 87 apple pickers and pays them each $8 per hour to pick apples, which he sells for $1.60 per box. If Frank is maximizing profit, what is the marginal revenue product of the last worker he hired? What is that worker's marginal product?

1.6 [**Related to** Solved Problem 17.1 **on page 536**] Complete the following table for Terrell's Televisions:

Number of Workers (L)	Output of Televisions per Week (Q)	Marginal Product of Labor (television sets per week) (MP)	Product Price (P)	Marginal Revenue Product of Labor (dollars per week)	Wage (dollars per week) (W)	Additional Profit from Hiring One More Worker (dollars per week)
0	0	_____	$300	_____	$1,800	_____
1	8	_____	300	_____	1,800	_____
2	15	_____	300	_____	1,800	_____
3	21	_____	300	_____	1,800	_____
4	26	_____	300	_____	1,800	_____
5	30	_____	300	_____	1,800	_____
6	33	_____	300	_____	1,800	_____

   a. From the information in the table, can you determine whether this firm is a price taker or a price maker? Briefly explain.

   b. Use the information in the table to draw a graph like Figure 17.1 on page 535 that shows the demand for labor by this firm. Be sure to indicate the profit-maximizing quantity of labor on your graph.

1.7 State whether each of the following events will result in a movement along the market demand curve for labor in electronics factories in China or whether it will cause the market demand curve for labor to shift. If the demand curve shifts, indicate whether it will shift to the left or to the right and draw a graph to illustrate the shift.

   a. The wage rate declines.

   b. The price of televisions declines.

   c. Several firms exit the television market in China.

   d. Chinese high schools introduce new vocational courses in assembling electronic products.

1.8 Baseball writer Rany Jazayerli assessed the Kansas City Royals outfielder Jose Guillen as follows: "Guillen has negative value the way his contract stands." How could a baseball player's contract cause him to have negative value to a baseball team?

Source: Rany Jazayerli, "Radical Situations Call for Radical Solutions," www.ranyontheroyals.com, June 6, 2009.

17.2 The Supply of Labor, pages 538–540

LEARNING OBJECTIVE: Explain how people choose the quantity of labor to supply.

Summary

As the wage increases, the opportunity cost of leisure increases, causing individuals to supply a greater quantity of labor. Normally, the labor supply curve is upward sloping, but it is possible that at very high wage levels, the supply curve might be backward bending. This outcome occurs when someone with a high income is willing to accept a somewhat lower income in exchange for more leisure. We find the market labor supply curve by adding up the quantity of labor supplied by each worker at each wage, holding constant all other variables that might affect the willingness of workers to supply labor. The most important variables that shift the labor supply curve are increases in population, changing demographics, and changing alternatives.

 MyEconLab   Visit www.myeconlab.com to complete these exercises online and get instant feedback.

Review Questions

2.1 How can we measure the opportunity cost of leisure? What are the substitution effect and the income effect resulting from a wage change? Why is the supply curve of labor usually upward sloping?

2.2 What are the three most important variables that cause the market supply curve of labor to shift?

Problems and Applications

2.3 Daniel was earning $65 per hour and working 45 hours per week. Then Daniel's wage rose to $75 per hour, and as a result, he now works 40 hours per week. What can we conclude from this information about the income effect and the substitution effect of a wage change for Daniel?

2.4 A columnist writing in the *Wall Street Journal* argues that because "hourly wages in real terms" rose, the "price of time" also rose. What is the "price of time"? Is the columnist correct that when real hourly wages rise, the price of time increases? Briefly explain.
Source: Brett Arends, "Spend Some Time, Save Some Money," *Wall Street Journal*, May 19, 2009.

2.5 Most labor economists believe that many adult males are on a vertical section of their labor supply curves. Use the concepts of income and substitution effects to explain under what circumstances an individual's labor supply curve would be vertical.
Source: Robert Whaples, "Is There Consensus among American Labor Economists? Survey Results on Forty Propositions," *Journal of Labor Research*, Vol. 17, No. 4, Fall 1996.

2.6 Suppose that a large oil field is discovered in Michigan. By imposing a tax on the oil, the state government is able to eliminate the state income tax on wages. What is likely to be the effect on the labor supply curve in Michigan?

2.7 A columnist in the *New York Times* notes that the U.S. labor supply "in the next decade is expected to expand at less than half the pace of the 1960s, 1970s and 1980s." What explains these changing growth rates in the U.S. labor supply?
Source: Eduardo Porter, "The Payoff in Delaying Retirement," *New York Times*, March 5, 2013.

2.8 State whether each of the following events will result in a movement along the market supply curve of agricultural labor in the United States or whether it will cause the market supply curve of agricultural labor to shift. If the supply curve shifts, indicate whether it will shift to the left or to the right and draw a graph to illustrate the shift.
a. The agricultural wage rate declines.
b. Wages outside agriculture increase.
c. The law is changed to allow for unlimited immigration into the United States.

17.3 Equilibrium in the Labor Market, pages 540–544

LEARNING OBJECTIVE: Explain how equilibrium wages are determined in labor markets.

Summary

The intersection between labor supply and labor demand determines the equilibrium wage and the equilibrium level of employment. If labor supply is unchanged, an increase in labor demand will increase both the equilibrium wage and the number of workers employed. If labor demand is unchanged, an increase in labor supply will lower the equilibrium wage and increase the number of workers employed.

 MyEconLab   Visit www.myeconlab.com to complete these exercises online and get instant feedback.

Review Questions

3.1 If the labor demand curve shifts to the left and the labor supply curve remains unchanged, what will happen to the equilibrium wage and the equilibrium level of employment? Illustrate your answer with a graph.

3.2 If the labor supply curve shifts to the left and the labor demand curve remains unchanged, what will happen to the equilibrium wage and the equilibrium level of employment? Illustrate your answer with a graph.

Problems and Applications

3.3 **[Related to the** Making the Connection **on page 542]** Over time, the gap between the wages of workers with college degrees and the wages of workers without college degrees has been increasing. Shouldn't this gap have increased the incentive for workers to earn college degrees, thereby increasing the supply of college-educated workers and reducing the size of the gap?

3.4 Reread the discussion on page 543 of changes in the salaries of software engineers. Use a graph to illustrate this situation. Make sure your graph has labor demand and supply curves for 2009 and 2013 and that the equilibrium point for each year is clearly indicated.

3.5 Sean Astin, who played Sam in *The Lord of the Rings* movies, wrote the following about an earlier film he had appeared in: "Now I was in a movie I didn't respect, making obscene amounts of money (five times what a teacher makes, and teachers do infinitely more important work)." Are salaries determined by the importance of the work being done? If not, what are salaries determined by?

Source: Sean Astin, with Joe Layden, *There and Back Again: An Actor's Tale*, New York: St. Martin's Press, 2004, p. 35.

3.6 A newspaper article summarizes a study showing that "a standout kindergarten teacher is worth about $320,000 a year. That's the present value of the additional money that a full class of students can expect to earn over their careers. This estimate doesn't take into account social gains, like better health and less crime." Why are even standout kindergarten teachers paid salaries much lower than $320,000?

Source: David Leonhardt, "The Case for $320,000 Kindergarten Teachers," *New York Times*, July 27, 2010.

3.7 In 541 A.D., an outbreak of bubonic plague hit the Byzantine Empire. Because the plague was spread by flea-infested rats that often lived on ships, ports were hit particularly hard. In some ports, more than 40 percent of the population died. The emperor, Justinian, was concerned that the wages of sailors were rising very rapidly as a result of the plague. In 544 A.D., he placed a ceiling on the wages of sailors. Use a demand and supply graph of the market for sailors to show the effect of the plague on the wages of sailors. Use the same graph to show the effect of Justinian's wage ceiling. Briefly explain what is happening in your graph.

Source: Michael McCormick, *The Origins of the European Economy: Communications and Commerce, A.D., 300–900*, New York: Cambridge University Press, 2001, p. 109.

3.8 [Related to the Making the Connection on page 544] If the incomes of veterinarians are falling, why has the number of students enrolling in schools of veterinary medicine in the United States not declined?

17.4	**Explaining Differences in Wages, pages 544–554**

LEARNING OBJECTIVE: Use demand and supply analysis to explain how compensating differentials, discrimination, and labor unions cause wages to differ.

Summary

The equilibrium wage is determined by the intersection of the labor demand curve and the labor supply curve. Some differences in wages are explained by **compensating differentials**, which are higher wages that compensate workers for unpleasant aspects of a job. Wages can also differ because of **economic discrimination**, which involves paying a person a lower wage or excluding a person from an occupation on the basis of irrelevant characteristics, such as race or gender. **Labor unions** are organizations of employees that have the legal right to bargain with employers about wages and working conditions. Being in a union increases a worker's wages about 10 percent, holding constant other factors, such as the industry the workers are in.

 MyEconLab   Visit **www.myeconlab.com** to complete these exercises online and get instant feedback.

Review Questions

4.1 What is a compensating differential? Give an example.

4.2 Define *economic discrimination*. Is the fact that one group in the population has higher earnings than other groups evidence of economic discrimination? Briefly explain.

4.3 In what sense do employers who discriminate pay an economic penalty? Is this penalty enough to eliminate discrimination? Briefly explain.

4.4 Is the fraction of U.S. workers in labor unions larger or smaller than in other countries?

Problems and Applications

4.5 Writing on the Baseball Prospectus Web site, Dan Fox argued: "What a player is really worth depends a great deal on the teams that are interested in signing him." Do you agree? Shouldn't a baseball player with a particular level of ability be worth the same to every team? Briefly explain.

Source: Dan Fox, "Schrodinger's Bat," www.baseballprospectus.com, May 17, 2007.

4.6 [Related to the Chapter Opener on page 533] A student remarks: "I don't think the idea of marginal revenue product really helps explain differences in wages. After all, a ticket to a baseball game costs much less than college tuition, yet baseball players are paid much more than college professors." Do you agree with the student's reasoning?

4.7 [Related to the Don't Let This Happen to You on page 546] Joe Morgan is a sportscaster and former baseball player. After he stated that he thought the salaries of Major League Baseball players were justified, a baseball fan wrote the following to Rob Neyer, a sports columnist:

> Mr. Neyer,
> What are your feelings about Joe Morgan's comment that players are justified in being paid what they're being paid? How is it ok for A-Rod [New York Yankees infielder Alex Rodriguez] to earn $115,000 per GAME while my boss works 80 hour weeks and earns $30,000 per year?

How would you answer this fan's questions?

Source: ESPN.com, August 30, 2002.

4.8 Buster Olney, a columnist for ESPN.com, wondered why baseball teams pay the teams' managers and general managers less than they pay most baseball players:

> About two-thirds of the players on the [New York] Mets' roster will make more money than [manager Willie] Randolph; Willie will get somewhere in the neighborhood of half of an average major league salary for 2007. But Randolph's deal is right in line with what other managers are making, and right in the range of what the highest-paid general managers are

making…. I have a hard time believing that Randolph or general manager Omar Minaya will have less impact on the Mets than left-handed reliever Scott Schoeneweis, who will get paid more than either the manager or GM.

Provide an economic explanation of why baseball managers and general managers are generally paid less than baseball players.

Source: Buster Olney, "Managers Low on Pay Scale," ESPN.com, January 25, 2007.

4.9 When Nick Saban agreed to leave his job as head coach of the Miami Dolphins National Football League team to take a job as head football coach at the University of Alabama, he received a salary of $4 million per year for eight years. Ivan Maisel, a columnist for ESPN.com, wondered whether Saban was worth such a large salary: "Is Saban eight times better than the coach who outmaneuvered Bob Stoops of Oklahoma on Monday night? Boise State paid Chris Petersen $500,000 this season—and he still hasn't lost a game." Might Saban still be worth a salary of $4 million per year to Alabama even if he is not "eight times better" than a coach being paid $500,000 at another school? In your answer, be sure to refer to the difference between the marginal product of labor and the marginal revenue product of labor.

Source: Ivan Maisel, "Saban Will Find Crowded Pond in Tuscaloosa," ESPN.com, January 3, 2007.

4.10 [Related to the Making the Connection **on page 546**] According to Alan Krueger, an economist at Princeton University, the share of concert ticket revenue received by the top 1 percent of all acts rose from 26 percent in 1982 to 56 percent in 2003. Does this information indicate that the top acts in 2003 must have been much better performers relative to other acts than was the case in 1982? If not, can you think of another explanation?

Source: Eduardo Porter, "More Than Ever, It Pays to Be the Top Executive," *New York Times*, May 25, 2007.

4.11 [Related to the Making the Connection **on page 546**] Why are there superstar basketball players but no superstar plumbers?

4.12 [Related to the Chapter Opener **on page 533**] Sam Goldwyn, a movie producer during Hollywood's Golden Age, once remarked about one of his stars: "We're overpaying him, but he's worth it."

  a. In what sense did Goldwyn mean that he was overpaying this star?

  b. If he was overpaying the star, why would the star have still been worth it?

4.13 Prior to the early twentieth century, a worker who was injured on the job could collect damages only by suing his employer. To sue successfully, the worker—or his family, if the worker had been killed—had to show that the injury was due to the employer's negligence, that the worker did not know the job was hazardous, and that the worker's own negligence had not contributed to the accident. These lawsuits were difficult for workers to win, and even workers who had been seriously injured on the job often were unable to collect any damages from their employers. Beginning in 1910, most states passed workers' compensation laws that required employers to purchase insurance that would compensate workers for injuries suffered on the job. A study by Price Fishback, of the University of Arizona, and Shawn Kantor, of the University of California, Merced, shows that after the passage of workers' compensation laws, wages received by workers in the coal and lumber industries fell. Briefly explain why passage of workers' compensation laws would lead to a fall in wages in some industries.

Source: Price V. Fishback and Shawn Everett Kantor, "Did Workers Pay for the Passage of Workers' Compensation Laws?" *Quarterly Journal of Economics*, Vol. 110, No. 3, August 1995, pp. 713–742.

4.14 The following table is similar to Table 17.2 on page 548, except that it includes the earnings of Asian males and females. Does the fact that Asian males are the highest-earning group in the table affect the likelihood that economic discrimination is the best explanation for why earnings differ among the groups listed in the table? Briefly explain your argument.

Group	Annual Earnings
Asian males	$60,253
White males	56,247
Asian females	46,371
White females	42,171
Black males	39,816
Black females	35,090
Hispanic males	32,516
Hispanic females	29,508

Source: U.S. Bureau of the Census, Table PINC-01, "Current Population Survey," *2013 Annual Social and Economic Supplement.*

4.15 During the 1970s, many women changed their minds about whether they would leave the labor force after marrying and having children or whether they would be in the labor force most of their adult lives. In 1968, the National Longitudinal Survey asked a representative sample of women aged 14 to 24 whether they expected to be in the labor force at age 35. Twenty-nine percent of white women and 59 percent of black women responded that they expected to be in the labor force at that age. In fact, when these women were 35 years old, 60 percent of those who were married and 80 percent of those who were unmarried were in the labor force. In other words, many more women ended up being in the labor force than expected to be when they were of high school and college age. What effect did this fact have on the earnings of these women? Briefly explain.

Source: Claudia Goldin, *Understanding the Gender Gap: An Economic History of American Women*, New York: Oxford University Press, 1990, p. 155.

4.16 Lawrence Katz, an economist at Harvard, was quoted in a newspaper article as arguing that differences between the incomes of male physicians and female physicians "are largely explained by individual choices." He also noted that discrimination could account for part of the gap "though it isn't clear how much."

  a. What did Katz mean by "individual choices"? How can individual choices result in differences between how much men and women are paid?

b. Why is it difficult to estimate how much of the gap between what men and women are paid is due to discrimination?

Source: Josh Mitchell, "Women Notch Progress," *Wall Street Journal*, December 4, 2012.

4.17 [Related to Solved Problem 17.4 **on page 549**] Use the following graphs to answer the questions:

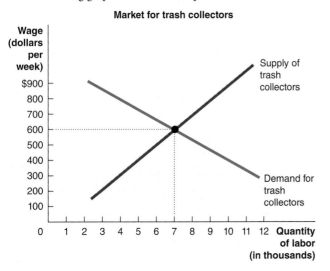

Market for trash collectors

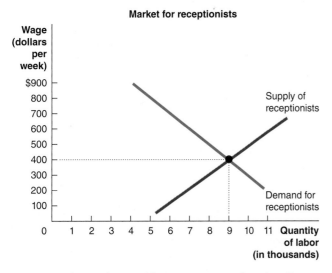

Market for receptionists

a. What is the equilibrium quantity of trash collectors hired, and what is the equilibrium wage?

b. What is the equilibrium quantity of receptionists hired, and what is the equilibrium wage?

c. Briefly discuss why trash collectors might earn a higher weekly wage than receptionists.

d. Suppose that comparable-worth legislation is passed, and the government requires that trash collectors and receptionists be paid the same wage, $500 per week. Now how many trash collectors will be hired and how many receptionists will be hired?

4.18 [Related to Solved Problem 17.4 **on page 549**] In most universities, economics professors receive larger salaries than English professors. Suppose that the government requires that from now on, all universities must pay economics professors the same salaries as English professors. Use demand and supply graphs to analyze the effect of this requirement.

4.19 [Related to the Making the Connection **on page 550**] Why might employers be more likely to interview a job applicant with a white-sounding name than an applicant with an African-American–sounding name? Leaving aside legal penalties, will employers who follow this practice incur an economic penalty? Briefly explain.

4.20 According to data from the Bureau of Labor Statistics, the unemployment rate among whites in June 2013 was 6.6 percent, while the unemployment rate among African Americans was 13.7 percent. If a news commentator concluded that economic discrimination is the best explanation for the difference in unemployment rates, would you agree? Briefly explain.

Source: U.S. Department of Labor, Bureau of Labor Statistics, *The Employment Situation—June 2013*, July 5, 2013.

4.21 Daniel Hamermesh is an economist at the University of Texas who has done a great deal of research on labor markets. According to an article in *Forbes*, Hamermesh writes that "below-average-looking men earn 17% less than those considered good-looking, while below-average-looking females earn 12% less than their attractive counterparts." Is this difference in earnings due to economic discrimination? Briefly explain.

Source: Susan Adams, "Does Beauty Really Pay?" *Forbes*, August 30, 2011.

4.22 Anthony Carnevale, director of the Center on Education and the Workforce at Georgetown University, recently noted that even among college graduates, unemployment rates can vary quite a bit. However, Carnevale also found that unemployment rates during 2010 and 2011 "were 9 to 10 percent for noncollege graduates, compared to 4.6 to 4.7 percent for college graduates 25 years or older." What could explain this difference in unemployment rates between college graduates and noncollege graduates?

Source: Gail MarksJarvis, "Costs vs. Benefits of College," *The Dallas Morning News*, June 30, 2013.

17.5 **Personnel Economics, pages 554–556**

LEARNING OBJECTIVE: Discuss the role personnel economics can play in helping firms deal with human resources issues.

Summary

Personnel economics is the application of economic analysis to human resources issues. One insight of personnel economics is that the productivity of workers can often be increased if firms move from straight-time pay to commission or piece-rate pay.

Review Questions

5.1 What is personnel economics?

5.2 What are the two ways that the productivity of a firm's employees may increase when a firm moves from straight-time pay to commission or piece-rate pay?

5.3 If piece-rate or commission systems of compensating workers have important advantages for firms, why don't more firms use them?

Problems and Applications

5.4 According to a study, the number of jobs in which firms used bonuses, commissions, or piece rates to tie workers' pay to their performance increased from an estimated 30 percent of all jobs in the 1970s to 40 percent in the 1990s. Why would systems that tie workers' pay to how much they produce have become increasingly popular with firms? The same study found that these pay systems were more common in higher-paid jobs than in lower-paid jobs. Briefly explain this result.

Source: Thomas Lemieux, W. Bentley MacLeod, and Daniel Parent, "Performance Pay and Wage Inequality," *Quarterly Journal of Economics*, Vol. 124, No. 1, February 2009, pp. 1–49.

5.5 Many companies that pay workers an hourly wage require some minimum level of acceptable output. Suppose a company that has been using this system decides to switch to a piece-rate system under which workers are compensated on the basis of how much output they produce. Is it likely that workers under a piece-rate system will end up choosing to produce less than the minimum output required under the hourly wage system? Briefly explain.

5.6 In most jobs, the harder you work, the more you earn. Some workers would rather work harder and earn more; others would rather work less hard, even though as a result they earn less. Suppose, though, that all workers at a company fall into the "work harder and earn more" group. Suppose also that the workers all have the same abilities. In these circumstances, would output per worker be the same under an hourly wage compensation system as under a piece-rate system? Briefly explain.

5.7 For years, the Goodyear Tire & Rubber Company compensated its sales force by paying a salesperson a salary plus a bonus, based on the number of tires he or she sold. Eventually, Goodyear made two changes to this policy: (1) The basis for the bonus was changed from the *quantity* of tires sold to the *revenue* from the tires sold; and (2) salespeople were required to get approval from corporate headquarters in Akron, Ohio, before offering to sell tires to customers at reduced prices. Explain why these changes were likely to increase Goodyear's profits.

Source: Timothy Aeppel, "Amid Weak Inflation, Firms Turn Creative to Boost Prices," *Wall Street Journal*, September 18, 2002.

5.8 **[Related to the** Making the Connection **on page 555]** What effect did the incentive pay system have on Safelite's marginal cost of installing replacement car windows? If all firms that replace car windows adopted an incentive pay system, what would happen to the price of replacing automobile glass? Who would ultimately benefit?

17.6 The Markets for Capital and Natural Resources, pages 556–559

LEARNING OBJECTIVE: Show how equilibrium prices are determined in the markets for capital and natural resources.

Summary

The approach used to analyze the market for labor can also be used to analyze the markets for other factors of production. In equilibrium, the price of capital is equal to the marginal revenue product of capital, and the price of natural resources is equal to the marginal revenue product of natural resources. The price received by a factor that is in fixed supply is called an **economic rent** (or a **pure rent**). A **monopsony** is a situation in which a firm is the sole buyer of a factor of production. According to the **marginal productivity theory of income distribution**, the distribution of income is determined by the marginal productivity of the factors of production individuals own.

 Visit **www.myeconlab.com** to complete these exercises online and get instant feedback.

Review Questions

6.1 In equilibrium, what determines the price of capital? What determines the price of natural resources? What is an economic rent?

6.2 What is a monopsony?

6.3 What is the marginal productivity theory of income distribution?

Problems and Applications

6.4 Adam operates a pin factory. Suppose Adam faces the situation shown in the following table and the cost of renting a machine is $550 per week.

   a. Fill in the blanks in the table and determine the profit-maximizing number of machines for Adam to rent. Briefly explain why renting this number of machines is profit maximizing.

   b. Draw Adam's demand curve for capital.

Number of Machines	Output of Pins (boxes per week)	Marginal Product of Capital	Product Price (dollars per box)	Total Revenue	Marginal Revenue Product of Capital	Rental Cost per Machine	Additional Profit from Renting One Additional Machine
0	0	_____	$100		_____	$550	
1	12		100			550	
2	21		100			550	
3	28		100			550	
4	34		100			550	
5	39		100			550	
6	43		100			550	

6.5 Many people have predicted, using a model like the one in panel (b) of Figure 17.12 on page 558, that the price of natural resources should rise consistently over time in comparison with the prices of other goods because the demand curve for natural resources is continually shifting to the right, while the supply curve must be shifting to the left as natural resources are used up. However, the relative prices of most natural resources have not been increasing. Draw a graph showing the demand and supply for natural resources that can explain why prices haven't risen even though demand has.

6.6 In 1879, economist Henry George published *Progress and Poverty*, which became one of the best-selling books of the nineteenth century. In this book, George argued that all existing taxes should be replaced with a single tax on land. Tax incidence refers to the actual division of the burden of a tax between buyers and sellers in a market (see Chapter 4). If land is taxed, how will the burden of the tax be divided between the sellers of land and the buyers of land? Illustrate your answer with a graph of the market for land.

6.7 The total amount of oil in the earth is not increasing. Does this mean that in the market for oil, the supply curve is perfectly inelastic? Briefly explain.

6.8 In a competitive labor market, imposing a minimum wage should reduce the equilibrium level of employment. Will this result still hold if the labor market is a monopsony? Briefly explain.

Public Choice, Taxes, and the Distribution of Income

Chapter Outline and Learning Objectives

Should the Government Use the Tax System to Reduce Inequality?

It wasn't a happy New Year for many American workers in January 2013 when Congress and President Barack Obama allowed a temporary reduction in the payroll tax used to fund the Social Security program to expire. As a result, the taxes paid by an average household increased by $1,000 per year. Income tax rates for individuals earning more than $400,000 and the tax rate on dividends and capital gains were also raised. Although the tax increases were used to help reduce the federal budget deficit, the increases were also intended to change the distribution of income.

During the 2012 presidential election campaign, President Obama and former Massachusetts Governor Mitt Romney debated whether changes in the tax system should be used to reduce income inequality. The president argued that tax cuts enacted during the early 2000s had increased the burden on individuals with low and moderate incomes, while the burden on the wealthy and on corporations had been reduced. He proposed to use the tax code to help reduce this inequality. Romney argued that increasing income inequality had not been caused by changes in taxes and that increasing taxes on individuals with high incomes was likely to reduce economic efficiency while having little effect on inequality.

The questions raised by the debate over taxes during the 2012 election campaign were not new. For example, Presidents John F. Kennedy and Ronald Reagan proposed significant cuts in income taxes that they claimed would enhance economic efficiency, while their opponents claimed that the tax cuts rewarded high-income taxpayers and increased income inequality. The design of the tax system and the criteria used to evaluate it are important issues. Has the tax code improved economic efficiency? Has the government, through its tax and other policies, had much effect on the distribution of income? We explore these questions in this chapter.

Sources: Jose Pagliery, "Smaller Paychecks Coming," www.cnnmoney.com, January 2, 2013; and Associated Press, "Deal Means Taxes Will Rise for Most Americans," *USA Today*, February 5, 2013.

Economics in Your Life

How Much Tax Should You Pay?

The government is ever present in your life. Just today, you likely drove on roads that the government paid to build and maintain. You may attend a public college or university, paid for, at least in part, by the government. Where does the government get its money? By taxing citizens. Think of the different taxes you pay. Do you think you pay more than, less than, or just about your fair share in taxes? How do you determine what your fair share is? As you read this chapter, try to answer these questions. You can check your answers against those we provide on **page 594** at the end of this chapter.

Public choice model A model that applies economic analysis to government decision making.

W e have seen that the government plays a significant role in helping the market system work efficiently by providing secure rights to private property and an independent court system to enforce contracts (see Chapter 2). We have also seen that the government itself must sometimes supply goods—known as *public goods*—that private firms will not supply (see Chapter 5). But how do governments decide which policies to adopt? In recent years, economists led by the late Nobel Laureate James Buchanan and Gordon Tullock, of George Mason University, have developed the **public choice model**, which applies economic analysis to government decision making. In this chapter, we will explore how public choice can help us understand how policymakers make decisions.

We will also discuss the principles that governments use to create tax policy. In particular, we will see how economists identify which taxes are most economically efficient. At the end of this chapter, we will discuss the extent to which government policy—including tax policy—affects the distribution of income.

18.1 LEARNING OBJECTIVE

Describe the public choice model and explain how it is used to analyze government decision making.

Public Choice

In earlier chapters, we focused on explaining the actions of households and firms. We have assumed that households and firms act to make themselves as well off as possible. In particular, we have assumed that households choose the goods they buy to maximize their utility and that firms choose the quantities and prices of the goods they sell to maximize profits. Because government policy plays an important role in the economy, it is also important to consider how government policymakers—such as senators, governors, presidents, and state legislators—arrive at their decisions. One of the key insights from the public choice model is that policymakers are no different than consumers or managers of firms: Policymakers are likely to pursue their own self-interest, even if their self-interest conflicts with the public interest. In particular, we expect that public officials will take actions that are likely to result in their being reelected.

How Do We Know the Public Interest? Models of Voting

It is possible to argue that elected officials simply represent the preferences of the voters who elect them. After all, it would seem logical that voters will not reelect a politician who fails to act in the public interest. A closer look at voting, however, makes it less clear that politicians are simply representing the views of the voters.

The Voting Paradox Many policy decisions involve multiple alternatives. Because the size of the federal budget is limited, policymakers face trade-offs. To take a simple example, suppose that there is $1 billion available in the budget, and Congress must choose whether to spend it on *only one* of three alternatives: (1) research on breast cancer, (2) subsidies for mass transit, or (3) increased border security. Assume that the votes of members of Congress will represent the preferences of their constituents. We might expect that Congress will vote for the alternative favored by a majority of the voters. In fact, though, there are circumstances in which majority voting will fail to result in a consistent decision. For example, suppose for simplicity that there are only three voters, and they have the preferences shown at the top of Table 18.1.

In the table, we show the three policy alternatives in the first column. The remaining columns show the voters' rankings of the alternatives. For example, Lena would prefer to see the money spent on cancer research. Her second choice is mass transit, and her third choice is border security. What happens if a series of votes are taken in which each pair of alternatives is considered in turn? The bottom of Table 18.1 shows the results of these votes. If the vote is between spending the money on cancer research and spending the money on mass transit, cancer research wins because Lena and David both prefer spending the money on cancer research to spending the money on mass transit. So, if the votes of members of Congress represent the preferences of voters, we have a clear verdict, and the money is spent on breast cancer research. Suppose, though,

Policy	Lena	David	Kathleen	**Table 18.1**
Cancer research	1st	2nd	3rd	**The Voting Paradox**
Mass transit	2nd	3rd	1st	
Border security	3rd	1st	2nd	

Votes	Outcome
Cancer research versus mass transit	Cancer research wins
Mass transit versus border security	Mass transit wins
Border security versus cancer research	Border security wins

that the vote is between spending the money on mass transit and spending the money on border security. Then, because Lena and Kathleen prefer spending on mass transit to spending on border security, mass transit wins. Now, finally, suppose the vote is between spending on cancer research and spending on border security. Surprisingly, border security wins because that is what David and Kathleen prefer. The outcome of this vote is surprising because if voters prefer cancer research to mass transit and mass transit to border security, we would expect that consistency in decision making would ensure that they prefer cancer research to border security. But in this example, the collective preferences of the voters turn out not to be consistent. The failure of majority voting to always result in consistent choices is called the **voting paradox**.

This example is artificial because we assumed that there were only three alternatives, there were only three voters, and a simple majority vote determined the outcomes. In fact, though, Nobel Laureate Kenneth Arrow of Stanford University has shown mathematically that the failure of majority votes to always represent voters' preferences is a very general result. The **Arrow impossibility theorem** states that no system of voting can be devised that will consistently represent the underlying preferences of voters. This theorem suggests that there is no way through democratic voting to ensure that the preferences of voters are translated into policy choices. In fact, the Arrow impossibility theorem indicates that voting might lead to shifts in policy that may not be efficient. For instance, which of the three alternatives for spending the $1 billion Congress will actually choose would depend on the order in which the alternatives happen to be voted on, which might change from one year to the next. So, with respect to economic issues, such as providing funding for public goods, we cannot count on the political process to necessarily result in an efficient outcome. In other words, the "voting market"—as represented by elections—may often do a less efficient job of representing consumer preferences than do markets for goods and services.

The Median Voter Theorem In practice, many political issues are decided by a majority vote. In those cases, what can we say about which voters' preferences the outcome is likely to represent? An important result known as the **median voter theorem** states that the outcome of a majority vote is likely to represent the preferences of the voter who is in the political middle. To take another simplified example, suppose there are five voters, and their preferences for spending on breast cancer research are shown in Figure 18.1. Their preferences range from Kathleen, who prefers to spend nothing on breast cancer research—preferring the funds to be spent on other programs or for federal spending to be reduced and taxes lowered—to Lena, who prefers to spend $6 billion.

In this case, David is the median voter because he is in the political middle; two voters would prefer to spend less than he does and two voters would prefer to spend more than he does. To see why the median voter's preferences are likely to prevail, consider first a vote between David's preferred outcome of spending $2 billion and a proposal to spend $6 billion. Because only Lena favors $6 billion and the other voters all prefer spending less, the proposal to spend $2 billion would win four votes to one. Similarly, consider a vote between spending $2 billion and spending $1 billion. Three voters prefer spending more than $1 billion and only two prefer spending $1 billion or less, so the

Voting paradox The failure of majority voting to always result in consistent choices.

Arrow impossibility theorem A mathematical theorem that holds that no system of voting can be devised that will consistently represent the underlying preferences of voters.

Median voter theorem The proposition that the outcome of a majority vote is likely to represent the preferences of the voter who is in the political middle.

MyEconLab Animation

Figure 18.1

The Median Voter Theorem

The median voter theorem states that the outcome of a majority vote is likely to represent the preferences of the voter who is in the political middle. In this case, David is in the political middle because two voters want to spend more on breast cancer research than he does and two voters want to spend less. In any vote between a proposal to spend $2 billion and a proposal to spend a different amount, a proposal to spend $2 billion will win.

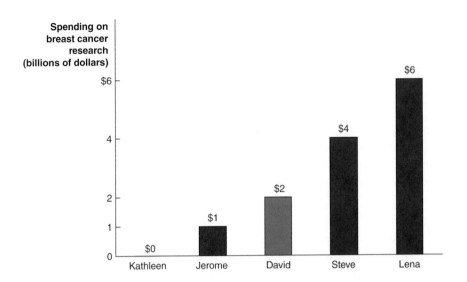

proposal to spend $2 billion will win three votes to two. Only the proposal to spend $2 billion will have the support of a majority when paired with proposals to spend a different amount. Notice also that the amount spent as a result of the voting is less than the amount that would result from taking the simple average of the voter's preferences, which would be $2.6 billion.

One implication of the median voter theorem is that the political process tends to serve individuals whose preferences are in the middle but not those individuals whose preferences are far away from the median. There is an important contrast between the political process, which results in collective actions in which everyone is obliged to participate, and the market process, in which individuals are free to participate or not. For instance, even though Kathleen would prefer not to spend government funds on breast cancer research, once a majority has voted to spend $2 billion, Kathleen is obliged to go along with the spending—and the taxes required to fund the spending. This outcome is in contrast with the market for goods and services, where if, for instance, Kathleen disagrees with the majority of consumers who like iPads, she is under no obligation to buy one. Similarly, even though Lena and Steve might prefer to pay significantly higher taxes to fund additional spending on breast cancer research, they are obliged to go along with the lower level of spending the majority approved. If Lena would like to have her iPad gold plated, she can choose to do so, even if the vast majority of consumers would consider such spending a waste of money.   MyEconLab Concept Check

Government Failure?

The voting models we have just looked at indicate that individuals are less likely to see their preferences represented in the outcomes of government policies than in the outcomes of markets. The public choice model goes beyond this observation to question whether the self-interest of policymakers is likely to cause them to take actions that are inconsistent with the preferences of voters, even where those preferences are clear. There are several aspects of the way the political process works that might lead to this outcome.

Rent Seeking   Economists usually focus on the actions of individuals and firms as they attempt to make themselves better off by interacting in markets. The public choice model shifts the focus to attempts by individuals and firms to engage in **rent seeking**, which is the use of government action to make themselves better off at the expense of others. One of the benefits of the market system is that it channels self-interested behavior in a way that benefits society as a whole. Although Apple developed the iPad to make a profit, its actions increased the well-being of millions of consumers. When Samsung introduced the Galaxy Tab to compete with the iPad, it was also motivated by the desire for profit, but it further increased consumer well-being by expanding the choice of tablets available. Rent seeking, in contrast, can benefit a few individuals or firms at the

Rent seeking Attempts by individuals and firms to use government action to make themselves better off at the expense of others.

expense of all other individuals and firms. For example, U.S. sugar firms have successfully convinced Congress to impose a quota on imports of sugar (see Chapter 9). The quota has benefited the owners of U.S. sugar firms and the people who work for them but has reduced consumer surplus, hurt U.S. candy companies and their workers, and reduced economic efficiency.

Because firms can benefit from government intervention in the economy, as the sugar companies have benefited from the sugar quota, they are willing to spend money to influence government policymakers. Members of Congress, state legislators, governors, and presidents need funds to finance their election campaigns. So, these policymakers may accept campaign contributions from rent-seeking firms and may be willing to introduce *special-interest legislation* on their behalf.

Logrolling and Rational Ignorance Two other factors help explain why rent-seeking behavior can sometimes succeed. It may seem puzzling that the sugar quota has been enacted when it helps very few workers and firms. Why would members of Congress vote for the sugar quota if they do not have sugar companies in their districts? One possibility is *logrolling*, which refers to the situation where a member of Congress votes to approve a bill in exchange for favorable votes from other members on other bills. For example, a member of Congress from Texas might vote for the sugar quota, even though none of the member's constituents will benefit from it. In exchange, members of Congress from districts where sugar producers are located will vote for legislation the member of Congress from Texas would like to see passed. As Pennsylvania Senator Pat Toomey put it after his attempt to eliminate the sugar quota was voted down: "They circle the wagons, work together, protect each others' interests." This vote trading may result in a majority of Congress supporting legislation that benefits the economic interests of a few while harming the economic interests of a much larger group.

But if the majority of voters are harmed by rent-seeking legislation, how does it get passed, even given the effects of logrolling? Consider another possible explanation for the survival of the sugar quota (see Chapter 9). Although total consumer surplus declines by $3.9 billion per year because of the sugar quota, when it is spread across a population of more than 300 million, the loss per person is only about $12.50. Because the loss is so small, most people do not take it into account when deciding who to vote for, and many people are not even aware that the sugar quota exists. Other voters may be convinced to support restrictions on trade because the jobs saved by tariffs and quotas are visible and often highly publicized, while the jobs lost because of these restrictions and the reductions in consumer surplus are harder to detect. Because becoming informed on an issue may require time and effort and the economic payoff is often low, some economists argue that many voters are *rationally ignorant* of the effect of rent-seeking legislation. In this view, because voters frequently lack an economic incentive to become informed about legislation, the preferences of voters do not act as a constraint on legislators voting for rent-seeking legislation.

Regulatory Capture One way in which the government intervenes in the economy is by establishing a regulatory agency or commission that is given authority over a particular industry or type of product. For example, no firm is allowed to sell prescription drugs in the United States without first receiving authorization from the Food and Drug Administration (FDA). Ideally, regulatory agencies will make decisions in the public interest. The FDA should weigh the benefits to patients from quickly approving a new drug against the costs that the agency may overlook potentially dangerous side effects of the drug if approval is too rapid. However, because the firms being regulated have a financial stake in the regulatory agency's actions, the firms have an incentive to try to influence those actions. In extreme cases, this influence may lead the agency to make decisions that are in the best interests of the firms being regulated, even if these actions are not in the public interest. In that case, the agency has been subject to *regulatory capture* by the industry being regulated. Some economists point to the Interstate Commerce Commission (ICC) as an example of regulatory capture. Although Congress has since abolished the ICC, for decades it determined the prices that railroads and long-distance trucking firms could charge to haul freight. Congress originally established the ICC to safeguard the interests of consumers, but some economists have argued that for many years the ICC operated to suppress competition, which was in the interests of the railroads and trucking firms rather than in the interests of consumers. Economists debate the extent to which regulatory capture explains the decisions of some government agencies.

The presence of externalities can lead to market failure, which is the situation where the market does not supply the economically efficient quantity of a good or service (see Chapter 5). Public choice analysis indicates that *government failure* can also occur. For the reasons we have discussed in this section, it is possible that government intervention in the economy may reduce economic efficiency rather than increase it. Economists disagree about the extent to which government failure results in serious economic inefficiency in the U.S. economy. Most economists, though, accept the basic argument of the public choice model that policymakers may have incentives to intervene in the economy in ways that do not promote efficiency and that proposals for such intervention should be evaluated with care.

MyEconLab Concept Check

Is Government Regulation Necessary?

The public choice model raises important questions about the effect of government regulation on economic efficiency. Can we conclude that Congress should abolish agencies such as the Food and Drug Administration (FDA), the Environmental Protection Agency (EPA), and the Federal Trade Commission (FTC)? In fact, most economists agree that these agencies can serve useful purposes. For instance, the EPA can help correct the effects of production externalities, such as pollution. Regulatory agencies can also improve economic efficiency in markets where consumers have difficulty obtaining the information they need to make informed purchases. For example, consumers have no easy way of detecting bacteria and other contaminants in food or determining whether prescription drugs are safe and effective. The FDA was established in the early twentieth century to monitor the nation's food supply following newspaper accounts of unsanitary practices in many meatpacking plants.

Although government regulation can clearly provide important benefits to consumers, we need to take into account the costs of regulations. Recent estimates indicate that the costs of federal regulations may be several thousand dollars per taxpayer. Economics can help policymakers devise regulations that provide benefits to consumers that exceed their costs.

MyEconLab Study Plan

MyEconLab Concept Check

The Tax System

However the size of government and the types of activities it engages in are determined, government spending has to be financed. The government primarily relies on taxes to raise the revenue it needs. Some taxes, such as those on cigarettes or alcohol, are intended to discourage what society views as undesirable behavior in addition to raising revenue. These are the most widely used taxes:

- *Individual income taxes.* The federal government, most state governments, and some local governments tax the wages, salaries, and other income of households and the profits of small businesses, which are typically taxed the same as wages and salaries. The individual income tax is the largest source of revenue for the federal government. Because low-income people are exempted from paying federal individual income taxes, in recent years nearly half of all households have paid no federal income tax.

- *Social insurance taxes.* The federal government taxes wages and salaries to raise revenue for the Social Security and Medicare systems. *Social Security* makes payments to retired workers and to disabled individuals. *Medicare* helps pay the medical expenses of people over age 65. The Social Security and Medicare taxes are often called *payroll taxes*. As the U.S. population has aged, payroll taxes have increased. By 2013, more than three-quarters of taxpayers paid a greater amount in payroll taxes than in federal income taxes. The federal government and state governments also tax wages and salaries to raise revenue for the unemployment insurance system, which makes payments to workers who have lost their jobs.

- *Sales taxes.* Most state and local governments tax retail sales of most products. More than half the states exempt food from the sales tax, and a few states also exempt clothing.

- *Property taxes.* Most local governments tax homes, offices, factories, and the land they are built on. In the United States, the property tax is the largest source of funds for public schools.

- *Excise taxes.* The federal government and some state governments levy excise taxes on specific goods, such as gasoline, cigarettes, and beer.

An Overview of the U.S. Tax System

Panels (a) and (b) of Figure 18.2 show the revenue sources of the federal, state, and local governments. Panel (a) shows that the federal government raises more than 75 percent of its revenue from the social insurance taxes and individual income taxes. Corporate income taxes and excise taxes account for much smaller fractions of federal revenues. In 2012, federal revenues of all types amounted to almost $2.7 trillion, or about $22,161 per household. Over the past 40 years, federal revenues as a share of gross domestic product (GDP—the value of all the goods and services produced in the U.S. economy) have typically remained in a fairly narrow range between 17 percent and 19 percent, with a low of 16 percent in 2009 and a high of 21 percent in 2000.

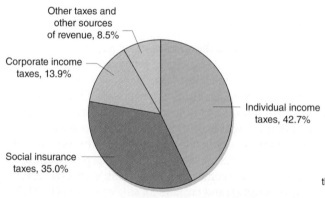

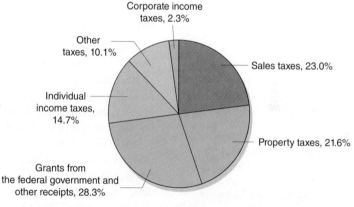

Tax	Amount (billions)	Amount per Household	Percentage of Total Tax Receipts
Individual income taxes	$9,453	$1,145	42.7%
Social insurance taxes	7,752	939	35.0
Corporate income taxes	3,075	372	13.9
Other taxes and sources of revenue	1,882	228	8.5
Total	$22,161	$2,683	100.0%

(a) Sources of federal government revenue, 2012

Tax	Amount (billions)	Amount per Household	Percentage of Total Tax Receipts
Grants from the federal government and other receipts	$585	$4,795	28.3%
Sales taxes	475	3,896	23.0
Property taxes	448	3,670	21.6
Individual income taxes	304	2,488	14.7
Other taxes	210	1,721	10.1
Corporate income taxes	48	395	2.3
Total	$2,070	$16,965	100.0%

(b) Sources of state and local government revenue, 2012

MyEconLab Animation

Figure 18.2   Federal, State, and Local Sources of Revenue, 2012

Individual income taxes are the most important source of revenue for the federal government, and social insurance taxes are the second most important source. State and local governments receive most of their revenue from sales taxes. State and local governments also receive large transfers from the federal government, in part to help pay for federally mandated programs.

Many local governments depend on property taxes to raise most of their tax revenue.

Note: Categories may not sum to totals because of rounding.

Source: U.S. Department of Commerce, Bureau of Economic Analysis, "National Income and Product Accounts of the United States," Tables 3.2 and 3.3, June 26, 2013.

Income	Tax Rate
$0–$8,925	10%
$8,926–$36,250	15
$36,251–$87,850	25
$87,851–$183,250	28
$183,251–$398,350	33
$398,351–$400,000	35
Over $400,000	39.6

Source: Internal Revenue Service.

Panel (b) shows that state and local governments rely on a different mix of revenue sources than does the federal government. In the past, the largest source of revenue for state and local governments was sales taxes. State and local governments also receive large grants from the federal government, which in 2012 were their largest source of revenue. These grants are intended in part to pay for programs that the federal government requires state and local governments to carry out. These programs, often called *federal mandates*, include the *Medicaid* program, which finances health care for many low-income people, and the Temporary Assistance for Needy Families (TANF) program, which provides financial assistance to poor families. During and after the 2007–2009 recession, the federal government temporarily increased its grants to local governments. Local governments also raise substantial revenue from property taxes. Many local school districts, in particular, rely almost entirely on revenues from property taxes. MyEconLab Concept Check

Progressive and Regressive Taxes

Regressive tax A tax for which people with lower incomes pay a higher percentage of their income in tax than do people with higher incomes.

Progressive tax A tax for which people with lower incomes pay a lower percentage of their income in tax than do people with higher incomes.

Economists often categorize taxes on the basis of the amount of tax people with different levels of income pay relative to their incomes. A tax is **regressive** if people with lower incomes pay a higher percentage of their income in tax than do people with higher incomes. A tax is **progressive** if people with lower incomes pay a lower percentage of their income in tax than do people with higher incomes. A tax is *proportional* if people with lower incomes pay the same percentage of their income in tax as do people with higher incomes.

The federal income tax is an example of a progressive tax. To see why, note first the important distinction between a tax rate and a tax bracket. A *tax rate* is the percentage of income paid in taxes. A *tax bracket* refers to the income range within which a tax rate applies. Table 18.2 shows the federal income tax brackets and tax rates for single taxpayers in 2013.

We can use Table 18.2 to calculate what Matt, a single taxpayer with an income of $100,000, pays in federal income tax. This example is somewhat simplified because we are ignoring the *exemptions* and *deductions* that taxpayers can use to reduce the amount of income subject to tax. For example, taxpayers are allowed to exclude from taxation a certain amount of income, called the *personal exemption*, that represents very basic living expenses. Ignoring Matt's exemptions and deductions, he will have to make the tax payment to the federal government shown in Table 18.3. Matt's first $8,925 of income is in the 10 percent bracket, so he pays $892.50 in taxes on that part of his income. His next $27,325 of income is in the 15 percent bracket, so he pays $4,098.75. His next $51,600 of income is in the 25 percent bracket, so he pays $12,900. His last $12,150 of income is in the 28 percent bracket, so he pays $3,402, which brings his total federal income tax bill to $21,293.25. MyEconLab Concept Check

On Matt's ...	Matt pays tax of ...
first $8,925 of income	$892.50
next $27,325 of income	4,098.75
next $51,600 of income	12,900.00
last $12,150 of income	3,402.00
His total federal income tax payment is	$21,293.25

Making the Connection
MyEconLab Video

Which Groups Pay the Most in Federal Taxes?

At the beginning of this chapter, we mentioned the ongoing debate over whether to increase taxes on people with high incomes. To evaluate this debate, it's useful to know how much each income group pays of the total taxes collected by the federal government. The following table shows projections for 2013 by the Tax Policy Center, with taxpayers divided into quintiles from the 20 percent with the lowest income to the 20 percent with the highest income. The last row also shows taxpayers whose incomes put them in the top 1 percent. Column (1) shows the percentage of total income earned by each income group. Column (2) shows the percentage of all federal taxes—including Social Security and Medicare payroll taxes—paid by each income group. Column (3) shows the average federal tax rate for each group, calculated by dividing total taxes paid by total income.

Income Category	Share of Total Income Earned (1)	Share of Total Federal Taxes Paid (2)	All Federal Taxes Paid as a Fraction of Income (Average Federal Tax Rate) (3)
Lowest 20%	4.2%	0.3%	3.8%
Second 20%	9.9	4.3	9.5
Third 20%	14.9	10.8	15.9
Fourth 20%	20.0	17.7	19.3
Highest 20%	51.5	66.7	26.1
Total	100.0%	100.0%	20.9%
Highest 1%	17.4	29.3	30.9

Note: Columns may not sum to precisely 100 percent due to rounding.
Source: Urban-Brookings Tax Policy Center, Tables T13-0035 and T13-0049, January 25, 2013.

The data in column (2) show that the 20 percent of taxpayers with the highest incomes pay 67 percent of federal taxes, which is greater than their 52 percent share of total income earned, as shown in column (1). Only taxpayers in the highest quintile pay a larger share of taxes than their share of income. Taxpayers whose incomes put them in the top 1 percent pay more than 29 percent of federal taxes. Many individuals in the lowest quintile of income, particularly those with children, receive tax credits from the federal government so that they in effect pay negative taxes. Column (3) indicates that average tax rates rise as income rises.

If we look at just the federal individual income tax considered separately from the payroll tax and other federal taxes, the results are similar. In 2013, taxpayers in the top 1 percent of the income distribution were projected to earn 17 percent of all income while paying 43 percent of all federal individual income taxes. The top 20 percent earned 52 percent of income while paying 84 percent of individual taxes. The bottom 40 percent of the income distribution earned 14 percent of income but actually paid *negative* 4 percent of federal individual income taxes when taking into account tax credits, such as the child tax credit.

We can conclude that the federal taxes are progressive. Whether the federal tax system should be made more or less progressive remains a source of political debate.

Your Turn: Test your understanding by doing related problem 2.9 on page 597 at the end of this chapter.

MyEconLab Study Plan

Marginal and Average Income Tax Rates

The fraction of each additional dollar of income that must be paid in taxes is called the **marginal tax rate**. The **average tax rate** is the total tax paid divided by total income. When a tax is progressive, as is the federal income tax, the marginal and average tax rates

Marginal tax rate The fraction of each additional dollar of income that must be paid in taxes.

Average tax rate Total tax paid divided by total income.

differ. For example, in Table 18.3 on page 576, Matt had a marginal tax rate of 28 percent because that is the rate he paid on the last dollar of his income. But his average tax rate was:

$$\left(\frac{\$21,293.25}{\$100,000}\right) \times 100 = 21.29\%.$$

His average tax rate was lower than his marginal tax rate because the first $87,850 of his income was taxed at rates below his marginal rate of 28 percent.

The marginal tax rate is a better indicator than the average tax rate of how a change in a tax will affect people's willingness to work, save, and invest. For example, if Matt is considering working longer hours to raise his income, he will use his marginal tax rate to determine how much extra income he will earn after taxes. He will ignore his average tax rate because it does not represent the taxes he must pay on the *additional* income he earns. The higher the marginal tax rate, the lower the return he receives from working additional hours and the less likely he is to work those additional hours.   MyEconLab Concept Check

The Corporate Income Tax

The federal government taxes the profits earned by corporations under the *corporate income tax*. Like the individual income tax, the corporate income tax is progressive, with the lowest tax rate being 15 percent and the highest being 35 percent. Unlike the individual income tax, however, where relatively few taxpayers are taxed at the highest rate, many corporations are in the 35 percent tax bracket.

Economists debate the costs and benefits of a separate tax on corporate profits. The corporate income tax ultimately must be paid by a corporation's owners—who are its shareholders—or by its employees, in the form of lower wages, or by its customers, in the form of higher prices. Some economists argue that if the purpose of the corporate income tax is to tax the owners of corporations, it would be better to do so directly by taxing the owners' incomes rather than by taxing the owners indirectly through the corporate income tax. Individual taxpayers already pay income taxes on the dividends and capital gains they receive from owning stock in corporations. In effect, the corporate income tax "double taxes" earnings on individual shareholders' investments in corporations. An alternative policy that avoids this double taxation would be for corporations to calculate their total profits each year and send a notice to each shareholder, indicating the shareholder's portion of the profits. Shareholders would then be required to include this amount as taxable income on their personal income tax. Under another alternative, the federal government could continue to tax corporate income through the corporate income tax but allow individual taxpayers to receive corporate dividends and capital gains tax-free.   MyEconLab Concept Check

International Comparison of Corporate Income Taxes

In recent years, several countries have cut corporate income taxes to increase investment spending and growth. Table 18.4 compares corporate income tax rates in several high-income countries. The tax rates given in the table include taxes at all levels of government. So, in the United States, for example, they include taxes imposed on corporate profits by state governments as well as by the federal government. The table shows that several countries, including Italy, Germany, and Ireland, significantly reduced their corporate income tax rates between 2000 and 2012. Ireland, in particular, has been successful in using lower corporate income tax rates to attract foreign corporations to locate facilities there. Lower tax rates have led Microsoft, Intel, and Dell, among other U.S. firms, to base some of their operations in Ireland. The table also shows that corporate income tax rates are higher in the United States than in other high-income countries.

The relatively high U.S. corporate tax rate has led many large U.S. firms with significant sales in foreign countries to avoid returning profits earned in those countries back to the United States. By keeping their profits overseas, these U.S. firms do not have to pay U.S. taxes on them, although the funds are also not available to be spent in the United States. As a result, many large U.S. firms pay a marginal tax rate well below the 40 percent rate indicated in Table 18.4.   MyEconLab Concept Check

Country	Tax in 2000	Tax in 2012
France	37%	33%
Germany	52	29
Ireland	24	13
Italy	41	31
Japan	42	38
Spain	35	30
Sweden	28	26
United Kingdom	30	24
United States	40	40

Table 18.4

Corporate Income Tax Rates around the World

Source: KPMG, *KPMG's Corporate and Indirect Tax Survey, 2012.*

Evaluating Taxes

We have seen that to raise revenue, governments have available a variety of taxes. In selecting which taxes to use, governments take into account the following goals and principles:

- The goal of economic efficiency
- The ability-to-pay principle
- The horizontal-equity principle
- The benefits-received principle
- The goal of attaining social objectives

The Goal of Economic Efficiency   We can briefly review the effect of taxes on economic efficiency (see Chapter 4). Whenever a government taxes an activity, it raises the cost of engaging in that activity, so less of that activity will occur. Figure 18.3 uses a demand and supply graph to illustrate this point for a sales tax. A sales tax increases the cost of supplying a good, which causes the supply curve to shift up by the amount of the tax. In the figure, the equilibrium price rises from P_1 to P_2, and the equilibrium quantity falls from Q_1 to Q_2. When a good is taxed, less of it is produced.

The government collects tax revenue equal to the tax per unit multiplied by the number of units sold. The green-shaded rectangle in Figure 18.3 represents the government's tax revenue. Although sellers appear to receive a higher price for the good—P_2—the price they receive after paying the tax falls to P_3. Because the price consumers pay has risen, consumer surplus has fallen. Because the price producers receive has also fallen, producer surplus has fallen. Some of the reduction in consumer surplus and producer surplus becomes tax revenue for the government. The rest of the reduction in consumer

MyEconLab Animation

Figure 18.3

The Efficiency Loss from a Sales Tax

This figure reviews the discussion of the efficiency loss from a tax (see Chapter 4). A sales tax increases the cost of supplying a good, which causes the supply curve to shift up, from S_1 to S_2. Without the tax, the equilibrium price of the good is P_1, and the equilibrium quantity is Q_1. After the tax is imposed, the equilibrium price rises to P_2, and the equilibrium quantity falls to Q_2. After paying the tax, producers receive P_3. The government receives tax revenue equal to the green-shaded rectangle. Some consumer surplus and some producer surplus become tax revenue for the government, and some become deadweight loss, shown by the yellow-shaded triangle. The deadweight loss is the *excess burden* of the tax.

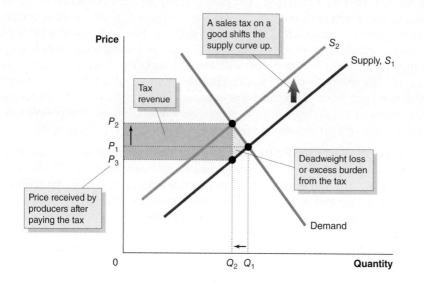

Excess burden A measure of the efficiency loss to the economy that results from a tax having reduced the quantity of a good produced; also known as the deadweight loss.

surplus and producer surplus is equal to the deadweight loss from the tax and is shown in the figure by the yellow-shaded triangle. The deadweight loss from a tax is known as the *excess burden* of the tax. The **excess burden** is a measure of the efficiency loss to the economy that results from the tax having reduced the quantity of the good produced. *A tax is efficient if it imposes a small excess burden relative to the tax revenue it raises.*

Economists believe that to improve the economic efficiency of a tax system, the government should reduce its reliance on taxes that have a high deadweight loss relative to the revenue raised. The tax on interest earned from savings is an example of a tax with a high deadweight loss because savings often comes from income already taxed once. Therefore, taxing interest earned on savings from income that has already been taxed is essentially double taxation.

There are other examples of significant deadweight losses of taxation. High taxes on work can reduce the number of hours an individual works, as well as how hard the individual works or whether the individual starts a business. In each case, the reduction in the taxed activity—here, work—generates less government revenue, and individuals are worse off because the tax encourages them to change their behavior.

Taxation can have substantial effects on economic efficiency by altering incentives to work, save, or invest. A good illustration of this effect can be seen in the large differences between annual hours worked in Europe and in the United States. Europeans typically work fewer hours than do Americans. According to an analysis by Nobel Laureate Edward Prescott of Arizona State University, this difference was not always present. In the early 1970s, when European and U.S. tax rates on income were comparable, European and U.S. hours worked per employee were also comparable. Prescott finds that virtually all of the difference between labor supply in the United States and labor supply in France and Germany since that time is due to differences in their tax systems.

The administrative burden of a tax represents another example of the deadweight loss of taxation. Individuals spend many hours during the year keeping records for income tax purposes, and they spend many more hours prior to April 15 preparing their tax returns. The opportunity cost of this time is billions of dollars each year and represents an administrative burden of the federal income tax. For corporations, complexity in tax planning arises in many areas. The federal government also has to devote resources to enforcing the tax laws. Although the government collects the revenue from taxation, the resources spent on administrative burdens benefit neither taxpayers nor the government.

Wouldn't tax simplification reduce the administrative burden and the deadweight loss of taxation? The answer is "yes." So why is the tax code complicated? In part, complexity arises because the political process has resulted in different types of income being taxed at different rates, requiring rules to limit taxpayers' ability to avoid taxes. In addition, interest groups seek to pay lower taxes, while the majority of taxpayers, who do not benefit from these "tax loopholes," find it difficult to organize a drive for a simpler tax system.

The Ability-to-Pay Principle The *ability-to-pay principle* holds that when the government raises revenue through taxes, it is fair to expect a greater share of the tax burden to be borne by people who have a greater ability to pay. To follow this principle, the government should attempt to achieve *vertical equity* by raising more taxes from people with high incomes than from people with low incomes. The federal income tax is consistent with the ability-to-pay principle. The sales tax, in contrast, is not consistent with the ability-to-pay principle because low-income people tend to spend a larger fraction of their income than do high-income people. As a result, low-income people will pay a greater fraction of their income in sales taxes than will high-income people.

The Horizontal-Equity Principle The *horizontal-equity principle* states that people in the same economic situation should be treated equally. Although this principle seems desirable, it is not easy to follow in practice because it is sometimes difficult to determine whether two people are in the same economic situation. For example, two people with the same income are not necessarily in the same economic situation. Suppose one person does not work but receives an income of $50,000 per year entirely from interest received on bonds and another person receives an income of $50,000 per year from working at two jobs 16 hours a day. In this case, we could argue that the two people are in different economic situations and should not pay the same tax. Although policymakers and economists usually consider horizontal equity when evaluating proposals to change the tax system, it is not a principle they can easily follow.

The Benefits-Received Principle According to the *benefits-received principle,* people who receive the benefits from a government program should pay the taxes that support the program. For example, if a city operates a marina that private boat owners use, the government can raise the revenue to operate the marina by levying a tax on the boat owners. Raising the revenue through a general income tax that both boat owners and non–boat owners pay would be inconsistent with the benefits-received principle. Because the government has many programs, however, it would be impractical to identify and tax the beneficiaries of every program.

The Goal of Attaining Social Objectives Taxes are sometimes used to attain social objectives. For example, the government might want to discourage smoking and drinking alcohol. Taxing cigarettes and alcoholic beverages is one way to help achieve this objective. Taxes intended to discourage certain activities are sometimes called *sin taxes.*
MyEconLab Concept Check   MyEconLab Study Plan

Tax Incidence Revisited: The Effect of Price Elasticity

18.3 LEARNING OBJECTIVE

Understand the effect of price elasticity on tax incidence.

Tax incidence The actual division of the burden of a tax between buyers and sellers in a market.

There is an important difference between who is legally required to send a tax payment to the government and who actually bears the burden of a tax (see Chapter 4). Recall that the actual division of the burden of a tax between buyers and sellers in a market is known as **tax incidence**. We can go beyond the basic analysis of tax incidence by considering how the price elasticity of demand and price elasticity of supply affect how the burden of a tax is shared between consumers and firms.

If the government imposes a 10-cent-per-gallon federal excise tax on gasoline, consumers will pay the majority of the tax because the elasticity of demand for gasoline is smaller than the elasticity of supply. In fact, we can draw a general conclusion: *When the demand for a product is less elastic than the supply, consumers pay the majority of the tax on the product. When demand for a product is more elastic than the supply, firms pay the majority of the tax on the product.*

Figure 18.4 shows why this conclusion is correct: D_1 is inelastic between points A and B, and D_2 is elastic between points A and C. With demand curve D_1, the 10-cent-per-gallon tax raises the market price of gasoline from \$4.00 (point A) to \$4.08 (point B) per gallon, so consumers pay 8 cents of the tax, and firms pay 2 cents. With D_2, the market price rises only to \$4.02 (point C) per gallon, and consumers pay only 2 cents of the tax. With demand curve D_2, sellers of gasoline receive only \$3.92 per gallon after paying the tax. So, the amount they receive per gallon after taxes falls from \$4.00 to \$3.92 per gallon, and they pay 8 cents of the tax.
MyEconLab Concept Check

Don't Let This Happen to You

Don't Confuse Who Pays a Tax with Who Bears the Burden of the Tax

Consider the following statement: "Of course, I bear the burden of the sales tax on everything I buy. I can show you my sales receipts with the 6 percent sales tax clearly labeled. The seller doesn't bear that tax. I do."

The statement is incorrect. To understand why it is incorrect, think about what would happen to the price of a product if the sales tax on it were eliminated. Figure 18.4 shows that the price of the product would fall because the supply curve would shift down by the amount of the tax. The equilibrium price, however, would fall by less than the amount of the tax. (If you doubt that this is true, draw the graph to convince

yourself.) So, the gain from eliminating the tax would be received partly by consumers in the form of a lower price but also partly by sellers in the form of a new price that is higher than the amount they received from the old price minus the tax. Therefore, the burden from imposing a sales tax is borne partly by consumers and partly by sellers.

In determining the burden of a tax, what counts is not what is printed on the receipt for a product but how the price of a product changes as a result of the tax.

MyEconLab Study Plan

Your Turn: Test your understanding by doing related problem 3.5 on page 598 at the end of this chapter.

Figure 18.4

The Effect of Elasticity on Tax Incidence

When demand is more elastic than supply, consumers bear less of the burden of a tax. When supply is more elastic than demand, firms bear less of the burden of a tax. D_1 is inelastic between points A and B, and D_2 is elastic between points A and C. With demand curve D_1, a 10-cent-per-gallon tax raises the equilibrium price from $4.00 (point A) to $4.08 (point B), so consumers pay 8 cents of the tax, and firms pay 2 cents. With D_2, a 10-cent-per-gallon tax on gasoline raises the equilibrium price only from $4.00 (point A) to $4.02 (point C), so consumers pay 2 cents of the tax. Because in this case producers receive $3.92 per gallon after paying the tax, their share of the tax is 8 cents per gallon.

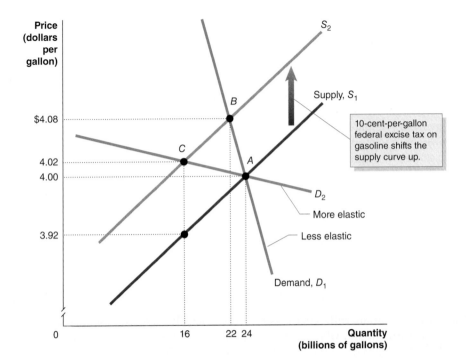

10-cent-per-gallon federal excise tax on gasoline shifts the supply curve up.

Will this consumer be paying part of Apple's corporate income tax when she buys an iPad or an iPhone?

Making the Connection

Do Corporations Really Bear the Burden of the Federal Corporate Income Tax?

During the 2012 presidential election campaign, hecklers at an Iowa appearance by former Massachusetts Governor Mitt Romney suggested that taxes on corporations be raised. Romney responded by saying, "Corporations are people, my friend." The hecklers responded, "No, they're not!" To which Romney responded, "Of course they are. Everything corporations earn ultimately goes to people. Where do you think it goes?" Romney was correct that corporations are legal persons in the eyes of the law. But what about the larger question: Who actually pays the corporate income tax? The incidence of the corporate income tax is one of the most controversial questions in the economics of tax policy. It is straightforward to determine the incidence of the gasoline tax using demand and supply analysis. Determining the incidence of the corporate income tax is more complicated because economists disagree about how corporations respond to the tax.

A study by the Congressional Budget Office stated:

A corporation may write its check to the Internal Revenue Service for payment of the corporate income tax, but the money must come from somewhere: from reduced returns to investors in the company, lower wages to its workers, or higher prices that consumers pay for the products the company produces.

Most economists agree that some of the burden of the corporate income tax is passed on to consumers in the form of higher prices. There is also some agreement that, because the corporate income tax reduces the rates of return received by investors, it results in less investment in corporations. This reduced investment means workers have less capital available to them. When workers have less capital, their productivity and their wages both fall (see Chapter 17). In this way, some of the burden of the corporate income tax is shifted from corporations to workers in the form of lower wages. Some studies have found that workers ultimately bear as much as 90 percent of the burden of the corporate income tax in the form of lower wages. The deadweight loss or excess burden from the corporate income tax is substantial. A study by the Congressional Budget Office estimated that this excess burden could equal more than half of the revenues raised by the tax. This estimate would make the corporate income tax one of the most inefficient taxes imposed by the federal government.

As a consequence, economists have long argued for reform of the system of double taxing income earned on investments that corporations finance by issuing stock. This income is taxed once by the corporate income tax and again by the individual income tax as profits are distributed to shareholders. Not surprisingly, discussion of the corporate income tax has played an important role in the ongoing debate in Congress over reforming the U.S. tax system.

Sources: Ashley Parker, " 'Corporations Are People,' Romney Tells Iowa Hecklers Angry over His Tax Policy," *New York Times*, August 11, 2011; Jennifer C. Gravelle, "Corporate Tax Incidence: A Review of Empirical Estimates and Analysis," Congressional Budget Office Working Paper 2011-01, June 2011; and Congressional Budget Office, "The Incidence of the Corporate Income Tax," CBO paper, March 1996.

Your Turn: Test your understanding by doing related problem 3.6 on page 598 at the end of this chapter.

MyEconLab Study Plan

Solved Problem 18.3

MyEconLab Interactive Animation

The Effect of Price Elasticity on the Excess Burden of a Tax

Explain whether you agree with the following statement: "For a given supply curve, the excess burden of a tax will be greater when demand is less elastic than when it is more elastic." Illustrate your answer with a demand and supply graph.

Solving the Problem

Step 1: **Review the chapter material.** This problem is about both excess burden and tax incidence, so you may want to review the section "Evaluating Taxes," which begins on page 579, and the section "Tax Incidence Revisited: The Effect of Price Elasticity," which begins on page 581.

Step 2: **Draw a graph to illustrate the relationship between tax incidence and excess burden.** Figure 18.4 on page 582 is a good example of the type of graph to draw. Be sure to indicate the areas representing excess burden.

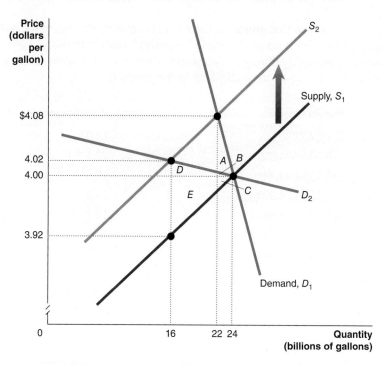

Step 3: **Use the graph to evaluate the statement.** As we have seen, for a given supply curve, when demand is more elastic, as with demand curve D_2, the fall in equilibrium quantity is greater than when demand is less elastic, as with demand curve D_1. The deadweight loss when demand is less elastic is shown by the area of the triangle made up of areas A, B, and C. The deadweight loss when demand is more elastic is shown by the area of the triangle made up of areas B, C, D, and E. The area of the deadweight loss is clearly larger when demand is more elastic than when it is less elastic. Recall that the excess burden of a tax is measured by the deadweight loss. Therefore, when demand is less elastic, the excess burden of a tax is *smaller* than when demand is more elastic. We can conclude that the statement is incorrect.

MyEconLab Study Plan

Your Turn: For more practice, do related problems 3.9 and 3.10 on pages 598–599 at the end of this chapter.

18.4 LEARNING OBJECTIVE

Discuss the distribution of income in the United States and understand the extent of income mobility.

Income Distribution and Poverty

In every country, some individuals will have very high incomes, and some individuals will have very low incomes. But how unequal is the distribution of income in the United States today? How does it compare with the distribution of income in the United States in the past or with the distribution of income in other countries today? What determines the distribution of income? And, to return to an issue raised at the beginning of this chapter, how does the tax system affect the distribution of income? These are questions we will explore in the remainder of this chapter.

Measuring the Income Distribution and Poverty

Tables 18.5 and 18.6 show that the distribution of income clearly is unequal. Table 18.5 shows that while 13 percent of U.S. households had annual incomes less than $15,000, the top 22 percent of households had incomes greater than $100,000. Table 18.6 divides the population of the United States into five groups, from the 20 percent with the lowest incomes to the 20 percent with the highest incomes. The fraction of total income received by each of the five groups is shown for selected years. Table 18.6 reinforces the fact that income is unequally distributed in the United States. The first row shows that in 2012, the 20 percent of Americans with the lowest incomes received only 3.2 percent of all income, while the 20 percent with the highest incomes received 51.0 percent of all income.

Table 18.6 also shows that over time, there have been some changes in the distribution of income. There was a moderate decline in inequality between 1936 and 1980, followed by an increase in inequality during the years after 1980. We will discuss some reasons for the recent increase in income inequality later in this chapter.

Table 18.5

The Distribution of Household Income in the United States, 2012

Annual Income	Percentage of All Households
$0–$14,999	13.0%
$15,000–$34,999	22.4
$35,000–$49,999	13.6
$50,000–$74,999	17.5
$75,000–$99,999	11.7
$100,000–$199,999	17.5
$200,000 and above	4.5

Note: Totals don't sum to 100 percent due to rounding.
Source: Carmen DeNavas-Walt, Bernadette D. Proctor, and Jessica C. Smith, U.S. Census Bureau, Current Population Reports, P60–245, *Income, Poverty, and Health Insurance Coverage in the United States: 2012,* Washington, DC: U.S. Government Printing Office, September 2013.

Year	Lowest 20%	Second 20%	Third 20%	Fourth 20%	Highest 20%
2012	3.2%	8.3%	14.8%	23.0%	51.0%
2000	3.6	8.9	14.8	23.0	49.8
1990	3.9	9.6	15.9	24.0	46.6
1980	4.3	10.3	16.9	24.9	43.7
1970	4.1	10.8	17.4	24.5	43.3
1960	3.2	10.6	17.6	24.7	44.0
1950	3.1	10.5	17.3	24.1	45.0
1936	4.1	9.2	14.1	20.9	51.7

Table 18.6

How Has the Distribution of Income Changed over Time?

Sources: Carmen DeNavas-Walt, Bernadette D. Proctor, and Jessica C. Smith, U.S. Census Bureau, Current Population Reports, P60–245, *Income, Poverty, and Health Insurance Coverage in the United States: 2012*, Washington, DC: U.S. Government Printing Office, September 2013; U.S. Census Bureau, *Income in the United States, 2002*, P60–221, September 2003; and U.S. Census Bureau, *Historical Statistics of the United States, Colonial Times to 1970*, Washington, DC: U.S. Government Printing Office, 1975.

The Poverty Rate in the United States Some of the discussion of the distribution of income focuses on poverty. The federal government has a formal definition of poverty that was first developed in the early 1960s. According to this definition, a family is below the **poverty line** if its annual income is less than three times the amount necessary to purchase the minimum quantity of food required for adequate nutrition. In 2013, the poverty line was $23,550 for a family of four. Figure 18.5 shows the **poverty rate**, or the percentage of the U.S. population that was poor during each year between 1960 and 2012. Between 1960 and 1973, the poverty rate declined by half, falling from 22 percent to 11 percent of the population. In the past 40 years, however, the poverty rate has declined very little. In 2012, it was actually higher than it was in 1966.

Different groups in the population have substantially different poverty rates. Table 18.7 shows that while the overall poverty rate in 2012 was 15.0 percent, the rates among women who head a family with no husband present, among black people, and among Hispanic people were much higher. The poverty rates for white and Asian people, as well as for families headed by married couples, were below average.　MyEconLab Concept Check

Poverty line A level of annual income equal to three times the amount of money necessary to purchase the minimum quantity of food required for adequate nutrition.

Poverty rate The percentage of the population that is poor according to the federal government's definition.

Explaining Income Inequality

The novelists Ernest Hemingway and F. Scott Fitzgerald supposedly once had a conversation about the rich. Fitzgerald said to Hemingway, "You know, the rich are different from you and me." To which Hemingway replied, "Yes. They have more money." Although witty, Hemingway's joke doesn't help answer the question of why the rich have

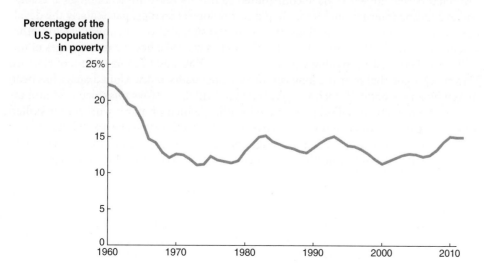

MyEconLab Animation

Figure 18.5

Poverty in the United States, 1960–2012

The poverty rate in the United States declined from 22 percent of the population in 1960 to 11 percent in 1973. Over the past 30 years, the poverty rate has fluctuated between 11 and 15 percent of the population. **Source:** Carmen DeNavas-Walt, Bernadette D. Proctor, and Jessica C. Smith, U.S. Census Bureau, Current Population Reports, P60–245, *Income, Poverty, and Health Insurance Coverage in the United States: 2012*, Washington, DC: U.S. Government Printing Office, September 2013.

All people	15.0%
Female head of family, no husband present (all races)	30.9
Blacks	27.2
Hispanics	25.6
Asians	11.7
White, not Hispanic	9.7
Married couple families (all races)	6.3

Note: Hispanics can be of any race.
Source: Carmen DeNavas-Walt, Bernadette D. Proctor, and Jessica C. Smith, U.S. Census Bureau, *Current Population Reports,* P60–245, *Income, Poverty, and Health Insurance Coverage in the United States: 2012,* Washington, DC: U.S. Government Printing Office, September 2013.

Human capital The accumulated knowledge and skills that workers acquire from formal training and education or from life experiences.

more money. One answer to the question of why incomes differ is given by the *marginal productivity theory of income distribution* (see Chapter 17). In equilibrium, each factor of production receives a payment equal to its marginal revenue product. The more factors of production an individual owns, and the more productive those factors are, the higher the individual's income will be.

For most people, of course, the most important factor of production they own is their labor. Therefore, the income they earn depends on how productive they are and on the prices of the goods and services their labor helps produce. Baseball player Zack Greinke earned a salary of $17 million in 2013 because he is a very productive player, and his employer, the Los Angeles Dodgers, can sell tickets and television rights to the baseball games Greinke plays in for a high price. Individuals who help to produce goods and services that can be sold for only a low price earn lower incomes.

An individual's productivity depends in part on his or her **human capital**, which refers to the accumulated knowledge and skills that workers acquire from formal training and education or from life experiences. Human capital is not equally distributed across workers. For example, some people have degrees in software engineering that prepare them for high-paying jobs, while other people drop out of high school and are prepared only for lower-paying jobs.

Many people own other factors of production beyond just their labor. For example, many people own capital by owning stock in corporations or by owning shares in mutual funds that buy the stock of corporations. Ownership of capital is not equally distributed, and income earned from capital is more unequally distributed than income earned from labor. Some people supply entrepreneurial skills by starting and managing businesses. Their income is increased by the profits from these businesses.

We saw in Table 18.6 that income inequality has increased during the past 30 years. Two factors that appear to have contributed to this increase are technological change and expanding international trade. Rapid technological change, particularly the development of information technology, has led to the substitution of computers and other machines for unskilled labor. This substitution has caused a decline in the wages of unskilled workers relative to other workers. Lawrence Katz and Claudia Goldin of Harvard University argue that over the long run income inequality in the United States has been driven by a race between technological change, which destroys unskilled jobs and increases the returns to skilled jobs, and education, which prepares workers for skilled jobs. Rising educational attainment between 1910 and the 1970s narrowed the income distribution by reducing the relative wages of skilled workers. Educational attainment in the United States since the 1970s has increased more slowly, leading to rising relative wages of skilled workers.

Expanding international trade has put U.S. workers in competition with foreign workers to a greater extent than in the past. This competition has caused the wages of unskilled workers to be depressed relative to the wages of other workers. Some economists have also argued that the incomes of low-income workers have been depressed by competition with workers who have immigrated to the United States.

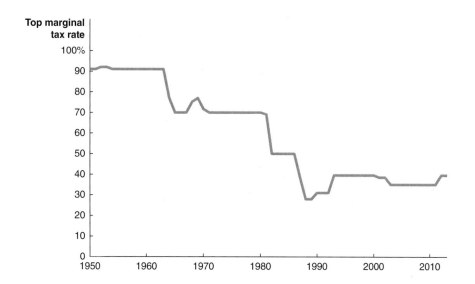

MyEconLab Animation

Figure 18.6

The Top Marginal Income Tax Rate in the United States, 1950–2013

The top marginal tax rate has varied dramatically since 1950, while the distribution of income has changed much less.
Sources: Urban Institute and the Brookings Institution, Tax Policy Center.

As Figure 18.6 shows, federal income tax rates have changed dramatically during the years covered in Table 18.6. For example, the top marginal income tax rate was 91 percent in the 1950s; it declined to 70 percent in the 1960s and to 28 percent in the 1980s. The rate then rose to 39.6 percent in the 1990s before declining to 35 percent in 2003 and rising back to 39.6 percent in 2013. Economists debate the effect of the tax system on income inequality. The values in Table 18.6 show the distribution of income *before* people have paid taxes, so they don't directly reflect the effect of the tax system on inequality. As we have seen, the federal income tax system is progressive, with higher-income people paying a larger percentage of their income in taxes than do lower-income people. Therefore, the after-tax distribution of income is more equal than the pretax distribution of income. Some economists argue, though, that the after-tax distribution of income could be made more equal if top marginal rates were to rise to the higher levels that prevailed prior to the 1980s. Higher-income people are more likely than lower-income people to own assets, such as stocks and bonds, and the returns people receive on their financial assets often receive favorable tax treatment. For example, people who own stock in corporations receive dividend payments and earn *capital gains* if they sell the stock for a profit. Both dividends and capital gains are taxed at rates that are lower than the top marginal individual income tax rates. Raising taxes on dividends and capital gains could potentially reduce the after-tax inequality of incomes.

Other economists are skeptical that raising taxes is an efficient way to reduce income inequality. These economists argue that higher marginal tax rates will discourage work, saving, and investment, thereby slowing economic growth and increases in incomes for all groups. Similarly, higher taxes on dividends and capital gains will reduce incentives to save and invest. They also argue that past periods of high marginal tax rates have seen higher-income people devote time and money to *tax avoidance*, which involves searching for provisions of the tax code that will allow individuals to reduce their tax payments. Resources spent on tax avoidance add to the excess burden of the tax code. The debate over the effects of the tax code on income inequality will undoubtedly continue.

Finally, like everything else in life, earning an income is subject to good and bad luck. A poor person who becomes a millionaire by winning the state lottery is an obvious example, as is a person whose earning power drastically declines as a result of a debilitating illness or accident. So, we can say that as a group, the people with high incomes are likely to have greater-than-average productivity and own greater-than-average amounts of capital. They are also likely to have experienced good luck. As a group, people with low incomes are likely to have lower-than-average productivity and own lower-than-average amounts of capital. They are also likely to have been unlucky.   MyEconLab Concept Check

Making the Connection
MyEconLab Video

What Explains the 1 Percent?

In the past few years, concerns about increasing inequality have often focused on the top 1 percent of the income distribution. During 2012, the "Occupy Wall Street" movement, which held demonstrations against income inequality in New York and other cities, used the slogan "We are the 99%" to indicate what they saw as the unfair advantages the 1 percent received at the expense of the rest of the population. Research by Emmanuel Saez of the University of California, Berkeley, has used data from income tax returns to look at changes in the share of income earned by the top 1 percent. As the blue line in the following graph shows, the top 1 percent earned between 18 and 24 percent of total income from 1913 through the late 1920s. (The red line is discussed below.) The share then began a long decline, dropping below 9 percent in the 1970s before rising again, reaching 20 percent in the past few years.

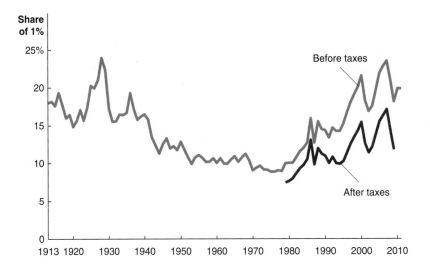

Economists, political commentators, and policymakers have debated two questions connected with the increased share of income the top 1 percent earn: (1) What explains the increase? and (2) Does the increase require a change in economic policy?

Saez and colleagues believe that reductions in marginal tax rates in the United States have increased the share of the top 1 percent, but in an indirect way. They argue that lower rates increase the incentive for CEOs of top corporations and other very high income earners to bargain for larger salaries. Saez and colleagues note that the top 1 percent of income earners have also increased their share of total income in other countries, such as Canada, the United Kingdom, and Australia, where top marginal tax rates have been reduced. The top 1 percent has experienced smaller increases in their income share in the countries of Western Europe where reductions in top marginal tax rates have been smaller. Saez and colleagues also note that the deregulation of financial markets has increased the earnings of investment bankers, fund managers, CEOs of private equity firms, and other top managers of financial firms. Finally, they argue that notions of fairness or "pay codes" that in the past limited the pay of top managers relative to the pay of other employees of firms have become less widely followed.

Other economists see the increased share of income earned by the top 1 percent as the result of market forces. We saw in the chapter on labor markets that economists have recognized a *superstar effect*, where changing technology has increased the income of the most famous entertainers and athletes (see Chapter 17). Steven Kaplan of the University of Chicago and Joshua Rauh of Stanford have argued that the superstar effect also applies in many other areas, where the incomes of top earners in law firms, financial firms, private and public corporations, and elsewhere have increased relative to average incomes in those fields. Because the superstar effect is so widespread, Kaplan and Rauh argue that it cannot be explained by factors such as the improved bargaining power of top earners or a breakdown in notions of fairness about pay differences within firms. They have analyzed the list of the wealthiest Americans from *Forbes* magazine and found that compared with the list in the 1980s, the currently wealthy are much *more* likely to be the first in their family to run a firm and much *less* likely to have been born into a wealthy family.

Whatever the reasons for the increase in the share of income the 1 percent earn, does the increase matter? First, note that in the previous graph, the blue line shows the share of income received by the 1 percent *before taxes*. The red line shows data prepared by the Congressional Budget Office for the years 1979–2009 on the share of income received by the 1 percent *after taxes*. The red line shows that the share has been significantly reduced by taxes; it will likely be reduced further in future years as a result of the increase in marginal tax rates instituted in 2013. Still some economists and policymakers are concerned that the increase in the share of income earned by the 1 percent is damaging to the country for several reasons: The higher incomes of the 1 percent may give them disproportionate political influence through campaign contributions. Some political commentators have argued that very high income people have used this political influence to push for changes to laws and regulations that have further increased their incomes. Some economists have argued that countries with high levels of income inequality have lower growth rates than do countries with more equal distributions of income. Finally, some political commentators have argued that rising income inequality can lead to political unrest, as shown by the Occupy Wall Street movement.

Other economists and policymakers are skeptical that the rising share of income the 1 percent earn has resulted in significant political problems and they worry that further increases in marginal tax rates may reduce work, saving, and investment, thereby reducing economic growth.

The debate over the 1 percent clearly has a substantial normative element as differing political viewpoints play a large role in policy proposals. Undoubtedly, the debate over income inequality will continue in the years to come.

Sources: Emmanuel Saez and Thomas Piketty, "Income Inequality in the United States, 1913–1998," *Quarterly Journal of Economics*, Vol. 118, No. 1, May 2003, pp. 1–39 [data updated through 2011 on Saez's Web site: http://elsa.berkeley.edu/~saez/; the series used includes capital gains]; Facundo Alvaredo, Anthony B. Atkinson, Thomas Piketty, and Emmanuel Saez, "The Top 1 Percent in International and Historical Perspective," *Journal of Economic Perspectives*, Vol. 27, No. 3, Summer 2013, pp. 3–20; Steven N. Kaplan and Joshua Rauh, "It's the Market: The Broad-Based Rise in the Return to Top Talent," *Journal of Economic Perspectives*, Vol. 27, No. 3, Summer 2013, pp. 35–56; and Congressional Budget Office, *The Distribution of Household Income and Federal Taxes, 2008 and 2009*, Supplemental Data, August 10, 2012.

Your Turn: Test your understanding by doing related problems 4.8 and 4.9 on page 600 at the end of this chapter.

MyEconLab Study Plan

Showing the Income Distribution with a Lorenz Curve

Figure 18.7 presents the distribution of income using a **Lorenz curve**, which shows the distribution of income by arraying incomes from lowest to highest on the horizontal axis and indicating the cumulative fraction of income earned by each fraction of households on the vertical axis. If the distribution of income were perfectly equal, a Lorenz curve would be a straight line because the first 20 percent of households would earn 20 percent of total income, the first 40 percent of households would earn 40 percent of total income, and so on. Panel (a) of Figure 18.7 shows a Lorenz curve for the actual distribution of income in the United States in 1980 and another curve for the distribution of income in 2012, using the data from Table 18.6. We know that income was distributed more unequally in 2012 than in 1980 because the Lorenz curve for 2012 is farther away from the line of equal distribution than is the Lorenz curve for 1980.

Panel (b) illustrates how to calculate the *Gini coefficient*, which is one way of summarizing the information provided by a Lorenz curve. The Gini coefficient is equal to the area between the line of perfect income equality and the Lorenz curve—area *A* in

Lorenz curve A curve that shows the distribution of income by arraying incomes from lowest to highest on the horizontal axis and indicating the cumulative fraction of income earned by each fraction of households on the vertical axis.

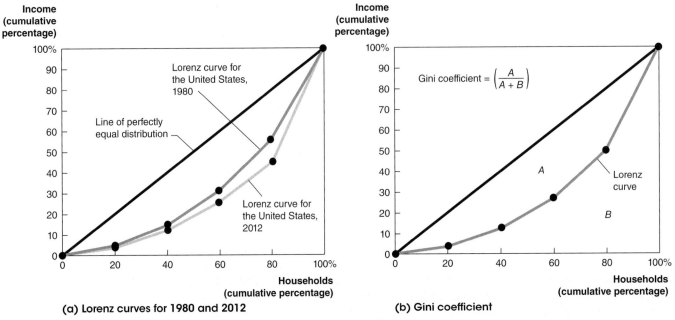

(a) Lorenz curves for 1980 and 2012

(b) Gini coefficient

MyEconLab Animation

Figure 18.7 **The Lorenz Curve and Gini Coefficient**

In panel (a), the Lorenz curves show the distribution of income by arraying incomes from the lowest to the highest on the horizontal axis and indicating the cumulative fraction of income by each fraction of households on the vertical axis. The straight line represents perfect income equality. Because the Lorenz curve for 1980 is closer to the line of perfect equality than the Lorenz curve for 2012, we know that income was more equally distributed in 1980 than in 2012. In panel (b), we show the Gini coefficient, which is equal to the area between the line of perfect income equality and the Lorenz curve—area A—divided by the whole area below the line of perfect equality—area A plus area B. The closer the Gini coefficient is to 1, the more unequal the income distribution.

panel (b)—divided by the whole area below the line of perfect equality—area A plus area B in panel (b). Or:

$$\text{Gini coefficient} = \left(\frac{A}{A + B}\right).$$

If the income distribution were completely *equal*, the Lorenz curve would be the same as the line of perfect income equality, area A would be zero, and the Gini coefficient would be zero. If the income distribution were completely *unequal*, area B would be zero, and the Gini coefficient would equal 1. Therefore, the greater the degree of income inequality, the greater the value of the Gini coefficient. In 1980, the Gini coefficient for the United States was 0.403. In 2012, it was 0.477, which tells us again that income inequality increased between 1980 and 2012. MyEconLab Concept Check

Problems in Measuring Poverty and the Distribution of Income

The measures of poverty and the distribution of income that we have discussed to this point may be misleading for two reasons. First, these measures are snapshots in time that do not take into account *income mobility*, which refers to changes in an individual's or a family's income over time. Second, they ignore the effects of government programs meant to reduce poverty.

Income Mobility in the United States We expect to see some income mobility. When you graduate from college, your income will rise as you assume a new job. A family may be below the poverty line one year because the main wage earner is unemployed but may rise well above the poverty line the next year, when that wage earner finds a job. A medical student may have a very low income for several years but a very high income after graduating and establishing a medical practice. It is also true that someone might have a high income one year—perhaps from making a very profitable investment in the stock market—and have a much lower income in future years.

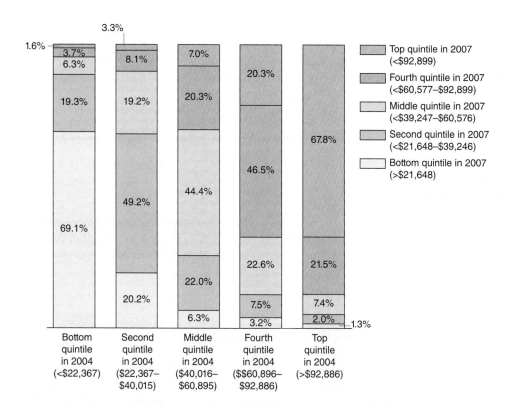

MyEconLab Animation

Figure 18.8

Income Mobility in the United States, 2004–2007

Each column represents one quintile—or 20 percent—of households, arranged by their incomes in 2004. Reading up the column, we can see where the households that started in that quintile in 2004 ended up in 2007. Only 69 percent of the households that were in the bottom quintile of income in 2004 were still in the bottom quintile in 2007. Only 68 percent of the households that were in the top quintile of income in 2004 were still in the top quintile in 2007.

Note: Incomes are in 2007 dollars to correct for the effects of inflation.

Source: U.S. Census Bureau, "Dynamics of Economic Well-Being: Movements in the U.S. Income Distribution, 2004–2007," *Current Population Reports*, P70–124, March 2011.

Statistics on income mobility are more difficult to collect than statistics on income during a particular year because they involve following the same individuals over a number of years. A study by the U.S. Census Bureau tracked the incomes of the same households for each year from 2004 to 2007. Figure 18.8 shows the results of the study. Each column represents one quintile—or 20 percent—of households, arranged by their incomes in 2004. Reading up the column, we can see where the households that started in that quintile in 2004 ended up in 2007. For example, the bottom quintile (the first column) consists of households with incomes of less than $22,367 in 2004 (all values are measured in 2007 dollars to correct for the effects of inflation). About 69 percent of these households were still in the bottom quintile in 2007. Only a small number—1.6 percent—had moved all the way to the top quintile, but more than one-quarter had moved into either the second quintile or the middle quintile. At the other end of the income distribution, of those households in the top income quintile—with incomes of $92,886 or more—in 2004, only two-thirds were still in the top quintile in 2007. Given the relatively short time period involved, this study indicates that there is significant income mobility in the United States.

The U.S. economy experienced rapid growth between 2004 and 2007, which may have increased the degree of income mobility. However, an earlier study by Peter Gottschalk of Boston College and Sheldon Danziger of the University of Michigan also provides evidence of significant income mobility. In that study, only 47 percent of people who were in the lowest 20 percent of incomes in 1968 were still in the lowest bracket in 1991. More than 25 percent had incomes in 1991 that put them in the middle- or higher-income brackets. Of those people who were in the highest-income bracket in 1968, only 42 percent were still in the highest bracket in 1991. Almost 8 percent of this group had fallen to the lowest-income bracket.

Some economists and policymakers are concerned, though, that the extent of economic mobility in the United States may have declined over time and that mobility may now be lower in the United States than in Canada and Western Europe. For example, a study by Markus Jäntti, of Stockholm University in Sweden, and colleagues found that 42 percent of American males who began life in the bottom quintile of the income distribution remained there as adults. In contrast, only 25 percent of Danish males and 30 percent of British males born into the bottom quintile remained there as adults.

Finally, another study by the U.S. Census Bureau found that of people who were poor at some time during the years 2004–2006, about half were in poverty for four months or less. Of the people who were poor in January 2004, only about 23 percent remained in poverty every month through December 2006. Only 2.8 percent of the U.S. population was poor every month during those three years.

Solved Problem 18.4

MyEconLab Interactive Animation

Are Many People in the United States Stuck in Poverty?

Evaluate the following statement:

> Government statistics indicate that about 15 percent of the population is below the poverty line. The fraction of the population in poverty has never dropped below 10 percent. Therefore, more than 10 percent of the population must cope with very low incomes year after year.

Solving the Problem

Step 1: **Review the chapter material.** This problem is about income mobility, so you may want to review the section "Income Mobility in the United States," which begins on page 590.

Step 2: **Use the discussion in this chapter to evaluate the statement.** Although it is true that the poverty rate in the United States is never below 10 percent, it is not the same 10 percent of the population that is in poverty each year. This chapter discusses one U.S. Census Bureau study that showed that only about 69 percent of the people who were in the lowest 20 percent of the income distribution in 2004 were still in the lowest 20 percent in 2007. Another census study of the years from 2004 to 2006 showed that only 2.8 percent of the U.S. population was poor every month during those three years. Poverty remains a problem in the United States, but fortunately, the number of people who remain in poverty for many years is much smaller than the number who are in poverty during any one year.

Sources: U.S. Census Bureau, "Dynamics of Economic Well-Being: Poverty 2004–2006," *Current Population Survey*, P70–123, March 2011; and U.S. Census Bureau, "Dynamics of Economic Well-Being: Movements in the U.S. Income Distribution, 2004–2007," *Current Population Reports*, P70–124, March 2011.

MyEconLab Study Plan

Your Turn: For more practice, do related problem 4.15 on page 600 at the end of this chapter.

The Effect of Taxes and Transfers A second reason the conventional statistics on poverty and income distribution may be misleading is that they omit the effects of government programs. Because of government programs, there is a difference between the income people earn and the income they actually have available to spend. The data in Tables 18.5 and 18.6 show the distribution of income before taxes are paid. We have seen that at the federal level, taxes are progressive, meaning that people with high incomes pay a larger share of their incomes in taxes than do people with low incomes. Therefore, income remaining after taxes is more equally distributed than is income before taxes. The tables also do not include income from *transfer payments* individuals receive from the government, such as Social Security payments to retired and disabled people. The Social Security system has been very effective in reducing the poverty rate among people older than 65. In 1960, 35 percent of people over age 65 in the United States had incomes below the poverty line. By 2012, 9 percent of people over age 65 had incomes below the poverty line.

Individuals with low incomes also receive noncash benefits, such as food stamps, free school lunches, and rent subsidies. The government's Supplemental Nutrition Assistance Program, more commonly called the *food stamp program*, has been a particularly important noncash benefit. Under this program, individuals with low incomes can buy, at a discount, coupons to purchase food in supermarkets. In 2013, more than 47 million people participated in this program, at a cost to the federal government of more than $75 billion. Because individuals with low incomes are more likely to receive transfer payments and other benefits from the government than are individuals with high incomes, the distribution of income is more equal if we take these benefits into account.   MyEconLab Concept Check

Income Distribution and Poverty around the World

How does income inequality in the United States compare with income inequality in other countries? Table 18.8 compares the ratio of total income received by the 20 percent of the population with the lowest incomes and the 20 percent with the highest incomes in several countries. The countries are ranked from most unequal to least unequal. As the table shows, poor countries, such as Bolivia and Paraguay, typically have more unequal distributions of income than does the United States. The distribution of income in the United States is less equal than in some moderate-income countries, such as Chile and Argentina, but it is more equal than in other moderate-income countries, such as Brazil. The United States has the most unequal distribution of income of any high-income country in the world. Of course, we must be careful with such comparisons because transfer payments are not counted in income. For example, the Social Security and Medicare systems in the United States are much more generous than the corresponding systems in Japan but less generous than those in France and Germany.

Although poverty remains a problem in high-income countries, it is a much larger problem in low-income countries. The level of poverty in much of sub-Saharan Africa, in particular, is a human catastrophe. In 2013, the poverty line in the United States for a family of four was an annual income of $23,550, but economists often use a much lower threshold income of $1 per day when calculating the rate of poverty in poor countries. As Table 18.9 shows, by this measure, according to estimates by Maxim Pinkovskiy of MIT and Xavier Sala-i-Martin of Columbia University, poverty declined from about 27 percent of the world population in 1970 to 5 percent in 2006, the most recent year for which statistics are available. The greatest reduction in poverty has taken place in Asia. In East Asia, which includes China, the poverty rate dropped spectacularly from about 60 percent in 1970 to less than 2 percent in 2006. In South Asia, which includes India, poverty rates dropped from 20 percent to less than 3 percent. Even in sub-Saharan Africa, poverty

Country	Ratio of Income Received by Highest 20% to Income Received by Lowest 20%
Bolivia	27.8
Brazil	20.6
Paraguay	17.3
United States	15.9
Chile	13.5
Argentina	11.3
Canada	11.2
China	10.1
Italy	5.6
United Kingdom	5.3
France	4.6
Germany	4.5
Sweden	3.6
Japan	3.0

Table 18.8

Income Inequality around the World

Sources: The World Bank, Eurostat, and Statistics Canada.

Table 18.9

Poverty Has Declined Dramatically around the World Since 1970

Region	Percentage of the Population in Poverty	
	1970	2006
World	26.8%	5.4%
East Asia	58.8	1.7
South Asia	20.1	2.6
Middle East and North Africa	8.4	5.2
Latin America	11.6	3.1
Sub-Saharan Africa	39.9	31.8

Source: "Percentage of the Population in Poverty," by Xavier Sala-i-Martin and Maxim Pinkovskiy, from "Parametric Estimations of the World Distribution of Income," National Bureau of Economic Research Working Paper 15433, October 2009. Copyright © 2009 by Xavier Sala-i-Martin and Maxim Pinkovskiy. Reprinted by permission.

decreased from 40 percent in 1970 to 32 percent in 2006. Why has poverty fallen dramatically more in Asia than in Africa? The key explanation is that the countries of Asia have had higher rates of economic growth than have the countries of sub-Saharan Africa. Recent economic research demonstrates a positive relationship between economic growth and the incomes of lower-income people.

MyEconLab Study Plan

MyEconLab Concept Check

Continued from page 569

Economics in Your Life

How Much Tax Should You Pay?

At the beginning of this chapter, we asked you to think about where government gets the money to provide goods and services and about whether you pay your fair share of taxes. After reading this chapter, you should see that you pay taxes in many different forms. When you work, you pay both individual income taxes and social insurance taxes on your income. When you buy gasoline, you pay an excise tax, which, in part, pays for highways. When you buy goods at a local store, you pay state and local sales taxes, which the government uses to fund education and other services. Whether you are paying your fair share of taxes is a normative question. The U.S. tax system is progressive, so higher-income individuals pay more in taxes than do lower-income individuals. In fact, as we saw in the *Making the Connection* on page 577, people in the lowest 40 percent of the income distribution pay no federal individual income tax at all. You may find that you will not pay much in federal income taxes in your first job after college. But as your income grows during your career, so will the percentage of your income you pay in taxes.

Conclusion

The public choice model provides insights into how government decisions are made. The decisions of policymakers will not necessarily reflect the preferences of voters. Attempts by government to intervene in the economy may increase economic efficiency, as when governments take actions to deal with externalities, but they may also lead to government failure and a reduction in economic efficiency.

A saying attributed to Benjamin Franklin states that "nothing in this world is certain but death and taxes." But which taxes? As we saw at the beginning of this chapter, politicians continue to debate whether the government should use the tax system and other programs to reduce the level of income inequality in the United States. The tax system represents a balance among the principles of economic efficiency, ability to pay, paying for benefits received, and achieving social objectives. Those favoring government intervention to reduce inequality argue that it is unfair for some people to have much higher incomes than others. Others argue that income inequality largely reflects higher incomes resulting from greater skills and from entrepreneurial ability, and that higher taxes reduce work, saving, and investment.

Many economists are skeptical of tax policy proposals intended to significantly reduce income inequality. They argue that a market system relies on individuals being willing to work hard and take risks, with the promise of high incomes if they are successful. Taking some of that income from them in the name of reducing income inequality reduces the incentives to work hard and take risks. As we saw in Chapter 1, policymakers are often faced with a trade-off between economic efficiency and equity. Ultimately, whether policies to reduce income inequality should be pursued is a normative question. Economics alone cannot decide the issue.

Visit MyEconLab for a news article and analysis related to the concepts in this chapter.

Chapter Summary and Problems

Key Terms

Arrow impossibility theorem, p. 571

Average tax rate, p. 577

Excess burden, p. 580

Human capital, p. 586

Lorenz curve, p. 589

Marginal tax rate, p. 577

Median voter theorem, p. 571

Poverty line, p. 585

Poverty rate, p. 585

Progressive tax, p. 576

Public choice model, p. 570

Regressive tax, p. 576

Rent seeking, p. 572

Tax incidence, p. 581

Voting paradox, p. 571

 18.1 **Public Choice, pages 570–574**

LEARNING OBJECTIVE: Describe the public choice model and explain how it is used to analyze government decision making.

Summary

The **public choice model** applies economic analysis to government decision making. The observation that majority voting may not always result in consistent choices is called the **voting paradox**. The **Arrow impossibility theorem** states that no system of voting can be devised that will consistently represent the underlying preferences of voters. The **median voter theorem** states that the outcome of a majority vote is likely to represent the preferences of the voter who is in the political middle. Individuals and firms sometimes engage in **rent seeking**, which is the use of government action to make themselves better off at the expense of others. Although government intervention can sometimes improve economic efficiency, public choice analysis indicates that *government failure* can also occur, reducing economic efficiency.

MyEconLab   Visit **www.myeconlab.com** to complete these exercises online and get instant feedback.

Review Questions

1.1 What is the public choice model?

1.2 What is the difference between the voting paradox and the Arrow impossibility theorem?

1.3 What is rent seeking, and how is it related to regulatory capture?

1.4 What is the relationship between market failure and government failure?

Problems and Applications

1.5 Will the preferences shown in the following table lead to a voting paradox? Briefly explain.

Policy	Lena	David	Kathleen
Cancer research	1st	2nd	3rd
Mass transit	2nd	1st	1st
Border security	3rd	3rd	2nd

1.6 Many political observers have noted that Republican presidential candidates tend to emphasize their conservative positions on policy issues while running for their party's nomination, and Democratic presidential candidates tend to emphasize their liberal positions on policy issues while running for their party's nomination. In the general election, though, Republican candidates tend to downplay

their conservative positions and Democratic candidates tend to downplay their liberal positions. Can the median voter theorem help explain this pattern? Briefly explain.

1.7 Briefly explain whether you agree with the following argument:

> The median voter theorem will be an accurate predictor of the outcomes of elections when a majority of voters have preferences very similar to those of the median voter. When the majority of voters have preferences very different from those of the median voter, the median voter theorem will not lead to accurate predictions of the outcomes of elections.

1.8 An article in the *Economist* magazine made the following observation: "Public-choice economics assumes that government figures are merely human." What are the implications of this assumption for understanding government policy?
Source: "The Voice of Public Choice," *Economist*, January 19, 2013.

1.9 An article in the *Economist* magazine on the work of James Buchanan made the following observation: "It was important … to understand the ways that government could fail systematically."

   a. What does government failure mean in this context? How does public choice theory help us to understand how government could fail systematically?

   b. The same article notes that: "Rent-seeking is a very useful concept to have around when thinking about policy." What is rent seeking? Why is the concept useful when thinking about policy?
Source: "Don't Hate the Player, Hate the Game," *Economist*, January 17, 2013.

1.10 Is the typical person likely to gather more information when buying a new car or when voting for a member of the House of Representatives? Briefly explain.

1.11 Nobel Laureate James Buchanan, who was one of the key figures in developing the public choice model, wrote: "The relevant difference between markets and politics does not lie in the kinds of values/interests that persons pursue, but in the conditions under which they pursue their various interests." Do you agree with this statement? Are there significant ways in which the business marketplace differs from the political marketplace?
Source: James M. Buchanan, "The Constitution of Economic Policy," *American Economic Review*, Vol. 77, No. 3, June 1987, p. 246.

The Tax System, pages 574–581

18.2

LEARNING OBJECTIVE: Understand the tax system in the United States, including the principles that governments use to create tax policy.

Summary

Governments raise the funds they need through taxes. The most widely used taxes are income taxes, social insurance taxes, sales taxes, property taxes, and excise taxes. Governments take into account several important objectives when deciding which taxes to use: efficiency, ability to pay, horizontal equity, benefits received, and attaining social objectives. A **regressive tax** is a tax for which people with lower incomes pay a higher percentage of their incomes in tax than do people with higher incomes. A **progressive tax** is a tax for which people with lower incomes pay a lower percentage of their incomes in tax than do people with higher incomes. The **marginal tax rate** is the fraction of each additional dollar of income that must be paid in taxes. The **average tax rate** is the total tax paid divided by total income. When analyzing the effect of taxes on how much people are willing to work, save, or invest, economists focus on the marginal tax rate rather than the average tax rate. The **excess burden** of a tax is the efficiency loss to the economy that results from a tax having reduced the quantity of a good produced.

MyEconLab   Visit **www.myeconlab.com** to complete these exercises online and get instant feedback.

Review Questions

2.1 Which type of tax raises the most revenue for the federal government? Which type of tax raises the most revenue for state and local governments?

2.2 In 2012, Congress and President Barack Obama passed legislation raising tax rates on families earning $450,000 or more. Did this change in the law make the U.S. tax system more progressive or less progressive? Be sure to provide a definition of *progressive tax* and *regressive tax* in your answer.

2.3 What is the difference between a marginal tax rate and an average tax rate? Which is more important in determining the effect of a change in taxes on economic behavior?

2.4 Briefly discuss each of the five goals and principles governments consider when deciding which taxes to use.

Problems and Applications

2.5 Why does the federal government raise more tax revenue from taxes on individuals than from taxes on businesses?

2.6 On April 1, 2009, a 62-cent increase in the federal cigarette tax went into effect. The following data are from the Gallup-Healthways Well-Being Index for 2008:

Percentage Who Smoke, by Annual Household Income

Income	Percentage Who Smoke
Less than $12,000	34%
$12,000–$35,999	28
$36,000–$59,999	22
$60,000–$89,999	16
$90,000+	13

Based on these data, would the federal cigarette tax be considered progressive or regressive? Be sure to define *progressive tax* and *regressive tax* in your answer.
Source: Lydia Saad, "Cigarette Tax Will Affect Low-Income Americans Most," *Gallup, Inc.*, April 1, 2009.

2.7 Many state governments use lotteries to raise revenue. If we think of a lottery as a type of tax, is a lottery likely to be progressive or regressive? What data would you need to determine whether the effect of a lottery is progressive or regressive?

2.8 Use the information in Table 18.2 on page 576 to calculate the total federal income tax paid, the marginal tax rate, and the average tax rate for people with the following incomes. (For simplicity, assume that these people have no exemptions or deductions from their incomes.)
   a. $25,000
   b. $125,000
   c. $300,000

2.9 **[Related to the** Making the Connection **on page 577]** President Barack Obama proposed legislation that Congress failed to enact that would have included the so-called "Buffett Rule," named after billionaire Warren Buffett, who noted that he was paying a lower tax rate than his secretary. The Buffett Rule would set a new tax rate for those earning incomes of more than $1 million per year.
   a. Looking at the table on page 577 for the percentage of federal taxes paid by the different income categories, is Mr. Buffett's situation of paying a lower tax rate than his secretary typical of the highest 1 percent of U.S. income earners?
   b. According to an article in the *New York Times*: "[Buffett's] income comes mostly from his investments, which are taxed at the capital gains rate of 15 percent. His secretary is most likely paid a salary and bonus, which would be taxed as ordinary income, at a rate that goes as high as 35 percent." What are capital gains? Which goals and principles of evaluating taxes are relevant to considering whether the federal government should continue to tax capital gains at a lower rate than ordinary income? Briefly explain.
Source: Paul Sullivan, " 'Buffett Rule' Is More Complicated Than Politics Suggest," *New York Times*, September 23, 2011.

2.10 Currently, the Social Security and Medicare programs are funded by payroll taxes rather than by the federal personal income tax. In 2013, the payroll tax for Social Security was 12.4 percent on wage, salary, and self-employment income up to $113,700. (Half of the tax is collected from employers and half from employees.) Above that income level, the tax dropped to zero. The Medicare tax was 2.9 percent on all wage, salary, and self-employment income. Some economists and policymakers have proposed eliminating the payroll tax and shifting to funding Social Security and Medicare out of the federal personal income tax. Would this proposal make the federal income tax system as a whole more progressive or less progressive? Briefly explain.

2.11 Almost all states levy sales taxes on retail products, but about half of them exempt purchases of food. In addition, virtually all services are exempt from state sales taxes. Evaluate these tax rate differences, using the goals and principles of taxation on pages 579–581.

2.12 Suppose the government eliminates the income tax and replaces it with a consumption tax. With a consumption tax, individuals pay a tax on only the part of their income they spend rather than save. Think about the effect of this change on the market for automobiles. Can you necessarily tell what will happen to the price and quantity of automobiles? Briefly explain.

2.13 Use the following table to answer the questions:

Annual Income	Tax Liability
$15,000	$0
30,000	4,500
45,000	11,250
60,000	21,000
75,000	30,000

    a. What is the average tax rate at each income level?

    b. Based on these data, is the tax progressive or regressive? Briefly explain.

    c. Is it possible based on these data to determine the marginal tax rate of someone earning $65,000 per year? Briefly explain.

 18.3 **Tax Incidence Revisited: The Effect of Price Elasticity, pages 581–584**
LEARNING OBJECTIVE: Understand the effect of price elasticity on tax incidence.

Summary

Tax incidence is the actual division of the burden of a tax. In most cases, buyers and sellers share the burden of a tax levied on a good or service. When the elasticity of demand for a product is smaller in absolute value than the elasticity of supply, consumers pay the majority of the tax on the product. When the elasticity of demand for a product is larger in absolute value than the elasticity of supply, sellers pay the majority of the tax on the product.

MyEconLab   Visit **www.myeconlab.com** to complete these exercises online and get instant feedback.

Review Questions

3.1 What does *tax incidence* mean?

3.2 Briefly discuss the effect of price elasticity of supply and demand on tax incidence.

Problems and Applications

3.3 According to the 2004 *Economic Report of the President*, "The actual incidence of a tax may have little to do with the legal specification of its incidence." Briefly explain what this statement means and discuss whether you agree with it.

3.4 According to the 2004 *Economic Report of the President*, "Another crucial principle [of tax incidence] is that only people can pay taxes. Businesses and other artificial entities cannot pay taxes." Do you agree that businesses cannot pay taxes? Don't businesses pay the federal corporate income tax? Briefly explain.

3.5 **[Related to the** Don't Let This Happen to You **on page 581]** According to an article in the *New York Times*, during 2009 some New Yorkers were deciding to buy existing condominiums (condos) rather than newly constructed condos. One reason given was the following: "[Some buyers] seek to avoid the 1.825 percent transfer tax that buyers must pay on a brand-new condo. (In resales, the seller pays the tax.)" Analyze this reason for buying a resale rather than a new condo.
Source: Teri Karush Rogers, "Mint Condition, Low Miles," *New York Times*, May 29, 2009.

3.6 **[Related to the** Making the Connection **on page 582]** Use a demand and supply model for the labor market to show the effect of the corporate income tax on workers. What factors would make the deadweight loss or excess burden from the tax larger or smaller?

3.7 According to an article in the *New York Times*, when the French government imposed a new tax on sales of beer, it estimated that the retail price of beer would rise by the equivalent of 6 cents per half pint. A spokesman for the beer industry argued that the actual increase in price would be 25 cents per half pint. Discuss the differences between the French government's and the beer industry's estimates of the price elasticity of demand for beer.
Source: Aurelien Breeden, "Beer Lovers Fear an Unequal Tax Bite in Wine Country," *New York Times*, November 26, 2012.

3.8 Governments often have multiple objectives in imposing a tax. In each part of this question, use a demand and supply graph to illustrate your answer.

    a. If the government wants to minimize the excess burden from excise taxes, should these taxes be imposed on goods that have price elastic demand or goods that have price inelastic demand?

    b. Suppose that rather than minimizing excess burden, the government is most interested in maximizing the revenue it receives from the tax. In this situation, should the government impose excise taxes on goods that have price elastic demand or on goods that have price inelastic demand?

    c. Suppose that the government wants to discourage smoking and drinking alcohol. Will a tax be more effective in achieving this objective if the demand for these goods is price elastic or if the demand is price inelastic?

3.9 **[Related to** Solved Problem 18.3 **on page 583]** Use the following graph of the market for cigarettes to answer the questions:

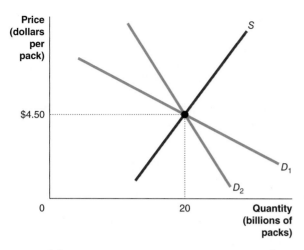

a. If the government imposes a 10-cent-per-pack tax on cigarettes, will the price consumers pay rise more if the demand curve is D_1 or if the demand curve is D_2? Briefly explain.

b. If the government imposes a 10-cent-per-pack tax on cigarettes, will the revenue the government collects be greater if the demand curve is D_1 or if the demand curve is D_2? Briefly explain.

c. If the government imposes a 10-cent-per-pack tax on cigarettes, will the excess burden from the tax be greater if the demand curve is D_1 or if the demand curve is D_2? Briefly explain.

3.10 **[Related to** Solved Problem 18.3 **on page 583]** Explain whether you agree with the following statement: "For a given demand curve, the excess burden of a tax will be greater when supply is less price elastic than when it is more price elastic." Illustrate your answer with a demand and supply graph.

3.11 Suppose the government decides to tax sales of pizzas. Use the following graph to answer the questions:

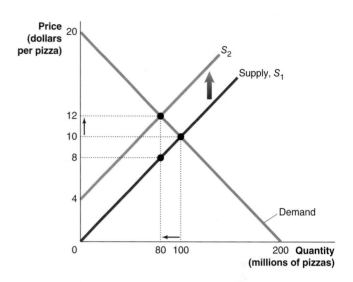

a. How much of a per unit tax did the government impose on pizzas?

b. Before the tax, what price do consumers pay for pizza? How does the price consumers pay change after the tax?

c. Before the tax, what price do sellers receive? How does the price sellers receive change after the tax?

d. Are consumers or producers bearing a greater burden of this tax? Briefly explain.

 Income Distribution and Poverty, pages 584–594

LEARNING OBJECTIVE: Discuss the distribution of income in the United States and understand the extent of income mobility.

Summary

In the United States, there was some decline in income inequality between 1936 and 1980, and there has been some increase in income inequality between 1980 and today. A **Lorenz curve** shows the distribution of income by arraying incomes from lowest to highest on the horizontal axis and indicating the cumulative fraction of income earned by each fraction of households on the vertical axis. About 15 percent of Americans are below the **poverty line**, which is defined as the annual income equal to three times the amount necessary to purchase the minimum quantity of food required for adequate nutrition. Over time, there has been significant income mobility in the United States. The United States has a more unequal distribution of income than do other high-income countries. The **poverty rate**—the percentage of the population that is poor—has been declining in most countries around the world, with the important exception of Africa. The *marginal productivity theory of income distribution* states that in equilibrium, each factor of production receives a payment equal to its marginal revenue product. The more factors of production an individual owns and the more productive those factors are, the higher the individual's income will be.

Review Questions

4.1 Discuss the extent of income inequality in the United States. Has inequality in the distribution of income in the United States increased or decreased over time? Briefly explain.

4.2 Define *poverty line* and *poverty rate*. How has the poverty rate changed in the United States since 1960?

4.3 What is a Lorenz curve? What is a Gini coefficient? If a country had a Gini coefficient of 0.48 in 1960 and 0.44 in 2014, would income inequality in the country have increased or decreased?

4.4 Describe the main factors economists believe cause inequality of income.

4.5 Compare the distribution of income in the United States with the distribution of income in other high-income countries.

4.6 Describe the trend in global poverty rates.

Problems and Applications

4.7 **[Related to the** Chapter Opener **on page 569]** In a column in the *Washington Post*, Robert J. Samuelson wrote: "As for what's caused greater inequality, we're also in the dark. The Reagan and Bush tax cuts are weak explanations, because gains have occurred in pretax incomes.... Up to a point, inequality is inevitable and desirable."
   a. What are pretax incomes?
   b. Do you agree with Samuelson's argument that income inequality may be inevitable and desirable?
   Source: Robert J. Samuelson, "The Rich and the Rest," *Washington Post*, April 18, 2007.

4.8 **[Related to the** Making the Connection **on page 588]** In a speech, Federal Reserve Chairman Ben Bernanke made the following observation: "Although we Americans strive to provide equality of economic opportunity, we do not guarantee equality of economic outcomes, nor should we." If the federal government wanted to, how could it "guarantee equality of economic outcomes"? If the government succeeded in making the distribution of income completely equal, what would be the benefits, and what would be the costs?
   Source: "Remarks by Chairman Ben S. Bernanke before the Greater Omaha Chamber of Commerce, Omaha, Nebraska," February 6, 2007.

4.9 **[Related to the** Making the Connection **on page 588]** In an article in the *Wall Street Journal*, Edward Lazear of Stanford University was quoted as saying: "There is some good news.... Most of the inequality reflects an increase in returns to 'investing in skills.'" Why would it be good news if it were true that most of the income inequality in the United States reflected an increase to returns in investing in skills?
   Source: Greg Ip and John D. McKinnon, "Bush Reorients Rhetoric, Acknowledges Income Gap," *Wall Street Journal*, March 26, 2007.

4.10 Use the following Lorenz curve graph to answer the questions:

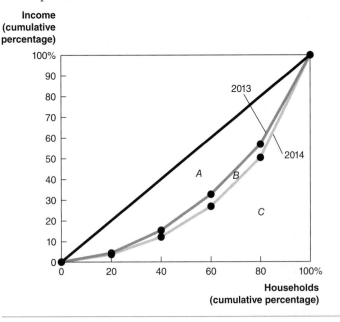

a. Did the distribution of income become more equal in 2014 than it was in 2013, or did it become less equal? Briefly explain.
b. If area $A = 2,150$, area $B = 250$, and area $C = 2,600$, calculate the Gini coefficient for 2013 and the Gini coefficient for 2014.

4.11 Draw a Lorenz curve showing the distribution of income for the five people in the following table.

Name	Annual Earnings
Lena	$70,000
David	60,000
Steve	50,000
Jerome	40,000
Lori	30,000

4.12 Why do economists often use a lower poverty threshold for low-income countries than for high-income countries such as the United States? Is there a difference between *relative* poverty and *absolute* poverty? Briefly explain.

4.13 Suppose that a country has 20 million households. Ten million are poor households that each have labor market earnings of $20,000 per year, and 10 million are rich households that each have labor market earnings of $80,000 per year. If the government enacted a marginal tax of 10 percent on all labor market earnings above $20,000 and transferred this money to households earning $20,000, would the incomes of the poor rise by $6,000 per year? Explain.

4.14 A U.S. Census Bureau report showed that 46 percent of households living below the poverty line owned their own homes, 76 percent lived in dwellings with air-conditioning, about 75 percent owned cars, and 62 percent had cable or satellite television reception. All these levels are considerably higher than they were for households below the poverty line a generation ago, but the official poverty rate is virtually unchanged over this period, as Figure 18.5 on page 585 shows. Going back to the official definition of poverty, how could ownership and purchases of these goods by the poor become more common while the poverty rate stayed the same?

4.15 **[Related to** Solved Problem 18.4 **on page 592]** Evaluate the following statement: "Policies to redistribute income are desperately needed in the United States. Without such policies, the roughly 15 percent of the population that is currently poor has no hope of ever climbing above the poverty line."

GLOSSARY

A

Absolute advantage The ability of an individual, a firm, or a country to produce more of a good or service than competitors, using the same amount of resources.

Accounting profit A firm's net income, measured as revenue minus operating expenses and taxes paid.

Adverse selection The situation in which one party to a transaction takes advantage of knowing more than the other party to the transaction.

Allocative efficiency A state of the economy in which production is in accordance with consumer preferences; in particular, every good or service is produced up to the point where the last unit provides a marginal benefit to society equal to the marginal cost of producing it.

Antitrust laws Laws aimed at eliminating collusion and promoting competition among firms.

Arrow impossibility theorem A mathematical theorem that holds that no system of voting can be devised that will consistently represent the underlying preferences of voters.

Asset Anything of value owned by a person or a firm.

Asymmetric information A situation in which one party to an economic transaction has less information than the other party.

Autarky A situation in which a country does not trade with other countries.

Average fixed cost Fixed cost divided by the quantity of output produced.

Average product of labor The total output produced by a firm divided by the quantity of workers.

Average revenue (AR) Total revenue divided by the quantity of the product sold.

Average tax rate Total tax paid divided by total income.

Average total cost Total cost divided by the quantity of output produced.

Average variable cost Variable cost divided by the quantity of output produced.

B

Balance sheet A financial statement that sums up a firm's financial position on a particular day, usually the end of a quarter or year.

Barrier to entry Anything that keeps new firms from entering an industry in which firms are earning economic profits.

Black market A market in which buying and selling take place at prices that violate government price regulations.

Bond A financial security that represents a promise to repay a fixed amount of funds.

Brand management The actions of a firm intended to maintain the differentiation of a product over time.

Budget constraint The limited amount of income available to consumers to spend on goods and services.

Business strategy Actions that a firm takes to achieve a goal, such as maximizing profits.

C

Cartel A group of firms that collude by agreeing to restrict output to increase prices and profits.

Centrally planned economy An economy in which the government decides how economic resources will be allocated.

Ceteris paribus **("all else equal") condition** The requirement that when analyzing the relationship between two variables— such as price and quantity demanded—other variables must be held constant.

Circular-flow diagram A model that illustrates how participants in markets are linked.

Coase theorem The argument of economist Ronald Coase that if transactions costs are low, private bargaining will result in an efficient solution to the problem of externalities.

Collusion An agreement among firms to charge the same price or otherwise not to compete.

Command-and-control approach A policy that involves the government imposing quantitative limits on the amount of pollution firms are allowed to emit or requiring firms to install specific pollution control devices.

Common resource A good that is rival but not excludable.

Comparative advantage The ability of an individual, a firm, or a country to produce a good or service at a lower opportunity cost than competitors.

Compensating differentials Higher wages that compensate workers for unpleasant aspects of a job.

Competitive market equilibrium A market equilibrium with many buyers and sellers.

Complements Goods and services that are used together.

Constant returns to scale The situation in which a firm's long-run average costs remain unchanged as it increases output.

Consumer surplus The difference between the highest price a consumer is willing to pay for a good or service and the actual price the consumer pays.

Cooperative equilibrium An equilibrium in a game in which players cooperate to increase their mutual payoff.

Copyright A government-granted exclusive right to produce and sell a creation.

Corporate governance The way in which a corporation is structured and the effect that structure has on the corporation's behavior.

Corporation A legal form of business that provides owners with protection from losing more than their investment should the business fail.

Coupon payment An interest payment on a bond.

Cross-price elasticity of demand The percentage change in the quantity demanded of one good divided by the percentage change in the price of another good.

D

Deadweight loss The reduction in economic surplus resulting from a market not being in competitive equilibrium.

Demand curve A curve that shows the relationship between the price of a product and the quantity of the product demanded.

Demand schedule A table that shows the relationship between the price of a product and the quantity of the product demanded.

Demographics The characteristics of a population with respect to age, race, and gender.

Derived demand The demand for a factor of production; it depends on the demand for the good the factor produces.

Direct finance A flow of funds from savers to firms through financial markets, such as the New York Stock Exchange.

Diseconomies of scale The situation in which a firm's long-run average costs rise as the firm increases output.

Dividends Payments by a corporation to its shareholders.

Dominant strategy A strategy that is the best for a firm, no matter what strategies other firms use.

Dumping Selling a product for a price below its cost of production.

E

Economic discrimination Paying a person a lower wage or excluding a person from an occupation on the basis of an irrelevant characteristic such as race or gender.

Economic efficiency A market outcome in which the marginal benefit to consumers of the last unit produced is equal to its marginal cost of production and in which the sum of consumer surplus and producer surplus is at a maximum.

Economic growth The ability of an economy to produce increasing quantities of goods and services.

Economic loss The situation in which a firm's total revenue is less than its total cost, including all implicit costs.

Economic model A simplified version of reality used to analyze real-world economic situations.

Economic profit A firm's revenues minus all its costs, implicit and explicit.

Economic rent (or pure rent) The price of a factor of production that is in fixed supply.

Economic surplus The sum of consumer surplus and producer surplus.

Economic variable Something measurable that can have different values, such as the incomes of doctors.

Economics The study of the choices people make to attain their goals, given their scarce resources.

Economies of scale The situation when a firm's long-run average costs fall as it increases the quantity of output it produces.

Elastic demand Demand is elastic when the percentage change in the quantity demanded is *greater* than the percentage change in price, so the price

elasticity is *greater* than 1 in absolute value.

Elasticity A measure of how much one economic variable responds to changes in another economic variable.

Endowment effect The tendency of people to be unwilling to sell a good they already own even if they are offered a price that is greater than the price they would be willing to pay to buy the good if they didn't already own it.

Entrepreneur Someone who operates a business, bringing together the factors of production—labor, capital, and natural resources—to produce goods and services.

Equity The fair distribution of economic benefits.

Excess burden A measure of the efficiency loss to the economy that results from a tax having reduced the quantity of a good produced; also known as the deadweight loss.

Excludability The situation in which anyone who does not pay for a good cannot consume it.

Expansion path A curve that shows a firm's cost-minimizing combination of inputs for every level of output.

Explicit cost A cost that involves spending money.

Exports Goods and services produced domestically but sold in other countries.

External economies Reductions in a firm's costs that result from an increase in the size of an industry.

Externality A benefit or cost that affects someone who is not directly involved in the production or consumption of a good or service.

F

Factor market A market for the factors of production, such as labor, capital, natural resources, and entrepreneurial ability.

Factors of production Labor, capital, natural resources, and other inputs used to produce goods and services.

Fee-for-service A system under which doctors and hospitals

receive a payment for each service they provide.

Fixed costs Costs that remain constant as output changes.

Free market A market with few government restrictions on how a good or service can be produced or sold or on how a factor of production can be employed.

Free riding Benefiting from a good without paying for it.

Free trade Trade between countries that is without government restrictions.

G

Game theory The study of how people make decisions in situations in which attaining their goals depends on their interactions with others; in economics, the study of the decisions of firms in industries where the profits of a firm depend on its interactions with other firms.

Globalization The process of countries becoming more open to foreign trade and investment.

H

Health care Goods and services, such as prescription drugs, consultations with a doctor, and surgeries, that are intended to maintain or improve a person's health.

Health insurance A contract under which a buyer agrees to make payments, or *premiums*, in exchange for the provider agreeing to pay some or all of the buyer's medical bills.

Horizontal merger A merger between firms in the same industry.

Human capital The accumulated knowledge and skills that workers acquire from formal training and education or from life experiences.

I

Implicit cost A nonmonetary opportunity cost.

Imports Goods and services bought domestically but produced in other countries.

Income effect The change in the quantity demanded of a good that

results from the effect of a change in the good's price on consumers' purchasing power, holding all other factors constant.

Income elasticity of demand A measure of the responsiveness of the quantity demanded to changes in income, measured by the percentage change in the quantity demanded divided by the percentage change in income.

Income statement A financial statement that shows a firm's revenues, costs, and profit over a period of time.

Indifference curve A curve that shows the combinations of consumption bundles that give the consumer the same utility.

Indirect finance A flow of funds from savers to borrowers through financial intermediaries such as banks. Intermediaries raise funds from saves to lend to firms (and other borrowers).

Inelastic demand Demand is inelastic when the percentage change in quantity demanded is *less* than the percentage change in price, so the price elasticity is *less* than 1 in absolute value.

Inferior good A good for which the demand increases as income falls and decreases as income rises.

Interest rate The cost of borrowing funds, usually expressed as a percentage of the amount borrowed.

Isocost line All the combinations of two inputs, such as capital and labor, that have the same total cost.

Isoquant A curve that shows all the combinations of two inputs, such as capital and labor, that will produce the same level of output.

L

Labor union An organization of employees that has a legal right to bargain with employers about wages and working conditions.

Law of demand The rule that, holding everything else constant, when the price of a product falls, the quantity demanded of the product will increase, and when the price of a product rises, the quantity demanded of the product will decrease.

Law of diminishing marginal utility The principle that consumers experience diminishing additional satisfaction as they consume more of a good or service during a given period of time.

Law of diminishing returns The principle that, at some point, adding more of a variable input, such as labor, to the same amount of a fixed input, such as capital, will cause the marginal product of the variable input to decline.

Law of supply The rule that, holding everything else constant, increases in price cause increases in the quantity supplied, and decreases in price cause decreases in the quantity supplied.

Liability Anything owed by a person or a firm.

Limited liability The legal provision that shields owners of a corporation from losing more than they have invested in the firm.

Long run The period of time in which a firm can vary all its inputs, adopt new technology, and increase or decrease the size of its physical plant.

Long-run average cost curve A curve that shows the lowest cost at which a firm is able to produce a given quantity of output in the long run, when no inputs are fixed.

Long-run competitive equilibrium The situation in which the entry and exit of firms has resulted in the typical firm breaking even.

Long-run supply curve A curve that shows the relationship in the long run between market price and the quantity supplied.

Lorenz curve A curve that shows the distribution of income by arraying incomes from lowest to highest on the horizontal axis and indicating the cumulative fraction of income earned by each fraction of households on the vertical axis.

M

Macroeconomics The study of the economy as a whole, including topics such as inflation, unemployment, and economic growth.

Marginal analysis Analysis that involves comparing marginal benefits and marginal costs.

Marginal benefit The additional benefit to a consumer from consuming one more unit of a good or service.

Marginal cost The additional cost to a firm of producing one more unit of a good or service.

Marginal product of labor The additional output a firm produces as a result of hiring one more worker.

Marginal productivity theory of income distribution The theory that the distribution of income is determined by the marginal productivity of the factors of production that individuals own.

Marginal rate of substitution (*MRS*) The rate at which a consumer would be willing to trade off one good for another.

Marginal rate of technical substitution (*MRTS*) The rate at which a firm is able to substitute one input for another while keeping the level of output constant.

Marginal revenue (*MR*) The change in total revenue from selling one more unit of a product.

Marginal revenue product of labor (*MRP*) The change in a firm's revenue as a result of hiring one more worker.

Marginal tax rate The fraction of each additional dollar of income that must be paid in taxes.

Marginal utility (*MU*) The change in total utility a person receives from consuming one additional unit of a good or service.

Market A group of buyers and sellers of a good or service and the institution or arrangement by which they come together to trade.

Market demand The demand by all the consumers of a given good or service.

Market-based reforms Changes in the market for health care that would make it more like the markets for other goods and services.

Market economy An economy in which the decisions of households

and firms interacting in markets allocate economic resources.

Market equilibrium A situation in which quantity demanded equals quantity supplied.

Market failure A situation in which the market fails to produce the efficient level of output.

Market power The ability of a firm to charge a price greater than marginal cost.

Marketing All the activities necessary for a firm to sell a product to a consumer.

Median voter theorem The proposition that the outcome of a majority vote is likely to represent the preferences of the voter who is in the political middle.

Microeconomics The study of how households and firms make choices, how they interact in markets, and how the government attempts to influence their choices.

Minimum efficient scale The level of output at which all economies of scale are exhausted.

Mixed economy An economy in which most economic decisions result from the interaction of buyers and sellers in markets but in which the government plays a significant role in the allocation of resources.

Monopolistic competition A market structure in which barriers to entry are low and many firms compete by selling similar, but not identical, products.

Monopoly A firm that is the only seller of a good or service that does not have a close substitute.

Monopsony The situation in which a firm is the sole buyer of a factor of production.

Moral hazard The actions people take after they have entered into a transaction that make the other party to the transaction worse off.

N

Nash equilibrium A situation in which each firm chooses the best strategy, given the strategies chosen by other firms.

Natural monopoly A situation in which economies of scale are

so large that one firm can supply the entire market at a lower average total cost than can two or more firms.

Network externalities A situation in which the usefulness of a product increases with the number of consumers who use it.

Noncooperative equilibrium An equilibrium in a game in which players do not cooperate but pursue their own self-interest.

Normal good A good for which the demand increases as income rises and decreases as income falls.

Normative analysis Analysis concerned with what ought to be.

O

Oligopoly A market structure in which a small number of interdependent firms compete.

Opportunity cost The highest-valued alternative that must be given up to engage in an activity.

P

Partnership A firm owned jointly by two or more persons and not organized as a corporation.

Patent The exclusive right to a product for a period of 20 years from the date the patent is filed with the government.

Patient Protection and Affordable Care Act (ACA) Health care reform legislation passed by Congress and signed by President Barack Obama in 2010.

Payoff matrix A table that shows the payoffs that each firm earns from every combination of strategies by the firms.

Perfectly competitive market A market that meets the conditions of (1) many buyers and sellers, (2) all firms selling identical products, and (3) no barriers to new firms entering the market.

Perfectly elastic demand The case where the quantity demanded is infinitely responsive to price and the price elasticity of demand equals infinity.

Perfectly inelastic demand The case where the quantity demanded is completely unresponsive to price and the price elasticity of demand equals zero.

Personnel economics The application of economic analysis to human resources issues.

Pigovian taxes and subsidies Government taxes and subsidies intended to bring about an efficient level of output in the presence of externalities.

Positive analysis Analysis concerned with what is.

Poverty line A level of annual income equal to three times the amount of money necessary to purchase the minimum quantity of food required for adequate nutrition.

Poverty rate The percentage of the population that is poor according to the federal government's definition.

Present value The value in today's dollars of funds to be paid or received in the future.

Price ceiling A legally determined maximum price that sellers may charge.

Price discrimination Charging different prices to different customers for the same product when the price differences are not due to differences in cost.

Price elasticity of demand The responsiveness of the quantity demanded to a change in price, measured by dividing the percentage change in the quantity demanded of a product by the percentage change in the product's price.

Price elasticity of supply The responsiveness of the quantity supplied to a change in price, measured by dividing the percentage change in the quantity supplied of a product by the percentage change in the product's price.

Price floor A legally determined minimum price that sellers may receive.

Price leadership A form of implicit collusion in which one firm in an oligopoly announces a price change and the other firms in the industry match the change.

Price taker A buyer or seller that is unable to affect the market price.

Principal–agent problem A problem caused by agents pursuing their own interests rather than the interests of the principals who hired them.

Prisoner's dilemma A game in which pursuing dominant strategies results in noncooperation that leaves everyone worse off.

Private benefit The benefit received by the consumer of a good or service.

Private cost The cost borne by the producer of a good or service.

Private good A good that is both rival and excludable.

Producer surplus The difference between the lowest price a firm would be willing to accept for a good or service and the price it actually receives.

Product market A market for goods—such as computers—or services—such as medical treatment.

Production function The relationship between the inputs employed by a firm and the maximum output it can produce with those inputs.

Production possibilities frontier (*PPF*) A curve showing the maximum attainable combinations of two products that may be produced with available resources and current technology.

Productive efficiency A situation in which a good or service is produced at the lowest possible cost.

Profit Total revenue minus total cost.

Progressive tax A tax for which people with lower incomes pay a lower percentage of their income in tax than do people with higher incomes.

Property rights The rights individuals or firms have to the exclusive use of their property, including the right to buy or sell it.

Protectionism The use of trade barriers to shield domestic firms from foreign competition.

Public choice model A model that applies economic analysis to government decision making.

Public franchise A government designation that a firm is the only legal provider of a good or service.

Public good A good that is both nonrival and nonexcludable.

Quantity demanded The amount of a good or service that a consumer is willing and able to purchase at a given price.

Quantity supplied The amount of a good or service that a firm is willing and able to supply at a given price.

Quota A numerical limit a government imposes on the quantity of a good that can be imported into the country.

R

Regressive tax A tax for which people with lower incomes pay a higher percentage of their income in tax than do people with higher incomes.

Rent seeking Attempts by individuals and firms to use government action to make themselves better off at the expense of others.

Rivalry The situation that occurs when one person consuming a unit of a good means no one else can consume it.

S

Scarcity A situation in which unlimited wants exceed the limited resources available to fulfill those wants.

Separation of ownership from control A situation in a corporation in which the top management, rather than the shareholders, controls day-to-day operations.

Short run The period of time during which at least one of a firm's inputs is fixed.

Shortage A situation in which the quantity demanded is greater than the quantity supplied.

Shutdown point The minimum point on a firm's average variable cost curve; if the price falls below this point, the firm shuts down production in the short run.

Single-payer health care system A system, such as the one in Canada, in which the government provides health insurance to all of the country's residents.

Social benefit The total benefit from consuming a good or service, including both the private benefit and any external benefit.

Social cost The total cost of producing a good or service, including both the private cost and any external cost.

Socialized medicine A health care system under which the government owns most of the hospitals and employs most of the doctors.

Sole proprietorship A firm owned by a single individual and not organized as a corporation.

Stock A financial security that represents partial ownership of a firm.

Stockholders' equity The difference between the value of a corporation's assets and the value of its liabilities; also known as *net worth*.

Substitutes Goods and services that can be used for the same purpose.

Substitution effect The change in the quantity demanded of a good that results from a change in price making the good more or less expensive relative to other goods that are substitutes.

Sunk cost A cost that has already been paid and cannot be recovered.

Supply curve A curve that shows the relationship between the price of a product and the quantity of the product supplied.

Supply schedule A table that shows the relationship between the price of a product and the quantity of the product supplied.

Surplus A situation in which the quantity supplied is greater than the quantity demanded.

T

Tariff A tax imposed by a government on imports.

Tax incidence The actual division of the burden of a tax between buyers and sellers in a market.

Technological change A change in the ability of a firm to produce a given level of output with a given quantity of inputs.

Technology The processes a firm uses to turn inputs into outputs of goods and services.

Terms of trade The ratio at which a country can trade its exports for imports from other countries.

Total cost The cost of all the inputs a firm uses in production.

Total revenue The total amount of funds a seller receives from selling a good or service, calculated by multiplying price per unit by the number of units sold.

Trade The act of buying and selling.

Trade-off The idea that, because of scarcity, producing more of one good or service means producing less of another good or service.

Tragedy of the commons The tendency for a common resource to be overused.

Transactions costs The costs in time and other resources that parties incur in the process of agreeing to and carrying out an exchange of goods or services.

Two-part tariff A situation in which consumers pay one price (or tariff) for the right to buy as much of a related good as they want at a second price.

U

Unit-elastic demand Demand is unit elastic when the percentage change in quantity demanded is *equal to* the percentage change in price, so the price elasticity is equal to 1 in absolute value.

Utility The enjoyment or satisfaction people receive from consuming goods and services.

V

Variable costs Costs that change as output changes.

Vertical merger A merger between firms at different stages of production of a good.

Voluntary exchange A situation that occurs in markets when both the buyer and the seller of a product are made better off by the transaction.

Voluntary export restraint (VER) An agreement negotiated between two countries that places a numerical limit on the quantity of a good that can be imported by one country from the other country.

Voting paradox The failure of majority voting to always result in consistent choices.

W

Wall Street Reform and Consumer Protection Act (Dodd-Frank Act) Legislation passed during 2010 that was intended to reform regulation of the financial system.

World Trade Organization (WTO) An international organization that oversees international trade agreements.

COMPANY INDEX

Key terms and the page on which they are defined appear in **boldface**

CREDITS

Photo

Cover, Lucadp/Shutterstock

Front matter, *page vii(t)*, Courtesy of Glenn Hubbard; *page vii(b)*, Courtesy of Tony O'Brien

Chapter 1, *page 2*, Véronique Burger/Science Source/Photo Researchers, Inc.; *page 14*, Burger/Phanie/SuperStock

Chapter 2, *page 36*, Stephen Lam/Reuters/Landov; *page 49*, Rolf Bruderer/Corbis/Glowimages; *page 51B*, Mikael Damkier/Shutterstock; *page 51L*, Elena Elisseeva/Shutterstock; *page 51R*, MBI/Alamy; *page 51T*, JupiterImages; *page 53*, Pawel Kopczynski/Reuters/Landov; *page 57*, AF archive/Alamy

Chapter 3, *page 68*, Ariel Skelley/Blend Images/Corbis; *page 73*, Wavebreak Media/Thinkstock; *page 74*, Eric Audras/Alamy; *page 77*, Susanna Bates/EPA/Landov

Chapter 4, *page 100*, Susanna Bates/EPA/Landov

Chapter 5, *page 136*, Ungnoi Lookjeab /Shutterstock; *page 145*, Natacha Pisarenko/AP Images

Chapter 6, *page 170*, Bill Aron/Science Source/Photo Researchers, Inc.

Chapter 7, *page 204*, Seth Joel/Getty Images; *page 219*, White House Photography

Chapter 8, *page 236*, Reuters/Landov

Chapter 9, *page 270*, Rainier Ehrhardt /AP Images; *page 282*, David Ball/Alamy; *page 289*, Joerg Boethling/Alamy; *page 292*, Daniel Acker/Bloomberg/Getty Images

Chapter 10, *page 304*, Mark Lennihan/AP Images; *page 316*, Gianni Baldizzone/Corbis; *page 325*, Jay Paul/The New York Times/Redux Pictures; *page 327*, Bebeto Matthews/AP Images

Chapter 11, *page 350*, Brennan Linsley/AP Images; *page 353*, Katie N. Gardner/The Washington Post/Getty Images; *page 354*, Damon Higgins/ZUMA Press/Corbis; *page 359*, Ria Novosti/Alamy; *page 369*, Everett Collection Inc./Alamy; *page 386*, Rich Kane/Icon SMI 781/Newscom

Chapter 12, *page 390*, Michael Nolan/Robert Harding; *page 412*, Alex Segre/Alamy

Chapter 13, *page 424*, Lou Linwei/Alamy; *page 434*, Robert Alexander/Archive Photos/Getty Images; *page 438*, Steve Helber/AP Images; *page 440*, Studiomode/Alamy

Chapter 14, *page 450*, Robyn Beck/AFP/Getty Images; *page 461*, David Butow/Corbis; *page 468*, Damian Dovarganes/AP Images

Chapter 15, *page 476*, Katja Heinemann/Aurora Photos/Robert Harding; *page 479*, Paul Sakuma/AP Images; *page 481*, Jason DeCrow/Invision/AP Images; *page 482*, Roussel Bernard/Alamy; *page 494*, Migstock/Alamy

Chapter 16, *page 506*, Katja Kreder/imagebroker/Alamy; *page 515*, Bruce Newman/AP Images

Chapter 17, *page 532*, Rob Carmell/Cal Sport Media/Newscom; *page 546*, Jeson Szenes/EPA/Newscom; *page 551*, Ronnie Kaufman/Larry Hirshowitz/Alamy; *page 555*, Courtesy of Safelite Auto Glass

Chapter 18, *page 568*, Jason Reed/Reuters /Landov; *page 582*, Amy Sussman/Corbis

Text

Chapter 1, *page 5*, John Hechinger, "FBI Presses Banks to Boost Security as Robberies Rise," *Wall Street Journal*, October 8, 2002.

Chapter 5, *page 141*, Ronald H. Coase, "The Problem of Social Cost," *Journal of Law and Economics*, Vol. 3, October, 1960, pp. 1–44.

Chapter 6, *page 180*, Table 6.2, Estimated Real-World Price Elasticities of Demand, Kelly D. Brownell and Thomas R. Frieden, "Ounces of Prevention—The Public Policy Case for Taxes on Sugared Beverages," *New England Journal of Medicine*, April 30, 2009; Sheila M. Olmstead and Robert N. Stavins, "Comparing Price and Non-Price Approaches to Urban Water Conservation," Resources for the Future, Discussion paper 08-22, June 2008; Jonathan E. Hughes, Christopher R. Knittel, and Daniel Sperling, "Evidence of a Shift in the Short-Run Price Elasticity of Gasoline Demand," *Energy Journal*, Vol. 29, No. 1, January 2008;

Robert P. Trost, Frederick Joutz, David Shin, and Bruce McDonwell, "Using Shrinkage Estimators to Obtain Regional Short-Run and Long-Run Price Elasticities of Residential Natural Gas Demand in the U.S.," George Washington University Working Paper, March 13, 2009; Lesley Chiou, "Empirical Analysis of Competition between Wal-Mart and Other Retail Channels," *Journal of Economics and Management Strategy*, Vol. 18, No. 2, Summer 2009; Judith Chevalier and Austan Goolsbee, "Price Competition Online: Amazon versus Barnes and Noble," *Quantitative Marketing and Economics*, Vol. 1, No. 2, June 2003; Henry Saffer and Frank Chaloupka, "The Demand for Illicit Drugs," *Economic Inquiry*, Vol. 37, No. 3, July 1999; "Response to Increases in Cigarette Prices by Race/Ethnicity, Income, and Age Groups—United States, 1976–1993," *Morbidity and Mortality Weekly Report*, July 31, 1998; James Wetzel and George Hoffer, "Consumer Demand for Automobiles: A Disaggregated Market Approach," *Journal of Consumer Research*, Vol. 9, No. 2, September 1982; Jerry A. Hausman, "The Price Elasticity of Demand for Breakfast Cereal," in Timothy F. Bresnahan and Robert J. Gordon, eds., *The Economics of New Goods*, Chicago: University of Chicago Press, 1997; Christopher J. Ruhm, et al., "What U.S. Data Should Be Used to Measure the Price Elasticity of Demand for Alcohol," *Journal of Health Economics*, Vol. 31, No. 16, December 2012; Susan Dynarski, Jonathan Gruber, and Danielle Li, "Cheaper By the Dozen: Using Sibling Discounts at Catholic Schools to Estimate the Price Elasticity of Private School Attendance," NBER Working Paper 15461, October 2009; and U.S. Department of Agriculture, Economic Research Service.

Chapter 8, *page 253*, Michael Lewis, "The End," *Portfolio*, December 2008.

Chapter 10, *page 317*, Gary Becker and Kevin M. Murphy, *Social Economics*, Cambridge: Harvard University Press, 2000, p. 9.

Chapter 12, *page 409*, Sharon M. Oster, *Modern Competitive Analysis*, Third Edition, New York: Oxford University Press, 1999.

Chapter 13, *page 439*, Peter F. Drucker, *Management: Tasks, Responsibilities, Practices*, New York: Harper & Row, 1974, pages 63–64.

We use **business examples** to explain economic concepts. This table highlights the topic and **real-world** company introduced in the chapter-opening vignette and revisited throughout the chapter. This table also lists the companies that appear in our *Making the Connection* and *An Inside Look* features.